Encyclopedia
of
Concert Music

ENCYCLOPEDIA

of

CONCERT MUSIC

by

DAVID EWEN

HILL AND WANG · NEW YORK

To

NICOLAS SLONIMSKY,
a dedicated encyclopedist,
with admiration and affection

Preface

The *Encyclopedia of Concert Music*—a companion volume to the *Encyclopedia of the Opera* published in 1955—is an attempt by the editor to collate within a single volume all such information about serious concert music as will enrich the listening experience of concertgoers and record collectors.

This information covers many areas.

I. THE MUSIC. This volume presents a guide to, and an analysis of, approximately 1,500 of the best-known compositions in all branches of instrumental music, past and present (with the exception of the semi-classical or "pop" variety): symphonies, tone poems, overtures, and other orchestral works; concertos; music for solo instruments; chamber music.

While vocal and choral music do not come within the scope of this volume, some exceptions had to be made. There are works in the symphonic repertory that have vocal or choral sections, and they had to be considered: Mahler's Symphony No. 2, Beethoven's Ninth Symphony, and Brahms' Alto Rhapsody, for example.

Besides this, the editor felt strongly that certain choral masterworks are basic to the repertory of symphony orchestras. Their exclusion from this book would have represented a serious gap to most music lovers. Consequently—even though this volume has not covered choral music as such—discussions have been included of about fifteen of the most important choral works of the past: Handel's *Messiah,* for example, Bach's B minor Mass, and Mozart's Requiem.

From the field of opera, only those excerpts, episodes, overtures, preludes, or entr'actes that belong to the orchestral repertory have been considered. By the same token, only those ballets that have contributed suites to the orchestral repertory are commented upon.

II. THE COMPOSERS. There are here over three hundred biographies of the world's foremost composers—not merely the facts of their lives and careers but also an estimate of their style and place in music history, and a listing of their major instrumental works. At the end of each biography will be found a reference to all works by that composer discussed in other parts of the book.

III. PERFORMERS AND PERFORMANCES. The biographies of musical performers in this volume embrace more than 150 conductors and 250 instrumentalists. In addition, brief histories are provided for over a hundred symphony orchestras, chamber music ensembles, two-piano teams, music festivals, and summer concert series (European as well as American), and the foremost auditoriums in which these performances take place.

IV. MUSICAL TERMS. Over five hundred technical terms are explained. All leading musical instruments and all the basic techniques of musical composition are described.

V. HISTORY AND BACKGROUNDS OF MUSIC. In addition to general articles on various aspects of music history (History and Structure of the Symphony Orchestra, Program Music, History of Concerts and Recitals, History of Conducting, and so forth), this volume explains all the important trends, movements, and schools of composers of the past three centuries: from homophony through Impressionism and Expressionism and the twelve-tone technique; from Baroque and Rococo to jazz and Concrete Music. The physiognomy of more than 125 forms of music is described together with the principal works in each of these forms.

VI. THEORIES AND THEORISTS OF MUSIC. Numerous biographies are devoted to leading theorists of music from Zarlino to Joseph Schillinger and Heinrich Schenker, with a discussion of their main contributions. Also the biographies embrace many important teachers, critics, historians, and musicologists.

VII. LITERARY AND ARTISTIC SOURCES. There are several hundred listings of the world's foremost writers from Aeschylus to Thomas Mann and the instrumental works that their literary creations inspired. A comprehensive article on Painters and Paintings does a similar service for art.

VIII. SPECIAL ARTICLES. Certain general subjects that throw additional light on specific aspects of music, music-making, and music history are treated in special articles. They include Humor in Music, National Anthems in Music, Jazz and the Blues in Serious Music, Negro Music, and History of Program Notes.

This book is designed for the layman who has only an elementary acquaintance with the technical phases of music. Consequently, wherever possible, material is presented in simple, non-technical language. Nevertheless, an effort has been made to adhere throughout to the highest principles of musical scholarship. Some of the basic biographical facts found in this book come from first-hand sources: birth and death certificates; programs and newspaper criticisms; information provided by the musicians themselves. In this, the editor has profited no end from material generously provided him by Nicolas Slonimsky, material gathered over a period of many years from all parts of the world. Where names, dates, or other facts in this volume differ from those appearing in other music reference works they do so because in the opinion of the editor the evidence he consulted made the changes necessary.

D. E.

Little Neck, N. Y.

Encyclopedia
of
Concert Music

A

A–B–A. Symbol indicating a three-part (ternary) form in which the third part is a repetition of the first.

Abduction from the Seraglio (Die Entfuehrung aus dem Serail), Overture to The. Overture to a comic opera by Mozart, with libretto by Gottlieb Stephanie, adapted from a text by Christoph Bretzner for an earlier opera by Johann André. Mozart's opera (the first significant one in the German language) was introduced in Vienna on July 16, 1782. The vivacious overture sets the mood of gaiety that prevails throughout the work. The opening, saucy melody for strings is the main theme. This overture is characterized by frequent alternations between loud and soft passages, by sudden changes of key, and by an occasional exotic idiom which in Mozart's time was identified as Turkish.

Abegg Variations (Thème sur le nom Abegg, or Variations in F Major). Schumann's first composition for piano, and first opus (1830). Meta Abegg was an attractive young lady whom the composer met at a ball in Mannheim, Germany, and to whom he dedicated this piece. In her honor he derived his opening theme from the letters of her name: A, B (German for "B-flat"), E, G, G. While Schumann's dedication reads "à Mlle. Pauline d'Abegg, Comtesse," the young lady was not a countess, and her given name was not Pauline. This work is of special interest as one of the rare compositions of its period to use for variations an original theme rather than a popular tune or opera aria. It also merits consideration for the finale, with its cross accents, syncopations and exciting rhythms.

Abendroth, Hermann, conductor. Born Frankfort-on-the-Main, Germany, Jan. 19, 1883; died Jena, Germany, May 29, 1956. After studying theory with Ludwig Thuille and piano with Anna Langen-han-Hirzel, Abendroth became a bookseller. In 1903 he served his conducting apprenticeship with the Munich Orchestral Society. Recognition came in Cologne where, in 1915, he started conducting the Gurzenich concerts, and, in 1918, he was appointed general music director. From 1934 to 1942 he conducted the Gewandhaus Orchestra in Leipzig and was director of the Conservatory. After World War II, he became Director General of Music in East Germany, principal conductor of the Weimar State Orchestra and director of the Musikhochschule. From 1949 until his death he was musical director of the Leipzig Radio.

Absolute Music. As opposed to "program music," any music not requiring a literary or pictorial association or a program for its full appreciation, but whose interest is derived entirely from its form and musical content.

Absolute (or Perfect) Pitch. The specific pitch of a note. A musician with a faculty for absolute pitch can identify any sounded note by its pitch name without consulting an instrument or printed music.

Academic Festival Overture (Akademische Festouvertuere). Concert overture by Brahms, op. 80 (1880), written to acknowledge an honorary degree of Doctor of Philosophy conferred on him by the University of Breslau on May 11, 1879. The overture was first performed in Breslau on Jan. 4, 1881, the composer conducting. The work opens with a brisk subject for violins followed by a more subdued passage for the violas. We then hear several German student songs. The most important, in the order of their appearance, are: *Wir hatten gebauet ein stattliches Haus* in three trumpets; *Der Landesvater* in second violins; *Was kommt dort von der Hoeh,* or *Fuchslied,* in bassoons accompanied by violas and

3

cellos; and finally the famous *Gaudeamus igitur* presented at the conclusion of the overture by the full orchestra.

Acadian Songs and Dances (Virgil Thomson). *See: Louisiana Story.*

Accelerando. Increase in velocity.

Accent. Emphasis by increased intensity on a tone or chord.

Acciaccatura. An ornament of short duration, sounded together with the ornamented note but immediately released while the latter is held.

Accidental. A symbol of a sharp, flat, or natural placed before a note to raise or lower the pitch.

Accompaniment. That part of a musical setting which has a subsidiary or supporting role.

Accompanist. Performer of the accompaniment, usually on the piano.

Accordare. To tune.

Acoustics. The science of sound.

Action. The mechanism of a piano, organ, or harp, in which the sound of the strings or pipes is controlled by the fingers.

Ad Libitum (or **A Piacere**). A term found before a passage leaving tempo, expression, and at times even the instrumental medium, to the discretion of a performer. Also a passage that may be omitted.

Adagietto. A tempo somewhat faster than Adagio, of which it is the diminutive.

Adagio. A very slow and leisurely tempo, but not as slow as Largo.

Adagio for Strings. (1) By Samuel Barber, op. 11 (1936). It originated as the slow movement of his String Quartet in B minor, but was subsequently transcribed by the composer for string orchestra. In the latter version it was first performed by the NBC Symphony under Toscanini on Nov. 5, 1938. A single theme, heard immediately in first violins, dominates the composition. Other groups of instruments refer to it, treat it canonically, then develop it into a powerful climax. At the end of the piece, the theme reverts to its former serene mood.

(2) By Guillaume Lekeu (1891). It was inspired by a poem by Georges Vanor, a motto from which appears in the published score: "The pale flowers of memory." This work, which is in an elegiac mood, is scored for divided strings, except for double basses. (The composer also wrote it for string quartet.) A melancholy subject is presented in the opening measures. A secondary melody for solo violin intensifies the poignancy of the music, after which the opening subject returns to end the work.

Adelaide Concerto. For violin and orchestra, in D major, attributed to Mozart. He was said to have written it in May 1766, when he was only ten, and dedicated it to Adelaide, daughter of Louis XV of France. The work was supposed to have lain forgotten for a century and a half. In 1933 the house of Schott in Mainz, Germany, published it in an edition by Marius Casadesus, with three cadenzas by Paul Hindemith. In this version it was performed by Yehudi Menuhin. Musicologists are now convinced that this is not authentic Mozart.

Adieux, L'Absence, et Le Retour, Les. *See:* Sonata—*Beethoven.*

Adonais. *See:* Shelley, Percy Bysshe.

Adventures in a Perambulator. Suite for orchestra by John Alden Carpenter (1915), introduced in Chicago on May 19, 1915, Frederick Stock conducting. The music literally follows an amusing program provided by the composer and describing the experiences of a child as it is being wheeled around in its perambulator. The titles of the respective movements provide the clue to their programmatic content: I. *En Voiture;* II. *The Policeman;* III. *The Hurdy Gurdy;* IV. *The Lake;* V. *The Dogs.* VI. *Dreams.*

There are witty interpolations of popular melodies. In the *Hurdy Gurdy* section, Irving Berlin's *Alexander's Ragtime Band* is quoted; and in the *Dogs* movement we hear snatches of *Ach, du lieber Augustin* and *Where, Oh Where, Has My Little Dog Gone?.*

Aeolian Harp Etude. *See:* Etude—*Chopin.*

Aeolian Mode. A Gregorian mode corresponding to our scale from "A" to "A" on the white keys of the piano.

Aeschylus, Greek tragic poet. Born Eleusis, Greece, 525 B.C.; died Gela, Sicily, 456 B.C. His tragedies inspired many instrumental compositions. Among these dramas are the following:

Agamemnon: Ildebrando Pizzetti (orchestral prelude).

Epithalamium: Ildebrando Pizzetti (orchestral prelude).

Oresteia: Incidental music by Max von Schillings.

The Persians: Incidental music by Henri Sauguet.

Prometheus Bound: Marion Bauer (music for two pianos and flute); Karl Goldmark (concert overture). Incidental music by Arthur Honegger.

Afternoon of a Faun, The (L'Après-midi d'un faune). Orchestral prelude by Debussy (1894), first performed in Paris on Dec. 23, 1894, Gustave Doret conducting. It was inspired by a poem by the Symbolist, Stéphane Mallarmé. Debussy originally planned to use the poem as the basis of a triptych, consisting of a prelude, an interlude, and a finale, but completed only the prelude. This was the composer's first masterwork for orchestra. The principal theme is immediately given by the solo flute to evoke Mallarmé's half-real, misty world of the faun. The latter is lying half-asleep, dreaming he has been visited by nymphs. Upon awakening, he tries to recall his vision and becomes emotionally overwrought; then once again he succumbs to his half-sleep and delightful dreams. Besides the opening flute melody, two other musical subjects are of interest: a passionate song for oboe, and a monologue for solo violin. At the conclusion the music dissolves into mist, and the faun's unreal world evaporates. This composition has been successfully used as a ballet score. The ballet was introduced in Paris by the Ballet Russe on May 29, 1912. The choreography was by Nijinsky, whose portrayal of the faun was one of his triumphs.

Aglavaine et Sélysette. *See:* Maeterlinck, Maurice.

Agamemnon. *See:* Aeschylus.

Agathe Sextet. *See:* Sextet—*Brahms.*

Age of Anxiety, The. *See:* Symphony—*Bernstein.*

Age of Gold, The. Ballet suite for orchestra by Shostakovich, op. 22 (1929), derived from an "industrial ballet" introduced in Leningrad on Oct. 26, 1930. The ballet was a satire on capitalism,

Fascism, and "bourgeois psychology." The text (by A. V. Ivanovsky) concerned an athletic meet in a non-Soviet city during a trade exhibit. The captain of a visiting Soviet soccer team falls in love with a foreign young lady who turns out to be a Fascist. For his suite Shostakovich drew four sections from the ballet score: I. Introduction; II. Adagio; III. Polka; IV. Russian Dance. The most popular numbers are the third and fourth, often performed independently of the other two sections. The Polka caricatures the Geneva Disarmament Conference. A saucy tune is here projected by the xylophone, followed by a brass-band melody first for tuba and trumpets, then for full orchestra. The Russian Dance is virtually a travesty on band music, with its accordion-like sonorities and excessive use of percussion. Both pieces have been transcribed for solo piano, two pianos, four pianos, and violin and piano. The opening Introduction highlights a lilting waltz, while the ensuing Adagio has an appealing melody for solo saxophone.

Age of Steel, The (Le Pas D'Acier). Ballet suite for orchestra by Prokofiev, op. 41a (1925), derived from his ballet score. The ballet was introduced in Paris by the Ballet Russe on June 7, 1927. The text, by Giorgi Yakulov, glorified the growth of Soviet industrialization. Prokofiev's music sought to portray factory noises, and the rhythms of machines in motion, through shrill dissonances and varied rhythmic patterns. One critic described the music as "an apotheosis of machinery." The score, nevertheless, makes use of Russian melodies to characterize the chief protagonists—a comical sailor, a commissar, and a working woman. The symphonic suite has six parts: I. Train of Men Carrying Bags; II. Sailor with Bracelet and Working Women; III. Reconstruction of Scenery; IV. The Factory; V. The Hammer; VI. The Final Scene.

Agitato. Agitated.

Agon. Ballet suite for orchestra by Stravinsky (1957). The ballet was commissioned by the Rockefeller Foundation and was introduced by the New York City Ballet in New York on Dec. 1, 1957. The orchestral suite consists of the entire eighteen-minute ballet score, rather than excerpts; it was first played at a symphony concert at the Hollywood Bowl on June 17, 1957. "Agon" is a Greek term for a contest or struggle; in the ballet the word is used to connote a dance competition. The ballet itself is non-representational—devoid of plot, costumes, or décor. The music is equally pure and bare, entirely stripped of non-essentials. The writing is linear, but a strong rhythm prevails. The principal dances used by Stravinsky in his score (Sarabande, Galliard, and Bransle) were found by him in a mid-17th-century dance manual.

Ajax. *See:* Sophocles.

Ala and Lolli (Prokofiev). *See: Scythian Suite.*

Alastor. *See:* Shelley, Percy Bysshe.

Albéniz, Isaac, composer. Born Camprodón, Spain, May 29, 1860; died Cambo-Bains, Pyrenees, May 18, 1909. He entered the Madrid Conservatory in his eighth year. Several years later he ran away from home and earned his way playing the piano in Spain and America. He was back in Spain in 1875, then pursued formal music study at the Conservatories in Brussels and Leipzig. After several years touring as concert pianist, including appearances with Anton Rubinstein in America and Europe, Albéniz went to Paris in 1893. There he earned his living teaching, while studying privately with Vincent d'Indy and Paul Dukas. During this period he met and became a friend of Felipe Pedrell, Spanish musicologist, who convinced him of the artistic and musical significance of Spanish folksong and dance. It was owing to Pedrell's influence upon him that Albéniz decided to become a serious composer of national Spanish music. His *Rapsodie espagnole* for orchestra was introduced in Barcelona in 1895; *Catalonia,* a suite for orchestra (originally for piano), was given in Paris in 1899. Serious illness sent Albéniz back to his native land in 1900 and he remained there for the rest of his life. Between 1906 and 1909 he completed his masterwork, *Iberia,* for the piano.

Albéniz' best music is for the piano and includes the four books of *Iberia,* 2 Spanish suites, 6 Spanish Dances, *Suite española* (including the popular *Sevillana*), *Cantos de España* (including *Córdoba*), *Navarra* (completed by D. de Séverac), and the famous Tango in D major. He drew his inspiration from Spanish subjects: his country's geography, people, and folklore. His music is filled with the warm and sinuous melodies, pulsating rhythms, and brilliant harmonic colors of Andalusian folksongs and dances. He became the first major creative figure in the Spanish national school, which was soon to include Enrique Granados, Joaquin Turina, Manuel de Falla, and Manuel Infante.

See: Iberia.

Albert, Eugene D'. *See:* D'Albert, Eugene.

Alberti Bass. A term for a broken chord accompaniment in classical keyboard music. It was named after the composer, Domenico Alberti (born Venice, Italy, about 1710; died Formio, Italy, about 1740), who made extensive use of it.

Alborada. *See:* Aubade.

Alborada del Gracioso (Ravel). *See: Miroirs* (2).

Album for the Young (Album fuer die Jugend), children's pieces for piano by Schumann, op. 68 (1848). Schumann had written an earlier set of children's pieces in 1838 entitled *Scenes from Childhood* (which see). The *Album* consists of 43 miniatures about children's games, thoughts, moods, fancies, stories—all written *for* children rather than *about* children, as had been the case with the earlier *Scenes.* All miniatures in the *Album* are elementary in technique, simple in approach, unsophisticated in content. The most popular pieces are the following: No. 2, *Soldier's March (Soldatenmarsch),* which has been transcribed for orchestra; No. 7, *Little Hunting Song (Jaegerliedchen);* No. 8, *Wild Horseman (Wilder Reiter),* which was made into an American popular song; No. 10, *Happy Farmer* or *Merry Peasant (Froehlicher Landmann);* No. 12, *Knight Rupert (Knecht Rupprecht);* No. 31, *War Song (Kriegslied).*

Albumblatt (Album Leaf). A brief, artistically slight piece, usually for the piano, carrying the implication of a dedication in an autograph album. Beethoven's *Für Elise* is designated both an Albumblatt and a Bagatelle. Some of the best examples of Albumblaetter can be found in a set by Schumann, op. 124 (1832-1845). Of its 20 pieces the following are special favorites: No. 4, *Waltz (Walzer)*; No. 5, *Fantastic Dance (Fantasietanz)*; No. 16, *Slumber Song (Schlummerlied)*; and No. 17, *Elf (Elfe)*.

Liszt's Albumblatt in E major (about 1841) and Albumblatt in Waltz Form (1842) are also interesting examples of this type. Richard Wagner wrote an Albumblatt, for violin and piano, in E-flat major (1875) and three Albumblaetter for piano (1861).

Alceste, Overture To. Overture to an opera by Gluck, introduced in Vienna on Dec. 26, 1767. The libretto, by Ranieri Calzabigi, was based on the tragedy by Euripides. The overture opens with dramatic chords for full orchestra. A slow and stately melody is then stated by the strings and is developed with intensity. The music progresses with dramatic sweep. After a repeat of the opening chords, earlier material is recalled.

Alfvén, Hugo, composer. Born Stockholm, Sweden, May 1, 1872. After attending the Stockholm Conservatory he received a government stipend to study the violin with César Thomson in Brussels, and another to travel for three years in Germany and France. Returning to his native land, he taught composition and orchestration at the Stockholm Conservatory. From 1910 to 1939 he was musical director of the Royal University at Upsala, a period in which he also led the University Chorus in concerts throughout Europe and appeared as guest conductor with orchestras in London, Vienna, and Scandinavia. In recognition of his services to Swedish music he was honored with the Wuerttemberg Gold Medal and the Swedish medal "Litteris et Artibus."

His best music is for orchestra, his most famous composition being the Swedish rhapsody, *Midsummer Vigil* (*Midsommarvaka*). He wrote two other Swedish rhapsodies, five symphonies, several shorter works for orchestra, and a violin sonata.

See: Midsummer Vigil.

Alice in Wonderland. *See:* Carroll, Lewis.

Alkestis. *See:* Euripides.

Alla Breve. An indication at the head of a composition to double the speed so that four-to-a-bar becomes two-to-a-bar.

Allargando. A term indicating slackening of the tempo and broadening of the style.

Allegretto. Somewhat quickly, slower than Allegro.

Allegro. Fast and lively, faster than Andante but slower than Presto.

Allemande. A dance presumably of German origin, usually in moderate quadruple rhythm and binary form. It has a free-flowing ornamented melody. It often appears as a first movement of the late Baroque suite.

Alma Brasileira (Villa-Lobos). *See:* Chôros.

Alpine Symphony. *See:* Symphony—*Richard Strauss.*

Also Sprach Zarathustra (Richard Strauss). *See: Thus Spake Zarathustra.*

Altered Chords. Chords with one or more of the notes of the prescribed key altered by one or more accidentals.

Alto Clef. A clef now used primarily for viola music, indicating middle C on the middle (third) line of the staff.

Alto Rhapsody. Rhapsody for alto voice, men's chorus, and orchestra by Brahms, op. 53, first performed publicly in Jena, Germany, on March 3, 1870, with Pauline Viardot-Garcia as soloist and Ernst Naumann conducting. This is a setting of three verses from Goethe's *Harzreise im Winter*. The somber poetry struck a responsive chord with Brahms, for during this time he himself was despondent, suffering from a frustrated love affair. His musical setting is suffused with melancholy, and at times despair—particularly in the first two verses, each for alto voice and orchestra. In the third verse (where the music shifts from C minor to C major) the clouds disperse and the work ends on a strong note of optimism. Here the setting is for men's chorus in addition to the alto soloist and the orchestra.

Altschuler, Modest, conductor. Born Mogilev, Russia, Feb. 15, 1873. He studied at the Conservatories in Warsaw and Moscow. After settling in the United States he founded the Russian Symphony

Orchestra in New York in 1903 to promote the music of contemporary Russians, its first concert taking place on Jan. 7, 1904. During the next fifteen years this organization introduced to the United States major works by Ippolitov-Ivanov, Liadov, Rachmaninoff, and Scriabin, among others; also such eminent Russian performing artists as Mischa Elman, Josef Lhévinne, and Scriabin. From 1919 Altschuler lived in Florida and California, conducting various minor orchestras and teaching.

Alt Wien (Godowsky). *See: Triakontameron.*

Amadeus String Quartet. A chamber music ensemble organized in London in 1947. Its members are Norbert Brainin and Siegmund Nissel, violins; Peter Schidloff, viola; and Martin Lovett, cello. After appearances throughout Europe, the Amadeus Quartet made a highly successful début in the United States, in Newark, N.J., on Jan. 29, 1953.

Amar String Quartet. *See:* Hindemith, Paul.

Amati. A family of violin makers in Cremona, Italy, in the 16th and 17th centuries. Some of their instruments are still used by world-famous virtuosos. The first of the Amatis was Andrea (born probably Genoa, Italy, 1530; died there, 1611), who helped evolve the violin from the old viol. His two sons, Girolamo and Antonio, continued producing violins, making several structural changes. The greatest of the Amatis was Niccolò, son of Girolamo (born Cremona, Italy, Dec. 3, 1596; died there April 12, 1684). In his shop such celebrated craftsmen as Andrea Guarneri and Antonio Stradivari received their apprenticeship.

America. An epic rhapsody (sometimes designated a symphony) by Ernest Bloch (1927), first performed by the New York Philharmonic on Dec. 20, 1928, Walter Damrosch conducting. *America* won first prize (by unanimous decision of the judges) in a contest for an American symphonic work sponsored by the journal, *Musical America.* The prize consisted of $3,000 in cash, and performances by several major American orchestras. One day after the première in New York, the rhapsody was simultaneously given in Chicago, Philadelphia, Boston, and San Francisco. The work is dedicated to the memory of Abraham Lincoln and Walt Whitman. A Whitman quotation appears in the score: "O America, because you build for mankind I build for you." It is in three sections: I. 1620. The Soil—The Indians—The Mayflower—The Landing Pilgrims; II. 1861-1865. Hours of Joy—Hours of Sorrow; III. 1926. The Present—The Future. The Indian element is pronounced in the first movement, but fragments of other types of themes appear. Among the latter are the opening phrases of the hymn, *Old Hundredth,* and an English march. In the second movement are heard fragments of several patriotic songs, war songs, Negro Spirituals, Creole folksongs and even Stephen Foster's *Old Folks at Home.* The finale opens with a syncopated subject suggesting the jazz age. Once again Bloch quotes Negro songs, the *Old Hundredth,* and this time *Yankee Doodle* as well. At the climax, an anthem is sung by a chorus, beginning with the words, "America! America! Thy name is in my heart." (The audience is invited to participate in the singing.) This is the focal point of the entire work. Previously this anthem theme had appeared as a recurring motto: in the opening of the first movement; the closing of the second movement; and in the syncopated introduction to the third.

American Festival Overture. Concert overture by William Schuman (1939), introduced by the Boston Symphony under Koussevitzky on Oct. 6, 1939. The opening three-note phrase imitates a call familiar in the New York City streets in the 1910's and 1920's: "Wee-awk-ee," used to convoke boys for play. The extension of this subject forms the first part of the overture. The middle section is a fugue whose subject is presented by violas; it is first found in strings alone, later for woodwind alone, finally for strings and woodwind together. The climax leads to the concluding section in which earlier material is extended.

American in Paris, An. Tone poem for orchestra by George Gershwin (1928), first performed by the New York Philharmonic under Walter Damrosch on

Dec. 13, 1928. The music describes the emotional responses of an American as he strolls along a Paris boulevard. The composition opens with a "walking theme" in strings and oboes, descriptive of the stroll; sounds of actual Parisian taxi horns punctuate the orchestration. As the American passes a famous Parisian night spot, a music hall tune appears in the trombone. A more vigorous walking theme is then given by the clarinet. A solo violin passage is the transition to the work's main melody—a blues song for muted trumpet. This, and a Charleston melody for two trumpets, speak for the American's nostalgia for home. The tone poem ends with a final robust statement of the blues song.

American Quartet. *See:* Quartet— *Dvořák.*

Amor Brujo, El (Love, the Magician). Ballet suite for orchestra by Manuel de Falla (1914), derived from his ballet score. The ballet was introduced in Madrid on April 15, 1915—scenario by Martinez Sierra derived from an old Andalusian gypsy tale. Candela loves Carmelo but they are haunted by the ghost of Candela's dead husband. In order to pursue their affair undisturbed, Candela and Carmelo find a gypsy girl to occupy the time and interests of the jealous ghost. The orchestral suite was introduced in Madrid, under the direction of Fernandez Arbós, one year after the première of the ballet. It contains twelve numbers, the ballet's principal music: I. Introduction and Scene; II. The Gypsies —Evening; III. Scene of Sorrowing Love (with backstage voice); IV. The Homecomer; V. Dance of Terror; VI. The Magic Circle; VII. Ritual Fire Dance; VIII. Scene; IX. Song of the Will-o'-the-Wisp; X. Pantomime; XI. Dance of the Game of Love (with backstage voice); XII. Morning Chimes. When performed without voice, the vocal parts are assigned to a wind instrument, usually the horn.

The *Ritual Fire Dance* has become popular apart from the ballet or the suite; it is now familiar not only in its original orchestral version but also in transcriptions for solo piano (by the composer), two pianos, violin and piano, and cello and piano.

Amoroso. Lovingly, a term allowing for emotionalization or sentimentalization in the performance of a passage.

Anacreon, Overture To. Overture to an opera by Luigi Cherubini. The opera was introduced at the Paris Opéra on October 4, 1803 when it was a fiasco, mainly owing to an absurd libretto by R. Mendouze. The overture is a stately work in the Classic style. It opens with a majestic slow section (Largo assai). The main Allegro section contains several themes from the opera. The orchestration includes an English horn, an instrument not often encountered in Cherubini's day.

Andaluza (Granados). *See:* Spanish Dances (1).

Andante. Slow.

Andante Cantabile. A tempo marking found as the slow movement of several compositions, indicating "slow and singing." The beautiful and sentimental slow movement of Tchaikovsky's String Quartet in D major, op. 11 (1871), is one of the most popular pieces with this marking. It has been transcribed by Fritz Kreisler for violin and piano and viola and piano; it has also been adapted for flute and piano, and for string orchestra.

Andante Favori (Beethoven). *See: Waldstein Sonata* in Sonata—*Beethoven.*

Andantino. Somewhat slow, but faster than Andante, of which it is a diminutive.

Andersen, Hans Christian, poet and writer of fairy tales. Born Odense, Denmark, April 2, 1805; died Copenhagen, Aug. 4, 1875. Andersen's fairy tales inspired the following orchestral compositions: Harry Farjeon's *Hans Andersen Suite;* Gyorgy Kósa's *Fairy Tale Suite;* Vitezslav Novák's tone poem, *Eternal Longing;* Bernard Rogers' *Characters from Hans Christian Andersen,* for small orchestra; and Stravinsky's tone poem *The Song of the Nightingale* and ballet suite, *The Fairy's Kiss.*

Andromache. *See:* Euripides, Racine.

Animato (or **Animé**). Spirited, animated.

Anitra's Dance (Grieg). *See: Peer Gynt Suite.*

Ann Arbor Festival. A music festival held annually in May at Ann Arbor, Michigan,, sponsored by the Musical Society of the University of Michigan. It was initiated in 1893 with Verdi's Requiem. From 1893 to 1904 the Boston Festival Orchestra was conducted by Emil Mollenhauer. From 1905 to 1935 the Chicago Symphony was led by Frederick Stock, and since 1935 the participating orchestra has been the Philadelphia Orchestra, first under Stokowski and later under Ormandy. Outstanding symphonic and choral music of the past and present are given with the cooperation of the University of Michigan Choral Union and noted soloists. Guest conductors participate.

Années de Pèlerinage (Years of Pilgrimage). Three sets of tone pictures for piano by Liszt inspired by his travels. The first, called *First Year,* was stimulated by Switzerland (1835-1836), and embraces nine pieces. The most celebrated of these is the fourth, *Au Bord d'une source,* an impressionistic setting of a spring and the feelings it arouses in a poet. Also notable are the sixth and seventh pieces, *Vallée d'Obermann* and *Églogue,* inspired respectively by the poets Obermann and Byron. To the ninth piece, *Les Cloches de Genève,* the composer appended an epigraph from Byron's *Childe Harold.*

The *Second Year,* inspired by Italy (1838-1839), has seven pieces, of which the following are among the best known: the fifth, *Sonetto del Petrarca,* inspired by the 104th sonnet of Petrarch; the seventh, *Fantasia quasi sonata après une lecture du Dante,* inspired by Dante. Also of interest are the first, *Sposalizio,* based on a bell theme and used in conjunction with a hymn-like melody; and the third, *Canzonetta del Salvator Rosa,* a popular Italian song to which Liszt added a rich harmonization.

The *Third Year* (1877) consists of random pieces. Generally speaking, this set is inferior to the other two, though it does contain a notable item in *Les Jeux d'eaux à la Villa d'Este,* one of the most vivid examples of impressionistic writing before Debussy.

Annunzio, Gabriele D'. *See:* D'Annunzio, Gabriele.

Anouilh, Jean, playwright. Born Bordeaux, France, June 23, 1910. The fol-lowing composers wrote incidental music to his plays: Norman Demuth (*Médée*); Darius Milhaud (*Le Bal des voleurs, Le Voyageur sans bagage*); Francis Poulenc (*Léodardia, Le Voyageur sans bagage*).

Ansermet, Ernest, conductor. Born Vevey, Switzerland, November 11, 1883. He attended a college in Lausanne, and subsequently taught mathematics in a high school. His music study took place in Geneva with Ernest Bloch, in Germany with Arthur Nikisch, and in Paris with Francesco de Lacerda. In 1914 he began conducting in Montreux. One year later he initiated a three-year period as symphony conductor in Geneva, at the same time serving as musical director of the Ballet Russe de Monte Carlo, with which he led many provocative premières. In 1918 he founded the Orchestre de la Suisse Romande in Geneva; under his guidance it became one of Europe's most celebrated symphony orchestras. He has remained since then its principal conductor, leading notable performances of many modern works. He also appeared as guest conductor of major European orchestras. From 1924 to 1927 he was conductor of the Buenos Aires Symphony; in 1936 and 1937, he was guest conductor at the Hollywood Bowl and Ravinia Festival in the United States. He is the author of *Le Geste du chef d'orchestre* (1943) and *Débat sur l'art contemporain* (1948). He made several transcriptions for orchestra, including Debussy's *Six epigraphes antiques.*

Antar Symphony. *See:* Symphony—*Rimsky-Korsakov.*

Antheil, George, composer. Born Trenton, N. J., July 8, 1900; died New York City, Feb. 12, 1959. He studied music with Constantin von Sternberg, Ernest Bloch, and at the Settlement School in Philadelphia. In 1922 he toured Europe as pianist, becoming notorious for his programs of ultra-modern music. He soon abandoned the concert stage to settle in Paris and devote himself to composition. During this period his writing was so unorthodox and iconoclastic that he was termed "bad boy of music." His most provocative and publicized composition was the *Ballet mécanique,* scored for anvils, airplane propellers, electric bells, automobile horns, and 16 player pianos; the composer described it as "a mechanistic dance of life." It was first performed in Paris on June 19, 1926, and the following April given in Carnegie Hall, New York. After returning to the United States in the early 1930's, Antheil deserted serious composition to write music for the movies. When he resumed creative work in 1939, he renounced his one-time experimentations for music traditional in technique and structure, romantic in feeling, and orthodox in approach. His works include 6 symphonies, concertos for violin and for piano, various shorter orchestral works (including *Over the Plains, Specter Waltz, Hot Time Dance, Serenade for Strings, McKonkey's Ferry,* and *The Rivers*), 3 string quartets, 2 violin sonatas, and 4 piano sonatas. He is the author of an autobiography, *Bad Boy of Music* (1945).

Anticipation. In harmony, the appearance of one or more notes of a chord before the emergence of the chord itself.

Antony and Cleopatra. *See:* Shakespeare, William.

Apaches, Les. *See:* Société des Apaches.

Apollon Musagète (Apollo, Leader of the Muses). Ballet suite for strings by Stravinsky (1928). The ballet, with choreography by Adolph Bolm, was introduced in Washington, D.C. on April 27, 1928. It consists of two tableaux. The first presents the birth of Apollo, and the second, his inspiration of the Muses. The score is neo-classic in the style of 17th-century French ballet composers: simple, economical, tight-lipped in emotional restraint. It is scored for strings in six parts, the cellos being subdivided. It opens slowly and quietly with a fluid ascending melody descriptive of Apollo's descent to earth. The tempo quickens and the rhythmic drive becomes more pronounced as Apollo dances in turn with Calliope, Polyhymnia, and Terpsichore (Pas d'action, Pas de deux, Coda). In the sonorous conclusion, Apollo leads the Muses to Parnassus.

Appalachian Spring. Suite for orchestra by Aaron Copland derived from his ballet score. Copland wrote this music for Martha Graham, to her choreography based on a poem by Hart Crane, and the ballet was introduced in Washington, D.C. on Oct. 30, 1944. The orchestral suite was performed for the first time by the New York Philharmonic under Rodzinski on Oct. 4, 1945. There are seven sections, played without interruption: I. Introduction of the characters. II. Sudden burst of unison strings, marking the beginning of the action. The sentiment here combines elation with religious feeling. III. Duo for the bride and her intended, a passionate scene. IV. The revivalist and his flock. The feeling is folk-like with echoes of country fiddlers and suggestions of square dances. V. Solo dance of the bride. The extremes of joy and fear are here voiced. VI. Transition scene in which the music recalls that of the introduction. VII. Scenes of daily activity for the bride and her farmer-husband. A Shaker theme is heard, followed by five variations. The theme, played by solo clarinet, is derived from an actual Shaker melody, *Simple Gifts.* VIII. Coda. The married couple is left alone in a new home. Music with reverent overtones is presented by muted strings. The final measures recall the opening music of the introduction.

Appalachian Spring received both the Pulitzer Prize in music and the award of the New York Music Critics Circle.

Appassionata (or Appassionato). Passionately.

Appassionata Sonata. *See:* Sonata—*Beethoven.*

Appoggiatura. Grace note, embellishment.

Apprenti Sorcier, L' (Dukas). *See: Sorcerer's Apprentice, The.*

Après-midi d'un faune, L' (Debussy). *See: Afternoon of a Faun, The.*

Après un lecture du Dante (Liszt). *See: Années de Pèlerinage (Second Year).*

Arabesque (or Arabesk). Originally a fanciful bit of ornamentation in ancient and Renaissance art. Schumann adapted the term for music to designate a composition in which the melodic line is highly ornamented, and which often ends with a poetic epilogue; structurally it resembles a rondo. Schumann's Arabesque in C major, op. 18 (1839), Debussy's Arabesques in E major and G major (1888), and Medtner's Three Arabesques, op. 7

(1905) are characteristic examples of this form.

Arbeau, Thoinot. See: Capriol Suite.

Arbós, Enrique Fernández, violinist and conductor. Born Madrid, Spain, Dec. 24, 1863; died San Sebastian, Spain, June 2, 1939. As a boy he entered the Madrid Conservatory. After that, through a royal grant, he spent four years at the Brussels Conservatory. After additional study of the violin with Joseph Joachim in Berlin he toured Europe as violin virtuoso. In 1883 he became concertmaster of the Berlin Philharmonic, and in 1889 of the Glasgow Symphony Orchestra. He also taught the violin at the Madrid Conservatory, and from 1894 to 1916 at the Royal College of Music in London. In 1904 he was appointed conductor of the Madrid Symphony, an organization that proved influential in developing a musical culture in Spain. While holding this post, Arbós filled engagements as guest conductor with major orchestras in Europe and America, where he helped promote Spanish music. In December 1933 his 70th birthday was celebrated throughout Spain. With the outbreak of civil war in Spain he went into retirement. He made a skillful orchestral adaptation of five sections from Albéniz' Iberia.

Archduke Trio. See: Trio—Beethoven.

Arco. In string music an indication that the bow is again to be used after a plucked string (pizzicato) passage.

Arcueil, École d'. A school of contemporary French composers founded by Erik Satie. The name came from the district near Paris where Satie was living at the time. Its principal members, besides Satie, were Roger Desormière and Henri Sauguet. Its main esthetic principle was a return to simplicity and economy.

Arensky, Anton, composer. Born Novgorod, Russia, Aug. 11, 1861; died Terijoki, Finland, Feb. 25, 1906. His parents, excellent musicians, early directed him to music. He studied with Rimsky-Korsakov at the St. Petersburg Conservatory, from which he was graduated with honors. From 1882 to 1894 he was professor of harmony and counterpoint at the Moscow Conservatory. He was conductor of the Russian Choral Society from 1889 to 1896, and of the Imperial Chapel in St.

Petersburg from 1895 to 1901. Dissipation undermined his health until he contracted consumption and had to be confined in a sanatorium, where he died.

Arensky's works for orchestra include 2 symphonies, a concerto for the violin and one for the piano, Fantasy on Russian Folksongs, and one of his most popular compositions, Variations on a Theme by Tchaikovsky for string orchestra. He was, however, at his best in the more intimate forms of chamber and piano music. In this field he produced 2 string quartets, a piano quintet, a piano trio written in memory of Tchaikovsky, 4 suites for 2 pianos, and smaller pieces for piano solo. His work often reminds us of Tchaikovsky and Rimsky-Korsakov. But he had a pleasing melodic gift and a sound technique.

See: Variations on a Theme by Tchaikovsky.

Aristophanes, writer of comedies. Born Athens, Greece, about 450 B.C.; died about 380 B.C. His plays have been the source of many instrumental compositions. These plays include the following:

The Birds: Incidental music by Georges Auric, John Knowles Paines, C. Hubert Parry, and Goffredo Petrassi.

The Frogs: Granville Bantock (Comedy Overture for The Frogs). Incidental music by C. Hubert Parry.

Lysistrata: Leo Ornstein (suite). Incidental music by Reinhold Glière, Engelbert Humperdinck.

Plutus: Incidental music by Darius Milhaud.

The Wasps: Overture and incidental music by Vaughan Williams.

The Women's Festival: Granville Bantock (Overture to a Greek Tragedy).

Arlésienne, L' (The Woman of Arles). Suite for orchestra by Bizet (1872), adapted from his incidental music to the Provençal play of the same name by Alphonse Daudet. The first performance of the play with Bizet's music took place in Paris on Oct. 1, 1872. Bizet himself adapted four sections of this incidental music into a suite for orchestra. The suite was introduced in Paris on Nov. 10, 1872. I. Prelude, a march adapted from an old Provençal minuet. II. Minuet. III. Adagietto, a religious type of melody for strings. IV. Carillon, a description of the celebration of the feast of St. Eloi by Provençal peasants. The tolling of carillon bells is reproduced by horns against a vigorous melody for strings.

After Bizet's death, Ernest Guiraud adapted other sections of Bizet's incidental music into a second suite. This is less often heard than the first. It has four sections: I. Pastorale; II. Intermezzo; III. Minuet; IV. Farandole. The fourth movement is the most interesting, a lively Provençal dance.

Arpeggio. Consecutive, rather than simultaneous, playing of the ascending or descending notes of a chord.

Arrangement. *See:* Transcription.

Arrau, Claudio, pianist. Born Chillán, Chile, Feb. 6, 1903. A prodigy who gave his first concert when he was five, Arrau was financed by the Chilean government to study in Europe. After attending the Stern Conservatory in Berlin as a pupil of Martin Krause, he made his Berlin début when he was eleven, then performed elsewhere in Germany and in Scandinavia. Two years later he won the Ibach Prize, the first of several awards that included the Liszt Prize (twice), the Schulhoff Prize, and the Geneva International Prize. In 1918 he toured Europe, and in 1921 South America. His American début took place in New York on Nov. 14, 1923. In 1935 he presented a series of 12 concerts in Berlin and Vienna devoted to the entire keyboard literature of Bach. From 1925 to 1940 he was professor of the piano at the Stern Conservatory, and in 1940 he founded a piano school in Santiago, Chile. He returned to the United States for a tour in 1941, and established his permanent residence in America.

Art of the Fugue (Die Kunst der Fuge). A set of 16 fugues, 4 canons, 2 fugues for 2 claviers, and a final unfinished fugue, all of them on one and the same theme, by Johann Sebastian Bach, written in the last year of his life (1749). It was left uncompleted owing to the composer's death. It is believed that Bach never intended this work for performance; except for two of the fugues, he did not even specifically designate the instrument or instruments for which it was intended. In all probability, he planned it to instruct others by example on the many ways a given theme could be treated fugally and canonically; possibly, too, it was his attempt at the end of his life to test his own creative powers in fugal writing. Nevertheless, the work is monumental both technically and artistically, representing Bach at the apex of his contrapuntal genius. It was published posthumously at the end of 1750 or beginning of 1751. Since only a few copies were sold, the copper plates were disposed of for a pittance in 1756, by Bach's son, Carl Philipp Emanuel.

When given in the concert hall today, this work is most often played on piano or harpsichord. Several transcriptions exist, notably for two pianos (Erwin Schwebsch), string quartet (Roy Harris and M. D. Herter Norton), and orchestra (Hermann Diener, Paul Graener, Wolfgang Graeser).

Arthurian Legends. British epic tales of the 12th and 13th centuries written in medieval French and centered around the exploits of Arthur (6th-century British chieftain) and his knights of the Round Table in Camelot. Orchestral works by the following composers were inspired by these legends: Arnold Bax (*Tintagel,* tone poem); Frederick Bridge (*Morte d'Arthur,* overture); Ernest Chausson (*Viviane,* tone poem); Edward Burlingame Hill (*Launcelot and Guinevere,* tone poem); Paul Ladmirault (incidental music to *Tristan et Iseult*); Edward MacDowell (*Lancelot and Elaine,* tone poem); Eugene Marty (*Merlin enchanté,* tone poem); Ludomir Rogowski (*A Celtic Legend,* symphonic pictures); and Wagner (*Prelude and Love Death* and the *Liebesnacht* from his music drama *Tristan and Isolde*).

As You Like It. *See:* Shakespeare, William.

Ascension, L' (The Ascension). Four "symphonic meditations" for orchestra by Olivier Messiaen (1934), introduced in Paris under the direction of Charles Munch in 1945. Messiaen originally wrote it as a suite for piano or organ. His inspiration was the Scriptures. Each of the four sections bears a title and subtitle derived from Scriptural or liturgical sources. I. *Majesty of Christ Beseeching*

His Glory of His Father. This is a hymn-like section scored for brass and woodwind (*Très lent et majestueux*). II. *Serene Hallelujahs of a Soul that Longs for Heaven.* Here the music has an archaic quality, and the mood is spiritual (*Pas trop modéré et clair*). III. *Hallelujah on the Trumpet, Hallelujah on the Cymbal.* The full orchestra gives voice to uninhibited joy (*Vif et joyeux*). IV. *Prayer of Christ Ascending to His Father.* This part is scored for strings alone, an unspecified number of muted first violins, five unmuted solo second violins, five solo violas, and two solo cellos (*Extrêmement lent, ému et solennel*).

Ase's Death (Grieg). *See: Peer Gynt Suite.*

Aspen Music Festival. An annual summer festival in Aspen, Colo., directed by Izler Solomon. Festival concerts take place several times a week in the amphitheater featuring a symphony orchestra directed by Solomon, famous concert artists, and chamber music groups. This festival is an outgrowth of the Goethe Bicentennial celebrated at Aspen in 1949. Its success led to the formation of a regular summer festival, and to a music school whose faculty was made up mainly of performing artists. The director was Walter P. Paepcke, chairman of the Aspen Institute for Humanistic Studies. In the fall of 1954, the Music Associates of Aspen was organized to control the policies of both the festival and the music school. The Festival honored Stravinsky in 1957, Hindemith in 1958, and the Bach family in 1959.

Assai. Very.

Assonance. Agreement of sounds.

Athalie. (1) Incidental music by Mendelssohn, op. 74 (1844-1845), for Racine's tragedy. The play, with Mendelssohn's music, was first performed in Charlottenburg, Berlin, on Dec. 1, 1845. The Overture and the *War March of the Priests* are the most familiar sections from the score. The overture opens solemnly. The first main theme is a melody for flutes and clarinets against harp and string accompaniment. A dramatic development ensues rising to a climax for full orchestra.

(2) *See:* Racine, Jean Baptiste.

Atonality. Absence of tonality or key centre.

Attacca. An indication at the end of a movement that the next movement is to follow without interruption.

Attack. The manner or act of beginning a phrase or composition.

Atterberg, Kurt, composer. Born Gothenburg, Sweden, Dec. 12, 1887. Before specializing in music he studied engineering. For many years (up to 1940) he worked in the Register Bureau at the Royal Patent Office. All this while music was a favorite avocation. After attending the Stockholm Conservatory and studying composition in Germany with Max von Schillings, he returned to Sweden and engaged in composition, conducting, and the writing of music criticism. A government subsidy finally enabled him to dedicate himself completely to music. In 1940 he became secretary of the Royal Academy of Music in Stockholm. He attracted world attention (and notoriety) in 1928 with his Sixth Symphony, which won the first prize of $10,000 in a competition conducted by Columbia Records to commemorate Schubert's centenary. After many of the world's foremost orchestras performed the symphony, Atterberg confessed his work was intended as a hoax on so-called musical connoisseurs.

Other major works, however, were of more serious purpose; they placed him in the front rank of contemporary Swedish composers. No other Swedish composer has been so extensively published or performed. Atterberg adheres to traditional techniques and structures, and favors a Romantic approach. Some of his best works are nationalistic, deriving their melodic and rhythmic materials from Swedish folk music. His compositions include 8 symphonies, 9 orchestral suites, various concertos for solo instruments and orchestra, several tone poems, *A Vaermland Rhapsody* for orchestra (one of his most popular works), 2 string quartets, and various other smaller chamber-music and orchestral works.

See: Vaermland Rhapsody, A.

Attwood, Thomas, organist and composer. Born London, England, Nov. 23, 1765; died Chelsea, England, March 24, 1838. After serving as a boy chorister in the

Chapel Royal, he pursued music study in Italy with Filippo Cinque and Gaetano Latilla, and in Vienna with Mozart. After returning to London in 1787 he held various organ posts. In 1791 he became music tutor to the Duchess of York, and in 1795 to the Princess of Wales. In 1813 he helped found the Royal Philharmonic Society, conducting some of its concerts. As a composer, he was famous for his operas and church music, but he also produced many sonatas and exercises for the piano.

Aubade (or **Alborada**). Morning music, or a morning serenade, usually instrumental and of light character. Many composers have written short pieces for the piano designated "aubades." Among those who wrote aubades for orchestra are: Constant Lambert (*Aubade héroïque,* for small orchestra); Edouard Lalo (two aubades, for small orchestra); Charles Martin Loeffler (*La Bonne Chanson,* described as an "orchestral aubade"). The opening movement of Rimsky-Korsakov's *Capriccio espagnol* is an alborada. Ravel's *Alborada del gracioso* is famous.

Aubert, Louis, composer. Born Paramé, Ille-et-Vilaine, France, Feb. 19, 1877. He attended the Paris Conservatory, where his teachers included Gabriel Fauré, Paul Vidal, and Vincent d'Indy, and where he received many prizes. After his graduation, he concertized in France as pianist. But he soon deserted the concert stage for composition. During World War I he was organist of the St. Hippolyte Church in Paris, and for many years was a member of the faculty at the Paris Conservatory. Aubert is not a prolific composer but what he has written shows sound craftsmanship, is poetic in content, and atmospherically effective. Though most strongly influenced by Fauré, some of his music has a pronounced Spanish character. His orchestral music includes the famous Habanera, Fantasy in B minor for piano and orchestra, *Suite brève, Offrande,* and *Le Tombeau de Chateaubriand;* he also wrote a piano quintet, violin sonata, and *Trois esquisses* and *Sillages,* for piano.

See: Habanera (2).

Au Bord d'une source (Liszt). *See: Années de pèlerinage (First Year).*

Auden, Wystan Hugh, poet. Born York, England, Feb. 21, 1907. Leonard Bernstein's symphony, *The Age of Anxiety,* was based on Auden's poem of the same name. One of Auden's poems is set to music in Benjamin Britten's *Spring Symphony.* Britten wrote incidental music to two plays written collaboratively by Auden and Christopher Isherwood, *The Ascent of F. 6.* and *On the Frontier.*

Auer, Leopold, violinist and teacher. Born Veszprém, Hungary, June 7, 1845; died Loschwitz, Germany, July 15, 1930. He was one of the most eminent violin teachers of his generation. After attending the Vienna Conservatory, he studied for five years privately with Joseph Joachim. For a period he was concertmaster of orchestras in Duesseldorf and Hamburg. From 1868 to 1917 he was professor of the violin at the St. Petersburg Conservatory, where his pupils included Heifetz, Elman, and Zimbalist. While occupying this post, he conducted orchestral concerts with the Russian Musical Society, appeared as solo violinist both in concerts and at the court of the Czars, and founded and played first violin in the St. Petersburg Quartet. He left Russia in 1917, finally settling in the United States. In 1926 he was appointed head of the violin department of the Institute of Musical Art in New York. One year later he assumed a similar post at the Curtis Institute. He made many transcriptions for the violin; wrote cadenzas for several famous violin concertos; and was the author of an autobiography, *My Long Life in Music* (1923), and several texts on violin playing. Tchaikovsky originally dedicated his violin concerto to Auer, but when Auer suggested certain alterations, Tchaikovsky changed his dedication to Adolf Brodsky.

Augmentation. The repetition of a melodic theme by lengthening the value of each of the notes, as opposed to "diminution."

Augmented. Intervals that are a semitone greater than major or perfect intervals; chords containing augmented intervals.

Augusteo Orchestra. A symphony orchestra in Rome, Italy, founded in 1908 for the Santa Cecilia Academy. It derived its name from the Augusteo auditorium in which it gave its concerts until 1936. Winter concerts take place at the Teatro Argentina, and summer concerts at the Basilica di Massenzio. The orchestra has most often operated under a system of guest conductors, although in 1953-1955 Fernando Previtali was principal conductor. It appeared with success at the Edinburgh Festival in 1948.

Auric, Georges, composer. Born Lodève, France, Feb. 15, 1899. He was a member of "Les Six," or "The French Six" (which see). His musical education took place at the Paris Conservatory and Schola Cantorum. He first came to prominence when his early works were performed in conjunction with those of the other members of the "French Six" immediately after World War I. Auric is known principally for his ballets, songs, and music for French and American motion pictures. He also wrote incidental music for many plays. His main instrumental works include a *Fox Trot, Nocturne, Overture,* and the *Phèdre Suite,* all for orchestra; also a violin sonata, trio for oboe, clarinet, and bassoon, 2 piano sonatas, and several impromptus for piano.

Aurora's Wedding (Tchaikovsky). *See: Sleeping Beauty.*

Aus meinem Leben. *See:* Quartet—*Smetana.*

Authentic Cadence. Harmonic sequence in which a dominant chord is followed by a tonic.

B

Baal Shem. Suite for violin and piano (or orchestra) by Ernest Bloch (1923). Baal Shem was a Hebrew seer, head of a Hasidic sect prominent in Poland in the late 18th century. To the Hasid, joy, redemption, and pleasure were all godly; religious worship was occasion for ecstatic revelry. Hasidic music had the passion and at times frenzy that permeated the Hasid's practice of his religion; and these qualities are found in Bloch's Suite. There are three movements. I. *Vidui* (Contrition) is a plaintive melody telling of the return to the fold of a repentant sinner. II. *Nigun* (Melody) is an improvised song in the style of a cantorial chant of the synagogue. III. *Simchas Torah.* "Simchas Torah" is a Hebrew holiday celebrating the delivery of the Torah to Moses and the Hebrew people. The Hasid celebrated this holiday with abandon, which spirit has been caught in Bloch's music.

Baba-Yaga. Fairy tale for orchestra by Anatol Liadov, op. 56 (1904). The composer wrote three fairy tales ("tableaux musicaux"). The other two are *The Enchanted Lake* and *Kikimora.* Baba-Yaga is a witch who inhabits a hut surrounded by a fence made up of human bones. Her flight through the air is realistically portrayed in the sweeping rhythms and soaring melodies of Liadov's music.

Bacchanale. An orgiastic dance of no special form performed by a corps de ballet. The bacchanales from Saint-Saëns' *Samson and Delilah* and Wagner's *Tannhäuser,* both operas, are often presented at symphony concerts.

Bacchantes. *See:* Euripides.

Bacchus and Ariadne (Bacchus et Ariane). Ballet suites for orchestra by Albert Roussel, op. 43 (1930), derived from his ballet score. The ballet, scenario by Abel Hermant, was introduced in Paris on May 22, 1931. It describes festivities on the island of Naxos attending Theseus, slayer of the Minotaur, and his beloved, Ariadne. During this celebration, Bacchus seizes Ariadne, who then forgets Theseus and abandons herself to her new lover.

Roussel prepared two suites from his ballet score, the second of which is the one more often performed. This second suite was introduced in Paris under Charles Munch's direction on Nov. 26, 1936. The published score provides the following programmatic note: "Introduction. Awakening of Ariadne. She looks around her, surprised. She rises, runs about looking for Theseus and his companions. She realizes that she has been abandoned. She climbs with difficulty to the top of the rock. She is about to throw herself in the stream. She falls into the arms of Bacchus, who has appeared from behind a boulder. Bacchus resumes with the awakened Ariadne the dance of her dreaming. Bacchus dances alone. The Dionysiac spell. A group marches past. A faun and a bacchante present to Ariadne the golden cup into which a cluster of grapes has been pressed. Dance of Ariadne. Dance of Ariadne and Bacchus. Bacchanale."

Bach, Carl Philipp Emanuel, composer. Born Weimar, Germany, March 8, 1714; died Hamburg, Germany, Dec. 14, 1788. The second son of Johann Sebastian Bach (and Maria Barbara), Carl Philipp Emanuel had only a single music teacher, his father. His academic education took place at the Thomasschule in Leipzig and at the University in Frankfort-on-the-Oder. In the latter city he founded a choral group that introduced some of his early works. When he was twenty-four he settled in Berlin, where he devoted himself to playing the clavier and to composition. In 1740 he was engaged by Frederick the Great as court musician, a post he retained for 27 years. In 1767 Bach became cantor of the Johanneum in Hamburg, and directed music in several other Hamburg churches.

Carl Philipp's clavier virtuosity and his more than 700 compositions were so famous that in his lifetime, and for some years thereafter, whenever the name of Bach was mentioned it was he who was meant, and not his now more celebrated father. A sound workman with a respect for formal structure, Carl Philipp Emanuel filled his music with fresh lyrical ideas and ingratiating harmonies. He was a significant historic figure in the transition period from the polyphonic era preceding him to the homophonic era that followed. He was probably the most important composer of piano music of his generation. In helping to crystallize the sonata form and the *galant* style of writing for the piano, his influence on both Haydn and Mozart was profound, as both of them freely acknowledged. Bach's musical output embraces 18 symphonies, 52 concertos for piano (or clavier) and orchestra, together with many other concertos for solo instruments and orchestra; almost 100 trios; numerous sonatas for two instruments and accompaniment; over 70 sonatas for clavier, the most famous found in the six sets entitled "For Connoisseurs and Amateurs"; and many smaller pieces for piano, the most popular being the *Solfeggietto*. Bach was also the author of a significant treatise on clavier playing, *Versuch ueber die wahre Art das Klavier zu spielen,* reissued in New York in 1949 as *Essay on the True Art of Playing Keyboard Instruments.*

See: Concerto—*C. P. E. Bach;* Sonata —*C. P. E. Bach.*

Bach, Johann Sebastian, composer. Born Eisenach, Germany, March 21, 1685; died Leipzig, Germany, July 28, 1750. For seven generations the Bachs were a family of professional musicians. Johann Sebastian was the youngest son of Johann Ambrosius, one of Eisenach's most highly regarded musicians, and Elisabeth Laemmerhirt. Since both parents died when Johann Sebastian was nine, the boy was adopted by his older brother, Johann Christoph, church organist. The five years the boy spent with his brother was a trying period since Johann Christoph was a miser and a tyrant. In 1700 the boy was freed from his brother's tyranny by becoming a choirboy in Lueneburg. He now dedicated himself passionately to musical activities by studying the violin, organ, and clavier, and writing his first compositions. On several occasions he walked miles on foot to hear musical performances—thirty miles to Hamburg for an organ recital by Johann Reinken, sixty miles to Celle for concerts of French music.

On Aug. 14, 1703, Bach was appointed

organist at Arnstadt. There he wrote his first church cantatas and some music for the clavier. He visited Luebeck to hear the organ and instrumental concerts arranged by Dietrich Buxtehude, Germany's eminent organist and composer. Inspired to imitation by Buxtehude, Bach would now often interpolate fanciful improvisations into his own organ performances, which disturbed the Arnstadt churchgoers no end. When Bach left Arnstadt to assume a new post in Muehlhausen, in 1707, there were few regrets at his departure. At this time, Bach married his cousin, Maria Barbara, on Oct. 17, 1707.

In 1708 Bach received his first major appointment: court organist and chamber musician to Duke Wilhelm Ernst in Weimar. He remained here nine years, a period in which he developed into one of the most distinguished organists of his time, particularly brilliant in the art of improvisation. It was during this period that Bach wrote many of his great organ works. Yet despite his formidable accomplishments, Bach was not appreciated either by his employer or by his fellow townspeople. His employer thought so little of him that he bypassed him when an appointment had to be made for Kapellmeister in 1716.

Bach's next post brought him in 1717 to Coethen, where for six years his duties required him to lead an orchestra and write music for the court concerts. A second great creative period now unfolded for Bach in which he completed many instrumental masterworks, including the *Brandenburg Concertos,* the orchestral suites, and most of his famous solo sonatas and suites.

Bach's first wife died at Coethen in the summer of 1720, after having borne him seven children (only four of whom survived). One year later Bach remarried. His second wife was Anna Magdalena Wuelcken (or Wilcken), daughter of the town trumpeter; she became the mother of 13 more Bach children.

Bach's last significant post was assumed in May 1723 when he was appointed cantor of the St. Thomas School (Thomasschule) in Leipzig. His duties included the playing of the organ, leading performances at church, and writing music for its services. He also trained the choir and taught a boy's class in Latin and music. Though his professional life was continually harassed by annoyances and conflicts with church and university authorities, he remained in Leipzig 27 years. Despite his many duties and severe personal problems he was able to create an incomparable repertory of choral music—cantatas, chorales, motets, as well as such gigantic works as the Mass in B minor, the *Passion According to St. John,* and the *Passion According to St. Matthew.*

Towards the end of his life, Bach suffered from failing eyesight. An operation performed by Dr. John Taylor (who had also operated on Handel) was unsuccessful, and blindness set in. Before his infirmity made him completely helpless, Bach worked tirelessly on the *Art of the Fugue* and his last 18 chorale preludes. Ten days before his death, his eyesight returned momentarily. But he was soon stricken again, this time by a paralytic stroke. Three days after his death he was buried in the churchyard of St. John in Leipzig. His grave was left unidentified, and its exact location long remained unknown. In 1894, when excavations were made to extend the church's foundations, Bach's remains were recovered and identified. They were then reburied in a sarcophagus beneath the church.

Although Bach was considered during his lifetime the finest organist of his day, his genius as a composer was recognized by very few for about 75 years. In that time there were several musicians (among whom were Mozart, Beethoven, and Mendelssohn) who admired him; but even they could not recognize the true magnitude of his genius since little of his enormous output was available. A revaluation of Bach's music first began to take place in 1829 when Mendelssohn led a performance of *The Passion According to St. Matthew*—the first such performance since the work had been introduced in Bach's day. Four years later, the *Passion According to St. John* was revived. In 1850, initiated by Schumann, the Bach Gesellschaft was formed in Leipzig to publish all of Bach's works. It took half a century and 46 volumes to complete this vast project, which finally succeeded in throwing the full light of recognition on the fabulous range of Bach's achievement. The formation of several Bach societies to promote performances of his music further helped to spread the gospel of Bach throughout Europe.

The reason why Bach's music remained so long buried in obscurity was that he had come at the end of a musical epoch, that of polyphony. During the last decades of Bach's life arose the dawn of the new era of homophony. Since Bach's music was mostly in a polyphonic style, his contemporaries and immediate successors considered him old-fashioned, a part of a dead tradition. But what a later generation came to realize, and what is universally accepted today, is that Bach's music is the summit of the polyphonic era. The techniques and structures of polyphony were brought by him to their ultimate development, yielding music so noble in thought, so majestic in concept, and so overpowering in creative force that its full impact on the music world, though belated, was cyclonic.

But Bach was not merely the apex of one epoch; he was also the base of another. While the flowering of homophony came after him, we find in his works a glimpse of the future. Page after page in Bach is filled with melodic writing of the highest inspiration, set against a harmonic accompaniment.

The following are Bach's principal instrumental compositions:

Chamber Music: 3 sonatas for unaccompanied violin; 3 partitas for unaccompanied violin; 6 sonatas, or suites, for unaccompanied cello; 6 sonatas for violin and clavier; 3 sonatas for cello and clavier; 3 sonatas for flute and clavier; 4 trio-sonatas; *The Musical Offering (Musikalisches Opfer)*.

Orchestra: 6 *Brandenburg Concertos;* 4 suites; various concertos for solo instruments and orchestra (violin, two violins, clavier, two, three, and four claviers, and others).

Organ. Little Organ Book (Orgelbuechlein), passacaglia, chorale preludes, toccatas, preludes, fugues, fantasias, and so forth.

Clavier (clavichord or harpsichord):

Chromatic Fantasy and Fugue; 6 *English Suites;* 6 *French Suites;* 6 Partitas; *Italian Concerto; Goldberg Variations; The Well-Tempered Clavier.*

See: *Art of the Fugue; Capriccio on the Departure of a Beloved Brother;* Chorale Prelude; *Christmas Oratorio;* Chromatic Fantasy and Fugue; Concerto —*J. S. Bach; English Suites;* Fantasia; French Suites; Fugue; *Goldberg Variations;* Inventions; *Italian Concerto; Little Notebook of Anna Magdalena; Little Organ Book;* Mass in B minor; *Musical Offering;* Partita; Passacaglia; *Passion According to St. John; Passion According to St. Matthew;* Sonata—*J. S. Bach;* Suite —*J. S. Bach;* Toccata; *Well-Tempered Clavier.*

Bach, John Christian, composer. Born Leipzig, Germany, Sept. 5, 1735; died London, England, Jan. 1, 1782. He was the youngest son of Johann Sebastian Bach (and Anna Magdalena), and was known as the "English Bach" because of his long residence and success in London. After his father's death, the boy, aged fifteen, lived in Berlin for four years and studied with his half-brother, Carl Philipp Emanuel. In 1756, John Christian left for Italy. There he studied with Padre Martini, was converted to Catholicism, and devoted himself to the study and writing of ecclesiastical music. He also wrote and had produced many operas which made him so famous that, in 1762, he was called to London to write for the Italian Opera. His success there brought him, a year later, the post of music master to the Queen, which he retained until his death. Like his half-brother, Carl Philipp Emanuel, John Christian was a prolific composer. His vast output includes almost 50 symphonies, 31 *sinfonie concertante,* 13 overtures, and 37 concertos for clavier and orchestra; also numerous works for various chamber-music combinations and 38 sonatas for the clavier. While less inventive and original than his half-brother, he was nevertheless a significant forerunner of Haydn and Mozart in clarifying the sonata form and establishing the Classic style.

Bach, Wilhelm Friedemann, composer. Born Weimar, Germany, Nov. 22, 1710; died Berlin, Germany, July 1, 1784. He was the second child and oldest son of Johann Sebastian (and Maria Barbara). At ten he began studying music with his father; then, for a year, he was a violin pupil of Johann Gottlieb Graun. His academic education took place at the Lutheran School in Coethen, and at the Leipzig University. From 1733 to 1747 he was organist of the Sophienkirche in Dresden, and from 1747 to 1764 at the Marienkirche in Halle. A proud, impulsive, and somewhat eccentric man, Wilhelm Friedemann deserted the last post because he felt he was not sufficiently appreciated. From 1774 to the end of his life he lived in Berlin, where he taught music and gave organ concerts. Like his brothers, Carl Philipp Emanuel and John Christian, he was a fertile composer; and, like them, he helped usher in the age of homophony with instrumental works in which the sonata form was established and the art of melodic writing advanced. His compositions included 9 symphonies, 5 clavier concertos together with other concertos for solo instruments and orchestra, trios, 9 clavier sonatas and many smaller keyboard pieces including fantasias, fugues, and preludes.

Bachauer, Gina, pianist. Born Athens, Greece, May 21, 1913. She was graduated from the Athens Conservatory with honors, then studied the piano with Alfred Cortot and Rachmaninoff. In 1933 she won the Gold Medal of Honor in an international competition for pianists in Vienna. Her début as a mature artist took place with the Athens Symphony in 1935, after which she made many appearances in her native land, France, and Italy. During World War II she gave over 600 concerts for the armed forces in the Near East. Her return to the professional concert stage, and her début in England, took place simultaneously on Jan. 21, 1946 when she appeared as soloist with the New London Symphony directed by Alec Sherman, whom she married in 1951. Her American début took place in New York on Oct. 29, 1950.

Bachaus (or **Backhaus**), **Wilhelm,** pianist. Born Leipzig, Germany, March 26, 1884. For five years he attended the Leipzig Conservatory, then studied privately with Eugène d'Albert. His concert career was launched in 1900. In 1905 he won the Rubinstein Prize; and on January 5, 1912 he made his American début as soloist with the New York Symphony. After World War I, he toured the music world, achieving international recognition as a trenchant interpreter of Classic and Romantic German music, particularly that of Beethoven and Brahms. He remained in Germany during World War II, but after the war settled in Switzerland. He returned to the United States for a tour in 1954 after an absence of 28 years.

Bachianas Brasileiras. Nine suites, mostly for orchestra, by Heitor Villa-Lobos (1930-1945). The "Bachiana Brasileira" is a form devised by the composer to combine the style of Johann Sebastian Bach with the personality of Brazilian folk music.

The second and fifth are perhaps the most popular. The second (1930), for orchestra, is in four movements: I. Prelude, or *Song of the Hoodlum;* II. Aria, or *Song of Our Country;* III. Danza, or *Woodland Memory;* IV. Toccata, or *The Little Train of Caipira.* Of special interest here are the second and fourth movements. The former is a tender folksong for solo cello, and the latter a realistic picture of a little train coursing through the Brazilian countryside.

The fifth (1938-1945), for voice and an orchestra of cellos, has two parts: I. Aria; II. Danza. The Aria is one of the most popular pieces by the composer: a three-part song in which the flanking parts consist of a sensual folk melody sung merely to the syllable "ah"; the middle part, which has a text, is more virile. Seven years after writing this Aria, the composer added to it the rhythmic Danza as a contrast.

The other *Bachianas Brasileiras* are: No. 1, for orchestra (1930); No. 3, for piano and orchestra (1938); No. 4, for piano solo (1930-1936); No. 6, for flute and bassoon (1938); No. 7, for orchestra (1942); No. 8, for orchestra (1944); No. 9, for vocal orchestra (1945).

Backhaus, Wilhelm. *See:* Bachaus, Wilhelm.

Badinerie (or **Badinage**). A trifle, frivolity. A piece of music in a frivolous vein, often in quick 2/4 time. It was occasionally used as a concluding movement of the Baroque suite, as in Bach's Suite in B minor, for orchestra.

Badura-Skoda, Paul, pianist. Born Vienna, Austria, Oct. 6, 1927. He studied the piano with Otto Schulhoff, Viola Therns, and Edwin Fischer, besides attending the Vienna Conservatory for two years. In 1947 he won the Austrian Music Competition which, in June of that year, brought him a début performance with the Vienna Symphony. In 1948 he won the Bartók Competition in Budapest, and in 1949 the International Music Competition in Paris. In 1949 he made successful appearances with the Vienna Philharmonic. In 1950-1951 he toured Italy, Scandinavia, and England; in 1952, Australia; and, in 1953, South America. During this period he was acclaimed at the Salzburg Festival and the Bach Festival in Vienna. His North American début took place in Toronto, Canada, on Nov. 1, 1952. His first appearance in the United States came six days later with the Cincinnati Symphony.

Bagatelle. A trifle, a brief musical composition for the piano, slight in content. This term first assumed prominence with Beethoven, who wrote 27 such piano pieces, unpretentious structurally and esthetically. His most famous bagatelle (sometimes also designated as an Albumblatt) is *Fuer Elise* (1810), a piece familiar to piano students everywhere. Saint-Saëns wrote a set of six Bagatelles, op. 3 (1856). Many contemporary composers have written bagatelles for the piano. Among them are Jean Absil (op. 61), Béla Bartók (Fourteen Bagatelles, op. 6), Ernst Dohnányi (*Winterreigen*, op. 13), Paul Juon (Eight Easy Bagatelles, op. 36), Vietezslav Novák (op. 5), Alan Rawsthorne, and Sibelius (Six Bagatelles, op. 97).

Anton Webern wrote Six Bagatelles, for string quartet, op. 9 (1913), in his characteristic atonal style. Each is a miniature; the longest takes only about a minute to perform, while the shortest is of only a few seconds' duration. In each there is a passing suggestion of a thematic subject rather than a fully developed melodic idea.

Bailly, Louis, violist. Born Valenciennes, France, June 13, 1882. He was graduated from the Paris Conservatory, then founded and played in the Capet Quartet. From 1917 to 1924 he was violist of the Flonzaley Quartet. After 1924 he played with the Elman and Curtis String Quartets. He also gave recitals, and appeared as soloist with major orchestras. In 1925 he joined the faculty of the Curtis Institute, and remained there many years. After World War II he made his home in Canada, where he joined the faculty of the Pelletier School of Music in Montreal.

Baiser de la fée, Le (Stravinsky). *See: Fairy's Kiss, The.*

Balakirev, Mily, composer. Born Nizhny-Novgorod, Russia, Jan. 2, 1837; died St. Petersburg, Russia, May 29, 1910. He helped found, and was a significant member of, the famous national school of Russian music, "The Five." He demonstrated unusual ability for music from childhood on as a student of several teachers, including John Field. In 1853 he entered the University of Kazan as a student of mathematics. While a University student, he earned his living for two years teaching music. In the autumn of 1855 he went to St. Petersburg, where he decided to devote himself completely to musical activity. A meeting with Glinka, father of Russian nationalism, infected him with enthusiasm for Russian folk music and aroused in him the ambition to write music of national character. He succeeded in transferring his own ideals and ambitions to four other Russian composers—Cui, Mussorgsky, Rimsky-Korsakov, and Borodin. They banded together for the common aim of producing music in the style of folk songs and dances, and inspired by Russian culture and backgrounds. On May 24, 1867, Balakirev led a concert in St. Petersburg devoted mainly to the music of these five composers, and it was on this occasion that the Russian critic, Vladimir Stassov, dubbed them "The Mighty Five."

Meanwhile, in 1862, Balakirev made a trip to the Caucasus; the folk music he found there he soon utilized for several major works, including *Russia* and *Tamara,* for orchestra, and *Islamey,* for piano. In 1862 he was appointed assistant director of the Free School of Music in St. Petersburg (becoming its director in 1868); and in 1863 he became conductor of the Free School Orchestra. From 1883 to 1885 he was conductor of the Court Chapel. Long a sufferer from emotional disturbances, and at one time the victim of a nervous breakdown, Balakirev became after 1895 a recluse, obsessed by religious mania.

He was more significant as an influence than as a composer. As the founder of the Russian national school, and as the one who stimulated and gave direction to his fellow composers, he played a major role in the development of Russian music. A few of his works are happy realizations of this national ideal, but it was left to his colleagues to achieve significance and greatness with Russian folk idioms. Besides compositions already mentioned, Balakirev wrote 2 symphonies, 2 piano concertos, several overtures, an octet, a septet, a string quartet, Sonata in B-flat minor for piano, and smaller piano pieces including mazurkas, nocturnes, waltzes, scherzos.

Balakirev issued a collection of 40 Russian folksongs in 1866, and edited the works of Glinka.

See: Islamey; Russia; Tamara.

Ballad of Reading Gaol. Tone poem for orchestra by Jacques Ibert (1921), introduced in Paris on Oct. 22, 1922, Gabriel Pierné conducting. Its source was Wilde's poem describing the abuses inflicted upon inmates of an English prison. The composer's first successful composition, it is in three episodes played without interruption. The first is as light and gay as the steps of the prisoner allegedly were in Wilde's opening lines. The second episode is filled with arabesques as the condemned man is haunted by fantasies and visions. The last part is a tragic prayer for a man about to meet his doom.

Ballade. A composition, usually for the piano, which has the narrative character of a ballad. Without having a specific program, it appears to be telling a story. There exist some examples of ballades for orchestra: for example, Hamish MacCunn's *The Ship o' the Fiend* and Sir Arthur Somervelle's *Helen of Kirkconnel.*

Henri Vieuxtemps wrote a *Ballade and Polonaise* for violin and piano, op. 38. Nevertheless, since Chopin, the ballade has been favored for the piano. The following are some of the most significant of such ballades.

BRAHMS. Four ballades are gathered in op. 10 (1854); a fifth is found in *Six Pieces,* op. 118 (1893). The first Ballade, in D minor, is based on the famous Scottish ballad, *Edward.* The Ballades in D major and B major, op. 10, nos. 2 and 4, are contemplative in mood; those in B minor, op. 10, no. 3, and G minor, op. 118, no. 3, are dramatic and stormy.

CHOPIN. All four ballades by Chopin are believed to have been inspired by poems of Adam Mickiewicz, Polish patriot, but the precise source of the fourth ballade has never been identified. One of the finest of these ballades is No. 1 in G minor, op. 23 (1835), based on *Konrad Valenrod.* It depicts the battle of the Christian Knights and pagan Lithuanians. Schumann considered it the "most daring, the most spirited" of Chopin's works. The second Ballade, in F major, op. 38 (1839), inspired by *Le Lac de Willis,* is marked by dramatic contrasts between tenderness and passionate conflicts. The third, in A-flat major, op. 47 (1841), is derived from *Undine,* and has a beautiful lyrical section. To James Gibbons Huneker, the fourth, in F minor, op. 52 (1842), had "irresistible . . . witchery." It boasts a long, expansive melodic line.

FAURÉ. The Ballade in F-sharp major, op. 19 (1881), is poetic and contemplative. It originated as a composition for piano solo, but the composer later adapted it for piano and orchestra, the version in which it is more familiar. In the adaptation the work's serenity and classic repose profits from Fauré's delicate and graceful instrumentation.

GRIEG. The Ballade in G minor, op. 24 (1875), is one of the composer's masterworks for piano solo. It consists of a beautiful Norwegian melody, which is subjected to variation treatment.

LISZT. The Ballades in D-flat major and B minor (1853) contrast affecting lyricism with rhythmic strength, and are in the composer's popular theatrical style.

Ballet mécanique. *See:* Antheil, George.

Bal martiniquais, Le. Suite for orchestra by Darius Milhaud (1944), first performed by the New York Philharmonic under the composer's direction on Dec. 5, 1945. Based on Martinique folk lore, *Le Bal martiniquais* derives its musical material from the folk tunes of the French West Indies. There are two sections: I. Chanson Creole, a slow folk melody; II. Beguine, a dynamic dance similar to the rhumba. This orchestral composition originated as two songs carrying the single title of *La Libération des Antilles.* Before orchestrating it, the composer had adapted the two songs for two pianos.

Baltimore Symphony Orchestra. An orchestra founded in Baltimore, Maryland, in 1916 under a municipal subsidy. Its first concert took place on Feb. 11, 1916, under Gustave Strube, who remained conductor until 1930. Since then the principal conductors have been George Siemonn, Ernest Schelling, Howard Barlow, Werner Janssen, Reginald Stewart, and Massimo Freccia.

Bamberg Symphony Orchestra. An orchestra founded in Bamberg, Germany, soon after the end of World War II, comprising former members of the Prague Philharmonic. Hans Knappertsbusch and Clemens Krauss were its first conductors. Joseph Kleiberth has been one of the principal conductors since 1949. The orchestra made a successful tour of England in 1957.

Band. An instrumental group. In the United States the term is usually applied to an ensemble made up either entirely or largely of wind instruments.

Bantock, Sir Granville, composer. Born London, England, Aug. 7, 1868; died there, Oct. 16, 1946. He entered the Royal Academy of Music in 1889; after a single term he became the first recipient of the Macfarren Scholarship for composition. After leaving the Academy he founded and edited *The New Quarterly Musical Review;* he also conducted orchestras in the provinces. Beginning in 1897 he led the Tower Orchestra in New Brighton for four years, his programs helping to promote new English music. In 1898 he founded the New Brighton Choral Society, and a few years later he became conductor of the Liverpool Philharmonic. In 1900 he was appointed principal of the Birmingham Music Institute, and in 1907 professor of music at Birmingham University. He was knighted in 1933.

Bantock first attracted notice as a composer with an overture, *Pierrot of the Minute.* Oriental and Scottish influences were important in his style after that. His writing was sensuous and at times exotic, with rich harmonies and a spacious lyricism. He wrote several symphonies (including the *Hebridean, Pagan,* and *Celtic*); 6 tone poems; 4 poems for cello and orchestra; various shorter orchestral compositions (including *Scottish Rhapsody, Pierrot of the Minute, Comedy Overture for The Frogs, Overture to a Greek Comedy, Two Heroic Ballads, Comedy Overture to The Birds, Old English Suite,* and *Four Chinese Landscapes*); sonatas for solo instruments (violin, cello, viola) and piano; String Quartet in C minor; and various compositions for the piano (including *Twelve Silhouettes, Dramatic Lyrics and Romances, Twelve Dramatic Poems, Arabian Nights,* and *Memories of Sapphire*).

Bar. A measure.

Barber, Samuel, composer. Born West Chester, Pa., March 9, 1910. The nephew of Louise Homer, Metropolitan Opera contralto, Barber revealed his musical precociousness by writing piano pieces when he was seven, and at twelve performing the organ at church services. In his fourteenth year he entered the Curtis Institute; in 1928 he received the Bearns Prize for composition. In 1932 he completed his first orchestral work, the *Overture to The School for Scandal;* in 1935 the New York Philharmonic introduced his *Music for a Scene from Shelley.* Between 1935 and 1937 he received the Pulitzer Traveling Scholarship twice as well as the American Prix de Rome. In Italy he completed his Symphony in One Movement, introduced in Rome in 1936 and one year later becoming the first American work performed at the Salzburg Festival. Toscanini introduced two Barber orchestral works in 1938 with the NBC Symphony: Adagio for Strings and Essay for Orchestra, No. 1. During World War II, Barber served in the Air Force, which commissioned him to write his Second Symphony. After the war he received a Guggenheim Fellowship, and the New York Music Critics Circle Award for his Cello Concerto. In 1947 and 1948 he was a consultant at the American Academy in Rome. In 1958 he received the Pulitzer Prize in music for his opera, *Vanessa*, introduced that year by the Metropolitan Opera and performed that summer at the Salzburg Festival. He also received in 1958 the Henry Hadley medal from the National Association for American Composers and Conductors for "exceptional services to American music."

Barber has written 2 symphonies, 2 Essays for Orchestra, a violin concerto, a cello concerto, *Capricorn Concerto* for flute, oboe, trumpet, and strings, various shorter works for orchestra (*Overture to The School for Scandal, Music for a Scene from Shelley,* Adagio for Strings, *Souvenirs,* ballet suite from *Medea*); also a string quartet, a serenade for string quartet, a sonata for cello and piano, *Summer Music* for woodwind quintet, and a sonata and *Excursions,* for the piano.

He allows himself to be disciplined by traditional forms and idioms, but without smothering his natural romantic impulses. Most of his music is lyrical, emotional, poetic; in his later works modern techniques and idioms are successfully employed.

See: Adagio for Strings; Concerto—*Barber;* Essay for Orchestra, Nos. 1 and 2; *Medea,* ballet suite; *Music for a Scene from Shelley;* Sonata—*Barber;* Symphony—*Barber.*

Barber of Seville, Overture to The (Il Barbiere di Siviglia). Overture to the opera buffa classic by Rossini. The opera was introduced in Rome on Feb. 20, 1816; the libretto, by Cesare Sterbini, was based on *Le Barbier de Seville* and *Le Mariage de Figaro,* both by Beaumarchais. The vivacious overture is so completely in the happy spirit of the comic opera that it comes as a shock to learn it had been written for another of Rossini's operas, and had been used by the composer for several other stage works, tragedies as well as comedies. A slow introduction highlights a melody for violins. Four chords then lead to the

main section whose principal theme is a vivacious little tune for strings doubled by piccolo. A second subject is also gay; it is first presented in oboe and clarinet, and then by a horn. A Rossini crescendo leads to the development of both themes, and the overture ends with a spirited coda.

Barbirolli, Sir John, conductor. Born London, England, Dec. 2, 1899. When he was eleven he made his début as a cellist in London. In 1912 he received a scholarship for the Royal Academy of Music, where he remained five years specializing in the cello. He later became a cellist of the Queen's Hall Orchestra. After World War I, he toured Europe with the International String Quartet. In 1925 he founded and directed the Barbirolli Chamber Orchestra, and in 1926 he appeared as conductor of the British National Opera. Appearances with the Royal Philharmonic of London and the London Symphony led to his appointment as principal conductor of the Scottish Orchestra. From then until 1937 he led not only that orchestra but also the Northern Philharmonic, and from 1937 to 1943 he was conductor of the Leeds Symphony. From 1936 to 1941 he was principal conductor of the New York Philharmonic, in succession to Toscanini, at whose recommendation he had been engaged. From 1943 to 1958 he was music director of the Hallé Orchestra in Manchester which he helped to reorganize. He was knighted in 1949, and a year later received a gold medal from the Royal Philharmonic of London. On Dec. 29, 1958, he returned as a guest conductor to the New York Philharmonic after an absence of over 17 years to begin a fourteen-week American tour. Barbirolli adapted music by Pergolesi into a Concerto for Oboe and Orchestra, and several pieces from the *Fitzwilliam Virginal Book* into the *Elizabethan Suite,* for orchestra.

Barcarolle. A boat song of Venetian gondoliers, originally a vocal form, but subsequently adapted for piano music. Its main characteristic is a melody in slow 6/8 time, its rhythm simulating the swaying of the gondola in the water.

Chopin's Barcarolle in F-sharp minor, op. 60 (1846), is his only composition in this form, and is popular. Fauré wrote 13 barcarolles, the best of which are No. 2 in G major, op. 41 (1885), and No. 4 in A-flat major, op. 44 (1886). Anton Rubinstein wrote two fine barcarolles: in F minor, op. 30, no. 1, and G minor, op. 50, no. 3. One of Tchaikovsky's best-loved piano pieces, *June*—the sixth number in the suite, *The Months*, op. 37a (1876)—is also a barcarolle; it has been transcribed for orchestra, for string quartet, and for two pianos. The popular Barcarolle from Act 2 of Offenbach's opera, *The Tales of Hoffmann*, appears in various instrumental transcriptions: orchestra, violin and piano, cello and piano, piano solo, and organ.

Barer, Simon, pianist. Born Odessa, Russia, Sept. 1, 1896; died New York City, April 2, 1951. He attended the St. Petersburg Conservatory—a pupil of Annette Essipov and Felix Blumenfeld—winning the Rubinstein Prize in 1918. He then launched his first concert tour. In 1929 he left Russia and settled in Berlin. He made his London début in 1934, and his American début in New York on Nov. 9, 1936. He died of a heart attack while performing the Grieg Piano Concerto on the stage of Carnegie Hall.

Barlow, Howard, conductor. Born Plain City, Ohio, May 1, 1892. While pursuing his academic education, he studied music privately with various teachers, principally the piano with Cornelius Rybner. In 1919 he made his début as conductor in Peterboro, N.H. In 1927 he was appointed conductor of the CBS Symphony. His association with radio continued from that time on, first as musical director of the Columbia Broadcasting System until 1943, then as conductor of the Firestone Hour over radio and then television. From 1939 to 1943 he was conductor of the Baltimore Symphony, and from 1943 to 1945 a conductor of the New York Philharmonic.

Baroque Style. A highly ornamented and predominantly contrapuntal style of composition that governed music between the late 16th and early 18th centuries. The second quarter of the 18th century saw the final fulfillment of the Baroque style and the beginning of the *galant* style. Domenico Scarlatti, Johann Sebastian Bach, and Handel were the last great figures in Baroque music.

Barque sur l'océan, Une (Ravel). *See: Miroirs.*

Barraud, Henry, composer. Born Bordeaux, France, April 23, 1900. In 1926 he entered the Paris Conservatory, where he was a pupil of Paul Dukas and Louis Aubert. Barraud first came to prominence as a composer in Paris in the middle 1930's, with performances of his *Poème* and the *Concerto da Camera*, both for orchestra. In 1937 he served as director of music at the Paris Exposition, and in the same year he led several performances at the Opéra-Comique. During World War II he served in the French army. After the defeat of France, he was a member of the Resistance movement. His war experiences led to the writing of one of his principal orchestral works, *Offrande à une ombre*. After the liberation of France he became director of music of the Radiodiffusion Française. Barraud's most effective musical writing has been in a neo-gothic vein, with a strong leaning towards quasi-archaic melodies and modal harmonies. Besides works already mentioned he wrote 3 symphonies, a piano concerto, *Suite pour un comédie de Musset* for orchestra, preludes for strings, a string quartet, two series of piano preludes, and impromptus for piano.

Barrère, Georges, flutist. Born Bordeaux, France, Oct. 31, 1876; died Kingston, New York, June 14, 1944. He attended the Paris Conservatory, then began his professional career as a member of the Modern Society of Wind Instruments. After playing the flute in the Colonne Orchestra and in the orchestra of the Paris Opéra, he came to the United States in 1905 and from then until 1928 was first flutist of the New York Symphony. During this period he appeared as soloist with the orchestra; organized and played in the Ensemble of Wood Instruments; and founded and conducted the Barrère Little Symphony. In 1937 he played with the Barrère-Britt Concertino. He was decorated with the order of Chevalier of the Legion of Honor in 1934.

Barrie, Sir James, playwright and novelist. Born Kirriemuir, Scotland, May 9,

1860; died Scotland, June 19, 1937. His famous fantasy for children, *Peter Pan,* was the inspiration for a tone poem by Ernst Toch and a string quartet by Sir Henry Walford Davies; Fini Henriques and Leonard Bernstein wrote incidental music for it. Lehman Engel wrote incidental music for *A Kiss for Cinderella;* Sir Alexander Mackenzie, for *The Little Minister;* and Norman O'Neill for *Mary Rose, A Kiss for Cinderella,* and *Quality Street.*

Bartered Bride, Overture to The (Prodána Nevěsta). Overture to the Bohemian folk opera by Smetana, with libretto by Karel Sabina. It was introduced in Prague on May 30, 1866. The lively overture opens with the first theme in violins, violas, cellos, and woodwind in unison, against accompanying chords in brass and timpani. After this subject has been developed fugally, carried to a climax, and repeated, a brief second theme is heard in the oboe. A melodious idea is then presented by violins and cellos, whereupon the first theme is repeated, elaborated upon, and makes its final appearance in the coda.

For other orchestral excerpts from the opera see *Dance of the Comedians,* Furiant, Polka.

Bartlett and Robertson. A duo-piano team made up of Ethel Bartlett and Rae Robertson, in private life wife and husband. Ethel Bartlett was born in London, England, on June 6, 1900; Rae Robertson, in Inverness, Scotland, on Nov. 29, 1898. They met as students at the Royal Academy of Music in London and were married in 1923. In 1927 they began their professional career as a two-piano team, one of the first to give such concerts in England. They made their American début in 1928, after which they toured the world. Many composers wrote major works for them including Arnold Bax, Arthur Bliss, Cyril Scott, Alexander Tansman, and William Walton. The partnership was dissolved with the death of Robertson in Los Angeles, California, on November 4, 1956, after which Ethel Bartlett devoted herself to teaching the piano.

Bartók, Béla, composer. Born Nagyszentmiklos, Hungary, March 25, 1881; died New York City, Sept. 26, 1945. He completed writing a set of piano pieces when he was nine, and a year later made a local début as pianist. In 1894 the family moved to Bratislava, where he studied piano with László Erkel. From 1899 to 1903 he attended the Budapest Music Academy; while still a student he wrote a patriotic symphony, *Kossuth.*

After leaving the Academy, Bartók supported himself by teaching the piano and making transcriptions. During this period he first interested himself in Hungarian folk music, making in 1905 the first of several trips to remote regions of his country in search of folksongs. In time he discovered a wealth of indigenous folksongs and dances, unknown to the rest of the world, which he edited and helped publish.

This immersion in Hungary's folk music influenced his creative development. Before 1905 he wrote mostly in a Romantic vein, influenced by Brahms, Liszt, and Richard Strauss. After 1905 he evolved a personal identity by absorbing many of the attributes of Hungarian folk music. His style became complex and discordant, rhythmically barbaric, exotic in its use of unusual scales. The strangeness of his writing kept his music from general acceptance. For many years he labored in obscurity, earning his living as professor of the piano at the Music Academy. He served as his own propagandist by touring Europe as piano soloist in his own works; he paid his first visit to the United States in 1927. Gradually, he managed to win the approval of discriminating musicians; but the general public remained aloof for a long time.

When World War II erupted in Europe, Bartók made his home in the United States. For a while he was engaged by Columbia University to do research there. These were unhappy years for him. Forced to live and work in a strange land, he felt isolated and lonely. Most of the time he was also suffering physically from leukemia. The fact that so few of his works were performed was a continual source of frustration. Yet, despite such unhappy circumstances, he was able to complete several major works: various concertos for solo instruments and orchestra or for orchestra alone. Here emotion and poetic feeling brought a new humanity to his formerly recondite style. These last works did much to establish Bartók's fame with the general public, almost immediately following his death.

Bartók's principal instrumental compositions are the following:

Chamber Music: 6 string quartets; 2 sonatas for violin and piano; 2 rhapsodies for violin and piano; *Contrasts* for violin, clarinet, and piano; Sonata for violin solo.

Orchestra: Dance Suite; Music for Strings, Percussion, and Celesta; Divertimento; 3 concertos for piano and orchestra; Concerto for Violin and Orchestra; Concerto for Viola and Orchestra; Concerto for Orchestra.

Piano: Mikrokosmos; Sonata; bagatelles, elegies, sketches, rondos, studies.

See: Concerto—*Bartók;* Divertimento; Dance Suite; *Mikrokosmos;* Music for Strings, Percussion, and Celesta; Quartet —*Bartók;* Rhapsody.

Baruffe Chiozzotte, Le, Overture (*The Quarrels of the People of Chiozza*). Concert overture by Leone Sinigaglia, op. 32 (1907), introduced in Milan under Toscanini's direction in the spring of 1907. It was based on the famous 18th-century comedy by Carlo Goldoni. This spirited piece of music opens with an ebullient subject for full orchestra. A serene subsidiary idea then provides contrast. The second main theme is a folksong first heard in the oboe, then in the first violins. As the tempo quickens, the music grows increasingly vivacious; the woodwind and violins treat a chattering figure with amusing effect. The return first of the song, and then of the first theme, leads to a brief concluding coda.

Barzin, Leon, conductor. Born Brussels, Belgium, Nov. 27, 1900. He came to the United States as an infant. After studying with private teachers in America and Europe—and principally the violin with Eugène Ysaÿe—he became in 1919 a violinist in the New Symphony Orchestra in New York. When this organization merged with the New York Philharmonic two years later, Barzin became assistant solo violist, and in 1925 solo violist. He left the orchestra in 1929 to become assistant conductor of the American Orchestral Association. When this orchestra was reorganized, and renamed the National Orchestral Association, Barzin became its principal conductor, holding this post until 1958. From 1938 to 1940 he was principal conductor of the Hartford Symphony and from 1948 to 1958 principal conductor of the New York City Ballet. In 1958 Barzin went to live in Paris, where he became a conductor of the Pasdeloup Orchestra.

Barzun, Jacques, historian and writer on music. Born Paris, France, Nov. 30, 1907. He came to the United States when he was twelve, and since then has become an American citizen. He was graduated from Columbia University in 1927, and in 1932 received there his doctorate in history. In 1927 he joined the history department at Columbia. In 1958 he was appointed Provost of the University. He is the author of *Berlioz and the Romantic Century* (1950) and *Music in American Life* (1956), editor of *New Letters of Berlioz* (1954), and translator of Berlioz's *Evenings with the Orchestra* (1956). His book *Darwin, Marx, Wagner: Critique of a Heritage* (1941) has a section on Wagner, while *Romanticism and the Modern Ego* (1943) contains significant material on the Romantic movement in music.

Basel Chamber Orchestra. *See:* Sacher, Paul.

Basel Concerto. *See:* Concerto—*Stravinsky.*

Bass Viol (or Contrabass). *See:* Doublebass.

Basso Continuo (or Figured Bass). *See:* Thorough Bass.

Bassoon. The lowest in pitch of the woodwind instruments. It has a double reed and a double tube. The contrabassoon, or double bassoon, has the lowest pitch among bassoons.

Bate, Stanley Richard, composer. Born Plymouth, England, Dec. 12, 1911. He attended the Royal College of Music in London where his teachers included Vaughan Williams and Arthur Benjamin. A traveling scholarship enabled him to complete his music study in Paris with Nadia Boulanger and in Berlin with Paul Hindemith. He first attracted attention as composer with a Concertino for Piano and Orchestra and two ballets. In 1940-1941 he toured Australia as pianist. In 1942 he visited the United States, where he performed his Second Piano Concerto with the New York Philharmonic. In 1945 he gave several concerts of his own music in Brazil. His works include 4 symphonies, 2 sinfoniettas, 3 piano concertos, a cello concerto, a harpsichord concerto, 2 string quartets, various sonatas for solo instruments and piano, and 9 piano sonatinas.

Baton. A stick used by the conductor to beat time in directing an orchestra. The first successful use of the baton is attributed to Louis Spohr when he appeared as guest conductor of the Royal Philharmonic in London on March 6, 1820. *See:* Conducting.

Battery. The percussion instruments of an orchestra.

Battle Symphony, or **The Battle of Vittoria (Wellingtons Sieg,** oder **Die Schlacht bei Vittoria).** An orchestral composition (*not* a symphony) by Beethoven, op. 91 (1813), first performed in Vienna on Dec. 8, 1813. One of the composer's less distinguished works, this "symphony" is a programmatic composition in which are imitated the sounds of thundering cannon and firing muskets, and in which there appear quotations from such popular anthems as *God Save the King* and *Rule Britannia.* The work is divided into two sections: I. *The Battle;* II. *Victory Symphony.* The work was originally written for an instrument called the panharmonicon and invented by Maelzel—a mechanical brass band, the instruments being blown through a bellows, and the notes controlled by a revolving brass cylinder with pins.

Bauer, Harold, pianist. Born Kingston-on-Thames, England, April 28, 1873; died Miami, Florida, March 12, 1951. He began his professional career in music as a violinist after having studied with Adolf Pollitzer. In or about 1892 his interest shifted to the piano. He took some piano lessons with Graham Moore, then became a private pupil of Paderewski. In 1893 he toured Russia, then established his reputation with successful appearances in Madrid and Paris, and guest perform-

ances with the Concertgebouw and Berlin Philharmonic orchestras. He made his American début in December 1900 as soloist with the Boston Symphony. In 1914 he made America his permanent home, becoming a citizen seven years later. In 1918 he organized the Beethoven Association, which gave seasonal concerts of chamber music in New York; he remained its president until its dissolution in 1940. His tours as piano virtuoso carried him throughout the world; he was also a guest performer with leading chamber-music groups. A musician of highest ideals, he had a vast repertory ranging from 17th- and 18th-century music for harpsichord and clavichord to the works of moderns, particularly of Debussy, whom he helped to popularize. He transcribed numerous works for the piano and was the author of an autobiography, *Harold Bauer: His Book* (1948).

Bax, Sir Arnold, composer. Born London, England, Nov. 8, 1883; died Cork, Ireland, Oct. 3, 1953. For several years, beginning in 1900, he attended the Royal Academy of Music in London as a pupil of Tobias Matthay and Frederick Corder. Recognition as a composer first came in 1909, with the tone poem, *The Faery Hills,* the first of several works influenced by Celtic lore and Irish poetry. Other compositions, however, while not of Celtic inspiration, were equally Romantic in spirit and poetic in content. Bax was knighted in 1937, and in 1941 was named Master of the King's Music. He was the author of an autobiography, *Farewell My Youth* (1943). His compositions include 7 symphonies, a cello concerto, a violin concerto, various tone poems (including *The Faery Hills, The Garden of Fand, Tintagel, November Woods, The Tale the Pine Trees Knew, The Happy Forest*), various overtures (including *Romantic Overture, Overture to a Picaresque Comedy, Overture to Adventure,* and *Rogues' Comedy Overture*), 3 string quartets, 3 violin sonatas, 2 cello sonatinas, octet, oboe quintet, piano quintet, piano quartet, 4 piano sonatas, and many smaller pieces for the piano.

See: Overture to a Picaresque Comedy; Tintagel.

BBC Symphony. A symphony orchestra

created by the British Broadcasting Company in London during the 1930-1931 season with Adrian Boult as conductor. Boult remained principal conductor until 1950, when he was succeeded by Sir Malcolm Sargent. Rudolf Schwartz became conductor in 1957. The orchestra has made many tours of Europe and Scandinavia.

Beat. Pulsation, part of a measure.

Beck, Conrad, composer. Born Schaffhausen, Switzerland, June 16, 1901. He attended the Zurich Conservatory, then studied privately with Arthur Honegger and Ernst Lévy in Paris. In 1939 he became radio conductor in Basel. A neo-Classicist with a strong bent for contrapuntal writing, Beck has become a leading composer in Switzerland by virtue of his 6 symphonies, piano concerto, viola concerto, concerto for harpsichord and string orchestra, concertino for clarinet, bassoon, and orchestra, 4 string quartets, 2 violin sonatas, 2 cello sonatas, 2 string trios, and various pieces for the piano.

Beecham, Sir Thomas, conductor. Born St. Helens, England, April 29, 1879. He is the son of the wealthy manufacturer of Beecham's Pills. His musical training was haphazard. Except for some piano instruction at the Rossall School in Lancashire, and lessons in theory at Wadham College, Oxford, he was mostly self-taught. He left Oxford without a degree, after which he organized an amateur orchestra in Huyton. In the same town he made his professional début as conductor by substituting for Hans Richter with the Hallé Orchestra. In 1902 he became a conductor of the Kelson Truman Opera Company. After making his London début with the Queen's Hall Orchestra in 1905, he founded the New Symphony in London and the Beecham Symphony. With both organizations he was a powerful propagandist for English composers, and especially for Delius.

Between 1910 and 1919 Beecham devoted himself mainly to opera, first as founder of the Beecham Opera, then as director of Covent Garden. His personal fortune depleted by his varied musical activities, he announced his retirement from music in 1919. But four years later he returned to the baton with an orchestral performance in London. From this time on he was indefatigable in directing both operas and symphonic music in all parts of the world. His American début took place with the New York Philharmonic in 1928. In 1932 he founded the London Philharmonic and became artistic director of Covent Garden. Just before World War II he once again announced his retirement; once more it proved temporary. From 1941 to 1943 he was principal conductor of the Seattle Symphony, and in 1942 he made his début at the Metropolitan Opera in New York. Five years later he helped found a new symphony orchestra in London; he toured the United States with it in 1949. Besides being a remarkable conductor—an outstanding interpreter of Handel, Mozart, and Delius—Beecham has been a dynamic and at times provocative figure whose influence on music-making in England during the past half century can hardly be overestimated. For these services to English music he was knighted in 1914 and received a baronetcy in 1916. He is the author of an autobiography, *A Mingled Chime* (1943), and has adapted music by Handel into several orchestral suites, including *The Origin of Design, Il Pastor Fido Suite, The Great Elopement,* and *The Gods Go A-Begging.*

Beethoven, Ludwig van, composer. Born Bonn, Germany, Dec. 16, 1770; died Vienna, Austria, March 26, 1827. Ludwig's father, Johann, was a singer in the Electoral Chapel in Bonn. A drunkard and martinet, he subjected the child Beethoven to despotic discipline in an effort to train him into a musical *Wunderkind.* Ludwig's childhood, consequently, was unhappy, and was spent among scenes of drunkenness, in a setting of poverty, and with a ruthless father who subjected him to physical abuse. Nevertheless he made excellent progress in music, and was able to make a concert appearance when he was eight. But he was no Mozart; and Johann's efforts to reap financial rewards from his son's gifts proved unsuccessful.

In 1781 Beethoven acquired his first important teacher in Christian Gottlob

Neefe, court organist. Neefe recognized Beethoven's genius and stood ready to encourage and nurse it. When Beethoven was fourteen, Neefe appointed him his assistant as court organist, and one year later arranged for the boy to take over his post as cembalist at opera performances. "If he goes as he has begun," wrote Neefe in 1783, "he will certainly become a second Mozart."

In 1787 Neefe encouraged Beethoven to go to Vienna, then Europe's musical capital. Beethoven stayed only a few weeks, long enough to impress Mozart with his talent at improvisation. "You will some day make a big noise in the world," Mozart is reputed to have said. Beethoven might have remained longer in Vienna but for the fact that his mother was dying of tuberculosis. He was at her side when she died, her death robbing him of the only real tenderness he ever knew. After her death, Father Johann became so increasingly intemperate in his drinking that in 1789 he was dismissed from his chapel post. To Ludwig now fell the responsibility of supporting the family and maintaining some semblance of order at home. He worked at court and gave private lessons. He also wrote music which made an impression on such influential people in Bonn as the Breunings and the Waldsteins, who from that time on remained his devoted friends and patrons. Even Haydn was enthusiastic. Passing through Bonn on his way from London in 1792, Haydn saw the score of a Beethoven cantata. "You have great talent," the master told him, "and you must come to Vienna and study with me."

In November 1792 Beethoven left Bonn for good (his father died a few months later). He now settled permanently in Vienna, where he soon started studying with Haydn. But teacher and pupil did not get along. Beethoven's ungovernable genius, which played havoc with schoolbook rules, and his boorish manners upset the master. And to Beethoven, Haydn appeared too academic, too much the traditionalist. The young man turned to other teachers, principally to Johann Georg Albrechtsberger and Antonio Salieri; but the former, too, was intolerant of his independence of thought and iconoclasm.

Nevertheless, Beethoven made his way quickly in Vienna. In a few years' time he became one of its most famous musicians. In high places his genius was recognized—in the palaces of Prince Lobkowitz and Prince Lichnowsky, and the home of Baron van Swieten. He was also favored by titled people as a teacher of the piano; and as a composer he received many commissions. When he made his first public appearance in Vienna with two concerts, in March 1795, his improvisations led one critic to speak of him as "the giant among pianoforte players." At another Vienna concert, on April 20, 1800, Beethoven made his bow as symphonist with the première of his First Symphony.

He was a musician of considerable stature and even greater promise when tragedy struck hard. In 1801 Beethoven realized he was going deaf. His despair found expression in 1802 in the "Heiligenstadt Testament" (so called because it was written while the composer was living in Heiligenstadt, a suburb of Vienna). "For me," he wrote, giving voice to his immeasurable grief, "there can be no recreation in the society of my fellows, refined intercourse, mutual exchange of thought. . . . I must live like an exile." But despair gave way to resignation; and renunciation of society uncovered within him new spiritual resources. Separated from the world of sound, he found strength to put down on paper the turbulent music within his mind and heart, music like a hurricane breaking down the dykes of classical structures and conventions. A great creative period gradually unfolded for him. The period of apprenticeship was past. Now came a second period in which he became more daring in his harmonic writing, more expansive in his lyricism, freer and more spacious in his use of form, and most of all more personal and poetic in his expression. "I am now making a fresh start," he himself said and proceeded to produce masterwork after masterwork: the *Eroica*, Fourth, and Fifth symphonies; the *Appassionata, Moonlight,* and *Waldstein* piano sonatas; the *Kreutzer* violin sonata; the fourth piano concerto; the violin concerto; the Rasoumovsky Quartets. He was well aware of his giant powers. "With whom," he inquired, "need I be afraid of measuring my strength?"

As the years passed, and as silence enveloped him completely, he became increasingly arrogant, irritable, unreasonable in his demands on friends, suspicious, even insulting. Yet friends clung to him, forgave him his tantrums and insults, tolerated his moods and whims. Recognizing him as a Titan, they always stood ready to help him, and in 1809 some of them arranged for him a generous annual pension.

While he never lacked sympathetic friends, he never found a woman who could give herself completely to him. He was drawn to many women, often felt himself to be in love. The women he chose were generally out of his reach either because they were too young or too high in social station. The anguish of unrequited love is expressed in a document found in a secret drawer of his desk after his death. It is a letter to his "immortal beloved"—a flaming, poignant, and at times tortured love message in which he pours out his heart without restraint. Biographers have tried solving the mystery of this "immortal beloved." Was she Giulietta Guicciardi, to whom the composer dedicated his *Moonlight Sonata?* Or Theresa von Brunswick, for whom he wrote the *Appassionata?* Or the poetess friend of Goethe, Bettina Brentano? The mystery has never been solved, and there is reason to believe that the identity of the woman is unknown because Beethoven did not have any one woman in mind but was addressing himself to an imaginary love or to all womankind.

Between 1812 and 1818 Beethoven's demoniac creative drive slackened. But powers so long held in check were once again released, beginning with the *Hammerklavier Sonata,* for piano. A new creative period now began for Beethoven —his third, and in some respects his richest. The logic of his structures grew subtle and complex; his language became freed of convention as he allowed his style and technique full freedom of movement and expression. His poetic thinking acquired an almost other-worldly radiance and spirituality—new for music. This was the period of the *Missa Solemnis,* the *Ninth Symphony,* and the last piano sonatas and string quartets.

Beethoven's last public appearance took place in Vienna on May 7, 1824, when he led the première of his Ninth Symphony. In 1826 he contracted pneumonia which developed into dropsy and jaundice. In his sick bed he received gifts from different parts of Europe. He signed his will on March 23, 1827; received his last sacrament a day later; and after another day lapsed into unconsciousness. He died during a thunderstorm on March 26. On the day of his funeral (March 29) thousands lined the streets of Vienna to pay him their last respects.

Beethoven came at the dusk of the Classical era that had produced Haydn and Mozart. From their hands he received the forms of the symphony, concerto, quartet, and sonata, to which he brought formidable extension of structure, incomparable enrichment of harmonic and melodic language, and a new profundity of musical thought. Through Beethoven, music acquired a new concept of poetic, even philosophic, expression; a new capacity to express abstract ideas as well as feelings. Thus Beethoven not only helped bring one epoch to a magnificent conclusion, but he also helped to usher in the new era of Romanticism.

The following are Beethoven's principal instrumental works:

Chamber Music: 16 string quartets; *Grosse Fuge,* for string quartet; 4 piano quartets; 9 piano trios; 5 string trios; 10 sonatas for violin and piano; 5 sonatas for cello and piano; 2 wind octets; Septet in E-flat major; 3 string quintets.

Orchestra: 9 symphonies; 5 piano concertos; Concerto for Violin and Orchestra; Concerto for Violin, Cello, Piano, and Orchestra; 2 Romances, for violin and orchestra; *Coriolan Overture; Fidelio Overture; Leonore Overture,* Nos. 1, 2, 3; incidental music to *Egmont* (including the famous Overture); incidental music to *Prometheus* (including Overture); incidental music to *The Ruins of Athens* (including the popular *Turkish March*);

Consecration of the House Overture (Die Weihe des Hauses); minuets, laendler, contredanses, German dances.

Piano: 32 sonatas (also 6 easy sonatas and sonatinas); Variations on a Waltz by Diabelli; Thirty-Two Variations; *Andante Favori* in F major; bagatelles, ecossaises, rondos, waltzes.

See: Bagatelles; *Battle Symphony;* Choral Fantasy; Concerto—*Beethoven; Consecration of the House;* Contredanse; *Coriolan Overture; Ecossaise; Egmont Overture; Fidelio Overture;* German Dances; *Jena Symphony; Leonore Overture,* Nos. 1, 2, 3; Minuet; *Missa Solemnis; Prometheus Overture;* Quartet—*Beethoven;* Romance; *Ruins of Athens;* Septet; Sonata—*Beethoven;* Symphony—*Beethoven;* Trio—Beethoven; *Turkish March;* Variations on a Waltz by Diabelli.

Beethoven Society (New York). *See:* Bauer, Harold.

Beinum, Eduard van, conductor. Born Arnhem, Holland, Sept. 3, 1901; died Amsterdam, Holland, April 12, 1959. He was born to a family which had produced professional musicians for generations. From 1918 to 1921 he attended the Amsterdam Conservatory, then for a decade conducted various orchestras and choral groups in Holland. In 1931 he became Mengelberg's assistant conductor with the Concertgebouw Orchestra. Beginning in 1938 he shared the post of first conductor, and in 1945 he became the third musician to be its principal conductor. Between 1946 and 1949 he also conducted the London Philharmonic. His American début took place with the Philadelphia Orchestra on Jan. 8, 1954. In the fall of that year he returned to the United States to direct the Concertgebouw Orchestra on its first American tour. In the fall of 1956 he became principal conductor of the Los Angeles Philharmonic, holding this post without relinquishing his duties in Holland until his death there during a rehearsal. He was the recipient of many honors, including Chevalier of the Legion of Honor from France, the Order of the Star of the North from Sweden, and the Order of the Dannebrog from Denmark.

Benjamin, Arthur, composer. Born Sydney, Australia, Sept. 18, 1893. In 1911 he settled in London, where for three years he attended the Royal College of Music. He returned to Australia after World War I and for two years was professor of piano at the Sydney Conservatory. But in 1921 he was back in London, from then on his permanent home. In 1924 his string quartet received the Carnegie Award. In 1926 he became a member of the faculty of the Royal College of Music, where Benjamin Britten was one of his pupils. From 1941 to 1946 he was principal conductor of the Vancouver Symphony. In some of his compositions he has utilized a popular West Indian style, as in his successful *Two Jamaican Pieces* and *Caribbean Dance,* both for orchestra. In other works, like the symphony and the violin concerto, modern techniques and idioms predominate. His works include also an *Overture to an Italian Comedy, Prelude to a Holiday, Red River Jig, Cotillon,* and *From San Domingo,* all for orchestra; an oboe concerto adapted from Cimarosa; a flute concerto adapted from Domenico Scarlatti; and a *Concerto quasi fantasia,* for piano and orchestra; various sonatinas for solo instruments and piano; *Elegy, Waltz and Toccata,* for viola and piano; and numerous pieces for the piano including *Three New Fantasies, Two Jamaican Street Songs,* and *Chinoiserie.*

See: Overture to an Italian Comedy; Two Jamaican Pieces.

Bennett, Robert Russell, composer. Born Kansas City, Mo., June 15, 1894. After studying harmony in Kansas City with Carl Busch, he came to New York in 1916 and worked as copyist for the publishing house of G. Schirmer. After World War I he inaugurated his career as orchestrator of Broadway musical comedies which has continued to the present time. In the early 1920's he went to Europe and studied composition with Nadia Boulanger. His Symphony No. 1, in 1927, received honorable mention in a contest sponsored by the journal *Musical America; Sights and Sounds* and the *Abraham Lincoln Symphony,* both completed in 1929, received prizes in a competition conducted by R.C.A. Bennett subsequently wrote several serious works in a jazz style, but he did not abandon writing in a more orthodox idiom. His principal works for orchestra, besides those already mentioned, include the *American Ballade* (a fantasia on Stephen Foster's melodies), Eight Etudes, *The Four Freedoms Symphony, Overture to an Imaginary Drama*, a piano concerto, a violin concerto, and a symphony; Concerto Grosso (in a jazz style) for band; his chamber music includes a violin sonata, *Hexapoda* for violin and piano, a symphony for five woodwinds, and *Six Souvenirs* for two flutes and piano.

Bennett, Sir William Sterndale, conductor, teacher, and composer. Born Sheffield, England, April 13, 1816; died London, England, Feb. 1, 1875. He attended the Royal Academy of Music in London where he wrote the Piano Concerto in D minor, whose successful performances in London and Cambridge attracted the interest of Mendelssohn. In 1837, Bennett went to Leipzig, where he became intimate with both Mendelssohn and Schumann, and achieved his first major success as composer with the Piano Concerto in C minor and *The Naiades Overture*, both introduced by the Gewandhaus Orchestra early in 1837. After returning to England he earned his living playing the piano and teaching, all the while continuing to compose. Strongly derivative from the German Romantics, his music is now mostly dated. Bennett is perhaps best remembered as conductor and teacher. From 1856 to 1866 he was principal conductor of the Royal Philharmonic of London. In 1856 he was also appointed professor at Cambridge, and in 1866 he became Principal of the Royal Academy of Music. He was knighted in 1871, and after his death was buried in Westminster Abbey, near Purcell's tomb. His compositions include a symphony, several orchestral overtures, four piano concertos, and numerous chamber music works and piano pieces.

Benvenuto Cellini, Overture to. Overture to an opera by Berlioz, op. 23. The opera was introduced at the Paris Opéra on Sept. 10, 1838. The libretto, by Leon de Wailly and August Barbier, was based on Cellini's autobiography. The overture begins with a spirited theme. A second subject is slow and stately (coming from the Cardinal's monologue in the opera, *À tous péchés pleine indulgence*). A third subject is lyrical and emotional, derived from the love duet of Cellini and Teresa.

Berceuse. Cradle song, originally a vocal form but subsequently adapted for instrumental music. It is characterized by a tender, lullaby-like melody. Chopin's Berceuse in D-flat major for piano, op. 57 (1843), has such a melody set against a swaying rhythm suggesting a rocking cradle. Fauré wrote a sensitive berceuse, for violin and piano, op. 16 (1880). Liszt's Berceuse, for piano, is in two versions, one written in 1854, the other eight years later. The popular Berceuse from Benjamin Godard's opera, *Jocelyn*, is familiar in numerous transcriptions: for violin and piano; cello and piano; viola and piano; orchestra; and cello and orchestra.

Berceuse Elégiaque. Tone poem for orchestra by Ferruccio Busoni, op. 42 (1909). It originated as a piano piece, but when Busoni's mother died, he transcribed it for orchestra as a tribute to her memory. It is in the orchestral version that the work is heard most often. The title page of the published score bears a picture of a mother at the side of her child's cradle; in the background hovers the figure of a man following a coffin. The score carries the following statement: "The man sings to the dead mother the same song he had heard from her as a child and which had followed him through a lifetime and undergone a transformation."

Berg, Alban, composer. Born Vienna, Austria, Feb. 9, 1885; died there, Dec. 24, 1935. Though he began writing music in his fifteenth year, he did not receive any formal instruction until early manhood. While working as a government official he met Arnold Schoenberg. As a result of Schoenberg's influence, Berg gave up his job to begin studying with the older man. Berg's first works were a piano sonata and a string quartet, written in 1908 and 1910 respectively. With Five Songs With Orchestra, in 1912, Berg began assuming his teacher's atonal style. During World War I, Berg served in the

Austrian army. After the war he completed his masterpiece, the expressionist opera, *Wozzeck*. Like Schoenberg, Berg progressed from atonalism to the twelve-tone technique, a style in which he produced the *Lyric Suite* for string quartet, a remarkable violin concerto, and a second opera, *Lulu*. Other works include the Three Pieces for Orchestra, Four Pieces for clarinet and piano, and a Chamber Concerto for piano, violin, and 13 wind instruments. Berg succeeded in bringing romantic feeling and a fresh lyricism to the austere style of atonality and the mathematical precision of the twelve-tone technique. Berg, a sickly man all his life, was finally the victim of blood poisoning caused by an abscess on his back.
See: Concerto—*Berg; Lyric Suite*.

Bergmann, Carl, conductor. Born Ebersbach, Germany, April 12, 1821; died New York City, Aug. 16, 1876. For over twenty years he was conductor of the New York Philharmonic. He completed music study in Germany with private teachers. In 1850 he came to the United States, joining the cello section of the Germania Orchestra, of which he became conductor a few months later. In 1855 he was appointed one of the conductors of the New York Philharmonic and from 1862 to 1876 he was its sole conductor. A pioneer in promoting Wagner's music in America, Bergmann's programs included the American premières of many excerpts from that master's music dramas.

Bériot, Charles de, violinist and composer. Born Louvain, Belgium, Feb. 20, 1802; died Brussels, Belgium, April 8, 1870. After studying violin with a local teacher he made a public appearance in his ninth year. He entered the Paris Conservatory when he was nineteen. His career as a mature virtuoso began in Paris in 1821. In 1826 he made his début in London, then toured Europe, often in joint concerts with the singer, Mme. Malibran, whom he married in 1835. In 1836 he went into temporary retirement owing to despondency over his wife's death. He emerged from that retirement in 1840. From 1843 to 1852 he was director of the violin classes at the Brussels Conservatory. He was forced to resign this post because of failing eyesight, and in 1858

he became totally blind. A prolific composer for the violin, Bériot is remembered by violin students for his 7 concertos and 11 sets of variations, which make excellent teaching material; he also edited a useful book of violin studies.

Berkshire Symphonic Festival. An annual summer festival at Tanglewood (setting of Hawthorne's *Tanglewood Tales*) in Lenox, Massachusetts. The principal concerts are given by the Boston Symphony under Charles Munch and guest conductors. This festival was inaugurated in 1934 when Henry Hadley led a series of orchestral concerts on the Dan Hanna estate in nearby Stockbridge. In August 1936 the Boston Symphony under Koussevitzky gave several concerts on Margaret Emerson's estate in Stockbridge. When the grounds of Tanglewood were presented to the Boston Symphony by Mrs. Gorham Brooks in 1937, the Berkshire Symphonic Festival became an annual event, with series of concerts under Koussevitzky. In 1938 an open-air shed was built; in 1940, the Berkshire Music Centre, directed by Koussevitzky, was opened on the grounds to train music students in the performing and creative phases of music. In 1941 a special opera house and a small concert auditorium were added. During World War II the activity was curtailed to include only several concerts of music by Bach and Mozart led by Koussevitzky. In 1946 full operations were resumed, and the regular festival symphony series was prefaced by a cycle of concerts devoted to Bach and Mozart. Since the war, this festival has become the major musical event of its kind in the United States. Koussevitzky remained artistic director until his death in 1951, when he was succeeded by Charles Munch, with Aaron Copland as associate director.

Berlin Philharmonic Orchestra. A symphony orchestra founded in Berlin, Germany, in 1882 with Joseph Joachim and Karl Klindworth as conductors. Its artistic significance dates from 1897, when Arthur Nikisch became principal conductor. Nikisch held this post until 1922, when he was succeeded by Wilhelm Furtwaengler, who continued as musical director until World War II. During the war the orchestra was temporarily disbanded, but in 1945 it was reorganized with a subsidy from the West Berlin Senate and Furtwaengler returned as principal conductor. Upon Furtwaengler's death he was succeeded by Herbert von Karajan. The Berlin Philharmonic made its first tour of the United States early in 1955, conducted by von Karajan.

Berlioz, Hector, composer. Born Côte-Saint-André, France, Dec. 11, 1803; died Paris, March 8, 1869. His father, a physician, tutored Hector in the sciences. Then in 1821 he sent him to Paris to study medicine. There, in 1824, Berlioz received a degree in science. Music had been a major interest from childhood on; Berlioz now determined to engage in music professionally. Promised support from his father if he could prove his talent within a reasonable period, Berlioz entered the Paris Conservatory, where his teachers included Jean François Lesueur and Anton Reicha. Under their guidance he completed a Mass, performed in Paris on July 10, 1825. Lesueur told him: "You have genius." Nevertheless, Berlioz twice failed to gain the Prix de Rome, a circumstance that led his father to withdraw all financial help. Berlioz now supported himself by giving private lessons and working as choirmaster.

In the fall of 1827, a visiting Shakespeare company from England appeared at the Odéon in Paris. Berlioz saw a performance of *Hamlet,* and immediately fell in love wtih Henrietta Smithson, the actress who played Ophelia. He now attended every performance in which she appeared; he deluged her with ardent love letters which she did not answer. To impress her with his talent he arranged a concert of his works on May 26, 1828, which she did not attend. His unrequited love led him further to write a major work for orchestra reflecting his turbulent emotions. It proved to be his first masterwork, the *Symphonie fantastique,* a huge success when introduced in Paris on Dec. 5, 1830. But to Berlioz this was a hollow victory because Henrietta Smithson had ignored the concert.

In October 1830 Berlioz finally received the Prix de Rome. The three years spent at the Villa Medici in Rome were unhappy, since he did not like Italy and chafed under the rigid regimen imposed upon him. Back in Paris in 1832, he discovered that Henrietta Smithson was again in the city. He arranged a new performance of his symphony in her honor, this time with her in the audience. They now had their first meeting, which was followed by a stormy courtship and culminated in marriage on Oct. 3, 1833. Their relationship was disastrous from the beginning. After the birth of a son, they decided to separate. Berlioz, however, did not marry again until Henrietta died in 1854; his second marriage—to Marie Recio in 1854—was no more successful than the first.

The success of the *Symphonie fantastique* brought Berlioz a patron in Paganini. The legendary violinist had recently become interested in the viola. He commissioned Berlioz to write for him a major work with a viola obbligato. Since what Berlioz produced was not a virtuoso piece to set off the talent of the performer but a poetic symphony, *Harold en Italie,* inspired by Byron's *Harold in Italy,* Paganini lost all interest. The work was introduced in Paris on Nov. 24, 1834, without the virtuoso's patronage. But four years later Paganini was so moved by this music that he sent Berlioz a gift of 20,000 francs.

Berlioz now undertook another large work for orchestra, a dramatic symphony, *Romeo and Juliet,* in which he nostalgically recalled his own once tempestuous love for Henrietta. Performed at the Paris Conservatory on Nov. 4, 1839, the symphony was a triumph. Wagner, then unknown, was in the audience; he wrote "it took me by storm and impetuously fanned the flame of my personal feeling for music and poetry."

Beginning in 1842, Berlioz made several tours of Germany, Austria, England, and Russia, conducting programs of his own music. While on one of these trips, in 1846, he completed the dramatic legend, *The Damnation of Faust,* begun many years earlier; when introduced at the Opéra-Comique on Dec. 6, 1846, it was a failure.

In 1852 Berlioz was invited by Liszt to Weimar to participate in a Berlioz

Week. It was a "pyramidal success," as Berlioz himself described it. A second Berlioz Week was celebrated in Weimar three years after that. Still another signal honor came to him in 1856, when he was elected a member of the Institut de France.

Berlioz' last years were unhappy. His second marriage proved a failure; the death of his only son of yellow fever, in 1867, was another shattering blow. He himself was suffering from nervous ailments, aggravated by a trip to Russia. In March 1868, in Nice, he had an attack of cerebral congestion. Broken in health, he returned to Paris, where he died the following year.

Berlioz was the first of music's great Romantics. His music was like his life—often passionate and febrile, and in the large design. His pictorial and programmatic writing, his vast architectonic structures and the ardor of his emotions represented a permanent break with the Classical past. He carried music to new horizons with his use of literary subjects, his love of fantasy, and his remarkable innovations in orchestration. He was one of music's great pioneers: the apostle of program music (though program music had existed before his time); the originator of the *Leitmotif* (or as he called it, the "idée fixe"), whose influence on Wagner was so far-reaching; and the first of modern orchestrators.

His principal orchestral works are: *Symphonie fantastique; King Lear,* overture; *Rob Roy,* overture; *Roman Carnival Overture (Le Carnival romain); Le Corsaire,* overture; *Harold in Italy,* symphony with solo viola; *Romeo and Juliet,* dramatic symphony.

See: *Benvenuto Cellini Overture; Damnation of Faust;* Requiem—*Berlioz; Roman Carnival Overture; Romeo and Juliet;* Symphony—*Berlioz.*

Bernstein, Leonard, composer, conductor, and pianist. Born Lawrence, Mass., Aug. 25, 1918. After studying the piano with Helen Coates and Heinrich Gebhard, he took courses in music at Harvard University with Walter Piston and Edward Burlingame Hill. After graduating from Harvard in 1939 he attended the Curtis Institute as a pupil of Fritz Reiner, Isa-

belle Vengerova, and Randall Thompson; during the summers of 1940 and 1941 he studied conducting with Koussevitzky at the Berkshire Music Centre. Through Koussevitzky's influence, he was appointed assistant conductor to Artur Rodzinski with the New York Philharmonic in 1943, even though up to then he had never led a major orchestra. When Bruno Walter suddenly became indisposed and could not conduct a Sunday afternoon performance of the New York Philharmonic on Nov. 14, 1943, Bernstein substituted for him without the benefit of a single rehearsal, making such a profound impression that his unscheduled début was reported not only on the front page of the *New York Times* but also in its editorial columns. After that Bernstein was several times called upon to serve as guest conductor of the New York Philharmonic. In 1944-1945 he also appeared with seven other major American orchestras. In 1945 he was appointed principal conductor of the New York City Symphony, a post he held for three seasons. In May 1946 he scored a triumph at the International Music Festival in Prague; in 1947 he made the first of many outstanding appearances in Palestine (later Israel), and conducted in major European cities. In 1953 he became the first American-born conductor to lead performances at La Scala in Milan; and in the fall of 1958 the first to become music director of the New York Philharmonic.

Bernstein scored his first success as a composer with his initial orchestral work, the *Jeremiah Symphony,* introduced in Pittsburgh in 1944, and selected by the New York Music Critics Circle as the best new American work of the season. Later major works for orchestra include a second symphony, *The Age of Anxiety,* which received the Hornblit Award after its première by the Boston Symphony in 1949, the Serenade for Violin, String Orchestra, and Percussion, the ballet-suite *Fancy Free,* and *Facsimile: A Choreographic Essay.* Other instrumental works include the Overture to *Candide,* a clarinet sonata, and two sets of *Anniversaries* for piano. Bernstein has also been successful in writing music of more popular appeal, including the scores for several Broadway musical comedies, including *On the Town, Wonderful Town,* and *West Side Story.*

Bernstein also achieved recognition as pianist, often in performances of concertos whose orchestral accompaniments he conducted from the keyboard. He has lectured on musical subjects for the "Omnibus" Program over television, has written analytical notes for the recordings of Music Appreciation Records; since 1951 has been in charge of the conducting class at the Berkshire Music Centre; and since 1957 has led concerts for children with the New York Philharmonic. In 1958 he received the Alice M. Ditson Award for distinguished services to American music.

See: Serenade for Violin, Strings, and Percussion; Symphony—*Bernstein.*

Big Ben. Variation-fantasy for orchestra by Ernst Toch, op. 62 (1934), introduced by the Boston Symphony under Richard Burgin on Dec. 20, 1934. The composer was stimulated into writing this work after crossing Westminster Bridge in London one foggy night and hearing the chiming of Big Ben. The Big-Ben motif appears at the opening of this variation-fantasy in a slightly altered form. After that comes a series of variations, the last of which is brought to a climax and leads into a fugue. A transitional section brings on a final statement of the chime motif.

Biggs, Edward Power, organist. Born Essex, England, March 29, 1906. The award of the Thomas Threlfall Organ Scholarship enabled him to attend the Royal College of Music in London, from which he was graduated with highest honors in several categories in 1929. He made his début as organist in London in the same year, then embarked on a six-month tour of the United States during which he gave over 200 concerts. In 1932 he established permanent residence in the United States, becoming a citizen. He was appointed organist and music director of the Harvard Church in Cambridge, Massachusetts, and official organist of the Boston Symphony. His concerts of organ music at Harvard made him famous. Since 1942 he has been broadcasting over the Columbia Broadcasting System network, and in 1945-1946 he became the first organist to perform over the air all of Bach's organ music. In 1952 he received a citation from the National Association of Composers and Conductors for his service to American music, having given frequent performances of American compositions over the radio, including works written for him by Roy Harris, Walter Piston, Howard Hanson, and Quincy Porter, among others.

Billy the Kid. Ballet suite for orchestra by Aaron Copland (1938), adapted from the ballet score. Commissioned by the Ballet Caravan, *Billy the Kid* was first given by that company in Chicago on Oct. 16, 1938. The book was by Lincoln Kirstein, and choreography by Eugene Loring. Both the scenario and Copland's music were derived from the folklore of the American cowboy. The ballet traces the picaresque history of Billy the Kid up to the time of his capture by a posse. Copland's suite, adapted three years after the première of the ballet, has six sections: I. *The Open Prairie;* II. *Street in Frontier Town;* III. *Card Game at Night;* IV. *Gun Battle;* V. *Celebration After Billy's Capture;* VI. *The Open Prairie.* The music is enlivened by the interpolation of several famous cowboy melodies, including *Git Along, Little Dogie, Old Chisholm Trail, Goodbye, Old Paint,* and *Oh, Bury Me Not on the Lone Prairie.*

Binary Form. A pattern consisting of two principal sections.

Binary Measure. A measure with two beats.

Bingham, Seth, organist and composer. Born Bloomfield, N.J., April 16, 1882. He studied music in the United States with Horatio Parker, and in Paris with Vincent d'Indy, Charles Widor, and Alexandre Guilmant. He was graduated from Yale University in 1904, and from 1908 to 1919 he was a member of its music faculty. From 1919 to 1954 he was instructor, then associate professor of music, at Columbia University. He has made many appearances in organ recitals, and is the composer of several notable works for orchestra (including *Wall Street Fantasy, Symphonic Fantasy, Memories of France,* and *Connecticut Suite*), various concertos, and numerous pieces for the organ (including hymns, psalms, hymn-preludes, and carol canons).

Bird Quartet. See: Quartet—Haydn.

Birds, The. See: Aristophanes.

Birds, The (Gli Uccelli). Suite for small orchestra by Ottorino Respighi (1927), introduced in 1927 in São Paulo, Brazil, the composer conducting. In 1934 the music was used for a ballet presented at the Rome Opera. Respighi drew his thematic material from music by four 17th- and 18th-century composers which he adapted freely. The suite has five sections: I. Prelude (Preludio), based on a piece by Bernardo Pasquini; II. The Dove (La Colomba), based on Jacques de Gallot; III. The Hen (La Gallina), based on Rameau's popular La Poule; IV. The Nightingale (L'Usignuolo), based on an anonymous English composition; V. The Cuckoo (Il Cucu), based on Pasquini. In the Prelude themes used in later movements are briefly presented. In The Nightingale, Respighi deliberately parodies the Forest Music from Wagner's music drama Siegfried in an accompanying passage. The concluding The Cuckoo makes brief reference to a main theme in the Prelude.

Birthday of the Infanta, The. (1) Ballet Suite for orchestra by John Alden Carpenter (1919), adapted from the composer's ballet score. The ballet was introduced in Chicago on Dec. 23, 1919. Eleven years later the composer prepared his orchestral suite. The ballet text was derived from Oscar Wilde's famous tale in which a 16-year-old Spanish Infanta is surprised at her birthday party by a performance by jugglers, dancers, and other diversions. The Infanta is so enchanted by a dance by a misshapen dwarf, Pedro, that she throws her handkerchief at him. After the party Pedro sees himself in the mirror and is horrified by the way he looks, and the effect these looks must have had on the Infanta. He begins his grotesque dance anew, then falls dead, holding tightly to the Infanta's handkerchief. The suite is in three parts: I. The Guest; II. The Infanta; III. Games.

(2) Ballet Suite for orchestra by Mario Castelnuovo-Tedesco (1947), introduced by the New Orleans Symphony on Jan. 28, 1947, Massimo Freccia conducting.

The suite was based on the tale of Oscar Wilde, and is in seven parts: I. Fanfare; II. Sarabande of the King of Spain; III. Pavane of the Infanta; IV. Ronde of Las Meninas; V. Minuet of the Rose; VI. Dance of the Mirror; VII. Epilogue.

(3) See: Wilde, Oscar.

Bitonality. Simultaneous use of two different keys.

Bizet, Georges, composer. Born Paris, France, Oct. 25, 1838; died Bougival, France, June 3, 1875. He attended the Paris Conservatory, receiving the Prix de Rome in 1857. He embarked on a career as opera composer with a one-act opéra-comique, Le Docteur miracle, produced in Paris in 1857. Though most famous as a composer for the stage—especially for his masterwork, Carmen—Bizet also wrote some significant instrumental music, of which the best are his Symphony in C major, the incidental music to Daudet's L'Arlésienne, and a four-hand piano suite of children's pieces, Jeux d'enfants. Other instrumental works include La Chasse d'Ossian, the overture Patrie, and the symphony Roma, all for orchestra; and numerous pieces for the piano including Trois esquisses musicales, preludes, waltzes, caprices, variations, and nocturnes. In 1869 he married Geneviève Halévy, daughter of his professor at the Conservatory; and three years after that he first became famous through his L'Arlésienne music. He died three months after the première of his opera, Carmen.

See: Carmen; Symphony—Bizet.

Bjørnson, Bjørnstjerne, dramatist, novelist, and poet. Born Kvikne, Norway, Dec. 8, 1832; died Paris, France, April 26, 1910. Grieg's orchestral suite, Sigurd Jorsalfar, op. 56, is made up of significant sections from his incidental music to that play by Bjørnson. Johan Svendsen wrote a concert overture to the same play. Johan Halvorsen wrote incidental music for King Sverre and Rikard Nordraak for Maria Stuart in Scotland.

Blacher, Boris, composer. Born Newchwang, China, Jan. 3, 1903. After receiving his early academic and musical schooling in the Far East he came in his 19th year to Berlin, where he attended the High School of Music. From 1926 on he earned his living in Berlin through music—as copyist, orchestrator, and performer in motion pictures. A ballet, *Festival in the South (Fest im Sueden)*, introduced at Cassel in 1937, was his first major success, given in about 50 German theaters. He wrote several more ballets after that before undertaking his first opera, *The Princess Tarakanova (Fuerstin Tarakanova)*, first given in Wuppertal in 1941. His later operas made him a leading figure in post-war Germany, especially *Romeo and Juliet, Prussian Fairy Tale (Preussisches Märchen)* and *Abstrakte Oper No. 1*. In 1948 he was appointed professor at the High School of Music in Berlin, and in 1953 its director. In his instrumental music Blacher has occasionally utilized the twelve-tone technique, but he is best known for a system of his own creation called "variable meters," a system of irregular rhythms worked out on a set of mathematical formulas; a rhythm row is chosen for a composition in advance. His works for orchestra include a symphony, 2 piano concertos, a viola concerto, a tone poem *Hamlet, Variations on a Theme by Paganini,* a divertimento, a partita, a concertino for string orchestra, *Study in Pianissimo,* and *Music for Cleveland.* Other instrumental works include 3 string quartets, flute sonata, violin sonata, 2 piano sonatinas, piano sonata, and *Ornaments,* the last both for the piano and for orchestra.

Black Key Etude *See:* Etude—*Chopin.*

Blanik (Smetana). *See: Má Vlast.*

Bliss, Sir Arthur, composer. Born London, England, Aug. 2, 1891. After receiving degrees from Pembroke College, Cambridge, he attended the Royal College of Music in London, where his teachers included Gustav Holst and Vaughan Williams. He first achieved recognition as a composer soon after World War I with two unusual works. One was the Rhapsody for soprano and tenor (vocalizing on the single syllable "ah" throughout the work), flute, English horn, string quartet, and bass, completed in 1919, and introduced the following year in Salzburg. The other was *Rout,* for voice and ten instruments, a satiric work, with a text made up of meaningless syllables, first heard in Lon-

don in the year of its composition (1920). Between 1923 and 1925 Bliss lived in California, the first of several extended visits to the United States, some of them in conjunction with assignments to write music for motion pictures. He was in the United States at the outbreak of World War II as professor of music at the University of Southern California. From 1942 through 1944 he was music director of BBC. He was knighted in 1950, and in 1953 made Master of the Queen's Music. While Bliss has never avoided experimentation, his music always has a strong emotional base. His main concern is beauty of sound and poetic expressiveness, always in well formed structures. His main instrumental works include *A Colour Symphony, Introduction and Allegro, Music for Strings,* the ballet suite *Checkmate, Discourse,* and *Edinburgh Overture,* all for orchestra; a piano concerto, two-piano concerto, and violin concerto; 3 string quartets, oboe quintet, clarinet quintet, viola sonata, and various shorter works for piano.
See: Checkmate.

Blitzstein, Marc, composer. Born Philadelphia, March 2, 1905. His musical training took place at the Curtis Institute, with Alexander Siloti in New York, Nadia Boulanger in Paris, and Arnold Schoenberg in Berlin. He is best known for his works for the stage, particularly those on social-conscious texts of his own writing. But he has also produced some notable instrumental music. During World War II he served in the Air Force, which commissioned him to write his tone poem *Freedom Morning* and his symphony *The Airborne.* Other instrumental works include a piano concerto, *Variations* and *Lear: A Study,* both for orchestra; a string quartet and Serenade for string quartet; piano sonata, piano suite, and *Percussion Music* for piano.

Bloch, Ernest, composer. Born Geneva, Switzerland, July 24, 1880. He began studying music in his fourteenth year with Jaques-Dalcroze and Louis Rey. Later study took place with Eugène Ysaÿe in Brussels, and in Germany with Ivan Knorr and Ludwig Thuille. In 1902 he completed the Symphony in C-sharp minor. Failure to get it performed proved so discouraging that Bloch decided to settle down in Geneva as a shopkeeper. But while working in his father's store he did not desert music. He conducted several subscription concerts and completed a few major works, including an opera, *Macbeth*. It was introduced by the Opéra-Comique in Paris in 1910, attracting the interest of Romain Rolland, who made a special trip to Geneva to meet the composer. Largely owing to Rolland's advice, Bloch gave up business to concentrate on music.

His apprentice years over, Bloch entered upon his first fruitful creative phase, the Hebrew period in which he aspired to write music expressing his racial backgrounds. As he put it: "It is the Jewish soul that interests me, the complex, glowing, agitated soul that I feel vibrating through the Bible." He wrote *Two Psalms,* for soprano and orchestra, *Psalm 22,* for baritone and orchestra, *Three Jewish Poems* for orchestra, and two other works in which he achieved full maturity, *Schelomo* and the *Israel Symphony*.

Early in 1916 Bloch visited the United States as conductor of the Maud Allan dance troupe. When his organization went bankrupt, Bloch was stranded, but several important musicians came to his help by arranging performances of his works. Presentation of his music by the Flonzaley Quartet, the Philadelphia Orchestra, the Boston Symphony, and the Society of Friends of Music in New York helped to introduce him to the American public. In 1919 his reputation in the United States was further enhanced with the winning of the Elizabeth Sprague Coolidge Prize of $1,000 for his Suite for Viola and Piano.

Now a composer of established reputation, Bloch was appointed director of the Cleveland Institute in 1920. During the five years he held this post he completed several important compositions, notably the Concerto Grosso No. 1, and the Piano Quintet. In 1925 he transferred his teaching activity to San Francisco, where, two years later, he completed the epic rhapsody *America,* with which he won first prize in a national contest sponsored by *Musical America*.

An endowment by a San Francisco patron enabled him to give up teaching in 1931 and devote himself completely to composition. For a few years he lived in Switzerland, where he completed the *Sacred Service,* introduced in New York on April 11, 1934. After reestablishing his home in the United States in 1934, Bloch produced other ambitious works. Most of these no longer were in a Hebraic style or on Hebraic subjects. But like his Hebrew compositions, they are all characterized by a rhapsodic style, spacious structures, passionate speech, and stirring emotion.

Since 1943, Bloch has lived in Oregon. For several summers he taught classes in composition at the University of California in Berkeley. In 1942 he received a gold medal from the American Academy of Arts and Letters. Five years later he was given the New York Music Critics Circle Award for his String Quartet No. 2, and in 1954 he became the first composer to receive this same award in two different categories in the same season (for the String Quartet No. 3 and Concerto Grosso No. 2). An Ernest Bloch Society was formed in 1937 to promote his music.

His daughter, Suzanne (born Geneva, Switzerland, Aug. 7, 1907), has distinguished herself as a performer on the lute and other old instruments.

These are Bloch's principal instrumental compositions:

Chamber Music: 5 string quartets; 2 piano quintets; 3 suites for unaccompanied cello, 2 for unaccompanied violin, and 1 for unaccompanied viola; 2 violin sonatas; Suite, for viola and piano; *Baal Shem,* for violin and piano (or orchestra).

Orchestra: Three Jewish Poems; Three Psalms; Schelomo, for cello and orchestra; *Israel Symphony;* 2 concerti grossi; *America; Helvetia; Voice in the Wilderness,* for cello and orchestra; *Evocations;* Concerto for Violin and Orchestra; *Suite symphonique; Concerto symphonique; Scherzo fantasque,* for piano and orchestra; *In Memoriam;* Concertino for flute, viola, and strings; *Suite hebraïque,* for viola and orchestra; *Sinfonia breve;* Symphony for Trombone and Orchestra; Symphony in E-flat major; *Suite modale,* for flute and orchestra; *The Last Two Poems,* for flute and orchestra; *Four Episodes,* for chamber orchestra.

See: *America; Baal Shem;* Concerto— *Bloch;* Concerto Grosso—*Bloch;* Quartet —*Bloch;* Quintet—*Bloch;* Symphony— *Bloch; Voice in the Wilderness.*

Blom, Eric, music critic. Born Bern, Switzerland, Aug. 20, 1888; died London, England, April 11, 1959. Early in life he settled in England, becoming a British subject. From 1919 to 1926 he contributed program notes for the Queen's Hall concerts. He was music critic of the *Birmingham Post* from 1931 to 1946, and after 1949 of the *Observer.* From 1937 to 1950 and again after 1954 he edited *Music and Letters.* He edited *Everyman's Dictionary of Music* and the enlarged, 5th edition of Grove's *Dictionary of Music and Musicians.* He was the author of many books on music, among which are *Stepchildren of Music* (1923), *The Romance of the Piano* (1927), *Mozart* (1935), *Music in England* (1942), and *Some Great Composers* (1944). He was also the compiler of *The Music Lover's Miscellany* (1935).

Bloomfield, Theodore, conductor. Born Cleveland, Ohio, June 14, 1923. He studied at the Oberlin Conservatory, the Juilliard School of Music, and with Pierre Monteux in Maine. He made his conducting début with the New York Little Symphony in 1945. One year later he was chosen from over a hundred applicants as apprentice and assistant to George Szell with the Cleveland Orchestra. From 1947 to 1952 he was conductor of the Cleveland Little Symphony, which he organized. He made his European début in 1952 with performances of opera and symphony in Italy. During that summer he toured Germany in piano recitals under the auspices of the United States State Department. He subsequently made guest appearances as conductor in Vienna, Brussels, Monte Carlo, Switzerland, and Spain. From 1955 to 1958 he was conductor of the Portland Symphony in Oregon. In 1959 he became principal conductor of the Rochester Philharmonic.

Blue-Bird, The. *See:* Maeterlinck, Maurice.

Blues. A jazz idiom derived from the Negro songs of lamentation. The blues is characterized by a twelve-bar melody, divided into three four-bar phrases; the "blue note," a flatted third or seventh in the diatonic scale; "breaks" in the melody permitting the singer to interpolate exclamations. Blues are found in symphonic music, notably in Gershwin's *Rhapsody in Blue* and *An American in Paris,* Gould's *Interplay,* Symphony No. 3, and Concerto for Orchestra, and Ravel's Violin Sonata and Piano Concerto in G major.

Boccherini, Luigi, composer. Born Lucca, Italy, Feb. 19, 1743; died Madrid, Spain, May 28, 1805. He studied music in his native city and in Rome. He then played the cello in theater orchestras and in a band in Lucca. A local concert of his sonatas performed by Filippo Manfredi, the composer accompanying, proved so successful that a tour of Lombardy and France followed, culminating with a triumphant appearance in Paris in 1768. Between 1782 and 1786 Boccherini toured Germany, and in 1787 he was appointed chamber composer to the king of Prussia, Frederick William II, holding this post for a decade. When his royal patron died in 1797, Boccherini settled in Spain, living there for several years in obscurity and poverty. There came a temporary recess from want when he was patronized by the Ambassador of the French republic at Madrid, for whom he wrote many chamber-music works. But Boccherini's last years were dismal, all his efforts to relieve his poverty through hack work proving futile.

As a contemporary of Haydn and Mozart, Boccherini helped establish both the form and the style of the Classic concerto and string quartet. He also opened new horizons for chamber music by devising the combinations of the string quintet and string sextet. He was a facile and prolific composer who lacked the power of invention of either Haydn or Mozart. Nevertheless, he possessed a gift for ingratiating melody and harmony, and an aristocratic sense of style. His Concerto for Cello and Orchestra in B-flat major, op. 34, is still popular in the repertory. His equally popular "Minuet" comes from his string quintet in E major, op.

13, no. 5. Boccherini wrote 20 symphonies, 4 cello concertos, 125 string quintets, 102 string sextets, 60 string trios, 2 octets, 16 sextets, and numerous sonatas.

Bodanzky, Artur, conductor. Born Vienna, Austria, Dec. 16, 1877; died New York City, Nov. 23, 1939. He attended the Vienna Conservatory and made his conducting début in Vienna in 1900. Though he subsequently became famous as a conductor of operas in Austria, in London, and at the Metropolitan Opera in New York, he was also active in symphonic music. From 1916 to 1931 he was the conductor of the Society of Friends of Music in New York. In 1919 he helped found the New Symphony Orchestra in New York, which he conducted three seasons. When that orchestra merged with the New York Philharmonic in 1922 Bodanzky became one of the guest conductors of the latter organization for a single season.

Boecklin, Arnold, painter. *See:* Painters and Painting.

Boehm, Joseph, violinist and teacher. Born Budapest, Hungary, March 4, 1795; died Vienna, Austria, March 28, 1876. He was one of the most significant violin teachers of the 19th century. After studying with his father and Pierre Rode, he made his début at Budapest in 1803. In 1815 he scored his first successes as a mature artist in Vienna. In 1819 he became professor of the violin at the Vienna Conservatory, holding this post until 1848. From 1821 to 1868 he played in the Imperial Orchestra. His long list of famous pupils over half a century included Joseph Joachim, Leopold Auer, Heinrich Ernst, Eduard Reményi, Joseph Hellmesberger, and Eduard Rappoldi. He also wrote many instructive pieces still used by violin students.

Boehm, Theobald, flutist and inventor. Born Munich, Germany, April 9, 1794; died there Nov. 25, 1881. He was the inventor of the famous Boehm flute. After becoming celebrated as a flute virtuoso and performer at the court in Munich, he opened a factory in that city in 1828 to construct flutes along new designs. He devised the Boehm system which utilized a new method of fingering; the holes of the flute were cut in correct acoustical position, controlled by open-standing keys closed automatically by rings fitted over the fingerholes. After considerable study and experimentation he invented the Boehm flute by 1847, a cylindrical instrument with parabolic head joint, fifteen holes, and twenty-three keys and levers. This instrument is now in general use.

Bolero. A Spanish dance in 3/4 time usually accompanied by castanets. It has two sections, each repeated. As a musical form it was originated by Sebastian Cerezo in 1780. Chopin wrote an interesting Bolero in C major for piano, op. 19 (1833). Most generally boleros are for orchestra, and the most celebrated of these is that by Maurice Ravel (1928), written for the dancer, Ida Rubinstein, who introduced it in Paris on Nov. 22, 1928. When Ravel's *Bolero* received its American première by the New York Philharmonic under Toscanini on Nov. 14, 1929, it created a sensation. Soon after that the composition achieved a vogue throughout the country. It was performed by every major American orchestra; was made into numerous arrangements; received jazz treatment; was introduced in a Broadway revue; and lent its name to a motion picture. Ravel's *Bolero* has a sustained, gradual crescendo. Its theme is in two parts. The first is introduced by flute, then clarinet; the second, by bassoon, then clarinet. As different sections of the orchestra take over the melody and its continuation the sonority develops until a tremendous climax is achieved by full orchestra; all the while a subtle background is created by a side drum emphasizing the bolero rhythm.

Bolet, Jorge, pianist. Born Havana, Cuba, Nov. 15, 1914. He attended the Curtis Institute on a scholarship, as a pupil of David Saperton, then made his American début in New York in 1933. One year later the Cuban government financed a European tour. After returning to the United States he was appointed Rudolf Serkin's assistant at the Curtis Institute. In 1937 he received the Naumburg Award, and in 1938 the Josef Hofmann Award from the Curtis Institute. During World War II he served in the United States Army. Resuming his concert activity after the war, he became one of five American musicians invited for a four-week tour of Western Germany as guests of the German Republic in 1954, the first time a foreign government served as host to American artists.

Bonne Chanson, La. Poem for orchestra by Charles Martin Loeffler (1901), introduced as *Poem* by the Boston Symphony under Gericke on April 2, 1902. Many years later the composer reorchestrated and renamed it, and in its new and definitive version it was given by the Boston Symphony under Monteux on Nov. 1, 1918. The work is based on the fifth poem of Paul Verlaine's *La bonne chanson,* beginning with the line "before you fade and disappear, pale morning star." The tone poem opens with serene music describing the early dawn and the disappearance of the morning star. The main theme is then heard in the strings. After an Allegro section, described by the composer as "the lark mounting skyward with the day," the serene opening is brought back. There is an intensification of feeling and a mounting surge of emotion before the full orchestra announces the bursting light of the golden sun.

Bonnet, Joseph, organist. Born Bordeaux, France, March 17, 1884; died Sainte-Luce-sur-Mer, Quebec, Aug. 2, 1944. He was graduated from the Paris Conservatory with first prize in organ. In 1906 he was appointed organist of the St. Eustache Church, where he remained until 1940 and where his organ recitals became world famous. During this period he also taught organ at the Paris Conservatory and made many successful tours of Europe. His American début took place in New York on Jan. 30, 1917. He subsequently made several transcontinental tours of the United States, where he settled permanently in 1940. From 1940 until his death four years later he taught organ at the Quebec Conservatory. He wrote many works for the organ, and edited the *Historical Organ Recitals* made up of music he performed in a five-concert historical series at the Hotel Astor in New York in 1917, and later in several other cities.

Boris Godunov. A folk opera by Mussorgsky, with libretto by the composer based on a drama by Alexander Pushkin. It was first performed in St. Petersburg on Feb. 8, 1874. For orchestral excerpt *see:* Polonaise. *See also:* Pushkin, Alexander.

Borodin, Alexander, composer. Born St. Petersburg, Russia, Nov. 11, 1833; died there, Feb. 27, 1887. Though unusually precocious in music he did not plan to become a professional musician. In 1856 he was graduated from the Academy of Medical and Physical Sciences with highest honors. For two years after that he served in a military hospital, and for three additional years he studied in Europe on a government subsidy. In November 1862 he returned to St. Petersburg, becoming professor of chemistry at the Academy. His friendship with Balakirev aroused his ambition to write national Russian music. He completed his first symphony in 1867, successfully introduced in St. Petersburg under Balakirev on Jan. 16, 1869. From then on, Borodin divided his energies equally between science and music. As a scientist he lectured, taught, translated treatises, and did valuable research. As a composer, he identified himself with the national group, "The Russian Five," producing music whose roots were deeply embedded in the soil of Russian folksong and dance, and which derived its inspiration from Russian backgrounds and culture. Like his colleagues he was best in writing music with a text or program which absorbed stylistic traits of Russian folk music. But unlike them he liked to blend his Russian idioms with Oriental rhythms, melodies, and instrumental colors. Borodin died of a burst aneurism while celebrating the Carnival of 1887. His most important instrumental works include 3 symphonies, the tone poem *In Central Asia,* 2 string quartets, and the *Petite Suite* for piano.

See: In Central Asia; Polovtsian Dances; Quartet—*Borodin;* Symphony—*Borodin.*

Bossi, Marco Enrico, organist, teacher, and composer. Born Salò, Brescia, Italy, April 25, 1861; died at sea, Feb. 20, 1925. The son of an organist, Bossi received his musical training at the Liceo Musicale in Bologna and at the Milan

Conservatory. In 1881 he began a long and successful career as organist at the Como Cathedral. He was also eminently successful as a teacher. From 1891 to 1895 he was professor of organ and theory at the Naples Conservatory; from 1896 to 1902, director of the Benedetto Marcello Conservatory in Venice; from 1902 to 1912, director of the Liceo Musicale in Bologna; and from 1916 to 1923, director of the Santa Cecilia in Rome. He died aboard the *De Grasse* after a successful tour of the United States as organist. A prolific composer, he was at his best in writing for the organ, producing over 50 such compositions, including sonatas, scherzos, pieces, and a concerto with orchestra. His orchestral and chamber music is of less interest.

His son, Renzo (born Como, Italy, April 9, 1883), has distinguished himself as a composer, professor of composition at the Verdi Conservatory in Milan, and as a conductor at La Scala. His best works are his operas; but he has also written a symphony, a violin concerto, and various other orchestral and chamber-music compositions.

Boston Pops Orchestra. An orchestra made up of members of the Boston Symphony which gives popular concerts at Boston in May and June under the direction of Arthur Fiedler. It was an outgrowth of the Music Hall Promenade Concerts inaugurated in 1885 under Adolf Neuendorff's direction. When this orchestra moved to Symphony Hall in 1900 its concerts became known as the "Symphony Hall Pops," and after that merely as "Boston Pops." Arthur Fiedler assumed his office in 1930. One year earlier, he had inaugurated outdoor concerts with members of the Boston Symphony on the banks of the Charles River, from then on known as the Esplanade Concerts.

Boston Symphony Orchestra. One of the world's foremost symphony orchestras, founded in Boston, Massachusetts, in 1881 by Colonel Henry Lee Higginson. It gave its first concert at the Boston Music Hall on Oct. 22, 1881, George Henschel conducting. Henschel remained its principal conductor the first three seasons. Among the most important later permanent conductors were Wilhelm Gericke, Arthur Nikisch, Emil Paur, Karl Muck, Max Fiedler, Henri Rabaud, Pierre Monteux, Serge Koussevitzky, and Charles Munch. The Boston Symphony acquired its present auditorium, Symphony Hall, on Sept. 15, 1900.

The orchestra celebrated its 50th anniversary on Oct. 10, 1931, with its first conductor, Henschel, returning to lead the same program (except for one number) with which the orchestra had begun its existence. In 1952 the Boston Symphony made its first tour of Europe; and in 1956 it became the first American orchestra to perform in the Soviet Union, and the second to appear at the Edinburgh Festival. For jubilee celebrations of the orchestra, leading composers have written special works, among these being Aaron Copland, Igor Stravinsky, Arthur Honegger, Paul Hindemith, Serge Prokofiev, Ottorino Respighi, and Albert Roussel.

Bottesini, Giovanni, double-bass player and conductor. Born Crema, Italy, Dec. 22, 1821; died Parma, Italy, July 7, 1889. He was admitted to the Milan Conservatory when he was fourteen. Since the only opening there was in double-bass, he came to study that instrument. Even as a student he revealed remarkable talent for the double-bass. He gave his first concert in Crema in 1840, then toured Italy several times. In 1846 he went to Havana as principal double-bass player in its symphony orchestra. He gave his first New York concert in 1848, and made his first London appearance a year later. His recitals succeeded in bringing artistic significance to the double-bass as a solo instrument. He subsequently turned to conducting, directing opera performances in Paris, Palermo, Cairo, London, and Barcelona; in 1871, on invitation from Verdi, he led the world première of *Aida* in Cairo. Bottesini wrote many works for the double-bass, including fantasies on operas and the *Carnival of Venice*.

Boulanger, Nadia, teacher and conductor. Born Paris, France, Sept. 16, 1887. Her musical training took place at the Paris Conservatory, where she won several prizes and the second Prix de Rome. She has appeared as guest conductor of many of the world's leading orchestras. In 1936 and 1937 she led programs of French music over the BBC, and in 1937 became the first woman ever to conduct an entire program with the Royal Philharmonic Society of London. Her American début as conductor took place with the Boston Symphony in 1938. She has distinguished herself most of all as a teacher of composition both privately and at various music schools and universities, including the Paris Conservatory, Ecole Normale de Musique, and American Conservatory at Fontainebleau. Among her pupils were Jean Françaix, Aaron Copland, Roy Harris, Igor Markevitch, Walter Piston, and Virgil Thomson. During World War II she lived in the United States, where she devoted herself to lecturing and teaching. After the war she became director of music for Monaco, where, in 1956, she conducted the concert at the marriage ceremonies of Prince Rainier and Grace Kelly. She has written several works for orchestra and for the piano, and incidental music for D'Annunzio's *The Dead City*.

Boulez, Pierre, composer. Born Montbrison, France, March 26, 1925. After being graduated from the Paris Conservatory in 1945, where he was a pupil of Messiaen, he studied privately with René Leibowitz. In 1948 he became conductor of a theater orchestra in Paris, and in 1952 he visited the United States as conductor of the French Ballet. Boulez belongs in the vanguard of French modernists who have exploited the most advanced techniques and styles. Much of his writing is in the twelve-tone technique; he has also produced Concrete Music. His instrumental compositions include a *Symphonie concertante* for piano and orchestra; *Polyphonie X* for 17 instruments; a flute sonata; 2 piano sonatas; and a string quartet.

Boult, Sir Adrian, conductor. Born Chester, England, April 8, 1889. After receiving a degree from Christ Church, Oxford, he attended the Leipzig Conservatory. Arthur Nikisch influenced him to become a conductor. Boult made his baton début at Liverpool in 1914, and achieved his first success with the Royal Philharmonic in London in 1918. He then made guest appearances with major European orchestras, distinguishing himself in contemporary English music, and especially in the music of Elgar. In 1924 he was appointed conductor of the City of Birmingham Orchestra. Six years later he became musical director of the BBC, and soon after that he founded the BBC Symphony. Though he resigned his directorial post with the BBC in 1942, he remained principal conductor of the Orchestra until 1950. In 1935 he led a program of British music at the Salzburg Festival, and in the same year he made his American début with the Boston Symphony. He was knighted in 1937 for his services to British music. In 1950 he became conductor of the London Philharmonic, resigning in 1956 to become honorary musical adviser. In 1957 he toured the Soviet Union with that orchestra. He is the author of *A Handbook on the Technique of Conducting* (1921).

Bourgeois gentilhomme, Le. Suite for orchestra by Richard Strauss, op. 66 (1912), derived from the composer's incidental music to the Molière comedy, produced in Stuttgart on Oct. 25, 1912. The suite is in nine sections: I. Overture; II. Minuet; III. The Fencing Master; IV. Entrance and Dance of the Tailors; V. The Minuet of Lully; VI. Courante; VII. Entrance of Cleonte; VIII. Intermezzi: Dorante and Dorimente, Count and Marquise; IX. The Dinner.

The overture is a portrait of Jourdain, the wealthy bourgeois determined to become a gentleman. After a classic minuet there comes a movement satirizing Jourdain's attempts at fencing. This spirit of burlesque is maintained in the fourth part, while the classic style of old dances is revived in the fifth and sixth sections. Entrance of Cleonte alternates between solemnity and gaiety in music adapted from Lully. The *Intermezzi* evoke the world of Louis XIV. The concluding section is an amusing travesty which quotes from Wagner's music drama, *The Rhinegold,* to describe the Rhine salmon, and from Strauss' own *Don Quixote* to speak about the roast mutton.

Bourrée. An old dance of either Spanish or French origin, usually in 2/4 or 4/4 time. It is in two parts, each repeated.

Bourrée fantasque. For piano by Emmanuel Chabrier (1891); a tribute to the composer's province of Auvergne, where the Bourrée is believed to have originated. This composition has an undercurrent of humor and a feeling for the grotesque. It is perhaps best known in Felix Mottl's orchestration, a version first performed in Karlsruhe in 1897. The work was also orchestrated by Charles Koechlin.

Boutique fantasque, La. Ballet suite for orchestra by Ottorino Respighi (1918), freely adapted from Rossini's piano pieces from *Les Péchés de vieillesse.* The ballet, choreography by Leonide Massine, was introduced by the Ballet Russe in London on June 5, 1919.

Bow. An implement used for stringed instruments with which the performer is able to control the vibration of the strings. The modern bow was developed by François Tourte between 1775 and 1780.

Bowing. Manner in which a bow is applied to the strings by a performer, and in which a passage should be played.

Boyce, William, composer. Born probably London, England, about 1710; died Kensington, London, Feb. 7, 1779. He was a boy chorister at St. Paul's Cathedral. After studying the organ with Maurice Greene he was appointed organist of Oxford Chapel in 1734. Though early afflicted by partial deafness, his career was not seriously hampered. He became organist of St. Michael's in Cornhill in 1736, and in 1749 at All Hallows Great and Less, retaining both posts until 1768-1769, when deafness compelled him to withdraw from active participation in music. Meanwhile, in 1758, he became one of three organists at the Chapel Royal. After his retirement he settled in Kensington and dedicated himself to the editing of an anthology of Church music. He died nineteen years after his retirement and was buried in St. Paul's Cathedral. Though most famous for his church music, Boyce wrote eight charming symphonies that are sometimes revived and have been recorded. He also wrote 12 overtures, 12 violin sonatas, and many pieces and duets for harpsichord. He produced a considerable amount of incidental music for plays by Shakespeare, Dryden, Garrick, Richard Steele, and others.

Boyd Neel String Orchestra. *See:* Neel, Boyd.

Brahms, Johannes, composer. Born Hamburg, Germany, May 7, 1833; died Vienna, Austria, April 3, 1897. Born to parents in humble circumstances, Brahms spent his childhood in abject poverty. He was exceptionally gifted in music, and early was taught the piano by Otto Cossel. When Brahms was ten he acquired his first important piano teacher in Eduard Marxsen. His progress now proved so rapid that he was able to give a public recital when he was fourteen. After that he supported himself by doing hack work and teaching the piano; but at the same time he did serious composition, completing songs, piano pieces, and a piano trio.

In 1853 Brahms became the accompanist of the Hungarian violinist, Eduard Reményi. Through him, Brahms came to know many prominent musicians, including Joseph Joachim, and Robert and Clara Schumann, all of whom befriended him. Robert Schumann was so impressed by Brahms' talent that he arranged for the publication of his three piano sonatas and some songs and for his appearance as pianist at the Gewandhaus in Leipzig. Schumann also published an article in the *Neue Zeitschrift fuer Musik* (Oct. 28, 1853) paying high tribute to the young man. The bond between Brahms and the Schumanns remained close. When Robert Schumann was consigned to an asylum, Brahms spent two years near Clara, administering to her needs and helping her care for her children; after Schumann's death, Brahms remained one of her most devoted friends.

In 1857 Brahms was appointed part-time music master to the Prince of Lippe-Detmold. In the three years he held this post he completed his first orchestral works: two serenades and the First Piano Concerto, the latter a failure when introduced at Hanover in 1859 with Joachim conducting and Brahms as soloist. Between 1860 and 1863 Brahms led a women's choir in Hamburg, a period in which he revealed rapidly expanding creative powers through the composition of 2 piano quartets, a sextet, and the Variations on a Theme by Handel for piano. "This is Beethoven's heir!" exclaimed Joseph Hellmesberger when he saw the manuscript of the G minor Piano Quartet.

His failure to get a post as musical director of the Hamburg Philharmonic led Brahms to leave the city and settle permanently in Vienna in 1863, his home for the rest of his life. In the fall of that year he became conductor of the Vienna Singakademie. After that he taught piano for a living until he was able to support himself from his music. From 1871 until 1874 he was musical director of the Gesellschaft der Musikfreunde.

Creatively he was growing all the time. His compositions became increasingly ambitious in structure and scope. His musical speech was continually enriched with poetic accents. His thoughts deepened and matured. With *A German Requiem* he achieved the first major success of his career upon its first performance in its entirety at Bremen in 1868, the composer conducting. There was also acclaim for his first important work for orchestra, Variations on a Theme by Haydn, at Vienna in 1873. In 1876 he completed his first symphony. That work, followed by three others in the same form between 1887 and 1894, placed him at the head of German symphonic composers, the most important symphonist since Beethoven.

Now recognized as one of music's masters, not only in Vienna but abroad, Brahms was surrounded by admirers and disciples among whom were some of the foremost musicians of that age. And he was the recipient of many honors. In 1879 the University of Breslau conferred on him a doctorate in philosophy. In 1886 he was made knight of the Prussian Ordre pour le mérite. In 1889 he was given the honorary freedom of the city of Hamburg. And in 1890 the Emperor of Austria bestowed on him the Order of Leopold.

Though comparatively affluent, Brahms continued to live simply in a small three-room apartment in Vienna until the end of his life; his summers were usually spent in the nearby mountain districts of Vienna. Through the years he came to love several women—including Clara Schumann—but he never married.

Brahms was a giant figure at the culmination of the Romantic era. But he was a Romantic who preferred writing within Classical forms, and within a style that was pure and objective, avoiding programmatic implications. For this he was severely criticized by the many followers of Wagner and Liszt, who considered him behind the times. But other contemporaries, equally distinguished, recognized him as a master and a genius—a composer who had succeeded in fusing the best elements of Classicism and Romanticism. To soundly constructed forms Brahms brought a wealth of poetic thought and feeling. If he had the Classicist's respect for tradition, he also had the Romanticist's lack of inhibitions in giving free rein to his emotions. He added little to musical development, but he did bring to music a majesty of expression, a grandeur, a profundity of introspective thought, and a stirring emotion few composers have equalled.

The following are Brahms' principal instrumental compositions:

Chamber Music: 2 string sextets; 2 string quintets; Piano Quintet in F minor; Clarinet Quintet in B minor; 3 string quartets; 3 piano quartets; 3 piano trios; 3 violin sonatas; 2 cello sonatas; 2 clarinet sonatas; Clarinet Trio in A minor.

Orchestra: 4 symphonies; 2 piano concertos; Concerto in D minor, for violin and orchestra; Concerto in A minor, for violin, cello, and orchestra; 2 serenades; Variations on a Theme by Haydn (also for two pianos); *Academic Festival Overture* (*Akademische Festouvertuere*); *Tragic Overture* (*Tragische Ouvertuere*); Hungarian Dances.

Organ: 11 chorale preludes.

Piano: 3 sonatas; Variations on a Theme by Handel; Variations on a Theme by Paganini; capriccios, intermezzos, rhapsodies, waltzes, ballades, Hungarian Dances for piano duet, and so forth.

See: Alto Rhapsody; Academic Festival Overture; Ballade; Capriccio; Concerto—*Brahms; Hungarian Dances; Im-*

promptu; Intermezzo (3); Quartet— *Brahms;* Quintet—*Brahms;* Requiem— *Brahms;* Rhapsody; Serenade—*Brahms;* Sextet; Symphony—*Brahms; Tragic Overture;* Trio—*Brahms;* Variations on a Theme by Handel; Variations on a Theme by Haydn; Variations on a Theme by Paganini; Waltz.

Brailowsky, Alexander, pianist. Born Kiev, Russia, Feb. 16, 1896. He studied piano mainly in Vienna with Theodor Leschetizky. Soon after the end of World War I, he made his début in Paris, after which he toured Europe, the Near East, the Far East, and Australia. In 1924 he presented in Paris a cycle of 6 concerts devoted to all of Chopin's 169 works; he subsequently performed a similar cycle in Brussels, Zurich, Mexico City, and several times in New York. Also in 1924 —on November 19—he made his American début in New York City. He has achieved world recognition as one of the foremost living interpreters of Chopin's music.

Brain, Aubrey, horn player. Born London, England, July 12, 1893. The son of a horn player, Aubrey received a scholarship for the Royal College of Music in 1911. In the same year he became first horn of the New Symphony Orchestra, and in 1912 of the London Symphony, with which he toured the United States with Arthur Nikisch as conductor. After playing first horn with the orchestra of Covent Garden, Brain was appointed first horn of the BBC Symphony, holding this post until his health forced him to retire in 1945. From 1923 on he was professor at the Royal Academy of Music.

His son, Dennis, also distinguished himself as a horn player (born London, England, May 17, 1921; died Hatfield, England, Sept. 1, 1957). He studied horn with his father at the Royal College of Music, after which he played horn with the Busch Chamber Orchestra, the Royal Philharmonic of London, and with many outstanding chamber-music ensembles. He also appeared as soloist with leading orchestras, often in major works written for him by Benjamin Britten, Paul Hindemith, and others. For a decade, and up to the time of his death in an auto acci-

dent, he was first horn of the Philharmonia Orchestra.

Brand. *See:* Ibsen, Henrik.

Brandenburg Concertos. A set of 6 concerti grossi for orchestra by Johann Sebastian Bach. *See:* Concerto Grosso— *J. S. Bach.*

Brass Band. *See:* Band.

Brass Instruments. Instruments of the horn, trumpet, trombone, and tuba families that form part of a symphony orchestra or band.

Braut von Messina, Die. *See:* Schiller, Friedrich von.

Bravura. An ornamental passage calling for exceptional skill on the part of a performer; a virtuoso style.

Bravo. A cry of approbation by an audience; it originated in Italy but was subsequently heard in concert auditoriums throughout the world.

Bridal Procession. March for orchestra in Act 3 of Rimsky-Korsakov's opera *Le Coq d'or. See also: Coq d'or, Le, Suite.*

Bride of Lammermoor. *See:* Schiller, Friedrich von.

Bridge. A piece of wood supporting the strings of a stringed instrument and transmitting the vibrations of the strings to the belly of the instrument.

Bridge, Frank, composer and conductor. Born Brighton, England, Feb. 26, 1879; died Eastbourne, England, Jan. 10, 1941. Though trained as a violinist at the Royal College of Music in London, Bridge first distinguished himself as violist in such outstanding chamber-music groups as the Joachim Quartet and English String Quartet. This experience in chamber-music performances led to the writing of his first significant works, between 1905 and 1915: the *Fantasy Quartet,* the String Quartet in E minor, *Fantasy Trio,* String Quartet in G minor, and String Sextet. It is through his chamber music that Bridge is most often represented on present-day concert programs, though he did write abundantly and skilfully for orchestra and for the piano. His earlier works were Classical in structure and traditional in idiom; but in the middle 1920's he became more daring in harmony and tonality. For many years Bridge appeared as guest conductor of English orchestras. When he visited the

United States in 1923—and again in 1934 and 1938—he was guest conductor of major American orchestras in programs made up mainly of his own music. His orchestral music includes tone poems (among them *Isabelle* and *Summer*), *Lament* for strings, a suite *The Sea, Rebus, Vignettes, Dance Rhapsody,* and *Dance Poem.* He also wrote, in addition to the chamber works mentioned above, a fourth string quartet, 2 piano trios, a piano quintet, and *Sir Roger de Coverly* (for string quartet, also for orchestra), and numerous works for the piano including a sonata, *Three Poems, A Fairy Tale,* and *Improvisations for the Left Hand.*

Bridge Passage. A transitional section leading either from one main theme to another, or from one movement to the next.

Brigg Fair. (1) Orchestral rhapsody by Frederick Delius (1907), first performed in Liverpool on Jan. 18, 1908. It is built from an old English folksong from Lincolnshire discovered by Percy Grainger, to whom Delius dedicated this composition. In it, the song appears in the oboe, then is elaborated upon. The entire work maintains a pastoral character.

(2) *See:* Grainger, Percy.

Brio. Vigor.

Britt, Horace, cellist. Born Antwerp, Belgium, June 18, 1881. He attended the Paris Conservatory, a pupil of Jules Delsart and Albert Lavignac. After additional study with André Caplet he made his début as cellist with the Lamoureux Orchestra at Paris in 1897. He then toured Europe and the Far East, and made his American début in 1907 as soloist with the Chicago Symphony. From then on, he appeared throughout the music world in recitals, as soloist with orchestras, and guest performer with major chamber-music groups. He also made several appearances as conductor. He has taught the cello at the Curtis Institute, the National Conservatory of Mexico, and Middlebury Music Centre.

Britten, Benjamin, composer. Born Lowestoft, England, Nov. 22, 1913. Remarkably gifted in music from childhood on,

he completed a symphony, 6 string quartets, 10 piano sonatas, and numerous smaller works by the time he was sixteen. Some of the melodic material from this *juvenilia* was gathered into his *Simple Symphony* in 1934. His academic education took place at Gresham's School, Holt; his music study, with Frank Bridge, and from 1930 to 1933 at the Royal College of Music in London, where his teachers included John Ireland, Arthur Benjamin, and Harold Samuel.

Britten first attracted interest with compositions performed at festivals of the International Society for Contemporary Music between 1934 and 1938. These included the *Fantasy Quartet,* a suite for violin and piano, and most significantly the Variations on a Theme by Frank Bridge for orchestra. Two concertos, one for piano and the other for violin, added to his reputation.

In 1939 Britten visited the United States, where he lived several years and completed some major works, including the *Sinfonia da Requiem,* for orchestra. He returned to his native land in 1942. Soon after the end of World War II he became famous throughout Europe for operas that brought him to a leading position among England's composers. The first of these, *Peter Grimes* (commissioned by the Koussevitzky Foundation), was a sensation when introduced in London in 1945.

Though his greatest strength lies in his music for the stage, Britten has also produced many distinguished works for orchestra and various instrumental combinations. He also successfully adapted the music of Rossini into two orchestral suites, *Matinées musicales* and *Soirées musicales.* Britten is an eclectic composer who has written skilfully in many different styles from Germanic Romanticism to Expressionism. He is a remarkable craftsman who is the master of any idiom he undertakes, and who is able to bring to his writing a strong gift for lyric expression. In 1953 he was awarded the Companionship of Honor by the British government for services to English music.

The following are Britten's principal instrumental works:

Chamber Music: 2 string quartets; *Fantasy Quartet;* Suite for violin and piano; *Lacrymae* (reflections on a song by John Dowland), for viola and piano; *Six Metamorphoses after Ovid,* for oboe solo.

Orchestra: Simple Symphony; Variations on a Theme by Frank Bridge; Piano Concerto in D major; *Mont Juic,* suite of Catalan dances (with Lennox Berkeley); Violin Concerto in D minor; *Canadian Carnival; Sinfonia da Requiem; Diversions on a Theme* for piano (left hand) and orchestra; *Matinées musicales,* suite after Rossini; *Soirées musicales,* suite after Rossini; *Scottish Ballad,* for two pianos and orchestra; *A Young Person's Guide to the Orchestra; An Occasional Overture; Spring Symphony,* for solo voice, chorus, and orchestra; *Divertimento; Gloriana,* symphonic suite based on the opera.

See: Four Sea Interludes; Passacaglia; *Scottish Ballad; Sinfonia da Requiem;* Variations on a Theme by Frank Bridge; *Young People's Guide to the Orchestra.*

Brodsky, Adolf, violinist. Born Taganrog, Russia, March 21, 1851; died Manchester, England, Jan. 22, 1929. A prodigy, he was financed by local patrons to study the violin in Vienna with Joseph Hellmesberger, and after that at the Vienna Conservatory. Following his graduation he joined the Hellmesberger Quartet as violinist; he also played in the Vienna Royal Opera orchestra and toured as virtuoso throughout Europe. In 1881 he presented in Vienna the world première of Tchaikovsky's Violin Concerto. Besides winning renown as violinist, Brodsky had a fruitful career as teacher, first at the Moscow Conservatory, then at the Leipzig Conservatory. In Leipzig he founded the Brodsky String Quartet (with Hugo Becker, Hans Sitt, and Julius Klengel), which became famous throughout Europe. In 1891 he came to the United States, where for several years he was concertmaster of the New York Symphony. He returned to Europe in 1894, becoming concertmaster of the Hallé Orchestra and director of the Manchester Royal College of Music. In 1892 he was honored with the Norwegian Order of St. Olaf.

Brodsky String Quartet. *See* above.

Broken Chords. Arpeggios.

Broken Octaves. Successive alternation of higher and lower tones of a series of octaves.

Bruch, Max, composer. Born Cologne, Germany, Jan. 6, 1838; died Friedenau, near Berlin, Germany, Oct. 2, 1920. He began composing when he was eleven, and by the time he was fourteen he had completed a symphony (performed in Cologne in 1852) and a string quartet which won a prize. On receiving the Mozart Prize from Frankfort-on-the-Main, he studied for four years with Karl Reinecke and Ferdinand Hiller. He first attracted attention with an opera, *Die Loreley,* and a choral work, *Frithjof.* For several years Bruch conducted orchestral concerts in Cologne; after that he served as Kapellmeister to Prince Schwarzburg in Sondershausen. In 1878 he was appointed director of the Stern Choral Society in Berlin. From 1880 to 1883 he was conductor of the Liverpool Philharmonic, and from 1883 to 1890 of the Breslau Orchestral Society. In 1883 he visited the United States, leading choral groups in programs of his own works. In 1891 he became professor of composition at the Berlin High School of Music, holding this post until his retirement in 1910. In 1908 he was honored with the Prussian Order, Pour le mérite.

Bruch is a Romanticist who brought a pleasing lyricism (often grounded in folk music) and an astute technique to his best works. But his melodic and harmonic writing have greater charm and facility than originality. He remains alive in the contemporary concert repertory by virtue of his excellent Violin Concerto in G minor, the *Kol Nidrei* for cello and orchestra, and the *Scottish Fantasy* for violin and orchestra. He wrote two other violin concertos, 3 symphonies, a two-piano concerto, 2 string quartets, 3 piano trios, *Swedish Dances* for violin and piano, and pieces for piano, two and four hands.

See: Concerto—*Bruch; Kol Nidrei.*

Bruckner, Anton, composer. Born Ansfelden, Austria, Sept. 4, 1824; died Vienna, Austria, Oct. 11, 1896. The son of a schoolmaster, Bruckner was trained as a teacher. But he also began music study early, first with a cousin, then at the secular school of St. Florian. After completing his academic education in Linz, he began his teaching career in Windhaag, and in 1845 received an appointment at the St. Florian School. While fulfilling these teaching duties, he played the organ, acquiring a reputation for his virtuosity and skill at improvisation; he also started serious composition. By 1853 he decided to abandon schoolteaching for music. Settling in Vienna, he studied counterpoint with Simon Sechter. In 1856 he was appointed organist of the Linz Cathedral, where he remained for about a dozen years. At the same time he also conducted a Vienna choral society, beginning in 1860; with that group he made his official bow as composer by directing the première of his *Ave Maria* on May 12, 1861.

Hearing Wagner's opera *Tannhaeuser* was a turning point in his life. He became one of Wagner's most devoted disciples. In 1865 he made a pilgrimage to Munich to attend the première of *Tristan and Isolde;* on this occasion he met the master and fell humbly on his knees before him. This worship of Wagner affected his style of composition, which now absorbed Wagner's mannerisms besides emulating the master's dramatic expressiveness.

In 1867 Bruckner was appointed court organist in Vienna, and in 1868 he became professor at the Vienna Conservatory, where he remained many years. He lived in Vienna for the rest of his life, dividing his time between teaching and composition. He had to wait a long time for recognition as a composer. His First Symphony, introduced in Linz in 1868, was a failure; so was the Third Symphony in Vienna in 1877. This public and critical hostility to Bruckner continued for several years while anti-Wagner and pro-Brahms forces in Vienna made him the helpless butt of their abuse.

His first taste of approval came in 1881 when Hans Richter gave the première of Bruckner's Fourth Symphony in Vienna. Even greater approbation came to him in Leipzig at the première of his Seventh Symphony in 1884. Later presentations of the Seventh Symphony

under Felix Mottl, Karl Muck, and Hermann Levi helped spread Bruckner's fame throughout Austria and Germany. He now became the recipient of major honors, including an honorary degree from the University of Vienna in 1891, and an imperial insignia from the Emperor of Austria in 1894.

Bruckner's nine symphonies are an indestructible monument in orchestral music. He had obvious weaknesses as a composer. He was garrulous; he had a tendency towards vast structures and a partiality for grandiloquent utterances; he liked to pile detail upon detail and ornament upon ornament with disconcerting profusion. And too often he was an echo of Wagner. Yet he could also bring to his music an other-worldly serenity, poetry, mysticism, and ingratiating charm. His best symphonies are rewarding experiences for the discriminating music-lover able and willing to separate gold from dross. Besides his symphonies Bruckner wrote an orchestral Overture in G minor, a string quartet in F major, *Intermezzo* for string quintet, and various preludes and other pieces for the organ.

See: Symphony—*Bruckner.*

Bruennhilde's Immolation. Closing scene of Wagner's music drama *The Twilight of the Gods* (*Goetterdaemmerung*) with which the *Ring of the Nibelungs* cycle is brought to a cataclysmic conclusion. Discovering she is the cause of Siegfried's death, Bruennhilde orders a funeral pyre built for the burning of his body. Into these flames she angrily throws the accursed Ring. The music of the Immolation scene begins at this point, as, summoning her horse, Bruennhilde bids farewell and calls upon Wotan and the other gods to witness her grief. In orchestral presentations, her magnificent song of farewell is assumed mainly by strings. Mounting her horse she rides to her death in the flames. Now in rapid succession come the motifs of the "Magic Fire," "Rhine," "Rhinemaidens," and finally "Valhalla." The river Rhine rises and swells. The Rhinemaidens carry Hagen to his death as he tries to retrieve the Ring. Valhalla collapses, and the gods meet their doom.

Budapest String Quartet. One of the

world's most distinguished chamber-music ensembles, organized in Kolozvar, Hungary, on Dec. 19, 1917. During its initial tours the members were Emil Hauser, Imre Poganyi, Istvan Ipolyi, and Harry Son. When the Quartet made its American début in New York on Feb. 3, 1931, Joseph Roisman replaced Poganyi, and Mischa Schneider took over for Son. Since then its personnel has changed several times, but never its integrity and high standards. With Joseph Roisman, Jac Gorodetzky, Boris Kroyt, and Mischa Schneider it has toured the music world. Its American television début took place on Oct. 27, 1957.

Buelow, Hans von, pianist and conductor. Born Dresden, Germany, Jan. 8, 1830; died Cairo, Egypt, Feb. 12, 1894. He began to study music seriously in his ninth year with Friedrich Wieck, Schumann's father-in-law, and continued later with several other teachers in Leipzig. But he was originally directed to law rather than music. While attending the University of Leipzig, which he had entered in 1848, he studied counterpoint with Moritz Hauptmann. The première of Wagner's opera, *Lohengrin,* under Liszt's direction in 1850 impelled von Buelow to abandon law for music. After studying the piano with Liszt, he toured Central Europe as piano virtuoso for the first time in 1853. Two years later he was appointed head of the piano department of the Stern Conservatory in Berlin. He retained this post nine years, inaugurating there outstanding concerts. During this period, in 1857, he married Cosima, Liszt's daughter. In 1864, von Buelow was appointed court pianist to Ludwig II of Bavaria and conductor of the Royal Opera in Munich, where his performances of Wagnerian music dramas (including the world premières of *Tristan and Isolde* and *The Mastersingers*) were of historic significance. In 1867 he was also named director of the Munich Conservatory. When Cosima von Buelow and Wagner fell in love, von Buelow divorced his wife and saw her marry Wagner, with whom she had been living illicitly for several years. Despite his bitterness towards Wagner as a man, his enthusiasm for Wagner's music remained

undiminished and he never relaxed his efforts in promoting it. Von Buelow now toured Europe as concert pianist more extensively than before, achieving world recognition as one of music's most trenchant intellects and one of the most formidable piano virtuosos. In 1873 he appeared for the first time in England, and in 1875-1876 he toured the United States, giving 139 concerts. In 1878 he became Kapellmeister at the Court of Hanover, and in 1880 he was appointed Court Music Director to the Duke of Meiningen. For the next five years he directed such outstanding orchestral concerts in Meiningen that its orchestra became one of the most celebrated in Europe. After resigning from this post in 1885 he again appeared throughout Europe both as pianist and conductor. In 1894 declining health sent him to Egypt, where he died. Von Buelow made transcriptions for the piano of works by Berlioz and Wagner, and prepared new editions of Beethoven's sonatas and Cramer's etudes.

Buerger, Gottfried August, poet. Born Molmserwende, Germany, Jan. 1, 1748; died Goettingen, Germany, 1794. His famous narrative poem, *Lenore,* based on German folk lore, was the inspiration for a tone poem of the same name by Henri Duparc and for Joachim Raff's Symphony No. 5. César Franck's tone poem, *Le Chasseur maudit,* was based on Buerger's ballad, *Der wilde Jaeger.*

Bull, John, composer. Born Somersetshire, England, about 1562; died Antwerp, Belgium, March 12 or 13, 1628. He was an early master of keyboard music. From 1572 to 1578 he was educated at the Chapel Royal. In 1582 he became organist of the Hereford Cathedral; in 1585 he was admitted as a member of the Chapel Royal, becoming its organist in 1591. From 1596 to 1607 he was professor of music at Gresham College. Beginning with the turn of the 17th century, he toured the Continent as virtuoso on the organ and virginals. In 1611 he entered the service of Prince Henry, but two years later he left England for good and settled in Belgium, where in 1617 he became organist of the Antwerp Cathedral, a post he held until his death. The circumstances surrounding his departure from England are enshrouded in mystery. The 200 or so compositions Bull wrote for keyboard instruments are among the most significant of his era—historically important in developing a technique of keyboard performance and an instrumental style of writing. His music embraces many preludes, fantasies, pavanes, and variations for the virginals and for the organ; among his most familiar works are *The King's Hunt, Queen Elizabeth's Pavane,* and the *Walsingham* Variations. He also wrote about 50 works for viols, but these are of lesser interest.

Bull, Ole, violinist. Born Bergen, Norway, Feb. 5, 1810; died Lyso, Norway, Aug. 17, 1880. He studied the violin as a child but made little headway until a hearing of Paganini at Paris in 1831 inspired him to renewed efforts at mastering the instrument. Largely self-taught, he made his début in Paris on April 18, 1832. He subsequently toured the music world several times, including five tours of the United States between 1843 and 1879. Besides being an outstanding virtuoso, he was also an astute showman and a magnetic personality; his fame rivalled that of Paganini. In 1870 he married an American, Sara Chapman Thorp (his second wife), who wrote his biography in 1886. An ardent nationalist, Bull encouraged Norwegian composers to write national music and was responsible for founding a theater of national drama in Bergen, and a Conservatory in Christiania (now Oslo). He wrote many compositions for the violin, including 2 concertos, and many small pieces and variations; his music, however, is now rarely performed.

Bulwer-Lytton, Edward George Earle, novelist and dramatist. Born London, England, May 25, 1803; died Torquay, England, Jan. 18, 1873. Among the instrumental compositions inspired by Bulwer-Lytton's novels or plays were the following: Edward MacDowell's poem for piano, *The Brook* (a movement from his suite, *Four Little Poems,* op. 32); John Philip Sousa's orchestral suite, *The Last Days of Pompeii;* and Wagner's overture to his opera *Rienzi.*

Burgin, Richard, violinist and conductor. Born Warsaw, Poland, Oct. 11, 1892. After studying the violin with Isidor Lotto, Joseph Joachim, and Leopold Auer, he made his début as soloist with the Warsaw Philharmonic on Dec. 7, 1903. In 1907 he toured Europe and the United States. From 1912 to 1920 he was concertmaster of several important European orchestras, including the Warsaw Philharmonic and the Oslo Symphony. Since 1920 he has been the concertmaster, and since 1927 also the assistant conductor, of the Boston Symphony. He has often conducted performances of the Boston Symphony and other major American orchestras. From 1951 to 1956 he was the principal conductor of the Portland (Maine) Symphony. He is married to the concert violinist, Ruth Posselt.

Burkhard, Willy, composer. Born Évilard-sur-Bienne, Switzerland, April 17, 1900; died Zurich, Switzerland, June 18, 1955. He studied at the Bern Conservatory, and in Germany and Paris with various teachers including Max d'Ollone and Siegfried Karg-Elert. In 1924 he began teaching in Bern, becoming professor at the Conservatory four years later. In 1942 he moved to Zurich, where he taught at the Conservatory until his death. A prolific composer, he was a modernist who combined the most advanced techniques and idioms with contrapuntal writing and harmonies derived from church modes. In 1950 he received the Schweizer-Tonkuenstlerverein Prize for composition. His works include a symphony, a concerto for strings, 2 violin concertos, Symphony in One Movement, a Toccata and a Sonata da camera, both for orchestra, 2 string quartets, a piano trio, violin sonata, cello sonata, and a Serenade for eight instruments.

Burleigh, Cecil, violinist and composer. Born Wyoming, N.Y., April 17, 1885. For three years he studied music in Berlin with Anton Witek, Max Grunberg, and Hugo Leichtentritt. Later music study took place in the United States with Émile Sauret, Felix Borowski, Leopold Auer, and Ernest Bloch. In the early 1920's he began a career as concert violinist. During this period he completed several major works, including 3 violin concertos (one of which received a prize in Chicago in 1916) and 2 tone poems. In the early 1930's he lapsed into a period of creative inactivity from which he emerged in 1940 with *Leaders of Men*, a suite for orchestra. At this time he repudiated most of the works written before 1930. Among his principal works since 1940 are *From the Muses* and a trilogy of symphonies entitled *Creation, Prophecy*, and *Revelation*, all for orchestra; 2 string quartets entitled *Illusion* and *Transition;* and *American Processional* for violin and piano.

Burleske. For piano and orchestra in D minor by Richard Strauss (1885), introduced in Eisenach, Germany, on June 21, 1890; Eugène d'Albert was the soloist, and the composer conducted. This work is a happy excursion into burlesque humor and improvisation. It opens in unorthodox fashion with the principal theme announced by the timpani. The timpani play a prominent role throughout the work, and at times engage in conversation with the solo piano.

Burney, Charles, music historian. Born Shrewsbury, England, April 7, 1726; died Chelsea, England, April 12, 1814. He was early trained as organist and in his boyhood played in several churches. For nine years Burney served as organist at St. Margaret's at King's Lynn. In 1770 he toured France and Italy to gather material for a music history. The result was *The Present State of Music in France and Italy* (1771), written in diary form. In 1772 he undertook a second tour, after which he published *The Present State of Music in Germany, the Netherlands and the United Provinces* (1773). The *General History of Music* was published between 1776 and 1789, and was reissued in a new edition in London and New York in 1935. Burney's historical writings are of great importance in the literature on music, and to this day are a valuable source of information about 18th-century music.

Burns, Robert, poet. Born Alloway, Scotland, Jan. 25, 1759; died Dumfries, Scotland, July 21, 1796. Burns' *Tam o' Shanter* was the inspiration for a symphonic ballad by George Chadwick, a concert overture by Learmont Drysdale, and a

tone poem by Ian Whyte—all three bearing the same name as the poem. Sir Alexander Mackenzie's *Scottish Rhapsody, No. 3*, was also inspired by *Tam o' Shanter*, while his *Scottish Rhapsody, No. 2*, is a musical tribute to the poet.

Busch, Adolf, violinist. Born Siegen, Germany, Aug. 8, 1891; died Guilford, Vt., June 9, 1952. He was the brother of Fritz Busch (see below). He studied music with Willy Hess and Bram Eldering at the Cologne Conservatory, and at Bonn with Hugo Grueters. In 1912 he became concertmaster of the Vienna Konzertverein; in 1918 he was appointed head of the violin department of the Berlin High School of Music; and in 1919 he formed a string quartet bearing his name which became famous throughout Europe. Meanwhile he concertized as violin virtuoso extensively, besides making notable appearances with chamber-music groups and distinguished artists, including the pianist, Rudolf Serkin, who subsequently became his son-in-law. Busch made his American début in 1931 with the New York Philharmonic Orchestra conducted by Toscanini. Though an Aryan, he renounced his native land in 1933 because of his disapproval of the Nazi regime. He now became a Swiss citizen and helped to found the Lucerne Festival. In the fall of 1939 he toured the United States with the Busch Quartet. He then made his home in Guilford, Vermont, where, with Rudolf Serkin, he helped organize the Marlboro School of Music. He also became an American citizen. Busch wrote many works for orchestra and for chamber-music groups. His principal works include a symphony, various concertos, a *Comedy Overture* and Variations and Fugue on a Theme by Mozart, both for orchestra, a piano quintet, string quartet, and piano trio.

Busch, Fritz, conductor. Born Siegen, Germany, March 13, 1890; died London, England, Sept. 14, 1951. He was the brother of Adolf Busch (see above). He attended the Cologne Conservatory, a pupil of Fritz Steinbach and Otto Klauwell among others. He began his career as conductor in 1909 at the Riga Municipal Theater, after which he led orchestral concerts in Bad Pyrmont and Berlin.

In 1918 he conducted a successful Reger festival with the Berlin Philharmonic in Jena. Though he subsequently achieved fame in opera, first at the Dresden Opera, then at Glyndebourne (which he helped to organize) and at the Metropolitan Opera, he was also a noted symphony conductor. It was in the latter capacity that he made his American début with the New York Symphony in 1927. He also led orchestral concerts with the State Radio in Copenhagen. He left Germany for good in 1933 because of his disapproval of the Nazi regime and subsequently appeared in South America, England, the United States, and Edinburgh. He is the author of an autobiography, *Pages from a Musician's Life* (1949).

Busoni, Ferruccio, pianist and composer. Born Empoli, Italy, April 1, 1866; died Berlin, Germany, July 27, 1924. He came from a family of professional musicians. After receiving preliminary training in music he made his début as a pianist at the age of eight in Trieste, after which he toured Europe. He then studied composition with Wilhelm Mayer at Graz. In 1888-1889 he joined the faculty of the Helsingfors Conservatory. One year later he received an appointment at the Moscow Conservatory, and from 1891 to 1893 he taught at the New England Conservatory in Boston. During the latter period he made his first appearance as pianist in the United States, with the Boston Symphony. Returning to Europe, he made several successful tours, then established himself in Berlin, where he spent several years in intensive study of the piano. In his later tours he received acclaim throughout the world for his brilliant bravura style in the tradition of Anton Rubinstein as well as for his trenchant musicianship. He was serving as director of the Liceo Musicale in Bologna when World War I broke out. Busoni went to live in Zurich, where he devoted himself to composition. After the war he made triumphant tours as pianist in all parts of Europe, and occupied the chair in composition at the Royal Academy of Arts in Berlin. His last work was an opera, *Doktor Faust,* which he was prevented from finishing by his death. One of the most penetrating musi-

cal minds of his generation, Busoni brought to his compositions and piano performances profundity of thought, complete mastery of technique, and a restless intelligence that made him seek out new methods and approaches. Since many of his works are efforts to prove a theory or solve a specific technical problem, they are frequently exercises in intellectual processes rather than deeply felt music. For this reason their appeal to the general public is limited. Busoni's name appears most often on concert programs in conjunction with his brilliant transcriptions for the piano of works by Johann Sebastian Bach. He also prepared new editions of Bach's *Well-Tempered Clavier* and some of Liszt's piano music. Busoni's principal instrumental works include 2 symphonic suites, *Comedy Overture (Lustspielouvertuere), Turandot Suite, Berceuse élégiaque, Indian Fantasy (Indianische Fantasie),* and *Rondo arlecchinesco,* all for orchestra; various concertos for solo instruments and orchestra (including the excellent Concerto in D major for violin and orchestra); 2 string quartets and 2 violin sonatas; and numerous pieces for the piano, including 6 sonatinas, 24 preludes, *Elegies,* and *Indian Diary.*

See: *Berceuse élégiaque; Comedy Overture; Indian Fantasy;* Sarabande.
Butterfly (Grieg). See: *Lyric Pieces.*
Butterfly Etude. See: Etude—*Chopin.*
Buxtehude, Dietrich, organist and composer. Born Oldesloe, Denmark, about 1637; died Luebeck, Germany, May 9, 1707. He was early given instruction on the organ by his father. Between 1657 and 1660 he held various minor posts as church organist. When he was thirty he went to Luebeck, where on April 11, 1668, he became organist at St. Mary's. There he became famous for his organ concerts, which attracted pilgrims from all parts of Europe (including Bach in 1703 and Handel in 1705). In 1673 he inaugurated Sunday evening concerts (*Abendmusiken*), given the five Sundays preceding Christmas; outstanding organ and choral music was performed in these, among the earliest public concerts given anywhere.

Buxtehude's importance as instrumental composer rests in his remarkable works for organ, in which he opened new vistas by developing and solidifying major forms and crystallizing a pure instrumental style. He was one of the most notable predecessors of Johann Sebastian Bach in this field—setting the artistic stage for that master. Buxtehude's organ music includes many chorale preludes, chaconnes, passacaglias, fantasias, fugues, toccatas, and so forth.

Byrd, William, composer. Born probably Lincolnshire, England, 1543; died Stondon, Essex, England, July 4, 1623. In 1563 he was appointed organist of Lincoln Cathedral. Six and a half years later he became Gentleman of the Chapel Royal, assuming in 1572 the post of organist, which he shared with Thomas Tallis. His first publication was also shared with Tallis, a volume of motets (1575). After Tallis' death in 1585, Byrd became the leading musical figure in England. He published his first volume of madrigals in 1588, and in 1590 began writing his first important pieces for the virginals. Byrd is most famous for his choral and vocal music, but his instrumental music also has interest. With John Bull he was responsible for establishing a school of music in England which helped crystallize an instrumental style. Byrd's more than 100 compositions for the virginals were among the first in this field to suggest both the technical and the artistic possibilities of keyboard music. They include preludes, voluntaries, courantes, pavanes, galliards, airs, varia-

tions, grounds, and fantasies—the most popular being the *Earl of Salisbury* Pavane and Galliard, *Sellinger's Round, Wolsey's Wilde,* and the *Earl of Oxford's March.* Gordon Jacob adapted three of Byrd's virginal pieces (*The Bells, Earl of Oxford's March,* and *Wolsey's Wilde*) into a suite for orchestra.

Byron, George Gordon Noel, Lord, poet. Born London, England, Jan. 22, 1788; died Missolonghi, Greece, April 19, 1824. The following poems and poetical dramas by Byron were the source of instrumental compositions (where titles of compositions are not given they are the same as Byron's):

Childe Harold: Berlioz (*Harold in Italy*); Liszt (*Les Cloches de Genève* for piano from *Années de pèlerinage*).

The Corsair: Berlioz (concert overture); Vitezslav Novák (concert overture).

The Lament of Tasso (Liszt's tone poem for orchestra, *Tasso*).

Manfred: Henry Bishop (incidental music); Anatoli Bogatirev (Variations and Suite, for piano); Adam Carse (orchestral prelude); William Howard Glover (concert overture); Alexander Mackenzie (incidental music); Friedrich Nietzsche (*Manfred Meditation,* for piano); Vitezslav Novák (Ballad in E minor, for piano); Schumann (incidental music, including a famous Overture); Tchaikovsky (*Manfred Symphony*).

Ode to Napoleon: Arnold Schoenberg (ode for narrator and orchestra).

C

Cacophony. A discord, an unpleasant combination of tones.

Cadence. Termination of a phrase, section, or movement.

Cadenza. A florid and usually an unaccompanied passage for a solo instrument near the end of a movement of a concerto. Cadenzas are intended to dis-

play the virtuosity of the performer and are built from the basic thematic material of the movement in which they appear. Originally these cadenzas were improvised by the performer during the actual concert. But later on it became habitual for performers to interpolate into the concerto cadenzas previously written for it by the composer, the performer, or some other musician. In some of Mozart's and Beethoven's piano concertos, and in the piano concertos of Brahms and Schumann, the cadenzas are by the composers themselves; this is also true of most contemporary concertos. Cadenzas for piano concertos by Mozart and Beethoven were written by Clara Schumann, Saint-Saëns, Anton Rubinstein, Edwin Fischer, Ernst Dohnányi, Karl Reinecke, among many others. Beethoven wrote a cadenza for Mozart's Piano Concerto in D minor, K. 466. For the Beethoven Violin Concerto there are cadenzas by Joseph Joachim, Fritz Kreisler, and Leopold Auer, among others. Joachim wrote cadenzas for the violin concertos of Mendelssohn and Brahms.

Cadman, Charles Wakefield, composer. Born Johnstown, Pa., Dec. 24, 1881; died Los Angeles, Calif., Dec. 30, 1946. During boyhood, he studied music in Pittsburgh with Emil Paur and Leo Oehmler, and in his sixteenth year became an organist there. Cadman early interested himself in the music of the American Indian. He not only did considerable research among Omaha Indians, but he also lectured extensively on the subject, and completed several successful works utilizing melodies and rhythms of American Indian music. These works include his extraordinarily popular song, *From the Land of the Sky-Blue Water,* an opera *Shanewis* (performed at the Metropolitan Opera in 1918), and various instrumental works including the *Thunderbird Suite,* for orchestra. After 1926, Cadman abandoned this idiom, but his later works remained identifiably American in their melodic and rhythmic content now derived from the music of the Negro, the cowboy, or the folk music of the Kentucky mountains. His most significant later orchestral works are the *Dark Dancers of the Mardi Gras, Suite on American Folktunes, Aurora Borealis* for piano and orchestra, *Pennsylvania, Huckleberry Finn Goes Fishing,* and a symphony. He also wrote a piano quintet, piano trio, violin sonata, piano sonata, and pieces for the violin.

Cage, John, pianist and composer. Born Los Angeles, Calif., Sept. 5, 1912. He is an innovator in writing non-thematic, non-harmonic music emphasizing percussion; in creating works for the "prepared piano"; and in exploring unorthodox sounds. After studying the piano with Fannie Dillon in Los Angeles and Lazare Lévy in Paris, he took lessons in theory and composition with Arnold Schoenberg and Henry Cowell among others. Vitally interested from the first in percussive music, he wrote many works that emphasized rhythm alone; these included *Constructions, Imaginary Landscape, Amores,* and a piano concerto. He also devised the "prepared piano," which achieved unique percussive effects and sonorities through the attachment of bits of metal, wood, rubber, and so forth to the strings of the piano from the damper point. He completed numerous compositions for the prepared piano. He also explored broader fields of sound in *Williams Mix* and *Construction in Metal* by combining various bell tones, utilizing different recordings of various non-musical sounds picked up on magnetic tape, and using such novel procedures as dipping a vibrating cymbal into a bowl of water. A work entitled *Four Minutes and Thirty-Three Seconds* consists entirely of silent "music," with the pianist merely sitting at the piano without playing anything. A cross-section of his most important music over a period of a quarter of a century was given in New York on May 16, 1958. Cage has taught music at various schools and colleges and has written many articles about his novel procedures and approaches. In 1949 he received a Guggenheim Fellowship and the Award of the Society of Arts and Letters.

Calm Sea and Prosperous Voyage (Meeresstille und glueckliche Fahrt). Concert overture in D major by Mendelssohn, op. 27 (1832), first performed at Leipzig in 1835 under the composer's direction. The source was two short poems by Goethe, *The Calmness of the Sea* and *A Prosperous Voyage.* The overture is in two sections. The first, Adagio, begins with a motto theme in the basses. Full harmonies in the strings against a wind accompaniment describe the calm sea. A figure in the flute leads to a subject for flute and wind with a background of plucked strings: a picture of the sea voyage. The second section (*Molto allegro vivace; Allegro maestoso*) is dominated by a song for the cellos. In the coda the safe arrival is portrayed. Edward Elgar quotes from this overture in the 13th variation of his *Enigma Variations.*

Camera. A term found in 17th- and 18th-century sonatas and concertos to designate a secular composition.

Cameron, Basil, conductor. Born Reading, England, Aug. 18, 1884. He studied the violin in Berlin with Joseph Joachim and Leopold Auer, and composition with Max Bruch. He then joined the violin section of the London Symphony. From 1912 to 1916 he was music director in Torquay, where he led notable Wagner and Richard Strauss festivals. After World War I he made successful appearances in Brighton and Harrogate, and from 1923 to 1930 was conductor of the Hastings Municipal Orchestra. Between 1928 and 1931 he also led the Royal Philharmonic of London. He made his American début with the San Francisco Symphony in 1930, then until 1932 was with Issai Dobrowen co-conductor of that orchestra. From 1932 to 1938 he was principal conductor of the Seattle Symphony. After returning to England he conducted the London Promenade Concerts and appeared as guest conductor with leading European orchestras.

Campanella, La (The Bells). Final (third) movement of Paganini's Concerto No. 2 in B minor, for violin and orchestra, op. 7. Here harmonics in the violin are combined with bells in the orchestra. Liszt transcribed this movement for the piano, including it in his *Etudes d'exécution transcendante d'après Paganini* (the "Paganini Etudes"). *See:* Etude—*Liszt.*

Campoli, Alfredo, violinist. Born Rome, Italy, Oct. 20, 1906. His father, a professor at the Santa Cecilia Academy, was his only teacher. In 1911 the family settled in London. Campoli began concertizing in his tenth year, winning several awards and medals. He subsequently achieved success throughout Europe as a violin virtuoso. In London he also conducted an orchestra which he founded. During World War II he played the violin

for British troops. His concert career was resumed after the war with extended tours of Europe, Australia, New Zealand, India, and in Hong Kong and Singapore. He also performed regularly over the BBC, and made many recordings. His American début took place with the New York Philharmonic on Dec. 5, 1949.

Canon. A contrapuntal style or composition in strict imitation. The subject or melody, presented by one voice or instrument, is imitated strictly by one or more other voices or instruments. *Three Blind Mice* and *Frère Jacques* are familiar examples of canons.

Cantabile. Singing style.

Cantelli, Guido, conductor. Born Novara, Italy, April 27, 1920; died off Orly airfield, France, Nov. 23, 1956. He attended the Milan Conservatory where, in his last year, he led one of its orchestral concerts. His official début as a conductor took place in 1941 with a performance of Verdi's opera, *La Traviata,* in Novara. For the next two years Cantelli conducted performances of opera and symphonic music throughout Italy. During World War II he was interned in concentration camps in Germany and Italy because of his opposition to the Fascist-Nazi axis. After the war he renewed his activity as a conductor. Between 1946 and 1948 he performed in Belgium and Austria. He was discovered by Toscanini, who invited him to the United States to conduct the NBC Symphony. Cantelli made an impressive American début with that orchestra on Jan. 1, 1949. For the next two seasons he returned to the United States to direct the NBC Symphony, and beginning with 1951 he led each year a part of the season of the New York Philharmonic. He also appeared with other major orchestras in America and Europe, and scored substantial successes at festivals in Salzburg, Lucerne, Edinburgh, Venice, and elsewhere. He was en route to the United States for appearances with the New York Philharmonic when he was killed in a crash just as his plane took off from Orly Field outside Paris.

Cantilena. A melody, or air.

Canzona (Canzone). An instrumental composition of the 16th century in contrapuntal style and usually in several sections.

Canzonetta. A short song; a form sometimes found in instrumental music, as in the second movement of Mendelssohn's String Quartet No. 1.

Capet, Lucien, violinist and teacher. Born Paris, France, Jan. 8, 1873; died there Dec. 18, 1928. After attending the Paris Conservatory he became concertmaster of the Lamoureux Orchestra in 1896. He subsequently toured Europe as a violin virtuoso. He organized his first string quartet in 1893. Beginning in 1903, the ensemble (which now included Capet and Touret as violins, Henri Casadesus, viola, and Louis Hasselmans, cello) achieved renown throughout Europe, especially for its performances of Beethoven's last quartets. In 1911 the Capet Quartet represented French quartet-playing at the Beethoven festival in Bonn. From 1907 on, Capet was a member of the faculty of the Paris Conservatory, where his career as professor of violin and chamber music was both long and distinguished.

Capet Quartet. *See:* above.

Caplet, André, conductor. Born Le Havre, France, Nov. 23, 1878; died Paris, France, April 22, 1925. He attended the Paris Conservatory, winning the Prix de Rome in 1901. He directed a performance of his own *Marche solenelle* for orchestra at the Villa Medici on April 18, 1903. After returning to Paris he led performances of opera and symphonic music. Debussy regarded him so highly that in 1911 he selected him to conduct *Le Martyre de Saint-Sébastien.* Caplet became one of Debussy's most intimate friends; orchestrated some of his piano works, including *Children's Corner;* made piano arrangements of *La Mer* and *Le Martyre de Saint-Sébastien.* From 1910 to 1914 he was principal conductor of the Boston Opera Company. After World War I he led the Pasdeloup and other major French orchestras. He was a composer in an impressionist style. His best orchestral works are the tone poem *Le Masque de la mort rouge,* after Poe, and *Epiphanie* for cello and orchestra; his chamber music includes *Conte fantastique* for harp and string quartet

(also after Poe), *Suite persane* for ten instruments, a piano quintet, and *Sonata da chiesa* for violin and organ.

Capriccio. A caprice. In 17th- and 18th-century harpsichord music it was often used as a synonym for fantasia—for example, Johann Sebastian Bach's *Capriccio on the Departure of a Beloved Brother* discussed below. As a type of piano music it was developed by Brahms as a short composition, whimsical in mood and light in character. Brahms wrote seven such pieces: 4 in *Eight Pieces,* op. 76 (1878); 3 in *Fantasien,* op. 116 (1892). One of the most popular of these is that in B minor, op. 76, in which the main staccato melody is contrasted by a graceful lyrical subject. Contrast between buoyant lyricism and dramatic power characterizes another famous Brahms Capriccio, that in D minor, op. 116.

In orchestral music, a capriccio is usually a potpourri of popular melodies, as in Rimsky-Korsakov's *Capriccio espagnol* and Tchaikovsky's *Capriccio italien* discussed below.

Stravinsky's Capriccio, for piano and orchestra, revives one of the original concepts of the capriccio as a fantasia, with fugato passages. Stravinsky completed it in 1929, and it was first performed in Paris on Dec. 6, 1929, Ernest Ansermet conducting and the composer as soloist. (I. Presto. II. *Andante rapsodico.* III. *Allegro capriccioso.*) The first and last movements are ironic; the second, rhapsodic. In the first movement the main idea is rhythmic, presented by piano and timpani after a vigorous introduction. Following several other terse, and at times dance-like, subjects, the movement ends with a return of the vigorous introduction. The second movement opens with a dialogue between piano and woodwind. A cadenza for piano and flute solo leads to the finale which overflows with dance, and occasionally jazz, ideas.

Capriccio Espagnol (Spanish Caprice). Caprice for orchestra by Rimsky-Korsakov, op. 34 (1887), introduced in St. Petersburg on Nov. 12, 1887, the composer conducting. This five-movement work is an elaboration of popular Spanish melodies. I. *Alborada,* or morning song, has two main subjects, both given by the orchestra. II. Variations. A theme for horns and five variations. III. *Alborada.* The opening melody returns changed in pitch and instrumentation. IV. *Scene and Gypsy Dance.* This part consists of five cadenzas. V. *Fandango asturiano.* A vigorous dance presented by trombones is contrasted with a secondary subject in woodwind. The Capriccio ends with a final statement of the melody of the first movement.

Capriccio Italien (Italian Caprice). Caprice for orchestra by Tchaikovsky, op. 45 (1880), first performed in Moscow on Dec. 18, 1880, Nicholas Rubinstein conducting. The melodic material came from some Italian folk tunes heard by the composer during a visit to Italy, and others he picked up in various publications. The work opens with an orchestral fanfare, a bugle call sounded each morning at the barracks of the Royal Cuirassiers. Two Italian melodies follow. The first is a tender song for strings; the other, a jaunty tune for oboe. A change of tempo leads to march music, and the work ends with a whirling tarantella.

Capriccio on the Departure of a Beloved Brother (Capriccio sopra la lontananza del suo fratello dilettissimo). A caprice for clavier by Johann Sebastian Bach (1704), written when his brother, Johann Jakob, departed for Poland. This is an early example of program music, opening with a tonal description of the traveler's friends trying to dissuade him from undertaking so arduous a journey. The argument develops into a lively and humorous fugue. Then comes a "Lament," as friends speak of their grief at the impending departure. Finally the sound of a postillion's horn is heard. To a fugal treatment of this motif, the coach stumbles along on its journey.

Capriccio and Pastorale. Tausig's modern piano arrangement of two harpsichord sonatas by Domenico Scarlatti: E major, L. 375 ("Capriccio") and D minor, L. 413 ("Pastorale"). *See:* Sonata—*Scarlatti.*

Capriccioso. In a playful, whimsical style.

Caprice. (1) A short composition in quick tempo characterized by unusual effects in melody, rhythm, modulation, and so forth, calculated to surprise the listener. While Paganini's Caprices are the most popular, several composers preceded him in writing works of that type for the violin. In 1733 Pietro Locatelli completed *L'Arte del violino,* op. 3, a set of 24 violin caprices; before the end of the 18th century, Federico Fiorillo published a set of 36 violin caprices. Paganini's 24 Caprices for unaccompanied violin, op. 1 (1820), are sometimes referred to as a lexicon of violin technique in general and Paganini's technique in particular—so remarkably do they exploit the technical resources of the violin, including arpeggios, tremolos, staccatos, octave passages, double and triple stops, harmonics, trills, and so forth. But these caprices are not merely technical exercises in violin playing. They are often filled with such imagination and poetic fancy that they are as important artistically as they are pedagogically. These are some of the most important of Paganini's Caprices: No. 9, in E major, *La Chasse,* so called because the theme in double stops sounds like a horn call; No. 13, in G minor, *Le Rire du diable,* which uses a demoniac and mocking melody; No. 20, in D major; and the most famous of them all, No. 24, in A minor, a series of variations on the opening melody. This last Caprice has been used as the starting point of major works by other composers: Brahms (Variations on a Theme by Paganini, for piano); Boris Blacher (Variations on a Theme by Paganini, for orchestra); Rachmaninoff (Rhapsody on a Theme by Paganini, for piano and orchestra). Luigi Dallapiccola wrote *Sonata canonica* for piano, based on several Paganini Caprices. Schumann and Liszt transcribed some of the Paganini Caprices for the piano. Several musicians have provided the Caprices with a piano accompaniment, including Georges Enesco, Fritz Kreisler, and Mario Pilati.

(2) A composition in modified sonata or rondo form, as in Mendelssohn's *Three Caprices* for piano, op. 33 (1833-1834): A minor, E major, B-flat minor.

(3) A transcription of, or a fantasia on, a composition by another composer,

as in Saint-Saëns' *Caprice on Danish and Russian Airs,* op. 79 (1887), for flute, oboe, clarinet, and piano; and his *Caprice on the Airs de Ballet from Gluck's Alceste,* for piano solo. (4) A potpourri of popular melodies. *See: Capriccio espagnol, Capriccio italien.*

Caprice Basque (Sarasate). *See:* Spanish Dances (2).

Caprice Poétique (Liszt). *See:* Etude—*Liszt.*

Capriol Suite. Suite of 16th-century French dances for orchestra by Peter Warlock (pseudonym for Philip Heseltine). He scored it for string orchestra in 1926, but two years later rewrote it for full symphony. All his dance melodies but one were derived from the *Orchésographie* of Thoinot Arbeau (1519-1595). Thoinot, a French priest, was a devotee of dancing. He compiled his study in 1589 (translated into English in 1925) to provide performing details about dances of his period; he also included some 50 dance tunes. The text is in the form of dialogues between Arbeau and a lawyer named Capriol, who feels dancing is important to his legal practice. The lawyer's name provided Warlock with the title of his suite, which has six sections: I. *Basse-danse;* II. *Pavane;* III. *Tordion;* IV. *Bransles;* V. *Pieds-en-l'air;* VI. *Mattachins.*

Card Game or **Card Party (Jeu de Cartes).** Ballet-suite in three "deals" by Stravinsky (1936), written on commission from the American Ballet which introduced it in New York on April 27, 1937, the composer conducting. The orchestral suite as performed at symphony concerts consists of the ballet score without alterations or interruption. It has the following divisions: I. Introduction; *Pas d'action;* Dance of the Joker; Little Waltz. II. Introduction; March; Variation of the Four Queens; Variation of the Jack of Hearts, and Coda, March and Ensemble. III. Introduction; Waltz-Minuet; Presto (Combat Between Spades and Hearts); Final Dance (Triumph of the Hearts). All the characters in the ballet are cards in a poker game. The composer explains: "At each deal the situation is complicated by the endless guile of the perfidious Joker, who believes himself invincible. . . . During the first deal one of the players is beaten, but other two remain with even 'straights,' although one of them holds the Joker. In the second deal, the hand which holds the Joker is victorious, thanks to the four Aces, who easily beat four Queens. Now comes the third deal. The action grows more and more acute. This time it is a struggle between three flushes. Although at first victorious over one adversary, the Joker, strutting at the head of a sequence of Spades, is beaten by a 'royal flush,' in Hearts. This puts an end to his malice and knavery."

Carmen. An opera by Georges Bizet (1875), libretto by Henri Meilhac and Ludovic Halévy. It was introduced at the Opéra-Comique in Paris on March 3, 1875. Melodic material from this well loved opera has often been utilized for instrumental works. Among these compositions are: Ferruccio Busoni's Sonatina No. 6, *Fantasy on Carmen,* for piano; Abram Chasins' *Fantasia on Themes from Carmen,* for two pianos; Vladimir Horowitz's *Carmen Fantasia,* for piano; Pablo de Sarasate's *Carmen Fantasia,* for violin and piano; Franz Waxman's *Carmen Fantasia,* for violin and orchestra (originally used in the motion picture *Humoresque*).

Orchestra suites made up of excerpts from the opera are sometimes presented at symphony concerts. These consist of various combinations of the following parts: Preludes to the four acts; *Aragonaise;* Changing of the Guard; Dragoons of Alcala; Habanera; Micaëla's Air; March of the Smugglers; *Danse bohème.*

Carnaval (Schumann). *See: Carnival.*

Carnaval da Venise. *See: Carnival of Venice.*

Carnaval de Pesth (Liszt). *See: Hungarian Rhapsodies.*

Carnaval des animaux (Saint-Saëns). *See: Carnival of the Animals.*

Carnaval romain, Le (Berlioz). *See: Roman Carnival Overture.*

Carnegie Hall. The most important concert auditorium in the United States, situated at 57th Street and Seventh Avenue in New York City. It was built largely from funds supplied by Andrew

Carnegie, and opened as The Music Hall with a five-day music festival between May 5 and 9, 1891, in which Tchaikovsky appeared as guest conductor. In 1898 the auditorium was renamed Carnegie Hall to honor the man whose funds made it possible. For the next half century and more it was the scene of performances by the world's foremost concert artists, chamber-music groups, and orchestras. It was the principal home of the New York Symphony up to the time of its dissolution, and of the New York Philharmonic. Its history was written by Ethel Peyser, *The House That Music Built* (1936), and a motion picture based on its history and including many notable concert artists and the New York Philharmonic entitled *Carnegie Hall* was released in 1946.

Carnival. (1) Concert overture for orchestra by Dvořák, op. 92 (1891). The composer originally planned this work as the second of a cycle of three overtures collectively entitled *Nature, Life, and Love.* All three works were introduced simultaneously in Prague on April 20, 1892, the composer conducting. Rich with Bohemian dance rhythms and folk colors, this overture is exuberant music except for a haunting melody for solo violin and English horn, the heart of the piece. Dvořák provided the following program: "The wanderer . . . reaches the city at nightfall, where a carnival of pleasure reigns supreme. On every side is heard the clangor of instruments, mingled with shouts of joy and the unrestrained hilarity of people giving vent to their feelings in the songs and dance tunes."

(2) Suite for piano (*Carnaval*), by Schumann, op. 9 (1835), subtitled by the composer "little scenes in four notes." The four notes are A-flat (in German "As"), E-flat (in German "Es"), C, and B natural (in German "H"). The four letters in varied order spell out the name "Asch," a little town in Bohemia, home of Ernestine von Fricken, with whom Schumann was in love at the time. This work is a picture of a gay carnival in a series of short scenes, played without interruption. It opens with *Préambule,* evoking the festive atmosphere of the carnival. *Pierrot* and *Arlequin* follow, portraits of two clowns long favored in European masquerades. This is followed by *Valse noble,* a sentimental waltz tune, and two self-portraits of the composer—*Eusebius,* his dreamy, poetic self, and *Florestan,* his more dynamic and decisive side. After this appears *Coquette,* a sketch of a flirtatious girl whose attempts find an answer in the ensuing *Réplique.* In *Sphinxes* the composer poses a puzzle: two different anagrams of "Asch." (This part is usually omitted.) *Papillons* now recreates the flight of butterflies. (A more popular Schumann piano piece, also named *Papillons,* has no relation to this section.) A brief episode, *Lettres dansantes,* is followed by *Chiarina,* a tribute to Clara Wieck. Two more portraits are now drawn. One is *Chopin,* in the style of a Chopin nocturne; the other, *Estrella,* is Ernestine von Fricken. In *Reconnaissance* we get the joy of reunion, while in *Pantalon et Colombine* two characters famous in Italian comedy are depicted. Dance music is briefly exploited in *Valse allemande,* which leads to a brief passage of virtuoso character entitled *Paganini. Aveu* is a passionate avowal, and *Promenade* a lilting waltz. After a turbulent section named *Pause* we come to the final part, *Marche des Davidsbuendler contre les Philistins.* Its heroic music speaks of the victory of the champions of idealism and true art over the materialists. The latter are symbolized by a trite waltz tune whose theme is derived from the *Grossvater Tanz,* a favorite of middle-class 19th-century German families.

Four Russian composers (Rimsky-Korsakov, Liadov, Glazunov, and Nicholas Tcherepnin) collaborated in orchestrating *Carnival;* this score was used for a ballet still popular in the repertory, and first introduced by the Ballet Russe in Paris on June 4, 1910, choreography by Michel Fokine.

Carnival of the Animals, The (Le Carnaval des animaux). Suite for two pianos and orchestra by Saint-Saëns (1886), subtitled "a grand zoölogical fantasy." The composer wrote it as a musical joke, and it was first performed privately for the Saint-Saëns family (two pianos without orchestra). Saint-Saëns did not allow the work to be performed publicly or published. The suite has 14 sections. I. *Introduction and Royal March of the Lion* (*L'Introduction et marche royale du lion*). An opening fanfare is followed by a march which reproduces realistically a lion's roar. II. *Hens and Cocks* (*Poules et coqs*). The hen's cackle is imitated by piano and strings, and the cock's call by a clarinet. III. *Mules* (*Hémiones*). This section is for two unaccompanied pianos. The rigid rhythms and unchanging dynamics are said to be a satire on pianists who play more correctly than musically. IV. *Tortoises* (*Tortues*). Two melodies from Offenbach's *Orpheus in the Underworld* are quoted here. V. *The Elephant* (*L'Eléphant*). This clumsy animal is depicted by a ponderous melody in the double-bass incongruously set off against a gracious waltz rhythm in the piano. A theme from Berlioz' *The Damnation of Faust* is interpolated. VI. *Kangaroos* (*Kangourous*). While this is a picture of kangaroos, the halting rhythms are also meant to suggest the chatter of concertgoers during a performance. VII. *Aquarium*. A melody in flute and violin describes the fish, while arpeggio figures in the piano suggest the water. VIII. *Personages With Long Ears* (*Personnages à longues oreilles*). These animals are actually donkeys, portrayed in a melody with leaping intervallic skips. IX. *Cuckoo in the Woods* (*Le Coucou au fond des bois*). The melody of the cuckoo appears in the clarinet against a secondary subject in the piano. X. *Aviary* (*Volière*). The flight and the singing of birds is recreated. XI. *Pianists* (*Pianistes*). A beginning pianist struggles with his scales. In the opinion of the composer these are deserving members of the zoological family. XII. *Fossils* (*Fossiles*). Four familiar melodies are quoted: from Rossini's *The Barber of Seville* and the composer's own *Danse macabre,* and two French folk songs. XIII. *The Swan* (*Le Cygne*). This is the most celebrated section of the suite, one of the composer's most beautiful melodies—a gentle song in the cello describing the serene movement of a swan on the water. This is the

only part of the suite the composer allowed to be played and published in his lifetime. It was made world-famous by the ballerina, Pavlova. XIV. *Finale* (*Final*). All characters return for a final bow.

Ogden Nash, the American humorist and poet, wrote delightful verses for each section of this suite. This version calls for a narrator as well as the two pianos and orchestra.

Carnival of Venice (Carnaval da Venise). (1) A popular Italian tune heard by Paganini in Venice, which he subsequently used for a set of twenty variations for unaccompanied violin, op. 10, describing scenes and episodes of the Venetian festival. His performance of this composition did much to popularize the melody throughout Europe. Other and later composers also used this melody for variation treatment, among them being Julius Schulhoff (piano), Giovanni Bottesini (double bass), and Vincenzo Tommasini (orchestra).

(2) Variations for orchestra by Vincenzo Tommasini (1928), first performed by the New York Philharmonic Orchestra under Toscanini on Oct. 10, 1929. This work is based on Paganini's variations on the famous Italian melody.

Carpenter, John Alden, composer. Born Park Ridge, Ill., Feb. 28, 1876; died Chicago, Ill., April 26, 1951. The son of wealthy parents, Carpenter was able to get a comprehensive academic and musical education. He first studied music in Chicago, then with John Knowles Paine at Harvard, from which he was graduated in 1897. Later music study took place in Rome with Edward Elgar and in Chicago with Bernard Ziehn. Meanwhile he entered his father's prosperous Chicago business firm (mill, railroad, and ship supplies) and until his retirement in 1936 successfully combined a business career with one in music. Carpenter first attracted notice as a composer with a violin sonata introduced by Mischa Elman in 1912. His best-known work for orchestra, *Adventures in a Perambulator,* came in 1915; his successful jazz ballet, *Skyscrapers,* was introduced a decade later. Other major works for orchestra include 2 symphonies, the suite *The*

Birthday of the Infanta, Patterns for piano and orchestra, the tone poem *Sea-Drift*, a piano concerto, *Dance Suite, The Seven Ages,* and *Carmel Concerto.* He also wrote a piano quintet and a string quartet. In 1921 he was made knight of the French Legion of Honor and in 1947 he received a gold medal from the National Institute of Arts and Letters for "distinguished services to music."

See: *Adventures in a Perambulator; Birthday of the Infanta* (1); *Sea Drift; Seven Ages; Skyscrapers.*

Carreño, Maria Teresa, pianist. Born Caracas, Venezuela, Dec. 22, 1853; died New York City, June 12, 1917. When she was eight she gave several concerts in New York and Boston. Serious study of the piano then began with Louis Gottschalk, and continued in Europe with George Matthias and Anton Rubinstein. Her career as a mature artist began with sensational performances in Europe in 1865. From 1890 on she was ranked with the foremost women pianists of all time. She combined phenomenal technique, dramatic fire, and a profound musicianship. She also distinguished herself as a singer, as a conductor, and as the composer of music for the piano and a string quartet. She married four times, her husbands including the violinist Émile Sauret (with whom she gave sonata recitals) and the distinguished pianist-composer, Eugène d'Albert. In 1938 her remains were shipped from New York to her native land.

Carroll, Lewis (born **Charles Lutwidge Dodgson**), mathematician and writer. Born Daresbury, England, Jan. 27, 1832; died Guildford, England, Jan. 14, 1898. Carroll's two classics for children— *Alice in Wonderland* and *Through the Looking Glass*—were the inspiration for Edgar Stillman Kelley's *Alice in Wonderland* and Deems Taylor's *Through the Looking Glass,* both orchestral suites. Richard Addinsell wrote incidental music for two different stage presentations of *Alice in Wonderland.*

Carvalho, Eleazar, conductor and composer. Born Iguatu, Brazil, July 28, 1912. Before becoming a musician he entered upon a career as a seaman. But while attending the naval academy he studied composition; and while serving in the Brazilian Navy he played in brass bands. After being discharged from the Navy he became assistant conductor to Eugen Szenkar with the Brazilian Symphony, where he made his début as conductor in 1941. For the next few seasons he conducted performances of that orchestra, as well as several operatic presentations at the Municipal Theater. He came to the United States in 1946 to study conducting with Koussevitzky at the Berkshire Music Centre. His North American début took place with the Boston Symphony on Dec. 19, 1947. Since then he has made many guest appearances with leading American orchestras besides serving as principal conductor of the Brazilian Symphony. He occupies a permanent chair in the Brazilian National Academy of Arts, and in 1958 he became head of the orchestral division of the Berkshire Music Centre. Though Carvalho has written a symphony, 3 overtures, 2 string quartets, 2 piano trios, and a violin sonata, he is best known for his operas.

Casadesus, Henri. *See:* Society of Ancient Instruments.

Casadesus, Robert Marcel, pianist. Born Paris, France, April 7, 1899. He came from a family of famous musicians. His uncle was Henri Casadesus, founder of the Society of Ancient Instruments. Entering the Paris Conservatory when he was thirteen, he remained there several years, winning first prizes in piano playing and harmony. His concert career began with a successful début at Paris in 1922, after which he toured Europe, North Africa, and South America. His first appearance in the United States took place on Jan. 20, 1935, with the New York Philharmonic. His performances throughout the world after that placed him among the foremost French pianists of his time. In 1934 he became head of the piano department at the American Conservatory in Fontainebleau, and for a few years beginning with 1945 he served there as director. From 1942 to 1947 he conducted classes in piano in Great Barrington, Mass., and in 1945-1946 he lectured at Princeton. He is the composer of 2 symphonies, 4 concertos, various sonatas, 3 quintets, and numerous works for the piano including 6 sonatas, etudes, and 24 preludes. He has written cadenzas for piano concertos by Beethoven and Mozart, and edited Cimarosa's piano sonatas. In 1958 he was the only non-German to be awarded the Brahms medal by the city of Hamburg on the occasion of the 125th anniversary of that composer's birth. His wife, the former Gaby L'Hote, is also a pianist, who has appeared with him in performances of two-piano music.

Casals, Pablo, cellist and conductor. Born Vendrell, Spain, Dec. 29, 1876. The son of a church organist, Casals early received instruction on the piano, organ, and violin. While earning his living during his boyhood playing in a café ensemble, he studied the cello with José García at the Municipal School in Barcelona. It was there that Casals made his concert début in 1891. In 1894 he went to Madrid, where he attended the Royal Conservatory, a pupil of Jesús de Monasterio and Tomás Bretón. In that city he played the cello in various theater, opera, and casino orchestras; performed in a string quartet he had founded; and was soloist with the Madrid Symphony conducted by Bretón. In 1895 he went to Paris, where he played in the Paris Opéra orchestra, and in 1897 taught the cello at the Paris Conservatory. His success as a virtuoso can be said to date from Nov. 12, 1899, when he appeared as a soloist with the Lamoureux Orchestra in Paris in Lalo's Cello Concerto. He was a sensation. A tour of Europe followed, and in 1901-1902 he made the first of many tours of the United States. Wherever he played he was honored for his aristocratic interpretations of the cello literature (and particularly for the solo suites of Johann Sebastian Bach, which he was responsible for popularizing for the first time). No less remarkable was his fantastic technique, with which it was said cello performance had entered upon a new era.

In 1919 Casals founded a symphony orchestra in Barcelona, directing its first concert on Oct. 13, 1920. This organization not only gave seasonal concerts but also special performances for workers at nominal prices. His success led other European symphony orchestras to invite him as guest conductor. Casals made his conducting début in America with the New York Symphony in 1922.

When civil war broke out in 1936, Casals continued to pursue his varied musical activities in Barcelona while siding passionately with the Loyalists. After Franco's victory, he left his native land for good. He settled in the French town of Prades, near the Spanish border, where he devoted himself to study and teaching. He vowed never again to play the cello in public as long as Franco remained in power in Spain. He kept that vow for many years. But when the bicentennial of Bach's death was commemorated in 1950, Casals was prevailed upon by his friends to emerge from his retirement and become the central figure in a festival of Bach's music in Prades. During that festival, in June 1950, Casals played the cello publicly for the first time in several years; he also conducted a chamber orchestra. From then on this festival became an annual summer event, held either in Prades or nearby Perpignan, with Casals as its dominating personality. Later festivals were devoted to Beethoven, Mozart, Schubert, and Brahms, as well as to Bach; some of the world's outstanding instrumentalists collaborated with Casals in these performances.

Late in 1956 Casals announced that his permanent home would henceforth be in Puerto Rico, though he still planned to spend several months a year in Europe to appear at the Prades Festival and fulfil some teaching commitments. In honor of his 80th birthday, a festival devoted to Bach, Mozart, and Schubert was organized by the Puerto Rican government, with Casals scheduled to appear as cellist and conductor. While rehearsing for this event Casals suffered a heart attack, which made his participation in the festival impossible. Nevertheless, the festival took place between April 22 and May 8, 1957. At the second Puerto Rico festival the following year, Casals was well enough to make his scheduled appearances. Casals made his first reappearance in the United States in thirty years on Oct. 24, 1958, when he performed a Bach solo suite in the General Assembly Chamber of the United Nations in celebration of United Nations Day. Casals appeared in a scene in the motion picture *Windjammer*, released in 1958.

Casella, Alfredo, composer, pianist, and conductor. Born Turin, Italy, July 25, 1883; died Rome, Italy, March 5, 1947. In 1896 he entered the Paris Conservatory, where he won prizes in piano playing and composition. His first major works were 2 symphonies, written between 1905 and 1907. In 1909 he achieved his first success with an orchestral rhapsody, *Italia*. For several years he was a member of the faculty at the Paris Conservatory. Returning to Italy in 1915, he assumed a dominating role in Italian music. He taught piano at the Santa Cecilia Academy in Rome; he toured Italy as pianist and conductor, usually in performances of contemporary music; he wrote criticisms; he founded a magazine devoted to modern music, *Musica d'Oggi;* he organized societies promoting the music and interests of the modern composer; he prepared editions of piano works by Bach, Mozart, and Chopin; he did valuable research in old Italian music. His American début took place in Philadelphia on Oct. 28, 1921, when he appeared in the triple role of pianist, conductor, and composer. He subsequently made several more tours of the United States, conducting major orchestras, and appearing as pianist in his own works. In 1926 he served as one of the two principal conductors of the State Symphony Orchestra in New York, and in 1927-1929 he was the conductor of the Boston Pops Orchestra.

He was in the vanguard of that Italian group of composers which aspired to restore Italy's long lost prestige in instrumental music. He wrote in many styles with equal skill—Impressionism, polytonality, neo-Classicism—but was probably most successful in the last of these. His neo-Classical works are clear, precise, transparent, a skilful blend of old forms and approaches with modern idioms.

Casella's open espousal of the Fascist cause in Italy alienated many of his admirers outside that country. After Italy entered World War II, Casella suffered both physical deprivations and poor health. But he continued working industriously to the end of his life. He orchestrated Balakirev's *Islamey* and some of Albéniz' piano music. He wrote an autobiography, *Music in My Time* (1955). The following are Casella's principal instrumental compositions.

Chamber Music: 2 cello sonatas; Concerto for string quartet; Serenata; Sinfonia.

Orchestra: 3 symphonies; *Italia; Notte di Maggio; Elegia eroica; La Giara;* Partita, for piano and orchestra; *Scarlattiana,* for piano and orchestra; *Paganiniana;* various concertos (violin; cello; trio and orchestra; strings, piano, and percussion).

Piano: Sonatina; *Eleven Pieces for Children; Due canzoni italiane;* Six Studies.

See: Giara, La; Italia; Paganiniana; Scarlattiana.

Cassadó, Gaspar, cellist and composer. Born Barcelona, Spain, Sept. 30, 1897. He began studying the cello at seven, and at nine gave a public concert that brought him a scholarship for study abroad. He then studied for several years in Paris with Pablo Casals. Cassadó's career as virtuoso began with a European tour soon after the end of World War I. His American début took place on Dec. 10, 1936, with the New York Philharmonic Orchestra. After World War II Cassadó established his home in Florence, becoming professor of the cello at the Accademia Musicale Chigiana in Siena.

Cassadó's best known compositions include the *Catalonian Rhapsody* for orchestra, a cello concerto, several string quartets, piano trios, cello sonatas and smaller pieces for the cello. He also made transcriptions for cello and orchestra of a Mozart horn concerto, Schubert's Arpeggione Sonata, and Weber's Clarinet Concerto.

Cassation. An 18th-century orchestral or chamber-music composition, like a serenade or divertimento, made up of several movements. Haydn and Mozart wrote cassations for various combinations of instruments.

Casse-noisette (Tchaikovsky). *See: Nutcracker Suite.*

Castanets. Percussion instruments believed to be of Spanish origin, often used in Spanish compositions, and to accompany Spanish dances. They consist of two small pieces of wood connected by a string. A pair is held in each hand and manipulated to provide various rhythms.

Castelnuovo-Tedesco, Mario, composer. Born Florence, Italy, April 3, 1895. He attended the Cherubini Royal Institute in Florence, where Ildebrando Pizzetti exerted a profound influence upon him. While there Castelnuovo-Tedesco wrote several small pieces for the piano. His first major work, composed in 1920, was *Fioretti,* a setting of three verses by St. Francis of Assisi for voice and orchestra. His first success arrived with an opera, *La Mandragola,* based on the comedy by Machiavelli, which won the Italian Prize in 1926. Performances of his major orchestral works, and two violin concertos, gave him a prominent place among contemporary Italian composers. He left Italy in 1939 and came to the United States, where he made his American début as piano soloist with the New York Philharmonic on November 2 in the American première of his Second Piano Concerto. He has since settled in California, where he has become an American citizen and written music for the motion pictures.

Three important influences affected his creative development: Shakespeare, Hebrew backgrounds, and the Bible. However, since coming to the United States he has completed several major works reflecting American influences. In 1958 he received from Italy the David Campari Prize for his opera, *The Merchant of Venice.* He has written an autobiography, *A Life of Music,* completed in 1957.

His principal works for orchestra include numerous concert overtures to plays by Shakespeare, 2 violin concertos (*The Lark* and *The Prophets*), 2 piano concertos, 2 guitar concertos, a cello concerto, Symphonic Variations for violin and orchestra, *Poem* for violin and orchestra, *Indian Songs and Dances,* *Humoresques on Foster's Themes, An American Rhapsody, Noah's Ark,* and a suite, *The Birthday of the Infanta.* Among his chamber music compositions are 2 string quartets, 2 piano quintets, 2 piano trios, various sonatas, a guitar quintet, and a Concertino for harp and seven instruments. He has also produced numerous pieces for the piano including *Cipressi, Alt Wien, Chorals on Hebrew Melodies, Candide,* and a sonata.

See: Birthday of the Infanta (2); *Concerto—Castelnuovo-Tedesco; Taming of the Shrew; Twelfth Night.*

Caston, Saul, conductor. Born New York City, Aug. 22, 1901. He studied the trumpet with Max Schlessberg while attending high school. In his seventeenth year he became trumpeter for the Philadelphia Orchestra. Four years later he was elevated to first trumpet, and in 1936 to the post of associate conductor. He was principal conductor of the Reading Symphony in Pennsylvania from 1941 to 1945, and since 1945 principal conductor of the Denver Symphony, which he helped to elevate to a position of national significance.

Cathédrale engloutie, La. *See:* Prelude—*Debussy.*

Cat's fugue. *See:* Sonata—*Scarlatti.*

Cat's waltz. *See:* Waltz—*Chopin.*

Caucasian Sketches. Suite for orchestra by Ippolitov-Ivanov, op. 10 (1895). Its first performance took place in Moscow on Feb. 5, 1895, the composer conducting. The work was inspired by the composer's contact with Caucasian folk music during a visit to Tiflis. It is filled with Oriental melodies and vivid orchestral colors. Direct in melodic appeal and rhythmic cogency, it has become the composer's most popular composition, and a favorite on "pop" programs. It is in four parts: I. *In the Mountain Pass;* II. *In the Village;* III. *In the Mosque;* IV. *March of the Sirdar.*

Cavalleria rusticana. An opera by Pietro Mascagni. The libretto, by Guido Menasci and Giovanni Targioni-Tozzetti, is based on a play by Giovanni Verga. The opera was first performed in Rome on May 17, 1890. For orchestral excerpt, *see:* Intermezzo.

Cavatina. An instrumental composition

with a sustained melody of songlike character. Raff's Cavatina in A-flat major for violin and piano, op. 85, no. 3, is popular. The slow movement of Beethoven's String Quartet in B-flat major, op. 130, is also a Cavatina.

Celesta. A keyboard instrument invented by Auguste Mustel in Paris. The keys activate hammers which strike steel plates over resonators. The celesta, with a range of four octaves from middle C up, has a delicate, pure tone. Tchaikovsky used it effectively in the *Dance of the Sugarplum Fairy* in the *Nutcracker Suite.*

Cello. Contraction of violoncello.

Cembalo. Contracted form of clavicembalo. A harpsichord.

Cervantes, Miguel de, novelist, dramatist, and poet. Born Alcalá de Henares, Spain, Oct. 9, 1547; died Madrid, Spain, April 23, 1616. He was the author of *Don Quixote,* the famous novel about the self-styled knight errant of La Mancha. The following are some composers of orchestral music inspired by this classic (all compositions listed without specific titles are named *Don Quixote*): Robert Delaney (symphony); Oscar Esplá (tone poem); Eugeniusz Morawski (tone poem); Henry Purcell (incidental music to *The Comical History of Don Quixote*); Jean Rivier (*Ouverture pour Don Quichotte*); Anton Rubinstein (orchestral humoresque, or portrait); Richard Strauss (tone poem); Jaromir Weinberger (orchestral scherzo). In addition, Alexander Mackenzie wrote an orchestral overture, *Cervantes.*

Chabrier, Emmanuel, composer. Born Ambert, France, Jan. 18, 1841; died Paris, France, Sept. 13, 1894. Trained for law, he completed his studies in 1862 and for the next eighteen years filled a government post in Paris in the Ministry of the Interior. Meanwhile he studied music with private teachers and started composition. In 1877 one of his operettas, *L'Étoile,* was produced in Paris. A performance of Wagner's music drama, *Tristan and Isolde,* in Munich in 1880 inspired him to give up his government post and devote himself exclusively to music. In 1881 he published *Pièces pittoresques* for piano (four of these pieces

were later orchestrated and renamed *Suite pastorale*). Three months later he spent a three-month holiday in Spain which inspired him to write his first major orchestral work, *España,* a sensation when introduced at Paris in 1884. But Chabrier was most successful in writing for the piano, a medium for which he wrote not only *Pièces pittoresques* but also *Habanera, Bourrée fantasque,* and *Trois valses romantiques* for two pianos. Gaiety and laughter—and a partiality for the unexpected or the grotesque—are some of the qualities of Chabrier's best music which make him a significant precursor of Erik Satie. His occasional harmonic daring and subtle tonal relationships also make him an important predecessor of Debussy and Ravel. Besides *España* and *Suite pastorale,* Chabrier's orchestral music includes *Joyeuse marche.*

During the last two years of his life Chabrier suffered from paralysis, and in his last days his mind was affected.

See: Bourrée fantasque; España; Gwendoline, Overture; Habanera—Chabrier; Joyeuse marche; Valses romantiques.

Chaconne. A slow and stately dance, probably of Spanish origin, in 3/4 time. It sometimes appears as a movement in the Baroque suite (or partita), as is the case with the celebrated Chaconne for solo violin by Bach. As a form of instrumental music it was first developed for the organ by such early masters as Frescobaldi and Buxtehude. As an instrumental composition, it is usually characterized by a four-measure theme constantly repeated in the bass, while variations are spun above it. The chaconne is so similar to the passacaglia that the two terms were for a long time used interchangeably.

The following are some of the most famous compositions in the chaconne form.

J. S. BACH. The Chaconne, which is the final movement of the Partita in D minor for unaccompanied violin, is probably the most famous work in this form. A majestic melody in full chords is subjected to 31 variations. "The master's spirit," wrote Philipp Spitta, "inspires the instrument to express the inconceivable;

at the end . . . the music swells like organ-tone, and at times one hears a whole chorus of violins." Bach's Chaconne has been transcribed for piano by Busoni; for piano left hand by Brahms; for guitar by Segovia; and for orchestra by Stokowski. Mendelssohn wrote a piano accompaniment for it in 1854.

HANDEL. One of Handel's best keyboard compositions is the Chaconne in G major from the *Suites de pièces,* or *Lessons,* for harpsichord, volume 2. Handel also wrote a second harpsichord Chaconne, in F minor.

PURCELL. The Chaconne in G minor is for a chamber-music ensemble (four viols) rather than harpsichord. It has been transcribed for orchestra by William G. Whittaker.

VITALI. The Chaconne in G minor, for violin and piano, is among violinists second in popularity only to that of Bach. Ottorino Respighi transcribed it for orchestra; Luigi Silva, for cello and piano; and Alfonso Gibilaro for strings and organ.

Chadwick, George Whitefield, composer. Born Lowell, Mass., Nov. 13, 1854; died Boston, Mass., April 4, 1931. In 1872 he entered the New England Conservatory, where his teachers included Dudley Buck and George E. Whiting. Financial difficulties compelled him to give up music and become a clerk in an insurance firm. But in 1876 he returned to music study, and two years later was a pupil in Leipzig of Karl Reinecke and Salomon Jadassohn. For his graduation exercise he wrote *Rip van Winkle,* an overture for orchestra, introduced at the Leipzig Conservatory on June 20, 1879; it has become one of his most popular works. After studying the organ with Josef Rheinberger in Munich he returned to the United States in 1880, making his home in Boston, where he became organist of the South Congregational Church. For many years he was also professor of composition and orchestration at the New England Conservatory, and from 1897 on was its director. Chadwick was a traditional composer whose music owed a strong debt to German Romanticism, and in its orchestration to Wagner. Occasionally he made tentative efforts to inject an American element into his writing, particularly through the introduction of Negro melodies; later in life he also revealed a tendency towards modern idioms. His works for orchestra include 3 symphonies, several overtures (including *Melpomene, Rip Van Winkle,* and *Adonais*), *Symphonic Sketches* (which includes the popular *Jubilee* and *Noël*), *Aphrodite, Tam o'Shanter,* and *Theme, Variations and Fugue* for organ and orchestra. He also wrote 5 string quartets and a piano quintet.

See: Jubilee.

Chamber music. Music written for performance in an intimate auditorium, for small combinations of instruments. This category includes sonatas, trios, quartets, quintets, sextets, octets, and so forth.

Chant du rossignol, Le (Stravinsky). *See: Song of the Nightingale, The.*

Chantecler, Le. *See:* Rostand, Edmond.

Chanticleer. Concert overture by Daniel Gregory Mason (1926), introduced by the Cincinnati Symphony on Nov. 23, 1928, Fritz Reiner conducting. A motto from Thoreau's *Walden* appears in the published score: "I do not propose to write an ode to dejection, but to brag as lustily as a chanticleer in the morning, standing up on his roost, if only to wake my neighbors up." The overture's first principal theme, in the trumpet, simulates the crow of the chanticleer. Two other subjects—one for the woodwind, the other for four horns—are intended to suggest the joy inspired by Nature. After the return of the chanticleer motif, a slow, meditative section, dominated by a theme for solo bassoon, appears; it is followed by a subject for solo horn and muted strings.

Charfreitagszauber (Wagner). See *Good Friday Spell.*

Chasins, Abram, pianist and composer. Born New York City, Aug. 17, 1903. He studied the piano with Bertha Tapper, Ernest Hutcheson, and Josef Hofmann. In 1924 he was appointed to the piano faculty of the Curtis Institute, where he gave annual recitals from 1928 to 1934. He made his official concert début on Jan. 18, 1929, in the première of his own First Piano Concerto with the Philadelphia Orchestra. For the next half dozen years he toured Europe and America as concert pianist. From 1932 to 1938 he conducted weekly series of radio broadcasts in which he performed and analyzed piano works. In 1943 he was appointed music consultant of WQXR, New York, and in 1947 he became its director. As a composer, Chasins first became successful with piano miniatures, the most notable being *Three Chinese Pieces*, in 1925 (*A Shanghai Tragedy, Flirtation in a Chinese Garden,* and *Rush Hour in Hong Kong*). In 1931 he became the first American performed by Toscanini when the latter introduced *Parade* and an orchestration of *Three Chinese Pieces* with the New York Philharmonic. Other major works include 2 piano concertos, 24 piano preludes, *Narrative* for piano, and *Period Suite* for orchestra. He is the author of *Speaking of Pianists* (1957) and co-author of *The Cliburn Legend* (1959).

Chasse, La (*The Hunt*). (1) *See:* Symphony—*Haydn.* The same nickname is sometimes applied to Haydn's string quartet in B-flat major, op. 1, no. 1.

(2) *See:* Caprice (1).

Chasseur maudit, Le (*The Wild Huntsman*). Tone poem by César Franck (1883), introduced in Paris on March 31, 1883. Inspired by a ballad by Gottfried August Buerger, it is in four sections. The composer provided his own program. In the first part, the huntsman prepares for the chase. A hunting subject for horns tells about the rider. The chase takes place in the second part; a solemn chant in the cellos goes unheeded by the huntsman. In the third part, he is alone, his horse refusing to move, his horn incapable of emitting a sound. First the bass tuba, then the brass choir, project a solemn subject. In the concluding part, the huntsman, pursued by demons and tortured by flames, flees across abysses and through the air.

Chausson, Ernest, composer. Born Paris, France, Jan. 20, 1855; died Limay, France, June 10, 1899. He was trained for the law, and did not receive formal instruction in music until his twenty-fifth year, when he entered the Paris Conservatory. There his teachers included Jules Massenet and César Franck, the latter

exerting upon him a far-reaching influence. Dissatisfied with the strict regimen at the Conservatory and with its emphasis on tradition, he left it to study privately with Franck. His first publication (two songs) came in 1878. But recognition did not come until the end of his life, with the première of his symphony in B-flat, in 1891. His reputation was subsequently enhanced by two masterworks: Concerto for Piano, Violin, and String Quartet, and the *Poem* for violin and orchestra. He was at the height of his creative powers and on the eve of winning acceptance as one of France's major composers when he met his fatal end by losing control on a bicycle. Chausson, like his teacher Franck, was dedicated to the highest ideals of his art. He belonged to the French Romantic school which brought to music a sensitive feeling for beauty of sound, and an emotional reserve. With Chausson, as with Franck, these qualities were often combined with a touch of melancholy, and sometimes of mysticism. The delicacy and refinement of his style led some critics to regard him as a forerunner of Impressionism. His most famous works are his symphony, *Poem,* and concerto. He also wrote several shorter works for orchestra (*Viviane, Solitude dans les bois,* and *Soir de fête*), a piano quartet, piano trio, and several compositions for the piano (including *Cinq fantaisies, Quelques danses,* and *Paysage*).

See: Concerto—*Chausson; Poem;* Symphony—*Chausson.*

Chávez, Carlos, composer and conductor. Born Mexico City, June 13, 1899. Self-taught in music, he began serious composition in his eighteenth year. A personal identity did not emerge in his writing until he became interested in native Mexican folk music and instruments, of both of which he made an extensive study. Native Mexican elements began appearing in his works in the 1920's, especially in the ballets *New Fire* and *H.P.* During this period, Chávez traveled throughout Europe, then lived for several years in New York City. After returning to his native land he founded the National Symphony Orchestra in Mexico City in 1928 and conducted it for many years. From 1928 to 1934 he was director of the National Conservatory, which he helped to modernize, and from 1933 to 1953 he was head of the Department of Fine Arts. In these various offices, he became one of Mexico's most influential musicians. Since 1937 he has visited the United States many times, appearing as guest conductor of principal orchestras; in 1958 he was appointed to the Charles Eliot Norton professorship at Harvard. He was a recipient of a Guggenheim Fellowship in 1938. In Chávez' music we find the austere simplicity of melody, challenging contrasts of mood, primitive rhythms, often archaic idioms, and the percussive strength of indigenous Mexican music. These elements are incorporated into a style that makes full use of contemporary harmonic and instrumental techniques. His orchestral works include 6 symphonies, the most popular of which are the *Sinfonía de Antígona* and *Sinfonía India*, a *Sinfonía Proletaria* for chorus and orchestra, a piano concerto, violin concerto, harp concerto, concerto for 4 horns, Toccata for percussion instruments, *Xochipilli-Macuilxochitl* for Mexican orchestra, and *Caracas*. He also wrote 3 string quartets, a sonata for 4 horns, *Energía* for 9 instruments, 10 piano preludes, and 3 piano etudes.

See: *Sinfonía de Antígona; Sinfonía India.*

Checkmate. Ballet-suite for orchestra by Arthur Bliss (1937). The ballet, with choreography by Ninette de Valois, was introduced in Paris on June 15, 1937. The setting is a chessboard, and the ballet involves the pawns in a life and death struggle, symbols of the lust of human beings in actual life. Bliss' suite, derived from the ballet score, has six sections: I. Dance of the Four Knights; II. Entry of the Black Queen; III. The Red Knight; IV. Ceremony of the Red Bishops; V. Death of the Red Knight; VI. Finale—Checkmate.

Cherubini, Luigi, composer. Born Florence, Italy, Sept. 14, 1760; died Paris, France, March 15, 1842. He studied music with his father and Giuseppe Sarti. Cherubini's fame rests on his operas. He is often represented on symphony programs with the overtures to the most famous of them. Occasionally his pleasing and melodious Symphony in D major is revived. Cherubini also wrote 6 string quartets, a quintet, and 6 piano sonatas. From 1822 until his death he was the director of the Paris Conservatory.

See: *Anacreon, Overture to; Water Carrier, Overture to The.*

Chest of viols. A 16th- and 17th-century term designating a set of viols of varying sizes, usually six in number, kept in a special chest in some English households.

Chevillard, Camille, conductor. Born Paris, France, Oct. 14, 1859; died Chatou, France, May 30, 1923. He was the son of a distinguished cellist (Alexander Chevillard), and son-in-law of the famous conductor, Charles Lamoureux. Chevillard attended the Paris Conservatory. In 1886 he became assistant conductor to Lamoureux, helping him prepare the first Paris performance of Wagner's opera, *Lohengrin.* He subsequently married Lamoureux's daughter and often substituted for his father-in-law as conductor of the Lamoureux Orchestra. In 1897 he succeeded his father-in-law as head of the orchestra. From 1907 on he was professor of instrumental music at the Paris Conservatory. He was also the organizer of, and performer in, the Trio Chevillard-Hayot-Salmon. In 1903 he received the Prix Chartier for chamber music, and in 1916 was elected president of the Société française de musique de chambre. He was made an Officier de l'Instruction publique and Chevalier of the Legion of Honor.

Chicago Symphony Orchestra. Third oldest existing symphony orchestra in the United States. It was founded in Chicago, Ill., its first concert taking place on Oct. 7, 1891, Theodore Thomas conducting. Thomas remained principal conductor until his death in 1905. For the first 15 years the ensemble was known as the Chicago Orchestra, and from 1896 to 1912 as the Theodore Thomas Orchestra. It acquired a new auditorium in 1904, Orchestra Hall, built for it by popular subscription. Ownership of this auditorium made the orchestra self-supporting. In 1912 it assumed its present name. Since Thomas, its principal conductors have been Frederick Stock, Désiré Défauw, Artur Rodzinski, Rafael Kubelik, and Fritz Reiner.

Childe Harold. *See:* Byron, George Noel Gordon, Lord.

Children's Corner. Suite of children's pieces for piano by Debussy (1908), written for the composer's daughter, Chou-Chou. Debussy provided English titles for the work as a whole and for its respective movements because he wished to suggest games an English governess might play with a French child. In six brief movements, the suite evokes the world of a child: I. *Doctor Gradus ad Parnassum,* a satire on five-finger exercises; II. *Jimbo's Lullaby,* crooned by a child to a toy elephant named Jimbo; III. *Serenade for the Doll;* IV. *The Snow is Dancing;* V. *The Little Shepherd;* VI. *Golliwogg's Cakewalk,* the most famous movement, derived from the cakewalk, a dance popular in America in the 1890's. This movement satirically quotes from Wagner's *Tristan and Isolde.* The entire suite was orchestrated by André Caplet.

Chopin, Frédéric François, composer. Born Zelazowa Wola, Poland, Feb. 22, 1810; died Paris, France, Oct. 17, 1849. Chopin was six when he began studying the piano with Albert Zwyny. One year later he made a public appearance. He also started composition early, publishing a polonaise and having one of his marches performed by a military band, both when he was only seven. In 1823 he entered the Warsaw High School. During his three years there, he studied music privately with Joseph Elsner, director of the Warsaw Conservatory. Upon leaving high school in 1826, Chopin became a full-time student at the Conservatory, from which he was graduated with honors in 1829. In the summer of that year, Chopin visited Vienna, giving two highly successful concerts in which he introduced several of his works. He left Poland a second time, in November 1830, never again to return. This second journey was less happy than the first, since he failed to interest publishers, and his concerts found both the audiences and the critics apathetic. While in Vienna, Chopin heard that his native country had risen in revolt against Russia. His first impulse was to return home and join in

the battle, but the advice of his mother and friends finally dissuaded him. He remained in Vienna a few months more, then embarked on a journey across Germany to Paris. He sublimated his patriotism in his music, which for some time now had begun to assume a Polish identity. One of these pieces was the so-called "Revolutionary Etude," in C minor, op. 10, no. 12, inspired by the news that the Russians had retaken Warsaw in 1831.

Chopin arrived in Paris early in September of 1831, intending to pass through on his way to London. But Paris remained his permanent home for the rest of his life. He gave his first public concert on Feb. 26, 1832, performing his F minor Piano Concerto. He soon began moving in the most influential musical and social circles in Paris, becoming a favorite of the salon, and a much sought-after teacher for the children of the rich. His compositions for the piano began to find an enthusiastic public, and were eagerly accepted by French publishers; these works included waltzes, nocturnes, etudes, mazurkas, and polonaises.

His personal life was permanently affected when, in 1837, he met the celebrated woman novelist, Georges Sand. He was at first strongly repelled by her masculinity, her lack of physical appeal, and her unsavory moral reputation. But repeated meetings impressed him with her brilliant wit and dynamic personality. Before long they were inseparable, hopelessly involved emotionally with each other. They were together during the summer of 1838 at Sand's home in Nohant; and that winter they went off to the island of Majorca. The Majorcan holiday did not turn out to be the idyl they had expected. The weather was miserable, and the food poor. They incurred the suspicion of the townspeople. And Chopin's health, ever delicate, broke down under such trying conditions; he became a victim of nightmare and hemorrhages. When they finally left Majorca, Chopin was a virtual invalid. The only compensation of this sordid experience for Chopin was the writing of one of his masterworks, the Preludes.

Back in Nohant and Paris, Chopin's

strength returned. He now was able to produce several of his most ambitious compositions, including his Sonata in B-flat minor (with the Funeral March), the F minor Fantaisie, ballades, and impromptus. For two years his creative output was impressive; but then his health once again deteriorated. He broke with Sand permanently in 1847. Chopin's last public appearance took place in Paris on Feb. 16, 1848. After that, despite his poor health, he toured England and Scotland. Back again in Paris in 1849, he was so weak that he became a recluse. He died the following Fall and was buried in the Père Lachaise cemetery in Paris.

Chopin wrote 169 works, of which only a handful are not for solo piano. Thus he is the only great composer to make piano music his creative world. In that world he was a sovereign. So greatly did he extend piano technique, so successfully did he realize new sonorities and dynamics, and so remarkably did he evolve a style that belonged to the piano alone that it can be said that modern piano writing and technique originated in his music. All subsequent composers for the piano were inevitably influenced by him, even when their own styles were radically different.

If Chopin is the only great composer to devote himself almost exclusively to the piano, he is also the only great composer to have concentrated mainly on the smaller forms. He knew his limitations. He was incapable of coping successfully with the demands made by large structures in the way of development and variation; and he was uncomfortable in sustaining a thought to the dimensions required by larger works. (His large works—the 2 piano concertos, the 3 sonatas—consist mostly of smaller ideas strung together.) He therefore preferred working within more modest molds. To these molds he brought a perfection of form, original and poetic thought, an abundant lyricism decorated with the most magical embellishments, an aristocratic and personal rhetoric, and a grace and refinement and elegance of style that place him with music's élite. Most of his compositions are masterworks, even if

miniatures; few composers maintained such a consistently high standard.

An outstanding trait of much of his music is its national Polish character. He is the first major composer to introduce Slavic musical expression into Western music. In many of his compositions we find the distinctive qualities of Polish folksong and dance, elevated to a vital and living art. It is the Polish patriot who speaks in the polonaises and mazurkas, just as it is the Romanticist whose musings are found in the nocturnes and ballades.

Chopin's works for solo piano include 4 ballades, 24 etudes, 4 impromptus, 55 mazurkas, 11 polonaises, 24 preludes, 4 scherzos, 3 sonatas, 15 waltzes, and rondos, ecossaises, variations, a barcarolle, a berceuse, fantasies, and a tarantella. He also wrote a Rondo in C major for two pianos, 2 piano concertos, a piano trio, and a cello sonata.

See: Barcarolle; Berceuse; Concerto—Chopin; Impromptu; Mazurka; Nocturne; Polonaise; Prelude—Chopin; Scherzo; Sonata—Chopin; Waltz—Chopin.

Chopsticks. A child's tune for piano, in waltz-time, which derived its name from the fact that it is played with two forefingers (resembling Chinese chopsticks). An interesting set of variations on this tune was written collectively by four Russian composers in 1880 (Borodin, Cui, Liadov, and Rimsky-Korsakov). For the second edition of these variations, Liszt contributed one of his own.

Choral Fantasy (Chorfantasie). For piano, chorus, and orchestra, in C minor, by Beethoven, op. 80 (1808). Its première took place in Vienna on Dec. 22, 1808, the composer playing the piano part in one of his last important public appearances as pianist. In two sections (Adagio and Finale), it foreshadows Beethoven's later and more mature writing in the Ninth Symphony. The second part includes variations on Beethoven's early song, *Gegenliebe.*

Choral Symphony. See: Symphony—Beethoven.

Chorale prelude. A short composition for organ based on a chorale, or German Protestant hymn-tune. It was first developed in the 16th century by Jan Sweelinck; was structurally advanced by Buxtehude and others; and brought to its final technical and artistic development by Johann Sebastian Bach. Bach wrote 46 chorale preludes in *The Little Organ Book* (*Orgelbuechlein*), besides many others.

Bach was the last great master to deal with the chorale prelude except for Brahms, who wrote 11 pieces for organ in this style, op. 122 (1896).

Chord. A combination of three or more tones.

Chôros. A musical form conceived by Heitor Villa-Lobos, in which he wrote 15 compositions between 1920 and 1929. The "chôros" is a popular Brazilian dance played by a street band; consequently to Villa-Lobos the form signified popular Brazilian music synthesizing different modalities of Brazilian, Indian, and popular music. Villa-Lobos' works in this form are for various instruments. No. 1 is a guitar solo; No. 2, a duet for flute and clarinet; No. 3, for winds (including saxophone) and male chorus; No. 4, for horns and trombones; No. 5, for piano solo; No. 6, for orchestra; No. 6-bis, for violin and cello; No. 7, for chamber orchestra; No. 8, for two pianos and orchestra; No. 9, for orchestra; No. 10, for chorus and orchestra; No. 11, for piano and orchestra (actually a piano concerto); No. 12, for orchestra; No. 13, for two orchestras and band; No. 14, for large orchestra, military band, and mixed chorus. The series ends with an unnumbered work entitled *Introdução aos Chôros* for orchestra.

Nos. 5, 6, and 10 are heard most often. No. 5 is entitled *Alma Brasileira,* and is a three-part piano piece. The flanking parts are rhythmic, while the middle section is lyrical in the vein of a Brazilian folksong. No. 6, scored for orchestra, guitar, and native percussion instruments, is a polyphonic treatment of several Brazilian folk and popular melodies, opening with a sad subject for flute. No. 10, for chorus and orchestra, represents (in the composer's words) "the reaction of a civilized man to stark nature . . . Little by little his humanity asserts itself; there are living people in this land, even though they are savages. Their music is full of nostalgia and of love; their dances are full of rhythm."

Chotzinoff, Samuel, writer on music. Born Vitebsk, Russia, July 4, 1889. In 1912 he was graduated from Columbia College in New York, where he attended the music classes of Daniel Gregory Mason. For a while he was piano accompanist to several important virtuosos, including Heifetz and Zimbalist. From 1925 to 1930 he was music critic of the *New York World,* and from 1934 to 1941 of the *New York Post.* In 1937 he was responsible for bringing Toscanini back to the United States to conduct the NBC Symphony, which had been created for him. Since 1938 Chotzinoff has been music consultant, then general music director, of the National Broadcasting Company, in which capacity he was the producer of the NBC Symphony broadcasts. His books are *Eroica,* a novelized life of Beethoven (1930); *A Lost Paradise,* an autobiography (1955); and *Toscanini: An Intimate Portrait* (1956).

Chout. Ballet suite for orchestra by Prokofiev, derived from his ballet score, op. 21 (1915-1920). The ballet was introduced in Paris by the Ballet Russe on May 17, 1921. The composer derived his text from an old Russian fairy tale about a *chout* (a buffoon) who manages to outwit seven other buffoons, together with a village priest and a rich merchant. The buffoon pretends to kill his wife, and then brings her back to life. When seven other buffoons try to work this trick they discover to their horror that they cannot revive their wives. To escape their wrath, the *chout* disguises himself as a female cook, and is chosen as wife by a rich merchant. The *chout* manages to escape, convincing the merchant that the cook he has hired and chosen for a wife has been transformed into a goat. To avoid scandal, the merchant pays off the *chout,* who then joins his wife and friends in a general celebration. The orchestral suite has 12 sections: I. The Clown and His Wife (*Andantino scherzando*); II. Dance of the Buffoons' Wives (Andantino; *Allegretto ma non troppo*); III. The Buffoons Kill Their Wives (Fugue; *Allegro sostenuto;* Vivace); IV. The Buffoon Masquerades as a Young Girl (*Andan-*

tino innocente); V. Third Entr'acte (*Un poco andante*); VI. Dance of the Buffoons' Daughters (*Moderato scherzando; Vivace*); VII. The Arrival of the Merchant, Dance of Obeisance, and Choice of the Fiancée (*Andante gravissimo; Andantino; Allegretto espressivo; Andante maestoso*); VIII. In the Bedroom of the Merchant (*Moderato tranquillo*); IX. The Young Girl Is Transformed Into a Goat (*Moderato con agitazione*); X. Fifth Entr'acte and Burial of the Goat (*Lento con tristezza*); XI. The Quarrel of the Buffoon and the Merchant (*Allegro marziale*); XII. Final Dance (Moderato; Allegretto).

Christmas Concerto. *See:* Concerto Grosso—*Corelli.*

Christmas Oratorio. By Johann Sebastian Bach (1734), first performed during the Christmas season at Leipzig in 1734. Unlike the traditional oratorio, this one does not unfold a dramatic story, but consists of a series of 6 church cantatas intended for performance during the period from Christmas to Epiphany. Much of the text is drawn from the Nativity sections of St. Luke and St. Matthew.

The elegiac and pastoral orchestral introduction to the second part tells the waiting shepherds of the birth of Christ. Sometimes called *Pastoral Symphony*, it has the rhythm of a siciliana, and consists of a tender melody for strings interrupted by a chanting commentary by the woodwind.

Chromatic. Said of tones foreign by a semitone to the key or chord in which they appear. Chromatic music consequently employs accidentals frequently. A chromatic scale is built of 12 half steps.

Chromatic Fantasy and Fugue. For clavier, by Johann Sebastian Bach (1723). The title comes from the chromatic modulations in the fantasy, and from the fact that the subject of the fugue is also chromatic. Free in form, rhapsodic in feeling, this composition opens with a dramatic recitative that leads into a fantasia section characterized by runs and arpeggios. The three-part fugue begins quietly, then develops to a climax.

Church Windows (Vetrate di chiesa). Suite of four symphonic impressions by Ottorino Respighi (1926), introduced by the Boston Symphony under Koussevitzky on Feb. 25, 1927. In attempting to convey in tones the impressions made upon him by the stained-glass windows of churches, Respighi recreates a medieval spirit through the use of ecclesiastical modes. There are four movements. I. The Flight into Egypt. The little caravan carries the Treasure of the World. II. The Archangel Michael. Michael, with flaming sword, drives the rebellious angels from heaven. III. The Matin of Saint Chiara (St. Claire). Saint Claire, gravely sick, laments she could not attend matins at the church at Portiuncula. She is miraculously transported there. IV. St. Gregory the Great. St. Gregory blesses the throng, represented in all his splendor at ceremonial services.

Ciccolini, Aldo, pianist. Born Naples, Italy, Aug. 15, 1925. After attending the Naples Conservatory he made his début at Naples in 1942. Six years later he won the Santa Cecilia Prize for piano playing, and in 1949 the Long-Thibaud Prize in Paris. In 1949 he made an extended tour of Europe and South America. His American début took place with the New York Philharmonic in Carnegie Hall on Nov. 2, 1950.

Cimarosa, Domenico, composer. Born Aversa, Italy, Dec. 17, 1749; died Venice, Italy, Jan. 11, 1801. He attended the Santa Maria di Loreto Conservatory in Naples on a scholarship, after which he wrote his first opera buffa. His fame rests on his comic operas, the most celebrated of which is *The Secret Marriage* (*Il Matrimonio segreto*). Cimarosa is less famous as an instrumental composer, but he did produce some pleasing sonatas for harpsichord and 2 flute concertos. The Cimarosa Concerto for Oboe and Strings sometimes appearing on symphony programs was not written in that form by the composer. It is a free adaptation by Arthur Benjamin of 4 harpsichord sonatas by Cimarosa (No. 23 in A minor; No. 24 in C major; No. 29 in C minor; and No. 31 in G major).

Cimento dell' Armonia e dell' Inventione, Il. *See:* Concerto Grosso—*Vivaldi.*

Cincinnati Symphony Orchestra. A symphony orchestra founded in Cincinnati, Ohio, in 1895 with three series of concerts directed by Frank van der Stucken, Anton Seidl, and Henry Schradieck. For 12 seasons after that, Frank van der Stucken was principal conductor. In 1907 the orchestra disbanded rather than submit to what the management considered unreasonable demands by the American Federation of Musicians. Two years later it was reorganized, and Leopold Stokowski became principal conductor. Since Stokowski, the principal conductors have been Ernest Kunwald, Eugène Ysaÿe, Fritz Reiner, Eugene Goossens, Thor Johnson, and Max Rudolf. The orchestra performs in Music Hall.

Circus Polka. For orchestra by Stravinsky (1942), written as a ballet for elephants. In this version it was introduced at the Ringling Brothers Barnum and Bailey Circus at Madison Square Garden, New York, in the opening performance of the 1942 circus season. The ballet was directed by George Balanchine, and staged by John Murray Anderson. Stravinsky's amusing score includes a grotesque adaptation of Schubert's *Marche militaire*. The first concert performance took place on Jan. 14, 1944, the composer conducting the Boston Symphony.

Clair de lune. (1) A piece for the piano by Debussy from *Suite bergamasque* (which see).

(2) *See also: Masques et bergamasques* (Fauré).

Clarinet. A woodwind instrument with a cylindrical bore and a single reed mouthpiece. It has a virile tone, and a range of about three and a half octaves. The clarinet most often used is that in B-flat, but the clarinet in A, the bass clarinet, and the E-flat clarinet are also employed. The tonality of a composition dictates which clarinet is preferable: compositions with sharps usually utilize the A-clarinet; those with flats, the B-flat.

Classical Period. An era that is generally considered to begin with the death of Johann Sebastian Bach in 1750 and end in the first decade of the 19th century with Beethoven. The Classical period in music was characterized by respect for rules and forms, precision of expression,

clarity of writing, and restraint in emotion.

Classical Symphony. *See:* Symphony—*Prokofiev.*

Clavecin. French for harpsichord.

Clavicembalo. *See:* Cembalo.

Clavichord. A small keyboard instrument, precursor of the modern piano, in use from the 16th to 18th centuries. It was rectangular in shape, thus being the prototype of the square piano. Its weak, metallic tone, capable of delicacy of expression, was produced by metal tangents striking the strings.

Clavier. Literally keyboard. Before the 19th century, the term was used in German-speaking countries for any stringed keyboard instrument. It was also used for a time and in some regions to mean the clavichord specifically.

Clavieruebung. A collective title for a series of keyboard works by Johann Sebastian Bach published serially between 1726 and 1742. Part 1 contains the Partitas; Part 2, the *Italian Concerto* and *Overture in the French Manner;* Part 3, chorale preludes, four duets, and a prelude and fugue (the *St. Anne Fugue*) for the organ; Part 4, *Goldberg Variations.*

Clef. A sign at the beginning of a staff indicating pitch. Two clefs are used in piano music: the "G clef" in the treble and "F clef" in the bass. In viola music, the "C" clef is used.

Clementi, Muzio, pianist and composer. Born Rome, Italy, Jan. 23, 1752; died Evesham, England, March 10, 1832. He studied piano, thorough-bass, and counterpoint with local teachers, completing his music study in London, where his career as concert pianist began triumphantly in 1770. In the next dozen years, Clementi established his fame as one of Europe's foremost piano virtuosos. In Vienna, in 1781, he was invited by the Austrian Emperor to engage Mozart in a "musical duel," finally judged a draw. Between 1782 and 1802 Clementi devoted himself to varied musical activities. He achieved renown as a teacher of the piano, his many pupils including John Field, J. B. Cramer, Ignaz Moscheles, Friedrich Kalkbrenner, and Giacomo Meyerbeer. Clementi also interested himself in the manufacture of pianos, to which he devoted himself almost exclusively after 1810. He is most often remembered as composer for his more than 60 piano sonatas, which have become valuable in piano pedagogy. Even more important in the field of piano study is his volume of approximately 100 etudes entitled *Gradus ad Parnassum* (1817), which helped establish the backgrounds for the modern art of piano performance. Tausig has coupled this work with Chopin's Etudes as the "two works in musical literature which are entirely indispensable to the pianist." Clementi also wrote a number of delightful symphonies, long forgotten, but resuscitated in 1917. Alfredo Casella edited two of these (C major, D major) and introduced them in Turin and Rome, respectively, in 1935 and 1936.

Cleveland Orchestra. A symphony orchestra organized in Cleveland, Ohio, in 1902 by the Musical Arts Association of Cleveland, with Nikolai Sokoloff as principal conductor. In 1929 it was permanently endowed, and from then on was supported by an annual maintenance fund. After Sokoloff the principal conductors have been Artur Rodzinski, Erich Leinsdorf, and its present music director, George Szell. Szell was responsible for establishing a workshop for young conductors and creating the post of apprentice conductor in order to train young conductors. The orchestra acquired its present home, Severance Hall, in 1931. In 1957 it made a successful tour of Europe under Szell.

Cliburn, Van, pianist (born **Cliburn, Harvey Lavan, Jr.).** Born Shreveport, La., July 12, 1934. He studied piano with his mother, making his début in his twelfth year as soloist with the Houston Symphony. His only other teacher was Rosina Lhevinne at the Juilliard School of Music. In 1954 he won the Edgar N. Leventritt Award, which brought him an appearance with the New York Philharmonic under Mitropoulos. He made concert tours of the United States in 1955 and 1956. In April 1958 he attracted world attention by winning first prize in the Tchaikovsky competition for pianists in Moscow, and with it the rhapsodic praises of leading Soviet musicians and

the adulation of Soviet music lovers. He successfully repeated this prize-winning performance in May of the same year, in two concerts at Carnegie Hall, New York, and single appearances in Philadelphia and Washington, D.C., always to sold-out houses. On this occasion he became perhaps the first American musician to receive a ticker-tape parade up Broadway on May 20, 1958. Now a major concert attraction, Cliburn made an extended tour in 1958-1959, fully confirming the earlier impressions that he was one of the most formidable young piano virtuosos to appear since World War II.

Cloches à travers les feuilles (Debussy). *See: Images* (2).

Clock Symphony. *See:* Symphony— *Haydn.*

Clouds, The. *See:* Aristophanes.

Cluytens, André, conductor. Born Antwerp, Belgium, March 26, 1905. Cluytens received his musical instruction at the Antwerp Conservatory, from which he was graduated in his nineteenth year with honors in piano, harmony, counterpoint, and fugue. From 1927 to 1932 he was conductor of the Antwerp Royal Theater. In 1932 he settled permanently in France, where at first he led opera performances in the provinces, then joined the conducting staffs of the Opéra and the Opéra-Comique in Paris. As a symphony conductor he distinguished himself as principal conductor of the Paris Conservatory Orchestra, to which post he was appointed in 1949. After 1950 he made many guest appearances with major European orchestras. When the Vienna Philharmonic made its first tour of the United States in 1956, Cluytens was one of two men selected as conductors. He made his American début with that orchestra in Washington, D.C. on November 4.

Coates, Albert, conductor. Born St. Petersburg, Russia, April 23, 1882; died Capetown, South Africa, Dec. 11, 1953. His musical education took place at the Leipzig Conservatory, and he received his first training as conductor as assistant to Arthur Nikisch at the Leipzig Opera. Though best known as a conductor of operas, Coates also distinguished himself in symphonic music. In 1918 he became principal conductor of the London Symphony. He made his American début on Dec. 30, 1920, as guest conductor of the New York Symphony Society. From 1923 to 1925 he was principal conductor of the Rochester Philharmonic, which he had helped to organize. He subsequently was often heard in guest performances with other major American orchestras. In 1946 he settled in South Africa, where he served as conductor of the Johannesburg Symphony and as a member of the music faculty at the University of South Africa in Capetown.

Cockaigne. Concert overture for orchestra by Elgar, op. 40 (1900), first performed in London on June 20, 1901, the composer conducting. Subtitled "In London Town," this overture is a tonal picture of the city in the time of Edward VII— its sights and sounds as absorbed by two lovers taking a stroll. They enter a church, then exchange love messages in a park. The martial sound of a band and the religious music of a church organ form part of the music's texture.

Coda. Concluding section in a movement of an instrumental work.

Codetta. A brief coda.

Cohen, Harriet, pianist. Born London, England, Dec. 2, 1895. She received a scholarship for the Royal Academy of Music when she was twelve, and one year later made her concert début. Her first appearance as a mature artist took place at London in 1920. Several tours followed, including performances at a modern music festival at Salzburg in 1924, the presentation of her first all-Bach program in 1925, and her American début at Chicago in October 1930. Besides achieving worldwide acclaim for her performances of Bach, Miss Cohen has won accolades for her presentation of modern music. She was responsible for the English premières of works by Ravel, Bloch, Kodály, Schoenberg, and Manuel de Falla; and for the American premières of concertos by Arnold Bax, Vaughan Williams, and William Walton, the first two written for her. During World War II she played extensively for the British troops. During the London blitz her home was destroyed and she received several injuries, including loss of vision in one eye. Nevertheless, she continued to concertize. In 1938 she was made Dame Commander of the British Empire. She is the author of *Music's Handmaiden* (1936).

Col Legno. "With the wood," a term in string music indicating the use of the back of the bow on the strings instead of the hair.

Colas Breugnon, Overture to. Overture to an opera by Dmitri Kabalevsky. The libretto, by V. Bragin, is based on a story by Romain Rolland. The opera was introduced in Leningrad on Feb. 22, 1938. The sparkling music of this brief overture is intended to portray the principal character, Colas Breugnon, a Burgundian craftsman of the 16th century, whose view of life in general, and his immediate surroundings in particular, was softened by good spirits and continual laughter. The musical foundation of the overture is an energetic and gay theme representing Breugnon himself. Though heard often by itself on symphony programs, this overture is also a part of a suite prepared by the composer from his opera score. The other sections are three orchestral entr'actes entitled *People's Rebellion*, *People's Calamity*, and *People's Festival*.

Coleridge-Taylor, Samuel, composer. Born London, England, Aug. 15, 1875; died Croydon, England, Sept. 1, 1912. He was the son of a Negro physician. He studied music at the Royal Academy of Music with Charles Villiers Stanford and J. F. Bridge among others. His Symphony in A minor, on Negro themes, introduced in London in 1898, was his first major work to attain performance. Soon after this he was acclaimed for his choral trilogy, *Hiawatha*, which became world famous. Between 1900 and 1907 he was the conductor of the Rochester Choral Society in England. In 1903 he also founded a string orchestra in Croydon which became celebrated. During this period, in 1904, he paid the first of three visits to the United States conducting concerts of his own works. His best works abound in the use of Negro melodies and African rhythms. Among his orchestral compositions are an *African Suite, Symphonic Variations on an African Air, Bamboula,* the already mentioned Symphony in A, a violin concerto, and Ballade for piano and orchestra. He also wrote a clarinet quintet and string quartet.

Collines d'Anacapri (Debussy). *See:* Preludes—*Debussy.*

Colonne, Édouard (born **Colonne, Judas**), conductor. Born Bordeaux, France, July 23, 1838; died Paris, France, March 28, 1910. He attended the Paris Conservatory, then played the violin with the Paris Opéra orchestra and the Lamoureux Quartet. In 1873 he helped found the Concerts National, which gave significant concerts in Paris, including many French premières. Subsequently these performances became known as the Concerts du Châtelet and after that the Concerts Colonne. As conductor of his own orchestra, Colonne was responsible for provocative and exciting programs which included premières of many works by leading French composers, including Édouard Lalo, Jules Massenet, and César Franck; he also led a monumental festival of all of Berlioz' orchestral and choral works. In 1878 Colonne became director of orchestral concerts at the Paris Exposition, and in 1896 he paid the first of several visits to London as guest conductor. In 1905 he appeared with the New York Philharmonic. He also gave successful concerts in Russia and Portugal.

Colonne Orchestra (Concerts Colonne). Symphony orchestra founded in Paris in 1873 as Concerts National by Édouard Colonne (in collaboration with G. Hartmann) at the Odéon. Upon Hartmann's withdrawal in 1874, these concerts were called Concerts du Châtelet, since they were given at the Châtelet Theater under Colonne's direction. Subsequently, the orchestra assumed the name of its founder and conductor. Upon Colonne's death in 1910, Gabriel Pierné was appointed principal conductor, holding the post until his own death in 1933. Since Pierné, the principal conductors of the orchestra have been Paul Paray, Charles

Munch, and Gaston Poulet. The orchestra toured Europe several times and in 1947 appeared at the Edinburgh Festival.

Combat between David and Goliath. *See:* Kuhnau, Johann.

Comedians, The. Suite for orchestra by Dmitri Kabalevsky, op. 26 (1938), derived from his incidental music to *The Inventor and the Comedians,* a children's play produced in Moscow. The play concerned a group of wandering comedians, and their experiences as they travel from town to town performing at fairs, in public squares, and so forth. Kabalevsky's music is light and tuneful, and has proved popular at children's and "pop" concerts as well as on regular symphony programs. The suite, introduced in Moscow in 1940, has ten brief sections: I. Prologue; II. Galop; III. March; IV. Waltz; V. Pantomime; VI. Intermezzo; VII. Little Lyrical Scene; VIII. Gavotte; IX. Scherzo; X. Epilogue.

Comedy of Errors. *See:* Shakespeare, William.

Comedy Overture (Lustspielouvertuere). Concert overture by Ferruccio Busoni, op. 38 (1897, revised 1904). The main theme appears in strings without preliminaries; the second subject is subsequently presented by the clarinet. A new section leads to the development. In the recapitulation the second theme is worked over in cellos and basses over a pedal point in the timpani. The composition ends with a lively coda.

Comedy Overture on Negro Themes. Concert overture by Henry F. Gilbert (1910), first performed in New York City by the Municipal Symphony in Central Park on Aug. 17, 1910. The main melodic material consists of three Negro folksongs. The first is a Bahaman tune; the second a roustabout melody from the Mississippi wharves, *I'se Gwine to Alabamy;* the third, *Old Ship of Zion,* is used as the subject of a fugue.

Comes Autumn Time. Concert overture by Leo Sowerby (1916), one of the composer's most popular works. It was introduced by the New York Symphony Society in 1918, Walter Damrosch conducting. Its inspiration was Bliss Carman's poem, *Autumn*. The overture opens exuberantly with a lively theme in bass clarinet, horns, and low strings. A woodwind transition brings on the second main idea by flutes and celesta against a delicate background of harp and clarinet. The first subject receives attention in the development, while in the recapitulation the second theme returns before the first. A brilliant coda, based on the second theme, gives the overture a lively finish.

Common Chord. A chord consisting of a major or minor triad.

Common Time. Popular term for 4/4 time.

Comodo. Leisurely.

Compass. Range; the two extremes in the notes of an instrument.

Compound Interval. An interval in which the distance between the two notes exceeds an octave, as opposed to "simple interval."

Con Amore. Tenderly, with sentiment.

Con Anima. Spirited.

Con Brio. With fire, spirit.

Con Moto. With motion, fluidly.

Con Sordino. With a mute.

Concert. A performance by an artist or a group of artists before a paying or invited public. The first public concerts were believed to have taken place in London in 1672, when a violinist, John Banister, and other performers gave daily concerts for six years first at his home, then in other places. In one of his advertisements Banister referred to his performance as "concerted music," the first use of the word "concert" in conjunction with one of these events. Banister's series was succeeded in London by those instituted by Thomas Britton in or about 1678, which continued weekly for about 35 years.

Among the earliest concerts on the Continent were the *Abendmusiken,* "Evenings of Music," inaugurated by Buxtehude in Luebeck in 1673. These became so celebrated that many musicians (including Bach and Handel) made pilgrimages to Luebeck. About 1700, public concerts were given in Germany, Switzerland, and Sweden by the Collegia Musica, while in France concerts were instituted in 1725 by the

Concert Spirituel (which see).

O. G. Sonneck's researches into the early musical life of the United States have disclosed that concert performances took place in the Colonies, both in Boston and Charleston, S.C., in 1731; the first series of subscription concerts was organized in Charleston in 1732; and the first concert in New York City dates from 1736.

Concert Etude. *See:* Etude.

Concert Overture. *See:* Overture.

Concertante. (1) A term used for a style of writing for instrumental ensemble in which one or more solo instruments have brilliant parts.

(2) A concerto for two or more instruments and orchestra.

(3) *See also: Sinfonia concertante.*

Concertgebouw Orchestra. A symphony orchestra founded in Amsterdam, Holland, in 1883 with Wilhelm Kes as principal conductor. Five years later the orchestra acquired its present auditorium, the Concertgebouw. Willem Mengelberg succeeded Kes in 1894, remaining principal conductor until World War II. Discredited for having collaborated with the enemy during the war, Mengelberg was removed from his post and succeeded by Eduard van Beinum. In 1958 George Szell joined van Beinum as principal conductor. The orchestra made many tours of Europe; its first tour of the United States took place in the fall of 1954 under van Beinum.

Concertino. (1) In the concerto grosso, the solo instrument or instruments as opposed to the "ripieno," the rest of the orchestra.

(2) A small concerto, bearing the same relation to the concerto that a sonatina does to a sonata. It is slighter in structure, its movements are shorter, and the development sections are either abbreviated or completely eliminated. Franz Clement wrote 25 concertinos for violin and orchestra in the early 19th century. Carl Maria von Weber's tuneful Concertino for Clarinet and Orchestra in C minor, op. 26 (1811), is still sometimes performed; Weber also wrote a Concertino for Horn in E minor, op. 45 (1806, rescored 1815). The concertino form, however, has achieved its

greatest popularity among 20th-century composers.

The following are some of the best-known and most frequently heard concertinos by 20th-century composers.

JEAN FRANÇAIX. The Concertino for Piano and Orchestra (1934) was introduced in Paris on Dec. 15, 1934, with the composer as soloist and Jean Morel conducting the Lamoureux Orchestra. (I. *Presto leggiero.* II. *Lent.* III. *Allegretto.* IV. *Allegretto vivo.*) The work begins with a forceful subject for solo piano, the basic idea of a movement that maintains a capricious attitude. In the slow movement, which is only thirty bars long, the piano presents a haunting tune against strings. The third movement has a jazz-like melody for trumpet, and the finale is a rondo in which the abandoned mood of the preceding movement is maintained.

EUGENE GOOSSENS. The Concertino for Double String Orchestra (1927) is unusual in that no solo instrument is prominent. It originated as an octet, then was rescored for double string orchestra. In the latter version it was introduced in New York City on Dec. 18, 1929. While in a single movement, this composition has three sections (*Allegro moderato, Andante espressivo,* and *Allegro*). The basis of the Concertino is a rhythmic figure presented early in the first movement; it becomes the spine of the concluding section. The melody of the slow movement has the character of a folksong. Just before the conclusion of the finale there comes an interruption, followed by a change of key and tempo in music of sinister character; but this mood is of only brief duration and the work ends in a lively vein.

HONEGGER. The Concertino for Piano and Orchestra (1924) was introduced in Paris on May 23, 1925; Andrée Vaurabourg (the composer's fiancée, and later his wife) was the soloist and Koussevitzky conducted. This music is light, jaunty, and filled with popular music-hall tunes (I. *Allegro molto moderato.* II. *Larghetto sostenuto.* III. *Allegro*). A dialogue between piano and orchestra ushers in the first movement. A synco-

pated theme is then given by the piano. The development is in fugal style. In the second movement a pleasing melody appears in the piano against orchestral embellishments. The finale opens percussively: the violinists strike the strings with the back of their bows. A syncopated, jazz-like idea is then heard in the piano, and a secondary subject, also of music-hall flavor, is given by violas and bassoons.

IBERT. The *Concertino da Camera,* for alto saxophone and orchestra (1935) was introduced in Barcelona at the International Society for Contemporary Music Festival on April 20, 1936. Modern harmonic and rhythmic resources are here combined with the concerto grosso structure in music that often has an infectious sense of humor (I. *Allegro con moto.* II. Larghetto. III. *Animato molto*). In the first two movements the main melodic material is presented by the saxophone; the first movement ends with a wittily conceived fugato section. The second and third movements blend into a single integrated piece of music, despite contrasts of mood.

Concertmaster. The leader of the first violin section in a symphony orchestra. He assists the conductor in solving any technical problem that may arise in the music for violins; he helps train the violin section; and he performs any solo violin passages that may appear in the score.

Concerto. A large work usually for one but sometimes for two or more solo instruments and orchestra, highlighting both the individuality of the solo instrument or instruments and the virtuosity of the performer or performers. Most concertos are in three movements. The first is usually in some variety of sonata form. The second is slow and lyrical, sometimes in three-part song form, sometimes in variation form. The third is lively, gay, or vigorous, usually in rondo form. Most concertos have cadenzas for the first and last movements, and many have one for all three movements.

The word "concerto" began to appear in the 16th century, but it was not used consistently in its modern sense until instrumental concertos by Giuseppe Torelli appeared in 1686. In 1714 Corelli published a set of 12 concerti grossi for two violins, cello, and strings, the foundation upon which all subsequent works in the concerto-grosso style rest.

The concerto grosso (which see) was the forerunner of the solo concerto. (Concertos for orchestra discussed below are usually an extension and modernization of the concerto-grosso form.) Early masters of the concerto grosso soon began writing compositions in which a single solo instrument, instead of a group of solo instruments as had been the case with the concerto grosso, was contrasted against and balanced with the accompanying orchestra. Thus the concerto for solo instrument and orchestra came into existence. However, these early concertos are essentially concerti grossi in style and structure, even though the solo instrument is allowed more individuality than heretofore, and even though both Bach and Handel began introducing cadenza passages.

Johann Sebastian Bach was one of the first important composers to write a clavier concerto. But the concerto, as the term is understood today, does not make its appearance until Mozart, who finally crystallized the form, and filled that form with a heretofore unprecedented intensity and variety of expression; Mozart also helped liberate the solo instrument. But while with Mozart we are often made aware of the virtuosity of the soloist, with Beethoven virtuosity always gives way to the poetic content of the music. With the Romantic composers who followed Beethoven, the concerto acquired a greater elasticity of form, and an intensified emotional ardor in the musical content; at the same time the writing for the solo instrument acquired new dash and brilliance.

The principal works in the concerto literature are discussed below.

CARL PHILIPP EMANUEL BACH. The Concerto in D major for string orchestra by Carl Philipp Emanuel Bach often presented at symphony concerts is ac-

tually an adaptation. Bach's concerto, also in D major, was scored for a quartet of viols. Koussevitzky commissioned Maximilian Steinberg to adapt the work for a modern chamber orchestra, and this version was published in 1911 (I. *Allegro moderato*. II. *Andante lento molto*. III. Allegro). The first movement consists of two robust themes; the slow movement has an elegiac melody; and the finale is in three-part song form.

JOHANN SEBASTIAN BACH. Bach wrote his clavier concertos in the 1730's for performance by his pupils or sons. Most are transcriptions of other works, sometimes of his own violin concertos. The Concerto No. 1 in D minor is a favorite with present-day audiences. The composer himself was partial to it, since he used material from it in 2 church cantatas. The basic melodic material is usually found in the orchestra, while the solo instrument generally provides filigree trimmings (I. Allegro. II. Adagio. III. Allegro). The first movement opens with a vigorous six-bar subject for unison orchestra; this is the main subject. The second movement has a soaring minor-mode melody in the orchestra. The finale is introduced with a swiftly moving twelve-bar idea. After a final statement of this theme, in the solo instrument, there appears a short cadenza.

In the Concerto No. 5 in F minor (I. Allegro. II. Largo. III. Presto) the first movement opens with a robust fourteen-bar passage for clavier and orchestra; at its termination, the clavier embarks upon an expressive section of its own. After a return of the opening vigorous section, a second sensitive thought is introduced. The slow movement is a spacious aria-like melody decorated with figures in the strings. The finale is energetic music in triple time which receives a dramatic workout.

Two of Bach's concertos for two claviers and orchestra are adaptations of violin concertos. The exception is the Concerto in C major (I. Allegro. II. *Adagio ovvero Largo*. III. Fuga). The first movement is built from two succinct phrases: the initial two bars of the opening virile subject for claviers and orchestra, and the first two bars of a subsequent idea for two solo claviers. The orchestra is dispensed with in the slow movement, which is built entirely from a broad melody for the solo instruments. The finale is a fugue on a sprightly subject.

The Concerto for Three Claviers and Orchestra in C major (I. Allegro. II. Adagio. III. Allegro) first presents in the opening movement the three solo instruments in unison in opposition to the orchestra; then new material is introduced. The slow movement opens with a polyphonic section for strings alone, after which the three claviers appear with the main theme; towards the end of the movement the solo instruments are heard in a cadenza characterized by unusual chromatic harmonies. The finale treats its thematic material fugally, with each of the three solo players allowed to exhibit his virtuosity. The movement opens and closes with a vigorous passage for solo instruments and orchestra.

The Concerto for Four Claviers and Orchestra in A minor is an adaptation of a concerto by Vivaldi: the Concerto in B minor for four violins and orchestra, op. 3, no. 10. Besides changing the key of the original Vivaldi composition, Bach filled out the harmonic structure of the solo instruments and contributed a measure of his own in the finale. Otherwise the music is basically Vivaldi's (I. Allegro. II. Largo. III. Allegro). The dynamic rhythmic figure with which the first movement opens, and the brief commentary to it provided by the four instruments, is the main thematic material. The second movement is in three-part song form, its middle section consisting of broken arpeggios in the four claviers, unaccompanied. The finale then enters without interruption.

See also: Italian Concerto.

Bach wrote his violin concertos between 1717 and 1723 during his stay in Coethen. These are the earliest violin concertos to survive in the standard repertory. As was the case with his clavier concertos, the solo instrument is often used to embellish the material provided by the orchestra.

The Concerto in A minor (I. Allegro. II. Andante. III. *Allegro assai*) begins with a vivacious twenty-four bar theme in the orchestra made up of two sections, each with a self-sufficient motif; the first part appears and reappears throughout the movement in counterpoint to the solo instrument. The second movement is a flowing melody against a persistent ground bass, to which the solo instrument provides decorations. In the finale we see the composer's skill at contrapuntal writing, with the opening orchestral passage presenting the main theme fugally.

The Concerto in E major (I. Allegro. II. Adagio. III. *Allegro assai*) is a work of such exuberance that Johann Nicolaus Forkel described it as "full of an unconquerable joy of life." The basis of the first movement is the three sharply accented quarter notes with which it opens; midway in the movement the solo instrument spins an eloquent melody. The slow movement is a freely treated chaconne, its main subject presented immediately in the bass while over it soars a melody of compelling beauty. A virile subject for orchestra heard at the opening of the finale sets into motion a momentum that continues throughout the movement.

The Concerto for Two Violins and Orchestra in D minor is one of the composer's most sublime works in the concerto form (I. Vivace. II. *Largo ma non tanto.* III. Allegro). In the first movement the two solo instruments share a bold three-bar subject, treated fugally. A second subject is then used contrapuntally to this initial idea. The slow movement is music of radiant beauty in which, once again, the melody is treated canonically by the two instruments. The concerto ends dynamically with a forceful statement shared fugally by the two solo instruments, but midway a contrast is provided by a haunting melody first heard in the first violin.

A Concerto for Violin, Oboe and Orchestra in D minor is an attempt by modern editors to restore the original form of the Concerto for Two Claviers and Orchestra in C minor (I. Allegro. II. Adagio. III. Allegro). The first movement opens with an orchestral preface after which the two solo instruments enter with the main melody. The slow movement is a majestic song presented in imitation by the two solo instruments against a pizzicato string accompaniment. The finale begins without interruption with a brisk orchestral section, followed by the entrance of the two solo instruments who then discourse at length on this topic.

For Bach's concertos for orchestra (Brandenburg Concertos) *see:* Concerto grosso—*J. S. Bach.*

SAMUEL BARBER. Barber's Concerto for Cello and Orchestra, op. 22 (1945), was introduced by Raya Garbousova and the Boston Symphony under Koussevitzky on April 5, 1946. It received the New York Music Critics Award (I. *Allegro moderato.* II. *Andante molto sostenuto.* III. *Molto allegro e appassionata*). In the first movement, the principal theme appears in the English horn after two introductory measures, while the second major subject is shared by the solo instrument and strings. The slow movement is a lyrical exchange between the solo cello and the orchestra; the main melody is heard after a single introductory measure. The finale is mostly made up of virtuoso material for the solo instrument; but it also includes a sensitive lyrical passage for the cello.

BARTÓK. Béla Bartók wrote three piano concertos. The second (1931) is filled with primitive rhythms, is constructed from fragmentary themes, and erupts with orgiastic sounds (I. Allegro. II. Adagio; Presto. III. *Allegro molto*). The first movement, in sonata form, opens with a trumpet motif, following which the solo piano arrives with the first theme. The second theme, also in the solo piano, is heard after an extended development of the first. In this movement the orchestration dispenses with the strings. The second movement opens and closes with a chorale-like melody to which, midway, an exciting and primitive presto section provides dramatic relief. The primitive forces of this section are again released in the finale as percussive strength is contributed by piano and timpani.

The Concerto No. 3 came fourteen years later. It was first performed in Philadelphia by György Sándor and the Philadelphia Orchestra on Feb. 8, 1946, Ormandy conducting (I. Allegretto. II. *Adagio religioso.* III. Allegro). Written in the last year of the composer's life, this concerto is a personalized message to his wife, and is filled with strong emotion. The first movement is in sonata form, the principal theme given by the piano; the second theme is more decorative. A horn passage is the transition for both the development and the recapitulation. In the slow movement a stately theme for strings leads to a Bach-like chorale in the piano; midway there appears an agitated trio. The finale is a scherzo whose heart is a complex fugue.

Bartók's Concerto for Violin and Orchestra is one of the composer's masterworks (1938). It was introduced in Amsterdam on April 23, 1939, Zoltán Székely soloist and Mengelberg conducting. (I. *Allegro non troppo.* II. *Andante tranquillo.* III. *Allegro molto*). Whereas in earlier piano concertos Bartók used mainly fragmentary thematic subjects he here employs full grown, spacious melodies; but the passion, intensity, and dramatic thrust are not abandoned. In the first movement, in sonata form, the first theme is in a Romantic style, while the second employs a twelve-tone row. This movement opens with a vigorous, march-like subject. The slow movement boasts one of the composer's most ingratiating melodies, which is subjected to six variations. In the finale, a rondo, material of the first movement reappears in altered form. This movement is in a savage mood and is filled with demoniac Hungarian dance rhythms.

The Concerto for Orchestra is one of Bartók's most popular works, and one of his best. He wrote it in 1943, about two years before his death, on a commission from the Koussevitzky Foundation. Its première took place in Boston on Dec. 1, 1944, with Koussevitzky conducting the Boston Symphony. It has five movements, the two outer ones being in sonata form, while the middle one consists of brief episodes (I. *Andante non troppo; Allegro vivace.* II. *Allegro scherzando.* III. *Elegia: Andante non troppo.* IV. *Intermezzo interrotto:* Allegretto. V. *Presto).* In the first movement a melancholy mood prevails. The first theme is immediately given by lower strings; the second follows in a flute, then a trumpet. The mood lightens in the second movement, subtitled, "The Game of the Couples." Five pairs of winds (bassoons, oboes, clarinets, flutes, and muted trumpets) present five different thematic subjects representing the five couples; a brief brass chorale serves as a transition between the different themes. The first subject of the first movement becomes the material from which the elegiac third movement is constructed. This is followed by a buoyant intermezzo. The concerto concludes with an energetic rondo in Hungarian style, whose development section consists of a fugue.

BEETHOVEN. Beethoven wrote five piano concertos. The first three are in the classical style of Mozart, with only the third concerto allowing Beethoven's independence of structure and thought to assert itself. Concerto No. 1 in C major, op. 15 (1797), was written after the second concerto, but its earlier publication has brought it the designation of "first." Its première took place in Vienna on April 2, 1800, the composer appearing as soloist. Concerto No. 2 in B-flat, op. 19 (1795), was introduced in Vienna on March 29, 1795, the composer as soloist. Both these works are so direct in appeal, so simple and forthright in construction, and so filled with engaging lyricism that their effect on audiences is immediate.

It is in the Concerto No. 3 in C minor, op. 37 (1800), that the composer outgrows the model established by Mozart and begins to assert his own original personality. The composer himself introduced this work in Vienna on April 5, 1803 (I. *Allegro con brio.* II. Largo. III. Allegro). In it Beethoven endows the solo instrument with new breadth and dimension, while providing the orchestra with an altogether new symphonic scope. In the first movement the main theme, typically Beethoven in

its athletic drive, appears at once in unison strings. The second theme then is stated by clarinets, and repeated by violins. After the extended orchestral preface is over, the solo instrument appears with three C major scale passages, after which it discusses the principal material dramatically. The movement ends with an extended cadenza. In the slow movement a stately melody is presented by the piano, then repeated by muted strings. This is followed by an effective lyrical subject, treated decoratively by both solo instrument and orchestra, and a brief episode for the woodwind against piano arpeggios. A brief cadenza concludes the movement. The finale is a vivacious rondo with some striking enharmonic passages for the solo instrument. The movement ends impetuously with a presto coda in which some fresh material is introduced.

The last two Beethoven piano concertos are masterworks that carry the concerto to dramatic power and expressive eloquence it had heretofore not known. The Concerto No. 4 in G major, op. 58 (1806), was first performed publicly by the composer in Vienna on Dec. 22, 1808. Virtuosity now makes way for artistic expression (I. *Allegro moderato.* II. *Andante con moto.* III. Vivace). The first movement opens in unorthodox fashion with the piano quietly presenting four measures of the first theme. Only then does the orchestra appear with a discourse in which this theme, and a second subject for the strings, are presented and developed. In working out these ideas in piano and orchestra there is spaciousness of design and a grandeur of speech which, for want of a better term, we must describe as "Beethovenian." The second movement is an eloquent dialogue between piano and orchestra—the orchestra speaking in strong and almost defiant accents while the piano replies submissively. The finale is a rondo in which the piano immediately engages the first theme, then emerges with a second episode after the orchestra had taken up this initial material. The work ends with a coda in which the tempo accelerates to presto.

The Concerto No. 5 in E-flat major, op. 73 (1809), is known as the "Emperor," a name probably bestowed upon it by some later publisher who wished to point up its majestic content. The first public performance took place in Leipzig on Nov. 28, 1811, Friedrich Schneider, soloist (I. Allegro. II. *Adagio un poco mosso*. III. Allegro). A powerful chord introduces the first movement, after which the piano presents a rhapsodic passage. There follows a one-hundred bar section for the orchestra in which two main themes are presented. The development that follows is of epical dimensions. After a dramatic climax, there comes a brief pause followed by the solo instrument in a cadenza written out by the composer, in which the elevated thought of preceding pages still predominates. The second movement opens with a stately melody for strings. The piano comments on this subject in a reflective and improvisational manner, before repeating it against plucked strings. Two bars before the end of the movement there comes a hint of the main theme of the finale. In rondo form, this last movement is full of vivacity.

The Concerto in D major, op. 61 (1806), is Beethoven's only violin concerto. It was introduced in Vienna by Franz Clement on Dec. 23, 1806 (I. *Allegro ma non troppo*. II. Larghetto. III. Allegro). The first movement is prefaced by a symphonic introduction in which the main themes are presented by the woodwind. The solo instrument then appears with ascending octaves after which there takes place a monumental working out, by both orchestra and solo instrument, of the principal themes. The soloist often decorates the main melodies with filigree. The second movement is a sustained song in muted strings to which the solo instrument provides trimming; then the solo instrument presents a second lyrical subject before the original material is recalled. A spirited theme in solo violin brings on the third movement, a rondo, in which the second subject (also heard in the solo violin) is a sentimental melody.

The Concerto in C major, for piano, violin, cello, and orchestra, op. 56 (1805), is the composer's only concerto for more than one solo instrument; it is his attempt to revive and modernize the concerto-grosso form. It was first performed in Vienna in 1807. Though completed in Beethoven's middle period, this work reaches back stylistically to his first three piano concertos. The main interest lies in its fresh, ingratiating lyricism, rather than in dramatic developments and poetic speech (I. Allegro. II. Largo. III. *Rondo alla polacca*). The work opens with an orchestral introduction in which the main themes are presented: the first in cellos and basses; the second, more lyrical, in first violins. A restatement of this material occurs when the three solo instruments make their appearance. The development and recapitulation follow traditional lines. In the second movement, a beautiful melody unfolds in solo cello, accompanied by the piano. After it is repeated by clarinets and bassoons, the solo instruments reappear to comment upon it. The finale, in rondo form, enters without interruption, with a lively tune in polonaise style in the solo cello. The other solo instruments discuss it, after which they are joined by the orchestra.

ALBAN BERG. Berg's Violin Concerto (1935) is in the twelve-tone technique. It was introduced by Louis Krasner in Barcelona on April 19, 1936. Berg planned it as a requiem to a young girl (daughter of Mahler's widow by a second marriage), and her presence is felt throughout this poignant music (I. Andante; Allegro. II. Allegro; Adagio). In the first movement she is described in several pleasing themes, one in the style of an Alpine folksong, another in that of a Viennese waltz. The music grows more emotional in the second movement as the composer speaks of the girl's death and tells of the deliverance of her soul. As her soul achieves peace, Berg quotes a chorale by Bach: *Es ist genug* from the cantata *O Ewigkeit, du Donnerwort.*

This concerto proved to be Berg's own threnody, for it was his last work. Even as he was completing it, he knew he was dying; as he turned the manuscript over to his wife he remarked softly, "Es ist genug" ("It is enough").

Berg's Chamber Concerto, for piano, violin, and 13 wind instruments (1925), was introduced at the Frankfort Music Festival on July 2, 1927. Berg wrote it with his teacher, Schoenberg, in mind. Feeling that Schoenberg, himself, and another of Schoenberg's disciples, Anton Webern, represented a kind of trinity of atonal music, Berg constructed his music with the number "three" predominating. There are three movements: I. *Epigraphe.* II. Adagio. III. *Rondo ritmico con introduzione.* The instrumental group is made up of three units (keyboard, strings, wind). The rhythmic and harmonic construction carries out this pattern of threes. In the first movement the composer creates a kind of musical anagram made up of letters from the names of three atonal composers; this anagram is presented in three different themes. The slow movement is in three-part song form, while in the finale material from the earlier movements is repeated in three combinations.

ERNEST BLOCH. The Concerto for Violin and Orchestra (1938) received its première in Cleveland on Dec. 15, 1938, Joseph Szigeti soloist, Dimitri Mitropoulos conducting. (I. *Allegro deciso.* II. Andante. III. *Deciso).* The first movement opens with a virile theme of American-Indian character, stated by four horns, oboes, and clarinets. The second main theme is feminine and more expressive, a *dolce espressivo* section in solo violin. But the rhapsodic character of the entire movement, and its virility, are derived from the first, Indian, theme, which arrives at a powerful climax with the aid of trumpets, timpani, and cymbals. The movement ends with an extended cadenza. A simple diatonic melody in the orchestra ushers in the second movement, following which the violin appears with a dreamlike song. Other thematic ideas, mostly in the violin, maintain an idyllic mood. The finale is by turns tragic and turbulent, marked by piercing dissonances. The thematic material here bears a family relationship to that of the first movement; and the tender, expressive melody of the first movement is recalled.

BOCCHERINI. The Concerto in B-flat major for cello and orchestra, op. 34, is most often performed in an edition by Friedrich Gruetzmacher published in 1900. Gruetzmacher also prepared the first-movement cadenza (I. *Allegro moderato.* II. *Adagio non troppo.* III. Allegro). The first movement opens with an orchestral introduction in which the principal material appears. The solo instrument then takes over this material and embellishes it with figurations and variations. The slow movement consists of a soaring, singing melody for the solo instrument. The finale, a rondo, begins with a lively subject in the upper register of the solo instrument. The lightness of spirit thus imposed is continued throughout the movement.

BRAHMS. Brahms wrote two concertos for piano and orchestra. When the Concerto No. 1 in D minor, op. 15 (1856), was introduced in Hanover on Jan. 22, 1859 (the composer was soloist, and Joseph Joachim conducted), it was a dismal failure. Brahms had originally planned it as a symphony, then tried to revamp it into a sonata for two pianos. His final compromise was to transform it into a piano concerto (I. Maestoso. II. Adagio. III. *Allegro non troppo).* A dramatic subject in strings introduces the first movement. This is followed by two contemplative melodies. After a return of the initial theme, the piano recalls all three subjects, then enters upon a new spacious melody of rhapsodic feeling. The agitation and passion of the opening subject, however, is the prevailing mood of the movement. Above the second movement the composer wrote the following inscription: "Benedictus qui venit in nomine Dei." The entire movement is an elegy whose main theme appears first in strings and bassoons; an equally emotional second idea is subsequently stated by the clarinets. The finale, in rondo form, releases animal energy, but before this movement ends, a cadenza introduces a welcome atmosphere of contentment.

The Concerto No. 2 in B-flat major, op. 83, came a dozen years later, a product of the composer's full maturity (1881). It was introduced in Budapest on Nov. 9, 1881, with the composer as soloist, and Alexander Erkel conducting. It is a work of such spacious dimensions, and so monumental in concept, that it is sometimes called a symphony with piano. It has four, instead of the more usual three movements (I. *Allegro non troppo.* II. *Allegro appassionato.* III. Andante. IV. *Allegretto grazioso*). The main theme of the first movement appears at once in the first horn. A transition in the piano leads to a large section for orchestra in which the first subject reappears, followed by a second one in the violins. After both themes are developed by solo instrument and orchestra, a second spacious orchestral section introduces the extended development. The opening horn theme brings on the recapitulation, and the movement ends with a large coda in which the material from the first orchestral section is reviewed. The second movement is a scherzo, its principal theme first heard in the solo piano, then repeated by the full orchestra. The trio section begins with a sharply accented idea in the violins. The slow movement is one of Brahms' most eloquent pages, beginning with a solo cello melody which the composer also used for his song, *Immer leiser wird mein Schlummer.* A second melody, first heard in piano and clarinet, is equally poignant. After the movement ends with a brief coda, a dynamic finale, rich in Hungarian rhythms and melodies, follows.

Brahms completed only a single concerto for the violin, that in D major, op. 77 (1878). It was introduced in Leipzig on Jan. 1, 1879, with Joseph Joachim as soloist and the composer conducting (I. *Allegro ma non troppo.* II. Adagio. III. *Allegro giocoso, ma non troppo vivace*). The first movement has a hundred-bar orchestral preface in which the main lyrical subject is immediately presented by cellos, violas, bassoons, and horns; a secondary idea follows in the oboe. After a *marcato* section in the strings, the soloist enters with detailed passage work. The development of both main themes is involved and at times stormy; an idyllic moment arrives after the cadenza with a return of the opening melody in the solo instrument. The second movement opens

with a beautiful song for oboe. After it has been repeated by the solo instrument the latter proceeds to a second eloquent melody. The finale, in rondo form, is Hungarian in its vital rhythms and passionate melodies. A brief cadenza leads to a marchlike coda.

The Concerto in A minor for violin, cello, and orchestra, op. 102 (1887), is Brahms' last effort in the concerto form and is in the style of a concerto grosso. It was first heard publicly in Cologne on Oct. 18, 1887, with Joseph Joachim and Robert Hausmann as soloists, and the composer conducting (I. Allegro. II. Andante. III. *Vivace non troppo*). After a four-bar orchestral prelude to the first movement, the two solo instruments engage in a brief interlude. Now an extended orchestral passage presents the main material: a vigorous first theme in the full orchestra, and a more tender subject in the woodwind. The second movement is a meditative song which Walter Niemann has described as a "great ballade, steeped in the rich, mysterious tones of a northern evening atmosphere." The main thought comes in octaves in the two solo instruments after an introductory four-note passage in horns and woodwind. In the finale a delightful gypsy tune is heard in the cellos, then repeated by the violins. The secondary subject in clarinets and bassoons to a rising arpeggio accompaniment also has a pronounced gypsy flavor.

BRUCH. The Concerto No. 1 in G minor, for violin and orchestra, op. 26 (1866), is one of a handful of works by which the composer is remembered. It was introduced in Coblenz on April 24, 1866, with Otto von Koenigsloew as soloist, and the composer conducting (I. *Allegro moderato.* II. Adagio. III. *Allegro energico*). A soft drum roll introduces the orchestral preface, whose material bears no relation to that of the rest of the first movement. A highly rhythmic first theme then appears in the solo violin; the expressive second subject that follows is shared by the solo instrument and an oboe. Passage work, and development of these ideas, lead to a cadenza which blends directly into the slow movement. The latter is a spacious melody for the solo instrument in long, sustained phrases; this is followed by a second melody in the orchestra, with figurations in the solo violin. An intriguing rhythmic phrase appears in the introduction to the finale. This is the germ of a vigorous melody soon presented by the solo violin. The second theme, passionate and intense, is played by the full orchestra and then taken up by the soloist. Both subjects are worked out energetically and culminate in a brilliant coda.

CASTELNUOVO-TEDESCO. Castelnuovo-Tedesco wrote two violin concertos. The second is the more popular. It is entitled *The Prophets* (1932) and it was introduced in New York on April 12, 1933, by Jascha Heifetz with the New York Philharmonic Orchestra conducted by Toscanini. Each of the three movements bears the name of a Hebrew prophet of whom it is a tonal representation: I. *Isaiah*. II. *Jeremiah*. III. *Elijah*. The composer explains that his aim was to "glorify the splendor of the past days and the burning inspiration which enflamed the 'envoys of God,' the Prophets. The violin seemed to me particularly adapted to personify, as protagonist, the free and vivid eloquence of the Prophets, while the orchestra, in the multiform aspects of the symphonic texture, could evoke all the voices of the surrounding world: voices of people, voices of Nature, voices of God." The composer derived some of his thematic material from a collection of Jewish-Italian melodies, edited by Federico Consolo, and published in Florence in or about 1870.

CHAUSSON. The Concerto in D major, for piano, violin, and string quartet, op. 21 (1891), is one of the composer's major works. It was introduced by Eugène Ysaÿe and his ensemble in Brussels on March 4, 1892 (I. *Décidé*. II. *Sicilienne*. III. *Grave*. IV. *Très animé*). The first movement has two principal ideas: the first is a sustained melody for solo violin; the other, a virile subject for piano. In the second movement, the entire ensemble presents a beautiful melody allowed to grow and expand in emotional intensity. The third movement injects a somber mood, its music being mostly a duet for violin and piano. But exuberance and healthy animal spirits characterize the finale, which, structurally, is a gigue-toccata.

CHOPIN. Chopin's two piano concertos came early in his career. The Concerto No. 1 in E minor, op. 11 (1830), actually was his second concerto, but it was the first to be published. The Concerto No. 2 in F minor, op. 21, preceded it by a year.

The Concerto No. 1 was introduced in Warsaw on Oct. 11, 1830, with the composer as soloist (I. *Allegro maestoso*. II. Larghetto. III. Vivace). The first movement has a rhapsodic orchestral introduction in which the two main themes make their appearance. The first is energetic and is presented by the first violins; the second is an effeminate, lyrical song for strings. It is to the second subject that the composer is more partial in working out his ideas. The second movement, a Romanza, is a poetic discourse beginning with twelve measures of introduction in muted strings. The piano then chants an eloquent melody which the composer intended to convey the impression of "a fine moonlit spring night." The concluding movement is a spirited rondo, beginning with a robust exchange between strings and wind. The piano then contributes two other subjects, one a sprightly dancelike tune, the other a powerful theme accompanied by delicate figures in the strings.

The Concerto No. 2 was first performed at a concert in which Chopin made his début both as composer and pianist, in Warsaw, on March 17, 1830 (I. Maestoso. II Larghetto. III. *Allegro vivace*). The opening movement has two exposition sections. The first is for orchestra, and introduces the two main themes, one for strings, the other for oboe. In the second exposition, given by the piano, these themes are repeated. In the development the first theme is discussed at length. Chopin uses his slow movement to unfold a soulful song, whose main idea is found in the piano after six introductory measures. The finale has a fiery spirit, both themes having the character of a mazurka.

DVOŘÁK. Dvořák wrote his violin Concerto in A minor, op. 53 (1880), for Joseph Joachim, who made so many suggestions to the composer that it took Dvořák almost two years to complete it. It was not Joachim who introduced it, but Franz Ondříček, in Vienna on Dec. 3, 1883. The material is rhapsodic in the composer's most grateful Slavic style (I. *Allegro ma non troppo*. II. *Adagio ma non troppo*. III. *Allegro giocoso ma non troppo*). The concerto opens dramatically with the main theme vigorously projected by the orchestra. After this has been amplified, the violins introduce the second main theme in octaves to a contrapuntal background by the woodwind. The solo instrument reviews both these ideas, then introduces a third subject of its own. The slow movement, which follows the first without pause, is a Romanza and consists of Bohemian folk material. The first melody is heard in the solo violin to a woodwind accompaniment. After this theme is taken over by the woodwind, the solo violin presents the second theme. There is still a third motif, played by the orchestra following some passage work in the violin. A rhapsodic section for violin finally leads to a return of all three themes. The finale is a rondo, also made up of three melodies, all of them of Bohemian folk character, and all first appearing in the solo violin.

The Concerto in B minor, for cello and orchestra, op. 104 (1895), was written during Dvořák's stay in the United States. Its first performance took place in London on March 16, 1896, with Leo Stern as soloist, and the composer conducting. Whereas the violin concerto was of unmistakable Bohemian identity, the cello concerto uses American folk materials (I. Allegro. II. *Adagio ma non troppo*. III. *Allegro moderato*). An extended orchestral introduction presents the two main themes of the first movement; the second, in the solo horn against strings, is in the style of a Negro Spiritual. After the appearance of the solo instrument, both themes are worked out, often with interesting embellishments by the solo cello. Two expressive melodies dominate the second movement. The first is stated by the clarinet against an oboe and bassoon accompaniment; the other is presented by the strings after the solo cello has repeated the opening subject. The en-

tire movement has deep emotional content, and is of affecting tenderness. The finale, on the other hand, is a joyous outburst, opening with a strong rhythmic theme that leads to the first principal melody, which sounds like a peasant dance. The second theme, in the clarinet with embellishments by the solo cello, is also spirited. The concerto concludes, as the composer has explained, "like a breath, with reminiscences of the first and second movements; the solo dies away to a pianissimo; then there is a crescendo, and the last measures are taken up by the orchestra, ending stormily."

ELGAR. Elgar's Violin Concerto in B minor, op. 61 (1910), is a personal work to which the composer committed some of his most endearing thoughts and deepest feelings. It is romantic, rhapsodical, with impressive flights of poetic fancy. It also boasts some interesting innovations. It was introduced in London by Fritz Kreisler on Nov. 10, 1910. (I. Allegro. II. Andante. III. *Allegro molto*). In the first movement the solo violin appears simultaneously with the concluding bars of a long orchestral introduction. All the basic melodic material is found in this introduction, the most important being the phrase with which the concerto opens. The slow movement is a serene, affecting, lyrical page, its main thought a placid melody for orchestra to which the solo violin soon supplies an effective countersubject. In the third movement Elgar uses an accompanied cadenza (defying the tradition that dictates that cadenzas be unaccompanied). He also borrows his melodic material from the first two movements. The major new subject is a brilliant passage for the orchestra, which is then extended by the solo violin; a secondary idea is a quiet and reflective melody for the solo violin.

FALLA. The Concerto for Harpsichord, Flute, Oboe, Clarinet, Violin, and Cello (1926) was written for the famous harpsichordist, Wanda Landowska, who introduced it in Barcelona on Nov. 5, 1926, Pablo Casals conducting. This music, while in a neo-Classic style, is often a subtle evocation of Spain, its music, and people (I. Allegro. II. Lento. III. Vivace). In the first movement the harpsichord simulates a strumming guitar, providing a compelling rhythm to several folk-like melodies. The second movement makes one think of a processional, the melodic material deriving its style from plainsong. Varied Spanish dance rhythms contribute momentum to the finale.

FRANÇAIX. Jean Françaix's Piano Concerto (1934) was introduced in Berlin on Nov. 8, 1936, with the composer as soloist (I. Allegro. II. Andante. III. Scherzo. IV. Allegro). The concerto is slender in structure and consistently light in mood. The first movement is built from four brief and sprightly subjects. The mood in the second movement becomes somewhat pensive as an expressive melody is projected by the piano. In the ensuing scherzo all three main ideas are first stated by the piano. The gaiety and abandon of the finale are derived from four vivacious tunes, brilliantly exploited by the solo instrument and orchestra.

GERSHWIN. Gershwin's only piano concerto, in F (1925), was completed a year after his celebrated *Rhapsody in Blue*. It was commissioned by the New York Symphony Society, which introduced it under Walter Damrosch's direction, with the composer as soloist, on Dec. 3, 1925. The work is a successful effort to embody jazz idioms and techniques within the classical form of the concerto (I. Allegro. II. Andante. III. *Allegro agitato*). An eight-measure Charleston motif, shared by timpani and woodwind, introduces the first movement. The main section consists of three main ideas: a racy theme first stated by a bassoon, then repeated by the orchestra; a delicate melody for the piano; and a sedate waltz for strings. The second movement has an atmosphere of mystery as muted trumpet presents a sensitive melody against nebulous harmonies in the clarinets. A jazzy theme in the piano follows, accentuated by a brisk rhythm in the strings. Then a second idea is developed, and a transition in the piano leads to a cadenza, in which a new thought is introduced. This thought soon becomes enlarged into a sensual melody for the strings. The finale is a gay, ebullient eruption of color and rhythm. Material from earlier movements is recalled, then a climax is achieved with a dramatic

restatement of the second theme of the first movement. The concerto ends after a brief coda.

GLAZUNOV. The Concerto in A minor, for violin and orchestra, op. 82 (1904), was introduced in London on Oct. 17, 1905, with Mischa Elman as soloist. The three movements are played without interruption (I. Moderato. II. *Andante sostenuto*. III. Allegro). The first principal subject of the first movement is a sentimental melody for the solo violin accompanied by clarinets and bassoons. The solo violin subsequently also introduces the romantic second theme against a string background. A broad G-string melody in the solo violin is the heart of the slow movement. Its poetic mood is temporarily broken by an *agitato* section in which the solo instrument is assigned figuration passages. After a cadenza, the spirited finale arrives, dominated by a dialogue between solo violin and trumpets.

CARL GOLDMARK. The Concerto No. 1 in A minor, for violin and orchestra, op. 28 (1878), is a pleasing melodic work that makes few demands on the listener. It was first performed in Nuremberg on Oct. 28, 1878, with Johann Lauterbach as soloist (I. *Allegro moderato*. II. Andante. III. Moderato; Allegretto). The first movement begins with an attractive little theme which, however, is not one of the main subjects. The principal subjects come somewhat later in the solo violin, the second being a sensitive song above a soft string accompaniment. In the development, the orchestra treats the opening little theme fugally. The slow movement opens with a fifteen-bar introduction in muted strings; the solo violin then emerges with a poignant melody, the main material of the movement. A middle section, *poco animato*, provides a change of mood. In the finale, the first theme appears in the solo violin after a five-bar introduction. It is elaborated upon, then the solo violin appears with a soaring melody in octaves. A third lyrical subject is stated, accompanied by violas. The concerto ends after a brief cadenza.

GOULD. The Concerto for Orchestra (1944) was commissioned by the Kulas

Fund and introducted in Cleveland on Feb. 1, 1945, Golschmann conducting. Popular idioms are used extensively in what the composer called "a show piece for the modern symphony orchestra" (I. Moderately Fast, With Drive and Vigor. II. Slowly, with Stately Lyricism. III. Fast, with Gusto). The work begins with a kind of toccata movement, filled with vigorous statements. This is followed by a lyrical movement, opening with a brief trumpet solo, and dominated by a blues section. The finale is in an abandoned mood, its main theme developed over a persistent boogie-woogie rhythm.

GRIEG. The Concerto in A minor, for piano and orchestra, op. 16 (1868), was introduced in Copenhagen on April 3, 1869, with Eduard Neupart as soloist (I. *Allegro molto moderato.* II. Adagio. III. *Allegro moderato molto e marcato*). A drum roll and a vigorous descending passage for piano introduces the first movement. The first main theme is given quietly by the woodwind. After some development, the melody is taken over by the piano. A tripping figure for piano and orchestra brings on the second theme: a tranquil dialogue for cellos and woodwind. Both main themes are worked out. After a vigorous recall of the first theme, the cadenza improvises upon it rhapsodically. The second movement is a haunting folksong melody for muted strings. An interlude arrives with an improvisational section for piano, to which the strings provide a gentle commentary. Then the opening song returns powerfully in piano and orchestra. There is no pause before the eruption of the finale. A virile introduction evokes several folk-dance melodies, two of them given by the piano. A melody is sung by the flute, repeated by the piano, and then taken over by piano and orchestra. Scale passages lead to the coda, in which the first dance theme is elaborated. The flute song now is heard in trumpet, woodwind, cellos, and violas, against piano arpeggios. It receives a last forceful statement, then the concerto ends with two strong chords.

HANDEL. Handel produced four sets of concertos for organ and orchestra. Two were published in his own time (1738,

1740), and two posthumously (1760, 1797). These works are generally in three or four movements. In a three-movement work, two fast sections flank a slow one; when there are four movements, the pattern is slow-fast-slow-fast. Some of these concertos were outgrowths of organ improvisations with which Handel entertained audiences at intermission time in performances of his oratorios. Consequently, it is not unusual to find in some of these concertos quotations from other Handel compositions. For example, Concerto No. 13 in F major, *The Cuckoo and the Nightingale,* is made up of transcriptions of other instrumental pieces by Handel: the first and last movements from the Trio Sonatas Nos. 5 and 6, and a movement from the Concerto Grosso, op. 6, no. 9. The name "Cuckoo and the Nightingale" comes from the bird calls in the second movement.

The Organ Concerto No. 10, in D minor, op. 7, no. 4, is one of the most popular of these works. This is a four-movement composition (I. Adagio. II. Allegro. III. Adagio. IV. Allegro). In the first movement we hear a solemn melody, while the second movement generates power. In the third movement, the orchestra steps aside to permit the solo organ to discourse eloquently with an improvisation. The finale is spacious in design, filled with majestic statements.

The Handel organ concertos are sometimes heard in other versions, notably for harpsichord and orchestra. The set, op. 4, was designated by the composer as for either organ or harpsichord. No. 6 of that set is marked as for harp or organ.

The Concerto in D major for organ and orchestra, frequently heard at symphony concerts, is an adaptation by Sir Hamilton Harty of a concerto found in the Handel Gesellschaft edition, vol. 47. This adaptation was first performed in London on Oct. 9, 1933, Sir Hamilton Harty conducting (I. Adagio. II. *Allegro moderato.* II. Adagio. III. *Allegro con brio*).

HAYDN. The Concerto in D major for piano or harpsichord and orchestra, op. 21 (1783), is the composer's best-known concerto for a keyboard instrument (I. Vivace. II. Larghetto. III. *Allegro assai*).

In the first movement the main themes appear in the orchestral introduction. The first is a lyrical subject for strings, and the second a melody for strings supplemented by woodwind. The solo instrument then takes up both ideas, which are amplified and repeated. The slow movement is a song first presented by the violins, then taken over in extended form by the solo instrument. The finale is a rondo in Hungarian style.

The Concerto in D major (1783) is the only cello concerto by Haydn to survive, and it is one of his masterworks. For a long time it was suspected that this work was written not by Haydn but by one of his pupils. But such doubts about the authenticity of this Haydn composition have been completely dispelled (I. *Allegro moderato*. II. *Adagio*. III. *Allegro*). Its joyous opening in the strings is followed by a graceful lyrical subject for oboes and clarinets. The solo instrument repeats and elaborates upon these melodies. The slow movement is made up of three themes, all introduced by the solo cello. The first is a stately dance subject; the second, a mobile melody treated imitatively by the bassoons; the third, also of lyric character, precedes the return of the first melody and the concluding cadenza. The finale, a rondo, is a gay episode in which the main melody, first heard in the cello, has the character of a folk dance.

HINDEMITH. The Concerto for Piano and Orchestra (1945) was commissioned by the pianist Jesús María Sanromá, who introduced it in Cleveland, Feb. 27, 1947, George Szell conducting (I. Moderately Fast. II. Slow. III. Medley on the Medieval Dance, *Tre Fontane*). The first movement amplifies three ideas. The first is presented by the clarinet at the opening; the second is more lyrical and appears in clarinets and bass clarinet; the third is stated by muted trumpet. The second movement is in three-part song form. The flanking sections are dominated by two themes, the initial one in cellos and bass clarinet in unison, and the other in piano. The middle part consists of a theme for piano, soon repeated by horn. The heart of the finale is a 14th-century dance tune discovered by the composer.

This tune appears at the opening of the movement in the piano. After being transformed into a march and a waltz, the tune returns in piano and orchestra to bring the concerto to its conclusion.

The Concerto for Viola and Small Orchestra (1935) is entitled *Der Schwanendreher* ("The Organgrinder"), because the finale quotes an old German melody, *Seid ihr nicht der Schwanendreher*. This is only one of several old German folksongs quoted. The concerto was introduced in Amsterdam on Nov. 14, 1935, with the composer as soloist, and Mengelberg conducting (I. *Langsam; Maessig bewegt mit Kraft*. II. *Sehr ruhig*. III. *Maessig schnell*). The composer added the following program note to his score: "A minstrel, joining a merry company, displays what he has brought back from foreign lands: song serious and gay, and finally a dance piece. Like a true musician he expands and embellishes the melodies, preluding and improvising according to his fancy and ability. This medieval scene was the inspiration of the composition." In the first movement the old folksong, *Zwischen Berg und tiefem Tal*, appears in the horns. In the second, two folksongs are presented: *Nun laube, Lindlein, laube*, a duet for solo viola and harp; and *Der Gutzgauch auf dem Zaune sass*, which is presented fugally. In the finale, *Seid ihr nicht der Schwanendreher* is subjected to five variations.

KABALEVSKY. The Concerto No. 2 in G minor, for piano and orchestra, op. 23 (1935), is one of the composer's most frequently performed orchestral compositions (I. *Allegro*. II. *Andante*. III. *Allegro molto*). The first movement is essentially virile, with a strong opening subject, but the second theme has a pronounced lyric character. The slow movement is in a funereal mood. The finale has the style of a toccata, its main thought being a variation of the first theme from the opening movement.

For the Concerto for Violin and Orchestra, op. 48 (1948), the composer received the Stalin Prize for the second time. It is dedicated to "Soviet youth" and is a consistently forceful composition (I. *Allegro molto e con brio*. II. *Andantino cantabile*. III. *Vivace gio-*

coso). The concerto received a double première, in Moscow and Leningrad, on Oct. 29, 1948. The first movement is traditional in form and its melodic content is lively and vigorous. A broad romantic melody initiates the slow movement, contrast being provided by a sharply rhythmic theme of capricious character. The finale is consistently gay, its light character emphasized in a cadenza in which the composer makes a hasty, witty reference to Mendelssohn.

KHATCHATURIAN. The Concerto for Piano and Orchestra (1935) is one of the most popular works in the contemporary piano-concerto repertory. It was introduced in Moscow on July 5, 1937, with the composer as soloist (I. *Allegro ma non troppo e maestoso*. II. *Andante con anima*. III. *Allegro brillante*). The percussive first movement is ushered in by a strong, primitive orchestral introduction. This is followed by the first theme in the piano, which maintains this savage mood. The second theme has an Oriental character; it is first heard in the oboe, then in an extended form in the piano. An Oriental atmosphere is also evoked in the second movement, with a languorous melody in the piano against a background of low notes in the flute. A second theme, also for flute, continues this exotic mood. The finale reverts to the savage intensity and passion of the first movement. After a few thundering piano chords, a solo trumpet presents a spirited melody; this is later developed with considerable power. After a return of the trumpet melody, the main theme of the first movement recurs in the brass. The coda reviews the main themes of both the first and third movements.

LALO. The Concerto in D minor, for cello and orchestra (1876), was first performed in Paris on Dec. 9, 1877. Adolphe Fischer was the soloist and Pasdeloup conducted (I. Prelude: Lento; *Allegro maestoso*. II. Intermezzo: *Andante con moto*. III. Andante; *Allegro vivace*). A slow eight-bar introduction in the first movement leads to an improvisation in the cello. A brief dialogue then ensues between cello and orchestra. The main section now unfolds with a presentation of both main themes in the solo instru-

ment. The slow movement leads from a twelve-bar orchestral introduction to an emotional first theme in the solo instrument. After a change of key, a virile second theme is assigned to the solo cello. The finale is a rondo, much of whose music consists of brilliant bravura passages for the soloist.

LISZT. Liszt wrote two piano concertos, of which the first, in E-flat major, op. 22 (1849), is the more popular. Liszt himself introduced it in Weimar on Feb. 17, 1855, Berlioz conducting. Early in its history this work was derisively described by Eduard Hanslick as "the triangle concerto" because the composer used the then unorthodox triangle in the scherzo (I. *Allegro maestoso*. II. *Quasi adagio; Allegretto vivace*. III. *Allegro animato; Allegro marziale animato*). A powerful subject for strings begins the first movement. This is the first main theme; the second, of greater lyric interest, is introduced by the piano, and is then taken over by the clarinet. The second movement is begun by a poetic subject in muted basses and cellos. After this material has been amplified, a new idea appears in the solo flute against a sustained trill in the piano. The clarinet provides a transition to a scherzo section which ends with the return of the solo flute melody, once again against a piano trill. The finale, as the composer explained, is "merely an urgent recapitulation of the earlier subject matter with quickened livelier rhythms and contains no new motifs." The theme with which the concerto opened is also enlisted to bring the work to its conclusion.

The Concerto No. 2 in A major (begun in 1839 and revised in 1849 and later) is romantic where the first had been dramatic. Its première took place in Weimar on Jan. 7, 1857; Hans von Bronsart was the soloist, and the composer conducted. Designated by its composer as a "symphonic concerto" to point up its symphonic character, the work is in a single movement with one dominant melody, a pensive song (*Adagio sostenuto assai*) first heard in the woodwind after which it is adorned by arpeggios from the solo piano. A cadenza leads to a more brilliant section which culminates in a stormy climax. There then appears the suggestion of a second theme in the strings, but it soon makes way for the return of the opening romantic melody, which is discoursed upon in a kind of rambling fashion, returning now in one guise, now in another.

MACDOWELL. The Concerto No. 2 in D minor, for piano and orchestra, op. 23 (1885), is one of the composer's most significant works. Its première took place in New York City on March 5, 1889, with the composer as soloist and Theodore Thomas conducting (I. *Larghetto calmato; Poco più mosso e con passione.* II. *Presto giocoso.* III. *Largo; Molto allegro*). A brief dialogue between muted strings and solo piano opens the first movement. A subject for woodwind and second violins then leads to a statement of the first main theme by the piano— a broadly romantic melody. After this idea has been discussed, the cellos present the second theme. In the ensuing development, the music alternates between lyrical exuberance and dramatic surges. The second movement is an elfin-like scherzo, puckish in mood. A first sprightly idea is stated by woodwind and strings; a second one, more vigorous, is heard in the horns. A slow introduction for cellos and bassoons, answered by piano and woodwind, serves as a preface to the finale. A monologue by the piano leads to the allegro section, in which the major subject is introduced by the woodwind. Virtuoso passages for piano, and agitated commentary by the orchestra, give this finale dash and brilliance.

FRANK MARTIN. The Concerto for Seven Winds and Orchestra (1949) has been successfully performed in most of the world's music capitals; it is one of the major works in the 20th-century repertory. Its première took place in Bern, Switzerland, on Oct. 25, 1949, Luc Balmer conducting. (I. Allegro. II. Adagietto. III. *Allegro vivace*). A single motto theme recurs throughout the work. In the first movement this episodic subject serves as an introduction to each of the seven wind instruments, which make their entrance in the following order: oboe, clarinet, horn, trumpet, trombone, bassoon, and flute. Two important sub-jects follow: the first is developed by the flute after being introduced by the clarinet; and the second is stated by the trombone. At the conclusion of this movement, the seven wind instruments return in the same order in which they first appeared. An expressive melody for violins is the core of the slow movement. The finale, in free rondo form, opens and closes with a gay scherzo-like idea; a secondary subject is played by the trumpet.

MENDELSSOHN. The Concerto No. 1 in G minor, op. 25 (1831), is the more popular of Mendelssohn's two concertos for the piano. The composer himself introduced it in Munich on Oct. 17, 1831 (I. *Molto allegro con fuoco.* II. Andante. III. *Molto allegro e vivace*). There are two main themes in the first movement. One is agitated, the other lyrical; both are first presented in the solo instrument. A fanfare for horns and trumpets and a brief cadenza make way for the slow movement, a dreamy melody introduced by violas and cellos, and then repeated with some embellishments by the piano. A second fanfare sets the stage for the virtuoso music of the finale.

Mendelssohn wrote only one violin concerto, but it is surely one of the best loved in the entire repertory. The Concerto in E minor, op. 64 (1844), was introduced in Leipzig on March 13, 1845, by Ferdinand David with Niels Gade conducting. The composer wanted the three movements to be played without pause, but it is now habitual to introduce a slight pause between the first two movements (I. *Allegro molto appassionato.* II. Andante. III. *Allegretto non troppo; Allegretto molto vivace*). The first movement opens with only a single measure for orchestra to preface the presentation of the first main theme by the violin. After that subject has been amplified, the second theme is presented by the orchestra, and then in the solo violin. There is still a third important melody, this one in clarinets and flutes over a sustained "G" in the solo violin. The development follows more or less formal procedures before the recapitulation and a brief cadenza. An eight-bar introduction for orchestra in the second movement leads into one of Mendelssohn's most beautiful melodies. Midway in the movement there appears a turbulent section for orchestra, but before long the opening radiant song reappears. A fourteen-bar transition is the bridge to the finale. The first subject is vivacious, and it is found in the violin. Two more significant ideas are presented and discussed. The first is a robust melody for full orchestra, and the second a lyrical passage for solo violin. The latter soon becomes a contrapuntal background for orchestra when the first theme is recalled by solo violin. After a vigorous presentation of the second theme, the coda arrives to end the concerto.

MOZART. Most of the twenty or so piano concertos written by Mozart are worth listening to. Half a dozen are masterworks, the most advanced concertos in structure and content up to that point.

The Concerto in F major, K. 459 (1784), is consistently light in mood, the touch graceful, the tone intimate (I. Allegro. II. Allegretto. III. *Allegro assai*). The first movement is mainly made up of the delicate subject for strings with which it opens; the subsidiary material includes a canonic passage for flute and bassoon against piano figurations, and a gentle tune shared by strings and winds before being taken over by the piano. The development of this material has a breadth not often encountered in the concerto literature of this period. The movement ends with a cadenza and a brief coda. The expressive slow movement has two contrasting subjects: the first opens the movement, the second is presented by the oboe. The mood passes nimbly to gaiety in the finale in which are found some effective contrapuntal passages and some brilliant virtuoso sections for the piano.

The Concerto in D minor, K. 466 (1785), is at times dramatic, at times turbulent, and at times melancholy. Once again we note that never before had such deeply personal utterances and such intensity of emotion found a voice in concerto literature (I. Allegro. II. Romanze. III. *Allegro assai*). The orchestral introduction to the first movement is somber; here we find an agitated first theme heard at once, followed by a darkly brooding second subject in oboes and bassoons. At first the piano expresses a soft comment of its own, but then it elaborates upon the two main subjects and soon is joined by the orchestra. The emotional upheaval does not subside in the development. A brief piano solo leads to the recapitulation. The second movement highlights a pastoral melody in the piano. After the entrance of the orchestra, the piano presents a second melody. Thus far the mood is gentle and subdued, but midway there comes an outburst of deep feeling in piano and woodwind. Tranquillity is restored with a recapitulation of the opening pastoral melody. The finale is a rondo in which the prevailing restlessness and agitation of preceding movements continue almost to the very end, when there is a sudden change of key and the emergence of a sprightly new tune in the woodwind. The brief coda helps retain this bright atmosphere.

The Concerto in C major, K. 467 (1785), combines brilliant virtuosity with poetic statements (I. Allegro maestoso. II. Andante. III. *Allegro vivace assai*). The first movement opens with a bright march-like melody, the first theme; the second theme is a melody of haunting beauty for violins. After the piano enters with broken phrases, it contributes a beautiful melody of its own. The development contains many bravura passages for the solo instrument. The slow movement is one of the composer's supreme lyrical inspirations. A thirty-six bar melody of surpassing eloquence for violins and violas, against a background of triplets in other strings, opens the movement. To Alfred Einstein this was music "like an ideal aria freed of all the limitations of the human voice." The finale, in rondo form, is based on a dashing subject for orchestra, repeated by the piano. The gaiety continues through the movement in music that sparkles like new-minted coin.

The Concerto in A major, K. 488, and the Concerto in C minor, K. 491, were both written in 1786, but they are opposites in mood and feeling. The A major Concerto is for the most part ebullient and jovial; the C minor Concerto is generally tragic. The A major Concerto (I. Allegro. II. Andante. III. Presto) has an irrepressibly good-humored first movement. The first theme, in the strings, repeated by the woodwind, has a carefree air; so does the second theme, first heard in violins before being repeated by bassoons and flute. The piano embarks on a statement of the first subject which is completed by the orchestra. Some decorative passages lead to a recall of the second theme by the piano. After this idea is repeated by the orchestra, it is given filigree decoration by the piano. The second movement temporarily abandons this light mood for deeply moving music. The first melody is presented by the piano, followed by a second, moving, lyrical passage for orchestra. The entire movement is then maintained on a high plane of eloquence. But the gaiety of the first movement returns in the finale, the opening eight-bar theme in the piano sounding an exclamation of delight that sets the mood for the music that follows.

The tragic character of the Concerto in C minor (I. Allegro. II. Larghetto. III. Allegretto) is at once established with a melancholy subject for strings punctuated by woodwind chords. The sorrow deepens with the second theme, also in the strings. When the piano makes its first entry, it is with a new idea, a tender soliloquy serving as a preface to a recall of the two earlier subjects. The piano repeats the soliloquy, after which the development section unfolds majestically; always the tragic overtones are prominent, particularly in the agitated passages for the piano. The slow movement is in the form of a rondo. It opens with an elegiac three-part song. Two sections follow, each equally poignant; after each, the three-part song is recalled. The finale is a theme and variations, with the theme presented immediately by the strings. In the variations the music passes from vigor to serenity; but with the last powerful variation we are reminded for the last time that this concerto has tragic implications.

The Concerto in D major, K. 537 (1788), is often called the "Coronation Concerto," because the composer played it in Frankfort in September 1790 during the festivities attending the coronation of Leopold II. If this music is less passionate or personal than the preceding C minor Concerto it is nonetheless music in the grand design and of high inspiration (I. Allegro. II. Larghetto. III. Allegretto). The first movement presents two light-hearted themes in the orchestral opening. The piano appears with the first of these ideas. After the orchestra recalls part of the second, there follows some brilliant virtuoso music. The piano then presents a beautiful melody. The slow movement arrives with a simple, stately melody for the piano, repeated by the orchestra. After a countersubject is heard, a new section is introduced by the piano; the opening melody is then repeated. In the finale, a rondo, the vivacious opening theme is at once stated by the piano, and repeated by the orchestra. Some subsidiary thoughts follow, after which the piano sings a soaring melody. Dramatic pages then provide contrast, but the concerto ends vivaciously.

The Concerto in B-flat major, K. 595 (1791), was Mozart's last piano concerto. As Alfred Einstein said of it, it "stands at the gate of heaven, at the door of eternity" (I. Allegro. II. Larghetto. III. Allegro). The opening movement presents a suave melody for violins following a one-bar introduction; the second theme follows in the strings. When the piano appears, it is with its own version of these two subjects. The development is spacious, and mainly concerned with the first theme, which also serves to bring on the recapitulation. The slow movement provides a majestic melody for unaccompanied piano, repeated by the orchestra. After this melody has been amplified, the piano arrives with a new subject. An orchestral passage introduces the piano with still another beautiful melodic discourse. The whole movement has a subdued emotional character. The finale, a rondo, presents an animated idea in the piano. A twenty-five bar orchestral section follows. The piano then presents the second main theme. There are two other subsidiary melodies in a movement that has wit and at times bravura brilliance.

Mozart's Concerto for Two Pianos and

Orchestra in E-flat major, K. 365 (1779-1780), is famous and popular. Otto Jahn has explained that the composer had no intention to make the two solo instruments independent of each other. "The players emulate each other in the delivery of the melodies and passages, sometimes together, sometimes in succession, often breaking off in rapid changes and interruptions; the melodies are sometimes simply stated, sometimes with variations so divided between the two instruments that neither can be said to have the advantage over the other" (I. Allegro. II. Andante. III. Allegro). In the first movement the principal theme appears at once, a vigorous subject with a downward octave leap. After that comes an important subsidiary theme in violins and violas, with horns joining in at the end of the phrase. The second movement is a tranquil melody to which the two pianos provide interesting figurations. The finale, in rondo form, is an outburst of gay feelings, though midway in the movement a more somber mood is temporarily interpolated.

Mozart wrote five violin concertos between April and December 1775, all of which can be accepted without reservations as authentic. Other violin concertos attributed to Mozart are of doubtful origin, as for example the so-called *Adelaide Concerto* (which see).

Two violin concertos are among Mozart's greatest works. The Concerto No. 4 in D major, K. 218 (1775), is in three movements (I. Allegro. II. *Andante cantabile*. III. *Andante grazioso; Allegro ma non troppo*). The first movement begins with a martial subject developed by the orchestra. The solo violin arrives with a lyrical second theme. As both ideas are worked out, the solo violin is often assigned bravura passages. A cadenza and an eight-bar orchestral tutti close the movement. The slow movement consists of two beautiful melodies. The first is stated by the orchestra and repeated by the violin. After a change of key, the second is presented by the violin to a harmonic background of the orchestra. The finale is a two-section rondo. The first section boasts an aristocratic melody for the violin. Livelier music follows.

The second section begins with an exchange between solo violin and the violins of the orchestra. After a cadenza, the first graceful subject is recalled for the last time.

The Concerto No. 5 in A major, K. 219, was also completed in 1775 (I. *Allegro aperto*. II. Adagio. III. *Tempo di minuetto*). An orchestral introduction presents the two main themes. After the solo violin sings a soulful six-bar melody, it embarks on a reflection of the first vigorous theme. The solo violin later also discourses on the second theme. A brief development and recapitulation lead to the cadenza and then the coda. The second movement again introduces the basic material in an orchestral preface. When the violin appears it repeats both themes and embellishes them. An exalted mood is sustained throughout the movement. The finale is unusual in that it is a rondo in the tempo of a minuet. Midway the minuet is abandoned to permit the presentation of a sensual pseudo-Turkish melody by the solo violin. But the minuet melody soon reappears to provide the concerto with a graceful conclusion.

Mozart wrote numerous concertos for various instruments other than piano and violin. For the most part, he assigned his more personal thoughts and deeper feelings to his piano and violin concertos. Other concertos are usually virtuoso music to set off the technical capabilities of the instrument and performer. But Mozart's gift of melody and of evoking gay and infectious moods are never absent.

These concertos wear their hearts, and lovely melodies, on their sleeves. They are all easy to listen to, and are readily assimilated and appreciated at first hearing. Among the most frequently performed of these compositions are: Concerto in C major, for flute, harp, and orchestra, K. 299 (1778); Concerto No. 1 in G major, for flute and orchestra, K. 313 (1778); Concerto No. 2 in D major, for flute and orchestra, K. 314 (1778); Concerto in B-flat major, for bassoon and orchestra, K. 191 (1774); Concerto in A major, for clarinet and orchestra, K. 622 (1791); Concerto in D major, for horn and orchestra K. 412 (1782); and

Concerto in E-flat major, for horn and orchestra, K. 447 (1783).

See also: Sinfonia concertante.

PAGANINI. Paganini wrote three violin concertos, of which only the first has remained in the repertory. The second concerto, in B minor, op. 7, is remembered only for its second movement, *Ronde à la clochette.* As *La Campanella* this movement is often played as a violin solo, or in the piano transcription by Liszt.

There is a bit of confusion about the key of the Concerto No. 1, op. 6. It is most often designated as D major, but it was written in E-flat major. The reason is that the composer often tuned his violin half a tone higher, making the music of this concerto sound as if it were in the more brilliant key of E-flat while playing it in the more comfortable key of D major (I. *Allegro maestoso.* II. Adagio. III. *Allegro spiritoso*). The first movement opens with an orchestral preface in which the main themes are given. The principal one is a soulful melody for the violins. After the solo violin appears, it indulges in virtuoso passages before addressing itself to the main lyrical subject. This movement is filled with pyrotechnical writing for the solo instrument. The beautiful song of the second movement, heard in the solo violin, follows a brief orchestral introduction. This song is said to have been inspired by the stage performance of a prison scene which moved the composer. The finale, in rondo form, is again, like the first movement, dazzling virtuoso music. This concerto is often played in adaptations by August Wilhelmj and Fritz Kreisler, in each of which only the first movement is given, and that in a truncated form and revised orchestration.

PIZZETTI. The *Concerto dell' Estate* for orchestra (1928) is a successful merger of modern harmonic and melodic techniques with the concerto grosso format. The work was introduced in New York on Feb. 28, 1929, Toscanini conducting. (I. *Mattutino.* II. *Notturno.* III. *Gagliarda e finale*). Five themes comprise the material of the first movement, three appearing early and in rapid succession. After the first three themes have been extended, a fourth subject is heard in a solo oboe, and the fifth in the full orchestra. The lyric slow movement is a poetic song for unaccompanied violins, while the vigorous accents and rhythms of the finale revive an old Italian dance.

POULENC. The Concerto for Piano and Orchestra (1949) was introduced by the Boston Symphony on Jan. 6, 1950, with the composer as soloist and Charles Munch conducting. Poulenc treats the piano not as a solo instrument but almost like one of the instruments of the orchestra (I. Allegretto. II. *Andante con moto.* III. *Rondeau à la française*). In the first movement, the first theme is a rhythmic subject presented by the piano; the second theme, of greater lyric interest, is stated by the English horn against piano arpeggios. The dominant thought of the second movement is a pensive subject for strings accompanied by a quartet of horns. In the finale, a lively little tune is presented by the piano, unaccompanied. This is followed by a quotation of an old French melody, *À la claire fontaine,* which sounds like Stephen Foster's *Swanee River.*

The Concerto in D minor, for two pianos and orchestra (1932), is filled with witty, and at times ironic, statements. The première took place in Venice on Sept. 5, 1932, with the composer and Jacques Fevrier as soloists (I. *Allegro ma non troppo.* II. Larghetto. III. Finale). Two strong chords open the first movement and lead into a virtuoso passage for the first piano. After the second piano has taken over this material, a gay, staccato four-note phrase is presented, followed by a tune in popular style for woodwind and solo horn. Midway in the movement there is heard a sentimental passage for the two pianos, followed by a development of earlier melodies. There is no recapitulation section; the coda consists mainly of a short melody in muted strings against accompanying pianos. A sentimental song initiates the second movement in the pianos. The mood changes as the tempo and intensity increase, but the gentle character of the opening melody is soon brought back. The finale is made up of a jig tune, a march melody, and several music-hall tunes, all of them combined into a movement filled with contagious fun and wit.

PROKOFIEV. Prokofiev wrote five piano concertos—the first in D-flat major, op. 10, in 1911. He achieved full maturity with Concerto No. 3 in C major, op. 26 (1921), introduced by the composer in Chicago on Dec. 16, 1921, Frederick Stock conducting (I. Andante; Allegro. II. Andantino. III. *Allegro ma non troppo*). There is a short, quiet introduction to the first movement after which an unaccompanied clarinet presents the first main theme. A change of tempo takes place, then the first subject is reviewed by the piano. A chordal passage for the piano leads to an expressive second theme in the oboe to a pizzicato accompaniment. After an extended development the movement sweeps to a climax. The first theme now recurs loudly in the orchestra, with the piano soon joining in. Brilliant treatment is then given to both main ideas and a crescendo brings the movement to a dramatic conclusion. The second movement consists of a theme heard in the orchestra, and five variations. After the fifth variation, the theme is repeated by the orchestra with piano adornments. A staccato theme for bassoons and pizzicato strings opens the finale. This theme is soon amplified by the piano, then built up into a climax. A subsidiary subject is then introduced by woodwinds and answered by the piano. Virtuoso passages for the piano ensue, and the concerto ends with a forceful coda.

Almost as popular as the Third Concerto is the Concerto No. 5 in G major, op. 55 (1932). Prokofiev actually wrote this work in 1918 but the manuscript was lost when the composer first left Russia. In 1932 he rewrote the work from preserved sketches and in this version it was introduced in Berlin on Oct. 31, 1932, with the composer as soloist (I. *Allegro con brio*. II. *Moderato ben accentuato*. III. Allegro. IV. Larghetto. V. *Vivo più mosso*). The composer provided his own analysis: "The first movement . . . though not in the sonata form . . . is the main movement of the concerto. It fulfills the function of a sonata form and is in the spirit of the usual sonata form.

. . . The second movement has a march-like rhythm. . . . The third movement is a toccata . . . a precipitate, displayful movement of much technical brilliance and requiring a great virtuosity; it is a toccata for orchestra as much as for the piano. The fourth . . . is the lyrical movement. . . . It starts off with a soft, soothing theme; grows more and more intense in the middle portion, develops breadth and tension, then returns to the music of the beginning. The finale has a decided classic flavor. The coda is based on a new theme, which is joined by the other themes of the finale. There is a reference to some of the material of the preceding movements."

Prokofiev wrote two violin concertos. The first, in D major, op. 19 (1913), was one of his earliest masterworks. It was introduced in Paris on Oct. 18, 1923, with Marcel Darrieux as soloist (I. Andantino. II. *Scherzo vivacissimo*. III. Moderato). The work is often played without interruption. A tender song for solo violin opens the concerto. After the violin engages upon some virtuoso passages, the flute recalls the opening melody with embroidery by the violin. The violin then indulges in some forceful embellishments on this subject, often supported by the orchestra. In the ensuing scherzo, the violin presents a flashing melody characterized by athletic leaps from low to high registers, by glissandi and harmonics. This movement is in the grotesque or whimsical vein for which the composer is famous. A spacious melody for the solo instrument introduces the finale, in which brilliance and virtuosity are featured. Towards the end of the movement the tender theme of the opening movement returns in the violins of the orchestra; as the solo instrument repeats this idea in trills in an upper register the concerto comes to its conclusion.

The Concerto No. 2 in G minor, op. 63 (1935), was introduced in Madrid on Dec. 1, 1935, Robert Soetens soloist. More romantic than its predecessor, this work is filled with spacious melodies and rich emotion (I. *Allegro moderato*. II. *Andante assai*. III. *Allegro ben marcato*). This emphasis on broad lyricism is immediately apparent in the expressive song for solo violin unaccompanied with which the first movement opens. Later on, the solo violin also presents the second, equally lyrical subject. In the development the main theme appears in lower strings of the orchestra after which the solo violin takes up the second theme. The opening theme is amplified in the coda. In the slow movement, the solo violin is heard in an extended song against a pizzicato background. While other episodic material is subsequently presented, this melody is the heart of the movement. The coda, in which the solo violin takes over the opening accompaniment in a pizzicato passage, ends with a brief duet for clarinet and solo double bass. The finale is a mixture of rondo and sonata components, in which strong rhythmic passages alternate with satiric comments. The opening subject is forcefully stated by the solo violin. A later important thought is introduced by the solo violin on the G string. A dramatic coda, in which the violin is accompanied only by the bass drum and lower strings, comes as a conclusion.

RACHMANINOFF. The Concerto No. 2 in C minor, op. 18 (1901), is surely one of the best-loved piano concertos in the modern repertory. It came a decade after the composer's first concerto, in F-sharp minor, op. 11—and at a crucial period in his life. He had just recovered from a nervous breakdown and a seizure of melancholia and inertia that followed. With the Second Concerto his will to live and work was revived. Certainly never before, and rarely afterward, did he pour into one of his works such a wealth of lyricism, poignant sentiment, seductive moods, and sensitive beauty. The concerto was introduced in Moscow on Oct. 27, 1901, the composer appearing as soloist (I. Moderato. II. *Adagio sostenuto.* III. *Allegro scherzando*). It opens with nine unaccompanied crescendo chords in the piano. The strings then appear with a rhapsodic subject against piano arpeggios—the first main theme. The second subject, a yearning melody gently touched by melancholy, is subsequently stated by the piano. The development comes after a loud restatement of the first theme; here we get not only

a passionate, intense working out of the two basic subjects but also a new idea of march-like character in the orchestra. As this new idea gathers strength it is finally projected powerfully by the piano. A return of the first main theme brings on the recapitulation, which in turn leads to the coda. The second movement is a nocturne-like song in the composer's most sensitive lyric style. It first appears in the flute, then in the clarinet, and finally in the piano. Contrasting material is offered in the middle section. After a brief cadenza the opening song is brought back. A short orchestral introduction precedes the main section of the finale, a strong, arresting theme for the piano. This is soon followed by a haunting melody for oboe and violas, supported by clarinet and horns. This theme is given considerable attention before the movement reaches a climax with a fugato section. A short cadenza then leads to a final repeat of this melody in the full orchestra against piano chords.

The Concerto No. 3 in D minor, op. 30 (1909), was written for the composer's first tour of the United States. He introduced it in New York on Nov. 28, 1909, with Walter Damrosch conducting the New York Symphony (I. *Allegro ma non tanto.* II. Adagio. III. *Alla breve*). After two introductory measures the piano accompanied by strings and bassoon appears with a theme of Slavic character. This theme is repeated by horn and violas, after which the second subject is softly stated by strings and answered by the piano. This material is worked out passionately, often with rhapsodic breadth, as the piano achieves virtuoso brilliance. The development ends with a piano cadenza against reminders of the first theme in flute, oboe, clarinet, and horn (one of the rare instances in which a cadenza is accompanied). After the piano repeats the first, Slavic melody, the recapitulation restores all earlier material. The slow movement is an intermezzo with two main melodies, the first in woodwinds repeated by strings, the second in the clarinet and bassoon against a waltz rhythm in the strings. The finale opens with a vigorous subject in triplets in the piano. Energetic chords lead to another basic idea, divided between piano and strings. Important material from the first movement is recalled before a *pianissimo* phrase in the piano leads to a forceful restatement of the two main themes of the finale.

The Concerto No. 4 in G minor, op. 40 (1926), was introduced by the composer in Philadelphia on March 18, 1927, Leopold Stokowski conducting (I. *Allegro vivace*. II. Largo. III. *Allegro vivace*). There is a six-bar orchestral introduction before the piano states the first eloquent theme. After the presentation of some subsidiary material, the piano enters with the second theme. The development is rhapsodic, with considerable emphasis on bravura passages for the solo instrument. The slow movement has for its main melody a melancholy Russian song in the strings, repeated by the piano. An agitated section comes midway in the movement, followed by a new idea in the piano accompanied by clarinets. Then the beautiful Russian song comes back to end the movement. The finale follows without pause. Two new robust themes and some material from earlier movements provide the principal ideas.

RAVEL. Ravel's two piano concertos (one of them for left hand alone) are his last major works. The Concerto in G major (1931) was conceived as a "concerto in the strict sense, written in the spirit of Mozart and Saint-Saëns," as the composer explained. Marguerite Long introduced it in Paris on Jan. 14, 1932, the composer conducting (I. *Allegramente; Andante a piacere*. II. *Adagio assai*. III. Presto). The work is in a consistently light vein with an occasional spicing of jazz condiments. The first movement opens in a happy frame of mind with a saucy tune for piccolo. The movement progresses vivaciously to a slow section in which a main theme is presented by the piano against scales and runs in the woodwind. The slow movement is a sustained song in the style and spirit of a Bach arioso. This is first stated by the piano; when the orchestra takes over, the piano provides the embellishments. The finale is enlivened with the spirit of jazz. The principal subject is a blues song for orchestra against a syncopated rhythm in the piano.

The Concerto for Left Hand (1931) was written for the one-armed Viennese pianist, Paul Wittgenstein, who introduced it in Vienna on Nov. 27, 1931. Though in a single movement, the work has three sections: I. Lento; II. Allegro; III. Lento. It makes extensive use of jazz idioms. An introductory section presents two main themes, one in the contrabassoon, the other in the horns. These are built up powerfully. The piano then enters with strong chords after which it engages in an improvisation climaxed by a cadenza. There then appears a jazz section built up from melodic material from the first section. The more restful mood of the introduction is then recalled, but the concerto ends with an outburst of energy.

ANTON RUBINSTEIN. The Concerto No. 3 in G major for piano and orchestra, op. 45, is one of the composer's most popular works in the larger forms (I. *Moderato assai*. II. Moderato. III. *Allegro non troppo*). The first movement opens with a melody for the violins. The piano arrives in the fifth measure with a cadenza. After the orchestra repeats the first subject, the piano introduces a new theme with orchestral accompaniment. Another principal melody is soon heard in the clarinet, and then taken over by the piano; a phrase from this theme is enlarged into an expansive lyric passage which receives considerable prominence in the development section. The second movement begins with a phrase for muted strings and woodwind. The piano appears with a subject to which the strings provide answer. After a change of tempo and key, the piano arrives with a new expressive melody. Later on the orchestra recalls the first theme to background comments by the piano, and the movement ends with a final recall of the expressive melody. In the finale two new ideas are combined with themes recalled from earlier movements.

SAINT-SAËNS. Saint-Saëns wrote five piano concertos. The most popular is the second, in G minor, op. 22 (1868). It was introduced in Paris on May 6, 1868, with the composer as soloist and Anton

Rubinstein conducting (I. *Andante sostenuto*. II. *Allegretto scherzando*. III. *Presto*). The first movement opens unorthodoxly with an extended cadenza for the piano. A forceful subject then is introduced by the orchestra and answered by a lyrical passage in the piano. Virtuoso passages for the piano lead to a recall of the lyric passage, this time by the orchestra. A piano cadenza brings on a restatement of the first forceful idea by the orchestra. There is no slow movement, the second having the character of a scherzo. A rhythmic dance-like melody is presented by the piano, which is soon joined by the orchestra. A second theme, in the orchestra, appears against piano arpeggio figures. The finale has an impetuous drive, and generates a feeling of excitement. The first theme sounds like an Italian folk dance, and the second is also virile and rhythmic. After the first theme is repeated, both ideas are developed. Finally a chorale-like episode, in the woodwind, appears against piano trills.

Among Saint-Saëns' violin concertos, the third, in B minor, op. 61 (1880), is the one most often performed. It was written for Pablo de Sarasate, who introduced it in Paris on Jan. 2, 1881 (I. *Allegro non troppo*. II. *Andantino quasi allegretto*. III. *Molto moderato e maestoso; Allegro non troppo*). The traditional three-movement form is here used with considerable flexibility. The first theme of the first movement appears without preliminaries, in the solo violin accompanied by strings and timpani. Passage work leads to the second theme in the solo violin. In the development section the first theme gets prominent treatment, while the second is discussed in the brief recapitulation. Once again it is the first theme that receives attention in the extended coda. The second movement has the character of a barcarolle. After a three-bar introduction, the principal melody appears in the solo violin to woodwind accompaniment. The solo violin also contributes the second main theme. The finale opens with an introduction, after which the solo violin introduces both main themes, the second a passionate subject against chords in the winds. After

a dramatic development of the first theme, muted strings state a chorale-like melody, soon repeated by the solo violin. In the concluding coda the chorale-melody gets extended treatment.

Saint-Saëns wrote two cello concertos. The Concerto No. 1 in A minor, op. 33 (1873), is the more popular. It was introduced in Paris on Jan. 19, 1873, with Auguste Tolbecque as soloist. The work is played without interruption. It opens (*Allegro non troppo*) with the main theme in the solo cello against a sixteenth-note accompaniment by second violins and violas. After this idea is taken over by other instruments, the solo cello returns with the second theme, a tranquil melody. A turbulent section follows, highlighted by virtuoso passages for the cello. After a recall of the two main ideas, an *Allegretto con moto* section appears. Here muted strings present a minuet-like dance theme against a countermelody in the solo cello. After a cello cadenza, old material is brought back, and some new episodes are introduced. A forceful statement by the violins of the first principal theme leads to a quickening of tempo and an expansion of sonority (*Come prima, un peu moins vite*). An altogether new thought is suddenly introduced by the solo instrument to conclude the concerto.

SCHUBERT. For the Concerto in A minor, for cello and orchestra, *see*: Sonata—*Schubert*.

SCHUMANN. Though the Concerto in A minor, for piano and orchestra, op. 54, was completed in 1845, it originated four years earlier as a *Fantasie* for piano and orchestra. In extending this earlier work into a concerto, the composer used the original material as a first movement of fantasia character, appending to it two additional movements. In this final version, the concerto was introduced in Dresden on Dec. 4, 1845. Clara Schumann was the soloist and Ferdinand Hiller conducted (I. *Allegro affettuoso*. II. *Andante grazioso*. III. *Allegro vivace*). A loud chord and a three-bar descending passage for piano opens the first movement. The winds then present the principal theme. It is repeated by the piano and developed and varied by both piano and orchestra. This fantasia-like movement is crowded with other lyric ideas, and dramatized by contrasts of tempo, tonality, and rhythm. An extended piano cadenza leads to a coda in which the main theme is utilized. The second movement, an intermezzo, shares a staccato melody between piano and strings; the core of this movement is a soaring song for the cellos accompanied by piano arpeggios. Just before the end of the movement, the main theme of the first movement is hurriedly recalled. The finale now enters without pause, and with a forceful statement by the piano. The first principal subject follows, a syncopated theme for strings. The opening forceful theme now becomes the subject of a fugato passage which, in turn, leads to a fantasia section introducing some new lyric thoughts. The concerto ends with a return of the finale's first two principal ideas.

The Concerto in A minor, for cello and orchestra, op. 129 (1850), was first performed in Leipzig on June 9, 1860, with Ludwig Ebert as soloist, four years after the composer's death. That concert commemorated the 50th anniversary of Schumann's birth. The three movements are played without interruption (I. *Nicht zu schnell.* II. *Langsam.* III. *Sehr lebhaft*). Four introductory measures in woodwinds and pizzicato strings bring on the first main theme, a lyrical subject for solo cello. The second theme is heard in the orchestra before it receives elaboration by solo cello. Both themes are developed and lead into a coda. The solo instrument then provides a transition to the second movement, whose main thought is a graceful romanza for solo cello. A six-measure passage for cello introduces the lively finale, in which a virile first theme is presented by the solo cello after a crescendo in the orchestra. Following some passage work in the solo instrument, the cello brings on the second theme. All this material is then developed, after which the orchestra recalls the first theme. The concerto ends with a cadenza for the cello.

SHOSTAKOVICH. Shostakovich has written two piano concertos. The Concerto in C minor, op. 35 (1933), while of early vintage, is one of the composer's most popular works. It was introduced in Leningrad on Oct. 15, 1933, with the composer as soloist (I. *Allegro moderato.* II. Lento. III. Moderato. IV. *Allegro con brio*). The work is scored for strings and solo trumpet. The latter opens the first movement with a jaunty tune soon taken over by the strings, then by strings and piano. The violin provides a transition to the second main theme, which is presented by the piano. In the working out of this material, contrapuntal writing is exploited; a feeling of mockery and burlesque prevails throughout. The return of the first theme in the violins introduces the recapitulation section. In the second movement, the first melody is found in the violins against a ground bass. This is answered by a subsidiary subject in the unaccompanied piano. The tempo quickens, and the sonority increases, to achieve a climax. The trumpet now recalls the first theme, and the movement is brought to completion by the piano. The third movement is a twenty-nine bar intermezzo in which two piano cadenzas (one accompanied) are prominent. The finale begins with a brief theme for piano, after which the violins present the first principal subject. In the ensuing development the feeling of satire and burlesque are strongly accented, the trumpet serving as a kind of clown in these gay proceedings. An extended cadenza for the piano leads to a concluding coda in which the mocking voice of the trumpet predominates.

Shostakovich dedicated his Concerto in A minor for violin and orchestra, op. 99 (1955), to David Oistrakh. Oistrakh gave the première performance in Leningrad on Oct. 29, 1955 (I. Nocturne. II. Scherzo. III. Passacaglia. IV. Burlesca). In the first movement (Moderato) the main thought appears in the violin; it is a spacious song in shifting meters against a bassoon background. The scherzo (Allegro) passes from an airy theme for flute and bass clarinet, with interpolations by the solo instrument, to a more dramatic section. The passacaglia of the third movement (Andante) is built upon an ostinato figure in cellos and basses; the cadenza gives considerable attention to this figure. In the finale, a burlesque mood is invoked with a gay dance tune in the orchestra.

SIBELIUS. Sibelius wrote only one concerto. That one, for the violin, is a rhapsodic work, rich in lyricism and romantic ardor. The Concerto in D minor, op. 47 (1903), was introduced in Berlin on Oct. 19, 1905, with Carl Halir as soloist (I. *Allegro moderato.* II. *Adagio di molto.* III. *Allegro ma non tanto*). A plaintive melody for solo violin, accompanied by muted strings, opens the first movement. After this melody has been developed, the orchestra provides a transition to the second theme, an expansive lyrical thought for the violin. The second movement is deeply poetic. Five measures in the woodwinds lead to a haunting song for the solo instrument. After the orchestra has offered contrasting material, the violin reappears with the first melody. The finale, in rondo form, begins with four strongly rhythmic measures in timpani and basses. The solo violin then contributes an equally forceful idea, the main theme. The second theme, which resembles a Finnish folksong, is given by violins and cello. The movement then proceeds vigorously with some dynamic passage work for the violin and two robust orchestral tutti. The coda consists of octave passages in the violin against a background of the first theme.

SPOHR. Of Spohr's nineteen violin concertos, the Concerto No. 9 in D minor, op. 55 (1820), is the one most likely to receive performance today. (I. Allegro. II. Adagio. III. Rondo). Spohr himself introduced it in Quedlinburg on Oct. 14, 1820. The work is consistently melodious. In the first movement the solo violin presents the two main themes after an orchestral introduction; one subject is of chromatic construction, while the second is a flowing melody. The slow movement is in a serene mood with two expressive and mobile melodies prominent. The finale exploits brilliant virtuoso writing for the violin.

Also sometimes heard is the Concerto No. 8 in A minor, op. 47 (1816). This is somewhat of a curiosity. Subtitled "Vocal Scene" (*Gesangsscene*), it is an attempt on the part of the composer to adapt the violin concerto-form into an operatic scene in which the violin takes the place of the human voice. This operatic style is most in evidence in the slow movement, a three-part song form. To give the work greater integration, Spohr had the three movements played as one (I. *Allegro molto.* II. Adagio. III. *Allegro molto*), thus foreshadowing the one-movement concerto of a later period.

STRAVINSKY. Stravinsky has written a piano concerto (1924) scored for winds, double basses, and timpani; it was introduced in Paris on May 22, 1924, with the composer as soloist and Koussevitzky conducting. He has also written a violin concerto in D major (1931), first performed in Berlin on Oct. 23, 1931, with Samuel Dushkin as soloist and the composer conducting. But his most successful efforts within the concerto form have been two works for orchestra alone in which he revived the old concerto grosso form. The first is the Concerto in E-flat major (1938), named the *Dumbarton Oaks* because it was dedicated to the owner of the Dumbarton Oaks estate in Washington, D.C. The work was introduced there under the direction of Nadia Boulanger on May 8, 1938 (I. *Tempo giusto.* II. Allegretto. III. *Con moto*). The second concerto for orchestra, in D major (1946), is called the *Basel Concerto* because it was commissioned by the Basel Chamber Orchestra, which introduced it under Paul Sacher's direction on Jan. 21, 1947 (I. Vivace. II. Arioso. III. Rondo). Both works are in the composer's neo-Classic style with strict adherence to the form and structure of the concerto grosso and its partiality to contrapuntal (often fugal) writing. In the *Dumbarton Oaks* the three movements are played without interruption. Fugal writing brings the first and third movements to a climactic point, while the second movement has a serene, classic beauty. The slow movement of the *Basel Concerto* is also of classic design; a sustained melody is presented in first violins and cellos. The outer movements have rhythmic drive and astringent thematic ideas. The *Basel Concerto* music was used for the ballet *The Cage,* choreography by Jerome Robbins, introduced in New York by the New York City Ballet on June 10, 1951.

SZYMANOWSKI. Szymanowski wrote two excellent violin concertos. The first, op. 35 (1918), was introduced in Warsaw in 1922 with Emil Mlynarski as soloist and Gregor Fitelberg conducting. While in three sections (I. Vivace. II. Andantino. III. Vivace), this work is in a single movement. In the first section the two principal themes, both highly lyrical, are presented respectively by the solo violin and the violins of the orchestra. In the second section an accompanied cadenza for the viola separates two significant musical thoughts. The two main ideas of the concluding section are first presented separately, then combined contrapuntally. The first melody of the second section is quietly recalled by the solo violin to end the concerto.

The Concerto No. 2, op. 61 (1933), was written for the violinist Paul Kochanski, who introduced it in Warsaw on Oct. 6, 1933. It is in a single movement. After a brief orchestral introduction, in which various members of the orchestra take turns in presenting the main theme, the solo violin appears with the second theme, which soon is repeated by the orchestra. The emotions become intensified. A cadenza leads into a new section which opens with forceful rhythms and continues with a soaring lyrical passage. All earlier material is now developed, and then achieves a forceful climax.

See: Sinfonia concertante.

TCHAIKOVSKY. Only the first of Tchaikovsky's three piano concertos is now played, but that work is one of the most popular in the entire repertory. The Concerto No. 1 in B-flat minor, op. 23 (1875), received its world première in the United States, on Oct. 25, 1875. Hans von Buelow was the soloist with the Boston Symphony Orchestra. (I. Allegro non troppo e molto maestoso; Allegro con spirito. II. Andante semplice. III. Allegro con fuoco.) In view of the universal appeal of this work it is interesting to note that when the composer first played it at a private audition for his friend and admirer Nicholas Rubinstein the latter condemned it violently and refused to have anything to do with it.

The first movement begins with a long introduction whose sweeping first theme in the strings against powerful piano chords is one of the composer's most famous melodies. Curiously enough, this impressive subject is never again used in the movement. The main section has two themes: a vitally rhythmic folk tune for piano (which, it is said, the composer heard a blind beggar sing in the Ukraine); and a lyrical subject first stated by horns and woodwinds, and then assumed by the piano. The second movement begins with a tender song for the flute. After a second melody in oboe and clarinet, a sweeping waltz, said to have been adapted from a French song, is presented by violins and cellos. Unbridled energy is released in the finale with a rhythmic folk dance in the piano. A contrast comes from a haunting folk-like song in the violins accompanied by the horns. In the coda, the composer returns to his first vigorous dance tune.

The Concerto in D major, for violin and orchestra, op. 35 (1878), is the composer's only violin concerto (I. Allegro moderato. II. Andante. III. Allegro vivacissimo). Like the composer's first piano concerto, it suffered unhappy early experiences before winning world acceptance. First Tchaikovsky's patroness, Mme. von Meck, expressed her disapproval of the work. Then the violinist and teacher, Leopold Auer, to whom the work was dedicated, refused to perform it because he objected to some of its technical features. Finally when the concerto was introduced in Vienna on Dec. 14, 1881, with Adolf Brodsky as soloist and Hans Richter conducting, Vienna's leading music critic, Eduard Hanslick, was annihilating in his criticism. Yet the composer had complete faith in this work, and his faith has been fully justified.

There is an extended introduction for the solo instrument in the first movement. When the orchestra enters it presents the hint of a first theme, which is finally unfolded by the solo violin. A sentimental melody for the solo violin is the second main subject. The second movement consists of an eloquent song first stated by muted violins. After the solo violin appears with a second haunting theme, the first is brought back for elaboration. The finale appears without pause. It opens with a sharply accented sixteen-bar introduction. The violin enters with a short cadenza before playing the first main theme, which has the vitality of a Russian peasant dance; a second theme, also heard in the violin, has greater melodic than rhythmic interest.

VIEUXTEMPS. Vieuxtemps wrote seven violin concertos. The most popular is the fourth, in D minor, op. 31 (1850), introduced in Paris in 1851 with the composer as soloist. The work is in four movements (I. Andante; Moderato. II. *Adagio religioso*. III. Vivace. IV. Andante; Allegro). A short, somewhat dramatic orchestral preface precedes the entrance of the solo violin on a sustained high note. It then embarks on a recitative. Following some virtuoso passages it presents a soaring melody against an orchestral countersubject. A brilliant cadenza and presentation of the early dramatic material by the orchestra concludes this movement. A sustained note in the horn leads to the slow movement, in which a solemn mood is projected by two horns and two bassoons, the horns sustaining the melody. After the appearance of the violin, it embarks upon a spiritual song. Later in the movement the violin takes over the opening solemn theme in an upper register to endow it with radiance, while the orchestra supplies an eloquent contrapuntal background. The scherzo movement makes use of a waltz-melody in its first section, and a kind of hunting motif in the trio. The finale has martial character. Material from the concerto's opening movement is recalled by the orchestra in a slow introduction. Later on in the movement, other earlier material is also reviewed.

VIOTTI. Only one of Viotti's twenty-nine violin concertos is still performed. It is No. 22, in A minor (I. Moderato. II. Adagio. III. *Agitato assai*). Though written towards the end of the 18th century, this concerto has so rich an orchestration and is so advanced in its use of the sonata form that it is sometimes called one of the earliest of the "modern" violin concertos. It also has

throughout an ingratiating lyricism. The first movement opens with a short orchestral introduction terminating with the appearance of the solo violin in a serene melody. After a brief transition, the violin presents the second theme, a soaring melody. A ten-measure introduction in the second movement precedes a beautiful song for the violin. The finale, in rondo form, opens with the violin presenting the main theme. An orchestral section then leads to a second theme, also in the violin.

VIVALDI. While Vivaldi's set of concertos, op. 8, *Il Cimento dell' armonia e dell' inventione,* are actually violin concertos, they retain so many of the characteristics of the concerto-grosso form that they are discussed under that category. *See:* Concerto grosso—*Vivaldi.*

WALTON. Sir William Walton's Concerto for Violin and Orchestra (1939) was introduced by the Cleveland Orchestra under Artur Rodzinski on Dec. 7, 1939. The soloist was Jascha Heifetz, for whom this work was written (I. *Andante tranquillo*. II. *Presto capriccioso à la napolitana*. III. Vivace). The concerto opens with a sustained slow section after which the solo instrument presents a spacious melody. Though dramatic episodes are later injected, the poetic and tranquil mood of the opening section remains dominant in the movement. The lively second movement consists of a vigorous folk dance, a Neapolitan melody, and a waltz. In the finale, a subject in the lower strings is not only the first theme of the movement but also the material from which subsequent themes are developed.

The Concerto for Cello and Orchestra (1956) was written for Gregor Piatigorsky, who introduced it with the Boston Symphony, Charles Munch conducting, on Jan. 25, 1957 (I. Moderato. II. *Allegro appassionato*. III. Lento; *Allegro molto;* Lento). The first movement is highly lyrical, dominated by a broad, flowing song in the solo cello over divided strings and harp chords. The second movement, on the other hand, has rhythmic vitality, the solo cello presenting a kind of perpetual-motion theme which sets the entire movement into rapid motion. The concerto has no slow movement. But the finale opens with an extended Lento section in which a beautiful melody for the solo cello is prominent. This is followed by an *Allegro molto* section made up of a theme and four improvisations. An epilogue based on ideas from the first and third movements brings the work to a slow and stately conclusion.

WIENIAWSKI. The Concerto No. 2 in D minor, op. 22, is the more popular of Wieniawski's two violin concertos (I. *Allegro moderato.* II. *Andante non troppo.* III. *Allegro moderato con fuoco;* Allegro). The first-movement orchestral introduction presents the main theme in the strings and a suggestion of a subsidiary theme in the horn. The solo instrument then plays the first theme, and embarks on the second accompanied by the cellos. The movement has no cadenza. The second movement, connected to the first by a twelve-bar clarinet solo, is a Romance—one of the most beautiful pages of lyricism in Romantic violin literature. The gypsy-like main melody of the finale is stated by the solo violin after being hinted at in a solo cadenza. A second principal melody also has a strong Hungarian character and is introduced by the solo violin in double stops.

Concerto Grosso. Forerunner of the concerto for one or more instruments and orchestra. The concerto grosso is a compisition for two or more instruments and orchestra, in several movements, popular at the end of the 17th century and in the first half of the 18th. Arcangelo Corelli established the general structure and style. Two or more instruments, called the "concertino," are either combined with or set against the rest of the orchestra, which is designated the "ripieno." This form continued to interest composers through Vivaldi, Bach, and Handel. With the evolution of the solo concerto, the concerto grosso passed out of general use. But it has occasionally been revived through the years. Beethoven's Concerto for Violin, Cello, Piano, and Orchestra is a carryover of the old concerto-grosso idea into the 19th century; so is Brahms' Concerto for Violin, Cello, and Orchestra. Heinrich Kaminski, a 20th-century composer, attempted to revive the concerto grosso by writing several major works in that style between 1922 and 1936. Other 20th-century composers also resuscitated the form successfully, among these being Béla Bartók, Ernest Bloch, Jacques Ibert, Bohuslav Martinu, Ildebrando Pizzetti, and Igor Stravinsky.

Some basic works in the concerto grosso repertory are discussed below.

JOHANN SEBASTIAN BACH. The six concerti grossi of Bach are known as the Brandenburg Concertos because they were commissioned by the Margrave of Brandenburg in or about 1720. Each calls for a different set of solo instruments, the third one being an exception in that in place of solo instruments there is a partition of the orchestra into three parts. Bach's Brandenburg Concertos are in three movements, two vigorous ones flanking a lyrical one. Deviations from this pattern can be found in the first and third concertos. The first has an extended minuet movement as finale, and the third is made up merely of two fast movements separated by two slow chords. It is believed that Bach intended these chords to be the basis of an improvisation by the harpsichord player. Some conductors have made it a practice to play here a slow movement from some other Bach composition.

These are the six Brandenburg Concertos: No. 1, in F major, for violin, three oboes, bassoon, two horns, strings, and harpsichord (I. Allegro. II. Adagio. III. Allegro. IV. Menuetto); No. 2, in F major, for trumpet, oboe, flute, violin, strings, and harpsichord (I. Allegro. II. Andante. III. *Allegro assai*); No. 3, in G major, for three violins, three violas, three cellos, double bass, and harpsichord (I. Allegro. II. Allegro); No. 4, in G major, for violin, two flutes, strings, and harpsichord (I. Allegro. II. Andante. III. Presto); No. 5, in D major for solo harpsichord, flute, violin, and strings (I. Allegro. II. *Affettuoso.* III. Allegro); No. 6, in B-flat major, for strings without violins, and harpsichord (I. Allegro. II. *Adagio ma non tanto.* III. Allegro).

The second and fifth concertos are of special interest. The second has unusual tone colorations through the use of a quartet of high pitched instruments, including a trumpet. Some of the most effective passages in the first and last movements come from the arabesques woven around the main themes by the solo trumpet. The second movement is a spiritual melody, in flute, oboe, and violins accompanied by cellos and harpsichord. The fifth concerto is notable for the prominence it gives to the solo harpsichord, particularly in the spacious, rhapsodic cadenza in the first movement.

There are some individual points of interest in the other concertos. In the first, the minuet finale is a series of sections comprising a minuet for full orchestra, a trio for oboes and bassoon, a return of the minuet in the full orchestra, a polacca for strings, a repetition of the minuet, a second trio, for horns and oboes, and a final repetition of the minuet.

The structure of the third concerto deserves attention. Three string choirs are used, each divided into three (three violins, three violas, three cellos). Sometimes the three instruments within their respective choirs are used in unison, and sometimes they are split up as separate voices. The breaking-up and amalgamation of these choirs, and their components, provide remarkable variety.

In the fourth concerto the emphasis is on lyricism, especially in the noble slow movement; Bach transcribed this concerto grosso as a Clavier Concerto in F major.

It is the scoring that is somewhat unusual in the sixth concerto, and which endows it with its at times somber coloration. This work is for strings and harpsichord but the violins are omitted and an old instrument, the viola da gamba (forerunner of the cello), added. The gambas, however, are dispensed with in the slow movement.

BARTÓK. *See:* Concerto for Orchestra under Concerto—*Bartók*.

BEETHOVEN. *See:* Concerto for Violin, Cello, Piano, and Orchestra under Concerto—*Beethoven*.

BLOCH. In the Concerto Grosso No. 1 (1925) Bloch tried to prove to his pupils that it is possible for a composer to write so-called "modern music" within a classical form. This work was introduced in Cleveland on June 1, 1925, the composer conducting (I. Prelude: *Allegro energico e pesante.* II. Dirge: *Andante moderato.* III. Pastoral: *Assai lento;* Allegro. IV. Fugue: Allegro). The first movement is built almost entirely from a single strong and sharply accented subject, with which the work opens. The slow movement is a melancholy song for string choir, developed with powerful emotional impact. The third movement is in a lighter style, with the sprightly rhythms of a rustic dance prominent. The concerto concludes with a fugue in a modern style.

Bloch's Concerto Grosso No. 2 (1952) was introduced in London by the BBC Symphony under Sir Malcolm Sargent on April 11, 1953 (I. Maestoso; Allegro. II. Andante. III. Allegro. IV. *Tema con variazioni*). Bloch has offered the following analysis: "The first two movements are connected. In the third the solo quartet separates only briefly from the main body of the strings, but otherwise the classical alternation of the two groups is maintained, following the style of the concertino and ripieno. The finale is a theme with four variations, the theme being a simple descending chromatic scale, resulting in a sort of free passacaglia."

BRAHMS. *See:* Concerto for Violin, Cello and Orchestra in Concerto— *Brahms*.

CORELLI. It was with the twelve concerti grossi, op. 6 (1714) that the concerto grosso form and style were crystallized. The composer filled these compositions with such a wealth of melodic ideas, such effective contrasts of color and movement, and such technical skill in combining and contrasting the solo instruments with the orchestra, that his concerti grossi became the models for his contemporaries and successors.

The work most often heard is the Concerto Grosso No. 8 in G minor, called the "Christmas Concerto" ("Fatto per la Notte di Natività"). This work is made up of six short contrasting movements (I. Vivace; Grave. II. Allegro. III. Adagio; Allegro. IV. Vivace. V. Allegro. VI. Pastorale: Largo). It is the concluding movement that brought this work its specific title. This is a "Pastorale" in a religious mood, a musical reflection of the scene at Christ's cradle in Bethlehem. This "Pastorale" was the prototype of similar religious orchestral pieces found in such choral masterworks as Handel's *Messiah* and Bach's *Christmas Oratorio*.

ELGAR. *See:* Introduction and Allegro.

HANDEL. The twelve concerti grossi gathered in op. 6 (1739) appeared about twenty years after Bach's Brandenburg Concertos, and are among the greatest works in this form. They are not Handel's only concerti grossi. He produced a set of six works in op. 3, in or about 1734, and in 1736 a Concerto Grosso in C major for oboe and strings. Handel's contact with Corelli and his music, during a visit to Italy in the early 18th century, first inspired him to write his concerti grossi. While Handel's works are modeled after Corelli, they contain an abundant lyricism, an ambitious structure, and a subtlety of construction that place them on a higher esthetic level than those of Corelli. Handel's twelve concerti grossi in op. 6 are in the following keys: No. 1, G major; No. 2, F major; No. 3, E minor; No. 4, A minor; No. 5, D major; No. 6, G minor; No. 7, B-flat major; No. 8, C minor; No. 9, F major; No. 10, D minor; No. 11, A major; and No. 12, B minor.

The fifth and sixth concertos are often performed. The fifth is in six short movements (I. Larghetto. II. Allegro. III. Presto. IV. Largo. V. Allegro. VI. *Un poco larghetto*). The first movement is slow and stately, and is succeeded by a brisk fugal section. The third movement is almost capricious in tone, and provides a sharp contrast to the eloquent, almost sombre, Largo that follows. The fifth movement has rhythmic vitality and the sixth is a graceful minuet.

The sixth concerto is in five movements (I. *Larghetto e affettuoso*. II. *A tempo giusto*. III. Larghetto. IV. Allegro. V. Allegro). The first movement is slow and majestic. This is followed by a four-part fugue on a chromatic subject. The third movement is a musette, one of Handel's loveliest melodies set against a drone

bass. The concerto ends with two vigorous allegro movements.

IBERT. *See: Concertino da Camera* under Concertino—*Ibert*.

MARTINU. The Concerto Grosso (1937) was first performed by the Boston Symphony under Koussevitzky on Nov. 14, 1941, and is scored for two pianos and chamber orchestra (I. *Allegro non troppo*. II. Lento. III. Allegretto). The first movement is constructed out of a germ-theme of half a measure which, in the composer's words, "binds the different developments of the other motives and which appears in the most diversified form up to the end." The second movement is an expressive melody for cellos and other strings. The third movement is a lively excursion with the two pianos setting forth the main themes, which are repeated by the orchestra to ornamental figures in the pianos.

PIZZETTI. *See: Concerto dell' Estate* under Concerto—*Pizzetti*.

STRAVINSKY. *See: Dumbarton Oaks Concerto* and *Basel Concerto* under Concerto—*Stravinsky*.

VIVALDI. Vivaldi wrote hundreds of concertos and concerti grossi. Among the latter are two sets of exceptional interest. One, op. 3, is entitled *Estro armonico* (*Harmonic Inspiration*), and was published about 1716. The second, op. 8 (date of publication unknown), bears the title *Il Cimento dell' armonia e dell' inventione* (*The Trial of Harmony and Invention*). The most celebrated work in the op. 3 set is the Concerto No. 11, in D minor. There are three movements: I. Maestoso. II. Largo. III. Allegro. The first is vigorous, its powerful opening figure built up with telling force. The second movement is contemplative, set against an even rhythm. The finale is in the style of the first movement. A vigorous phrase set against strong chords is worked up dramatically and with striking contrasts. This concerto is sometimes presented today in modern transcriptions, the most popular being those by Alexander Siloti and Stokowski.

While the op. 8 set are essentially violin concertos, they retain so many of the characteristics of the concerto grosso that it is advisable to discuss them here.

In op. 8 will be found four famous concertos collectively entitled *The Four Seasons* (*Le quattro stagioni*). Each work is devoted to a season of the year; each has an unidentified sonnet at its head to provide a clue to its programmatic content. This quartet of compositions is one of the earliest successful efforts at literal program music, each of the four works resembling a tone poem. *Spring* (*La Primavera*), in E major, begins ebulliently in the full orchestra, and soon launches into several descriptive passages: trills in three solo violins simulate the song of birds; running figures of sixteenths in violins suggest the murmur of playing fountains. The concluding part is a pastoral dance. *Summer* (*L'Estate*), in B-flat, recreates the voices of the cuckoo, turtle dove, and goldfinch. *Autumn* (*L'Autunno*), in F major, begins with a picture of merrymaking farmers at harvest time. A slow section provides a complete change of pace with a description of their peaceful slumber. *Winter* (*L'Inverno*), in F minor, is even more realistic. Staccato passages imitate the chattering of teeth in the cold, while running figures in strings remind us of the shiver brought on by the chilling snows. The gentle slow section tells of the peace of sitting by the fireside while the vigorous finale recalls that the winter can also bring joy. *The Four Seasons* has been transcribed for modern orchestra by Bernardino Molinari.

Concert Spirituel. An organization for public musical performances founded in 1725 during the reign of Louis XV. The first Concert Spirituel took place on March 18, 1724, Anne Phi.idor conducting, and the program including works by Corelli and Michel Delalande. The Concert Spirituel continued to function until 1791, presenting about twenty concerts a year. Among its principal conductors were Jean Joseph Mouret, Antoine Dauvergne, and Pierre Montan Berton.

Concerts Colonne. *See:* Colonne Orchestra.

Concerts Lamoureux. *See:* Lamoureux Orchestra.

Concerts royaux. Four suites for harpsichord, or various instruments, by Couperin-le-Grand, written for his Sunday evening concerts at the court of Louis XIV. A unity of tonality is maintained among the respective pieces of each suite.

Concertstueck. *See: Konzertstueck.*

Concitato. Disturbed, agitated.

Concord. A combination of sounds pleasing to the ear, as opposed to discord.

Concord Sonata. *See:* Sonata—*Ives.*

Concours International Eugène Ysaÿe. *See:* Queen Elizabeth of Belgium International Music Competition.

Concrete Music (Musique Concrète). Music consisting of various kinds of sounds recorded on tape and sometimes including distortions or alterations of sounds already recorded. Composition of concrete music thus consists of the selection of different sounds and their electronic manipulation, and the emphasis is on rhythm and color. This creative process was developed under the auspices of the Club d'Essai of the Radiodiffusion française in the late 1940's. One of the pioneers was Pierre Schaeffer, who wrote a ten-movement symphony in which sounds heard by a solitary man are recorded, and arranged in rhythmic patterns (*Symphonie pour un homme seul*). Other French composers have written concrete music, among these being Olivier Messiaen and Pierre Boulez.

Conducting. The art and technique of leading a group of performers. The qualities making up a great conductor are a commanding personality, sensitive ear, retentive memory, consummate command of the music he is directing, a sure feeling for tempo and rhythm, a sensitivity for style enabling him to penetrate into the heart of a composition to comprehend its subtlest message.

Until the mid-19th century, the conductor's main function was to beat time; thus the Germans often spoke of him as a "time-beater" (*Taktschlaeger*). Time-beating had existed for centuries, and its methods were many and varied. In the 18th century time-beating was usually assigned to a performer on the organ or harpsichord. Handel and Johann Sebastian Bach, for example, conducted their performances while seated at the organ or harpsichord, suggesting the tempo with nods of the head or quick gestures of the hand.

But even time-beaters occasionally exerted their will in an effort to give shape and design to the music they were directing. Bach, Handel, Haydn, and Beethoven were such time-beaters, injecting their own concepts of tempo, phrasing, and nuance into the performance. Early conductors like Johann Wenzel Stamitz of the Mannheim Orchestra were also inflexible in imposing their own musical values and concepts upon their musicians.

A milestone in conducting history came with the introduction of the baton. Freed from the necessity of playing an instrument while beating time, the conductor could concentrate on his men and on the stylistic details of the music they were performing. It was Louis Spohr, distinguished German violinist, who is credited with being the first to make the baton popular. This happened in 1820, when he appeared as a guest conductor of the Royal Philharmonic Orchestra in London. The baton helped change the conductor from a time-beater to an interpreter. The first conductors who rose to the new artistic demands made upon them were Felix Mendelssohn in Germany, Hector Berlioz in France, Franz Liszt in Weimar, Sir Michael Costa in England, and Hans von Buelow in Meiningen. These men helped develop the techniques of modern conducting, including the science of indicating the beat with the baton, and tempo, rhythm, and nuances with movements of the left hand. They also helped crystallize the art of orchestral interpretation. Fastidious rehearsals now became the rule as the conductor became a painstaking analyst, dissecting for his men the technical and stylistic details of a musical work, as he meticulously led them through the problems of tempo, phrasing, balance, dynamics, and interpretation.

Now a re-creator in the finest sense of the term, the conductor became a performer on the most complex musical instrument in the world: the symphony orchestra. In the closing decades of the 19th century, and in the first years of the 20th, many distinguished conductors throughout the world helped advance the art of conducting, proving themselves to be musical interpreters of the first magni-

tude. Among those who were particularly distinguished were Arthur Nikisch, Karl Muck, Hans Richter, Gustav Mahler, Felix Weingartner, Arturo Toscanini, Bruno Walter, Wilhelm Furtwaengler, and Serge Koussevitzky, to mention only a representative handful.

Consecration of the House, Overture (Die Weihe des Hauses). Concert overture by Beethoven, op. 124 (1822), written for the opening of the Josephstadt Theater in Vienna on Oct. 3, 1822. A slow introduction leads to an allegro in fugal style; the principal melody appears in the woodwind against pizzicato strings.

Consecutive intervals. The progression of parallel fifths or octaves, a practice condemned by the theoreticians but sometimes followed by composers.

Consolations. Six pieces for piano by Liszt (1850). They are brief mood pictures in a sentimental, tender, ardent, passionate, or religious vein. The most popular is No. 3, in D-flat major (*Lento placido*), a serene and reflective piece of music. It has been transcribed for violin and piano by Nathan Milstein.

Console. The part of the organ at which the player sits, comprising the manuals, drawstops, and pedals—as distinct from the pipes, bellows, and motor.

Consonance. A pleasing combination of sounds, as opposed to dissonance.

Consort (or Concert). A term used in the 16th and 17th centuries to designate a set of instruments; also several instruments playing together.

Consort of viols. *See:* Chest of viols.

Continuo. In 17th- and 18th-century performance, the accompanying figured bass part on a keyboard or plucked string instrument.

Contrabass. A bass viol with a range an octave lower than the cello's. Also called the double bass.

Contrabasso. Italian for double bass.

Contrabassoon. A large bassoon, whose range is an octave lower than the regular bassoon's.

Contrapuntal. Relating to counterpoint.

Contrary motion. In counterpoint the movement of simultaneous voices in opposite directions.

Contredanse. A lively old English dance in 2/4 or 6/8 time popular in 18th-century France, where it was known as "contredanse anglaise," and subsequently introduced into Germany. The form was appropriated for instrumental music. Mozart wrote numerous contredanses including a set of four, K. 267 (1777), a set of three, K. 535a (1788), a set of five, K. 609 (1791), and two popular contredanses with the names of *Das Donnerwetter* and *La Bataille*, K. 534 and 535 (1788). Beethoven wrote twelve contredanses, op. 141 (1801). The seventh, in E-flat, is a melody particularly favored by the composer since he used it in the finale of his *Eroica Symphony*, the finale to his music to *Prometheus*, and in the Piano Variations, op. 35.

Converse, Frederick Shepherd, composer. Born Newton, Mass., Jan. 5, 1871; died Boston, Mass., June 8, 1940. After studying piano with local teachers, he attended Harvard, from which he was graduated with honors in 1893. Additional music study took place with Carl Baermann and George Chadwick, and at the Royal College of Music in Munich. Returning to the United States, he was a member of the faculty of the New England Conservatory from 1899 to 1901. His first significant works for orchestra came between 1900 and 1903, including the tone poems *Festival of Pan* and *Endymion's Narrative* and the concert overture, *Euphrosyne*. From 1901 to 1907 he was professor of music at Harvard. During this period major works brought him national recognition as a composer, the most significant being *The Mystic Trumpeter* in 1905, and in 1906 an opera, *The Pipe of Desire*, the first by an American composer to be given at the Metropolitan Opera. In 1921 Converse returned to teaching at the New England Conservatory, and from 1930 to 1938 served as its director. Converse was a traditional composer with a healthy respect for Classical style and structure, but also with a strong Romantic bent. After 1927 he often turned to American scenes and backgrounds for material for major works. His orchestral music includes 6 symphonies, many tone poems and overtures (including *Festival of Pan, Endymion's Narrative, Euphrosyne, The Mystic Trumpeter, Ave atque vale, Song*

of the Sea, Elegiac Poem, Flivver Ten Million, California, Ormazd, and *American Sketches*). He also wrote 3 string quartets, a piano trio, and a cello sonata.

Coolidge, Elizabeth Sprague, music patron. Born Chicago, Ill., Oct. 30, 1864; died Cambridge, Mass., Nov. 4, 1953. Throughout her mature years she was indefatigable in promoting musical performances and encouraging musical creation. In 1918 she established a chamber-music festival in Pittsfield, Mass. In 1925 she founded the Elizabeth Sprague Coolidge Foundation at the Library of Congress in Washington, D.C., providing for performances of concerts and festivals, awards for important new music given at these events, and the financing of some of the library's musicological endeavors; she also paid for the erection of a concert auditorium at the Library. Other benefactions included the award of a music building to Yale University, and the creation of the Elizabeth Sprague Coolidge medal for distinguished services to chamber music. In 1936 she provided funds for the formation of the Coolidge String Quartet, which for many years gave distinguished performances of chamber music in America and Europe; its members were William Kroll, Nicolai Berezowsky, Nicholas Moldavan, and Victor Gottlieb. She herself was a talented amateur pianist and composer.

Coolidge String Quartet. *See:* Coolidge, Elizabeth Sprague.

Copland, Aaron, composer. Born Brooklyn, N.Y., Nov. 14, 1900. After studying piano with local teachers and harmony with Rubin Goldmark, he entered the American School of Music in Fontainebleau in 1921. He later studied composition privately with Nadia Boulanger in Paris. His first major work was the Symphony for Organ and Orchestra in 1924, introduced the following January by the New York Symphony Society. This work attracted the interest of Koussevitzky, who undertook to promote Copland's career by commissioning him to write *Music for the Theatre* in 1925, and introducing his Piano Concerto (with the composer as soloist) a year later. In 1925 and 1926, Copland was the recipient of a Guggenheim Fellowship, the first given to a composer. In 1930 he won an award of $5,000 from RCA Victor for the *Dance Symphony*. His compositions of this period progressed from the jazz idioms of *Music for the Theatre* and the Piano Concerto to a complex and recondite style and ultramodern techniques. But he soon became convinced he had lost touch with his audience and made a deliberate effort to write more simply and emotionally. He achieved a major success with his first large work in this new simplified style, *El Salón México* in 1936. From that time on he continued writing in a more or less easily assimilable style which often exploits American popular or folk idioms. He also, however, continued to produce works in his more abstract style. He has written functional music for performance by school children, and music for the stage, motion pictures, and radio. In his later works intended for wide consumption there has been no lowering of artistic standards. On the contrary: in this vein he has produced some of his most significant works, the works by which he is most likely to be remembered. Among them are his ballet *Appalachian Spring*, which received both the Pulitzer Prize in music and the New York Music Critics Circle Award in 1945; and the Symphony No. 3, recipient of the Boston Symphony Award of Merit and the New York Music Critics Circle Award in 1946.

Besides being one of the best-known living American composers, Copland has been an indefatigable champion of American music. He has written numerous articles and has often appeared as lecturer; he has served as executive director of the League of Composers; he has been founder and director of several organizations and festivals dedicated to contemporary American music. He has also taught composition at the Berkshire Music Centre in Tanglewood, where he serves as head of the composition department and chairman of the faculty. He is the author of *What to Listen for in Music* (1939), *Our New Music* (1941), and *Music and Imagination* (1952). In 1956 he received an honorary doctorate from Princeton University.

These are Copland's principal instrumental compositions.

Chamber Music: Vitebsk Trio; Two Pieces, for string quartet; Sonata for Violin and Piano; Piano Quartet.

Orchestra: 3 symphonies; *Music for the Theatre;* Concerto for Piano and Orchestra; *Symphonic Ode; Short Symphony; Statements; An Outdoor Overture; El Salón México; Quiet City,* suite; *Our Town,* suite; *Lincoln Portrait; Danzón Cubano; Appalachian Spring,* ballet suite; *Letters from Home; Billy the Kid,* ballet suite; *Rodeo,* ballet suite; Concerto for Clarinet and Orchestra; *The Red Pony,* suite; *Preamble,* for speaker and orchestra; *Canticle of Freedom,* for chorus and orchestra; *Orchestral Variations.*

Piano: Variations; Sonata; Piano Fantasy.

See: *Appalachian Spring; Billy the Kid; Salón México, El; Lincoln Portrait; Red Pony, The;* Symphony—*Copland.*

Coq d'or, Le, Suite (The Golden Cockerel). Suite for orchestra by Rimsky-Korsakov adapted from his opera. The opera was introduced in St. Petersburg on Oct. 7, 1909. The text, by Vladimir Bielsky, is based on a tale by Pushkin. The golden cockerel, which possesses a gift for prophecy, is presented to King Dodon by his astrologer. Eventually the cockerel brings death to both the astrologer and the king. The suite is made up of four sections: I. Introduction and Prologue; Slumber Scene and Warning of the Cockerel. II. Prelude and Scene at the Palace from Act. 2. III. Dance of King Dodon and the Queen of Shemakha. IV. Prelude; Bridal Procession, and Death of King Dodon.

See also: *Bridal Procession.*

Cor anglais. *See:* English horn.

Corelli, Arcangelo, violinist and composer. Born Fusignano, Italy, Feb. 17, 1653; died Rome, Italy, Jan. 8, 1713. He was a giant figure in the early history of Italian instrumental music. He received intensive musical instruction in Bologna. In 1671 he established himself in Rome, where he played the violin at the French Church and later in the orchestra of the Teatro Capranica. By 1672 he had established his reputation as a virtuoso, honored by the social elite of Rome. He received the patronage of Cardinal Pietro Ottoboni, at whose palace Corelli directed Monday evening concerts for many years. In the closing years of his life, Corelli's fame was eclipsed by that of younger performers and composers. He died a bitter man.

Corelli was a leader in a school of Italian violin composers and performers that helped establish both the technique and the style of violin playing. As a composer, Corelli was among the first to develop the structure of the sonata and the concerto grosso; to realize a purely instrumental style of writing liberated from choral or vocal techniques. Thus he helped to lay the foundations upon which subsequent composers of orchestral, chamber, and solo violin music built their own musical structures. His principal works comprise sonatas for two instruments and figured bass, opp. 1-4; sonatas for violin and figured bass, op. 5; and concerti grossi for string orchestra, op. 6.

Several interesting orchestral works have been arranged from Corelli's music. From his volume of sonatas, op. 5, Enrique Arbós arranged a suite for strings, and John Barbirolli, a concerto grosso and the Concerto in F major for oboe and orchestra.

See: Concerto grosso—*Corelli; Folia, La.*

Coriolan, Overture. Concert overture by Beethoven, op. 62 (1807). Its inspiration was not the Shakespeare tragedy, but a German play by Heinrich Josef von Collin. The overture was probably introduced at a subscription concert in Vienna in March 1807. The main theme, in strings, portrays the hero, Coriolanus. The gentler traits of his personality are described in a secondary subject, a beautiful melody for strings. The stress of a hero's life is then dramatically unfolded in the development, while the hero's death is depicted in the coda.

Coriolanus. *See:* Shakespeare, William.

Cornet. Member of the horn or trumpet family. It has a cupped mouthpiece, a comparatively short brass conical tube, and three valves with piston. It is pitched in B-flat. Since valved trumpets were rarely used in French orchestras in the 19th century, French composers from Berlioz on used cornets. To this day, French orchestras often include two cornets and two trumpets; where compositions require three trumpets, one is supplanted by a cornet. Outside France, trumpet parts are sometimes played on the cornet. Stravinsky has made effective use of the cornet in *Petrouchka* and *The Story of a Soldier.*

Coronation Concerto. *See:* Concerto—*Mozart.*

Corsair, The. *See:* Byron, George Noel Gordon, Lord.

Cortot, Alfred, pianist. Born Nyon, Switzerland, Sept. 26, 1877. The son of French parents, he was brought to Paris in his childhood. After attending the Paris Conservatory, where he won first prize in piano playing, he made his concert début in 1896 as soloist with the Colonne Orchestra. He then achieved major successes with performances of several of Beethoven's piano concertos with the Colonne and Lamoureux Orchestras in Paris. His success was further solidified by a European tour. Between 1898 and 1901 he was assistant conductor to Felix Mottl and Hans Richter at the Bayreuth Festival. Now a Wagner enthusiast, he founded in 1902 in Paris the Association des Concerts A. Cortot, which he conducted for two years in performances of Wagner's music. In the next few years he also led choral and orchestral performances in Paris, as well as several seasons of popular concerts in Lille. The piano, however, was not neglected. He appeared as a virtuoso throughout Europe, achieving acclaim for his remarkable performances of French music and of Chopin and other Romantics. He also made notable appearances in chamber music: sonata recitals with Jacques Thibaud, and trio concerts with Thibaud and Pablo Casals. On Oct. 18, 1918, Cortot made his American début in New York as soloist with the visiting French Symphony Orchestra conducted by André Messager. One season later he returned to the United States for a second tour, an occasion upon which he played all five Beethoven concertos with the New York

Symphony. In 1907 Cortot was appointed instructor of piano at the Paris Conservatory, becoming head of the department a decade later. In 1919 he helped found the Ecole Normale de Musique in Paris, of which he became director and where he conducted master classes in piano. Cortot has edited Chopin's etudes, preludes, and ballades. Two of his scholarly works on the piano have been translated into English: *French Piano Music* (1932) and *Alfred Cortot's Studies in Music Appreciation* (1937).

Cortot has been made Commander of the Legion of Honor and Knight of the Order of Isabella La Catolica.

Costa, Sir Michael, conductor. Born Naples, Italy, Feb. 4, 1806; died Hove, England, April 29, 1884. He was trained at the Naples Conservatory. In 1829 he went to England, where he spent most of his time. Between 1842 and 1882 he distinguished himself as conductor at various English festivals, and with the Royal Philharmonic Society of London. He brought both the technique and the art of conducting to an advanced stage of development, and helped lift the Royal Philharmonic to a dominant position among Europe's orchestras. He was knighted in 1869, and in 1871 appointed director of music at Her Majesty's Opera.

Counterpoint. The combination of two or more independent melodic lines.

Couperin, François (Le Grand), composer. Born Paris, France, Nov. 10, 1668; died there Sept. 12, 1733. Couperin was born into a family that for generations had produced celebrated musicians. To single him out from the others he is known as "le grand" ("the great one"). His first teacher was his father, from whom he inherited the post of organist at St. Gervais in 1685, retaining it until his death. He also studied with Jacques-Denis Thomelin. In 1693 Couperin competed for and won the post of organist at the Chapel Royal. He soon became a favorite of Louis XIV—music master to the princes, performer for the king, and director of the Sunday evening concerts, for which he wrote many of his instrumental works. Couperin retired from all court activity in 1715 and lived quietly

in Paris, devoting himself to composition and to arranging concerts at his home.

Couperin's pieces for harpsichord are a monument in early instrumental music. They established a keyboard style and technique for French music. At the same time they introduced a variety of expression and an aptness of programmatic writing unknown in French instrumental music at the time. Couperin's sonatas and suites for various combinations of instruments laid the groundwork of French chamber music. This chamber music includes *La Superbe,* trio sonata; *La Sultane,* quartet-sonata; *Concerts royaux; Les Goûts réunis,* for unspecified instruments and accompaniment; *L'Apothéose de Lully,* for two violins and accompaniment; *L'Apothéose de Corelli; Le Parnasse,* for two violins and accompaniment; and *Les Nations,* trio sonatas and suites. For harpsichord, Couperin wrote the *Pièces de clavecin* and the Appendix to *L'Art de toucher le clavecin;* and for organ, the Masses, *Pour paroisses* and *Pour les couvents.*

Richard Strauss adapted several of Couperin's harpsichord pieces into a Divertimento for small orchestra, op. 86. Darius Milhaud made a transcription for orchestra of two movements from Couperin's *La Sultane,* calling it *Overture and Allegro.*

See: *Pièces de clavecin.*

Courante. A two-section dance of French origin. It is in triple rhythm and is characterized by its polyphonic style and dotted rhythms. It was often used as a movement in the Baroque suite.

Courboin, Charles Marie, organist. Born Antwerp, Belgium, April 2, 1886. A child prodigy at the organ, Courboin gave his first organ recital when he was nine; at twelve, filled an organ post at Notre Dame College in Antwerp; and at sixteen was appointed organist of the Antwerp Cathedral. He studied music at the Conservatories of Antwerp and Brussels. After touring Europe, in 1904 he settled permanently in the United States, where he soon held a leading position among American organists. For ten years he was organist at St. Paul's in Oswego, N.Y. He subsequently held other organ posts besides giving many concerts in public auditoriums and over the radio. He has also been an important designer of organs. In 1920 he became the only organist to receive the Order of the Crown from Belgium.

Cowell, Henry Dixon, composer. Born Menlo Park, Calif., March 11, 1897. He was at first too poor to pay for lessons, and taught himself music. He acquired his first piano when he was fourteen, and at once began experimenting with unusual chords. His first public appearance took place in San Francisco on March 12, 1912, in a concert of his own works. When he was seventeen he entered the University of Southern California, where for several years he took some music courses. After World War I he attended the Institute of Applied Music in New York. All the while he was writing pieces for the piano in a highly personal and provocative style. In some of his works he used "tone clusters," groups of notes produced by striking the keyboard with the elbow or forearm. He also appropriated techniques from violin music, such as harmonics, muted tones, and pizzicatos, achieved by plucking the strings of the piano. These compositions were presented by him in numerous piano recitals throughout the United States and Europe in the 1920's, arousing considerable controversy. A Guggenheim Fellowship in 1930 and 1931 enabled him to pursue musicological studies in Berlin. Since 1933, Cowell has deserted his experimental idioms for more formal procedures. In his later works he has often been strongly influenced by American folk sources, particularly American hymnody, folk and country tunes of British origin, and Celtic folksongs and dances.

With Leon Theremin, Cowell invented the Rhythmicon, an instrument capable of projecting sixteen different rhythms. He has been an indefatigable champion of modern American music through his numerous articles and lectures; through the founding of magazines, recording companies, and musical societies. During World War II he served as chief music editor of the O.W. I., in charge of music used in all broadcasts. In 1948 he received a grant from the American Academy of Arts and Letters, and in 1957-1958 he made a tour of the world collecting material on folk music. He is the author of *New Musical Resources* (1930) and a biography of Charles Ives (1954).

His compositions for the piano in the tone-cluster technique include such pieces as *Advertisement, Antinomy, Tiger,* and *Sinister Resonance.* For orchestra, he has written 14 symphonies, 8 *Hymns and Fuguing Tunes,* and a number of smaller works including *Old American Country Set, Tales of Our Countryside, Celtic Set, Big Sing, Fiddler's Jig, Music: 1957,* and *Ongaku.* He has also written some chamber music, including a violin sonata, *Tall Tale* for brass sextet, *United Quartet,* and *Ostinati with Chorales* for oboe (or clarinet) and piano.

See: Hymn and Fuguing Tune, No. 2; Tales of Our Countryside.

Cowen, Sir Frederick, conductor and composer. Born Kingston, Jamaica, Jan. 29, 1852; died London, England, Oct. 6, 1935. He was brought to England when he was four. There he studied music with Sir John Goss and Sir Julius Benedict, and gave several piano recitals. Later music study took place at the Leipzig and Stern Conservatories. He was the conductor of the Royal Philharmonic of London from 1888 to 1892 and again from 1900 to 1907, and of the Liverpool Philharmonic from 1896 to 1913. Besides being one of England's leading conductors he was also a prolific composer. He often employed a light, graceful, and at times fanciful style which was particularly effective in music describing delicate subjects and fairy tales. His works include 6 symphonies, a piano concerto, two suites, two sets of old English dances, and several tone poems. He was knighted in 1911.

Cracovienne. *See: Krakowiak.*

Cramer, Johann Baptist, pianist and composer. Born Mannheim, Germany, Feb. 24, 1771; died London, England, April 16, 1858. The son of a famous musician, Wilhelm Cramer, Johann was brought to England as an infant. England remained his permanent home. He studied the piano in London with J. D. Benser and J. S. Schroeter. On April 5, 1781, Cramer made his public début as pianist in London. Further study took place with Muzio Clementi, after which Cramer toured Europe and was acclaimed. In 1813 he helped found the Royal Philharmonic Orchestra of London, which he conducted for several seasons besides appearing with it as piano soloist. He also distinguished himself as professor of the piano at the Royal Academy of Music, and as a publisher of music with the firm of J. B. Cramer and Company which he founded in 1824. He wrote 7 piano concertos, over one hundred piano sonatas, and many smaller piano pieces. He is remembered chiefly for his excellent piano studies, the *Grosse Praktische Pianoforte Schule,* in five parts (1815); the last part, *84 Studies,* op. 50, has become indispensable to piano students everywhere. Anton Schindler wrote that Beethoven regarded these studies as "the chief basis of all genuine piano playing." Cramer's *100 Progressive Etudes* also have pedagogic value.

Creation, The (Die Schoepfung), oratorio by Haydn (1798), introduced in Vienna on April 29, 1798, the composer conducting. Though written in the last years of the composer's life, this was his first oratorio; and to it he confided his most profound religious feelings. He himself revealed that he had never been so pious as when he wrote this music. "Daily I fell on my knees and begged God to vouchsafe me strength for the fortunate outcome of my work."

The text, drawn from *Genesis* and Milton's *Paradise Lost,* was written by a certain Lidley or Lidell, and was translated into German by Gottfried van Swieten. It had originally been intended for Handel, who never got around to writing the music. Johann Peter Salomon, the impresario, suggested to Haydn that he take over this text for his first oratorio, possibly an oratorio in a Handelian style.

Haydn's prelude is a remarkable programmatic tone poem describing the resolution of chaos into order, darkness into light. In the first three sections of the oratorio the six days of Creation are unfolded in music that often achieves telling majesty and eloquence. But *The Creation* as a whole is not a sustained masterwork. Too much of its musical realism approaches the naive, and there are many perfunctory passages. But at its best, *The Creation* is music of inspiration, and its finest pages surely entitle it to a place of honor among the world's great oratorios. The cream of the music can be found in the following passages: the two mighty choruses, *And the Spirit of God* and *The Heavens are Telling;* the baritone aria, *Rolling in Foaming Billows;* the tenor song, *In Native Worth;* the deservedly famous pastoral for soprano, *In Verdure Clad;* the effective recitative of Raphael, *Be Fruitful All;* and the long and inspired duet of Adam and Eve, with interpolated choruses.

Création du monde, La (The Creation of the World). Ballet suite for orchestra by Darius Milhaud (1922), first performed in Paris by the Swedish Ballet on Oct. 25, 1923. The ballet scenario by Blaise Cendrars sees the creation of the world through the eyes of an aborigine. The action takes place on a darkened stage with many of the dancers, on stilts, representing herons and various other animals. Milhaud derived his inspiration from a visit in 1922 to Harlem, where he was fascinated by the music of Negro jazz bands. The score of his ballet is in a jazz idiom—one of the earliest serious works to employ this style with artistic success. The suite derived from the ballet score comprises an overture and five sections. For each of the sections there is a note in the published score. I. The Chaos Before Creation. Giant deities of Creation hold council. II. The Confused Mass Begins to Move. Suddenly a tree appears, and then various animals. III. The Animals Join in a Dance. Two bodies emerge limb by limb from the central mass. IV. The Pair Perform a Dance of Desire. The remaining mass dissolves into human beings who join in a frenetic round to the point of vertigo. V. The Crowd Disappears in Little Groups. The Negro Adam and Eve, left behind, embrace in a lasting kiss. It is Springtime.

Creatures of Prometheus (Beethoven). *See: Prometheus, Overture.*

Credendum. For orchestra by William Schuman (1955), introduced by the Cincinnati Symphony on Nov. 4, 1955, Thor Johnson conducting. This work was commissioned by the United States National Commission for UNESCO. It opens with a stately prelude subtitled "Declaration," and proceeds with a gentle chorale, at first scored for strings. A dramatic climax is reached and the work ends with a powerfully rhythmic scherzo-like finale.

Crescendo. Gradual increase in volume.

Creston, Paul (born Joseph Guttoveggio), composer. Born New York, N.Y., Oct. 10, 1906. He studied piano and composition with local teachers while attending public and high school, but much of his early music education came from reading theoretical treatises. His first composition was *Five Dances* for piano in 1932, and recognition came in 1940 with his First Symphony, introduced by the Philadelphia Orchestra under Ormandy and the recipient of the New York Music Critics Circle Award. Meanwhile in 1938 and 1939 he received a Guggenheim Fellowship. In 1941 and 1943 he was given citations of merit from the National Association for American Composers and Conductors, of which he was elected president in 1956; in 1943 he received a grant from the American Academy of Arts and Letters, and in 1945 the Ditson Fund Award. Since 1940 his principal works have been performed in many countries. His music has a fullness of lyricism, a warmth of feeling, and a disposition towards ingenious rhythmic patterns that make it fall pleasantly on the ear. His orchestral works include 5 symphonies, a piano concerto, violin concerto, *Threnody, Prelude and Dance, Pastorale and Tarantella, Poem* for harp and orchestra, *Dance Overture, Frontiers,* Toccata, *Invocation and Dance,* and Partita for flute, violin, and strings. He also wrote a string quartet; a violin and piano suite; a suite for piano, flute, and viola; a piano sonata; and several smaller pieces for the piano including *Five Little Dances, Prelude and Dance,* Nos. 1 and 2, *Seven Theses,* six preludes, and five two-part inventions.

See: Dance Overture; Frontiers.

Cristofori, Bartolommeo di Francesco, inventor of the pianoforte. Born Padua, Italy, May 4, 1655; died Florence, Italy, Jan. 27, 1731. He achieved renown early in Padua as a manufacturer of harpsichords. Called to Florence by Prince Ferdinand de' Medici, he invented the pianoforte there in or about 1711. It was over four octaves in range, with hammer action. He called it "gravecembalo col piano e forte" to point up the fact that the dynamics could pass from soft to loud according to the pressure on the keys, an effect impossible to obtain on the harpsichord.

Cross rhythm. The simultaneous use of different rhythms.

Crotchet. Quarter note; a quarter of the time value of the whole note.

Csardas. *See:* Czardas.

Cuckoo and the Nightingale, The. *See:* Concerto—*Handel.*

Cui, César, composer. Born Vilna, Russia, Jan. 18, 1835; died St. Petersburg, Russia, March 24, 1918. Trained as an engineer, he attended the School of Military Engineering in St. Petersburg, where he subsequently served as professor. He became an authority on military fortifications, writing several treatises on that subject, and serving as instructor for members of the royal family, including Nicholas II himself. Music had always been a major interest. A meeting with Balakirev, in 1857, encouraged him to begin composition. With Balakirev, Rimsky-Korsakov, Borodin, and Mussorgsky he helped form the national school of composers now identified as the "Russian Five" or the "Mighty Five," whose influence on Russian musical culture was decisive. Cui's national ideals were best realized in his operas, though none have survived. Here, as in his orchestral and piano works, he was a facile melodist who lacked a strong identity; he was too derivative to provide sustained interest. If he is remembered at all as a composer it is for a comparative trifle, *Orientale,* one of twenty-four pieces for violin and piano collectively entitled *Kaleidoscope,* op. 50. His orchestral works include 4 suites, *Tarentelle,* and *Marche solennelle.* He also wrote polonaises, impromptus, mazurkas, and other piano pieces.

Curtis String Quartet. A chamber-music ensemble founded by Mrs. Mary Louise Curtis Bok in 1927. It made its début in New York City in 1928 as the Swastika Quartet, so-named after Mrs. Bok's estate; it acquired its present name in 1932. It has performed extensively throughout the United States, making its first tours of Europe in 1936 and 1937. It has also performed series of concerts with outstanding educational institutions and at the Library of Congress, in Washington, D.C. Of its present members, only Jascha Brodsky, first violin, has been with the Quartet since its inception. Max Aronoff, violist, joined the group after its first season. The other two members are Enrique Serratos, second violin, and Orlando Cole, cello.

Curzon, Clifford, pianist. Born London, England, May 18, 1907. He began taking piano lessons when he was five, and at twelve was the youngest pupil ever admitted to the Royal Academy of Music in London. After subsequent piano study with Tobias Matthay and Katharine Goodson, he made his first public appearance in 1923 as one of three soloists in a London performance of a Bach Concerto for Three Pianos. He started concertizing in England in 1925, and in the same year joined the faculty of the Royal College of Music, where he remained until 1937, when he was made a Fellow of the Academy. Hearing a recital by Artur Schnabel convinced him he needed more study. For two years he worked with Schnabel in Berlin, then studied in Paris with Wanda Landowska and Nadia Boulanger. He resumed his concert career in 1930 with recitals and appearances with major orchestras in Europe. His American début took place in New York on Feb. 26, 1939. He was engaged to tour the country the following season, but the outbreak of World War II prevented him from returning. When he was again able to tour the United States, in 1947, he was acclaimed as one of England's leading pianists. Curzon has also distinguished himself in performances of chamber music with leading ensembles.

Cyclic form. A technique, utilized especially by César Franck, in which the same thematic material is used in more than one movement of a work, for purposes of structural unification.

Cyclops. *See:* Euripides.

Cymbals. Two round metal plates which are struck and permitted to vibrate. A cymbal roll can also be produced by striking one of the cymbals with a drum stick. Cymbals are part of the percussion family of the symphony orchestra.

Cymbeline. *See:* Shakespeare, William.

Cyrano de Bergerac. *See:* Rostand, Edmond.

Czardas (or Csardas). A Hungarian folk dance in duple time, characterized by quick syncopations. It consists of a slow section called "lassu" alternating with a rapid one, "friss." A characteristic work in this form is the popular *Hungarian Czardas Scenes,* for violin and piano, op. 13, by Jenö Hubay. The intermezzo movement of Zoltán Kodály's *Háry János* suite is a czardas. There is also a czardas in Tchaikovsky's *Swan Lake.*

Czech Philharmonic Orchestra. A symphony orchestra organized in Prague, Bohemia, with members of the National Theater Orchestra. It gave its first concert on Jan. 4, 1896, Antonin Dvořák conducting. In 1901 it became completely independent of the National Theater. The orchestra first achieved renown between 1903 and 1908 when it was conducted by Vilem Zemánek. In 1925 it became subsidized by the State and by the city of Prague. Among its principal conductors since Zemánek have been Vaclav Talich, Rafael Kubelik, and Karel Ancerl.

Czerny, Carl, teacher of the piano. Born Vienna, Austria, Feb. 20, 1791; died there, July 15, 1857. After receiving some preliminary instruction on the piano from his father, he studied with Beethoven for three years, beginning in 1800. He also profited from the advice and direction given him by Muzio Clementi and Johann Nepomuk Hummel. He was only fifteen when he launched his teaching career by accepting Beethoven's nephew as a pupil. Though Czerny made some successful concert appearances as a pianist, he concentrated his activity on teaching the piano, becoming one of the most celebrated teachers in Europe; among his many pupils were Liszt, Theodor Kullak, and Sigismond Thalberg. A prolific composer—he wrote about a thousand compositions, including symphonies, concertos, overtures, and chamber and piano music—Czerny is most famous for his many piano studies and exercises which have become an essential tool for piano students throughout the world.

D

Da Capo. "From the beginning." An indication that a section of a composition is to be repeated from the beginning.

D'Albert, Eugène, pianist and composer. Born Glasgow, Scotland, April 10, 1864; died Riga, Latvia, March 3, 1932. Two years after entering the National Training School in London, where his teachers included Ernst Pauer and Arthur Sullivan, he made his début as a pianist. Winning the Mendelssohn Prize in 1881 enabled him to study with Hans Richter in Vienna and Liszt in Weimar. After a successful performance of his own piano concerto on Oct. 24, 1881 in London, he made several tours of Europe and the United States. His first visit to the United States took place in 1889-1900, when he appeared in joint recitals with Pablo de Sarasate. When not on tour he lived mainly in Germany, where he renounced his British birth and became a German citizen. In 1895 he was appointed court director in Weimar, and in 1907 director of the Berlin High School of Music. D'Albert was the composer of 2 piano concertos, a cello concerto, a symphony, an orchestral suite, 2 string quartets, a piano sonata, a piano suite, and other instrumental compositions.

Dallapiccola, Luigi, composer. Born Pisino, Italy, Feb. 3, 1904. He studied music principally at the Cherubini Institute in Florence, where, since 1934, he has been a member of the faculty. In 1950 and 1952 he taught a master class in composition at the Berkshire Music Centre in Tanglewood, and in 1956-1957 he was a member of the music department of Queens College, New York. He made his American début as composer-pianist over the NBC network on Aug. 16, 1952, in the American première of his *Little Concerto,* for piano and orchestra. Most of Dallapiccola's major works are in the twelve-tone technique, but he also sometimes incorporates into his writing stylistic elements from Impressionism and neo-Classicism. His most important orchestral works are a Partita, *Two Pieces,* two divertimenti for violin and chamber orchestra derived from music by Tartini and called *Tartiniana,* a rhapsody for cello and orchestra, Variations, *Piccola musica notturna,* and *Concerto per la notte di natale dell' anno.* He also wrote *Two Pieces* for violin and piano, *Chaconne, Intermezzo and Adagio* for solo cello, and *Sonata canonica, Hymns,* and *Quaderno musicale di Anna Libera* for piano.

Dallas Symphony Orchestra. A symphony orchestra organized in Dallas, Texas, in 1901 by Hans Kreissig. Since then its principal conductors have been Walter J. Fried, Carl Venth, Paul van Katwijk, Jacques Singer, Antal Dorati, Walter Hendl, and Paul Kletzki. In 1956 the orchestra acquired a new home in the State Fair Auditorium.

Damnation of Faust, The (La Damnation de Faust). Dramatic legend by Berlioz, op. 24 (1846), based on Goethe's epic poem. In 1828 Berlioz had completed eight scenes from Goethe's *Faust,* but after that discarded the project of setting the poem to music. In 1846, while touring Eastern Europe, he returned to it, using some of his earlier material and adding a considerable amount of new music to a text mostly his own. When this work was introduced as an oratorio at the Opéra-Comique in Paris on Dec. 6, 1846, it was a failure. As an opera, it was introduced in Monte Carlo on Feb. 18, 1903. Three orchestral excerpts from this "legend" are often heard at symphony concerts. I. *Minuet of the Will-o'-the-Wisps* (*Menuet des feux-follets*). This is a graceful dance melody for woodwind and brass, followed by a trio. After a repetition of the minuet theme comes a mocking subject in piccolo, flute, and oboe. The minuet melody returns twice more, the second time interrupted after each phrase by chords in the orchestra. This music appears in the scene in which Mephisto calls on evil spirits and will-o'-the-wisps to surround Marguerite's house. II. *Dance of the Sylphs* (*Danse des sylphes*). Here a waltz melody for violins depicts the dancing of gnomes and sylphs in Faust's dreams. III. *The Rakóczy March*. This stirring Hungarian march is based on a folk melody. The main march theme appears softly in the woodwind and is followed by a trumpet fanfare. A countertheme then is presented by the strings. Both ideas are worked out, with the first Hungarian melody growing in sonority until it erupts triumphantly in the full orchestra. The inclusion of a Hungarian march in *Faust* is made plausible by having Faust wander about in Hungary.

Damrosch, Walter, conductor. Born Breslau, Germany, Jan. 30, 1862; died New York City, Dec. 22, 1950. He was the son of Leopold Damrosch (born Posen, Germany, Oct. 22, 1832; died New York City, Feb. 15, 1885), founder and, until his death, conductor of the New York Symphony Society and the first conductor of Wagner operas at the Metropolitan Opera. Walter Damrosch was only five when his family came to the United States. Subsequently he returned to Germany, where he studied music with Felix Draeseke and Hans von Buelow. He assisted his father at rehearsals of the New York Symphony Society and the Oratorio Society of New York, and took over the direction of both these organizations when his father died. He remained principal conductor of the New York

Symphony until 1928, when it merged with the New York Philharmonic Orchestra; then, for a single season, he was a guest conductor of the New York Philharmonic. During this period he was also active as conductor of opera at the Metropolitan Opera and with his own company. In 1926 he entered the field of radio, becoming a pioneer in directing symphony concerts over the air and in presenting music-education programs for children. He retired as conductor of the NBC Music Appreciation Program in 1942, and as musical adviser of NBC in 1947. As a conductor, both in the concert hall and over the radio, Damrosch was a major influence in developing a musical culture in the United States. He appeared in two motion pictures, both times as himself: *The Star Maker* and *Carnegie Hall.* He was the author of an autobiography, *My Musical Life* (1923).

Walter Damrosch's brother, Frank Heino (born Breslau, Germany, June 22, 1859; died New York City, Oct. 22, 1937), was a distinguished music educator. From 1897 to 1905 he was director of music of the New York City public schools. In 1905 he founded, and from then until his death directed, the Institute of Musical Art in New York.

Dance Overture. Concert overture by Paul Creston (1954), introduced in Miami, Fla., on April 24, 1955. It was commissioned by the National Federation of Music Clubs for its biennial convention. This work is in four sections, each idealizing a national dance rhythm: Spanish bolero, English country dance, French loure, and American square dance. Creston selected these four specific countries because at different epochs these countries ruled the state of Florida, where the National Federation of Music Clubs had chosen to hold its convention.

Dance Suite. Suite for orchestra by Béla Bartók, one of the composer's earliest successes (1923). It was written for a festival held in Budapest to celebrate the 50th anniversary of the merging of Buda and Pesth. The Suite was first performed in Budapest on Nov. 19, 1923. The six movements are played without interruption (I. Moderato. II. *Allegro molto.* III. *Allegro vivace.* IV. *Molto tranquillo.*

V. *Comodo*. VI. Allegro). A kind of ritornello serves as a connecting link between the end of the movements and is developed climactically at the end of the composition. The entire work is rich with Magyar dance rhythms and with folk melodies built from Hungarian scales.

Dance of the Apprentices. A spirited dance performed by apprentices and their girls during the prize-singing contest festivities in Act 3, Scene 2 of Wagner's music drama, *The Mastersingers.*

Dance of the Blessed Spirits. A beatific dance, with flute solo, describing the radiance of the Elysian fields in Act 3 of Gluck's opera *Orpheus and Eurydice.* It is also popular in transcriptions for violin and piano (Fritz Kreisler), cello and piano (Heinrich Grünfeld), and piano solo (Giovanni Sgambati).

Dance of the Buffoons, or **Tumblers.** Dance in Act 3 of Rimsky-Korsakov's opera *The Snow Maiden.*

Dance of the Camorristi. An orchestral tarantella from Act 3 of Ermanno Wolf-Ferrari's opera, *The Jewels of the Madonna.* With this music the Camorrists enjoy a revel in their hideout.

Dance of the Comedians. A Bohemian folk dance in Act 3 of Smetana's folk opera, *The Bartered Bride.* This is the music with which acrobats of a traveling troupe of performers entertain Bohemian villagers in the town square.

Dance of the Furies. The demoniac dance in Hades in Act 2 of Gluck's opera, *Orpheus and Eurydice.*

Dance of the Seven Veils. The sensual dance of Salomé before King Herod which climaxes Richard Strauss' opera, *Salomé.* The music begins dramatically with propulsive rhythms and outcries in the orchestra. After this initial agitation subsides, a dance motif emerges in viola and flute. The music grows increasingly passionate as Salomé goes through her lascivious motions. The second dance melody is the heart of the composition. It is a slow, voluptuous melody for the strings. From this point on the music grows increasingly intense until a thunderous climax erupts in the full orchestra. The final motions of the dance are depicted by trills in the woodwind and tremolo strings. With an irresistible drive,

the music rushes to a precipitous conclusion.

Dance of the Sylphs (Berlioz). *See: Damnation of Faust, The.*

Dance of the Tumblers (Rimsky-Korsakov). *See: Dance of the Buffoons.*

Dances of Galánta. Suite for orchestra by Zoltán Kodály (1934). Though written for the 80th anniversary of the Budapest Philharmonic, its world première took place in the United States, in Philadelphia on Dec. 11, 1936. As the composer has explained, Galánta is a small Hungarian town where as a child he first heard "orchestral sonorities" in the form of a gypsy band. These gypsy bands helped preserve the old Hungarian traditions in music. To continue that tradition, the composer took his main thematic material from this ancient music. The work is made up of five gypsy dances played without interruption. It opens sedately with a solo cello passage, but the pace is soon accelerated by woodwinds and strings. As one dance leads to the next, the tempo increases until the music becomes a veritable tonal orgy. Each dance is independent of the other, but integration of the whole is achieved through a continual repetition of thematic material.

Dances of Marosszék. Suite for piano, and also for small orchestra, by Zoltán Kodály (1929). The orchestral version was first performed in Dresden on Dec. 28, 1930, Fritz Busch conducting. Marosszék is a Hungarian town whose folksongs and dances provided Kodály with his material for this work, which comprises six folk dances, and is in the form of a rondo. The main subject is a melody for violas and cellos against chords in the wind.

Danish State Radio Orchestra. A symphony orchestra founded in Copenhagen in 1925 with a radio ensemble and with Launy Grondahl as conductor. It was expanded in 1931 for more ambitious radio and concert work with Fritz Busch and Nikolai Malko as conductors. Since then its principal conductors have been Erik Tuxen and Thomas Jensen. The orchestra toured England in 1950, the United States in 1952, and made successful appearances at the Edinburgh Festival in 1950 and 1954.

D'Annunzio, Gabriele, poet, novelist, and dramatist. Born Francaville al mare, Italy, March 12, 1863; died Gardone Riviera, Italy, March 1, 1938. Enrico Toselli's tone poem, *Il Fuoco*, was inspired by the drama of the same name. Incidental music to other plays was written by Nadia Boulanger (*La Città morta*), Debussy (*Il Misterio di S. Sebastiano*), Arthur Honegger (*Phèdre*), and Ildebrando Pizzetti (*La Nave, La Pisanelle*).

Danse Macabre. (1) Tone poem for orchestra by Saint-Saëns, op. 40 (1874), first performed in Paris on Jan. 24, 1875, Édouard Colonne conducting. The composer transcribed it for two pianos, and Liszt for solo piano. The program, derived from a poem by Henri Cazalis, is literally followed by the music. The hour of midnight strikes (harp). Death tunes his violin. An orgiastic dance follows, its main theme given by flute. Death contributes a dance of his own, as a xylophone simulates the rattle of bones. In these frenetic proceedings the strains of the *Dies irae* are interpolated. Suddenly a cock crows, announcing dawn. The dance dies out; the ghostly dancers fade.

(2) See: *Totentanz.*

Danses Concertantes. Suite for small orchestra by Igor Stravinsky (1941), first performed in Los Angeles, Feb. 8, 1942, Werner Janssen conducting. Though this music has been used for a ballet, produced by the Ballet Russe de Monte Carlo in New York on Sept. 10, 1944, with choreography by George Balanchine, it is actually concert music not originally intended for choreographic treatment. The composer aspired in this music to comment on various types of dances. In doing so he had recourse to his natural bent for wit and parody. There are five sections: I. *Marche-Introduction;* II. *Pas d'action;* III. *Thème Varié;* IV. *Pas de deux;* V. *Marche-Conclusion.*

Danses Espagnoles (Sarasate). *See:* Spanish Dances (2).

Danses Villageoises. *See:* Grétry, André.

Dante Alighieri, poet. Born Florence, Italy, May 1265; died Ravenna, Italy, Sept. 14, 1321. This celebrated Italian poet,

and his masterwork *The Divine Comedy*, inspired numerous instrumental compositions. These include: Granville Bantock's tone poem, *Dante* (later revised as *Dante and Beatrice*); Conrado del Campo's *La divina comedia*, for orchestra; Arthur Foote's symphonic prologue, *Francesca da Rimini;* Enrique Granados' tone poem, *La divina comedia;* Paul von Klenau's three symphonic fantasies on Dante; Liszt's *A Dante Symphony,* and the *Dante Sonata* for piano; Quinto Maganini's *Concerto after Dante,* for chamber orchestra; Piotyr Rytel's tone poem, *Dante's Dream;* Charles Villiers Stanford's *Three Rhapsodies from Dante,* for piano; Tchaikovsky's orchestral fantasy, *Francesca da Rimini;* and William Wallace's tone poem, *The Passing of Beatrice.*

Dante Sonata (Liszt). *See: Années de pèlerinage.*

Dante Symphony. *See:* Symphony—*Liszt.*

Danzas Españoles (Granados). *See:* Spanish Dances (1).

Danzas Fantasticas. Suite for orchestra by Joaquín Turina (1920), first performed in Madrid in March 1921. The composer appended a quotation to each movement to suggest its content. I. *Exaltation.* "It was like the features of some incomparable picture, moving within the calyx of a blossom." II. *Musing.* "The strings of a guitar sounding laments of a nature that remind one of nothing so much as the weight of sorrow." III. *Orgy.* "The perfume of flowers is intermingled with the odor of camomile, and the bouquet of tall chalices filled with incomparable wine. From this, like an incense, the dance rises."

Daphnis and Chloe. Ballet suites for orchestra by Maurice Ravel (1911). The ballet, with a scenario by Michel Fokine based on a Greek pastoral said to be by Longus, was introduced in Paris by the Ballet Russe on June 8, 1912. From this ballet score the composer prepared two orchestral suites, or, as he designated them, "series of orchestral fragments." The second is the more famous, an unqualified masterwork (I. Daybreak. II. Pantomime. III. General Dance). The following program note appears in the published score. "Daphnis lies stretched before the grotto of the nymphs . . .

Herdsmen enter seeking Daphnis, and Chloe. She appears, at last, encircled by shepherdesses. The two rush into each other's arms. Daphnis observes Chloe's crown. His dream was a prophetic vision; the intervention of Pan is manifest. The old shepherd, Lammon, explains that Pan saved Chloe in remembrance of the nymph, Syrinx, whom the gods loved. Daphnis and Chloe mime the story of Pan and Syrinx. . . . He plucks some stalks, fashions a flute, and plays on it a melancholy tune. Chloe comes out and imitates with her dance accents of the flute. The dance becomes more and more animated. In mad whirlings, Chloe falls into the arms of Daphnis . . . A group of young men come on the stage. Joyous tumult. A general dance."

Suite No. 1 also comprises three sections: Nocturne; II. Interlude; III. Warlike Dance. Once again the published score provides the program. "The nymph comes to life and leaves her pedestal. Others descend, come together, and begin a slow and mysterious dance. They see Daphnis . . . Reanimating him and leading him to the rock, they invoke the god Pan . . . Daphnis kneels in supplication. All is dark. Behind the scene voices are heard, far off at first. And now there is dim light. The pirates' camp is disclosed . . . The pirates, laden with booty, run to and fro. Torches are brought which at last throw a strong light on the stage."

Both orchestral suites are subtly constructed from many episodic thematic ideas, and gain much of their effect from the masterful orchestration and the sensitive feeling for impressionistic colors and atmosphere.

David, Ferdinand, violinist and teacher. Born Hamburg, Germany, Jan. 19, 1810; died Kolsters, Switzerland, July 14, 1873. After completing the study of the violin with Louis Spohr and composition with Moritz Hauptmann in Leipzig, David made his début as concert violinist in that city. During the next few years he appeared in recitals, as guest artist with orchestras and chamber-music ensembles; he was particularly successful in Russia in 1835. In 1836, on Mendelssohn's recommendation, he became concertmaster of the Gewandhaus Orchestra, holding this post until his death. He was also a distinguished professor of the violin at the Leipzig Conservatory from its founding in 1843; among his pupils were Joseph Joachim and August Wilhelmj. A friend of Mendelssohn, David advised the composer about technical details in his famous Violin Concerto; and it was David who introduced it in Leipzig in 1845. David himself wrote 5 violin concertos, together with other pieces for the violin, and 2 symphonies and several string quartets. He is famous for his *Violin School,* a useful volume of exercises for the violin student; also for his collection of violin masterpieces, *Die Hohe Schule des Violinspiels.* David edited many violin compositions for educational purposes.

Davidov, Carl, cellist and composer. Born Goldingen, Courland, March 15, 1838; died Moscow, Russia, Feb. 26, 1889. He studied mathematics but finally abandoned it for music. He received his musical training in St. Petersburg and Leipzig. His début as cello virtuoso took place in Leipzig on Dec. 15, 1839. After a highly successful appearance in Leipzig in 1859 he was appointed first cellist of the Gewandhaus Orchestra and professor at the Leipzig Conservatory. In 1862 he went to St. Petersburg, where he became first cello of the Russian Music Society, professor and later director of the St. Petersburg Conservatory. All the while he concertized throughout Europe and Russia. His works include 4 cello concertos, several orchestral compositions, and many small pieces for the cello and for the piano. He also wrote a book of exercises for the cello.

Davidsbuendler (League of David). An imaginary music society created by Schumann to espouse the cause of contemporary music and to fight against musical Philistines. Schumann's music contains references to this society, notably the *Davidsbuendlertaenze* (see below) and in the finale of *Carnaval.*

Davidsbuendlertaenze (Dances of the League of David). Suite of 18 pieces for the piano by Schumann, op. 6 (1837). These are actually not dances but a series of characteristic pieces, or little dialogues, about Philistinism in music, between Florestan and Eusebius. At various points in his music Schumann interpolated interesting verbal notations. At the end of the eighth piece he noted: "Here Florestan made an end, and his lips quivered painfully." Before the eighteenth number he wrote: "Quite superfluously Eusebius remarked as follows; but all the time great bliss spoke from his eyes." These pieces range from quiet meditation to sentimental expressions of love, from brooding sadness to irrepressible gaiety. The suite ends with a passage made up of twelve low C's to designate the striking of midnight and the end of festivities.

Davies, Sir Henry Walford, composer and organist. Born Oswestry, England, Sept. 6, 1869; died Wrington, England, March 11, 1941. He attended the Royal College of Music, where he taught counterpoint from 1895 to 1903. He held several minor posts as organist before becoming principal organist of Temple Church in London in 1898. Between then and 1927, when he became organist of St. George's Chapel in Windsor, he received recognition throughout England as an organ virtuoso. He also led several notable English choral groups, such as the Bach Choir. From 1919 to 1926 he was professor of music at the University of Wales. He was knighted in 1922, and in 1934 he succeeded Sir Edward Elgar as Master of the King's Music. As a composer he is best known for his choral music; but he also wrote a considerable amount of orchestral and chamber music. His principal works for orchestra include a Symphony in G, *Children's Symphony*, Suite in C, *Festival Overture, Parthenia Suite, Memorial Suite,* and *Big Ben Looks On.* He also wrote a quintet and a chamber-music suite, *Peter Pan.*

Death and the Maiden Quartet. *See:* Quartet—*Schubert.*

Death and Transfiguration (Tod und Verklaerung). Tone poem for orchestra by Richard Strauss, op. 24 (1889), introduced in Eisenach on June 21, 1890, the composer conducting. A poem by Alexander Ritter serves as its program; but it is important to note that the poem was written after the music. "In the little room . . . lies a sick man on his bed. But just now he has wrestled despairingly

with Death . . . But Death does not long grant sleep and dreams to his victim. Cruelly, he shakes him awake, and the fight begins afresh . . . Sunk back, tired of battle, sleepless as in a fever-frenzy, the sick man now sees his life pass before his inner eyes. First the morning red of childhood. Then his saucier play of youth, till he ripens to man's fight, and now burns with the hot lust after the higher prizes of life. Cold and sneering, the world sets barrier upon barrier in the way of his achievement. And so he pushes forward, so he climbs. Then clangs the last stroke of Death's iron hammer . . . But from heavenly spaces sounds mightily to greet him what he yearningly sought for here: deliverance from the world, transfiguration of the world."

Though played without interruption, the tone poem has four sections. The first, *Sleep, Illness, Reverie,* serves as a slow introduction. A syncopated subject in second violins and violas symbolizes Death, and a melody for oboe speaks for youth. The turbulent section that follows is *Fever and Struggle with Death.* Here the transfiguration theme is given by trombones, cellos, and violas. In the third section—*Dreams, Childhood, Memories, Death*—the dying man recalls his early struggles, then engages in a bitter struggle with Death. Harps and tam-tam tell of his defeat. The finale is the "Transfiguration," which opens with the transfiguration theme in the horns. The theme grows passionate, but then succumbs to the deliverance and final transfiguration.

Death of Tintagiles, The. *See:* Maeterlinck, Maurice.

De Bériot, Charles. *See:* Bériot, Charles de.

Debussy, (Achille-) Claude, composer. Born Saint-Germain-en-Laye, France, Aug. 22, 1862; died Paris, France, March 25, 1918. From 1874 to 1884 he attended the Paris Conservatory, a pupil of Antoine Marmontel, Émile Durand, and Ernest Guiraud. In the summers of 1881 and 1882 he was the household pianist for Mme. von Meck, Tchaikovsky's patroness. In 1884 he won the Prix de Rome. His stay in Italy was unhappy, since he disliked the country and was upset by the severe criticisms levelled at him by the Conservatory authorities for the musical compositions he was required to send in. Without completing the prescribed three years, Debussy returned to Paris. There, at its cafés, he came into contact with the then current movements in French poetry and painting: Symbolists like Stéphane Mallarmé, and Impressionists like Édouard Manet and Pierre August Renoir. Their fresh, provocative ideas on poetry and art coincided with his own urge to open for music new horizons of expression. Given further direction in his musical thinking by the iconoclastic composer, Erik Satie, Debussy clarified his own mission and arrived at a style with which he was to revolutionize the French musical art. By adopting and exploiting certain technical devices—the whole-tone scale, unresolved discords, movement of chords independent of a tonal center, and new concepts of tone color and form—and by perfecting a style that combined refinement and delicacy with the most subtle feeling for nuance and color, Debussy arrived at musical Impressionism. Like Renoir and Manet in their paintings, he sought out the most elusive moods and the most sensitive atmospheres, to express the feelings and impressions aroused in him by a given subject rather than trying to present the subject itself. His music concerned itself less with emotion than with mood and effect. As the first great painter in music, Debussy became not only an innovator whose influence was to be felt by an entire generation, but also a creator of preeminent significance.

The first works in which his new style achieved full maturity were the Quartet in G major, introduced in 1893, and the orchestral prelude *The Afternoon of a Faun* (*L'Après-midi d'un faune*), a year later. After that came a succession of compositions that made their composer one of the most exciting new voices in French music and a fiercely disputed figure; a man who became something of a cult to his admirers and the object of vituperative criticism to his enemies. These works included major compositions for orchestra, for piano, for voice, and the opera, *Pelléas and Mélisande*.

In the last decade of his life, Debussy

suffered from cancer, for which he had to undergo two painful and debilitating operations. Physical suffering was combined with other problems and frustrations, including financial duress brought on by the outbreak of World War I, and his bitter disappointment in failing to gain a seat at the Académie de France. His death came when his morale and fortunes were at their lowest ebb. He was given a drab funeral because of the war, and his passing was virtually unnoticed.

Debussy's principal instrumental works follow.

Chamber Music: Quartet in G major; Rhapsody for saxophone and piano (or orchestra); Rhapsody for clarinet and piano; sonatas for cello and piano, for flute, viola, and harp, and for violin and piano.

Orchestra: Printemps; The Afternoon of a Faun (*L'Après-midi d'un faune*); *Danses sacrée et profane,* for harp and strings; Nocturnes; La Mer; Images.

Piano: Petite suite, for piano duet; 2 *Arabesques; Suite bergamasque; Pour le piano; Estampes; L'Isle joyeuse; Masques; Images; Children's Corner; La Plus que lent;* Preludes; Etudes; *Six épigraphes antiques,* for piano duet; *En blanc et noir,* for two pianos.

See: Afternoon of a Faun, The; Arabesque; Children's Corner; Estampes; En blanc et noir; Etude—*Debussy; Isle joyeuse, L'; Images; Mer, La;* Nocturne (2) —*Debussy;* Prelude—*Debussy;* Quartet—*Debussy;* Sonata—*Debussy.*

Deceptive cadence. A cadence in which a dominant chord is not followed by the tonic.

Deciso. Boldly, vigorously.

Decrescendo. *See:* Diminuendo.

Defauw, Désiré, conductor. Born Ghent, Belgium, Sept. 5, 1885. He attended Ghent Conservatory when he was eight, and was graduated with first prize in violin playing. He then performed throughout Europe as a violin virtuoso and as member of the Allied String Quartet. Turning to conducting, he led orchestral concerts at the Théâtre des Marais in Brussels and the symphony concerts of the Antwerp Royal Conservatory. He resigned both posts in 1925 to become professor at the Royal Conservatory in Brussels. He also served as music director of the National Institute of Radio, with which he conducted radio symphony concerts. He made his American début as conductor with the NBC Symphony on Dec. 9, 1939. From 1943 to 1947 he was principal conductor of the Chicago Symphony. Since then he has conducted the Grand Rapids Symphony in Michigan, and the Bloomington Normal Symphony in Indiana.

De Falla, Manuel. *See:* Falla, Manuel de.

Delicato. Delicately.

Deliciae basilienses. *See:* Symphony—*Honegger.*

Delius, Frederick, composer. Born Bradford, England, Jan. 29, 1862; died Grez-sur-Loing, France, June 10, 1934. The son of a prosperous wool merchant, Delius was first trained for business. For two years he worked in his father's establishment. In 1884 he came to Solano, Florida, where he purchased and supervised an orange plantation. Here he began studying the violin by himself and counterpoint and harmony with Thomas F. Ward. In 1886 he returned to Europe to attend the Leipzig Conservatory. His suite for orchestra, *Florida,* completed in 1886 impressed Grieg, then visiting Germany. Grieg used his influence on Delius' father to have the young man financed for a musical career. In 1888 Delius settled in Paris, where he wrote several ambitious works, including operas, and a *Legend* for violin and orchestra which became his first published work. On May 30, 1899, there took place in London the first concert devoted entirely to Delius' music.

In 1897 Delius married Jelka Rosen; they made their home in the little French town of Grez-sur-Loing, where Delius remained for the rest of his life. Henceforth he lived more or less the life of a recluse, devoting himself to composition. At this time he completed a series of works for orchestra which placed him in the vanguard of contemporary British composers. Delius was an Impressionist whose best works consisted of subtle and sensitive tone pictures; his music was the serene, contemplative and emotionally restrained expression of an artist who had divorced himself from the world outside his villa.

Recognition came slowly. It arrived first in Germany. In England, Delius won acceptance largely through the devoted efforts of Sir Thomas Beecham, whose continual performances of Delius' works over a period of more than two decades finally convinced the English public he was a composer of the first rank.

In the 1920's Delius' health began disintegrating. At first he was struck by paralysis, then by total blindness. But his infirmities did not arrest the flow of his music. Engaging the services of Eric Fenby as a musical secretary, Delius continued producing important works. When, in October 1929, Sir Thomas Beecham led a six-day festival of Delius' music in London, the composer was brought into the auditorium on a wheelchair to receive the greatest ovation of his career. Oxford presented him with an honorary degree; the King made him Companion of Honor; and the City of Bradford gave him the freedom of the city. Less than five years later he was dead.

The following are Delius' principal instrumental compositions.

Chamber Music: 3 violin sonatas; String Quartet; Cello Sonata.

Orchestra: Concertos for various solo instruments and orchestra (piano; violin; cello); *Over the Hills and Far Away; Paris: The Song of a Great City; Brigg Fair; In a Summer Garden;* 2 *Dance Rhapsodies; On Hearing the First Cuckoo in Spring; Summer Night on the River; North Country Sketches; Eventyr; A Song Before Sunrise; A Poem of Life and Love; A Song of the High Hills; A Song of the Summer.*

See: Brigg Fair; Eventyr; In a Summer Garden; On Hearing the First Cuckoo in Spring; Paris; Song of the High Hills, A; Song of Summer, A; Summer Night on the River; Walk to Paradise Garden, The.

Dello Joio, Norman, composer. Born New York City, Jan. 24, 1913. After attending the Institute of Musical Art and Juilliard Graduate School he studied composition with Paul Hindemith at the Berkshire Music Centre in Tanglewood, and organ privately with his godfather, Pietro Yon. In 1942 he received the Town Hall Composition Award for his *Magnificat,* for orchestra. He was given Guggenheim Fellowships in 1944 and 1945, a grant from the American Academy of Arts and Letters in 1946, the New York Music Critics Circle Award for *Variations, Chaconne and Finale* for orchestra in 1948, and the Pulitzer Prize in music for *Meditations on Ecclesiastes* in 1956. From 1944 to 1950 he was on the music faculty of Sarah Lawrence College in Bronxville, N.Y. In 1947 he toured Poland as a pianist in programs of his own works. Dello Joio writes in a neo-Classic style which prefers such old forms and materials as the ricercare, passacaglia, and chaconne, and Gregorian modes. These, however, are adapted to 20th-century techniques and idioms. His orchestral music includes a piano concertino, harp concerto, clarinet concerto, Sinfonietta, *American Landscape, Ricercare* for piano and orchestra, *Concert Piece, Variations, Chaconne and Finale, Three Symphonic Dances, Serenade, New York Profiles, Epigraph, Concert Music, Variations on a Theme*, and *Meditations on Ecclesiastes*. He also wrote a flute trio, Capriccio for violin and piano, *Duo Concertante* for cello and piano, 3 piano sonatas, and preludes and nocturnes for piano.

See: Meditations on Ecclesiastes; Ricercare; *Variations, Chaconne and Finale.*

Delvincourt, Claude, music educator and composer. Born Paris, France, Jan. 12, 1888; died Bivio di Albinia, Italy, April 5, 1954. He attended the Paris Conservatory, winning the Prix de Rome in 1913. During World War I he saw active service and was seriously wounded. After the war, he divided his activity between teaching and composition. After serving as director of the Versailles Conservatory, he held a similar post with the Paris Conservatory from 1941 until his death, which occurred in an automobile accident. As a composer he was most successful in his stage works, but he also wrote 2 orchestral suites, a violin sonata and other chamber-music works, piano pieces, and music for motion pictures.

Demisemiquaver. A thirty-second note.

Dent, Edward Joseph, musicologist and teacher. Born Ribston, England, July 16, 1876; died London, England, Aug. 22, 1957. He was educated at Eton and Cambridge. In 1902 he became Fellow of King's College at Cambridge, and from 1926 on was professor of music there. He also lectured at Cornell University in Ithaca, N.Y., in 1937. He helped organize the International Society for Contemporary Music in 1922, serving as its president up to 1938, and again in 1945. In 1931 he was appointed president of the Société Internationale de Musicologie. His lectures on music at Cambridge and his many articles in leading publications exerted a far-reaching influence; so did his music reviews in *The Athenaeum* (later *The Nation and Athenaeum*). He wrote biographies of Busoni (1933) and Handel (1934), *Music of the Renaissance in Italy* (1934), and books on opera. He also contributed articles to important dictionaries and encyclopedias.

De Pachmann, Vladimir. *See:* Pachmann, Vladimir de.

Demetrius. *See:* Schiller, Friedrich von.

De Sabata, Victor. *See:* Sabata, Victor de.

Des pas sur la neige. *See:* Prelude—*Debussy.*

Detroit Symphony Orchestra. An orchestra founded in Detroit, Mich., in 1914, with Weston Gales as conductor. Gales continued as conductor until the 1917-1918 season, supplemented by several guest conductors. One of these, Ossip Gabrilowitsch, served as principal conductor of a greatly enlarged orchestra and program of activity from 1918 until 1935, when he was succeeded by Victor Kolar. When the orchestra was reorganized in 1943, Karl Krueger became principal conductor. Three years later, the Detroit Symphony acquired its new home, Music Hall, dedicated with a symphony concert on Oct. 24, 1946. Krueger left the orchestra in 1949, when it was temporarily disbanded. It was again revived and reorganized in 1951, and in 1952 Paul Paray become conductor.

Development. (1) Elaboration of a theme or subject, or enlargement of a musical section.

(2) Middle section of the sonata form, preceded by the exposition, and followed by the recapitulation.

Devil's Trill Sonata (Il Trillo del diavolo). Sonata in G minor for violin and piano by Giuseppe Tartini (1713). Tartini revealed that his inspiration for this music came from a dream in which he heard the devil play a beautiful melody. "The work which this dream suggested," he went on to say, "is doubtless the best of my compositions." The sonata opens with a Larghetto in two-part song form. A brief trill leads to a Grave section. A series of staccato figures and trills introduce a second Grave section. The sonata ends with a spirited finale in which the trill that gave the sonata its name is prominent. This sonata is often performed in an edition by Fritz Kreisler. Liszt transcribed it for the piano.

Diabelli Variations (Beethoven). *See:* Variations on a Waltz by A. Diabelli.

Diamond, David, composer. Born Rochester, N.Y., July 9, 1915. He attended the Cleveland Institute of Music, Eastman School of Music, and the Dalcroze School in New York. After that he studied composition privately with Roger Sessions in New York and Nadia Boulanger in Paris. Among his early works is a *Psalm* for orchestra, introduced by the San Francisco Symphony. In 1938, 1941, and again in 1958, he received Guggenheim Fellowships, and in 1942 the American Academy in Rome Award. Many other honors have come his way, including the New York Music Critics Circle Award for *Rounds* and the Third String Quartet, the Paderewski Award in 1943, and a grant from the National Academy of Arts and Letters in 1944. A prolific composer, he has produced abundantly in all the instrumental forms. He has written 6 symphonies, 2 violin concertos, a cello concerto, and a concerto for chamber orchestra, and many shorter orchestral works (including *Elegy, The Enormous Room, Rounds, Romeo and Juliet, Timon of Athens: A Symphonic Portrait,* music for the *Tempest, Sinfonia Concertante,* and *The World of Paul Klee*). He has also written a piano sonata, 4 string quartets, piano quartet, concerto for string quartet, violin sonata, cello sonata, clarinet quintet, and piano trio.

See: Rounds.

Diapason. (1) Greek name for an octave. (2) A fundamental organ stop.

Diaphony. Greek term for dissonance as opposed to *symphonia,* or consonance. The term is also applied to medieval two-part polyphony.

Diatonic. Consisting of the tones of any major or minor key without any foreign sharps, flats, or naturals.

Dickens, Charles, novelist. Born Landsport, England, Feb. 7, 1812; died Gadshill, England, June 9, 1870. One of Dickens' most celebrated novels, *Pickwick Papers,* was the inspiration for the following instrumental works: Debussy's *Hommage à S. Pickwick, Esquire,* for piano, from the second book of preludes; Hans Gál's *A Pickwickian Overture,* for orchestra; Joseph Holbrooke's string quartet No. 3, *Pickwick Club;* and Norman O'Neill's incidental music to *Mr. Pickwick.* Dickens was also the stimulus for Jørgen Bentzon's Symphony No. 1 ("on motifs from Dickens") and Felix White's *A Dickens Notebook,* for piano.

Diémer, Louis, pianist and teacher. Born Paris, France, Feb. 14, 1843; died there Dec. 21, 1919. He attended the Paris Conservatory, where he won first prizes in piano, harmony, and fugue. After his graduation he scored major successes as a pianist in appearances with leading French orchestras. In 1889 he performed a monumental historical series of piano music in Paris. His interest in old music led him to help organize the Société des Anciens Instruments in Paris and to edit *Clavecinistes français.* From 1887 until his death he was a distinguished professor of the piano at the Paris Conservatory.

Dieren, Bernard van, composer. Born Rotterdam, Holland, Dec. 27, 1884; died London, England, April 24, 1936. He studied music in Germany and Holland. In 1909 he made his home permanently in London, where he wrote music criticisms for newspapers and magazines and devoted himself to composition. His music was advanced in technique and idiom and was most highly regarded by Cecil Gray and several other leading English musicians. His works include 4 string quartets, *Sonata Tyroica* for violin and piano, a choral symphony on Chinese texts, *Overture to an Ideal Comedy,* and pieces for the piano. He was the author of *Down Among the Dead Men* (1935).

Dies irae. A plainsong sequence whose

musical origin is unknown, with text by Thomas of Celano of the 13th century. This melody has been interpolated into many instrumental compositions, including Berlioz' *Symphonie fantastique;* Khatchaturian's Symphony No. 2; Liszt's *Totentanz;* Rachmaninoff's *Etude tableau* in C major, op. 39, no. 2, *Isle of the Dead,* and *Rhapsody on a Theme by Paganini;* Saint-Saëns' *Danse macabre;* Tchaikovsky's *Manfred.*

Diminished. (1) Intervals a semitone smaller than perfect or minor intervals.

(2) Chords including one or more diminished intervals.

Diminished seventh. A chord made up of bass, minor third, diminished fifth, and diminished seventh.

Diminuendo (or **Decrescendo**). Diminishing in sonority.

Diminution. Repetition of a theme by shortening the duration of each note, as opposed to augmentation.

D'Indy, Vincent. *See:* Indy, Vincent d'.

Discord. An inharmonious combination of tones.

Dissonant Quartet. *See:* Quartet—*Mozart.*

Dittersdorf, Karl Ditters von (born **Karl Ditters**), composer and violinist. Born Vienna, Austria, Nov. 2, 1739; died Castle Rothlhotta, Bohemia, Oct. 24, 1799. He studied the violin with private teachers, then played in the orchestra of St. Stephen's Cathedral and the private orchestra of Prince von Hildburghausen. The Prince arranged for him to study composition with Giuseppe Bonno, and violin with Trani. In 1761 Dittersdorf toured Italy with Gluck in joint concerts, and in 1764 he and Gluck performed at the coronation ceremonies of Archduke Joseph at Frankfort. In 1764 Dittersdorf became Kapellmeister for the Bishop of Grosswardein. When that orchestra was disbanded five years later, Dittersdorf assumed a similar post with Count von Schaffgotsch, Bishop of Breslau. Dittersdorf, who was made Knight of the Golden Spur in 1770 and given a title of nobility, worked for the Bishop until the latter's death in 1795, after which he served at the home of Count von Stillfried in Neuhaus, Bohemia. A prolific composer, Dittersdorf was at his best in oratorios and comic operas. But he was

productive in other fields as well. His instrumental music includes over a hundred symphonies, 35 concertos, 12 string quintets, 14 string trios, 17 violin sonatas, 30 piano sonatas, and many divertimentos, string quartets, and so forth. While he lacked the invention of Haydn and Mozart, he was an important influence in the early evolution of Classical style and form. Occasionally, his symphonies boasted effective tone painting.

Divertimento. A form popular in the late 18th century, actually a suite in a light style; it usually has more than four movements. Haydn and Mozart, who wrote many divertimentos, used this term interchangeably with serenade, so that it is often difficult to make a distinction between the two. The following are some of the representative compositions in this form:

BARTÓK. The Divertimento for String Orchestra (1939) is an interesting experiment in endowing this 18th-century structure with 20th-century idioms. It was introduced in Basel, Switzerland, on June 11, 1940 (I. *Allegro non troppo.* II. *Molto adagio.* III. *Allegro assai.*). An energetic theme is the main subject of the first movement and is given varied treatment; syncopated rhythms and dissonances provide spice, and abrupt contrasts of rhythm and tonality contribute surprise. The slow movement is emotional, with an affecting song in the muted violins against a background of chattering basses; the second theme, in violas, has a folk character. In the finale there is an outburst of gaiety carried to a whirlwind climax.

HAYDN. Some of Haydn's earliest quartets and symphonies were actually divertimentos. His most successful use of this form, however, is found in a set of six compositions for flute, two horns, string quartet, and bass, op. 31 (1775). In these divertimentos there are only three movements; and they are distinguished for their expressive, at times deeply emotional, slow movements; also for their skillful use of the theme and variations technique.

MOZART. Mozart wrote numerous divertimentos for string trio, string quartet, wind instruments, and mixed instrumental combinations. The Divertimento No. 15 in B-flat major, K. 287, is often heard. It is scored for strings and two horns and is in six short movements (I. Allegro. II. *Andante grazioso*. III. Minuet. IV. Adagio. V. Andante. VI. *Allegro molto*). Of especial interest are the second movement, six variations on a graceful theme; the beautiful melody of the fourth movement; and the finale, which makes witty use of a popular South-German tune.

The Divertimento No. 11 in D major, K. 251 (1776), for oboe, two horns and strings, was written to honor the twenty-fifth birthday of the composer's sister (I. *Allegro molto*. II. Minuet. III. Andantino. IV. Minuet. V. Rondo. VI. *Marcia alla francese*). In the opinion of Alfred Einstein, Mozart was here trying to remind his sister of their happy days in France together. The term "alla francese" appears in the first and concluding movements, suggesting a French style of writing.

Divertimento No. 16 in D major, K. 334 (1779), for two horns and strings, is actually in six movements, but it is a general practice now to present only four: I. Allegro; II. Andante; III. Minuet; IV. Allegro. The most famous movement is the third, one of the composer's most popular minuets, and one often heard in various transcriptions, notably for violin and piano.

Divertissement. (1) French equivalent of divertimento, a group of instrumental numbers combined into a suite.

(2) A fantasia on given melodies.

(3) Suite for orchestra by Jacques Ibert (1930), introduced in Paris on Nov. 30, 1930. This is music with a strong bent for satire (I. Introduction. II. *Cortège*. III. Nocturne. IV. Valse. V. *Parade*. VI. Finale). The saucy introduction sets the mood of levity that prevails throughout the work. In the second movement a few introductory bars usher in a march theme for strings; this is followed by a second march subject for trumpet. Towards the end of this section there appears a quotation from Mendelssohn's popular *Wedding March*. The next movement is a twenty-six bar mood picture, followed by a satirical waltz in which

Johann Strauss' *Blue Danube* is referred to. *Parade* brings back the march-like character of the second movement with interesting dynamics. The suite ends with a boisterous movement in which the main melody sounds like an Offenbach can-can. Here the piano adds to the hilarity by interpolating strident, dissonant harmonies.

Divine Comedy, The. *See:* Dante Alighieri.

Divine Poem, The. *See:* Symphony—Scriabin.

Divisi. A term indicating the division into two or more parts of a group of performers normally playing in unison.

Dobrowen, Issai, conductor. Born Nizhny Novgorod, Russia, Feb. 27, 1893; died Oslo, Norway, Dec. 9, 1953. He attended the Moscow Conservatory, from which he was graduated in 1911 with the Great Gold Medal. After additional study of the piano in Vienna with Leopold Godowsky, he made his conducting début at the Moscow Grand Theater. Though he subsequently achieved his greatest successes in opera, and mainly in the Russian repertory, he was also a significant symphonic conductor. From 1931 through 1933 he was principal conductor of the San Francisco Symphony, and in 1937 he was appointed permanent conductor of the then recently founded Palestine Symphony. He also appeared as guest with major European and American orchestras. During World War II he went to live in Scandinavia, where he achieved some of the most impressive successes of his career in opera and symphony.

Doctor Gradus ad Parnassum (Debussy). *See:* Children's Corner.

Dodecaphony. Synonym for twelve-tone music. *See:* Schoenberg, Arnold.

Dohnányi, Ernst von, composer, pianist, and conductor. Born Pressburg, Hungary, July 27, 1877. He attended the Budapest Academy, where his teachers included Stefan Thomán and Hans Koessler, and from which he was graduated in 1897. After completing two major works—a piano quintet and a symphony—he continued study of the piano with Eugène d'Albert. Dohnányi made his début as a pianist in Berlin on Oct. 1, 1897, after which he toured Europe and the United States. From 1908 to 1911 he was professor of the piano at the Berlin High School for Music. In 1919 he was appointed director of the Budapest Conservatory, and in 1934 director of the Budapest Landesakademie. Dohnányi was also principal conductor of the Budapest Philharmonic for about thirty years, and one of the conductors of the State Symphony in New York in 1926. In 1949 he settled permanently in the United States, becoming a member of the music faculty at Florida State College in Tallahassee.

Dohnányi is most often represented on concert programs by compositions of his early manhood. These are Romantic works filled with a spontaneous lyricism, in which his indebtedness to Brahms is pronounced. He never quite succeeded in achieving a personal identity; his music has remained true to the German Romantic traditions of the late 19th century. But his finest works maintain interest because of their craftsmanship, interesting instrumentation, and freshly conceived melodies. His most famous compositions are the *Variations on a Nursery Song* for piano and orchestra, the Suite in F-sharp minor for orchestra, and *Ruralia Hungarica* for piano and also for orchestra. Other orchestral compositions include 2 symphonies, 2 violin concertos, 2 piano concertos, a harp concertino and *Minutes symphoniques*. He also wrote 2 piano quintets, 3 string quartets, a sextet, a cello sonata, and a violin sonata; his many pieces for the piano include bagatelles, rhapsodies, etudes, humoresques, pieces, *Winterreigen*, and *Variations on a Hungarian Folksong*.

See: Suite—*Dohnányi; Variations on a Nursery Song.*

Dolce. Sweetly.

Dolente (or **Doloroso**). Sad, sorrowful.

Dolly. Suite of six pieces for children, for piano duet, by Gabriel Fauré, op. 56 (1893). Its movements are: I. *Berceuse;* II. *Mi-a-ou;* III. *Le Jardin de Dolly;* IV. *Kitty-Valse;* V. *Tendresse;* VI. *Le Pas espagnol.* It was orchestrated by Henri Rabaud and used as music for a ballet.

Dolmetsch, Arnold, instrument maker and musical antiquarian. Born Le Mans, France, Feb. 24, 1858; died Haslemere,

England, Feb. 28, 1940. He came from a family of professional musicians and instrument makers, and early was directed to music. He studied the violin in Brussels with Henri Vieuxtemps, after which he attended the Royal College of Music in London, where his interest in old music was encouraged by George Grove. In 1899 he discovered a manuscript cache of old English music at the British Museum, an event that decided him to dedicate himself henceforth to the seeking out of old music in manuscript and to construct the types of instruments for which it was originally intended. In 1890 he gave his first concert of old music in London, on instruments of his own construction. From 1905 to 1909 he worked for Chickering in Boston, and from 1911 to 1914 for Gaveau in Paris, assisting in the production of harpsichords, clavichords, lutes, and viols from old pictures and descriptions. He also published *The Interpretation of the Music of the 17th and 18th Centuries* (1915). In 1914 he made his home in Haslemere, where after World War I he built modern recorders. In 1925 he initiated there festivals of old music on old instruments in which he, his wife, and their children participated up to the time of his death. In 1928 the Dolmetsch Foundation was organized to promote old music.

Doloroso. *See: Dolente.*

Domestic Symphony. *See:* Symphony— *Richard Strauss.*

Dominant. (1) Fifth note of a scale or key.

(2) Chord built on the fifth note.

Dominant seventh. Chord on the fifth degree of the key, made up of a major triad plus a minor third.

Don Carlos. *See:* Schiller, Friedrich von.

Don Giovanni, Overture to. Overture to an opera by Mozart. The libretto, by Lorenzo da Ponte, was based on a play by Giovanni Bertati. The opera received its first performance in Prague on Oct. 29, 1787. The overture opens with thirty measures of portentous music foretelling the doom of Don Giovanni. This music reappears in the opera's closing scene. The mood of the overture then lightens; the vivacious themes that follow portray different facets of the Don's personality, and provide a clue to some of his adventures.

For another orchestral excerpt from this opera *see:* Minuet.

Don Juan. Tone poem for orchestra by Richard Strauss, op. 20 (1889), first performed in Weimar on Nov. 11, 1889, Hans von Buelow conducting. This was Strauss' second tone poem, its inspiration being a poem by Nicolaus Lenau. Strauss himself provided no specific program for his music beyond explaining that his Don Juan was "no hotblooded man eternally pursuing women" but a man "longing to find a woman who to him is incarnate womanhood and to enjoy in the one all the women on earth whom he cannot possess as an individual." Strauss goes on to say: "Because he cannot find her . . . at last disgust seizes hold of him and this disgust is the devil come to fetch him."

An upward sweep of the strings, with which the tone poem opens, depicts Don Juan's ardor. His longing is then expressed in a tender passage for strings. Various love episodes follow, highlighted by a passionate song for the oboe, repeated by the clarinet. The music grows more sensual as Don Juan passes from love to debauchery. A dissonant chord appears at the climax to be followed by a sudden silence. A quivering orchestral passage tells of the Don's disgust.

Don Quixote. (1) Tone poem for orchestra by Richard Strauss, op. 35 (1897), introduced in Cologne on March 8, 1898, Franz Wuellner conducting. Subtitled by the composer "Fantastic Variations on a Theme of Knightly Character," this tone poem is in three sections: Introduction, Theme and Variations, and Finale. Don Quixote is represented by a solo cello; his squire, Sancho Panza, by tenor tuba and bass clarinet, and later by solo viola. In the introduction Don Quixote is found in his study poring over his chivalric lore. After an opening subject for the woodwind, a lyrical theme appears in the strings. Unrelated chords tell of the Don's growing confusion, and dissonant chords suggest his imminent madness. The theme and variations section now appears. The theme has a mock heroic character; it is presented by the solo cello and is a description of Don Quixote. A comic idea

in tenor tuba and bass clarinet represents Sancho Panza. In the ensuing ten variations we witness the varied exploits of the knight errant: the fight with the windmills; the battle with sheep which appear to him like a mighty army (muted brass simulate the bleating of the animals); the skirmish with a band of pilgrims; the appearance of Dulcinea in a vision; the Don's search for the Ideal Woman (the latter found in a melody for solo cello interrupted by a cadenza for harp and strings); the attempted flight through the air on a wooden horse (in this section Strauss introduces a wind machine); a voyage on a boat believed by the Don to have been sent him by supernatural powers (the orchestra presents a barcarolle melody); the encounter with the monks; the Don's defeat at the hands of one of his townsmen disguised as the Knight of the White Moon. The Don returns home disillusioned. In the finale, his death is described. The Don Quixote theme in the cello is touched by tragedy. Consonant chords create a serene setting as the Don passes away peacefully.

(2) *See:* Cervantes, Miguel de.

Dorati, Antal, conductor. Born Budapest, Hungary, April 9, 1906. He was graduated in 1924 from the Budapest Academy, where his teachers included Béla Bartók and Zoltán Kodály; he was one of the youngest men ever to receive a degree there. He served his conducting apprenticeship with several opera companies and with opera performances over the French National Radio. From 1934 to 1940 he was principal conductor of the Ballet Russe, with which he toured Europe and the United States. His American début as symphony conductor took place in Washington, D.C., in December 1937 with the National Symphony. In 1941 he settled permanently in the United States, becoming a citizen in 1947. After leading various ballet and opera organizations, he became principal conductor of the newly reorganized Dallas Symphony in 1945. Under his leadership it became an orchestra of national significance. In 1949 he succeeded Dimitri Mitropoulos as principal conductor of the Minneapolis Symphony, becoming its music director in

1955. He also appeared in Europe and South America.

Dorian Fugue. Johann Sebastian Bach's Fugue in D minor which follows a toccata in the same key. The fugue suggests the Dorian mode without being written strictly in that tonality.

Dorian mode. A medieval scale similar to that on the piano beginning and ending with "D" and utilizing only the white keys.

Double-bass (or **Contrabass,** or **Bass Viol**). The largest in size, and the lowest in pitch, of the violin family. Its strings from low to high are E-A-D-G, and its range is from E in the third octave below middle C up to about middle C.

Double bassoon (or **Contrabassoon**). *See:* Bassoon.

Double concerto. A concerto for two instruments and orchestra, for example Bach's Concerto for Two Violins and Orchestra, or Brahms' Concerto for Violin, Cello and Orchestra.

Double counterpoint (or **invertible counterpoint**). Counterpoint in which two themes are played simultaneously, and which can be inverted so that the treble can become the bass, and the bass the treble.

Double fugue. A fugue in which subject and countersubject appear simultaneously.

Double stop. Two tones played simultaneously on a string instrument.

Dowland, John, lutenist and composer. Born Ireland, December 1562; died London, England, Jan. 21, 1626. He went to England in or about 1578, and two years later went on to Paris, where he entered the service of the English Ambassador to France. After a period of study with Luca Marenzio, he served as lutenist for the King of Denmark from 1598 to 1609. He later was lutenist in England for Lord Walden and Charles I. He was one of the foremost lutenists of his generation. As a composer, Dowland is most famous for his songs, or "ayres." But he also wrote pieces for the lute, remarkable for their harmonic as well as melodic inventiveness. His most important instrumental work is *Lachrymae, or Seven Teares Figured in Seven Passionate Pavans,* for lute, viols, or violins, in five parts (1605); an edition in modern notation was issued in London by Peter Warlock in 1927.

Down beat. The downward movement of a conductor's arm which designates the first beat of a bar.

Downes, Olin, music critic. Born Evanston, Ill., Jan. 27, 1886; died New York City, Aug. 22, 1955. After studying piano with Carl Baermann, music history with Louis Kelterborn, and music appreciation with J. P. Marshall, he served as music critic of the *Boston Post* from 1906 to 1924; and from 1924 until his death he was music critic of the *New York Times.* He was also active as lecturer and radio commentator. His books include *The Lure of Music* (1918), *Symphonic Broadcasts* (1931), *Symphonic Masterpieces* (1935). A collection of his criticisms for the *New York Times* was published posthumously, edited by his widow, Irene Downes, *Olin Downes on Music* (1957).

Dragonetti, Domenico, double-bass player. Born Venice, Italy, April 7, 1763; died London, England, April 16, 1846. One of the most celebrated double-bass virtuosos of his generation, Dragonetti turned to this instrument after studying the violin and guitar. He made such progress on the double-bass that by the time he was thirteen he was engaged for the orchestra of the Teatro San Benedetto in Venice. He then played the double-bass at St. Mark's Cathedral, and held many important posts not only in Italy but also in Russia and England for over half a century. He possessed remarkable technical skill, and with it a consummate musicianship and a rare gift for sight reading. He was a personal friend of both Haydn and Beethoven. During the Beethoven festival in Bonn in 1845 he played in the double-bass section of the orchestra. Berlioz reported that he rarely heard the double-bass part of the Scherzo of Beethoven's Fifth Symphony played as nimbly as Dragonetti played it. Dragonetti wrote many works for his instrument, including a concerto that has been recorded.

Dresden, Sem, composer and teacher. Born Amsterdam, Holland, April 20, 1881; died The Hague, Holland, July 31, 1957. After studying with various teachers, including Bernard Zweers and Hans

Pfitzner, he became music critic of several important Dutch newspapers, serving in this capacity from 1918 on. From 1924 to 1929 he was director of the Royal Conservatory at The Hague, and from 1929 to 1937 of the Amsterdam Conservatory. He returned to the Conservatory at The Hague in 1937, helping to reorganize it after World War II. In 1945 he was appointed a member of the State Commission for Orchestra and Opera by the Dutch government. Dresden was one of Holland's most distinguished 20th-century composers. He was originally influenced by the German Romantics of the late 19th century, but he soon achieved a personal style that was economical, precise, and characterized by a subtle rhythm derived from the music of the polyphonic era. His orchestral works include numerous concertos for various solo instruments and orchestra (violin; oboe; organ; piano; flute), together with a Sinfonietta for clarinet and orchestra, and Variations. He was also the composer of 3 sextets for piano and winds, 2 cello sonatas, a flute sonata, a string quartet on old Dutch melodies, a sonata for violin solo, and a suite for cello solo.

Dresden State Orchestra. A symphony orchestra in Dresden, Germany, which first became prominent under the direction of Ernst von Schuch, its principal conductor from 1877 to 1914. Fritz Busch was principal conductor from 1922 to 1933, and from 1934 until World War II the orchestra was led by Karl Boehm. After World War II the orchestra was reorganized and Rudolf Kempe was appointed conductor. It has toured Europe several times.

Drone bass. A sustained tone suggesting the drone of a bagpipe.

Drum. A percussion instrument in which sound is produced by striking a skin stretched tightly over a frame. The drums most often encountered in symphony orchestras are the timpani (or kettledrums), bass drum, and side drum.

Drum Roll Symphony. *See:* Symphony—*Haydn.*

Duerer, Albrecht, painter. *See:* Painters and Paintings.

Duet. A composition for two instruments; also for two players at one keyboard instrument.

Dukas, Paul, composer. Born Paris, France, Oct. 1, 1865; died there, May 17, 1935. He attended the Paris Conservatory, where he won several prizes and the second Prix de Rome. After a period of military service he devoted himself to composition, first attracting notice with *Polyeucte,* a concert overture successfully introduced in Paris in 1892. Success came with the work by which he is still most often remembered, the orchestral scherzo, *The Sorcerer's Apprentice* (*L'Apprenti sorcier*) in 1897. Never a prolific composer, Dukas after 1910 destroyed most of the little he had produced. His best music is fastidious in workmanship, and often has a classic serenity. In 1910 he became professor of orchestration, and in 1927 professor of composition, at the Paris Conservatory. In 1918 he succeeded Debussy as member of the Conseil de l'Enseignement Supérieur, and a few months before his death he was made a member of the Académie des Beaux-Arts. Besides the compositions already mentioned, Dukas' instrumental works include a symphony, the dance poem *La Péri,* a piano sonata, various smaller pieces for the piano (including Variations, Interlude and Finale on a theme by Rameau and *Prélude élégiaque*), and *La Villanelle,* for horn and piano.

See: Sorcerer's Apprentice, The.

Duke, Vernon (born **Vladimir Dukelsky**), composer. Born Pskov, Russia, Oct. 10, 1903. Revolution broke out in Russia while he was attending the Kiev Conservatory. The Dukelsky family fled and came to the United States in 1921 by way of Constantinople. For a while he earned his living by filling various menial jobs. In 1924 he returned to Europe, where he was discovered by Serge Diaghilev and Koussevitzky. During the next decade, following his return to the United States, Duke was extensively performed by the Boston Symphony under Koussevitzky. Until the middle 1950's, Duke used his original name of Vladimir Dukelsky for all his serious compositions, reserving the pseudonym of Vernon Duke for his popular songs and lighter scores for Broadway and Hollywood. But since then he has assumed the legal name of Vernon Duke for all his music, serious as well as popular. He is the author of an autobiography, *Passport to Paris* (1955). His major orchestral works include 3 symphonies, a cello concerto, violin concerto, *Ode to the Milky Way*, and Ballade for piano and orchestra. He also wrote a string quartet, a violin sonata, and several other compositions for chamber-music combinations, as well as a sonata, *Surrealist Suite*, and *Serenade to San Francisco*, all for piano.

Dumbarton Oaks Concerto. *See:* Concerto—*Stravinsky.*

Dumka (plural Dumky). A Russian term signifying a "passing thought." As used by Dvořák it designates a slow and elegiac piece of music. Dvořák's Trio in E minor is called the "Dumky Trio." Dvořák also wrote *dumky* for the piano: *Dumka and Furiant* in C minor, op. 12, and *Dumka* in D minor, op. 35. Tchaikovsky wrote a *Dumka* for the piano, op. 59. There is also a *Dumka* in Alexander Tansman's *Four Polish Dances*, for orchestra.

Dupré, Marcel, organist and composer. Born Rouen, France, May 3, 1886. He began studying the organ when he was seven. At ten he performed from memory several Bach preludes and fugues at the Rouen Exhibition. He then attended the Paris Conservatory, receiving many prizes and the Prix de Rome in 1914. Two years later he was appointed organist of Notre Dame in Paris. He resigned six years after that to devote himself to concert work. Early in 1920 he performed over 200 works by Bach in ten recitals, all from memory. On Nov. 18, 1921, he made his American début in New York, following this with a tour of the United States in which he gave 94 concerts in 85 cities. In 1934 he succeeded Widor as organist of St. Sulpice in Paris, and the following spring he officiated at the wedding of the Duke of Windsor (formerly Edward VIII of England) to Wallis Warfield Simpson. In 1947 he was appointed director of the American Conservatory at Fontainebleau, France, and in 1954 director of the Paris Conservatory. He wrote many pieces for the organ, including symphonies, concertos, and educational works. At his recitals he often improvised four-movement symphonies on themes provided him by musicians in the audience.

Dur. German for major, as opposed to "moll" for minor.

Dushkin, Samuel, violinist. Born Suwalki, Poland, Dec. 13, 1897. A child prodigy, he toured Europe in his tenth year, and one year after that came to the United States, where he attended the Music School Settlement in New York. He then returned to Europe to attend the Paris Conservatory, and after that to study privately with Fritz Kreisler and Leopold Auer. After World War I he toured Europe, and in 1924 made his American début as soloist with the New York Symphony. A friend of Stravinsky, he has often appeared with the composer in joint recitals devoted to Stravinsky's works. He also made violin transcriptions of several Stravinsky compositions and presented the world première of a violin concerto written for him by Stravinsky.

Dusk of the Gods, The (Wagner). *See: Ring of the Nibelungs, The; Twilight of the Gods, The.*

Dussek, Jan (Johann) Ladislav, composer and pianist. Born Cáslav, Bohemia, Feb. 12, 1760; died Saint-Germain-en-Laye, France, March 20, 1812. He began to study the piano when he was five, and the organ at nine. As a chorister in a Minorite Church in Iglau he received music instruction at a Jesuit college, where he subsequently became organist. He then settled in Prague, receiving there a degree from the University. He now planned to enter the church, but an Austrian artillery officer persuaded him to engage professionally in music instead. For a while, Dussek was organist in a leading church in Bergen-op-Zoom. In 1762 he settled in Amsterdam, achieving there a leading position in its musical life as composer, pianist, and teacher. Still dissatisfied with himself, he proceeded to Hamburg for further study, with Carl Philipp Emanuel Bach. A piano recital at Berlin in 1784 put him in the front rank of European piano virtuosos of that period, a position he solidified with tours of Germany, Russia, Poland, France, and England. From 1788 to 1792 he lived in London, where he opened a music shop which ruined him financially and compelled him to flee to Germany to escape debtor's prison. He gave many concerts in Germany, and entered the service of several powerful patrons, both in that country and in France. Illness finally compelled him to retire to Saint-Germain-en-Laye, where he died.

Dussek's most significant music is for the piano. While none of these compositions appear any longer on concert programs, they are still used advantageously by piano students. Dussek helped advance piano style and technique at a time when the piano was still in its infancy; in some of his sonatas he anticipated the keyboard style of such later masters as Beethoven, Schumann, and Liszt. He wrote 12 piano concertos, almost 40 piano sonatas and many sonatinas, rondos, waltzes, variations, fantasies, and so forth. He also wrote piano quintets, quartets, trios, and violin sonatas.

Dvořák, Antonin, composer. Born Mühlhausen, Bohemia, Sept. 8, 1841; died Prague, Bohemia, May 1, 1904. Dvořák's father, an innkeeper, planned to have his son follow in his footsteps. As a boy, Dvořák was sent to Zlonice to study German. There he acquired his first sympathetic teacher in Antonin Liehmann, who taught him the organ, piano, and viola. In 1857 Dvořák entered the Prague Organ School, where he remained two years. He then found a job as violist in the orchestra of the National Theater, where he remained for more than a decade. From 1873 to 1877 he was organist of St. Adalbert's Church. On March 9, 1873, his first ambitious work—*Hymnus* for chorus and orchestra—was introduced in Prague; and in 1875 he won the Austrian State Prize for a symphony.

While working in the National Theater orchestra he came to know its conductor, Bedrich Smetana. The latter aroused in Dvořák enthusiasm for Bohemian national music. Dvořák now destroyed many of his early compositions, in which he had imitated the German Romantics and especially Wagner, and started writing Bohemian music. In this new vein he produced among other compositions a comic folk opera and a set of vocal duets entitled *Airs from Moravia;* the latter brought him an annual stipend from the Austrian State Commission.

One of the members of that Commission was Brahms, who now became interested in Dvořák. Through Brahms, Dvořák acquired a powerful publisher in Simrock, and succeeded in getting major performances for his compositions. Also on Brahms' urging, Simrock commissioned Dvořák to write a set of *Slavonic Dances* similar to Brahms' own *Hungarian Dances*. These *Dances* proved so popular throughout Europe that they established Dvořák's reputation. He was now besieged by commissions for new music and invitations to conduct his works with major orchestras everywhere. When, in 1884, he appeared in London for three concerts devoted entirely to his compositions he was given a tumultuous ovation.

In 1892 Dvořák came to the United States to fill the post of director of the National Conservatory in New York. He remained three years, a period in which he became interested in the musical idioms of the American Indian and Negro. He was inspired to write several major works in those styles, including his celebrated *Symphony from the New World* and the *American Quartet*. Homesickness finally drove him back to Bohemia in 1895. Six years later he became director of the Prague Conservatory, a post he held until the end of his life. As the most eminent musician in Bohemia he was honored by becoming the first musical figure to receive an appointment to a life membership in the Austrian House of Lords. He died of an apoplectic stroke, and his funeral on May 5, 1904, was decreed a national day of mourning.

His greatest music is that in which he projected Bohemian landscapes, feast days, ceremonies, folksongs, and dances. But he was also able to produce significant works in which the Bohemian element is not pronounced. His music is Romantic, filled with lyrical thoughts of surpassing charm, infectious rhythms, sensitive feelings, and an unfailing capacity to project beauty. These works are embedded in the soil of German Romanticism, especially the Romanticism of Brahms; and this is true whether Dvořák was writing Bohemian music or music of an American character.

The following are Dvořák's principal instrumental compositions.

Chamber Music: 13 string quartets (including the famous *American Quartet*); 3 string quintets (including the Quintet in E-flat major); 5 piano trios (including the *Dumky Trio*); 2 piano quintets; string sextet; violin sonata; violin sonatina.

Orchestra: 7 published symphonies (including the *Symphony from the New World*); various concertos (violin; cello; piano); *Symphonic Variations; Three Slavonic Rhapsodies; Slavonic Dances;*

My Home; Legends; Scherzo capriccioso; three overtures collectively entitled *Nature, Life and Love* (*In Nature's Realm, Carnival,* and *Othello*); 5 tone poems based on ballads by K. J. Erben (*The Water Sprite, The Midday Witch, The Golden Spinning Wheel, The Wood Dove,* and *Heroic Song*).

Piano: Silhouettes; Theme and Variations; Suite; *dumky,* waltzes, mazurkas, and humoresques (including the popular Humoresque op. 101, no. 7).

See: Carnival; Concerto—*Dvořák;* Humoresque; *In Nature's Realm; Legends; Nature, Life and Love;* Quartet—*Dvořák;* Quintet—*Dvořák; Scherzo capriccioso; Slavonic Dances; Slavonic Rhapsodies;* Symphony—*Dvořák;* Trio—*Dvořák.*

Dynamics. Intensity of sound, degrees of loudness or softness.

E

Earl of Oxford's March. *See:* Byrd, William.

Earl of Salisbury Pavane and Galliard. *See:* Byrd, William.

École des femmes, L'. *See:* Molière.

Ecossaise. A dance in 2/4 or 3/4 time said to be of Scottish origin, though this is doubtful. It has been used as a form of piano music with a Scottish character. Beethoven wrote 7 ecossaises in E-flat (1823-1825) and an eighth in G major (date unknown). Three ecossaises by Chopin are gathered in op. 72 (1826). Schubert wrote numerous piano pieces in this form between 1815 and 1826; some are found in opp. 18, 33, and 67.

Edinburgh International Festival of Music and Drama. A leading music festival of Europe, organized in Edinburgh, Scotland, in 1947 by Mrs. John Christie and Rudolf Bing; the latter was artistic director. Bing's success at Edinburgh led to his appointment in 1950 as general manager of the Metropolitan Opera in New

York; he was succeeded by Ian Hunter. The first festival began on August 24 and continued until September 13, its program of activity embracing opera, ballet, drama, and 20 concerts of orchestral, chamber, and solo music. Many orchestras, chamber-music groups, and soloists came from other parts of Europe. Variety of program has continued as one of the major attractions of this festival. In 1951 the festival became the first in Europe to invite a major American symphony orchestra to participate, the New York Philharmonic under Dimitri Mitropoulos. The Boston Symphony under Charles Munch performed at the 1956 festival.

Egk, Werner, composer. Born Auchsesheim, Germany, May 17, 1901. Though he received some music instruction in Augsburg and Munich, he was virtually self-taught. He planned a literary career but a visit to Italy decided him to turn to music professionally. Making his home in Munich, he devoted himself mainly to composition, achieving his first successes with radio music, incidental music for plays, and several operas. He was also active as conductor in Munich and Berlin. In 1949 he settled in Berlin and from 1950 to 1953 was director of the High School of Music. Egk brings to his musical writing the rhythmic and harmonic style of Stravinsky and the contemporary French. He has a fine gift for orchestration, and a rich lyricism which is sometimes colored by folksong. His orchestral music includes *Georgica* (three peasant pieces), *Geigenmusik* for violin and orchestra, *Allegria*, *Orchestersonate*, and *Franzoesische Suite* based on Rameau.

Egmont Overture. Concert overture by Beethoven, op. 84 (1810). This is a part of the incidental music written for the Goethe tragedy and commissioned by Joseph Hartl, director of the Vienna court theaters. The tragedy, with Beethoven's music, was performed for the first time in Vienna on May 24, 1810. Besides the overture, the incidental music comprises 9 numbers: four orchestral entr'actes; two songs for soprano; music describing the death of Clärchen; a "melodrama"; and a finale. Only the overture has remained popular. It opens with a majestic statement by violins speaking of Egmont's heroism in liberating the Netherlands from Spanish rule. A second forceful subject later appears in the strings. These melodies are developed dramatically, and a powerful climax is reached. The coda consists of a fanfare for full orchestra.

Eight Russian Folksongs. Suite for orchestra by Anatol Liadov, op. 58 (1906). This is one of several works by the composer influenced by his researches into Russian folk music. I. Religious Chant. This melody, heard in English horn and bassoons, is said to have been sung by children in religious processions. II. Christmas Carol. A gentle melody, presented by oboes and clarinets, tells about Christmas fairies who appear at dawn in a golden sled drawn by six reindeer. III. Plaintive Melody. This is a village song for solo voice. IV. Scherzo: I Danced With a Mosquito. This humorous episode for muted strings suggests the buzzing of the mosquito while rhythmic figures in the woodwind provide the basic dance

tune. V. Legend of the Birds. In this song the voices of birds are imitated. VI. Cradle Song. This is a melancholy berceuse for strings (without the double-basses). VII. Round Dance. A lively dance appears in strings, piccolo, and tambourine. VIII. Village Dance Song. The song of the finale is associated with the crowning of the May Queen, and is a vibrant melody for full orchestra meant to accompany village dancing.

Eine kleine Nachtmusik (A Little Night Music). Serenade in G major for string orchestra by Mozart, K. 525 (1787). It was originally written as a string quintet. While most serenades are in five movements, this one is only in four; it is believed that an additional minuet has been lost (I. Allegro. II. Romanze. III. Menuetto. IV. Allegro). The first movement is gay and brisk, with two light themes and no development to speak of. In the Romanze a sentimental melody is followed by two vivacious sections; after each of these the melody is repeated. A graceful and formal minuet and a vivacious rondo are the two concluding movements.

Ein' feste Burg ist unser Gott. A setting by Martin Luther of the 46th Psalm. It became the battle song of the Reformation and since then has entered the Protestant hymn book. Johann Sebastian Bach adapted the melody for an organ prelude. Several instrumental compositions quote this hymn: Debussy's *En Blanc et noir,* for two pianos; Mendelssohn's *Reformation Symphony;* Meyerbeer's overture to *Les Huguenots;* Joachim Raff's overture, *Ein' feste Burg;* and Wagner's *Kaisermarsch.*

Ein musikalischer Spass (Mozart). *See: Musical Joke, A.*

Einem, Gottfried von, composer. Born Bern, Switzerland, Jan. 24, 1918. The son of an Austrian military attaché, he was brought to Austria as a child. Frequent attendance at the Salzburg festivals, and personal meetings with Toscanini and Bruno Walter, encouraged him to become a musician. He went to Berlin in 1938 and for a short while worked as coach at the Berlin State Opera and in Bayreuth. Arrested by the Gestapo, he was incarcerated for several months. After his release he studied composition for two years with Boris Blacher. His first important work to be performed was the Capriccio for orchestra in 1943; this was followed by the Concerto for Orchestra and a ballet, *Princess Turandot*. In 1945 he settled in Salzburg, where he completed an opera that made him famous, *Dantons Tod*, introduced at the Salzburg festival in 1947. Early in 1953 Einem paid a visit to the United States as guest of the American State Department; on that occasion the New York Philharmonic under Mitropoulos gave the American première of his *Orchestra Music*. Besides the works already mentioned, Einem's orchestral compositions include a Serenade for double string orchestra, *Meditations, Symphonic Scenes*, and Ballade. He also wrote a violin sonata.

Einstein, Alfred, musicologist. Born Munich, Germany, Dec. 30, 1880; died El Cerrito, Calif., Feb. 13, 1952. He was a cousin of the renowned scientist, Albert Einstein. Alfred Einstein studied law before deciding on music as a career. After studying music at the Munich University he was appointed in 1913 music critic of the Munich *Post*. In 1918 he became editor of the *Zeitschrift für Musikwissenschaft*. After settling in Berlin in 1927 he served for six years as music critic of the *Berliner Tageblatt*. He left Germany upon the rise of the Nazi regime, and for several years lived in England and elsewhere. In 1938 he made the United States his permanent home, becoming a citizen, and from 1939 until his death was professor of music history at Smith College. In 1949-1950 he was visiting professor at Yale and Princeton. One of Einstein's most distinguished contributions to music scholarship was his revision of the Koechel catalogue of Mozart's works (1937), now a definitive authority for the chronology of Mozart's compositions. Among Einstein's books are a study of Mozart (1945), *A Short History of Music* (1936), *Greatness in Music* (1941), *Music in the Romantic Era* (1947), and *Schubert: A Musical Portrait* (1950).

Eisenberg, Maurice, cellist. Born Koenigsberg, Germany, Feb. 24, 1900. He came to the United States in childhood, then attended the Peabody Conservatory in Baltimore. For an extended period he played the cello in the Philadelphia Orchestra and the New York Symphony. He then went to Europe, attending the Leipzig Conservatory and the École Normale de Musique in Paris; he also studied privately with Pablo Casals. His concert début took place at Paris in 1926, after which he toured Europe and the United States. From 1930 to 1937 he was head of the Casals class at the École Normale. He was also head of the cello departments of the New York College of Music, the Philadelphia Musical Academy, and since 1953 at the Longy School of Music in Cambridge, Mass. He is the artistic director of the International Cello Center in London and author of *Cello Playing Today* (1957).

El Corpus en Sevilla (Albéniz). *See: Iberia* (1).

Electra. *See:* Euripides, Sophocles.

Electronic Music. Music or musical sounds produced by electrophonic instruments through electromagnetic vibrations converted into soundwaves by means of a loudspeaker, or through various electronic devices. *See:* Concrete Music.

Elegy. (1) A short sad poem usually lamenting the passing of a person. In music it connotes a short composition of melancholy character commemorating someone deceased. One of the most familiar works in this form is the *Élégie* of Jules Massenet. This piece originated as the *Invocation* from the incidental music to *Les Érinnyes* (1873). The composer later adapted it for voice, cello, and piano to lyrics by E. Gallet, calling it *Élégie*. One of Heinrich Ernst's most successful smaller works for violin is the *Élégie,* op. 10. Gabriel Fauré's *Élégie* in C minor, for cello and piano, op. 24 (1883), is also very popular.

(2) Tone poem for orchestra by Deems Taylor (1946), introduced by the Indianapolis Symphony under Fabien Sevitzky on Dec. 6, 1946. A horn solo introduces a dirge-like melody in the strings. The second subject comes after a descending subsidiary melody; in this section will be found the main theme of the composition, a lyric passage which the composer interprets as "suggestive of youth and naïveté." From time to time the opening

dirge breaks in, but the lyric idea is allowed full freedom of expression and is followed by two variations. After a climax, the dirge melody returns in trumpets, and finally concludes the work serenely on the G string in the violins.

Though the son of the organist of Worcester Cathedral, Edward Elgar was at first directed to law. When he was sixteen he was sent to London to begin law studies, but he soon abandoned them to return to his native city and engage in musical activities. He later studied the violin in London with Adolf Pollitzer. Soon after his marriage to Caroline Alice Roberts in 1889, he undertook serious composition, completing an oratorio and a concert overture. Then, settling in Malvern, he produced several choral works, which were well received at various English festivals. Success finally came with two major works, still among Elgar's most celebrated compositions. The first was the *Enigma Variations* for orchestra, introduced in London in 1899; the other an oratorio, *The Dream of Gerontius,* based on the poem by Cardinal Newman, given its première at the Birmingham Festival on Oct. 3, 1900, Hans Richter conducting. From the beginning of the 20th century, Elgar assumed a dominating position in English music, being regarded by many as the most significant creative musical figure produced in England since Henry Purcell in the 17th century. In 1902 he was invited by the government to write the music for the coronation of Edward VII. In 1904 he was knighted. One year later, when he paid his first visit to the United States, he received an honorary doctorate from Yale University. Later honors included an appointment as Master of the King's Music in 1924, and a baronetcy in 1931.

The death of his wife in 1920 brought on a period of creative sterility which persisted for fourteen years. He returned to composition in 1934 with a hymn for the recovery of the then ailing King George V. He then started sketching a third symphony, which he did not live to complete.

Elgar was a derivative composer whose works often echo the styles of Brahms, Wagner, Delibes, and several others. Yet he was able to tap veins of beauty and compelling emotion. At his best he had considerable dignity and charm. He was a Romanticist who lived in and was inspired by the past. He was the musical spokesman of an age—the Edwardian—that died long before he himself did. His major instrumental compositions follow.

Chamber Music: String Quartet; Piano Quintet.

Orchestra: 2 symphonies; *Froissart; Enigma Variations (Variations on an Original Theme); Pomp and Circumstance,* marches; *Cockaigne; In the South;* Introduction and Allegro for string quartet and string orchestra; *Elegy,* for strings; Concerto in B minor, for violin and orchestra; *Falstaff;* Concerto in E minor, for cello and orchestra.

See: Cockaigne; Concerto—*Elgar; Enigma Variations; Falstaff;* Introduction and Allegro; *In the South; Pomp and Circumstance;* Symphony—*Elgar.*

Elijah. Oratorio by Mendelssohn, op. 70 (1846), first performed at the Birmingham Festival in England on Aug. 26, 1846, the composer conducting. The text, by the composer and Pastor Julius Schubring, is in two sections. In the first, Elijah invokes a drought in Israel to punish the people for forsaking God and following Baal. Elijah then effects his miracles and destroys Baal's prophets. In the second part, enemies rise to destroy Elijah. After suffering tribulations at the hands of Jezebel, he receives the protection of the Lord who conducts him to heaven in a flaming chariot.

If *Elijah* possesses some of the dramatic elements of opera, as has often been said, it is because this is what the composer had intended. "In such a character as that of Elijah," he wrote, "it seems to me that the dramatic should predominate—the personages should be introduced as acting and speaking with fervor." Certainly the oratorio opens in a dramatic vein: a spirited one-sentence recitative by Elijah announcing the drought, followed by a dirge-like overture. Cries of anguish in the chorus then intensify the theatrical effect. This effect is soon developed further through stirring recitatives, extended dialogues, and rolling choruses.

But the lyrical element is not absent, and it is in its lyricism that the oratorio presents its noblest music: in Elijah's poignant aria, *It Is Enough;* the aria of the Angel, *O Rest in the Lord;* and Obadiah's song, *If With All Your Hearts.*

Eliot, Thomas Stearns, poet. Born St. Louis, Mo., Sept. 26, 1888. He became a naturalized British citizen in 1927, and won the Nobel Prize for literature in 1948. Lehman Engel, Wolfgang Fortner, and Darius Milhaud each wrote incidental music for Eliot's poetical drama, *Murder in the Cathedral,* and Quincy Porter wrote incidental music for *Sweeney Agonistes.* Eliot's *The Hollow Men* was the inspiration for a work for trumpet and orchestra by Vincent Persichetti.

Elizabethan Suite (Barbirolli). *See: Fitzwilliam Virginal Book.*

Elman, Mischa, violinist. Born Stalnoye, Russia, Jan. 20, 1891. He began studying the violin with Alexander Fiedelmann as a child, making a public appearance when he was only five. In 1901 he began studying with Leopold Auer in St. Petersburg. His professional début took place in Berlin on Oct. 14, 1904, and his American début in New York on Dec. 10, 1908, with the Russian Symphony Orchestra. Since then Elman has performed in all parts of the civilized world and has been universally acclaimed as one of the foremost violin virtuosos of the 20th century. He has made numerous transcriptions for the violin and has written several minor compositions for that instrument.

Embouchure. (1) The mouthpiece of a wind instrument.

(2) The adjustment of tongue and lips to produce a tone from a wind instrument.

Emperor Concerto. *See:* Concerto—*Beethoven.*

Emperor Quartet. *See:* Quartet—*Haydn.*

En blanc et noir. Suite for two pianos by Debussy (1915). Each movement suggests a picture in black and white. I. *Avec emportement.* This movement is dedicated to Serge Koussevitzky, and carries the following quotation from Gounod's *Romeo and Juliet:* "He who keeps his place and does not join the ring silently confesses to some disgrace." The main theme is a waltz developed with rhythmic vitality. It is believed that this section was intended by the composer as an ironical commentary on people like himself who, through some physical defect, could not join his fellow countrymen in the war against Germany. II. *Lent sombre: sourdement tumultueux.* Dedicated to a French lieutenant killed in World War I, this movement bears a quotation from François Villon's ballade, *Contre les ennemis de la France.* The piece begins solemnly, grows agitated, then achieves what the composer describes as "purification" through the quotation of Luther's hymn, *Ein' feste Burg.* III. Scherzando. Here the music is dedicated to Stravinsky and is preceded by a quotation from Charles, Duke of Orleans: "Winter, you are nothing but a villain." The tempo is slow, and in the opinion of some this music is meant to describe a chateau in a bleak setting smitten by raging storms. An old castellan is recounting some gruesome legend. Then the storm subsides and the setting again becomes peaceful.

Enchanted Lake, The (Le Lac enchanté). A "fairy tale" for orchestra by Anatol Liadov, op. 62 (1909), first performed in St. Petersburg on Feb. 21, 1909. Liadov completed three fairy-tales for orchestra, the other two being *Baba-Yaga* and *Kikimora.* While *The Enchanted Lake* has no specific program, the writing is so vividly pictorial that it is not difficult to provide an interpretation of the music. An undulating figure for muted strings, the principal theme, suggests the magic lake. Later on the water nymphs who inhabit the lake are depicted in vivacious, rhythmic figures.

Encore. The cry of an audience in English-speaking countries for the repetition of a composition. The term used in France is "bis."

Endymion. *See:* Keats, John.

Energico. Energetic.

Enesco, Georges, composer, violinist, and conductor. Born Liveni, Rumania, Aug. 19, 1881; died Paris, France, May 4, 1955. A prodigy violinist, Enesco was admitted to the Vienna Conservatory even though under age. After that he attended the Paris Conservatory, where his teachers included Jules Massenet, Gabriel Fauré, and André Gedalge, and where he won several prizes. He was only fifteen, and only a Conservatory student, when a concert of his own works was given in Paris, on June 11, 1897. A year later the Colonne Orchestra in Paris introduced his *Poème roumain,* and in 1899 he initiated his professional career as violin virtuoso with a European tour. He soon achieved recognition as a violinist of the first rank and was appointed court violinist to the Queen of Rumania. He also scored a major success as composer in 1906 when his First Symphony was introduced, and in 1908 when his two Rumanian Rhapsodies were performed for the first time. Just before World War I, Enesco returned to his native land to assume a position of first importance in its musical life, as conductor, composer, violinist, and teacher. After the war he returned to Paris to make it a permanent residence, from which point he set off on extended tours. His American début took place on Jan. 2, 1923, in New York when he appeared with the Philadelphia Orchestra in the triple role of composer, conductor, and violinist. During World War II Enesco lived on a farm in Rumania, devoting himself to creative work. He returned to the United States after an absence of almost a decade, for a five-month tour in 1946. The last years of his life were spent in Paris. Though he refused to compromise with the Communist regime in Rumania, he was the recipient there of many posthumous honors. The village of his birth was renamed Enescu, a bust of him was erected in a public park, and the name of the Rumanian State Philharmonic was changed to the Georges Enesco Philharmonic.

The following are Enesco's major instrumental compositions.

Chamber Music: 3 violin sonatas; 2 string quartets; piano quartet; string quintet; octet.

Orchestra: Poème roumain; 3 symphonies; 3 suites; violin concerto; 2 Rumanian Rhapsodies; *Overture on Motifs in the Rumanian Character; Poème symphonique; Symphonie de chambre.*

Piano: 2 suites; sonata.

See: Rumanian Rhapsodies; Suite—Enesco.

Engel, Carl, musicologist. Born Paris, France, July 21, 1883; died New York City, May 6, 1944. After attending the Munich Conservatory and studying composition with Ludwig Thuille, he settled in the United States in 1905, later becoming a citizen. From 1909 to 1921 he was editor and musical adviser for the Boston Music Company. From 1922 to 1934 he was chief of the music division of the Library of Congress, in Washington, D.C. From 1929 to 1932, and again from 1934, he was president of G. Schirmer, Inc., and from 1929 until his death, editor of *The Musical Quarterly.* He was a founder, and in 1937-1938 president, of the American Musicological Society; the first chairman of the Committee on Musicology of the American Council of Learned Societies; and in 1935 vice-president of the Friends of Music at the Library of Congress. He was the author of *Alla Breve* (1921) and *Discords Mingled* (1931).

English horn. An instrument of the oboe family, pitched a fifth below the oboe.

English Suites. A set of 6 suites for piano by Johann Sebastian Bach. He wrote another set of 6 suites for piano entitled *French Suites.* The reason why these works are designated "English" and "French" has never been authoritatively determined. The *English Suites* differ from the *French* in that each is prefaced by a prelude; in the *French Suites* the dances are shorter and of slighter musical content.

The 6 *English Suites* are as follows: No. 1, A major; No. 2, A minor; No. 3, G minor; No. 4, F major; No. 5, E minor; No. 6, D minor. The third is especially famous, boasting a beautiful and stately fourth movement (Sarabande) followed by a delightful Gavotte.

Enharmonic. Said of tones or chords that differ in name or notation but are the same, or almost the same, in sound, as for example D-sharp and E-flat.

Enigma Variations (Variations on an Original Theme). By Sir Edward Elgar, op. 36 (1899), introduced in London on June 19, 1899, Hans Richter conducting. The composer here achieved his first major success, which remains to this day one of his most celebrated works. Elgar planned it as a portrait of fourteen intimate friends, each represented by a variation. To identify these people, he set down initials or a nickname before each variation. The work has been designated an "Enigma" because of a belief that it contains a "hidden theme." This theme is never actually stated, and is often intended as a "silent accompaniment" to the variations. Nobody has yet been able to identify the theme. The guesses range from *Auld Lang Syne* to a motif from Wagner's music drama, *Parsifal.*

The composition opens with an eloquent melody for strings. Fourteen variations follow. I. C.A.E. (Elgar's wife, Alice). The melody is touched with tenderness. II. H.D.S.-P. (H. D. Stuart-Powell). Stuart-Powell was a pianist; this variation points up his habit of exercising his fingers before he began playing. III. R.B.T. (Richard Baxter Townshend). Townshend was an amateur actor. A mocking subject for woodwind pokes fun at the actor's ability to change his full-sounding voice to falsetto whenever he impersonated old men. IV. W.M.B. (William M. Baker). The music here is headstrong, with timpani and trumpets predominating. V. R.P.A. (Richard P. Arnold). The music, by turns moody and vivacious, depicts different facets of the personality of Matthew Arnold's son. VI. Ysobel (Isabel Fitton). A viola is assigned a soulful melody in tribute to an amateur violist. VII. Troyte (Arthur Troyte Griffith). Griffith had an excitable nature, which is reflected in this music. VIII. W.N. (Winifred Norbury). A gracious and charming lady is depicted by a sedate version of the theme in the clarinets. IX. Nimrod (August Jaeger). This section, one of the most beautiful in the entire work, makes brief reference to Beethoven's *Sonata pathétique,* in deference to Jaeger, who used to talk to Elgar eloquently about Beethoven during their long walks. X. Dorabella (Miss Penny). Miss Penny had the physical defect of halting speech, simulated in the halting, somewhat capricious strains of this section. XII. G.R.S. (George Robertson Sinclair). This variation is believed to be

more a picture of Sinclair's dog than of Sinclair himself—especially of the dog when he jumps into the water and takes his usual swim. XII. B.G.N. (Basil G. Nevinson). An emotional solo for the cello tells us what instrument Nevinson used to play. XIII. **** (Lady Mary Lygon). A romanza describes an ocean voyage. The clarinet quotes from Mendelssohn's overture, *Calm Sea and Prosperous Voyage.* XIV. E.D.U. This is believed to be a self-portrait. "Edu" stands for "Edoo," a nickname by which Elgar was often called. At first the music speaks of illusions and frustrations. Then with the appearance of the organ, Elgar's faith in himself, life, and art are asserted. Themes from Variations 1 and 9 are recalled. A charming presto concludes the composition.

En Saga. Tone poem by Sibelius, op. 9 (1892, revised 1901), first performed in Helsingfors on Feb. 16, 1893, the composer conducting. This was Sibelius' first major work for orchestra, the first in which he became the musical voice for Finnish nationalism. The tone poem opens with a horn call above string tremolos and arpeggios. The first subject, initially hinted at, is unfolded in bassoons against string arpeggios. This theme is developed, and following a climax, another main thought is projected by the violas. Once again the ideas are enlarged and brought to a climactic point. A pastoral section now appears in which an idyllic melody for solo clarinet is prominent. A third climax leads to a tranquil ending.

Ensemble. A group of performers or a combination of instruments.

Entfuehrung aus dem Serail, Overture to Die (Mozart). *See: Abduction from the Seraglio, Overture to The.*

Entrance of the Gods into Valhalla. The closing scene of Wagner's music drama, *The Rhinegold,* from the tetralogy, *The Ring of the Nibelungs.* Valhalla, citadel of the gods, has been built by the giants, Fafner and Fasolt. This majestic music accompanies the gods as they enter their new abode. The musical material of this excerpt is made up principally of the "Rainbow" and "Valhalla" motifs, the latter a majestic utterance in the horns, with which this excerpt ends.

Éolides, Les. Tone poem for orchestra by César Franck (1876), introduced in Paris on May 13, 1877. This is Franck's first tone poem, and his first major orchestral composition. It was inspired by a poem of Leconte de Lisle addressed to the Éolides, "the floating breezes of the skies . . . that caress the hills and plains with freakish kisses." The germinal idea is a short chromatic phrase built up effectively in a freely constructed symphonic movement.

Epithalamium. *See:* Aeschylus.

Equal temperament. A method of tuning now in use in which the octave is divided into 12 equal parts. The first important practical application of this method is found in Bach's *Well-Tempered Clavier.*

Equale. A composition for two or more instruments of the same kind.

Ernst, Heinrich Wilhelm, violinist and composer. Born Bruenn, Moravia, May 6, 1814; died Nice, France, Oct. 8, 1865. He attended the Vienna Conservatory and made his first concert tour when he was sixteen. In 1832 he settled in Paris, devoting himself for the next few years to study and concert work. He firmly established his reputation as a virtuoso with a succession of triumphant tours between 1838 and 1850. In 1855 he went to live in London. He wrote many works for the violin, including fantasias and variations on well-known airs and opera melodies. Among his surviving works are the Concerto in F-sharp minor for violin and orchestra, op. 23 (*Pathétique*), the *Carnival of Venice,* and *Élégie.*

Eroica Symphony. *See:* Symphony—*Beethoven.*

Eroica Variations. Variations for piano in E-flat major by Beethoven, op. 35 (1802). The melody used here is from the finale of the *Eroica Symphony.* This subject was also used by the composer for a contredanse and in his music to *Prometheus.*

Erotik (Grieg). *See: Lyric Pieces.*

Erskine, John, author and educator. Born New York City, Oct. 5, 1879; died there June 1, 1951. Erskine's fame rests mainly on his accomplishments as professor of English at Columbia University and on several best-selling novels. But he was also active in music. He was a competent pianist who made several guest appearances with American orchestras; was president of the Juilliard School of Music from 1928 to 1937, and president of the Juilliard Music Foundation from 1948 until his death. He also wrote several books on music, including a young people's biography of Mendelssohn, *Song Without Words* (1941), a history of the New York Philharmonic Orchestra (1943), *What Is Music?* (1944), and *My Life In Music* (1950). He was editor of *A Musical Companion* (1935).

Escales (Ports of Call). Suite for orchestra by Jacques Ibert (1922), introduced in Paris on Jan. 6, 1924. This is the composer's most frequently performed work for orchestra. Each of the three movements represents a Mediterranean port. I. Rome-Palermo. This music is in Italian style. An Italian melody for flute appears in the second measure. II. Tunis-Nefta. Against a marked rhythm in divided strings and timpani, the oboe presents a melancholy oriental melody. III. Valencia. This movement features a Moorish melody in the strings, developed in an improvisatory manner.

España (Spain). Rhapsody for orchestra by Emmanuel Chabrier (1883), introduced in Paris on Nov. 4, 1883. This, the composer's first successful work, was inspired by a holiday in Spain. A tone picture of a colorful land, the rhapsody is based on several Spanish dances, including a jota and a malagueña. A third principal subject, a robust melody for trombones, is original with the composer. These themes are treated so freely that the composition has the character of a fantasia. The Parisian waltz-king, Émile Waldteufel, used the principal melodies from this rhapsody for one of his most celebrated waltzes, also entitled *España.*

Espressivo. Expressively.

Essay for Orchestra, Nos. 1 and 2. By Samuel Barber (1937, 1942). The first *Essay* was introduced by the NBC Symphony on Nov. 5, 1938, Toscanini conducting; the second, by the New York Philharmonic under Bruno Walter on April 16, 1942. Each is a short orchestral composition attempting to carry over into music the literary form of the essay by developing some reflective ideas. The first *Essay* opens with a pregnant motif in the lower strings; this is developed and grows in volume and intensity. A martial figure in the brass leads to a scherzo-like section for strings and woodwinds. The brass figure returns and brings with it, at the very end, the main theme. The second *Essay* begins with a flute solo. The other themes follow: a sweeping one for violas and a short one for brasses. A concluding fugue combines all three ideas.

Essipoff (Essipova), Anna, pianist and teacher. Born St. Petersburg, Russia, Feb. 13, 1851; died there, Aug. 18, 1914. She was first a pupil, then the wife, of Theodor Leschetizky. She made her début as a concert pianist in St. Petersburg, then made many tours of Europe and the United States; between 1870 and 1885 she gave over 600 concerts. From 1893 until her death she was a distinguished professor of the piano at the St. Petersburg Conservatory; Serge Prokofiev was one of her many students there.

Estampes (Engravings). A set of three pieces for the piano by Debussy (1903), first performed in Paris by Ricardo Viñes on Jan. 9, 1904. I. *Pagodes.* This is music built from a pentatonic scale; its exoticism is heightened by a dissonant ending. II. *Soirée dans Grenade.* This portrait of Granada in the evening was the composer's first attempt to create a Spanish background and setting in his music. The rhythm is that of a habanera; towards the end of the piece, the strumming of a mandolin is simulated. III. *Jardins sous la pluie.* This picture of gardens in the rain utilizes two French folk songs: *Nous n'irions plus au bois* and *Do, do, l'enfant do.* The image of the rain-drenched, wind-swept garden is evoked by rushing arpeggio figures and rapid changes of tonality.

Estro armonico, L' (Harmonic Inspiration). *See:* Concerto Grosso—*Vivaldi.*

Etude. An exercise for a solo instrument, attempting to solve some specific technical problem. Students of piano, violin, cello, and so forth have cut their teeth on such pedagogical etudes. The most famous for the piano were produced by Cramer, Clementi, Czerny, Hummel, Kalkbrenner, and Moscheles, among others; for the violin, by Jean Charles Dancla, Ferdinand David, Kreutzer, and Rode; for cello, by Davidov and Popper.

Many serious composers have lifted the etude out of the class of pedagogy into the category of art by writing pieces (usually for the piano) that, while ostensibly treating a technical problem, actually treat that problem with such artistic amplitude that the piece becomes a serious musical composition rather than an exercise. To differentiate these pieces from exercises they have acquired the designation of "concert etudes."

The following are some of the basic concert etudes for the piano.

CHOPIN. Chopin was one of the first significant composers to produce concert etudes. His etudes include exercises in thirds, sixths, octaves, arpeggios, the chromatic scale, and syncopation. But Chopin's creative genius brought artistic stature to these pieces by endowing them with the same poetic insight, imagination, and variety of expression he brought to all other forms of piano music. Chopin wrote 27 etudes. Twelve are found in op. 10 (1829-1832); 12, in op. 25 (1832-1836); three are without opus numbers, having been published posthumously. The following are the most popular: E major, op. 10, no. 3, distinguished for its elegant melody, and regarded by the composer himself as one of the best in this *genre;* G-flat, op. 10, no. 5, called the "Black Key Etude," since it employs only the black keys; C minor, op. 10, no. 12, the "Revolutionary Etude," so designated because of its martial character, having been inspired by the news in 1831 that the Russians had taken Warsaw; A-flat, op. 25, no. 1, the "Aeolian Harp Etude," which Schumann described as "an undulation of the A-flat major chord . . . exquisitely entangled in the harmony"; G-flat, op. 25, no. 9, known as the "Butterfly Etude," because of its delicate, graceful mobility; A minor, op. 25, no. 11, the "Winter Wind Etude," the name derived from its sweeping, surging sounds.

DEBUSSY. Towards the end of his life, Debussy completed two books of piano etudes, six in each book (1915). He dedicated them to Chopin's memory. These are pieces intended to train the performer in such technical problems as thirds, fourths, sixths, octaves, chromatic intervals, grace notes, reiterated notes, contrasted sonorities, arpeggios, and chords. Within the framework of such formal exercises, Debussy successfully incorporated his own Impressionistic style. The pieces abound with the composer's personal use of rhythm, harmony, tone color, and dynamics.

LISZT. Liszt wrote many concert etudes in which he extended the resources of piano writing while indulging in dramatic or atmospheric expositions. There are 12 pieces in the *Études d'exécution transcendante* (1851), the most interesting being the fourth and fifth, respectively entitled *Mazeppa* and *Feux-follets*. These are studies in contrast. The first is brilliant, stormy, bravura music, while the other is a sensitive, exquisite tone picture.

There are 6 pieces in *Études d'exécution transcendante d'après Paganini,* or more tersely, the *Paganini Etudes* (1838). These utilize melodic ideas from various Paganini compositions, but mainly from his Caprices for solo violin. The most popular of these etudes is the third in A-flat minor, *La Campanella*. Its source was the *Rondo à la clochette* movement from Paganini's Concerto in B minor for violin and orchestra.

Three more pieces appear in the *Études de concert,* or *Caprices poétiques* (1848), the best of these being the delicate study in F minor entitled *La Leggierezza* and the lyrical composition in D-flat known as *Un Sospiro.*

Both of the *Études de concert* (1863), entitled *Waldesrauschen* and *Gnomenreigen,* are famous.

RACHMANINOFF. *See: Études-tableaux.*
SCHUMANN. *See: Études symphoniques.*
SCRIABIN. Scriabin wrote 24 etudes. One is found in *Three Pieces,* op. 2; 12, in op. 8; 8 more in op. 42; and 3, in op. 65. As was the case with other piano works by this composer, the earlier pieces (through op. 8) are strongly influenced by Chopin and Liszt. The writing becomes bolder and the feeling more esoteric in the op. 42 group; while the 3 in op. 65 are completely unorthodox in their use of harmonic progressions and tonalities, and in the subtlety of their lyricism.

SZYMANOWSKI. The Twelve Etudes, op. 33 (1917), were mainly influenced by Scriabin, in their complex chordal structure and subtlety of rhythm. These pieces are not actually exercises but brief tonal impressions. While each is self-sufficient, they were written and assembled by the composer with a view to their atmospheric and stylistic relationship to one another. For this reason the composer preferred having these etudes played as a group and without interruption.

Études de concert. *See:* Etude—*Liszt.*
Études d'exécution transcendante, and Études d'exécution transcendante d'après Paganini. *See:* Etude—*Liszt.*
Études symphoniques. For piano by Schumann, op. 13 (1834). This work was an effort to endow the concert etude with symphonic dimensions. It is not, however, a series of studies but a single integrated composition in the form of a theme and variations. The theme is a majestic melody played softly at the opening of the composition. Twelve variations follow in which the theme is altered so freely that it often is not recognizable. A single melodic phrase or a rhythmic or harmonic fragment of the original theme is enough to give wings to the composer's imagination and to set him soaring into new realms of thought. The dynamic subject that introduces the final variation comes from an opera by Heinrich Marschner. The reason for this quotation is that the *Études symphoniques* is dedicated to the celebrated English musician, William Sterndale Bennett, who was an admirer of Marschner.

Études-tableaux. Pieces for the piano by Rachmaninoff. Six are found in op. 33 (1911), and 9 in op. 39 (1917). In addition, the composer wrote two others in 1911 intended for op. 33 but which he finally insisted must remain unpublished; they were issued posthumously in 1948. The "etude tableau" is a miniature in either binary or ternary form in which a virtuoso's regard for piano technique is combined with a poet's interpretation of a picture or a scene. However, in only five instances did the composer reveal what picture or scene he had in mind. This was in a communication to Ottorino Respighi, who orchestrated the five pieces. The Etude in E-flat major, op. 33, no. 4, represents a scene at a fair; the C major, op. 39, no. 2, the sea and sea-gulls (it has been transcribed for violin and piano by Jascha Heifetz); the A minor, op. 39, no. 6, the fairy tale of Little Red Riding Hood; the C minor, op. 39, no. 7, a funeral march; the D major, op. 39, no. 9, an oriental march. In op. 39, no. 2, the composer gives prominent treatment to the *Dies irae.*

Eurhythmics. A system of musical training created by Emile Jaques-Dalcroze at the Geneva Conservatory. It combines bodily exercises and physical action with musical rhythm, thus coordinating a feeling for rhythm and physical movement. In subsequent training, musical compositions are interpreted through these physical reactions.

Euripides, dramatist. Born Salamis Greece, 480 B.C.; died Pella, Greece, 406 B.C. One of the greatest of the classical tragic dramatists, Euripides was the author of over 75 plays. Those for which incidental music has been written in modern times include: *Andromache* (George Kazasoglou); *The Bacchantes* (Willem Pijper, Ernst Toch); *Cyclops* (Willem Pijper); *Electra* (Walter Damrosch, Dimitri Mitropoulos); *Hecuba* (Darius Milhaud, Constantine Nottara); *Hippolytus* (Granville Bantock, Dimitri Mitropoulos); *Iphigenia in Aulis* (Walter Damrosch, André Jolivet); *Iphigenia in Tauris* (Giorgio Federico Ghedini, Petro Petridis, Charles Wood); *Medea* (Walter Damrosch, George Kazasoglou); *Orestes* (George Kazasoglou); *Phoenician Women* (Michael Gnessin); *Rhesus* (Ernest Walker); *The Trojan Women* (Louis Coerne, John Foulds, Virgil Thomson).

Euryanthe, Overture to. Overture to the German Romantic opera by Carl Maria von Weber, introduced in Vienna on Oct. 25, 1823. The libretto, by Helmina von Chézy, was based on the 13th-century romance, *L'Histoire de Gérard de Nevers.* The overture opens dramatically. After eight measures, the wind instruments present the first theme. After this idea has been worked out, a loud chord and a cello passage lead to a second theme, a beautiful melody for strings. The dramatic opening returns, followed by a moment of silence. A Largo section for muted strings is succeeded by a fugal interlude and a restatement of the two main themes.

Eusebius. *See:* Florestan and Eusebius.

Euterpe. One of the nine muses in Greek mythology, patroness of music.

Eventyr (Once upon a Time). Tone poem for orchestra by Frederick Delius (1917), introduced in London on Jan. 11, 1919, Henry J. Wood conducting. "Eventyr" means "adventure," and the inspiration for the tone poem was a Norwegian fairy tale. Delius' music evokes a fanciful world of Norwegian spirits, hobgoblins, and so forth. It opens with an eerie twenty-bar introduction, after which a fantastic theme is heard in the bassoons and repeated by other woodwinds. The second subject, in the strings, gains intensity through the imposition of an expressive contrapuntal subject. After several climactic moments, the fantastic fairy world is created. It is dominated by a descending chromatic theme for strings, celesta, and harp. A return of earlier material is succeeded by a serene closing section in which the fairy spirits vanish.

Evocación (Albéniz). *See: Iberia* (1).

Exposition. That section of the sonata form or fugue in which the thematic material is first presented.

Expression. The sum of nuances of dynamics, duration, phrasing, and so on in a musical performance, too subtle to be indicated in the music and consequently left to the judgment of the performing artist.

Expressionism. A style striving to penetrate to the very essence of a subject by expressing it in abstract terms, as in atonality.

Extempore. Extemporaneous.

Extemporization. *See:* Improvisation.

F

Façade. Two suites for orchestra by William Walton (1926, 1938). They originated in 1922 as a "melodrama" for reciting voice and seven instruments, consisting of an overture, sixteen poems, and interlude based on abstractionist poems by Edith Sitwell. When introduced in London on June 12, 1923, the poems were recited in sing-song fashion, the voice emerging from the megaphone-shaped mouth of a mask painted on a curtain. Walton's music, like Miss Sitwell's poems and the performance, proved so provocative and attracted so much attention and criticism that overnight the little-known composer became famous. In a successful revival of the "melodrama" in London on April 27, 1926, a revised and expanded version of the score was presented.

From the complete work the composer prepared two suites for symphony orchestra. The first is in five movements: I. Polka; II. Waltz; III. Swiss Yodelling Song; IV. Tango Pasodoble; V. Tarantella Sevillana. There are six movements in the second suite: I. Fanfare; II. Scotch Rhapsody; III. Country Dance; IV. Noche Española; V. Popular Song; VI. Foxtrot. Walton's music is a delightful excursion into burlesque, parody, wit, satire, and tongue-in-the-cheek sentimentality. There are witty quotations: from Rossini's *William Tell Overture* in the Swiss Yodelling Song; from Mozart's *Don Giovanni* in the Tarantella Sevillana; of popular English tunes in the Polka and Tango Pasodoble. Jazz is used with a dash of mockery in the Popular Song and Foxtrot. The more recognizable attributes of the polka, waltz, and tarantella are irreverently distorted.

Façade was also adapted into a ballet. With choreography by Frederick Ashton, it was successfully produced in London on April 26, 1931.

Fairy tale. A short composition for the piano devised by Nicolas Medtner. Without being programmatic, such a piece has such narrative character and dramatic interest that it appears to be telling a story from the world of fantasy. Medtner wrote 30 such compositions between 1905 and 1929 (opp. 8, 9, 14, 20, 26, 34, 35, 42, and 51). Here, as Leonid Sabaneyev has written, were caught "the poetry of ancient heroic legends, and most of all an echo of the underworld of Nibelungs, gnomes, and mountain kings." The most popular of these fairy tales are: B-flat minor, op. 20, no. 1 (transcribed for violin and piano by Jascha Heifetz); B minor, op. 20, no. 2; E minor, op. 34, no. 2; and F minor, op. 42, no. 1.

Fairy's Kiss, The (Le Baiser de la Fée). Ballet suite (or divertimento) for orchestra by Igor Stravinsky (1928), based on music by Tchaikovsky. Stravinsky's suite was derived from his score to a ballet introduced by Ida Rubinstein in Paris on Nov. 27, 1928, the composer conducting. Stravinsky wrote his own ballet scenario, based on a fairy tale by Hans Christian Andersen, *The Ice Maiden.* The Andersen tale concerns a kiss planted by a fairy on a child's cheek at its birth. Twenty years later, the fairy returns to kiss the child, now become a man, an takes him off with her. Stravinsky's scor utilizes the following material by Tchaikovsky: *Lullaby in the Storm,* from *Children's Songs,* op. 54, with which the suite opens and ends; Humoresque, for piano, op. 10, no. 2; *Nata Valse,* from Six Pieces for piano, op. 51; and *A Peasant Plays the Harmonica,* from *Children's Album,* op. 39.

The suite is in four parts. I. *Sinfonia* (Andante; Allegro; Vivace). The fairy kisses the child and disappears. II. Swiss Dances—Waltz (*Tempo giusto; Poco più nto*). A village fair is described; the child, now grown into manhood, is being betrothed. III. Scherzo (Moderato; *Allegretto grazioso*). The fairy leads the young man to a mill where his betrothed is playing round games with her friends. IV. *Pas de deux* (Adagio). The young man and his betrothed are described. Variation (*Allegretto grazioso*). The Betrothed. Coda (Presto). The young man is left alone as his betrothed leaves to try on her wedding veil.

Falla, Manuel de, composer. Born Cádiz, Spain, Nov. 23, 1876; died Alta Gracia, Argentina, Nov. 14, 1946. After preliminary music instruction with local teachers in Cádiz, he attended the Madrid Conservatory. There he came under the influence of Felipe Pedrell, musical scholar and nationalist. Pedrell aroused in Falla the ambition to become a composer and to write Spanish music. Falla completed a Spanish opera, *La Vida breve,* which in 1905 won first prize in a competition sponsored by the Madrid Academy of Fine Arts. In that same year he also won the Ortiz y Cussó prize for piano playing. From 1907 to 1914 he lived in Paris. During this period he wrote little but spent his time absorbing musical experiences and receiving advice and encouragement from leading French musicians, including Ravel and Debussy. A set of four piano pieces, *Pièces espagnoles,* was introduced in Paris by Ricardo Viñes in 1908; and in 1913 performances of *La Vida breve* in Nice and at the Opéra-Comique in Paris brought him recognition. Just before the beginning of World War I, Falla returned to Spain. For several years he wandered about, then in 1921 settled in Granada, his home for the next 17 years. In 1915 he completed and had performed two of his most famous compositions: *Nights in the Gardens of Spain* (*Noches en los jardines de España*), for piano and orchestra, and the ballet, *El Amor brujo.* Later compositions further extended his reputation as one of the foremost exponents of Spanish nationalism in music. These works included the ballet *The Three-Cornered Hat* (*El Sombrero de tres picos*) and the Concerto for Harpsichord, Flute, Oboe, Clarinet, and Cello.

In his effort to create national music, Falla did not (like so many of his fellow countrymen) attempt the reproduction of the externals of Spanish life, its sights and sounds. Instead, being a mystic, he sought to interpret the very essence and soul of his country and its people. Up to about 1919 his style was dominated by the idioms of Andalusian folk music, but in subsequent works he was more strongly influenced by the music of the Spanish classical era.

In 1939, disillusioned by the Franco regime which he had originally supported and which in 1938 had elevated him to the post of president of the Institute of Spain, Falla left his country for good and went to live in Argentina. There he devoted himself to the writing of a major work for chorus, solo voices, and orchestra, *La Atlántida,* which was left uncompleted at his death. Falla wrote only a handful of instrumental works. Besides those already mentioned, there were *Fanfare* for wind instruments, *Homages* (*Homenajes*) for orchestra, and some pieces for the piano.

See: Amor brujo, El; Concerto—*Falla; Homages; Nights in the Gardens of Spain; Three-Cornered Hat, The.*

False accent. Accentuation on a normally weak beat in the bar.

False cadence. An interrupted or imperfect cadence.

False relation. A chromatic contradiction between two notes in a chord or in two adjacent chords.

Falstaff. "Symphonic study" for orchestra by Sir Edward Elgar, op. 68 (1913). It was written for and introduced at the Leeds Festival in England on Oct. 1, 1913. The hero of this study comes from Shakespeare's *Henry IV* (Parts 1 and 2) and *Henry V,* rather than from *The Merry Wives of Windsor.* Though in a single movement, the work has four sections, subtitled: I. Falstaff and Prince Henry; II. Eastcheap—Gadshill—The Boar's Head, Revelry and Sleep; III. Falstaff's March—The Return Through Gloucestershire—The New King—The Hurried Ride to London; IV. King Henry's Progress—The Repudiation of Falstaff and His Death.

Falstaff is represented by five different

152

themes, four in the first section, the fifth in the second. The first, and principal, theme arrives at once and describes Falstaff "in a great old age," in the composer's words, "mellow, frank, gay, loose, unprincipled and luxurious." The other four ideas are respectively a brief motif for clarinet followed by a chord for horns and an answering chord in the strings; a subject for high woodwind; an upward crescendo for cellos; and, finally, a "boastful and vociferous" theme.

Fancy Free. Ballet-suite for orchestra by Leonard Bernstein (1944), derived from the score to a ballet introduced in New York on April 18, 1944. *Fancy Free,* choreography by Jerome Robbins, concerned the exploits of three sailors on leave in quest of girls. The orchestral suite has six movements: I. Dance of the Three Sailors; II. Scene at the Bar; III. Pas de deux; IV. Pantomime; V. Three Variations (Galop, Waltz, Danzon); VI. Finale.

Fanfare. A passage for trumpets to attract attention. It is usually built from the notes of a simple chord. More generally, this term is used for a short passage for brass. William Walton's *Façade* Suite No. 2 opens with a satiric treatment of a fanfare.

Fantasia (Fantasy, or **Fantaisie).** An instrumental composition, free in form and in the presentation and development of its thematic material. It originated in the 16th century as a contrapuntal composition for lute and for organ. The early organ masters—notably Frescobaldi and Froberger—developed and amplified this structure, whose highest artistic and technical peak was achieved with Johann Sebastian Bach. Fantasias were also written for the piano, for orchestra, and occasionally for other instruments.

The following are some representative fantasias for various media.

J. S. BACH. Among Bach's most celebrated fantasias is the Fantasia and Fugue in G minor for organ. Here the fantasia section is spacious in form, and filled with rhapsodic utterances. The ensuing fugue is often designated "the great" to distinguish it from another famous G minor fugue known as "the little." Bach's best-known fantasia for clavier is that which appears in the *Chromatic Fantasy and Fugue.*

CHOPIN. The Fantaisie in F minor for piano, op. 49 (1841), is a masterwork inexorable in its structural logic and outstanding for the grandeur of its expression and its emotional depth. The Fantaisie-Impromptu in C-sharp minor (1834), published posthumously, is an interesting attempt at combining the fantasy form with that of the impromptu. Its beautiful main melody was borrowed for the popular song, *I'm Always Chasing Rainbows.*

HAYDN. The Fantasia in C, for piano, published in 1789, is striking for its surprising changes of key. It is filled with light and gay moods in Haydn's most ingratiating manner.

MOZART. The Fantasia in C minor, K. 475 (1785), is one of the composer's most significant works for solo piano. It is music rich in contrasts—opening and closing in a dramatic, almost tragic vein and including several rich lyrical passages. The composer intended this work to be performed in conjunction with his piano Sonata in C minor, K. 457 (1784) and originally they were published together. Another outstanding Mozart Fantasia for piano is that in D minor, K. 397 (1782).

PAGANINI. *See: Fantasia on the G String.*

PURCELL. Purcell wrote three-part and four-part fantasias for strings which are among the finest in the early chamber music literature. In the celebrated five-part *Fantasia on One Note,* the viola sustains the note "C" while the other instruments weave melodies around it.

SCHUBERT. The Fantasy in F minor, op. 103, for piano four hands, is one of the composer's keyboard masterworks (1828). As his biographer, Heinrich Kreissle von Hellborn, wrote, it is "remarkable for wealth and beauty of melody . . . startling modulations, and a certain moderation in the treatment of various themes. Schubert has written no second work in this style to be compared with it in the delicate fancies here displayed." The four movements are played without interruption (I. *Allegro molto moderato.* II. *Largo.* III. *Scherzo.* IV. *A.*

legro vivace). The main theme is a haunting melody which appears in the opening measures of the first movement and recurs in the finale.

See also: Wanderer Fantasy.

SCHUMANN. The Fantasy in C major, op. 17 (1836), is of epic structural dimensions and equally spacious writing. The following lines by Friedrich August Wilhelm von Schlegel appear in the published score: "There is one gentle note for the secret listener through all the tones that sound in earth's fitful dream." The work has three uninterrupted movements (I. *Il tutto fantastico ed appassionata; Im Legendenton.* II. *Moderato con energia.* III. *Lento sostenuto; Un poco più mosso*). The first movement is turbulent. "I do not think," Schumann wrote to his future wife, Clara, "I ever wrote anything more impassioned . . . It is a profound lament over you." That lament is found midway in the movement, but it is prefaced by agitation. This section is followed by march music within the structure of a rondo. The concluding movement is elegiac.

VAUGHAN WILLIAMS. Vaughan Williams wrote several fantasias. The Fantasia on *Greensleeves,* for orchestra (1929), is, as its title implies, an elaboration of the famous English folksong, *Greensleeves.* The Fantasia on Christmas Carols, for baritone, chorus, and orchestra (1912) and Fantasia on Sussex Folk Tunes, for cello and orchestra (1930), are also occasionally performed. But the composer's most celebrated work in the fantasia form, and one of his masterpieces, is the Fantasia on a Theme by Thomas Tallis (see below).

Fantasia on a Theme by Thomas Tallis. For double string orchestra (string quartet and string orchestra) by Ralph Vaughan Williams (1910), first performed at the Three Choirs Festival in Gloucester on Sept. 6, 1910. The fantasia is based on the third of eight tunes by Thomas Tallis (16th century) from his Metrical Psalter of Matthew Parker, Archbishop of Canterbury. The Tallis theme appears first in the orchestra against violin tremolos, following a brief introduction. The violins repeat the melody, then the two orchestras (one muted) develop the idea

before passing it on to the solo instruments. After considerable transformation and enlargement, this melody is brought to a powerful climax. The melody then reappears in a solo violin against a contrapuntal subject in a solo viola.

Fantasia on One Note. *See:* Fantasia—*Purcell.*

Fantasia on the G String. A set of pyrotechnical variations for violin and piano by Paganini. The theme is by Rossini, *Dal tuo stellato soglio,* and comes from his opera *Mosè in Egitto.* As the title of the Paganini fantasia implies, the entire work is performed on the G string.

Fantasia quasi sonata après une lecture du Dante (Liszt). *See: Années de pèlerinage.*

Fantasiestuecke. A set of eight small pieces for the piano by Schumann, op. 12 (1837). Their contrasting moods express the opposing natures of Eusebius and Florestan (which see). In the first four pieces the moods alternate; in the last four, they are combined. The gentle Eusebius appears in the first piece, *Des Abends,* a picture of a tranquil night, and in the third, *Warum?* Florestan is portrayed in the second, *Aufschwung* with its energetic rhythmic drive, and in the fourth, *Grillen,* a whimsical piece. The last four numbers are *In der Nacht, Fabel, Traumes Wirren,* and *Ende vom Lied.* All the above titles were added by Schumann after he had written the music.

Fantastic Symphony. *See:* Symphony—*Berlioz.*

Farewell Symphony. *See:* Symphony—*Haydn.*

Farm Journal. Suite for chamber orchestra by Douglas Moore (1947), introduced by the Little Orchestra Society in New York on Jan. 19, 1948, Thomas Scherman conducting. The four movements are entitled *Up Early, Sunday Clothes, Lamplight,* and *Harvest Song.*

Farnaby, Giles, composer. Born Truro, England, about 1560; died London, England, November 1640. Little is known of his life beyond the facts that he received a degree from Oxford in 1592 and in 1598 published his first volume (a set of vocal canzonets). Though essentially a vocal composer, Farnaby wrote pieces for the virginals significant in the early history of English instrumental music. Over 50 of these compositions are found in the *Fitzwilliam Virginal Book.*

Faschingsschwank aus Wien (Carnival Jest from Vienna). Suite for piano by Schumann, op. 26 (1839), inspired by the composer's visit in 1838 to Vienna. The work is in five uninterrupted parts. The first has themes and rhythms of folk character which recreate the bustle of carnival time. In this part, Schumann interpolates a quotation from the *Marseillaise,* which at that time was forbidden to be performed in Austria; and it is probably for this quotation that the entire composition was called by the composer a "jest." The second part is a romanza. The third is a scherzo with virtuoso passages. The fourth, an intermezzo, has a soaring melody set against accompanying triplets. The finale carries the Carnival revelry to a frenzied climax.

Fauré, Gabriel-Urbain, composer. Born Pamiers, France, May 12, 1845; died Paris, France, Nov. 4, 1924. He attended the Ecole Niedermeyer in Paris for about a decade. There Saint-Saëns was one of his teachers, and a vital influence. After that Fauré filled several minor posts as organist in Rennes and Paris. During the Franco-Prussian War he served in the French Army. After the war he wrote some songs on poems by Verlaine and Baudelaire, and then several chamber-music works which are still popular, among them the Sonata No. 1 in A major for violin and piano and the Piano Quartet in C minor. In 1877 he was appointed second organist at the Madeleine Church, becoming principal organist 19 years later. While filling this post he completed many major works for piano and chamber-music groups, and his first large work, the Requiem, in 1886.

Fauré also distinguished himself as a teacher, first as professor of composition at the Ecole Niedermeyer and the Paris Conservatory, and from 1905 to 1920 as the director of the latter institution. His influence was felt by an entire generation of French musicians; among his many pupils were Florent Schmitt, Nadia Boulanger, Maurice Ravel, Georges Enesco, Louis Aubert, and Roger-Ducasse. Recognized as one of France's leading musi-

cians, Fauré was elected to the Académie des Beaux-Arts in 1909, made Commander of the Legion of Honor in 1910, and in 1922 was given a testimonial at the Sorbonne University by national decree.

During his last two decades, Fauré suffered from failing hearing which finally became complete deafness. He tried concealing this deformity from even close friends, but by 1920 realized he could no longer fulfil his duties as director of the Paris Conservatory, and resigned.

Fauré was perhaps at his best in the smaller forms and more intimate media: songs, piano pieces, chamber music. His was a personal art: sensitive, delicate, refined, expressing a restrained and classic beauty. His later music is more elusive in its appeal than his earlier works, owing to its overrefinement of writing and subtle construction. But Fauré's later works are by no means less distinguished, and at times they are touched by a spiritual incandescence that set them apart from the rest of his production.

The following are Fauré's major instrumental compositions.

Chamber Music: 2 piano quintets; 2 piano quartets; 2 violin sonatas; 2 cello sonatas; Piano Trio; String Quartet.

Orchestra: Symphony; Ballade for piano and orchestra; *Pelleas and Melisande,* suite; Fantaisie, for piano and orchestra; Pavene; Romance, for violin and orchestra; *Masques et bergamasques,* suite.

Piano: Valse-caprices; Dolly; Huit pièces brèves; impromptus, waltzes, nocturnes, barcarolles.

See: Ballade—*Fauré;* Barcarolle; *Dolly; Masques et bergamasques;* Nocturne; *Pelleas and Melisande;* Prelude—*Fauré;* Quartet—*Fauré;* Quintet—*Fauré;* Sonata —*Fauré.*

Faust. *See:* Goethe, Johann Wolfgang von; Lenau, Nikolaus.

Faust Overture, A (Eine Faust Ouvertuere). Concert overture by Wagner (1840), first performed in Dresden on July 22, 1844, the composer conducting. This is one of the few symphonic works by Wagner that is still performed. Its inspiration was the epic poem by Goethe. A melancholy introduction, in which the main thematic material is presented, suggests the despair of the aging Faust, contemplating his lost youth. An incisive staccato chord introduces the main body of the overture. The main theme is now heard in violins over harmonies in bassoons and horns. The second theme is later presented by the flute. Both subjects are expanded, and the overture ends with a brief coda.

Faust Symphony, A. *See:* Symphony—*Liszt.*

Feast at Solhaug, The. *See:* Ibsen, Henrik.

Fermata. A symbol indicating a long pause.

Feroce. Fiercely.

Fervente. Fervently.

Festin d'araignée, Le (The Spider's Banquet). Ballet suite for orchestra by Albert Roussel, op. 17 (1912). The ballet, with text by Gilbert de Voison based on Fabre's *Studies of Insect Life,* was introduced in Paris on April 3, 1913. The ballet suite for symphony orchestra was performed for the first time in New York on Oct. 23, 1914, Walter Damrosch conducting; it is one of the composer's most frequently played compositions. There are five sections. I. Prelude. A garden on a summer afternoon is here depicted. II. Entrance of the Ants. The ants industriously explore the garden and finally land on a rose petal. III. The Dance of the Butterfly. The butterfly dances into a spider's web where it meets death after a brief struggle. IV. Hatching of the Ephemera; Dance of the Ephemera. The hatching is celebrated with a frenetic dance. V. Funeral March of the Ephemera. All insects join in a solemn funeral procession for the dead ephemera.

Festivals (Debussy). *See: Fêtes;* Nocturnes.

Festspielhaus. *See:* Salzburg Festival.

Fête-Dieu à Séville (Albéniz). *See: Iberia* (1).

Fêtes. The second of three Impressionistic tone poems for orchestra by Claude Debussy collectively entitled Nocturnes (which see).

Feu d'artifice (Stravinsky). *See: Fireworks.*

Feuermann, Emanuel, cellist. Born Kolomea, Poland, Nov. 22, 1902; died New York City, May 25, 1942. As a child he studied the cello in Vienna, giving successful concerts when he was only eleven. Additional study took place later in Leipzig with Julius Klengel. Feuermann taught the cello in Leipzig until 1930, when he became head of the cello department of the Berlin High School of Music. All this while he made concert appearances throughout Europe. He left Germany in 1933 and settled in Vienna, but after the *Anschluss* he came to the United States, where he later became a citizen. Meanwhile, his American début took place in New York on Jan. 2, 1935, when he appeared as soloist with the New York Philharmonic, Bruno Walter conducting. Until his untimely death, Feuermann appeared throughout Europe and the United States, not only in recitals and with symphony orchestras but also with leading chamber-music ensembles.

Feuerzauber (Wagner). *See: Wotan's Farewell* and *Magic Fire Scene.*

Feux-Follets. *See:* Etude—*Liszt.*

Fidelio, Overture to. One of four overtures by Beethoven for his opera, *Fidelio.* (The other three are *Leonore Overture,* Nos. 1, 2, and 3.) Beethoven wrote the *Fidelio Overture,* op. 72, for a Vienna revival of his opera in 1814. (For the chronology of all four overtures *see: Leonore Overture,* No. 3.) The opera, libretto by Joseph Sonnleithner and Georg Friedrich Treitschke, was first performed in Vienna on Nov. 20, 1805. The *Fidelio Overture* uses none of the thematic material found in the three *Leonore Overtures.* It opens with a vigorous four-measure passage for full orchestra, which leads into a melody for horns. Two themes are prominent in the main body. The first comes in the horn and is answered by a clarinet; the second appears in the strings. A presto section developing a phrase from the first theme provides a dramatic conclusion.

Fiedler, Arthur, conductor. Born Boston, Mass., Dec. 17, 1894. He studied the violin with his father and with Willy Hess in Berlin. In 1915 he joined the viola section of the Boston Symphony, remaining there fifteen years. In 1925 he formed, and for several years conducted, the Boston Sinfonietta, the first such organization in the United States. He founded summer Esplanade concerts in Boston in 1929. Since 1930 he has been the conductor of the Boston Pops Orchestra. He has also appeared as guest conductor with other American and European orchestras. In 1954 he was made Chevalier of the Legion of Honor.

Fiedler, Max, conductor. Born Zittau, Germany, Dec. 31, 1859; died Stockholm, Sweden, Dec. 1, 1939. From 1887 to 1880 he attended the Leipzig Conservatory. In 1902 he was appointed a member of the faculty of the Hamburg Conservatory, and in 1903 its director. In 1904 he became conductor of the Hamburg Philharmonic. He made successful appearances with the New York Philharmonic in 1905-1906 and with the London Symphony in 1907; from 1908 to 1912 he was principal conductor of the Boston Symphony. From 1916 to 1933 he conducted the Essen Symphony Orchestra in Germany. After that he confined himself to guest appearances in Germany, Sweden, and at Beethoven festivals in Bonn.

Field, John, pianist and composer. Born Dublin, Ireland, July 26, 1782; died Moscow, Russia, Jan. 23, 1837. He studied the piano with Tommaso Giordani, who arranged for his début in Dublin in 1792. After settling in London in 1794, Field became apprentice, pupil, and protégé of Muzio Clementi, under whose guidance his career as virtuoso unfolded, first in England, then in the rest of Europe. In 1803 Field went to Russia, where he remained for several decades, enjoying high esteem as pianist and teacher. Both his health and his fortune were depleted by his dissolute way of life. In an effort to rehabilitate himself, Field toured the leading European capitals between 1832 and 1834. By the time he returned to Russia his health gave way completely. Though little known as a composer, and rarely performed, Field holds an important place in the growth and evolution of piano music. He wrote 7 piano concertos, 4 piano sonatas, and many smaller pieces, including 18 nocturnes (a form he created). He was one of the earliest of Romantics, whose impact on later

piano composers was profound. He both anticipated and influenced Chopin. His smaller pieces often suggested stylistic mannerisms found in later Romantics. As Liszt noted, Field's works "cleared the way for all subsequent efforts appearing under the names of Songs Without Words, impromptus, ballades, and the like."

Four piano pieces by Field were orchestrated as a symphonic suite by Sir Hamilton Harty: I. Polka; II. Nocturne; III. Slow Waltz; IV. Rondo.

See: Nocturne.

Fiesko. *See:* Schiller, Friedrich von.

Fifth. An interval between two notes separated by five diatonic tones, and consisting of three whole tones and a semitone.

Figuration. Ornamental passage.

Figurato. Free, florid.

Figured bass (or **Basso continuo**). *See:* Thorough bass.

Figured melody. A melody embellished with florid ornaments.

Fille aux cheveux de lin, La. *See:* Prelude —*Debussy.*

Finale. Concluding movement of a large composition in several movements.

Finck, Henry Theophilus, music critic. Born Bethel, Mo., Sept. 22, 1854; died Rumford Falls, Me., Oct. 1, 1926. He was graduated from Harvard with highest honors in 1876, after which he lived in Europe for several years studying philosophy and psychology. Back in the United States he became music critic of the New York *Evening Post* in 1881, holding this position for more than 40 years. In 1888 he was appointed to the faculty of the National Conservatory in New York. Finck wrote several books, including *Chopin and Other Essays* (1889), *Grieg and His Music* (1909), and *Richard Strauss* (1917). He also wrote his autobiography, *My Adventures in the Golden Age of Music* (1926).

Fine. End.

Fingal's Cave Overture (or **Hebrides Overture**). Concert overture by Mendelssohn, op. 26 (1830, revised 1832), introduced in London on May 14, 1832, Thomas Attwood conducting. A seascape in tones, this overture was inspired by a walking trip in the Scottish Highlands.

The opening theme came to Mendelssohn while he visited the caves of Staffa; it is heard in lower strings and bassoons and depicts the rolling waves at the mouth of the cave. After an extended treatment of this theme, a second subject is given by cellos and bassoons. The development section pays considerable attention to the first theme.

Fingerboard. That part of a string instrument on which the strings are stopped by the fingers.

Fingering. The science or technique of applying fingers to keys, strings, holes, or valves of a musical instrument.

Finlandia. Tone poem for orchestra by Sibelius, op. 26 (1899, revised 1900), first performed in Helsinki on July 2, 1900, the composer conducting. This is one of the composer's earliest works, and one of his most stirring national creations; to the Finnish people it is a second national anthem. So strongly national is *Finlandia* that for a long time people believed it was made up of actual Finnish folk tunes. But all the musical material is Sibelius' own. The work opens with a forceful statement in the brass, followed by a tender section for woodwind. There then comes a melody for strings, almost like a supplication. The storm and stress of struggle now dramatize the music before there enters the most famous melody of the composition—a prayer, first presented by woodwinds, then repeated by strings. A fiery section culminates in a climax in which the defiance of a people against tyranny is proudly proclaimed.

Fioritura. An embellishment, or ornament, to a melody.

Fire Symphony. *See:* Symphony—*Haydn.*

Firebird, The (L'Oiseau de feu). Three ballet suites for orchestra by Igor Stravinsky, derived from the score to a ballet successfully introduced in Paris by the Ballet Russe on June 25, 1910. This was the work with which the composer first achieved prominence. The ballet text was derived from an old Russian legend recounting the adventures of Ivan Czarevitch (son of the Czar). He captures, then frees, the Firebird, who rewards him with one of his magic feathers. Czarevitch comes into conflict with the evil Kastchei, who holds thirteen beautiful

princesses as prisoners. But the magic feather protects him. The Firebird helps Czarevitch destroy the Kastchei and free the princesses, one of whom becomes the Czarevitch's bride.

The second is the most popular of the three suites for orchestra prepared by the composer. It has six sections. I. Introduction. An eerie atmosphere is evoked with a theme for strings in low register and a somber subject in the woodwind against harmonics in violins and cellos. II. Dance of the Firebird. An undulating theme in strings and woodwind simulates the sinuous movements of the Firebird's dance. III. Dance of the Princesses. A graceful melody is presented by the oboe with harp accompaniment. IV. Dance of the Kastchei. By contrast, this movement offers a demoniac and savage dance. V. Berceuse. This is a gentle lullaby for the bassoon. VI. Finale. The last movement opens with a soft melody for horn solo against tremolo strings. From this point on, the music gains in intensity and excitement until a feverish section for strings brings the suite to a dramatic conclusion.

Fireworks (Feu d'artifice). Fantasy for orchestra by Stravinsky (1908). This is the composer's third orchestral work, written as a gift to his teacher, Rimsky-Korsakov, on the occasion of the marriage of the master's daughter, Sonia, to Maximilian Steinberg. The première took place in St. Petersburg on Feb. 6, 1909, Alexander Siloti conducting. The entire work is built from a four-bar melody, first given in fragments bar by bar, and after that treated canonically.

Fireworks Music (Handel). *See: Royal Fireworks Music, The.*

Firkušný, Rudolf, pianist. Born Napajedla, Czechoslovakia, Feb. 11, 1912. He attended the Brünn Conservatory, where his teachers included Josef Suk and Leoš Janáček. On June 14, 1920, he made his first concert appearance, in Prague, after which he toured Europe for several years. After additional piano study at the Master School in Prague and privately with Artur Schnabel, he made his American début in New York on Jan. 13, 1938, and in 1943 his first tour of South America. He has since distinguished himself not only in the Classical and Romantic repertory, but also in modern music, being responsible for the premières of major works for the piano by Bohuslav Martinu, Howard Hanson, and Gian Carlo Menotti, among others. He has also made notable appearances with leading chamber-music ensembles.

First inversion. In harmony, a chord in which the bass takes the third: for example, the first inversion of the chord CEG is EGC.

First Piano Quartet. A quartet of pianists comprising Vladimir Padwa, Frank Mittler, Adam Garner, and Edward Edson. The team was organized in 1941 in the United States, making its first appearances over the radio. Since then the ensemble has concertized extensively throughout the world and has made many recordings. Their programs are made up mostly of their own transcriptions.

Fischer, Edwin, pianist. Born Basel, Switzerland, Oct. 6, 1886. He studied at the Basel and Stern Conservatories. From 1905 to 1914 he was professor of piano at the Stern Conservatory and up to 1935 he held a similar post at the Berlin High School for Music. Meanwhile he achieved fame throughout Europe as a piano virtuoso, especially in the works of Bach and Mozart. He also gained prominence as conductor of a chamber orchestra which he founded, and with the Bach Verein in Munich.

Fistoulari, Anatol, conductor. Born Kiev, Russia, Aug. 20, 1907. His father was his first teacher. He made his first appearance, as a prodigy conductor, in Kiev when he was only eight. During World War I he settled in Paris, where he later conducted Russian operas starring Feodor Chaliapin. He conducted the Ballet Russe, with which he toured the United States in 1937 and 1939. During World War II he served in the French army. When France fell, he fled to England, which has since been his permanent home and in which he has conducted extensively, notably performances of the London Philharmonic. His wife, Anna, is the daughter of Gustav Mahler.

Fitelberg, Gregor, composer and conductor. Born Dvinsk, Latvia, Oct. 18, 1879; died Katowice, Poland, June 10, 1953. He attended the Warsaw Conservatory, then played the violin in the Warsaw Philharmonic, which he conducted for the first time in 1908. When World War I broke out he went to live in Russia, where, until 1921, he conducted symphony concerts. From 1921 to 1923 he conducted the Ballet Russe in Paris. After 1923, he distinguished himself as a principal conductor of the Warsaw Philharmonic and a guest conductor of other leading European orchestras. He was a passionate spokesman for contemporary Polish music, and an outstanding interpreter of Szymanowski's orchestral works. From 1942 to 1945 he lived in the United States. After World War II, he returned to Poland, where he conducted the Polish Radio and, in 1951, was recipient of the Polish State Prize. He was the composer of 2 symphonies, a violin sonata (which won the Paderewski Award in 1896), *Polish Rhapsody* for orchestra, a tone poem *In der Meerestiefe,* and some chamber music.

His son, Jerzy, was also a gifted composer, mainly in a contrapuntal style (born Warsaw, Poland, May 20, 1903; died New York City, April 25, 1951). He received his musical training from his father and at the Berlin High School for Music. In 1936 he received the Elizabeth Sprague Coolidge Award for a string quartet. He lived in the United States from 1940 until his death. His major works for orchestra include 3 suites, a concerto for orchestra, 2 violin concertos, and many shorter compositions; he also wrote 5 string quartets, 2 violin sonatas, and a sonata and sonatina for two violins and piano.

Fitzwilliam Virginal Book. The most significant collection of Elizabethan keyboard music, preserved in the Fitzwilliam Museum in Cambridge, England. It had been presented to Cambridge in 1816 by Viscount Fitzwilliam. Little of the early history of this collection is known, but the belief that it was once owned by Queen Elizabeth is false. (For a long time the collection was even known as "The Queen Elizabeth's Virginal Book.") The collection was first published by Breitkopf & Haertel in Germany in monthly installments between 1894 and 1899, edited by J. A. Fuller Maitland and W. Barclay Squire. It was finally assembled into two volumes. It is a remarkable repository of 17th-century English music by such masters as William Byrd, Giles Farnaby, Orlando Gibbons, John Bull, and Thomas Morley. John Barbirolli's *Elizabethan Suite* and Max Ettinger's *Alt-Englische Suite,* both for orchestra, are made up of orchestral transcriptions of pieces from this collection.

Five, The. *See:* Russian Five, The.

Five Pieces for Orchestra. By Arnold Schoenberg, op. 16 (1908), introduced in London on Sept. 3, 1912, Henry J. Wood conducting. At that time the program described this music as "experiments in dissonance." Here the composer finally abandons his former Romantic and Wagnerian tendencies for an atonal style in which he was to produce some of his most provocative works. The titles of the pieces provide some clue to their meaning: I. *Presentiments (Vorgefuehle)*; II. *The Past (Vergangenes)*; III. *The Changing Chord (Der wechselnde Akkord)*; IV. *Peripetia* (a Greek term indicating a sudden reversal of dramatic action); V. *The Obbligato Recitative (Das obligate Rezitativ)*. At the première performance this work provoked laughter and hissing. The critics also proved hostile. The *Daily Mail* inquired: "Why . . . should the ears of the . . . audience be tortured with scrappy sounds and perpetual discord?" Only Ernest Newman was tolerant: "I take leave to suggest that Schoenberg is not the mere fool or madman that he is generally supposed to be."

Flat. Symbol denoting the lowering of a note by half a step.

Flautando (or **flautato**). Production of flute-like sounds on the violin either through harmonics or by bowing over the fingerboard with the tip of the bow.

Fleisher, Leon, pianist. Born San Francisco, Calif., July 23, 1928. After studying the piano with Lev Shorr and Artur Schnabel, he made a successful appearance with the San Francisco Symphony in 1943; one year later he toured the United States. In 1952 he won first prize in the Queen Elizabeth of Belgium International Music Competition. After returning to the United States in 1954, he made extended tours throughout the world.

Flesch, Carl, violinist and teacher. Born Moson, Hungary, Oct. 9, 1873; died Lucerne, Switzerland, Nov. 14, 1944. He studied the violin with Jakob Gruen in Vienna and Martin Pierre Joseph Marsick at the Paris Conservatory. His first public appearance took place in Vienna in 1895, after which he was heard throughout Europe. From 1897 to 1902 he was professor of violin at the Bucharest Conservatory and chamber virtuoso to the Queen of Rumania. In 1909 he gave a notable series of concerts in Berlin tracing the history of violin music. In 1913 he made his first tour of the United States. He conducted master classes in violin in Berlin, Amsterdam, and from 1924 to 1928 at the Curtis Institute of Music. He is the author of several treatises on music and studies in violin technique; of the latter the most important is *The Art of Violin Playing* (1919). He also edited many violin compositions by Beethoven, Brahms, Mozart, and others.

Fliegende Hollaender, Overture to Der (Wagner). *See: Flying Dutchman, Overture to The.*

Flonzaley Quartet. One of the most notable chamber-music ensembles of the early 20th century. It was founded in New York City in 1902 by Edward J. De Coppet, with Adolfo Betti and Alfred Pochon, violins, Ugo Ara, viola, and Iwan d'Archambeau, cello. The name "Flonzaley" was taken from that of De Coppet's summer villa in Switzerland where the quartet first rehearsed. The Quartet made a triumphant tour of Europe and the United States in 1904. From then on it performed throughout the world, setting a standard of chamber-music performance which other ensembles would henceforth reach for. From 1917 to 1924 Louis Bailly filled the viola chair; he, in turn, was succeeded by Félicien d'Archambeau. The Quartet was disbanded in 1928 after a farewell tour that ended in London on April 14.

Florence May Music Festival (Maggio musicale fiorentino). A major music festival held each May in Florence, Italy.

Though opera is featured most prominently, the festival has also presented notable symphony concerts by local and visiting ensembles under outstanding conductors; also concerts of chamber music and recitals by famous virtuosos. The first festival took place in 1933; the second, in 1935. In 1937 the Italian government subsidized it, and from then on it became an annual event, except for the years of World War II. The orchestra of the Florentine May Music Festival, conducted by Adone Zecchi, toured the United States in the fall and winter of 1957.

Florestan and Eusebius. Imaginary characters invented by Schumann. He used these names as pseudonyms in his critical writings; and at times he personified himself through these characters in his compositions (as in *Carnaval* or *Davidsbündlertänze*). Florestan and Eusebius are opposites in temperament and personality. The former is dynamic and passionate, the latter, a dreamer.

Flower Maiden Scene (Wagner). *See: Klingsor's Magic Garden and Flower Maiden Scene.*

Flute. A wind instrument in which an air column is set into vibration by air blown across a mouth hole near the end of the tube. Together with its associate, the piccolo, the flute has the highest register of the woodwind instruments. *See also:* Boehm, Theobald.

Flying Dutchman, Overture to The (Der fliegende Hollaender). Overture to the opera by Wagner, first performed in Dresden on Jan. 2, 1843. Wagner's own libretto was based on an old legend adapted by Heinrich Heine. The overture opens with a stormy passage that leads to the Dutchman theme in horns and bassoons. The storm returns and is dissipated by the appearance of a beautiful motif from Senta's famous ballad. After a rousing sailor's dance the motif from Senta's ballad is enlarged and finally sounded by full orchestra.

Folia. An old Spanish or Portuguese dance in 3/4 time. Its melody became extremely popular and was used by many composers including Corelli.

Folia, La. Sonata for violin and accompaniment (or figured bass) by Arcangelo Corelli. This is the twelfth and most popular composition in a set of sonatas, op. 5. Structurally this work is not a sonata, but a set of variations on the popular *folia* melody. Rachmaninoff used this same melody for his Variations on a Theme by Corelli, for piano.

Foote, Arthur, composer. Born Salem, Mass., March 5, 1853; died Boston, Mass., April 8, 1937. He was graduated in 1874 from Harvard, where he studied composition with J. K. Paine. He later studied the organ with B. J. Lang. From 1878 to 1910 he was the organist of the First Unitarian Church in Boston, a period in which he wrote some distinguished chamber music performed by the Kneisel Quartet. His first large work for orchestra was the Suite in E major, introduced by the Boston Symphony in 1886, and still popular. The Boston Symphony also presented some of his later orchestral works; on the occasion of his 80th birthday it devoted an entire program to him. In 1899 he was elected a member of the American Academy of Arts and Sciences. From 1909 to 1912 he served as president of the American Guild of Organists, which he had helped to found.

Foote favored traditional structures and idioms, to which he brought a consummate craftsmanship and a fine feeling for well-sounding melodies and harmonies. His principal works for orchestra include 3 suites, *Night Piece* for flute and orchestra, the overture *In the Mountains,* the tone poem *Francesca da Rimini, Four Characters after Omar Khayyam,* and a Serenade in E. He also wrote 3 string quartets, 2 piano trios, a piano quintet, piano quartet, violin sonata, and cello sonata.

See: Suite—*Foote.*

Forelle Quintet, Die. *See:* Quintet—*Schubert.*

Forest Murmurs (Waldweben). Episode in Act 2 of Wagner's music drama *Siegfried* from the *Ring of the Nibelungs.* It is a pastoral poem for orchestra recreating the calls of birds and the murmur of forest trees. Siegfried, reclining under a tree, listens to the music of the forest and muses about his mysterious past. The whispering of the leaves is reproduced by the strings. Various leitmotifs trace the course of his shifting reverie: the "Volsung" theme (clarinets, then bassoons and horns); the "love-life" theme representing Siegfried's mother (cellos, violas, and double basses); and so forth. The murmur of the forest is then combined with the theme of the forest-bird (oboe, flute, and clarinet). The section ends with a recapitulation of some of the leitmotifs, principally those of Siegfried, the forest-bird, and fire.

Forlane. A lively Italian dance in 6/4 time or 6/8 time. It was used as a movement in J. S. Bach's orchestral Suite in C major.

Form. The structure of a musical composition; the arrangement of melody, harmony, counterpoint, rhythm, and so forth into an organic unity. The binary (two-section) or ternary (three-section) forms are among the most elementary; and the sonata form is among the most advanced.

Forte. Loud. The various degrees of loudness are designated by *mezzo-forte* (moderately loud), *più forte* (louder), and *fortissimo* (very loud).

Foss, Lukas, composer (born Lukas Fuchs). Born Berlin, Germany, Aug. 15, 1922. He studied music in Berlin with Julius Goldstein, and in Paris with Noël Gallon, Felix Wolfes, and Lazare Lévy. In 1937 he came to the United States, of which he later became a citizen. After attending the Curtis Institute and the Berkshire Music Centre he received a Pulitzer Scholarship in 1942. Recognition as a composer came in 1944 with a major work for chorus and orchestra, *The Prairie.* In 1945 he became the youngest composer ever to receive a Guggenheim Fellowship, and in 1950 he was awarded a Fulbright Fellowship for travel in Italy. After returning from Rome he became, in 1953, professor of composition at the University of California in Los Angeles. Foss has also appeared as concert pianist and conductor; for several years beginning with 1944 he was the official pianist of the Boston Symphony. His principal works for orchestra include 2 piano concertos, an oboe concerto, Symphony in G, *Symphony of Chorales, Song of Anguish* for

baritone and orchestra, *Song of Songs* for soprano and orchestra, *Pantomime, A Parable of Death* for narrator, tenor, chorus, and orchestra, and *Recordare.* Among his chamber-music compositions are a string quartet, violin sonata, Capriccio for cello and piano, and Three Pieces for violin and piano.

Foster, Stephen Collins, composer. Born Lawrenceville (now Pittsburgh), Pa., July 4, 1826; died New York City, Jan. 13, 1864. Some of Foster's best-loved songs have been used in orchestral compositions. Among these works are: Robert Russell Bennett's *American Ballade;* Mario Castelnuovo-Tedesco's *Humoresques on Foster's Themes;* Lucien Cailliet's *Memories of Stephen Foster;* and Werner Janssen's *Foster Suite.* Ernest Bloch quoted *Old Folks at Home* in *America;* John Alden Carpenter *Massa's in de Cold, Cold Ground* in *Skyscrapers;* Aaron Copland and Elie Siegmeister, *Camptown Races* in *A Lincoln Portrait* and *Prairie Legend,* respectively.

Fountains of Rome (Fontane di Roma). Tone poem for orchestra by Ottorino Respighi (1916), first performed in Rome on March 11, 1917, Antonio Guarnieri conducting. This work consists of impressionistic pictures of images evoked for the composer by four of Rome's most famous fountains at different times of the day. I. The Fountain of Valle Giulia at Dawn. This describes cattle "in the fresh, damp mists of a Roman dawn." Bits of pastoral melodies in woodwind and brass culminate in a melody for oboe, repeated by clarinet. A loud horn call above trills brings on the second picture. II. The Fountain of the Triton in the Morning. This gay music portrays a dance of naiads and tritons. One dance tune is heard in flutes, clarinets, and harp; another, in the violins. III. The Fountain of Trevi at Midday. This solemn music represents a procession of sirens and tritons headed by Neptune's chariot. The music gains in intensity and sonority until it becomes a triumphant outcry; then the sonority decreases and the section ends with a call in horn and trumpets. IV. The Fountain of the Villa Medici at Dusk. "The air is full of the sound of tolling bells, birds twittering, leaves rustling." The violins present a melody against harp glissandos. This is followed by other brief themes in flute, horn, and violins. The first melody returns to conclude the tone poem in a tranquil mood.

Four Legends (Sibelius). *See: Swan of Tuonela, The.*

Four Norwegian Moods. Suite for orchestra by Igor Stravinsky (1942), first performed by the Boston Symphony on Jan. 14, 1944, the composer conducting. While the music is based on actual Norwegian folk melodies, the composer has emphasized that he used this material only "as a rhythmic and melodic basis." He goes on to explain that this composition is "purely a mode, a form or manner of style without any assumption of ethnological authenticity."

Four Roman Sketches. Suite for piano by Charles Tomlinson Griffes, op. 7 (1916). The most famous movement is the first, *The White Peacock* (which see), more familiar as an orchestral tone poem than in its original piano version. The other three movements are *Nightfall, The Fountain of Acqua Paola,* and *Clouds.*

Four Sea Interludes. Four interludes for orchestra by Benjamin Britten from his opera *Peter Grimes.* The opera, introduced in London on June 7, 1945, made the composer world-famous; the libretto, by Montagu Slater, is based on a poem by George Crabbe. The four interludes, sometimes presented on symphony programs, are as follows: I. Dawn. Heard between the prologue and Act I, this music is a description of the somber atmosphere of a little fishing town at dawn as fishermen begin their day's tasks. II. Sunday Morning. This is another atmospheric picture, a transition into Act 2. It is Sunday, and church bells are ringing. III. Moonlight. This episode leads into Act 3 and depicts a fishing village street scene at night. IV. The Storm. Occurring between scenes 1 and 2 of Act 1, this vivid and dramatic music portrays a storm as it lashes through the village.

Four Seasons, The. *See:* Concerto Grosso —*Vivaldi.*

Four Temperaments (Hindemith). *See: Theme with Variations according to the Four Temperaments.*

Four Tone Poems after Boecklin (Vier Tondichtungen nach Arnold Boecklin). Suite for orchestra by Max Reger, op. 128 (1913), first performed in Essen on Oct. 12, 1913, the composer conducting. Each of the four movements was inspired by a Boecklin painting: I. *The Hermit with the Violin (Der geigende Eremit);* II. *Among the Play of the Waves (Im Spiel der Wellen);* III. *The Isle of the Dead (Die Toteninsel);* IV. *Bacchanale.*

Fournier, Pierre, cellist. Born Paris, France, June 24, 1906. He attended the Paris Conservatory, where he was a pupil of André Hekking. His concert début took place in Paris in 1925. From then on, he made many tours of Europe, achieving considerable popularity. In 1939 he gave 32 concerts in Berlin alone. From 1937 to 1939 he was professor of cello and chamber music at the Ecole Normale de Musique in Paris, and from 1941 to 1949, professor of the cello at the Paris Conservatory. He made his first tour of the United States in 1948, and of South America in 1949. Between 1948 and 1950 he appeared at major European festivals. He was made Chevalier of the Legion of Honor in 1953.

Fourth. An interval between two notes separated by four diatonic tones, consisting of two whole tones and a semitone.

Françaix, Jean, composer. Born Le Mans, France, May 23, 1912. Françaix's early musical training took place at the Le Mans Conservatory, of which his father was director; then at the Paris Conservatory, where in 1930 he received first prize in piano playing. He also studied harmony and counterpoint with Nadia Boulanger. He first attracted attention with his Bagatelles for string quartet, performed at the International Society for Contemporary Music in Vienna in 1932. In the same year Pierre Monteux introduced in Paris Françaix's Symphony. A Concerto and Concertino, both for piano, in 1934 and 1937 respectively, added appreciably to his rapidly growing fame. A neo-Classic composer strongly influenced by Stravinsky, Françaix is partial to slight forms, economical statements, and spare harmonies and instrumentation. His best works are often touched with irony. He made his American début in New York on Feb. 11, 1938, in his own Piano Concerto. His Serenade for Twelve Instruments, written in 1934, was successfully used as the music for a ballet entitled, *À la Françaix,* introduced by the New York City Ballet in 1951. Besides the orchestral works already mentioned Françaix wrote seven waltzes collectively entitled *Les Bosquets de Cythère,* a Symphony for Strings, and a rhapsody for viola and wind instruments. His chamber music includes a sonata for two violins and cello, piano trio, woodwind quintet, string quartet, saxophone quartet, woodwind trio, *Variations sans thème* for cello and piano, trumpet sonatina, and a Quintet for violin, cello, viola, harp, and flute.

See: Concertino—*Françaix;* Concerto —*Françaix.*

Francesca da Rimini. (1) Symphonic fantasia by Tchaikovsky, op. 32 (1876), introduced in Moscow on March 9, 1877, Nicholas Rubinstein conducting. Inspired by the fifth canto of Dante's *Inferno,* this music tells the tragic love story of Paolo and Francesca. The composer himself provided a program for his music. I. Introduction: The gateway to the Inferno. Tortures and agonies of the condemned. II. Francesca tells the story of her tragic love for Paolo. III. The Turmoil of Hades. Conclusion. The three parts are played without interruption. The turbulent underworld is evoked in the opening and closing sections. The main melody is a song, for clarinet against pizzicato strings, in which Francesca tells of her love .

(2) *See:* Dante Alighieri.

Francescatti, Zino, violinist. Born Marseilles, France, Aug. 9, 1905. After some study of the violin with his father he made his first public appearance at the age of five; in his tenth year he was acclaimed for his performance of the Beethoven Concerto; and when he was twenty his reputation was firmly established with a successful début in Paris. His subsequent performances throughout Europe placed him in the front rank of contemporary French violinists. He made

his American début on Nov. 8, 1939, as soloist with the New York Philharmonic. Since then he has appeared throughout the world of music.

Francis of Assisi (born **Giovanni Francesco Bernardone**), monk and preacher. Born Assisi, Italy, about 1182; died there Oct. 3, 1226. The founder of the Roman Catholic order of Franciscans, Francis of Assisi and his writings were the inspiration of several musical compositions; among them are Mario Castelnuovo-Tedesco's *Tre Fioretti,* for voice and orchestra; Giorgio Ghedini's *Cantico del sole,* for voice and string orchestra; Liszt's legend for piano, *St. Francis Preaching to the Birds;* Charles Martin Loeffler's *Canticum Fratris Solis,* for voice and chamber orchestra; Charles Tournemire's tone poem for orchestra, *Saint Françoise d'Assise;* and Hermann Wetzler's symphonic legend for orchestra, *Assisi.*

Franck, César, composer. Born Liège, Belgium, Dec. 10, 1822; died Paris, France, Nov. 8, 1890. At the Liège Conservatory, Franck concentrated on the piano. He was on a concert tour when he was only eleven, and at thirteen won the Conservatory first prize in piano. In 1837 he entered the Paris Conservatory. Though a brilliant student—winning prizes in piano, fugue, and organ playing—he was withdrawn from the Conservatory in 1842 because his father wanted him to become a virtuoso. Between 1842 and 1844 Franck made several tours as a pianist. But recognizing his shortcomings as a virtuoso he decided to devote himself to composition. His first major work was *Ruth,* a biblical eclogue, introduced at the Conservatory in 1846. From then on he continued working devotedly at composition; but he also played the organ and taught piano and solfeggio. In 1858, after having held various minor organ posts, he became principal organist of Sainte Clotilde, a position he occupied until the end of his life. In 1872 he was appointed professor of organ at the Paris Conservatory. There he was responsible for creating a new interest in absolute music. Many pupils came under his influence and were inspired by him, among them being Gabriel Pierné, Vincent d'Indy, and Ernest Chausson. A humble man who dedicated himself to the highest principles of his art, Franck lived for many years an obscure existence. The masterworks he was producing failed to gain him any appreciable recognition. Inadequate performances of major works did much to alienate his public and critics. Between 1873 and 1877 several important compositions were introduced in Paris: an oratorio, *The Redemption; Variations symphoniques,* for piano and orchestra; and *Le Chasseur maudit,* for orchestra. All suffered severely from poor performances. Even the première of his now-famous Symphony, in 1889, was a fiasco. A small group of faithful pupils and disciples knew his true value as a composer and teacher. Other contemporaries regarded him as an obscure, somewhat eccentric musician whose importance rested more on his organ playing (which was truly remarkable) than on his compositions.

Not until the last year of his life did he receive any measure of public recognition. This happened on April 19, 1890, with the première of his String Quartet, acclaimed by both audience and critics. His death, the following winter, was brought on by pleurisy.

Franck was a Romanticist who worked within classical structures. Maturity as a creator came to him comparatively late (not until his fifty-second year). But once it came, he was able to produce a succession of works in which his creative power kept growing all the time. To his greatest music he brought poetic beauty, serenity, profound religious feeling, and at times mysticism and spirituality. His music was like the man who created it— at peace with the world, consecrated to God and art.

He had some individual mannerisms as a composer. He had a tendency to reduce melodies to fragments, to use shifting harmonies and rapid modulations, and to indulge in rambling improvisations. He was also partial to a structural technique of his own creation, the "cyclic form." This technique employs melodic fragments called "generative phrases" which are permitted to grow into fully developed melodies. Unity of structure is achieved through the recapitulation in the later movements of a large work of material from earlier ones.

The following are Franck's principal instrumental compositions.

Chamber Music: Piano Quintet in F minor; Violin Sonata in A major; String Quartet in D major.

Orchestra: Les Eolides; Le Chasseur maudit; Les Djinns; Variations symphoniques, for piano and orchestra; Symphony in D minor; *Psyché.*

Organ: 44 *Petites pièces,* for harmonium; *Offertory on a Breton melody;* Andantino; *L'Organiste,* 55 pieces for harmonium; Three Chorales.

Piano: Les Plaintes d'une poupée; Prelude, Chorale and Fugue; *Danse lente;* Prelude, Aria and Finale.

See: Chasseur maudit, Le; Eolides, Les; Prelude, Chorale and Fugue; *Psyché;* Quartet—*Franck;* Quintet—*Franck;* Sonata—*Franck;* Symphony—*Franck; Variations symphoniques.*

Frankenstein, Alfred, music critic. Born Chicago, Ill., Oct. 5, 1906. He received his academic education at Yale and the University of Chicago, while studying music privately. From 1931 to 1934 he was assistant music critic of the Chicago *American,* and from 1932 to 1934 instructor in music at the University of Chicago. In 1935 he was appointed lecturer at Mills College, California. Since 1934 he has been the principal music critic of the San Francisco *Chronicle,* and the program annotator for the San Francisco Symphony. Always a penetrating student of art, as well as of music, he received a Guggenheim Fellowship in 1947 to write a book on American still-life painting. In 1957 Frankenstein established an annual award, "Fund for Second Performances," to encourage conductors to repeat contemporary works which have had only a single performance.

Franko, Sam, violinist and conductor. Born New Orleans, La., Jan. 20, 1857; died New York City, May 6, 1937. He studied the violin in Europe with Joseph Joachim and Henri Vieuxtemps, among others. After returning to the United States he played the violin in the Mendelssohn Quartet, the Theodore Thomas Orchestra, and the New York Philharmonic. In an effort to destroy the prejudice then existing against American-born musicians he organized in 1894 the American Symphony, composed entirely of native musicians. With this organization he gave distinguished concerts of old music, including many works heard for the first time in the United States. Franko was also a distinguished violin teacher, arranger of 17th- and 18th-century music, and transcriber of music for the violin. He was the author of an autobiography, *Chords and Discords* (1938).

His brother, Nahan (born New Orleans, La., July 23, 1861; died Amityville, Long Island, June 7, 1930), was a pioneer in promoting free concerts in New York. He studied the violin in Europe with Joseph Joachim and August Wilhelmj, then played in leading orchestras in America and Europe. He was the first American-born conductor to serve at the Metropolitan Opera in New York. In 1907 he founded the Franko Orchestra, which for two decades gave free concerts in New York and was responsible for inaugurating city-sponsored concerts in the public parks.

Freccia, Massimo, conductor. Born Florence, Italy, Sept. 19, 1906. His musical training took place at the Florence Conservatory and with Franz Schalk in Vienna. In 1930 and 1931 he filled minor engagements as conductor in Europe. From 1933 to 1935 he was principal conductor of the Budapest Philharmonic. In the latter year he conducted distinguished performances with the La Scala Orchestra in Milan. He made his American début at the Lewisohn Stadium in New York on July 17, 1938. From 1939 to 1943 he was principal conductor of the Havana Philharmonic; from 1944 to 1952 of the New Orleans Symphony; and from 1952 to 1958 of the Baltimore Symphony.

Frederick II, the Great, king of Prussia, patron of music and amateur flutist. Born Berlin, Germany, Jan. 24, 1712; died Potsdam, Germany, Aug. 17, 1786. He studied the flute with Gottlieb Hayne and Johann Joachim Quantz. When Frederick ascended the throne in 1740 he established a court orchestra, and in 1742 added to it a well equipped opera house. From 1740 to 1767 he employed Carl Philipp Emanuel Bach at court as harpsichordist. Throughout his life, Frederick played the flute daily, and wrote numerous compositions for that instrument, including several sonatas; his compositions were published in three volumes by Breitkopf & Härtel (1889).

Freischuetz, Overture to Der. Overture to the German Romantic opera by Carl Maria von Weber, introduced in Berlin on June 18, 1821. The libretto, by Friedrich Kind, was based on a folk tale. After some introductory measures there is a stately subject for four horns accompanied by strings. The main section of the overture presents the principal theme in the strings; this is a spacious melody representing the heroine, Agathe. The Agathe melody reappears in the closing coda.

French horn. A brass instrument, lower in register than the trumpet, but higher than the trombone. The length of its tube, which is coiled in circles, may be extended by means of valves. A wide bell expands from one end, while the other end has a funnel-shaped mouth. The tone is romantic and stately.

French overture. *See:* Overture.

French Six, The. *See: Six, Les.*

French Suites. A set of six suites for piano by Johann Sebastian Bach. For a discussion of these works as distinct from six other compositions for piano entitled English Suites, *see: English Suites.* The six French Suites are: No. 1, D minor; No. 2, C minor; No. 3, B minor; No. 4, E-flat; No. 5, G major; No. 6, E major. Characteristic of this group of works is the graceful and delicate sixth suite, whose movements are: I. Allemande; II. Courante; III. Sarabande; IV. Gavotte; V. Polonaise; VI. Bourrée; VII. Gigue.

Frescobaldi, Girolamo, organist and composer. Born Ferrara, Italy, Sept. 1583; died Rome, March 1, 1643. He was a pupil of Luzzasco Luzzaschi in Ferrara. In 1607 he was appointed organist at Santa Maria in Trastevere in Rome, and in 1608 he became the organist of St. Peter's. He received a leave of absence from the latter cathedral in 1628. For the next five years he served as court organist in Florence. After that he returned to his post at St. Peter's, where he remained for the rest of his life. Frescobaldi was one of the most distinguished organists of his generation. His first appearance at St. Peter's was said to have attracted 30,000 music lovers. In his many works for organ he was one of the first to realize an instrumental style, and to express in it warm feeling and a personal lyricism. He helped to clarify and establish such important organ forms as the toccata, partita, and fugue. In doing so, he helped set the stage for Johann Sebastian Bach.

Fricsay, Ferenc, conductor. Born Budapest, Hungary, Aug. 9, 1914. He attended the Budapest Musical Academy, where his teachers included Béla Bartók and Zoltán Kodály. In 1936 he made his conducting début in Szeged, then achieved recognition as conductor of the Budapest Opera. He made numerous appearances throughout Europe as guest conductor both in opera and symphonic music. In 1949 he became principal conductor of the RIAS Orchestra in West Berlin. He made his American début on Nov. 13, 1953, with the Boston Symphony. In the fall of 1954 he was appointed principal conductor of the Houston Symphony in Texas. However, he conducted only a few concerts, then resigned his post owing to differences with the management over artistic policies.

Fried, Oscar, conductor. Born Berlin, Germany, Aug. 10, 1871; died Moscow, Russia, July 1941. He attended the Berlin High School of Music after which he studied composition with Engelbert Humperdinck in Frankfort-on-the-Main. After playing the horn in various orchestras he was appointed principal conductor of the then recently organized Bluethner Orchestra in 1908. He appeared as guest conductor throughout Europe and Russia, and became the first German conductor to direct concerts in Paris after World War I. In 1925 he was made permanent conductor of the Berlin Symphony. He made his American début with the New York Symphony in 1928. After the rise of the Nazi regime he left Germany and settled in Tiflis, where he became a So-

viet citizen and led opera performances.

Friedberg, Carl, pianist. Born Bingen, Germany, Sept. 18, 1872; died Merano, Italy, Sept. 8, 1955. He attended the Conservatory at Frankfort-on-the-Main where his teachers included Clara Schumann. His concert career began in 1892 when he appeared as soloist with the Vienna Philharmonic, Gustav Mahler conducting. Between 1893 and 1914 he taught piano at the Conservatories in Frankfort and Cologne. During this period he concertized throughout Europe. His American début took place in New York on Nov. 2, 1914. He became professor of the piano at the Institute of Musical Art, and subsequently head of the piano department at the Juilliard School of Music.

Friedheim, Arthur, pianist. Born St. Petersburg, Russia, Oct. 26, 1859; died New York City, Oct. 19, 1932. While attending the University of St. Petersburg he studied the piano with Anton Rubinstein. He also studied with Liszt, whose secretary and disciple he became, as well as one of the most authoritative interpreters of his piano music. Friedheim made his first tour of the United States in 1891, and in 1897 he joined the faculty of Chicago Musical College. He traveled several times around the world giving concerts. In 1911 he was a principal participant at Liszt festivals in America and Europe. He settled permanently in the United States in 1915 and devoted himself to teaching and concert work.

Friedman, Ignaz, pianist. Born Podgorze, Poland, Feb. 14, 1882; died Sydney, Australia, Jan. 26, 1948. He made several appearances as a child prodigy, then studied in Vienna with Guido Adler and Theodor Leschetizky, and in Leipzig with Hugo Riemann. He made his first concert tour of Europe in 1905 and was immediately acclaimed for his performances of Chopin. In 1920 he made his début in the United States. For the next decade and a half he toured the world, giving almost 3,000 performances by the time he died. He edited all of Chopin's works besides writing many pieces for the piano and making numerous transcriptions.

Friends of Music. A musical society organized in New York City in 1913 by

Mrs. Harriet Lanier to present Sunday afternoon concerts of unusual music. The first concert took place on Dec. 7, 1913, under Franz Kneisel's direction. Artur Bodanzky, after directing some of its performances for several years, became permanent conductor in 1921, and held this post until the Society was disbanded a decade later. The Society was responsible for many distinguished world, American, and New York premières, among which were Arnold Schoenberg's first *Kammersymphonie,* Gustav Mahler's Eighth Symphony and *Das Lied von der Erde,* Arthur Honegger's *King David,* and Ernest Bloch's *Schelomo* and *Israel Symphony.* The Society was also responsible for the revival of many long-neglected choral and orchestral masterworks of the 17th and 18th centuries.

Froberger, Johann Jacob, organist and composer. Born Stuttgart, Germany, May 18, 1616; died Héricourt, France, May 7, 1667. After studying the organ with his father, Froberger became a court organist at Vienna in 1637. He remained there until 1657, except for leaves of absence. During one of these he stayed three and a half years in Italy studying with Frescobaldi; in several others he toured Europe as organ virtuoso. In his last years he was music master to the Duchess Sybille of Wuerttemberg. Froberger wrote many works for organ and harpsichord: suites, fantasias, canzonas, ricercari, toccatas, caprices, and so on. These were significant in solidifying these instrumental forms (particularly the keyboard suite, which he is said to have created) and in crystallizing an instrumental style.

Frog Quartet. *See:* Quartet—*Haydn.*

Frogs, The. *See:* Aristophanes.

From My Life. *See:* Quartet—*Smetana.*

From the Fields and Groves of Bohemia (Smetana). *See: My Country.*

From the New World Symphony. *See:* Symphony—*Dvořák.*

Frontiers. Tone poem for orchestra by Paul Creston (1943). It was commissioned by André Kostelanetz, who introduced it in Toronto on Oct. 14, 1943. In three sections (played without interruption), this music tells of the great western migration in the United States a century ago. The work is based on a single theme, first heard in a muted trumpet.

Fuer Elise (Beethoven). *See:* Bagatelle.

Fugato. A passage in fugal style.

Fughetta. A little fugue.

Fugue. The most complex of contrapuntal forms. It is usually for three, four, or five "voices" (or contrapuntal parts). In the first section of the fugue, called the exposition, the theme of the fugue, called the "subject," is presented by each voice in turn. After the subject is stated by the first voice it is repeated a fifth higher or a fourth lower by the second voice, while the first voice continues with a counter-subject. The third voice then presents the subject an octave higher or lower than the first, and additional voices, if any, enter similarly. The exposition is followed by a free development in which there are usually episodes, modulations, restatements of the material with the voices entering in a different order, and the theme may be subjected to all sorts of changes such as augmentation, diminution, inversion, and so on. Two devices frequently employed near the end are the stretto, in which the voices follow one another so closely as to overlap, and the pedal point, in which the bass sustains a single tone while other voices are active above it.

Fundamental bass. The root of a chord, or root notes in a series of chords.

Funerailles. Seventh piece in the piano suite, *Harmonies poétiques et religieuses* by Liszt (1849). This threnody, one of the most eloquent in the piano literature, may have been written in memory of Chopin, who died the month it was written. Some believe it was meant to honor Liszt's friends victimized by the recent revolution in Europe. In any event, personal grief finds voice in this music. A short dramatic section leads to the funeral march. The trio has tender feeling. A secondary martial theme is then stated and built up into a climax. The main funeral music and its trio are now repeated. The work ends with a final statement of the second martial theme.

Funeral March. The two most famous funeral marches in music are movements from larger works. One is the second movement of Beethoven's Symphony No.

3, the *Eroica;* the other is the third movement of Chopin's Sonata No. 2 in B-flat minor, for piano. Beethoven's piano sonata No. 12 in A-flat major, op. 26, also has a third-movement funeral march; this is popular not only in its original version, but also in transcriptions for orchestra and for brass band. The music for *Siegfried's Death* in Wagner's music drama *The Twilight of the Gods* from *The Ring of the Nibelungs* cycle is not actually a funeral march but funeral music. *See also: Funerailles.*

Fuoco. Fire.

Furiant. A fiery Bohemian dance in 3/4 time marked by cross rhythms. One of the most popular examples of this dance in orchestral music is an interlude in Act 2 of Bedrich Smetana's folk opera, *The Bartered Bride.* Other Bohemian composers, including Antonín Dvořák, also interpolated furiants into their symphonic and chamber-music compositions, or wrote independent pieces in this form.

Furtwaengler, Wilhelm, conductor. Born Berlin, Germany, Jan. 25, 1886; died Baden Baden, Germany, Nov. 30, 1954. He was eight when he began studying music in Munich with Max von Schillings and Josef Rheinberger. After serving his apprenticeship as conductor with several minor German and Swiss orchestras, he was appointed conductor of opera and symphonic music in Mannheim. Several other posts, in Vienna, Berlin, and Frankfort, led in 1922 to his appointment as Arthur Nikisch's successor as principal conductor of the Leipzig Gewandhaus Orchestra and the Berlin Philharmonic. He rapidly assumed a preeminent position among Germany's conductors. On Jan. 3, 1925, he made a sensational début in the United States as guest conductor of the New York Philharmonic. He returned to the United States for the next three seasons to fill guest engagements with that orchestra. He also appeared throughout Europe, directing both opera and symphonic music; in 1931 he made his first appearance at the Bayreuth Festival.

Furtwaengler became a controversial figure in Germany soon after the Nazis assumed power. At first he was embraced by the new rulers and given the significant appointments of Deputy President of the Reich Chamber of Music, director of the Berlin State Opera, and principal conductor of the Bayreuth Festival. But he soon aroused the enmity of Nazi officials by his insistence on performing Hindemith's *Mathis der Maler,* which the Nazis considered antagonistic to their ideology. As a result of this altercation, Furtwaengler was forced to resign all his posts. But six months later he was restored to favor, once again to be a leading musical figure in Germany. After the *Anschluss,* he also became the Director of Musical Life in Vienna.

His intimate associations with the Nazi regime made Furtwaengler *persona non grata* in the United States after the war, even though he was officially absolved of pro-Nazi activities in 1946. Several attempts to bring him back to the United States, first as conductor of the New York Philharmonic, then of the Chicago Symphony, collapsed in the face of public opposition. But his musical position in Europe remained unchallenged; his performances in all parts of Europe, and at leading festivals, were musical events of first significance.

In 1955 Furtwaengler was finally permitted to return to the United States to direct the Berlin Philharmonic on its first tour of America, but he died before this tour materialized. Whatever might still be the reaction to Furtwaengler's political associations in the turbulent era in Germany preceding and during World War II, there can be no question of his musical significance. He was a giant figure, an interpreter of immense scholarship and profound insight. He was the author of *Concerning Music* (1953).

Fux, Johann Joseph, composer and theorist. Born Hirtenfeld, Styria, 1660; died Vienna, Austria, Feb. 14, 1741. Little is known of his early life and musical training. After serving as organist at the Schottenkirche in Vienna he became court composer in 1698. He later was appointed Kapellmeister at St. Stephen's, assistant Kapellmeister at court, and from 1713 until his death full Kapellmeister there. He was the composer of over 400 works, few of which were published; none are still performed. He is remembered for his *Gradus ad Parnassum*, a scholarly treatise on counterpoint (1725) which as recently as 1943 was republished in an English translation as *Steps to Parnassus*. Fux wrote it in Latin, in the form of a dialogue between teacher and pupil. It has two sections, the first theoretical, and the second practical.

G

G Clef. Treble clef.

Gabrieli, Andrea, organist and composer. Born Venice, Italy, about 1520; died there, 1586. He studied the organ with Adrian Willaert. From 1566 to 1585 he was second organist at San Marco, and first organist after that. He was one of the most celebrated organ virtuosos and teachers of his time, and the composer of many organ pieces including canzoni and ricercari which are historically significant.

His nephew, Giovanni Gabrieli, was also a distinguished organist and composer (born Venice, Italy, about 1557; died there, Aug. 12, 1612). He was a pupil of his uncle, whom he succeeded as second organist of San Marco in 1585. His instrumental compositions exerted a far-reaching influence on his Italian contemporaries, and through his German pupils on the early development of German instrumental music; they include canzoni, sonatas, fantasias, toccatas, and ricercari.

Gabrilowitsch, Ossip, pianist and conductor. Born St. Petersburg, Russia, Feb. 7, 1878; died Detroit, Mich., Sept. 14, 1936. He attended the St. Petersburg Conservatory, where his teachers included Anton Rubinstein, Anatol Liadov, and Alexander Glazunov, and from which he was graduated with the Rubinstein Prize. From 1894 to 1896 he studied with Theodor Leschetizky in Vienna. His concert career began in Berlin in 1896 and was followed by a European tour. He made his American début in New York on Nov. 12, 1900. On several occasions, both in Europe and America, he gave cycles of concerts tracing the evolution of piano music from Bach to the 20th century. In 1909 he married Clara Clemens, concert contralto and daughter of Mark Twain; he often appeared with her in joint concerts. Meanwhile in 1906 he launched a new career as conductor in Paris, Vienna, and Manchester. From 1910 to 1914 he conducted the Konzertverein Orchestra in Munich. After establishing permanent residence in the United States, where he later became a citizen, he made his American début as conductor in New York in 1917. From 1918 until his death he was the principal conductor of the Detroit Symphony. Despite his success as conductor he continued appearing as concert pianist until the end of his life.

Gade, Niels, composer. Born Copenhagen, Denmark, Feb. 22, 1817; died there, Dec. 21, 1890. He was the creator of the modern school of Scandinavian composers. He was taught the violin by several local teachers, then made his début at Copenhagen in 1833. He attended a music school connected with the court orchestra, studying composition with A. P. Berggreen, who awakened his enthusiasm for Danish folk music and poetry. Gade's first work to attract notice, and from then on one of his best-known compositions, was *Echoes from Ossian* (*Nachklaenge von Ossian*), awarded first prize by the Copenhagen Musical Society, successfully performed in Copenhagen in 1841, and published in Germany. His Symphony in C minor scored another major success when Mendelssohn introduced it at Leipzig in 1843. Gade was now granted a government subsidy enabling him to travel to Germany and

Italy. Mendelssohn invited him to conduct several concerts of the Gewandhaus Orchestra; on Mendelssohn's death in 1847, Gade succeeded him as permanent conductor. He returned to Denmark in 1848, from then on occupying a commanding position in Danish music as composer, director of the Copenhagen Conservatory (which he helped found), and conductor of the Copenhagen Musical Society. In 1876 the government bestowed on him a life pension. In his music Gade successfully combined German Romantic tendencies with Danish nationalism. He wrote 8 symphonies, 6 overtures, a violin concerto, various shorter works for orchestra, 2 string quintets, 3 violin sonatas, string octet, string quartet, piano sonata, and numerous shorter pieces for piano and for organ.

Galant Style (Galanter Stil). An elegant, graceful, homophonic style of writing music developed about the middle of the 18th century.

Galanteries. In the 18th-century suite any movements that were not essential to the structure but were interpolated. Movements like the minuet, gavotte, bourrée, loure, polonaise, air, and passepied were regarded as *galanteries* since they were not basic to the classic suite form.

Galliard. An old, spirited dance usually in triple time.

Galuppi, Baldassare (Il Buranello), composer. Born Burano, Italy, Oct. 18, 1706; died Venice, Italy, Jan. 3, 1785. He studied music with his father, and with Antonio Lotti in Venice. In 1748 he became assistant chapelmaster at St. Mark's, becoming full chapelmaster in 1762. He also was the director of the Conservatorio degli Incurabili, and from 1766 to 1768 was court musician in Russia. Galuppi was most famous for his operas. He also wrote some instrumental music for the harpsichord, for organ, and for stringed instruments. Robert Browning wrote a poem *To a Toccata of Galuppi,* but the specific work he had in mind was never identified.

Gamut. Range of a voice or an instrument; also a scale.

Ganz, Rudolph, pianist, conductor, and teacher. Born Zurich, Switzerland, Feb. 24, 1877. After attending the Zurich Conservatory he studied the piano in Berlin with Ferruccio Busoni. In December 1899 he appeared as soloist with the Berlin Philharmonic. After a European tour, he came to the United States in the fall of 1900, serving for five years as head of the piano department of the Chicago Musical College. His American début as pianist took place in Chicago on May 10, 1902. He now made the United States his permanent home, and applied for citizenship. His concert tours were extensive, and his programs were enlivened by a consistent interest both in modern music and in the forgotten piano literature of the past. From 1921 to 1927 he was the principal conductor of the St. Louis Symphony; from 1938 to 1949 he was conductor of the Young People's Concerts of the New York Philharmonic, and for a great part of that time of similar concerts of the San Francisco Symphony. He also appeared as guest conductor of major American orchestras. In 1927 he was appointed vice president of Chicago Musical College. He became president in 1933, and president emeritus in 1954.

Gaspard de la nuit. Suite for piano by Maurice Ravel (1908), first performed in Paris on Jan. 9, 1909, by Ricardo Viñes (I. *Ondine.* II. *Le Gibet.* III. *Scarbo*). The first movement is the most popular; delicate broken chords reproduce the sound of flowing water. The second is a musical picture of a gallows in which a persistent pedal point is prominent. *Scarbo* is a scherzo describing a tiny, grotesque, elfin creature.

Gastein Symphony. A symphony reputedly written by Schubert during a visit to Gastein, in the Austrian Salzkammergut, in August-September 1825. It is mentioned in several letters by Schubert's friends, but the manuscript has never been found. One theory suggests that the Grand Duo for piano four hands, op. 140, is a version of the *Gastein Symphony.* (It has been orchestrated by Joseph Joachim, Anthony Collins, and several others.)

Gatti, Guido Maria, musicologist. Born Chieti, Italy, May 30, 1892. He founded *La Rassegna musicale* in 1928 and has since then been its editor. In 1925 he helped found the Teatro di Torino, where performances of symphonic music and opera were given until 1931. He also helped found the Florence May Music Festival in 1933. For several years he has been secretary of the International Music Congress which he helped to organize. With Andrea Della Corte he edited the *Dizionario di musica* (1925). He is the author of *Musicisti moderni d'Italia e di fuori* (1920) and a biography of Ildebrando Pizzetti (1934), which has been translated into English.

Gaubert, Philippe, flutist, conductor, and composer. Born Cahors, France, July 3, 1879; died Paris, France, July 8, 1941. He attended the Paris Conservatory, where he won first prize in flute in 1894 and the second Prix de Rome in 1905. After playing the flute in several French orchestras he was appointed in 1919 professor of the flute at the Paris Conservatory. From 1919 to 1938 he was principal conductor of the Conservatory Orchestra. He also conducted at the Paris Opéra. In 1938 he was made Commander of the Legion of Honor. His compositions include a symphonic suite, tone poem, violin concerto, symphony, 4 symphonic tableaux, and piano pieces.

Gavotte. A two-part dance form of French origin, each part repeated. It is in 4/4 time, beginning on the third beat. It is often found in the Baroque suite. A popular gavotte for orchestra appears as an entr'acte in Act 2 of Ambroise Thomas' opera *Mignon*. Serge Prokofiev has been particularly fond of the gavotte form, using it as a movement for his *Classical Symphony*, in the *Cinderella* ballet, and in several of his piano collections (Ten Pieces, op. 12; Four Pieces, op. 32; Three Pieces, op. 95).

Gayane (or Gayaneh). Two ballet suites for orchestra by Aram Khatchaturian, derived from the score of a folk ballet introduced in Molotov on Dec. 9, 1942; it received the Stalin Prize in 1943. The libretto, by K. N. Derzhavin, has for its setting a collective farm where Gayane, the heroine, is married to Giko, a traitor. Giko becomes a smuggler and tries to set the farm afire; the farm is saved through the heroism of a Red commander, Kazakov. After Giko is arrested, Gayane and

Kazakov fall in love and marry. From his ballet score the composer extracted 13 folk dances which he devided into two suites. These dances are varied in mood, some of them barbaric, some exotic, some sensitively lyrical. Suite No. 1 includes Saber Dance, Dance of Ayshe, Dance of the Rose Maidens, Dance of the Kurds, Lullaby, Dance of the Young Kurds, Variations, and Lezghinka. Suite No. 2 includes Russian Dance, Introduction, Gayane's Adagio, and Fire.

The most celebrated single number is the Saber Dance, which has been transcribed for piano and orchestra, and piano solo.

Gazza Ladra (The Thieving Magpie), Overture to La. Overture to an opera buffa by Rossini. The opera, libretto by Giovanni Gherardini based on *La Pie voleuse* by d'Aubigny and Caigniez, was introduced in Milan on May 31, 1817. The overture opens with rolls in the side drum, leading to the presentation of the main melody. This is a march-like subject for full orchestra. The allegro section that follows is built mainly from a delicate melody for strings and a saucy tune shared by strings and woodwind. The overture arrives at a climax with a characteristic Rossini crescendo.

Gebrauchsmusik. Functional music, a term devised by Paul Hindemith for pieces of utilitarian purpose, such as music for radio, for theater or movies, educational compositions, and works meant for amateur performance. Such functional music was produced by other 20th-century composers, including Kurt Weill and Darius Milhaud.

Geister Trio. *See:* Trio—Beethoven.

Geminiani, Francesco, violinist and composer. Born Lucca, Italy, December 1687; died Dublin, Ireland, Sept. 17, 1762. After studying the violin with Arcangelo Corelli and Alessandro Scarlatti, he played in the Lucca Orchestra from 1707 to 1710, and from 1711 to 1714 in an opera orchestra in Naples. In 1714 he settled in England, where he acquired an outstanding reputation as a virtuoso. There he wrote some theoretical works, including *The Art of Violin Playing* (1730), one of the earliest such methods ever published. In 1733 he gave concerts in Dublin and helped to establish there a concert auditorium. He began living permanently in that city in 1759, and became music master to Count Bellamont. As a violinist, Geminiani helped carry on traditions established by Corelli and his school; and through his compositions he advanced the technique of violin performance. He wrote 18 violin concertos, 24 violin sonatas together with various sonatas for other solo instruments, concerti grossi, trios, and piano pieces.

Gericke, Wilhelm, conductor. Born Schwanberg, Austria, April 18, 1845; died Vienna, Austria, Oct. 27, 1925. He attended the Vienna Conservatory. After serving his conducting apprenticeship in Linz and as Hans Richter's assistant at the Vienna Opera, he was appointed in 1880 conductor of the Gesellschaft concerts in Vienna, and of the Singverein. He was principal conductor of the Boston Symphony from 1884 to 1889, and from 1898 to 1906. In 1906 he went into retirement.

German dance (Deutscher Tanz, or **Deutsche,** or **Teutsche).** A slow country dance in 3/4 time, usually with the accent on the first beat. It became popular in Germany and Austria in the 18th century. It was evolved from the laendler and was a precursor of the waltz. Beethoven wrote 12 German Dances, op. 40 (1785). Mozart's numerous German Dances were written between 1787 and 1791 and bear the following Koechel numbers: 509, 536, 567, 571, 586, 600, 602, and 605. Schubert also wrote numerous German Dances: 54 for piano solo between 1815 and 1824. Some were transcribed for orchestra, and some for violin and piano; five are for strings and horn (1813).

German Requiem, A. *See:* Requiem—*Brahms.*

Gershwin, George, composer and pianist. Born Brooklyn, N.Y., Sept. 26, 1898; died Hollywood, Calif., July 11, 1937. He studied the piano with Charles Hambitzer, and in his sixteenth year was employed as staff pianist at Remick's, publisher of popular songs. Later music study took place privately with Edward Kilenyi, Henry Cowell, and Joseph Schillinger. In 1918 he produced his first song hit, *Swanee;* in 1919 his first Broadway musi-

cal comedy, *La, La, Lucille.* He soon achieved outstanding success as a stage composer. One of these productions, *Of Thee I Sing,* became the first musical comedy to win the Pulitzer Prize for drama. Though in his boyhood he attempted serious composition, he did not write a major work for the concert hall until commissioned to do so by the popular bandleader, Paul Whiteman. The work was the *Rhapsody in Blue,* introduced by Paul Whiteman and his Orchestra in New York on Feb. 12, 1924. This was a successful attempt to introduce popular musical elements within an ambitious symphonic structure, and proved a powerful influence in inducing major composers everywhere to write compositions in a symphonic-jazz style. The *Rhapsody in Blue* made Gershwin world-famous and wealthy. From this time on he successfully ploughed two fields of music, the popular and the serious. In serious music he completed a piano concerto, the *Second Rhapsody,* the tone poem *An American in Paris, Cuban Overture,* piano preludes, *Variations on I Got Rhythm* for piano and orchestra, and the opera *Porgy and Bess* which, while originally not successful, became world-famous after the composer's death. Gershwin died following a brain operation.

See: American in Paris, An; Concerto—*Gershwin;* Prelude—*Gershwin; Rhapsody in Blue.*

Gesangszene. *See:* Concerto—*Spohr.*

Geschoepfe des Prometheus, Die (Beethoven). *See: Prometheus, Overture.*

Gevaert, François Auguste, teacher and theoretician. Born Huysse, Belgium, July 31, 1828; died Brussels, Belgium, Dec. 24, 1908. He attended the Ghent Conservatory, winning the Prix de Rome. He achieved fame as an opera composer before he turned to teaching. In 1871 he became director of the Brussels Conservatory, where he conducted distinguished orchestral concerts and historical cycles. His treatises on instrumentation and orchestration became staples in musical pedagogy. These are the *Traité général d'instrumentation* (1863) and the *Cours méthodique d'orchestration* (1890).

Gewandhaus Orchestra. Symphony orchestra in Leipzig, Germany, and one of the most distinguished in Europe. The name "Gewandhaus" comes from the auditorium in which the concerts take place. The orchestra originated as "Das grosse Concert" in 1743 with a private performance directed by Friedrich Doles. The activity of the orchestra was interrupted during the Seven Years War, but its regular schedule was resumed in 1763. Johann Adam Hiller was conductor from 1763 to 1785. In 1781 the orchestra rented a floor in the old Gewandhaus. It first achieved artistic significance under the direction of Mendelssohn between 1825 and 1843. Since that time its principal conductors have included Ferdinand Hiller, Niels Gade, Julius Rietz, Karl Reinecke, Arthur Nikisch, Wilhelm Furtwaengler, Bruno Walter, Hermann Abendroth, and Fritz Konwitschny. The orchestra moved into its present auditorium, the Gewandhaus, on March 26, 1885.

Ghedini, Giorgio, composer and teacher. Born Cuneo, Italy, July 11, 1892. He was graduated from the Bologna Liceo Musicale in 1911. In 1918 he began teaching composition at the Turin Liceo Musicale. From 1938 to 1941 he taught composition at the Parma Conservatory; and from 1941 on at the Milan Conservatory where, a decade later, he became director. His principal works for orchestra include *Marinaresca e Baccanale, Architecture, Concerto dell' Albatro* for narrator and orchestra (based on Herman Melville's *Moby Dick*), *Canzoni,* various concertos (piano; two pianos; violin; flute and violin; two cellos). He also wrote a violin sonata and a piano quartet. He has transcribed numerous works by old Italian masters.

Giara, La (The Jug). Ballet suite for orchestra by Alfredo Casella (1924), adapted from his ballet introduced in Paris on Nov. 19, 1924. The text is based on a Sicilian tale by Luigi Pirandello. A hunchback, attempting to mend a huge jug, gets himself imprisoned within. When peasants dance around the jug and make merry, the owner sends it rolling down the hill until it smashes and releases the prisoner. The suite is in two sections. The first consists of a Prelude and Sicilian Dance; the second, of a Nocturne, Dance of Nela, Entrance of Peasants and Brindisi, General Dance, and Finale.

Gibbons, Orlando, composer and organist. Born Oxford, England, December 1583; died Canterbury, England, June 5, 1625. He became organist of the Chapel Royal in 1605, in 1619 chamber musician to the king, and in 1623 organist at Westminster Abbey. Though most famous for his vocal music, Gibbons also wrote pieces for keyboard instruments, and pavanes, fantasias, and galliards for strings. These are significant in the early history of English instrumental music.

Gide, André, poet, dramatist, and writer. Born Paris, France, Nov. 22, 1869; died there, Feb. 19, 1951. He won the Nobel Prize for literature in 1947. Gide's *Le Voyage d'Urien* was the source of two works for orchestra: Charles Koechlin's *Hymne à la jeunesse* and Jean Rivier's *Le Voyage d'Urien.* Arthur Honegger wrote incidental music for *Saul;* Henri Sauguet for *Le Retour de l'enfant prodigue;* and Florent Schmitt for Gide's adaptation of Shakespeare's *Antony and Cleopatra.*

Gieseking, Walter, pianist. Born Lyons, France, Nov. 5, 1895; died London, England, Oct. 26, 1956. While attending Hanover Conservatory, a pupil of Karl Leimer, he gave a series of concerts in 1915 devoted to all the Beethoven sonatas. He served in the German army during World War I. On returning to the concert stage he performed in Germany and Paris, soon distinguishing himself for his remarkable interpretations of Debussy, Ravel, and the moderns. His American début took place in 1926. In subsequent appearances throughout the world he firmly established a reputation as one of the foremost virtuosos of his time, an incomparable performer of Scarlatti, Mozart, and Debussy among others. Gieseking remained in Germany throughout World War II. At first blacklisted by the American Military Government, he was finally cleared in 1947 and allowed to concertize. A projected tour of the United States in 1949, the first in eleven years, was frustrated when Gieseking was threatened by investigation by the American Immigration Service and the Department of Justice. But he was finally allowed to tour the country in 1953. He died of a heart attack after an emergency operation.

Gigue (English **Jig**). A spirited two-part dance form of Italian origin in 3/8, 6/8, or 6/4 time. It is often found as a concluding movement of the Baroque suite.

Gilbert, Henry Franklin Belknap, composer. Born Somerville, Mass., Sept. 26, 1868; died Cambridge, Mass., May 19, 1928. He attended the New England Conservatory, where he studied composition with Edward MacDowell and violin with Emil Mollenhauer. For several years he engaged in business, but a hearing of Gustave Charpentier's opera, *Louise,* in 1900 sent him back to music. He soon interested himself in American folk and popular music, completing in 1903 a suite based on three minstrel-show tunes entitled *Americanesque.* He subsequently became enthusiastic over the folk music of the American Negro, an idiom in which he produced his first major success in 1910, *Comedy Overture on Negro Themes,* and later the *Negro Rhapsody,* both for orchestra. Other subsequent works utilized also the folk idioms of the American Indian and the Creole. *The Dance in Place Congo* was given at the International Festival of Contemporary Music at Frankfort-on-the-Main, Germany, on July 1, 1927; though an invalid, Gilbert attended that performance. Other orchestral works by Gilbert not mentioned above include *Three American Dances, Two Episodes,* and the symphonic prologue *Riders to the Sea.*

See: *Comedy Overture on Negro Themes.*

Gilels, Emil, pianist. Born Odessa, Russia, Oct. 19, 1916. He studied the piano with Jacob Tkach, Bertha Ringold, and at the Odessa Conservatory. He completed his studies at the Moscow Conservatory. In 1936 he won second prize in an international competition for pianists in Vienna, and in 1938 first prize at the Queen Elizabeth of Belgium International Competition in Brussels. Several tours of the Soviet Union brought him to an imposing place among Soviet musicians. In 1946 he received the Stalin Prize. He scored personal triumphs at a festival in Prague in 1948, the Florence May Music Festival

in 1951, and at the Berlin Embassy during the Conference of Foreign Ministers in 1954. His American début took place in Philadelphia on Oct. 3, 1955, when he appeared as soloist with the Philadelphia Orchestra. This was followed by a tour of the United States, Mexico, and Canada. Since 1936 Gilels has been professor of piano at the Moscow Conservatory. His brother-in-law is Leonid Kogan, Soviet concert violinist.

Gilman, Lawrence, music critic. Born Flushing, N.Y., July 5, 1878; died Franconia, N.H., Sept. 8, 1939. Mostly self-taught in music, he held various posts as editor and music critic before becoming music critic of the New York *Herald Tribune* in 1923, a post he held until his death. He was also program annotator for the concerts of the New York Philharmonic and the Philadelphia Orchestra. His principal books are: *Phases of Modern Music* (1904); *Edward MacDowell* (1905, revised 1909); *The Music of Tomorrow* (1906); *Stories of Symphonic Music* (1907); *Nature in Music* (1914); *Music and the Cultivated Man* (1929); and *Toscanini and Great Music* (1938).

Ginastera, Alberto, composer. Born Buenos Aires, Argentina, April 11, 1916. He was graduated from the National Conservatory of Buenos Aires in 1938, and in 1953 he was appointed professor there. In 1946-1947 he visited the United States on a Guggenheim Fellowship and was honored with a concert of his works in New York by the League of Composers. His major compositions combine national tendencies with advanced idioms, and include *Pampeana No. 3* for orchestra (introduced by the Louisville Orchestra in Kentucky in 1954); a string quartet and other chamber music; *12 American Preludes, Creole Dance Suite,* and a sonata, for piano.

Giocoso. Joyful.

Girl with the Flaxen Hair, The (Debussy). *See: Fille aux cheveux de lin, La;* Prelude—*Debussy.*

Giusto. Precise or exact.

Glazunov, Alexander, composer. Born St. Petersburg, Russia, Aug. 10, 1865; died Paris, France, March 21, 1936. He began studying the piano at nine, and at thirteen wrote his first large works. In 1879 he met Balakirev, who encouraged him to continue his music study with Rimsky-Korsakov, under whose guidance Glazunov wrote his first symphony, acclaimed when introduced in St. Petersburg in 1882. By 1900 Glazunov had written many of the works by which he is most often represented today on concert programs. He wrote little after 1914, and nothing that added appreciably to his importance. Glazunov was a traditionalist who remained faithful to the national principles of the "Russian Five." Oblivious of all experimental tendencies, he preferred to write music orthodox in structure, pleasing in melodic and harmonic content, and rich in emotion.

In 1899 Glazunov made his first appearance as conductor, at the Paris Exposition, where he performed his tone poem *Stenka Razin* with outstanding success. In that same year he launched a fruitful career as teacher by becoming professor of instrumentation at the St. Petersburg Conservatory, where from 1905 to 1928 he was director. Glazunov left Russia for good in 1928 and went to live in Paris. He visited the United States in 1929, making his début in Detroit on Nov. 21 as guest conductor of the Detroit Symphony.

The following are his principal instrumental works:

Chamber Music: 7 string quartets; *Five Novelettes,* for string quartet; string quintet; *In modo religioso,* for brass quartet.

Orchestra: 8 symphonies; 2 violin concertos (including the famous Concerto in A minor, op. 82); 2 overtures on Greek themes; *Stenka Razin; The Sea; Oriental Rhapsody; Carnival; Valses de concert; Scènes de ballet; From the Middle Ages; Ouverture solenelle; Symphonic Prelude in Memory of Gogol; Finnish Fantasy; Cortège solenelle; A Karelian Legend; The Seasons,* ballet suite.

Piano: 2 sonatas; etudes, waltzes, preludes, fugues, nocturnes, mazurkas, impromptus.

See: Concerto—*Glazunov; Seasons, The; Stenka Razin;* Symphony—*Glazunov.*

Glière, Reinhold, composer. Born Kiev, Russia, Jan. 11, 1875; died Moscow, Russia, June 23, 1956. He did not receive formal musical training until his twentieth year, when he entered the Moscow Conservatory, where his teachers included Ippolitov-Ivanov, Taneiev, and Arensky, and where he won a gold medal in composition. From 1905 to 1907 he lived and studied in Germany. The influence of Germanic Romanticism is discernible in his first major works: a tone poem, *The Sirens,* and his second symphony. Success came to him first in 1911 with his third symphony, *Ilia Mourometz,* in which earlier Romantic tendencies were skilfully combined with Russian nationalism. After the Revolution in Russia, Glière's compositions often glorified the Soviet regime. In this vein he wrote one of his most celebrated works, the ballet *The Red Poppy,* introduced in Moscow in 1927. Glière won the Stalin Prize twice, in 1948 for his fourth string quartet, and in 1950 for the ballet *The Bronze Horseman.* For about a decade, beginning with 1939, he was chairman of the organizing committee of the Union of Soviet Composers. A month before his death he toured the Soviet Union in concerts of his own works. Glière enjoyed a rich career as teacher, first as professor and director of the Kiev Conservatory, and from 1920 until his death as member of the faculty of the Moscow Conservatory. Besides 3 symphonies, Glière wrote the following works for orchestra: *Cossacks of Zaporozh, Trizna, Friendship of Nations, Victory Overture,* and several concertos (harp; cello; horn; coloratura soprano). He also wrote 3 string sextets, 4 string quartets, a string octet, and over two hundred compositions for piano.

See: Russian Sailors' Dance; Symphony —*Glière.*

Glinka, Michael, composer. Born Novosspasskoye, Russia, June 1, 1804; died Berlin, Germany, Feb. 15, 1857. While attending a private school in St. Petersburg from 1818 to 1822 he studied the piano with John Field and Carl Meyer and violin with Carl Böhm. Poor health sent him in 1823 to the Caucasus, where he studied orchestration and harmony by himself and where he first interested himself in Russian folk music. From 1824 to 1827 he worked in the Ministry of Communications in St. Petersburg without abandoning his musical activities. After that came a period of travel in Italy and Germany, and some study of theory with Siegfried Dehn in Berlin. In Russia, he associated himself with leading literary and artistic groups. He was now fired with the ambition of writing music with a strong Russian identity, and deriving its inspiration and material from Russian backgrounds and people. He completed two operas which laid the foundations of Russian national opera: *A Life for the Czar* and *Russlan and Ludmilla,* produced in 1836 and 1842 respectively. Here, and in later operas, he became the first composer in Russia to realize a national art, thus setting the stage for the "Russian Five," who were inspired and influenced by him. In his last years Glinka lived in France and Spain, where he wrote some orchestral music. His death came suddenly in Berlin, where he was buried; but a few months later his body was brought back to St. Petersburg.

The following are Glinka's major instrumental compositions:

Chamber Music: 2 string quartets; septet; viola sonata; *Trio Pathétique.*

Orchestra: Symphony in B-flat major; *Overture-Symphony on Russian Themes; Valse-Fantaisie; Jota aragonesa; Kamarinsakaya; Festival Polonaise.*

Piano: Waltzes, variations, fugues, nocturnes, impromptus, mazurkas.

See: Kamarinskaya; Life for the Czar, A, Overture; Russlan and Ludmilla, Overture.

Glissando. A continuous tone, produced by sliding from one pitch to another and obtainable on keyboard and bowed string instruments as well as the harp, trombone, xylophone, etc.

Glockenspiel. Percussion instrument of bells tuned to a diatonic scale and played from a keyboard.

Gluck, Christoph Willibald, composer. Born Erasbach, Bavaria, July 2, 1714; died Vienna, Austria, Nov. 15, 1787. He came in 1736 to Vienna, where he was employed by Prince Ferdinand Lobkowitz. Another patron, Prince Melzi, took him to Italy, where he studied with G. B. Sammartini and wrote his first opera. He was back in Vienna seven years later, there to become Kapellmeister at the Court. He wrote several operas which opened new vistas for dramatic music, among them *Orpheus and Eurydice* and *Alceste,* performed in 1762 and 1767 respectively. He later achieved triumphs in Paris with *Iphigenia in Aulis* and *Iphigenia in Tauris,* introduced in 1774 and 1779. Though Gluck wrote some overtures for orchestra (sometimes designated as symphonies) and trio sonatas, he is essentially a composer for the stage. When he is represented on concert programs it is usually through overtures to his operas, or suites adapted by other musicians from his opera scores. One of the most popular of such suites is the Ballet Suite arranged by Felix Mottl. It opens with introductory music from Gluck's ballet *Don Juan.* After that come the Air Gai and Lento from *Iphigenia in Aulis,* Dance of the Blessed Spirits from *Orpheus and Eurydice,* and Musette and Sicilienne from *Armide.* Another Ballet Suite was arranged by François Gevaert, comprising Air, Danse, Tambourin, and Chaconne from *Iphigenia in Aulis* and Musette from *Armide.*

See: Alceste, Overture; Dance of the Blessed Spirits; Dance of the Furies; *Iphigenia in Aulis, Overture.*

Gnomenreigen. *See:* Etude—Liszt.

Godfrey, Sir Dan, conductor. Born London, England, June 20, 1868; died Bournemouth, England, July 20, 1939. After attending the Royal College of Music in London he settled in Bournemouth in 1892. In 1894 he founded a symphony orchestra there which he directed until his retirement in 1934, his programs continually espousing the cause of contemporary British music. He was knighted in 1922. He was the author of an autobiography, *Memories and Music* (1924).

Godowsky, Leopold, pianist, teacher, and composer. Born Soshly, Poland, Feb. 13, 1870; died New York City, Nov. 21, 1938. He was a child prodigy pianist who made his first public appearance when he was nine, after which he toured Poland and Germany. For two years he attended the Berlin High School of Music. He made his American début in Boston on Dec. 7, 1884. After some additional study with Camille Saint-Saëns in Paris, he performed extensively throughout Europe and the United States. When he returned to the United States in 1890, he became a member of the faculty of the New York College of Music. A year later he married an American woman, Frieda Saxe, and became an American citizen. From 1895 to 1900 he was head of the piano department of the Chicago Conservatory. A recital in Berlin on Dec. 6, 1900, established his reputation as a performer of searching intelligence and a profound sense of musical values. From 1909 to 1914 he conducted a master class in piano at the Vienna Academy. In 1914 he decided to live permanently in the United States, where he resumed his activity as teacher of the piano besides making concert appearances throughout the world. A slight paralysis of the left hand brought his concert career to an end in 1930, but he continued functioning fruitfully as teacher and composer. As composer, Godowsky confined himself to the piano, developing the resources and technique of piano performance more than almost any other composer since Debussy. His principal works include several suites, the most significant being *Triakontameron* (in which the popular *Alt Wien* is found), *Java, Renaissance* (dance pieces adapted from the works of Rameau, Lully, Corelli, and others), *Walzermasken* (24 studies in three-quarter time), and *Miniatures* (24 pieces for four hands). He also wrote a sonata (E minor) and many smaller pieces for the piano, some for left hand alone. He made transcriptions for the piano, and edited studies for the piano by Carl Czerny and others. He arranged Chopin etudes for the left hand alone, and wrote paraphrases of Weber's *Perpetual Motion* and *Invitation to the Dance* and several Johann Strauss waltzes.

See: Triakontameron.

Goehr, Walter, conductor. Born Berlin, Germany, May 28, 1903. He received his musical training at the Berlin High School for Music and with Arnold Schoenberg. From 1933 to 1938 he was director of the Columbia Gramophone Company in England, with which he made numerous orchestral recordings. In 1943 he was appointed conductor of Morley College Choir and Concert Society. From 1946

to 1949 he was conductor of the BBC Theatre Orchestra. Since then he has appeared in guest performances with most of the important European orchestras.

Goethe, Johann Wolfgang von, poet, dramatist, and novelist. Born Frankfort, Germany, Aug. 28, 1749; died Weimar, Germany, March 22, 1832. The following are among the works by Goethe that inspired instrumental compositions (where titles of compositions are not given they are the same as the original source).

Egmont: Beethoven (incidental music, including a famous overture).

Faust: Berlioz (*The Damnation of Faust*); Ferruccio Busoni (*Mephistopheles' Song,* for voice and orchestra; *Sarabande* and *Cortège,* two orchestral studies for his opera *Doktor Faust*); Felix Draeseke (piano sonata); Alberto Ginastera (overture); Hans Henze (*Chor der Gefangener Trojer,* for chorus and orchestra); André Jolivet (*Hélène et Faust,* radio music); Charles Koechlin (*Nuit de Walpurgis classique,* tone poem); Eduard Lassen (incidental music); Liszt (*A Faust Symphony*); Mahler (Symphony No. 8, which uses a part of the final scene); Wagner (*A Faust Overture*).

Goetz von Berlichingen: Paul Dukas (overture); Paul Graener (symphonic march).

Harzreise im Winter: Brahms (Alto Rhapsody).

Hermann und Dorothea: Schumann (overture).

Pandora: Conrad Beck (incidental music); Eduard Lassen (incidental music).

Stella: Ernst Krenek (*Stella's Monolog,* concert aria with orchestra).

Der Triumph der Empfindsamkeit: Ernst Krenek (incidental music).

Goethe's ballad, *Der Zauberlehrling,* was the source and program of Paul Dukas' orchestral scherzo, *The Sorcerer's Apprentice.* Mendelssohn's overture, *Calm Sea and Prosperous Voyage,* was inspired by two short Goethe poems, *The Calmness of the Sea* and *A Prosperous Voyage.*

Goldberg, Simon, violinist. Born Wloclawek, Poland, June 1, 1909. After studying the violin in Warsaw, and in Berlin with Carl Flesch, he made his concert début at Berlin in 1923 as soloist with the Berlin Philharmonic. In 1925 he became concertmaster of the Dresden Philharmonic, and from 1929 to 1933 he held a similar post with the Berlin Philharmonic. On Feb. 10, 1938, he made his American début in New York. He was touring the Orient when World War II broke out. For almost three years he was interned by the Japanese. He resumed his concert activity in 1947 with extensive performances in Europe and the United States.

Goldberg Variations. A set of 30 variations for piano by Johann Sebastian Bach (1736). It was written for Count von Kayserling, Russian envoy to Saxony. A victim of insomnia, the Count had Johann Gottlieb Goldberg play the clavier for him each night at bedtime to help induce slumber. For these nocturnal performances, the Count commissioned Bach to write a peaceful work. For his main theme, Bach selected an aria—a slow and stately Sarabande. The ensuing variations maintain the peaceful character of the main melody. Some are gentle and pastoral; others, sombre. The composer's consummate mastery in the art of variation is here evident. The composition ends with a repetition of the opening aria.

Golden Sonata. Sonata No. 9 in F major, for two violins and accompaniment, by Henry Purcell. It can be found in a set of 12 sonatas published posthumously in 1697. It has never been explained why this specific work is called "golden."

Goldmark, Carl, composer. Born Keszthely, Hungary, May 18, 1830; died Vienna, Austria, Jan. 2, 1915. When he was fourteen Goldmark became a pupil of Leopold Jansa in Vienna, and from 1847 to 1848 he attended the Vienna Conservatory. When the Revolution of 1848 closed the Conservatory, Goldmark began earning his living by playing the violin in theaters, teaching piano, and writing music criticisms. Two concerts of his works, one in Vienna and the other in Budapest, failed to raise him from his obscurity and poverty. Recognition did not come until 1865, when his *Sakuntala Overture* was successfully introduced in Vienna. A decade later his fame was solidified by the premières of his *Rustic Wedding Symphony* (*Laendliche Hochzeit*) and his opera, *The Queen of Sheba.*

A master of technique, Goldmark was a Romanticist who brought ingratiating harmonies and melodies, together with a vivid orchestration, to his best writing.

His principal instrumental works follow:

Chamber Music: 2 piano trios; piano quintet; violin sonata; cello sonata; Suite in E-flat, for violin and piano.

Orchestra: 2 symphonies (including the *Rustic Wedding*); *Sakuntala Overture;* Concerto in A minor, for violin and orchestra; *Im Fruehling; Der gefesselte Prometheus; In Italien; Aus Jugendtagen.*

See: Concerto—*Goldmark; Sakuntala Overture;* Symphony—*Goldmark.*

Goldmark, Rubin, composer and teacher. Born New York City, Aug. 15, 1872; died there, March 6, 1936. He was the nephew of Carl Goldmark (see above). After studying music privately in New York while attending the College of the City of New York, he went to Vienna, where he attended the Conservatory. His music study was completed at the National Conservatory in New York, where his teachers included Antonín Dvořák and Rafael Joseffy. For a period he taught piano and theory there, but poor health sent him to Colorado, where for six years he was director of the Colorado College Conservatory. In 1902 he returned to New York, devoting himself to teaching and lecturing. From 1924 until his death he was head of the composition department at the Juilliard School. Among his many pupils were Abram Chasins, George Gershwin, and Aaron Copland. Goldmark was a founder of The Bohemians, a New York club for musicians, serving as its president for many years. His principal orchestral compositions include the *Requiem* for orchestra (based on Lincoln's Gettysburg Address), *Negro Rhapsody, The Call of the Plains,* and *Hiawatha.*

Goldsand, Robert, pianist. Born Vienna, Austria, March 17, 1911. He received his musical training in Vienna from Mrs. H. Rosenthal and Joseph Marx. He was only ten when he made his first concert appearance in Vienna. His American début took place in New York on March 21, 1927. Five years later he gave a series of concerts in New York tracing the evolution of piano music. In 1933 he made his first tour of South America. He went into temporary retirement in Austria in 1935 to devote himself to more study. When he returned to the United States in 1939 he re-established his home there permanently and later became a citizen.

Golliwogg's Cakewalk (Debussy). *See: Children's Corner.*

Golschmann, Vladimir, conductor. Born Paris, France, Dec. 16, 1893. After attending the Schola Cantorum in Paris he played the violin in several Paris orchestras. In 1919 he founded the Concerts Golschmann in Paris which for several years specialized in modern works and premières. He also appeared as guest conductor of major European orchestras and served as a principal conductor of the Ballet Russe and Swedish Ballet. He first came to the United States in 1924 as conductor of the Swedish Ballet. At this time he made his American début as symphony conductor with the New York Symphony. From 1928 to 1931 he was principal conductor of the Scottish Orchestra in Glasgow, and from 1931 to 1957 of the St. Louis Symphony. In 1958 he was appointed musical adviser of the Tulsa Philharmonic in Oklahoma.

Gong. A percussion instrument used in the symphony orchestra for special effects. It hangs in a wooden frame and is struck in the center. It has a solemn, almost awesome tone. The gong has been effectively employed by Tchaikovsky in the *Symphonie pathétique* and Richard Strauss in *Death and Transfiguration,* among others.

Good Friday Spell (Charfreitagszauber). An episode in Act 3 of Wagner's music drama, *Parsifal.* Parsifal is recognized as a new knight of the Holy Grail, and is bathed in preparation for his entry into the Grail Castle. He notices that the surrounding meadows are radiant, and is informed by Gurnemanz that the spell of Good Friday is at hand. The orchestra describes that spell in music that is spiritual and otherworldly. The main subject is an incandescent melody for the oboe.

Good-Humored Ladies, The (Le Donne di buon umore). Ballet suite for orchestra by Vincenzo Tommasini (1917), based on music by Domenico Scarlatti. The suite was adapted from a ballet intro-

duced in Rome on April 12, 1917. The story, based on a comedy by Goldoni, is played in a carnival, and the plot concerns the amatory diversions of a Count disguised as a woman. The suite has five sections: I. Presto; II. Allegro; III. Andante; IV. *Tempo di ballo;* V. Presto. These are the sonatas by Scarlatti scored by Tommasini: G major, L. 388; D major, L. 361; B minor, L. 33; G major, L. 209; G minor, L. 499; D major, L. 463; and F major, L. 385.

Goodson, Katharine, pianist. Born Watford, England, June 18, 1872; died London, England, April 14, 1958. Her study of the piano took place at the Royal Academy of Music in London and with Theodor Leschetizky in Vienna. She made a successful début in London on Jan. 16, 1897. Her tours of Europe that followed placed her with the foremost British women pianists of her day. Her American début took place in Boston on Jan. 18, 1907, when she appeared as soloist with the Boston Symphony.

Goossens, Sir Eugene, conductor and composer. Born London, England, May 26, 1893. He came from a family of noted musicians. Both his grandfather and father were prominent conductors in London. His brother, Leon, is a celebrated oboist. Two sisters are professional harpists. Eugene's musical training took place at the Bruges Conservatory, Liverpool College of Music, and the Royal College of Music in London. For some years he played the violin in the Queen's Hall Orchestra and Philharmonic String Quartet. In 1921 he founded his own orchestra which presented concerts in London for several seasons. During this period he also made guest appearances with important European orchestras, the Ballet Russe, and the Carl Rosa Opera Company. From 1923 to 1931 he was principal conductor of the Rochester Philharmonic Orchestra in Rochester, N.Y., and from 1931 to 1946 of the Cincinnati Symphony. In 1947 he settled in Sydney, Australia, as conductor of the Sydney Symphony and director of the New South Wales Conservatory. He resigned from both posts in 1956. He was knighted in 1955. He is the author of an autobiography, *Overture and Beginners* (1951).

Goossens has been a prolific composer in all forms. Modern techniques, and at times an Impressionist style, are combined with traditional contrapuntal and melodic idioms. He has a polyglot style which once tempted Cyril Scott to say that Goossens could be "witty, grotesque, hard, soft, pathetic, exotic, and passionate." Goossens' works for orchestra include 2 symphonies, oboe concerto, *Fantasy Concerto* for piano, piano concertino, concertino for double orchestra, *Nature Poems,* Sinfonietta, and *Lyric Poem* for violin and orchestra. He has also written 2 string quartets, 2 violin sonatas, a sextet, and several suites for the piano.

See: Concertino—*Goossens.*

Gordon, Jacques, violinist. Born Odessa, Russia, March 7, 1899; died Hartford, Conn., Sept. 15, 1948. In 1912 he was graduated from the Odessa Conservatory. Just before the outbreak of World War I he established permanent residence in the United States, where he became a citizen, and studied the violin with Franz Kneisel. From 1921 to 1930 he was concertmaster of the Chicago Symphony, and in 1921 he founded the Gordon String Quartet. He established a summer colony in Falls Village, Conn., where each summer he taught violin and chamber music and where his Quartet gave concerts. In 1938 he received the Elizabeth Sprague Cooiidge Award for "highest achievement in chamber music."

Gossec, François, composer and conductor. Born Vergnies, Belgium, Jan. 17, 1734; died Passy, France, Feb. 16, 1829. As a boy chorister at Notre Dame in Antwerp he studied music intensively. In 1751 he went to Paris, where he was employed by Rameau's patron, La Pouplinière, for whom he directed an orchestra and wrote symphonies. During this period he issued his first publication, a set of violin sonatas. In 1762 he went to work for Prince de Conti, who encouraged him to write operas, a field in which Gossec achieved particular eminence. He also became famous as teacher and conductor. In 1770 he founded the Concerts des Amateurs which introduced

many Haydn symphonies to Paris. In 1773 he became director of the Concert Spirituel in Paris, and from 1780 to 1785 was a conductor at the Opéra. In 1784 he helped found a school of singing, which fifteen years later became the Paris Conservatory, where Gossec served as inspector and professor of composition. During the French Revolution he was one of its most important musical spokesmen. He led the band of the National Guard and wrote numerous works commemorating major events of the revolution. He continued to hold a high position in French music even after the revolution. He produced a considerable amount of charming instrumental music, including over 30 symphonies and numerous chamber-music works. The clarity of his form, the fluidity of his style, and the grace of his lyricism were emulated by many of his contemporaries and successors. He was also a bold innovator in orchestration, sometimes anticipating Berlioz in using unusual effects and timbres; he helped introduce horns and clarinets into the official orchestral family. Gossec's ever-popular Gavotte, familiar in numerous transcriptions, comes from his opera *Rosine.*

Goetterdaemmerung (Wagner). *See: Twilight of the Gods, The; Ring of the Nibelungs, The.*

Gottschalk, Louis Moreau, pianist and composer. Born New Orleans, La., May 8, 1829; died Rio de Janeiro, Brazil, Dec. 18, 1869. He was one of the first American-born concert pianists. He attended the Paris Conservatory from 1841 to 1846, then studied privately with Berlioz. In April 1844 he made his Paris début as pianist and was hailed by Chopin. He then toured Europe, scoring major successes in Spain. In 1853 he returned to the United States, giving his first American concert at Niblo's Gardens in New York on Feb. 10, 1853. After that he toured the country many times, often performing his own compositions, and occasionally conducting mammoth orchestras. In 1855-1856 he gave 80 concerts in New York alone, and from 1856 to 1861 he made several extensive tours of the West Indies. He died in South America of yellow fever, in the course of a long and successful tour. Gottschalk wrote many works for the piano, including numerous salon pieces which were favorites with piano students in the 19th century. These pieces included *The Last Hope, The Dying Poet, The Banjo, Creole Ballads,* and *Cuban Dances.* He also wrote a symphony and some smaller works for orchestra (*Montevideo,* and *Escenas campestres cubanas*). He often introduced into his writings the rhythms and idiom of Creole and Negro folksongs and dances. Several of his compositions were used for a ballet, *Cakewalk,* introduced by the New York City Ballet on June 12, 1951; the score was adapted and orchestrated by Hershy Kay.

Goetz von Berlichingen. *See:* Goethe, Wolfgang von.

Gould, Glenn, pianist. Born Toronto, Canada, Sept. 25, 1932. He was graduated from the Toronto Royal Conservatory in 1950, after having made his concert début as soloist with the Toronto Symphony on Jan. 14, 1947. His début in the United States took place in Washington, D.C., on Jan. 2, 1955; soon after that he attracted national attention with his brilliant recording of Bach's *Goldberg Variations.* An entire program was assigned to Gould at the second annual Stratford (Ontario) Festival on Jan. 9, 1956, when he appeared as pianist, composer, and conductor. He made his first extended tour of the United States in 1956-1957, and his European début took place on April 28, 1957, as soloist with the Berlin Philharmonic, Herbert von Karajan conducting. A few months later he became the first North American concert pianist to tour the Soviet Union.

Gould, Morton, composer. Born New York City, Dec. 10, 1913. He entered the Institute of Musical Art on a scholarship when he was eight; at thirteen he studied piano with Abby Whiteside; and at fifteen he completed a two-year course in theory and composition at New York University. He made numerous appearances as a child prodigy pianist. Later on, he earned his living playing the piano in motion-picture theaters and on vaudeville circuits. For three years he was staff pianist at the Radio City Music Hall, New York. He first attracted interest as a composer when he was eighteen with the *Chorale and Fugue in Jazz* introduced by the Philadelphia Orchestra under Stokowski. In his twenty-first year he started a long and fruitful association with radio, as conductor and arranger, becoming an outstandingly popular radio personality. All the while he continued writing serious compositions which were performed by leading American and European musical organizations. Gould has been at his best in exploiting American popular and folk idioms, which he has done with extraordinary skill. He has also written music for the stage and motion pictures. A prolific composer, his main works are for orchestra, and include 3 symphonies, *Foster Gallery, Spirituals, Cowboy Rhapsody,* a viola concerto, a concerto for orchestra, *Minstrel Show, Philharmonic Waltzes, Serenade of Carols, Family Album, Tap Dance Concerto, Dance Variations, Inventions* for four pianos and orchestra, *Showpiece, Sante Fe Saga, Jekyll and Hyde Variations, Declaration Suite, Rhythm Gallery,* and *Dialogue* for piano and orchestra.

See: Concerto—*Gould; Spirituals.*

Gounod, Charles François, composer. Born Paris, France, June 17, 1818; died there, Oct. 18, 1893. He attended the Paris Conservatory and after that became a composer of operas, achieving his first major success with his masterwork, *Faust,* in 1869. While best known for his operas, and secondarily for his religious and choral music, Gounod also wrote a considerable amount of instrumental music. Of the last about all that is still performed is a slight piece for orchestra, *Funeral March of a Marionette.* Other music for orchestra includes 2 symphonies, *Marche romaine, Marche religieuse,* and *Saltarello.* For piano, Gounod wrote many waltzes, scherzos, romances, preludes, and marches. He also wrote a string quartet and a piano quintet.

Goyescas. Two books of three pieces each for the piano by Enrique Granados (1911). Each composition interprets some painting by Goya, and the six pieces together represent a musical portrait of 18th-century Madrid as the painter knew it. Granados himself introduced the suite in Barcelona, on March 11, 1911. He subsequently used three of the pieces for his opera, *Goyescas*. The most popular numbers from this collection are: No. 1, *Los Requiebros;* No. 3, *El Fandango del Candíl;* No. 4, *Quejas o la Maja y el Ruiseñor.*

Grace Note. Ornament written in small notation.

Gradus ad Parnassum. (1) A series of about a hundred exercises for piano by Muzio Clementi (1817).

(2) *See:* Fux, Johann Joseph.

Graffman, Gary, pianist. Born New York City, Oct. 19, 1928. He attended the Curtis Institute of Music for about a decade, a pupil of Isabelle Vengerova. In 1947 he won first prize in the Rachmaninoff Fund Contest, which brought him a nationwide tour and a recording contract. In 1949 he received the Leventritt Award, and in 1950 a Fulbright fellowship for study in Europe. Since 1951 he has made appearances throughout Europe and the United States.

Grainger, Percy, pianist and composer. Born Melbourne, Australia, July 8, 1882. Appearances as a child prodigy pianist enabled him to finance his music study in Germany with Ferrucio Busoni and James Kwast. In 1900 he made a successful concert début in London, following this with a tour of Great Britain, New Zealand, Australia, and South Africa. At Grieg's request he gave the first performance of the A minor Concerto in England in 1907. Largely through Grieg's influence, Grainger became interested in English folk music. He soon produced a succession of arrangements and adaptations of British folksongs which are among his most popular compositions. These include *Molly on the Shore, Shepherd's Hey, Mock Morris, Country Gardens, Brigg Fair, Handel in the Strand, Londonderry Air, English Dance,* and *Irish Tunes from County Derry.* Grainger made his American début as pianist in New York on Feb. 11, 1915. He has since remained a permanent resident of the United States and for many years was active as concert pianist and lecturer.

Granados, Enrique, composer. Born Lé-

rida, Spain, July 27, 1867; died aboard *Sussex,* March 24, 1916. He studied piano in Barcelona with Francisco Jurnet and Joan Baptista Pujol and composition with Felipe Pedrell. In 1887 he went to Paris, where he continued piano study with the younger Charles de Bériot. Granados' début as a mature pianist took place in Barcelona on April 20, 1890, after which he performed throughout Europe. Inspired by his teacher, Pedrell, he began composing music national in spirit and content. His first opera, *Maria del Carmen,* was introduced at Madrid in 1898. After that he wrote several more operas, the most significant being *Goyescas.* He also wrote abundantly for the piano, pieces in which he combined Spanish national idioms with the full resources of keyboard technique; he is sometimes referred to as the creator of modern Spanish music for the piano. His most significant pieces for the piano are assembled in the four volumes of Spanish Dances (*Danzas españoles*), in *Six Pieces on Spanish Popular Songs,* and in the two books of *Goyescas* on which his opera was based.

Granados came to the United States in 1916 to attend the world première of his opera, *Goyescas,* at the Metropolitan Opera. He delayed his return to Europe to perform for President Wilson at the White House. Thus he was aboard the *Sussex,* sailing from Folkestone to Dieppe, when it was torpedoed by German U-boats during World War I.

See: Goyescas; Intermezzo; Spanish Dances (1).

Grand Canyon Suite. Suite for orchestra by Ferde Grofé (1930), first performed in Chicago by Paul Whiteman and his orchestra on Nov. 22, 1931. This five-movement suite is a tonal tour of one of America's natural wonders. I. *Sunrise.* A roll of the timpani leads to the principal melody in muted trumpet against a chordal accompaniment. II. *The Painted Desert.* An air of mystery is projected with ominous chords. After a lyric section, the mysterious setting of the opening measures returns. III. *On the Trail.* This is the most famous movement of the suite. The stumbling progress of a burro is described in a halting rhythm against which a cowboy tune is heard. IV. *Sunset.* A series of animal calls lead to a beautiful melody describing a sunset over the Canyon. V. *Cloudburst.* A summer storm erupts, after which the Canyon reverts to its former tranquil self.

Grande pâque russe, La (Rimsky-Korsakov). *See: Russian Easter Overture.*

Gray, Cecil, writer on music. Born Edinburgh, Scotland, May 19, 1895; died Worthing, England, Sept. 9, 1951. He studied music with private teachers including Bernard van Dieren and Granville Bantock. In 1915 he settled in London, where five years later he founded with Philip Heseltine *The Sackbut.* For many years Gray was active as music critic of *The Nation and Athenaeum, The Daily Telegraph,* and *The Manchester Guardian.* His most important books are: *A Survey of Contemporary Music* (1924); *History of Music* (1928); *Sibelius* (1931); *Sibelius: The Symphonies* (1935); *Predicaments* (1936); *The Forty-Eight Preludes and Fugues of Bach* (1938); and *Contingencies* (1947).

Greensleeves. An English folksong often adapted for concert music. The song itself probably dates from the early 16th century and is mentioned by Shakespeare in *The Merry Wives of Windsor.* It became a party tune of the Cavaliers in the 17th century; and in the United States, in 1957, it was adapted into a popular song. The best-known concert arrangement is an orchestral fantasia by Ralph Vaughan Williams, also entitled *Greensleeves* (1929); he had previously used the song in his opera, *Sir John in Love.* In the last movement of the *St. Paul Suite,* Gustav Holst uses this melody as a contrapuntal background.

Gretchaninov, Alexander, composer. Born Moscow, Russia, Oct. 25, 1864; died New York City, Jan. 3, 1956. He had comparatively little musical training when he entered the Moscow Conservatory in his seventeenth year. He was not happy there and soon transferred to the St. Petersburg Conservatory, where he found a sympathetic teacher in Rimsky-Korsakov. Under the guidance of Rimsky-Korsakov, Gretchaninov completed a string quartet that won a prize and a symphony that Rimsky-Korsakov introduced in 1895.

For six years, Gretchaninov taught music in St. Petersburg. His poverty led him back to Moscow, where he finished his first opera, *Dobrina Nikitch,* a major success at its première in 1903 with Feodor Chaliapin in the principal role. Gretchaninov subsequently devoted himself to writing songs and church music, proving himself a master in both fields. In instrumental music he was also extraordinarily prolific, producing 5 symphonies, concertos, suites, and shorter works for orchestra, 4 string quartets, 2 piano trios, 2 violin sonatas, 2 clarinet sonatas, cello sonata, septet, and a library of music for the piano, including numerous compositions for children. His works are traditional in idiom and structure, and more Germanic than Russian in style. In 1925 Gretchaninov left the Soviet Union and settled in Paris. Between 1929 and 1936 he made five trips to the United States, then settled there permanently in 1939. His last public appearance took place in New York on Oct. 5, 1954, in a concert devoted entirely to his music.

Grétry, André Ernest, composer. Born Liège, Belgium, Feb. 8, 1741; died Montmorency, France, Sept. 24, 1813. After studying in Italy with Giovanni Battista Casali, Grétry wrote his first opera, *Le Vendemmiatrici,* successfully produced at Rome in 1765. He then went to Paris, where he wrote over 50 operas and comic operas, a field in which he won renown. During the French Revolution he allied himself with the new regime by writing many popular works reflecting its ideology. The municipality of Paris named a street after him and later placed his statue in the Opéra-Comique. When the Paris Conservatory was founded in 1795 he became one of its Inspectors; and at the inauguration of the Institut de France he was elected a member. Upon the restoration of the monarchy, Grétry changed allegiance and remained a powerful figure in French music. Napoleon honored him with a pension and the Legion of Honor. Grétry lived his last years in the home formerly inhabited by Jean Jacques Rousseau, in Montmorency.

Both as composer and theorist, Grétry was most significant in the field of opera.

But he was also the composer of many delightful orchestral and instrumental works which afford pleasant listening whenever revived. These works include 6 symphonies, 6 quartets, 6 piano sonatas, and several trios and divertissements.

A charming orchestral suite, *Danses villageoises,* arranged by Frans Ruehlmann, comprises six dances from five Grétry operas: *Danse rustique* from *Richard Coeur-de-Lion; Gavotte et Danse en Rond* from *Colinette à la Cour;* Gigue from *L'Epreuve villageoise;* Entr'acte from *La Rosière de Salency;* and Contredanse from *L'Embarras de richesses.*

Other ballet suites for orchestra derived from Grétry's music were arranged by Felix Mottl and Selmar Meyrowitz.

Grieg, Edvard, composer. Born Bergen, Norway, June 15, 1843; died there, Sept. 4, 1907. By the time Grieg was twelve he was able to play the piano competently and had completed his first composition, *Variations on a German Theme* for piano. Ole Bull, the famous Norwegian violinist, urged Grieg's parents to send the boy to the Leipzig Conservatory, which he attended for several years. In 1860 Grieg was stricken by pleurisy, which permanently damaged his left lung and created respiratory troubles from which he henceforth suffered. After a period of rest in Bergen, he returned to Leipzig and remained there until spring of 1862. Then he went back to Bergen, and in 1863 participated there in several concerts in which some of his compositions were introduced. Discouraged by his inability to gain a government stipend, he settled for several years in Copenhagen. There his friendship with two composers—Niels Gade and Rikard Nordraak—proved a decisive influence. Gade encouraged him to continue serious composition by undertaking a symphony; Nordraak directed Grieg towards musical nationalism. Grieg's first work to show a national character was the *Humoresques* for piano, op. 6, dedicated to Nordraak. Grieg also collaborated with Nordraak in organizing the Euterpe Society to sponsor Scandinavian music.

Grieg was traveling in Italy in 1865 when he heard that Nordraak had died suddenly in Paris. His grief brought on physical collapse. Following his recovery, Grieg wrote a piano work in memory of his friend, and at the same time strengthened his resolve to carry on the esthetic principles and musical ideals promulgated by him. Returning to Scandinavia, Grieg arranged in Christiania (now Oslo) the first concert ever devoted entirely to Norwegian music, on Oct. 15, 1866; on this program Grieg himself was represented by two piano sonatas and the *Humoresques.* In 1867 he helped launch the Norwegian Academy of Music. He also became conductor of the Harmonic Society, with which he often helped promote Scandinavian music.

On June 11, 1867, Grieg married Nina Hagerup, a gifted singer. They settled in Christiania, where Grieg became active as teacher, conductor, pianist, composer, and propagandist for Norwegian music. His own works now began to attract attention. In 1869 Liszt wrote him from Rome praising Grieg's Sonata in F major for violin and piano. In the same year Grieg received a small government subsidy enabling him to travel to Italy; there he met Liszt, who expressed unqualified enthusiasm for Grieg's Piano Concerto in A minor.

Now a major musical figure in Norway, Grieg was appointed to the Swedish Academy in 1872, and to the Leyden Academy one year after that. His reputation began to spread to all parts of Europe. In the fall of 1880 he made an extended concert tour of Germany and Holland; only his poor health prevented him from filling other concert commitments in England and France. Now a man of some means, Grieg fulfilled a lifelong dream in 1885 by acquiring a beautiful villa, Troldhaugen, six miles outside Bergen, his home for the rest of his life. From then on, pilgrims from all parts of the world beat a path to his villa to pay him homage.

Many honors came his way, including honorary degrees from Oxford and Cambridge, and election to the French Academy of Arts in 1890. His sixtieth birthday, in 1903, was a national holiday in Norway. In Leipzig, they erected a bust and placed it in the entrance of the Gewandhaus.

His last public appearance took place at London in May 1906 when he conducted two concerts of his own works. He was about to pay another visit to England the following year when he suffered a heart attack in Bergen. A few days later he died in his sleep. He was given a state funeral, and his ashes (at his own request) were buried in a grotto near Troldhaugen.

Grieg is Norway's greatest composer, its most eloquent musical voice. He drew his inspiration from Norway's history, geography, culture, and folklore. In his works are interpreted the forests and fjords of his native land, its people and customs, its traditions. He rarely quoted folk melodies; but he created music that absorbed stylistic elements of Norwegian folksongs and dances so successfully that this music seems to be authentic folk art.

He was perhaps at his best in his miniatures for the piano; it is for this reason that Hans von Buelow once described him as the "Chopin of the North." But he could also be completely at ease in works of larger design, able to produce integrated masterworks within the more ambitious forms of the sonata and the concerto.

The following are Grieg's principal instrumental works.

Chamber Music: 3 violin sonatas; string quartet; cello sonata.

Orchestra: Concerto in A minor, for piano and orchestra; *In Autumn; Two Elegiac Melodies* and *Holberg Suite* for string orchestra; Norwegian Dances; *Peer Gynt,* two suites; *Sigurd Jorsalfar; Symphonic Dances; Lyric Suite.*

Piano: Sonata; *Lyric Pieces; Moods; Norwegian Mountain Tunes; Norwegian Peasant Dances;* ballades, humoresques, *Albumblätter.*

See: Concerto—*Grieg; Holberg Suite; Lyric Pieces;* Norwegian Dances; *Peer Gynt,* Suites; *Sigurd Jorsalfar;* Sonata—*Grieg.*

Griffes, Charles Tomlinson, composer. Born Elmira, N.Y., Sept. 17, 1884; died New York City, April 8, 1920. In his adolescence he went to Berlin to specialize in the piano. There he was urged

by Engelbert Humperdinck to devote himself to composition. In 1907 Griffes returned to the United States, and from 1908 until his death taught music at the Hackley School in Tarrytown, N.Y. Creative work was consigned to the late hours of the night, a practice largely responsible for undermining his health. Between 1918 and 1920 several important musical organizations performed some of his works, including the Philadelphia Orchestra, New York Symphony, and the Flonzaley Quartet; but these performances did little to lift him out of his poverty and obscurity. His early death from pneumonia was believed to have been caused by the strain of copying out the parts of his score, *The Pleasure Dome of Kubla Khan,* for its première performance by the Boston Symphony late in 1919. Griffes was a sensitive Impressionist who filled his music with poetic statements and freshly conceived melodies and harmonies. He was growing creatively through the years; his premature death at the age of thirty-six robbed the American scene of one who might have become a major composer. Besides his most celebrated orchestral work, the tone poem *The Pleasure Dome of Kubla Khan,* his major works include a *Poem* for flute and orchestra, *Two Sketches on Indian Themes* for string quartet, *Three Tone Pictures* for wind instruments and harp; a piano sonata, *Fantasy Pieces,* and *Four Roman Sketches,* all for piano. *The White Peacock,* one of the *Four Roman Sketches,* is well known in its orchestral version.

See: Four Roman Sketches; Pleasure Dome of Kubla Khan, The; Poem (2); *White Peacock, The.*

Griller String Quartet. An English chamber-music ensemble organized in 1929 by four students of the Royal Academy of Music in London. Its members were Sydney Griller and Jack O'Brien, violins; Philip Burton, viola; and Colin Hampton, cello. After appearing for a decade throughout England and the Continent in over 800 concerts, the Quartet made its American début in New York on Feb. 5, 1939. The Quartet was temporarily disbanded during World War II when its members joined the British army; but it resumed musical activity after the war in all parts of the world. **Grofé, Ferde,** composer. Born New York City, March 27, 1892. After studying piano, violin, and harmony with his mother, and viola with his father, he played the viola for ten years in the Los Angeles Philharmonic. In his last year with that orchestra he began playing in jazz bands, and making excellent orchestrations of current popular songs. In 1919 he went to work for Paul Whiteman's Orchestra as pianist and arranger. For the next half-dozen years all of Whiteman's numbers were arranged by Grofé, including Gershwin's *Rhapsody in Blue.* In 1924 Grofé wrote his first work in a large form, *Broadway at Night;* and in 1931 he achieved his first major success as a composer with the *Grand Canyon Suite,* still his most popular work. Grofé left Whiteman's employ in 1927 to embark on his own career as conductor. He made numerous appearances in concert auditoriums and over the radio. He was also active as a composer, producing such works for orchestra as the *Mississippi Suite, Metropolis, Three Shades of Blue, Tabloid, Hollywood Suite, Aviation Suite,* and *Hudson River Suite.* He belongs with those composers who have successfully used American popular idioms in serious music.

See: Grand Canyon Suite.

Grosse Fuge. *See:* Quartet—*Beethoven.*

Ground bass (or **basso ostinato**). A theme or figure repeated in the bass throughout a composition.

Grove, Sir George. Musical amateur and compiler of a celebrated music dictionary. Born London, England, Aug. 13, 1820; died London, England, May 28, 1900. Early in life he was a civil engineer who helped erect the Crystal Palace in London. A devoted musical amateur, he immersed himself in musical interests from 1865 on. For forty years he wrote the program notes for concerts at the Crystal Palace. In 1882 he helped found the Royal College of Music, serving as its director until 1894. In 1867, with Arthur Sullivan, he unearthed a precious cache of manuscripts by Schubert in Vienna, all of it hitherto unknown. From 1868 to 1883 he was editor of the *Mac-*

millan Magazine. He visited the United States in 1878, and in 1883 was knighted. He is most famous for his *Dictionary of Music and Musicians,* originally in four volumes (1879-1889). The second edition, in five volumes, was edited by J. A. Fuller-Maitland (1904-1910); the third and fourth, also in five volumes, was edited by H. C. Colles (1928-1940). A completely revised and reset fifth edition appeared in 1954 in nine volumes, edited by Eric Blom. Grove was also the author of *Beethoven and His Nine Symphonies* (1884).

Gruenberg, Louis, composer. Born Brest-Litovsk, Poland, Aug. 3, 1884. He came to the United States as an infant. After studying the piano with Adele Margulies, he returned in 1903 to Europe, where he attended the Vienna Conservatory and studied piano privately with Ferruccio Busoni. He embarked on a career as concert pianist, making his début as soloist with the Berlin Philharmonic in 1912. But he soon made an even more auspicious bow as composer when his tone poem, *The Hill of Dreams,* won a prize of $1,000. In 1919 he was back in the United States, where he soon produced several works with which he assumed a prominent position among American composers. The most ambitious and significant of his works are the opera, *Emperor Jones,* based on Eugene O'Neill's play, and introduced at the Metropolitan Opera in 1933; and a violin concerto written for and introduced by Jascha Heifetz in 1944. He also wrote 5 symphonies, 2 piano concertos, various shorter works for orchestra (*The Enchanted Isle, Jazz Suite, Music to an Imaginary Ballet, Nine Moods, Dance Rhapsody, Music to an Imaginary Legend, Variations on a Pastoral Theme, Americana*), 2 piano quintets, 2 string quartets, a violin sonata, violin suite, *Diversions* for string quartet, and *Daniel Jazz,* for tenor and eight instruments. His music has passed through several changes of style: Impressionism, jazz, and finally a modern idiom in which advanced devices of rhythm, harmony, and tonality are employed.

Grumiaux, Arthur, violinist. Born Villers-Perwin, Belgium, March 21, 1921. He was graduated from the Conservatory of Charleroi when he was eleven, after which he studied violin with Alfred Dubois and Georges Enesco. His début as a mature artist took place in Belgium just before the outbreak of World War II, and after he had won the Prix Vieuxtemps and the Belgian National Competition. During the war years, Grumiaux played the violin in a string quartet and taught violin at the Brussels Conservatory. His career on the concert stage as violin virtuoso was resumed after the war with appearances throughout Europe. He made his American début in Baltimore, Md., on Jan. 18, 1952.

Guadagnini. An 18th-century family of violin makers which followed methods and techniques established by Stradivari. Lorenzo Guadagnini (about 1695-1745) was the first member of this family to make violins; these were modeled after the Stradivari. His son, Giovanni Battista (1711-1786), was the most celebrated member of the family, and his instruments are justly famous to this day. Giovanni's three sons—Giuseppe, Gaetano, and Lorenzo—also made violins, though with less brilliant results than their father. The tradition of instrument-making was passed on by these three sons to several more generations of Guadagninis.

Guarneri. A 17th- and 18th-century family of Italian violin makers. The most famous was Giuseppe (1698-1744) known as "Del Gesù," to distinguish him from his father, also named Giuseppe (1666-1740). The younger Giuseppe's fame and skill were surpassed only by Stradivari. His instruments are characterized by their beautiful tone.

Guido d'Arezzo (Guido Aretinus), theoretician and teacher. Born Arezzo, Italy, about 990; died Pomposa, Italy, May 17, 1050. He was a Benedictine monk who revolutionized musical notation. He introduced four-line staves which for the first time established certainty of pitch in notation. He is also the inventor of solmization: calling the notes of the scale "do, re, mi" and so forth.

Guilmant, Alexandre, organist and composer. Born Boulogne-sur-mer, France, March 12, 1837; died Meudon, France, March 29, 1911. He studied the organ with private teachers and at sixteen became organist of a cathedral in Boulogne. He went to Paris in or about 1863 where he inaugurated the organs at St. Sulpice and Notre Dame. From 1871 to 1901 he was the organist at the Trinité. His reputation as one of Europe's leading organists was further enhanced through concert tours in Europe, and in the United States in 1893. In 1894 he helped found the Schola Cantorum, where he was professor of organ; in 1896 he also became professor of organ at the Paris Conservatory. Guilmant wrote over a hundred compositions for organ, including 2 symphonies for organ and orchestra, 8 sonatas, and 25 sets of pieces. He edited *L'École classique de l'orgue* and, with André Pirro, *Archives des maîtres de l'orgue,* which revived many long-forgotten masterworks.

Guiraud, Ernest, composer and teacher. Born New Orleans, La., June 23, 1837; died Paris, France, May 6, 1892. He went to Paris as a boy and attended the Paris Conservatory, receiving the Prix de Rome in 1859. As a composer he was later most active in opera, but he did write several orchestral suites, an overture, and a Caprice for violin and orchestra introduced by Pablo de Sarasate. He also arranged *L'Arlésienne Suite* No. 2 from Bizet's incidental music to the play of Daudet after Bizet's death. He had a fruitful career as professor of harmony, accompaniment, and advanced composition at the Paris Conservatory; his pupils included Debussy and Charles Martin Loeffler.

Guitar. A plucked string instrument belonging to the lute and zither families. It has six strings, a flat back, and sides curving inward. The guitar has entered the modern concert hall mainly through the efforts of several distinguished performers, the most notable being Andrés Segovia. Many contemporary composers have written major works specifically for Segovia, among them being Castelnuovo-Tedesco and Manuel Ponce. Segovia himself made many transcriptions from the classical literature for the guitar.

Gulda, Friedrich, pianist. Born Vienna, Austria, May 16, 1930. For five years he attended the Vienna State Academy, and when he was sixteen he won the International Pianists' Competition at Geneva. He made his début as soloist with the Orchestre de la Suisse Romande, Ernest Ansermet conducting, after which he toured Europe. He scored successes at the Prague Music Festival in 1947 and the Festival of Vienna a year later. His American début took place in New York in 1950. In 1956 he made the first of several appearances as a jazz pianist, but without abandoning his more serious concert activity.

Gurre Lieder. *See:* Schoenberg, Arnold.

Guy-Ropartz, Joseph, composer. Born Giungamp, Côtes-du-Nord, France, June 15, 1864; died Lanloup, France, Nov. 22, 1955. He attended the Paris Conservatory, and later studied privately with César Franck, whose influence on him was profound. For many years Guy-Ropartz was director of Conservatories in Nancy and Strasbourg, after which he went into retirement. In his music the Breton influence is prominent. Many of his best works were inspired by Breton scenes and legends, and some utilize authentic Breton folk idioms. His major works include 5 symphonies, shorter works for orchestra (*Soir sur les chaumes, La Chasse du Prince Arthur, Les Landes, Scènes bretonnes*), 5 string quartets, 3 violin sonatas, 2 cello sonatas, string trio, and piano trio.

Gwendoline, Overture to. Overture to an opera by Emmanuel Chabrier. The opera, in which the composer was strongly influenced by Wagner, has a text by Catulle Mendès based on a medieval legend; it was introduced in Brussels on April 10, 1886. The overture is essentially a portrait of the leading male character, Harald. It opens with a stormy theme of Danish character. After a transition which speaks of the concern of Harald's beloved, Gwendoline, for his safety, there appears a tender passage quoting the love music of the second act. The overture ends in the same vigorous mood in which it opened.

Gymnopédies. Suite of three pieces for the piano by Erik Satie (1888), each a slow and solemn dance with unusual progressions and novel harmonies. The title was derived from *gymnopedia*, a festival in ancient Sparta in which naked youths celebrated their gods by dancing and singing. The first and third dances of this suite were orchestrated by Debussy. The entire work was inspired by a decoration on a Greek vase.

Gypsy Airs (Zigeunerweisen). For violin and piano by Pablo de Sarasate, op. 20, no. 1. This is one of the most popular works in the violin repertory—a skilful fantasia on varied gypsy melodies, some sentimental, some pyrotechnical.

H

Hába, Alois, composer. Born Vizovice, Moravia, June 21, 1893. He has specialized in writing quarter-tone music. He studied music at the Prague Conservatory, the Vienna Academy, and the Berlin High School for Music. Boyhood associations with Bohemian folk music, with its subtle deviations from pitch, and subsequent interest in oriental music early led him to experiment with quarter-

tone music. He founded a class in quarter-tone music at the Prague Conservatory; devised his own music notation; invented instruments capable of performing his works. Another technical trait of his writing is "athematic" music, a continuous flow of musical sound without definitely stated subjects. Besides his operas his major works include 10 string quartets, 3 wind nonets, various fantasies and suites for solo instruments and piano, or unaccompanied solo instruments, a violin concerto, Symphonic Fantasy for piano and orchestra, overture, *Symphonic Music,* 5 piano suites, 10 piano fantasies, 2 piano sonatas, and smaller pieces for piano. Hába has also written some essays on quarter-tone music. His brother, Karel (born Vizovice, May 21, 1898), is also a composer of quarter-tone music.

Habanera. A slow dance in 2/4 time said to have originated in Cuba but long popular in Spain. Debussy's *La Puerta del Vino* from piano Preludes, Book 2, and *La Soirée dans Grenade* from *Estampes,* for piano, are in this form. The following are some other compositions in the habanera rhythm and style.

LOUIS AUBERT. Aubert's Habanera is a tone poem for orchestra (1919), introduced in Paris on March 22, 1919, Rhené-Baton conducting. While utilizing the habanera rhythm, this work is not essentially an evocation of that popular dance. It is more directly a musical interpretation of the following lines by Baudelaire: "Let me smell your hair, to bury in it my whole face . . . If you could only know all that I see, all that I feel, all that I hear in your hair. My soul travels on this perfume like the soul of other men on music."

CHABRIER. Habanera, for piano (1885), makes effective use of the characteristic rhythm of the dance. The work has been orchestrated by Felix Mottl.

RAVEL. One of the most popular habaneras for violin and piano is Ravel's *Pièce en forme de habanera.* It originated as, and is a transcription of, the composer's Vocalise, for voice and piano. It has also been transcribed for cello and piano.

Ravel also wrote a Habanera for two pianos (1896). This is the first movement of a two-movement suite entitled *Les Sites auriculaires.* (The second movement is *Entre cloches.*) This suite, the composer's first work to be performed, was introduced by Ricardo Viñes and Marthe Dron in Paris on March 5, 1898. The Habanera was later adapted by the composer for orchestra as the third movement of his *Rapsodie espagnole* (which see).

See also: Havanaise; Spanish Dances (2).

Habeneck, François Antoine, violinist and conductor. Born Mézières, France, Jan. 22, 1781; died Paris, France, Feb. 8, 1849. After attending the Paris Conservatory, he served there as assistant professor of violin from 1808 to 1816 and as professor from 1825 to 1848. He is best known as a conductor, a pioneer in popularizing Beethoven's symphonies in France. In 1828 he founded the Société des Concerts du Conservatoire (Paris Conservatory Orchestra), which he conducted for twenty years. He also led orchestral performances at the Tuileries.

Hadley, Henry Kimball, conductor and composer. Born Somerville, Mass., Dec. 20, 1871; died New York City, Sept. 6, 1937. After attending the New England Conservatory he went to Europe for further study of composition and counterpoint. He served his apprenticeship as conductor in Europe between 1905 and 1909. In the latter year he was appointed permanent conductor of the Seattle Symphony in the State of Washington; from 1911 to 1915 he was principal conductor of the San Francisco Symphony; from 1915 to 1922, associate conductor of the New York Philharmonic; and from 1929 to 1932, conductor of the Manhattan Symphony. He also made numerous guest appearances with other major orchestras in America and Europe. As a composer, Hadley was a traditionalist who leaned perhaps too heavily on German Romanticism to permit him any degree of individuality. He was a facile writer and a good craftsman, but lacked a personal approach. His works for orchestra include 5 symphonies, several tone poems (*Salomé, Lucifer, The Ocean*), overtures (*In Bohemia, Aurora Borealis, Herod, Alma Mater*), a concertino for piano and orchestra, and a suite, *Streets of Pekin.* He also wrote 2 string quartets, 2 piano trios, and a piano quintet.

Hadow, Sir William Henry, writer on music. Born Ebrington, England, Dec. 27, 1859; died London, England, April 8, 1937. His academic education took place at Malvern College, and Worcester College, Oxford. Music study was pursued in Germany and London. For many years Hadow was associated with Worcester College, first as fellow and tutor, then proctor, and after that university examiner. From 1909 to 1919 he was principal of Armstrong College in Newcastle-on-the-Tyne, and in 1919 he became chancellor of Sheffield University. As a writer on music he first distinguished himself with *Studies in Modern Music* (1892, 1895). His later books include the following: *A Croatian Composer* (1897), *Music* (1924), and *Collected Essays* (1928). He was the editor of the *Oxford History of Music* to which he contributed its fifth volume, *The Viennese Period* (1904).

Haffner Serenade. *See:* Serenade—*Mozart.*

Haffner Symphony. *See:* Symphony—*Mozart.*

Haieff, Alexei, composer. Born Blagoveschensk, Russia, Aug. 25, 1914. As a child he settled with his family in Harbin, Manchuria, where his musical training began. In 1931, the family settled in the United States, where Alexei attended the Juilliard School on a scholarship. He later studied composition privately with Nadia Boulanger. In 1941 he won the Lili Boulanger Memorial Award and a medal from the American Academy of Rome; in 1946 and 1949 a Guggenheim Fellowship; in 1947 and 1948 the American Prix de Rome; and in 1952, the New York Music Critics Circle Award for his piano concerto. Haieff is a neo-Classical composer strongly influenced by Stravinsky; but a romantic infusion brings to his writing a definite personal character. His orchestral works include 2 symphonies, violin concerto, piano concerto, Divertimento for small orchestra, and *Ballet in E,* for orchestra. He also wrote a violin suite, a two-piano sonata, 3 Bagatelles for oboe and bassoon, a Serenade for piano, oboe, clarinet, and bassoon, a piano sonata, and various smaller pieces for piano and for harpsichord.

Hale, Philip, music critic. Born Norwich, Vt., March 5, 1854; died Boston, Mass., Nov. 30, 1934. He was graduated from Yale in 1876, after which he practiced law, a period in which he also studied piano with John Kautz and played the organ in a church. In 1882 he abandoned law for music, continuing his music study in Germany with Josef Rheinberger, and in Paris with Alexandre Guilmant. After his return to the United States he worked for several years as organist and conductor. In 1890 he turned to music criticism by writing for the Boston *Post.* From 1891 to 1903 he was music critic of the Boston *Journal,* and from 1903 until his death for the Boston *Herald,* becoming one of the most distinguished music critics of his time. From 1901 on he also wrote the analytical notes for the concerts of the Boston Symphony. The best of these have been collected by John N. Burk in *Philip Hale's Boston Symphony Programme Notes* (1935).

Hallé, Sir Charles, pianist and conductor. Born Hagen, Westphalia, April 11, 1819; died Manchester, England, Oct. 5, 1895. He made his début as pianist when he was only four. Later on he studied the piano in Darmstadt and Paris, after which he concertized in France and England. In 1848 he settled in Manchester, where two years later he became conductor of the Gentleman's Concerts. In 1857 he formed his own orchestra there for performances at the Exhibition. From 1858 on the Hallé Orchestra gave concerts in Manchester, becoming one of England's major symphonic organizations. From 1883 on, Hallé also conducted the Liverpool Philharmonic. In 1890 and 1891 he toured Australia, and in 1895, South Africa. He was knighted in 1888, and in 1893 was appointed the first principal of the newly founded Royal College of Music in Manchester.

Hallé Orchestra. Symphony orchestra founded in Manchester, England, in 1857 for performances at the Manchester Exhibition, the first concert taking place on Jan. 30. In 1858 it began presenting series of concerts in Manchester each season, then made tours of cities in North England. Hallé led the orchestra until his death, after which the Hallé Concerts Society was formed to perpetuate and finance the organization. Since Hallé, its principal conductors have been Frederick H. Cowen, Hans Richter, Michael Ball-ing, Sir Hamilton Harty, and Sir John Barbirolli. The orchestra celebrated its centenary in 1957, an occasion for which Vaughan Williams wrote *Flourish for Glorious John* in honor of its conductor, Barbirolli.

Hambourg, Mark, pianist. Born Boguchar, Russia, May 31, 1879. Taken to England in childhood, he studied piano there with his father, and subsequently became a British subject. From 1891 to 1894 he studied with Theodor Leschetizky in Vienna, and in 1894 he launched his career as a mature artist with a performance in Vienna. He made his first tour of Australia in 1895, and the first of several tours of the United States in 1899-1900. His brothers, Jan and Boris, were also distinguished musicians. Jan (born Voronezh, Russia, Aug. 27, 1882; died Tours, France, Sept. 29, 1947) was a violinist who made appearances throughout Europe and the United States. Boris (born Voronezh, Russia, Jan. 8, 1884; died Toronto, Canada, Nov. 24, 1954) was a cellist who toured Europe and the United States. He then settled in Toronto, where he helped found and was principal of the Hambourg Conservatory. In 1924, Boris Hambourg was instrumental in organizing the Hart House String Quartet with Geza de Kresz and Harry Adaskin, violins, and Milton Blackstone, viola. For many years this Quartet made successful tours of Canada, Europe, and the United States.

Hamburg Philharmonic Orchestra. A symphony orchestra founded in Hamburg, Germany, in 1828 by Friedrich Wilhelm Grund, who served as principal conductor until 1862. Its leading conductors after that were J. Stockhausen, Julius von Bernuth, Richard Barth, Siegmund von Hausegger, Karl Muck, Eugen Jochum, and Joseph Keilberth. The orchestra performs in the principal concert auditorium of the city, the Musikhalle.

Hamlet. (1) Overture-fantasia by Tchaikovsky, op. 67a (1888), first performed in St. Petersburg on Nov. 24, 1888, the composer conducting. An expressive melody for cellos and violins in the introductory section tells of Hamlet's grief over his father's death. After the midnight hour is struck, and the presence of the ghost suggested by wind instruments against tremolos, the main section of the fantasia is presented. The first theme is in a disturbed mood and represents Hamlet; a more tender second subject speaks for Ophelia. After a march section for the brasses, both main themes are worked out dramatically. In the coda the Ophelia melody and the march subject are effectively recalled. The overture ends softly with a final statement of the Hamlet theme.

(2) *See:* Shakespeare, William.

Hammerklavier Sonata. *See:* Sonata— *Beethoven.*

Handel, George Frideric, composer. Born Halle, Saxony, Feb. 23, 1685; died London, England, April 14, 1759. His music study began in Halle with Friedrich Zachau, after which he served as organist at the Domkirche. In 1703 he went to Hamburg, then an active opera center, playing the violin in the Opera orchestra and writing and producing his first opera, *Almira.* In 1706 he went to Italy, where he became acquainted with the compositions of Corelli which became models for his own instrumental writing. In 1710 he was appointed Kapellmeister in Hanover. Soon after this appointment he took a leave of absence to make his first visit to England. There he became famous for his operas. He returned to Hanover to fulfill his duties as Kapellmeister, but in 1712 he was back in London, this time to remain in England for good and to achieve recognition there as one of that country's most celebrated musicians. Queen Anne made him court composer. When the Elector of Hanover succeeded her to the throne Handel became his royal music master. From 1717 to 1720 Handel served as music master for the Duke of Chandos in Cannons. In 1720 he was back in London, filling the post of artistic director of the newly founded Royal Academy of Music, for which he wrote several important operas. Now at the height of his success, Handel was a favorite of both royalty and the general public. But he also had important enemies who resented him because he was a foreigner, a musical tyrant, and a man of boorish manners. Gathering around the powerful Earl of Burlington, these enemies joined forces to destroy him. They invited to London the popular Italian opera composer, Giovanni Maria Bononcini, to offset Handel's popularity. Bononcini scored a triumph with his operas, but when Handel countered with *Ottone* his rival met permanent defeat. But this victory for Handel was short-lived. The triumph of John Gay's *The Beggar's Opera* in 1728 threw into shade more serious endeavors and sent Handel's Academy into bankruptcy. Handel now went into partnership with John Jacob Heidegger to form a new opera company for which he wrote several new works. But he could not win back his public. When a rival company, sponsored by the Prince of Wales, drew from Handel his best singers, he conceded defeat and turned his enormous energies and gifts to another branch of composition—the oratorio—in which he was destined to scale the heights. The greatest of these oratorios was the *Messiah*, introduced at Dublin in 1742. It helped rehabilitate Handel's fortunes and his position in English music. While working on his last oratorio, *Jephtha*, Handel suddenly went blind. An operation proved unsuccessful. Nevertheless, Handel continued writing music, giving organ concerts, and directing performances of his oratorios. It was while directing *Messiah* at Covent Garden that he collapsed with his last, fatal illness. He died a few days later and was buried in Westminster Abbey.

To the concerto grosso form Handel brought artistic fulfillment by infusing it with noble melodies, rich harmonies, and varied moods while extending its structure. His various concertos and suites may lack the majesty he poured into his oratorios, but they are beautifully constructed and rich in musical thought. His main instrumental works include 6 concerti grossi, op. 3; 12 concerti grossi, op. 6; *Water Music* and *Royal Fireworks Music* for orchestra; various concertos for solo instruments and orchestra; numerous sonatas for various solo instruments and accompaniment; trio sonatas; and many suites, fugues, and smaller pieces for the harpsichord.

See: Concerto—*Handel;* Concerto Grosso—*Handel; Harmonious Black-*smith, The; Messiah; Royal Fireworks Music; Suite—*Handel; Water Music.*

Handel Variations (Brahms). *See:* Variations on a Theme by Handel.

Hannikainen, Tauno, conductor. Born Jyväskylä, Finland, Feb. 26, 1896. From 1914 to 1917 he attended the Helsinki Conservatory, subsequently studying the cello with André Hekking and Pablo Casals. In 1927 he was appointed conductor of the Turku Symphony. He made his American début on June 30, 1938, by conducting a special concert commemorating the 300th anniversary of the settling of Delaware by the Finns. He then appeared as guest of several major American symphony orchestras. From 1942 to 1946 he was principal conductor of the Duluth Symphony in Minnesota, and from 1947 to 1951 assistant conductor of the Chicago Symphony. Since 1951 he has been principal conductor of the Helsinki Symphony in Finland. In 1953 he received the decoration of Commander of the Order of the Finnish Lion.

Hanslick, Eduard, music critic. Born Prague, Czechoslovakia, Sept. 11, 1825; died Baden, Austria, Aug. 6, 1904. He attended the Universities of Prague and Vienna, studying law and philosophy, and received his doctorate in 1849. He studied music privately. In 1856 he became lecturer, and in 1861 professor of esthetics and music history at the University of Vienna. His career as music critic started in 1848 on the *Wiener Zeitung.* He continued writing music criticisms for the *Presse* and the *Neue freie Presse* up to 1895, his provocative and often brilliant pieces exerting a profound influence on Viennese musical life. An advocate of absolute music, he was a passionate champion of Brahms and an equally virulent antagonist of Wagner. It is believed Wagner created the villainous role of Beckmesser in *The Mastersingers* with Hanslick in mind, even going so far at first as to plan calling the character Hans Lick. Among Hanslick's most important books are *The Beautiful in Music* (1854), *Geschichte des Concertwesens in Wien* (1869), and *Aus dem Concertsaal* (1870). He also wrote an autobiography, *Aus meinem Leben* (1894). A collection of his criticisms was published in the

United States in 1950 under the title of *Vienna's Golden Years of Music: 1850-1900.*

Hanson, Howard, composer, conductor, and educator. Born Wahoo, Neb., Oct. 28, 1896. After receiving his musical training at Luther College in Wahoo, the Institute of Musical Art in New York, and Northwestern University, he was appointed professor of theory and composition at the Conservatory of Fine Arts associated with the College of the Pacific in San José, Calif. He was soon promoted there to the post of dean. In 1921 he became the first music fellow of the American Academy in Rome. In Italy he completed his first major work, the *Nordic Symphony,* introduced in Rome under his own direction in 1923. After returning to the United States in 1924 he became director of the Eastman School of Music in Rochester, N.Y., holding this post since then with distinction. He has organized and led an annual festival of American music in Rochester which has been responsible for the performance of over 1,000 works (many premières) by more than 600 composers. Hanson has also appeared as guest conductor of leading American and European orchestras, in which capacity he again proved himself a propagandist for American music. As composer, Hanson is most famous for his symphonies. His style is Classical in its adherence to traditional structures, but Romantic in emotional responses and expressive lyricism. His restraint in the use of harmonic colors and dynamics and his occasional indulgence in somber moods have led some critics to describe him as an "American Sibelius." In 1944 his Fourth Symphony became the first work in that form to win the Pulitzer Prize in music. His major orchestral works include 5 symphonies, various concertos (organ; piano), the tone poem *Pan and the Priest, Lux Aeterna,* Fantasy for String Orchestra, Serenade for Flute, Harp and Strings, *Fantasy Variations on a Theme of Youth* for piano and strings, *Mosaics,* and *Elegy in Memory of Serge Koussevitzky.*

See: Symphony—*Hanson.*

Hardy, Thomas, novelist and poet. Born Upper Brockhampton, England, June 2, 1840; died Dorchester, England, Jan. 11, 1928. Hardy's *The Return of the Native* was the source of Gustav Holst's tone poem, *Egdon Heath,* and *Wessex Tales* was the inspiration of Henry Balfour Gardiner's *The Shepherd Fennel's Dance,* for orchestra, one of the composer's most popular works.

Harmonic minor. A minor scale in which, ascending or descending, the sixth step is minor and the seventh major.

Harmonics. Flutelike sounds on a string instrument produced by placing the finger lightly on the string instead of pressing the string down firmly.

Harmonie der Welt, Die (The Harmony of the World). Symphony by Paul Hindemith (1951). Like another of this composer's symphonies, *Mathis der Maler,* this one was adapted from an opera score. The opera, *Die Harmonie der Welt,* has for its central character the astronomer, Johann Kepler. The symphony, first performed in Basel, Switzerland, on Jan. 24, 1952, Paul Sacher conducting, has three movements. I. *Musica Instrumentalis.* This movement discusses Kepler's physical evolution and his unhappy childhood. The first main theme is a broad subject for brass, repeated by woodwind and strings. This leads to a march melody. A fugal section brings on an epilogue in which the march melody is further discussed. II. *Musica Humana.* Here the spiritual evolution of Kepler is described. In the first part of the movement the main melodic material is characterized by the interval of a fourth. The second section is brought on by an oboe solo. After a climax for full orchestra, the first section is recalled. The epilogue that follows was described by the composer as a "depressed dance." III. *Musica Mundana.* This movement consists of a passacaglia with twenty-one variations, prefaced by an extended fugal section.

Harmonious Blacksmith, The. Fourth movement of Handel's Suite No. 5 in E major for harpsichord (1720). It is most often performed independently of the larger work. *The Harmonious Blacksmith* consists of an eight-bar melody in two parts, followed by five simple variations. The title "Harmonious Blacksmith" was created not by the composer but by a publisher in Bath, England, who issued the movement as a separate composition in 1822. This publisher came upon his title through the circumstance that a Bath blacksmith often sang the Handel tune and thus came to be known as "the harmonious blacksmith." The story that Handel conceived his melody in a blacksmith's shop during a storm is apocryphal.

Harmony. The science of combining notes into chords, and chords into progressions.

Harold in Italy. *See:* Symphony—*Berlioz.*

Harp. A stringed instrument played by plucking the strings with the fingers of both hands. It has forty-six strings. The C notes are colored red, and the F, blue. Seven pedals help raise the tones of the scale by one or two semitones.

Harp Quartet. *See:* Quartet—*Beethoven.*

Harpsichord. A precursor of the piano. The tone is thin and sensitive, produced by strings plucked by quills rather than struck by hammers as is the case with the piano.

Harris, Roy, composer. Born Lincoln County, Okla., Feb. 12, 1898. He acquired the elements of music by himself. Later on he studied harmony at the University of California, and composition privately with Arthur Farwell. His first works to be performed were a suite for string quartet, *Impressions of a Rainy Day,* and an Andante for orchestra, both in 1926. In that year he went to Paris, where he stayed for three years, studying composition with Nadia Boulanger and completing several ambitious chamber-music works. After returning to the United States, his *Symphony: 1933* was introduced by the Boston Symphony under Koussevitzky in 1934. His Third Symphony, Third String Quartet, and a piano quintet placed him among the most significant composers to appear in America since the end of World War I. From 1934 to 1938 he was head of the composition department at the Westminister Choir School, in Princeton, N.J. Since then he has held many posts either as teacher or as composer-in-residence: at Cornell University, Colorado College, Pennsylvania Women's College, and Indiana University, among other places.

During World War II he was head of the music section of the Office of War Information.

Harris has shown a predilection for forms of the past: fugue, passacaglia, toccata, and so forth. He has also been partial to polyphony and modal harmonies. Yet his music remains contemporary and American. It is broad in concept, with spaciously arched melodies; it is dynamically forceful in its exploitation of asymmetrical rhythms. He has been prolific, having produced for orchestra 7 symphonies, various concertos (violin; piano; two pianos; trio and orchestra), various shorter works (*When Johnny Comes Marching Home, Three Symphonic Essays, Challenge, American Creed, Memories of a Child's Sunday, Kentucky Spring, Cumberland Concerto, Symphonic Epigrams, Ode to Consonance, Reverie and Dance*), and a Fantasy for piano and orchestra. In the field of chamber music he has produced 3 string quartets, piano sextet, piano quintet, string sextet, piano trio, *Three Variations on a Theme* for string quartet, and *Soliloquy and Dance* for viola and piano. His piano compositions include a sonata, *Little Suite, Children at Play,* and *Ten American Ballads.*

See: Symphony—*Harris.*

Harrison, Guy Fraser, conductor. Born Guildford, England, Nov. 6, 1894. After attending the Royal College of Music in London, he was appointed in 1913 organist of the Episcopal Cathedral in Manila, the Philippines. He held this post six years, then settled in the United States, where for several years he taught organ and piano at the Eastman School of Music, and was conductor of the Eastman Theater Orchestra. In 1929 he was appointed conductor of the newly-founded Rochester Philharmonic; while holding this post he made many appearances as guest conductor of American orchestras. In 1951 he became principal conductor of the Oklahoma City Symphony.

Hart House String Quartet. *See:* Hambourg, Mark.

Harty, Sir Hamilton, conductor. Born Hillsborough, Ireland, Dec. 4, 1879; died Brighton, England, Feb. 19, 1941. He early received from his father a thorough training in music. After holding various posts as church organist in Ireland, he went to London in 1900 and soon made his mark as a piano accompanist. He made his début as a conductor with the London Symphony. From 1920 to 1933 he was principal conductor of the Hallé Orchestra in Manchester. After that he appeared as guest conductor with leading European orchestras. He made his American début in 1931, and in 1934 toured Australia. He was knighted in 1925, and in 1934 received a gold medal from the Royal Philharmonic Society of London. Harty was the composer of many orchestral works, including an *Irish Symphony*, a violin concerto, *Comedy Overture*, and a tone poem *With the Wild Geese*. He is most often represented on symphony programs by his admirable modern orchestral adaptations of two Handel suites, *Water Music* and the *Royal Fireworks Music*.

Háry János. Suite for orchestra by Zoltán Kodály (1925), adapted from the score to his opera introduced in Budapest on Oct. 16, 1926. The libretto, by Béla Paulini and Zsolt Harsányi, has for its hero a character famous in Hungarian folklore: a boastful, pompous fellow given to telling fantastic tales which he insists are true. In the opera, this character (Háry János) tells about falling in love with Marie Louise, wife of Napoleon. In an ensuing war between Austria and France, Háry defeats the enemy singlehanded. He returns to Vienna in triumph, and rejects Marie Louise for his boyhood sweetheart, Orzse.

The suite, one of the composer's most frequently performed works for orchestra, has six movements. I. Prelude: The Fairy Story Begins. An orchestral glissando in the opening bar imitates a sneeze: it is a Hungarian superstition that if a person sneezes while telling a tale, the story must be true. The sentimentality and roving imagination of Háry are caught in a tender melody first in cellos and basses, later developed by the strings. II. The Viennese Musical Clock. Háry is in Vienna, listening to the chimes of a musical clock in front of the imperial palace. A little tune is presented by woodwinds, horns, piano, and chimes; this is followed by a march theme for trumpets and percussion. III. Song. This is a folk melody speaking of Háry's love for Orzse. IV. The Battle and Defeat of Napoleon. This is a battle scene. A brief quotation of the *Marseillaise* (sounding almost like a lament) announces the defeat of the French. V. Intermezzo. This is a fiery czardas. VI. Entrance of the Emperor and his Court. A fanfare introduces march music of pomp and ceremony. Háry is brought in triumph before the Austrian Emperor.

Haskil, Clara, pianist. Born Bucharest, Rumania, Jan. 7, 1895. She made her concert début at the age of seven. She later attended the Paris Conservatory, where her teachers included Alfred Cortot and Gabriel Fauré, and studied piano privately with Ferruccio Busoni. Her concert tours after that brought her to a leading position among the women pianists of her day; she was also heard in distinguished sonata recitals with Georges Enesco, Pablo Casals, and Eugène Ysaÿe. Her American début took place in 1956.

Havanaise (Habanera). For violin and piano by Saint-Saëns, op. 83 (1887), one of the composer's most popular works for violin. It utilizes the rhythm of the habanera.

Haydn, Franz Joseph, composer. Born Rohrau, Austria, March 31, 1732; died Vienna, Austria, May 31, 1809. When Haydn was only five his unusual talent for music made an impression on Johann Mathias Franck, a professional musician and relative. Franck took the boy into his own household for two years and gave him a comprehensive training in harmony, counterpoint, solfeggio, and harpsichord. In 1740, Haydn was accepted for the renowed choir of St. Stephen's in Vienna, with which he remained nine years. During that time he attended the choir school. When his voice broke in his seventeenth year he was dismissed. For a while he taught music, performed on the harpsichord, and did hack work. But at the same time he continued studying by himself, and pursued serious composition. His.

first permanent job came when he was hired by the famous singing teacher and composer, Nicola Porpora, as accompanist and house servant. In this post Haydn had the opportunity to meet some of Vienna's foremost musicians and most influential patrons. One of the latter was Baron Karl von Fuernberg who in 1755 engaged Haydn to conduct performances at his palace in Weinzierl and write music for these concerts. In this office Haydn wrote numerous orchestral works (divertimentos, nocturnes, serenades) together with his first symphony and first dozen string quartets.

In 1758 Haydn was appointed Kapellmeister to Count Ferdinand Maximilian Morzin. He held this post two years, writing abundantly for orchestra and various chamber-music groups. Feeling financially secure, Haydn married Maria Anna Keller in 1760. It was an unhappy marriage from the beginning. Anna was a shrew, incapable of understanding her husband's genius or being sympathetic to his warm and sensitive nature. They parted after a few years. Anna died nine years before Haydn.

When financial difficulties compelled Count Morzin to disband his orchestra in 1761, Haydn was engaged as second Kapellmeister by Prince Paul Anton Esterházy at Eisenstadt. In 1766 the Esterházys built a new palace to rival Versailles, where Haydn was elevated to the post of first Kapellmeister. He remained in the Esterházy employ for many years, directing all the musical performances at the palaces, and writing for these concerts an abundant library of music in every possible form. He reached full maturity as a composer of symphonies, sonatas, and quartets; and his reputation spread to all parts of Europe. He did not travel much from Esterház; when he did it was usually to visit Vienna where, beginning in 1781, there developed a unique and devoted friendship between himself and the young Mozart.

When Haydn left his post with the Esterházys in 1790 he settled in Vienna. Now one of the most honored musicians in Europe, he was engaged by Johann Peter Salomon to go to London to direct orchestral concerts and write some new symphonies. Haydn paid two such visits to London, in 1791 and 1794; for these visits he wrote twelve symphonies, which are among his greatest (the so-called "London" or "Salomon" symphonies). On both occasions he was the man of the hour, fêted at balls, banquets, and river excursions, and honored, on the first trip, by a degree from Oxford.

After his second London visit, Haydn spent the rest of his life in a suburb of Vienna. In the dusk of a long and rich career he was still destined to produce two masterpieces, both of them oratorios: *The Creation* and *The Seasons*. He was also honored by the Minister of the Interior with a commission to write the Austrian National Anthem, introduced in all of Austria's theaters on the Emperor's birthday on Feb. 12, 1797.

Haydn made his last public appearance on March 2, 1808, at a performance of *The Creation*. About ten weeks later he was dead. All of Vienna's churches held special services.

Haydn was a giant figure in the early Classical era. When he was born, music had only just passed from polyphony to homophony; at the time of his death homophony was in full flower. Through Haydn, the structures of the sonata, symphony, concerto, and quartet were amplified and solidified. Instrumentation was enriched, as the modern symphony orchestra came into existence. The expressive content of musical writing was deepened. New concepts of variation and thematic development had been arrived at.

Up to his last works, Haydn kept growing, continued bringing to his writing new techniques, new harmonic devices, new instrumental colors, new nuances and overtones. When his day ended, a new century was at hand, not only in the calendar but also for music. It was the age of Beethoven, and music's emancipation. Haydn and Mozart, more than any other composers, had helped to usher in that age.

The following are Haydn's principal instrumental compositions.

Chamber Music: 82 string quartets; 35 piano trios; 18 string trios; 125 trios for other instrumental combinations; sonatas, duos, quintets, sextets, divertimentos, nocturnes, cassations.

Orchestra: 104 symphonies; 15 piano concertos; 3 violin concertos; 2 cello concertos; 2 horn concertos; other concertos; marches, notturnos, German dances, divertimentos.

Piano: 52 sonatas; various smaller pieces including the *Andante con variazioni* (Variations in F minor) and Fantasia in C major.

See: Concerto—*Haydn; Creation, The;* Fantasia—*Haydn;* Quartet—*Haydn; Seven Last Words of the Saviour on the Cross, The;* Sonata—*Haydn;* Symphony—*Haydn; Toy Symphony;* Variations in F minor.

Haydn Quartets (Mozart). *See:* Quartet—*Mozart.*

Haydn Variations (Brahms). *See:* Variations on a Theme of Haydn.

Hebrides Overture (Mendelssohn). *See: Fingal's Cave Overture.*

Heckelphone. A modern woodwind instrument of the oboe family invented by Wilhelm Heckel in 1904. It has a baritone register. Its tube has a conical bore and it is played with a double reed. The Heckelphone has been used effectively by Richard Strauss and Delius.

Hecuba. *See:* Euripides.

Heifetz, Jascha, violinist. Born Vilna, Russia, Feb. 2, 1901. He began studying the violin with his father when he was three. At eight he was graduated from the Vilna School of Music. One year later he entered the St. Petersburg Conservatory, where Leopold Auer prepared him for the concert stage. An appearance in St. Petersburg on April 30, 1911, launched his professional career. Fame came a year later with sensational performances in Berlin, Vienna, and Leipzig. After a tour of Scandinavia and the Orient he came to the United States, making his début in New York on Oct. 27, 1917. Acclaim was immediate. Since then Heifetz has lived in the United States and has become an American citizen. He has made many tours of the world; he is everywhere regarded as one of the foremost violinists of the 20th century. He has been responsible for many world premières of notable contemporary concertos, including those by

William Walton, Louis Gruenberg, Robert Russell Bennett, Erich Wolfgang Korngold, and Castelnuovo-Tedesco. He has also made many transcriptions for the violin, the most popular of which is *Hora Staccato* by Gheorghe Dinicu.

Hejre Kati. *See:* Hubay, Jenö.

Hekking, André, cellist. Born Bordeaux, France, July 30, 1866; died Paris, France, Dec. 14, 1925. He studied with Charles de Bériot and at fifteen toured Spain. By the time he settled in Paris in 1909 as a teacher of the cello he had achieved renown throughout Europe as a virtuoso. In 1918 he joined the faculty of the Paris Conservatory, becoming professor a year later. He later also served as professor of cello at the American Conservatory in Fontainebleau.

His brother, Anton (born The Hague, Holland, Sept. 7, 1856; died Berlin, Germany, Nov. 18, 1935), was also a distinguished performer on and teacher of the cello. He was first cellist of the Boston Symphony from 1889 to 1891, and of the New York Symphony from 1895 to 1898. After 1898 he was professor of the cello at the Stern Conservatory in Berlin.

Their cousin, Gérard (born Nancy, France, Aug. 12, 1879; died Paris, France, June 5, 1942), was first cellist of the Concertgebouw Orchestra from 1903 to 1914, and from 1927 until his death professor of the cello at the Paris Conservatory.

Heldenleben, Ein (Richard Strauss). *See: Hero's Life, A.*

Heller, Stephen, pianist and composer. Born Budapest, Hungary, May 15, 1813; died Paris, France, Jan. 14, 1888. He appeared as a boy prodigy, then after study with Anton Halm, toured Austria and Germany from 1828 to 1830. A nervous breakdown necessitated his withdrawal from the concert stage for several years, a period in which he renewed his study. In 1838 he settled in Paris, where he became famous as a teacher of the piano. His concert appearances, while few and far between, were distinguished events. Heller was a prolific composer for the piano, producing over 150 works, including 4 sonatas, 3 sonatinas, tarantellas, laendler, barcarolles, waltzes, mazurkas, etudes, scherzos, preludes, and so forth. Many of these pieces were so popular in Heller's time that the eminent French scholar, François Joseph Fétis, considered Heller a finer poet of the piano than Chopin. Heller's compositions, however, have fallen out of favor in the concert hall and are remembered today only by piano students.

Hellmesberger, Joseph, violinist. Born Vienna, Austria, Nov. 23, 1828; died there, Oct. 24, 1893. The son of Georg Hellmesberger, a distinguished Viennese professor of the violin, Joseph attended the Vienna Conservatory where he studied the violin with his father. From 1851 to 1877 he was professor of the violin at the Conservatory, and from 1877 its director. He held other important musical posts in Vienna, as conductor of the Gesellschaft der Musikfreunde concerts, soloist at the Court Chapel, and as court conductor. He was also the founder and first violinist (until 1877) of the Hellmesberger Quartet, which became one of Europe's leading chamber-music ensembles, responsible for bringing belated recognition to Beethoven's last quartets and for introducing some of Brahms' chamber masterworks.

His son, Joseph Jr. (born Vienna, Austria, April 9, 1855; died there April 26, 1907), played second violin in the Hellmesberger Quartet from 1875 on, and in 1887 took over his father's first-violin chair. He was also professor of the violin at the Vienna Conservatory from 1878 on.

Hellmesberger Quartet. *See* above.

Helmholtz, Hermann von, scientist. Born Potsdam, Germany, Aug. 31, 1821; died Berlin, Germany, Sept. 8, 1894. Professor of physics at the University of Berlin from 1871 on, Helmholtz published a valuable study on acoustics important to musicians: *On the Sensations of Tone as a Physiological Basis for the Theory of Music* (1863). Amplifying theories previously set forth by Rameau, Tartini, and others, Helmholtz made a study of musical tones and realized formulas for all kinds of consonant and dissonant tone effects besides establishing laws governing tone colors.

Hemidemisemiquaver. A sixty-fourth note.

Hen, The (La Poule). (1) *See:* Symphony—*Haydn.*

(2) A descriptive piece for the harpsichord (in G minor) by Rameau, a movement from *Nouvelle suite de pièces de clavecin.* It was freely arranged and orchestrated by Ottorino Respighi in *The Birds.*

Henderson, William James, music critic. Born Newark, N.J., Dec. 4, 1855; died New York City, June 5, 1937. He studied music with private teachers. After being graduated from Princeton in 1876 he became the music critic of the *New York Times,* holding that post until 1902, when he was appointed to the *New York Sun,* where he remained for the rest of his life. Besides his activities as a music critic, he lectured on music history. His most important books are *The Story of Music* (1889), *How Music Developed* (1898), *Preludes and Studies* (1891), *What Is Good Music?* (1898), and *Modern Musical Drift* (1904). He died by suicide.

Hendl, Walter, pianist and conductor. Born West New York, N.J., Jan. 12, 1917. After studying the piano with Clarence Adler, he attended the Curtis Institute on a scholarship; there he was a student of David Saperton in piano and Fritz Reiner in conducting. In 1941 and 1942 he studied conducting with Koussevitzky at the Berkshire Music Centre. After World War II he appeared as piano soloist with various orchestras and was guest conductor of the Pittsburgh Symphony and the Boston Pops Orchestra. From 1945 to 1948 he was associate conductor of the New York Philharmonic. From 1949 to 1958 he was principal conductor of the Dallas Symphony, after which he became associate conductor of the Chicago Symphony. In 1953 he was also appointed music director of the Chautauqua Symphony. He also appeared as guest conductor in South America, Europe, the Philippines, and with the Symphony of the Air in the Orient. In 1953 he received the Alice M. Ditson Award for "distinguished services to American music."

Henriot, Nicole, pianist. Born Paris, France, Nov. 23, 1925. She entered the

Paris Conservatory at twelve, at fourteen won first prize in piano, and at fifteen made her concert début with the Pasdeloup Orchestra. She then made many appearances in France and Belgium. During World War II she was a member of the Resistance, for which she was later decorated with the Badge of the Commandos, an honor earned by few civilians. She returned to the concert stage after the war and on Jan. 29, 1948, made her American début as soloist with the New York Philharmonic.

Henry IV, Henry V, and Henry VIII. *See:* Shakespeare, William.

Henschel, Sir George, conductor. Born Breslau, Germany, Feb. 18, 1850; died Aviemore, Scotland, Sept. 10, 1934. In 1867 he entered the Leipzig Conservatory, where his teachers included Ignaz Moscheles and Carl Reinecke. He subsequently attended the Berlin Royal Conservatory. He began his professional career as a singer, achieving prominence both on the concert stage and in opera. In 1881 he was appointed conductor of the then newly organized Boston Symphony, holding that post three years. In 1886 he founded the London Symphony, serving as its conductor for a decade; from 1893 to 1895 he was the conductor of the Scottish Orchestra. He also distinguished himself as a teacher, first at the Royal College of Music in London, then at the Institute of Musical Art in New York, and after 1914 privately. In his 80th year he helped the Boston Symphony celebrate its 50th season by performing in Boston the identical program (with one exception) he had conducted fifty years earlier at the orchestra's first concert. He was knighted in 1914. Henschel was the author of *Personal Recollections of Johannes Brahms* (1907) and *Musings and Memories of a Musician* (1918).

Herbeck, Johann Franz von, conductor. Born Vienna, Austria, Dec. 25, 1831; died there, Oct. 28, 1877. He was virtually self-taught in music. In 1859 he became professor at the Vienna Conservatory. From 1875 on he was the conductor of the Gesellschaft der Musikfreunde concerts, from 1866 to 1871 court conductor, and from 1871 to 1875 principal conductor of the Court Opera. He was an influential figure in Viennese musical life for half a century.

Herbert, Victor, composer and conductor. Born Dublin, Ireland, Feb. 1, 1859; died New York City, May 26, 1924. He received his musical education at the Stuttgart Conservatory in Germany. After studying the cello privately with Bernhard Cossmann, he played in symphony orchestras and appeared as soloist throughout Europe. In 1886 he married the prima donna, Theresa Foerster. When she joined the Metropolitan Opera company in New York, Herbert became a member of the cello section of its orchestra. In 1893 he succeeded Patrick S. Gilmore as bandmaster of the 22nd Regiment Band. From 1898 to 1904 he was principal conductor of the Pittsburgh Symphony. After 1904 he made occasional appearances as guest conductor of the New York Philharmonic, and was director of his own salon orchestra. Herbert is famous for his many delightful operettas successfully produced on Broadway. But he was also a serious composer. Besides two operas, he wrote 2 cello concertos and numerous orchestral works, including *Hero and Leander, Irish Rhapsody, Suite romantique, Woodland Fancies, Pan Americana, Columbus,* and *Suite of Serenades.*

Hero's Life, A (Ein Heldenleben). Tone poem by Richard Strauss, op. 40 (1899), first performed at Frankfort-on-the-Main, on March 3, 1899, the composer conducting. This work is a tonal autobiography. Strauss' protagonist is a hero like himself, surrounded by antagonism and cabals, which he overcomes successfully. Strauss even quotes several of his works in a section intended to point up the hero's accomplishments. The tone poem, while played without interruption, has six sections. The first introduces the hero, his theme heard at once—a bold, sweeping melody for strings and horn. As this theme is altered, we get a glimpse of the hero's varied personality. The hero's adversaries appear in the second part; the petty enemies are portrayed by a sardonic passage for the woodwind. The hero replies with a gentle subject for muted cellos and brasses. A brass fanfare suggests the imminence of battle, in which a gentle respite is provided through a vision of the hero's beloved in a tender melody for violins. The third section is the love music of the hero and his beloved, the woman represented by a solo violin. A trumpet flourish introduces the fourth section, a battle between the hero and his enemies in which he proves victorious. In the fifth part, the hero sums up his achievements. The "works of peace" motif is given by the trumpet, after which Strauss steps into the shoes of his hero by quoting from his own works: fragments from *Macbeth, Don Juan, Death and Transfiguration, Don Quixote,* the song *Traum durch die Daemmerung,* and part of his opera *Guntram.* In the last part the hero takes leave of the world, as a beautiful subject rises from the strings. The solo violin brings back the image of his beloved, then tells of the flight of the hero's soul to the beyond. The hero subject is now heard for the last time. After a powerful climax, the hero is laid to rest with solemn music.

Heroic Polonaise (Chopin). *See:* Polonaise.

Hertz, Alfred, conductor. Born Frankfort-on-the-Main, Germany, July 15, 1872; died San Francisco, Calif., April 17, 1942. After completing his music study at the Raff Conservatory he held several posts as opera conductor in Germany. From 1902 to 1915 he was conductor of the German repertory at the Metropolitan Opera. After that he concentrated on orchestral music, serving as principal conductor of the San Francisco Symphony from 1915 to 1930. In 1922 he helped organize summer concerts at the Hollywood Bowl in California, where he conducted over a hundred concerts.

Heseltine, Philip (Peter Warlock), composer and writer on music. Born London, England, Oct. 30, 1894; died there, Dec. 17, 1930. His critical writings appeared under his own name; but for his musical compositions he assumed the pseudonym of Peter Warlock. He took courses in music at Eton and subsequently profited from the advice and guidance of Delius and Bernard van Dieren. In 1920 he helped found the music journal *Sackbut,* which he edited for a year. He interested himself in old music and allowed it to influence his own composition. His best-known work is the *Capriol Suite,* an orchestral adaptation of 16th-century dances. Though his best compositions were vocal, he wrote a Serenade for String Orchestra (for Delius' 60th birthday) and *An Old Song* for woodwind and strings. He was the author of a biography of Delius (1923), many of whose orchestral works he transcribed for piano. He committed suicide after a siege of melancholia.

See: Capriol Suite.

Hess, Dame Myra, pianist. Born London, England, Feb. 25, 1890. She attended the Royal Academy of Music on a scholarship, from 1902 to 1907, a pupil of Tobias Matthay. She then made a sensational début in London on Nov. 15, 1907, as soloist with Thomas Beecham's orchestra. After extended tours of Europe, she made her American début in New York on Jan. 17, 1922. In 1936 she was made Commander of the Order of the British Empire in recognition of her position as one of the leading women pianists of the world. With the outbreak of World War II, she organized concerts at the National Gallery in London to help maintain civilian morale. By the time the war ended she had arranged 1,698 such concerts in which over a thousand artists had participated. For such services she was made Dame Commander of the Order of the British Cross by George VI in 1941. On Oct. 12, 1946, she returned to the American stage after an absence of almost eight years.

Hess, Willy, violinist. Born Mannheim, Germany, July 14, 1859; died Berlin, Germany, Feb. 17, 1939. His father was his first important teacher. In 1865 Hess came to the United States, where his career as violin virtuoso began with appearances with the Theodore Thomas Orchestra. He returned to Germany in 1872 to tour Europe, then to study for two years with Joseph Joachim. From 1888 to 1895 he was concertmaster of the Hallé Orchestra; from 1895 to 1903 of the Gurzenich concerts in Cologne; and from 1904 to 1910 of the Boston Symphony. He also distinguished himself as a teacher of the violin at the Conservatories of Rotterdam and Cologne, at the Royal Academy of Music, and the Berlin High School for Music. He was the head of several distinguished chamber music ensembles including the Gurzenich, Hess, and Halir String Quartets.

Heward, Leslie, conductor. Born Littletown, England, Dec. 8, 1897; died Birmingham, England, May 3, 1943. In 1917 he entered the Royal College of Music in London on a scholarship. While there he served as music master at Eton and organist at a garrison church in Windsor. In 1921 he made his début as a conductor in London. From 1924 to 1927 he was music director of the South African Broadcasting Corporation and conductor of the Capetown Orchestra. In 1930 he succeeded Adrian Boult as principal conductor of the City of Birmingham Orchestra.

Hexachord. Six consecutive notes in a diatonic scale.

Hiawatha. *See:* Longfellow, Henry Wadsworth.

Higginson, Henry Lee, banker and music patron. Born New York City, Nov. 18, 1834; died Boston, Mass., Nov. 15, 1919. He was the founder of the Boston Symphony. He attended Harvard, then studied music in Vienna from 1856 to 1860. He later became a member of the banking house of Lee, Higginson and Company. In 1881 he provided an endowment to organize and support the Boston Symphony. He directed its policies for the next thirty-five years, after which he relinquished his control to a board of directors.

Hill, Edward Burlingame, composer and teacher. Born Cambridge, Mass., Sept. 9, 1872. The grandson of a former president of Harvard University, and the son of one of its chemistry professors, Hill attended Harvard, where he took music courses with J. K. Paine, and from which he was graduated *summa cum laude*. After an additional period of studying music with George Chadwick at the New England Conservatory and with Charles Marie Widor in Paris he joined the music faculty of Harvard in 1908. From 1928 to 1934 he was head of the music

department, then continued as professor until his retirement in 1940. Hill wrote many works for orchestra and chamber-music groups, traditional in harmony and lyricism. He first attracted attention in 1917 and 1922 with two programmatic orchestral suites based on Robert Louis Stevenson's *A Child's Garden of Verses* and entitled *Stevensoniana*. Other orchestral works include 3 symphonies, piano concerto, violin concerto, concertino for string orchestra, Sinfonietta for string orchestra, Suite for string orchestra, Music for English Horn and Orchestra, *Diversion* for small orchestra, and concerto for two flutes and orchestra. His chamber music includes a sextet for winds and piano, piano quartet, clarinet quintet, flute sonata, clarinet sonata, and sonata for two clarinets and piano.

Hiller, Ferdinand, pianist, conductor, and composer. Born Frankfort-on-the-Main, Germany, Oct. 24, 1811; died Cologne, Germany, May 10, 1885. He studied music with Aloys Schmitt and Johann Nepomuk Hummel. In 1827 he went with Hummel to Vienna, where he published a string quartet and visited Beethoven at his death bed. From 1828 to 1835 he lived in Paris. There he performed the French première of Beethoven's *Emperor Concerto,* and for several years taught piano at Choron's Institute of Music. Between 1837 and 1841 he made several trips to Italy, and in Germany conducted several concerts of the Gewandhaus Orchestra. In 1847 he was appointed municipal conductor for the city of Duesseldorf, and in 1850, for Cologne. In the latter city he helped found the Cologne Conservatory, which he directed for the rest of his life. He was a prolific composer who was influenced by Mendelssohn. His compositions include 3 symphonies, 3 overtures, 3 piano concertos, a violin concerto, 5 string quartets, 5 piano quartets, 5 piano trios, 3 piano sonatas, and various smaller piano pieces. He also wrote several texts on harmony and counterpoint, a biography of Beethoven (1871), *Aus dem Tonleben unsere Zeit* (1871), and *Kuenstlerleben* (1880).

Hills of Anacapri, The. *See:* Prelude—*Debussy.*

Hilsberg, Alexander (born **Alexander**

Hillersberg), violinist and conductor. Born Warsaw, Poland, April 24, 1900. He was taught the violin by Leopold Auer at the St. Petersburg Conservatory. In 1917 he went to Tomsk, West Siberia, where he taught violin at the Conservatory. For four additional years he lived in Harbin, Manchuria, teaching violin there and playing in a string quartet. In 1923 he settled in the United States, later becoming a citizen. He joined the Philadelphia Orchestra in 1926, and was associated with it for twenty years, first as violinist, then as concertmaster, and from 1945 on as associate conductor. During this period he taught the violin at the Curtis Institute and, in 1947, became conductor of the Curtis Institute Symphony and head of the orchestra department. His official début as conductor had taken place in the summer of 1935 at the Lewisohn Stadium in New York, but his first major success came in 1950 when he conducted the Philadelphia Orchestra in New York. He has also appeared as guest conductor of other major American orchestras, and since 1952 has been the principal conductor of the New Orleans Symphony.

Hindemith, Paul, composer. Born Hanau, Germany, Nov. 16, 1895. As a boy, he attended Hoch's Conservatory in Frankfort-on-the-Main, while earning his living playing the violin in café and theater orchestras. After completing his studies he became a violinist with the Frankfort Opera orchestra, and in 1915 was appointed its concertmaster. During the eight years he served in the latter post, he also helped found the Amar String Quartet (with Licco Amar and Walter Caspar violins, Paul Hindemith viola, and Maurice Frank, cello). This Quartet became famous throughout Europe for its performances of new chamber music and its participation in festivals of modern music. It was for this group that Hindemith wrote some of his early chamber-music works, including the Second String Quartet in F minor, introduced at the Donaueschingen Festival in 1921. Other compositions soon enhanced his reputation in Germany. Among them were the *Kammermusik,* Nos. 1 and 2, first performed at the Donaueschingen and Ven-

ice festivals in 1922 and 1925 respectively; a clarinet quintet and string trio introduced at Salzburg in 1923 and 1925; and a provocative opera, *Cardillac,* whose première took place at Dresden in 1926. During this same period Hindemith also wrote functional pieces intended for mass consumption and designed for such media as the radio, pianola, theater, motion pictures, and schools; a special term was coined in Germany for these practical Hindemith works, "Gebrauchsmusik," "functional music."

By 1933 Hindemith was generally recognized in Germany as one of its major creative figures and most influential musicians. He had completed over 50 works which were among the most vital being produced in Germany. He was also professor of composition at the Berlin High School of Music and a member of the renowned German Academy. Nevertheless, when the Nazi regime came to power, it frowned upon him. For one thing, he was married to a Jewess; for another, he had played chamber music and had made recordings with Jewish artists. Most serious of all, his music was regarded as "degenerate." The Nazi powers were particularly disturbed by his opera, *Mathis der Maler,* whose text concerned the defeat of German liberalism during the Peasants War. When Wilhelm Furtwaengler insisted on giving the première of this opera, in spite of official opposition, he was temporarily deprived of all his conducting posts; and Hindemith was compelled to leave the country.

After a year and a half in Turkey, where he helped reorganize its musical life, Hindemith came to the United States, making his American début in Washington, D.C., on April 10, 1937, in a performance of his own unaccompanied viola sonata. He now made his permanent home in America and applied for citizenship. In America, Hindemith was active not only as a composer, but also as a teacher. He has been a member of the music faculty at Yale, and has conducted master classes in composition at the Berkshire Music Centre in Tanglewood and at Harvard.

In 1949 Hindemith paid his first visit

to Germany in about fifteen years; he was given a hero's welcome, and had a street named after him. In 1953 he went to live in Switzerland, assuming a teaching position at the University of Zurich, and making appearances in different parts of Europe as conductor in his own music.

Hindemith has produced an abundant library of music in all forms. His writing employs polyphony so consistently that he is sometimes called a 20th-century Bach. His music is frequently dissonant and atonal. The relationships between contrapuntal voices are guided by a system of degrees of tension and relaxation which is explained in Hindemith's theoretical writings. In his later works there has been a growing tendency towards simplicity, clarity, and directness of expression. Nevertheless, his music is always subtle and complex, not easily assimilable at first hearing. His remarkable craftsmanship and the inexorable logic of thought, however, command immediate respect.

In 1954 Hindemith received the Sibelius Award of $35,000. He is the author of *The Craft of Musical Composition* (1941) and several other textbooks, *J. S. Bach: Heritage and Obligation* (1952), and *A Composer's World* (1952).

The following are his principal instrumental compositions.

Chamber Music: Kammermusik, Nos. 1-7; 7 string quartets; 2 string trios; clarinet quintet; various sonatas for solo instruments and piano; various solo sonatas.

Orchestra: Konzertmusik, for brass and strings; various concertos (piano; cello; flute, oboe, clarinet, bassoon, harp; horn; clarinet; trumpet and bassoon; orchestra); *Mathis der Maler,* symphony; *Der Schwanendreher,* for viola and orchestra; *Trauermusik,* for viola and string orchestra; *Philharmonic Concerto; Symphonic Dances;* Symphony in E-flat major; *Theme With Variations According to the Four Temperaments,* for piano and orchestra; *Symphonic Metamorphosis on Themes by Carl Maria von Weber; Symphonia Serena; Sinfonietta in E; Nobilissima Visione; Die Harmonie der Welt,* suite from the opera.

Piano—Ludus Tonalis; sonatas, etudes, dance pieces.

See: Concerto—*Hindemith; Kammermusik; Konzertmusik; Ludus Tonalis; Nobilissima Visione;* Quartet—*Hindemith; Symphonic Metamorphosis on Themes by Carl Maria von Weber;* Symphony—*Hindemith; Theme with Variations According to the Four Temperaments.*

Hippolytus. *See:* Euripides.

Histoire du soldat, L' (A Soldier's Tale). Ballet suite for orchestra by Igor Stravinsky (1918), adapted from his score to a ballet meant "to be read, played and danced." The ballet was introduced in Lausanne, Switzerland, on Sept. 28, 1918. The text, by C. F. Ramuz, is built around a soldier returning from the wars who meets a devil disguised as a benign old man. The soldier trades his violin for a book able to answer all his questions. This book arouses in the soldier an insatiable Wanderlust. After extensive travels and many adventures, the soldier returns home, where he is seized by the devil. The orchestral suite is in nine parts: I. Soldier's March; II. Soldier's Violin; III. Pastorale; IV. Royal March; V. Little Concerto; VI. Three Dances; VII. Devil's Dance; VIII. Grand Chorale; IX. Triumphal March of the Devil. The suite opens with a grotesque march tune which is contrasted with a lyrical passage for solo wind instruments against sustained notes in the strings. After two brief contrasting sections there comes a rowdy burlesque on a military band; trombone and trumpet provide embellishments against a steady rhythm. The fifth part boasts a predominantly Russian melody, while the three dances of the sixth section are a tango for violin, clarinet, and percussion, a satirical waltz, and a ragtime tune. Rhythmic motor energy characterizes the devil's dance of the seventh part, and is followed by a sedate section in polyphonic style. The finale is a virtuoso exercise in polymeters in which percussion is emphasized.

Hofmann, Josef, pianist. Born Podgorze, Poland, Jan. 20, 1876; died Los Angeles, Calif., Feb. 16, 1957. He studied piano with his father, then made sensational appearances as a child prodigy throughout Europe. His American début, in New York on Nov. 29, 1887, was hailed as an outstanding exhibition of piano virtuosity. An extended American tour followed, interrupted after 42 concerts by the Society for Prevention of Cruelty to Children. Young Hofmann now returned to Europe, withdrew from the professional stage and for the next six years devoted himself to intensive study with Moritz Moszkowski and Anton Rubinstein. He returned to the concert platform in 1894 with performances in Germany. In 1896 he toured Russia and Scandinavia, now the sovereign artist in full maturity and with a phenomenal command of technique. In 1898 he also paid a return visit to the United States, which now became his permanent home (he became a citizen in 1926). While touring the concert world as one of the preeminent pianists of the 20th century, Hofmann also filled the post of head of the piano department of the Curtis Institute from 1924 to 1926 and director of the Curtis Institute from 1926 to 1938. His golden jubilee as pianist was celebrated in New York with a gala concert on Nov. 28, 1937; his last appearance on any concert stage took place in New York on Jan. 16, 1946. He then went into retirement in California. Hofmann wrote several works for orchestra, and for the piano, some of them under the pseudonym of Michel Dvorsky.

Holberg Suite. Suite for piano by Edvard Grieg, op. 40 (1884), later adapted by the composer for string orchestra (1886). Here Grieg paid tribute to the famous Danish writer, Ludvig Holberg, on the occasion of the bicentenary of his birth. Since Holberg lived in the 17th century, Grieg wrote a classical suite, but without deserting his own romantic tendencies. It opens with a Prelude, in which a forceful theme is set against a nervous rhythm. Three classical dances follow: Sarabande, Gavotte, and Musette. After an Air in the lyrical style of a Norwegian folksong, the suite ends with another classical dance, a Rigaudon.

Holland Music Festival. A festival inaugurated in Amsterdam, The Hague, and Scheveningen, Holland, in June 1949 with performances of symphonic, chamber, and solo music, together with operas and choral masterworks. Since that time, the annual one-month summer festival in Holland has been one of Europe's most distinguished music events. The main orchestras of Holland participate. But the festival has also played host to leading foreign orchestras. Distinguished Dutch chamber-music groups and virtuosos have been supplemented by visiting organizations and artists. The Holland Festival has featured cycles of concerts commemorating the 70th and 75th birthdays of Igor Stravinsky, the 60th birthday of Arthur Honegger, and the 40th anniversary of Gustav Mahler's death.

Hollywood Bowl Concerts. Summer concerts held annually in July and August in the Hollywood Bowl, an open-air stadium in Hollywood, Calif. These concerts have been described as "Symphonies Under the Stars." They were instituted under the patronage of W. A. Clarke in 1922 with a five-week season conducted by Alfred Hertz. In 1925 a policy of guest conductors was instituted which brought to the orchestra (members of the Los Angeles Philharmonic) the world's most distinguished conductors and soloists.

Hollywood String Quartet. A quartet founded in 1947 in Hollywood, Calif., with Felix Slatkin and Paul Shure, violins, Alvin Dinkin, viola, and Eleanor Aller, cello. For several years this Quartet confined itself primarily to recordings. In 1957 it performed the last five quartets of Beethoven at the Edinburgh Festival, and on March 6, 1958, it made its New York début.

Holst, Gustav (born Gustavus Theodore von Holst), composer. Born Cheltenham, England, Sept. 21, 1874; died London, England, May 25, 1934. After attending the Royal College of Music in London, where he was a pupil of Charles Villiers Stanford, Holst played the trombone in various orchestras. In 1903 he began a career as a teacher which, through the ensuing years, brought him to the St. Paul's Girls' School as music master, to Morley College as music director, and to the Royal College of Music in London as professor of composition. In 1923 he visited the United States, where he delivered several lectures at the University of Michigan at Ann Arbor. After returning to England, his health deteriorated appreciably, compelling him to give up all activities save composition. However he was able to pay a return visit to the United States in 1932 to appear as guest conductor of the Boston Symphony in a program of his own works and to lecture at Harvard. Holst passed through several phases as a composer. The first was the "Sanskrit period," in which his music was influenced by the poetry and mysticism of Eastern philosophy, and in which he imitated the exotic scales and irregular rhythms of Eastern music. During this period he wrote several works for the stage, together with a tone poem, *Indra*, and an oriental suite for orchestra, *Beni Mora*. This phase ended in or about 1913, when Holst began writing Western music strongly stamped with his own individuality. It was at this time that he completed two works by which he is most often represented on symphony programs today, the *St. Paul's Suite* and *The Planets*. Soon after the end of World War I, Holst's writing acquired greater austerity, his style grew terser and more economical, and his emotion more restrained. At this time he also began experimenting with freer tonality and nonharmonic counterpoint. Besides compositions already mentioned, Holst's works for orchestra include the *Cotswolds* for orchestra, *The Mystic Trumpeter* for soprano and orchestra, *Song of the Night* for violin and orchestra, *Somerset Rhapsody*, *Japanese Suite*, *Fugal Overture*, *Egdon Heath*, *Brook Green*, *Scherzo*, *Lyric Movement* for viola and orchestra, and a concerto for two violins and orchestra. He also wrote some pieces for piano and a Terzetto for flute, oboe, and viola.

See: Planets, The; St. Paul's Suite.

Homages (Homenajes). Suite for orchestra by Manuel de Falla (1920-1933), introduced in Buenos Aires in 1939. In 1929 Falla was invited to write a piece of music as a tribute to Debussy for the Debussy Issue of *La Revue musicale* in Paris. He wrote *Homage*, an elegy for guitar (subsequently transcribed by the composer for piano). In the ensuing decade, Falla wrote three additional homages, orchestrated all four, and assembled them into a suite. The four movements are: I. Fanfare in the Name of E. F. Arbós; II. To Claude Debussy; III. To Paul Dukas; IV. Pedrilliana. The first movement opens with a muffled drum roll. The melody that follows has a basic motif made up of three notes, the initials of Arbós' name ("E," "F," and "A"). The second movement imitates a strumming guitar through pizzicato strings and harmonics. A quotation from Debussy's *Soirée dans Grenade* is interpolated. The third movement bears the inscription "Hope of Life." The wholetone scale is here used effectively, while the main theme has the character of a plainchant. In the finale, Falla quotes from Felipe Pedrell's opera, *La Celestina*. The music of this movement is colorful with lively shifting rhythms, cross accents, and vivid orchestration.

Homer, Greek epic poet who lived about the 9th century B.C., but whose specific dates of birth and death are unknown. His epics, *The Iliad* and *The Odyssey*, were the sources for the following instrumental compositions: Guido Guerrini's tone poem *L'Ultimo viaggio di Odisseo;* Henry Hadley's overture, *Hector and Andromache;* Frederick Jacobi's *Impressions from the Odyssey*, for violin and piano; Roger-Ducasse's *Ulysse et les sirènes*, a tone poem with women's voices; and Karol Szymanowski's *Metopes*, for piano.

Homophony. A musical style in which a single melody and its harmony is emphasized, as opposed to polyphony where two or more melodies appear simultaneously.

Honegger, Arthur, composer. Born Le Havre, France, March 10, 1892; died Paris, France, Nov. 27, 1955. He studied music at the Zurich Conservatory and with Vincent d'Indy, André Gedalge, and Charles Marie Widor at the Paris Conservatory. His début as a composer took place at Paris in 1916 with some songs. This was followed two years later by an all-Honegger concert, also in Paris. But Honegger did not become known to the general musical public until late that year, when his name was linked with those of five other young French composers into an avant-garde school labeled as "Les Six" or "The French Six" (*see: Six, Les*). Though Honegger never completely subscribed to the artistic aims attributed to the "Six," his identification with this group made him a provocative figure whose music received wide circulation. The oratorio (or "dramatic psalm") based on a drama by René Morax, *King David* (*Le Roi David*), was successfully introduced in a dramatic version at Mézières, Switzerland, on June 11, 1921. Two years later Honegger reorchestrated it and adapted it for concert performance, and in this version it received successful performances in Switzerland, Paris, Rome, and New York. This work is in a neo-Handelian style (though with occasional excursions into atonal writing). Other and later works are more modern in idiom. Among these are the provocative and cacophonous *Pacific 231* for orchestra, the First Symphony, and a cello concerto, which are filled with linear counterpoint, free and forceful rhythms, and dissonant harmonies.

During World War II Honegger lived in seclusion in Paris while secretly serving as a link in the Resistance movement. He found escape from war's realities in his creative work. He now tapped in his writing new veins of humanity, compassion, pathos, mysticism, and religious feeling. This new manner first became evident in his Symphony for Strings in 1941. This work, and the symphonies that followed it, belong with Honegger's most important compositions, and are the works by which he is most often represented on concert programs.

Honegger first visited the United States in 1929, appearing as guest conductor of several major orchestras in his own works. He returned for another visit in 1949 to conduct a master class in composition at the Berkshire Music Centre at Tanglewood, but owing to poor health was incapable of fulfilling his obligations.

These are Honegger's principal instrumental works.

Chamber Music: 3 string quartets; piano quartet; sonatas for various solo instruments and piano; sonatinas for various solo instruments and piano.

Orchestra: 5 symphonies; *Pastorale d'été; Horace victorieux; Pacific 231, Rugby;* piano concertino; cello concerto; *Mouvement symphonique No. 3; Concerto da camera,* for flute, English horn, and strings; *Prelude, Arioso and Fughetta on the Name of Bach,* for strings; *Nocturne; L'Appel de la montagne; Sérénade à Angelique; Prelude, Fugue and Postlude; Suite archaïque; Monopartita.*

Piano: Prélude et danse; Sept pièces brèves; Le Cahier romand; Hommage à Albert Roussel.

See: Concertino—*Honegger; Pacific 231; Pastorale d'été;* Symphony—*Honegger.*

Hoogstraten, Willem van, conductor. Born Utrecht, Holland, March 18, 1884. He studied the violin in the Conservatories of Cologne and Prague, and received his conducting apprenticeship in Hamburg, Krefeld, and The Hague. After achieving his first successes in Vienna and Salzburg he came to the United States in 1921. From 1922 to 1938 he appeared each summer at the Lewisohn Stadium in New York, besides making guest appearances during the winter season with other major American orchestras. From 1923 to 1925 he was associate conductor of the New York Philharmonic, and from 1925 to 1937 he was principal conductor of the Portland Symphony in Oregon. He was conductor of the Mozarteum concerts in Salzburg from 1939 to 1945, and after World War II he conducted the Stuttgart Philharmonic. For many years, he was married to the concert pianist, Elly Ney.

Hopak (or **Gopak**). A spirited Russian dance with two beats to the measure. A celebrated orchestral example is found in Act 3 of Mussorgsky's opera, *The Fair at Sorochinsk.*

Horenstein, Jascha, conductor. Born Kiev, Russia, May 6, 1898. He left Russia at the age of six, and from 1911 to 1919 lived in Vienna, where he studied violin with Adolf Busch and composition with Franz Schreker. His début as a conductor took place at Vienna in 1923. In 1928 he was appointed director of the Duesseldorf Opera. After the Nazis came to power, he made his home in Paris. He was now heard in guest performances with major orchestras in France, Warsaw, the Soviet Union, Palestine, Australia, and New

Zealand. After World War II, he performed extensively in the United States and South America as well as Europe. When the National Symphony of Mexico made its first tour of the United States in the fall of 1958, Jascha Horenstein appeared as one of its conductors.

Horn. *See:* French horn.

Hornpipe. A dance in common time of English origin, sometimes used by English composers of the 17th century as a movement of the suite. Handel utilized it in his *Water Music,* and as the concluding movement of his Concerto Grosso No. 7 in B-flat major. Purcell used the hornpipe as a movement of his Suite No. 7 in D minor, for harpsichord.

Horn-Signal Symphony. *See:* Symphony —*Haydn.*

Horowitz, Vladimir, pianist. Born Kiev, Russia, Oct. 1, 1904. He attended the Kiev Conservatory as a pupil of Felix Blumenfeld, and was graduated with highest honors when he was seventeen. In 1922 he made his concert début in Kharkov, a performance that proved so successful that he was asked to give twelve more concerts in that city. He then toured Russia, and in 1925 performed throughout Europe. His formidable technique electrified audiences everywhere. Horowitz made his American début as soloist with the New York Philharmonic on Jan. 12, 1928. His performances throughout the world after that gave him a commanding position among contemporary piano virtuosos. After 1950 he was forced by a nervous ailment to reduce the number of his concert appearances appreciably. Horowitz married Toscanini's daughter, Wanda, in 1933.

Horszowski, Miecyzslaw, pianist. Born Lemberg, Poland, June 23, 1892. He studied the piano at the Lemberg Conservatory and with Theodor Leschetizky in Vienna. In 1901 he gave an impressive début performance in Vienna, following this with a tour of Europe and the United States. After an additional period of study he returned to the concert stage as a mature artist in 1913. Since then he has been heard extensively in recitals, as guest with orchestras and chamber music ensembles, and in joint recitals with Casals, Ravel, and Szymanowski. Since 1940

his permanent home has been in the United States.

Hovhaness, Alan, composer. Born Somerville, Mass., March 8, 1911. He attended the New England Conservatory, where he studied composition with Converse, and in 1942 the Berkshire Music Centre at Tanglewood. He subsequently became organist of the St. James Church in Watertown, Mass., and teacher of composition at Boston University. Of Armenian descent, Hovhaness has from the beginning been influenced by his studies in Armenian folk music. His musical style has absorbed near-Eastern influences in its orchestral coloration, partiality for florid melodies, tranquil moods, exotic personality, and excursions into religious and spiritual thought. In 1940 he destroyed virtually everything he had written up to that time, almost a thousand works; but being a prolific composer, he has since produced a formidable library of music. He first achieved recognition with a concert devoted entirely to his works in New York on Feb. 7, 1947. His orchestral music includes 3 symphonies, 7 concertos for orchestra, 2 Armenian rhapsodies, 5 piano concertos, violin concerto, trumpet concerto, and many shorter works (*Psalm and Fugue, By the Fountain* for flute and strings, *Haroutiun, Sosi, Vosdan, Ad Lyram, Mysterious Mountain, Khaldis, Tower Music, Alleluia and Fugue, The Flowering Peach*). His chamber-music works include *Adana, Invocation to Vahakn, Upon Enchanted Ground, October Mountain,* quartet for flute, oboe, cello, and piano, viola suite, and harp sonata. He also wrote many pieces for the piano, including *12 Armenian Folksongs.*

Hubay, Jenö, violinist and composer. Born Budapest, Hungary, Sept. 15, 1858; died Vienna, Austria, March 12, 1937. After studying with his father, he received a government subsidy in his thirteenth year to study with Joseph Joachim in Berlin. Returning to Hungary in 1876, he gave many concerts throughout that country. In 1878 he scored a major success in Paris as soloist with the Pasdeloup Orchestra. After further study with Henri Vieuxtemps, he succeeded him as head of the violin department at the Brussels Conservatory, where he remained until

1886. After 1886 he assumed a similar post with the Budapest Conservatory, and from 1919 to 1934 served as its director. During his long and distinguished teaching career he did not abandon the concert stage. He was also the head of several distinguished string quartets bearing his name, the first in Brussels, another in Budapest. In 1907 he was knighted by the Hungarian government. Hubay wrote numerous works for the violin, including several concertos, a sonata, and smaller pieces. Some of the last were derived from Hungarian folksongs and dances and have become popular in the violin repertory. The most important of these shorter works are five sets of pieces collectively entitled *Hungarian Czardas Scenes* (opp. 13, 18, 32, 33, and 83) for violin and piano. Here will be found the popular *Hejre Kati,* op. 32, no. 4; Hungarian Rhapsody, op. 18, no. 3; and *Waves of Balaton,* op. 33, no. 5.

Huberman, Bronislaw, violinist. Born Czenstochowa, Poland, Dec. 19, 1882; died Nant-sur-Corsier, Switzerland, June 15, 1947. After making appearances as a child prodigy, Huberman studied the violin with Isidor Lotto in Warsaw and Joseph Joachim in Berlin. On Jan. 12, 1895, he scored such a sensation at Adelina Patti's farewell concert, in Vienna, that he was required to give twelve concerts. In 1895 he was praised by Brahms for his performance of that master's Violin Concerto. In 1896-1897 he made his first tour of the United States; and in 1909 he was invited by the city of Genoa to play on Paganini's violin at the Town Hall there. From 1934 to 1936 he taught at the Vienna State Academy. In 1936 he was a major influence in the founding of the Palestine Symphony, made up mostly of Jewish refugees from Europe. His last public appearance took place in New York in December 1945. He was the author of *Aus der Werkstatt des Virtuosen* (1912).

Huettenbrenner, Anselm, composer. Born Graz, Austria, Oct. 13, 1794; died Ober-Andritz, Austria, June 5, 1868. A trained musician, Huettenbrenner was a prolific composer of symphonies, overtures, quartets, sonatas, and so forth. All of these are forgotten. But Huettenbrenner's name has survived because of his friendship with Schubert. His book, *Fragments from the Life of the Lied Composer, Franz Schubert* (1906), was an important source of information for all subsequent Schubert biographers. From 1823 to 1865 Huettenbrenner owned the manuscript of Schubert's *Unfinished Symphony* without releasing it to the world. It is sometimes suspected that Schubert wrote a complete symphony and that one reason why Huettenbrenner withheld this work from performance was that he had lost the manuscript of the last two movements.

Hugo, Victor, dramatist, novelist, and poet. Born Besançon, France, Feb. 26, 1802; died Paris, France, May 22, 1885. A leading figure in the French Romantic movement, Hugo wrote many works that have inspired instrumental compositions. These compositions include: César Franck's tone poem, *Ce qu'on entend sur la montagne,* and *Les Djinns* for piano and orchestra; Benjamin Godard's *Symphonie orientale* (partly after Hugo); Ernest Guiraud's *Chasse fantastique* for orchestra; Liszt's tone poems *Ce qu'on entend sur la montagne* and *Mazeppa;* Edward MacDowell's *Les Orientales* for piano; and Mendelssohn's overture, *Ruy Blas.*

Léo Delibes wrote incidental music for *Ruy Blas* and Jules Massenet for *Notre Dame de Paris.*

Hummel, Johann Nepomuk, pianist and composer. Born Pressburg, Germany, Nov. 14, 1778; died Weimar, Germany, Oct. 17, 1837. As a child he demonstrated such remarkable talent for the piano that Mozart accepted him as a pupil and had him live with him for two years. In 1787 Hummel made his début at a concert in Dresden in which Mozart appeared as conductor. Hummel toured Europe in 1788; during this period he received some additional instruction from Muzio Clementi in London. After returning to Vienna in 1793 he devoted himself to still further study with Haydn and Salieri. He then resumed his concert career with ever mounting success. His skill at extemporization was regarded second only to that of Beethoven; and the elegance of his piano playing was described by Czerny as a "revelation." From 1804 to 1811

Hummel was Kapellmeister to Prince Esterházy, a post previously held by Haydn. After returning to Vienna he taught piano and gave concerts for five years. In 1816 he was appointed court Kapellmeister in Stuttgart, and from 1819 until his death he held a similar post in Weimar. A prolific composer, Hummel produced over 150 works for the piano, including concertos, sonatas, fantasias, waltzes, rondos, and variations. He is perhaps most famous for his *Piano School,* or *Anweisung zum Pianofortespiel* (1828), one of the earliest texts advocating a rational system of fingering. Czerny and Liszt were among Hummel's pupils.

Humor in Music. Through the years, composers have achieved comic effects in music through various means. Comedy is sometimes produced by introducing the unexpected, as in the second movement of Haydn's *Surprise Symphony,* where a loud chord comes without warning after a quiet passage. The exaggeration of the tone quality or the unique personality of a musical instrument, and unusual couplings of instruments can yield humor: the xylophone in Shostakovich's Polka from *The Age of Gold;* the double bass in Stravinsky's *Pulcinella;* the high squeal of the clarinet in Richard Strauss' *Till Eulenspiegel;* the juxtaposition of violin and piccolo in Mozart's German dance, *The Canary.* Pert melodies and rhythms, unorthodox harmonies, unexpected modulations, and jazz techniques are often a rich source of wit and satire, as in Mozart's *A Musical Joke,* Stravinsky's Capriccio, some of the piano concertos of Jean Françaix and Francis Poulenc, Satie's *Parade,* and Milhaud's *Le Boeuf sur le toit.* Satie became music's humorist par excellence by using the most quixotic titles for, and interpolating the most capricious instructions within, his various piano pieces. Unusual quotations of music by other composers is often an effective way of being funny in music, as in Walton's *Façade,* Ibert's *Divertissement,* and Stravinsky's *Petrouchka.* Finally, perhaps the most efficacious method of achieving humor in music is to treat an amusing program realistically in the way Beethoven did in a piano capriccio, *Rage Over the Lost Penny,* Dukas in *The Sor-*

cerer's Apprentice, Prokofiev in *Lieutenant Kije* and *Peter and the Wolf,* and Saint-Saëns in *The Carnival of Animals.*

Humoresque. A slight and small piece, generally for the piano, usually of whimsical character. The most celebrated piece in this form is by Antonín Dvořák: the seventh in a set of eight Humoresques, op. 101 (1894). It is familiar not only in its original version but also in transcriptions. A popular humoresque by Tchaikovsky is found in *Nocturne and Humoresque,* for violin and piano, op. 10 (1871). Grieg's Humoresques, op. 6, were his first efforts at writing national music. Paderewski's celebrated Minuet was designated by the composer as a "humoresque de concert." Ernst von Dohnányi, Rachmaninoff, and Sibelius are other composers who wrote excellent humoresques for the piano. Schumann's Humoreske in B-flat major, op. 20 (1839), does not comply with the generally accepted meaning of the term, being a suite of five connected movements.

Huneker, James Gibbons, music critic. Born Philadelphia, Pa., Jan. 31, 1860; died Brooklyn, N.Y., Feb. 9, 1921. He studied piano with George Mathias in Paris and Rafael Joseffy in New York, and for a period was Joseffy's assistant at the National Conservatory in New York. After serving an apprenticeship as music critic on various journals between 1891 and 1897, he became art critic of the *New York Sun.* In 1917 he became music critic of the Philadelphia *Press.* From 1918 until 1919 he was the music critic of the *New York Times* and from 1919 until his death of the *New York World.* His various books on music contain some of the most penetrating critical writing in the United States of the time. These books include: *Mezzotints in Modern Music* (1899), *Melomaniacs* (1902), *Overtones* (1904), *Ivory Apes and Peacocks* (1915), and biographies of Chopin (1900) and Liszt (1911). His autobiography, *Steeplejack* (1919), is a rich source of information about musical activity in New York in Huneker's day.

Hungarian Czardas Scenes. See: Hubay, Jenö.

Hungarian Dances. Four books of 21 dances for the piano by Brahms. He is sued the first two books as piano duets in 1869, and for solo piano in 1872; the last two books were published as piano duets in 1880. Brahms orchestrated three of these dances, Nos. 1, 3, and 10. Eduard Reményi, the Hungarian violinist, had introduced the young Brahms to Hungarian folk music. Taken with these spirited, fiery, and at times languorous melodies, Brahms adapted many of them, providing them with his own inventive harmonies. The most popular of Brahms' Hungarian Dances is No. 5 in F-sharp minor, famous in its original version and in transcriptions. Other popular Hungarian dances are: No. 1 in G minor; No. 2, in D minor; No. 3, in F major; No. 4, in F minor; No. 6, in D-flat major; No. 7, in A major; and No. 17 in F-sharp minor.

Hungarian Fantasy. For piano and orchestra by Liszt (1860). It is actually an adaptation for piano and orchestra of the composer's Hungarian Rhapsody No. 14, for piano solo (1852). A solemn slow section opens the piece. After a piano cadenza there arrives a rapid section filled with the fiery rhythms and sensual gypsy melodies of Hungarian folk music. A graceful interlude leads to the conclusion.

Hungarian Quartet. A chamber-music ensemble founded at Budapest, Hungary, in 1935 with Zoltán Szekely and Sandor Vegh, violins, Denes Koromzay, viola, and Vilmos Palotai, cellist. (Alexander Moskovsky subsequently replaced Sandor Vegh.) This Quartet has appeared throughout the world, distinguishing itself particularly in the modern repertory. Béla Bartók, Willem Pijper, and Castelnuovo-Tedesco are some of the composers who wrote pieces for this organization.

Hungarian Rhapsody. (1) A form successfully exploited by Liszt, who wrote 19 such works between 1846 and 1885. Liszt himself explained that in using the rhapsody form for these nationalistic works, he wanted to express "certain states of the soul in which are summarized the ideals of the nation" and to emphasize the "fantastically epic element" of this music. The Liszt Hungarian Rhapsody consists of effective contrasts between slow and sensual music (called *lassan*) and frenetic, theatrical music (called *friskan*). Dramatic effect is achieved not only through the alternation of opposing moods but also through theatrical changes of rhythm, tempo, and dynamics. Liszt's Hungarian Rhapsodies are replete with actual Hungarian melodies, dances, and rhythms, the result of the composer's researches into Hungarian folk music.

The most famous of these Rhapsodies is No. 2 in C-sharp minor (1847), probably the most widely known piece of music by this composer. In its exciting changes of pace and mood, and in its theatrical climaxes, it is characteristic of this *genre* as a whole.

Here are some other popular Liszt Hungarian Rhapsodies: No. 9 in E-flat major, *Carnaval de Pesth;* No. 12 in C-sharp minor; No. 13 in A minor (also adapted by the composer into the *Hungarian Fantasy,* for piano and orchestra); and No. 15 in A minor, *Rakóczy March.*

Six of Liszt's Hungarian Rhapsodies were transcribed for orchestra by the composer and Franz Doppler: Nos. 2, 5, 6, 9, 12, and 14.

(2) *See:* Hubay, Jenö.

Hunt Quartet. *See:* Quartet—*Mozart.*

Hutcheson, Ernest, pianist. Born Melbourne, Australia, July 20, 1871; died New York City, Feb. 9, 1951. He studied piano with private teachers in Australia while making appearances as a child prodigy. In his fourteenth year he entered the Leipzig Conservatory; he subsequently completed his piano study in Weimar with Bernhard Stavenhagen. From 1898 to 1900 he taught piano at the Stern Conservatory in Berlin, a period in which he also successfully launched his career as virtuoso throughout Europe. In 1900 he settled in the United States, becoming a citizen. From 1900 to 1912 he was head of the piano department of Peabody Conservatory in Baltimore. In 1924 he became dean of the Juilliard Graduate School and in 1933 also dean of the Institute of Musical Art. From 1937 to 1945 he was president of the Juilliard School of Music. His concert activity was not abandoned. In 1915 and 1919 he presented concerts in New York featuring three concertos in a single performance, an unusual procedure at the time. In the early 1920's he devoted a series of seven recitals in New York to the history of piano music. Subsequently he performed all the major piano concertos in a series of coast-to-coast radio concerts. He was the author of *The Literature of the Piano* (1948).

Hymn and Fuguing Tune, No. 2. For string orchestra by Henry Cowell (1944), inspired by old American hymn tunes. This composition was first performed by the NBC Symphony in March 1944, Henri Nosco conducting. Like others in a similar vein, it was inspired by the *Southern Harmony,* an old hymn book, which Cowell had an opportunity to inspect. Cowell began to wonder how this music would sound if modern resources were applied to it. He then proceeded to write a series of compositions, all entitled *Hymn and Fuguing Tune,* in which his own musical material was based on American hymnology. The most popular of this set is the second. The melodies here are entirely Cowell's, but, as he explains, his music "pays respect to the early American modal religious musical style, containing severe simplicity of rhythm and form and many open chords incidental to fervent flowing polyphony."

Hymne. For large orchestra by Olivier Messiaen (1945), first performed by the New York Philharmonic on March 13, 1947, Leopold Stokowski conducting. The composer explains that this work is based on two themes. "The first theme ends with a burst of winds . . . The second theme, more dreamy, and very singing . . . utilizes only violins and violas soli. The middle development is polymodal, alternating with opposing the more belligerent first theme and more passionate second theme. The final development resumes the martial character and the polymodality of the first development, and concludes on a joyous fanfare of brass."

I

Iberia. (1) Suite of 12 pieces, in four books, for piano by Isaac Albéniz (1906-1909). Each book was separately introduced by Blanche Selva, in Paris and Saint-Jean-de-Luz, between 1906 and 1909. Book I contains *Evocacíon,* an Andalusian song contrasted with the rhythm of a jota; *El Puerto,* which describes a fiesta in a Spanish seaport; and *El Corpus en Sevilla* (or *Fête-Dieu à Séville*), the most famous number in the entire suite, which evokes a picture of an ecclesiastical procession in a Spanish street. In Book II will be found *Rondeña,* inspired by a dance popular in the city of Ronda, a variant of the fandango; *Alméria,* a picture of the Mediterranean seaport of that name, in a jota-like melody set against the rhythm of a tarantas, a dance indigenous to that town; and *Triana,* which depicts the gypsy suburb of Seville in a haunting gypsy song and dance. In Book III are: *El Albaicín,* which catches the spirit of a Seville suburb in a number characterized by the lyricism and rhythms of a gypsy song and dance; *El Polo,* based on a poignant Andalusian folksong of the same name; and *Lavapiés,* a piece filled with excitement, evoking the atmosphere of a popular section of Madrid. The fourth and last book contains *Málaga,* in the rhythm of a dance that actually originated in that city; *Jérez,* modeled after the gypsy dance, the soleares, whose melody is full of intriguing figurations; and *Eritaña,* in which vivacious rhythms, contrasting with tender strains of melody, depict a tavern in the outskirts of Seville.

Evocacíon, El Puerto, El Corpus en Sevilla, Triana, and *El Albaicín* have become popular in transcriptions for orchestra by Enrique Fernández Arbós. Stokowski also made an orchestral adaptation of *El Corpus en Sevilla.*

(2) The second in a set of three piano

pieces for orchestra collectively entitled *Images,* by Debussy. *See: Images* (2).

Ibert, Jacques, composer. Born Paris, France, Aug. 15, 1890. His study of music was sporadic until his twenty-first year, when he entered the Paris Conservatory. There, for several years, he studied under André Gedalge, Roger-Ducasse, and Gabriel Fauré. After World War I he continued his music study with Paul Vidal, winning the Prix de Rome in 1919. In Italy he completed two large works for orchestra: a tone poem, *The Ballad of Reading Gaol,* based on Oscar Wilde's poem, and *Escales,* an orchestral suite still one of his most famous compositions. In 1937 Ibert became the first musician to become director of the Académie de France in Rome, holding this post until 1955. After World War II he divided his activity between Paris and Rome by becoming assistant director of the Paris Opéra. From 1955 to 1957 he was full director of the combined management of the Paris Opéra and Opéra-Comique. In 1950 he visited the United States to conduct a master class in composition at the Berkshire Music Centre in Tanglewood. His compositions embrace two opposing styles. One is light and satirical; the other, neo-Impressionistic, with subtle moods and delicate effects. His orchestral works include various concertos (cello and wind instruments; flute; *Louisville Concerto* for orchestra), the tone poem *Ballad of Reading Gaol,* the suite *Escales, Féerique, Divertissement, Overture for a Fête, Suite élisabethaine, Capriccio, Impressions of Paris, Symphonie concertante* for oboe and strings, *Concertino da camera* for saxophone and small orchestra. He also wrote several suites for piano including *Histoires,* in which will be found the popular *The Little White Donkey.*

See: Ballad of Reading Gaol, The; Concertino—Ibert; Escales, Les.

Ibsen, Henrik, playwright and poet. Born Skien, Norway, March 20, 1828; died Christiania (now Oslo), Norway, May 23, 1906. One of the first social dramatists, Ibsen was the author of many plays which have been the source of instrumental compositions. Among these plays are the following (where titles of

compositions are not given they are the same as the play):

Brand: Gerhard Schjelderup (tone poem). Incidental music by Ture Rangström.

The Feast at Solhaug: Incidental music by Hans Pfitzner, and Hugo Wolf.

John Gabriel Borkman: Hjalmar Borgstrøm (tone poem).

Lady from the Sea: William Wallace (suite for orchestra).

Peer Gynt: Grieg (two suites for orchestra). Incidental music by Grieg, Harald Saeverud, and Johann August Söderman.

Idée fixe. A term devised by Berlioz to designate a recurring theme or *Leitmotiv.*

Idyl. A term borrowed from poetry to denote a musical composition of pastoral character, as for example, Leoš Janáček's *Idyl* for orchestra or Edward MacDowell's *Forest Idyls* for piano.

Ilia Mourometz. *See:* Symphony—*Glière.*

Iliad, The. *See:* Homer.

Im Walde (In the Forest). A programmatic symphony, No. 3, by Joseph Joachim Raff, op. 153 (1869). This work enjoyed a considerable vogue in the 19th century, but is now rarely revived.

Images. (1) A set of three symphonic sketches by Debussy (1906-1912). The first sketch is entitled *Gigues,* and it was introduced in Paris on Jan. 26, 1913, André Caplet conducting. The main gigue melody appears in the solo oboe d'amore, following a twenty-bar introduction. A melody of Scottish character in bassoons is the second principal theme. The third and concluding sketch is *Ronde de printemps,* first performed in Paris on March 2, 1910, the composer conducting. This is the least frequently performed of the three sketches. The published score carries the following identifying line: "Long live the month of May! Welcome to May with its savage banner."

The second and middle sketch is the most famous, almost always performed independently of its companion pieces. This is *Ibéria,* first heard in Paris on Feb. 20, 1910, Gabriel Pierné conducting. There are three sections. I. *In the Streets and Byways (Par les rues et par les chemins*). After an outburst of rhythm and tonal colors, there appears the first main theme, a sprightly tune for two clarinets against a rhythmic background in a tambourine, and a harmonic setting for oboes and bassoons. After a change of tempo, a second main subject is presented: a march-like melody for four unison horns. II. *The Perfumes of the Night* (*Les Parfums de la nuit*). A sensual melody for muted divided violins and violas is the opening theme. After glissandos and chromatic runs, a new haunting song is played by the oboe, with harmonies in divided violas and strings. Momentarily, a melody from the first movement is recalled. Then a powerful climax is built up. After a repetition of previously stated material, the section ends with a solemn tolling of bells. III. *The Morning of a Festival Day* (*Le Matin d'un jour de fête*). This section arrives without pause. The dominant idea is a march-like melody developed with compelling force. Throughout this section, themes from earlier movements are recalled. Then the section comes to a dynamic close with an acceleration of the tempo and a monumental building up of the sonority.

(2) Two sets of pieces for the piano by Debussy (1905-1907). The first set includes *Reflets dans l'eau* (*Reflections in the Water*) with undulating melodic figures and nebulous progressions suggesting the shimmering images on the water; *Hommage à Rameau* (*Homage to Rameau*), a tribute to the 18th-century French master in a graceful musical composition of classic design; and *Mouvement* (*Movement*), in which a feeling of perpetual motion is created through a succession of rapid triplets. The second set also has three numbers. The first is *Cloches à travers les feuilles* (*Bells Through the Leaves*), an impression of the sound of bells muffled by the leaves of a forest. The middle number is *Et la lune descend sur le temple* (*And the Moon Descends on the Temple*), which evokes an exotic, at times archaic, atmosphere. The final piece is *Poissons d'or* (*Goldfish*), inspired by a piece of oriental lacquer on which was painted a picture of goldfish in a stream. The music

suggests the movement of the fish in the water with rising and falling arpeggios and a rapid movement of scale passages.

Imitation. In counterpoint, a phrase or theme repeated by another "voice" usually at a lower or higher pitch.

Imperfect cadence. *See:* Perfect cadence.

Imperfect interval. *See:* Perfect interval.

Imperial Symphony. *See:* Symphony—Haydn.

Impressionism. A term in music derived from 19th-century painting, describing a style seeking to express feeling, and the impression a subject or idea arouses, rather than the subject or idea itself. In Impressionism the composer strives for delicate effects, subtle colors, nebulous suggestions. The word "Impressionism" has one of two origins. One is a painting of a sunrise over the sea, *Une Impression*, by Claude Monet; the other is a quotation from a catalogue for an exhibition of Édouard Manet's paintings in 1867 which explains the artist's aim as one of rendering "impressions." In music, this term is most often associated with Claude Debussy, who crystallized an impressionist style of composition and made it famous.

Impromptu. A composition in extended song form for piano, giving the suggestion of an improvisation. It became famous with Schubert. The following are some of the more notable compositions in this form:

CHOPIN. Chopin wrote four important impromptus: in A-flat, op. 29, no. 1; F-sharp, op. 36, no. 2; G-flat, op. 51, no. 3; and C-sharp minor, op. 66, better known as "Fantaisie impromptu." The impromptu in A-flat (1837) is perhaps the most popular—a pensive, poetic piece of music with intermittent contrasts of dramatic episodes. The *Fantaisie impromptu* (1834) is also celebrated, particularly since its main melody was used for a popular American song.

FAURÉ. Fauré wrote 5 impromptus for piano. A sixth, in D-flat major, op. 86, is merely a transcription of a piece originally for harp. The 5 impromptus are: E-flat major, op. 25; F minor, op. 31; A-flat, op. 34; D-flat-C-sharp major, op. 91; and F-sharp minor, op. 102. The

Impromptu No. 2, in F minor (1883), one of the best of this group, is notable for sensitive lyricism and inventive use of harmony and tone colors.

SCHUBERT. Schubert's 8 impromptus for the piano are virtually songs for the piano. It is doubtful that the composer himself applied the term "impromptu" to these pieces, the general belief being that this was done for him by his publishers. Four of these pieces are found in op. 90 (1827), four more in op. 142 (1827). All are gems. The Impromptus in B-flat major, op. 142, no. 3 boasts one of Schubert's loveliest melodies. Schubert himself liked it so well that he used it again for his incidental music for *Rosamunde,* and for the slow movement of his A minor string quartet. In the piano impromptu the melody undergoes a series of variations. The Impromptu in A-flat, op. 142, no. 3, is also highly lyrical, consisting of a minuet and trio. The Impromptu in E-flat, op. 90, no. 2, is a bravura piece with an expressive intermezzo section while the Impromptu in F minor, op. 142, no. 4, has a fanciful, almost capricious, mood.

SCHUMANN. Schumann produced 2 impromptus. The *Impromptu on a Theme by Clara Wieck,* op. 5 (1833), consists of a series of variations. A second impromptu appears as the first number of *Albumblaetter,* op. 124 (1832-1845).

Improvisation (or Extemporization). A performance without preconceived plan.

In a Summer Garden. Fantasy for orchestra by Frederick Delius (1908), first performed in London on Dec. 11, 1908, the composer conducting. Two quotations, appended to the published score, provide a clue to its emotional content. One is a couplet by Dante Gabriel Rossetti: "All are my blooms; and all sweet blooms of love. To thee I gave while Spring and Summer sang." The other (of unknown authorship) is: "Roses, lilies, and a thousand scented flowers. Bright butterflies, flitting from petal to petal. Beneath the shade of ancient trees, a quiet river with water lilies. In a boat, almost hidden, two people. A thrush is singing in the distance." This composition is constructed out of several important themes. The first appears in the woodwind, then strings; the second, in the English horn; a third is a beautiful melody for violas against figures in the woodwind and chords in lower strings. This material is worked out vigorously but a new theme in the violins, repeated by woodwind, provides emotional respite.

In Central Asia. Orchestral sketch by Borodin (1880), written as music for a "tableau vivant" commemorating the 25th anniversary of the reign of Alexander II. This was one of the 12 compositions commissioned from Russian composers to accompany tableaux describing major events in the Czar's reign. Borodin provided the following program for his music: "Through the silence of the steppes of Central Asia are heard the strains of a peaceful Russian song. Sounds of horses and camels come from the distance, approaching ever nearer, and with them the strains of a haunting Eastern melody. A caravan is crossing the desert escorted by Russian soldiers . . . [and] disappears into the distant horizon. The song of the Russians blends with that of the Orientals in a common harmony, until both fade away from the plains." The peaceful Russian song is heard in solo clarinet, while the haunting Eastern melody is given by the English horn. Both themes are combined contrapuntally, then allowed to fade away as the composition ends with the tones of a lonely flute and the dying voices of flute and violins.

In Nature's Realm (In der Natur). Concert overture for orchestra by Dvořák, op. 91 (1891), one of three overtures of a cycle collectively entitled *Nature, Life and Love.* All three were introduced in Prague on April 28, 1892, the composer conducting. *In Nature's Realm* reflects the composer's love of Nature, and the reverent feelings that love inspired. The main theme, sometimes designated as "Nature's motif," appears in the clarinet and is repeated by the full orchestra. An ensuing vigorous section describes the joy "which all Nature proclaims." A more subdued melody, in strings, speaks of the "more quiet gladness of the beholder."

In the Hall of the Mountain King (Grieg). *See: Peer Gynt Suite.*

n the South (Alassio). Concert overture
y Edward Elgar, op. 50 (1903), intro-
luced at an Elgar festival in London on
March 16, 1904, the composer conduct-
ng. Written one spring when the composer was vacationing in the valley of
Andorra, this work reflects the compos-
r's love of nature. The following quota-
ion appears in the published score: "A
and which *was* the mightiest in its old
ommand and *is* the loveliest; wherein
vere cast the men of Rome. Thou art the
arden of the world." The overture be-
ins with a sprightly tune for clarinet,
orns, violins, and cellos. This subject
eceives vigorous treatment and enlarge-
nent before the appearance of a pastoral
ection for woodwind and muted strings,
 description of a shepherd and his flock.
The overture after that alternates between
tress and tranquillity, considerable prom-
nence being given to the shepherd's mel-
dy. A solo in the viola leads to the re-
apitulation section.

n the Steppes of Central Asia (Borodin).
See: In Central Asia.

ncidental Music. Music written for per-
ormance with a spoken drama but in-
idental to the play. Bizet's incidental
nusic to Daudet's *L'Arlésienne,* Grieg's
or Ibsen's *Peer Gynt,* and Mendelssohn's
or Shakespeare's *A Midsummer Night's
Dream* are popular examples.

ncredible Flutist, The. Ballet suite for
orchestra by Walter Piston (1938)
adapted from his score to a ballet intro-
luced by Hans Wiener at a concert of
he Boston Pops Orchestra in Boston on
May 30, 1938. The orchestral suite was
played for the first time on Nov. 22,
1940, by the Pittsburgh Symphony, Fritz
Reiner conducting. The ballet—text by
he composer and Hans Wiener—de-
cribes a market place pulsating with
activity and made colorful by the arrival
of a circus. A flutist charms snakes and
women. A rich widow flirts with a merchant, faints when she is discovered by
her lover, and is revived by the flutist's
music. Then the circus leaves the square
and the excitement dies down. The suite
has 13 sections: I. Introduction; II. Siesta
Hour in the Marketplace and Entrance
of the Vendors; III. Dance of the
Vendors; IV. Entrance of the Customers;

V. Tango of the Four Daughters; VI.
Arrival of Circus and Circus March; VII.
Solo of the Flutist; VIII. Minuet—Dance
of the Widow and Merchant; IX. Spanish
Waltz; X. Eight O'Clock Strikes; XI.
Siciliano—Dance of the Flutist and the
Merchant's Daughter; XII. Polka; XIII.
Finale.

Indeciso. Italian for capricious.

Indian Fantasy (Indianische Fantasie).
For piano and orchestra by Ferruccio
Busoni, op. 44 (1913), introduced in
Zurich in January 1916, Volkmar An-
dreae conducting. The work is based upon
American-Indian melodies and rhythms
supplied the composer by Natalie Curtis
Burlin, an American writer on Indian
lore. The music provides a picture of the
North American prairies, and is in three
sections. I. Fantasy. An orchestral introduction leads into an extended piano
solo. After the return of the orchestral
introduction, the main themes are given
and followed by variations. II. Canzona.
Two songs are prominent. III. Finale. A
theme from the first section is recalled,
with three new Indian melodies introduced.

Indian Suite. For orchestra by Edward
MacDowell, op. 48 (1892), first per-
formed in New York City by the Boston
Symphony on Jan. 23, 1896. This was
the composer's second suite for orchestra.
As its name indicates, it makes use of
American Indian melodies and rhythms.
There are five sections. I. Legend. Two
themes, both for horns, are prominent.
One is virile, the second tender. II. Love
Song. The main melody was derived
from a tribal love song of Iowa Indians.
III. In War Times. This is martial music
of primitive strength. IV. Dirge. A poignant threnody is introduced by solemn
tolling bells. V. Village. Two Iroquois
melodies are exploited. The first appears
in plucked strings; the other in flute and
piccolo with string and woodwind accompaniment.

Indianapolis Symphony Orchestra. A
symphony orchestra founded in Indianapolis, Ind., in 1929 by Ferdinand Schaefer,
who was its principal conductor until
1937. After Schaefer the principal conductors were Fabien Sevitzky and Izler
Solomon. Since 1943 the orchestra has

been subsidized by a municipal grant. Its concerts take place in the Murat Theatre.

Indy, Vincent d', composer. Born Paris, France, March 27, 1851; died there, Dec. 2, 1931. As a boy, he studied piano with Louis Diémer and Antoine Marmontel, and harmony with Albert Lavignac. His studies were interrupted by the Franco-Prussian War, in which he saw active service. After the war he began studying with César Franck, both privately and at the Paris Conservatory, where he won the first accessit in organ playing in 1875. Franck's influence upon him was decisive. A second powerful influence was that of Wagner, but this was felt most strongly in d'Indy's operas.

In 1871 d'Indy helped Franck found the Société Nationale de Musique in Paris, dedicated to the presentation of new French music; when Franck died in 1890, d'Indy succeeded him as president. Between 1872 and 1876, d'Indy was organist at St. Leu, and from 1873 to 1878 he was chorusmaster and timpanist with the Colonne Orchestra. On May 15, 1875, that orchestra introduced d'Indy's first symphony, *Jean Hunyade.* Major works for orchestra were given in Paris between 1886 and 1897, including *Le Chant de la cloche* (which won the City of Paris prize in 1885), the *Symphony on a French Mountain Song (Symphonie cévenole sur un chant montagnard français), Istar,* and the tone poem *Summer Day on the Mountain (Jour d'été à la montagne).* In these and other compositions d'Indy reveals the impact the personality and art of Franck had had upon him. Much of d'Indy's best music, like that of his teacher, has spiritual overtones and nobility of concept. Structurally, it owes a debt to Franck in its exploitation of the cyclical form. But d'Indy also brought to his writing a detachment, objectivity, and subtle intellectual processes, together with emotional control, that we do not find often in Franck; and in his anticipation of Impressionist harmonies and advanced orchestration he was years ahead of Franck.

In 1893 d'Indy was invited by the French government to serve on a com-

mittee to reform the Paris Conservatory. His program was so revolutionary that it antagonized the Conservatory professors, who banded against him. The reform movement was shelved for several years. Meanwhile, in 1894, d'Indy helped organize the Schola Cantorum, soon to become one of Paris' leading music schools. Both as a teacher and as its director, d'Indy influenced an entire generation of young French musicians. After 1912 he combined his activity at the Schola Cantorum with duties as professor of conducting at the now-reformed Paris Conservatory. Among his pupils were Arthur Honegger, Erik Satie, Albert Roussel, and Georges Auric.

Besides his contributions as teacher and composer, d'Indy was also distinguished as a conductor, editor, writer, scholar, and lecturer. As a conductor he made notable appearances in France, Spain, and Russia; his American début took place on Dec. 1, 1905, with the Boston Symphony. He was the author of biographies of Franck (1906) and Beethoven (1911), among other books. In 1892 he was made Chevalier of the Legion of Honor, and in 1912, Officier.

The following are d'Indy's principal instrumental works:

Chamber Music: 3 string quartets; 2 piano trios; piano quintet; string sextet; violin sonata; cello sonata.

Orchestra: Wallenstein, symphonic trilogy; *Symphony on a French Mountain Song (Symphonie cévenole sur un chant montagnard français); Istar;* Symphony No. 2 in B-flat major; *Summer Day on the Mountain (Jour d'été à la montagne); Souvenirs; Sinfonia brevis; Poème des rivages; Diptyque méditerranéen;* Concerto for Piano, Flute, Cello and String Orchestra.

See: Istar; Summer Day on the Mountain; Symphony—*d'Indy.*

Infante, Manuel, composer. Born Osuna, Spain, July 29, 1883; died Paris, France, April 1958. After studying piano and composition with Enrique Morera, he settled in Paris in 1909; there through the years he presented numerous concerts of Spanish music. In his own works, the Spanish national element was predominant. His most significant works are for piano and include a suite for two pianos; also, for solo piano, *Gitanerias, Sevillana, El Vito, Trois danses andalouses,* and *Pochades andalouses.*

Inghelbrecht, Désiré Émile, conductor and composer. Born Paris, France, Sept. 17, 1880. After attending the Paris Conservatory he made his conducting début with the Société Nationale. In 1908 he led orchestral performances in Paris, emphasizing modern works, and achieved recognition as an outstanding interpreter of Debussy. In 1919 he founded the Pleyel Concerts, famous for its programs of old music, and in 1928 he became principal conductor of the Pasdeloup Orchestra. Since then he has conducted radio concerts of the National Orchestra, which he founded in his capacity as director of the State Radio. He has also distinguished himself as a conductor of opera and ballet. As a composer, he is best known for his ballets. His best works are the *Symphonie brève,* the Quintet for harp and strings, and *Suite Petite-Russienne* and *La Nursery* for piano.

Interlude. A brief section connecting two movements; or a piece of orchestral music in an opera or play; or an instrumental sequence for organ between two choruses.

Intermezzo. (1) A term used interchangeably with entr'acte to designate a piece of orchestral music in opera played during the lowering of the curtain to designate the passage of time. The most popular of these intermezzos are those by Enrique Granados from *Goyescas,* Pietro Mascagni from *Cavalleria rusticana,* and Ermanno Wolf-Ferrari from *The Jewels of the Madonna.*

(2) In symphonic music, a short movement serving as a transition between two larger ones, as in Schumann's Symphony No. 4.

(3) In piano music, a short movement or transition between two larger sections, as in Beethoven's *Waldstein Sonata.* But the most familiar application of "intermezzo" to piano music is as a short piece with no definite form expressing a passing thought. Brahms' 18 Intermezzos for piano contain some of his most personal thoughts. Three were published separately as op. 117 (1892); four are found

in Eight Pieces, op. 76 (1878); four, in Six Pieces, op. 118 (1893); three, in Four Pieces, op. 119 (1893). Brahms' Intermezzos traverse the gamut of emotion from tragedy (E-flat major, op. 118, no. 6) to light-hearted gaiety (C major, op. 119, no. 3). Two of the most popular of these pieces are those in E-flat major, op. 117, no. 9, a cradle song inspired by the Scottish ballad, *Lady Anne Bothwell's Lament;* and E minor, op. 119, no. 2, a poignant love song.

Schumann wrote 6 intermezzos for piano, op. 4 (1832). Each contains two basic melodic ideas, the first repeated after the second.

International Society for Contemporary Music. A society promoting contemporary music and composers in annual festivals. It was founded in 1922 in Salzburg, Austria. Compositions performed at these annual festivals are selected by an international committee. Edward J. Dent was first president of the Society, and the first festival took place at Salzburg in 1923. The locale of each festival has shifted annually from city to city: Venice, Prague, Zurich, Frankfort, Vienna, Geneva, and so forth. During World War II it was held in New York (1941) and San Francisco (1942). After a five-year hiatus, the Festival resumed operations in 1947 at London. In 1938, Edwin Evans succeeded Dent as president, and Evans in turn has been succeeded by Edward Clark.

Interval. Distance in pitch between two tones.

Intonation. The quality of faithfulness to pitch in musical tones.

Introduction. A prefatory passage to a musical composition, or to a movement of a sonata, symphony, and so forth. It varies in length from a few chords to a fully developed section.

Introduction and Allegro. (1) For string quartet and string orchestra by Edward Elgar, op. 47 (1905), introduced in London on March 8, 1905. Written in the style of a classic concerto grosso, this work utilizes the string quartet as the traditional "concertino," with the rest of the orchestra serving as the "ripieno." The opening subject is given by the quartet and strings, followed by a second theme in the quartet. After some development, a Welsh melody is heard in a solo viola, with which the introduction ends. A change of key from minor to major brings on the Allegro section. Here the previously stated themes are enlarged, while a new subject appears in the solo quartet. After a fugato section, the composition ends with a recollection of the Welsh melody by quartet and strings.

(2) For harp, string quartet, flute, and clarinet by Maurice Ravel (1906). It was written for the harpist, Micheline Kahn, who helped to introduce it in Paris on Feb. 22, 1907. The introduction opens with a delicate duet for flute and clarinet. This is followed by the principal subject, a lyrical passage for cello, accompanied by violin, flute, and clarinet. After the latter theme is dramatized through acceleration of tempo and enlargement of the sonority, the Allegro enters without interruption, opening with an extended harp solo. The flute takes up this idea, and other instruments follow suit. After a detailed development, a harp cadenza brings back some basic melodies.

Introduction and Rondo Capriccioso. For violin and orchestra by Saint-Saëns, op. 28 (1863), introduced in Paris by Pablo de Sarasate on April 4, 1867. The theme of the introduction is a slow, somewhat melancholy melody for solo violin. A forceful chord brings on the *Rondo capriccioso* section. After three measures, the solo violin presents the main theme; the solo instrument is also responsible for introducing the subsidiary subject. After some virtuoso passages, and a return of the first main theme, a new idea is stated loudly by the orchestra, and repeated by the violin. All this material is then discoursed upon, often with brilliant embellishments by the violin.

Invention. A short piece for the clavier made famous by Johann Sebastian Bach. He wrote two sets intended as educational pieces for his sons, "a guide for clean performance," as he himself explained, "with special emphasis on the cultivation of a cantabile style of playing and the acquisition of a strong foretaste of composition." Each set consists of 15 pieces. The first set is made up of two-part inventions—or inventions with two contrapuntal voices;

the second set, of three-part inventions (Bach called these "symphonies"). They are not only valuable pedagogically, particularly important as preparation for the mastery of Bach's more complex polyphonic works for the piano, but they are charming pieces, so much so that they are occasionally included on concert programs.

Inversion. Two notes of an interval turned upside down. In harmony, it consists of changing the tones of a chord by having the bass note assume a position other than the root. In a melodic line, it consists of reversing the intervals. In counterpoint, inversion means changing the relative position of the two melodic lines.

Invertible counterpoint. *See:* Double Counterpoint.

Invitation to the Dance (Aufforderung zum Tanz). "Rondo brillant" in D-flat major for piano by Carl Maria von Weber (1819). This is one of the earliest successful attempts at integrating several different waltz melodies into a cohesive composition, prefaced by an introduction, and concluding with an epilogue; this form was subsequently used effectively by the Viennese waltz kings. This composition is most familiar through the orchestral transcription of Berlioz or Felix Weingartner. Berlioz' version, the one heard most often, was intended as ballet music for an 1841 performance in Paris of Weber's opera *Der Freischuetz*. This transcription opens with a gentle dialogue between cello and woodwind: A young man is asking the lady for a dance. Various waltz melodies follow as the couple engages in the dancing. At the conclusion of the piece, the opening slow section is repeated: the gentleman is thanking the lady for having danced with him.

Ionian mode. A Gregorian mode similar to the C major scale.

Iphigenia in Aulis. *See:* Euripides.

Iphigenia in Aulis (Iphigénie en Aulide), Overture to. Overture to an opera by Gluck, introduced at the Paris Opéra on May 19, 1774. The libretto, by Bailli du Roullet, was based on a drama by Racine, in turn derived from Euripides. The overture opens with stately music described by Wagner as an invocation for deliverance from affliction. Two main themes appear in the principal section: a forceful melody for orchestra (the assertion of the will, according to Wagner) and a sentimental song for violins (representing Iphigenia). Since in the opera the overture does not have a formal ending but leads into the opening scene, various composers have prepared concert endings. The one used most often is by Wagner in which the opening stately theme is recalled against the background of a phrase from the first forceful subject. The overture ends with a last repetition of this forceful subject.

Iphigenia in Tauris. *See:* Euripides.

Ippolitov-Ivanov, Michael, composer. Born Gachina, Russia, Nov. 19, 1859; died Moscow, Russia, Jan. 28, 1935. He attended the St. Petersburg Conservatory from 1875 to 1882, a pupil of Rimsky-Korsakov. He then became director of the Tiflis Music School and conductor of its orchestra. In Tiflis he became interested in the folk music of that region, writing an authoritative study on that subject, *On the National Songs of Georgia.* In 1893 he went to Moscow, where he was appointed professor at its Conservatory; from 1906 to 1922 he was its director. He also held important conducting posts with the Moscow Choral Society and the Moscow Private Opera. His most famous composition is the *Caucasian Sketches,* for orchestra. Other orchestral works include a Sinfonietta, overtures (*Spring, Medea*), suites (*Iveria, In the Steppes of Turkmenia,* and *Catalonian Suite*), 2 symphonies, *Armenian Rhapsody,* a tone poem *Mtsyry,* and *Musical Scenes of Uzbekistan.* He also wrote a piano quartet, string quartet, and violin sonata.

See: Caucasian Sketches.

Ireland, John, composer. Born Bowden, England, Aug. 13, 1879. He entered the Royal College of Music at London in 1893, remaining there eight years. In 1905 he received a bachelor's degree in music from the University of Durham. One year later he completed his first ambitious composition, the *Phantasy Trio.* In 1909 he received the Cobbett Prize for the Sonata in D minor, for violin and

piano; and in 1913, his first major orchestral work, *The Forgotten Rite,* was written. While completing these and later compositions, Ireland held various posts as organist and teacher. For many years he taught composition at the Royal College of Music, where his pupils included Benjamin Britten. When World War II broke out, Ireland was living quietly on the island of Guernsey, from which he managed to escape just before its invasion by the Nazis. Ireland's earlier works reveal two significant influences. One is his love of nature, the other literature (especially the writings of Arthur Machen and English poetry). His later music tends towards greater simplicity and economy, the harmonic and orchestral textures having been refined. But Romantic tendencies have not been abandoned. His orchestral music includes a symphonic rhapsody, *Mai-Dun, A London Overture, Concertino Pastorale, Epic March, Overture Satyricon,* and a piano concerto. In chamber music he has produced 2 piano trios, 2 violin sonatas, cello sonata, *Fantasy Sonata* for clarinet and piano as well as the *Phantasy Trio.* He has also written many pieces for the piano including preludes, dances, *Sarnia,* and *Three Pastels.*

Isherwood, Christopher. *See:* Auden, Wystan Hugh.

Islamey. Oriental fantasy for piano by Balakirev, the composer's most famous composition. It was inspired by a trip in 1862 to the Caucasus, whose folk music provided the composer with his melodic and rhythmic materials. Two oriental melodies are prominent. They are freely developed, often against a rich harmonic background, and just as often decorated with brilliant virtuoso passage work. *Islamey* has been transcribed for orchestra by Alfredo Casella.

Isle joyeuse, L' (The Happy Island). For piano by Debussy (1904), first performed in Paris by Ricardo Viñes on Feb. 18, 1905. Debussy originally planned this piece as a movement of his *Suite bergamasque.* He finally decided to issue it as an independent work. His inspiration was Watteau's *Embarquement pour Cythère.* Debussy's music is characterized by sensitive tone colorations and ingenious rhythmic patterns.

Isle of the Dead (Toteninsel). Tone poem for orchestra by Rachmaninoff, op. 29 (1907), first performed in Moscow on May 1, 1909, the composer conducting. The inspiration was a painting by Arnold Boecklin in which a small boat, carrying a flag-draped coffin and a mourner, is proceeding to a grim island. An undulating figure in 5/8 meter suggests the movement of the water; this subject courses throughout the entire composition. A funereal melody is then presented by the horn. The gloomy atmosphere is intensified by a brief passage for solo violin and a theme for divided strings. The cello suddenly interpolates a quotation from the medieval hymn, *Dies irae.* After a powerful development, the music reverts to the quiet and funereal opening mood.

For other works inspired by the same painting *see:* Painters and Painting.

Israel Philharmonic Orchestra. A symphony orchestra in Israel founded as the Palestine Symphony in 1936 largely through the efforts of Bronislaw Huberman, its personnel made up mostly from musicians who had fled from Fascist persecution in Europe to Palestine. The first concert took place in Tel Aviv on Dec. 26, 1936, Toscanini conducting (his first visit to the Near East). For the next decade the orchestra was directed by some of the world's leading conductors. For a number of years it had no principal conductor, but was directed by two resident conductors, Michael Taube and George Singer. In 1946 the orchestra changed its name to Palestine Philharmonic, and after the establishment of the State of Israel in 1948 to Israeli Philharmonic. In 1951 it toured the United States, and in 1955 Europe. In 1957 the orchestra acquired the Frederic R. Mann Auditorium, named after the Philadelphia philanthropist who had provided the funds for the building. The orchestra gave its first concert in its new home in September 1957, Leonard Bernstein conducting. Jean Martinon was appointed permanent conductor of the orchestra in 1959.

Israel Symphony. *See:* Symphony—*Bloch.*

Istar. Symphonic variations for orchestra by Vincent d'Indy, op. 42 (1896), introduced at an Ysaÿe Concert in Brussels on Jan. 10, 1897. Its inspiration was the Babylonian poem, *Istar's Descent into Hades.* The Daughter of Sin passes through seven gates in her progress to Istar. At each gate she removes one of her garments until, at the seventh gate, she disrobes completely and enters the "immutable land" nude. While structurally *Istar* is a theme and variations, it departs from accepted procedures by presenting its theme after, not before, the variations. The first variation offers an oriental melody in the first horn; the woodwinds reply with a countertheme. In the six ensuing variations, fragments of the main theme are suggested. Only when Istar passes through the seventh gate does the main theme finally emerge, a melody in octaves.

Istesso tempo, L'. The same speed.

Istomin, Eugene, pianist. Born New York City, Nov. 26, 1925. He attended the Curtis Institute, a pupil of Rudolf Serkin and Mieczyslaw Horszowski. In 1943 Istomin won the Philadelphia Youth Contest, which led to his début as soloist with the Philadelphia Orchestra, Eugene Ormandy conducting. This was followed by an appearance with the New York Philharmonic, under Artur Rodzinski, brought on by the winning of the Leventritt Award. Performances throughout the United States were followed by a European tour in 1950 which included appearances with Pablo Casals at the Prades Festival. He also appeared in other areas, including the Far East in 1956, and at the Casals Festival in Puerto Rico in 1957, 1958, and 1959.

Italia. Rhapsody for orchestra by Alfredo Casella (1909), first performed in Paris on April 23, 1910, the composer conducting. This was Casella's first successful work for orchestra. It reflects Sicilian and Neapolitan life and makes use of Italian folk melodies. The opening theme is a song often heard in the province of Caltanisetta. This is followed by a tune from Sicilian sulphur mines; a stately hymn heard on Good Friday processions in Caltanisetta; and, as a finale, three popular Italian melodies, *Funiculi, funiculà,* Mario Costa's *Lariulà,* and Paolo Tosti's *Amarechiare.*

Italian Caprice (Tchaikovsky). *See: Capriccio italien.*

Italian Concerto. For solo clavier by Johann Sebastian Bach, published in 1735 in part 2 of his *Clavieruebung.* It derives its name from the fact that the composer here attempted writing for solo keyboard a concerto in the style then established for solo instrument and orchestra by such Italian masters as Arcangelo Corelli. Bach's concerto is in three movements (I. Allegro. II. Andante. III. Presto), the most interesting being the middle one, a soulful, rhapsodic melody in which the homophonic period of the late 18th century is clearly foreshadowed.

Italian Overture. *See:* Overture.

Italian Serenade. For string quartet by Hugo Wolf (1887). The composer originally planned this work as the first movement of an orchestral suite. He wrote fragments of two other movements which were never completed. Then he wrote it as a one-movement composition for string quartet entitled Serenade in G major. Five years after that he scored it for small orchestra. The main melody is an Italian folksong formerly played in Italy on a pastoral instrument called the "piffero."

Italian Symphony. *See:* Symphony—*Mendelssohn.*

Italian Woman in Algiers (L'Italiana in Algeri), Overture to The. Overture to a comic opera by Rossini introduced at Venice in 1813. The libretto is by Angelo Anelli. The overture opens with a slow section in which a tender melody for oboe is dominant. After a Rossini crescendo, the main body of the overture arrives with a jolly tune for woodwinds. The second theme, for oboe, is also bright. After both melodies are developed and recapitulated, the overture ends with a dramatic crescendo.

Iturbi, José, pianist and conductor. Born Valencia, Spain, Nov. 28, 1895. After studying the piano with Joaquin Malats in Barcelona, he attended the Paris Conservatory, from which he was graduated with honors when he was seventeen. From 1919 to 1923 he was head of the piano department at the Geneva Conservatory. In 1923 he launched his career as a piano virtuoso with a successful performance in London; this was followed by a tour of Europe. He made his American début in 1928 as soloist with the New York Philharmonic. He was so successful that the following season he was engaged to give 77 concerts throughout the United States, five of them in Carnegie Hall. Iturbi has also distinguished himself as a conductor, a field in which he made his début at Mexico City in 1933. In 1934 he made guest appearances with American orchestras, and from 1936 to 1947 he was principal conductor of the Rochester Philharmonic. After that he appeared throughout the world as both pianist and conductor. His sister, Amparo (born Valencia, Spain, March 12, 1899), is also a concert pianist. She has appeared with her brother in performances of two-piano music.

Ivanhoe. *See:* Scott, Sir Walter.

Ives, Charles Edward, composer. Born Danbury, Conn., Oct. 20, 1874; died New York City, May 19, 1954. His father was a Civil War bandmaster who had experimented with new musical systems and acoustics; it is from him that Charles received both his first musical training and a lifelong passion for exploring new musical horizons. After additional music study with Dudley Buck, Harry Rowe Shelley, and Horatio Parker, Ives became the organist of a Danbury church. In 1908 he was graduated from Yale. He then entered the insurance business, a field in which he achieved success. Up until 1930 he combined insurance with musical composition, most of the latter being done on holidays or late at night. In his earliest songs, dating from 1894, Ives already experimented with unusual polytonal combinations; and in his first quartet and symphony, in 1896, he made audacious use of unusual harmonies and rhythms. His first major work was the Third Symphony, written between 1901 and 1904. It was not performed until forty years later, when it received the Pulitzer Prize in music, and an award from the New York Music Critics Circle. Ives continued producing important works, each increasingly daring in idiom and technique. All were ignored by his contemporaries, so much so that Ives remained for many years an obscure and unknown figure in American music, his works collecting dust on the shelf. But these compositions were many years ahead of their time. Ives used polyrhythms before Béla Bartók; polytonality before Darius Milhaud; quarter tones before Alois Hába; tone clusters before Henry Cowell. If he was ultramodern even before the era of the ultramoderns, he was also an American composer long before Americans took to writing American music. His inspiration came from American customs, culture, scenes, politics, holidays, and history. In its strength and individuality, brusqueness and severity, this music was completely independent of European styles. Most of Ives' best-known works were completed in the early 1900's, all before 1920. After withdrawing from business in 1930, he lived the life of a recluse in Connecticut, fastidiously avoiding contact with the world outside. Even when he finally received public recognition in old age, he preferred to ignore it, still maintaining aloofness from the press, photographers, admiring visitors, and even professional musicians. His major works include 4 symphonies, 2 orchestral sets (including *Three Pieces in New England*), 2 overtures for orchestra, 5 violin sonatas, a string quartet, and 2 piano sonatas (including the *Concord*).

See: Three Places in New England; Sonata—*Ives;* Symphony—*Ives.*

J

Jacobi, Frederick, composer. Born San Francisco, Calif., May 4, 1891; died New York City, Oct. 24, 1952. He studied music in the United States with Rubin Goldmark, Rafael Joseffy, and Ernest Bloch; and in Europe at the Berlin High School for Music. His first significant works, influenced by his researches in the music of the American Indian, include the *String Quartet on Indian Themes,* and *Indian Dances* for orchestra. This phase was followed by another in which Jacobi's style became Hebraic in its employment of the melodic, rhythmic, and spiritual values of Jewish religious music. In this vein he wrote the Sabbath Evening Service, *Hagiographia* for string quartet and piano, and *Two Pieces in the Sabbath Mood,* for orchestra. While Jacobi continued writing Hebraic works for the rest of his life, he also produced other works representing a skilful synthesis of Classical, Romantic, and modern tendencies. Besides compositions already mentioned, Jacobi wrote 2 symphonies, various concertos for solo instruments and orchestra (cello; piano; violin), a piano concertino, various shorter works for orchestra or for solo instruments and orchestra, 2 string quartets, and numerous compositions for the piano.

Jacobi had a fruitful career as a teacher of composition at the Juilliard School of Music in New York and the Julius Hartt Musical Foundation in Hartford, Conn.

Jadassohn, Salomon, teacher. Born Breslau, Germany, Aug. 13, 1831; died Leipzig, Germany, Feb. 1, 1902. His musical education took place at the Leipzig Conservatory, and privately with Liszt, among others. In 1852 he settled in Leipzig where he remained for the rest of his life, first as a teacher of music, and from 1871 on as professor of composition and instrumentation at the Leipzig Conservatory. His texts on harmony, canon, fugue form, and counterpoint have been widely translated, and have been used by leading conservatories.

Jamaican Rhumba (Benjamin). *See: Two Jamaican Pieces.*

Janáček, Leoš, composer. Born Hukvaldy Moravia, July 3, 1854; died Ostrau, Czechoslovakia, Aug. 12, 1928. After studying music in Bruenn and at the Prague Organ School he settled in Bruenn in 1875 as a teacher of music. Three years later he visited Vienna and Leipzig for additional study at their Conservatories. Returning to his native land, he became a dominating figure in its musical life. He established and conducted orchestral concerts; he founded, and later directed, the Organ School and the Conservatory of Bruenn. In 1896 he paid the first of several visits to Russia, when his interest in Russian literature and language was aroused; the Russian influence was soon felt in his musical writing. A second important creative influence was the folk music of Moravia, of which he made an exhaustive study. Stimulated by Moravian folk music, Janáček created his own musical system derived from folk elements in which melody and rhythm were molded after the inflections and rhythms of speech. This new style was crystallized in his operas, especially in his masterwork, *Jenufa;* but it is also evident in his orchestral and chamber music. In instrumental music his principal works are a Suite for string orchestra, *Idyl* for string orchestra, a rhapsody *Taras Bulba,* a Sinfonietta, and *The Ballad of Blanik,* 2 string quartets, piano trio, violin sonata, *Fairy Tale* for cello and piano, and *Youth* for wind sextet. He also wrote several works for piano including a sonata, *Moravian Dances,* and *National Dances of Moravia.*

See: Sinfonietta; *Taras Bulba.*

Janssen, Werner, conductor and composer. Born New York City, June 1, 1899. In 1921 he was graduated from Dartmouth College with the degree of Bachelor of Music. He then received additional music instruction from Frederick Converse, George Chadwick, and Arthur Friedheim. In 1930 he won the Prix de Rome for composition. While in Italy he began his career as conductor with guest appearances with the Royal Orchestra of Rome. Janssen made his American début as guest conductor of the New York Philharmonic on Nov. 8, 1934. From 1937 to 1939 he was principal conductor of the Baltimore Symphony, from 1946 to 1947 of the Utah Symphony, from 1947 to 1949 of the Portland Symphony in Oregon, and from 1952 to 1954 of the San Diego Orchestra in California. In 1940 he founded, and since then has conducted, the Janssen Symphony, with which he toured South America in 1941.

In his compositions Janssen has made effective use of popular and jazz styles and techniques. His most popular works are for orchestra and include *New Year's Eve in New York, Louisiana Symphony, Dixie Fugue,* and *Foster Suite.*

Jaques-Dalcroze, Émile, teacher and composer. Born Vienna, Austria, July 6, 1865; died Geneva, Switzerland, July 1, 1950. A comprehensive training in music took place in Paris with Léo Delibes, in Vienna with Anton Bruckner, and at the Geneva Conservatory. In 1892 he was appointed professor of harmony at the Geneva Conservatory. It was there that he first evolved his system of eurhythmics, coordinating music with physical movement. Recognition of his method came in 1905. In 1910 he organized an Institute for teaching rhythmical movement in a town near Dresden, Germany; and in 1914 he founded the Jaques-Dalcroze School in Geneva. Schools teaching his methods were subsequently founded in London, Paris, Berlin, Vienna, Stockholm, and New York. The Jaques-Dalcroze method of eurhythmics, in the words of its originator, strove to "create by help of rhythm, a rapid and regular current of communication between brain and body, and to make feeling for rhythm a physical experience." The system was elaborated upon in two publications translated into English as *The Eurhythmics of Jaques-Dalcroze* (1917) and *Rhythm, Music and Education* (1922). Jaques-Dalcroze was also the author of an autobiography, *Souvenirs* (1942).

Jardins sous la pluie (Debussy). *See: Estampes.*

Jazz. A style of American popular music which reached its heyday in the 1920's. It evolved from the ragtime music of Negro bands popular in New Orleans, St. Louis, and Chicago. Among the characteristics differentiating jazz from other forms of American popular music are its marked syncopations against a steady four-beat rhythm; prominence of certain "blue" notes (minor thirds, flatted sevenths);

characteristic "breaks," or improvised comments by solo instruments; and the cultivation of strange and original tone colors through the unorthodox use of wind instruments. The repertory of serious music abounds in works in which jazz techniques and styles are successfully exploited. The following are some composers, European as well as American, who have used jazz with serious purpose: Georges Auric (*Adieu New York*, fox trot for piano); Robert Russell Bennett (*Charleston Rhapsody*, for orchestra; Concerto Grosso for orchestra and jazz band; Variations on a Theme by Jerome Kern for orchestra; March for two pianos and orchestra); Leonard Bernstein (*Fancy Free*, ballet suite; *The Age of Anxiety*, symphony); John Alden Carpenter (*Skyscrapers*, ballet suite); Aaron Copland (*Music for the Theatre* for orchestra; Concerto for Piano and Orchestra); George Gershwin (*Rhapsody in Blue;* Concerto for Piano and Orchestra; *An American in Paris;* Second Rhapsody for orchestra; *Variations on I Got Rhythm* for piano and orchestra; piano preludes); Morton Gould (Symphony No. 3; *Chorale and Fugue in Jazz; Swing Sinfonietta; Boogie-Woogie Etude* for orchestra; *Interplay* for piano and orchestra); Ferde Grofé (*Grand Canyon Suite, Shades of Blue,* and *Metropolis,* all for orchestra); Louis Gruenberg (*Daniel Jazz,* for tenor and eight instruments; *Jazz Suite* for orchestra); Paul Hindemith (*Kammermusik* No. 1); Arthur Honegger (Concertino for Piano and Orchestra); Charles Ives (*Central Park in the Dark,* for orchestra); Werner Janssen (*New Year's Eve in New York* for orchestra); Constant Lambert (*Rio Grande* for orchestra); Rolf Liebermann (Concerto for Jazz Band and Orchestra); Charles Martin Loeffler (*La bonne chanson;* and *Clowns*); Frank Martin (*Foxtrot,* for two pianos); Robert McBride (*Swing Stuff,* for clarinet and piano; *Jam Session* for wind quintet; *Strawberry Jam* for orchestra); Darius Milhaud (*La Création du monde,* ballet suite; *Rag Caprice* for piano and orchestra; *Le Boeuf sur le toit,* ballet suite; and *Caramel Mou,* a shimmy for jazz band); Marcel Poot (*Jazz Music*); Maurice Ravel (Concerto for Piano, Left Hand, and Orchestra; Sonata for Violin and Piano); Erik Satie (*Parade*); Igor Stravinsky (*Ragtime,* for eleven instruments; *Ragtime,* for piano; *Ebony Concerto; L'Histoire du soldat*); William Walton (*Façade,* suites).

Brandeis University in Waltham, Mass., commissioned six American composers to write serious musical works in a jazz style for its festival in 1957. These composers were: Harold Shapero, Milton Babbitt, George Russell, Jimmy Giuffre, Charles Mingus, and Gunther Schuller.

Jean-Christophe. A cyclical musical novel by Romain Rolland (1905-1913). It was responsible for bringing its author the Nobel Prize for literature. The novel traces the personal history of a fictional contemporary German composer and describes his artistic struggles. Episodes from this novel were the source of two tone poems for orchestra by Charles Koechlin, both entitled *Le Buisson ardent.*

Jena Symphony. A symphony attributed to Beethoven, discovered in 1909 in the archives of a Jena concert society and published by Breitkopf and Haertel in 1911. It is now known to have been written by Friedrich Witt.

Jeremiah Symphony. See: Symphony—Bernstein.

Jeu de cartes (Stravinsky). *See: Card Game.*

Jeune France, La. A group of 20th-century French composers that included Olivier Messiaen, Daniel-Lesur, Yves Baudrier, and André Jolivet. They made their collective appearance at a concert in Paris on June 3, 1936, an occasion upon which they issued a manifesto expressing their dedication to "the dissemination of works, youthful, free, as far removed from revolutionary formulas as from academic formulas." An avowed mission was the establishment of deeper spiritual values in music, "a living music . . . with nothing less than sincerity, generosity, and artistic good faith."

Jeunesse d'Hercule, La (The Youth of Hercules). Tone poem by Saint-Saëns, op. 50 (1877), first performed in Paris on Jan. 28, 1877. The score explains that "Hercules on his entrance upon life saw two roads . . . that of pleasure and that of virtue. Insensible to the seduction of nymphs and bacchantes, the hero chooses the paths of struggle and combat, at the end of which he catches a glimpse of the reward of immortality, through the flames of the funeral pyre." The tone poem opens with muted violins against other strings and woodwind. A roll of the timpani introduces the first subject in the strings. The second theme is later given by flute and clarinet. A quick section for flute leads to a return of the first idea which is now brought to a powerful climax. The second idea is recalled by woodwind, harp, and horns. It is the first subject that brings the music to its conclusion.

Jeux d'eau (The Fountain). For piano by Ravel (1901), introduced in Paris by Ricardo Viñes on April 5, 1902. It was inspired by the sound of water in streams, cascades, and fountains. The composer's stimulus came from a line by H. de Regnier: "A river god laughing at the waters as they caress him." This is one of Ravel's earliest piano pieces, and it was revolutionary in its exploration of new piano sonorities, resonances, and colors. Its influence on Ravel's contemporaries, Debussy included, was profound.

Jeux d'eaux à la Villa d'Este, Les (Liszt). *See: Années de pèlerinage.*

Jig. *See:* Gigue.

Joachim, Joseph, violinist, teacher, and composer. Born Kittsee, Pressburg, Germany, June 28, 1831; died Berlin, Germany, Aug. 15, 1907. A child prodigy, he made his first public appearance when he was seven. In 1841 he began studying the violin in Vienna with Miska Hauer and G. Hellmesberger the elder. Performances in Leipzig and London in 1843 and 1844 were so successful that extensive tours of Europe were undertaken. Nevertheless, feeling the need for more study, Joachim settled in Leipzig, where he studied with Ferdinand David and remained until 1849. There he became intimately associated with Mendelssohn and Schumann. In his last years in Leipzig he took over Ferdinand David's chair as concertmaster of the Gewandhaus Orchestra. In 1849 Joachim was appointed concertmaster of the Weimar Orchestra, then conducted by Liszt; and in 1854 he as-

sumed the post of solo violinist and conductor for the court at Hanover. In 1868 he went to live in Berlin, becoming head of the newly formed department of the Hochschule fuer ausuebende Tonkunst at the Royal Academy of Arts. Through his activity as teacher he helped make Berlin a center of violin instruction for half a century; students from all parts of the world came to Berlin to study with him. All the while he kept on giving concerts in Germany and England, where his preeminence among the violinists of his generation was never questioned. His interpretations of the violin concertos of Bach, Beethoven, Mendelssohn, and Brahms became the criterion by which all other performances were measured. Joachim was also the founder and first violinist of the Joachim Quartet, one of Europe's major chamber-music groups for more than 30 years. He first created it in Berlin in 1869 with Ernest Schiever, violin, Heinrich de Ahna, viola, and Wilhelm Muller, cello. When ill health prevented Joachim from playing further with his Quartet in 1907 his place was taken by Carl Halir; after Joachim's death, the name of the organization was changed to the Halir Quartet.

Joachim wrote numerous works for orchestra and for solo instruments with orchestra. His style was derived from that of Brahms and Schumann. His best known work is the *Hungarian Concerto* in A major for violin and orchestra, op. 11, but even this is not often performed. His cadenzas for the violin concertos of Mozart, Beethoven, and Brahms are still played. Three volumes of his letters were edited by Andreas Moser and Johann Joachim (1911-1913), and a volume of his letters to Brahms was edited by Moser (1908).

Joachim Quartet. *See* above.

Joan of Arc. The 15th-century French heroine and martyr, whose leadership of the French compelled the English to lift the siege of Orleans and who was finally burned at the stake, was the inspiration for several notable instrumental compositions: Jean Absil's tone poem, *Jeanne d'Arc;* Moritz Moszkowski's symphony, *Joan of Arc;* Jean Rivier's tone poem, *Paysage pour Jeanne d'Arc;* Manuel

Rosenthal's suite, *Jeanne d'Arc;* Henri Sauguet's *Dix images pour une vie de Jeanne d'Arc;* and Leo Smit's tone poem, *Joan of Arc.*

See also: Schiller, Friedrich von (*Die Jungfrau von Orleans*).

Jochum, Eugen, conductor. Born Babenhausen, Germany, Nov. 1, 1902. He studied piano and organ at the Augsburg Conservatory and conducting with Sigmund von Hausegger in Munich. After serving an apprenticeship as coach and conductor in opera houses in Kiel and Mannheim, he was appointed principal conductor of the Duisburg Opera in 1930. This marked the beginning of a fruitful career in opera which included performances in major German and Austrian theaters, including the Bayreuth Festival. Jochum has also distinguished himself as a symphony conductor. From 1932 to 1934 he was conductor of the Radio Orchestra in Berlin, and from 1934 to 1945 principal conductor of the Hamburg Philharmonic. In 1949 he helped organize the Radio Symphony in Munich, which he has since conducted with distinction. On Nov. 13, 1958, he made his American début with the Los Angeles Philharmonic. Two of his brothers are professional musicians. Georg Ludwig (born Babenhausen, Dec. 10, 1909) is also a conductor and since 1946 director of the Duisburg Conservatory. Otto (born Babenhausen, March 18, 1898) was director of the Augsburg Conservatory from 1949 to 1952, and is a composer.

Johnson, Thor, conductor. Born Wisconsin Rapids, Wis., June 10, 1913. He was graduated from the University of North Carolina in 1934, then received his Master's degree at the University of Michigan. Later on he studied conducting in Europe with Bruno Walter, Felix Weingartner, and Nikolai Malko. In 1937 he was appointed assistant professor of music at the University of Michigan, where he conducted the Little Symphony of Ann Arbor. During the summers of 1940 and 1941 he studied conducting with Koussevitzky at the Berkshire Music Centre in Tanglewood. While serving in the United States Army during World War II he helped organize and directed

the first all-soldiers' orchestra. After the war he became conductor of the Juilliard School of Music Orchestra. From 1947 to 1957 he was principal conductor of the Cincinnati Symphony. In 1955 he conducted the Symphony of the Air on a tour of the Orient. In 1958 he was appointed director of orchestral activities at Northwestern University in Evanston, Ill. In the same year he was the recipient of the Laurel Leaf Award of the American Composers Alliance for "distinguished service to contemporary music," a service that included conducting 115 world premières.

Jolivet, André, composer. Born Paris, France, Aug. 8, 1905. He engaged in literature, drama, and art before concentrating on music. For many years he studied composition with Paul Le Flem and Edgard Varèse. In 1936 he helped found a new school of French composers identified as "La Jeune France," which sought a revaluation of music in terms of more spiritual values. Jolivet combines religious and mystical concepts with a highly unorthodox musical style exploiting atonality and formerly untried sonorities and instrumental effects. He also explores a seemingly limitless range of rhythmic and dynamic effects. Jolivet has appeared as conductor, and in 1945 he was made director of music of the Comédie-Française. His orchestral works include several concertos (piano; harp; bassoon; Ondes Martenot), *Symphonie de danses, Suite delphique,* trumpet concertino, flute concertino, and *Suite transocéane.* He also wrote a string quartet, a Serenade for oboe and piano, and a *Petite Suite* for flute, viola, and harp, and several compositions for the piano including a sonata.

Jonas, Maryla, pianist. Born Warsaw, Poland, May 31, 1911. She made her first public appearance at the age of nine as soloist with the Warsaw Philharmonic. She later studied privately with Paderewski and Emil Sauer. In 1932 she won the Chopin Prize, and in 1933 the Beethoven Prize in Vienna. During her first tour of Europe she was acclaimed as one of Europe's outstanding women pianists. During World War II she was interned in a concentration camp by the Nazis. Though her father, husband, mother, and brother were all killed by the Nazis, she managed to escape and find a new home in Rio de Janeiro, where she finally returned to the concert stage. She made a highly successful début in the United States on Feb. 25, 1946.

Jongen, Joseph, composer. Born Liège, Belgium, Dec. 14, 1873; died Sart-lez-Spa, Belgium, July 12, 1953. His entire musical schooling took place at the Liège Conservatory. After winning the Belgian Prix de Rome in 1897, he achieved recognition as a composer with a symphony and piano quartet written between 1900 and 1903. For many years he was professor of harmony and counterpoint at the Brussels Conservatory, and from 1925 to 1939 served as its director. Jongen wrote music in virtually every form except opera. His style is Impressionistic and poetic, strongly influenced by Debussy and Franck. His principal orchestral works include 3 suites, concertos (violin; cello; piano; harp), Symphony, trumpet concertino, Suite for viola and orchestra, *Symphonie concertante* for organ and orchestra, and various shorter works including *Lalla-Roukh, Deux Rondes wallonnes, Suite in the Olden Style,* and *In Memoriam.* In chamber music he wrote 3 string quartets, 3 piano trios, 2 quintets for wind instruments, piano quintet, quartet for saxophones, and numerous sonatas for various solo instruments and piano, among many other works; and for piano, a sonata, sonatina, 24 preludes, as well as various etudes, pieces, mazurkas, ballades, and so forth.

Jordá, Enrique, conductor. Born San Sebastian, Spain, March 24, 1911. After studying with local teachers he began conducting performances in his parish church when he was only twelve. At eighteen he went to Paris, where he studied harmony and composition with Paul Le Flem, conducting with Frans Rühlmann, and organ with Marcel Dupré. From 1937 to 1939 he conducted the Basque Ballet. In 1938 he made so successful a début as symphony conductor in Paris that he was invited to Brussels to give several performances. From 1940 to 1945 he was principal conductor of the Madrid Symphony, and beginning with 1945 he made many guest appearances with leading European orchestras. He was principal conductor of the Capetown Symphony in South Africa from 1947 to 1951. His North American début took place at San Francisco in 1952 with the season's opening concert of the San Francisco Symphony. In 1954 he was appointed principal conductor of that organization.

Joseffy, Rafael, pianist and teacher. Born Hunfalu, Hungary, July 3, 1852; died New York City, June 25, 1915. He attended the Leipzig Conservatory, then studied piano in Berlin with Carl Tausig and profited from the guidance and advice of Liszt. In 1870 he made a brilliant début in Berlin. In 1879 he established permanent residence in the United States, making that year his American début with the Leopold Damrosch Orchestra in New York. He was subsequently heard throughout the United States. He was also a distinguished teacher of the piano, a member of the faculty of the National Conservatory in New York from 1888 to 1906. He was the author of a volume of piano studies, *School of Advanced Piano Playing* (1902), and editor of pedagogical works by other musicians. He made many transcriptions for the piano of works by Bach, Gluck, Schumann and others, and was the editor of a 15-volume edition of Chopin's complete works.

Jota. A Spanish dance in quick 3/4 time, accompanied by castanets. Examples of a jota in symphonic music can be found in Manuel de Falla's *Three-Cornered Hat* (Final Dance) and in Glinka's *Jota aragonesa.*

Jota Novarra (Sarasate). *See:* Spanish Dances (2).

Jour d'été à la montagne (d'Indy). *See: Summer Day on the Mountain.*

Joyeuse, La. A rondeau for harpsichord in D major by Rameau in *Pièces de clavecin* (1724). *See:* Rameau, Jean Philippe.

Joyeuse Marche. For orchestra by Emmanuel Chabrier. It originated as a piano piece entitled *Marche française,* written in 1888 for the Bordeaux Conservatory as an exercise in sight-reading. When it was found too difficult for this purpose, the composer orchestrated and renamed it. In this new and definitive version it was introduced in Paris by the Lamoureux Orchestra on Feb. 16, 1890. This music, in the composer's best humorous and exuberant style, is believed to be a description of a group of drunken musicians staggering homeward. The main theme, which appears in the solo oboe after a brief orchestral flourish, is light and capricious; a secondary subject, in violins, is boisterous and gay.

Jubilee. For orchestra by George Chadwick (1895). It is the first section of a suite, *Symphonic Sketches*, which was introduced in Boston on Feb. 7, 1908, Karl Muck conducting. The music is in a spirited carnival mood, opening with a vivacious subject for full orchestra. The main theme is a song for woodwind and horn. The opening idea serves as the principal material for the sprightly coda with which the composition ends.

Jubilee (Jubel) Overture. Concert overture in E major by Carl Maria von Weber, op. 59 (1818), written to celebrate the 50th anniversary of the ascension to the throne of the King of Saxony. A slow introduction, emphasizing the basses, leads to the main section, where the principal theme is loudly stated by full orchestra. A subsidiary idea follows, light and vivacious, and given considerable prominence in the free fantasia development. After a recall of both main themes, the winds present the anthem *God Save the King* against a string accompaniment.

Julius Caesar. *See:* Shakespeare, William.

Jullien, Louis Antoine, conductor. Born Sisteron, France, April 23, 1812; died Paris, France, March 14, 1860. The son of a bandmaster, Jullien attended the Paris Conservatory. In 1836 he led orchestral concerts at the Jardin Turc in Paris. His insolvency led him to flee France. Settling in London, he founded his own orchestra in 1839 with which he presented concerts for many years. In his attempt to popularize music he combined popular and semi-classical compositions with masterworks, often presenting these

with monster-sized ensembles. His unquestioned gift at conducting was combined with eccentricity and partiality to quixotic stunts. He would conduct Beethoven's music with a jeweled baton while wearing gloves; and he would use the most extravagant gestures and showman methods while conducting. In 1853 he toured the United States with his orchestra. Various unfortunate investments once again threw him into debt. When he returned to Paris in 1859 he was arrested and imprisoned. He was soon released, but a few months afterwards he was consigned to an insane asylum. Though primarily a charlatan, he was nevertheless a significant influence in developing both in America and England an interest in serious music.

Jungfrau von Orleans, Die. *See:* Schiller, Friedrich von.

Juon, Paul, composer. Born Moscow, Russia, March 6, 1872; died Vevey, Switzerland, Aug. 21, 1940. He attended the Moscow Conservatory and the Berlin High School for Music, winning the Mendelssohn scholarship at the latter institution. For a while he taught at the Baku Conservatory, but then settled in Berlin, where from 1906 to 1934 he was professor at the High School for Music. Through the influence of the Berlin publisher, Schlesinger, his early works were published and performed, most notably a symphony introduced successfully at Meiningen in 1903. Juon combined German structures and techniques with Slavic rhythms and melodies. In 1919 he was elected to the Berlin Academy of Arts and won the State Beethoven Prize. His principal works for orchestra include a symphony, 2 violin concertos, a symphonic fantasy on Danish folksongs (*Vaegtervise*), *Episodes concertantes*, and a Serenade. He also wrote 2 piano quintets, 3 string quartets, 2 piano trios, 2 violin sonatas, 2 cello sonatas, a viola sonata, 2 divertimentos, and numerous pieces for the piano including waltzes, bagatelles, preludes, capriccios, and a sonatina.

Jupiter Symphony. *See:* Symphony—Mozart.

K

Kabalevsky, Dmitri, composer. Born St. Petersburg, Russia, Dec. 30, 1904. When he was fourteen his family moved to Moscow, where he attended first the Scriabin Music School, then the Moscow Conservatory, from which he was graduated with honors in 1929. After teaching composition at the Scriabin School, Kabalevsky was appointed teacher of composition at the Moscow Conservatory in 1932, a post he still holds. Kabalevsky completed his first symphony in 1930, and enjoyed a major success with his second symphony, introduced at Moscow in 1934 and soon after that heard throughout the world. Kabalevsky became one of the most honored musicians in the Soviet Union, a member of the Presidium of the Organizing Committee of the Union of Soviet Composers in 1939. In 1940 he received the Order of Merit, and after that he was three times honored with the Stalin Prize. After World War II he toured Europe in concerts of his own works. Kabalevsky is a traditionalist who, within accepted structures, gives preference to well sounding melodies and harmonies and vigorous rhythms. He has produced 4 symphonies, several concertos (piano; cello; violin), two orchestral suites (*The Comedians, Pictures for Romeo and Juliet*), 2 string quartets, 3 piano sonatas, 2 piano sonatinas, and 24 preludes for piano.

See: *Colas Breugnon, Overture; Comedians, The;* Concerto—*Kabalevsky;* Sonata—*Kabalevsky;* Symphony—*Kabalevsky.*

Kajanus, Robert, conductor. Born Helsingfors, Finland, Dec. 2, 1856; died there, July 6, 1933. He attended the Conservatories in Helsingfors and Leipzig, then studied privately with Johan Svendsen in Paris. In 1881 he made his début as conductor in Dresden in a program of his own works. He returned to Finland, where in 1886 he founded the Philharmonic Society Orchestra, which he conducted annually in concerts that helped popularize for Finland the music of masters and the moderns; he was responsible for the Finnish première of Beethoven's Ninth Symphony. Kajanus also appeared as guest conductor throughout Europe, where he introduced many Finnish compositions. In 1900 he was invited by the French government to direct a Finnish program at the World Exposition in Paris. He was particularly distinguished as an interpreter of Sibelius, who dedicated to him *Pohjola's Daughter.* From 1897 to 1926 he was director of music at the University of Helsingfors. He went into retirement in 1926.

Kalevala. The national epic of Finland, made up of folk and heroic songs, probably the work of many poets over a period of several generations. The first significant collection was made in 1822. The most important edition is that of Elias Lönnrott (1835), containing over 10,000 verses. His second edition (1849) is the best-known form of the epic; it has 23,000 verses in eight-syllable trochaic and alliterative verses without rhyme. The word "Kalevala" means the "land of Kaleva," Kaleva being an ancient cultural hero of Finland. The main characters of the poem are Kaleva's three sons, Vainämoinen, Ilmarinen, and Lemminkaïnen. The *Kalevala* was the inspiration of several important instrumental works by Sibelius, including the *Four Legends* (in which will be found the celebrated *The Swan of Tuonela*), *Pohjola's Daughter,* and *Kyllikki,* the last being three lyric pieces for the piano. Other Finnish composers were also inspired by the *Kalevala.* Among these were: Robert Kajanus (*Aino,* a symphony); Uuno Klami (*Kalevala Suite* for orchestra and *Lemminkaïnen,* an orchestral scherzo); and Leevi Madetoja (*Kullervo,* tone poem).

Kalinnikov, Vassily, composer. Born Voin, Russia, Jan. 13, 1866; died Yalta, Russia, Jan. 11, 1901. After receiving training at the music school of the Moscow Philharmonic Society he played the bassoon in theater orchestras and served as assistant conductor of the Italian Opera. Tuberculosis compelled him to spend winters in Odessa, and to abandon all musical activity except composition. He scored a major success with his First Symphony which, after its première at Kiev in 1897, was performed throughout Europe; it is still his most popular work. Kalinnikov died at the age of thirty-five and before he could fulfil the promise of his first symphony. He also completed a second symphony, in A major, an orchestral suite, *Two Symphonic Sketches,* and *Two Intermezzi* for orchestra, together with a string quartet and some piano pieces.

See: Symphony—*Kalinnikov.*

Kalkbrenner, Friedrich, pianist and composer. Born near Cassel, Germany, Nov. 1785; died Deuil, France, June 10, 1849. For four years he attended the Paris Conservatory, graduating in 1802 with first prizes in piano and harmony. After some additional study in Vienna he made his first concert appearances between 1805 and 1806 in Berlin, Munich, Stuttgart, and Paris. From 1814 to 1823 he lived in London, where he was successful as teacher and performer. In 1824 he went to Paris where he also achieved considerable popularity for his salon pieces for the piano. Most of these are now forgotten, but his etudes for the piano are still used profitably by piano students.

Kamarinskaya. Fantasy for orchestra by Glinka (1848). Originally entitled "Wedding Song and Dance Song," this composition is made up of two folksongs heard by the composer at a Russian wedding. One is a marriage song, *Over the Hills, the High Hills,* presented in the strings after a few introductory measures. The other, a dance song, *Kamarinskaya,*

is played by first violins after a short development of the first melody. In Tchaikovsky's diary (July 9, 1888) he noted that in this orchestral work Glinka intended "a simple, humorous trifle" but succeeded in producing a "little masterpiece, every measure of which is the outcome of enormous creative power."

Kammermusik. (1) German for chamber music.

(2) Seven works for chamber orchestra, or for solo instrument and chamber orchestra, by Paul Hindemith. These works are such a successful fusion of counterpoint and modern idioms that they were once described in Germany as "Brandenburg Concertos—upside down." It is with these compositions that Hindemith first attracted attention to his powerful creative individuality. The seven works are as follows: No. 1, for chamber orchestra, op. 24, no. 2 (1922); No. 2, for piano and 12 solo instruments, op. 36, no. 1 (1924); No. 3, for cello and 10 solo instruments, op. 36, no. 2 (1925); No. 4, for violin and chamber orchestra, op. 36, no. 3 (1925); No. 5, for viola and chamber orchestra, op. 36, no. 4 (1927); No. 6, for viola d'amore and chamber orchestra, op. 46, no. 1 (1930); No. 7, for organ and chamber orchestra, op. 46, no. 2 (1930).

Kammersymphonie (Chamber Symphony). For 15 solo instruments by Schoenberg, op. 9 (1906), introduced in Vienna on March 31, 1913. This work represents a transition from the composer's earlier methods to later ones. It is one of the last by Schoenberg to utilize tonality, and one of his first to suggest his subsequent atonal writing and even the twelve-tone technique. The first main theme is given by the horn and built from fourths; it recurs throughout the composition. After a melody for horn, a brief motif leads into a cadence which in turn is the preface to a second important subject suggesting the twelve-tone style. The development of these basic ideas, and some subsidiary material, is concise. This work is scored for 10 wind instruments and 5 strings. Each instrument is regarded by the composer as a solo instrument, accorded full individuality. The composer later rescored this work for full orchestra, op. 9-b (1935). He also composed a Second Chamber Symphony, op. 38 (1939).

Kansas City Philharmonic. A symphony orchestra founded in Kansas City, Mo., in 1933 by Karl Krueger. Krueger remained principal conductor until 1943, when he was succeeded by Efrem Kurtz. Hans Schwieger has been principal conductor since 1948. The orchestra performs in Music Hall.

Kapell, William, pianist. Born New York City, Sept. 20, 1922; died near San Francisco, Calif., Oct. 29, 1953. He was a pupil of Olga Samaroff in Philadelphia, after which he attended the Juilliard School in New York. In 1940 he won the Philadelphia Youth Contest, which brought him an appearance with the Philadelphia Orchestra. Winning the Naumburg Foundation Award enabled him to make his début recital in New York on Oct. 28, 1941, a performance that brought him the Town Hall Endowment Series Award. In 1942 Kapell made his first concert tour of the United States. In 1945 he became the first American instrumentalist invited to tour Australia since World War II, and two years after that he made his first tour of Europe. A versatile artist, equally distinguished in all styles and schools, Kapell was particularly brilliant in contemporary concertos by Khatchaturian, Prokofiev, and Rachmaninoff. He was returning from a two-month tour of Australia when his plane crashed into a mountainside near Half Moon Bay, only a few minutes away from his San Francisco destination. He was killed instantly.

Kapellmeister. German for conductor. Originally the term referred to the director of the musical establishment of a court or church or cathedral.

Karajan, Herbert von, conductor. Born Salzburg, Austria, April 5, 1908. He studied the piano at the Mozarteum in Salzburg, and conducting with Franz Schalk. His conducting début took place at Salzburg in 1927, after which he filled minor opera posts in Ulm and Aachen. In 1937 a guest appearance with the Berlin Philharmonic proved so successful that he was assigned to reorganize the symphony concerts of the Berlin State Opera Orchestra, which he directed from 1938 to 1945. After World War II he emerged as one of the most important conductors to appear since the war. He conducted the concerts of the Vienna Philharmonic; was a member of the board of directors reorganizing the Salzburg Festival; was made artistic director of the Gesellschaft der Musikfreunde in Vienna. In 1950 he directed the International Bach Festival in Vienna, and in 1951 the entire *Ring* cycle of Wagner at the Bayreuth Festival. He also scored major successes at the Salzburg and Lucerne festivals, became conductor of the Berlin Philharmonic, and of the London Philharmonia Orchestra with which he toured Europe and made numerous recordings. When the Berlin Philharmonic made its first tour of the United States in 1954, Karajan substituted for the recently-deceased Wilhelm Furtwaengler as its conductor, making his American début in Washington, D.C. late in February 1955. Karajan returned to the United States in the fall of 1955 for a transcontinental tour of the Philharmonia Orchestra of London; and during the 1958-1959 season he made his first appearance with an American orchestra as guest conductor of the New York Philharmonic. In 1954 Karajan succeeded Furtwaengler as musical director of the Berlin Philharmonic, a lifetime appointment. Soon after that he was also appointed musical director of the Vienna State Opera and the Salzburg Festival.

Katims, Milton, violist and conductor. Born Brooklyn, N.Y., June 24, 1909. He studied viola and conducting with various teachers including Seth Bingham and Leon Barzin. He made his début as violist in 1934 with the Wallenstein Sinfonietta over the radio. In 1943 he was appointed by Toscanini first violist of the NBC Symphony, and four years after that he conducted that orchestra in several concerts. Beginning with 1952 he made guest appearances as conductor throughout the United States, Europe, and Israel. In 1954 he was appointed principal conductor of the Seattle Symphony. From 1946 to 1953 he taught a master class in viola at the Juilliard School of Music.

Keats, John, poet. Born London, England, Oct. 31, 1795; died Rome, Italy, Feb. 23, 1821. Many of Keats' poems were the inspiration for instrumental compositions. These compositions include: Frank Bridge's tone poem, *Isabella;* Benjamin Britten's Serenade for voice and orchestra (7th part); Frederick Converse's tone poem, *Endymion's Narrative;* Arthur Hinton's orchestral suite, *Endymion;* Edward MacDowell's tone poem, *Lamia;* Sir Alexander Mackenzie's ballad for orchestra, *La Belle Dame sans Merci;* and Ernst Toch's dramatic prelude, *Hyperion.* In addition, Sir Hubert Parry wrote incidental music for *Proserpine.*

Keilberth, Joseph, conductor. Born Karlsruhe, Germany, April 19, 1908. After studying music with private teachers in his native city, Keilberth became coach and conductor at the Karlsruhe State Theater. From 1940 to 1945 he was principal conductor of the Prague Philharmonic and a conductor of the Berlin Philharmonic, and from 1945 to 1951 he was conductor at the Dresden State Opera. In 1951 he helped found the Bamberg Philharmonic, which he has since directed, and with which he toured Europe, Cuba, and Mexico. He has also appeared as guest conductor of major orchestras throughout Europe. He made his American début in New York on April 4, 1954.

Kell, Reginald, clarinetist. Born York, England, June 8, 1906. He attended the Royal College of Music in London. In 1932 he was appointed first clarinetist of the then recently founded London Philharmonic Orchestra. He subsequently held a similar post with other notable English orchestras including the London Symphony, Liverpool Philharmonic, and the Royal Philharmonic Society. From 1935 to 1948 he taught the clarinet at the Royal Academy of Music in London. In 1948 Kell established permanent residence in the United States, where he devoted himself to concert work and teaching. Kell has appeared as soloist with major orchestras and chambermusic ensembles.

Kelley, Edgar Stillman, composer. Born Sparta, Wis., April 14, 1857; died New York City, Nov. 12, 1944. He studied music in the United States with Clarence Eddy and other teachers and at the Stuttgart Conservatory in Germany. After returning to the United States in 1880, he played the organ in San Francisco, taught music, wrote music criticisms, and conducted a light opera company. From 1902 to 1910 he taught piano and composition in Berlin and from 1910 until his death was dean of the department of composition at the Cincinnati Conservatory. His first important work was *Aladdin,* an orchestral tone poem in an oriental style. In later works the influence of German post-Romanticism is apparent. Other orchestral works include the suite *Alice in Wonderland, New England Symphony, Israel, Eldorado, The Pit and the Pendulum,* and *Gulliver: His Voyage to Lilliput.* He also wrote a string quartet and piano quintet.

Kempff, Wilhelm, pianist. Born Jueterbog, Germany, Nov. 25, 1895. After studying the piano with his father, and composition with Robert Kahn, he established a reputation as a concert pianist with several successful tours of Europe; one of the features of his concerts was his improvisations. He became particularly famous for his interpretation of Beethoven's sonatas. From 1924 to 1930 he taught piano at the Stuttgart High School for Music. Since 1955 he has made his home in Ammerland, Austria.

Kentner, Louis, pianist. Born Karvin, Hungary, July 19, 1905. From 1911 to 1922 he attended the Academy of Music in Budapest. In 1912 he made his professional début in Budapest, and while still a Conservatory student gave a series of concerts in that city devoted to all the Beethoven piano sonatas. After leaving the Academy he toured Europe, proving himself a vigorous propagandist for contemporary Hungarian piano music. In 1935 he settled in England (later becoming a British subject), where he distinguished himself for his cycles devoted either to a single composer or to a single work like the *Well-Tempered Clavier* of Bach or Liszt's *Années de pèlerinage.* In his concerts in and out of England he also identified himself with contemporary British music, giving premières of works by

William Walton, Michael Tippett, Alan Rawsthorne, and others. In 1954 he toured India with Yehudi Menuhin (his brother-in-law), and in 1956 the Far East. He made a highly successful American début in New York on Nov. 28, 1956.

Kettledrums (or **Timpani**). The principal percussion instrument of the symphony orchestra. Kettledrums come in various sizes and are tuned to specific pitches, according to the requirements of the music being played. They are normally struck by two drumsticks of flexible cane with felt-covered heads. The pitch of the drums can be adjusted by tightening or loosening screws on the rim.

Key. Lever of the mechanism of a musical instrument (keyboard or wind), operated by the performer's fingers; also a series of tones or a scale whose center or point of rest is the tonic from which the key derives its name.

Key Signature. Group of sharps or flats found immediately after the clef at the beginning of each staff, indicating the key of the composition or of a section of it.

Keyboard. Series of black and white keys on the piano or organ.

Keyboard instrument. Any musical instrument manipulated by a keyboard, such as a harpsichord, piano, or organ.

Keynote. The tonic.

Khatchaturian, Aram, composer. Born Tiflis, Russia, June 6, 1903. He did not begin intensive music study until 1923, when he entered the Gniessen Music School in Moscow. Six years later he enrolled in the Moscow Conservatory, where his teachers included Nikolai Miaskovsky and Sergei Vassilenko. He first attracted interest with his First Symphony, introduced at Moscow in 1935; even greater success came with his Piano Concerto, in 1937, which first made him famous outside the Soviet Union. In 1939 he received the Order of Lenin, and in 1940 and 1942 the Stalin Prize. Despite these honors, he was one of many leading composers in the Soviet Union to be violently denounced by the Central Committee of the Communist Party in 1948 for "bourgeois formalism" and "antipopular trends." Yet his music has always had a wide appeal and is easily assimilated at first hearing. His style and idioms are modeled after the highly rhythmic folk dances and the dramatic and improvisational lyricism of the folk songs of Armenia and Transcaucasia. Like the other major Soviet composers, Khatchaturian has completely rehabilitated his position in Soviet music since 1948. In 1954 he conducted a concert of his own works in London. He has also made similar appearances in other European capitals. His major works include 2 symphonies, two orchestral suites derived from his ballet *Gayane*, various concertos (piano; violin; cello; violin and cello), *Russian Fantasy* for orchestra, incidental music to *Masquerade, Overture—Poem* for orchestra, a string quartet, string trio, violin sonata, and some pieces for the piano.

See: Concerto—*Khatchaturian; Gayane; Masquerade;* Symphony—*Khatchaturian.*

Khovantschina, Prelude To. A prelude for orchestra to an opera by Mussorgsky. The libretto was by the composer and Vladimir Stassov, and the opera was introduced in St. Petersburg on Feb. 21, 1886, by an amateur group. The prelude is a landscape which the composer entitled "Dawn on the Moskava River." It consists of a folk melody and five variations. To Oskar Riesemann these variations simulate the tendency of Russian singers to vary the folksong they are performing with each successive stanza.

An entr'acte from *Khovantschina*—appearing before Act 4, Scene 2—is also a concert favorite. This is also a landscape, picturing the vast expanses of the Siberian plains. A bleak, gloomy melody for solo trumpet and violins is the main subject.

Khrennikov, Tikhon, composer. Born Elets, Russia, June 10, 1913. He studied music in Moscow at the Gniessen School and the Conservatory. While at the latter institution he completed a piano concerto which was performed and acclaimed. His First Symphony, finished in 1935, was even more successful and made him known for the first time outside the Soviet Union. In 1936 he was graduated from the Moscow Conservatory. Soon thereafter he assumed an important place in Soviet music with his Second Symphony and an opera, *The Storm*. Other works include incidental music to *Much Ado About Nothing* and *Don Quixote* and some piano pieces.

Kikimora. A fairy tale for orchestra by Anatol Liadov, op. 63 (1909). The composer wrote three such fairy tales, the other two being *Baba-Yaga* and *The Enchanted Lake*. *Kikimora* has a specific program which appears in the published score. "Kikimora (the phantom) is brought up by a sorceress in the mountains. In her youth she is beguiled from early morning to late at night by the tales of foreign lands told by the sorceress' Magic Cat. . . . In seven years the phantom grows up. . . . Kikimora makes all manner of noises from morning to night, then whistles and hisses from early evening to midnight. Then the phantom spins until daylight—and spins and stores up evil in her mind against all mankind." An introductory section in muted lower strings leads to a lugubrious strain in English horn, flute, and oboe over tremolo strings. This theme is elaborated upon, then a presto section brings the work to a dramatic end.

Kinderscenen (Schumann). *See: Scenes from Childhood*.

Kindertotenlieder (Songs for Dead Children). A cycle for voice and orchestra by Gustav Mahler (1902), first performed by the New York Philharmonic on Jan. 26, 1910, the composer conducting. It consists of five elegies by Friedrich Rueckert, a few of many he wrote on the death of his two children. When Mahler's little daughter died of scarlet fever in 1906 he became obsessed with a feeling of guilt that never left him, that her death had been precipitated by his writing this work. The *Kindertotenlieder* is so filled with personal grief that it almost seems as if the composer here anticipates his own later tragedy. The five elegies, which pass from resignation to subdued pathos to outright tragedy are: I. *Once more the sun would gild the morn;* II. *Ah, now I know why oft I caught you gazing;* III. *When my mother dear;* IV. *I think oft they've gone abroad;* V. *In such a tempest*.

Kindler, Hans, cellist and conductor. Born Rotterdam, Holland, Jan. 8, 1892; died Watch Hill, R.I., Aug. 30, 1949. He won first prizes in piano and cello at the Rotterdam Conservatory. When he was seventeen he appeared as cello soloist with the Berlin Philharmonic. Two years later he was appointed professor of the cello at the Scharwenka Conservatory in Berlin. Later on he played the cello in the orchestra of the Berlin Royal Opera and appeared as virtuoso throughout Europe. From 1914 to 1920 he was first cellist of the Philadelphia Orchestra. He resigned this post to resume his concert activity, giving over one hundred concerts in the United States and Europe in a single year, besides performances in India and Java. He made his conducting début at Philadelphia in 1927. In 1931 he helped found the National Symphony Orchestra in Washington, D.C., which he conducted until 1948. In 1939 he received the Elizabeth Sprague Coolidge medal for distinguished services to chamber music.

King David. *See:* Honegger, Arthur.

King Lear. *See:* Shakespeare, William.

King's Hunt. *See:* Bull, John.

Kirkpatrick, Ralph, harpsichordist. Born Leominster, Mass., June 10, 1911. He completed his academic education at Harvard, after which he went to Europe on a traveling fellowship to study harpsichord with Wanda Landowska and Arnold Dolmetsch among others. In 1933-1934 he taught the harpsichord at the Mozarteum in Salzburg, and in 1934 he joined the faculty of the Jaques-Dalcroze School in New York. His American début as harpsichordist took place in New York in 1934. Three years later he helped inaugurate an annual festival of old music at the Governor's Palace in Williamsburg, Va. In 1937 a Guggenheim Fellowship enabled him to do research in the techniques and styles of musical performance in the 17th and 18th centuries. He subsequently did research in the life and music of Domenico Scarlatti which resulted in a definitive biography (1953) and a recording and edition of 60 Scarlatti sonatas. In 1944 he made the first of many transcontinental tours of the United States, and since

1947 he has been performing in various countries. He has been a member of the music faculty of Yale since 1940.

Kiss for Cinderella, A. *See:* Barrie, Sir James.

Klavier. German for keyboard or a keyboard instrument, such as the harpsichord, piano, or clavichord.

Kleiber, Erich, conductor. Born Vienna, Austria, Aug. 5, 1890; died Zurich, Switzerland, Jan. 27, 1956. While studying music privately and at the Prague Conservatory, he pursued a comprehensive academic course of studies in Vienna and Prague. In 1912 he became conductor of the Darmstadt Opera. In the ensuing years he became famous as an opera conductor at the Berlin State Opera and the National Theater in Prague among other European theaters. At the same time he made guest appearances with leading European symphony orchestras. He made his American début as a symphony conductor with the New York Philharmonic on Oct. 2, 1930. When, in 1935, Wilhelm Furtwaengler was compelled by the Nazi officials to resign his musical posts in Germany, Kleiber withdrew from his opera post with the Berlin State Opera in protest and left the country. From 1935 to 1949 he led opera and symphony performances in South America. From 1944 to 1947 he was principal conductor of the Havana Philharmonic. After 1949 he returned to Europe, where he became principal conductor, then music director, of the Berlin State Opera in East Germany. He left this post in protest against interference by the Communist authorities with the artistic policies of the company.

Kleine Nachtmusik, Eine (Mozart). *See: Eine kleine Nachtmusik.*

Klemperer, Otto, conductor. Born Breslau, Germany, May 14, 1885. He received his musical training at the Hoch Conservatory in Frankfort and with Xaver Scharwenka, James Kwast, and Hans Pfitzner in Berlin. His apprenticeship as conductor was served under Oskar Fried and Gustav Mahler. The latter recommended him for the post of conductor at the German National Theater in Prague in 1907, and after that for the Hamburg Opera. In 1917 Klemperer be-

came director of the Cologne Opera; it was in that city that he conducted his first orchestral concerts. From 1924 to 1926 he was musical director of the Berlin Volksoper and from 1927 to 1933 of the Berlin State Opera. He achieved world recognition in opera, especially in the modern repertory. But he was also an important symphony conductor. He made his American début on Jan. 24, 1926, with the New York Symphony Society and from 1933 to 1939 was music director of the Los Angeles Philharmonic. In 1939 he was operated upon for a tumor on the brain. After a long period of convalescence he resumed his career with extensive appearances both in opera and symphonic music in Europe. From 1947 to 1950 he was principal conductor of the Budapest Opera.

Klenau, Paul von, conductor and composer. Born Copenhagen, Denmark, Feb. 11, 1883; died there, Aug. 31, 1946. His musical education took place mainly at the Berlin High School for Music with Max Bruch, in Munich with Ludwig Thuille, and at Stuttgart with Max von Schillings. After returning to his native land he devoted himself to conducting and composition. In 1922 he founded, and up to 1930 directed, the Copenhagen Philharmonic. During this period he made many guest appearances with major European orchestras. He was a vigorous propagandist for contemporary music, and an outstanding interpreter of Delius. As a composer, he is best known for his operas; but he also wrote 3 symphonies, 3 orchestral fantasies after Dante, and other orchestral, chamber, and piano compositions.

Klengel, Julius, cellist. Born Leipzig, Germany, Sept. 24, 1859; died there, Oct. 27, 1933. He studied cello with Emil Hegar and theory and composition with Salomon Jadassohn. He was only fifteen when he joined the cello section of the Leipzig Gewandhaus Orchestra. He remained with that orchestra fifty years, becoming first cellist in 1881. Meanwhile, in 1875, he began an equally active career as cello virtuoso. He also distinguished himself as a teacher, being appointed in 1881 Royal Professor of the cello at the Leipzig Conservatory. He wrote many works for the cello, including a concerto for cello and orchestra, a concerto for two cellos and orchestra, and a concerto for violin, cello, and orchestra.

Kletzki, Paul (born **Pawel Klecki**), conductor. Born Lodz, Poland, March 21, 1900. After completing his studies in Poland and Berlin he played the violin in the Lodz Philharmonic from 1914 to 1919. In 1921 he settled in Berlin as violinist and teacher, and for several years after 1933 he lived in Italy. After the end of World War II he made many appearances as guest conductor of European orchestras and in Israel. In 1954 he was appointed principal conductor of the Liverpool Philharmonic. His American début took place with the Cincinnati Symphony on Jan. 17, 1958. Later the same year he was engaged as principal conductor of the Dallas Symphony.

Klindworth, Karl, pianist and conductor. Born Hanover, Germany, Sept. 25, 1830; died Stolpe, Germany, July 27, 1916. He studied piano mostly by himself, and for two years with Liszt in Weimar. In 1854 he settled in London, where he remained fourteen years, conducting orchestras, appearing as piano virtuoso, and organizing chamber-music concerts. In 1868 he went to Russia, where for a decade or so he served as professor of the piano at the Moscow Conservatory; during this period he issued a piano transcription of Wagner's complete *Ring* cycle. In 1882 he became one of the conductors of the Berlin Philharmonic Orchestra and the principal conductor of the Wagner Verein. He also established a music school in Berlin in 1884 which continued operation until 1893, when it merged with the Scharwenka Conservatory. In 1897 Klindworth went into retirement in Potsdam. He edited Beethoven's piano sonatas, rescored Chopin's F minor Piano Concerto, and made a transcription for two pianos of Schubert's C major Symphony, and for four hands of Tchaikovsky's *Francesca da Rimini.*

Klingsor's Magic Garden and Flower Maiden's Scene. The sensual music from Act 2 of Wagner's music drama, *Parsifal.* Klingsor, the magician, has put Kundry under his spell, and she must seduce Parsifal. The scene suddenly changes to a magic garden filled with beautiful women. When Parsifal appears, the women, dressed in flowers, surround him with song and dance and try to entice him. But when the guileless Parsifal resists their advances, Klingsor hurls at him a magic spear which momentarily remains suspended in mid-air. Parsifal seizes it, makes the sign of the cross, and the magic garden disintegrates.

Kneisel, Franz, violinist. Born Bucharest, Rumania, Jan. 26, 1865; died New York City, March 26, 1926. After attending the Bucharest Conservatory, where he won first prize in violin, he entered the Vienna Conservatory in 1879, once again to win first prize. On Dec. 31, 1882, he made his professional début as soloist with the Vienna Philharmonic. He came to America in 1885, making his American début as soloist with the Boston Symphony on Oct. 31, 1885. From 1885 to 1903 he was concertmaster of the Boston Symphony. From 1903 he devoted himself primarily to solo appearances and performances with the Kneisel Quartet, which he had founded in 1886. The original members of this Quartet were Kneisel himself and Emmanuel Fiedler violins, Louis Svecenski viola, and Fritz Giese, cello. Though the personnel changed through the years, the Kneisel Quartet with Kneisel as first violinist remained one of America's most distinguished chamber music ensembles. It gave its last concert on April 3, 1917, then disbanded. Kneisel was also active as conductor, and was an eminent teacher of the violin. In 1905 he was appointed professor at the Institute of Musical Art in New York, becoming head of the violin department in 1917.

Kneisel Quartet. *See* above.

Knipper, Lev, composer. Born Tiflis, Russia, Dec. 16, 1898. His principal music study took place with Reinhold Glière in Moscow and Philip Jarnach in Berlin. He first attracted attention as a composer with a tone poem, *The Legend of the Plaster Garden,* written in 1924, then introduced by the Philadelphia Orchestra under Stokowski. After that he wrote copiously for orchestra, his main works including 13 symphonies, a violin concerto, various suites, and several shorter works (*Two Preludes on Iranian Themes, Maku, Sia,* and *Fantasy on Two Balkar Themes*).

Knorr, Iwan, teacher. Born Mewe, Germany, Jan. 3, 1853; died Frankfort, Germany, Jan. 22, 1916. After attending the Leipzig Conservatory he lived several years in Russia as a teacher of composition. He settled in Frankfort in 1883, becoming a member of the faculty of the Hoch Conservatory, and in 1908 its director. He was an influential teacher whose pupils included Ernest Bloch, Hans Pfitzner, Ernst Toch, and Cyril Scott.

Knoxville: Summer of 1915. For soprano and orchestra by Samuel Barber (1947), introduced by the Boston Symphony under Koussevitzky, Eleanor Steber soloist, on April 9, 1948. This is a setting of a text by James Agee. The following motto appears under the title in the published score. "We are talking of summer evenings in Knoxville, Tennessee, in the time that I lived there so successfully disguised to myself as a child." The musical setting of the poem is in arioso style with a freely varied metrical beat and is in four sections played without interruption (I. *Andante un poco mosso;* II. *Allegro agitato;* III. Allegretto; IV. Maestoso).

Kochanski, Paul, violinist. Born Odessa, Russia, Sept. 14, 1887; died New York City, Jan. 12, 1934. He was a pupil of Emil Mlynarski at the Warsaw Conservatory. In 1901 he was appointed concertmaster of the Warsaw Philharmonic. Two years later he entered the Brussels Conservatory, where, as a pupil of César Thomson, he won the grand prize in violin. For several years he made successful tours of Europe. From 1907 to 1913 he was professor of violin at the Warsaw Conservatory, and in 1913 he succeeded Leopold Auer at the St. Petersburg Conservatory. In 1919 he left Russia. His American début took place in New York on Feb. 14, 1921, as soloist with the New York Symphony. Three years later he joined the violin faculty of the Juilliard School, where he remained for the rest of his life. He also continued his career as concert violinist, distinguishing

himself for his promotion of modern works for the violin, especially those by Karol Szymanowski. Kochanski was made Chevalier of the Legion of Honor. He transcribed numerous works for the violin.

Kodály, Zoltán, composer. Born Kecskemet, Hungary, Dec. 16, 1882. He entered the Budapest Academy when he was eighteen. Through his fellow student, Béla Bartók, he became vitally interested in Hungarian folk music. With Bartók he did extensive research in this field over a period of many years, uncovering thousands of folksongs and dances. Kodály received his doctorate in music with a thesis on folk music, *Strophic Structure in the Hungarian Folksong* (1906). As was the case with Bartók, Kodály was influenced by Hungarian folk styles and idioms, incorporating some of these elements into his own writing. The modal quality of his tonality, the narrative structure of his lyricism, the brusqueness of his accentuation, the tendency to repeat certain melodic and rhythmic phrases—these are some of the qualities of Kodály's works that originate in Hungarian folksongs and dances. Kodály first achieved prominence as a composer with the *Psalmus Hungaricus* for chorus and orchestra, written in 1923 to honor the 50th anniversary of the union of Buda and Pest. Introduced in Budapest on Nov. 19, 1923, it was a success, and soon performed in major music centers. Two years after that came Kodály's most celebrated composition, the opera *Háry János,* an orchestral suite from which is his most frequently heard work. From 1907 on Kodály taught composition at the Budapest Academy, and for a brief period after 1919 he was also its director. He paid his first visit to the United States in 1946 as delegate to the Congress of International Confederation of Authors Societies held in Washington, D.C. During this visit he appeared as guest conductor with leading American orchestras in his own compositions.

The following are Kodály's principal instrumental works:

Chamber Music: 2 string quartets; cello sonata; Serenade for two violins and viola.

Orchestra: Summer Evening; Theater Overture; Dances of Marosszék (also for piano); *Dances of Galánta; Háry János,* suite; *Peacock Variations;* Concerto for Orchestra; *Funeral Music for the Dead of the War;* Viola Concerto; Concerto for String Quartet and Orchestra.

See: Dances of Galánta; Dances of Marosszék; Háry János; Peacock Variations; Summer Evening.

Koechel, Ludwig Ritter von, naturalist and musicographer. Born Stein, Austria, Jan. 14, 1800; died Vienna, Austria, June 3, 1877. He was a professional botanist and mineralogist. But he became famous in music in 1862 by compiling the first complete and detailed chronological catalogue of Mozart's works, *Chronologisch-thematisches Verzeichniss.* His catalogue numbers are still used to identify Mozart's works.

Koechlin, Charles, composer. Born Paris, France, Nov. 27, 1867; died Canaden, France, Dec. 31, 1950. He did not begin serious music study until his twenty-second year, when he entered the Paris Conservatory, where he remained seven years. After leaving the Conservatory, he lived a retired existence, devoting himself completely to composition. Many of his best orchestral and chamber-music works were influenced by Gabriel Fauré; but he has assumed varied styles ranging from the traditional and the Romantic to the atonal and polytonal. He was exceptionally prolific. His most representative compositions for orchestra included several symphonies, many tone poems (*La Course de printemps, Vers la voûte étoilée, Sur les flots lointains, Méditation de Purun Baghât, La Cité nouvelle rêve d'avenir, Le Buisson ardent, La Loi de la jungle, Les Bandar-Loge,* and *Le Docteur Fabricus*), and numerous shorter compositions. He also wrote many works for various chamber-music groups, including 3 string quartets, a woodwind trio, and various sonatas, and pieces for the piano and for the organ.

Kogan, Leonid, violinist. Born Dniepropetrovsk, Russia, Nov. 14, 1924. He was graduated in 1948 from the Moscow Conservatory, where his principal teacher of the violin had been Abram Yampol-sky. Meanwhile, in 1940, he made his professional début. In 1951 he won first prize in the Queen Elizabeth of Belgium International Competition. A comprehensive tour of the Soviet Union followed, after which Kogan performed throughout Europe, and in South America and Canada. His American début took place in Boston on Jan. 10, 1958, as soloist with the Boston Symphony. Kogan is married to the sister of Emil Gilels, Soviet pianist. He serves as professor of violin at the Moscow Conservatory and has made many chamber-music appearances with Gilels and Mstislav Rostropovich.

Kol Nidrei. For cello and orchestra by Max Bruch, op. 47 (1880), first performed in Leipzig on Oct. 20, 1881, with A. Fischer as soloist with the Gewandhaus Orchestra. The *Kol Nidrei* is a traditional Hebrew melody sung on the eve of the Day of Atonement, the holiest in the Jewish calendar. Bruch bases his principal melody on this old synagogal chant. It is first heard simply in the solo cello, after which it is varied. A second main melody, this time Bruch's own, is then offered by the orchestra and repeated by the solo instrument.

Kolar, Victor, conductor. Born Budapest, Hungary, Feb. 12, 1888; died Detroit, Mich., June 16, 1957. He attended the Prague Conservatory, a pupil of Otakar Ševčík and Antonín Dvořák. From 1905 until 1920 he played the violin in the Pittsburgh Symphony and New York Symphony, and from 1920 to 1941 served first as assistant conductor then as principal conductor of the Detroit Symphony. He wrote a symphony, several tone poems and orchestral suites; one of the last, *Americana,* won first prize in a contest sponsored by the Illinois State Teachers Association in 1914.

Kolisch Quartet. A distinguished chamber-music group founded in Vienna in 1922 by the violinist, Rudolf Kolisch (born Klamm, Austria, July 20, 1896). It was originally called the Vienna String Quartet but in 1928 assumed the name of its founder and first violinist. Its personnel comprised Kolisch and Felix Khuner violins, Jenö Lener, viola, and

Benar Heifetz, cello. After touring Europe several times, the Quartet made its American début in Washington, D.C., in 1945. An unusual feature of this ensemble is that it performed its repertory from memory; another is the fact that Kolisch plays the violin left-handed owing to an early injury to his left hand. The Quartet was responsible for the premières of major works by Alban Berg, Béla Bartók, Arnold Schoenberg, Anton Webern, and others. It was reorganized in 1939 and disbanded in 1942, after which Kolisch played in other chamber-music groups, including the Stradivarius and Pro Arte Quartets.

Kolodin, Irving, music critic. Born New York City, Feb. 22, 1908. After completing music study at the Institute of Musical Art, he became a music critic on the *Brooklyn Eagle,* and in 1932 assistant to W. J. Henderson on the *New York Sun.* From 1937 to 1949 he was first critic on the *Sun,* after which he was appointed music editor of the *Saturday Review.* His books include *New Guide to Recorded Music* (1950), *Orchestral Music* (1955) and *Musical Life* (1958). He was also editor of *The Composer As Listener* (1940, revised 1957).

Konzertmusik. (1) German for concert music.

(2) A number of compositions for various instrumental combinations by Paul Hindemith. *Konzertmusik,* op. 41 (1927), is for a wind band; op. 49 (1931), for piano, brass, and harps; op. 50 (1931), for strings and brass. The last is the one most often heard. It was commissioned for the 50th anniversary of the Boston Symphony, which introduced it on April 3, 1931, under Koussevitzky. It is in two parts. The first, "Moderately Fast, with Force," opens powerfully in unison trumpets and trombones; the second theme is for unaccompanied brass. The forceful accompaniment to the opening subject becomes the principal idea elaborated upon by the strings. The movement ends with a return of the opening strong subject. The second part, "Lively, Slowly, Lively," is a three-voice fugue, its subject first stated in the violins, then taken over by violas, cellos, and basses.

Konzertstueck (or **Concertstueck**). German for concert piece, an extended composition for solo instrument (usually piano) and orchestra. One of the most popular works in this form is the *Konzertstueck* in F minor for piano and orchestra by Carl Maria von Weber, op. 79 (1821). It was introduced in Dresden on June 25, 1821, the composer appearing as soloist. The music portrays the era of the Crusades, and its four movements set forth a specific program (I. *Larghetto affettuoso.* II. *Allegro passionato.* III. *Tempo di marcia.* IV. *Presto giocoso*). In the first movement "the lady sits in her tower . . . gazes sadly in the distance," wondering if she will ever again see her knight, gone these many years in the Holy Land. In the second movement she sees a vision of her knight lying deserted on a battlefield. The third movement presents "knights and squires of the Cross of the Crusaders, banners waving, acclamations of the people." The lady sees her knight and falls into his arms. In the finale the happiness of the lovers is described.

Korngold, Erich Wolfgang, composer. Born Bruenn, Austria, May 29, 1897; died Hollywood, Calif., Nov. 29, 1957. He was the son of the influential Viennese music critic, Julius Korngold (born Brünn, Austria, Dec. 24, 1860; died Hollywood, Calif., Sept. 25, 1945). Erich was exceptionally precocious, starting composition at the age of three. A pantomime completed when he was eleven was performed by the Vienna State Opera, and a piano sonata, written two years after that, was successfully given in Europe and the United States. Korngold achieved his principal successes as a mature composer in the field of opera. In 1936 he left Austria for good and made his home permanently in the United States, where he wrote a considerable amount of music for the motion pictures; he twice won Academy Awards for his screen music. His instrumental works in a more serious vein are distinguished for their integrity and craftsmanship. They include a Symphony in F-sharp, Sinfonietta, various concertos (left-hand piano; violin; cello), *Sursum corda* and *Tomorrow,* both for orchestra, incidental music to *Much Ado About*

Nothing, 2 string quartets, piano quintet, sextet, violin sonata, and piano sonata. **Kostelanetz, André,** conductor. Born St. Petersburg, Russia, Dec. 22, 1901. After attending the St. Petersburg Conservatory, he was appointed assistant conductor of the Imperial Opera in that city. He came to the United States in 1922 and later became a citizen. In 1929 he made his American début as a conductor over the radio networks. In 1930 he initiated a long and rich association with the Columbia Broadcasting System, over whose network he conducted many performances of semi-classical music. He has appeared as guest conductor with the foremost orchestras of Europe both in the serious and the semi-classical repertory. For these performances he has commissioned new works from leading American composers, including Aaron Copland, William Schuman, Virgil Thomson, and Ferde Grofé. During World War II, Kostelanetz led concerts in all theaters of war, for which he was awarded the Asiatic-Pacific ribbon by the United States Army. In 1938 he married the prima donna, Lily Pons.

Koussevitzky, Serge, conductor. Born Vishny-Volotchok, Russia, July 26, 1874; died Boston, Mass., June 4, 1951. When he was fourteen he entered the Moscow Philharmonic School, where he specialized in the double bass. He then played that instrument in the Imperial Orchestra and concertized throughout Russia and Europe, achieving recognition as one of the world's foremost double bass virtuosos. In 1905 he married Natalie Ushkov, daughter of a wealthy merchant. He made his first appearance as a conductor in Berlin on Jan. 23, 1908. In that same year he founded in Russia the Editions Russes de Musique, a publishing house devoted to new Russian music. A year later he organized a symphony orchestra in Moscow. He soon became one of Russia's most influential and dynamic conductors, introducing the works of many new composers, including Stravinsky and Scriabin. In 1910 he made the first of several tours down the Volga, performing with his orchestra in villages and towns that had never before heard a concert. His significant place in Russian music

was fully recognized by the new regime in Russia in 1917, which appointed him director of the State Symphony Orchestra. But in 1920 Koussevitzky lost faith in the Communist regime and left his native land for good to live in Paris. There he created the Concerts Koussevitzky, which for four years introduced to French audiences new music by both Russian and French composers. In 1924 Koussevitzky was appointed principal conductor of the Boston Symphony. The quarter of a century for which he held this post was one of the richest in the history of that orchestra—remarkable not only for the dynamic quality of Koussevitzky's performances in a varied repertory but also for his indefatigable sponsorship of new music, and particularly new American music. The list of his world premières is almost a cross-section of the most significant creative activity in music of that period. But his service to new music did not end there. In 1942 he organized the Koussevitzky Music Foundation, which from then on commissioned new works from the world's foremost composers. Other notable achievements by Koussevitzky in the United States included the growth of the Summer Berkshire Festival in Lenox, Mass., and, on July 8, 1940, the opening on these festival grounds of the Berkshire Music Centre, which immediately became an important summer school of music.

Koussevitzky became an American citizen in 1941. Five years after the death of his wife, Natalie, Koussevitzky married his secretary and niece, Olga Naoumoff. Koussevitzky retired as music director of the Boston Symphony in 1949, approximately two years before his death.

Koussevitzky Music Foundation. A foundation for commissioning new musical works. It was created by Koussevitzky in 1942. Among the many composers who have received commissions from the Foundation are Benjamin Britten (who wrote his world-famous opera, *Peter Grimes,* through this endowment), Igor Stravinsky, Bohuslav Martinu, Béla Bartók, William Schuman, Darius Milhaud, Aaron Copland, Heitor Villa-Lobos, Howard Hanson, David Diamond, Gian Francesco Malipiero, and Arnold Schoenberg.

Krakowiak (or **Cracovienne**). A Polish country dance usually in 2/4 time with syncopations in the even bars. It derives its name from its point of origin—Cracow, Poland. Chopin wrote an effective work in this form for piano and orchestra, op. 14 (1828). Paderewski was especially partial to it, writing six such pieces: op. 3 (1884); op. 5, nos. 1 and 3 (1884); op. 9, nos. 1 and 5 (1884); and *Cracovienne fantastique* in *Humoresques de concert,* op. 14, no. 6.

Krasner, Louis, violinist. Born Cherkassy, Russia, June 21, 1903. He received his musical training at the New England Conservatory, and in Europe with Carl Flesch, Lucien Capet, and Otakar Ševčík. From 1944 to 1949 he was concertmaster of the Minneapolis Symphony, and from 1949 professor of violin and chamber music at Syracuse University. He has concertized throughout the world and was responsible for the world premières of concertos by Alban Berg (which he commissioned) and Arnold Schoenberg.

Kraus, Lili, pianist. Born Budapest, Hungary, April 3, 1905. She began music study in her sixth year at the Budapest Academy where her teachers included Béla Bartók and Zoltán Kodály. After graduating with highest honors in piano, she studied piano privately with Artur Schnabel. She toured Europe extensively, distinguishing herself for her performances of Mozart and contemporary composers. During a world tour in 1942 she was apprehended by the Japanese and interned for three years. After liberation, she was flown by the British forces to Australia, where she made two tours in 1946 and 1947. In 1948 she returned to Europe and became a British subject. Thereafter she made several tours of Europe, South America, and the United States.

Krauss, Clemens, conductor. Born Vienna, Austria, March 31, 1893; died Mexico City, Mexico, May 16, 1954. After attending the Vienna Conservatory he served apprenticeship as a conductor with opera companies in Brünn and Riga. From 1923 to 1927 he was conductor of the Tonkuenstler Konzerte in Vienna. From 1924 to 1929 he was artistic director of the Frankfort Opera, a period in which he also led orchestral performances at the Museum. His later opera posts included the Vienna State Opera, Berlin State Opera, Bavarian State Opera in Munich, and the Bayreuth Festival. But he was also active in symphonic music, leading guest concerts with major European orchestras. He made his American début as guest conductor of the Philadelphia Orchestra in 1929. He was touring South America and Mexico when he was fatally stricken. His wife, Viorica Ursuleac, is a famous opera and concert singer. He often appeared as her piano accompanist at recitals.

Krehbiel, Henry Edward, music critic. Born Ann Arbor, Mich., March 10, 1854; died New York City, March 20, 1923. He studied law in Cincinnati, but abandoned it for journalism by becoming music critic of the Cincinnati *Gazette* in 1874. From 1880 until his death he was the music critic of the New York *Tribune,* an influential figure in the development of American musical culture, and in spreading to Americans the gospel of Wagner, Brahms, Tchaikovsky, and Dvořák. For many years he was program annotator for the New York Philharmonic. His most important books (outside the field of opera) include: *The Philharmonic Society of New York* (1892), commemorating that orchestra's 50th anniversary; *How to Listen to Music* (1896); *Music and Manners in the Classical Period* (1898); and *The Pianoforte and Its Music* (1911). He was translator and editor of Thayer's *Life of Beethoven* (1921) and American editor of the second edition of *Grove's Dictionary of Music and Musicians* (1904-1910).

Kreisler, Fritz, violinist and composer. Born Vienna, Austria, Feb. 2, 1875. He appeared as a child prodigy in Vienna, then attended the Conservatories of Vienna and Paris. In his twelfth year he received the Grand Prix for violin at the Paris Conservatory. One year later he toured the United States in joint recitals with the pianist, Moriz Rosenthal, making his American début in Boston on Nov. 9, 1888. After returning to Vienna he decided to abandon music. For several years he studied medicine at the Vienna Academy. Then, tiring of medicine, he prepared for and passed army examinations with highest honors, serving for a year as officer of an Uhlan regiment. Then, deciding finally to return to the violin, he went through an intensive period of training. His return début took place at Berlin in March 1899, but it was still some time before he achieved recognition. This first occurred in the United States between 1901 and 1903. These performances, and subsequent appearances in Europe, were acclaimed. The grace and charm of his style, his penetrating musical perception, and his over-all culture and humanity gave him a position of first importance among the violinists of his generation.

In the early part of World War I Kreisler served with his Austrian regiment and was wounded in Lemberg. After recovery, he came back to the United States, using his concert appearances to raise money for Austrian war relief. Upon American entry into the war, his position became embarrassing. After some unpleasant episodes at his concerts he went into temporary retirement. He emerged from that retirement only after the war had ended, with a recital in New York in 1919. For the next two decades he maintained his status as one of the world's most highly honored and beloved performers.

Just before World War II Kreisler became a French citizen, and in 1943 an American citizen. Meanwhile, in 1941, he was struck by a motor vehicle while crossing a New York street. After a long illness and slow convalescence, he returned to the concert stage. Near the end of World War II he went into complete and permanent retirement.

Kreisler wrote a library of charming pieces for the violin, staples in the repertory. Among the most popular of these are: *Caprice viennois, La Gitana, Liebesfreud, Liebesleid, Marche miniature viennoise, The Old Refrain, Polichinelle Serenade,* Praeludium and Allegro, Recitative and Scherzo Caprice, *Chanson Louis XIII et Pavane,* Rondino on a Theme of Beethoven, *Schoen Rosmarin, Shepherd's Madrigal, Sicilienne et Rigaudon,* and *Tambourin chinois.* Some of these pieces were at first presented by Kreisler as "transcriptions" of classics by masters like Couperin, Francoeur, Pugnani, Mar-

tini, and others in order to gain for them a wider circulation and greater audience interest. In 1935 Olin Downes, the music critic, tried to trace the origin of the Praeludium and Allegro supposedly by Pugnani. Only then did Kreisler confess that not only this piece, but also most of the others masquerading under the names of old masters and supposedly only arranged by him were of his own creation. For this deception, which for many years had fooled both audiences and critics, Kreisler was severely criticized at the time.

Kreisler also wrote a string quartet in A minor, a violin concerto in the style of Vivaldi, and several excellent cadenzas for the violin concertos of Beethoven, Brahms, Mendelssohn, and Mozart.

Kreisleriana. Cycle of pieces for the piano by Schumann, op. 16 (1838). The title was derived from the name of Johannes Kreisler, a Kapellmeister who was the hero of fantastic tales by E. T. A. Hoffmann in *Fantasiestuecke in Callots Manier.* Schumann's cycle consists of eight fantasies, each a separate entity yet bearing such a subtle relation to the others that they can best be appreciated if played in proper sequence. They alternate passionate moods (nos. 1, 3, 5, 7) with slow lyrical pages (Nos. 2, 4, 6).

Krenek, Ernst, composer. Born Vienna, Austria, Aug. 23, 1900. Between 1916 and 1922 he studied composition with Franz Schreker. He then wrote some string quartets and symphonies that made a good impression. When success came it arrived with an opera in a jazz idiom, *Jonny spielt auf!,* introduced in Leipzig on Feb. 11, 1927. He wrote two more operas in a jazz style, then abandoned this vein for chamber and orchestral music influenced by Schubert's lyricism. A few years later came a new change of idiom, and one to which he has since remained faithful: twelve-tone technique.

Krenek first visited the United States as conductor of the Salzburg Opera Guild. After the *Anschluss* he left Austria for good and returned to America where, in 1945, he became a citizen. He has been a member of the music faculty of several universities and conservatories in the United States. From 1950 on he made several tours of Europe conducting programs of his own works. He is the author of *Music Here and Now* (1939) and a text on twelve-tone technique, *Studies in Counterpoint* (1940). Krenek is a highly prolific composer. His orchestral compositions include 5 symphonies, various concertos (piano; violin; two pianos; violin and piano), Capriccio for cello and chamber orchestra, and numerous shorter works (Theme and Eighteen Variations, Adagio and Fugue, *Symphonic Pieces, I Wonder as I Wander, Eleven Transparencies,* and *Tricks and Trifles*). He also wrote 8 string quartets, violin sonata, harp sonata, viola sonata, 2 sonatas for unaccompanied violin, sonata for unaccompanied viola, suite for unaccompanied cello, as well as other chamber music and 6 piano sonatas, sonatinas, bagatelles, variations, and other pieces for the piano.

Kreutzer, Rodolphe, violinist. Born Versailles, France, Nov. 16, 1766; died Geneva, Switzerland, Jan. 6, 1831. He studied violin with his father, and at the age of 16 became first violin in the royal chapel of Marie Antoinette. He later became violinist in the Théâtre Italien orchestra, and professor of violin at the newly founded Conservatory, both in Paris. In 1797 he toured Italy, Germany, and the Netherlands, his performances attracting considerable acclaim. In 1798, in Vienna, he met Beethoven, who dedicated to him the *Kreutzer Sonata,* which he never played. In 1801 he became solo violinist at the Paris Opéra; in 1802, soloist at the chapel of the First Consul; in 1806, violinist to the Emperor; and in 1815 Maître de la Chapelle for Louis XVIII. From 1816 to 1824 he was conductor at the Académie de Musique. A broken arm compelled him to give up violin playing and teaching in 1826. The last years of his life were embittered by his declining fame and influence. Kreutzer wrote many operas famous in his day, together with 19 violin concertos, 15 string quartets, 15 string trios, and many other smaller instrumental compositions. His most celebrated work is *40 Études, ou Caprices, pour le violon,* which has been adopted by schools and teachers the world over and is one of the foundations of every violinist's training.

Kreutzer Sonata. *See:* Sonata—*Beethoven.*

Krips, Josef, conductor. Born Vienna, Austria, April 8, 1902. He received his musical training at the Vienna Academy. He underwent his first experiences in conducting with several minor opera companies, then as musical director in Dortmund. From 1926 to 1933 he was musical director in Karlsruhe. He then achieved popularity as conductor of the Vienna State Opera and the Salzburg Festival and as professor at the Vienna Academy of Music. During the *Anschluss* he relinquished all his posts, but after the war he returned to the Vienna State Opera. He also made guest appearances with major European symphony orchestras. In 1950 he was appointed principal conductor of the London Symphony, retaining this post five years. In 1953 he was appointed musical director of the Cincinnati May Festival, and in 1954 principal conductor of the Buffalo Philharmonic in New York.

Krueger, Karl, conductor. Born Atchison, Kan., Jan. 19, 1894. He received his academic education at the Universities of Kansas and Heidelberg. At the same time he studied music with private teachers in New York and Boston, and finally conducting with Arthur Nikisch, Felix Weingartner, and Franz Schalk. After serving as conductor of the Vienna State Opera and the Vienna Philharmonic, Krueger was appointed principal conductor of the Seattle Symphony in Washington in 1926. In 1933 he was appointed principal conductor of the Kansas City Philharmonic, and in 1943 of the reorganized Detroit Symphony. He remained in Detroit until its orchestra was temporarily disbanded in 1949. He then founded and directed the short-lived All-American Art Orchestra for radio broadcasts. He is the author of *The Way of the Conductor* (1958).

Kubelik, Jan, violinist. Born Michle, Bohemia, July 5, 1880; died Prague, Czechoslovakia, Dec. 5, 1940. He received his training on the violin at the Prague Conservatory with Otakar Ševčík. His performance at the Conservatory, while he was still a student, drew attention to his impressive technique. Upon his professional début in Vienna on Nov. 26, 1898, he was described by one critic as "a second Paganini." A tour of Hungary, Italy, France, and England brought him to an impressive position among violinists of his time. He made his first tour of the United States in 1901-1902. In 1903 he married a Hungarian countess, after which he became a Hungarian citizen. During the next quarter of a century he toured the United States many times, besides performing in every other music center of the world. Kubelik was the composer of 6 violin concertos, a symphony, and many smaller items for the violin. He also wrote cadenzas for the violin concertos of Beethoven, Brahms, Mozart, Paganini, and Tchaikovsky.

Kubelik, Rafael, conductor. Born Býchory, Bohemia, June 29, 1914. He is the son of Jan Kubelik (see above). After receiving violin instruction from his father he attended the Prague Conservatory, from which he was graduated in 1933 as violinist, conductor, and composer. On Jan. 24, 1934, he made his début as a conductor with the Czech Philharmonic. For three years beginning with 1936 he was acting conductor of that orchestra, with which he toured England and Belgium in 1937; from 1942 to 1948 he was its artistic director. After World War II he appeared as guest conductor throughout Europe and in Russia. He left his native land for good when the Communists seized control, and went to live in London. In 1949 he was appointed conductor of the Concertgebouw Orchestra of Amsterdam, and in November of the same year he made his American début as guest conductor of the Chicago Symphony. From 1950 to 1953 he was principal conductor of the Chicago Symphony, and in 1955 he became musical director of Covent Garden. When the Concertgebouw Orchestra made its first tour of the United States in 1955, Kubelik was one of its conductors.

Kuhnau, Johann, organist and composer. Born Geising, Germany, April 6, 1660; died Leipzig, Germany, June 5, 1722. His musical schooling took place in Dresden and Zittau. In the latter city he was appointed cantor. In 1682 he went to Leipzig, where he remained for the rest of his life. While there he completed the study of law at the University, but with-

out abandoning musical activities. In 1684 he became organist at the Thomasschule, and four years after that he founded a Collegium Musicum for the presentation of public concerts. For thirteen years Kuhnau followed both the practice of law and music. In 1701, however, he renounced law for good and became cantor of the Thomasschule, holding this post for the rest of his life. As cantor, Kuhnau led performances at the Thomasschule while devoting himself to composition. Besides producing many admirable choral works, he also wrote numerous pieces for the clavier; it is with these pieces that he achieved prominence in music history, particularly the set of six sonatas called *Musicalische Vorstellung einiger Biblischer Historien* (*Musical Representation of Some Bible Stories*). The lucidity of Kuhnau's instrumental writing, the grace with which his thematic material is presented and developed, his fine feeling for architectonic construction, and his occasional use of contrasting themes gave his sonatas pioneer significance in the era preceding Bach.

The *Biblische Historien* set is an outstanding example of early program writing and tone painting. Especially famous is the sonata from this set called *The Combat Between David and Goliath* (*Der Streit zwischen David und Goliath*). It is in six parts: I. The Bravado of Goliath; II. The Terror of the Israelites and Their Prayer to God; III. David's Courage Before the Terrible Enemy; IV. The Dispute and the Slinging of the Stone by David; V. The Plight of the Philistines; VI. Paeans of Victory by the Israelites.

Kujawiak. A mazurka originating in the district of Kuawy, Poland. Wieniawski's Kujawiak for violin and piano in A minor, op. 3, is popular. Alexander Tansman interpolated a kujawiak in his *Four Polish Dances* for orchestra.

Kullak, Theodor, pianist and teacher. Born Krotoschin, Germany, Sept. 12, 1818; died Berlin, Germany, March 1, 1882. After studying the piano in Berlin and with Czerny in Vienna, he was appointed court pianist to the King of Prussia in 1846. Four years later he helped found a conservatory in Berlin, and in 1855 he established in Berlin his own music school, the Neue Akademie der Tonkunst, or Kullak's Academy. He wrote many salon pieces for the piano. He is most famous for his pedagogical works, including the *Materialien für den Elementar-Unterricht* and the *Schule des Oktavenspiel.*

Kunst der Fuge, Die (J. S. Bach). *See: Art of the Fugue, The.*

Kunsthaus. *See:* Lucerne Festival.

Kunwald, Ernst, conductor. Born Vienna, Austria, April 14, 1868; died there, Dec. 12, 1939. After studying music with Julius Epstein, Hermann Graedener, and Theodor Leschetizky in Vienna, and for a year at the Leipzig Conservatory, he made his conducting début in 1895 with the Rostock Opera. From then until 1912 he led opera and orchestral performances in Germany, directing the Berlin Philharmonic from 1907 to 1912. He made his American début in 1906 with the New York Philharmonic. From 1912 to 1917 he was principal conductor of the Cincinnati Symphony, and from 1914 of the May Music Festival in that city. During World War I he was arrested in the United States as an enemy alien. Returning to Germany in 1919, he became conductor of symphony concerts in Königsberg, where from 1922 on he was general music director. From 1928 to 1931 he was the principal conductor of the Berlin Symphony. After that he confined his performances to guest appearances throughout Germany and Austria. Kunwald was also an excellent pianist who appeared both in recitals and as guest performer with chamber-music ensembles.

Kurtz, Efrem, conductor. Born St. Petersburg, Russia, Nov. 7, 1900. His musical training took place at the St. Petersburg Conservatory and the Stern Conservatory in Berlin. In 1920 he made his conducting début by substituting for Arthur Nikisch at a performance of the dancer, Isadora Duncan. In 1924 he was appointed conductor of the Stuttgart Orchestra. After nine years in this post he became a principal conductor of the Ballet Russe. His American début as symphony conductor took place at the Lewisohn Stadium, New York, in July 1939. He made distinguished guest appearances with other American orchestras, then served as principal conductor of the Kansas City Philharmonic from 1943 to 1948. From 1948 to 1954 he was principal conductor of the Houston Symphony in Texas. In 1955 he became principal conductor of the Liverpool Philharmonic in England.

L

Lac de Cygnes, Le (Tchaikovsky). *See: Swan Lake.*

Laendler. A slow peasant dance originating in the "Landel" district of Austria north of the Ems River. It was the predecessor of the waltz. Mozart wrote 6 Laendler, K. 606 (1791); Beethoven, 5 Laendler, op. 169 (1801); Schubert wrote almost fifty, some gathered in opp. 18a and 171, others published posthumously. Several later Romantic composers, including Liszt, Karl Reinecke, and Joachim Raff, also wrote laendler, but by that time the form had lost much of its original identity.

Laendliche Hochzeit. *See:* Symphony—*Goldmark.*

Lalla Roukh. *See:* Moore, Thomas.

Lalo, Edouard, composer. Born Lille, France, Jan. 27, 1823; died Paris, France, April 22, 1892. He attended the Conservatories in Lille and Paris. In 1855 he became violist of the Armingaud-Jacquard Quartet, which gave notable concerts of German music in France. His first publication was some songs in 1848-1849. In

1867 he won third prize for an opera, *Fiesque*, in a national competition. Between 1872 and 1875 he came to prominence with a *Divertissement* for orchestra introduced at Paris in 1872, and a violin concerto and the *Symphonie espagnole* for violin and orchestra, both written for Pablo de Sarasate, who introduced them in 1872 and 1874 respectively. The crowning work of his career was the opera, *Le Roi d'Ys*, introduced at the Opéra-Comique in Paris in 1888 and soon after that heard throughout Europe and in the United States. The last years of Lalo's life were unhappy. He was a victim of paralysis, and he further suffered from disappointment at not being elected to the Institut de France. But he was not without honors, having been made Officer of the Legion of Honor in 1888, and later awarded the Prix Monbinne by the Académie des Beaux-Arts. Lalo was a composer of highest principles whose writing always has distinction of form, elegance of style, and grace of expression. Besides compositions already mentioned he wrote a cello concerto, piano concerto, Symphony in G minor, Scherzo, and *Rapsodie norvégienne* all for orchestra, and a string quartet, 3 piano trios, violin sonata, cello sonata and several other chamber-music works.

See: Concerto—*Lalo; Roi d'Ys, Le; Symphonie espagnole.*

Lambert, Constant, composer and conductor. Born London, England, Aug. 23, 1905; died there, Aug. 21, 1951. He attended the Royal College of Music, where his teachers included R. O. Morris and Vaughan Williams. He was still a conservatory student when Diaghilev, the ballet impresario, commissioned him to write a score for the Ballet Russe. Lambert's ballet, *Romeo and Juliet,* the first score commissioned by Diaghilev from an English composer, was produced at Monte Carlo in 1926. One year later, Lambert completed his first important work for orchestra, *Music for Orchestra.* He became famous for *Rio Grande,* a major work for chorus, orchestra, and solo piano based on a poem of Sacheverell Sitwell, a substantial success when introduced in Manchester, England, on Dec. 12, 1929. It was particularly admired for

its brilliant use of jazz idioms. In 1931 Lambert became musical director of the newly established ballet company at the Sadler's Wells Theatre in London, holding this post sixteen years; this company presented two of Lambert's ballets, *Horoscope* and *Apparitions*. Besides his performances with this company in Europe and the United States, Lambert appeared as guest conductor of symphony orchestras in London and on the Continent. He was also a trenchant music critic, and author of a provocative book, *Music Ho!* (1934). His principal instrumental compositions, besides those already referred to, include *Elegiac Blues* for small orchestra, *Horoscope,* ballet suite for orchestra, *Aubade héroïque* for orchestra, incidental music to *Hamlet,* a concerto for piano and nine instruments, and a piano sonata.

Lament of Tasso, The. *See:* Byron, George Noel Gordon, Lord.

Lamia. *See:* Keats, John.

Lamond, Frederic, pianist. Born Glasgow, Scotland, Jan. 28, 1868; died Stirling, Scotland, Feb. 21, 1948. He attended the Raff Conservatory in Frankfort, then studied privately with Hans von Buelow and Liszt. His professional début took place in Berlin on Nov. 17, 1885. Appearances in Vienna, London, and other European centers helped establish his authority and scholarship, especially in the piano works of Beethoven. In 1896 he made his first tour of Russia, and in 1899 of France. In 1904 he made his home in Berlin, where he lived during World War I. After the war he resumed his concert activity and became professor of the piano at the Conservatory in The Hague. He made the first of several tours of the United States in 1922; in 1923 and 1924 he conducted master classes in piano at the Eastman School of Music in Rochester, N.Y. During World War II he lived in England and taught piano at the Scottish National Academy.

Lamoureux, Charles, conductor. Born Bordeaux, France, Sept. 28, 1834; died Paris, France, Dec. 21, 1899. He attended the Paris Conservatory, then played the violin for several years in Parisian orchestras. In 1860 he founded a society for the advancement of chamber music in

Paris which was responsible for many notable premières. In 1862 he formed the Lamoureux Quartet. After serving as assistant conductor of the Paris Conservatory Orchestra for five years, he became a principal conductor at the Opéra-Comique and the Paris Opéra. In 1881 he founded the Lamoureux Orchestra (see below). As its conductor, he established his reputation as an interpreter of outstanding authority and remarkable gifts, a passionate propagandist for Wagner, many of whose music dramas he introduced to France in concert versions. He also championed the cause of modern French music by presenting premières of works by Paul Dukas, César Franck, Vincent d'Indy, Edouard Lalo, Saint-Saëns, and many others.

Lamoureux Orchestra (Concerts Lamoureux). An important symphony orchestra founded at Paris in 1881 by Charles Lamoureux as the Nouveaux Concerts. Its first concert took place on October 23. Lamoureux remained principal conductor until his death, when his post was inherited by his son-in-law, Camille Chevillard. Among later principal conductors were Paul Paray, Eugène Bigot, André Cluytens, Jean Martinon, and Igor Markevitch.

Landowska, Wanda, harpsichordist and pianist. Born Warsaw, Poland, July 5, 1877. She was graduated as a pianist from the Warsaw Conservatory when she was fourteen, after which she studied composition in Berlin with H. Urban. Even before she launched her career as a piano virtuoso she became interested in the harpsichord and its music. Her researches in European libraries helped uncover many long-forgotten masterworks which she subsequently popularized in her many concerts on the harpsichord. In 1900 she settled in Paris, where, until 1913, she taught the harpsichord and the music of the 16th and 17th centuries at the Schola Cantorum. She gave her first public harpsichord recital in 1903, and from then on appeared in Europe and Russia in concerts in which she often played both the harpsichord and the piano. From 1913 until the outbreak of World War I she taught the harpsichord at the

Berlin High School for Music. During World War I she was interned by the Germans. In 1919 she gave master classes in the harpsichord at the Basel Conservatory. She made her American début in Philadelphia on Nov. 20, 1923, as soloist with the Philadelphia Orchestra in a program made up of three concertos, two for the harpsichord and one for the piano. In 1925 she purchased a villa in Saint-Leu-la-Forêt, near Paris, where she opened a school for harpsichord playing and music called the Ecole de Musique Ancienne. Two years later she built on those grounds an auditorium for lectures and concerts. Each summer, up to 1939, she gave weekly concerts of old music which attracted audiences from all parts of the world. When the Nazis occupied Paris, she fled and finally came to the United States, since then her permanent home. The Nazis confiscated her priceless collection of old instruments and her library of over 10,000 volumes. Landowska made her first American reappearance in fourteen years in New York on Feb. 21, 1942. Since then she has lived in Lakeville, Conn., where she has devoted herself to teaching and recording. Her scholarship and consummate art have helped to revive interest in the harpsichord among several contemporary composers, including Manuel de Falla and Francis Poulenc, who wrote major compositions for her use. Landowska is the author of *Music of the Past* (1909); she has made transcriptions for the piano of works by numerous composers; and she has written cadenzas for concertos by Haydn and Mozart.

Lanier, Sidney, poet and flutist. Born Macon, Ga., Feb. 3, 1842; died Lynn, N.C., Sept. 7, 1881. He studied the flute in his boyhood and for several years, from 1873 on, was first flutist of the Peabody Symphony in Baltimore. But he distinguished himself outside music. In brilliant essays, he was a pioneer in adult education and in championing the underprivileged; he lectured on English literature; he was a sensitive poet. His poems occasionally treat musical subjects, as for example, *To Beethoven* and *To Wagner;* at times they are filled with musical analogies, as in *The Symphony.* His health undermined by imprisonment during the Civil War, he finally became a victim of consumption.

La Pouplinière, Alexandre. *See:* Pouplinière, Alexandre Jean-Joseph, Le Riche de la.

Largamente. In a broad, free, and full style.

Largando. Broadening.

Larghetto. Slow, but not as slow as largo.

Largo. A slow and stately tempo, slower than adagio.

Largo Quartet. *See:* Quartet—*Haydn.*

Lark Ascending, The. Romance for violin and orchestra by Vaughan Williams (1914), introduced in London on June 14, 1921, Adrian Boult conducting. This sensitive picture of nature is a lyric fantasy in which folk tendencies are combined with mystical feelings. It was inspired by a poem by George Meredith.

Lark Quartet. *See:* Quartet—*Haydn.*

Laudon Symphony. *See:* Symphony—*Haydn.*

Leader. British term for concertmaster.

Leading Tone. Seventh note of the major, or the harmonic minor scale.

Leading Seventh. Chord of the minor seventh on the leading tone.

League of Composers. An organization in New York devoted to the promotion of modern music. It was founded in 1923 by several members of the International Guild. The first executive board consisted of Arthur Bliss, Stephan Bourgeois, Louis Gruenberg, Minna Lederman, Leo Ornstein, Mrs. Arthur M. Reis, Lazare Saminsky, and Mrs. Maurice Wertheim. The League has each season presented several concerts devoted to new American and foreign music, much of it premières; it has commissioned new works from important composers; it has sponsored radio and stage presentations of new works; it has given receptions to musicians visiting the United States and those making notable contributions to modern music. From 1924 to 1947 it issued a quarterly, *Modern Music,* edited by Minna Lederman.

Leclair, Jean Marie, l'aîné, violinist and composer. Born Lyons, France, May 10, 1697; died Paris, France, Oct. 22, 1764. He went to Turin in 1722 as ballet master but was induced to study the violin

seriously. In 1728 he settled in Paris, where he played the violin at court, in the Opéra orchestra, and with the Concert Spirituel. After 1736 he devoted himself mainly to composition. He returned to Paris after a visit to Holland and was murdered under mysterious circumstances. One of the earliest masters of French violin music, he helped create an instrumental style that was French in grace and sensitivity, as opposed to the somewhat more emotional content of the Italian masters. He brought to violin writing a richer harmonic interest, a greater skill in writing double stops, a wider range of dynamics, and greater flexibility of tempo than hitherto encountered in French music. His main works include 48 violin sonatas, as well as violin concertos, concerti grossi, and trios.

Legato. Smooth and connected from one note to the next, as opposed to staccato.

Legend (Légende). A composition that by its narrative character suggests a story or a poem. Liszt wrote two legends for piano (1866): *St. Francis' Sermon to the Birds* (*St. François d'Assise prédicant aux oiseaux*) and *St. Francis Walking on the Waves* (*St. François de Paule marchant sur les flots*). The first contrasts the chirping of the birds with a hymn-like melody representing the sermon. In the second, the ebb and flow of the water is portrayed realistically. The composition as a whole has a delicate impressionistic character. Henri Wieniawski's *Légende* for violin and orchestra, op. 17, is popular. Though possessing no program it has such a pronounced narrative character that it appears to be telling a tale.

Legends. (1) A set of ten compositions for orchestra by Dvořák, op. 59 (1881). The composer originally wrote them for piano four hands, but they became so popular that his publisher commissioned him to orchestrate them. Two are particularly famous: No. 7, an infectious piece with lively dance rhythms (*Allegretto grazioso*), and No. 8, which has an idyllic atmosphere (*Un poco allegretto grazioso quasi andantino*).

(2) A set of four tone poems by Sibelius, op. 22 (1893-1895). They are I. *Lemminkaïnen and the Maidens;* II.

Lemminkaïnen in Tuonela; III. *The Swan of Tuonela;* IV. *Lemminkaïnen's Homeward Journey.* All four derive their program from the *Kalevala,* and relate the adventures of Lemminkaïnen, warrior-hero described as the "Achilles of Finnish mythology." The third tone poem, *The Swan of Tuonela* (which see), is frequently performed.

Leggiero (or **leggiadro**). Lightly, gracefully; in piano performance indicating a light pressure on the keys particularly in rapid passages.

Leggierezza, La. *See:* Etude—*Liszt.*

Leginska, Ethel (born **Ethel Liggins**), pianist and conductor. Born Hull, England, April 13, 1886. After studying the piano at the Hoch Conservatory in Frankfort and with Theodor Leschetizky in Vienna, she made her début in London, and then toured Europe. Her American début took place on Jan. 20, 1913. Her dynamic personality and brilliant technique made her a favorite of the concert hall in Europe and America. She then became interested in conducting, and founded and led several women's orchestras in Boston and Chicago. She also made guest appearances with major American symphony orchestras. In 1939 she went to live in Los Angeles, where she devoted herself to teaching the piano.

Legno (col legno). Italian for "wood" ("with the wood"). An indication in string music for the performer to play on the strings with the back of the bow.

Leibowitz, René, conductor and composer. Born Warsaw, Poland, Feb. 17, 1913. When he was thirteen, his family went to live in Paris. From 1930 until 1933 he studied composition with Arnold Schoenberg and Anton Webern, under whose influence he started writing in the twelve-tone technique. His compositions include a symphony, chamber concerto for violin, piano, and 17 instruments, chamber concerto for 9 instruments, wind quintet, violin sonata, string quartet, Variations for orchestra, chamber symphony for 12 instruments, and a piano sonata. He has also made many appearances in Paris as a conductor, and is the author of a text on the twelve-tone technique (1949) and of the study, *Schoenberg et son école* (1947).

Leinsdorf, Erich, conductor. Born Vienna, Austria, Feb. 4, 1912. After attending the Vienna Academy he became assistant to Bruno Walter and Toscanini at the Salzburg Festival in 1934 and 1935. In 1936 he conducted opera and orchestral performances in Italy. He made his American début on Jan. 21, 1938, at the Metropolitan Opera. The following season he took over the direction of the entire Wagner repertory. In 1943 Leinsdorf left the Metropolitan to devote himself to symphonic music. He was principal conductor of the Cleveland Orchestra from 1943 to 1947, and of the Rochester Philharmonic from 1947 to 1956. For a single season, in 1956, he was musical director of the New York City Opera. Early in 1957 he returned to the Metropolitan Opera as musical adviser and guest conductor. He also made numerous guest appearances in Europe, America, and Israel.

Leipzig Gewandhaus Orchestra. *See:* Gewandhaus Orchestra.

Leise. Softly, gently.

Lekeu, Guillaume, composer. Born Heusy, France, Jan. 20, 1870; died Angers, France, Jan. 21, 1894. He received his academic education at a high school in Poitiers and at the University of Paris. He began to study music seriously in Paris: harmony with Gaston Vallin and composition with Vincent d'Indy. In 1891 he won the second Belgian Prix de Rome. During the next three years he completed several works giving evidence of a powerful creative gift. But death came from typhoid in his twenty-fourth year before that gift could develop. His most famous works are an Adagio for Strings and a violin sonata. Other works include two symphonic studies (*Chant de triomphale délivrance* and *Hamlet*), *Epithalame* for strings, trombone, and organ, Introduction and Adagio for brass, *Fantaisie symphonique sur deux airs angevins,* a string quartet, a piano quartet and cello sonata (both completed by d'Indy), piano trio, and piano sonata.
See: Adagio for Strings (2).

Lenau, Nikolaus (Nikolaus Niembsch von Strehlenau), poet. Born Csátad, Hungary (now Rumania), Aug. 13, 1802; died Vienna, Austria, Aug. 22, 1850.

His dramatic poem *Faust* was the source of the following instrumental works: Liszt's *Mephisto Waltz* and *Der naechtliche Zug,* two orchestral works collectively entitled *Two Episodes from Lenau's Faust;* Liszt's *Third Mephisto Waltz* and *Mephisto Polka,* both for piano; Henri Rabaud's tone poem, *La Procession nocturne.* Richard Strauss' tone poem *Don Juan* was based on Lenau's poem of the same name.

Lener Quartet. A distinguished chamber-music ensemble founded in 1918 by the violinist Jenö Léner (born Szabadka, Hungary, June 24, 1894; died New York City, Nov. 4, 1948). The other members were Joseph Smilovits violin, Sandor Roth viola, and Imre Hartmann cello. The Quartet made its bow in Vienna in 1920, in Paris in 1921, in London in 1922, and in the United States in 1929. It continued giving concerts in the United States and Europe until the beginning of World War II, when it disbanded. Three of the members then settled in Mexico, while Léner continued living in New York up to the time of his death, occasionally participating in chamber-music performances with other ensembles.

Leningrad Symphony. *See:* Symphony—*Shostakovich.*

Lent. Slow.

Lentando. Retarding.

Lento. A slow tempo between andante and largo.

Leonore Overtures, Nos. 1, 2, and 3. Three overtures by Beethoven, opp. 138, 72a, and 72b respectively, for his opera *Fidelio.* A fourth overture is called *Fidelio Overture* (which see). The opera, with a libretto by Josef Sonnleithner and George Treitschke, was introduced in Vienna on Nov. 20, 1805. The first of the *Leonore Overtures* to be written was No. 2, the one used for the opera's première. No. 3 was written for a revival of the opera in Vienna in 1806. No. 1 is a simplification and condensation of No. 3, written in 1807 for a projected performance of the opera in Prague which did not materialize. In present-day performances of the opera, it is customary to give the *Fidelio Overture* before Act 1, and *Leonore Overture No. 3* between scenes 1 and 2 of Act 2. The *Leonore*

Overtures Nos. 1 and 2 are now never presented with the opera, but occasionally performed at symphony concerts.

The most celebrated of these overtures is No. 3, one of the composer's unqualified masterworks for orchestra. A stately introduction leads to the first theme, in clarinet and bassoon; this is Florestan's aria from the opera, *In des Lebens Fruehlingstagen* in Act 2. A dramatic development section is succeeded by the second theme, first heard in horns, then repeated by first violins and flute. Another dramatic working-out of the material follows. Offstage fanfares in the trumpet, announcing the arrival of the Prime Minister at the dungeon, are answered by the strings playing Leonore's song of gratitude for the delivery of her husband. The triumph of Leonore in saving her husband from unjust imprisonment is then joyously described in the coda.

Leschetizky, Theodor, pianist and teacher. Born Lancut, Poland, June 22, 1830; died Dresden, Germany, Nov. 14, 1915. He received piano instruction from his father, then became a pupil of Carl Czerny in Vienna. He was only fifteen when he started teaching the piano on a full-time schedule, but he did not neglect his own musical education. In 1852 he settled in Russia, and from 1862 to 1878 was professor of the piano at the St. Petersburg Conservatory. During this period he toured Europe as pianist and conductor. He returned to Vienna in 1878 to develop his own piano school. After abandoning the concert stage in 1886 he achieved world recognition as one of the foremost piano teachers of his generation. His pupils included Ossip Gabrilowitsch, Mark Hambourg, Paderewski, and Artur Schnabel. One of his four wives, Anna Essipova, was herself a distinguished pianist and teacher.

Levant, Oscar, pianist. Born Pittsburgh, Pa., Dec. 27, 1906. He studied piano with private teachers in Pittsburgh, and in New York with Sigismund Stojowski. From 1928 on he was active as a composer for the Broadway stage and Hollywood screen. As a concert pianist, he first became known for his authoritative performances of George Gershwin's music, making his first public appearance in the summer of 1931 in Gershwin's *Rhapsody in Blue* at the Lewisohn Stadium in New York. In the early 1930's he resumed study of composition, with Joseph Schillinger, and between 1935 and 1937 was a pupil of Arnold Schoenberg. In 1938 he became known for his wit and wisdom on the radio program, "Information Please." After that he made many appearances over radio and television, and in motion pictures. Beginning with 1942 he toured the United States in recitals and as soloist with orchestras in the Classical, Romantic, and modern repertory. He is the author of a best-selling book, *A Smattering of Ignorance* (1940), and the composer of a piano concerto, string quartet, 2 piano sonatinas, and shorter works for orchestra.

Levitzki, Mischa, pianist. Born Krementchug, Russia, May 25, 1898; died Avon-by-the-Sea, N.J., Jan. 2, 1941. After studying the piano with Alexander Michaelowski in Warsaw, he made his début in Antwerp in his eighth year. He then came to the United States, where from 1906 to 1911 he attended the Institute of Musical Art in New York, a pupil of Sigismund Stojowski. He completed his piano study in 1915 at the Berlin High School for Music with Ernst von Dohnányi, receiving the Mendelssohn Prize. Before these studies ended, however, he performed throughout Europe and Scandinavia. He made his American début in New York on Oct. 17, 1916. Making his home now in the United States, he became an American citizen. He continued concertizing throughout the world up to the time of his death. He made many transcriptions for piano, prepared a cadenza for Beethoven's Piano Concerto No. 3, and wrote small pieces for the piano (including Valse in A, Gavotte, and *Valse tzigane*).

Lewisohn Stadium Concerts. Summer symphony concerts inaugurated on June 23, 1918, by Arnold Volpe at the Lewisohn Stadium adjoining the College of the City of New York. For the next three summers these concerts were primarily devoted to semi-classical favorites, and were conducted by Volpe, Walter Henry Rothwell, Victor Herbert, and Henry Hadley. With Willem van Hoogstraten,

principal conductor at the Stadium from 1921 to 1939, the concerts embraced a symphonic repertory no less ambitious than that undertaken by a winter organization. Some of the world's foremost conductors and soloists have appeared at these concerts. The orchestra is made up mainly of members of the New York Philharmonic but is called the Lewisohn Stadium Orchestra.

Lhévinne, Josef, pianist. Born Orel, Russia, Dec. 13, 1874; died New York City, Dec. 2, 1944. After studying with private teachers, and while attending the Moscow Conservatory, he made his début at Moscow in 1889 as guest artist with an orchestra conducted by Anton Rubinstein. In 1891 he was graduated from the Conservatory with highest honors, after which he toured Russia. Upon the advice of Anton Rubinstein, with whom he studied, he competed for and won the Rubinstein Prize in 1895. From 1902 to 1906 he was professor of the piano at the Moscow Conservatory. In 1906 he came to the United States, making his American début as soloist with the Russian Symphony Orchestra in New York on January 27. Lhévinne was immediately offered a contract for 150 appearances in the United States for the following season. Until the outbreak of World War I he continued concertizing both in the United States and Europe while holding a teaching post in Berlin. He was in Berlin when World War I broke out, and was interned for five years. In 1919 he became a resident, and later a citizen, of the United States. He continued giving concerts for the remainder of his life while teaching piano privately and at the Juilliard School of Music.

His wife, Rosina (born Kiev, Russia, March 28, 1880), is also a concert pianist and distinguished teacher. She and Josef Lhévinne met as students at the Moscow Conservatory and were married in 1899. In that year they also made their first appearance as a two-piano team. Josef and Rosina Lhévinne continued giving two-piano performances after that, celebrating the 40th anniversary of this artistic partnership with a Carnegie Hall concert on Jan. 14, 1939. Rosina has also given solo performances and for many years has taught piano both privately and at the Juilliard School of Music.

Liadov, Anatol, composer. Born St. Petersburg, Russia, May 10, 1855; died Novgorod, Russia, Aug. 28, 1914. He attended the St. Petersburg Conservatory, where he was a pupil of Rimsky-Korsakov. Expelled in 1876 for failure to attend classes, he was soon reinstated and in 1878 was graduated with high honors. He was then appointed teacher of theory at the Conservatory, subsequently attaining the position of professor, which he held until the end of his life. He was also active as composer, conductor, and as a scholar doing research in folk music. Creatively, Liadov was at his best in small and intimate forms such as songs, piano pieces, and adaptations of Russian folk tunes. But he also wrote a few effective orchestral fairy tales—the most famous being *Baba Yaga, The Enchanted Lake,* and *Kikimora*—which are beautifully orchestrated and constructed with consummate skill. Other orchestral works include the popular *Eight Russian Folksongs,* the tone poem *Fragments from the Apocalypse,* and an orchestral dirge *Nenie.* His many compositions for the piano include etudes, mazurkas, preludes, ballades, barcarolles, variations, canons, and so forth.

See: Baba Yaga; Eight Russian Folksongs; Enchanted Lake, The; Kikimora.

Liebermann, Rolf, composer. Born Zurich, Switzerland, Sept. 14, 1910. After studying conducting with Hermann Scherchen and composition with Vladimir Vogel, he directed various Swiss orchestras and became associated with the Swiss Radio Corporation. Liebermann first attracted attention as a composer in 1947 with *Furioso,* for orchestra, introduced at the Darmstadt Music Festival and described as "the first existentialist musical composition." He later became famous for several provocative operas, notably *Leonore 40/45,* first given at Bern in 1952. In 1949 he received the Konrad Ferdinand Prize from the city of Zurich. Liebermann is an atonal composer, many of whose works are in the twelve-tone technique. Besides compositions already mentioned, he wrote a symphony, *Poly-*

phonic Studies for orchestra, *Suite o Swiss Folk Melodies* for orchestra, Con certo for Jazz Band and Orchestra, *Mu sique* for narrator and orchestra, and piano sonata. He has made numerous ap pearances as conductor in France and a prominent German festivals.

Liebesnacht (Night of Love). Love due of Tristan and Isolde in Act 2 of Wag ner's music drama, *Tristan and Isolde* This excerpt is often heard in a sym phonic transcription, and includes Bran gaene's warning call followed by the sen suous love music. This love passag reaches a climax with the passionate mel ody which, at the end of Act 3, become the spine of Isolde's Love-Death music

Liebestod (Love Death). Isolde's song o death which concludes Wagner's musi drama, *Tristan and Isolde.* For more de tailed comment *see: Tristan and Isolde Prelude and Love Death.*

Liebestraum (Love's Dream). A popula piece for the piano in A-flat major b Liszt. It is the third in a set of three noc turnes for piano, all entitled *Liebes traeume* (1850). All three originated a songs—the third as *O lieb, so lang d lieben kannst,* lyric by Freiligrath. Th third *Liebestraum* is one of Liszt's mos celebrated piano works, and in its sen timentality and tenderness is characteris tic of the other two works in this form

Lied ohne Worte (Mendelssohn). *See Songs Without Words.*

Lied von der Erde, Das (The Song o the Earth). A cycle of six songs for tenor contralto, and orchestra by Gustav Mah ler (1908), introduced in Munich o Nov. 20, 1911, Bruno Walter conducting While described by the composer as а "symphony," it is essentially a voca suite, even though the voices are integra to the symphonic texture. Nevertheless this work is often given at symphon concerts and is one of Mahler's master pieces. The texts are old Chinese poems adapted into German by Hans Bethge I. *The Drinking Song of Earthly Woe* (*Das Trinklied vom Jammer der Erde*) poem by Li-Tai-Po, for tenor. This is ar epicurean drinking song over which hov ers the dark clouds of morbidity. II. *The Lonely One in Autumn* (*Der Einsame im Herbst*), poem by Chang-Tsi, for contralto. This is a nature picture, painted in drab, gray colors and evoking a bleak atmosphere. III. *Of Youth* (*Von der Jugend*), by Li-Tai-Po, for tenor. A song of youth, this music evokes oriental imagery in a picture of merrymakers reflected in the water. IV. *Of Beauty* (*Von der Schoenheit*), by Li-Tai-Po, for contralto. This is a song of love, as two lovers wander through the countryside which becomes enchanted because of their feelings. V. *The Drunken One in Spring* (*Der Trunkene im Fruehling*), by Li-Tai-Po, for tenor. Once again, as in the first poem, this is a drinking song, but again in a depressed mood. VI. *Awaiting a Friend* (*In Erwartung des Freundes*) by Mong-Kao-Jen, for contralto; and *The Farewell of a Friend* (*Der Abschied des Freundes*) by Wang-Wei, for contralto. The poets renounce happiness, seeing the world from the distorted vision of a drunken sleep.

Lieutenant Kije. Suite for orchestra by Prokofiev (1933) derived from the score to a motion picture released in 1934, a satire on militarism in Czarist Russia. Lieutenant Kije is a mythical character created by Czar Nicholas I when he misreads a military report. His aides, reluctant to tell the Czar he made a mistake, make believe that the Lieutenant is an actual person and fabricate all kinds of exploits to make him into a hero; eventually they conveniently kill him off. The orchestral suite has five sections. I. The Birth of Kije. This is a musical caricature of the "hero," who comes into being with a fanfare of cornets, roll of drums, and a mocking tune for fifes. II. Romance. A sentimental tune is presented by a tenor saxophone, describing our hero in love. III. Kije's Wedding. The pomp and ceremony of the hero's wedding are depicted. IV. Troika. As Kije regales himself in a tavern, a tavern song is played by the tenor saxophone. V. Burial of Kije. The death of the hero is presented. Fragments from the preceding movements recall his life and achievements. The suite then ends with the voice of a muted trumpet dissolving into air, even as does the character of Kije. The orchestral suite was given for the first time in Paris on Feb. 20, 1937, the composer conducting.

Life for the Czar, Overture to A. Overture to a folk opera by Glinka (1936). The libretto was by Baron von Rosen, and the opera was introduced in St. Petersburg on Dec. 9, 1836. The overture opens with a slow introduction dominated by a melody for oboe. The main section comes with a vigorous subject for first violins. After this thought has been elaborated upon, a second theme is presented by the clarinet. Development of both themes is brief, but the coda, in which the basic melodies are reviewed, is extended.

For another excerpt from this opera *see:* Mazurka.

Lincoln, Abraham, 16th President of the United States. Born Hardin County, Ky., Feb. 12, 1809; died Washington, D.C., April 15, 1865. Many American composers have found Lincoln an inspiration for major works. Among these composers are: Robert Russell Bennett (*A Lincoln Symphony*); Aaron Copland (*A Lincoln Portrait*); Rubin Goldmark (*Requiem*, for orchestra); Morton Gould (*Lincoln Legend*, for orchestra); Roy Harris (Symphony No. 6); Daniel Gregory Mason (Symphony No. 3); and Silas Gamaliel Pratt (*A Lincoln Symphony*).

Lincoln Portrait, A. For narrator and orchestra by Aaron Copland (1942). It was commissioned by André Kostelanetz, who introduced it in Cincinnati on May 14, 1942. The work has three sections, played without interruption. In the first part the composer has attempted to suggest (in his own words) "the mysterious sense of fatality that surrounds Lincoln's personality. Also near the end of this section something of his gentleness and simplicity of spirit. The quick middle section briefly sketches in the background of the times in which he lived. This merges into the concluding section where my sole purpose was to draw a simple but impressive frame about the words of Lincoln himself." In the last part, a narrator reads a text derived from Lincoln's letters and speeches, concluding with the final lines of the *Gettysburg Address*. To give this music a closer identity with Lincoln's times Copland quotes Stephen Foster's *Camptown Races* and the folk ballad, *Springfield Mountain*.

Linear counterpoint. Music in a contrapuntal style with the voices moving independently of harmonic relationships. This technique is employed by several important contemporary composers, notably Paul Hindemith.

Linz Symphony. *See:* Symphony—*Mozart.*

Lipatti, Dinu, pianist and composer. Born Bucharest, Rumania, March 17, 1917; died Geneva, Switzerland, Dec. 2, 1950. After studying the piano with Floria Musicesco, he won 2nd prize in an international contest for pianists at Vienna in 1934. His music study was completed in Paris with Alfred Cortot, Charles Munch, Paul Dukas, and Nadia Boulanger. From 1934 until his death he was head of the piano department of the Geneva Conservatory. He also toured Europe as a piano virtuoso, acclaimed for his fine sense of detail and consummate musicianship. Though rheumatoid arthritis made concert appearances increasingly difficult in the last years of his life—and forced him to cancel a projected tour of the United States—he achieved recognition as one of Europe's foremost pianists. He was also the composer of *Satrarii* for orchestra (recipient of first prize in the Enesco Competition in Rumania in 1933), a piano concerto in classical style, *Symphonie concertante* for two pianos and orchestra, and piano pieces.

Lipkin, Seymour, pianist and conductor. Born Detroit, Mich., May 14, 1927. He studied piano with Rudolf Serkin at the Curtis Institute, then made his professional début as pianist with the Detroit Civic Orchestra in February 1938. In 1945 he toured Europe with Jascha Heifetz under the auspices of the U.S.O., performing for the armed forces in 65 concerts. In 1948 he won the Rachmaninoff Fund Award, which brought him a national concert tour and a recording contract. He has also appeared as a conductor, after studying conducting with Koussevitzky at the Berkshire Music Centre, and serving as apprentice conductor with the Cleveland Orchestra in 1947-1948. In 1951 he joined the conducting faculty at the Berkshire Music Centre, and in 1958 made his New York début as conductor in a performance of Leonard Bernstein's *Trouble in Tahiti* with the New York City Opera Company.

List, Eugene, pianist. Born Philadelphia, Pa., July 6, 1918. His initial musical training took place in Los Angeles, where he made his début at the age of twelve with the Los Angeles Philharmonic. After additional study with Olga Samaroff in Philadelphia and at the Juilliard School in New York he made an impressive New York début on Dec. 19, 1935 in the American première of Shostakovich's Piano Concerto. He has since toured the world, and appeared in a motion picture, *Bachelor's Daughters.* As a member of the American armed forces he performed before Truman, Churchill, and Stalin at the Potsdam Conference in July 1945. He is married to the concert violinist, Carol Glenn.

Liszt, Franz, pianist and composer. Born Raiding, Hungary, Oct. 22, 1811; died Bayreuth, Bavaria, July 31, 1886. After receiving some instruction from his father, Liszt made his first public appearances as pianist in Hungary when he was nine. Several Hungarian noblemen raised a fund to send him to Vienna, where he remained several years, studying the piano with Carl Czerny and composition with Antonio Salieri. His Vienna début, on Dec. 1, 1822, was a sensation. In 1823 Liszt went to Paris, intending to enter the Conservatory. Denied admission because of a rule barring foreigners, he studied privately with Antonín Reicha and Ferdinand Paër. On March 8, 1824, he gave his first concert in Paris and at once became an idol of the city. That summer he also made highly successful appearances in London, where he was commanded to play for King George IV. He continued to concertize for the next few years through France, England, and Switzerland. Then, in 1827, the death of his father inspired pious resolutions. He now planned to turn his fortune over to his mother and abandon his career as piano virtuoso for more significant endeavors. First he turned to religion, then to politics, and after that to literature and philosophy. But soon after 1830 he returned to music, inspired by his intimate associations with Chopin, Berlioz, and Paganini. Chopin and Berlioz fired in him the ambition to write music like theirs, new, fresh, and adventurous with the Romantic spirit then sweeping Europe. This ambition he would fulfil later on. Meanwhile, the dazzling virtuosity of Paganini inflamed in him a passion to become the Paganini of the piano, the consummate master of the keyboard. He worked intensively on his technique for about two years. When he returned to the concert stage in 1833 he was immediately hailed as one of the greatest piano virtuosos of his day.

A two-year interruption in his concert activity was caused by a turbulent love affair with Countess d'Agoult. Though married and the mother of three children, the Countess ran away with Liszt in 1835 to Geneva, where for four years they lived together without the benefit of clergy, raising three children of their own, one of whom was Cosima, later the wife of Hans von Buelow and Wagner.

Liszt's second return to the concert stage was attended by triumphs everywhere. These were his *Wanderjahre*—the years between 1839 and 1847—when he covered half the world in remarkable concerts. In him showmanship was combined with profound musicianship; a fabulous technique with a majestic sense of style. It can be said that the modern piano virtuoso came into existence with him. Liszt was the first to attempt giving solo concerts, instead of calling upon the collaboration of an orchestra or assisting artists, confident he could hold the attention of an audience through an entire program.

His affair with Countess d'Agoult ended in or about 1839. Eight years later he was involved in a new *grand passion,* this time for Princess Carolyne von Sayn-Wittgenstein. A brilliant though somewhat eccentric woman, she exerted a profound influence on him through her strong bent for religion, mysticism, and literature. She went to live with him in Weimar when, in 1848, Liszt was appointed Kapellmeister to the Grand Duke. In Weimar Liszt devoted himself to music-making of the highest order, giving outstanding performances of opera and orchestral music which laid particular stress on new music and unrecognized composers. He became the stout champion of the *avant-garde* in music, especially of the music of Berlioz and Wagner. With remarkable courage he put on a revival of Wagner's *Tannhaeuser* and the world première of Wagner's *Lohengrin* at a time when that composer was a political exile, *persona non grata* with established authority in Europe.

By 1859 Liszt found the reaction in Weimar unfavorable to him and his music. There was resentment against his personal life and his continued espousal of new music. He resigned his post, and two years after that left Weimar. The desperate need for spiritual peace first awakened in him by Princess Carolyne now made him seek out religion as a refuge. He could not become a priest, though this was his crowning ambition at the time, because of his unsavory personal history. But he did manage to achieve minor orders. He submitted to the tonsure in 1865, and entered the Third Order of St. Francis of Assisi as abbé. But he did not desert music. He continued writing abundantly, especially for the piano. He also devoted himself to teaching the piano to students who came to him from all parts of the world.

In 1866 Wagner and Liszt came to the parting of ways as friends, for it was in that year that Liszt's daughter, Cosima, left her husband Hans von Buelow to live with Wagner, an act Liszt for a long time could not forgive. Wagner and Liszt were finally reconciled in 1872, thereby enabling Liszt to participate in the ceremonies attending the laying of the cornerstone of the Wagner festival theater in Bayreuth; and in succeeding years he was able to attend the Wagner festivals there. But Cosima would not forget or forgive. She denied her father permission to attend Wagner's funeral in 1883, or to visit her home after that.

The last honors came to Liszt in 1886 in England, where he gave several concerts, including one for Queen Victoria. Returning to Bayreuth to attend the Wagner Festival there he fell ill, and had to leave a performance of *Tristan and Isolde.* He died soon after that, a victim of pneumonia.

Both as a man and a musician, Liszt

had grandeur and greatness. Nevertheless as both virtuoso and composer he was invariably conscious of his audience, wooing it with dramatics, trivialities, superficial effects. Yet he was also capable of producing music filled with poetry and majesty. If he was a great composer with serious faults, he was also a composer whose influence cannot be overestimated. He invented the tone poem, or symphonic poem. He brought a new expansiveness and flexibility to musical structure, a new dramatic impact to orchestral and piano writing, new dimensions to harmonic and instrumental language, new vitality to program music, new resiliency to the use of Berlioz' "idée fixe." Those who followed him—masters like Richard Strauss—wrote the kind of music they did because of the example Liszt had previously set in his own works.

These are his principal instrumental compositions:

Orchestra: 12 tone poems (including *Les Préludes, Tasso,* and *Mazeppa*); 2 piano concertos; *Hungaria; Hamlet; A Faust Symphony; A Symphony to Dante's Divine Comedy; Two Episodes from Lenau's Faust; Second Mephisto Waltz; Hungarian Fantasy,* for piano and orchestra; *Totentanz,* for piano and orchestra.

Piano: Etudes d'exécution transcendante; 2 concert etudes; *Album d'un voyageur; Années de pèlerinage; Harmonies poétiques et religieuses;* 2 legends; Sonata; *Weihnachtsbaum;* 15 *Hungarian Rhapsodies; Consolations;* also ballades, *Albumblaetter,* caprices, *Liebestraeume,* laendler, mazurkas, czardas, and numerous transcriptions.

See: Années de pèlerinage; Concerto —*Liszt; Consolations;* Etude—*Liszt; Funerailles; Hungarian Fantasy; Hungarian Rhapsody; Legend; Liebestraum; Mazeppa; Mephisto Waltz; Préludes, Les;* Sonata—*Liszt;* Symphony—*Liszt; Tasso; Totentanz.*

Little Minister, The. *See:* Barrie, Sir James.

Little Notebook of Anna Magdalena, The (Notenbuch fuer Anna Magdalena). A compilation of elementary pieces for the clavier, together with some songs, mainly by Johann Sebastian Bach. These pieces were intended for pedagogical use. Anna Magdalena was Bach's second wife, who would often copy pieces of music in a notebook as exercises for herself and her children, or as examples of music intended for special occasions such as a wedding or a christening. Most of these pieces—including marches, minuets, musettes, and polonaises—are by Bach himself; but some are by other composers and consist of tunes popular at the time. The simple and delightful little minuets by Bach taught to young pianists today come from this collection.

Little Orchestra Society. A chamber orchestra founded at New York in 1947 by Thomas Scherman for the presentation of unusual programs, made up of premières, interesting revivals, and rarely given novelties. The Society presented its first concert in New York on Oct. 20, 1947. Scherman has been the conductor since then. Through the years he has never relaxed in his efforts to make his programs fresh and exciting, and has been responsible for many world and American premières, the resuscitation of many long-neglected masterworks (particularly in the field of opera, presented in concert versions). He has also forged new trails by allowing audiences to attend his final rehearsals; by inaugurating unusual children's concerts; by initiating Saturday morning sessions in which composers can come to him for examination of new works. The Society has made many tours of the East Coast of the United States. In the Spring of 1959 it toured the Far East, traveling over 24,000 miles and giving performances in Japan, Korea, Formosa, the Philippines, Thailand, Cambodia, and other parts of the Orient.

Little Organ Book (Das Orgelbuechlein). A collection of 46 chorale preludes by Johann Sebastian Bach. Many of these pieces were intended for the different seasons of the Church calendar, from Advent through Whitsuntide; a final group is concerned with the Christian life. Each chorale prelude is brief. The wide variety of mood and expressiveness of these chorale preludes led Albert Schweitzer to describe the *Orgelbuechlein* as "the lexicon of Bach's musical speech." Bach originally intended including 164 compositions in this collection, which he started writing at Weimar in 1717.

Little Russian Symphony. *See:* Symphony —*Tchaikovsky.*

Little Shepherd, The (Debussy). *See: Children's Corner.*

Little Train to Caipira, The (Villa-Lobos). *See: Bachianas brasileiras.*

Liverpool Philharmonic Orchestra. A symphony orchestra founded in Liverpool, England, in 1840. For the next nine years it presented annual series of concerts in the Lascelles Rooms. In 1849 it acquired a permanent auditorium, destroyed in 1933; its present home was built in 1939. Among its principal conductors have been Jacob Zeugheer, Julius Benedict, Max Bruch, Charles Hallé, Frederic H. Cowen, Malcolm Sargent, Hugo Rignold, and Efrem Kurtz. For several years, beginning with 1910, the orchestra operated under a system of guest conductors.

Locatelli, Pietro, violinist and composer. Born Bergamo, Italy, Sept. 3, 1695; died Amsterdam, Holland, March 30, 1764. He studied violin with Arcangelo Corelli in Rome, after which he entered upon a successful career as a virtuoso. From 1725 to 1732 he was solo violinist for the Landgrave of Hesse-Darmstadt in Mantua. He made his permanent home at Amsterdam in 1732, devoting himself to concert appearances as both violinist and conductor. He also wrote numerous compositions which were influential in the early development of the sonata, concerto, and concerto grosso. His Caprices for the violin helped enhance the technique of violin performance so greatly that Locatelli is sometimes spoken of as the father of modern violin virtuosity. His works include violin concertos, concerti grossi, and many quartets, trio sonatas, and sonatas for solo instrument and accompaniment or for unaccompanied violin.

See: Caprice (1).

Loeffler, Charles Martin, composer. Born Mulhouse, Alsace, Jan. 30, 1861; died Medfield, Mass., May 19, 1935. He studied music in Berlin with Friedrich Kiel and Eduard Rappoldi, and in Paris with Ernest Guiraud and Joseph Massart. After playing the violin in the Pasdeloup Orchestra in Paris he came to the United States in 1881 and joined the violin section of the Leopold Damrosch Orchestra. One year later he became second concertmaster of the Boston Symphony. In 1883 he toured the United States as a member of the Theodore Thomas Orchestra. His first major work, *The Nights in the Ukraine,* was introduced by the Boston Symphony in 1891. Most of his later orchestral music was also first performed by the Boston Symphony, including *Fantastic Concerto* for cello and orchestra, *Divertimento* for violin and orchestra, *La Mort de Tintagiles, La Villanelle du diable, Poem (La bonne chanson),* and his masterwork, *A Pagan Poem.* In 1903 he retired from the Boston Symphony to devote himself entirely to composition. Everything he wrote has distinction of craftsmanship and aristocracy of style, but he was at his best in a post-Impressionistic vein and in the creation of sensitive, poetic moods. Besides works already mentioned, he wrote *Memories of My Childhood* for orchestra, *Clowns* for jazz band, and *Evocation* for chorus and orchestra. He also wrote a Partita for violin and piano, a quintet for strings, and *Music for Four Stringed Instruments.*

See: Bonne Chanson, La; Memories of My Childhood; Pagan Poem, A.

Loeillet, Jean Baptiste, flutist, harpsichordist, and composer. Born Ghent, Belgium, Nov. 18, 1680; died London, England, July 19, 1730. Coming from a family of professional musicians, he became adept at the harpsichord, flute, and oboe at an early age. In 1705 he went to London, where he played flute and oboe in the Queen's Theatre orchestra. After 1710 he devoted himself to teaching, and to the presentation of weekly concerts at his home; both endeavors brought him a fortune. His virtuosity on the flute did much to popularize that instrument in England in his day, and he wrote many works for that instrument. He was not a particularly daring innovator or original thinker, but his music has enough grace and charm to warrant occasional revival. His works include flute sonatas, sonatas for various other solo instruments and harpsichord, and "lessons" and suites for the harpsichord.

Lohengrin, Preludes to Act 1 and 3. Preludes for orchestra in an opera by Wagner. The libretto, by the composer, was based on medieval legends; the opera was introduced in Weimar on Aug. 28, 1850, Liszt conducting. The spiritual music of the Prelude to Act 1 is intended to portray a heavenly vision in which angels carry the Holy Grail. A single theme, the Holy Grail motif, dominates the composition. It appears at first quietly high in the violins before being taken over by the other instruments. This subject is built up into a crescendo, its peak being an eloquent statement by trumpet and trombones. Then a decrescendo follows, dying out in a pianissimo for strings in the upper register.

The spirited Prelude to Act 3 speaks of the joy of Elsa and Lohengrin on the eve of their wedding. The Prelude opens with a robust theme for full orchestra. This is followed by another virile subject for cellos, horns, and bassoons in unison, and a march-like theme for wind.

London Philharmonic Orchestra. A symphony orchestra founded in London, England, in 1932 by Sir Thomas Beecham. Beecham directed this organization in London, the English provinces, and on the Continent. He relinquished his post as conductor during World War II, and for a period the orchestra was led by guest conductors. Sir Adrian Boult became principal conductor in 1950. The London Philharmonic was the first orchestra from Western Europe to tour Soviet Russia, appearing there in the fall of 1956 under Boult. In 1958 William Steinberg became musical director. The orchestra receives an annual subsidy from the Arts Council. This orchestra should not be confused with the historic Royal Philharmonic Society of London.

London Royal Philharmonic Society. *See:* Royal Philharmonic Society of London.

London String Quartet. An outstanding chamber-music ensemble of England, founded in 1908 with Albert Sammons and Thomas Petre, violins, H. Waldo Warner, viola, and C. Warwick Evans, cello. (Only the last named remained with the Quartet until its dissolution.)

The Quartet gave its first concert in London on Jan. 26, 1910, and made its first tour of the United States in the fall of 1920; during the American tour James Levey took over the first violin chair. The Quartet was disbanded in 1935.

London (or Salomon) Symphonies. *See:* Symphony—*Haydn.*

London Symphony. (1) *See:* Symphony—*Haydn.*

(2) *See:* Symphony—*Vaughan Williams.*

London Symphony Orchestra. A symphony orchestra founded at London in 1904 by seceding members of the Queen's Hall Orchestra. Its first concert took place on June 9, Hans Richter conducting. Richter remained principal conductor until 1911, when he was succeeded by Arthur Nikisch, with whom the orchestra toured the United States in 1912. Since Nikisch, the orchestra has been led mostly by guest conductors; among its more permanent conductors have been Willem Mengelberg, Hamilton Harty, and Josef Krips. The orchestra toured South Africa in 1956.

Long, Marguerite, pianist. Born Nimes, France, Nov. 13, 1878. She studied the piano with Antonin Emile Louis Marmontel, and from 1906 on was a distinguished member of the piano faculty at the Paris Conservatory. She also won acclaim as a concert performer, particularly as an interpreter of the music of Debussy and Ravel.

Longfellow, Henry Wadsworth, poet. Born Portland, Me., Feb. 27, 1807; died Cambridge, Mass., March 24, 1882. The following works for orchestra were based on or inspired by Longfellow's poems: Louis Coerne's tone poem, *Hiawatha;* Frederick Delius' tone poem, *Hiawatha;* Henry Gadsby's overture, *The Golden Legend;* Joseph Holbrooke's tone poem, *The Skeleton in Armour;* Marinus de Jong's tone poem, *Hiawatha;* Hugo Kaun's tone poems, *Hiawatha* and *Minnehaha;* Victor Kolar's tone poem, *Hiawatha.* Charles Villiers Stanford wrote incidental music for *The Spanish Student.*

Lopatnikoff, Nikolai, composer. Born Reval, Estonia, March 16, 1903. He studied music at the St. Petersburg Conservatory and in Germany with Ernst

Toch, Hermann Grabner, and Willi Rehberg. He first attracted attention as a composer with a string quartet and a piano concerto, introduced in Germany in 1924 and 1925. In the succeeding decade he achieved prominence through several major works for orchestra given at leading European festivals and in the United States by the Boston Symphony under Koussevitzky. Just before World War II Lopatnikoff came to the United States, becoming a citizen in 1944, and in 1945 professor of composition at the Carnegie Institute of Technology. He was the recipient of a Guggenheim Fellowship in 1945. His best music is in a neo-Classical style, with a strong disposition for linear writing. His major works for orchestra include 3 symphonies, 2 piano concertos, a violin concerto, Sinfonietta, *Opus Sinfonicum*, Concertino, Variations, Divertimento, and *Variazioni concertanti*. He also wrote 2 string quartets, string trio, cello sonata, sonata for piano, violin, and snare drum, *Variations and Epilogue* for cello and piano, and a piano sonata.

Los Angeles Philharmonic Orchestra. A symphony orchestra founded in Los Angeles, Calif., in 1919 by William Andrews Clarke. Walter Henry Rothwell was the first principal conductor. He held this post until 1927, when he was succeeded by George Schneevoigt. Later permanent conductors were Artur Rodzinski, Otto Klemperer, Alfred Wallenstein, and Eduard van Beinum. Besides its winter season at the Philharmonic Auditorium, the orchestra performs each summer at the Hollywood Bowl.

Louisiana Story. Two suites for orchestra by Virgil Thomson (1948) adapted from a score to a documentary motion picture produced by Robert Flaherty. The motion picture described the effect of an oil-development project in Louisiana on a single French-speaking family as seen through the eyes of a fourteen-year-old boy. In his music Thomson used melodic and rhythmic material derived from the songs and dances of the Acadian region. Of the two orchestral suites prepared by the composer from his motion-picture score, the first has been outstandingly successful. It was first performed by the Philadelphia Orchestra under Ormandy on Nov. 26, 1948. In 1949 it received the Pulitzer Prize in music. The suite has four sections. I. Pastoral. This is a picture of the bayou country, of a boy in his rowboat, and of the maneuvers of a dredge in oil-prospecting operations. II. Chorale. A boy playing in a tree with his pet raccoon is depicted. He sees the approach of a drill barge. III. Passacaglia. The boy's adventure robbing an alligator's nest of its eggs is described. The movement ends with the approach of the mother reptile. IV. Fugue. In the motion picture, this music accompanies the boy's efforts to capture an alligator. The second suite is entitled *Acadian Songs and Dances,* its music influenced by the polka and waltz rhythms of Cajun folk tunes and dances.

Louisville Orchestra. A symphony orchestra founded in 1937 at Louisville, Ky., which since then has been conducted by Robert Whitney. This orchestra has placed particular emphasis on contemporary music. In a ten-year period beginning with 1948 it presented 131 world premières. As part of its dynamic program to further the cause of modern composers, the orchestra has commissioned new works from some of the world's leading composers. In April 1953 the Rockefeller Foundation granted the orchestra an endowment of $400,000 "to stimulate, encourage and foster the creation, performance and recording of new musical works by living composers." A further grant of $100,000 followed later to help the recording aspect of the project.

Loure. A slow country dance in 6/4 time marked by sharp accentuations. It is sometimes found as a movement of the Baroque suite, as in Bach's French Suite No. 5 in G major for clavier.

Love for Three Oranges, Suite. A suite for orchestra by Prokofiev, op. 33a, derived from the score to an opera. The opera, with libretto by the composer based on a story by Gozzi, was written for and introduced by the Chicago Opera on Dec. 30, 1921. The orchestral suite has six sections: I. Les Ridicules; II. Scène infernale; III. Marche; IV. Scherzo; V. Le Prince et la princesse;

VI. La Fuite. Three sections are especially popular and are often given at symphony concerts independently of the others. The March, with its vivacious leaps in the melody, has become popular. The other two parts, Scherzo and *Scène infernale,* indulge in the composer's favorite moods of whimsy and the grotesque.

Love, The Magician (Manuel de Falla). *See: Amor brujo, El.*

Love-Death (Wagner). *See: Tristan and Isolde, Prelude and Love-Death.*

Love's Labor Lost. *See:* Shakespeare, William.

Luboschutz, Lea, violinist. Born Odessa, Russia, Feb. 22, 1887. She attended the Odessa School of Music and the Moscow Conservatory. Soon after her graduation from the Conservatory she made her concert début in Odessa, then toured Europe. Her American début took place on Nov. 15, 1907, with the Russian Symphony in New York. Upon returning to Russia she won first prize in a national competition for violinists. This led to additional study with Eugène Ysaÿe in Brussels, and a resumption of concert activity in Europe and the United States. From 1921 to 1925 she taught in conservatories in Berlin and Paris, and in 1927 she joined the violin faculty at the Curtis Institute in Philadelphia. She has appeared in trio performances with her brother Pierre, and her sister, Anna, and in joint recitals with her son, Boris Goldovsky, and with the famous piano virtuoso, Josef Hofmann. She went into retirement in 1953.

Luboschutz and Nemenoff. A distinguished two-piano team made up of Pierre Luboschutz, brother of Lea (see above), and Genia Nemenoff, in private life husband and wife. Pierre Luboschutz (born Odessa, Russia, June 17, 1894) was graduated from the Moscow Conservatory after which he received additional piano instruction in Paris. His professional début took place in 1912 in Moscow with the Koussevitzky Orchestra. After that he toured Europe and the United States in recitals, as soloist with major orchestras, and as the piano accompanist for Efrem Zimbalist and Gregor Piatigorsky among others.

Genia Nemenoff (born Paris, France, Oct. 23, 1908) was Luboschutz' pupil after having attended the Paris Conservatory. She made her concert début in Paris, then appeared in joint recitals with Pablo Casals. Luboschutz and Nemenoff were married in 1931. Soon after that they formed a duo-piano team, making a tour of Europe, and the United States in 1936-1937. Since then they have concentrated their activity on two-piano performances, with tours of Europe, the United States, Greece, Israel, and South Africa.

Lucerne Festival. A summer festival held annually in Lucerne, Switzerland. It was created in 1938 by Adolf Busch, Toscanini, and other notable musicians. The first festival lasted from July 16 to September 1, and included orchestral concerts conducted by Toscanini, Bruno Walter, Mengelberg, Fritz Busch, and Ernest Ansermet, together with choral music and chamber music. With the exception of 1940, the Lucerne Festival has taken place each summer; its program of activity embraces opera, choral music, chamber music, recitals, and symphony concerts. Some of the world's most famous conductors have appeared with the Schweizerisches Festspielorchester or with visiting symphonic ensembles. These orchestral concerts, as well as recitals by leading instrumentalists and singers, take place in the Kunsthaus, a new auditorium facing Lake Lucerne, near the Central Station.

Ludus Tonalis (Play of Tones). A set of 12 piano fugues in as many keys of the chromatic scale by Paul Hindemith (1943). Each fugue is preceded by a prelude and followed by a postlude, while each prelude-fugue-postlude is connected to the next by an interlude in dance form. Subtitled "studies in counterpoint, tonal organization, and piano playing," *Ludus Tonalis* is a forty-five minute work representing one of the composer's most skilful exercises in contrapuntal writing; it is often compared to Bach's *Well-Tempered Clavier.* The work was first performed in its entirety in New York on Feb. 15, 1944, by Willard MacGregor.

Lute. A plucked instrument with fretted

fingerboard, pear-shaped back, and concave sides, and usually with six strings. It was favored by troubadours, and was popular as both a solo and ensemble instrument in the Renaissance. Both Bach and Handel wrote pieces for the lute, but the instrument passed out of general use after the 17th century.

Lydian mode. A Gregorian mode corresponding to the scale from F to F on the white keys of the piano.

Lympany, Moura, pianist. Born Saltash, England, Aug. 18, 1916. She entered the Royal College of Music in London in her thirteenth year, the youngest student ever admitted there, and was graduated with highest honors. She then completed her piano study in Vienna with Paul Weingarten and in London with Tobias Matthay and Mathilde Verne. In 1938 she won second prize in the Queen Elizabeth Competition in Brussels (the first prize going to Emil Gilels), but made such an impression on one of the judges, Artur Rubinstein, that he induced his own Paris manager to promote her professional career. She toured Europe and South America before World War II. In 1945 she became the first British musician (with Adrian Boult) to perform in liberated Paris. One year later she represented her country at the Prague Music Festival. A successful début in the United States took place in New York on Nov. 28, 1948.

Lyric Pieces. A set of 66 piano pieces by Grieg, collected in 10 volumes, opp. 12, 38, 43, 47, 54, 57, 62, 65, 68, and 71 (1867-1901). Each piece is a miniature, and the pieces together are varied in mood and feeling, their emotional gamut ranging from the somber to the capricious, from the gay and the whimsical to the elegiac. Some are nature pictures; others portray different facets of Norwegian life. Among them will be found little dances, marches, folksongs. The most popular are: *To the Spring, Erotik, Lonely Wanderer,* and *Butterfly,* from op. 43; Nocturne and *March of the Dwarfs,* from op. 54; *Wedding Day at Troldhaugen,* from op. 65.

Grieg orchestrated four pieces from op. 54, naming the set *Lyric Suite* (1903). The movements are: I. *Shepherd's Lad;* II. *Norwegian Rustic Dance;* III. Nocturne; IV. *March of the Dwarfs.*

Lyric Suite. (1) See above.

(2) Suite for string quartet by Alban Berg (1926), in six movements: I. *Allegretto giovale;* II. *Andante amoroso;* III. *Allegro misterioso;* IV. *Adagio appassionato;* V. *Presto delirando;* VI. *Largo desolato.* The première performance was given by the Kolisch Quartet in Vienna on Jan. 8, 1927. This is the first work by Berg that employs the twelve-tone technique. Nevertheless it is highly lyrical: the second movement, for example, which carries recollections of a Viennese waltz, or the fourth movement, described by Erwin Stein as "the summit of lyric expression." In the finale, a melancholy movement, Wagner's *Tristan and Isolde* is quoted briefly in the cello. Structurally the *Lyric Suite* is characterized by the fact that a theme or idea from one movement reappears in the next for the sake of cohesion. Berg arranged three of the movements from this suite for chamber orchestra (1928): I. *Andante amoroso;* II. *Allegro misterioso;* III. *Adagio appassionato.* The orchestral version was introduced in Berlin on Jan. 21, 1929.

Lysistrata. *See:* Aristophanes.

Lytton. *See:* Bulwer-Lytton.

M

Ma Mère l'Oye (Ravel). *See: Mother Goose Suite.*

Macbeth. (1) Tone poem by Richard Strauss, op. 23 (1886-1890), introduced in Weimar, Oct. 13, 1890, the composer conducting. Despite the opus number, *Macbeth* is Strauss' first tone poem. He does not follow the action of the Shakespeare tragedy but presents a psychological portrait of the principal protagonists. The themes identifying Macbeth and Lady Macbeth are both forceful and agitated. That of Macbeth is set against a countertheme; that of Lady Macbeth is first heard in flutes and clarinets. A passionate outburst for strings and a sensitive melody for violins provide later contrast.

(2) *See:* Shakespeare, William.

MacDowell, Edward Alexander, composer. Born New York City, Dec. 18, 1861; died there, Jan. 23, 1908. After studying music with private teachers in New York, he attended conservatories in Paris and Frankfort. He remained in Germany for a time as piano teacher. While there he completed his first major works, performed both in Europe and the United States: *Modern Suite,* for orchestra; 2 piano suites; the first piano concerto, and a concert overture *Hamlet and Ophelia.* In 1888 he returned to the United States. That same year he made his first American concert appearance, as soloist with the Kneisel Quartet. Several years later he was the soloist with the Boston Symphony and the New York Philharmonic in performances of his two piano concertos. Other major works performed by the Boston Symphony helped to establish his reputation. When, in 1896, a music department was established at Columbia University, MacDowell was appointed its first professor. He held this post eight years, then resigned owing to bitter differences with the University authorities over the way the department should be run. A disintegration of brain tissues began to take place soon after this resignation, resulting in insanity in 1905. He died three years later. Shortly before his death an endowment was raised to sponsor the MacDowell Colony, a summer retreat for creative people at the composer's summer home in Peterborough, N.H.

Strongly influenced by the German Romantic movement of the late 19th century, MacDowell was a Romanticist who sought to express poetic concepts, and at times supernatural subjects, within soundly conceived structures. Despite the impact of German traditions upon his thinking and writing, he was one of the first American composers seeking and achieving a national identity. Among his major orchestral works are 2 piano concertos, 2 suites (including the *Indian Suite*), 2 tone poems (*Lancelot and Elaine* and *Lamia*), and the concert overture *Hamlet and Ophelia.* He wrote abundantly for the piano, including several sonatas (*Eroica, Norse, Tragica,* and *Keltic*) and suites (*Six Idyls after Goethe, Six Poems after Heine, Woodland Sketches, Sea Pieces, Fireside Tales, New England Idyls,* and *Moon Pictures*).

See: Concerto—*MacDowell; Indian Suite; Woodland Sketches.*

Macfarren, Sir George Alexander, educator and composer. Born London, England, March 2, 1813; died there, Oct. 31, 1887. He was graduated from the Royal College of Music, where from 1834 to 1875 he was a distinguished professor. In 1875 he became professor at Cambridge, and in 1876 principal of the Royal Academy. He was knighted in 1883. He was the composer of many operas and distinguished choral works and songs.

Mackenzie, Sir Alexander Campbell, educator and composer. Born Edinburgh, Scotland, Aug. 22, 1847; died London, England, April 28, 1935. He came from a long line of distinguished musicians. He studied music in Germany and, on a scholarship, at the Royal Academy of Music. From 1888 to 1924 he was principal of the Royal Academy. He was knighted in 1895. He was a prolific composer, whose best works are programmatic and occasionally filled with Scottish elements. Among his most popular works are the *Pibroch Suite* for violin and orchestra, *Scottish Concerto* for piano and orchestra, and 3 *Scottish Rhapsodies.* He also wrote a considerable amount of other orchestral music as well as compositions for chamber-music combinations and for piano.

MacMillan, Sir Ernest Campbell, conductor. Born Mimico, Ontario, Canada, Aug. 18, 1893. He received his academic education at the University of Toronto and his musical training with Alfred Hollins and Frederick Niecks at Edinburgh University. After World War I he settled in Toronto, where from 1926 to 1952 he was principal of the Toronto Conservatory, and from 1931 to 1956 conductor of the Toronto Symphony. He has appeared in United States in organ recitals and as guest conductor and is the author of several educational publications.

Maelzel, Johann Nepomuk, inventor. Born Regensburg, Germany, Aug. 15, 1772; died aboard ship, West Indies, July 31, 1838. After several years as a music teacher in Vienna he turned to the invention of automatic instruments. The Panharmonicon, for example, imitated strings, drums, clarinets, and so forth. He created an ear trumpet for Beethoven and induced him to write the *Battle Symphony* for the Panharmonicon. Eventually they went to court to decide who owned this piece of music, and a satisfactory compromise was finally reached. Maelzel appropriated the idea of the metronome from another inventor, named Winkel, and manufactured it in Paris in 1816. The second movement of Beethoven's Eighth Symphony, however, was not inspired by Maelzel's metronome, as is often claimed, but by another Maelzel invention, the Chronometer.

Maessig. In moderate tempo.

Maestoso. Majestic.

Maestro. Italian for master, a term of respect in Italy for a distinguished musician.

Maestro al cembalo. In the 17th and 18th centuries, the director of an orchestra who performed the continuo parts at the harpsichord from a figured bass, and who from his place at the harpsichord led the other performers.

Maestro di cappella. Originally the Italian equivalent of *Kapellmeister*—that is, the director of an entire musical establishment—but the term later came to mean conductor, specifically the conductor of musical performances in a church.

Maeterlinck, Maurice, author. Born Ghent, Belgium, Aug. 29, 1862; died Nice, France, May 6, 1949. He won the Nobel Prize for literature in 1911. The following of his plays were the source of instrumental compositions (where titles of compositions are not given they are the same as the play):

Aglavaine et Sélysette: Arthur Honegger (prelude for orchestra).

The Blue Bird (L'Oiseau bleu): Fritz Hart (*Thirteen Scenes from The Blue Bird,* for orchestra); Jaroslav Křička (concert overture). Also incidental music by Engelbert Humperdinck, Norman O'Neill, and Albert Wolff.

La Mort de Tintagiles: Adam Carse (overture); Charles Martin Loeffler (tone poem); Francesco Santoliquido (tone poem); Alexander Voormolen (prelude for orchestra).

Pelleas and Melisande: Arnold Schoenberg (tone poem). Also incidental music by Gabriel Fauré and Jean Sibelius.

Maggio musicale fiorentino. *See:* Florence May Music Festival.

Maggiore. Italian for major as opposed to minore for minor.

Magic Fire Scene (Wagner). *See: Wotan's Farewell and Magic Fire Scene.*

Magic Flute (Die Zauberfloete), Overture to The. Overture to an opera by Mozart, libretto by Johann Emanuel Schikaneder; the première took place in Vienna on Sept. 30, 1791. The overture opens with three solemn chords; in the opera they are heard before the *March of the Priests* and Sarastro's air, *O Isis.* A sedate introduction follows. After a change of tempo, a brisk melody appears in violins, then is subjected to fugal treatment, in the course of which it undergoes an involved, and at times a dramatic, development.

Mahler, Fritz, conductor. Born Vienna, Austria, July 16, 1901. He is the nephew of Gustav Mahler (see below). After attending the University of Vienna and completing his music study with Arnold Schoenberg, Alban Berg, and Guido Adler, he served his baton apprenticeship with light opera companies and summer orchestras. From 1930 to 1935 he was conductor of a radio orchestra in Copenhagen. In 1936 he came to the United States, since then his permanent home and the country of his citizenship. He held various posts with minor opera companies and orchestras before becoming conductor of the Erie Philharmonic in Pennsylvania in 1947. In 1953 he was appointed conductor of the Hartford Symphony in Connecticut. After World

War II he made many guest appearances in France, Poland, Scandinavia, and Switzerland.

Mahler, Gustav, composer and conductor. Born Kalischt, Bohemia, July 7, 1860; died Vienna, Austria, May 18, 1911. In 1875 he went to Vienna, where he attended the Conservatory. After his graduation, he led orchestras in small-town theaters and opera companies. A series of increasingly important appointments finally brought him to Europe's leading opera houses in Prague, Leipzig, Budapest, and, in 1897, the Vienna Court Opera. In the decade following 1897 Mahler's autocratic rule over the musical destiny of the Vienna Opera lifted that company to an imperial position among Europe's opera houses. During this period he also conducted the Vienna Philharmonic, proving himself no less remarkable as an interpreter of symphonic music than of opera, and just as intransigeant in his demands for ideal performances. Though he reached heights as a conductor, Mahler placed greater importance on his creative work. His first major work was the song cycle *Songs of a Wayfarer* (*Lieder eines fahrenden Gesellen*), between 1883 and 1885. In 1888 came his first symphony. In the next two decades he completed eight more symphonies as well as several eloquent song cycles with orchestra. His music was sometimes formidable in design, requiring massive forces; and usually he sought to fill it with lofty messages and programs. For these reasons when his major works were introduced in Austria and Germany he was subjected to considerable abuse. But rejection of his music was not his only cause for frustration. At the Vienna Opera he was confronted with so much obstruction in his attempt to maintain the highest possible artistic standards that in 1907 he resigned. Thereafter, most of his activity as conductor took place in New York. He made his American bow as conductor at the Metropolitan Opera on Jan. 1, 1908. The following season he combined his activity at the Metropolitan with the post of principal conductor of the New York Philharmonic. Long a victim of a heart condition, Mahler finally collapsed under the weight of these duties, in New York in 1911. He was taken to Paris for serum treatments, then on his own request he was transported to Vienna to die.

Mahler was the last of the German neo-Romantic symphonists. His vast orchestral structures are filled with personal feelings, questionings, doubts, and struggles with spiritual problems. The *Weltschmerz* from which he suffered continually can be found in his music as he used tones to probe the meaning of life and death, to uncover the mysteries of nature. He was, it is true, often bombastic and prolix, often extravagant in his emotional outpourings. But he was also capable of nobility and grandeur of thought, profundity of concept, and intensity of emotion. Thus his greatest symphonies, while uneven in quality, are always a rewarding esthetic and emotional experience. His principal works are for orchestra and include 9 symphonies and the song cycles with orchestra, *Songs of a Wayfarer* (*Lieder eines fahrenden Gesellen*), *The Song of the Earth* (*Das Lied von der Erde*), and *Songs of Dead Children* (*Kindertotenlieder*).

See: Lied von der Erde, Das; Kindertotenlieder; Symphony—*Mahler.*

Maier and Pattison. A two-piano team made up of Guy Maier (born Buffalo, N.Y., Aug. 15, 1892; died Santa Monica, Calif., Sept. 24, 1956) and Lee Pattison (born Grand Rapids, Wis., July 22, 1890). Their début took place at New York City in 1916. For the next fifteen years the team toured America and Europe, its success being largely responsible for stimulating interest in two-piano music in the United States. After disbanding as a team, Maier appeared in solo performances, and taught piano at the Juilliard School in New York and the University of California. Lee Pattison also gave solo performances, taught piano in schools and universities, and held some directorial posts in opera.

Major interval. An interval a semitone larger than the minor and a semitone smaller than the augmented.

Major scale. A scale with half steps between the third and fourth, and seventh and eighth degrees.

Malade imaginaire, Le. *See:* Molière.

Malaga (Albéniz). *See: Iberia* (1).

Malagueña. A Spanish dance with a melody that has the character of an improvisation; it originated in Malaga, Andalusia. Two of the most popular compositions in this form are Pablo de Sarasate's Malagueña, op. 21, no. 1, for violin and piano, and Ernesto Lecuona's Malagueña from *Suite Andalucía,* for piano.

Malcuzynski, Witold, pianist. Born Warsaw, Poland, Aug. 10, 1914. After attending the Warsaw Conservatory, he studied piano privately with Paderewski. In 1937 he won first prize in the Chopin Competition in Warsaw. Just before World War II he went to Paris, then when Paris was occupied by the Nazis he fled to South America, where he made an extended tour. His North American début took place in New York City in 1942. After World War II, he made two world tours, distinguishing himself particularly in Chopin. He was selected by the Kozsciusko Foundation to commemorate the centenary of Chopin's death in 1949 with a Carnegie Hall recital, and was one of two recitalists chosen to commemorate the same event in Paris.

Malinconia. Melancholy.

Malinconia, La. *See:* Quartet—*Beethoven.*

Malipiero, Gian Francesco, composer. Born Venice, Italy, March 18, 1882. For a single year he attended the Vienna Conservatory, then was a pupil of Enrico Bossi in Venice and Bologna. He first became interested in old Italian music in 1902; he subsequently completed valuable researches into this field and produced important editions of works by old Italian masters. In 1913 he went to Paris, where his personal contacts with Ravel, Debussy, Stravinsky, and Manuel de Falla helped him to extend his own artistic horizon. He now achieved a style in which specifically Italian features were skilfully combined with advanced harmonic and rhythmic techniques. Malipiero first achieved recognition when four of his compositions, submitted under various pseudonyms, won the first four prizes in a national competition in Italy just before World War I. His fame spread throughout Europe after that war with the performance of such notable works as the *Pause del silenzio,* introduced at Milan in 1913, *Impressioni dal vero,* first given in Rome in 1917, and a string quartet entitled *Rispetti e strambotti,* which won the Elizabeth Sprague Coolidge Prize in 1920, and was introduced in Amsterdam in 1923.

After World War I, Malipiero went to live in the little town of Asolo, not far from Venice. Since then he has industriously pursued his career as composer, writing many works in all media. He has also continued his researches into old Italian music, and he has taught a select number of private students. Once a week Malipiero emerged from his seclusion in Asolo to teach composition at the Benedetto Marcello Conservatory in Venice, of which he became director in 1939. During World War II he remained in Asolo, where he engaged in secret anti-Nazi activity. He is the author of *L'Orchestra* (1920), *Stravinsky* (1945), *La Pietra del bando* (1947), and an autobiography, *Così va lo mondo* (1946). His principal works for orchestra include 9 symphonies, concertos for various solo instruments and orchestra (piano; violin; cello; two pianos; violin, cello, and piano), numerous shorter works (*Pause del silenzio, Impressioni dal vero, La Cimarosiana, Variazioni senza tema* for piano and orchestra, *L'Esilio dell' eroe, Sette invenzioni, Concertante in eco, Fantasie di ogni giorni,* and *Vivaldiana*). His major chamber-music works include 7 string quartets (among them *Rispetti e strambotti, Stornelli e ballate,* and *Cantari alla madrigalesca*), *Ricercari* for 11 instruments, *Ritrovari* for 11 instruments, *Sonata a tre,* and *Sonata a cinque.* He also wrote many compositions for the piano.

See: Rispetti e strambotti; Symphony—*Malipiero.*

Malko, Nicolai, conductor. Born Brailov, Russia, May 4, 1883. He attended the St. Petersburg Conservatory, then studied conducting with Felix Mottl. In 1922 he organized a conducting class at the Moscow Conservatory, and from 1926 to 1928 was conductor of the Leningrad Philharmonic. He left Russia in 1928, appeared as guest conductor of leading

European orchestras, and organized conducting classes in Prague, Copenhagen, and Salzburg. He made his American début in Boston with the Boston Symphony in 1940. For over a quarter of a century he was principal conductor of the Danish State Radio. In 1954 he became conductor of the Yorkshire Orchestra in England, and in 1956 of the Sydney Symphony in Australia. He is the author of *The Conductor and his Baton* (1950).

Mallarmé, Stéphane, symbolist poet. Born Paris, France, March 18, 1842; died Fontainebleau, France, Sept. 8, 1898. His poems were the inspiration of Debussy's *The Afternoon of a Faun* and Paul Hindemith's *Hérodiade* for chamber orchestra.

Mancando (or Mancante). Dying or fading away.

Manfred. Concert overture by Schumann, op. 115, from the incidental music prepared by the composer for Byron's poetical drama (1848-1849). The incidental music comprises fourteen numbers besides the overture, and it was introduced at the Weimar Court Theater on June 13, 1852. The incidental music is rarely heard, but the overture is one of Schumann's best-known shorter works for orchestra. After three chords for orchestra, a brooding section depicts Manfred's torment. The tempo changes. Now it is Manfred's struggle that is described in a turbulent passage for violins. A contrasting subject speaks for Astarte, the woman wronged by Manfred. Once again Manfred's struggle is narrated in a stormy development of both main themes. Three trumpet chords, sometimes described as Manfred's guilt-theme, bring on a more placid section in which a portion of the Astarte melody is recalled. The overture ends quietly with a description of Manfred's death.

(2) *See:* Byron, George Noel Gordon, Lord.

(3) *See:* Symphony—*Tchaikovsky*.

Mann, Thomas, author. Born Luebeck, Germany, June 6, 1875; died Zurich, Switzerland, Aug. 12, 1955. He won the Nobel Prize for literature in 1929. A penetrating and knowledgeable music lover, Mann filled some of his novels and stories with musical discussions and char-

acters. *Buddenbrooks* contains a portrait of a musical prodigy. *Doctor Faustus* has for its hero a composer who employs the twelve-tone technique (for additional comment *see:* Schoenberg, Arnold). Gustav Mahler was the prototype for a principal character in *Death in Venice*. Music is also forcefully present in the short story, *Tristan,* and in the novels *Tonio Kroeger* and *The Magic Mountain.* Two essays on Wagner appear in Mann's *Essays of Three Decades* (1947).

Mannes, David, violinist, conductor, and educator. Born New York City, Feb. 16, 1866; died there, April 24, 1959. After pursuing the study of music in New York and Berlin and with Eugène Ysaÿe in Brussels he became a member of the violin section of the New York Symphony. During this period (1898) he married Clara Damrosch, daughter of Leopold Damrosch and sister of Walter (born Breslau, Germany, Dec. 12, 1869; died New York City, March 16, 1948). A gifted pianist, Clara joined her husband in sonata recitals for many years. After leaving the New York Symphony in 1912, Mannes inaugurated free orchestral concerts at the Metropolitan Museum of Art, conducting them until 1947.

Mannes was also a distinguished music educator, director of the Music School Settlement and the Music School Settlement for Colored People, both in New York, and from 1915 until his retirement in 1947 director (with his wife) of the David Mannes School of Music, which he founded (now the Mannes College of Music). He is the author of an autobiography, *Music Is My Faith* (1938).

Manns, Sir August, conductor. Born Stolzenberg, Germany, March 12, 1825; died London, England, March 1, 1907. After learning the elements of music from a local teacher and playing in various German orchestras, he went to London and in 1854 was appointed assistant conductor at the Crystal Palace. One year later he became principal conductor, and in 1856 he initiated the famous Saturday Concerts, which he conducted in almost 15,000 concerts over a period of forty-five years. He was knighted in 1903.

Manual. Keyboard of an organ.

Manzoni Requiem. *See:* Requiem—*Verdi*.

Maraca. A percussion instrument shaken like a rattle. It consists of a dried Cuban gourd filled with dried seeds or beads, and is found mainly in dance orchestras. It is used in Gershwin's *Cuban Overture*.

Marcando (or Marcato). With emphasis.

Marcello, Benedetto, composer. Born Venice, Italy, July 24, 1686; died Brescia, Italy, July 24, 1739. He studied music with Antonio Lotti and Francesco Gasparini, but because of his father's objections to music prepared for the law. He held many government positions, including one as member of the Council of Forty for 14 years. But musical activity was never abandoned. As a composer, his importance rests mainly on his choral music. But he also produced some instrumental works which are sometimes revived, including concerti grossi and various sonatas. The principal Conservatory in Venice is named after him.

March. A musical composition in 2/4, 4/4, or 6/8 time intended for marching. It is usually in three-part song form, the middle section being a trio. Music in the form and style of a march is often found in other instrumental compositions. There are funeral marches in Beethoven's *Eroica Symphony* and in his Piano Sonata in A-flat major, op. 26, and in Chopin's Piano Sonata No. 2. Wedding marches appear in Carl Goldmark's *Rustic Wedding Symphony* and in Mendelssohn's incidental music for *A Midsummer Night's Dream*. The most popular wedding march of all comes from Wagner's opera *Lohengrin*.

A so-called "Turkish" march is in Beethoven's incidental music to *The Ruins of Athens*. A popular Hungarian march, the *Rakóczy March,* is an orchestral episode from Berlioz' *The Damnation of Faust*. Tchaikovsky wrote a Slavic march for orchestra in *Marche slave,* and Schubert a military march for piano four hands in *Marche militaire,* op. 51, no. 1. There is a charming march of the dwarfs for piano in Grieg's *Lyric Pieces,* a march of little lead soldiers for orchestra in Gabriel Pierné's *Album pour mes petits amis;* and an orchestral funeral march for a marionette by Charles Gounod. Edward Elgar wrote five symphonic marches, collectively entitled *Pomp and Circumstance*. The American bandleader, John Philip Sousa, has been called the "march king" by virtue of his many popular marches for band, the most famous being *The Stars and Stripes Forever*.

Marchand, Louis, organist. Born Lyons, France, Feb. 2, 1669; died Paris, France, Feb. 17, 1732. After studying organ with his father he held various organ posts in Paris, including that at the Chapel Royal, becoming famous for his virtuosity and skill at improvisation. He left Paris under a cloud, and traveled throughout Germany. He was scheduled to engage Johann Sebastian Bach in an organ-playing contest in Dresden but failed to make an appearance. Finally permitted to return to Paris, he not only reestablished his former position as a leading organist of France but became even more famous than before. He wrote many pieces for the organ and harpsichord.

Marche slave. For orchestra by Tchaikovsky, op. 31 (1876), written for a benefit concert for Serbian soldiers wounded in the war against Turkey. This concert took place in St. Petersburg on Nov. 17, 1876, Nicholas Rubinstein conducting. The work is in three parts, played without interruption. In the first a short introduction leads to the main march melody for strings, a theme taken from an old Serbian folksong. The ensuing trio quotes two more folksongs and the Russian national anthem. The concluding section repeats the march music, but with loud and ringing accents, proclaiming the victory of the Serbs over the Turks.

Marcia alla turca. *See:* Turkish March.

Maria Stuart. *See:* Schiller, Friedrich von.

Maria Theresa Symphony. *See:* Symphony—*Haydn*.

Marimba. An instrument popular in southern Mexico. It consists of graduated pieces of tuned wooden blocks suspended on wooden resonators and played with drumsticks. It has a compass of five octaves. Concertos for marimba and orchestra have been written by Darius Milhaud and Paul Creston.

Markevitch, Igor, conductor and composer. Born Kiev, Russia, July 27, 1912. He was still an infant when his family settled in Vevey, Switzerland. There he studied the piano with Alfred Cortot.

When he was fourteen he went to Paris to continue his music study with Nadia Boulanger and Vittorio Rieti. He early demonstrated his creative talent by completing a *Sinfonietta* for orchestra when he was seventeen, and a piano concerto a year later, which were acclaimed in Paris and London. He realized an even more striking success with *Rebus,* a ballet suite for orchestra, introduced at Paris in 1931. Later works for orchestra include a Partita for piano and orchestra, *Introduction and Hymn,* and *Le nouvel âge.*

He also successfully pursued a career as conductor. After some study with Hermann Scherchen he made his baton début in his eighteenth year with the Concertgebouw Orchestra in Amsterdam. After World War II he made highly successful guest appearances with major European symphony orchestras and opera companies; he also toured South America and Israel, and participated in festivals at Salzburg, Vienna, Lucerne, Holland, and Berlin. In 1953 he settled in London, and a year later made his bow at Covent Garden. His American début took place on March 18, 1955, with the Boston Symphony. In 1957 he was appointed principal conductor of the Lamoureux Orchestra and made Knight of the Legion of Honor. When the National Symphony Orchestra of Mexico City made its first tour of the United States in the fall of 1958, Markevitch was one of its conductors.

Marmion. *See:* Scott, Sir Walter.

Marmontel, Antoine-François, pianist and teacher. Born Clermont-Ferrand, France, July 16, 1816; died Paris, France, Jan. 17, 1898. He attended the Paris Conservatory, where in 1837 he became instructor in solfège. From 1848 to 1887 he was head of the piano department, his many students including Georges Bizet, Debussy, and Vincent d'Indy. He wrote numerous texts on piano technique and style.

Marriage of Figaro (Le Nozze di Figaro), Overture to The. An overture to an opera buffa by Mozart. The libretto, by Lorenzo da Ponte, is based on Beaumarchais' *Le Mariage de Figaro,* and the opera was introduced in Vienna on May 1, 1786. The overture is light and gay, magically creating an opera-buffa atmosphere of vivacity. It opens with a soft, rapid passage for strings. This leads to a secondary subject for woodwinds. The lyrical second theme subsequently appears in the strings. The vivacious mood of the opening returns to end the overture.

Marsick, Martin Pierre Joseph, violinist and teacher. Born Jupille, Belgium, March 9, 1848; died Paris, France, Oct. 21, 1924. He attended the Conservatories in Liège and Brussels, and completed his violin study with Joachim in Berlin. His début at Paris in 1873 was an emphatic success, leading to extended tours of Europe, and in 1895-1896 of the United States. From 1892 on he was a distinguished professor of the violin at the Paris Conservatory, among his pupils being Carl Flesch and Jacques Thibaud.

Marteau, Henri, violinist and teacher. Born Reims, France, March 31, 1874; died Lichtenberg, Bavaria, Oct. 3, 1934. He made his début in his tenth year as soloist with the Vienna Philharmonic, Hans Richter conducting. He then attended the Paris Conservatory where, in 1892, he won first prize. In the same year he made his first tour of the United States. In 1894 he toured Sweden, and in 1897, Russia. In 1900 he was appointed professor of the violin at the Geneva Conservatory, and from 1908 to 1915 occupied a similar post at the Berlin High School for Music, succeeding Joachim. From 1915 to 1920 he lived in Sweden, where he became a citizen, conducted the Goeteborg Symphony, taught and played the violin, and was elected a member of the Swedish Academy of Music. After 1921 he taught the violin at several important European schools including the Conservatories of Leipzig and Dresden. His last public appearance took place in Sweden in 1934 on the occasion of his 50th anniversary as a concert artist. Throughout his career he was also often heard in distinguished performances of chamber music, often with ensembles he himself organized.

Martellato. Hammered. In string music, a hammering style of bowing.

Martin, Frank, composer. Born Geneva, Switzerland, Sept. 15, 1890. After studying music with Joseph Lauber he attended Geneva College. *Poèmes payens,* in 1911, was his first work to receive public performance. From 1923 to 1925 Martin lived in Paris, absorbing musical experiences. Returning to his native land, he soon became one of its most prominent musicians. From 1927 to 1937 he played piano and harpsichord with a chamber-music ensemble; he founded the "Technicum Moderne de Musique"; served as music critic on the *Tribune de Genève;* was director of the Jaques-Dalcroze Institute of the Geneva Conservatory. From 1952 to 1958 he taught at the Cologne Conservatory, after which he returned to Switzerland.

In his first works Martin was faithful to accepted traditions, writing music conservative in style and technique. After his stay in Paris he grew more audacious and experimented with the newer resources of tonality, harmony, and rhythm. After 1938 he achieved full maturity with a style fusing old and new elements and permitting him complete latitude of expression within traditional structures. In this last manner he wrote the works that brought him world recognition, including the *Petite symphonie concertante,* which has been successfully performed in many countries. Other orchestral works include a symphony, various concertos (piano; violin; harpsichord; seven wind instruments, percussion, and strings), *Rhythmes,* a Ballade for piano and orchestra and a Ballade for cello and orchestra, Etudes for string orchestra, and *Six Monologues from Jedermann.* In chamber music he produced 2 string quartets, 2 violin sonatas, piano quintet, piano trio (on Irish melodies), string trio, various ballades, and a Rhapsody for two violins, two violas, and double bass.

See: Concerto—*Martin; Petite symphonie concertante.*

Martinon, Jean, composer and conductor. Born Lyons, France, Jan. 18, 1910. He attended the Conservatories of Lyons and Paris. His first symphony and a *Symphonietta,* completed between 1934 and 1936, were successfully performed in Paris. In World War II he was a prisoner of war for two years; during his internment he completed *Psalm 136,* a major success when heard in Paris in 1942, and a year later awarded the City of Paris

Prize. After the war Martinon came to prominence as conductor as well. From 1944 to 1946 he was assistant conductor of the Concerts du Conservatoire in Paris. In 1946 he became principal conductor of the Bordeaux Orchestra, and after that of the Lamoureux Orchestra. In 1959 he was appointed music director of the Israel Philharmonic. He made his American début on March 29, 1957, with the Boston Symphony. His principal works for orchestra include the *Symphonietta, Concerto giocoso* for violin and orchestra, *Hymn à la vie, Concerto lyrique* for string quartet and small orchestra, and *Les Metamorphoses d'Ovide.* He also wrote a string quartet, string trio, piano trio, wind quintet, woodwind trio, violin sonatinas, and various compositions for piano including a sonatina.

Martinu, Bohuslav, composer. Born Polička, Bohemia, Dec. 8, 1890. His townspeople raised a fund to send him to the Prague Conservatory, from which he was graduated when he was twenty-three. From 1913 to 1923 he played the violin in the Czech Philharmonic. During this period he studied with Joseph Suk and completed his first large works, including the ballet *Istar* and *Vanishing Midnight* and the *Czech Rhapsody,* both for orchestra. From 1923 to 1940 he lived in Paris, where he was strongly influenced by contemporary French music and profited from the advice and criticism of Albert Roussel. His music now assimilated the economy, grace, and objectivity of modern French music, a vein in which he wrote *Half-Time* for orchestra (described as a "symphony of rhythm" and inspired by a football match), and *La Bagarre,* also for orchestra, a musical description of a crowd. After that Martinu's style experienced another radical change as Czech folk elements were absorbed into his writing. Some of the works reflecting this new tendency were the opera *The Miracle of Our Lady,* the ballet *Spaliček,* and a string sextet that won the Elizabeth Sprague Coolidge Award in 1932. Soon after the invasion of Paris by the Nazis, Martinu came to the United States, where he established residence and became a citizen. In the United States he proved even more productive than heretofore, writing numerous works which have been performed by the world's leading musical organizations. His many compositions for orchestra include 6 symphonies, various concertos (piano; violin; cello; viola; harpsichord; string quartet; two pianos; three pianos; flute and violin), *Duo concertante* for two violins and orchestra, *Sinfonia* for piano and orchestra, *Suite concertante* for violin and orchestra, *Toccata and Two Canzone* for piano and chamber orchestra, *Incantations* for piano and orchestra, and sundry other compositions including Partita, Concerto Grosso, *Tre Ricercari, Memorial to Lidice, Fantaisies symphoniques, The Rock, Frescoes after Piero della Francesca,* and *The Parables.* His chamber music embraces 6 string quartets, piano trios, a nonet, various sonatas, a piano quintet, string sextet, string quintet and string trio. Among his piano compositions are preludes, mazurkas, etudes, polkas, and other small pieces.

See: Concerto Grosso—*Martinu.*

Martucci, Giuseppe, composer and conductor. Born Capua, Italy, Jan. 6, 1856; died Naples, Italy, June 1, 1909. From 1867 to 1871 he attended the Naples Conservatory. After touring Italy and England as a piano virtuoso, he was appointed professor of the piano at the Naples Conservatory in 1880. One year later he made his début as a conductor in Naples and one year after that led a notable Wagner concert commemorating the master's recent death. His most notable achievements as conductor came in Bologna where, as director of the Conservatory from 1886 to 1902, he led concerts of old and new music and was a propagandist for Wagner; in 1888 he conducted the Italian première of *Tristan and Isolde.* From 1902 until his death he was director of the Naples Conservatory. Despite his admiration of Wagner he was in the vanguard of those Italian composers who were directing Italian music away from opera and towards the field of symphonic music. In all his works, his indebtedness to Wagner and Liszt is apparent. He wrote 2 symphonies, 2 piano concertos, *Quattro piccoli pezzi* for orchestra, 2 piano trios, a piano quintet, a

cello sonata, and some pieces for the piano.

Mason, Daniel Gregory, composer, teacher, and writer on music. Born Brookline, Mass., Nov. 20, 1873; died Greenwich, Conn., Dec. 4, 1953. He was the grandson of Lowell Mason (born Medfield, Mass., Jan. 8, 1792; died Orange, N.J., Aug. 11, 1872), a distinguished pioneer in the field of music education in the public schools, for many years a member of the Public Board of Education in Massachusetts. Daniel Gregory Mason's father, Henry, was one of the founders of the piano and organ manufacturing firm of Mason & Hamlin. Daniel's uncle was William Mason (born Boston, Mass., Jan. 24, 1829; died New York City, July 14, 1908), a celebrated concert pianist and one of the most distinguished piano teachers of his time in the United States.

Daniel Gregory was graduated from Harvard in 1895, after which he studied music with Ethelbert Nevin, George Chadwick, Arthur Whiting, and in France with Vincent d'Indy. In 1910 he joined the music faculty of Columbia University. In 1929 he was appointed professor, and some years later head of the music department, retiring as professor emeritus in 1942. As a composer, Mason first attracted attention with a piano quartet, written in 1912, and introduced by Gabrilowitsch and the Kneisel Quartet. In 1916 the Philadelphia Orchestra under Stokowski introduced his first symphony. His best-known composition, the festival overture *Chanticleer,* was introduced in 1928. Other works for orchestra include two more symphonies (the third being *A Lincoln Symphony*), Prelude and Fugue for piano and orchestra, and *Suite after English Folksongs.* In the field of chamber music he produced a piano quartet, *String Quartet on Negro Themes, Variations on a Theme of John Powell* for string quartet, and a Serenade for string quartet. Among his piano works are the suites *Country Pictures* and *Silhouettes,* together with preludes, an Impromptu, and a Ballade.

Mason also distinguished himself as a writer on music. His most important books are: *From Grieg to Brahms* (1902); *Beethoven and his Forerunners*

(1904); *The Romantic Composers* (1906); *Great Modern Composers* (1916); *Artistic Ideals* (1925); *The Quartets of Beethoven* (1927); *The Dilemma of American Music* (1928); *Tune in, America* (1931); and *The Chamber Music of Brahms* (1933). He was also the author of a book of reminiscences, *Music In My Time* (1938), and editor of *The Art of Music* (1917).

See: Chanticleer.

Masque of the Red Death. *See:* Poe, Edgar Allan.

Masquerade. Suite for orchestra by Aram Khatchaturian, derived from incidental music to a play by Mikhail Lermontov, produced in 1939. From this score the composer assembled five episodes into a suite which was introduced by the Moscow Radio Orchestra in 1944: I. Waltz; II. Nocturne; III. Romance; IV. Mazurka; V. Galop. The music is consistently light in style and filled with infectious melodies.

Masques et bergamasques. Suite for orchestra by Gabriel Fauré, op. 112 (1920). This work was derived from music for "an entertainment," text by René Fauchois inspired by a poem by Paul Verlaine. The "entertainment" was introduced in Monte Carlo on April 10, 1919. The suite consists of an overture, three dances, and two earlier works by Fauré —the Pavane for orchestra, op. 50 (1887), and the orchestral setting of the song on a text by Verlaine, *Clair de lune,* op. 46, no. 2 (1887).

Mass in B minor. One of the most celebrated Masses in all the choral literature and one of the crowning masterworks by Johann Sebastian Bach.

Bach completed two sections of the Mass in B minor, the Kyrie and Gloria, in 1733 as a "trifling example of my skill," for King Augustus III of Saxony when Bach sought the post of composer in the Saxon Royal Chapel. The other parts were completed five years later. There was no performance of the complete Mass in Bach's time. The première took place in Berlin in two performances, the first half on Feb. 20, 1834, and the second half a year later, on Feb. 12, 1835.

In structural design, the Mass in B minor is one of the most massive in the choral literature. Within the five traditional sections (Kyrie, Gloria, Credo, Sanctus and Benedictus, and Agnus Dei) there are 24 parts (6 arias, 3 duets, and 15 choruses) requiring three and a half hours for performance. This formidable edifice contains some of the most exalted music Bach ever wrote. Unlike his *Passion According to St. Matthew,* which is subjective in the approach of a devout Christian to his religion, the Mass in B minor is completely objective. Personal feelings are not permitted to intrude as Bach creates a mighty paean of praise to the greater glory of God. The most noble pages are the choral ones, beginning with the opening monumental Kyrie, which suggested to Albert Schweitzer "nations innumerable ever joining with one accord in this prayer for mercy." After this, the choral passages follow one another like giant tidal waves. Some are expressive of joy (the five-part Gloria); some are profoundly moving in their pathos (*Crucifixus*); some are titanic in their passion and strength (Sanctus and Credo). Of the arias the most eloquent are the *Laudamus Te* for mezzo soprano, Benedictus for tenor against a contrapuntal background of a solo violin, and the Agnus Dei for contralto. The *Dona nobis pacem* with which the Mass ends is not so much a humble plea for peace as a triumphant expression of thanksgiving.

Massenet, Jules Emile Frédéric, composer. Born Montaud, France, May 12, 1842; died Paris, France, Aug. 13, 1912. He attended the Paris Conservatory and won the Prix de Rome. Soon after returning from Rome his first opera, *La Grand'-Tante,* was produced at the Opéra-Comique in 1867. It was in the field of opera that Massenet became famous, especially for works like *Manon* and *Thaïs.* But he achieved his first success with incidental music to *Les Erinnyes* in 1873, a score that contains his perennially popular *Elégie.* Massenet wrote incidental music for other plays, by Hugo, Sardou, Racine, and others. From 1878 until his death he was professor of composition at the Paris Conservatory. He was also a member of the Académie des Beaux-Arts; he was the youngest man ever elected to that body. He was also made Grand Officer of the Legion of Honor. His principal works for orchestra include 7 suites (including *Scènes pittoresques* and *Scènes alsaciennes*), 3 concert overtures, piano concerto, *Fantaisie* for piano and orchestra, and shorter works. His famous *Meditation,* a staple in the violin repertory, comes from the opera *Thaïs,* where it appears as an orchestral entr'acte with violin obbligato preceding Act 2, Scene 1.

Mastersingers, The (Die Meistersinger von Nuernberg), Preludes to Acts 1 and 3. Orchestral preludes to an opera by Wagner, with libretto by the composer. The opera was introduced in Munich on June 21, 1868. The Prelude to Act 1 opens with the Mastersingers theme, a majestic march in full chords. The tender theme for woodwinds that follows is the motif of the "Banner of the Mastersingers." Later comes the popular "Prize Song" in the violins and the motif of "Love's Ardor" in strings. All these ideas, and others, are woven into a remarkable polyphonic fabric, after which the prelude ends with a resounding restatement of the opening Mastersingers theme in full orchestra.

The Prelude to Act 3 is deeply reflective music, a tonal portrait of the cobbler-philosopher Hans Sachs. A brooding song for cellos is the first main subject, the second part of which soon receives a fugato treatment. A sonorous chorale for brass is then presented, followed by a quotation of the "Prize Song." The brooding song that opened the prelude returns first in the entire orchestra, then more plaintively in strings, to conclude the prelude.

For other orchestral excerpts from *The Mastersingers,* see: *Dance of the Apprentices, Procession of the Mastersingers.*

Mathis der Maler (Mathias, the Painter). A "symphony" by Paul Hindemith (1934), introduced in Berlin on March 12, 1934, Furtwaengler conducting. The "symphony" was derived by the composer from his opera of the same name, libretto by the composer based on the life of the 16th-century painter, Mathias Gruenewald, and introduced in Zurich on May 28, 1938. During the Peasants War of 1524, the painter Gruenewald abandons his art to become a leader in the peasant uprising against the Church. After that he retires to Oldenwald, where he receives the visions that enable him to paint the panels for the Isenheim Altar.

The "symphony"—it is actually a suite—is in three parts. I. The Concert of the Angels. This is the overture of the opera, gentle music whose main theme is an old German folk tune heard throughout the opera (*Es sungen drei Engel*); it first appears in trombones in the eighth bar. II. The Entombment. This is an intermezzo in the sixth scene. Two themes are prominent: the first in muted strings and woodwind, and the second in the flute against pizzicato strings. III. The Temptation of St. Anthony. This is an intermezzo from the final scene. Part of the music consists of lively strains leading to a fugato; part, in a chorale for woodwind followed by still another chorale for brass.

It is this music that discredited both the composer and the conductor, Furtwaengler, with the Nazi regime. The subject of a peasant uprising was obnoxious to the Nazi authorities, who had allowed Furtwaengler to perform the orchestral suite while refusing him permission to conduct the opera itself. When Furtwaengler persisted in his demands to be allowed to present the opera he was removed from all his posts for several months. Hindemith was compelled to leave the country.

Matin, Le. See: Symphony—*Haydn.*

Matrimonio Segreto (The Secret Marriage), Overture to Il. An overture to an opera buffa by Domenico Cimarosa. The libretto, by Giovanni Bertati, was based on an English play by George Coleman the elder and David Garrick, *The Clandestine Marriage.* The opera was first produced in Vienna on Feb. 7, 1792. Its gay overture occasionally reminds us of Mozart, and at times even anticipates Rossini. Three chords precede a brisk subject which sets the overture into fleet motion. The vivacity continues until the end, even though a second principal subject, heard first in the strings, is in a gentler vein.

Matthay, Tobias, pianist and teacher. Born London, England, Feb. 19, 1858;

died High Marley, Surrey, England, Dec. 14, 1945. He attended the Royal Academy of Music, then from 1876 to 1925 was a member of its piano faculty, a professor from 1880 on. He made his début as a concert pianist at London in 1880. Fifteen years later he abandoned concert work to found his own piano school in London, and from 1925 devoted to it all his efforts as teacher. He was one of England's most distinguished teachers of the piano, the exponent of a touch method controlled by weight and relaxation. He wrote several texts expounding the theories of the "Matthay system" of piano technique, including *The Art of Touch* (1903), *Relaxation Studies* (1908), and *The Rotation Principle* (1912). He was also the composer of over a hundred works for the piano.

Mazeppa. (1) Tone poem for orchestra by Liszt (1828, revised 1837 and 1841), first performed in Weimar on April 16, 1854, the composer conducting. It is based on a poem by Victor Hugo, which the music follows with realistic literalness. (Musically it is based on Liszt's own piano study in *Etudes d'exécution transcendante*.) Mazeppa is a famous Asiatic chieftain who is tied to an untamed horse on which he rides for three days across the Ukrainian plains until the horse collapses. The tone poem opens with a short phrase for wind instruments leading to a virulent first subject describing Mazeppa; this first subject is heard in trombones, cellos, and double basses. After the theme is worked out, the sweeping ride across the plains is powerfully recreated in energetic dynamics and sonorities. The suffering of Mazeppa is depicted in an elegiac melody that provides contrast. After the return and the further enlargement of the Mazeppa theme, the tone poem ends in a peaceful atmosphere, with the music giving a vivid description of the birds encircling the victimized hero and horse.

(2) *See:* Etude—*Liszt.*

Mazurka. A Polish national dance in two or four sections, triple time, and with an accent usually on the second beat. Chopin wrote 55 mazurkas, which include some of his most significant national compositions. Generally speaking, these pieces are of an improvisational nature, free in form and varied in rhythm. They embody some of the salient features of the Polish folk dance, notably an inclination to build an entire section from a simple phrase or two simple alternating phrases, and an occasional use of medieval Church modes. These mazurkas are varied in mood. At times they are somber, at times ironical, at times contemplative, at times fiery. The following are the most popular: B-flat, op. 7, no. 1 (1831); A minor, op. 17, no. 4 (1833); B-flat minor, op. 24, no. 4 (1835); C-sharp minor, op. 30, no. 4 (1837); D major, op. 33, no. 2 (1838); B minor, op. 33, no. 4 (1838); C-sharp minor, op. 50, no. 3 (1841); F-sharp minor, op. 59, no. 3 (1845); C-sharp minor, op. 63, no. 3 (1846); A minor, op. 67, no. 4 (1846); and A minor, op. 68, no. 2 (1849).

The 20th-century Polish composer Karol Szymanowski wrote 22 mazurkas: 20 in op. 50 (1926) and two in op. 62 (1934). They reveal his indebtedness to Chopin, and are successful in combining the identifying characteristics of the Chopin mazurka with 20th-century harmonic and rhythmic techniques.

There is a popular mazurka for orchestra in Glinka's folk opera *A Life for the Czar,* and another in Tchaikovsky's ballet, *Swan Lake.*

Measure. A bar.

Medea. (1) Ballet suite by Samuel Barber, op. 23 (1946). The ballet was written for and introduced by Martha Graham, in New York City on May 10, 1946; it was originally called *The Serpent Heart* and later *Cave of the Heart.* Treatment of the Medea-Jason legend is not literal but serves, as the composer explains, "to project psychological states of jealousy and vengeance which are timeless." The orchestral suite prepared by the composer, and renamed *Medea,* was introduced in Philadelphia on Dec. 5, 1947, Eugene Ormandy conducting. It opens with a *Parodos* in which the characters make their appearance. A reflective and lyrical *Choros* then comments on the coming action. A dance of innocence represents *The Young Princess,* and a heroic dance, *Jason.* Now comes a second *Choros,* this time in a plaintive mood, which leads to

Medea's Dance of Vengeance. The *Kantikos Agonias* is filled with foreboding, then interrupted by Medea's return after she has murdered the Princess and her own children. In the concluding *Exodos* the various themes of the principal characters are woven together.

In 1955 Barber rewrote sections from the above suite and published them as *Medea's Meditation and Dance of Vengeance.* The new version was introduced at the Berkshire Music Festival in the summer of 1957.

(2) *See:* Euripides.

Mediant. Third note of the scale or key.

Meditations on Ecclesiastes, for string orchestra, by Norman Dello Joio (1957). The composer wrote this work on a commission from the Juilliard School of Music for the dancer, José Limon. In its original version it was presented with Limon's choreography on April 6, 1957, in New York, Frederick Prausnitz conducting. Since then it has been played by major symphony orchestras without the dance. It was awarded the Pulitzer Prize in music in 1957. The music is a setting of verses from the opening of Chapter 3 of the Book of Ecclesiastes and comprises twelve sections: an introduction, theme, and ten variations.

Medtner, Nicolas, pianist and composer. Born Moscow, Russia, Jan. 5, 1880; died London, England, Nov. 13, 1951. He was graduated from the Moscow Conservatory with highest honors in 1900. After winning the Rubinstein Prize he initiated his career as a concert pianist in 1902 with the first of several tours of Europe. He also distinguished himself as a professor of the piano at the Moscow Conservatory from 1902 to 1903, and again from 1918 to 1921. In 1921 he left Russia permanently and embarked on a world tour. His American début took place in Philadelphia on Oct. 31, 1924, when he performed one of his concertos with the Philadelphia Orchestra. In 1936 he established permanent residence in England.

Though Medtner wrote 3 piano concertos, several piano sonatas, and 3 violin sonatas, he is most famous for his smaller pieces for piano. He employed such fanciful titles as *Fairy Tales, Ro-*

mantic Sketches, Lyric Fragments, Forgotten Melodies, and *Mood Pictures.* But he also wrote numerous arabesques, novelettes, preludes, *moments musicaux,* dithyrambs, and marches. Because of his successful fusion of Classical traditions with Romanticism he has been called the "Russian Brahms." But he is more closely allied in spirit to Schumann, especially in his delicate poetic concepts, his subtle suggestions, and his flights of magical fancy.

See: Fairy Tale.

Meeresstille und glueckliche Fahrt (Mendelssohn). *See: Calm Sea and Prosperous Voyage.*

Meistersinger, Prelude to Die (Wagner). *See: Mastersingers, The.*

Melody. The succession of single musical tones in some logical scheme or pattern.

Memories of My Childhood. Tone poem for orchestra by Charles Martin Loeffler (1924), first performed in Evanston, Ill., on May 29, 1924. In this music Loeffler recalls his childhood in Russia and his memories of Russian folksongs and church. He derived his musical texture from the "Russian peasant song, the Yourod Litany prayer . . . fairy tales and dance songs," as the composer has explained. He goes on to say that the closing section "commemorates the death of Vasinka, an elderly Bayan, or storyteller, singer, maker of willow pipes upon which he played tunes of weird intervals."

Mendelssohn-Bartholdy, Felix, composer. Born Hamburg, Germany, Feb. 3, 1809; died Leipzig, Germany, Nov. 4, 1847. His grandfather, Moses, a distinguished philosopher, and his father, Abraham, a successful banker, were both of the Jewish faith. But during Felix's boyhood he and his immediate family—which included a sister, Fanny—were converted to Protestantism. On that occasion, Abraham added the name "Bartholdy" to distinguish himself and his family from the other Mendelssohns who had remained Jewish.

When Felix was three his family moved to Berlin, where his musical training began with Ludwig Berger and Karl Friedrich Zelter. He was exceptionally precocious, making a public appearance as pianist on Oct. 24, 1818. By the time he was twelve he had written several symphonies, operas, and numerous other works, which were performed at Sunday morning musicales held at his home. When the Mendelssohn family moved in 1825 to more spacious quarters in Berlin, a theater was built in the garden for these concerts. It was there that Mendelssohn introduced in a two-piano version his first masterwork, the Overture to *A Midsummer Night's Dream,* written when he was only seventeen. By this time he had also completed an opera that was performed in Berlin in 1827, his thirteenth symphony, and a considerable amount of chamber music.

One of the milestones in Mendelssohn's career came in 1829. Long a profound admirer of Johann Sebastian Bach, who was still languishing in neglect and obscurity, Mendelssohn sought to acquaint the world with the grandeur of that master's music. On March 11, 1829, in Berlin, he conducted the *Passion According to St. Matthew,* the first performance of that masterwork since Bach's own day. This concert was so successful that it was repeated. It is not too much to say that the revival of Bach throughout the world of music was set into motion by these performances.

A few weeks after this concert, Mendelssohn paid his first visit to England, where from this time on, he would be regarded with a veneration England had accorded to no foreign musician since Handel. He led the première of a new symphony (in C minor) and was elected honorary member of the Royal Philharmonic. After a tour of Scotland, Italy, and France he returned to London to introduce several important new works: the Piano Concerto in G minor; the *Capriccio brillant,* for piano and orchestra; and the *Fingal's Cave Overture,* which had been inspired by his recent visit to Scotland.

For six months, in 1833, Mendelssohn was musical director in Duesseldorf. In 1835 he was appointed principal conductor of the Gewandhaus Orchestra in Leipzig. During the five years he directed that orchestra he lifted it to a preeminent position among Europe's symphonic organizations and helped establish a new era in orchestral conducting. His personal life was as satisfying as his artistic career. On March 28, 1837, he married Cécile Jeanrenaud, a marital relationship that remained happy until the very end.

In 1841 Mendelssohn became head of the music department of a projected Academy of Arts in Berlin. Involved in petty court intrigues, he found a temporary avenue of escape in an invitation to England, where he now introduced his *Scotch Symphony* and made two command appearances at Buckingham Palace. Returning to Berlin, he discovered that the Academy of Arts project had been abandoned. He assumed an honorary post as Kapellmeister to the King, which carried no set duties and allowed him full freedom of activity. He now returned to Leipzig, making occasional appearances as conductor with the Gewandhaus Orchestra. In 1843 he helped found the Leipzig Conservatory, creating an outstanding faculty that included Schumann, Ferdinand David, and Ignaz Moscheles. He also paid two more visits to England: in 1846 to conduct the première of his oratorio, *Elijah;* and in 1847 to fill various engagements and give a command performance for Queen Victoria.

Always delicate in health, his many activities soon sapped his strength. The sudden death of his sister, Fanny, in 1847, was a crushing blow. From this time on he began to succumb to depression and fits. He died at the age of thirty-eight at the height of his creative powers.

In Mendelssohn is found a synthesis of the Classic and Romantic movements. He came upon the musical scene when Classicism was at an ebb, but in many of his compositions we still find an allegiance to Classical structure and to traditional harmonic and contrapuntal procedures. But his appearance also coincided with the dawn of Romanticism. Despite his pronounced Classical tendencies, he was one of music's first eminent Romanticists. He had the Romantic's love of the supernatural world of fairies and elves; Mendelssohn's delicate and graceful music often evokes for us a magic world of fantasy. He had the Romantic's gift for painting landscapes and for interpreting lyric poetry. If his art was a limited one in that it rarely tapped deeply into veins of emotion and human experience, it was nevertheless a sensitive art that seldom fails to enchant the listener.

The following are Mendelssohn's principal instrumental works:

Chamber Music: 6 string quartets; 2 string quintets; 3 piano quartets; 2 piano trios; 2 cello sonatas; violin sonata; string octet; piano sextet.

Orchestra: 5 symphonies (not including his early symphonies, but embracing the *Scotch, Italian,* and *Reformation* symphonies); 2 piano concertos; violin concerto; *A Midsummer Night's Dream,* suite; *Fingal's Cave* (or *Hebrides*) *Overture; Calm Sea and Prosperous Voyage* (*Meeresstille und glueckliche Fahrt*); *Ruy Blas,* overture; *Capriccio brillant,* for piano and orchestra; *Rondo brillant,* for piano and orchestra.

Organ: 6 sonatas; preludes and fugues.

Piano: 3 sonatas; *Seven Characteristic Pieces;* 8 books of *Songs Without Words* (*Lieder ohne Worte*); *Variations sérieuses; Rondo capriccioso; Kinderstuecke,* caprices, preludes and fugues, etudes, scherzos, preludes, variations, and so on.

See: Athalie; Concerto—*Mendelssohn; Calm Sea and Prosperous Voyage;* Caprice (3); *Elijah; Fingal's Cave; Midsummer Night's Dream, A;* Octet; Quartet—*Mendelssohn; Rondo capriccioso; Ruy Blas; Songs Without Words;* Symphony —*Mendelssohn; Variations sérieuses.*

Mengelberg, Willem, conductor. Born Utrecht, Holland, March 28, 1871; died Chur, Switzerland, March 21, 1951. He studied music at the Utrecht School of Music and the Cologne Conservatory. He was trained as a pianist, but an appointment in 1891 as music director for the city of Lucerne, Switzerland, turned him to conducting. After leading orchestral concerts for four years in that city, Mengelberg became principal conductor of the Concertgebouw Orchestra in Amsterdam in 1895. In the next few years he lifted that orchestra to a commanding position among Europe's symphonic organizations. In 1903 he made the first of many appearances in London. His American début took place with the New York Philharmonic on Nov. 11, 1905.

He returned to the United States in 1921 as guest conductor of the National Symphony in New York, then returned for eight consecutive seasons as conductor of the New York Philharmonic. After Holland was occupied by the Nazis, Mengelberg continued to conduct the Concertgebouw Orchestra in Amsterdam while cooperating with and expressing sympathy for the invaders. For this he was tried and convicted by the Netherlands Honor Council soon after the end of World War II. A gold medal previously presented him by Queen Wilhelmina was withdrawn and he was sentenced to exile until 1951. He went to live in Switzerland, where he led some orchestral performances, but never again returned to his native land.

Menges, Isolde, violinist. Born Hove, England, May 16, 1893. After studying the violin with her parents, for three years with Leopold Auer in St. Petersburg, and in Dresden, she made her début in London on Feb. 4, 1913. Her American début took place in New York on Oct. 21, 1916. She became prominent not only as a violin virtuoso but also as the head of the Menges Quartet. In 1931 she was appointed professor of the violin at the Royal College of Music in London. Her brother, Herbert (born Hove, England, Aug. 27, 1902), is a conductor. He has been principal conductor at the Sadler's Wells Opera and with the Southern Philharmonic in Southsea, England, and in 1947 made his American début with the CBS Symphony over the CBS radio network.

Mennin, Peter (born **Peter Mennini**), composer. Born Erie, Pa., May 17, 1923. He attended Oberlin Conservatory, where, as a student, he wrote a symphony and some chamber music. After World War II he completed his music study with Howard Hanson and Bernard Rogers at the Eastman School of Music; he also studied conducting with Koussevitzky at the Berkshire Music Centre in Tanglewood. He first attracted attention as a composer in 1945 by winning the first George Gershwin Memorial Award and the Bearns Prize with his second symphony, which was introduced that year in New York, Leonard Bernstein conducting. He later received an award from the American Academy of Arts, and two Guggenheim Fellowships. From 1947 to 1958 he was a member of the faculty of the Juilliard School in New York, and in 1958 was appointed director of the Peabody Conservatory in Baltimore. He is the composer of 7 symphonies, a violin concerto, *Folk Overture,* Fantasia for string orchestra, other short works for orchestra, a piano sonata, and pieces for the piano.

Meno. Less.

Meno Mosso. Not so fast.

Menotti, Gian Carlo, composer. Born Cadegliano, Italy, July 7, 1911. In 1927 he came to the United States, where he attended the Curtis Institute in Philadelphia and later became famous for his operas. Menotti's instrumental music is of lesser interest. It includes 2 ballets, a violin concerto, piano concerto, *Apocalypse* (a tone poem), some chamber music, and pieces for the piano. A suite from his ballet score, *Sebastian,* is sometimes performed on symphony programs.

Menuhin, Yehudi, violinist. Born New York City, April 22, 1916. When he was nine months old his family moved to San Francisco, where he started to study the violin at the age of four with Sigmund Anker. After additional study with Louis Persinger, he made his début in 1924 with the San Francisco Symphony, and gave his first New York performance in 1925. He then went to Europe to study with Adolf Busch and Georges Enesco, making his début with the Lamoureux Orchestra in a program comprising three concertos. On Nov. 25, 1927, he returned to New York with a sensational performance of the Beethoven Concerto. In 1929 he made an equally impressive début in London, and in 1934 he made a world tour covering 73 cities in 13 countries. In 1936 he went into temporary retirement for further study and self-evaluation. When he reappeared on the concert platforms of the world in 1938, he was a fully matured artist commanding the respect and admiration of audiences everywhere. During World War II he played concertos for the armed forces more than 500 times. Menuhin was made Chevalier of the Legion of Honor in 1948. Ten years later he joined the violin faculty of the Manhattan School of Music in New York. He made numerous appearances in sonata recitals with his sister, Hephzibah, a gifted pianist (born San Francisco, Calif., May 20, 1920).

Mephisto Waltz (The Dance at the Village Inn). For orchestra by Liszt (1861), first performed in Weimar under the composer's direction. This is the second of two pieces for orchestra entitled *Two Episodes from Lenau's Faust.* The first, *Midnight Procession (Der naechtliche Zug),* is rarely performed. The second, *Mephisto Waltz (Der Tanz in der Dorfschenke),* is deservedly popular—music of great emotional and dramatic impact, and so advanced harmonically that at times it anticipates Scriabin. The following lines from Lenau appear in the published score of the *Mephisto Waltz:* "There is a wedding feast in progress in the village inn, with music, dancing, carousing. Mephistopheles and Faust pass by, and Mephistopheles induces Faust to enter and take part in the festivities. Mephistopheles snatches the instrument from the hands of a lethargic fiddler and draws from it indescribably seductive and intoxicating strains. The amorous Faust whirls about with a full-blooded village beauty in a wild dance; they waltz in mad abandonment, out of the room, into the open, away to the woods. The sounds of the fiddle grow softer and softer, and the nightingale warbles his love-laden song." Two significant melodic ideas represent the dance at the inn and the seductive strains of Mephistopheles. The first is a strongly accented theme for cellos; the other, a passionate song for strings.

Mer, La (The Sea). A set of three symphonic sketches by Debussy (1905), first performed in Paris on Oct. 15, 1905, Chevillard conducting. Other than the descriptive titles for each of the sketches, the composer provided no specific program. I. *From Dawn to Noon on the Sea (De l'aube à midi sur la mer).* This sketch opens with an undulating figure suggesting the play of the waves. Throughout we get different images of the sea at different times of the day. The section ends with an impressive brass chorale. II. *Play of the Waves* (*Jeux de vagues*). The sport of the waves is suggested in melodic fragments altered by changes of tone color and rhythm. III. *Dialogue between the Wind and the Sea* (*Dialogue du vent et de la mer*). The sea no longer is playful, but elemental and powerful. String melodic figures in the whole-tone scale suggest the sea's immensity. Some hasty recollections of ideas from the first movement appear. One of these, the chorale melody, is built into a powerful climax. Undulating figures, depicting the movement of the waves, close the work just as they opened it. *La Mer* is such an integrated work, with each movement so dependent on the others for its effect, that it is impossible to play one section by itself. The first two sketches are played without interruption.

Mercury Symphony. *See:* Symphony—Haydn.

Messiaen, Olivier, composer. Born Avignon, France, Dec. 10, 1908. He is the son of the famous poetess, Cécile Sauvage. He was graduated with highest honors in virtually every department from the Paris Conservatory in 1930. In 1931 he became organist at the Trinité Church in Paris. In the early 1930's he helped organize a new school of young French composers which identified itself as "La Jeune France" (which see). It was with this group that he first attracted attention as a composer. From 1936 to 1939 he taught composition at the Schola Cantorum and the Ecole Normale de Musique, and from 1942 on he was a professor at the Paris Conservatory. During World War II he was a prisoner of war in Germany. After he was released he resumed his post at the Trinité.

Messiaen is an original and provocative composer. He has been especially preoccupied with rhythm (notably Hindu rhythms), the treatment of which he has developed into a complex science. In his music we find rhythmic fugues and canons, with different instruments carrying on their own rhythmic patterns. A huge symphony, *Turangalîla*—introduced in Boston by the Boston Symphony conducted by Leonard Bernstein on Dec. 2,

1949—employs a special rhythmic language, making use of "several new rhythmic principles," in the description of the composer, "including non-reversible rhythms, asymmetric rhythms, augmentations with several rhythmic identities, rhythmic modes, and so forth." Messiaen has even prepared a rhythm dictionary including the principal rhythms of the Western and Eastern worlds as well as Greek music.

Besides his preoccupation with rhythm, Messiaen's music is often filled with spiritual values and profound religious feeling. His best works are mystic, deriving their subjects from Catholic liturgy or the Scriptures. His melodies and modes often come from plainsong.

In 1949 Messiaen conducted a master class in composition at the Berkshire Music Centre at Tanglewood. He wrote several texts on harmony and solfeggio and *The Technique of My Musical Language* (1957). His works for orchestra include *Les Offrandes oubliées, Hymne, L'Ascension, Poèmes pour moi, Trois petites liturgies de la présence divine, Turangalîla,* and *Réveil des oiseaux* for piano and orchestra. Other major works include the *Quartet for the End of Time;* preludes, *La Vision de l'amen, Vingt regards sur l'enfant Jésus,* and *Mode de valeurs et d'intensité,* all for piano; and *Apparition de l'église éternelle, La Nativité du Seigneur, Les Corps glorieux,* and *Messe de la Pentecôte,* for organ.

See: Ascension, L'; Hymne.

Messiah. An oratorio by Handel (1742), first performed in Dublin on April 13, 1742, the composer conducting. He wrote it in less than twenty-five days in a white heat of inspiration, and often in a kind of spell. "I think God has visited me," he said simply when he finished. The première performance was a triumph—Handel's first in some years. On March 23, 1743, he introduced the work to London before an audience that included royalty. It was on this occasion that the still-existing tradition was begun of having the audience rise during the rendition of the *Hallelujah Chorus.* King George II was so stirred by this music that he spontaneously arose in his box, and he was followed by the rest of the audience, all of whom remained standing throughout the chorus.

Handel was justified in his lofty estimate of the *Messiah*. It is his masterwork, perhaps the best known and best loved oratorio ever written. The high level of its inspiration never falters as chorus after chorus and aria after aria follow one another in a seemingly unending procession of sublimity. Now the music touches compassion, and now it expresses profound grief; now it gives voice to joy, and now it is suffused with an other-worldly radiance that makes us understand why at one point during the composition Handel exclaimed: "I did think I did see Heaven before me and the great God himself!"

The text, the work of Charles Jennens, is adapted from the Scriptures. It is in three parts. The first speaks of the coming of the Messiah; the second, describes the suffering and death of Christ; and the last tells of the Resurrection. The score comprises 50 numbers. The overture is in the French style, beginning with a majestic slow section and concluding with a sprightly fugue. In the first section, these are some of the more memorable pages: the joyous arias for tenor and contralto respectively, *Every valley shall be exalted* and *O thou that tellest good tidings to Zion;* arias deeply moving for their tenderness and pity, such as *He shall feed His flock,* for contralto and soprano; the stirring choruses, *And the glory of the Lord* and *For unto us a Child is born;* and the famous Pastoral Symphony for orchestra in which the Nativity is described in a poignant melody for strings derived from a Calabrian melody.

The second part comes to a magnificent and unforgettable culmination with the justly famous *Hallelujah Chorus.* In this part we find passages touched with spirituality and radiance, such as the opening chorus, *Behold the Lamb of God,* a later chorus, *Surely He hath borne our griefs,* and a poignant aria for alto, *He was despised.*

The concluding section opens with one of the most elevated arias in the oratorio, *I know that my Redeemer liveth,* for soprano; and it ends with a magnificent chorus in three sections, beginning *Worthy is the Lamb.*

Mesto. Sad.

Metamorphosen. Study for 23 strings by Richard Strauss (1945), first performed in Zurich on Jan. 25, 1946, Paul Sacher conducting. Separate parts are assigned to 10 violins, 5 violas, 5 cellos, and 3 double basses. Solo instruments, groups of strings, and the entire ensemble are featured. The composition opens with funereal chords, reminiscent of the funeral march from Beethoven's *Eroica Symphony.* It ends with this same motif placed contrapuntally against the actual one by Beethoven. This funereal suggestion was inspired by the collapse of Germany in World War II. At the end of the manuscript the composer added the words, "In memoriam." Between beginning and end there appear two theme groups of three subjects each which receive elaborate development and variation.

Metamorphoses. *See:* Ovid.

Metamorphosis on Themes by Carl Maria von Weber (Hindemith). *See: Symphonic Metamorphosis on Themes by Carl Maria von Weber.*

Meter. Measurement of music according to a series of recurrent pulses.

Metopes. Three poems for piano by Karol Szymanowski, op. 29 (1915). "Metope" refers to the carvings on a Doric frieze. The inspiration for these three piano pieces is *The Odyssey,* and they aspire to project three scenes from that epic: I. The Island of the Sirens; II. Calypso; III. Nausicaa. The first two are tone pictures; the last describes the games of maidens in an abandoned dance.

Metronome. An instrument capable of emitting regular beats in any of a wide range of desired speeds. It is used by composers to designate the exact tempo of their compositions. Maelzel's chronometer and Winkel's metronome which Maelzel appropriated and patented as his own, are the earliest successful specimens.

Mezzo. Half. Thus mezzo forte means moderately loud, and mezzo piano, moderately soft.

Miaskovsky, Nikolai, composer. Born Novogeorgievsk, in Russian Poland, April 20, 1881; died Moscow, Russia,

Aug. 9, 1950. The son of an engineer, Miaskovsky was graduated from a St. Petersburg military school in 1899. All the while music had been an avocation, but a six months' course in harmony with Reinhold Glière decided him to concentrate on music exclusively. After preliminary study of harmony and counterpoint in St. Petersburg, he entered the Conservatory there, where from 1906 to 1911 his teachers included Liadov and Rimsky-Korsakov. After World War I he made his home in Moscow, where in 1921 he became professor of composition at the Conservatory, holding this post until his death; among his pupils there were Kabalevsky and Khatchaturian.

Miaskovsky was one of the most prolific symphonists of the 20th century, producing 27 works in that form. His early symphonies are personal and introspective with an occasional suggestion of mysticism. The influence of the Russian Revolution becomes evident in the more objective writing of the Seventh Symphony and later works. He began to receive stimulation from the achievements of the new regime. Eventually he became even utilitarian in his attempts to write music for the masses. Several of his last works were inspired by World War II. He was several times winner of the Stalin Prize: for the Symphony No. 21, his most celebrated composition; String Quartet No. 9; Cello Concerto; Symphony No. 27; and String Quartet No. 13. The last two received the award posthumously. When in February 1948 most Soviet composers were censured by the Central Committee of the Communist Party for "decadent formalism" Miaskovsky was severely criticized for introducing "inharmonious music" into the Soviet educational system.

Besides his 27 symphonies, Miaskovsky wrote for orchestra 2 Sinfoniettas, a violin concerto, a cello concerto, 2 tone poems (*Silence* and *Alastor*), a Serenata, *Concertino lirico, Salutatory Overture,* and *Slavic Rhapsody*. He also wrote 13 string quartets, 2 cello sonatas, 3 piano sonatas, a piano sonatina, and various other suites and smaller pieces for the piano including three albums of children's pieces.

See: Symphony—*Miaskovsky*.

Michelangelo Buonarroti. *See:* Painters and paintings.

Midi, Le. *See:* Symphony—*Haydn*.

Midsummer Night's Dream, A. Suite for orchestra by Mendelssohn derived from his incidental music to the Shakespeare comedy. Mendelssohn wrote the overture, op. 21, when he was seventeen (1826). Seventeen years later he was commissioned by King Frederick William of Prussia to prepare music for a projected performance of Shakespeare's play in a new royal theater in Potsdam. The composer now added to his overture of 1826, 13 new numbers, op. 61a. The suite, as given most often at symphony concerts, is made up of the Overture, and three excerpts from the incidental music: Nocturne, Scherzo, and Wedding March.

The overture is a masterpiece, music of enchantment, an amazing production for a boy of seventeen. It brings forth the fairy world of Shakespeare's play with the most exquisite delicacy. Four delicate chords immediately create that world; we are plunged into it with a fleet staccato passage for strings. The main subjects maintain this fanciful mood: a haunting horn melody; a broad lyrical theme shared by woodwind and strings; a bucolic dance for strings. The overture ends as it began, with four chords.

The Nocturne is a romantic melody for horn. The Scherzo carries us back to fairyland with its grace and delicacy. Both of its main themes are presented by woodwind and unison strings. The Wedding March is one of the two most popular pieces of music for weddings ever written (the other being that from Wagner's *Lohengrin*). It opens with a trumpet fanfare, after which comes the stately music of the march. There are two different trio sections.

Other orchestral episodes from Mendelssohn's incidental music are: Fairies' March; Intermezzo, or Entr'acte; Melodrama; Andante; *Allegro comodo* and *Marcia funèbre;* Bergomask Dance; Finale.

Midsummer Vigil (Midsommarvaka). Rhapsody for orchestra by Hugo Alfvén, op. 19 (1904). It is based on Swedish folksongs and dances, with an occasional use of dances from the Schleswig-Holstein region of Germany. The work describes a revel celebrated in Sweden during the St. John's Eve Festival. The highlight is a melody first heard in muted strings and English horn, then repeated by French horn. This rhapsody has been adapted into a ballet, *La Nuit de Saint-Jean,* introduced in Paris by the Swedish Ballet on Oct. 25, 1920.

Mignone, Francisco, composer. Born São Paulo, Brazil, Sept. 3, 1897. He attended the São Paulo Conservatory, and in 1918 made his bow as a composer with piano pieces introduced by him in a piano recital in his native city. A few months later his father conducted the première of one of his orchestral works, *Caramurú.* In 1920 a government subsidy enabled him to go to Italy for additional study. There he completed an opera, *O Contractador dos diamantes,* introduced in Rio de Janeiro in 1924; an orchestral episode from this opera, *Congada,* is Mignone's best-known composition. Mignone returned to his native city in 1929, becoming professor of harmony and piano at the São Paulo Conservatory; later he held a similar post with the Rio de Janeiro Conservatory. In 1941 he helped Villa-Lobos modernize the curriculum in Brazil's music schools. In 1942 he paid his first visit to the United States, making appearances as pianist and conductor. Mignone is one of Brazil's foremost composers. His music has an unmistakable Brazilian character, his style having assimilated the rhythms, melodies, colors, and exotic personality of Brazilian folk music. Among his leading works for orchestra, besides *Congada,* are *4 Fantasias brasileiras* for piano and orchestra, *Momus, Suite brasileira, Suite asturiana, Sinfonía de trabalho, Festa das Igrejas, Seresta* for cello and orchestra, and *Miudinho.* He also wrote a string sextet, violin sonata, sextet for piano and winds, piano sonata, and etudes and preludes for piano.

Mikrokosmos. Suite of piano pieces for children by Béla Bartók (1926-1927). Literally meaning "little world," *Mikrokosmos* consists of six books of 153 pieces. The work was intended to teach children modern idioms, including the five-tone scale, polytonality, polyrhythm, disso-

nance, and so forth. In the first four books are found exercises in particular technical problems designated in the titles: *Imitation and Counterpoint, Accompaniment in Broken Triads, Minor Sixths in Parallel Motion, Fifth Chords, Contrary Motion, Alternating Hands, Dotted Notes,* and so on. In the next two books are gathered examples of different types and styles of folk music of the Balkan countries. Throughout the six books there are also to be found such descriptive pieces as *Stumblings, Boating,* or *Wandering;* also pieces that imitate extra-musical sounds, such as *Buzzing* and *Clashing Sounds.*

Tibor Serly prepared an orchestral suite made up of several of these pieces, introduced in St. Louis on Nov. 20, 1943. There are eight sections: I. Prelude; II. Scherzando; III. Unisono; IV. Bourrée; V. Moto perpetuo; VI. Contrasts over Pedals; VII. Bulgarian Rhythm No. 4; VIII. Bulgarian Rhythm No. 5.

Milhaud, Darius, composer. Born Aix-en-Provence, France, Sept. 4, 1892. He attended the Paris Conservatory, a pupil of Vincent d'Indy and Paul Dukas among others. During his student years he wrote several chamber music works, and an opera, *La Brebis égarée,* performed at the Opéra-Comique in 1923, a decade after it was written. In 1917 he became an attaché to the French Legation in Brazil, under Paul Claudel, the French ambassador (a poet whose verses Milhaud had previously set to music). Milhaud became interested in the popular songs and dances of Brazil, an influence discernible in works like the popular *Saudades do Brasil.* In Brazil Milhaud also first became interested in American jazz, an idiom he soon was to use in several ambitious works including the ballets *La Création du monde* and *Le Boeuf sur le toit.*

In 1919, back in France, Milhaud became identified with a new school of French composers baptized as the "French Six," or "Les Six" (which see). Though he first achieved popularity as a member of this group, Milhaud disavowed any artistic kinship with the other members, all personal friends; Milhaud insisted on maintaining his own creative identity. That identity first revealed itself in music exploiting popular idioms, spiced with an ingratiating wit. But in the late 1920's and early 1930's his style became dissonant and polytonal. After that his writing acquired deeper emotional content as he began tapping ever more serious veins of expression. Together with a personalized lyricism, he now brought to his music an intensity of feeling, a concentration of speech, and an inexorable logic which, after Ravel's death, made him France's foremost composer.

During World War II, soon after the occupation of France by the Nazis, Milhaud came to the United States. For the next few years he taught at Mills College in California, and wrote many major works. Despite a crippling attack of arthritis, which henceforth confined him most of the time to a wheelchair, Milhaud did not relax his activities as teacher, composer, and conductor. After the war's end, he returned to France, where since 1947 he has been a member of the faculty at the Paris Conservatory. Since then he has divided each year between France and the United States. He is the author of an autobiography, *Notes Without Music* (1953), and of *Entretiens avec Claude Rostand* (1952).

Milhaud is an extraordinarily prolific composer. The following are some of his major instrumental works:

Chamber Music: 18 string quartets; 2 piano quintets; 2 string quintets; 2 violin sonatas; 2 viola sonatas; various suites and sonatinas; *Quatre visages* for viola and piano; *Elégie* for cello and piano; *Sept danses sur des airs palestiniens* for eight instruments; Duo for two violins; *Duo concertante* for clarinet and piano.

Orchestra: 8 symphonies; various concertos (piano; cello; violin; flute and violin; clarinet; two pianos; harp; marimba and vibraphone; trombone); *Saudades do Brasil; Protée,* two suites; 5 symphonies for small orchestra; *La Création du monde; Carnival d'Aix,* for piano and orchestra; *Concertino de printemps* for violin and orchestra; *Suite provençale; Cortège funèbre; Opus Americanum No. 2; Suite française; Four Sketches; Le Bal martiniquais; Kentuckiana;* suite for two pianos and orchestra; *Suite concertante*

for piano and orchestra; *Aspen Serenade; Ouverture méditerranéenne.*

Piano: 2 sonatas; various suites (*Scaramouche, Touches noires, Touches blanches, La Libertadora, La Muse ménagère, La Liberation des Antilles*).

See: Bal martiniquais, Le; Création du monde, La; Octet; *Protée;* Quartet—*Milhaud; Saudades do Brasil; Suite provençale;* Symphony—*Milhaud.*

Military Polonaise (Chopin). *See:* Polonaise.

Military Symphony. *See:* Symphony—Haydn.

Milstein, Nathan, violinist. Born Odessa, Russia, Dec. 31, 1904. He was a pupil of Leopold Auer at the St. Petersburg Conservatory and of Eugène Ysaÿe. Upon completing his studies in 1923 he toured Russia in solo performances and joint recitals with Vladimir Horowitz. In 1925 he went to Paris, where he made a highly successful début. He made his début in the United States with the Philadelphia Orchestra in October 1928. Since then he has become an American citizen. He has toured the world many times, and has been recognized everywhere as one of the foremost violinists of our time. He was the recipient of numerous awards and honors. In 1956 he was made Chevalier of the Legion of Honor.

Minneapolis Symphony Orchestra. An orchestra founded in 1903 in Minneapolis, Minn., by Emil Oberhoffer, who conducted the first concert on November 5. Oberhoffer was principal conductor until 1921. After that, the principal conductors included Henri Verbrugghen, Eugene Ormandy, Dimitri Mitropoulos, and Antal Dorati. In 1957 the orchestra toured the Near East. During the latter part of the Verbrugghen regime the orchestra moved to its present home, the Northrop Memorial Auditorium on the campus of the University of Minnesota.

Minore. Italian for minor, as opposed to "maggiore" for major.

Minuet. A graceful, stately dance of French origin, popular in European courts up to the middle of the 18th century. It is in three-part form, the third being a repetition of the first, and the second part a trio. The minuet sometimes appears as a movement in the Baroque suite; and in the Classical symphony it constituted usually the third movement until it was replaced by the scherzo.

The minuet has appeared in piano music as an independent composition. Two of the most popular examples of minuets for the piano is Beethoven's Minuet in G, one of a set of six composed in 1795, and Paderewski's *Menuet à l'antique,* the first of six pieces for piano collectively entitled *Humoresques de concert,* op. 14.

Popular minuets for orchestra are in Mozart's Divertimento No. 16 in D major, K. 334, and in his opera *Don Giovanni;* the Minuet of the Courtiers in Verdi's opera *Rigoletto;* and the entr'acte to Act 3 of Massenet's opera *Manon.* Boccherini's famous Minuet comes from his Quintet in E major, op. 13, no. 5. That of Giovanni Bolzoni appears in one of his string quartets.

Minuet of the Will-o-the-Wisp (Berlioz). *See: Damnation of Faust, The.*

Minute Waltz. *See:* Waltz—*Chopin.*

Miracle Symphony. *See:* Symphony—*Haydn.*

Miroirs. Suite for piano by Maurice Ravel (1905), consisting of five impressionistic pictures: I. *Noctuelles;* II. *Oiseaux tristes;* III. *Une Barque sur l'océan;* IV. *Alborada del gracioso;* V. *La Vallée des cloches.* The fourth is the most celebrated, a morning serenade ("Alborada") with a touch of buffoonery ("gracioso," meaning jester); it is a blend of Spanish rhythms and French irony. Ravel orchestrated this piece in 1912, a version first performed in Boston on Feb. 16, 1921, Monteux conducting. The second and third parts are also well known. *Oiseaux tristes* describes birds suffering from lassitude during the midday summer heat. *Une Barque sur l'océan* is a sensitive picture of the changing sea; this section has also been orchestrated by the composer.

Miroirs was performed for the first time in Paris by Ricardo Viñes on Jan. 6, 1906. Each movement is dedicated to a different member of the "Société des apaches," a group of young musicians with whom Ravel associated himself artistically at the time.

Mischakoff, Mischa, violinist. Born Pro-

skurov, Russia, April 3, 1895. He was a pupil of Leopold Auer at the St. Petersburg Conservatory. In 1922 he came to the United States and made his American début at the Lewisohn Stadium, New York, on July 27, 1923. He later became an American citizen. From 1924 to 1927 he was concertmaster of the New York Symphony. Since 1927 he has held a similar post with the Philadelphia Orchestra, Chicago Symphony, NBC Symphony, and Detroit Symphony.

Missa solemnis. A Mass in D by Beethoven, op. 123 (1818-1823), the composer's greatest choral work. Beethoven planned it for the installation of Archduke Rudolph as Archbishop of Olmuetz. But the work assumed such massive proportions that it was not ready for that ceremony; indeed, it required three additional years for completion. Three sections were heard for the first time in Vienna on May 8, 1824, the same concert in which Beethoven's Ninth Symphony was introduced.

The following words appear on the manuscript: "It comes from the heart—may it go to the heart." The Mass is in the five usual sections, here enormously extended in musical scope: I. Kyrie; II. Gloria; III. Credo; IV. Sanctus; V. Agnus Dei. Less devout in feeling than the Bach Mass in B minor, the *Missa solemnis* is the proud and at times defiant expression of a man who feels God within him, who feels it can be found in the creative process. After the opening Kyrie, which was once described as "all humanity joining in a universal liturgy," come several sections of passionate, even Herculean strength in which the human spirit asserts itself defiantly. But this music also dwells on an ethereal plane, especially in the *Benedictus* section of the Sanctus and in the closing Agnus Dei.

Mitchell, Howard, conductor. Born Lyons, Nebr., March 11, 1911. He attended the Peabody Conservatory in Baltimore and the Curtis Institute in Philadelphia, specializing in the cello. For a while he played the cello in the National Symphony in Washington, D.C. In 1944 he was appointed assistant conductor, and in 1948 he succeeded Hans Kindler as permanent conductor of that orchestra.

He made his first European appearances in 1955 in Belgium and Holland. He was three times honored by the National Music Council for his services to contemporary American music.

Mitropoulos, Dimitri, conductor. Born Athens, Greece, March 1, 1896. He was graduated from the Athens Conservatory with a gold medal in piano in 1918; he subsequently studied composition with Paul Gilson in Brussels and Ferruccio Busoni in Berlin. Returning to his native city in or about 1925, he became conductor of various Greek orchestras. He made a distinguished guest appearance in Berlin, with the Berlin Philharmonic on Feb. 27, 1930, in the dual capacity of conductor and piano soloist. This was followed by other successful appearances with other European orchestras and in 1934 by an extended tour of Italy, France, Belgium, Poland, and the Soviet Union. His American début took place with the Boston Symphony in January 1936. From 1937 to 1949 he was principal conductor of the Minneapolis Symphony, and from 1949 to 1957 of the New York Philharmonic Orchestra. In 1957-1958 he shared the role of principal conductor of the latter orchestra with Leonard Bernstein, and in 1958 he resigned to devote himself mainly to opera performances and guest appearances. He became an American citizen in 1946. In 1956 he received the Orfeo d'Oro Award from the city of Mantua.

Mixolydian mode. A Gregorian mode which corresponds to the scale from G to G on the white keys of the piano.

Mlynarski, Emil, conductor and educator. Born Kibarty, Poland, July 18, 1870; died Warsaw, Poland, April 5, 1935. At the St. Petersburg Conservatory he was a pupil of Leopold Auer and Anton Rubinstein among others. From 1901 to 1905 he was conductor of the Warsaw Philharmonic. After that he made many appearances with other European symphony orchestras and for several years was conductor of the Scottish Orchestra, with which he made annual visits to London. He was also a distinguished educator, for many years director of the Warsaw Conservatory. He taught conducting at the Curtis Institute in Philadelphia from 1929

to 1931. His first violin concerto won the Paderewski prize in 1898. He also wrote a second violin concerto, a tone poem *Polonia,* and some violin pieces.

Mode. A kind of scale. Also a classification of scales or keys, as "major mode" and "minor mode."

Moderato. Moderate in speed.

Modulation. Change in key or tonality.

Moiseiwitsch, Benno, pianist. Born Odessa, Russia, Feb. 22, 1890. He won the Rubinstein Prize at the Odessa Conservatory in his ninth year. After additional study with Theodor Leschetizky in Vienna he made his concert début in Reading, England, on Oct. 1, 1908. He then settled in that country, and in 1937 became a naturalized British subject. In 1909 he made the first of many extended tours which in two decades brought him many times to all parts of the civilized world. His American début took place in New York on Nov. 29, 1919. A musician of poetic temperament, he has distinguished himself mostly in the Classical and Romantic repertory, even though early in his career he paid considerable attention to modern music.

Moldau, The (Vltava). Tone poem for orchestra by Smetana (1874), the second of a cycle of six national tone poems collectively entitled *My Fatherland (Má Vlast).* The following program note appears in the published score of *The Moldau:* "Two springs pour forth their streams in the shade of a Bohemian forest, the one warm and gushing, the other cold and tranquil . . . The woodland brook, chattering along, becomes the river Moldau . . . It flows through the dense woods amid which the joyous sounds of the chase resound, and the call of the hunter's horn is heard ever nearer and nearer. It flows through verdant meadows and lowlands, where a marriage feast is being celebrated with song and dance. At eve, in its glimmering wavelets, wood nymphs and naiads hold revels, and in these waters many a fortress and castle are reflected which bear witness to the bygone splendor of knight-errantry and to martial fame vanished with days of yore."

The tone poem opens with a rippling figure in the flute against plucked strings.

The strings then produce an undulating figure suggesting the flow of the Moldau, above which arises a folk melody in the violins. Hunting calls for horn follow, and after that a peasant dance in the orchestra. The revels of nymphs and naiads is depicted by the flutes. A return of the Moldau melody is built into an impressive climax, then subsides to ebb away even as the river does on its way to the city of Prague.

Molière (born Jean Baptiste Poquelin), playwright. Born Paris, France, Jan. 15, 1622; died there, Feb. 17, 1673. Incidental music was written to the following plays by Molière: *Le Bourgeois gentilhomme* (Charles Gounod, an adaptation of music by Lully; Konstantin Listov; Erwin Schulhoff; Richard Strauss); *Don Juan* (Henri Sauguet); *L'Ecole des femmes* (Henry Purcell); *Les Fâcheux* (Georges Auric); *Les Fourberries de Scapin* (Henri Sauguet); *George Dandin* (Charles Eugène Sauzay); *Le Malade imaginaire* (André Jolivet; Ludomir Rozycki); *Le Médecin volant* (Darius Milhaud); *Le Misanthrope* (Norman Demuth); *Les Précieuses ridicules* (André Jolivet); *Le Sicilien* (Charles Eugène Sauzay); *Le Tartuffe* (Juriiaan Andriessen; Yuri Shaporin).

Pierre Capdevielle's *Moliéra* suite for orchestra was inspired by several of Molière's plays, while Milhaud paid a tribute to Molière in his *L'Apothéose de Molière* for harpsichord and strings.

Molinari, Bernardino, conductor. Born Rome, Italy, April 11, 1880; died there, Dec. 25, 1952. He attended the Santa Cecilia Academy in Rome. In 1912 he was appointed conductor of the Augusteo Orchestra in Rome, a post in which he achieved recognition as one of Italy's most important symphony conductors. After World War I he appeared as guest conductor of many important European orchestras. He made his American début with the St. Louis Symphony in January 1928. For the next decade he paid many visits to the United States as guest conductor. He edited and arranged music by several old Italian masters including Carissimi and Vivaldi.

Moll. German for minor, as opposed to "dur" for major.

Molto. Very.

Moment musical. A short composition for piano, usually in song form, and with an improvisational character. The term and form originated with Schubert, who wrote six such pieces, op. 94 (1823-1828). The *Moment musical No. 3* in F minor, (sometimes referred to as "Air russe"), is one of Schubert's best loved instrumental compositions, famous in various transcriptions, including one for violin and piano by Fritz Kreisler. The other Schubert *Moments musicaux* are: No. 1, C major; No. 2, A-flat major; No. 4, C-sharp minor; No. 5, F minor; and No. 6, A-flat major.

Rachmaninoff wrote several pieces for piano in this form, his six *Moments musicaux,* op. 16 (1896), being among his earliest compositions.

Monody. Homophony.

Monophony. Music consisting of a single melodic line without accompaniment.

Monothematic. Based on or employing only one theme.

Monteux, Pierre, conductor. Born Paris, France, April 4, 1875. He was graduated from the Paris Conservatory in 1896, and for a while played viola in the Colonne Orchestra. From 1911 to 1914 he conducted the Ballet Russe in several epoch-making premières including Stravinsky's *Petrouchka* and *The Rite of Spring* and Ravel's *Daphnis and Chloe.* In 1914 he founded in Paris the Société des concerts populaires which paid particular attention to new French and Russian music; between 1913 and 1914 he led performances at the Paris Opéra and Opéra-Comique. In 1916-1917 he made his first tour of the United States with the Ballet Russe. He was conductor of French operas at the Metropolitan Opera from 1917 to 1919, and principal conductor of the Boston Symphony from 1919 to 1924. In 1929 he founded, and up to 1938 directed, the Orchestre symphonique de Paris. From 1936 to 1952 he was principal conductor of the San Francisco Symphony. After leaving this post he made guest appearances with the Metropolitan Opera and leading American orchestras. During the European tour of the Boston Symphony in 1956 he led some of its concerts. He was made Commander of the Order of Nassau in 1950 and Commander of the French Legion of Honor in 1952.

Moonlight Sonata. *See:* Sonata—*Beethoven.*

Moór, Emanuel, pianist and inventor. Born Kecskemét, Hungary, Feb. 19, 1863; died Mont Pèlerin, Switzerland, Oct. 21, 1931. After making tours of Europe and America as a pianist and as director of the Concerts artistiques, he invented the Moór Duplex Piano, in which a double keyboard an octave apart facilitated the playing of octaves, tenths, and chromatic glissandos. His wife, Winifred Christie (born Stirling, England, Feb. 26, 1882), gave numerous performances in America and Europe on this piano.

Moore, Douglas Stuart, composer and educator. Born Cutchogue, N.Y., Aug. 10, 1893. His academic education took place at Yale, where he received degrees of Bachelor of Arts (1915) and Bachelor of Music (1917). After World War I he attended the Schola Cantorum in Paris and studied privately with Vincent d'Indy and Nadia Boulanger. While serving as director of music at the Cleveland Art Museum between 1921 and 1925 he was a pupil of Ernest Bloch. In 1925 he returned to Europe on a Pulitzer traveling fellowship, devoting himself to composition. In 1926 he joined the music department of Columbia University, where in 1940 he succeeded Daniel Gregory Mason as head of the department. He received a Guggenheim Fellowship in 1934, and in 1946 was elected president of the National Institute of Arts and Letters. In 1951 he received the Pulitzer Prize in music for his opera, *Giants in the Earth.* He is the author of *Listening to Music* (1932) and *From Madrigal to Modern Music* (1942). His principal works for orchestra include *The Pageant of P. T. Barnum, Moby Dick, Symphony of Autumn,* Symphony in A major, *Overture on an American Tune, Village Music, In Memoriam, A Farm Journal,* and *Cotillion Suite.* He also wrote a quintet for woodwinds and horn, clarinet quintet, piano trio, string quartet, and violin sonata.

See: Farm Journal, A.

Moore, Gerald, pianist. Born Watford, England, July 30, 1899. After a brief career as concert pianist, he became an accompanist, serving some of the world's foremost singers and instrumentalists, and raising accompanying to the status of an art. He has toured Europe and the United States in lecture-recitals, and in 1956 appeared with Sir Arthur Bliss and other English musicians in the Soviet Union. He is the author of *The Unashamed Accompanist* (1943) and *Singer and Accompanist* (1953).

Moore, Thomas, poet. Born Dublin, Ireland, May 28, 1779; died there, Feb. 25, 1852. Besides becoming famous as a poet, he was a noted singer of ballads. His metrical romance, *Lalla Rookh,* was the source of instrumental works, bearing the same name as the poem, by Granville Bantock (tone poem) and Joseph Jongen (tone poem). Sir William Sterndale Bennett wrote a fantasy overture, *Paradise and the Peri,* based on the second book of *Lalla Rookh;* Schumann's *Das Paradies und die Peri* for solo voices, chorus, and orchestra was also based on *Lalla Rookh.*

Mordent. An ornament consisting of a rapid progression from a note to one immediately lower and back again. In some old forms of the mordent there is more than one such oscillation.

Morendo. "Dying." Gradual decrescendo.

Morini, Erica, violinist. Born Vienna, Austria, Jan. 5, 1904. She studied with Otakar Ševčík in Vienna and made her début in October 1916. This was followed by appearances with the Gewandhaus Orchestra, Nikisch conducting, and a tour of Europe. She made her American début in New York on Jan. 26, 1921, with the New York Philharmonic. Since then she has been heard throughout the world and is recognized as one of the foremost women violinists of our day.

Mort de Tintagiles, La. *See:* Maeterlinck, Maurice.

Moscheles, Ignaz, pianist, conductor, and teacher. Born Prague, Bohemia, May 30, 1794; died Leipzig, Germany, March 10, 1870. He launched his professional career as a virtuoso and teacher of the piano in Vienna after completing his music study there with Antonio Salieri and Johann Georg Albrechtsberger. He became a friend of Beethoven, who admired him greatly; Moscheles prepared a piano arrangement of Beethoven's opera *Fidelio*. In 1821 he settled in London as pianist and teacher. He made his first appearances as conductor with the Royal Philharmonic in 1837. Eight years later he became principal conductor. A friend and former teacher of Mendelssohn, he was invited by that composer to become first professor of piano at the Leipzig Conservatory in 1846. For the next twenty years Moscheles was one of its most renowned teachers. He wrote many works for piano—including concertos, sonatas, and smaller pieces. But he is remembered for his pedagogical works, the most significant being *Twenty-Four Etudes,* op. 70 (1825-1826), and *Characteristic Studies,* op. 95. He was the author of *Fragments of an Autobiography* (1889) and translator into English of Anton Schindler's biography of Beethoven (1841). His correspondence with Mendelssohn was edited by his son (1888).

Mosso. Animated.

Moszkowski, Moritz, pianist and composer. Born Breslau, Germany, Aug. 23, 1854; died Paris, France, March 4, 1925. After attending the Dresden Conservatory, and the Stern Conservatory and Kullak Academy in Berlin, he launched a successful career as concert pianist with a recital in Berlin in 1873. By the time he established his residence in Paris in 1897 his reputation as a virtuoso was solidly established. As a composer, he is most famous for his two books of *Spanish Dances* for piano solo (also for piano duo). He also wrote many other pieces for the piano including waltzes, gavottes, etudes, a tarantella, and a humoresque. His more ambitious compositions include a piano concerto, violin concerto, symphony, and several shorter works for orchestra, such as the tone poem *Jeanne d'Arc.*

Mother Goose Suite (Ma Mère l'Oye). Suite of five children's pieces for orchestra by Ravel (1908). The composer originally wrote this work for piano four hands, a version in which it was introduced in Paris on April 20, 1910. In 1911

he orchestrated the suite for a ballet, produced in Paris on Jan. 28, 1912. The suite has five movements. I. *Pavane of Sleeping Beauty (Pavane de la belle au bois dormant).* A sensitive melody for flute, and a countersubject for muted horn and violas, is the basic material of this twenty-measure section. II. *Tom Thumb (Petit Poucet).* A quotation from Charles Perrault's fairy tale appears in the score: "He believed he could easily find his way by means of his bread crumbs, which he had scattered as he passed along; but to his surprise he could not find a single crumb, for the birds had come and eaten it up." The path followed by Tom Thumb is traced by a theme for solo oboe against muted strings; the music later simulates the chirping of the birds. III. *Little Ugly One, Empress of the Pagodas (Laideronnette, impératrice de pagodes).* The following quotation from Marie Catherine d'Aulnoy's *Le Serpentin vert* appears in the score: "She undressed and entered the bath. Immediately, the pagodas, male and female, began to sing and play on various instruments. . ." This music, with a march-like character, has an enchanting quality of fantasy. IV. *Conversations of Beauty and the Beast (Les Entretiens de la belle et de la bête).* A dialogue from a story by Jeanne Marie Leprince de Beaumont is found in the score. Beauty is at first represented by solo clarinet, and the beast by double bassoon. But as the music progresses, Beauty is characterized by solo flute, solo oboe, and solo violin; the beast by solo cello. V. *The Fairy Garden (Le Jardin féerique).* Sleeping Beauty, represented by the celesta, is awakened by Prince Charming to the jubilation of all the story-book characters and the Good Fairy.

Motif (or Motive). Brief musical subject.

Moto. Motion.

Moto perpetuo. *See:* Perpetual motion.

Motto theme. A theme that recurs in several movements or sections of a composition.

Moussorgsky, Modest. *See:* Mussorgsky. Modest.

Movement. An important and self-sufficient part of a larger musical composition.

Mozart, Wolfgang Amadeus, composer. Born Salzburg, Austria, Jan. 27, 1756; died Vienna, Austria, Dec. 5, 1791. From earliest childhood his musical powers were so remarkable that he has since become the touchstone by which musical talent is measured. He was the son of Leopold Mozart, 2nd Kapellmeister at the court of the Archbishop of Salzburg. When he was four he began to study the harpsichord with his father, soon giving awe-inspiring demonstrations of sight reading and improvisation. When he was five he wrote minuets; at seven he completed his first sonata; and at eight, his first symphony.

When he was six, he and his older sister, Maria Anna (herself a gifted harpsichordist), were taken by their father to perform at the Electoral Court in Munich. This visit was so successful and lucrative that the father was now encouraged to undertake several more tours. For the next few years the young Mozarts appeared throughout Europe; wherever they played they gathered accolades and lavish gifts. "A phenomenon like that of Mozart remains an inexplicable thing," said Goethe. During these voyages Mozart's career as a composer was advanced. In Paris, four violin sonatas were published; in London, his first symphonies were performed; in Vienna, the Emperor commissioned him to write an opera buffa. In 1770 the Mozarts embarked on an extensive tour of Italy. In Milan he received a commission to write an opera, *Mitridate, rè di Ponto,* successfully given on Christmas day of that year. In Bologna he was elected member of the Accademia Filarmonica, even though its rules denied this honor to anyone under twenty. Almost as if to give further evidence of his genius, in Rome he wrote down from memory—and after only two hearings—the complete score of Gregorio Allegri's celebrated *Miserere.*

The years between 1772 and 1777 were mainly spent in his native Salzburg, where he was employed by an Archbishop who had little understanding or appreciation of his genius. Treated like a menial servant, and often subjected to personal abuse, Mozart eagerly sought some appointment elsewhere in Europe. But he was doomed to disappointment. When he revisited Paris in 1778 he found that, since he no longer was a child prodigy, the public had lost interest in him. The sudden death of his mother, who had accompanied him there, added tragedy to frustration. Mozart returned to Salzburg to resume his drab and poorly paid post, but more determined than ever to make a permanent break. That break came in 1782 when Mozart accompanied the Archbishop and his entourage to Vienna. Denied permission to appear at a benefit performance, Mozart flew into a rage, denounced the Archbishop, and was dismissed. Free at last, Mozart settled in Vienna, his home for the remainder of his life. There he was soon commissioned by the Emperor to write an opera: *The Abduction from the Seraglio* (*Die Entfuehrung aus dem Serail*), first given in Vienna on July 16, 1782. Confident of his future, Mozart married Constanze Weber on Aug. 4, 1782. While waiting for some court appointment, he supported himself by giving concerts and lessons. He wrote symphonies, operas, concertos, string quartets which brought new dimensions to the art of music. A handful in Vienna recognized the grandeur of this music. One of these was Haydn, already the most celebrated composer in Europe. Haydn described Mozart as "the greatest composer I know either personally or by name."

Some recognition also came from Prague, where a triumphant première of his opera *Don Giovanni* took place on Oct. 29, 1787. Returning to Vienna, Mozart was finally engaged as court composer and chamber musician, in succession to Gluck, but at a sharply reduced annual salary, hardly enough to sustain him. In these final years his poverty was so intense that he was often reduced to begging his friends for financial assistance. Impoverished, often sick in body and spirit, just as frequently a victim of despair, Mozart nevertheless allowed nothing to interfere with his musical fecundity. Artistically and technically he was growing continually. The last year of his life—beset by sickness and worry—was one of his richest creatively. In that year he wrote, among other works, the opera *The Magic Flute* (*Die Zauber-floete*), the *Ave, verum corpus* for chorus, the B-flat major Piano Concerto, the E-flat major String Quintet, and the Requiem.

The unusual and dramatic circumstances surrounding the writing of the Requiem are recounted elsewhere (*see:* Requiem—*Mozart*). Here it is only necessary to recall that in writing this work on a commission, Mozart soon became convinced he was producing his own threnody. Often wracked with pain, he refused to spare himself as he tried to bring this work to its completion. And when further work on this music was beyond his depleted strength, he minutely explained to one of his pupils, Franz Xaver Suessmayr, how he wanted the Requiem to be completed. The afternoon before his death, Mozart asked three friends to join him in singing parts of the Requiem. That night he received extreme unction, and towards midnight he turned to the wall and died. He had a dismal funeral. A few friends attended services at the St. Stephen Cathedral, but because of the rain they did not follow the body to the grave; and Mozart's widow had been too grief-stricken even to attend the church services. Thus, unmourned, Mozart's body was consigned to a pauper's grave in the churchyard of St. Mark's, with neither a tombstone nor a cross to mark the place of burial.

There is no branch of music that has not been enriched by Mozart's genius. His vast output is as remarkable for its quality as for its quantity. He never lacked elegance of workmanship, dignity of style, and the best possible taste—even when he wrote pieces on order to please the ear. But when he searched his mind for deeper concepts and his heart for profounder emotions, his was a creative force as Titanic as that of Bach who preceded him or Beethoven who followed. When he chose, he could be gay, charming, seductive. But he could also be tragic, spiritual, and radiant as well. In his greatest works, whatever the medium, he not only brought musical Classicism to its ultimate development, tapping the fullest resources of his era in melodic and harmonic writing, in structure and

style. He was also a bold adventurer, continually traveling upon virgin trails and thus continually coming upon a brave, new world. Eric Blom said that in him "Classicism and romanticism meet, and . . . once and for all we see a perfect equilibrium between them." The iconoclasm of Beethoven could hardly have been possible if Beethoven had not first been influenced and directed by Mozart's music. Both in his advanced idioms, and in the profound human values with which he endowed his music, Mozart was the dawn of a new age.

His principal instrumental works are as follows:

Chamber Music: 7 string quintets; 26 string quartets; 2 piano quartets; 7 piano trios; 42 violin sonatas; quintets for a wind instrument and strings; quintet for piano and winds; flute quartets; oboe quartet; string trios; duets.

Orchestra: 49 symphonies; numerous concertos for solo instruments and orchestra (piano; violin; flute and harp; flute; horn; clarinet; two pianos; three pianos; bassoon); *Sinfonia concertante* for violin, viola, and orchestra; 31 divertimentos, cassations, and serenades; 25 minuets, German dances, and country dances; 9 marches; sonatas for organ and orchestra.

Piano: 23 sonatas (solo piano; two pianos; four hands); variations, fantasies, rondos, minuets, fugues, and so on.

See: Abduction from the Seraglio, The; Concerto—*Mozart;* Divertimento—*Mozart; Don Giovanni; Eine kleine Nachtmusik;* Fantasia—*Mozart; German Dances; Magic Flute, The; Marriage of Figaro, The;* Minuet; *Musical Joke, A;* Quartet—*Mozart;* Quintet—*Mozart;* Requiem—*Mozart;* Serenade—*Mozart; Sinfonia concertante;* Sonata—*Mozart;* Symphony—*Mozart.*

Mozartiana. Suite for orchestra by Tchaikovsky, op. 61 (1887), the fourth of the composer's orchestral suites. It was derived from four compositions by Mozart. I. Gigue. This two-section dance (each section repeated) originated as a piano piece, K. 574 (1789). II. Minuet. In two repeated sections, but without the traditional trio, this also came from a piano piece, K. 355 (1790). III. *Prayer*

(*Preghiera*). This is an adaptation of an adaptation: Tchaikovsky's orchestral version of Liszt's piano transcription of the choral motet, *Ave, verum corpus*, K. 618 (1791). IV. Theme and Variations. The source of this finale is the piano variations on a theme by Gluck, K. 455 (1784).

Much Ado about Nothing. *See:* Shakespeare, William.

Muck, Karl, conductor. Born Darmstadt, Germany, Oct. 22, 1859; died Stuttgart, Germany, March 3, 1940. He received an intensive academic education at the Universities of Heidelberg and Leipzig, specializing in classic philology, and receiving his doctorate in 1880. His principal training in music took place at the Leipzig Conservatory. He made his professional début with an appearance as piano soloist with the Gewandhaus Orchestra in Leipzig. But he soon turned to conducting, receiving an intensive apprenticeship with numerous opera companies in Germany and Austria. He first distinguished himself as a conductor of Wagner's music—a field in which he had few equals and no superiors—with the Angelo Neumann Opera Company beginning in 1886. In 1891 and 1892 he directed performances of the entire Wagner *Ring* cycle in Russia. In 1892 he was appointed principal conductor of the Berlin Opera, where he remained many years and was acclaimed as one of Europe's most profound interpreters of the operatic literature. While holding this post he also led distinguished symphony concerts in Berlin, and in various other German cities. For the remainder of his brilliant career he divided his activity between opera and symphonic music with equal eminence. From 1903 to 1906 he was the conductor of the Vienna Philharmonic, and from 1906 to 1908 and again from 1912 to 1918 conductor of the Boston Symphony. When the United States became involved in World War I, considerable hostility arose against Muck because he was a German and a known friend of the Kaiser. Finally in 1918 he was falsely accused of being a spy and was interned as an enemy alien until the end of the war. After returning to Europe he served as conductor of the Hamburg Philharmonic from 1922 to 1933 and led distinguished performances at the Bayreuth Festival.

Munch, Charles, conductor. Born Strasbourg, Alsace, Sept. 26, 1891. He came from a family of musicians. His father was a professor at the Strasbourg Conservatory; Albert Schweitzer, the renowned organist and humanitarian, is a distant relative. Munch attended Conservatories in Strasbourg and Paris, after which he studied the violin in Paris with Lucien Capet and in Berlin with Carl Flesch. After World War I he became professor of violin at the Strasbourg Conservatory and concertmaster of an orchestra in that city. From 1926 to 1929 he was concertmaster of the Gewandhaus Orchestra in Leipzig. After studying with Furtwaengler in Leipzig, Munch made his conducting début on Nov. 1, 1932, with the Straram Orchestra in Paris. Guest appearances with other major Paris orchestras followed, and in 1935 he became principal conductor of the Paris Philharmonic, which he founded. From 1938 to 1946 he was the conductor of the Paris Conservatory Orchestra. He made his American début in the United States on Dec. 27, 1946, with the Boston Symphony. In 1947-1948 he toured the United States as conductor of the visiting French Radio Orchestra. In 1949 he succeeded Koussevitzky as conductor of the Boston Symphony. In 1952 Munch led that orchestra during its first tour of Europe, and in the summer of 1956 at the Edinburgh Festival and in the Soviet Union. He is the author of *I Am a Conductor* (1955).

Municipal Auditorium. *See:* New Orleans Symphony, Oklahoma Symphony.

Murat Theatre. *See:* Indianapolis Symphony.

Murder in the Cathedral. *See:* Eliot, T. S.

Musette. An air in 2/4, 3/4, or 6/8 time of moderate tempo and pastoral mood and characterized by drone-like effects. The musette was popular in France in the 17th and 18th centuries. It derives its name from the instrument for which it was originally intended, a member of the bagpipe family. The musette is sometimes found as a movement of the Baroque suite, as in Bach's English Suites for clavier, Nos. 3 and 6.

Music for a Scene from Shelley. Composition for orchestra by Samuel Barber (1933), introduced by the New York Philharmonic on March 24, 1935, Werner Janssen conducting. The music was inspired by lines in Act 2, Scene 5 of Shelley's *Prometheus Unbound,* in which the poet indicates music. But the composer explains that his work is "really incidental music for this particular scene and has nothing at all to do with the figure of Prometheus." The composition opens with muted violins and violas, soon joined by muted horn. The orchestration becomes richer and more expressive. After a crescendo there appears a melody in octaves for strings. The music now gains in passion and intensity and is carried to a climax. Then the mystery of the opening measures returns, and the work ends with fading chords in the horns.

Music for Strings, Percussion and Celesta. By Béla Bartók (1936), introduced in Basel, Switzerland, on Jan. 21, 1937, Paul Sacher conducting. This composition is scored for two string quartets, percussion, double basses, and celesta, and is in four movements: I. *Andante tranquillo;* II. Allegro; III. Adagio; IV. *Allegro molto.* In the first movement the two quartets are merged into a single group. The principal theme appears pianissimo in violas against a percussive background; it is subsequently treated fugally by the other strings. The main subject of the second movement is stated pizzicato in the second string group, while the first offers a subsidiary subject. The third movement is a nocturne in a placid, at times mysterious, mood; and the energetic finale highlights a vigorous peasant dance in the Lydian mode.

Musical Joke, A (Ein musikalischer Spass). A satirical composition for strings and two horns by Mozart, K. 522 (1787). Subtitled in some editions *The Village Musicians (Die Dorfmusikanten),* this witty music was long considered a satire on inept performances by village musicians—filled as it is with dissonances, ungainly melodic ornaments, disorderly rhythms, and a hodgepodge of unrelated

melodies. Actually what Mozart here intended to do was to poke fun at ignorant composers who think themselves qualified to write symphonic music. The work has four brief movements: I. Allegro; II. Minuet; III. *Adagio cantabile;* IV. Presto.

Musical Offering, A (Musikalisches Opfer). A collection of contrapuntal compositions, all based on a single theme and set in the key of C minor, by Johann Sebastian Bach (1747). The composer conceived this work during a visit to the court of Frederick II in Potsdam. At that time the King provided Bach with a melody, upon which the master improvised a three-part fugue. Later on, Bach wrote down a six-part fugue on the same theme, and used it as material for a sonata for flute, violin, and bass, besides basing ten canons on it. He published the entire work in 1747 as a "Musical Offering" to the King. It was Bach's last chamber-music work, completed only three years before his death, and the only one he himself had published.

Musical Representation of Some Bible Stories. *See:* Kuhnau, Johann.

Musicology. The scientific study of or research in any aspect of music, and especially its history.

Musikalisches Opfer (J. S. Bach). *See: Musical Offering, A.*

Musique concrète. *See:* Concrete Music.

Musset, Alfred de, poet and playwright. Born Paris, France, Nov. 11, 1810; died there, May 1, 1857. The following composers have written incidental music for plays by de Musset: Louis Beydts (*Il ne faut jurer de rien*); Arthur Honegger (*Fantasio*); Jean Huré (*Fantasio*); Saint-Saëns (*On ne badine pas avec l'amour*); Henri Sauguet (*A quoi rêvent les jeunes filles*); Adone Zecchi (*Barberine*).

In addition, Henry Barraud wrote a suite, *Pour une comédie de Musset* and Daniel Lesur an *Overture for Alfred de Musset's Andrea del Sarto,* both for orchestra.

Mussorgsky, Modest, composer. Born Karevo, Russia, March 21, 1839; died St. Petersburg, Russia, March 28, 1881. He was directed to a military career, but while in uniform was stimulated

by Alexander Dargomizhsky and Balakirev to participate in musical activities.
After some study with Balakirev, Mussorgsky gave up the army for music in
1858. From then until 1861 he completed
a Scherzo for orchestra (introduced at
St. Petersburg in 1860), some piano
pieces, and fragments of a never completed symphony. Now a passionate advocate of musical nationalism, he associated himself with Balakirev, Cui, Rimsky-Korsakov, and Borodin in the national school soon identified as the "Russian Five" or "Mighty Five." In 1861,
upon the abolition of serfdom in Russia,
Mussorgsky lost the financial security he
thus far had enjoyed as the son of a
wealthy landowner. For the next few
years he worked as a clerk in the Ministry of Communications, relegating musical composition to the status of an avocation. During this period his health deteriorated rapidly as he became a victim
of nervous disorders, melancholia, and
alcoholism. Nevertheless he was able to
complete some masterworks, among these
his opera *Boris Godunov*. His physical
and moral disintegration became complete after 1873; just before his death
he gave indications of losing his mind.

Both as an innovator and as a creator
Mussorgsky produced his most important
work in operas. But he also wrote some
distinguished instrumental music, vital
with original harmonies, melodies, and
rhythms, and bearing a strikingly individual as well as national stamp. The
most significant of these are the orchestral tone poem *A Night on Bald Mountain* and the piano suite, *Pictures from
an Exhibition*, famous in orchestral transcriptions. Other instrumental works include *Intermezzo in modo classico* and
Triumphal March for orchestra; and various works for piano including *Children's
Games, Memories of Childhood,* and *On
the Southern Shore of Crimea.*

See: Khovantschina; Night on Bald
Mountain, A; Pictures at an Exhibition; Polonaise.

Mute. A device that muffles the tone of
an instrument.

My Fatherland (Má Vlast). A cycle of
six national tone poems for orchestra by
Smetana (1874-1879). The most famous
is the second, *The Moldau,* or *Vltava.*
The other five are: I. *Vitesgrad.* A portrait of Bohemia's past as symbolized
by an ancient citadel, stronghold of
kings. III. *Sarka.* The tale of the Amazon
who was first the sweetheart, then the
murderess, of the chieftain Ctirad. IV.
From the Fields and Groves of Bohemia.
A picture of Bohemian peasant and country life. V. *Tabor.* A representation of
the fortress of the Hussites, a city most
closely identified with Bohemian struggles for political and religious freedom.
VI. *Blanik.* A legend about Hussite war-
riors who sleep within the mountain
Blanik, but stand ready at any time to
rise from their sleep to defend their
country.

The entire cycle was performed for the
first time in Prague on Nov. 2, 1882.

N

Nabokov, Nicolas, composer. Born
Lubcha, Russia, April 17, 1903. He studied music at the Berlin High School for
Music with Ferruccio Busoni, and in
Stuttgart. After settling in Paris he
achieved recognition with a ballet oratorio, *Ode,* produced in Paris by the
Ballet Russe in 1928. In 1933 he came
to the United States, where he later became a citizen. One year after his arrival
his ballet *Union Pacific,* based on American popular and folk tunes, was introduced in the United States by the Ballet
Russe; in 1941 the New York Philhar-

monic gave the première performance of his *Sinfonia biblica*. Other and later orchestral works include various concertos (piano; flute; cello), *La Vita nuova* for voice and orchestra, and *Symboli chrestiani* for baritone and orchestra.

During and immediately after World War II, Nabokov served with various American agencies in Europe, including the morale division of the Strategic Bombing Survey; he was also advisor to Ambassador Murphy on cultural and Russian affairs. In the United States in 1947 he helped organize the Russian Broadcast Unit of the Voice of America, serving first as chief, then as music commentator. From 1947 to 1952 he was professor of music at Peabody Conservatory in Baltimore. In 1952 he was appointed secretary general of the Congress of Cultural Freedom. He is the author of a book of reminiscences, *Old Friends and New Music* (1951).

Nachez, Tivadar, violinist. Born Budapest, Hungary, May 1, 1859; died Lausanne, Switzerland, May 29, 1930. Awarded a traveling scholarship by the King of Hungary, he studied for three years with Joachim in Berlin, and for a year in Paris with Hubert Léonard. He made his first successful appearances as a violinist in Paris with major orchestras, after which he toured the Continent. He settled in London in 1889. Later on he lived for several years in Santa Barbara, Calif. His last public appearance was in a joint recital with Jacques Thibaud in 1926. He wrote several works for the violin based on Hungarian folksongs together with two concertos and a string quartet; he also edited two violin concertos by Vivaldi.

Napravnik, Eduard, conductor and composer. Born Býšt, Bohemia, Aug. 24, 1839; died St. Petersburg, Russia, Nov. 23, 1916. After completing music study at the School for Organists in Prague and privately with J. B. Kittl, he wrote his first symphony. In 1861 he was appointed director of the private orchestra of Prince Yussupov in St. Petersburg. Two years later he became organist of the imperial theaters. In 1867 he was appointed second conductor, and from 1869 until his death was principal con-

ductor, of the St. Petersburg Imperial Opera, where he led over 4,000 performances, including more than 80 premières. He was also a distinguished symphony conductor, director of the Russian Musical Society from 1869 to 1881, and guest conductor of the Philharmonic Society. His compositions, strongly influenced by Tchaikovsky, include 4 symphonies, *Fantasia on Russian Themes* for piano and orchestra, and another for violin and orchestra, an orchestral suite, various shorter works for orchestra (*National Dances, Vostok,* and *Solemn Overture*), 2 string quartets, string quintet, piano quartet, piano trio, and violin sonata.

Nardini, Pietro, violinist and composer. Born Leghorn, Italy, April 12, 1722; died Florence, Italy, May 7, 1793. After studying the violin with Tartini in Padua, he became solo violinist at the Stuttgart ducal palace in or about 1753, holding this post fifteen years. In 1767 he returned to Italy and settled in his native city, where he helped attend Tartini during the latter's last illness. After Tartini's death, in 1770, Nardini became director of music at the court of the Duke of Tuscany. Nardini was distinguished both as a violin virtuoso and as a composer for that instrument. He made notable advances upon Tartini in the development of the sonata form; but he lacked Tartini's intensity of feeling and aristocracy of style. Nardini's major works include 6 violin concertos (including the Concerto in E minor, which has survived), 6 violin sonatas, 6 sonatas for two violins, 6 flute trios, 6 solo violin sonatas, and 6 string quartets.

National Anthems in Instrumental Music. The following national anthems have been quoted (in part or in whole) in instrumental music:

Austria (Gott erhalte Franz den Kaiser): Haydn's *Emperor Quartet.*

France (Marseillaise): Debussy's piano prelude *Feux d'artifice;* Henri Litolff's *Robespierre Overture* for orchestra; Zoltán Kodály's *Háry János,* suite for orchestra; Liszt's *La Marseillaise,* for piano; Schumann's *Faschingsschwank aus Wien,* for piano; Tchaikovsky's *Overture 1812,* for orchestra.

Great Britain (God Save the King);

Beethoven's *Battle Symphony,* and *Seven Variations on God Save the King* for piano; Debussy's piano prelude *Hommage à S. Pickwick;* Paganini's *Variations on God Save the King,* for violin; Weber's *Jubilee Overture,* for orchestra.

Poland (Jeszcke Polska): Alexandre Tansman's *Polish Rhapsody,* for orchestra.

Russia (God Save the Czar): Tchaikovsky's *Marche Slave* and *Overture 1812,* both for orchestra.

United States (The Star-Spangled Banner): Victor Herbert's *American Fantasy* for orchestra.

National Gallery Concerts (London). *See:* Hess, Dame Myra.

National Symphony Orchestra. A symphony orchestra founded in Washington, D.C. in 1931 by Hans Kindler, who was its principal conductor until 1948, when he was succeeded by Howard Mitchell. The orchestra performs during the winter season at Constitution Hall, and has made numerous tours.

Natural. A musical symbol nullifying a sharp or flat.

Naturalism. *See:* Realism.

Nature, Life and Love. Cycle of three concert overtures for orchestra by Dvořák (1891-1892). The composer originally intended calling the three overtures *Nature, Life,* and *Love.* He finally decided to publish them separately and to call them *In Nature's Realm, Carnival,* and *Othello.* These overtures are discussed under their individual headings.

NBC Symphony. A symphony orchestra founded in 1937 for Arturo Toscanini by the National Broadcasting Company in the United States for performances over its radio network. It was trained for Toscanini by Artur Rodzinski. Its first concert took place on Nov. 13, 1937, Monteux conducting; Toscanini conducted it for the first time on Dec. 25, 1937. Toscanini remained its musical director until his retirement in 1954, but in that time the orchestra also performed under many distinguished guest conductors. After Toscanini's retirement, the National Broadcasting Company withdrew its support. The orchestra was reorganized, renamed Symphony of the Air, and gave concerts in New York and

elsewhere, including a tour of the Far East; it has been directed by guest conductors.

Neapolitan Sixth. In harmony the first inversion of the chord on the lowered supertonic. In C major, the Neapolitan sixth comprises F, A-flat, and D-flat.

Neel, Boyd, conductor. Born Blackheath, England, July 19, 1905. He was trained as a physician, but all the while he studied music with private teachers. In 1933 he founded the Boyd Neel String Orchestra, mostly with music students, giving successful performances not only in England but also on tour in France, Germany, and Holland, and in 1937 at the Salzburg Festival. He abandoned his musical activity during World War II, but in 1945 reorganized his orchestra, making tours of Australia, New Zealand, and in 1952 of Canada and the United States, as well as notable appearances at various European festivals. In 1953 he was appointed dean of the Royal Conservatory of Music in Toronto, Canada. He is the author of *The Story of an Orchestra* (1950).

Negro music. The style and idiom of American-Negro folk music have been successfully adapted for serious musical composition. Some of the orchestral works employing such a Negro style are: William L. Dawson's *Negro Folk Symphony;* Dvořák's *Symphony from the New World* and Cello Concerto; Henry F. Gilbert's *Comedy Overture on Negro Themes;* Rubin Goldmark's *Negro Rhapsody;* Morton Gould's *Spirituals;* John Powell's *Rapsodie nègre* for piano and orchestra; Gardner Read's *First Overture;* William Grant Still's *Afro-American Symphony;* and Lamar Stringfield's *Negro Parade.* Daniel Gregory Mason wrote a *String Quartet on Negro Themes.*

Neo-Baroque. A modern style of composition reverting to the contrapuntal methods of the 17th and 18th centuries, as in some of Hindemith's major works.

Neo-Classicism. A modern style of composition reverting to the Classical styles and forms of the 18th century, as in some of the principal works by Stravinsky and Hindemith.

Neo-Romanticism. The return to the Romantic methods, esthetic, and styles of the mid-19th century through the employment of ambitious forms and programmatic implications often of a philosophic nature, as in the symphonies of Bruckner and Mahler, or of typical Romantic technical procedures, as in the works of Rachmaninoff.

New England Triptych. Suite for orchestra by William Schuman (1956), commissioned and introduced by André Kostelanetz in Miami, Fla., on Oct. 28, 1956. This is a set of three pieces for orchestra derived from the music of William Billings, 18th-century American composer of psalms and fuguing tunes. Billings' music is used merely as a point of departure. The composer explains: "These pieces do not constitute a fantasy on themes of Billings, nor variations on his themes." The first movement is based on Billings' anthem, *Be Glad, Then America,* and rises to a powerful climax on the final Hallelujah. The second piece is an elaboration and embellishment upon *When Jesus Wept.* The final section comes from Billings' most famous hymn, *Chester,* so popular during the Revolutionary War that it was described as the *"Marseillaise* of the American Revolution." In this movement Schuman blends both the hymn-like and the march-like traits of the song.

Two earlier works by Schuman are adaptations of Billings' music: Overture for brass band, based on *Chester;* and the *William Billings Overture,* for orchestra.

New Orleans Symphony. An orchestra founded in New Orleans, La., in 1936 by several public-spirited citizens headed by Mrs. Joseph E. Friend and Lucy Benjamin Lemann. Its first concert was conducted by Arthur Zack. Zack and Ole Windingstad were the orchestra's first principal conductors. Massimo Freccia was conductor from 1944 to 1952, and Alexander Hilsberg since 1952. The orchestra performs in the Municipal Auditorium.

New Queen's Hall Orchestra. A symphony orchestra prominent in London from 1895 to 1927. It was founded as the Queen's Hall Orchestra under Henry J. Wood. On Jan. 30, 1897, it presented its first Saturday afternoon concert at that hall. A dispute within the orchestral ranks in 1904 led some members to resign and form the London Symphony. With replacements, the New Queen's Hall Orchestra, as it was now called, resumed operations under Wood. Besides its London concerts, the orchestra appeared at many English festivals. It was taken over by the BBC in 1927, many of its members then becoming the nucleus of the new BBC Symphony formed that year.

New Symphony Orchestra (London). *See:* Royal Albert Hall.

New World Symphony. *See:* Symphony—*Dvořák.*

New York Philharmonic Orchestra. The oldest existing orchestra in the United States. It was founded in New York City by Ureli Corelli Hill and several other musicians. The first concert took place in the Apollo Rooms in New York on Dec. 7, 1842. Several conductors participated at that concert: Hill, H. C. Timm, and D. G. Etienne. In 1852 Theodore Eisfeld became principal conductor, and from 1864 to 1872 Carl Bergmann held this post. After Bergmann, and up to 1903, its most important permanent conductors were Theodore Thomas, Anton Seidl, Emil Paur, and Walter Damrosch. Between 1903 and 1906 the orchestra was led by distinguished European guest conductors. This arrangement ended with the appointment of Vassili Safonov as principal conductor, a post he held until 1909. The orchestra's most important principal or permanent conductors after Safonov were Gustav Mahler, Willem Mengelberg, Wilhelm Furtwaengler, Arturo Toscanini, John Barbirolli, Artur Rodzinski, Dimitri Mitropoulos, and Leonard Bernstein. Though never a principal or permanent conductor, Bruno Walter was associated with the orchestra for more than thirty years as one of its major guest conductors, and in 1947 as musical adviser.

On several occasions the orchestra was amalgamated with other New York symphonic groups: with the National Symphony in 1921, the City Symphony in 1923, and the New York Symphony in 1928.

The orchestra performs in Carnegie Hall, and has made numerous tours, including several of Europe and South America. The first European tour took place in the spring of 1930 under Toscanini. Since 1930 its Sunday afternoon concerts (Saturday night concerts during 1958-1959) have been broadcast over the nationwide facilities of the Columbia Broadcasting System. Over the years, many of the world's foremost conductors have appeared with it.

New York Symphony Society. A major symphony orchestra founded in New York City by Leopold Damrosch in 1878, the first concert taking place at the old Steinway Hall on 14th Street, on November 9. When Dr. Damrosch died in 1885, his son, Walter, assumed direction, and remained its conductor until 1928, when the orchestra merged with the New York Philharmonic. In 1903 the orchestra was reorganized with funds provided by Harry Harkness Flagler. In 1920 it became the first American orchestra to tour Europe.

Newman, Ernest, music critic and musicologist. Born Liverpool, England, Nov. 30, 1868. He prepared for the Indian Civil Service, then engaged in business before turning to music as a profession. In 1903 he was appointed music instructor at the Midland Institute in Birmingham. Two years later he became music critic of the *Manchester Guardian,* and from 1906 to 1919 was music critic for the *Daily Post.* In 1919 he established his home in London, where a year later he became principal music critic of the *Sunday Times,* a post he held until 1958. In 1924-1925 he was guest critic for the New York *Post.* A trenchant critic and scholar, he has had a far-reaching influence on English musical life. His most important work is a four-volume biography, *Life of Richard Wagner* (1933-1946). Among his other significant books, outside the field of opera, are: *Musical Studies* (1905); *Elgar* (1906); *Richard Strauss* (1908); *A Musical Motley* (1919); *A Music Critic's Holiday* (1925); *The Unconscious Beethoven* (1927); *The Man Liszt* (1934). He edited Berlioz' *Memoirs* (1932).

Newmarch, Rosa (born **Rosa Jeaffreson),** writer on music. Born Leamington, England, Dec. 18, 1857; died Worthing, England, April 9, 1940. In 1880 she settled in London, where she began contributing articles to literary journals. Three years later she married Henry Charles Newmarch, from which time she used her married name for her writings. From 1897 on she did considerable research in Russian music, becoming one of the first English critics to propagandize it in the Western world. After 1915 she did a similar service for Slovakian music. From 1908 to 1920 she was program annotator for concerts of the New Queen's Hall Orchestra. Her principal books, outside the field of opera, are: *Tchaikovsky* (1900); *Henry J. Wood* (1904); *The Life and Letters of Tchaikovsky* (1908); *The Music of Czechoslovakia* (1942); and *The Concert-Goer's Library,* in six volumes (1928-1948).

Ney, Elly, pianist. Born Duesseldorf, Germany, Sept. 27, 1882. Her principal study of the piano took place in Vienna with Theodor Leschetizky and Emil Sauer. After winning the Ilbach and Mendelssohn Prizes she made her concert début in Vienna in 1905. From that time on she made many appearances throughout Europe and the United States, besides founding and performing with the Elly Ney Trio. She was married to the conductor, Willem van Hoogstraten, from 1911 to 1927. In 1939 she became director of the piano department at the Mozarteum in Salzburg; since the end of World War II she has been in retirement. She is the author of an autobiography, *Ein Leben fuer die Musik* (1952).

Niederschlag (or **Niedertakt).** German for downbeat, as opposed to "Aufschlag" or "Auftakt" for upbeat.

Nielsen, Carl August, composer. Born Noerre-Lyndelse, Denmark, June 9, 1865; died Copenhagen, Denmark, Oct. 2, 1931. For several years he attended the Copenhagen Conservatory, where he was a pupil of Niels Gade. Winning the Ancker Prize enabled him to travel a year in France and Italy. For five years he played the violin in the Copenhagen Royal Orchestra. After 1895 he dedicated himself to composition. Though little known outside of Denmark, Nielsen is one of its most important composers; his stature has grown considerably since his death. He used several different styles skilfully, including post-Romanticism, Impressionism, and polytonality. He is most famous for his symphonies, of which he wrote six, all beautifully orchestrated and often interesting for their expressive programmatic content. He also wrote various concertos (violin; flute; clarinet) and some shorter works for orchestra, including *Four Temperaments, Helios Overture, Pan and Syrinx,* and *Rhapsodic Overture,* as well as 4 string quartets, a woodwind quintet, 2 violin sonatas, and various pieces for the piano including humoresques, bagatelles, and a Theme and Variations.

From 1908 to 1914 he was the conductor of the Copenhagen Royal Orchestra, a period in which he also made guest appearances with other European orchestras. From 1915 to 1927 he was director of the Copenhagen Conservatory and conductor of the Musical Society. He was a Knight of the Dannebrog, and a member of the Stockholm Royal Academy.

Nietzsche, Friedrich Wilhelm, philosopher. Born Roecken, Germany, Oct. 15, 1844; died Weimar, Germany, Aug. 25, 1900. An amateur composer of several choral works, piano pieces, and songs, Nietzsche originally was a rabid supporter of Wagner's music, then an equally virulent enemy. Nietzsche's philosophical work, *Thus Spake Zarathustra,* was the inspiration for Jan Ingenhoven's *Symphonic Fantasy on Zarathustra's Nachtlied,* parts of Mahler's Symphony No. 3, and Richard Strauss' tone poem, *Thus Spake Zarathustra.* Conrado del Campo wrote a string quartet, *Las Horas de Nietzsche.*

Night on Bald Mountain, A. Fantasy for orchestra by Modest Mussorgsky (1867), based on Gogol's story, *St. John's Eve.* Reorchestrated and revised by Rimsky-Korsakov, it was first performed in St. Petersburg on Oct. 27, 1886. The following program appears in the published score: "A subterranean din of unearthly voices. Appearance of the Spirits of Darkness, followed by that of Tchernobog. Glorification of the Black God. The Black Mass. The Revelry of the Witches' Sabbath interrupted from afar by the bells of a little church, whereupon the spirits of evil disperse. Dawn breaks."

Bald Mountain is Mt. Triglav near Kiev on which, according to legend, each year on St. John's Eve (June 24) there is celebrated the Feast of St. John the Baptist. Witches, sorcerers, and evil spirits of all kinds participate in the revelry, presided over by Tchernobog, the Black God.

Violins in the upper register, and ejaculations by woodwinds, trombones, and bassoons, set an atmosphere of mystery in the opening measures. A spirited Russian dance follows. After the first outburst of revelry subsides, a softer section appears, highlighted by a gentle dance melody in woodwinds set against strings. Once again the revelry begins and grows frenetic. It comes to an abrupt halt. Church bells ring, and a sensitive melody for clarinet announces the arrival of dawn.

Nights in the Gardens of Spain (Noches en los jardines de España). For piano and orchestra by Manuel de Falla (1915), first performed in Madrid on April 9, 1916, Fernandez Arbós conducting, and M. Cubiles, soloist. Falla's music is derived from modes, rhythms, and melodies of popular Andalusian music; its orchestration often imitates effects produced by native Spanish instruments. The work is made up of three symphonic impressions of Spain. I. At the Generalife. This is a picture of the beautiful gardens near the Alhambra. The main melodic subject is exotic, heard in a solo viola in unison with the harp. After the appearance of the piano, the orchestra presents a second theme, which is soon developed by the solo instrument. The first haunting subject reappears throughout the movement, and for the last time in the coda in a horn *pianissimo.* II. A Far-Off Dance. The main dance melody is a rhythmic subject for flute and English horn. III. In the Gardens of the Sierra of Cordóba. This movement enters without pause, tremolo violins providing the transition. The music is abandoned and passionate throughout, sensual in melody and with exciting gypsy rhythms. The movement begins in an ominous mood, with a subject for high strings, punctuated by the woodwind. The piano provides an insistent rhythm that gains in intensity until the full orchestra erupts in a corybantic dance.

Nigun (Bloch). *See: Baal Shem Suite.*

Nikisch, Arthur, conductor. Born Szent-Miklós, Hungary, Oct. 12, 1855; died Leipzig, Germany, Jan. 23, 1922. In 1866 he entered the Vienna Conservatory, where he was at once placed in the highest class with pupils ten years his senior. While still a student there he played the violin in a performance of Beethoven's Ninth Symphony conducted by Wagner during the ceremonies dedicating the cornerstone of the festival theater in Bayreuth. Nikisch was graduated from the Conservatory in 1874. For a few years he played the violin in the Vienna Court Orchestra. In 1878 he became a coach at the Leipzig Opera, where he conducted his first opera performance on Feb. 11, 1878. In 1879 he was made first conductor. While serving at the Leipzig Opera he made several appearances in Germany as conductor of symphony concerts. From 1889 to 1893 he was principal conductor of the Boston Symphony. After returning to Europe he assumed in 1895 the two posts that he held until the end of his life and with which he won world renown, principal conductor of both the Gewandhaus Orchestra in Leipzig and the Berlin Philharmonic. He toured France, Russia, and Switzerland with the Berlin Philharmonic, and the United States in 1912 with the London Symphony. He was one of the most admired conductors of his generation, an electrifying and romantic personality who constantly sought out the poetic content of the music he conducted. He was one of the first conductors to direct all performances from memory. His son, Mitja, was a concert pianist (born Leipzig, Germany, May 21, 1899; died Venice, Italy, Aug. 5, 1936). He made his American début in New York on Oct. 23, 1923.

Nobilissima visione. Ballet suite for orchestra by Hindemith (1938), adapted from the score to his "choreographic legend," *St. Francis,* introduced in London by the Ballet Russe on July 21, 1938. The orchestral suite was performed for the first time in Venice in September 1938, and is in three sections: I. Introduction; Rondo. II. March. III. Passacaglia. The composer has provided the following analysis: "The introduction consists of the part of the original music during which the hero of the action is sunk in deep meditation. The Rondo corresponds to the music in the stage score for the mystic union of the Saint to Mistress Poverty . . . The music reflects the blessed peace and unworldly cheer with which the guests at the wedding participate in the wedding feast—dry bread and water only. The second movement pictures the march of a troop of medieval soldiers. First heard but distantly, their gradual approach is observed. The middle portion of the movement suggests the brutality with which these mercenaries set upon a traveling burgher and rob him. The third and closing movement corresponds to the portion of the ballet score representing the Hymn to the Sun. Here all the symbolic personifications of heavenly and earthly existence mingle in the course of the different variations with which the six-measure theme of the passacaglia is transformed."

Noches en los jardines de España (Falla). *See: Nights in the Gardens of Spain.*

Nocturne. A poetic, romantic instrumental composition in slow tempo. The name was derived from the Italian "notturno" of the 18th century, which referred to "night music," much in the same way that "serenata" was "evening music" and the aubade, "morning music." The term "notturno" was used by many composers during the Classical period, including Haydn and Mozart, as interchangeable with serenade and divertimento.

The nocturne, as a piece of "night music" for orchestra, appears in the Romantic literature, celebrated examples being found in Mendelssohn's *A Midsummer Night's Dream* suite and in Grieg's *Lyric Suite.* Debussy wrote three nocturnes for orchestra; but, as the composer explained, these are not concerned "with the form of the nocturne, but everything that this word induces in the way of a diversified impression and special lights."

As a composition for the piano, the nocturne originated with John Field, who wrote 18 such pieces. They are dreamy, romantic, and at times sentimental melodies, gracefully embellished, and presented against an undulating harmonic background. These are Field's finest nocturnes: No. 3 in A-flat major; No. 4, in A major; No. 5, in B-flat major (orchestrated by Sir Hamilton Harty); and No. 12, in G major.

It was Chopin who made the nocturne a form famous in piano literature. He wrote 20 such compositions, all of them stylistically and structurally influenced by Field; however, they have deeper poetic content and are most refreshingly contrasted in mood. Three nocturnes are found in op. 9 (1831); three in op. 15 (1831-1833); two each in op. 27 (1835), op. 32 (1837), op. 37 (1838-1839), op. 48 (1841), op. 55 (1843), op. 62 (1846); one in op. 72 (1847); and one was published posthumously. The most popular of these is the Nocturne in E-flat major, op. 9, no. 2, one of Chopin's most beautiful and poetic melodies. Other famous Chopin nocturnes are the A-flat major, op. 32, No. 2, used prominently in the ballet *Les Sylphides;* C-sharp minor, op. 27, no. 1; F-sharp major, op. 15, no. 2; and D-flat major, op. 27, no. 2.

Gabriel Fauré wrote 13 nocturnes for piano, stylistically derived from Chopin. But where the nocturne of Chopin was poetic and at times sentimental, with Fauré it often became filled with gloomy suggestions. Thus the Nocturne No. 11 in F-sharp major, op. 104, no. 1 (1913), is an elegy inspired by a friend's death; and Nocturne No. 13 in B minor, op. 119 (1921), is the deeply tragic expression of a composer who here bids farewell forever to the piano.

There is a delightful and popular nocturne in Tchaikovsky's Six Pieces, for piano, op. 19 (1873). It is the fourth number in the group and is in the key of C-sharp minor.

Nocturnes. A set of three Impressionistic tone poems for orchestra by Debussy (1893-1899). The first two were introduced in Paris on Dec. 9, 1900, and the complete set was played there on Oct. 27, 1901. For each of the three movements the composer provided a programmatic interpretation. I. *Clouds (Nuages).*

The "unchangeable appearance of the sky with the slow and solemn clouds dissolving in a gray agony tinted with white" is described. Quiet chords in the woodwinds depict the moving clouds. Three main themes follow: a sensitive melody for English horn; a song for solo viola; and a subject for flute and harp. II. *Festivals (Fêtes).* This is music "rich with movement, rhythm, dancing." A colorful procession is taking place. After the violins suggest a dance rhythm, the English horn and clarinets introduce a tune which, later on, returns in an altered form in flutes and oboes. An important subject is given by woodwind after trumpet and oboe calls, and receives detailed treatment. When a climax is reached, the procession is depicted in a march rhythm enunciated by harp, drums, and plucked strings. The mood changes with a song for oboe, and the music gently ebbs away. III. *Sirens (Sirènes).* This section describes "the sea and its innumerable rhythms . . . Then the song of the Sirens is heard." This section calls for eight mezzo-sopranos, who sing a wordless chant.

Nonet. A composition for 9 instruments. Schubert's *Eine kleine Trauermusik* (1812) is a nonet for two clarinets, two bassoons, contrabassoon, two horns, and two trombones. Very popular in the 19th century and still heard occasionally is the Nonet for woodwinds, horn, and strings by Louis Spohr. Villa-Lobos wrote a nonet for flute, oboe, clarinet, saxophone, bassoon, celesta, harp, and timpani, with a chorus as the ninth "instrument." A nonet by Bohuslav Martinu received its world première at the Salzburg Festival in 1959.

Norfolk Rhapsody, No. 1. Rhapsody in E minor for orchestra by Vaughan Williams (1905-1906), introduced at a Promenade Concert in London on Aug. 23, 1906. This was one of the composer's first successful attempts at writing nationalistic music. He actually wrote three Norfolk Rhapsodies, planning them as a single work to be entitled *Norfolk Folk Symphony.* But when he realized that his second and third rhapsodies were inferior, he abandoned this project. The first rhapsody used folk material native to King's Lynn, a district in Norfolk. It quotes such

Norfolk melodies as *The Captain's Apprentice, A Bold Young Sailor, The Basket of Eggs,* and *Ward the Pirate.*

Northrop Auditorium. *See:* Minneapolis Symphony.

Norwegian Dances. A set of four folk dances by Grieg, op. 35 (1881). It originated as a piano duet. The second of these dances, in A minor, is one of the composer's most popular pieces. The other three dances are in the keys of D minor, G major, and D major.

Notation. The use of written or printed symbols (notes) in the representation of music.

Note. A symbol representing a musical tone.

Notenbuch vor Anna Magdalena Bach. *See: Little Notebook of Anna Magdalena, The.*

Notre Dame de Paris. *See:* Hugo, Victor.

Notturno. *See:* Nocturne.

Nováček, Ottokar, violinist and composer. Born Fehértemplom, Hungary, May 13, 1866; died New York City, Feb. 3, 1900. He attended the Leipzig Conservatory, winning the Mendelssohn Prize upon his graduation in 1885. He then played the violin in the Gewandhaus Orchestra and with the Brodsky Quartet. In 1891 he went to Boston, where he joined the violin section of the Boston Symphony; in 1892-1893 he played the viola in the New York Symphony. A heart condition compelled him to abandon his career as a performer in 1899. Nováček wrote 3 string quartets, a piano concerto, 8 caprices for violin and piano, and many smaller violin pieces. Of the last the most famous is the *Perpetual Motion* for violin and orchestra.

Novaës, Guiomar, pianist. Born São João da Boã Vista, Brazil, Feb. 28, 1895. She made her public début as a pianist at the age of seven. A government grant enabled her to attend the Paris Conservatory, where for two years she studied with Isidor Philipp. In 1911 she made a successful début in Paris. When she made her North American début, in New York on Nov. 11, 1915, she was acknowledged as one of the foremost women pianists of her time. In 1956 she received the Order of Merit from the Brazilian government.

Novák, Vitězslav, composer. Born Kamenitz, Bohemia, Dec. 5, 1870; died Skutec, Slovakia, July 18, 1949. While studying law at the University of Prague he attended the Prague Conservatory, where his teachers included Dvořák. When he turned to composition his writing was influenced by Brahms and Liszt. But after the turn of the 20th century, he became a nationalist whose works adopted the style and personality of Bohemian folksongs and dances. In this style he produced some of his best-known works, including the tone poem *In the Tatra* and the *Slovakian Suite,* and the *Bohemian Dances* and *Slovakian Suite* for piano. But in some of his later works he assumed an Impressionistic style. In 1909 he was appointed professor of composition at the Prague Conservatory, becoming professor at the Master School in 1918, and director of the School in 1919. In 1946 he received the honorary title of National Artist from the Republic of Czechoslovakia. Besides works already mentioned, his principal compositions for orchestra include the overture *Maryša,* the tone poems *Of Eternal Longing* and *De Profundis, May Symphony, South Bohemian Suite,* and Serenade for small orchestra. He also wrote 2 string quartets, a piano quartet, a sonata for viola, cello, and piano, 6 sonatinas and various suites, eclogues, serenades, and bagatelles for piano.

Novelette. A short, romantic composition for piano, free in form and development. The form originated with Schumann in 1838, with 8 pieces, op. 21. Schumann also wrote an additional novelette in *Bunte Blaetter,* op. 99.

Schumann's first Novelette, in F major, contrasts a march melody with a lyrical trio. The second, in D major, is virtuoso music alternating with a reflective intermezzo. The third, in D major, is vivacious, with an almost farcical episode. The longest, and perhaps the best, of the novelettes is the eighth, in A and D major. This work is so copious in melodic ideas that it almost has the spaciousness of a suite. It includes two trios, and two beautiful lyrical passages, the first with the character of a ballade, and the other with that of a lied.

Nozze di Figaro, Overture to Le. *See:*

Marriage of Figaro, Overture to The.

Nuages (Debussy). *See: Nocturnes.*

Nut. A screw-like device with which the hair of a bow is tightened and loosened.

Nutcracker Suite (Casse-Noisette). Ballet suite for orchestra by Tchaikovsky, op. 71a (1892), adapted from the score to a ballet. The ballet scenario was based on Dumas' adaptation of E. T. A. Hoffmann's story, *The Nutcracker and the Mouse King.* A girl receives as a Christmas gift a nutcracker. She dreams it is a prince leading the toys to battle against the mice. The Prince conducts the girl to Jam Mountain in Arabia where she is greeted by the Sugarplum Fairy and entertained with games and dances.

The ballet was first performed in St. Petersburg on Dec. 18, 1892, the composer conducting. The suite was introduced in St. Petersburg on March 19, 1892.

The suite has eight sections. I. *Miniature Overture.* This brisk movement has two lively subjects; the instrumentation dispenses with the lower strings. II. March. The main theme is a saucy tune for clarinet, horn, and two trumpets. In the trio, a staccato melody is shared by woodwinds and strings. III. *Dance of the Sugarplum Fairy.* A delicate melody is presented by the celesta, one of the earliest examples in which this instrument is given such prominence in the symphony orchestra. IV. *Trepak.* This is a lively Russian dance with exciting rhythmic momentum. V. *Arabian Dance.* An exotic melody appears in the clarinet in the lower register. VI. *Chinese Dance.* An oriental melody is presented by flute and piccolo. VII. *Dance of the Flutes.* This is a delicate dance tune for flutes with a contrasting section for trumpets. VIII. *Waltz of the Flowers.* After an infectious melody for horns, continued by clarinets, two ingratiating themes are heard; the first is for strings, the other for flute and oboe. The waltz melody is repeated after each of these melodies.

O

Obbligato. An essential accompanying solo passage for an instrument.

Oberon, Overture to. Overture to the German Romantic opera by Carl Maria von Weber, introduced at Covent Garden in London on April 12, 1826. The libretto, by James Robinson Plance, was based on an old French romance. The overture opens with a horn call, answered by muted strings. A pastoral scene is created by descending figures in flutes and clarinets, and maintained by a serene melody for cellos. Loud chords lead to the main section in which the first theme is turbulent. After a return of the opening horn call, there appears the second main theme, a beautiful song for solo clarinet, repeated by strings. After this comes an excerpt from a famous aria, *Ocean, Thou Mighty Monster.* Earlier material returns for elaboration, and the overture ends with a final statement of *Ocean, Thou Mighty Monster.*

Oboe. A woodwind instrument with a conical tube and double reed mouthpiece. It has a poignantly sweet tone; in register it is lower than the flute but higher than the clarinet.

Octave. A consecutive series of seven degrees of the diatonic scale between two notes of the same name, or the interval between those two notes.

Octet. A musical composition for eight instruments. Mendelssohn's Octet in E-flat major, op. 20 (1825), is for four violins, two violas, and two cellos (I. *Allegro moderato.* II. Andante. III. *Allegro leggierissimo.* IV. Presto). It is famous primarily for its third movement—one of those delicate, magical scherzos for which the composer was famous. The first movement opens with an energetic motif for first violin that rises and descends with a contagious sweep against tremolos. The second principal subject appears in one of the violins and first viola with an attractive countermelody in another violin. The slow movement is in the rhythm of a siciliano and is made up of two pleasing tunes. The scherzo movement has already been commented upon. Here the composer appended a motto from Goethe's *Faust:* "Trails of cloud and mist brighten from above; breeze in the foliage and wind in the reeds—and everything is scattered." The finale has the character of a perpetual motion.

Schubert's Octet in F major, op. 166 (1824), is for two violins, viola, cello, double bass, clarinet, bassoon, and horn. All movements are filled with lovable Schubertian lyricism (I. Adagio; *Andante un poco mosso.* II. *Allegro vivace.* III. Andante. IV. Allegretto. V. *Andante molto;* Allegro). The opening movement is high-tensioned, but the ensuing Andante is an expression of ebullient feelings. The second movement is a light-footed scherzo, and the third, a folk melody with seven variations. This is followed by a graceful minuet. The finale begins in a mournful strain but, like the first movement, soon erupts into vivacious and joyful melodies.

The contemporary French composer, Milhaud, wrote an unusual Octet for four violins, two violas, and two cellos. But actually it is made up of two string quartets, each a self-sufficient work which can be played separately. *See:* Quartet—*Milhaud.*

Ode. Triptych for orchestra by Stravinsky (1943), commissioned by the Koussevitzky Foundation and dedicated to the memory of Koussevitzky's recently deceased wife, Nathalie. It was introduced by the Boston Symphony under Koussevitzky on Oct. 1, 1943. The first part is a *Eulogy,* a song in fugal treatment. A lively *Eclogue* follows, suggesting outdoor music. The composer here had in mind Tanglewood and the Berkshire Music Centre, which Nathalie cherished as the spiritual creations of her husband. The

concluding section is a serene melody entitled *Epitaph.*

Ode to Joy. *See:* Symphony—*Beethoven.*

Ode to Napoleon. For speaking voice, piano, and string orchestra by Arnold Schoenberg, op. 41b (1942), introduced by the New York Philharmonic on Nov. 23, 1944, Rodzinski conducting. This is a setting of a poem by Byron in which the poet denounces Napoleon as a tyrant. To Schoenberg the poem had particular significance and timeliness in 1942: Hitler then loomed as another and even more terrible Napoleon. Byron's indictment served Schoenberg as an attack against Nazi dictatorship. The narrator utilizes the declamation (*Sprechstimme*) which the composer had previously used in *Pierrot Lunaire* and other works. No indication of pitch is given in the score; the inflections are left to the discretion of the performer. The music itself is mainly in the twelve-tone technique, but used with less rigidity and austerity than heretofore. Napoleon is symbolized by a theme constructed from ascending fourths and descending minor seconds, whose severity suggests his ruthlessness. As in the Byron poem, George Washington appears as the personification of democracy. His theme is in inversion to that of Napoleon to demonstrate he is the very antithesis of the French tyrant. The composition achieves a climax with a majestic invocation to Washington.

Odnoposoff, Ricardo, violinist. Born Buenos Aires, Argentina, Feb. 24, 1914. In his fourteenth year he went to Berlin to study with Carl Flesch. There he became the first undergraduate to appear as soloist with the Berlin Philharmonic. In 1932 he won first prize in an international competition in Vienna, and in 1937 in the Queen Elizabeth of Belgium Competition. Appearances in Europe and South America followed. He made his North American début in New York in February 1944. His first tour of Australia took place in 1951, and a year later he was soloist at the Sibelius festival in Helsinki.

Odyssey, The. *See:* Homer.

Oedipus Trilogy. *See:* Sophocles.

Oiseau bleu, L'. *See:* Maeterlinck, Maurice.

Oiseau de feu, L' (Stravinsky). *See: Firebird, The.*

Oiseaux tristes (Ravel). *See: Miroirs.*

Oistrakh, David, violinist. Born Odessa, Russia, Sept. 30, 1908. He attended the Odessa Conservatory, where Pyotr Stolarsky was his only teacher and from which he was graduated in 1926. As a student he made many public appearances in Odessa; after his graduation he was heard in Moscow, Leningrad, and throughout the Ukraine. In 1930 he won first prize in a competition in Kharkov; in 1934 he once again placed first in a competition, this time in Leningrad; and in 1937 he received top honors at the Queen Elizabeth of Belgium Competition. Meanwhile he was giving performances in the Soviet Union, Turkey, and Warsaw.

He received the Stalin Prize in 1942. In 1951 he was acclaimed at the Florence May Music Festival; in 1953 he made sensational appearances in Paris; in 1955 he concertized in Japan and Germany. On Nov. 20, 1955, he made his American début with a recital at Carnegie Hall. He also made distinguished appearances in the Soviet Union with chamber music ensembles and has been professor of the violin at the Moscow Conservatory since 1939.

His son, Igor (born 1931), is also a distinguished violinist. He won competitions at Budapest in 1949 and Poznan in 1952. In 1953 he made his first tour of Europe. Father and son have occasionally appeared in performances of music for two violins.

Oklahoma Symphony Orchestra. An orchestra founded in 1937 in Oklahoma City, Okla. Victor Alessandro was principal conductor until 1951, when he was succeeded by Guy Fraser Harrison. The orchestra plays in the Municipal Auditorium and goes on annual tours throughout the state.

On Hearing the First Cuckoo in Spring. Tone poem for orchestra by Frederick Delius (1912), first performed in Leipzig on Oct. 2, 1913. This portrait of spring opens with a slow three-bar sequence. The first theme is an exchange of cuckoo calls, first in the oboe, then in divided strings. The serene mood thus established

is maintained by the second theme, a melody for first violins derived from a Norwegian folksong, *In Ola Valley.* The cuckoo calls return in the clarinet, and then the tone poem ends in a pastoral vein.

On the Steppes of Central Asia (Borodin). *See: In Central Asia.*

Ondine (Ravel). (1) *See: Gaspard de la nuit.*

(2) *See:* Prelude—*Debussy.*

Ondříček, Franz, violinist. Born Prague, Czechoslovakia, April 29, 1859; died Milan, Italy, April 13, 1922. He was graduated from the Prague Conservatory with highest honors, after which he embarked on a successful tour of Europe. After additional study with Joseph Massart at the Paris Conservatory in 1877 he scored major successes throughout Europe; in Vienna he presented the world première of Dvořák's Violin Concerto. Between October 1895 and April 1896 he gave 70 concerts in the United States. From 1908 to 1911 he was first violinist of the Ondříček String Quartet, which he had founded in Vienna and which achieved renown throughout Europe. From 1910 to 1919 he was director of the Vienna Conservatory which he had organized; and in 1919 he was appointed professor of the violin at the Prague Conservatory. He made his last public appearance in Geneva five days before his death. He prepared several valuable pedagogical works for the violin.

Open Tones. Tones produced on a string instrument when fingers are not pressed on the strings; and on a brass instrument without using the valves.

Opus. A work or composition; the number of a published work.

Oración del torero, La (The Prayer of the Bull Fighter). For string quartet by Joaquín Turina, op. 34 (1926). This one-movement composition begins with a prayer-like melody. The music grows more agitated, then the principal melody unfolds spaciously. After a climax, earlier thematic material is recalled. The main melody brings the composition to a subdued conclusion.

Oratorio. A large work for soloists, chorus, and orchestra whose text is derived from the Bible, and which tells a story without the use of either scenery or costumes. The recitative carries on the dramatic action, while the chorus is a commentator on or participant in episodes taking place. For a discussion of a few of the most famous oratorios in the choral literature *see: Creation, The* (Haydn), *Elijah* (Mendelssohn), and *Messiah* (Handel).

Orchestra. An ensemble of musical instruments, including strings. The word "orchestra" originated in ancient Greece where it referred to that part of the theater between the auditorium and the stage where the chorus performed its dancing. While there have been orchestras as long as there have been musical instruments, the symphony orchestra is a comparatively recent development. Orchestras said to exist in the 14th century, in the court of Edward IV, consisted merely of lutes, viols, flutes, drums, and a virginal. The orchestra used in Italy by Jacopo Peri for his opera *Euridice* (1600) consisted only of lutes and harpsichords. One of the first pioneers to change the structure of the orchestra and the technique of orchestra performance was the 17th-century Italian opera master, Claudio Monteverdi. For his opera *Orfeo* (1607) Monteverdi used an orchestral ensemble embracing viols, flute, cornetts, lutes, harpsichord, and harp, among other instruments. He used the orchestra prominently throughout his opera (the first composer to do so), to set the mood or intensify dramatic effect; to extend the range of his artistic expression he introduced new techniques into orchestral performance. With the extension of dynamics and tone colors, and through the employment on stringed instruments of such novel devices as tremolo and pizzicato Monteverdi suggested the artistic potential of the orchestra.

The organization of the orchestra now kept changing. After Monteverdi the most important developments took place with Jean-Baptiste Lully, also a distinguished composer of operas, who was one of the first to endow bowed strings with significance within the orchestral texture; also with Alessandro Scarlatti, another Italian opera master, one of the first composers to use the string quartet as the heart of the string section.

With Handel and J. S. Bach the strings acquired new richness and variety of treatment. Bach was also important in bringing new independence to the wind instruments and endowing them with a range of expression they had previously not known.

In his search for great dramatic truth in his operas, Gluck uncovered a still wider range of tone colors through his idiomatic use of instruments like the piccolo, trombone, and harp; also, through the assignment of new significance to the brass section and to such strings as viola and cello.

In 1745 Johann Wenzel Stamitz became leader of the court orchestra in Mannheim, Germany. Under his direction this orchestra became one of the most important in Europe. "No orchestra in the world ever surpassed the Mannheim orchestra," reported the historian, Charles Burney. Stamitz helped develop the technique of orchestral performance and succeeded in finally establishing the organization of the orchestra along a more or less permanent design. Except for minor changes the orchestra conducted by Stamitz was the ensemble for which Haydn and Mozart wrote their symphonies. The Mannheim orchestra consisted of between 40 and 50 members: 20 violins, 4 violas, 4 cellos, 2 basses, and two each of flutes, oboes, clarinets, bassoons, horns, trumpets, and timpani.

From this point on the evolution of the orchestra consisted in the continual introduction of new instruments, and the extension of technique in the performance of all instruments; also in the continual experimentation with tone coloration, dynamics, sonorities, and expressive effects. Beethoven brought new importance to the brass, timpani, and double bass while introducing into his instrumentation such less familiar instruments as the trombone, contrabassoon, and several percussion. Berlioz introduced further refinements and innovations in the treatment of various orchestral choirs and took advantage of the important improvements made in the wind instruments during the first half of the 19th century, such as the introduction of valves and pistons in horns and trumpets. Weber and Schubert often achieved new expressiveness in their string writing by dividing the strings into more parts than the traditional quartet. Meyerbeer and Rossini were among the first to use the bass clarinet and English horn respectively. Wagner devised his own brand of tubas for special effects.

By the end of the 19th century—with Brahms, Mahler, and Franck among other symphonists—the organization of the modern symphony orchestra became fully established. Henceforth composers might occasionally use novel or rare or exotic instruments for special effects, but the basic physiognomy of the orchestra was to remain unchanged.

The modern symphony orchestra comprises between 80 and 110 men who can be divided into four groups: strings, woodwind, brass, and percussion.

The string section is the heart of the orchestra. The composer assigns to it his most expressive passages. More than half of the orchestra consists of strings. Here, too, we find four basic units: violins (first and second), violas, cellos, and double basses, in descending order of pitch. At the head of each of these units is a "first-desk" man; that of the first violins is called "concertmaster" in the United States, "leader" in Britain. The string section includes one other instrument, the harp. An orchestra like the New York Philharmonic or Boston Symphony has about 70 strings: 17 first violins, 17 second violins, 12 violas, 12 cellos, 10 double basses, and 2 harps.

The woodwinds are next in importance. Once again in descending order of pitch they include the flute (and piccolo, a member of the flute family), oboe (and English horn), clarinet (and bass clarinet), and bassoon (and contrabassoon). A major symphony orchestra has 16 woodwinds: 3 flutes and a piccolo; 3 oboes and an English horn; 3 clarinets and a bass clarinet; 3 bassoons and a contrabassoon.

The brass is the third section. Here we find, in order of pitch, the trumpet, French horn, trombone, and tuba. There are 14 brasses in a major orchestra: 4 trumpets, 5 horns, 4 trombones, and 1 tuba.

The percussion is the last group, its major member being the timpani or kettledrums. Others in the percussion family include cymbals, triangle, celesta, xylophone, glockenspiel, bass drum, tubular chimes, and piano. A major symphony orchestra has 2 timpani players, two additional performers adept at several of the other percussions, and a staff pianist.

For a description of each of the above instruments, consult individual entries.

The customary placement of the various sections is as follows: first violins at the left of the conductor, and second violins at his right; violas and cellos behind the violins, with the double basses lined up in a row in the rear of the stage; woodwinds in the two rows behind violas and cellos; brasses, directly behind the woodwind; and the percussion behind the brasses.

Some conductors prefer varying this arrangement somewhat. One such familiar variation is to place all violins to the left of the conductor, with violas and cellos to his right. Some conductors also prefer altering the position of brass, percussion, and double basses to conform to the acoustics of a particular auditorium.

Orchestra Hall. *See:* Chicago Symphony.
Orchestral score. *See:* Score.
Orchestration. The science and art of arranging music for an orchestra to achieve tonal balance and contrasts in instrumental colors.
Orchestre de la Suisse Romande. A symphony orchestra founded in Geneva, Switzerland, in 1918 by Ernest Ansermet, who has been the principal conductor ever since. This orchestra has distinguished itself for its brilliant performances of 20th-century music, especially the music of Stravinsky.
Orestes. *See:* Aeschylus; Euripides.
Orfeo ed Euridice (Gluck). *See: Orpheus and Eurydice.*
Organ. The largest and most complex of keyboard instruments. The organ produces its sounds by means of pipes—varied in size, form, and material—through which air is compressed by means of electricity. The modern organ

has two, three, or four manual keyboards, and a pedal keyboard.

While music for the organ was written in the 15th century, it was not until the 17th century that organ music came into its own, with Johann Froberger, Girolamo Frescobaldi, Jan Sweelinck, Samuel Scheidt, and Dietrich Buxtehude. With Johann Sebastian Bach music for the organ and organ performance entered upon their greatest epoch.

Organ point (Pedal point). A bass tone held below moving voices.

Orgelbuechlein (J. S. Bach). *See: Little Organ Book.*

Ormandy, Eugene (born **Eugene Blau),** conductor. Born Budapest, Hungary, Nov. 18, 1899. He was the youngest pupil ever admitted to the Budapest Academy, where he studied violin with Jenö Hubay. A special decree by the Ministry of Education allowed him to graduate in his fourteenth year, and four years later he was appointed professor of violin at the Academy. He also gave recitals in Central Europe. In 1921 he came to the United States, where he later became a citizen. After playing the violin in and conducting motion-picture theater orchestras in New York, he led performances of symphonic music at summer concerts in New York and Philadelphia and over the radio in 1930 and 1931. He scored a major success when called upon to substitute for Toscanini with the Philadelphia Orchestra in 1931. From 1931 to 1936 he was principal conductor of the Minneapolis Symphony. In 1936 he was appointed associate conductor of the Philadelphia Orchestra, and in 1938 he succeeded Stokowski as its principal conductor. He also appeared as guest conductor with other major American orchestras, at the Metropolitan Opera, and at leading European festivals. In 1949 he led the Philadelphia Orchestra on its first tour of Europe, and in 1958 he scored a triumph in appearances with that orchestra in the Soviet Union. He was made Officer of the French Legion of Honor in 1952, and Knight of the Order of the White Rose of Finland in 1955.

Ornament. An embellishment of any sort, such as a grace note, trill, mordent, etc.

Ornstein, Leo, pianist and composer. Born Kremenchug, Russia, Dec. 11, 1895. From 1904 to 1906 he attended the St. Petersburg Conservatory, and after that the Institute of Musical Art in New York. On March 5, 1911, he made his début as a pianist in New York. For the next decade he concertized throughout the United States and Europe. His fame during this period rested mainly on the iconoclastic and dissonant music he wrote for the piano and featured at his concerts: the *Piano Sonata, Wild Man's Dance,* and *Poems of 1917.* He was one of the earliest modernists in America, an *enfant terrible* of music. After World War I his music lost its capacity to shock and startle, and his works fell into obscurity. He himself withdrew from the concert stage to devote himself to teaching at the Philadelphia Musical Academy, Temple University, and the Ornstein School of Music in Philadelphia. His works for orchestra include *Three Moods, The Fog, Lysistrata, Nocturne and Dance of Fates, Impressions of Chinatown, Prelude tragique,* a symphony, and a piano concerto. Among his other works are a piano quintet, string quartet, Six Preludes for cello and piano, and 2 piano sonatas.

Orpheus. (1) A Thracian musician celebrated in Greek legend. He is the hero of a famous story in which he goes to Hades to retrieve his dead wife, Eurydice.

(2) Ballet for orchestra by Stravinsky (1947). The scenario is a version of the Orpheus and Eurydice legend. The ballet was introduced in New York by the Ballet Society on April 28, 1948. The entire score without alteration is performed at symphony concerts. The first such performance took place in Boston on Feb. 11, 1949, the composer conducting. Throughout, the music maintains a classic austerity, is touched by Hellenic serenity and at times a sensitive melancholy. The published score provides the following program: "Orpheus weeps for Eurydice . . . Friends pass, bringing presents and offering sympathy. *Air de Danse.* Dance of the Angel of Death. Interlude (The Angel and Orpheus reappear in the gloom of Tartarus). *Pas des Furies* (their agitation and their threats). *Air de danse* (Orpheus). Interlude (the tormented

ouls in Tartarus stretch out their fettered rms towards Orpheus and implore him o continue his song of consolation). *Air e Danse* (Orpheus). *Pas d'action* Hades, moved by the song of Orpheus, grows calm. The Furies surround him, bind his eyes and return Eurydice to him). *Pas de deux* (Orpheus and Eurydice before the veiled curtain). Interlude. *Pas d'action* (the Bacchantes attack Orpheus, seize him, and tear him to pieces). Apotheosis of Orpheus. Apollo reappears. He wrests the lyre from Orpheus and raises his song heavenward."

Orpheus and Eurydice (Orfeo ed Euridice). An opera by Gluck, libretto by Ranieri di Calzabigi, and first performed in Vienna on Oct. 5, 1762. For orchestral excerpts *see: Dance of the Blessed Spirits; Dance of the Furies.*

Ostinato. Ground bass.

Othello. *See:* Shakespeare, William.

Ottava. Italian for octave.

Ours, L'. *See:* Symphony—*Haydn.*

Ouverture solennelle, 1812 (Tchaikovsky). *See: Overture 1812.*

Overtones. Tones of a higher pitch present in a regular series in every perfect musical sound.

Overture. An orchestral introduction to an opera, play, oratorio, and so forth (sometimes also called a prelude). In the Baroque era, suites for orchestra sometimes began with an overture. The earliest operas, in the 17th century, were often prefaced by sinfonias or toccatas. Alessandro Scarlatti established in his operas the "Italian overture": a three-part composition opening with an allegro, continuing with a slow section, and ending with a lively finale. The "French overture" appeared in France with Lully, after which it was employed in England by Handel and Purcell and elsewhere. This usually had two sections, the first slow and dignified; the second, lively and often in fugal style; sometimes there is a return to the music of the first section.

For his music dramas *Alceste* and *Iphigenia in Aulis,* Gluck wrote one-movement overtures which set the mood for the action that followed. Mozart's overtures frequently incorporated material used subsequently in the opera. After Mozart's day, many opera composers

either quoted in their overtures basic material from their operas, or used the overture to suggest the spirit of the opera. Opera overtures by composers from Mozart through Wagner are frequently performed at symphony concerts. (*See also:* Prelude.)

There is still another kind of overture, intended exclusively for concert performance, and consequently referred to as "concert overtures." In this category we find compositions like Brahms' *Tragic* and *Academic Festival* Overtures, Tchaikovsky's *1812 Overture,* and Schumann's *Manfred Overture,* among many others.

Overture 1812. Concert overture for orchestra by Tchaikovsky, op. 49 (1880). It was commissioned for the consecration of the Temple of Christ the Redeemer in Moscow, built as a memorial to Napoleon's defeat in Russia in 1812. The composer, consequently, decided to utilize for his music a program describing the historic events in Russia beginning with the Battle of Borodino and culminating with Napoleon's flight from Moscow. There is no record of a performance of this overture when the Temple was consecrated in 1881; it is generally believed that the première took place in Moscow on Aug. 20, 1882, Nápravník conducting. The overture has an introductory section in which the Russian hymn *God Preserve Thy People* is used. The main section gives a realistic picture of the Battle of Borodino, with quotations from the Russian national hymn and the *Marseillaise* to identify the two opposing armies. The Russian hymn appears as a climax to announce the victory of the Russians.

Since Tchaikovsky planned this work for outdoor performance, he indicated that the percussion section should include actual cannon to boom at specified intervals.

Overture on Russian Themes. The first of two concert overtures on Russian themes by Balakirev (1858). The other is called *Russia.* This early composition was Balakirev's first successful effort at writing nationalistic music; it was introduced in St. Petersburg in 1859. Three folksongs are used here. Two are familiar. *In the Field There Stood the Little*

Birch Tree (played by the clarinets) is also quoted by Tchaikovsky in the last movement of his Fourth Symphony. The second, *She Went to a Feast* (oboe against pizzicato strings), was used by Stravinsky in *Petrouchka.* The third song is *Lo, the White Birch Tree Stood Near the Field,* and is presented by flute and clarinet.

Overture to an Italian Comedy. Concert overture for orchestra by Arthur Benjamin (1936), first performed in London on March 2, 1937, Gordon Jacob conducting. A subtitle in the published score reads: "Sorry you've been troubled." The overture opens *fortissimo* with the first main subject in the woodwinds against pizzicato strings; the mood is lively. The dynamics change quickly and a soft melody is presented by a solo horn. After that comes a gay tune in thirds for two flutes which the trumpets soon take over (the score gives specific instructions that this theme should sound vulgar). The opening subject returns, and so does the "vulgar" melody in thirds. The overture ends in a spirited vein.

Overture to a Picaresque Comedy. Concert overture for orchestra by Arnold Bax (1931), introduced in Manchester in November 1931, Sir Hamilton Harty conducting. The composer explains: "This overture does not pretend to be the prelude to any particular play. It is simply a piece of music associated with some character as d'Artagnan or Casanova." There are two main themes, one light and mocking, the other stately.

Ovid (born *Publius Ovidius Naso*), poet. Born Sulmo, Italy, 43 B.C.; died Tomi (now Constantinople), A.D. 18. He was an outstanding poet of the Augustan era. His masterwork, the *Metamorphoses* —poems based on mythological subjects and classical legends—was the inspiration for nine symphonies by Karl Ditters von Dittersdorf and for Benjamin Britten's *Six Metamorphoses after Ovid* for oboe.

Ox Minuet. *See:* Quartet—*Haydn.*

Oxford Symphony. *See:* Symphony— *Haydn.*

P

Pachelbel, Johann, organist and composer. Born Nuremberg, Germany, August 1653; died there, March 3, 1706. He studied music in his native city, and with J. Kaspar Kerll in Vienna. In 1674 he became organist at St. Stephen's in Vienna. He later held organ posts in Erfurt, Stuttgart, and Nuremberg. Besides being one of the most notable organ virtuosos of his time, Pachelbel was an important composer, a precursor of Johann Sebastian Bach in the writing of music for organ. His chorales were distinguished for their rich harmonizations, and his toccatas and fugues for their virtuosity. He also wrote suites, fantasias, and variations for various instrumental combinations and pieces for the harpsichord.

Pachmann, Vladimir de, pianist. Born Odessa, Russia, July 27, 1848; died Rome, Italy, Jan. 6, 1933. His father, a gifted violinist and university professor, gave him his first music lessons. Further piano study took place at the Vienna Conservatory. In 1869 he returned to Russia, where he made his first professional appearances. For eight years after that he withdrew from the concert stage to devote himself to further study. Failing to meet his own severe standards after some performances in Germany, he once again went into retirement for further study, this time for two years. Three concerts in Vienna, and three more in Paris, in 1880, finally convinced him of his ability. From this time on he concertized throughout the world. He made his first tour of the United States in 1891.

Everywhere he was acclaimed as one of the world's foremost exponents of Chopin, to whom he dedicated most of his programs. In 1885 he was made Knight of the Order of Danebrog in Denmark, and in 1916 he received the Beethoven medal from the Royal Philharmonic of London. Extraordinary though his playing was, it was often marred by his eccentric stage behavior: extravagant facial grimaces, body gestures, and even audible comments.

Pacific 231. Tone poem for orchestra by Arthur Honegger (1923), introduced in Paris by the Koussevitzky Orchestra on May 8, 1924. This is one of three orchestral pieces intended by the composer as a suite; the other two are *Rugby* and *Mouvement symphonique No. 3. Pacific 231* became famous as an independent composition, its cacophony in imitating the noises of a locomotive making it in the 1920s a provocative piece of music. Abrupt rhythms and chords at the opening depict the train as it is first set into motion. We then feel the motor energy of a train hurtling through space at high speed. Dissonance is piled upon dissonance; the rhythms grow increasingly complicated. Ponderous chords and halting rhythms finally slow down the train to a halt.

Paderewski, Ignace Jan, pianist, composer, and statesman. Born Kurylówka, Poland, Nov. 18, 1860; died New York City, June 29, 1941. In 1878 he was graduated with highest honors from the Warsaw Conservatory, where for three years after that he taught piano. In 1881 he studied composition with Friedrich Kiel in Berlin and from 1884 to 1887 piano with Theodor Leschetizky in Vienna. Paderewski's first major concert appearance took place in Vienna in 1887, in a joint concert with the singer Pauline Lucca. After some distinguished appearances in Paris, he scored a triumph in Vienna, and at the Paris Exposition in 1889. On May 9, 1890, he made his first appearance in London; on Nov. 17, 1891, he made his American début in New York City, the first of 117 performances throughout the United States. After that he appeared in virtually every music center of the world, everywhere acclaimed

a Titan of the keyboard, and one of the foremost interpreters of Chopin's music. In 1909 he was appointed director of the Warsaw Conservatory.

During World War I Paderewski gave numerous concerts in Europe and America to raise money for Polish war victims. Now devoted to aiding his stricken country, he became the spokesman for and spiritual leader of his land and its people, traveling extensively to speak out for Polish independence. It was mainly through his giant efforts that President Wilson included Poland's liberation as the thirteenth of his famous fourteen points. In 1918-1919 Paderewski was the diplomatic representative to the United States of the new State of Poland, and in 1919 he became Poland's first premier. With Poland free, Paderewski abandoned politics and returned to music. His reappearance on the concert stage took place in 1922, when once again he assumed an imperial position among the pianists of his time.

The outbreak of World War II carried him back into the political arena. Besides raising his voice to condemn the Nazi attack on Poland, Paderewski became, in 1940, president of the Polish National Council, the parliament of the Polish government in exile. Once again his was an eloquent voice raised throughout the free world on behalf of his country's liberation. He did not live to see the war's end; but he did live to be the object of a week-long celebration throughout the United States from Feb. 15 to 22, 1941, to commemorate the 50th anniversary of his musical career in America.

Upon Paderewski's death in 1941, President Roosevelt ordered that he be given a state funeral at the Arlington National Cemetery. The Polish government decorated him with its highest military honor, the Cross of Virtuti Militari, one of many world-famous honors and awards that a grateful world had bestowed upon him during his lifetime.

Paderewski appeared as himself in a motion picture, *Moonlight Sonata*. In 1900 he created in the United States the Paderewski Fund, providing prizes once every three years for the best composition by a native American. The first awards were given in 1902 to Henry Hadley, Horatio W. Parker, and Arthur Bird. Later recipients included Gardner Read and Wallingford Riegger.

Paderewski wrote many works, mainly for the piano, Romantic in mood and style, and often intensely Polish in content and spirit. These works include a symphony, a piano concerto, *Polish Fantasy* for piano and orchestra, a violin sonata, a piano sonata, and numerous other piano works including *Polish Dances, Scènes romantiques, Tatra Album, Humoresques de concert* (in which will be found his popular *Menuet à l'antique*), *Variations and Fugue on an Original Theme, Variations and Fugue in E-flat minor,* impromptus, pieces, etudes, and intermezzi.

Paesaggi toscani (Tommasini). *See: Tuscan Landscapes.*

Pagan Poem, A. Tone poem for orchestra by Charles Martin Loeffler, op. 14 (1906), one of the composer's most famous works. He originally wrote it in 1901 for piano, winds, violin, and double bass; two years after that he rescored it for two pianos and three trumpets. The definitive version, for orchestra with piano obbligato, solo English horn, and three solo trumpets, was introduced by the Boston Symphony on Nov. 23, 1907, Karl Muck conducting. The literary source of this work was the eighth eclogue by Virgil, in which a Thessalian maiden uses magic to revive the ardor of her beloved, who has deserted her. Loeffler makes no attempt to follow this program literally, but strives to present moods and feelings suggested by the poem. The three solo trumpets are used backstage, once against a percussive background of piano and timpani, and again as a chromatic accompaniment to a declamation by English horn.

Paganini, Niccolò, violinist and composer. Born Genoa, Italy, Oct. 27, 1782; died Nice, Sardinia (now France), May 27, 1840. A violinist whose technical exploits have become legendary, Paganini was trained by a ruthless father to become a prodigy. After studies with Giovanni Servetto and Giacomo Costa, Paganini performed publicly for the first time in

Genoa when he was eight; at nine he made a formal concert début, also in Genoa. Additional study followed with Ferdinando Paër and Alexander Rolla, who prepared him for a concert tour of northern Italy. Billed as "the wonder child," Paganini electrified audiences with his remarkable digital exploits. At the turn of the 19th century, Paganini withdrew from the concert stage. But three years after that he returned both to the violin and to Genoa, and in 1805 made an official reappearance in a concert auditorium. From then until 1808, he filled numerous concert engagements in Italy, besides holding a post as solo concert violinist at the court of Lucca.

Successful though he had become by 1808, it was with a concert appearance in Milan in 1813 that his legendary career really began. So sensational was this performance that he was required to give 36 concerts in Milan alone. For the next decade and a half he was the most celebrated violinist in Europe, even though he did not leave Italy. His fantastic technique led some to suspect that he acquired his powers by being the son of the devil; a few of the more superstitious crossed themselves when they came into contact with him.

His delicate health, which necessitated numerous rest cures, made him reluctant to make appearances outside Italy. But in 1828 he was finally prevailed upon to tour Europe. Few concert performers of any period aroused such a fever of adulation as Paganini now did. In Vienna, Germany, Paris, England, and Scotland audiences were enraptured. Men and women followed him about. He became the man of the hour who had fashions and commodities named after him. Musicians outdid each other in singing his praises. "Paganini," said Schumann, "is the turning point in the history of virtuosity." Liszt exclaimed: "What a man! What a violin! What an artist!"

After returning to Italy, Paganini settled down on an estate in Parma. Towards the end of his life he lost his fortune by financing a gambling establishment in Paris. Worry and heartache finally combined to undermine his health; he died in Nice, where he had gone for a rest cure.

The violin literature of Paganini exploits fully his own remarkable powers as a virtuoso. This music abounds with pyrotechnics—harmonics, double and triple stops, simultaneous pizzicato and bow passages—with which the horizons of violin writing and playing were greatly extended. It can almost be said that the modern technique of violin performance was born with Paganini. To this day, his works are favored by virtuosos desirous of exhibiting their technical facility. While Paganini wrote some chamber music, he is remembered almost exclusively for his works for the violin. These include the celebrated Twenty-Four Caprices for unaccompanied violin; 3 violin concertos (the most famous being No. 1, in D minor, op. 6); and numerous pieces still alive in the repertory, among which are the *Fantasia on the G String,* the *Carnival of Venice* variations, *Perpetual Motion,* and *Witches' Dance* (or *Le Streghe*).

See: Campanella, La; Caprice—*Paganini;* Concerto—*Paganini; Fantasia on the G String; Perpetual Motion.*

Paganini Etudes. (1) Two sets of pieces for the piano by Schumann, op. 3 (1832) and op. 10 (1833), based on Paganini's Caprices for solo violin.

(2) *See:* Etude—*Liszt.*

Paganini Quartet. *See:* Temianka, Henri.

Paganini Rhapsody (Rachmaninoff). *See:* Rhapsody on a Theme of Paganini.

Paganini Variations (Brahms). *See:* Variations on a Theme by Paganini.

Paganiniana. Divertimento for orchestra by Alfredo Casella (1942), based on melodies by Paganini. Casella wrote this work in honor of the centenary of the Vienna Philharmonic, which introduced it in March 1942, Karl Boehm conducting. The work has four movements: I. *Allegro agitato;* II. *Polachetta;* III. *Romanza;* IV. Tarantella. In the first movement Casella portrays the "satanic spirit of the great violinist." Four main themes are derived from Paganini's Caprices Nos. 5, 12, 16, and 19. The second movement is in a melancholy vein, the material derived from Paganini's Quartet No. 4, for violin, viola, cello, and guitar. The main subject of the third-movement *Romanza* comes from an unpublished work; it

appears as a duet for solo violin and clarinet. The music of the finale is based on the Quartet used in the second movement and on an unpublished dance for violin and small orchestra.

Pagodes (Debussy). *See: Estampes.*

Paine, John Knowles, composer and educator. Born Portland, Me., Jan. 9, 1839; died Cambridge, Mass., April 25, 1906. He studied music principally in Portland and in Berlin, Germany. In 1862 he was appointed instructor of music at Harvard, becoming a full professor in 1875, a post he held until his death; he was the first to hold a chair in music in an American university. Among his pupils through the years were John Alden Carpenter, Richard Aldrich, E. B. Hill, Daniel Gregory Mason, Frederick S. Converse, Henry T. Finck, and Arthur Foote.

He first achieved recognition as a composer with his first symphony, introduced in 1876 by the Theodore Thomas Orchestra. His orchestral and choral works were subsequently performed by leading musical organizations. A Romanticist within Classical structures, Paine was strongly influenced by Brahms. Besides the symphony already mentioned, he wrote a *Spring Symphony, Duo Concertante* for violin, cello, and orchestra, and several shorter orchestral compositions (*The Tempest, An Island Fantasy,* and *As You Like It*). He also wrote a string quartet, a piano trio, and a violin sonata.

Painters and paintings (in instrumental music). The following painters, or their principal paintings, were the inspiration for instrumental compositions:

Arnold Boecklin: Andreas Hallen's tone poem, *The Isle of the Dead;* Hans Huber's Symphony No. 2; Giacomo Orefice's *Quadri di Boecklin,* for piano; Rachmaninoff's tone poem, *The Isle of the Dead;* Max Reger's suite for orchestra, *Four Tone Poems After Boecklin;* Heinrich Schulz' tone poem, *The Isle of the Dead;* Felix Weingartner's tone poem, *Die Gefilde der Seligen;* Felix Woyrsch's *Three Boecklin Fantasies,* for orchestra.

Sandro Botticelli: Respighi's *Trittico botticelliano,* for small orchestra.

Pieter Brueghel: Michel Brusselmans' *Bruegheliaanse Tonelen,* for orchestra.

Jacques Callot: Walton's overture, *Scapino.*

Benvenuto Cellini: Berlioz' overtures, *Roman Carnival* and *Benvenuto Cellini.*

Albrecht Duerer: Richard Mohaupt's *Stadtpfeifermusik,* for orchestra; George Templeton Strong's symphony, *Sintram.*

Piero della Francesca: Bohuslav Martinu's *The Frescoes of Piero della Francesca,* for orchestra.

Francisco Goya: Granados' *Goyescas,* for piano.

Mathias Gruenewald: Hindemith's symphony, *Mathis der Maler.*

Victor Hartmann: Mussorgsky's *Pictures at an Exhibition,* for piano.

William Hogarth: Arnold Collins' *Hogarth Suite,* for oboe and orchestra.

Hans Holbein: Hans Huber's Symphony No. 3; Liszt's *Totentanz,* for orchestra.

Michelangelo: Niels Gade's overture, *Michelangelo;* Liszt's *La Notte* from *Trois odes funèbres,* for orchestra; Fartein Valen's *Sonetto di Michelangelo,* for orchestra.

Raphael: Liszt's *Sposalizio* from *Années de pèlerinage,* for piano.

Rembrandt: Cornelis Dopper's Symphony No. 2.

Dante Gabriel Rossetti: Felix White's tone poem, *Astarte Syriaca.*

Thomas Rowlandson: Walton's overture, *Portsmouth Point.*

Andrea del Sarto: Daniel Lesur's tone poem, *Andrea del Sarto.*

Leonardo da Vinci: Ludomir Rozycki's symphonic prelude, *Mona Lisa Gioconda.*

Jean Antoine Watteau: Gustave Charpentier's *Serenade to Watteau,* for voice and orchestra; Debussy's *L'Isle joyeuse,* for piano.

Palestine Symphony Orchestra. *See:* Israel Philharmonic Orchestra.

Palestrina, Three Preludes to. Orchestral preludes prefacing each of the three acts of Hans Pfitzner's opera, *Palestrina.* The opera, described by the composer as a "musical legend," and set to his own libretto, was introduced in Munich on June 12, 1917. Its hero is the 16th-century Italian polyphonic composer, Palestrina, who (according to legend) saved the art of contrapuntal music from banishment by the Church by writing his famous *Missa*

Papae Marcelli. The three orchestral preludes, sometimes performed at symphony concerts, are among the opera's best pages. The Prelude to Act 1 (*Ruhig*) is solemn, opening with a soaring phrase symbolizing the personality of Palestrina and the creative process. The Prelude to Act 2 (*Mit Wucht und Wildheit*) is dramatic, depicting the turbulent events surrounding the Council of Trent. The Prelude to Act 3 (*Langsam, sehr getragen*) is peaceful, touched with radiance.

Palmgren, Selim, pianist and composer. Born Björneborg, Finland, Feb. 16, 1878; died Helsinki, Finland, Dec. 13, 1951. He attended the Helsingfors (Helsinki) Conservatory from 1895 to 1899, then studied in Germany and Italy. After returning to his native land he held several conducting posts. In 1912 he began touring Europe as a pianist; he made his first appearances in the United States in 1920-1921; from 1923 to 1926 he was a member of the faculty of the Eastman School of Music in Rochester, N.Y. From 1936 until his death he was professor of harmony and composition at the Sibelius Academy in Helsinki.

Though Palmgren wrote several works for orchestra, including *From Finland, The Seasons, Pastorale in Three Scenes, Ballad,* and *A Merry Overture,* his finest compositions are for the piano. These include five concertos (the most famous being the second, entitled *The River*), 2 sonatas, 24 preludes, *Finnish Lyric Pieces, Finnish Suite,* and *Light and Shade.* All show a consummate command of piano technique, and an exceptional gift at pictorial writing and at creating subtle atmospheric suggestions. Many have a pronounced national character.

Panharmonicon. *See:* Maelzel, Johann Nepomuk.

Papillons (Butterflies). A set of piano pieces by Schumann, op. 2 (1829-1831). A musical description of a ball or festivity, in several short and related pieces, *Papillons* was the precursor of the same composer's more important and ambitious *Carnival.*

Parade. Ballet suite by Erik Satie (1918), adapted from his score to a ballet introduced in Paris on May 18, 1917, by the Ballet Russe. It is a satire on itinerant entertainers who perform in city streets. After a brief overture, Satie's music describes the performances of a Chinese conjurer, acrobats, and a little American girl who imitates Charlie Chaplin. Satie incorporates into his music noises which, as he said, "are indispensable to the surrounding of each character with its own atmosphere. These noises imitate waves, typewriters, revolvers, sirens, airplanes, dynamos." These sounds were not used during the première of the ballet, owing to technical difficulties, and they are not heard in the ballet suite. Satie's music is noteworthy for its broad humor, touches of irony, and skilful use of American jazz idioms.

Paradise and the Peri. *See:* Moore, Thomas.

Paray, Paul, conductor. Born Le Tréport, France, May 24, 1886. He received his musical training at the Paris Conservatory and in 1911 was the recipient of the Prix de Rome. He initiated his career as a conductor after World War I, making his début in Paris on Feb. 29, 1920. For a period he served as assistant conductor of the Lamoureux Orchestra; then, in 1923, he succeeded Camille Chevillard as its principal conductor. In 1928 he was appointed conductor of symphony concerts in Monte Carlo; in 1933 he succeeded Gabriel Pierné as conductor of the Colonne Orchestra. He made his American début at the Lewisohn Stadium in New York on July 24, 1939. In 1944, after the liberation of Paris, he returned to his post with the Colonne Orchestra. Between 1945 and 1952 he made many appearances throughout the United States. In 1952 he became principal conductor of the Detroit Symphony. He was elected a member of the Institut de France in 1950, and made Chevalier of the Legion of Honor in 1957.

Parergon to the Symphonia Domestica. *See:* Symphony—*Richard Strauss.*

Paris, A Night Piece—The Song of a Great City. Nocturne for orchestra by Frederick Delius (1899), introduced in Germany in 1900, Hans Haym conducting. Delius' tribute to Paris was not intended as a realistic picture of that city but as a tonal representation of his own impressions. The work opens and closes with an effective slow melody for oboe. In between several Parisian street cries are interpolated.

Paris Conservatory Orchestra (Concerts du Conservatoire). A symphony orchestra affiliated with the Paris Conservatory, founded in 1828 by François Antoine Habeneck as the Société des Concerts du Conservatoire. Its first concert took place in the Conservatory auditorium on March 9, 1828. Habeneck remained principal conductor for twenty years. Later principal conductors included Narcisse Girard, G. Hainl, Jules Garcin, Paul Taffanel, Georges Marty, André Messager, Philippe Gaubert, Charles Munch, and André Cluytens. The orchestra has toured Europe, and gave successful performances at the Edinburgh Festival in 1949.

Paris Symphonies. *See:* Symphony— *Haydn.*

Paris Symphony. *See:* Symphony— *Haydn;* Symphony—*Mozart.*

Parker, Horatio William, composer and teacher. Born Auburndale, Mass., Sept. 15, 1863; died Cedarhurst, Long Island, N.Y., Dec. 18, 1919. He studied music in Boston with Stephen Emery, John Orth, and George Chadwick; after that, at the High School of Music in Munich, Germany, with Josef Rheinberger. Returning to the United States in 1885, he settled in New York, where he held various organ posts and taught counterpoint at the National Conservatory. In 1888 he was appointed organist and choral director of Trinity Church, Boston. From 1894 until his death he was professor of music at Yale University. There he was responsible for elevating the standards of music instruction in colleges and in awakening and stimulating the musical interests of the city of New Haven. As a composer he first attracted wide attention with an oratorio, *Hora novissima,* introduced in New York on May 3, 1893, and subsequently given at several music festivals. In 1901 he won the Paderewski Fund Award with a cantata, and in 1911 his opera *Mona* received a $10,000 prize from the Metropolitan Opera in New York. Parker was a strong adherent of conservative methods, and stylistically he leaned heavily on German post-Romanticism. His orchestral works include a symphony, organ concerto, *Venetian Overture, Collegiate Overture,* Scherzo, and *A Northern Ballad.* Other compositions include a string quartet, a string quintet, a suite for violin, cello, and piano, an organ sonata, and various pieces for organ and for piano. **Parry, Sir Charles Hubert,** composer and educator. Born Bournemouth, England, Feb. 27, 1848; died Knight's Croft, Rustington, England, Oct. 7, 1918. He began his music study at Eton College, then pursued it intensively at Exeter College, Oxford, with Sterndale Bennett and G. A. Macfarren, among others. Following his graduation from Exeter he engaged for several years in business activity. The English musicologist, Edward Dannreuther, persuaded him to return to musical activity and promoted some of his early works, the most significant being the Concerto in F-sharp minor for piano and orchestra, introduced in London in 1880. During the next decade Parry achieved recognition in England for his choral music and symphonies. In 1894 he succeeded Sir George Grove as director of the Royal College of Music, holding this post for the remainder of his life. From 1899 to 1908 he was professor of music at Oxford. One of England's most renowned musicians, Parry was knighted in 1898 and created a baronet in 1903. He was the author of a biography of Johann Sebastian Bach (1909) and *The Seventeenth Century* in the *Oxford History of Music* (1896). A prolific composer, his major works for orchestra include 5 symphonies, a piano concerto, various overtures, tone poems, and suites, and incidental music to plays by Aristophanes and Aeschylus. In chamber music he produced 3 string quartets, 2 violin suites, a cello sonata, and a string quartet, while for the piano he wrote 2 sonatas, Theme and Variations in D minor, *Sonnets and Songs Without Words,* and other suites.

Parsifal, Preludes to. Orchestral preludes to Acts 1 and 3 of Wagner's "stage-consecrating festival drama." With a libretto by the composer based on a medieval legend and a poem by Wolfram von Eschenbach, this music drama was introduced in Bayreuth on July 26, 1882. The mysticism, spirituality, and religious fervor that pervade the music drama are found in the first-act prelude. It opens with a quotation of the "Last Supper" motif in woodwinds and strings. This motif undergoes several changes in modality and instrumentation. After a momentary pause, the majestic "Grail Theme" (a version of the famous "Dresden Amen") is presented by brass, followed by a statement of the "Faith" motif in horns and trombones. Earlier motifs are now recalled and amplified; the principal new theme is the "Lance," which is built out of four notes of the "Last Supper" motif. A forceful projection of the "Faith" motif concludes the prelude.

The Prelude to Act 3 is suffused with the melancholy of the Knights of the Grail who have despaired of finding a savior. The main motifs are "Desolation," with which the prelude opens, and the "Straying" and "Pure Fool" motifs.

For other orchestral excerpts from *Parsifal, see: Good Friday Spell; Klingsor's Magic Garden and Flower Maiden's Scene; Transformation Scene.*

Partita. A term used in the 17th century interchangeably with suite for a composition comprising several dance movements. The most famous use of this term in instrumental music is found with Johann Sebastian Bach, who wrote 6 partitas for clavier and three for unaccompanied violin; all might just as accurately be described as suites.

The six clavier partitas are: No. 1 in B-flat major; No. 2, in C minor; No. 3, in A minor; No. 4, in D minor; No. 5, in G major; and No. 6 in E minor. Characteristic of these works is the fourth, which opens with a three-part overture, and includes an Allemande, Courante, Aria, Sarabande, Minuet, and Gigue.

The three partitas for unaccompanied violin, among the most sublime works written for that instrument, are: No. 1, in B minor; No. 2 in D minor; and No. 3 in E major. The Prelude to the third Partita is famous both in its original version and in various transcriptions. The most celebrated single movement from these works is the Chaconne from Partita No. 2 (*see:* Chaconne—*J. S. Bach*).

Several modern composers have revived the idea of the partita. Among these are: Alfred Casella (Partita for piano and orchestra, op. 42); Charles Martin Loeffler (Partita for violin and piano); Goffredo Petrassi (Partita for orchestra); Walter Piston (Partita for violin, viola, and organ); Ture Rangström (Partita for violin and orchestra); Gardner Read (Partita for orchestra, op. 70); and William Walton (Partita for orchestra).

See also: Suite (1).

Partitur (Partitura, or **Partition).** *See:* Score.

Pas d'acier, Le (Prokofiev). *See:* **Age of Steel, The.**

Pasdeloup, Jules Etienne, conductor. Born Paris, France, Sept. 15, 1819; died Fontainebleau, France, Aug. 13, 1887. He attended the Paris Conservatory. In 1848 he acquired a government post, but continued his musical activity. In 1851 he founded the Société des Jeunes Elèves du Conservatoire, at whose concerts many new contemporary French works were introduced. He extended the scope and activity of this organization by establishing Sunday afternoon concerts on Oct. 27, 1861, calling them the Concerts populaires de musique classique; this organization gave distinguished performances under Pasdeloup's direction until 1884. After 1884 Pasdeloup made several attempts to organize symphony concerts in Monte Carlo and Paris but without sustained success.

Pasdeloup Orchestra. A distinguished symphony orchestra in Paris founded by Jules Etienne Pasdeloup in 1861 as the Concerts populaires de musique classique. Pasdeloup conducted the orchestra until 1884 when it disbanded. In 1918, the orchestra was revived with Rhené-Baton as conductor and named the Pasdeloup Orchestra, or Concerts Pasdeloup. In 1934, Albert Wolff was appointed conductor; Leon Barzin became conductor in 1958. The orchestra gives its performances at the Salle Pleyel and the Palais de Chaillot.

Passacaglia. A form of instrumental music prominent in the 17th century. It originated as a slow Spanish dance. Its main characteristic is a recurrent theme in the bass with the treble providing vari-

ations. In form and style the passacaglia is so similar to the chaconne that the two names were used interchangeably by many composers. Girolamo Frescobaldi was the first master to write important passacaglias for organ. Buxtehude brought the form to its most advanced stage of structural development before Johann Sebastian Bach carried it to its ultimate evolution. Bach's most celebrated work in this form is the monumental Passacaglia in C minor. The main theme appears immediately in the bass, after which the treble provides a series of variations extraordinary for their wide gamut of emotion. The theme finally becomes the subject of a fugue which is the crown of the composition.

Handel wrote an excellent Passacaglia in his Suite No. 7 in G minor for harpsichord; this movement is perhaps best known in a transcription for violin and viola by Johan Halvorsen. A passacaglia-like section can be found in Beethoven's *Thirty-Two Variations* for piano, and the finale of Brahms' Fourth Symphony is a passacaglia. Examples of the passacaglia can also be found in later instrumental literature: for example in Max Reger's Introduction, Passacaglia and Fugue in E minor, for organ, op. 127; Wallingford Riegger's Passacaglia and Fugue, for orchestra; and in Benjamin Britten's opera *Peter Grimes,* where a passacaglia for orchestra appears between the two scenes of Act 2.

Passepied. An old dance said to have originated with sailors in Brittany. It resembles a minuet, though somewhat quicker in tempo, and begins on the last beat of the bar. It is in 3/4 or 3/8 time. The passepied was occasionally used as a movement of the Baroque suite.

Passion According to St. John. A monumental work for chorus, soloists, and orchestra by Johann Sebastian Bach. The Passion is an oratorio in which the text is solely concerned with the final suffering of Christ. We have two works by Bach in this form. Both are masterpieces and often presented at symphony concerts. The *St. John Passion* came first (1724); it was introduced in the year of its composition at the Thomasschule in Leipzig, the composer conducting. Bach himself prepared the text from the 18th and 19th chapters of *St. John,* and from older Passion material collated by Barthold Heinrich Brockes. This Passion places its emphasis on dramatic interest, and its strongest pages are found in such overpowering choruses as *Wer hat dich so geschlagen* and *Kreuzige,* and in many of the stirring recitatives. But, as Albert Schweitzer remarked, the work also has some "points of repose." Its lyrical passages, nevertheless, are generally of lesser significance and do not seem inevitable to the over-all structure. Three lyrical pages, however, are of particular interest: the famous aria for contralto *Es ist vollbracht;* the equally moving arioso for bass, *Betrachte, meine Seel',* and the radiant closing chorale, *Ach, Herr, lass dein lieb' Engelein.*

Passion According to St. Matthew. The second of Johann Sebastian Bach's Passions (1729), first performed at the Thomasschule in Leipzig on April 15, 1729, the composer conducting. The text is mainly by Christian Friedrich Hinrici, derived from the 26th and 27th chapters of *St. Matthew.* In contrast to the *St. John Passion,* the present work is not essentially dramatic, but is poised on a high spiritual plane; it is mostly devotional and reflective. The lyrical solo passages rather than the choruses are emphasized. Especially noble are such remarkable melodic passages as the alto aria *Buss' und Reu';* the soprano aria, *Blute nur;* the tenor recitative with chorus, *O Schmerz;* the contralto aria with violin obbligato, *Erbarme dich, mein Gott;* and the soprano aria, *Aus Liebe will mein Heiland sterben.* The choruses are also more generally emotional and affecting than stirring (even though a few, like the stirring *Barabbas,* have a powerful dramatic impulse). The most eloquent choruses are: the funereal opening, *Kommt, ihr Toechter;* the poignant *O Mensch bewein' dein' Suende gross* with which the first part comes to a conclusion; and the moving closing chorus, sometimes described as the most poignant lullaby ever written, *Wir setzen uns mit Traenen nieder.*

One way in which Bach highlighted the exalted feeling of the *St. Matthew*

Passion was by endowing the recitatives of Christ with orchestral accompaniments (likened to a halo around Christ's head), while in the *St. John Passion* these, like all other recitatives, are accompanied only by chords of a keyboard instrument.

The *St. Matthew Passion* is in two contrasting sections. The first is tender and contemplative; the second, tragic. In the first is described the conspiracy of the scribes and priests, Christ's anointment in the house of Simon, the Last Supper, the Agony in the Garden, and the Betrayal. In the second part unfold the scene before Caiaphas, Peter's denial, the judgment of Pontius Pilate, the death of Judas, the march to Golgotha, and the final Crucifixion and the death of Jesus.

Passione, La. *See:* Symphony—*Haydn.*

Pastoral Symphony. (1) *See below:* Pastorale.

(2) *See:* Symphony—*Beethoven.*

(3) *See:* Symphony—*Vaughan Williams.*

Pastorale. (1) An instrumental composition in which a simple melody acquires a pastoral character through the imitation of the elementary sounds of a shepherd's pipe, and is often accompanied by drone bass. The Pastoral Symphonies describing the Nativity in Handel's *Messiah,* J. S. Bach's *Christmas Oratorio,* and Corelli's *Christmas Concerto* are all pastorales.

(2) *See:* Capriccio and Pastorale (Scarlatti).

Pastorale d'été. Tone poem for small orchestra by Arthur Honegger (1921), introduced in Paris on Feb. 17, 1921. This reflective music is a mood picture made up of two themes. The first, for horn, appears after a three-bar introduction; the second is presented by the clarinet.

Pathetic Sonata. *See:* Sonata—*Beethoven.*

Pathetic Symphony. *See:* Symphony—*Tchaikovsky.*

Pattison, Lee. *See:* Maier and Pattison.

Pauer, Ernst, pianist and teacher. Born Vienna, Austria, Dec. 21, 1826; died Jugenheim, Germany, May 9, 1905. After completing the study of harmony, counterpoint, and piano with private teachers in Vienna, he made his public début as a pianist in 1842. In 1851 he settled in

London, where a decade later he distinguished himself for his series of concerts tracing the history of piano literature; he gave other such historical surveys in different parts of Europe in 1862, 1863, and 1867. In 1866 he was appointed pianist to the Austrian court, and from 1859 to 1864 was professor of piano at the Royal Academy of Music in London. In 1867 he became first professor of piano at the National Training School of Music in London; in 1878 he was appointed member, and in 1879 Examiner, of the Board of Musical Studies at Cambridge. He edited many masterworks of the Classical and Romantic eras; made numerous transcriptions and arrangements for children; and wrote several theoretical treatises. He went into retirement in Germany in 1896.

His son, Max (born London, England, Oct. 31, 1866; died Jugenheim, Germany, May 12, 1945), was also a successful concert pianist, who made a tour of the United States in 1913-1914. From 1908 to 1934 he was director of the High School of Music in Mannheim.

Paukenschlag Symphony. *See:* Symphony —*Haydn.*

Paukenwirbel Symphony. *See:* Symphony —*Haydn.*

Paur, Emil, conductor. Born Czernowitz, Bukovina, Aug. 29, 1855; died Mistek, Czechoslovakia, June 7, 1932. After attending the Vienna Conservatory, he became a violinist in the Vienna Court Orchestra, then in 1876 made his first appearance as a conductor in Cassel. After holding important posts as conductor in Mannheim and Leipzig he was appointed, in 1893, successor to Arthur Nikisch as principal conductor of the Boston Symphony. Five years later he assumed a similar post with the New York Philharmonic. In 1899 he became director of the National Conservatory in New York, a post previously held by Dvořák. He returned to Europe in 1903, conducting symphony concerts in Germany and England. In 1904 he returned to the United States, where for the next six years he conducted the Pittsburgh Symphony.

Pavane. A slow and stately court dance of Italian origin, but popular in France.

It is usually in three sections and in 4/4 time. It sometimes appears as a movement of the Baroque suite. Interesting uses of this dance form in later instrumental music can be found in Gabriel Fauré's poignant *Pavane,* op. 50, for chorus and orchestra (1887) and in Ravel's popular *Pavane for a Dead Infanta* (see below).

Pavane for a Dead Infanta (Pavane pour une Infante défunte). An elegy for piano by Ravel (1899), first performed in Paris by Ricardo Viñes on April 5, 1902. This slow and stately dance (the composer's first successful composition) was inspired by the death of a princess of the royal house in Spain. It is equally popular in an orchestration prepared by the composer.

Peacock Variations. For orchestra by Zoltán Kodály (1939), written in honor of the 50th anniversary of the Concertgebouw Orchestra in Amsterdam, which introduced it on Nov. 23, 1939, Willem Mengelberg conducting. This work is based on a Hungarian folksong, *Fly, Peacock, Fly,* which is stated after a brief introduction. Sixteen variations follow, presented without interruption.

Pedal. An appliance found on the organ, piano, harp, and some timpani, and operated by the foot.

Pedal note. In brass instruments, the first or fundamental note in a harmonic series.

Pedal point. *See:* Organ point.

Peer Gynt. *See:* Ibsen, Henrik.

Peer Gynt Suites. Two suites for orchestra by Grieg, adapted from his incidental music to the play by Ibsen, produced in Christiania (now Oslo) on Feb. 24, 1876. Grieg arranged his first suite, op. 46, in 1888; the second, op. 55, in 1891. The first is the more popular and comprises four movements. I. *Morning.* A morning in the mountains is described in a barcarolle-like melody. II. *Ase's Death.* This is an elegy for muted strings for Peer Gynt's mother. III. *Anitra's Dance.* A vivacious oriental dance in the tempo of a mazurka is here presented. IV. *In the Hall of the Mountain King.* This is a ponderous march melody in grotesque style.

The second suite also has **four** movements: I. *Ingrid's Lament;* II. *Arabian Dance;* III. *Peer Gynt's Homecoming;* IV. *Solveig's Song.* The last, a tender melody for muted strings depicting Peer Gynt's faithful beloved, is the most famous of these movements, and is often heard independently of the other parts.

Pelleas and Melisande. (1) Suite for orchestra by Gabriel Fauré, op. 80 (1898), adapted from the composer's incidental music for a London production of the Maeterlinck drama on June 21, 1898. This is one of Fauré's most often performed works for orchestra. (It preceded Debussy's opera on the same drama by four years.) The Suite has four parts. I. Prelude. This is the prelude to the play, atmospheric music that maintains a calm beauty. Two themes are prominent. The first is in the strings, and the second in solo cello, flute, and bassoons. II. *The Spinner (Les Fileuses).* Melisande is at her spinning wheel. The whir of the wheel is simulated by the strings as a background to several melodies for woodwind. III. Siciliana. This movement is often omitted. It is slow and stately music which Fauré originally wrote for cello and piano. IV. *The Death of Melisande.* This elegy opens with a tender melody for winds. The emotion grows more intense and the dynamics increase as the music progresses to a stirring climax.

(2) Tone poem by Arnold Schoenberg, op. 5 (1903), inspired by the Maeterlinck drama. Its first performance took place in Vienna on Jan. 26, 1905, the composer conducting. While played without interruption, this work has four sections. The introduction discusses Golaud's meeting with Melisande in the forest. A Scherzo follows which covers the scenes at the well, in the castle tower, and in the vault. An Adagio then speaks of the farewell of Pelleas and Melisande, while in the finale the music relates how Golaud waylays the lovers and murders Pelleas.

(3) Suite for orchestra by Sibelius, op. 46 (1905), derived from incidental music for the Maeterlinck drama at its first presentation in Finland in 1905. The music has unmistakably Finnish character, and the style is Romantic rather than Impressionistic. There are nine parts: I.

At the Castle Gate; II. Melisande; III. By the Sea. IV. A Fountain in the Park; V. The Three Blind Sisters; VI. Pastorale; VII. Melisande at the Spinning Wheel; VIII. Entr'acte; IX. Death of Melisande. A tenth number in the incidental music (Prelude to Act 4, Scene 2) has not been published and is not included in the suite.

Pennario, Leonard, pianist. Born Buffalo, N.Y., July 9, 1924. His professional début took place when he was twelve as soloist with the Dallas Symphony. In 1942 he entered the University of Southern California, where he studied piano with Guy Maier. During this period he made several appearances with leading American orchestras. After World War II he resumed his concert activity by giving 58 concerts throughout the United States in 1947. He made his first tour of Europe in 1951.

Pentatonic scale. A scale made up of five tones. There are many pentatonic scales in use by primitive and oriental peoples. The term is often employed for the specific scale that can be produced by playing five consecutive black keys on the piano beginning with F-sharp. This scale has been used effectively by many composers to suggest an oriental atmosphere.

Penthesilea. Symphonic poem by Hugo Wolf (1885), based on Kleist's tragedy. The three sections, played without interruption, bear specific titles: I. The Departure of Amazons for Troy; II. Penthesilea's Dream of the Feast of the Roses; III. Combats, Passions, Frenzy, Annihilation. A bold subject depicting Penthesilea, Amazon warrior, opens the tone poem. The main theme of this first section is a virile march melody. In the second movement, a tranquil melody for flute, oboe, and violins depicts Penthesilea's reverie. Two opposing traits of Penthesilea's personality are revealed in the finale: her will to conquer and her will to love. After the music develops into a climax the tone poem ends softly with a description of the heroine's death.

Percussion. A family of instruments in which the sound is produced by the process of striking. This family includes the timpani, drums, triangle, and so on.

Perfect cadence. A cadence that gives the feeling of rest or finality, as opposed to an imperfect cadence, which conveys the feeling of only temporary repose.

Perfect interval. The interval of the unison or prime, the fourth, the fifth, or the octave.

Pergolesi, Giovanni Battista, composer. Born Jesi, Italy, Jan. 4, 1710; died Pozzuoli, Italy, March 16, 1736. He is most famous for his operas, especially *La Serva padrona,* described as the first important opera buffa in history. But he also wrote orchestral works and chamber music as well as pieces for harpsichord. The authenticity of much of this music has been questioned, but some of it is undoubtedly by Pergolesi. His instrumental music is characterized by artistocratic lyricism and elegant workmanship. Some of his trio sonatas anticipated the sonata form. John Barbirolli adapted various instrumental melodies and themes by Pergolesi into a Concerto for Oboe and Strings.

Pergolesi was a pupil of Francesco Santini and Francesco Mondini, and of Gaetano Greco, Francesco Durante, and Francesco Feo at the Naples Conservatory. His first success was a music drama, *La Conversione di San Guglielmo d'Aquitania,* produced at Naples in 1731. During the next six years he wrote many stage works successfully given in Naples. He died of consumption at the age of twenty-six.

Period. A musical sentence, generally made up of two four-measure phrases.

Perlea, Jonel, conductor. Born Ograda, Rumania, Dec. 13, 1900. He studied music principally at the Leipzig Conservatory with Max Reger and Otto Lohse. His conducting début took place in Leipzig. From 1934 to 1944 he was music director of the Bucharest State Opera and director of the Bucharest Conservatory. During this period he made guest appearances in Vienna, Berlin, Warsaw, and Paris. After World War II he conducted performances with the Santa Cecilia Orchestra in Rome, and at La Scala in Milan, where he conducted until 1949. His American début took place with the San Francisco Symphony in the winter of 1949, and on December 1 of the same year he appeared for the first time at the Metropolitan Opera in New York. In

1955 he was appointed conductor of the Connecticut Symphony Orchestra, and subsequently director of the orchestra department of the Manhattan School of Music in New York.

Perpetual Motion (Perpetuum mobile, or Moto perpetuo). A brief instrumental composition built out of short notes of equal time value, and played rapidly to give the impression of continual motion. Paganini, Ferdinand Ries, and Ottokar Nováček wrote virtuoso *Perpetual Motions* for the violin; Mendelssohn and Weber, for the piano.

Persians, The. *See:* Aeschylus.

Pesante. Forcefully.

Peter and the Wolf. A symphonic fairy tale for narrator and orchestra by Prokofiev, op. 67 (1936). The work was intended to teach children the instruments of the orchestra; it was first performed on May 2, 1936, in Moscow at a children's concert. At the beginning of the piece the narrator explains: "Each character in the tale is represented by a different instrument in the orchestra: the bird by a flute; the duck by an oboe; the cat by a clarinet in the low register; grandpapa by the bassoon; the wolf by three French horns; Peter by the string quartet; and the hunter's rifle shots by the kettledrums and bass drums." The story then unfolds through the words of the narrator supplemented by music which consists of a series of leitmotifs, each representing a different character. Peter, for example, is depicted by an impish melody for strings; the wolf by a grim and dire theme; the motifs for the bird, duck, and cat vividly recreate in tones the personality of these animals. All the leitmotifs are adroitly woven together into a single fabric.

The story is a simple tale of a boy, Peter, who despite the warnings of his grandfather goes out into the meadow. There he meets the wolf, which has succeeded in scaring the life out of a cat, bird, and duck. But the wolf does not frighten Peter, who captures him, ties him up in a rope, and leads him off to the zoo.

Peter Grimes. An opera by Benjamin Britten, libretto by Montagu Slater based on *The Borough,* a poem by George

Crabbe, and introduced in London on June 7, 1945. For orchestral excerpts *see: Four Sea Interludes.*

Peter Pan. *See:* Barrie, Sir James.

Petite Symphonie Concertante. For harp, harpsichord, piano, and two string orchestras by Frank Martin (1945), introduced in Zurich on May 27, 1946, Paul Sacher conducting. This is the composer's most celebrated work, and the one with which he first achieved world recognition. Stylistically it is a successful merger of old procedures and techniques with the twelve-tone system. It is in two sections played without interruption; each, in turn, has two parts. The first section begins with an Adagio forty-six measures long in which all later thematic material is suggested. A brief transition leads to an Allegro constructed along symphonic lines. The second part again begins with an Adagio in which the main subject is a nineteen-measure statement by harp accompanied by harpsichord. This part leads into a dance-like finale.

Petrarch (born Francesco di Petrarco), poet. Born Arezzo, Italy, July 20, 1304; died Arqua, Italy, July 19, 1374. Petrarch's celebrated sonnets were the inspiration for the following instrumental compositions: Liszt's *Tre Sonetti del Petrarca* (47, 104, 123) in *Années de pèlerinage,* for piano; and the fourth movement of Arnold Schoenberg's Serenade, op. 24. Alonso de Mudarra, 16th-century Spanish lutenist, set several Petrarch sonnets for the lute.

Petrassi, Goffredo, composer. Born Zagarolo, Italy, July 16, 1904. The necessity of earning a living kept him from formal music study until his twenty-first year. He attended the Santa Cecilia Academy in Rome, where he received a diploma in composition in 1932. He first attracted interest with a Partita for orchestra, which won prizes in Italy and France, and was successfully introduced at the International Society for Contemporary Music Festival in Amsterdam on June 13, 1933. From neo-Classicism he passed on to the twelve-tone technique, an idiom in which he became one of Italy's most forceful creative figures in music. In 1939 he was appointed professor of composition at the Santa Cecilia

Academy, and from 1947 to 1950 was director of the Accademia Filarmonica Romana. Since 1950 he has been superintendant of the Teatro La Fenice in Venice. He paid his first visit to the United States in 1955 to attend the world première of his Fifth Concerto for Orchestra, written for the 75th anniversary of the Boston Symphony and introduced by that organization on Dec. 2, 1955, Charles Munch conducting. In the summer of 1956 he taught a master class in composition at the Berkshire Music Centre at Tanglewood. His works for orchestra include 5 concertos, a piano concerto, a passacaglia, a partita, a Prelude and Fugue for strings, a divertimento, and *Ouverture da concerto.* Among his chamber-music compositions are a *Sinfonia, Siciliana e Fuga* for string quartet, an *Introduzione e Allegro* for violin and eleven instruments, *Sonata da camera* for harpsichord and ten instruments, and *Dialogo angelico* for two flutes. He also wrote inventions, a toccata, and sundry other pieces for piano solo, and *Siciliana e marcetta* for piano duet.

Petri, Egon, pianist. Born Hanover, Germany, March 23, 1881. He originally studied the violin and played that instrument in the Dresden Royal Orchestra. Busoni persuaded him to devote himself to the piano. After a year of preparation with Busoni, he made his professional début as a pianist in Holland. His reputation was established with successful appearances in England and Germany and with two command performances for the Queen of Holland. From 1905 to 1911 he was professor of piano at the Manchester College of Music, and from 1921 to 1926 he held a similar post with the Berlin High School of Music. All the while he concertized throughout Europe. Between 1923 and 1928 he gave over 300 concerts in the Soviet Union, the first foreign artist invited there since the Revolution. His American début took place in New York on Jan. 11, 1932. From 1940 to 1946 he was pianist-in-residence at Cornell University, and from 1947 to 1957 he held the same post at Mills College. He returned to Europe in 1957 to teach piano at the Basel Academy of Music.

Petrouchka. Ballet suite for orchestra by Stravinsky (1911), adapted from the score to the ballet. The ballet, with a scenario by the composer and Alexandre Benois, was introduced in Paris on June 13, 1911, by the Ballet Russe. The setting is a Russian carnival in which the puppet Petrouchka is in love with a puppet ballerina. She in turn is attracted to a handsome puppet Moor. The carnival presents dances by nurses and coachmen, and a performance by a trained bear. Petrouchka interrupts a love scene between the ballerina and the Moor and is brusquely ejected. Later on, Petrouchka is killed by his rival. When the crowd becomes upset, the policeman calms them down by reminding them that Petrouchka is, after all, only a puppet.

The orchestral suite contains the following sections played without interruption: Carnival; the Magician; Russian Dance; Petrouchka; The Moor; Dance of the Ballerina; Nurses' Dance; The Bear and the Peasant Playing a Hand Organ; The Merchant and the Gypsies; The Dance of the Coachman and the Grooms; the Masqueraders; the Quarrel of the Moor and Petrouchka; the Death of Petrouchka.

It is customary to present this suite with some minor deletions. In the abbreviated version the suite usually begins with the brilliant Russian Dance for full orchestra. This is followed by the Petrouchka episode in which the agitated music speaks of the Moor's angry reaction to the puppet's intrusion into his love scene with the ballerina. A pleasing section for piano, soon joined by flute, introduces the ballerina, with whom Petrouchka is in love. But a loud clarinet cadenza reveals Petrouchka's rejection by the ballerina. The Carnival scene follows, alive with the bustle of crowds. In rapid succession there follow the Nurses' Dance, a lively theme for oboe, then horns, and finally the violins; the Bear and the Peasant section, with the bear represented by a ponderous rhythm in the tuba against a jaunty tune for clarinet in the upper register; the Merchant and the Two Gypsies, the accordion music of

the merchant imitated by oboe against plucked strings; and The Dance of the Coachmen, a vigorous Russian melody for trumpets and plucked strings. The suite ends with The Masqueraders, lively dance music for flute, piccolo, and bells.

Peu. Little.

Pfitzner, Hans, composer. Born Moscow, Russia, May 5, 1869; died Salzburg, Austria, May 22, 1949. He was trained at Hoch's Conservatory in Frankfort, and on May 12, 1893, led a concert of his own works in Berlin in which he was hailed as a major composer. Four years later he settled in Berlin, where for several years he taught composition at the Stern Conservatory. For the next few decades he was prominent both as conductor and teacher in Germany. As a composer, he achieved his greatest success with the opera *Palestrina,* introduced in Munich in 1917. In 1920 he was appointed Bavarian Music Director, and in 1925 he was decorated with an Award for Merit by the Prussian Academy of Arts and Sciences. During the early years of the Hitler regime in Germany, Pfitzner associated himself with Nazi ideologies. But a denazification court in Munich exonerated him in 1948. The war had left him financially destitute, from which condition he was finally rescued by a pension from the Vienna Philharmonic. He was one of the last exponents of Germanic Romanticism. He always remained faithful to the traditions established by Brahms and Wagner. His major instrumental works include 2 symphonies, various concertos for solo instruments and orchestra (piano; cello; violin), 3 string quartets, piano trio, piano quintet, and a violin sonata.

See: Palestrina, Preludes to.

Phèdre. *See:* Racine, Jean Baptiste.

Philadelphia Orchestra, The. A major symphony orchestra founded in Philadelphia, Pa., in 1900 with Fritz Scheel, conductor; its first concert took place on November 16. Scheel remained principal conductor until his death in 1907; during that period Richard Strauss and Felix Weingartner appeared as guest conductors. After 1907 the principal conductors were Karl Pohlig, Leopold Stokowski, and from 1938, Eugene Ormandy. In

Philadelphia, the orchestra performs in the Academy of Music. Besides annual series of concerts in New York, the orchestra has made several transcontinental tours. It toured Europe in 1949, 1955, and 1958; during that last trip it made its first appearances in the Soviet Union and other countries behind the Iron Curtain.

Philharmonia Orchestra. A symphony orchestra founded in London, England, in 1945 by Walter Legge for the purpose of making recordings. The orchestra soon gave distinguished performances in London under the direction of Sir Thomas Beecham, Herbert von Karajan, and other conductors. It also made notable appearances at the Lucerne and Edinburgh festivals, besides performing over the radio, for motion pictures, and for records. In 1952 it toured Austria, Germany, and Switzerland under Karajan; and in 1955 it toured the United States and Canada, once again with Karajan.

Philharmonic Auditorium. *See:* Los Angeles Philharmonic.

Philharmonic Hall. *See:* Liverpool Symphony Orchestra.

Philharmonic-Symphony Society of New York. *See:* New York Philharmonic Orchestra.

Philidor. A family of French musicians prominent from the middle of the 17th century to the end of the 18th. The name "Philidor" was bestowed on Michel Danican by Louis XIII. Jean, probably Michel's brother, was the first to assume "Philidor" as a permanent name; and his sons followed suit. One of his sons was André, known as "Philidor l'aîné" (place and date of birth unknown; died Dreux, France, Aug. 11, 1730). He played the oboe at the court of Louis XIV; wrote music for court functions; was librarian to the king; and collected a 57-volume anthology of court music in manuscript. François André Danican Philidor, youngest son of André, was the most celebrated member of this family (born Dreux, France, Sept. 7, 1726; died London, England, Aug. 24, 1795). He was renowned for his many operas and opéra-comiques beside his skill at playing chess.

Philipp, Isidor, pianist and teacher. Born Budapest, Hungary, Sept. 2, 1863; died

Paris, France, Feb. 20, 1958. He was taken to France when he was only three, and later became a French citizen. After attending the Paris Conservatory he concertized in Europe and made appearances with various chamber-music groups, including the Société des instruments à vent, which he had helped to found. From 1903 to 1934 he was professor of the piano at the Paris Conservatory. He paid several visits to the United States before settling there permanently in 1941. He wrote pedagogical works for the piano, made numerous transcriptions for one and two pianos, and was the author of *La Technique de Liszt* (1932).

Philosopher, The. *See:* Symphony—Haydn.

Phoenician Women, The. *See:* Euripides.

Phrase. The smallest formal division of a melody.

Phrasing. The art of marking off phrases of a musical composition, either through indications in the music, or by interpretation in the performance.

Phrygian mode. A Gregorian mode corresponding to the scale from E to E on the white keys of the piano.

Piacere, A. An indication in printed music that the tempo, style, and so forth is left to the discretion of the performer.

Piacevole. Smoothly; free of exaggerated expression.

Pianissimo. Very soft.

Piano. Soft.

Piano (or **Pianoforte**). A modern keyboard instrument in which the strings are struck by hammer action. It was evolved from the virginals and harpsichord, which used quills to pluck the strings, thereby producing a thin and delicate tone without sustaining power. Another ancestor of the piano is the clavichord, whose tone was produced by metal tangents striking the strings. This too was a weak tone. Makers of keyboard instruments long felt that a richer tone could be produced through some kind of hammer action on the strings. But the first experiments in this direction failed to allow the hammers to spring back quickly enough to let the strings vibrate. This problem was finally solved by Bartolommeo di Francesco Cristofori, an instrument maker active in Florence, who in the first decade of the 18th century devised a four-octave instrument in which the hammer action on the strings was controlled by the force applied by the fingers to clavier keys. He called his instrument "gravicembalo col piano e forte," a term soon contracted to "pianoforte," and after that to "piano."

Just as the piano of Cristofori was evolved from the virginals, harpsichord, and clavichord, so music for the piano developed from that written for the earlier keyboard instruments. A technique for writing music for these instruments, and a style individual to them, first appeared in England in the 17th century: miniatures (mostly popular dances, but occasionally also variations and fantasias) for the virginals by Thomas Morley, Orlando Gibbons, Thomas Tallis, William Byrd, and John Bull. In the mid-17th century music for keyboard instruments other than the organ was produced outside England: in France, by Jacques Champion de Chambonnières; in Italy, by Girolamo Frescobaldi. Thus the stage was set for several masters with whom music for the keyboard progresses to a new level of technical and artistic development: Johann Kuhnau in Germany; François Couperin-le-Grand in France; and Domenico Scarlatti in Italy. With Johann Sebastian Bach clavier music achieved such a high artistic status that from this time on the clavier would engage the most serious interest of major composers. During the Classical era that succeeded Bach, the "galant" style entered into the writing for the keyboard instrument with Carl Philipp Emanuel Bach, Haydn, and Mozart. It was during the lifetime of these composers that the piano gradually began displacing the clavichord and harpsichord. With its richer dynamic range, its more extended palette of colors, the piano demanded a manner of writing and performance different from the "galant" style. It was Beethoven who, with a new concept of piano sound, introduced an almost orchestral sonority and variety of color to piano music. With Beethoven the piano finally came into its own, and the harpsichord and clavichord became historical curiosities—reminders of a bygone era.

Nevertheless in the 20th century there took place a revival of interest in the harpsichord—largely due to the pioneer efforts of performers like Arnold Dolmetsch and Wanda Landowska—with the result that several important contemporary composers, among them Manuel de Falla, Frank Martin, and Francis Poulenc, have written major works for that instrument.

Piano quartet. *See:* Quartet.

Piano quintet. *See:* Quintet.

Piano trio. *See:* Trio.

Piastro, Mishel, violinist. Born Kerch, Russia, June 19, 1891. He was a pupil of Leopold Auer at the St. Petersburg Conservatory, from which he was graduated in 1910 with the first prize in violin playing. In that same year he made his professional début with the Koussevitzky Orchestra. Extended tours of Russia, Europe, and the Orient followed. On Oct. 3, 1920, he made his American début in New York. From 1925 to 1931 he was concertmaster of the San Francisco Symphony, and from 1931 to 1937 of the New York Philharmonic. He then founded, and conducted over the radio, the Longines Symphonette.

Piatigorsky, Gregor, cellist. Born Ekaterinoslav, Russia, April 20, 1903. He studied the cello with Alfred von Glehn at the Moscow Conservatory. In his fifteenth year he was appointed first cellist of the Moscow Imperial Orchestra. He left Russia in 1921 and from 1924 to 1928 was first cellist of the Berlin Philharmonic. Embarking on a career as a virtuoso, he made a successful tour of Europe and his American début on Dec. 29, 1929, with the New York Philharmonic. From then on he appeared throughout the world, acclaimed as one of the foremost cellists of the 20th century. He has commissioned and introduced many works for cello and orchestra, by William Walton, Hindemith, Castelnuovo-Tedesco, and others.

Since World War II he has been head of the cello department of the Curtis Institute in Philadelphia and director of chamber music at the Berkshire Music Centre in Tanglewood. In 1955 he was made Chevalier of the Legion of Honor, and in 1957 received the Gold Medal of the London Royal Philharmonic. He has established scholarships for composition and cello in several important conservatories in Europe and the United States.

Piccolo. A small flute, half the size of and an octave higher in range than the flute.

Pick-Mangiagalli, Riccardo, composer. Born Strakonice, Bohemia, July 10, 1882; died Milan, Italy, July 8, 1949. He attended the Verdi Conservatory in Milan, and completed his music study in Vienna. For a while he made appearances in Europe as a concert pianist. In 1914 he abandoned the concert stage for composition, achieving his first success in 1918 with a ballet, *Il Salice d'oro.* Among his subsequent works are a choreographic tone poem, *Il Carillon magico,* produced at La Scala in 1918, numerous orchestral works including *Ballata sinfonico, Notturno e rondo fantastico, Sortilegi,* Two Preludes, *Four Poems, Scene carnevalesche, Piccola suite,* Prelude and Fugue, Prelude and Symphonic Scherzo, *Variazioni coreografiche,* and a *Humoresque* for piano and orchestra. His style is traditional, with a partiality for contrapuntal writing and dance rhythms. From 1936 until his death he was director of the Milan Conservatory.

Pickwick Papers. *See:* Dickens, Charles.

Pictures at an Exhibition. Suite for piano by Mussorgsky (1874), inspired by a visit to a posthumous art exhibit in St. Petersburg of canvases by Victor Hartmann. With remarkable realism, and a brilliant capacity for catching in appropriate music the essence of each picture, Mussorgsky was able to create a major work for the piano. Though sometimes heard in this version, the suite is most famous in transcriptions for orchestra. The most popular of these is that of Maurice Ravel, commissioned by Koussevitzky, who introduced it in Paris with his orchestra on May 3, 1923. Other transcriptions were made by Granville Bantock, Lucien Cailliet, Leopold Stokowski, and Henry J. Wood.

Ravel's transcription, like the original, has eleven sections. I. Promenade. A stately walking subject is given by the brass, as the composer ambles along at the exhibition. II. Gnomes. A theme with halting rhythms describes the deformed creatures Hartmann drew for a toy nutcracker. III. The Old Castle. After a brief restatement of the walking theme, a melody evokes a picture of a medieval castle; this melody is first given by the bassoon, and repeated by saxophone against strings. IV. Tuileries. Once again the walking theme is heard. Then sprightly music, with brisk rhythms, tells of the play of children in the famous Parisian park. V. Bydlo. A "bydlo" is a Polish oxcart. Its stumbling motion is recreated in a heavy theme for solo tuba characterized by nervous rhythms. VI. Ballet of the Unhatched Chickens. Again we hear a brief restatement of the walking theme, after which the play and the movement of chickens (as they appear in a Hartmann design for a stage set) is depicted in witty music. VII. Samuel Goldenburg and Schmuyle. This movement is a portrait of two Jews. One is rich and pompous, represented by a strong theme in the basses. The other is poor and humble; consequently he is portrayed by a weak subject for muted trumpets. VIII. The Market Place at Limoges. Fleet melodic figures and leaping rhythms suggest the gossiping of housewives as they do their shopping. IX. Catacombs. Another statement of the walking theme is followed by somber, heavy, chordal music. X. A Hut on Fowl's Legs. The thematic material in this section has the character of Russian folksong. XI. The Great Gate at Kiev. The suite comes to a majestic conclusion with a richly orchestrated and sonorous description of a monument planned by Hartmann for Kiev.

Pièces de clavecin. Four volumes of pieces for the harpsichord by François Couperin-le-Grand (1713-1730). These pieces are of historical importance in crystallizing a keyboard style and technique. They are also significant esthetically for their wide variety of expression, perfection of structure, richness of harmony, and effectiveness of programmatic writing. They range from the satiric to the sentimental; many are picturesque and evocative; some are interpretative. They contain descriptions of the weather, bees and gnats, jugglers, gossip, court life, and sights in Parisian streets. They draw parallels between colors and moods, and characters. All in all they offer in music a cross-section of French life in the 18th century: customs, dress, habits, daily life, dances, popular tunes, and so forth. Structurally they include musettes, rondeaux, passacaglias, chaconnes, and themes with variations. The cream of the crop are: *Les Barricades mystérieuses, Le Carillon de Cythère, Les petits moulins à vent, Le Rossignol en amour, Soeur Monique,* and *Tic-toc-choc ou les Maillotins.*

Pièces de clavecin (and **Nouvelle Suite de Pièces de clavecin**), two sets of pieces for the harpsichord by Jean-Philippe Rameau. Together with Couperin's pieces discussed above, these sets helped lay the foundations of French piano music. These collections embrace dances: allemandes, sarabandes, gavottes, minuets, courantes, gigues, rigaudons, and so forth. They also include delightful mood pictures, descriptive scenes, and programmatic morsels. The most famous are: *La Poule, Les tendres plaintes, Les Soupirs, La Joyeuse,* and *Le Rappel des oiseaux.* Here Rameau was a daring innovator who arrived at new techniques of harpsichord performance. At the same time he contributed new tone colorations, harmonic brilliance, and a fine dramatic and pictorial sense.

Pierné, Gabriel, composer and conductor. Born Metz, France, Aug. 16, 1863; died Ploujean, France, July 17, 1937. From 1871 to 1882 he attended the Paris Conservatory, where his teachers included César Franck and Jules Massenet. In 1882 he won the Prix de Rome. After returning to Paris he succeeded Franck as organist of the Sainte Clotilde in Paris, retaining this post eight years. After a long apprenticeship as assistant conductor of the Colonne Orchestra, Pierné succeeded Edouard Colonne as principal conductor in 1910, and for a quarter of a century led the orchestra in concerts outstanding both for the authority and distinction of his direction and for its dedication to new French music. Upon his resignation in 1932, Pierné was made honorary president of the orchestra.

Meanwhile in 1925 he was elected member of the Académie des Beaux-Arts.

Pierné's first success as a composer came with an oratorio, *The Children's Crusade (La Croisade des enfants),* which received the City of Paris Prize following its première in Paris in 1905. A ballet, *Cydalise,* in 1923, was another major success. A conformist, Pierné was not concerned with experimentation but only with the projection of poetic beauty and sensitive moods in an elegant style. His principal works for orchestra include a piano concerto, *Ouverture symphonique, Marche solennelle, Pantomime, Poème symphonique* for piano and orchestra, *Les Cathédrales, Paysages franciscains, Ballet de cour, Divertissement sur un thème pastoral,* and *Gulliver au pays de Lilliput.* He also produced a violin sonata, cello sonata, piano quintet, and piano trio among other chamber-music works, and numerous pieces for the piano. He is perhaps best known for two miniatures often heard at pop concerts: *Entrance of the Little Fauns (Marche des petits faunes)* from *Cydalise* and *March of the Little Lead Soldiers (Marche des petits soldats de plomb)* from *Album pour mes petits amis,* for piano.

Pierrot Lunaire. An atonal composition for voice, piano, flute (or piccolo), clarinet (or bass clarinet), violin (or viola), and cello, by Arnold Schoenberg, op. 21 (1912). Its première took place in Berlin on Oct. 16, 1912, when it provoked a riot because of its unorthodox idiom. The music is an Expressionist setting of 21 short poems, called "melodramas," all decadent in their symbolism, by Albert Giraud. For these poems, Schoenberg produced an atonal and dissonant work in which the melodic line is more recitative than lyrical. The voice is required to perform in a style that is neither speech nor song but somewhere between the two: it is called "Sprechstimme." This is absolute music deriving its interest entirely from musical values, and often bearing no perceptible relation to the text. Thus, where one of the poems *(Serenade)* speaks of Pierrot playing the viola, the musical setting is for cello; and where the word pizzicato appears in the poem, the cello plays arco. The titles of the individual songs are: I. Moonstruck; II. Colombine; III. The Dandy; IV. A Pale Washerwoman; V. Waltz of Chopin; VI. Madonna; VII. The Sick Moon; VIII. Night; IX. Prayer to Pierrot; X. Theft; XI. The Red Mass; XII. The Song of the Gallows; XIII. Decapitation; XIV. The Crosses; XV. Homesickness; XVI. Outrage; XVII. A Parody; XVIII. Moonspot; XIX. Serenade; XX. Journey Home; XXI. Oh, Olden Fragrance.

Pijper, Willem, composer. Born Zeist, Holland, Sept. 8, 1894; died Leidschendam, Holland, March 19, 1947. Soon after his graduation from the Utrecht Music School in 1915, he completed his first symphony, introduced by the Concertgebouw Orchestra at Amsterdam in 1918, Mengelberg conducting. Here Pijper was influenced by the German post-Romantic school, most of all by Mahler. He soon abandoned traditional techniques and structures for a more radical approach. His music became polytonal, built from an abundance of germinal ideas which he called "germ cells." His most important work in this manner is the Symphony No. 3, introduced by the Concertgebouw under Monteux in 1926. Besides distinguishing himself as one of Holland's leading creative figures in music, Pijper also achieved importance as a music critic for various Dutch newspapers. He taught at the Amsterdam High School and Amsterdam Conservatory; from 1930 until his death he was director of the Rotterdam Conservatory. His major works include 3 symphonies, various concertos for solo instruments and orchestra (piano; cello; violin), Divertimento for piano and orchestra, *Six Symphonic Epigrams,* incidental music to various plays, 4 string quartets, 2 piano trios, 2 violin sonatas, a septet, sextet, 2 cello sonatas, flute sonata, wind quintet, 3 sonatinas for piano and a sonata for two pianos.

Pines of Rome (Pini di Roma). Tone poem for orchestra by Respighi (1924), introduced in Rome on Dec. 14, 1924, Molinari conducting. Like its companion piece, *The Fountains of Rome,* this work is in four sections played without interruption; each movement represents a different part of Rome, and the feelings aroused in the composer by these Roman landscapes. I. The Pines of the Villa Borghese. Children are playing games in the gardens, these games suggested by brief motifs in brass and woodwind. The music grows dissonant and the scene changes. II. The Pines Near a Catacomb. Shadows of pines spread across the entrance of the catacombs, from whose depths there arises a solemn hymn which soon melts into silence. Muted and divided strings evoke a serene scene as a religious hymn is intoned by the orchestra. III. The Pines of the Janiculum. A full moon lights up the profile of the pines on Janiculum Hill. A song of the nightingale pierces the silence. The evening scene is described by a clarinet solo; the nightingale's solo (reproduced by a recording of an actual bird song) appears against tremolo strings. IV. The Pines of the Appian Way. In a misty dawn on a portion of the Appian Way flanked by pines, a march rhythm is heard. The poet sees a vision of past glories and the advance of the army of the Consul towards Capitoline Hill; he hears the sound of blaring trumpets. Throughout this section the music gains in power and intensity, grows ever more lustrous in tone color, until a mighty crescendo is released.

Piston, Walter, composer. Born Rockland, Me., Jan. 20, 1894. In 1916 he was graduated from the Massachusetts Normal Art School. He then studied piano and violin with private teachers. After World War I he decided on music as a career, specializing in that subject at Harvard, from which he was graduated in 1924 *summa cum laude.* From 1924 to 1926 he studied composition in Paris with Nadia Boulanger on a John Knowles Paine Scholarship. After returning to the United States he joined the music faculty of Harvard, where since 1944 he has been professor. His American début as a composer took place when his *Symphonic Suite* was performed by the Boston Symphony in 1928. Since then his major works for orchestra have been performed by the leading symphonic organizations. He received the New York Music Critics Circle Award for his Second Symphony in 1945; the

Pulitzer Prize in music for his Third Symphony in 1948. Previously he had received a Guggenheim Fellowship and had been elected a member of the National Institute of Arts and Letters and the American Academy of Arts and Sciences. He is the author of textbooks on harmony, counterpoint, and orchestration. While Piston has favored Classical forms in his compositions, and has often been Romantic in style, he has incorporated into his writing advanced techniques including dissonant harmonies and linear counterpoint. His most popular work is the ballet suite for orchestra, *The Incredible Flutist.* Other works for orchestra include 7 symphonies, 2 symphonic suites, various concertos (violin; orchestra; viola), Concertino for piano and orchestra, Prelude and Fugue, *Sinfonietta,* Toccata, *Serenata,* and Fantasy for English Horn, Strings and Harp. His chamber-music compositions include 4 string quartets, piano trio, flute quintet, violin sonata, sonatina for violin and harpsichord, Divertimento for nine instruments, and Partita for violin, viola, and organ.

See: Incredible Flutist, The; Symphony —*Piston.*

Pitch. The exact position of a tone in the musical continuum, determined by the number of vibrations producing that tone.

Pittsburgh Symphony Orchestra. A symphony orchestra founded in 1895 in Pittsburgh, Pa. Its first concert took place on Feb. 27, 1896, Frederic Archer conducting. From 1898 to 1904 Victor Herbert was principal conductor, and from 1904 to 1910 Emil Paur. The orchestra was disbanded in 1910, but sixteen years later it was reorganized, functioning for the next decade under the direction of Elias Breeskin, Antonio Modarelli, and various guests. It was once again reorganized in 1937. Since then its principal conductors have been Fritz Reiner and William Steinberg. The orchestra performs at the Syria Mosque.

Più. More.

Pizarro. *See:* Sheridan, Richard Brinsley.

Pizzetti, Ildebrando, composer. Born Parma, Italy, Sept. 20, 1880. He was graduated with honors from the Parma Conservatory in 1901, after which he worked as assistant conductor of the Parma Opera. In 1907 began a long and fruitful career as a teacher. After serving first as professor of theory and composition, then as director, of the Florence Conservatory, he became the director of the Milan Conservatory in 1925. In 1936 he was appointed professor of composition at the Santa Cecilia Academy in Rome, and from 1948 to 1951 served as its director. Despite this sustained activity in musical education, Pizzetti is a prolific composer who early assumed a commanding position among contemporary Italian composers. Though probably best known for his operas, he is equally distinguished in his orchestral music. His creative life has had several important influences. The first was Gabriele d'Annunzio, in a period during which Pizzetti produced incidental music to many of d'Annunzio's plays. The second phase was biblical, the Bible providing him with the material and inspiration for many compositions. The final, and perhaps richest, phase was one in which his writing was influenced by Italian backgrounds and history. In each of these phases, Pizzetti's music has been rich in lyricism and strong in dramatic impact. Pizzetti first visited the United States in 1930, appearing as pianist and conductor in his own music. He is the author of *Musicisti contemporanei* (1914), *Intermezzi critici* (1921), *Paganini* (1940), and *La Musica italiana dell' 800* (1946).

His principal orchestral works include a symphony, violin concerto, cello concerto, *La Pisanella, La Nave, Concerto dell' estate, Rondo veneziano, Canti della stagione alta* for piano and orchestra, *Canzone di beni perduti,* and *Preludio a un altro giorno.* He has also written 2 string quartets, piano trio, violin sonata, cello sonata, piano sonata, and pieces for the piano.

See: Concerto—*Pizzetti; Rondo veneziano;* Sonata—*Pizzetti.*

Pizzicato. In string music, the plucking of a string.

Placido. Placidly.

Plagal Cadence. A perfect cadence in which the final tonic chord follows a subdominant chord.

Planets, The. Suite for orchestra by Gustav Holst, op. 32 (1916), performed in its entirety for the first time in London on Nov. 15, 1920, Albert Coates conducting. This music, the composer explains, has no connection with the deities of classical mythology but was suggested by the astrological significance of the planets. There are seven sections. I. *Mars, the Bringer of War.* This is martial music opening with strong rhythms and counterrhythms. The basic melody appears in trumpets and horns. II. *Venus, Bringer of Peace.* Music of gentler mood, this section opens with a soft horn call to which delicate music for flutes provides an answer. III. *Mercury, the Winged Messenger.* This is a scherzo whose effect is achieved by motor energy. IV. *Jupiter, Bringer of Jollity.* This gay music depicts an English country festival. The core is a forty-bar melody which has the character of an English folksong. V. *Saturn, Bringer of Old Age.* This movement introduces a peaceful interlude. VI. *Uranus, the Magician.* By contrast to the preceding section, this one is in a jolly mood. VII. *Neptune, the Mystic.* The entire movement is *pianissimo*, in an atmosphere of mystery. At the end of this section a hidden choir of women's voices sounds a sustained tone against a background of flutes and clarinets.

Pleasure Dome of Kubla Khan. Tone poem for orchestra by Charles Tomlinson Griffes (1920), first performed by the Boston Symphony on Nov. 28, 1919, Monteux conducting. The programmatic source of this work is the famous poem by Coleridge. The following description was provided by the composer: "The vague, foggy beginning suggests the sacred river, running 'through caverns measureless to man down to a sunless sea.' The gardens with fountains and 'sunny spots of greenery,' are next suggested. From inside come sounds of dancing revelry which increases to a wild climax and then suddenly breaks off . . . There is a return to the original mood, suggesting the sacred river and the 'caves of ice.' " A low chord in divided cellos and double basses brings up the picture of the "sacred river." After a quiet passage of chords, flute and oboe present a haunting melody, soon taken over by

the strings, describing the gardens and fountains. A dance revelry follows, occasionally interrupted by contemplative moods.

Pleyel, Ignace Joseph, composer and manufacturer of pianos. Born Ruppersthal, Austria, June 1, 1757; died Paris, France, Nov. 14, 1831. As a boy he studied the clavier with Johann Wanhal and composition with Haydn in Vienna. After holding various posts as Kapellmeister, and achieving success as pianist and conductor, he founded a firm for manufacturing pianos in Paris in 1807. It was an immediate success. It still exists under the name of Pleyel, Wolf et Cie. Managing this firm occupied Pleyel for the rest of his life. At the same time he wrote much music, producing 29 symphonies, 8 concertos, 7 *symphonies concertantes,* 45 string quartets, 6 flute quartets, and 6 piano sonatas, among other works.

Plow that Broke the Plains, The. Suite for orchestra by Virgil Thomson (1936) adapted from a score to a documentary film. The film touched upon the tragedy in the abuse of our natural resources, in the exploitation of the soil, and in the havoc caused by drought. The suite has six movements: I. Prelude; II. Pastorale (Grass); III. Cattle; IV. Blues (Speculation); V. Drought; VI. Devastation. This suite was described as follows by *Modern Music:* "A simple, uninterrupted progression toward destruction provides a strong unifying factor. From the opening movement, with its mournful, broad sweep, prophetic of waste, there is a gradual build up to the final 'Devastation.' This movement is very similar to the beginning, yet the careful sequence of events which leads to it results in a quite different feeling, of consummated rather than implied loss. On the way there is a subtle stroke in the unhappy, almost querulous gaiety of the 'Blues,' a fine piece of understatement, of making a slight, apparently dissimilar mood a symbol of something more deeply tragic."

Poco. Little.

Poe, Edgar Allan, poet and story writer. Born Boston, Mass., Jan. 19, 1809; died Baltimore, Md., Oct. 7, 1849. The following instrumental compositions are based on tales or poems by Poe: André Caplet's symphonic study *Le Masque de la mort rouge,* and his *Conte fantastique,* for harp and string quartet; Henry F. Gilbert's *The Island of Fay,* for piano; Josef Holbrooke's tone poems for orchestra, *Ulalume* and *The Masque of the Red Death,* and his *Israfel* (sextet for winds), *Aal Aaraaf* (sextet for strings), *Irene* (nonet for woodwind and strings), and *Ligeia* (clarinet quintet); Edgar Stillman Kelley's tone poem for orchestra, *The Pit and the Pendulum;* Nikolai Miaskovsky's tone poem *Nevermore,* based on *The Raven;* Eugeniusz Morawski's tone poems, *Nevermore* and *Ulalume;* and Florent Schmitt's symphonic study, *The Haunted Palace.*

Poem. (1) For violin and orchestra by Ernest Chausson (1896), introduced in Paris by Eugène Ysaÿe and the Colonne Orchestra on April 4, 1897. Free in form, and romantic in mood, this composition (as its name suggests) is richly poetic in its thematic material. It opens with a soaring song in the solo violin against an orchestral background. The second main subject, though somewhat more agitated than the first, is also poetic and lyrical, and also makes its first appearance in the solo instrument. The work ends with a return of the first subject in the full orchestra.

(2) For flute and orchestra by Charles Tomlinson Griffes (1918). This composition was written for the flutist, Georges Barrère, who introduced it in New York with the New York Symphony on Nov. 16, 1919. This work has been subjected to varied programmatic interpretations. To Walter Damrosch, who conducted the première performance, it was music of Grecian spirit; to an unidentified New York critic it possessed the "naive and elemental qualities of an Irish folk song." The solo flute spins a languorous melody in a composition whose style skilfully blends French Impressionism with Russian orientalism.

Poem of Ecstasy. *See:* Symphony— *Scriabin.*

Pohjola's Daughter. Symphonic fantasy by Sibelius, op. 49 (1906), first performed in St. Petersburg on Dec. 29, 1906, the composer conducting. Its pro-

grammatic source was the *Kalevala,* and its subject was the courtship of "the daughter of the North" by the hero minstrel from Pohja, Väinämöinen. He tries to win her by performing various heroic feats, in one of which he is grievously wounded. With the aid of an ancient man his wounds are finally healed. The fantasy opens with solemn chords describing Väinämöinen. As he sets forth on his journey the music gains in spirit and animation. The maiden is represented by a gentle melody for muted strings and harp. At first the music is in the woodwind and is eloquent as Väinämöinen speaks of his love; then it grows turbulent following the hero in the performance of his various feats. The work ends peacefully as Väinämöinen's wound is finally healed.

Poissons d'or (Debussy). *See: Images* (2).

Polacca. A polonaise in an ornate Italian style, yet retaining its Polish identity. Compositions or parts of compositions with a polonaise-like character are sometimes designated as "alla polacca," as for example in the last movement of Sibelius' Violin Concerto.

Polish Symphony. *See:* Symphony— *Tchaikovsky.*

Polka. A lively Bohemian folk dance in duple time, popular throughout Europe in the mid-19th century. The polka, as a form of instrumental music, was favored by many serious Bohemian composers. Smetana incorporated polkas in his tone poem *The Moldau,* in his string quartet *From My Life,* and in his folk opera *The Bartered Bride.* He also wrote numerous polkas for the piano: *Three Drawing Room Polkas* (1855); *Three Poetical Polkas* (1855); *Memories of Bohemia* (1861); and *Czech Dances,* which includes 4 polkas (1878). Zdeněk Fibich used a polka as a scherzo movement of his String Quartet in A major (1874). A successful modern use of the polka is found in Weinberger's opera *Schwanda* (see below).

Polka and Fugue. Two orchestral episodes from Jaromir Weinberger's folk opera, *Schwanda the Bagpipe Player* (*Schwanda der Dudelsackpfeifer*). This opera, libretto by Miloš Kareš, was successfully introduced in Prague on April

27, 1927. The Polka and Fugue—often coupled on symphony programs as a single composition—are the most famous excerpts from this opera. The Polka is found in Act 2, Scene 2; the fugue, in the closing scene. At the conclusion of the fugue, the composer ingeniously combines the spirited polka melody contrapuntally with the fugue subject.

Polonaise. A courtly Polish dance, popular outside Poland in the 18th century. It is characterized by marked syncopations, and accents on the half beat. It sometimes appears as a movement in the Baroque suite, as in J. S. Bach's Suite No. 2, for orchestra. Many composers after Bach wrote concert polonaises: Mozart, Beethoven, Weber, Schubert, Schumann, among others. The most celebrated use of this form in concert music is found with Chopin, who wrote 13 compositions, the first two in 1817. In these polonaises, Chopin spoke of both his fiery and dynamic patriotism and his poignant nostalgia for home. Twelve are for piano solo; the thirteenth, Introduction and Polonaise, op. 3 (1819-1820), is for cello and piano. These are the most popular polonaises: the "Military Polonaise" in A major, op. 40, no. 1 (1838), which has a martial air; the "Heroic Polonaise," in A-flat major, op. 53 (1842) and the "Revolt" or "Serbian" Polonaise in E-flat minor, op. 26, no. 2 (1835), both of which are virile and strong-fibered; and the Polonaises in C minor, op. 40, no. 2 (1839), and C-sharp minor, op. 26, no. 1 (1835), which are brooding and contemplative. Since Chopin's time several important composers have produced popular instrumental polonaises: Glazunov in *Scènes de ballet;* Mussorgsky in Act 3, Scene 1 of his opera, *Boris Godunov;* Tchaikovsky in the opening scene of Act 3 of his opera, *Eugene Onegin;* and Wieniawski's *Polonaise brillante* in D major for violin and piano, op. 4, a staple in the violin repertory.

Polovtsian Dances. A series of oriental dances for orchestra by Borodin from his opera, *Prince Igor.* The dances occur towards the end of Act 2, when Khan Konchak, ruler of the Polovtsi, entertains his captives, Prince Igor and the Prince's sons, with tribal dances. In the opera, the dances are accompanied by chorus as well as orchestra, but at symphony concerts the choral background is omitted. In the first dance a melody for flute and oboe introduces the procession of the royal captives. This is followed by the dance of savage men—a sprightly melody for clarinet against a descending phrase of four sharply accentuated notes; by the dance of the boys, in which war games are simulated by a forcefully syncopated melody for strings interrupted by clashes of the cymbal; and by the dance of the young girls, a sinuous oriental melody shared by violins and cellos. The dances come to a vertiginous conclusion as the dancers salute their leader.

Polymeter. *See:* Polyrhythm.

Polyphony. The sounding of two or more independent melodies simultaneously.

Polyrhythm (or Polymeter). The simultaneous use of different rhythms.

Polytonality. The simultaneous use of different keys.

Ponticello. Bridge of a stringed instrument. The designation "sul ponticello" indicates that the bow is to be drawn as close to the bridge as possible.

Popper, David, cellist. Born Prague, Czechoslovakia, June 16, 1843; died Baden, Austria, Aug. 7, 1913. He attended the Prague Conservatory, where he specialized in the cello. His début took place in Karlsruhe on March 29, 1865, after which he toured Europe several times, and served as chamber virtuoso to Prince Hohenzollern. From 1868 to 1873 he was first cellist of the Vienna Court Opera orchestra. He resigned this post to resume his career as a virtuoso. In 1896 he became a Hungarian citizen and assumed the post of professor of cello at the Budapest Royal Conservatory which he held until his death. Popper wrote many works for the cello including 4 concertos, 3 suites, a Requiem for three cellos, and many smaller pieces, as well as etudes and methods.

Portamento. Gliding in continuous sound from one tone to another.

Porter, Quincy, composer. Born New Haven, Conn., Feb. 7, 1897. He was graduated from Yale College in 1919, and from the Yale School of Music with prizes in composition in 1921. Meanwhile, in 1920, he went to Europe, where he studied composition with Vincent d'Indy and violin with Lucien Capet. From 1922 to 1928 he was a member of the faculty of the Cleveland Institute of Music, a period during which he studied composition with Ernest Bloch. In 1928 he returned to Paris on a Guggenheim Fellowship, remaining three years. He was professor of music at Vassar College from 1932 to 1938. From 1938 to 1942 he was dean of the New England Conservatory, and from 1942 to 1946 its director. In 1946 he assumed his present post as professor of music at Yale University; in 1958 he was named Master of Pierson College there.

Porter has distinguished himself as a virtuoso on the viola. But he is even more famous as a composer, particularly of chamber music. In this field his production includes 8 string quartets, 2 violin sonatas, piano quintet, clarinet quintet, a fugue for string quartet, a horn sonata, *Quintet on a Childhood Theme, String Sextet on Slavic Folk Tunes,* and several duos. His writing is always marked by spontaneity, freshness, emotional vitality. In 1943 he received the Elizabeth Sprague Coolidge medal for distinguished service to chamber music. In 1954 he won the Pulitzer Prize for his Concerto for Two Pianos and Orchestra. Other orchestral works are a symphony, *Music for Strings, Fantasy on a Pastoral Theme,* a viola concerto, a Fantasy for cello and small orchestra, and *New England Episodes.*

Portsmouth Point. Concert overture for orchestra by William Walton (1925), introduced in Zurich on June 22, 1926, Volkmar Andrae conducting. The music is a tonal representation of a print by Thomas Rowlandson depicting a busy waterfront scene at Portsmouth Point, a British naval arsenal opposite the Isle of Wight. For his musical material, the composer uses some 18th-century sailor tunes and dances. The overture opens with a syncopated subject for full orchestra. This is followed by a sailor's dance and other robust and strongly rhythmed sailor tunes. With rapidly changing tempo, syncopations, and dissonant harmonies, the composer successfully describes the feverish activity on the waterfront.

Position. In violin playing, the place occupied by the fingers of the left hand on the fingerboard. The first position covers a perfect fifth on each string, with the open string as the lowest note and the highest a fifth above, stopped by the little finger. All other positions normally comprise a fourth.

Potpourri. A term originating with J. B. Cramer indicating a piece of salon music combining several familiar but unrelated tunes, airs, or melodies into a medley.

Poule, La. (1) *See: Hen, The.*
(2) *See:* Symphony—*Haydn.*

Poulenc, Francis, composer. Born Paris, France, Jan. 7, 1899. While pursuing a comprehensive academic education, Poulenc for a long time relegated music to the status of a diversion. His friends persuaded him to study it seriously, raising a fund to pay for piano lessons with Ricardo Viñes. After World War I he studied composition with Charles Koechlin, under whose guidance he completed the first of his works to get published, *Rapsodie nègre,* for voice and chamber orchestra. It was not until his name became linked with those of Darius Milhaud, Louis Durey, Georges Auric, Arthur Honegger, and Germaine Tailleferre—representing the "French Six" or "Les Six" (*see: Six, Les*)—that he first achieved recognition. For a while, Poulenc produced music in the precise, economical, lean, and at times witty style alleged to be the prevailing idiom of "Les Six," a vein in which he produced such delightful works as his *Concert champêtre,* for harpsichord and orchestra, and the Concerto in D minor, for two pianos and orchestra. But the period immediately preceding World War II, and following it, saw his writing gain greater emotional intensity and depth of feeling, greater vehemence, and at times even pathos. It is in this vein that he produced some of his most important compositions, including a concerto for organ, strings, and timpani, a piano concerto, *Sinfonietta,* violin sonata, string quartet, and the opera *Les Dialogues des Carmélites,*

introduced at La Scala on Jan. 26, 1957.
In 1948 Poulenc paid his first visit to
the United States, touring in joint recitals with the baritone, Pierre Bernac.

Besides the works already mentioned,
Poulenc wrote sonatas for various instruments (two clarinets; clarinet and bassoon; horn, trumpet, and trombone), a
trio, a sextet, and *Suite française* for
chamber orchestra. He also produced
much music for the piano, including a
sonata for four hands, suites, impromptus, intermezzi, and improvisations.

See: Concerto—*Poulenc; Sinfonietta.*

**Pouplinière, Alexandre Jean-Joseph le
Riche de La,** music patron. Born Chinon,
France, July 26, 1693; died Paris, France,
Dec. 5, 1762. For several years, from
about 1727, Jean Baptiste Rameau lived
in his palace, directed his orchestra, and
taught him music. Rameau then used his
influence to have François Joseph Gossec
appointed as director of the palace concerts in 1751; under Gossec, this orchestra became famous. Le Pouplinière was
responsible for introducing Johann Stamitz to the Parisian music public in 1754-
1755; it was on Stamitz' advice that
horns, clarinets, and a harp were introduced into the La Pouplinière orchestra,
the first time these instruments were
made a regular part of a non-operatic
French orchestra.

Powell, John, composer and pianist. Born
Richmond, Va., Sept. 6, 1882. After being graduated from the University of
Virginia in 1901, he studied piano with
Theodor Leschetizky and composition
with Karel Navrátil in Vienna. His début
as a pianist took place in Berlin in 1908,
followed by tours of Europe. He returned
to the United States in 1912 to make his
American début as a pianist. For several
years after that Powell combined his activity as pianist with that of composer.
One of his most successful works was the
Rapsodie nègre for piano and orchestra
(inspired by Joseph Conrad's *Heart of
Darkness*) and introduced in New York
City on March 23, 1918. His interest in
and study of the folk music of Virginia
led him to write compositions like the
Sonate Virginianesque for violin and
piano, *Virginia Overture* for orchestra,
and the Symphony in A, the last intro-

duced in Detroit in 1947. The 25th anniversary of his professional career in the
United States was celebrated with a concert appearance in New York on Nov.
1, 1938. Besides the works mentioned
above, Powell also wrote a violin concerto, a string quartet, and a second violin
sonata.

Powell, Maud, violinist. Born Peru, Ill.,
Aug. 22, 1868; died Uniontown, Pa.,
Jan. 8, 1920. After studying the violin
with Henry Schradieck in Leipzig,
Charles Dancla in Paris, and Joseph
Joachim in Berlin, she initiated her
professional career as a violinist at Berlin in 1885 with the Berlin Philharmonic,
Joachim conducting. In that same year
she made her American début, with the
New York Philharmonic. She then toured
the United States, Europe, Russia, Scandinavia, and South Africa, assuming a
leading position among the women violinists of her time. In 1894 she founded the
Maud Powell String Quartet, with which
she appeared throughout the United
States. She was responsible for introducing to America many important works
for the violin, including concertos by
Dvořák, Saint-Saëns, Sibelius, Tchaikovsky, and Lalo. She was also the first
violinist to make recordings for Victor.

Prades Festival. *See:* Casals, Pablo.

Praeludium. German for prelude (which
see).

Prague Symphony. *See:* Symphony— *Mozart.*

Prelude (Praeludium or Vorspiel). A self-
sufficient composition serving to introduce
the main body of a composition, or a
group of numbers, or a second piece of
music. The term prelude is often used
interchangeably with overture to designate
an orchestral preface to an opera; but a
prelude usually has a less elaborate structure than an overture. Wagner, Puccini,
and other later composers of opera often
preferred a prelude to an overture to provide an atmospheric setting or mood to
the act that follows.

In keyboard literature of the Baroque
era, the prelude often is found as the
first movement of a suite, as in Bach's
English Suites. It also appears as a preface to another self-sufficient piece of music, as in Bach's *Well-Tempered Clavier,*

where each fugue is preceded by a prelude. The juxtaposition of prelude and fugue was a device favored by many composers after Bach, including Mendelssohn, Max Reger, and Shostakovich.

Beginning with Chopin, however, the piano prelude often appeared as a completely independent piece, introducing nothing, and of no special pattern, but usually painting a definite mood.

The following are some of the most familiar examples of preludes for the piano:

CHOPIN. Chopin was the first to make the prelude famous in piano literature. The Chopin prelude is a brief, independent piece of music without a set form; it voices a passing mood or emotion, and leaves with the listener the feeling that when the piece is finished much more could be said. Chopin wrote 26 such pieces, 24 in op. 28 (1836-1839), one in op. 45 (1841), and another published posthumously. Each of the preludes in op. 28 is in a different key. Most are in a tormented mood, reflecting the composer's mental and physical misery on the island of Majorca, where they were written. The most popular works in op. 28 are: No. 1, C major; No. 3, G major; No. 4, E minor; No. 6, B minor; No. 7, A major, prominently used in the ballet *Les Sylphides;* No. 15, D-flat major, better known as the "Raindrop," because a repetitious figure in the melody seems to suggest the beating of raindrops on the roof; No. 16, B-flat minor; No. 17, A-flat major; No. 22, G minor; and No. 24, D minor.

DEBUSSY. The 24 preludes of Debussy represent the quintessence of his Impressionist art. They are among his masterworks, and are collected in two books, twelve in each (1910-1913). To each prelude Debussy supplied a title, but since he did not want the title to influence the listener into conceiving programmatic implications for the music (and since the titles were frequently concocted after the music had been written), he put them at the end of the composition, rather than at the head. Where Chopin's preludes attempted to speak at times of stormy and melancholy moods, those by Debussy create an evanescent impression.

These preludes are as important pianistically as they are esthetically, for they evoke colors, nuances, suggestions rarely before achieved by means of a piano, and mainly through original harmonic tints and unusual effects in resonance.

The following are Debussy's most celebrated preludes: *The Hills of Anacapri* (*Les Collines d'Anacapri*), which has the personality of a Neapolitan folksong; *Footsteps in the Snow* (*Des pas sur la neige*), an awesome picture of an icebound scene; *The Girl With the Flaxen Hair* (*La Fille aux cheveux de lin*), a tender evocative melody, one of the most popular by Debussy; *The Engulfed Cathedral* (*La Cathédrale engloutie*), inspired by a Breton legend about the cathedral of Ys which is said to rise out of and return into the sea to the sounds of tolling bells and chanting priests.

All of the preceding preludes are found in Book I. In Book II, the following preludes are of special interest: *La Puerta del Vino* describing a historic gate at the Alhambra in Granada, Spain; *People On a Terrace at Moonlight* (*La Terrasse des audiences au clair de lune*) and *Ondine,* the first a sensitive picture of nighttime, the other of a nymph.

FAURÉ. Fauré wrote 9 piano preludes, op. 103 (1911), which are among his most mature works for a solo instrument. They are integrated and sensitive mood pictures, the best being No. 2, in C-sharp minor, with its delicately exotic atmosphere evoked through the use of the whole-tone scale; No. 5, in D minor, a turbulent outburst of emotion; and No. 6, in E-flat minor, which has an exquisite sensitivity of feeling and structure.

GERSHWIN. Gershwin wrote 5 jazz preludes for the piano, of which only three are often heard. They were written in 1926. The first, in B-flat major, is strongly rhythmic, deriving its material from the tango and Charleston. The second, in C-sharp minor, is a three-part blues. In the third, B-flat major, energetic rhythms once again predominate.

RACHMANINOFF. The 24 preludes of Rachmaninoff are among his best-loved pieces for the piano. Ten appear in op. 23 (1904); 13 in op. 32 (1910); and one in Five Pieces, op. 3 (1892). Two of these preludes are among the composer's most frequently performed compositions, familiar in their original version and in numerous transcriptions. The Prelude in C-sharp minor, op. 3, no. 2, is a dramatic piece of writing which opens and closes with a stately theme of solemn chords; this is contrasted with a stormy middle section. The Prelude in G minor, op. 23, no. 5, begins and ends with a brisk theme suggesting marching soldiers; the middle section has a sentimental lyric character.

SHOSTAKOVICH. In Shostakovich's 24 preludes, op. 34 (1933), we are continually made aware of the influence of Rachmaninoff. Each prelude is filled with the same kind of emotional impact, psychological interest, and nostalgic moods we find in the Rachmaninoff preludes. These are the most popular: No. 10, in C-sharp minor; No. 14, in E-flat minor; No. 15, in D-flat major; and No. 24, in D minor.

Prélude à l'après-midi d'un faune (Debussy). *See: Afternoon of a Faun, The.*

Prelude, Chorale and Fugue. For piano by César Franck (1884). The composer here attempted to revive the spirit of Bach. To Bach's polyphony, Franck contributes his own high-minded expression, and a feeling for mysticism. There are two principal melodic ideas in the prelude; the first is majestic, and the second vigorous. The chorale is serene and contemplative. The subject of the fugue is a descending chromatic theme.

Préludes, Les. Tone poem for orchestra by Liszt (1854), introduced in Weimar on Feb. 23, 1854, the composer conducting. It was inspired by Lamartine's *Méditations poétiques,* lines from which appear in the score to provide a program for the music: "What is life but a series of preludes to the unknown song whose initial solemn note is tolled by death? The enchanted dawn of every life is love; but where is the destiny on whose first delicious joys some storm does not break? . . . And what soul thus cruelly bruised, when the tempest rolls away, seeks not to rest its memories in the calm of rural life? Yet man allows himself not long to taste the kindly quiet which first attracted him to Nature's lap; but when the trum-

pet gives the signal he hastens to join his comrades no matter what the cause that calls him to arms. He rushes into the thick of the fight and amid the uproar of the battle regains confidence in himself and his powers."

The principal musical idea is a stately theme in the double basses, with which the work opens. It returns in several different guises and is developed before a new melody appears in four horns, strings, and harps, to express the happiness of love. After a climax, the main theme returns slightly varied, then a stormy passage erupts. Tranquillity is restored with a revival of the main theme by the oboe; with the suggestion of a country dance in the horn; and with a restatement of the love melody. Once again the music becomes disturbed, reaching into the dramatic coda with powerful impact. The main theme, again altered, returns to provide a majestic ending to the composition.

Les Préludes is one of 12 orchestral works for which the composer coined the term "tone poem" or "symphonic poem."

Prepared Piano. An ordinary piano to the strings of which dampers of metal, wood, rubber, or other materials are attached in carefully prepared positions to produce unusual color effects. John Cage, an American composer, originated this process and has written provocative works employing it.

Presto. Very fast, faster than allegro. Prestissimo is the fastest tempo in music.

Previtali, Fernando, conductor. Born Adria, Italy, Feb. 16, 1907. He attended the Verdi Conservatory in Turin, receiving degrees in piano, organ, cello, and composition. After being assistant conductor at the Florence May Music Festival for eight years, he was appointed in 1936 principal conductor of the RAI Symphony in Rome. He subsequently led opera performances at La Scala in Milan and in other major Italian cities, besides appearing in guest performances with major European orchestras. From 1953 to 1955 he was the principal conductor of the Santa Cecilia Orchestra; he has also been professor of conducting at the Academy. His American début took place with the Cleveland Orchestra on Dec.

5, 1955; on Dec. 5, 1957, he made his New York début with the New York Philharmonic.

Primitivism. The application of rhythmic, dynamic, and melodic elements of primitive music to sophisticated musical forms, as in many compositions by Stravinsky and Prokofiev.

Primo. First.

Primrose, Sir William, violist. Born Glasgow, Scotland, Aug. 23, 1903. He was a student of the violin at the Guildhall School of Music in London. In 1923 he made his début as a violinist with the Albert Hall Orchestra in London. From 1925 to 1927 he studied with Eugène Ysaÿe, who persuaded him to take up the viola. After several years of preparation, Primrose resumed his concert activity, this time as a violist, and achieved immediate success. From 1930 to 1935 he was violist of the London String Quartet. During this period he appeared in recitals and as soloist with major European orchestras. From 1937 to 1942 he was a first violist of the NBC Symphony. In 1955 he was appointed to the faculty of the Juilliard School of Music in New York. He commissioned Béla Bartók to write his viola concerto, which (though left unfinished by the composer's death) Primrose introduced to England; he also gave the American première of Walton's Viola Concerto. Primrose was knighted in 1953.

Prince Igor. An opera by Borodin, libretto by Vladimir Stassov based on an old Russian chronicle. The première took place in St. Petersburg on Nov. 4, 1890. For orchestral excerpts *see: Polovtsian Dances.*

Princesse lointaine, La. *See:* Rostand, Edmond.

Pro Arte String Quartet. A Belgian chamber-music ensemble founded in 1912 by Alphonse Onnou, violinist. The other three members were Laurent Halleux, second violin, Germain Provost, viola, and Robert Maas, cello. The Quartet made its début at Brussels in 1913. Within the next decade it was heard throughout Europe, distinguishing itself particularly in the modern repertory. Its American début took place at Washington, D.C., in 1926; a year later it per-

formed for President Coolidge at the White House. In 1932 King Albert bestowed on it the official title of Quatuor de la Cour de Belgique. The organization passed out of existence with the death of Onnou in 1940.

Procesión del Rocío, La. Tone poem for orchestra by Joaquín Turina, op. 9 (1912), first performed at Madrid in March 1913, Fernandez Arbós conducting. This is a tonal description of a religious procession held each June in Triana, a suburb of Seville. The work is in two parts played without pause. The first presents a picture of gay Triana, alive with song and dance and festivities. In the second part the colorful religious procession takes place. Prominent throughout is a religious melody which in the second part is built up powerfully. The work ends with a repetition of some of the song and dance motifs of Triana.

Procession of the Mastersingers. Majestic march music accompanying the entrance of the Mastersingers in Act 3, Scene 2, of Wagner's opera, *The Mastersingers.*

Procession nocturne, La (The Nocturnal Procession). Tone poem for orchestra by Henri Rabaud, op. 6 (1898), introduced in Paris on Jan. 15, 1899, Edouard Colonne conducting. The music is a setting of a poem by Nicolaus Lenau describing Faust's contemplation of a religious procession on a summer night. The work begins slowly and softly. A two-tone theme is presented by French horns, while rolls of the timpani suggest distant thunder. The strings appear with a brief syncopated subject to which the clarinet replies with a recall of the opening motif. There now is heard a flowing melody for the violins. This is soon followed by another main theme in flutes and clarinets. In the development, the placid mood thus far projected is disturbed by a *fortissimo* for full orchestra. The turmoil subsides and the music ends serenely.

Program music. Music that tells a story, describes a specific mood or situation, or depends upon a literary program, as opposed to absolute music. In program music extramusical sounds are often imitated for greater realism. Johann Kuhnau's *The Combat of David and Goliath* in the 17th century, and Couperin's harpsichord pieces and J. S. Bach's *Capriccio on the Departure of a Beloved Brother* in the 18th are a few early examples of instrumental program music. Program music, however, came into prominence only in the 19th century, with Berlioz, Liszt, Saint-Saëns, and Richard Strauss. **Program notes.** Descriptive analytical or historical notes in programs about music about to be performed. This practice is believed to have originated in England in 1768 with annotations by T. A. Arne; in Germany in 1783 with J. F. Reichardt, an eminent conductor who wrote his own annotations for the music he performed; and in the United States in Philadelphia in 1787 with a performance of Handel's *Hallelujah Chorus* from the *Messiah*. The practice of providing notes at concerts was stimulated in England by George Grove, who supplied such information for the Saturday concerts of August Mann at the Crystal Palace for forty years. In the United States, the writing of program notes was advanced by Philip Hale with his material for the concerts of the Boston Symphony from 1891 to 1934; by Henry E. Krehbiel, for many years the annotator of the concerts of the New York Philharmonic; and by Lawrence Gilman, whose program notes were used by the New York Philharmonic and the Philadelphia Orchestra from 1921 to 1939. Since then the principal program annotators in the United States have been Irving Kolodin, Louis Biancolli, Robert Bagar, John N. Burk, Alfred Frankenstein, Deems Taylor, Olin Downes, George H. L. Smith, Frederick Dorian, and Donald L. Engle.

Progression. The movement of one tone or chord to another.

Prokofiev, Serge, composer. Born Sontzovka, Russia, April 23, 1891; died Moscow, Russia, March 5, 1953. He entered the St. Petersburg Conservatory when he was thirteen. He remained there a decade, a pupil of Rimsky-Korsakov, Nicholas Tcherepnin, and Anatol Liadov. During his student days he composed prolifically, including such impressive and unconventional works as his first piano sonata, the *Suggestion diabolique* for piano, and his first piano concerto. He was graduated in

1914 with the Rubinstein Prize for the piano concerto.

His first major work for orchestra was the *Scythian Suite*, introduced in St. Petersburg on Jan. 29, 1916, the composer conducting. Its advanced harmonic and melodic thinking alienated critics and audiences; Glazunov fled from the concert auditorium in horror. A ballet, *Chout*, written for Serge Diaghilev and the Ballet Russe—and finally produced by that company in Paris on May 17, 1921—was a major success. Here and in subsequent works completed during the period of World War I, Prokofiev reached full maturity as a composer; these works included his First Violin Concerto, two piano sonatas, and the *Classical Symphony*. He also crystallized that individual style and manner which would henceforth identify him: the impudent leaps in the melody which injected into his lyricism an often mocking or satiric attitude; the unexpected alternation from the direct and the simple to the complex and the subtle; the plunge down to, or leap up to, unexpected tones; the juxtaposition of naive tunes with complex harmony; the use of orthodox chords in unorthodox progressions. These elements injected surprise and freshness into his music; but they did not keep him from projecting dramatic, meditative, or passionate moods with compelling creative force.

Prokofiev left the Soviet Union in 1918 to undertake a tour of the United States. He made his American début with a piano recital in New York on Nov. 20, 1918. While in Chicago, he was commissioned by the Chicago Opera to write a work for that theater; the result was *The Love for Three Oranges*, produced on Dec. 30, 1921.

After returning to Europe from his first American tour, Prokofiev established residence in Paris. During the next decade he made many concert tours of the world. He also completed major works with which his dominant position in contemporary music was firmly established: the ballet, *The Age of Steel* (*Le Pas d'acier*), given by the Ballet Russe in 1927; the third and fifth piano concertos; the second, third, and fourth symphonies.

By 1933 Prokofiev had become convinced that his place was back in his native land. After returning to the Soviet Union, where he was given a hero's welcome, he often expressed in his music Soviet ideology or Russian cultural and historic traditions. Among his most popular Soviet works are the *Lieutenant Kije* suite and the cantata *Alexander Nevsky* (both originating as scores for motion pictures), and the delightful children's symphonic fairy tale, *Peter and the Wolf*.

During World War II Prokofiev allied himself with the war effort by writing anti-fascist songs, military marches, and larger works in which the impact of the war on the Soviet people found eloquent interpretation; among the last were the Piano Sonata No. 7, the Fifth Symphony, and the opera *War and Peace*.

By the end of the war, Prokofiev was hailed in the Soviet as one of its leading cultural figures. He was the recipient of the Stalin Prize for his Seventh Piano Sonata, and of numerous other awards and public honors. Nevertheless, when the Central Committee of the Communist Party in 1948 announced the formation of a new music policy—away from modernism and experimentation and towards a popular folk style easily assimilated by the masses—Prokofiev did not escape violent attack for his cerebralism and "decadent formalism," and for his "negation of the basic principles of classical music." Prokofiev was specifically accused of failing to "reflect the greatness of our people . . . the unfeeling essence of his music is alien to reality." It took some time for Prokofiev to recover his position in Soviet music. But he finally succeeded in doing this with the oratorio *On Guard for Peace* (which condemned "Western warmongers" and praised the Soviet "international peace movement") and a symphonic suite, *Winter Bonfire*. These two compositions won for him the Stalin Prize in 1951. In that year his 60th birthday was celebrated with a special concert broadcast throughout the Soviet Union. His death of a cerebral hemorrhage two years after that was an occasion for national mourning.

The following are Prokofiev's principal instrumental compositions:

Chamber Music: 2 string quartets; 2 violin sonatas; sonata for two violins; flute sonata; *Overture on Hebrew Themes;* Quintet, for wind and strings.

Orchestra: 7 symphonies; 5 piano concertos; 2 violin concertos; 2 cello concertos; concerto for two pianos; *Scythian Suite; Age of Steel (Le Pas d'acier),* ballet suite; *Divertimento; Lieutenant Kije,* suite; *Romeo and Juliet,* three ballet suites; *Peter and the Wolf; Summer Day; Russian Overture; Symphonic Suite; Cinderella,* ballet suite; *Ode on the End of the War.*

Piano: 9 sonatas; sonatinas; *Suggestion diabolique; Sarcasmes; Visions fugitives; Pensées; Children's Suite; Suite of Waltzes;* Toccata; various pieces.

See: Age of Steel, The; Concerto—*Prokofiev;* Gavotte; *Lieutenant Kije; Love for Three Oranges,* Suite; Quartet—*Prokofiev; Peter and the Wolf; Romeo and Juliet* (2); *Scythian Suite;* Sonata—*Prokofiev; Suggestion diabolique;* Symphony—*Prokofiev; Visions fugitives.*

Proletarian music. Music by Soviet composers reflecting the ideology, the social and political interests, of the Soviet people, and written for mass consumption. Shostakovitch and Prokofiev are among many Soviet composers to write such music.

Promenade Concerts. Summer concerts of orchestral music given at the Royal Albert Hall, in London, England; the direction is shared by Sir Malcolm Sargent and Basil Cameron.

While promenade concerts were given in London since 1838, the series now referred to by that name originated in 1895 when Robert Newman, manager of the Queen's Hall Orchestra, inaugurated a series of orchestral concerts in his hall directed by Henry J. Wood. These promenade concerts continued without interruption under Wood's direction through World War I. They were temporarily discontinued during the air raids of World War II. Additional problems arose when Queen's Hall was destroyed in an air attack, and Sir Henry J. Wood died in 1944. But the concerts were resumed after the war at a new auditorium and under different leadership. An American equivalent of these concerts are those of the Boston Pops Orchestra under Arthur Fiedler.

Prometheus, Overture to. An overture to a ballet by Beethoven, op. 43 (1800). Besides the overture, the ballet music includes an introduction and 16 numbers. The ballet was introduced in Vienna on March 28, 1801. The overture is the only portion of the incidental music to survive in orchestral programs. Other parts are of interest because Beethoven subsequently used some of this material in later compositions: the *Pastoral Symphony;* the last movement of the *Eroica Symphony;* a contredanse; and the piano Variations, op. 35.

The Overture opens with a stately Adagio section in which a theme for woodwinds, horn, and strings is prominent. The Allegro begins with a brisk passage for violins; the second main subject in this section follows in the winds. Both themes receive vigorous development before they are repeated, and the work ends with a dramatic coda.

Prometheus: The Poem of Fire. *See:* Symphony—*Scriabin.*

Prometheus Bound. *See:* Aeschylus.

Prophets, The. *See:* Concerto—*Castelnuovo-Tedesco.*

Protée: Symphonic Suite No. 2. Suite for orchestra by Darius Milhaud (1919), adapted from incidental music to a satirical play by Paul Claudel. Claudel's play concerned the aged prophet Proteus who falls in love with a young girl on an island in the Aegean Sea. The orchestral suite was first performed in Paris on Oct. 19, 1920. It opens with an overture in tango-habanera rhythm and in a bitonal style. This is followed by a prelude and fugue for brass, a pastorale, a nocturne, and a finale making effective use of polytonality and complex rhythmic combinations.

Prussian Quartets. *See:* Quartet—*Haydn.*

Psalmus Hungaricus. *See:* Kodály, Zoltán.

Psyche. Tone poem for orchestra by César Franck (1888), introduced in Paris on March 10, 1888, in its original version as a symphony for chorus and orchestra. The composer later adapted it into a tone poem in four uninterrupted

sections. I. Psyche's Sleep. The clarinet against strings, presents the sleep motif. This is followed by the motifs of "longing" and "love," both in the strings. The sleep motif is given greatest prominence. II. Psyche Borne Away by the Zephyrs. Two themes predominate. The first describes the zephyrs and appears in muted strings, with clarinet and flute; the second characterizes Psyche. III. The Garden of Eros. The core of this section is the passionate love music built from the Eros theme; it is heard in woodwinds and horn against violin trills. IV. Psyche and Eros. This part portrays the happiness of the lovers. A succession of lyrical ideas are subtly woven into a single texture.

Puerta del Vino, La. *See:* Prelude—*Debussy.*

Puerto Rico Festival. *See:* Casals, Pablo.

Pugnani, Gaetano, violinist and composer. Born Turin, Italy, Nov. 27, 1731; died there July 15, 1798. After studying with Tartini, Pugnani became one of Italy's most distinguished violinists, a performer who carried on the traditions previously established not only by his teacher, but also by Corelli and Vivaldi. From 1752 to 1754 he was first violinist at the court of Sardinia, and after 1754 he toured Europe as solo violinist, scoring successes in Paris and London. He returned to Turin in 1770 to remain there for the rest of his life, filling the office of general music director of the Royal Chapel. He also devoted himself to teaching; one of his pupils was Viotti. Pugnani's instrumental compositions include 9 violin concertos, 12 symphonies, 3 sets of violin sonatas, together with numerous duos, trios, quartets, and quintets. Two pieces for violin long ascribed to him are actually by Fritz Kreisler, who had formerly been credited as being only a transcriber. They are *Praeludium and Allegro* and *Tempo di Minuetto.*

Pugno, Raoul, pianist and composer. Born Montrouge, France, June 23, 1852; died Moscow, Russia, Jan. 3, 1914. He received his musical instruction at the École Niedermeyer and at the Paris Conservatory. In 1871 he was appointed organist of the St. Eugène Church in Paris. His first successes as a composer came through his operettas and ballets. In 1893 he gave a piano recital at the Paris Conservatory in which he demonstrated for the first time his remarkable virtuoso powers. A triumphant tour of Europe followed, in which he was acclaimed for his penetrating performances of the music of Mozart. He was also a distinguished interpreter of the piano works of César Franck, which he helped to popularize. Pugno made numerous appearances in sonata recitals with Eugène Ysaÿe and with various chamber-music groups. His first tour of the United States took place in 1897-1898. Pugno taught harmony at the Paris Conservatory from 1892 to 1896, and from 1896 to 1901 he was professor of piano there.

Pulcinella. Suite for small orchestra by Stravinsky (1919), derived from the score to a ballet first introduced in Paris by the Ballet Russe on May 15, 1920. Pulcinella is a traditional character in the Neapolitan theater. In Stravinsky's ballet he is envied by his friends because all the girls are fond of him. They attack him, leave him for dead, then assume his costume so that they might make love to the girls. Pulcinella, however, is revived, but he is in no mood for vengeance. He is happy that they are keeping the girls busy since he wants to woo a specific one.

Stravinsky's ballet score is made up of material extracted from works written by or attributed to Pergolesi, the 18th-century Neapolitan composer of comic operas; Stravinsky had discovered this music in manuscript in Naples. He borrowed the melodies and dressed them in somewhat more modern harmonies and instrumentation. The orchestral suite was introduced in Boston on Dec. 22, 1922, Monteux conducting. It has eight short movements: I. Sinfonia (Overture); II. Serenata; III. Scherzino; IV. Tarantella; V. Toccata; VI. Gavotte (with two variations); VII. Duetto; VIII. Minuetto-Finale.

Stravinsky also adapted parts of his ballet score into two suites for violin and piano. One of these he called simply Suite (1925). It has five movements: I. Introduction; II. Serenata; III. Tarantella; IV. Gavotte (with two variations); V. Minuetto-Finale. The second he named

Suite Italiana (1933). It is in six movements: I. Sinfonia; II. Canzona; III. Danza; IV. Gavotte (with two variations); V. Scherzino; VI. Moderato; Allegro vivace.

Purcell, Henry, composer. Born probably London, England, about 1659; died Dean's Yard, Westminster, England, Nov. 21, 1695. One of England's greatest composers, Purcell is most famous for his music for the stage, and especially for his opera, *Dido and Aeneas.* But his instrumental music is also a landmark. In 1669 he became a chorister of the Chapel Royal, where he studied with John Blow. He left the choir in 1673 to become "keeper of the instruments." Four years after that he was appointed composer of the King's band, and in 1679 organist at Westminster Abbey. In 1682 he became one of three organists of the Chapel Royal. His works for various string instruments are a major contribution to English music. These fantasias for strings, and sonatas, are filled with creative imagination and bold techniques—particularly in concepts of major-minor relations and in harmonic progressions. To the elegant lyricism and the graceful style of the Italian masters who had preceded and influenced him, Purcell added a subtlety and variety of expression and an intensity of emotion not often encountered in the instrumental music of his time. His instrumental compositions include 22 sonatas in three or four parts for violins and bass (including the famous *Golden Sonata*); various sonatas for violin and figured bass; fantasias in three, four, and five parts for strings (including the celebrated *Fantasia on One Note*); overtures, chaconnes, and a pavane for strings; suites, toccatas, chaconnes, voluntaries, minuets, airs, gavottes, preludes, grounds, and so on for harpsichord.

See: Chaconne—*Purcell;* Fantasia—*Purcell; Golden Sonata.*

Pushkin, Alexander, poet. Born Moscow, Russia, June 6, 1799; died St. Petersburg, Russia, Feb. 10, 1837. He was Russia's foremost literary figure. The following composers wrote incidental music to his poetical dramas: Prokofiev (*Eugene One-*

gin, Boris Godunov); Yuri Shaporin (*Boris Godunov*); and Vissarion Shebalin (*Mozart and Salieri, The Miserly Knight,* and *The Stone Guest*). Nicholas Nabokov's overture, *Le Fiancé,* was based on

a Pushkin poem; Tchaikovsky's symphonic ballad, *The Voyevoda,* on Pushkin's translation of a ballad by Mickiewicz. Anatol Liadov wrote a *Polonaise in Memory of Pushkin,* for orchestra.

Q

Quadruple time. Four beats to a measure.

Quadruplet. Group of four notes to be played in the same time as three ordinary notes of the same value.

Quality Street. *See:* Barrie, Sir James.

Quantz, Johann Joachim, flutist and composer. Born Oberscheden, Germany, Jan. 30, 1697; died Potsdam, Germany, July 12, 1773. He received training on various musical instruments in Merseburg, and in counterpoint in Vienna and Rome. In 1718 he entered the employ of the King of Poland as oboist and violinist. During this period he took up the study of the flute with Pierre Buffardin. Quantz acquired an extraordinary technical command of that instrument. On a visit to Berlin in 1728 he enchanted the Crown Prince Frederick with his flute playing, and Frederick became his pupil. After Frederick ascended the throne in 1740 he engaged Quantz as court composer and conductor. Quantz wrote about 300 concertos for one and two flutes besides 200 other flute compositions. He also wrote a famous method on flute playing (1752).

Quarter note. Half of a half note.

Quarter rest. A rest of a quarter note's duration.

Quarter tone. Half of a semitone.

Quarter-tone music. Music constructed on intervals of half a semitone, the scale comprising 24 quarter tones instead of 12 semitones. Alois Hába has been a pioneer in writing and propagandizing quarter-tone music. An American pianist-composer, Hans Barth, constructed a two-manual quarter-tone piano for which he

wrote a concerto and several other compositions.

Quartet. A composition for four voices or instruments. The most familiar combination is the string quartet: two violins, viola, and cello. Many composers have also written quartets for piano, violin, viola, and cello (piano quartet). Occasionally music has been produced for other quartet combinations, such as oboe and strings, or flute and strings.

Quartets are usually in four movements, similar to those in a sonata or symphony. The first significant works for string quartet were written at the end of the 17th century by Tommaso Antonio Vitali and Alessandro Scarlatti. Haydn was the composer who crystallized the form and style of string-quartet writing; while its artistic potentialities were fully realized by Mozart and Beethoven.

The following are basic works in quartet literature:

BARTÓK. The six string quartets of Béla Bartók provide a panorama of his creative development. His first quartet, op. 7 (1908), is Romantic, its sensual lyricism and chromatic harmonies influenced by Wagner and Brahms, while its excursions into whole-tone writing reveal the influence of Debussy. Bartók's individuality, arrived at through the assimilation of techniques and idioms of Hungarian folk music, first asserts itself in the second quartet, op. 17 (1917). Here the style becomes virile and brusque, and—as in the *Allegro molto capriccioso* movement —rhythmically barbaric. This work is unusual in its structure by ending with a

Lento movement, of an almost funereal character. With the third quartet (1927) the composer abandons both the opus number as an identification and a tonality as a unifying element of style. Ten years separate the second and third quartets; in that time the composer had embarked upon Expressionism. The third quartet is atonal, with an occasional suggestion of the twelve-tone technique. Throughout, the thinking is severe and concentrated. The fourth quartet (1928) is even more concise in technique and abstract in thought. The first and last movements (Allegro, and Allegro molto) are entirely built from a six-note phrase found in the seventh bar of the first movement. The finale is a spirited Magyar dance, but the middle movements—the second (Prestissimo con sordino) and the third (Allegretto pizzicato)—are lighter in spirit and texture. In his last two quartets (1934, 1939) the composer moved back to a more or less consistent tonality. The writing is simpler, clearer, occasionally more lyrical; the approach more classical. The fifth quartet is especially interesting for its finale (Allegro vivace), an extraordinary network of polyphonic writing climaxed by an extended fugue. Impressive chorales are found in two slow movements (Adagio molto, and Andante). In the sixth quartet there are passages of sardonic humor, as in the Burletta movement. The finale (Mesto), on the other hand, is rich in poetic content. While at first the lyricism of this movement is touched with sadness, the music grows in intensity until at the conclusion one succumbs to a shuddering feeling of depression.

BEETHOVEN. Beethoven's 16 string quartets are among the masterworks to which he not only confided some of his most personal musings and profoundest feelings but in which he also often asserted most boldly his strong personality and independent thinking. Roughly speaking, these quartets fall into three groups. The first embraces the 6 works in op. 18 (1798-1800), sometimes referred to as the "Lobkowitz Quartets" after the Prince to whom they were dedicated. Here Beethoven still follows the Classic string-quartet structure and style inherited from Haydn and Mozart, but not without at times establishing his own creative identity or venturing into new directions. These six quartets are: No. 1, F major; No. 2, G major; No. 3, D major; No. 4, C minor; No. 5, A major; and No. 6, B-flat major, La Maliconia.

An unusual feature of the second quartet is the way Beethoven suddenly interpolates a scherzo episode into his slow movement (Adagio cantabile). The fourth quartet is unorthodox in that it has no slow movement; there is instead a scherzo opening with a fugato. The sixth quartet is called La Maliconia because this heading appears over the short slow introduction that prefaces the finale. This episode is years ahead of its time in its rich and deep expressiveness.

The second group of Beethoven's quartets begins with three works, op. 59 (1806), known as the "Rasoumovsky Quartets" after the Russian Ambassador to Austria who had commissioned them. This is music of Beethoven's mature second period, in which he reveals an impatience with classical order, symmetry and restraint, and with the modus operandi of his times. The form in these works is often so elastic and the procedures so unorthodox that the composer himself regarded this as music "for a later age." With this freedom of style and structure are also found poetic and dramatic moods, at times a turbulence of spirit, which often characterize the compositions of Beethoven's middle period.

Because these quartets were written for a Russian patron, Beethoven introduced a folksong in the finale of the first quartet (Allegro); and a Russian national theme, also used by Mussorgsky for the Coronation Scene of Boris Godunov, in the scherzo movement of the second quartet (Allegretto).

In the first quartet, in F major, all movements are in the sonata form. The second quartet, in E minor, has one of the composer's most incandescent and radiant slow movements (Molto adagio). The third quartet, in C major, has such consistent dramatic impact and vigor that it has become known as the "Heroic Quartet." Here, too, the slow movement

(*Adagio ma non troppo e molto cantabile*) has an exalted character.

To this second group also belong the Quartet in E-flat major, op. 74 (1809), and the Quartet in F minor, op. 95 (1810). The first is called the "Harp Quartet" because in the first movement (*Poco adagio;* Allegro) one of the themes imitates the sound of a harp through a pizzicato subject for the four instruments. Beethoven himself designated the F minor Quartet as "Serious," recognizing the prevailingly somber character of the first three movements; even the Scherzo, usually light in mood, has unusual sobriety.

The five quartets beginning with op. 127 and ending with op. 135 belong to Beethoven's last creative period. The composer now refuses to recognize structural or technical limitations while allowing full freedom to his thinking. The dramatic and poetic idea becomes so important to him that earlier concepts of lyricism and tonal beauty must be sacrificed; the last quartets are filled with brusque statements, harsh accents, unorthodox modulations and progressions. The formal presentation of principal themes and the practice of developing them must now give way to a new process in which one theme succeeds another, one idea (or fragment of an idea) is superimposed upon the next. The composer continually aspires to tap ever richer, ever deeper veins of thought, ever subtler and more elusive veins of feeling.

The Quartet in E-flat, op. 127 (1824), has a pastoral character, one of several Beethoven works to reflect his profound love of nature. Its theme-and-variations movement (*Adagio ma non troppo e molto cantabile*) is on that sublime plane of mysticism and spirituality that Beethoven's slow movements would henceforth inhabit. That spirituality and that mysticism are found in the Cavatina (*Adagio molto espressivo*) of the B-flat major Quartet, op. 130 (1825), written with such an overwhelming intensity of feeling that at one point the composer marked a passage as "agonized." The same qualities are found in the melancholy fugue (*Adagio ma non troppo e molto espressivo*) that opens the C-sharp

minor Quartet, op. 131 (1826), and i the other-worldly radiance of the twenty eight bar Adagio that precedes the finale And they are found in the profoun religious content of the *Molto adagi* movement of the A minor Quartet, o 132 (1825), written as a prayer c thanksgiving for the composer's recover from a serious illness.

Beethoven's last string quartet, in I major, op. 135 (1826), is something o an enigma. Over the slow theme of th finale (Grave) the composer wrote : question: "Must it be?" And over th first theme of the ensuing Allegro, h added: "It must be!" The meaning o these sentences has never been adequatel; explained, though trite interpretation have been provided by some of Bee thoven's friends and biographers. Th most probable explanation may lie in th fact that Beethoven realized that he wa here writing his last quartet (the word "last quartet" appear at the end of th manuscript) and he was both askin Fate whether this farewell was necessar and providing his own answer.

There is still one more work for strin quartet belonging to this last period: th *Grosse Fuge*, op. 133 (1825). This wa originally written as the last movement o the Quartet in B-flat major, op. 130. Be cause Beethoven's publishers considere this music too complex and abstrus they prevailed on him to write anothe finale for his quartet (consequently th finale of op. 130 is the last music th composer wrote for string quartet). Th *Grosse Fuge* was then issued as a sepa rate composition.

BLOCH. Ernest Bloch has written string quartets: the first in 1916; th second in 1945; the third in 1953; th fourth in 1954. The second is the on most often heard, though there is a grea deal of rewarding music in the others This second quartet was introduced i London by the Griller Quartet on Oct 9, 1946 (I. Moderato. II. Presto. III Andante. IV. Finale). The music through out is in an elevated sphere of eloquence The third movement has a religious aur; about it; its sustained and sinuous lyri line simulates a synagogal cantillation

The finale is a monumental passacaglia culminating in a formidable fugue.

BORODIN. Borodin's String Quartet No. 2 in D major (1881-1885) is at its best in the third movement, a Nocturne (Andante). Its expressive twenty-four bar melody is stated by the cello against syncopated chords. The rest of the Quartet is lyrical, and pronouncedly national. In the scherzo movement, the composer uses an infectious waltz melody in thirds for the violins.

BRAHMS. Brahms' three string quartets were completed in 1874 and 1875. Two are found in op. 51 (C minor and A minor). The third is in B-flat major, op. 67. The C minor Quartet is mostly a lugubrious work, filled with at times turbulent and at times resigned moods; its general character is yearning and pathetic. The work is well integrated. A brief theme heard at the beginning of the first movement (Allegro) returns in the Romanze (*Poco adagio e commodo*) and assumes significance in the finale (Allegro). The Quartet in A minor has a sensitively elegiac first movement (*Allegro ma non troppo*), which opens with a hauntingly poignant song for the violin. The slow movement is also solemn (*Andante moderato*) and highlighted by an eloquent exchange between violin and cello. But the third-movement Minuet and the fiery Hungarian character of the finale (*Allegro non assai*) provide a welcome change of feeling. The third quartet, in B-flat major, opens with a hunting fanfare—an animated subject that projects a feeling of happy spirits, maintained throughout the first movement (Vivace). The good humor continues for the rest of the quartet and flows especially abundantly in the finale (*Poco allegretto*) which consists of a lively melody and eight variations.

Brahms wrote three piano quartets: G minor, op. 25 (1861), A major, op. 26 (1862), and C minor, op. 60 (1875). The first two were his first large works to reveal his creative power. Both were introduced at Vienna in 1862 by the Hellmesberger Quartet, the composer playing the piano part. (The C minor Quartet is of less importance and interest.)

In both works the finales are vitalized by Hungarian folk-dance rhythms and melodies. The first quartet is more lyrical than the second. It boasts an atmospheric nocturne-like Intermezzo (*Allegro ma non troppo*), one of the composer's first intermezzos in his characteristic style; also a sensitive, richly poetic slow movement (*Andante con moto*). The second quartet is especially interesting for its structure and technique; in the use of variations in the development of the first movement (*Allegro non troppo*); and in the canonic writing in the trio section of the scherzo. In this quartet, as in the first, the finest music is found in the slow movement, a brooding nocturne (*Poco adagio*).

DEBUSSY. The Quartet in G minor, op. 10 (1893), was Debussy's first masterwork; it was introduced in Paris by the Ysaÿe Quartet on Dec. 29, 1893 (I. *Animé et très décidé*. II. *Assez vif et bien rythmé*. III. *Andantino doucement expressif*. IV. *Très modéré*). The first movement opens with a sharply accented subject, the motto of the entire work. This subject is subsequently contrasted with a lyrical passage for violin and viola. In the second movement the motto theme is altered rhythmically, in tempo, and in intervallic construction. Next comes a slow movement in which muted strings present a melancholy song; a second lyrical subject, in which violin and cello are prominent, appears midway. The finale is a virile presentation of the motto theme, first heard inverted in the violin after a one-bar introduction by the cello; this motto later becomes the heart of a fugato section.

DVOŘÁK. Dvořák's best-known string quartet is that in F major, op. 96 (1893), popularly known as the "American Quartet." It was written during the composer's stay in the United States, when he visited Spillville, Iowa, and met three Iroquois Indians who performed for him authentic American-Indian music. So impressed was Dvořák with this music that he composed several important works incorporating the American-Indian idiom. But in the Quartet, as elsewhere, Dvořák did not borrow his material directly from Indian sources but merely wrote original melodies "embodying the peculiarities of the Indian music," as he explained, developing them with "all the resources of modern rhythm, harmony, counterpoint and color" (I. *Allegro ma non troppo.* II. *Lento.* III. *Allegro molto vivace.* IV. *Vivace ma non troppo*). There are three Indian-like subjects in the first movement: the first in the viola, repeated by the first violin; the second, a duet for two violins; the third, in the first violin over chords in the other instruments. The second movement opens with an Indian-like song in the first violin, and ends with the same song in the cello. The last two movements are more Bohemian than American-Indian in their vivacious folk-dance rhythms.

FAURÉ. The String Quartet in E minor, op. 121 (1923), is Fauré's last chamber-music work, and his only string quartet. It is rich in spiritual content; technically, it is marked by unusual progressions, modulations, and thematic sequences, providing the work as a whole with an elusive, at times exotic, character (I. *Allegro moderato.* II. *Andante.* III. *Allegro*). The finest of the movements is the middle one, which has the kind of introspective thought we find in Beethoven's last quartets.

The Piano Quartet in G minor, op. 45 (1886), is one of Fauré's most significant chamber-music works with piano (I. *Allegro molto moderato.* II. *Allegro molto.* III. *Adagio ma non troppo.* IV. *Allegro molto*). The first movement begins with a passionate subject for unison strings, but the secondary theme is, by contrast, in a gentle mood. The second movement is a scherzo without trio, built from a perpetual-motion motto. This is followed by a slow movement in sonata form. An introduction presents a subject made up of a succession of fifths which sounds like tolling bells. This idea courses throughout the movement, sometimes as a background to a barcarolle-like melody first heard in the viola. A passionate finale is dominated by a long-phrased melody which Florent Schmitt once described as a "chorus of lost souls."

FRANCK. Franck's only string quartet, in D major, was one of his last compositions (1889); it was introduced in Paris on April 19, 1890 (I. *Poco lento;* Alle-

gro. II. Scherzo. III. Larghetto. IV. *Allegro molto*). The spine of the first movement is a contemplative melody; the development section includes an extended fugal section. The second movement is a light and infectious scherzo, which is followed by a noble slow movement in five sections. The finale begins with an introductory section in which earlier material is recalled. A variation of the first movement melody then brings on the main section in which a basic subject is derived from transitional material in the first movement. The coda once again revives most of the important themes from earlier movements. The quartet ends in a sublime mood with a final recollection of the spiritual slow movement.

HAYDN. Haydn's first string quartets are actually suites for four instruments, usually in four brief movements, two of them minuets. It took Haydn 17 years and 40 quartets before he helped establish a string-quartet form and a chamber-music style that laid the foundations upon which all later string-quartet writing would rest. This occurred with the six quartets op. 20 (1772), sometimes known as the "Sun Quartets" from the illustration on the title-page of an early edition. The fifth quartet, in F minor, is characteristic of the works in this group (I. *Allegro moderato.* II. *Menuetto.* III. *Adagio.* IV. *Fuga a due soggetti*). This work passes from the graceful serenity of the first movement and the whimsical and fanciful moods of the minuet to dramatic and at times tragic expression. The slow movement is more emotional than any previously encountered in Haydn's chamber music. The finale (a fugue with two subjects) has such tragic overtones that it carried for W. W. Cobbett a hint of the "dramatic impulses" generated in some of Beethoven's fugues.

Nine years later, Haydn wrote another set of six quartets, op. 33 These are known as the "Russian Quartets," because they are dedicated to the Grand Duke Paul of Russia. Haydn himself said that in these six works he was writing in "an entirely new manner." He was becoming more daring in his invention, more original in his technique, and more emotional in his expression. The second quartet, in E-flat major, and the third, in C major, are those most often performed. The Quartet in E-flat major is known as "The Joke," for its finale (Presto), in which Haydn tried to prove that women always talked during the performance of music by interpolating unexpected rests. The C major Quartet is identified as "The Bird," owing to the decorative grace notes on the main theme of the first movement (*Allegro moderato*) which gives the impression of chirping birds. Such an impression is once again carried out in the trio of the second-movement Scherzo, a duet between first and second violins. The slow movement (Adagio) is one of Haydn's most eloquent utterances, demonstrating how far he had progressed in the art of writing music rich with poetic overtones.

In 1781 Haydn became Mozart's friend. Personal contact with Mozart, and familiarity with the younger man's quartets (particularly those that Mozart dedicated to Haydn), had a profound effect on Haydn's creative development. Haydn, at the height of his powers, stood ready and willing to learn and profit from the genius of a man twenty-four years his junior. Through Mozart, Haydn arrived at greater flexibility of form, bolder techniques, profounder concepts, and increased individuality for each of the four instruments. The impact of Mozart on Haydn first becomes evident with the Quartet in D minor, op. 42 (1785). There followed a set of six quartets, op. 50 (1787), known as the "Prussian Quartets" because of their dedication to the King of Prussia. Here we find a new mastery of thematic development. Sir Donald Francis Tovey considered the third quartet, in E-flat major, one of Haydn's greatest creations (I. *Allegro con brio*. II. *Andante più tosto*. III. Allegretto. IV. Presto). This is a joyous work, all movements being in the major mode. In the first movement, special interest arises from the contrapuntal skill with which the first theme is amplified. The slow movement has a somewhat brisker pace and lighter spirit than most Haydn slow movements. What is unusual in the minuet is the fact that the same theme is used for both the minuet section and the trio.

The sixth quartet in this group, in D major, is known as "The Frog": in the finale (*Allegro con spirito*) the playing of the same notes alternately on neighboring strings produces a croaking effect.

In 1789 Haydn published three quartets, op. 54, and three more in op. 55 known as the "Tost Quartets" after the man to whom they were dedicated. Of special merit is the Quartet in F minor, op. 55, no. 2, "The Razor." Legend would have us believe that while shaving one day, Haydn exclaimed to a friend he would gladly give one of his quartets for a good razor. When the friend provided such a razor, he received this F minor Quartet in compensation. In this work Haydn reverses the usual order by utilizing a slow theme and variations as the first movement and a brisk Allegro as the second.

In 1790 came six more quartets, op. 64, the most famous of which is the fifth, in D major, "The Lark." The "lark" is found in the first movement, where the main melody rising in the first violin above an accompaniment of the other strings gives the impression of a lark's song.

Six quartets came between 1790 and 1793—three in op. 71, and three more in op. 74. They are dedicated to Count Apponyi and consequently are known as the "Apponyi Quartets." One of the interesting new features here is the addition of an introductory section to the first movements; another is the almost orchestral effect achieved in the writing for the four instruments.

The apex of the structure of Haydn's quartet music is the six works written in 1797 and 1798, op. 76. While all six quartets are masterworks of the first order, three deserve special attention because of the frequency with which they are performed. The second, in D minor, is especially notable for its integration. All four movements are in the same key and have a subtle thematic unity (I. Allegro. II. *Andante o più tosto allegretto*. III. *Menuetto*. IV. *Vivace assai*). This work derives its name of "Quinten" from the fact that the main theme of the first movement has intervals of fifths. This movement is dominated by a single subject. The slow movement is one of Haydn's most sublime pages. In the Minuet we find a canon, the two violins playing in octaves, echoed a bar later by the lower instruments also in octaves. The character of the music of this minuet movement has provided for it the nickname of "Hexen."

The third quartet, in C major, is the "Emperor," since the melody of the second movement (*Poco adagio cantabile*) is Haydn's own Austrian National Anthem, which he had written two years earlier. This melody is subjected to a series of variations. The slow movement is pleasing music, but Haydn's skill at architectonic construction is more evident in the first movement (Allegro), a spacious cathedral built from simple tones, a five-note motto with which the movement opens.

The fifth quartet, in D major, is sometimes designated as the "Largo Quartet" for its deservedly celebrated slow movement—radiant music, now pensive, now melancholy, and now of an otherworldly beauty.

Haydn's last two complete quartets, in G major and F major, op. 77, came in 1799. A quartet in B-flat major, op. 103 (1803), was never finished.

HINDEMITH. Hindemith's linear style was first crystallized in his String Quartet No. 3, op. 22 (1922), introduced in Baden-Baden, Germany, on Nov. 4, 1922 (I. Fugato. II. Quickly and Energetically. III. Calm and Flowing. IV. Lively). The first movement combines fugal writing with atonality. The ensuing Scherzo comes without a break and is characterized by its powerful momentum and irregular rhythms. The slow movement, the longest of the quartet, is singularly expressive. A brief fantasia-like section then leads without interruption into a spirited finale, in rondo form.

The String Quartet No. 5 in E-flat major (1943) is characteristic of the composer's later style. For one thing, Hindemith here specified a definite key, rarely found in his earlier compositions; for another, the thematic material, and its development, plays a more significant

role in this composition than contrapuntal procedures. This music reflects Hindemith's increasing bent for expressive lyricism and for greater simplicity and clarity of writing (I. Very Quiet and Expressive. II. Lively and Very Energetic. III. Quiet; Variations. IV. Broad and Energetic; *Allegretto grazioso*).

MENDELSSOHN. Mendelssohn's String Quartet in E-flat major, op. 12 (1829), is his first work in that form, and one of his best (I. Adagio; *Allegro non tardente*. II. Canzonetta. III. *Andante espressivo*. IV. *Molto allegro e vivace*). The first movement has a solemn seven-bar introduction; the main section presents two traditional themes of contrasting mood, the first passionate, the other serene and lyrical. Much of the popularity of this quartet is due to the delightful second movement, one of Mendelssohn's happy excursions into lyricism—light, graceful, infectious. The slow movement comes next, highlighted by a religious type of song. The vivacious finale then appears without interruption.

MILHAUD. Among the earlier string quartets of Darius Milhaud, the fourth is most characteristic of the composer's style at that time (1918). It was written during his residence in Rio de Janeiro (I. *Vif*. II. *Funèbre*. III. *Très animé*). The first movement has a pastoral character. The first subject is presented in two different tonalities, first separately, then together; a second subject appears after the development of the first, in the viola supported by the other instruments. The slow movement is in the style of a funeral march, and has a fugal exposition built on a new subject. The quartet ends with a joyous movement, whose first theme is given by both violins against a strong rhythm; the second subject is presented in two tonalities. After a dissonant climax, a third principal subject appears in the first violin and is repeated by the viola.

String Quartets Nos. 14 and 15 (1948-1949) are unusual in that they can be played separately as quartets, or combined into an octet. They were introduced in Oakland, Calif., on Aug. 10, 1949, by the Paganini Quartet, which presented them on the same program in both their quartet and octet versions. The two quartets are so designed as to be contrasts to each other. Thus the opening lively and highly accented subject of the 14th Quartet is juxtaposed with a flowing lyrical idea in the 15th. The slow movement has a sensitive melody in the 15th quartet while the 14th seems to serve as an accompaniment. In the finale, the syncopations of the 15th are set against the vigorous rhythmic music of the 14th. The three movements of both quartets are marked: I. *Animé;* II. *Modéré;* III. *Vif.*

MOZART. Mozart wrote his first string quartet—G major, K. 80 (1770)—when he was fourteen. Structurally it reveals the influence upon him of the Italian masters who preceded him, particularly G. B. Sammartini. This work is not a string quartet in the classic definition of the form, but more of a divertimento made up of four brief movements. This was followed by two sets of six string quartets, K. 155-160 (1772-1773), and K. 168-173 (1773). It is here that the string-quartet form becomes clarified for Mozart and where Mozart's indebtedness to Haydn is pronounced. For nine years after that Mozart took a vacation from the string quartet. When he returned to the form he was no longer the submissive follower of Haydn, but the leader to new worlds of artistic expression, achieving freedom of thought and style and a complete mastery of his technique. He made this return to quartet-writing with six works dedicated to Haydn, K. 387, 421, 428, 458, 464, 465 (1782-1785). So daring is Mozart's invention here, so unorthodox his techniques at times, so advanced his style, and so rich the working out of his materials that Haydn could only shake his head with bewilderment. He could not always understand the purpose of these innovations but he could tell Mozart's father: "I tell you before God and as an honest man—your son is the greatest composer I know, either personally or by name." The first of these quartets, in G major, is perhaps most remarkable for its finale (*Molto allegro*). Here we have two thematic groups. One consists of two fugue subjects, followed by a second group made up of two homophonic subjects. Thus Mozart sought for

and achieved a synthesis between the fugue and the sonata form. In the closing measures, the first fugue subject is juxtaposed against a homophonic accompaniment to create a harmonious unity between the homophonic and the fugal style. The skill of Mozart's contrapuntal writing also distinguishes the first movement (*Allegro vivace assai*), since each of the four instruments is permitted to achieve its own identity. The minuet, which is the second movement here, is interesting for its emotional, at times even tragic, trio section. The slow movement (*Andante cantabile*), introduced by a forceful open C in the cello, is in a sustained mood of quiet exaltation, the first principal melody appearing in the first violin.

There is even greater technical daring in the second of these "Haydn" quartets, in D minor. The first movement (Allegro) abounds with bold modulations and enharmonic changes—as, for example, in the transition from the exposition to the development section. The first subject is built on a descending scale; the second, on an ascending one. There is metric irregularity and a persistent rhythmic drive in the slow movement (Andante) which keeps it from plunging completely into desolation. The principal theme is heard at once; and it also brings the movement to its close. As had been the case with the first "Haydn" quartet, the Minuet movement has a tragic character, but here the tragedy is found more in the minuet section than in the trio; in the latter, Mozart makes what is for him an unusual use of pizzicato effects. The finale (*Allegro ma non troppo*) begins with a spirited *siciliano* melody, inspired by a theme previously used by Haydn in the finale of his Quartet, op. 33, no. 5. It proceeds with four variations on that theme, and ends with an agitated coda.

The third quartet, in E-flat, is perhaps most famous for its slow movement (*Andante con moto*), which makes extensive use of chromatic progressions in the major mode, and occasional excursions into dissonance for greater intensity of expression. The first movement (*Allegro ma non troppo*) opens with a placid subject in unison strings; the second theme has greater rhythmic vitality and helps inject a feeling of unrest into the movement. In the minuet, the courtly grace of the minuet proper is contrasted with a somewhat somber mood in the trio. The finale (*Allegro vivace*) is spirited, and though in the sonata form suggests a rondo.

The fourth quartet, in B-flat, has acquired the nickname of the "Hunt," owing to the opening subject of the first movement (*Allegro vivace assai*) where the violins suggest the call of a hunter's horn. The music of this entire movement has such vivacity and rhythmic robustness that it is not difficult to carry further this picture of a hunting scene. The minuet movement that follows is traditional. The slow movement after that (Adagio) is stately and deeply felt music, opening with gentle dignity and proceeding to a profoundly emotional second theme in the first violin against a pulsating background. The finale (*Allegro assai*) while in sonata form, has the character of a rondo. It opens with a folk-like tune in first violin and proceeds to a second principal theme, equally vivacious, and also found in the first violin.

A distinguishing feature of the fifth quartet, in A major, is the family relationship among the principal themes of all four movements. The first movement (Allegro) is in sonata form. The first theme, which resembles an Austrian waltz, appears in the first violin. The second subject is also Viennese in its grace and refinement. The Minuet that follows is of formal design; although it is the second movement in the original manuscript, nowadays it is sometimes played after the Andante. That slow movement consists of six variations on a stately melody. The finale (Allegro), while in sonata form, is based on a single main theme constructed upon a descending subject, and first heard in the first violin. This movement is so remarkable for its contrapuntal technique that Beethoven copied it out note for note.

The last of the "Haydn" quartets, in C major, has come to be known as the "Dissonance Quartet." In the opening of the first movement (Adagio; Allegro) there are false relations and chromatic progressions which veil the presence of a definite key. Such dissonances were so far ahead of the time that Haydn could only remark, when people complained about this passage, "If Mozart wrote it he must have a good reason to do so." But the key of C major asserts itself in the ensuing Allegro section. The slow movement (*Andante cantabile*) is romantic, one of those seemingly effortless and spontaneous flights of lyricism for which Mozart was incomparable. Nevertheless abrupt and at times subtle changes of meter endow even this movement with occasional surprise. The minuet movement is more earthy and vigorous than is usual; its trio is impassioned music. The finale (*Allegro molto*) maintains a consistent air of exuberance.

Four years after completing the six "Haydn" quartets, Mozart produced a set of three works, his last in the string-quartet form, K. 575, 589, 590 (1789-1790). They are dedicated to the King of Prussia, who commissioned them, and are consequently known as the "Prussian Quartets." Since the King was an amateur cellist, Mozart emphasized the cello in all three works; indeed, the first of them, in D major, gives such prominence to that instrument that it is now known as the "Cello Quartet." The other two quartets are in the keys of B-flat major and F major. The daring experiments and innovations of the "Haydn" quartets are not in evidence in these works. Here Mozart easily and spontaneously projects melodic and harmonic beauty, but without the emotional intensity and profound feeling we so often encounter in the six earlier quartets.

Mozart was the first major composer to write music for the combination of piano, violin, viola, and cello. He wrote two such works, both of surpassing excellence. The Quartet in G minor, K. 478 (1785), is one of his most dramatic works for a chamber-music ensemble, at times high-tensioned, at other times theatrical (I. Allegro. II. Andante. III. Rondo). In the first movement a vigorous subject for the four instruments has tragic overtones; a contrasting second subject, tinged with melancholy, is introduced by the piano and is subsequently treated canonically by the strings. In the development, the music receives dramatic treatment, achieving a climactic force in the coda. The lyrical second movement presents both melodic ideas in the piano; even here there is more than a passing suggestion of emotional disturbance. But the concluding rondo is, by contrast, an outburst of gaiety, marked by brilliant passage work for the piano.

The Piano Quartet in E-flat major, K. 493, came a year later (I. Allegro. II. Larghetto. III. Allegretto). The first movement is made up of three thematic groups, with the main subject of the movement found in the second group. It is this theme that receives extended attention in the development and the coda. The second movement is a Romanza in which piano and strings indulge in a gentle, lyrical conversation; a serene coda brings this movement to its conclusion. Healthy animal spirits abound in the finale, a rondo.

In writing quartets for unusual combinations of instruments, Mozart usually had some specific performer in mind. He wrote three flute quartets (flute, violin, viola, and cello) for Monsieur de Jean, a Dutch patron and amateur flute player who had commissioned them: D major, K. 285; G major, K. 285a; C major, K. 285b (1777-1778). Like the A major, K. 298, they are light and tuneful, and in all the flute assumes the function performed in the string quartet by the first violin. The Adagio movement of the D major quartet is particularly arresting for its sensitive lyrical beauty. The C major Quartet has only two movements. The A major Quartet has its main point of interest in the first movement (Andantino), in which a folk melody is subjected to four variations; in the finale, a rondo, Mozart uses a melody by Paisiello, *Che mi mostra*.

Much more original and compelling in its lyric beauty than any of the flute quartets is the Oboe Quartet in F major, K. 370 (1781), written for the oboist Friedrich Ramm. The first movement (Allegro) is consistently light-hearted, its principal jaunty themes assigned to the oboe. In the second movement (Adagio), dominated by a beautiful song for the oboe, there is an arresting cadenza for that instrument. The concluding rondo (*Allegro ma non troppo*) has some daring polyrhythmic writing with the oboe presenting melody and figurations in 4/4 time against a 6/8 background in the strings.

PROKOFIEV. Prokofiev's String Quartet No. 2 in F major, op. 92 (1942), was written during the early part of World War II. At the time the composer was vacationing in the East Caucasus, and the folk music of that area inspired this work and contributed to it some of its melodic and rhythmic material. (I. *Allegro sostenuto*. II. Adagio. III. Allegro). The main theme of the first movement has a Caucasian character; it is a headstrong subject which after an upward sweep descends to two sharply accented notes. The second theme is more lyrical, once again betraying the Caucasian influence. In the development, the first theme receives prominent treatment; the recapitulation is but an abbreviated presentation of the exposition. The second movement is dominated by a Caucasian love song played by the cello against oriental ornamentations in the other instruments. This song is touched with sadness, but after it has been fully presented, the music becomes gay; in the conclusion of the movement the melody returns divested of all sentimental feeling. The finale is vital with varying rhythms of Caucasian folk dances. However, the rhythmic momentum is arrested from time to time to allow for the interpolation of several affecting lyric passages. The rhythmic vigor of the opening section returns to end the quartet.

RAVEL. The Quartet in F major (1903) is Ravel's only string quartet, and the first of his major works that can be classed as an unqualified masterwork. It was introduced successfully in Paris on March 5, 1904 (I. *Allegro moderato*. II. *Assai vif*. III. *Très lent*. IV. *Vif et agité*). This music was strongly influenced by Debussy, who was so enchanted with it that he told the young composer: "Do not change one thing!" The first movement, in sonata form, is enhanced by decorative trills, tremolos, and pizzicato effects. A pizzicato section opens the scherzo movement that follows; midway there appears a broad lyrical passage. The slow movement, in which the Debussy influence is most in evidence, is rhapsodic in mood and melodious in style; on the other hand, the finale is passionate and turbulent.

SCHOENBERG. Of Schoenberg's four string quartets, the first (1905) is in the Romantic and at times Wagnerian style of his earliest works. In his second quartet (1908) he abandons tonality, and produces those astringent sounds, and assumes that precise and economical writing, which characterize all his music of this period. Here a female voice is interpolated in the last two movements. The third string quartet, op. 30 (1926), is one of his first important works in the twelve-tone technique (I. Moderato. II. Adagio. III. Intermezzo. IV. Rondo). In the first movement a rhythmic ostinato predominates, often as a background for the concise, energetic thematic material. The slow movement is in the form of a theme and variations. The lyric line of the third movement has austerity, while rhythmic energy is released in the finale. The Quartet No. 4, op. 37, came a decade later (1937). Two main themes are prominent in the first movement (*Allegro molto; Energico*). The first is virile, the second syncopated. The second movement (*Comodo*) resembles a Viennese laendler. This is followed by a Largo which opens with the four strings in unison as a preface to an exotic melody which sounds like the traditional Hebrew prayer, *Kol Nidrei*. The quartet ends with dynamic rhythmic drive (Allegro).

SCHUBERT. Two of Schubert's 15 string quartets are masterworks. The Quartet in A minor, op. 29 (1824), is the only one of his quartets published in his lifetime. Much of this music has an elegiac character (I. *Allegro ma non troppo*. II. Andante. III. Allegro. IV. *Allegro moderato*). The work opens with a sweet, sad song for the first violin, accompanied by a swaying figure in the second violin. The melancholy mood thus created is carried over in the second main theme. The development section concerns itself chiefly with the first theme. In the second movement, Schubert uses a melody of which he was so fond that he employed it in several other places (as an entr'acte in *Rosamunde,* and as a piano impromptu). One can understand this partiality. This is one of his most inspired lyric creations. The minuet opens with a single phrase in the low register of the cello, repeated by the other strings. This is the germ from which grows the somber principal minuet melody. The finale dispels all earlier gloom with a vivacious outburst of gay tunes and rhythms derived from Hungarian folk music.

The Quartet in D minor (1826) is subtitled *Death and the Maiden* (*Der Tod und das Maedchen*) because the composer's song of that name is used in the slow movement. A mood of tragedy pervades the whole work (I. Allegro. II. *Andante con moto*. III. *Allegro molto*. IV. Presto). The first movement opens with a dramatic subject often interpreted as a struggle with death; this struggle continues in the forceful first theme. The second theme, however, conveys a feeling of resignation. The second movement is a theme and variations. The theme is Schubert's song *Death and the Maiden,* from which the composer uses only the second half, in which Death speaks. After this melody is stated, five variations follow, several of them in a melancholy cast. The same elegiac mood persists in the scherzo that follows, especially in the trio section. And the feeling of despair is dramatized in the finale, which opens with a vertiginous tarantella subject and continues with a solemn melody for the four instruments; the latter recalls another Schubert song, *Erlkoenig,* whose subject is also a struggle with death.

Among Schubert's earlier quartets one of the most interesting is that in E-flat major, op. 125, no. 1 (1813). This work is so mature, and so far in advance of the style found in other youthful chamber-music works by Schubert, that for a long time the composition date of 1813 was doubted. The two middle movements (Adagio and Prestissimo) rank with Schubert's best works. The brief trio that precedes the slow movement has the peasant vigor of a laendler; and the slow movement sings of tranquil beauty. The first movement (*Allegro moderato*) has an abundance of lyricism, with three themes, all in the tonic, of equal importance. The finale (Allegro) is filled with the buoyant youthful spirit that is found in many early Schubert compositions.

Among other Schubert quartets often given is a one-movement work, the *Quartetsatz*, in C minor (1820). Since sketches were found for a second movement, it is apparent that the composer had intended the *Quartetsatz* to be the first movement of a complete quartet. This single movement has sufficient lyric interest to stand solidly on its own feet.

SCHUMANN. All three Schumann string quartets, op. 41, were completed within the space of a few weeks, in 1842: No. 1, A minor; No. 2, F major; No. 3, A major. The first of these is interesting for its free modulatory scheme. Though designated A minor, the key of F major appears in the first two movements (Allegro and Adagio); however the quartet ends in the key of A major. The slow movement is perhaps the most consistently inspired, alternating between deeply emotional melody and an agitated mood.

From certain points of view, the third quartet, which is the one heard most often, is the most impressive (I. *Andante espressivo; Allegro molto moderato.* II. *Assai agitato; Un poco adagio.* III. *Adagio molto.* IV. *Allegro molto vivace*). A unique structural characteristic of this work is that each of the four movements emphasizes certain intervals in the melodic line: in the first movement, fifths and fourths; in the second, fourths; in the third, sevenths; in the fourth, descending sixths. The first movement opens with an introspective introduction in which the falling fifth is prominent. This interval is the basis of the first main theme, appearing in the first violin. A subsidiary subject in common chords follows, and the main second subject, a lyrical thought, is then presented by the cello against soft staccato notes in the first violin. The second movement is in the style of a theme and variations, though the successive variations do not bear a strong resemblance to the main theme. The theme itself is of turbulent character, constructed from the interval of the fourth; it makes its initial appearance in the first violin.

The third movement opens with an ascending subject which soon develops into a haunting melody. This entire movement is melancholy, a feeling that is finally dissipated by the vigor of the finale. Here the first violin presents a strongly rhythmic theme. A new vital idea is then offered by the viola, and is soon taken over by the other instruments. Midway in the movement there is an extended episode, in gavotte rhythm, which the composer designated as "quasi trio" and which is highlighted by contrapuntal writing.

SHOSTAKOVICH. Shostakovich has written four string quartets, one of the most notable being the second, op. 69 (1943). It is unorthodox in material and structure (I. Overture. II. Recitative. III. Romance. IV. Waltz and Variations). In the first movement the use of a plagal cadence gives the first main theme an exotic character; the second principal melody appears high in the first violin against plucked strings. The second movement is contemplative, resembling a recitative by Bach. Passionate interludes break into the otherwise serene atmosphere of the Romance. The finale begins with a Russian waltz in the cello, and continues with several variations on this melody.

SMETANA. The autobiographical nature of Smetana's String Quartet No. 1 in E minor (1876) is evident not only in its subtitle, *From My Life* (*Aus meinem Leben*), but also in its detailed program prepared by the composer (I. *Allegro vivo appassionata.* II. *Allegro moderato à la polka.* III. *Largo sostenuto.* IV. Vivace). Two years before the completion of this work, the composer realized he was going deaf. This tragedy led him to review his past life and consider his future, a review and a consideration he finally put into this music. He goes on to explain that the first movement "depicts the love of art in my youth . . . and also a kind of warning of future misfortune." This movement opens with a forceful chord, followed by a descending melody for the viola which recurs throughout the quartet. The second theme is a tender melody suggesting the composer's youthful ardors. The second movement, the composer adds, recalls "the joyful dance of my youth when I composed dance music . . . and was known as a passionate lover of dancing." This movement is a polka, its main theme appearing after a few introductory bars. The third movement recollects "the bliss of a first love for the girl who afterward became my fathful wife." This is a love song touched with sadness. The finale describes "the discovery that I could treat the national element in music, and my joy in following this path until the catastrophe overwhelmed me, the beginning of my deafness." This part opens vivaciously, with both main themes of a Bohemian and Russian character. The terrifying prospect of deafness is suggested in the coda, where a high E in the first violin over a tremolo in the other strings simulates "the fatal whistling in my ear that . . . announced my deafness." Brief quotations of main ideas from earlier movements follow, before the movement comes to a solemn conclusion.

VILLA-LOBOS. Two of Villa-Lobos' string quartets are subtitled "Brazilian." The more popular is No. 6 in E minor, or the *Brazilian Quartet No. 2* (1938). The work has a national character (I. *Poco animato*. II. Allegretto. III. Andante. IV. *Allegro vivace*). The Brazilian color is found in the improvisational character of the thematic material of the first movement and its dynamic changes of tempo and mood. In the second movement the principal theme is of folksong character. There is subtle atmospheric painting in the third movement, intended as a picture of a Brazilian jungle. The fourth movement has the primitive rhythmic vigor found in much of Brazilian folk music.

Quartetto Italiano. A string quartet organized in 1945 in Reggio d'Emilia, Italy, under the name of "Nuovo Quartetto Italiano." Its members were: Paolo Borciani and his wife, Elisa Pegreffi, violins; Lionelle Forzanti, viola; and Franco Rossi, cello. In 1947 Perio Faruli succeeded Rossi as cellist. The ensemble has toured Europe, the Near East, the United States, and Canada, and has appeared at major festivals. An unusual feature is that it performs entirely from memory.

Quartetsatz. *See:* Quartet—*Schubert*.
Quasi. Italian for "like" or "as if." Beethoven designated his *Moonlight Sonata* as "Sonata quasi fantasia," to indicate that this work is like a fantasia.
Quatorze Juilliet, Le. *See:* Rolland, Romain.
Quattro Stagioni, Le. *See:* Concerto Grosso—*Vivaldi*.
Quatuor. French for quartet.
Quaver. An eighth note.
Queen, The. *See:* Symphony—*Haydn*.
Queen Elizabeth of Belgium International Music Competition (Concours international Eugène Ysaÿe). One of the most important competitions for performing artists of all nationalities, held annually each May in Brussels. Each year a different field of musical performance is emphasized. In 1959 the competition was restricted to violinists, in 1960 to pianists. Performers appear anonymously before a group of judges; the first prize is approximately $3,000. The competition was organized in 1937 by leading Belgian musicians headed by the Queen Mother Elizabeth to honor the late Eugène Ysaÿe. The first competition, for violinists, was won by David Oistrakh of the Soviet Union; the second, for pianists, was also won by a Soviet musician, Emil Gilels. Leon Fleisher, pianist, and Berl Senofsky, violinist, were the first Americans to win first prize in their respective categories.
Queen Elizabeth's Pavane. *See:* Bull, John.
Queen Mab Scherzo (Berlioz). *See: Romeo and Juliet* (1).
Queen's Hall. A leading concert auditorium in London, England, situated in Langham Place, Regent Street. It was opened on Dec. 2, 1893, with a concert conducted by Frederick H. Cowen. In 1895 the Queen's Hall Orchestra was founded in that auditorium for Promenade Concerts, and after that for regular concert series. The hall was modernized in 1937, and it was completely destroyed during a Nazi air raid on London on May 10-11, 1941.
Queen's Hall Orchestra. *See:* New Queen's Hall Orchestra.
Quinten Quartet. *See:* Quartet—*Haydn*.
Quintet. A composition for five instru-

ments. A popular combination is a string quartet and piano, first made significant by Schumann. There are, however, other quintet combinations. A string quintet usually comprises two violins, two violas, and a cello; sometimes there are two cellos and one viola with the two violins, a favorite combination with Boccherini. Another popular combination is string quartet and clarinet. Schubert's quintet, *The Trout (Die Forelle)*, is for the unusual grouping of violin, viola, cello, double bass, and piano. Quintets have also been written for various other instruments and strings as well as for various combinations of wind instruments.

The following are some of the best-known works in the quintet literature:

BAX. The Quintet for Oboe and Strings (1923) by Arnold Bax is a comparatively early work. It is in the Celtic style found in many of that composer's compositions (I. *Tempo molto moderato; Allegro moderato.* II. *Lento espressivo.* III. *Allegro giocoso*). Two main ideas are found in the first movement, the first for strings, the other for the oboe; the latter is ornamented and has an oriental character. The second movement is a song for violin in a Celtic style. Two lively themes, both heard first in the oboe, form the material for the finale.

BLOCH. More than thirty years separate Ernest Bloch's two piano quintets. The first (1923) remains the more popular of the two, and is one of the composer's masterworks (I. *Agitato.* II. *Andante mistico.* III. *Allegro energico*). The first movement opens with a robust theme for piano that sounds like the *Dies Irae;* it is set against a provocative quarter-tone accompaniment. This subject recurs throughout the composition. After a descending piano passage, the second subject appears in low strings. The first theme is then taken over by different instruments as the music grows now brusque, now plaintive, now passionate. The prevailing mood of the second movement is that of melancholy; a poignant melody is given to the strings against a strong rhythmic background. As this melody evolves, it becomes a kind of lamentation; a climax is finally reached with the violin in a high register against somber piano

chords. The finale is set into motion with a recall of the virile opening theme of the first movement. A turbulent mood follows, of an almost savage intensity; but it is finally arrested by a gentle song for the viola. And it is in that peaceful vein that the quintet finally ends.

BRAHMS. The Quintet in F minor, for piano and strings, op. 34 (1864), is a comparatively early work, and it is aflame with the ardor of early manhood. It took some time for this work to jell into its final form. Brahms planned it originally as a string quintet, then as a composition for two pianos. Finally he decided on the combination of a single piano and strings (I. *Allegro non troppo.* II. *Andante un poco adagio.* III. Allegro. IV. *Poco sostenuto*). The work abounds with thematic material. There are five main ideas in the first movement. The most important is the somewhat elegiac melody for piano and strings with which the movement opens, and the tender song for strings against decorative piano figures that follows. The beautiful second movement alternates reflective and sensual passages in the presentation of a folk-like melody. There are three major thoughts in the succeeding scherzo movement, sharply contrasted in rhythm and tonality. The finale is the longest and most complex movement, opening with an extended, expressive introduction which leads into the vivacious principal theme.

The Quintet in B minor, for clarinet and strings, op. 115 (1891), is the serene and introspective music of a man who seems to look back upon a rich and productive life, is quietly satisfied with what he has accomplished, and is resigned to the fact that the end must soon be near (I. Allegro. II. Adagio. III. Andantino. IV. *Con moto*). Resignation, but with a touch of sadness, appears in the main theme with which the first movement opens, a gentle melody for clarinet and strings. The entire movement has the same kind of autumnal mellowness. So has the slow movement, the basis of which is a song for clarinet against tremolo strings. While there is some vivacity in the scherzo, the feeling is restrained, and dabbed with soft colors. The finale presents a spacious melody which is subjected to a series of variations.

Brahms' two string quintets are opposites in mood and feeling. The first—F major, op. 88 (1882)—is gentle and tender, filled with the verdant freshness of springtime. The second—G major, op. 111 (1890)—is emotionally overwrought and fiery in spirit. The first is structurally interesting in that the second movement (*Grave ed appassionato*) is a merger of a slow movement and a scherzo; its main subject was derived from an earlier work by Brahms. The concluding movement merges the sonata and fugue forms. The high points of the second quintet are the bucolic Romance movement and the vitally cogent finale.

DVOŘÁK. The Quintet in A major, for piano and strings, op. 81 (1887), is one of the composer's most popular chamber-music works. It was written before his prolonged visit to the United States. In the richness of its tone colors, vitality of its rhythms, and rapidly changing moods, it is Slavic to its very marrow. Folk-dance rhythms predominate in the last two movements. The most interesting movement is the slow one—an elegy (*dumka*) for viola in the lower register with a counter melody high in the piano; the plangent mood is shattered by the eruption of a passionate folk dance.

The Quintet in E-flat major for strings, op. 97 (1893), was written during the composer's stay in the United States. While visiting Spillville, Iowa, he became acquainted with the music of the American Indian, an experience that proved so impressive that he wrote several major works employing that idiom, including this quintet. The composer did not actually quote American-Indian material but fashioned his own music after the style of Indian melodies and rhythms, developing them with the fullest resources of European harmony, counterpoint, and tonal colors. In the first two movements the beating of an Indian drum provides a provocative background. The Larghetto movement is a plangent Indian melody in the viola, followed by five variations. The concluding Rondo is gay music opening vigorously with a strongly accented subject; two subsidiary ideas have a pronounced American character.

FAURÉ. The Piano Quintet No. 2 in C minor, op. 115 (1921), by Gabriel Fauré opens (*Allegro moderato*) with a single bar for the piano. The viola then suggests the first theme, which finally becomes fully realized when the other instruments have entered. The second theme is energetic, consisting of rhythmic chords. The second movement is a vivacious scherzo (*Allegro moderato*). In the slow movement (*Andante moderato*) the music is melancholy, as the strings bring up at first a plangent four-bar subject. After a tender dialogue between violin and piano, the piano introduces a funereal melody. Agitation and rhythmic strength characterize the finale (*Allegro molto*).

FRANCK. The Piano Quintet in F minor (1878) marked Franck's return to chamber music after an absence of 35 years. It is in three movements, the usual scherzo being omitted (I. *Molto moderato quasi lento;* Allegro. II. *Lento con molto sentimento.* III. *Allegro non troppo ma con fuoco*). All three movements are in sonata form, and the first and third movements have an introduction and coda. A single theme appears and returns throughout the work, a Lento passage first heard as the second theme of the first movement.

MOZART. The Clarinet Quintet in A major, K. 581 (1789)—like Mozart's Clarinet Concerto—was written for the clarinetist Anton Stadler. In the quintet the clarinet is not used as a solo instrument but becomes the equal partner of the other instruments in projecting music often of elegiac character for which the poignant voice of the clarinet is so singularly appropriate (I. Allegro. II. Larghetto. III. Menuetto. IV. *Allegretto con variazioni*). The role of the clarinet in the first movement is mainly to provide decoration for the main melodies; in fact, the clarinet does not assume a principal theme until the 49th bar. The first main subject is at once given by the strings, the clarinet entering in the sixth bar with figurations. The second theme appears in the first violin against a formal accompaniment of chords and plucked strings in the basses. It is repeated, in the minor, by the clarinet. In the coda, the first main theme reappears in the strings. In the slow movement, the clarinet takes a dominant role, unfolding a tender song against an accompaniment of muted strings. There are two trios in the third-movement minuet. The first is presented by strings alone, and the second features an infectious waltz tune for the clarinet. In the finale, a simple melody is stated by the clarinet, and then undergoes a series of variations; the fifth of these, shared by violin and clarinet, temporarily transforms a formerly light-hearted mood into one charged with intense feeling. The light character is restored with the sixth variation which, in turn, leads to the coda.

Mozart wrote five quintets for strings. One of the most celebrated is that in G minor, K. 516 (1787). This is a work filled with tragic content, music which to W. W. Cobbett is filled "with the resignation of despair and a struggle with destiny" (I. Allegro. II. Menuetto. III. *Adagio ma non troppo.* IV. Adagio; Allegro). This emotional intensity is found not only in the two principal melodies of the first movement, but even in the Minuet. But it is in the third movement that the note of tragedy is sounded most eloquently, music of such profound emotional impact that it led Henri Ghéon to say it reached "a height not surpassed by Beethoven himself until his second period." The finale opens with similar gravity, but in the Allegro the gloom is dispelled and Mozart is finally able to voice a vigorous optimism.

The Quintet in E-flat major, K. 614, is the composer's last chamber-music work for strings, completed in the year of his death (1791). This, in contrast to the G minor String Quintet, reveals a lighter facet of Mozart's creative personality, and comprises music that is consistently graceful and charming (I. *Allegro di molto.* II. Andante. III. Menuetto. IV. Allegro). The first movement highlights a hunting theme. The second movement is a romanza type of song. The minuet has some of the vigor and abandon of an Austrian peasant dance, especially in the trio; and the finale is an irrepressible outpouring of jovial feelings.

SCHUBERT. The Quintet in A major, op. 114 (1819), is one of the first piano quintets ever written, but it is not for a traditional combination. The instruments here called for are a piano, violin, viola, cello, and double bass. This work is entitled *The Trout (Die Forelle)* because the fourth movement quotes Schubert's song of that name. Schubert wrote this quintet during one of the rare happy periods in his life, a walking trip in Upper Austria which brought him to the hospitable household of Sylvester Paumgartner in Steyr. The host suggested that he write a chamber-music work based on the song, *The Trout,* and Schubert graciously complied by sitting down and writing out the string parts of a new work; when this composition was introduced in Paumgartner's house, Schubert played the piano part from memory. The quintet is filled with so many joyous melodies, and overflows with so ebullient a spirit, that it is easy to find here a reflection of the composer's inner joy when he wrote it. One graceful melody follows another in a seemingly inexhaustible abundance; it is the melodies themselves, rather than any development or variation, that provide the principal interest. The work is in five, instead of the usual four, movements (I. *Allegro vivace.* II. Andante. III. Presto. IV. Andantino. V. *Allegro giusto*). The first movement brims over with infectious tunes, while the lyricism of the second movement has a touch of wistfulness. The third and fifth movements are in the style of Austrian or Hungarian peasant dances. The fourth movement is where *The Trout* will be found, treated to six variations.

The String Quintet in C major, op. 163 (1828), is one of Schubert's most deeply personal and tragic compositions. It came in the last year of his life, and actually was his last chamber-music work; it seems to carry a presentiment of his imminent death. Like Boccherini, Schubert here adds a second cello to a string quartet, instead of the usual second viola. There are four movements: I. *Allegro ma non troppo;* II. Adagio. III. Scherzo; IV. Allegretto. In the first movement the expression of the tragic can be found in the second theme, an elegy first presented by the two cellos, then repeated with greater intensity by the higher strings. Tragedy dominates the entire second movement, with a sorrowful song for the three middle voices, punctuated by pizzicati in the second cello, and a sad commentary by the first violin. The music grows increasingly poignant as the first violin and cello introduce a new grief-stricken melody against a tormented accompaniment. Momentarily this despair is relieved with the first part of the scherzo, melodically resembling a hunting call; but in the trio we are again plunged into the depths of despondency. The finale, however, represents a victory over despair and frustration with music enlivened by Hungarian dance rhythms and folk melodies.

SCHUMANN. The Quintet in E-flat major, op. 44 (1842), is the first important work written for the combination of piano and string quartet; and to this day it is one of the most popular piano quintets ever written (I. *Allegro brillante.* II. *Un poco largamente.* III. *Molto vivace.* IV. *Allegro ma non troppo*). The first movement opens vigorously with a sharply accented subject. This is soon succeeded by a tender melody. The second principal subject is an eloquent dialogue for cello and viola. The second movement suggests a march of funereal character; the theme is first heard in the first violin after a three-bar introduction by the piano. The second theme in the violin maintains this elegiac character, and is emotionally heightened by the stormy passage that follows. The main melody of the scherzo is an ascending scale passage. In this movement there are two trios, the ascending scherzo theme repeated after each. The forceful idea with which the finale opens dominates the entire movement. The movement ends with a fugue based on the main subjects of the first and fourth movements.

SHOSTAKOVICH. The Piano Quintet, op. 57 (1940), earned the Stalin Prize for its composer following its successful première in Moscow on Nov. 23, 1940 (I. Prelude and Fugue. II. Scherzo. III. Intermezzo). The opening prelude has three sections, but the principal thematic material is found in the first part, a Lento. The fugue subject is derived from one of these themes. This first movement combines classic stateliness of structure with modern harmonic idioms. The second movement has satiric overtones both melodically and rhythmically. The last movement has been designated as "ballet music with a march rhythm"; one of its melodies was borrowed by the composer —it is traditionally heard at Russian circuses to herald the arrival of the clowns.

Quintuple time. A measure of five beats with main accent on the first and third or fourth beats, depending on the division of the five notes into two plus three, or three plus two.

Quintuplet (or **Quintole**). A group of five notes to be played in the same time as four ordinary notes of the same value.

Quodlibet. A form of composition popular in the 16th and early 17th centuries, a kind of musical joke in which two or more well-known songs, often incongruous to each other either in their text or musical content, formed the basis of a polyphonic piece. The practice of singing quodlibets was popular at the Bach family gatherings. J. S. Bach included a quodlibet at the conclusion of his *Goldberg Variations.* Karl Reinecke revived the idea in the first variation of his Variations for Two Pianos, which combines a gavotte by Gluck with a musette from an *English Suite* by Bach.

R

Rabaud, Henri, composer and conductor. Born Paris, France, Nov. 10, 1873; died there, Sept. 11, 1949. He attended the Paris Conservatory, winning the Prix de Rome in 1894. He then founded and directed orchestras in Rome and Vienna devoted to the performance of French music. In 1908 he was appointed conductor at the Paris Opéra and Opéra-Comique, and from 1914 to 1918 was the musical director of the Opéra. In 1918 he succeeded Karl Muck as principal conductor of the Boston Symphony. After a single season there he returned to Paris and from 1922 to 1941 was director of the Paris Conservatory. He also directed performances at the Opéra and Opéra-Comique.

Rabaud completed his first major work, the First Symphony, in 1895; four years later he scored his first success with the orchestral tone poem, *La Procession nocturne.* His orchestral music after that was distinguished for elegance of style, refinement, good taste, and at times wit. It includes 2 symphonies, a cello concertino, *Allegro de concert* for violin and orchestra, *Eglogue, Divertissement sur des airs russes,* and incidental music to *The Merchant of Venice.* He is most famous for his comic opera, *Marouf.*

See: *Procession nocturne, La.*

Rabin, Michael, violinist. Born New York City, May 2, 1936. He received his first lessons from his father, a member of the New York Philharmonic, and continued his studies with Ivan Galamian. His début took place in New York in 1950. In 1952-1953 he made his first tour of Australia and New Zealand, in 1954-1955 of Europe, and in the summer of 1956, of Israel.

Rachmaninoff, Sergei, composer, pianist, and conductor. Born Oneg, Russia, April 1, 1873; died Beverly Hills, Calif., March 28, 1943. Though he revealed extraordinary talent for music from earliest childhood, he was an indolent student at the St. Petersburg Conservatory, which he entered in 1882. At the advice of his cousin, Alexander Siloti, Rachmaninoff was brought to Moscow in 1885. At the Moscow Conservatory he came under the influence of Nikolai Zverev, a severe taskmaster, who proved successful in disciplining the boy to systematic study and inflaming his passion for music. Rachmaninoff was graduated from the Moscow Conservatory as a pianist in 1891, and as a composer in 1892. While still a Conservatory student he wrote and published a set of five pieces for piano, op. 3, one of which was the Prelude in C-sharp minor, whose success was immediate, worldwide, and permanent. Upon graduating from the Conservatory he received a gold medal for his opera, *Aleko,* produced at Moscow in 1893. Despite such auspicious beginnings as a composer, Rachmaninoff's career did not progress smoothly. His First Symphony, introduced in 1897, was a fiasco, mainly owing to a miserable performance. This failure had a shattering impact on the young composer, who suffered a nervous breakdown, and after that depression and a stultifying inertia. But following some therapeutic treatment through autosuggestion, Rachmaninoff returned to composition. His Second Piano Concerto was a triumph when introduced in Moscow on Oct. 27, 1901; to this day it is one of his most celebrated works and a perennial favorite in the concerto literature.

Success revived in him the will to live and work; also the energy to function productively in several directions. He became conductor of opera at the Bolshoi Theater. He advanced his career as a concert pianist. In both endeavors he was surpassingly successful; in the first years of the new century he was one of the most celebrated musicians in Moscow. But composition, which he never abandoned, was his first love. Feeling that his busy musical and social schedule was depriving him of the time and relaxation he needed for creative work, Rachmaninoff resigned his conducting post in 1906, left Moscow, and settled in Dresden. He soon produced two major works for orchestra, the Second Symphony, and the tone poem, *The Isle of the Dead*.

In 1909 Rachmaninoff made his first tour of the United States as concert pianist. His début took place in Northampton, Mass., on Nov. 4, 1909. A few weeks later he appeared in New York as soloist with the New York Symphony in the world première of his Third Piano Concerto. After that he toured the country as both pianist and conductor.

From 1910 to 1917 Rachmaninoff lived in Moscow, where for two years he conducted the Philharmonic. On two occasions he was offered the principal conducting post of the Boston Symphony, and both times he declined. In 1918 he returned to the United States a second time, now to establish a permanent winter home there. (Summers were spent near Paris, and after 1932, in Lucerne, Switzerland.) Unsympathetic to the new regime in Russia he never again saw his native land. During winters he embarked on concert tours of the world, everywhere recognized as an aristocratic pianist who combined a masterful technique with profound musicianship. Occasionally he also appeared as a conductor, usually in his own works. Summers were generally dedicated to composition.

The 30th anniversary of his American début was celebrated at Philadelphia in 1939 with a cycle of three concerts by the Philadelphia Orchestra in which Rachmaninoff appeared in the triple role of pianist, conductor, and composer. This event was also commemorated with a concert at Carnegie Hall.

He was embarking on a tour of the United States as pianist, planned as his farewell to the concert stage, when he was stricken with his last, fatal illness in New Orleans. Brought back to his home in Beverly Hills, where he had been residing for several years, he died less than two months after his farewell tour had begun. A few weeks before he died he had become an American citizen.

Rachmaninoff was one of the preeminent musicians of the 20th century, both as a musical creator and as an interpreter. In his compositions he was a conservative, a traditionalist who wore Tchaikovsky's mantle. His music was Russian to its very core in the way Tchaikovsky's music was Russian, not because he aspired towards a nationalist expression or used folk idioms, but because he was a Russian, and everything he wrote was colored by his own background and temperament. It is perhaps due to the intrinsically Russian character of his music that it remained a favorite in the concert halls of the Soviet Union even though its composer was regarded as a political renegade.

Rachmaninoff preferred to produce an art in which he could voice his inmost feelings and subtlest moods. For this purpose, the structures and techniques of the past were completely serviceable. If he did not discover any new worlds of sound, he did succeed in bringing to the old world of music a wealth of beauty, sentiment, nostalgia, and at times melancholy.

The following are Rachmaninoff's principal instrumental compositions:

Chamber Music: Trio élégiaque; cello sonata; Six Pieces, for violin and piano; Two Pieces, for cello and piano.

Orchestra: 2 symphonies; 4 piano concertos; *The Rock; Caprice bohémien; The Isle of the Dead; Rhapsody on a Theme by Paganini,* for piano and orchestra; *Symphonic Dances.*

Piano: 2 sonatas; 2 suites; Variations on a Theme by Chopin; Variations on a Theme by Corelli; *Moments musicaux;* preludes; *études-tableaux;* duets.

See: Concerto—*Rachmaninoff; Études-Tableaux; Isle of the Dead; Moment musical;* Prelude—*Rachmaninoff; Rhapsody on a Theme by Paganini; Symphonic Dances;* Symphony—*Rachmaninoff;* Variations on a Theme by Chopin; Variations on a Theme by Corelli.

Racine, Jean Baptiste, poet and dramatist.

Born La Ferté-Milon, France, December 1639; died Paris, France, April 26, 1699. The following tragedies by Racine were the source of orchestral compositions:

Andromaque: Incidental music by Saint-Saëns.

Athalie: Incidental music by Mendelssohn, Jean Baptiste Moreau, and Johann Christian Schulz.

Britannicus: Incidental music by André Jolivet.

Esther: Incidental music by Jean Baptiste Moreau.

Iphigenia in Aulis: overture to the opera of the same name by Gluck.

Phèdre: Georges Auric (symphonic suite); Martin Lunssens (tone poem). Also incidental music by Massenet.

Raeuber, Die. *See:* Schiller, Friedrich von.

Raff, Joachim, composer. Born Lachen, Switzerland, May 27, 1822; died Frankfort, Germany, June 25, 1882. As a schoolteacher he received encouragement from Liszt and Mendelssohn which persuaded him to begin formal music study seriously. This took place with Hans von Buelow, and after that with Liszt. From 1850 to 1856 he was Liszt's secretary in Weimar. Raff's popularity as a composer began in 1858 with an overture, *Bernhard von Weimar;* in 1863 his first symphony, *An das Vaterland,* won first prize in a Vienna competition. His reputation continued to grow from that time on until he became one of Germany's most popular and widely performed composers in the last half of the 19th century. He was highly prolific, producing over 230 compositions. He had a pleasing lyric gift and a flair for projecting ingratiating moods. But he lacked originality or depth, and his works have lost interest for present-day concert audiences. When his best symphonies—No. 3, *Im Walde,* and No. 4, *Lenore*—are revived they prove hardly more than dated museum pieces. Ironically, Raff survives almost exclusively because of a slight piece for violin and piano, the Cavatina, op. 85, no. 3. Raff's major works include 11 symphonies, 3 orchestral suites, 5 overtures, various concertos, 8 string quartets, 4 piano trios, 5 violin sonatas among other chamber-music works, a piano sonata, 6 piano suites, 4 piano fantasies, and smaller pieces for the piano, including capriccios, scherzos, rhapsodies, and waltzes.

From 1877 until his death Raff was the director of Hoch's Conservatory in Frankfort.

Ragtime. An idiom in American popular music (jazz). It is syncopated piano music of Negro origin, characterized by a steady rhythm in the bass, in 2/4 or 4/4 time, with marked syncopations in the treble. Ragtime has been used with serious intent by several composers: John Alden Carpenter in *Adventures in a Perambulator,* for orchestra, in which he quotes Irving Berlin's *Alexander's Ragtime Band;* Darius Milhaud in *Rag* and *Caprices,* for piano and orchestra; Stravinsky in *Ragtime,* for piano; and in various symphonic jazz compositions by Robert Russell Bennett, George Gershwin, Morton Gould, and others (*see:* Jazz).

Raindrop Prelude. *See:* Prelude—*Chopin.*

Rakóczy March (Berlioz). (1) *See: Damnation of Faust, The.*

(2) *See: Hungarian Rhapsodies* (Liszt).

Rallentando. Getting slower.

Rameau, Jean-Philippe, composer and theoretician. Born Dijon, France, Sept. 25, 1683; died Paris, France, Sept. 12, 1764. The son of a church organist, Rameau was early taught the organ, harpsichord, and violin. In 1701 he traveled through northern Italy, earning his living as organist and violinist. After returning to France, he served as organist in Avignon and Clermont-Ferrand. During this period he began writing music for the harpsichord. About 1705 he settled in Paris, where he studied the organ with Louis Marchand and devoured every book he could find on theory. In 1706 he published his first book of *Pièces de clavecin,* pieces for the harpsichord. He first became prominent as a musical theoretician in 1722 with his monumental *Traité de l'harmonie,* even today a work of great value. Four years after that, he published a second volume, *Nouveau système de musique théorique.* He was one of the first theoreticians to evolve a system of building chords by thirds; to establish the law of inversion of chords; and to promote the principle of chord progression by a fundamental bass. Thus he can be said to have been the creator of the modern science of harmony.

In 1730 he came to the attention of the powerful patron, Riche de la Pouplinière, and became conductor of La Pouplinière's private orchestra and his organist. He was also writing works for the stage; his first opera to be performed was *Hippolyte et Aricie,* in 1733. Though he was a controversial figure in that field owing to his emphasis on harmony and orchestration rather than pleasing melodies, and on dramatic rather than lyrical interest—and though he became the center of a violent musical struggle in Paris in 1752 known as the "guerre des bouffons"—he was recognized as one of France's supreme composers for the theater; and he lived to see the full vindication of his provocative theories about the music drama.

His principal achievement in instrumental music was several volumes of pieces for the harpsichord: *Pièces de clavecin, Nouvelle suite de pièces de clavecin,* and transcriptions of five of his own pieces, *Pièces en concert.* Historically, the harpsichord music of Rameau represents the transition from the Baroque style of his day to the *galant* style that followed him.

Rameau also wrote *Pièces de clavecin en concert* for harpsichord, violin (or flute), and viol (or second violin). Here Rameau brought to the writing of chamber music a new enrichment of harmonic writing, a new independence to the harpsichord within a chamber-music format, and a fresh melodic gift.

Werner Egk's *Franzoesische Suite* for orchestra is based on pieces by Rameau.

See: Pièces de clavecin (and *Nouvelle Suite de Pièces de clavecin*); *Tambourin.*

Range. The compass between the lowest and highest notes of a melody or instrument or voice.

Rangström, Ture, composer. Born Stockholm, Sweden, Nov. 30, 1884; died there, May 11, 1947. One of Sweden's foremost 20th-century composers, Rangström studied music in Stockholm, and with Hans Pfitzner in Munich. He then began writing music criticisms for the Swedish papers. He also became active as a conductor. From 1922 to 1925 he led

the Göteborg Symphony. After 1931 he served as stage director for the Stockholm Opera. Though he first attracted attention as a composer with works in an Impressionist style, he achieved fame and maturity with music in which a Swedish character was prominent. His most celebrated work is the Symphony No. 2, *My Country,* written in 1919. He produced 3 other symphonies, together with numerous orchestral suites, overtures, and tone poems; among the last were *Dithyramb, Ode to Autumn, The Sea Sings,* and *Sotto Voce.* He also wrote a Partita for violin and orchestra, a Ballade for piano and orchestra, and incidental music to various plays. His chamber music includes a string quartet and several suites for violin and piano.

Rappel des oiseaux, Le (Rameau). *See: Pièces de clavecin* (and *Nouvelle Suite de Pièces de clavecin*).

Rapsodie espagnole (Ravel). *See: Spanish Rhapsody.*

Rapsodie nègre. *See:* Powell, John.

Rasoumovsky Quartets. *See:* Quartet—Beethoven.

Ravel, Maurice, composer. Born Ciboure, France, March 7, 1875; died Paris, France, Dec. 28, 1937. After studying music privately in Paris with Henry Ghys and Charles-René, he entered the Conservatory in 1889, remaining there 15 years. He was a brilliant student, even though he often shocked his teachers with his unorthodox musical procedures and his excursions into forbidden areas of harmony and tonality. While still attending the Conservatory he demonstrated his creative gifts. A *Menuet antique* for piano was his first published work; *Les Sites auriculaires,* for two pianos, was the first of his compositions to get performed publicly, in Paris on March 5, 1898. By 1901 he had written such celebrated pieces for the piano as *Pavane pour une Infante défunte* and *Jeux d'eau* (both successfully introduced in Paris in 1902); and by 1904 he had completed his remarkable String Quartet in F major, highly acclaimed when introduced at Paris in 1904.

Many eminent Parisian musicians now regarded him as an important composer, and were shocked at his failure to win the Prix de Rome in four attempts. A heated controversy ensued that split musical Paris into two hostile camps; as a result of this bitterness, Théodore Dubois had to resign his post as director of the Paris Conservatory. Hardly had this storm subsided when Ravel again found himself a storm center in 1907. Following a performance of his *Histoires naturelles* in that year, several critics denounced him for plagiarizing Debussy, pointing to Ravel's Impressionism, his partiality for exotic modes and scales, and even his selection of titles for his compositions. Other critics defended Ravel, insisting that similarities between Debussy and the younger man were only skin-deep, that Ravel had a distinct style and personality of his own.

Seemingly oblivious of the stir he was creating, Ravel continued producing major works, of such creative power and originality that even many of his severest critics were silenced and finally recruited into the camp of his admirers. Among these works were the *Spanish Rhapsody* (*Rapsodie espagnole*) and *Mother Goose Suite* (*Ma Mère l'oye*) both for orchestra; *Miroirs, Gaspard de la nuit,* and *Valses nobles et sentimentales,* for piano; and most important of all, the ballet *Daphnis and Chloe,* produced with outstanding success in Paris by the Ballet Russe in 1912.

During World War I Ravel drove an ambulance at the front. After the war he withdrew to a villa in Montfort l'Amaury, his home for the rest of his life. He continued producing important works, thus solidifying his position as one of France's leading composers of the 20th century. One of these compositions, *Bolero,* became one of the most popular orchestral pieces of the post-war period, a sensation wherever it was introduced.

Ravel visited the United States for the first time for a concert tour in 1928; his début took place in Boston on January 12 with the Boston Symphony. About four years after returning to France from this tour, he was a victim of an auto accident in Paris which affected his nervous system and eventually brought on partial paralysis. An operation on

Dec. 19, 1937, proved fatal, and Ravel died in the hospital.

During his apprenticeship as a composer, Ravel was profoundly influenced by Erik Satie and Debussy. Satie encouraged him in his first innovations and experiments, and fostered his partiality for irony and wit. Debussy brought Ravel to musical Impressionism. In the early 1900's Ravel helped create a new school of French music called the "Société des apaches," which proclaimed the gospel of Impressionism, continual experiment, and tolerance towards all creative styles. But as he grew in artistic maturity and acquired increasing technical assurance, Ravel achieved an identity of his own. His style, while still clearly Impressionistic, was disciplined by classical restraint, strengthened by a virile imagination, and spiced with an engaging wit.

Impressionism and wit were not the only veins he tapped successfully. He also wrote many works strongly influenced by Spanish folksong and dance, culture and geography, including a delightful comic opera, *L'Heure espagnole.* His works include several exploring the world of fantasy, and others exploiting the waltz. To whatever style or manner he addressed himself he brought a consummate technique, an aristocratic taste, and an inexhaustible imagination.

Besides his own compositions, Ravel was responsible for a brilliant transcription for orchestra of Mussorgsky's *Pictures at an Exhibition,* a favorite at symphony concerts.

The following are Ravel's principal instrumental works:

Chamber Music: String quartet; piano trio; violin sonata; *Introduction and Allegro* (for harp, string quartet, flute, and clarinet); *Tzigane,* for violin and piano (or orchestra).

Orchestra: Spanish Rhapsody (*Rapsodie espagnole*); *Daphnis and Chloe,* two ballet suites; *Alborada del gracioso; Mother Goose Suite* (*Ma Mère l'oye*); *La Valse; Bolero;* piano concerto; concerto for piano left-hand.

Piano: Pavane pour une Infante défunte; Jeux d'eau; Miroirs; Gaspard de la nuit; Valses nobles et sentimentales;

Le Tombeau de Couperin (also for orchestra); Sonatine.

See: Bolero; Concerto—*Ravel; Daphnis and Chloe; Gaspard de la nuit;* Habanera; *Introduction and Allegro* (2); *Jeux d'eau; Miroirs; Mother Goose Suite; Pavane pour une Infante défunte;* Quartet—*Ravel;* Sonatina; *Spanish Rhapsody; Tombeau de Couperin;* Trio—*Ravel; Tzigane; Valse, La; Valses nobles et sentimentales.*

Raven, The. *See:* Poe, Edgar Allan.

Ravinia Festival. A summer festival organized in 1936 at Ravinia Park, Ill., with a five-week season by the Chicago Symphony led by six conductors. For the first few seasons performances of orchestral music were supplemented by the interpolation of special feature nights and the appearance of eminent soloists. In 1940 chamber-music concerts were introduced, and in 1950 a new auditorium was constructed. Since then the program has been expanded to include orchestral, children's, chamber-music, and twilight concerts, together with performances of opera and ballet, jazz evenings, and presentations of dramatic readings and motion pictures. American music has often been emphasized, with Chicago composers commissioned to write new works, and other outstanding Americans asked to lead programs of their own works. In 1957 the season was extended from seven to nine weeks.

Rawsthorne, Alan, composer. Born Haslingden, England, May 2, 1905. Serious music study did not begin until he was twenty. From 1926 to 1930 he attended the Royal Manchester College of Music, after which he studied piano privately with Egon Petri. After serving on the music faculty of Darlington Hall, in South Devon, he settled in London in 1932 to devote himself to composition. A few years later he made an excellent impression with Theme and Variations, for two violins, introduced at the International Society for Contemporary Music Festival in London. These modern music festivals subsequently introduced other major works by Rawsthorne, including the *Symphonic Studies* in 1939, *Cortèges* in 1946, and the Concerto for String Orchestra in 1950 After World War II,

Rawsthorne's Symphony and Second Piano Concerto showed his style in its full maturity. Rawsthorne is essentially a Baroque composer whose stylistic roots are found in the soil of Bach and Corelli. Partial as he is to such old forms as the concerto grosso, toccata, variation, and fugue, to contrapuntal writing, and to the style of 18th-century dances, he is nevertheless also a modernist whose music is marked by an astringent lyricism and freedom of tonality. Besides compositions already mentioned, his orchestral works include 2 violin concertos, *Street Corner Overture,* an oboe concerto, and a *Concertante pastorale* for flute, horn, and strings. He also wrote a clarinet quintet, cello sonata, piano sonatina, and various smaller pieces for piano.

Razor Quartet. *See:* Quartet—*Haydn.*

Read, Gardner, composer. Born Evanston, Ill., Jan. 2, 1913. From 1932 to 1936 he attended the Eastman School of Music on a scholarship, a student of Howard Hanson, Bernard Rogers, and Paul White. In 1937 his first symphony won first prize in a contest sponsored by the New York Philharmonic, which introduced it on November 4. The Cromwell Fellowship in 1938 enabled him to travel for two years in Europe, Scandinavia, and the Near East, and to study with Pizzetti in Rome and Sibelius in Finland. Further study took place in 1941 with Aaron Copland at the Berkshire Music Centre at Tanglewood. After that he held teaching posts at the St. Louis Institute of Music, Kansas City Conservatory, and Cleveland Institute of Music. Since 1948 he has been composer-in-residence at the Boston University College of Music. In 1957 a grant from the United States State Department enabled him to tour Mexico as a lecturer and conductor.

Read has written over a hundred instrumental compositions, including 4 symphonies, a viola concerto, various tone poems (including *Night Flight, Pan e Dafni, The Temptation of St. Anthony*), various suites for orchestra (including *Driftwood Suite* and *Pennsylvania Suite*), numerous shorter orchestral pieces (including *Quiet Music, A Bell Overture, Toccata giocosa, Dance of the Locomotives,* and *Vernal Equinox*), Partita for small orchestra, and *Threnody* for flute and strings, together with a string quartet, piano quintet, *Sonata brevis* for violin and piano, and many works for the organ.

Realism. The reproduction of realistic effects or sounds in music, as in some of Richard Strauss' tone poems.

Recapitulation. In the sonata and fugue forms, that section in which the exposition is repeated.

Recital. A concert performance by a single performer or two performers. This term is believed to have been used for the first time in London on June 9, 1840, at the Hanover Square Rooms, advertising a performance by Liszt.

Recorder. A member of the flute family, prominent in the 16th and 17th centuries. It was generally made out of wood and in various sizes, each with a range of about two octaves. It has a cylindrical head, usually a beakshaped mouthpiece, and a body with eight finger holes. The recorder has been revived in our times. Among the first to do so was Arnold Dolmetsch, who manufactured a quartet of recorders in England and introduced them at the Haslemere Festival in 1926. His son, Carl, became an outstanding performer on this instrument. In 1937 the Society of Recorder Players was founded in England. The recorder has also enjoyed a revival of interest in the United States, mainly with amateur musicians. Among contemporary composers who have written compositions for the recorder are Paul Hindemith, Edmund Rubbra, and Lennox Berkeley.

Red Pony, The. Suite for orchestra by Aaron Copland (1948), adapted from a motion-picture score. The suite was first played on Oct. 30, 1948, by the Houston Symphony, Efrem Kurtz conducting. The central character of the motion picture, based on a story by John Steinbeck, is Jody, a boy who lives on a California ranch. The suite sees his world from his point of view, and is in six parts. I. Morning on the Ranch. The daily ranch activities are described. II. The Gift. Jody is overjoyed at getting a pony as a present. III. Dream March and Circus Music. The music here carries us into the nebulous world of Jody's dreams. IV. Walk to the Bunkhouse. Jody's admiration for the horsehand, Billy Buck, is portrayed. V. Grandfather's Story. One of the adventure tales Jody used to hear from his grandfather is here related tonally. VI. Happy Ending. The music of the first section is recalled as we return to the daily ranch chores.

Red Poppy, The (Glière). *See: Russian Sailors' Dance.*

Reed. The speaking or sounding part of some wind or keyboard instruments, often forming the mouthpiece as well. The material used is a reed-like plant, or reeds. Reeds fall into two categories, "free" and "beating." The former is found in the harmonium and concertina; the latter, in the clarinet and the organ. This second category is further divided into two groups: single and double reeds. The clarinet has a single reed, and the oboe and bassoon, double reeds.

Reflets dans l'eau (Debussy). *See: Images* (2).

Reformation Symphony. *See:* Symphony —*Mendelssohn.*

Reger, Max, composer. Born Brand, Germany, March 19, 1873; died Leipzig, Germany, May 11, 1916. Remarkably precocious, he made public appearances as pianist and church organist at the age of 13. In 1890 he entered the Sondershausen Conservatory to study with Hugo Riemann. A year later he followed Riemann to the Wiesbaden Conservatory where he remained until 1895 and began his career as a teacher of piano and organ. After a year of military service, he settled in Weiden to devote himself to composition. In 1901 he changed his home to Munich, where he became active as teacher, conductor, and pianist. From 1907 until the end of his life he was professor of composition at the Leipzig Conservatory. He achieved such eminence as a teacher that the King of Saxony conferred on him the honorary title of professor. From 1911 to 1915 he was also conductor of the renowned Meiningen Orchestra.

In his numerous works, Reger shows himself to be a formidable technician, one of the most scholarly and penetrating authorities on the theoretical aspects of music. An apostle of abstract music (though towards the end of his career he produced some programmatic compositions), Reger was a neo-Baroque composer partial to a contrapuntal style and often to structures of the past. His major works were in such old forms as the passacaglia, toccata, fugue, and variations. His principal compositions provide more of an intellectual stimulus to the listener than emotional pleasure.

The following are his chief instrumental compositions:

Chamber Music: 5 string quartets; 2 piano quartets; 2 piano trios; 2 string trios; 9 violin sonatas; 3 violin suites; 4 sonatas for unaccompanied violin; 14 preludes and fugues for unaccompanied violin; 4 cello sonatas; 3 suites for unaccompanied cello; 3 clarinet sonatas; piano quintet; clarinet quintet; and so on.

Orchestra: Sinfonietta; Serenade; *Variations and Fugue on a Theme by J. A. Hiller; Symphonic Prologue to a Tragedy; Comedy Overture; Concerto in the Old Style; Romantic Suite; Four Tone Poems after Boecklin; Ballet Suite; Variations and Fugue on a Theme by Mozart.*

Organ: 2 suites; 6 trios; *Fantasy and Fugue on B.A.C.H.; Symphonic Fantasy and Fugue; Variations and Fugue on an Original Theme;* various pieces including chorale fantasies, preludes and fugues, chorale preludes, variations, and so on.

Piano: 4 sonatinas; *Variations and Fugue on a Theme by Telemann; Variations and Fugue on a Theme by Bach; Variations and Fugue on a Theme by Beethoven,* for two pianos (also for orchestra); etudes, canons, waltzes, pieces, *Phantasiestuecke,* intermezzi, *Silhouettes,* and so on.

See: Four Tone Poems After Boecklin; Romantic Suite; Variations and Fugue on a Theme by Mozart.

Reine, La. *See:* Symphony—*Haydn.*

Reinecke, Carl, pianist, teacher, and conductor. Born Altona, Germany, June 23, 1824; died Leipzig, Germany, March 10, 1910. After intensive musical training on the piano and violin, he toured Europe as a concert pianist from 1842 to 1844, and from 1846 to 1848 served as court pianist in Copenhagen. His distinguished career as a teacher began at the Cologne Con-

servatory in 1851; and his conducting career was launched in 1854 with the Konzertgesellschaft in Barmen. In 1860 he settled in Leipzig as conductor of the Gewandhaus Orchestra, and as professor of piano and composition at the Conservatory. He resigned as conductor in 1895 but continued his activities at the Conservatory until 1902, serving as director of musical studies the last five years. All the while he concertized as pianist throughout Europe, achieving recognition for his remarkable interpretations of Mozart. He was the composer of over 200 works, including 3 symphonies, 4 piano concertos, various concert overtures, and a vast library of chamber, piano, and organ music. Except for some of his organ works, virtually nothing of his is now ever performed.

Reiner, Fritz, conductor. Born Budapest, Hungary, Dec. 19, 1888. He was graduated from the Budapest Academy of Music, where he received some training in conducting from Jenö Hubay. Between 1909 and 1914 he held posts as chorus master and conductor with various small opera companies. In 1914 he was appointed conductor of the Dresden Royal Opera, where his performances attracted wide attention. Immediately after World War I he led orchestral concerts in Rome and performances of the Wagner music dramas in Spain. From 1922 to 1931 he was principal conductor of the Cincinnati Symphony. In 1931 he became head of the orchestral division at the Curtis Institute. From 1931 to 1938 he made many appearances as guest conductor in Europe and the United States. From 1938 to 1948 he was principal conductor of the Pittsburgh Symphony, and since 1953 he has been principal conductor of the Chicago Symphony.

Relative key. A term designating the relationship between a major and a minor key with the same signature; for example, the relative minor of C major is A minor.

Relative pitch. The aural faculty of recognizing the pitch of any single note after hearing a second note whose pitch has been identified.

Reményi, Eduard, violinist. Born Miskolcz, Hungary, July 17, 1830; died San

Francisco, Calif., May 15, 1898. He attended the Vienna Conservatory, a pupil of Joseph Boehm. Involved in the Hungarian insurrection against Austria in 1848, he had to flee to the United States, where he launched his professional career as a violin virtuoso. In 1853 he returned to Europe, and in 1854 was appointed solo violinist to Queen Victoria in England. Receiving an amnesty from the Austrian Emperor in 1860, he returned to Hungary, where he received an appointment as solo violinist to the Austrian Emperor. Until the end of his life he continued appearing throughout the world, extolled for his electrifying personality, fantastic technique, and highly individualized interpretations. He was touring the United States when he died of apoplexy in San Francisco. He made many transcriptions for the violin, and wrote a violin concerto and some shorter pieces for the violin.

Remoortel, Edouard van, conductor. Born Brussels, Belgium, May 30, 1926. He received his early musical training in Conservatories in Brussels and Geneva; later music study took place with Camargo Guarnieri at the Academia Chigiana, and with Joseph Krips. He made his conducting début with the Concerts Populaires in Brussels when he was seventeen. This was later followed by successful guest appearances throughout Europe; within a decade he was heard with about 50 orchestras on four continents. From 1951 to 1958 he was the principal conductor of the Belgian National Orchestra. He made his American début with the National Symphony Orchestra in Washington, D.C., in December 1957. Beginning with the 1958-1959 season he filled the post of principal conductor of the St. Louis Symphony.

Renardy, Ossy (born **Oskar Riess**), violinist. Born Vienna, Austria, 1921. After studying with local teachers he made his début in Vienna on Oct. 27, 1933. Other concert appearances followed in Italy, culminating with a highly successful performance in Vienna in 1934 and a tour of the Baltic States and Europe. He made his American début in New York on Jan. 8, 1938. He has since become an Ameri-

can citizen. During World War II he served in the American armed forces, giving over 400 concerts for American troops.

Reprise. A repeat.

Requiem. A Mass for the dead, utilizing the liturgical text of the Mass with some changes. The Gloria and Credo sections of the Mass are omitted, while the *Dies irae* and other sections are introduced.

The following are a few important Requiems sometimes heard at symphony concerts.

BERLIOZ. The Requiem, or *Messe des morts* (1837), was the composer's own favorite among his works. It was commissioned by the French government for a special religious and military service. Owing to intrigues it was never given on that occasion; its première took place in Paris in December 1837 as a memorial for French soldiers killed during the then recent Algerian campaign. It achieved a major success. This is not a Requiem along traditional lines. Cast in a monumental design, it requires four small orchestras, a chorus of several hundred voices, four brass bands, an organ, and a tenor solo. Novel instrumental effects and unique harmonic colors are continually exploited. There are 10 sections: I. Requiem and Kyrie; II. *Dies irae;* III. *Quid sum miser;* IV. *Rex tremendae;* V. *Quaerens me;* VI. *Lacrymosa;* VII. Offertory; VIII. *Hostias;* IX. Sanctus; X. Agnus Dei. In its style, the work is more dramatic than religious, so much so that it has sometimes been called a "sacred drama." Its best pages are those in which overpowering effects are achieved through huge masses of sound and through staggering climaxes as in the *Dies irae* section with its cataclysmic *Tuba mirum.* Other pages bring up vivid dramatic pictures or give unforgettable expression to grandeur and terror, as in *Rex tremendae, Hostias,* and the Sanctus. But in the Offertory, with the *Domine Jesu Christe,* the composer succeeds in sounding a deeply religious note.

BRAHMS. *A German Requiem,* for soloists, chorus, and orchestra, op. 64 (1866), was inspired by the death of two people close to the composer: Schumann in 1856, and Brahms' mother in 1865. The fifth part, *Ye that Now are Sorrowful* was specifically written as a tribute to the composer's mother. When the Requiem was first given in its entirety—in Leipzig on Feb. 18, 1869, Carl Reinecke conducting—it scored a huge success. The work is called "A German Requiem" because unlike traditional Requiems it uses a German instead of a Latin text, prepared by the composer himself from the Lutheran Bible. There are 7 sections: I. *Blessed are They that Mourn;* II. *Behold All Flesh;* III. *Make Me to Know;* IV. *How Lovely is Thy Dwelling Place;* V. *Ye that Now are Sorrowful;* VI. *Here on Earth;* VII. *Blessed are the Dead.*

Far from being sorrowful, this music is by turns challenging, defiant, or gently resigned. There is peace and serenity in the first section, a beautiful dialogue between chorus and orchestra; and there is proud defiance in the second section in the throbbing timpani beats of the background music. Strength and optimism predominate in the third part, for baritone and chorus, only to yield again to contemplation and solace in the next two sections, especially in the beautiful fifth part, for soprano solo and chorus. Death is contemplated in the sixth section, while in the seventh we find expressed the victory of life over death.

FAURÉ. It is the peace that death brings, rather than its terror, which is emphasized in Fauré's Requiem, op. 48 (1887). Consequently in contrast to dramatic works like the Requiems of Berlioz and Verdi, this one is deeply religious and consistently maintains an emotional level of serenity and tranquillity. As Nadia Boulanger once said of this work: "No exterior effect alters its sober and rather severe expression of grief, no restlessness troubles its deep meditation, no doubt strains its spotless faith, its gentle confidence, its tender and tranquil expectancy." The work has 7 parts: I. Introit and Kyrie; II. Offertorium; III. Sanctus; IV. *Pie Jesus;* V. Agnus Dei; VI. *Libera Me;* VII. *In Paradisum.* The Requiem was introduced in Paris in January 1888.

MOZART. The Requiem in D minor, K. 626 (1791), was the composer's last work. He lived to complete only 12 of the 15 sections. His pupil, Franz Xaver Suessmayr, filled in some of the instrumentation for some of the 12 completed sections and had to provide music for the three other parts. Since there is no deterioration in creative power or eloquence in any part of the Requiem, there can be little doubt that Mozart gave his pupil detailed and minute instructions on how the work should be completed, providing all the basic material.

The dramatic events surrounding the writing of this Requiem are familiar, but they deserve review. One day, a stranger, dressed in gray and masked, came to Mozart to commission him to write a requiem. A basic provision of this commission was that Mozart must turn over the completed work without ever trying to uncover the identity of his patron. We now know that the patron was Count von Walsegg, who made it a practice to engage composers to write musical works which he then presented as his own. But to Mozart—then in the last year of his life, and sick in body and spirit—this stranger appeared like some messenger from another world urging him to write his own requiem. Consequently he worked with unparalleled intensity and passion to bring his requiem to completion before it was too late; and to this music he brought the spiritual exaltation, the otherworldly radiance, and the sublimity—these, and a sense of awe and terror as well—of one who has already looked at the face of death.

The Requiem opens in a gentle mood with seven measures of instrumental preface, followed by an equally serene section for chorus, intoning a prayer for the dead (*Requiem aeternam*). The first section rises to a climax in a double fugue. The feelings of the sinner in the presence of the final judgment are reflected in the turbulent music of the *Dies irae.* This is followed by the *Tuba mirum,* music of Judgment Day, for solo quartet and solo tenor trombone. A short orchestral introduction leads to the awesome *Rex tremendae majestatis* for full chorus; this, in turn is succeeded by music in a more suppliant mood, *Salva me.* Once again there is a sharp contrast of feeling in the simple eloquence of the *Recordare,* and the violent agitation of the *Confutatis* for chorus. The *Lacrymosa* which comes next is one of the most moving pages in the entire score, suffused with quiet, poignant grief. In *Domine Jesu,* the grief yields to terror, and in *Hostias* the terror turns to resignation. The ensuing Sanctus is climaxed by a fugue and is music of splendor and majesty; the Benedictus and Agnus Dei, on the other hand, have tenderness and compassion. The Requiem ends with the *Lux aeterna* in which the opening measures of the first section are repeated.

VERDI. The *Manzoni Requiem* (1874) is one of Verdi's rare excursions away from the operatic theater, the only one of his works not intended for the stage which is a consistent masterwork. He wrote it in memory of his friend, the novelist Alessandro Manzoni, and it was introduced in Milan on May 22, 1874, under the composer's direction. The work took the city by storm; it was soon given in different parts of Italy, often in unauthorized performances and in unorthodox versions. In 1875 Verdi made a triumphant tour of Europe conducting it. Such immediate popularity is easily understandable. This is deeply emotional music whose impact is inescapable. It opens in an elegiac vein with *Requiem aeternam,* a gentle plea for eternal rest, which reaches a climax with a fugue. But after that the work as a whole is more dramatic than lyrical, achieving great sweeps of power in parts of the *Dies irae* and the *Tuba mirum.* The dramatic element becomes even more pronounced in the exchange between basses and tenors in *Rex tremendae,* while a more lyrical, and at times operatic, element is introduced in the poignant *Recordare,* for soprano and mezzo soprano, the *Ingemisco* for tenor solo and *Confutatis* for bass solo, and the moving *Lacrymosa* for quartet and chorus. But a religious atmosphere is restored with the Sanctus, a monumental eight-part fugue for double choir which is succeeded by the Benedictus, in which a more tranquil treatment is given to the chief subject in the preceding fugue. The Agnus Dei is one of the peaks of the score, beginning with an exalted melody for soprano which is later repeated by chorus and orchestra in unison. Then comes the *Lux aeterna,* a graceful trio for mezzo-soprano, tenor, and bass. In the concluding section, *Libera me,* parts of the opening are recalled. After a powerful fugal chorus, the work ends in the same restrained and elegiac mood with which it began.

Resolution. The movement from dissonance to consonance.

Respighi, Ottorino, composer. Born Bologna, Italy, July 9, 1879; died Rome, Italy, April 18, 1936. He was graduated from the Bologna Liceo in 1899 with a diploma in violin. A period of travel followed in which he studied with Rimsky-Korsakov in St. Petersburg and Max Bruch in Berlin. From 1903 to 1908 he played the viola in the Mugellini Quartet, and made several appearances as concert violinist. Composition, however, was a principal interest. In 1902 a piano concerto was introduced in Bologna; and three years later his first opera, *Re Enzo,* was successfully given in the same city. Success came in 1917 with his tone poem *Fountains of Rome (Fontane di Roma),* introduced in Rome. This, and a later set of Roman tone pictures for orchestra —*Pines of Rome (Pini di Roma),* in 1924—have remained his most popular compositions. In 1913 Respighi was appointed professor of composition at the Santa Cecilia Academy in Rome, and from 1923 to 1925 he was its director. In 1932 he became a member of the Royal Academy of Italy. Respighi paid his first visit to the United States in 1925-1926, making his American début in New York City on Dec. 31, 1925, as soloist with the New York Philharmonic in the world première of his Piano Concerto in the Mixolydian Mode.

Respighi was a leading figure in the movement among 20th-century Italian composers to cultivate symphonic music. Though he himself wrote several successful operas, his works for orchestra and for chamber-music groups helped to create a kind of renascence of instrumental writing in Italy. Respighi has followed several directions. His most famous works are vivid in their pictorial suggestions, fully utilizing the resources of modern harmony and orchestration. But he has also written compositions utilizing old scales, modes, and plainchant; while in still other works he is a neo-Classicist.

The following are his principal instrumental compositions:

Chamber Music: 3 violin sonatas; string quartet; *Doric Quartet;* piano quintet.

Orchestra: Various concertos (*Concerto gregoriano,* for violin; Concerto in the Mixolydian Mode, for piano; *Concerto a cinque,* for oboe; trumpet, violin, double bass, piano and string orchestra); *Fountains of Rome (Fontane di Roma); Old Airs and Dances for the Lute; Pines of Rome (Pini di Roma); Church Windows (Vetrate di chiesa); Trittico botticelliano; The Birds (Gli Uccelli);* Toccata, for piano and orchestra; *Roman Festivals (Feste romane); Metamorphosen; Impresioni brasiliane.*

Piano: Three Preludes on Gregorian Melodies; Six Pieces, for children, for four hands.

See: Birds, The; Church Windows; Fountains of Rome; Pines of Rome.

Rest. A period of silence in a composition while the tempo is maintained.

Resurrection Symphony. *See:* Symphony *—Mahler.*

Revolt (or Serbian) Polonaise. *See:* Polonaise.

Revolutionary Etude. *See:* Etude— *Chopin.*

Revueltas, Silvestre, composer. Born Santiago Papasquiaro, Mexico, Dec. 31, 1899; died Mexico City, Oct. 5, 1940. His early musical training took place at the National Conservatory in Mexico City. In 1916 he visited the United States, where he continued his music study in Austin, Texas, and at the Chicago Musical College. During a second visit to the United States he studied the violin with Ottakar Ševčik. Returning to his native country in 1929, he was appointed assistant conductor of the Orquesta Sinfónica de Mexico. The permanent conductor of that orchestra, Carlos Chávez, encouraged him to turn for the first time to composition. In 1931 Revueltas completed his first major work, *Esquinas,* for orchestra, introduced that year in Mexico City under the composer's direction. He continued writing music while extending his activity as conductor by founding an orchestra in

Mexico City and serving on the faculty of the National Conservatory. In 1937 he went to Spain to supervise the cultural activities of the Loyalist government. After returning to Mexico he resumed his many musical activities. He was stricken by pneumonia in his forty-first year. Revueltas' music is national in spirit and content, often inspired by subjects derived from Mexican folklore. His most important works for orchestra are *Ventanes, Cuauhnahuac, Janitzio, Caminos, Colorines,* and *Homenaje a Federico García Lorca.* He also wrote 2 string quartets and 3 pieces for violin and piano. Since his death, his significance in Mexican music has gained increasing recognition, beginning with an all-Revueltas concert in Mexico City two months after he died. In 1958 Mexico inaugurated an annual international festival to honor him in his native city. Besides his concert music, Revueltas wrote music for ballets and motion pictures.

Rhapsody. In piano music, a composition elastic and free in form and rhapsodic in character, sometimes utilizing popular melodies. The piano form was created by a Bohemian composer, Václav Tomašek, but it first became famous with Liszt, who wrote 15 Hungarian Rhapsodies (which see). Brahms wrote 3 rhapsodies for piano which are not made up of popular melodies but which reflect the original Greek concept of the rhapsody as music of epic character. Two of these rhapsodies, in B minor and G minor, op. 79 (1879), are among Brahms' most significant piano compositions, music of great passion and dramatic impact. A third rhapsody, in E-flat major, op. 119, no. 4 (1893), is the composer's last work for the piano, and like the earlier rhapsodies a work of exceptional power. Brahms' conception of the piano rhapsody as a work of epic character was continued by Ernst von Dohnányi, who wrote four rhapsodies for piano, op. 11, the most popular of these being the third, in C major.

In orchestral music, the rhapsody is often a fantasia on popular melodies or tunes in a popular or folklike style. Notable examples can be found in Chabrier's *España,* Dvořák's *Slavonic Rhap-*

sodies, Enesco's *Rumanian Rhapsodies,* Gershwin's *Rhapsody in Blue,* Lalo's *Norwegian Rhapsody,* Ravel's *Spanish Rhapsody,* Vaughan Williams' *Norfolk Rhapsodies,* and so on.

There are also other kinds of orchestral rhapsodies, in which the dramatic and epic qualities are emphasized, and popular tunes are not used. Béla Bartók wrote two such rhapsodies for violin and orchestra. They originated as compositions for violin and piano (1929), but two years later the composer orchestrated the accompaniment. The first rhapsody was also arranged by the composer for cello and piano. Both rhapsodies are improvisations, and, like the Liszt rhapsodies, alternate between slow and fast moods. Both works are made up of two sections: the first section has a rhapsodic character and utilizes native Hungarian rhythms; the second highlights a tender melody which gains in effect through continual repetition.

Rhapsody for Alto, Men's Chorus and Orchestra (Brahms). *See: Alto Rhapsody.*

Rhapsody in Blue. For piano and orchestra by George Gershwin (1924), first performed by the Paul Whiteman Orchestra in New York, on Feb. 12, 1924, the composer at the piano. This is the work that made its composer worldfamous; it is also the work that made popular among many leading American and European composers the practice of incorporating jazz idioms and techniques within serious musical structures and with serious artistic intent. The rhapsody opens with a low trill in a clarinet, leading to a seventeen-note ascent at whose peak erupts a spicy tune. This is followed by a jaunty melody in the piano. Both themes are worked out. The most celebrated melody of the composition is a rhapsodic blues song in the strings, repeated by the full orchestra. A hasty recollection of the opening phrase of this melody in fast tempo brings on the finale, in which earlier material is recalled and which is concluded with a short and dramatic coda. The *Rhapsody in Blue* has been adapted for several ballets.

Rhapsody on a Theme of Paganini. For piano and orchestra by Rachmaninoff, op. 43 (1934). The composer's last work for piano and orchestra, it was introduced in Philadelphia on Nov. 7, 1934; Stokowski conducted, and the composer was soloist. While designated as a rhapsody, this work is actually a series of variations on the famous theme of Paganini from the Twenty-fourth Caprice for solo violin. The theme is only suggested by the orchestra in the nineteen-bar introduction. In the first variation, however, the violins present it. Twenty-three variations follow in which the theme is transformed with remarkable inventiveness—harmonically, melodically, rhythmically, atmospherically. In the seventh and tenth variations Rachmaninoff quotes the *Dies irae,* which is restated forcefully by brass and strings in the final variation. The eighteenth variation is one of Rachmaninoff's famous lyric passages, shared between solo piano and strings. At the end of the work, the Paganini melody is recalled a last time in a vigorous statement by the piano.

Rheinberger, Josef, organist and teacher. Born Vaduz, Liechtenstein, March 17, 1839; died Munich, Germany, Nov. 25, 1901. From 1851 to 1854 he attended the Munich Conservatory; he subsequently studied privately with Franz Lachner. In 1859 he became professor of the piano at the Munich Conservatory, and a year later professor of counterpoint. From 1860 to 1866 he served as organist of St. Michael's Church in Munich. When Hans von Buelow reorganized the Munich Conservatory in 1867, Rheinberger was made professor of organ and counterpoint, holding this post until his death. In 1877 he was appointed Royal Kapellmeister in Munich, and in 1894 he was raised to the rank of nobility. One of the most highly esteemed organists in Germany, and a teacher of equal renown, Rheinberger produced many works in all branches of composition, including symphonies, concertos, overtures, sonatas, string quintets, piano trios, a string quartet, and much music for the piano. But only his works for the organ have survived; these include 2 sonatas, 22 trios, monologues, meditations, fughettas, and characteristic pieces.

Rheingold, Das (Wagner). *See: Rhinegold, The; Ring of the Nibelungs, The.*

Rhené-Baton (born René Baton), conductor and composer. Born Courseulles-sur-mer, France, Sept. 5, 1879; died Le Mans, France, Sept. 23, 1940. After attending the Paris Conservatory, he conducted orchestras in Bordeaux and Angers between 1910 and 1912, and the first festival of French music ever held in Germany, in 1910. After 1912 he was a conductor of the Ballet Russe, which toured Europe and South America. In 1918 he became principal conductor of the Pasdeloup Orchestra in Paris; except for the hiatus of a few years, he held this post until 1932. Rhené-Baton wrote several orchestral compositions, including a suite, Prelude and Fugue, and Variations for piano and orchestra; also some compositions for the piano, including the suite *En Bretagne*.

Rhenish Symphony. *See:* Symphony—*Schumann.*

Rhinegold, The (Das Rheingold). The prelude, or first music drama, of Wagner's cycle, *The Ring of the Nibelungs.* For orchestral excerpts *see: Ring of the Nibelungs, The.*

Rhythm. The arrangement of notes in time; the patterns of short and long notes, accented and unaccented notes, formed by such an arrangement.

Rhythmicon. *See:* Cowell, Henry.

Ricci, Ruggiero, violinist. Born San Francisco, Calif., July 24, 1920. After studying the violin with Louis Persinger, he made his début in San Francisco at the age of six, and his first New York appearance on Oct. 20, 1929. His first tour of Europe took place in 1934, and in 1957 he made a tour of the world.

Ricercare. A type of instrumental music popular in the 16th and 17th centuries and derived from the vocal motet. Its principal characteristic is a fugal development of some germinal idea. Several modern composers have revived this style of writing, among them being Norman Dello Joio in his *Ricercari* for piano and orchestra (1946), introduced by the New York Philharmonic on Dec. 19, 1946, George Szell conducting, and Alexander Tansman, whose *Ricercari* for orchestra (1949) was first performed in St. Louis on Dec. 22, 1949, Vladimir Golschmann conducting. In the latter

composition, the finale consists of *Study in Boogie-Woogie,* perhaps as far as any composer can go in bringing 20th-century modernity to this old technique.

Richard II, Richard III. *See:* Shakespeare, William.

Richter, Hans, conductor. Born Raab, Hungary, April 4, 1843; died Bayreuth, Germany, Dec. 5, 1916. He attended the Vienna Conservatory from 1860 to 1865. After playing the horn for several years in the orchestra of the Kaernthnerthor Theater in Vienna, he went to live with Wagner in Lucerne in 1866, serving as his musical assistant. On Wagner's recommendation he became chorus master of the Munich Opera. In 1868-1869 he was court conductor under Hans von Buelow, and on March 22, 1870, he conducted the first Brussels performance of Wagner's opera *Lohengrin.* From 1871 to 1875 he was conductor of the Budapest Opera. In 1875 he was appointed to a similar post with the Vienna Royal Opera, and from that year on he also was the conductor of the Vienna Philharmonic. In 1876 Wagner invited him to Bayreuth to direct the first complete performance of the *Ring of the Nibelungs* at the first Wagner festival there. Richter remained principal conductor at Bayreuth until his retirement. Meanwhile, in 1877, he visited London and alternated with Wagner in directing a festival of the master's music. Upon his return to London two years later, Richter inaugurated orchestral performances which soon came to be known as the Richter Concerts. For twenty years (conducting without a score) Richter presented the greatest symphonic literature with surpassing musicianship and penetration. From 1897 to 1911 he was principal conductor of the Hallé Orchestra in Manchester. Richter led his last orchestral concert there on April 11, 1911, and his last opera performance (Wagner's *The Mastersingers*) at the Vienna Opera a year later. He then went into retirement in Bayreuth.

Richter, Svyatoslav, pianist. Born Zhitomir, Russia, March 20, 1914. Until he was twenty-two the only formal music instruction he received was some piano lessons from his father, a professor at the Odessa Conservatory. In his twenty-second year he went to Moscow, where he became a pupil of Henri Neuhaus. Three years later he made a sensational début in Moscow, performing Prokofiev's Sixth Sonata. Since then he has been ranked with the world's foremost interpreters of Prokofiev's piano music; he introduced several of that composer's last sonatas. In 1945 Richter won first prize in a piano competition in Moscow, and after that he concertized throughout the Soviet Union. His first appearance outside Russia took place at the Prague Festival in 1950.

Ride of the Valkyrie, The (Walkuerenritt). An orchestral prelude with chorus to Act 3 of Wagner's music drama, *The Valkyries* (*Die Walkuere*) from *The Ring of the Nibelungs*. This excerpt is a vividly realistic tone picture of storm and motion. Leaping rhythms and brilliant orchestral sonorities describe the aerial flight of the Valkyrie through the storm on their dashing steeds, as they carry their heroic dead to Valhalla.

Riegger, Wallingford, composer. Born Albany, Ga., April 29, 1885. After being graduated from the Institute of Musical Art in New York in 1907, he attended the Berlin High School of Music, studying the cello with Anton Hekking. For several years he conducted orchestras and opera companies in Germany. Returning to the United States in 1917, he held various teaching posts at Drake University in Des Moines, the Institute of Musical Art, and Ithaca University. In 1922 he received the Paderewski Fund Award for a piano trio, and in 1924 the Elizabeth Sprague Coolidge Prize for his choral setting of Keats' *La Belle Dame sans Merci*. His style became atonal after 1924, and from that point he progressed to the twelve-tone technique. His major works for orchestra include the *Study in Sonority* for ten violins or any multiple of ten, introduced by the Philadelphia Orchestra under Stokowski in 1929, and the Symphony No. 3, which won the New York Music Critics Award in 1948. Other works for orchestra include a fourth symphony, *New Dance,* Canon and Fugue, Passacaglia and Fugue, *Dance Rhythms,* and Variations. He has also produced a considerable amount of chamber music, including 2 string quartets, a violin sonatina, a piano quintet, and a nonet for brass.

Rienzi, Overture to. Overture to an early opera by Wagner. The libretto, by the composer, was based on a novel by Bulwer-Lytton. The opera was introduced at the Dresden Opera on Oct. 20, 1842. Trumpet calls introduce a slow section in which strings present the solemn music of Rienzi's prayer for his people. After this theme is repeated by woodwinds and brass, the main section of the overture unfolds, borrowing its material from the opera. The first main theme is the battle hymn from Act 1, in the brass, superimposed on the Rienzi prayer motif. A recall of the solemn introduction brings on material from the first-act finale, which, in the recapitulation section of the overture, is combined with a counter melody in the trombones. The stirring coda is made up mostly of the battle-hymn music.

Rieti, Vittorio, composer and teacher. Born Alexandria, Egypt, Jan. 28, 1898. He studied music in Italy, mostly with Ottorino Respighi and Alfredo Casella. In 1924 he attracted attention with the Concerto for Woodwinds and Orchestra, in which his neo-Classical tendencies were first crystallized; this work was introduced at the International Festival of Contemporary Music in Prague on May 31, 1924. One year later, his ballet, *Barabau,* was successfully given in London by the Ballet Russe, and the suite from *Noah's Ark* for orchestra was introduced at the International Music Festival in Prague. In 1939 he settled permanently in the United States, becoming a citizen. From 1950 to 1958 he was a member of the music faculty at Roosevelt College in Chicago, and since then at Queen's College, New York. He has written 5 symphonies, various concertos, several other orchestral works (*Due Pastorali* and *Introduzione e gioco delle ore*), 3 string quartets, a woodwind quintet and other chamber-music compositions, and numerous works for the piano including sonatas, a sonatina, suites, and preludes.

Rigaudon. A lively dance of French origin in three or four sections and in 2/4 or 4/4 time. The music usually begins on the third or fourth beat of the bar. It is sometimes found as a movement of the Baroque suite. An interesting 20th-century revival of this old dance form can be found in Ravel's *Le Tombeau de Couperin*, both for piano and for orchestra. Fritz Kreisler's *Sicilenne et Rigaudon* for violin and piano was written in the style of the 18th-century composer, François Francoeur.

Riisager, Knudåge, composer. Born Port Kunda, Estonia, March 6, 1897. He studied music with Otto Malling, Peder Gram, and Peder Möller. After being graduated from the University of Copenhagen in 1921 he went to Paris for additional study with Albert Roussel and Paul Le Flem. This and later visits to Paris influenced him to turn to the more advanced techniques of modern music. His first symphony, in 1925, was polytonal and polyrhythmic. After 1931 his advanced writing was blended with elements of the Baroque style, a tendency brought about after his study of counterpoint with Hermann Grabner in Leipzig. Beginning with the era of World War II and the Nazi occupation of Denmark, a strong national feeling appears in his music, and his works often exploit Danish folk melodies. For many years Riisager worked as a government official in the post of secretary, and later chief, of the Ministry of Finance. He resigned in 1950 to devote himself exclusively to composition. His major works include 4 symphonies, a violin concerto, variations, suites, overtures, and other compositions for orchestra (including *Shrove Time, Marche tartare, Primavera, Three Danish Carols,* Partita, *Targut Dance, Summer Rhapsody,* Chaconne, and *Sinfonia serena*). In the field of chamber music he produced 6 string quartets, 2 violin sonatas, and various concertinos and divertimentos. He also wrote a sonata and a sonatina for piano.

Rimsky-Korsakov, Nikolai, composer. Born Tikhvin, near Novgorod, Russia, March 18, 1844; died St. Petersburg, Russia, June 21, 1908. Since he was trained for a naval career, he received at first only a haphazard musical education. But all his life he was passionately devoted to music; from boyhood on he was a profound admirer of Glinka's operas and Russian folksongs and ecclesiastical music. When he was seventeen he met Balakirev, who fired him with his own musical enthusiasms and encouraged him to try writing a symphony. But Rimsky-Korsakov's full conversion to music had to wait a few years. In the fall of 1862 he set out on a two-and-a-half year cruise as naval officer. After returning to Russia he settled in St. Petersburg, where he became more closely associated with Balakirev, joining him, Mussorgsky, Borodin, and Cui in a national school henceforth identified as "The Five." He now completed his first symphony (the first such work by a Russian), successfully introduced in St. Petersburg on Dec. 31, 1865, Balakirev conducting. After that, Rimsky-Korsakov wrote ambitious works with a national character, among which were the *Antar Symphony* and his first opera, *The Maid of Pskov*. The latter was so well received in St. Petersburg in 1873 that the government finally relieved him of his naval duties so that he could concentrate on music. The special post of Inspector of Military Orchestras was created for him. During the next few years he led the concerts of the Free Music Society. His appearances as conductor outside Russia included performances at the World Exposition in Paris in 1889, and other, later performances in Paris and Brussels. He had also been appointed professor of composition and orchestration at the St. Petersburg Conservatory in 1871.

Between 1878 and 1881 he completed two more operas, and in the three-year period of 1887-1890 wrote some of his most famous orchestral compositions, including the *Russian Easter Overture* (*La grande pâque russe*), *Scheherazade,* and the *Capriccio espagnol*. Opera dominated his creative activity after 1894.

Rimsky-Korsakov belonged to that dedicated small group of Russian composers whose ideal was musical nationalism; his own music is Russian to its very marrow. His melodies often have the character of Russian folksongs; his harmonies are often derived from scales and modes of Russian church music; his orchestration has an oriental brilliance of color. A master of harmony and orchestration, he brought to his writing a technical assurance and skill not often encountered in the works of his colleagues in "The Five." The following are his principal instrumental compositions:

Chamber Music: 3 string quartets; string sextet; wind quintet; piano trio; Serenade for cello and piano.

Orchestra: 3 symphonies (including *Antar*); *Capriccio espagnol; Scheherazade; Russian Easter Overture (La grande pâque russe); Dubinushka;* piano concerto; *Fantasy on Russian Themes* for violin and orchestra.

See: Capriccio espagnol; Coq d'or; Russian Easter Overture; Scheherazade; Symphony—Rimsky-Korsakov.

Ring of the Nibelungs, The (Der Ring des Nibelungen). A cycle of four music dramas by Wagner embracing *The Rhinegold (Das Rheingold), The Valkyries (Die Walkuere), Siegfried,* and *The Twilight of the Gods,* or *The Dusk of the Gods (Die Goetterdaemmerung).* The composer designated this cycle as a trilogy, since he considered the first drama merely a prologue to the others. The *Ring* was written between 1853 and 1874 —librettos by the composer based on ancient Scandinavian, German, and Icelandic sagas—and its première took place at the first Bayreuth festival, between August 13 and 17, 1876. The following orchestral excerpts from the *Ring* cycle are discussed under their own headings: *The Rhinegold (Entrance of the Gods Into Valhalla); The Valkyries (The Ride of the Valkyries, Wotan's Farewell and Magic Fire Scene); Siegfried (Forest Murmurs); The Twilight of the Gods (Bruennhilde's Immolation, Siegfried's Death Music, Siegfried's Rhine Journey).*

Rio Grande, The. *See:* Lambert, Constant.

Ripieno. In the concerto grosso the full orchestra as opposed to the "concertino," or the solo instruments.

Rire de Diable, Le. *See:* Caprice (1).

Rispetti e strambotti. For string quartet by Malipiero (1920), first performed in Pittsfield, Mass., on Sept. 25, 1920; it received the Elizabeth Sprague Coolidge Award. "Rispetti" and "strambotti" are two old forms of Italian poetry. The first is a love message from a man to a lady; the second is a roundelay. In using such old Italian poetic forms, the composer produced music in which he interpreted the social, political, and religious backgrounds of the Renaissance. This is a single, coherent work built from many episodic melodic subjects. The two most significant themes depict the clergy and peasantry respectively. The first is a kind of plainchant; the other, a robust subject with astringent harmonies.

Ritardando (or Ritenuto). A gradual retarding of the tempo.

Rite of Spring, The (Le Sacre du Printemps). Ballet suite for orchestra by Stravinsky (1913), introduced in Paris by the Ballet Russe on May 29, 1913. While this music has no specific program, it aims to portray abstractly a ritual of pagan Russia—the adoration of Nature by primitive man. It is in two sections played without interruption; each section, in turn, has smaller subdivisions. I. The Fertility of the Earth. The composition opens with a tonal painting of the spring season. In a 75-bar introduction, a solo bassoon is heard in a sensitive theme in its high register. An atmosphere of mystery is heightened with the appearance of other woodwinds and the brass. The Ballet of the Adolescents presents sharply punctuated and incisive rhythms which simulate the stamping of feet in a primitive dance. The excitement mounts. Four trumpets play a solemn tune against a melodic dance fragment in the flute. Spring Rounds is introduced with a theme for unison clarinets and bass clarinets against flute trills. The solemn tune of the preceding section is recalled by a clarinet. Then comes The Games of Rival Tribes, a competition between two groups in fighting and gymnastics, described musically in dynamic and rhythmic patterns and rapidly changing meters. A strong subject for four tubas introduces the Sage, come to consecrate the soil. A primitive dance ends this first part. II. The Sacrifice. Delicate tone painting, pagan in spirit, and filled with gloom and mystery, introduces the second part. A solemn subject in the flute brings on the Mysterious Circle of the Adolescents.

There follow the Evocation of the Ancestors and the Ritual of the Ancestors, music made savage by astringent harmonies and forceful rhythms. The final sacrifice is at hand: the victim, chosen for the sacrifice, must dance herself to death. Even more frenetic and demoniac does the music now become as it reaches a point of frenzy, at which the rite comes to its conclusion with a shattering outburst in the full orchestra.

Cecil Gray described *The Rite of Spring* as "one of the most conspicuous landmarks in the artistic life of our period." Its dynamic and unorthodox rhythmic, tonal, and harmonic procedures have left an indelible mark on musical thought and writing throughout the world. Its première in Paris in 1913 was one of the most dramatic pages in the history of musical performance. The music had progressed no more than a few bars before the audience began responding with catcalls, foot-stamping, hissing, and shouts of disapproval. A heated battle developed in the theater with a violent exchange of blows and hot words; the audience divided itself into two battle camps. Ravel and Debussy shouted at the top of their voices that this was the music of a genius and should be listened to with reverence. Others, including many noted Parisian critics, shouted back that the work was just a colossal fraud. The criticisms that appeared in the press were equally savage. "It has no relation to music," said one critic; another exclaimed that "a crowd of savages . . . might have produced such noises." Acceptance of this music as a masterwork came slowly. The score still produced antagonism in the audience and press when it was introduced to the United States by the Boston Symphony in 1924. But in time recognition of its inherent power and originality and creative force was universal. Today, *The Rite of Spring* is one of the composer's most often performed orchestral works, and one of the most highly acclaimed.

Ritual Fire Dance (Falla). *See: Amor brujo, El.*

Rivier, Jean, composer. Born Villemonble, France, July 21, 1896. His early musical training was haphazard. After World War I, he spent four years at the Paris Conservatory. Performances of some of his orchestral music in Paris by leading conductors first brought him recognition. With Henry Barraud he helped create the school of young French composers called "The Triton," serving as its chairman from 1936 to 1940. In his music, Rivier has followed a middle path of compromise between the economy of the neo-Classicists and the modern harmonic and rhythmic adventures of the *avant-garde.* He has written for orchestra 5 symphonies, a piano concerto, violin concerto, viola concertino, *Burlesque* for violin and orchestra, *Ouverture pour un Don Quichotte,* Adagio for Strings, *Le Voyage d'Urien, Paysage pour une Jeanne d'Arc à Domrémy, Rapsodie provençale, Ouverture pour une drame,* and *Ballade des amants désespérés.* Besides some pieces for the piano, he also wrote 2 string quartets, string trio, viola sonatina, and other chamber music.

Since the end of World War II he has been professor of composition at the Paris Conservatory and a member of the committee of the French Radio.

Rob Roy. *See:* Scott, Sir Walter.

Robertson, Rae. *See:* Bartlett and Robertson.

Robin Hood Dell Concerts. Annual series of summer concerts by the Philadelphia Orchestra under various conductors in an open amphitheater in the Robin Hood Dell in Fairmount Park, Philadelphia, Pa. These concerts were inaugurated in 1930 on a cooperative basis, the first concert taking place on July 8, 1930, under Alexander Smallens. Distinguished soloists, and opera and ballet, have been featured. In 1958 an ensemble other than the Philadelphia Orchestra appeared there for the first time (the Cleveland Orchestra), substituting for the Philadelphia Orchestra while the latter organization was touring Europe.

Rochester Festival of American Music. An annual festival held each Spring in Rochester, N.Y., under the auspices of, and with the full facilities, of the Eastman School of Music, directed by Howard Hanson. The festival was an outgrowth of the American Composers Concerts inaugurated at Rochester in May 1925. The first festival of American music took place in the spring of 1931. Since then, the festival has presented over 1,500 works by more than 750 composers, many of them premières.

Rochester Philharmonic Orchestra. A symphony orchestra founded in 1923 in Rochester, N.Y., by George Eastman, with Albert Coates and Eugene Goossens as conductors. Coates remained a principal conductor until 1926, and Goossens until 1931. José Iturbi was principal conductor from 1936 to 1947, Erich Leinsdorf from 1947 to 1956, and Theodore Bloomfield since 1958.

Rococo. A style in instrumental music during the last half of the 18th century, placing emphasis on delicacy, refinement, grace, and classical restraint.

Rode, Pierre, violinist and composer. Born Bordeaux, France, Feb. 26, 1774; died Château de Bourbon, France, Nov. 25, 1830. After studying the violin, principally with Giovanni Battista Viotti, Rode made a successful début as a violinist in Paris in 1790, then toured Europe in 1794. He became professor of the violin at the Paris Conservatory when it was first opened. His major successes as a virtuoso came in Paris beginning with 1800, the year in which he was appointed solo violinist to Napoleon. From 1803 to 1808 he was solo violinist to Alexander I in Russia. For some years after that he lived in Paris, then in Berlin, finally going into retirement in Bordeaux. Beethoven wrote for him the Violin Sonata op. 96 and the *Romance,* op. 50. Rode wrote 13 violin concertos, 5 sets of quartets, 7 sets of variations, and three books of duos for two violins. He is remembered almost solely for his Twenty-Four Etudes, or Caprices, for violin which have become indispensable to the violin student. He wrote other violin etudes and a violin method.

Rodzinski, Artur, conductor. Born Spalato, Dalmatia (now Jugoslavia), Jan. 2, 1894; died Boston, Mass., Nov. 27, 1958. He was graduated from the University of Vienna with a degree in law. During this period he also received a doctorate in music following study with Franz Schalk, Franz Schreker, and Emil Sauer. He made his conducting début with the Lemberg Opera in 1921. For five years after that he was conductor of the Warsaw Opera and made guest appearances with the Warsaw Philharmonic. In 1926 Leopold Stokowski appointed him his assistant with the Philadelphia Orchestra. During the three-year period Rodzinski filled this post he was also head of the orchestra and opera departments at the Curtis Institute, and appeared as guest conductor of many American orchestras. From 1929 to 1933 he was principal conductor of the Los Angeles Philharmonic, and from 1933 to 1943 principal conductor of the Cleveland Orchestra. In 1936 he made successful appearances at the Salzburg Festival. In 1937 he helped organize the NBC Symphony for Toscanini, and served as one of its conductors. From 1943 to 1947 he was the conductor of the New York Philharmonic and in 1947-1948 of the Chicago Symphony. After that he established his home in Italy, conducting opera and orchestral performances in Europe and South America. He returned to the United States in 1958, after an absence of a decade, to conduct *Tristan and Isolde* with the Chicago Lyric Opera on Nov. 10.

Roger-Ducasse, Jean, composer. Born Bordeaux, France, April 18, 1873; died Le-Taillan-Médoc, France, July 20, 1954. He attended the Paris Conservatory, receiving the second Prix de Rome. While still a student he wrote a *Petite Suite* for orchestra, successfully performed at Paris in 1898. Two string quartets, a tone poem *Au Jardin de Marguérite,* and the mimodrama *Orphée* helped establish his reputation before World War I. A lifelong student of Bach, he was partial to a polyphonic technique, but in the sensitivity of his style and in his poetic thought he was also indebted to Fauré. In 1909 he was appointed inspector of the teaching of singing in the public schools of Paris, and from 1935 to 1940 he was professor of composition at the Paris Conservatory.

Among his principal orchestral works are the tone poem with chorus *Sarabande, Suite française, Prélude d'un ballet, Variations plaisantes sur un thème grave, Nocturne de printemps, Epithalame,*

Poème symphonique sur le nom de Fauré, and *Ulysse et les sirènes.* He also wrote 2 string quartets and various works for the piano including arabesques, études, preludes, barcarolles, and variations.

Rogers, Bernard, composer. Born New York City, Feb. 4, 1893. He studied composition with Ernest Bloch; attended the Institute of Musical Art, where he won the Loeb Prize in composition; then studied with Nadia Boulanger in Paris and Frank Bridge in London on a Pulitzer Traveling Scholarship and a Guggenheim Fellowship. In 1929 he became instructor of composition and orchestration at the Eastman School of Music. He has written abundantly in all forms, many of his works finding their inspiration either in the Bible or in exotic subjects. His opera *The Warrior* was produced by the Metropolitan Opera in 1947; in that same year he was elected member of the National Institute of Arts and Letters. He is the author of *The Art of Orchestration* (1951). He has written four symphonies, *Soliloquy* for flute and strings, *Soliloquy* for bassoon and strings, *Fantasy* for flute, viola, and orchestra, and various other orchestral compositions (including *The Dance of Salome, The Song of the Nightingale, The Plains, Three Landscapes, Characters from Hans Christian Andersen, Amphitryon Overture,* and *Dance Scenes*).

Roi David, Le. *See:* Honegger, Arthur.

Roi d'Ys, Overture to Le. Overture to an opera by Edouard Lalo, libretto by Edouard Blau based on a Breton legend. The opera was introduced at the Opéra-Comique in Paris on May 7, 1888. The overture is a summation of the action of the opera, which involves Mylio and the two daughters of the king of Ys, Rozenn and Margared, in a love triangle. In the introductory section of the overture a clarinet solo describes Mylio. The main section is brought on by a trumpet flourish. Here we get a tonal representation of Margared's jealousy of Rozenn in a turbulent theme; gentler music in the cello speaks of Rozenn. Margared's theme and Mylio's lyrical melody are used in the climactic conclusion.

Rolland, Romain, novelist, dramatist, and musicologist. Born Clamecy, France, Jan. 29, 1866; died Vézelay, France, Dec. 30, 1944. He won the Nobel Prize for literature in 1915 for *Jean-Christophe,* a novel about a musician. Rolland was educated at the Ecole Normale Supérieure in Paris and the Ecole Française in Rome. In 1896 he received the Prix Kastner-Bourgault for his doctoral thesis on the early history of opera. Many of the articles on various aspects of music history he wrote for French journals were collected and published in 1908 in two volumes, *Musiciens d'autrefois* and *Musiciens d'aujourd'hui.* He also published *Voyage musicale au pays du passé* (1920), a biography of Handel (1910), several volumes on Beethoven, and an autobiography, *Journey Within* (1947). All have been translated into English. An anthology of essays from some of the above books was published in New York in 1948 as *Essays on Music.*

In 1900 Rolland organized the first international congress for the history of music. Three years later he became president of the music section of the Ecole des Hautes Etudes Sociales, which he had helped to organize for the University of Paris. He resigned in 1909 to devote himself to writing, and from 1913 to 1918 he lived in Switzerland.

Rolland wrote several plays to which various composers have written incidental music: *Le Quatorze Juilliet* (collaboratively by Georges Auric, Arthur Honegger, Charles Koechlin, Daniel Lazarus, Darius Milhaud, and Albert Roussel); *Liluli* (Arthur Honegger); and *L'Esprit triomphant* (Alexander Tcherepnin). Dmitri Kabalevsky's *Colas Breugnon* Overture is from the opera of that title adapted from Rolland's novel. *See also: Jean-Christophe.*

Roman Carnival Overture (Le Carnaval Romain). Concert overture by Berlioz, op. 9 (1844), introduced in Paris on Feb. 3, 1844, the composer conducting. The composer originally planned this music as a prelude for the second act of his opera *Benvenuto Cellini,* but in 1843 he decided to make it an independent symphonic work even though it used some of the melodic material from that opera. The overture opens with a dashing figure for violins and violas with the rhythm, tempo, and character of a saltarello, a 16th-century Roman dance. Then comes the overture's main melody: a beautiful song for English horn. Still a third subject is a dance theme first presented softly, then allowed to increase in sonority. All three subjects are enlarged, and the opening saltarello theme returns to end the overture.

Roman Sketches (Griffes). *See: Four Roman Sketches.*

Romance (Romanza). An instrumental composition in the style of a romantic song. Beethoven wrote two lyrical Romances for violin and orchestra: No. 1 in G major, op. 40 (1803), and No. 2 in F major, op. 50 (1802). One of the most celebrated Romances in violin literature is the second movement of Henri Wieniawski's Concerto No. 2, for violin and orchestra. Anton Rubinstein's Romance in E-flat, op. 44, no. 1, in *Soirées de St. Pétersbourg,* is one of the composer's popular pieces for the piano, familiar also in transcriptions for orchestra. Tchaikovsky's Romance in F minor, op. 5 (1868), is well known in its original version for piano and in transcriptions; Tchaikovsky dedicated this sentimental melody to Désirée Artôt, with whom he was then in love. Schumann wrote three Romances for piano, op. 28 (1839): B-flat minor, F-sharp major, and B major. He also wrote three beautiful Romances for oboe and piano, op. 94 (1849). The slow movement of Mozart's Concerto No. 20 in D minor, for piano and orchestra, K. 466, is a Romanza.

Romantic Suite (Romantischer Suite). Suite for orchestra by Max Reger, op. 125 (1912), first performed in Dresden on Oct. 11, 1912, Ernst von Schuch conducting. This three-movement composition was inspired by verses by Joseph Freiherr von Eichendorff. I. Notturno. Based on *Nachtzauber,* this movement opens with a gentle motif for two flutes, repeated by muted and divided first violins. A broad melody for violins follows, and after that a brief subject for clarinet. II. Scherzo. The source is *Elfe,* and the music presents an elf-like melody in woodwinds over tremolo strings. Later in the movement, an in-

triguing waltz-like melody is played by the oboe, accompanied by strings and harp. III. This is a setting of *Morgengruss.* This section opens with the same theme with which the first movement is introduced. New material is soon stated, and developed with intensity: a melody for cellos and English horn, and a stronger subject for horns continued by the woodwind. After a powerful climax, a subdued section is given to three horns against string tremolos; the suite ends sonorously and dramatically.

Romantic Symphony. (1) *See:* Symphony—*Bruckner.*

(2) *See:* Symphony—*Hanson.*

Romanza Andaluza (Sarasate). *See: Spanish Dances* (2).

Romeo and Juliet. (1) *See:* Symphony—*Berlioz.*

(2) Three ballet suites for orchestra by Prokofiev, op. 64 (1935), adapted from the score to a ballet produced in Leningrad, Jan. 11, 1940. The second of these suites, op. 64-ter, is the most popular; it was introduced in Leningrad on April 15, 1937. There are seven movements. I. Montagues and Capulets. This is an ironical picture of the arrogant noblemen, contrasted by a trio depicting Juliet dancing with Paris. II. Juliet, the Maiden. A tender melody brings up a picture of the young girl; the development of this melody suggests her awakening to love. III. Friar Laurence. Two themes—one for bassoons, tuba, and harps; the other for cellos divided into three parts—offer a tonal study of the Friar. IV. Dance. This is a lively, highly rhythmic section. V. The Parting of Romeo and Juliet. This is the most extended movement of the suite, built mainly from a theme representing Romeo. VI. Dance of the West Indian Slave Girls. As Paris presents pearls to Juliet, slave girls perform a sensual dance. VII. Romeo at Juliet's grave. This finale gives voice to Romeo's terrible grief at Juliet's sepulchre.

The first suite, op. 64-bis, introduced in Moscow on Nov. 24, 1936, is also in seven parts. I. Dance of the People. A tarantella is taking place in the public square in Verona. II. Scene. The adherents of the houses of Capulet and

Montague, just before the outbreak of hostilities, is described. III. Madrigal. Romeo meets Juliet. IV. Minuet. This music accompanies a dance at the Capulet ball. V. Masques. Romeo, in disguise, invades the ball. VI. Romeo and Juliet. This is the music for the famous balcony scene. VII. The Death of Tybalt. The music realistically describes the duel.

The third suite, the one given least frequently—op. 101—was first heard in Moscow on March 8, 1946. It has six movements: I. Romeo at the Fountain; II. The Morning Dance; III. Juliet; IV. The Nurse; V. Morning Serenade; VI. Juliet's Death.

(3) Overture-Fantasy by Tchaikovsky (1869, revised 1870, 1880). The first version was introduced in Moscow on March 16, 1870, Nikolai Rubinstein conducting. A year later the composer revised the work completely, and a decade after that he revised it again. It is the third and final version that is now performed. The overture opens with a hymn for woodwinds describing Friar Laurence. A storm erupts in the orchestra to suggest the feud between the houses of Capulet and Montague. After this comes Romeo's glowing and radiant love music in English horn and muted violins, accompanied by plucked strings and syncopated horns. Juliet responds just as ardently, with an exquisite melody for muted, divided strings. This romantic mood is soon shattered by the return of the turbulent music of the family feud. As the music gains in agitation, the wondrous love music arises in the woodwind, then erupts eloquently in the full orchestra. The timpani, and a sudden silence, suggest dire foreboding. The imminent tragedy of the lovers is signalized by a violent eruption in the orchestra. A tender elegy is hymned for them. The overture ends with a last ominous roll of the timpani.

(4) See: Shakespeare, William.

Ronald, Sir Landon (born **Landon Russell**), conductor. Born London, England, June 7, 1873; died there, Aug. 14, 1938. The son of a popular composer and the brother of a noted impresario, Landon Ronald attended the Royal College of Music for five years. In 1890 he made his début as a pianist in London but soon after that he became a conductor for several minor opera companies and theaters in London and the provinces. In 1894 he toured the United States as the accompanist for the prima donna, Nellie Melba. In 1904 he was appointed principal conductor of the then newly formed London Symphony. Guest appearances with leading European orchestras added to his reputation as a conductor. In 1908 he became principal conductor of the New Symphony Orchestra in London; when this organization was renamed the Royal Albert Hall Orchestra he continued as conductor. From 1910 until his death he was also principal of the Guildhall School of Music. He wrote many compositions for orchestra, and for the piano, but only some songs became popular. He was the author of two autobiographical volumes, *Variations on a Personal Theme* (1922) and *Myself and Others* (1931). He was knighted in 1922.

Rondalla aragonesa (Granados). *See: Spanish Dances* (1).

Rondo. A form of instrumental music in which the principal subject is repeated several times. If this principal subject is represented by "A" and episodes by "B," "C," and so on, the rondo form can be represented as follows: A-B-A-C-A, or A-B-A-C-A-D-A, or A-B-A-C-A-B-A. The form is frequently found in sonatas, symphonies, and concertos as a last movement.

Rondo capriccioso. (1) For piano by Mendelssohn, op. 14. This is one of the composer's best works for the piano. It is in two sections. The first (Andante) is a broad and stately melody. A delightful contrast is provided by the second section (Rondo) which, with its lightness of touch and delicacy of movement, is in the style of the composer's most famous scherzos.

(2) *See: Introduction and Rondo capriccioso* (Saint-Saëns).

Rondo veneziano. For orchestra by Pizzetti (1929), introduced by the New York Philharmonic on Feb. 27, 1929, Toscanini conducting. The composer provided the following analysis: "This composition consists of three 'strophes,' preceded and followed by a ritornello (refrain); whence the title Rondo." The composer goes on to explain that the ritornello that opens and closes the work may be regarded as "an expression of the fundamental and immutable traits of the Adriatic city." The first strophe depicts "aristocratic Venice," and the middle strophe, "plebian Venice." The middle strophe is a sort of intermezzo "both idyllic and impassioned . . . Both the first and third strophes consist of two extensive periods, equally long, connected by an intermediate passage."

Root. In harmony the tone upon which a chord is built.

Ropartz, Guy. *See:* Guy-Ropartz, Joseph.

Rosamunde. Incidental music by Schubert (1823) to a play by Helmina von Chézy. This play, with Schubert's music, was given in Vienna on Dec. 20, 1823. Schubert's incidental music includes the following numbers: Overture; Entr'acte I, B minor; Ballet Music I, B minor; Entr'acte II, D major; Romanze; Chorus of the Spirits; Entr'acte III, B-flat major; Shepherd's Melody; Shepherd's Chorus; Hunting Chorus; Ballet Music II, G major.

The Overture is popular. Considerable confusion exists over its origin, since Schubert never wrote an overture expressly for *Rosamunde*. The one he used in 1823 was written in 1820 for his operetta, *Die Zauberharfe*. Later on, Schubert published, in piano-duet form, an overture that he called *Rosamunde;* but this work turned out to be an overture he had written in 1822 for another operetta, *Alfonso und Estrella*. It is the *Zauberharfe* Overture that is now designated as *Rosamunde*. It opens with a stately slow section in which the major theme is a graceful song for oboe and clarinet. In the Allegro section, the first violins present a jaunty tune. After it is developed, the woodwinds enter with a contrasting lyric subject.

Of the other incidental pieces, only two are familiar. The Ballet Music II, in G major, is in Schubert's happiest *gemuetlich* vein. It is popular in Fritz Kreisler's charming transcription for violin and piano. The Entr'acte II, in B-flat major, is one of Schubert's best-loved melodies. He liked it so well himself that he used

it again for the slow movement of his A minor String Quartet, and for his Impromptu in B-flat major, for piano.

Rosbaud, Hans, conductor. Born Graz, Austria, July 22, 1895. After attending Hoch's Conservatory in Frankfort, he was appointed in 1923 director of the Mainz School of Music, where he remained five years. Later he became conductor and head of the music department of the Frankfort Radio. After holding posts as music director of the cities of Muenster and Strasbourg, he went to Munich in 1945 to become conductor of the Konzertverein there. In 1948 he was appointed principal conductor of the Suedwestfunk Orchestra in Baden-Baden, which he soon raised to importance among German orchestras. Without abandoning this position, he served as conductor of the Tonhalle Orchestra in Zurich in 1952. He also appeared as guest conductor of other leading European orchestras and at prominent European festivals. He made his American début with the Chicago Symphony on Jan. 2, 1959.

Rosé, Arnold Josef, violinist. Born Jassy, Rumania, Oct. 24, 1863; died London, England, Aug. 25, 1946. After attending the Vienna Conservatory he made his début as violinist on Oct. 30, 1879, as soloist with the Gewandhaus Orchestra in Leipzig. From 1881 to 1938 he was the concertmaster of the Vienna Philharmonic and the Vienna Opera Orchestra. In 1883 he founded the Rosé Quartet, which achieved world fame for its performances of contemporary chamber music. It made its American début in Washington, D.C., on April 28, 1928. The other three members of this ensemble were P. Fischer, A. Ruzitska (later Morawetz), and F. Buxbaum (later J. Walther).

From 1909 to 1924 Rosé taught violin at the Vienna State Academy. After the *Anschluss* Rosé escaped to London, where he continued to appear with his Quartet until his death. He was married to Gustav Mahler's sister, Justine.

Rose, Leonard, cellist. Born Washington, D.C., July 27, 1918. He studied the cello mainly with his cousin, Frank Miller, solo cellist of the NBC Symphony, and with

Felix Salmond at the Curtis Institute. In 1938 he joined the cello section of the NBC Symphony, but a season later he went to Cleveland to become solo cellist of the Cleveland Orchestra. From 1943 to 1951 he was solo cellist of the New York Philharmonic. While holding these varied orchestral posts he appeared in recitals and as guest performer with major orchestras. After 1951 he pursued more actively his career as virtuoso in Europe and the United States. Rose has been a member of the faculty of the Juilliard School of Music in New York, and head of the cello department at the Curtis Institute in Philadelphia.

Rosenkavalier Waltzes. Waltzes for orchestra by Richard Strauss from his opera, *Der Rosenkavalier.* The libretto is by Hugo von Hofmannsthal, and the opera was introduced in Dresden on Jan. 26, 1911. In the composer's attempt to write a comic opera incorporating the best qualities of Mozart and Johann Strauss, he filled his score with delightful waltz sequences which contribute much of its intoxicating and buoyant spirit. Soon after the première of the opera, Strauss selected several of the best waltz tunes and combined them into a single integrated symphonic sequence. This waltz sequence represents some of the freshest and most infectious waltz writing since the time of Johann Strauss.

Rosenthal, Manuel, composer and conductor. Born Paris, France, June 18, 1904. He attended the Paris Conservatory from 1920 to 1924, specializing in the violin. He later studied composition privately with Ravel. In 1928 he received a fellowship of the American Foundation for the French Arts, and in 1936 he first achieved prominence as a composer with an orchestral suite, *Jeanne d'Arc,* successfully performed in Paris, then presented at the International Society for Contemporary Music Festival in London. In 1937 he was appointed associate conductor of the French National Radio, and from 1944 to 1947 he was its musical director. After World War II he appeared as guest conductor with important European orchestras. He made his American début on Nov. 6, 1946, over the CBS network. For a while he served as composer-in-resi-

dence at the College of Puget Sound in Tacoma, Wash., and from 1949 to 1951 he was conductor of the Seattle Symphony. After 1951 he resumed his activities as composer and conductor in Paris. His principal works are for orchestra and include a symphony, *Sérénade en quatre mouvements, Les petits métiers, La Fête du vin, Musique de table, Christmas Symphonies, Magic Manhattan,* and *Aesopi convivium.*

Rosenthal, Moriz, pianist. Born Lemberg, Austria (now Poland), Dec. 19, 1862; died New York City, Sept. 3, 1946. After attending the Lemberg Conservatory he studied the piano with Rafael Joseffy in Vienna. His Vienna début in 1876 was successful. For the next two years he continued to study with Liszt in Weimar and Rome, while making concert appearances in Europe and Russia. In 1880 he withdrew from all concert activity to study philosophy and esthetics at the University of Vienna. He returned from a four-year period of absence from the recital stage to give a concert in Vienna in 1884 in which his technical endowments, his style in the grand manner, and his mature interpretative concepts stamped him as one of the leading piano virtuosos of the time. His American début took place on Nov. 9, 1888, in a joint recital with Fritz Kreisler, then only fourteen. This was the first of 12 tours of the United States Rosenthal was to make during the next half-century; the golden jubilee of his career in America was celebrated at Carnegie Hall on Nov. 13, 1938. In that year Rosenthal established permanent residence in the United States.

He was a giant figure among the pianists of his time, one of the world's outstanding interpreters of Chopin. In 1912 he received the highest honor the Austrian government could bestow on a musician: appointment as Kammervirtuoso to the Emperor. Rosenthal was married to Hedwig Kanner-Rosenthal, a distinguished piano teacher (born Budapest, Hungary, June 3, 1882).

Rossini, Gioacchino, composer. Born Pesaro, Italy, Feb. 29, 1792; died Passy, France, Nov. 13, 1868. Rossini's immortality rests exclusively on his operas; none of his instrumental music, other than the overtures to some of the operas, has found a permanent place on present-day concert programs. These instrumental compositions include 5 string quartets, a woodwind quartet, 4 orchestral marches and an overture, variations for clarinet and orchestra, and a set of 186 pieces for the piano collectively entitled *Péchés de vieillesse*. When Rossini is represented on orchestral programs it is either through overtures to his famous operas, which are gems and representative of his creative genius; or through orchestral suites prepared by other composers from his various works. Of the last the most popular are two suites by Benjamin Britten entitled *Soirées musicales* and *Matinées musicales*, and two suites by Ottorino Respighi, *Rossiniana* and *La Boutique fantasque;* the last was adapted as an orchestral suite from Respighi's score for a ballet. Paganini transcribed one of Rossini's operatic melodies in his *Fantasia on the G String.*

See: *Barber of Seville, The; Boutique fantasque, La; Gazza ladra, La; Italian Woman in Algiers; Rossiniana; Semiramide; William Tell.*

Rossiniana. Suite for orchestra made up of four compositions by Rossini freely transcribed by Ottorino Respighi (1925). The music comes from Rossini's *Quelques Riens,* and consists of the following movements: I. Capri and Taormina (Barcarolle and Siciliana); II. Lament; III. Intermezzo; IV. Tarantella.

Rostal, Max, violinist. Born Teschen, Silesia, Aug. 7, 1905. After studying the violin with Arnold Rosé in Vienna and Carl Flesch in Berlin, he was appointed concertmaster of the Oslo Philharmonic, holding this post from 1917 to 1928. In 1925 he won the Mendelssohn Prize, after which he made numerous concert tours of Europe in recitals and as a member of the Rostal String Quartet. For two years he was Carl Flesch's assistant in Berlin, and from 1930 to 1933 professor of the violin at the Berlin State Academy. When the Nazi regime came to power, he settled permanently in London, becoming a British subject. There he has served as professor of the violin at the Guildhall School of Music and made many public appearances and recordings.

Rostand, Edmond, poet and dramatist. Born Marseilles, France, April 1, 1864; died Paris, France, Dec. 2, 1918. Rostand's most famous poetic drama, *Cyrano de Bergerac,* was the inspiration for orchestral works, all bearing the same name as the play, by the following: Josef Bohuslav Foerster (symphonic suite); Franz Rubinstein (overture); Albert Stoessel (symphonic portrait); and Johan Wagenaar (overture). Paul Bowles and Jean Nougues each wrote incidental music for it.

Incidental music for Rostand's *L'Aiglon* was written by Richard Addinsell; for *Le Bois sacré,* by Reynaldo Hahn. Ruth Gipps wrote an orchestral overture, and Jaroslav Křička incidental music, for *Chantecler. La Princesse lointaine* was the inspiration for a tone poem by Vincenzo Davico (*La Principessa lontana*), and an overture for orchestra by Nikolai Tcherepnin. Incidental music for that play was written by Gabriel Pierné, who also produced incidental music for *La Samaritaine.*

Rostropovich, Mstislav, cellist. Born Baku, Azerbaijan, Soviet Union, March 27, 1927. After attending the preparatory Seven-Years School for gifted musical children, he was a pupil of the Moscow Conservatory, from which he was graduated in 1948. As a Conservatory student he made his début in chamber-music performances with Leonid Kogan, Svyatoslav Richter, and Emil Gilels. In 1948 he became instructor, and in 1957 professor, at the Moscow Conservatory. In 1950 he won first prize in a cello competition at a festival in Prague. He first attracted attention as a virtuoso one year later in Moscow in a performance devoted to all six solo cello suites by Bach. He then made distinguished appearances throughout the Soviet Union, at the Florence May Music Festival, and in London and Paris. His American début took place in New York City on April 4, 1956; during this first American tour he presented the American première of Prokofiev's Second Cello Concerto.

Rothwell, Walter Henry, conductor. Born London, England, Sept. 22, 1872; died Santa Monica, Calif., March 12, 1927. He attended the Vienna Conservatory, and completed his music study in Munich with Ludwig Thuille and Max von Schillings. In 1895 he was appointed assistant to Gustav Mahler at the Hamburg Opera. From 1904 to 1908 he was conductor of the Savage Opera Company in the United States. He was the principal conductor of the St. Paul Symphony from 1908 to 1914. In 1919 he helped organize, and from then on until his death he directed, the Los Angeles Philharmonic.

Rouet d'Omphale, Le (Omphale's Spinning Wheel). Tone poem for orchestra by Saint-Saëns, op. 31 (1871), introduced in Paris on April 14, 1872. The program came from the legend of Hercules, who disguises himself as a woman to avoid unpleasant developments, then is put to the task of spinning by Omphale, Queen of Lydia. The sound of the whirring of the spinning wheel is imitated at the opening cf the tone poem by the strings. A solemn subject in the bass follows: Hercules' complaint at being subjected to the female chore of spinning. The music quickens in tempo and grows lively; then the rhythm of the whirring spinning wheel in the strings suggests that Hercules is back at his spinning.

Rounds. For string orchestra by David Diamond (1944), introduced by the Minneapolis Symphony on Nov. 24, 1944, Mitropoulos conducting. This work adapts to instrumental music the form of the vocal round. There are three sections: I. *Allegro molto vivace;* II. Adagio; III. *Allegro vigoroso.* In the first movement different choirs of strings enter canonically; this introduces the main melody in the violas. Diamond describes the middle movement as a "resting point"; it is lyrical and moody. The finale is a kind of fugal section in rondo form. A rhythmic device of the first movement is repeated to help "round out the entire work and unify the formal structure."

Rousseau, Jean Jacques, philosopher, musical theorist, and composer. Born Geneva, Switzerland, June 28, 1712; died Ermenonville, France, July 2, 1778. The celebrated philosopher was also an influential musican. He was the composer of a delightful comic opera, *Le Devin du village,* and an active participant in varied operatic activities and controversies of his day. But his musical endeavors extended into directions other than opera. For many years he earned his living copying music. He contributed articles on music to Diderot's Encyclopedia; proposed some refinements in the system of notation; and was the author of a *Dictionnaire de musique* (1767).

Roussel, Albert Charles, composer. Born Turcoing, France, April 5, 1869; died Royan, France, Aug. 23, 1937. He attended the Brest Naval School, then worked as a midshipman on an armored gunboat bound for Indo-China. By 1894 he had had enough of the sea, and decided to devote himself completely to music. After some instruction in organ and theory from Eugène Gigout in Paris, he attended the Schola Cantorum from 1898 to 1907; there he was a pupil of Vincent d'Indy in composition. In 1902 he was appointed instructor of counterpoint, holding this post about a dozen years. Soon after completing an impressionistic symphony, *Le Poème de la forêt,* introduced in Brussels in 1908, he returned to his first love, the sea, this time as a passenger. His visits to the ruins of old cities in India influenced his music; he now drew his inspiration from Eastern or oriental subjects and combined his formerly Impressionist style with oriental harmonies, melodies, and tone colors. His first success in this new style was a choral symphony, *Les Évocations,* inspired by India. A decade later he returned to Indian subjects for the setting and characters of a ballet opera, *Pâdmâvatî,* produced in Paris on June 1, 1923. Meanwhile he had completed the ballet, *Le Festin de l'araignée,* introduced at Paris in 1913; the orchestral suite from this score has become his most celebrated work.

In the middle 1920's, Roussel's style underwent still another transformation. Abandoning Impressionism and orientalism, he developed a neo-Classic idiom in which some of the outstanding works of his career were produced, notably the Suite in F major, for orchestra, and the third and fourth symphonies. Besides these and other works already mentioned, Roussel wrote for orchestra a piano concerto, a cello concertino, *Petite suite,* ballet suite from *Bacchus and Ariadne* (*Bacchus et Ariane*), *Sinfonietta,* and *Rapsodie flamande.* Other works include 2 violin sonatas, a string quartet, string trio, flute trio, piano suite, piano sonatina, and other piano pieces.

See: Bacchus and Ariadne; Festin d'araignée, Le; Suite—*Roussel;* Symphony —*Roussel.*

Rout. *See:* Bliss, Arthur.

Royal Albert Hall. A leading concert auditorium in London, planned as a memorial to the Prince Consort for the Exposition of 1851. It opened on March 29, 1871. In June of that year, Gounod led there a notable choral concert. The hall was later the scene of many distinguished concerts, and of performances by the Royal Albert Hall Orchestra. That orchestra was organized in 1905 by John Saunders as the New Symphony. In October 1909 it initiated a series of Sunday afternoon concerts at the Hall under Landon Ronald's direction; these concerts continued until 1919; then a new series of Sunday concerts was inaugurated at the Hall on Oct. 30, 1920. It was on this occasion that the orchestra assumed the name of the auditorium, but the ensemble was disbanded a few years later. When Queen's Hall was destroyed in a Nazi air attack in 1941, the Royal Albert Hall became London's main concert auditorium until the Royal Festival Hall was opened in 1951.

Royal Festival Hall. The principal concert auditorium in London, England, erected by the London County Council on the south bank of the Thames, west of Waterloo Bridge, the site of the 1951 Exposition. It opened on May 3, 1951, with a concert by the BBC Symphony, the Royal Philharmonic of London, and the London Symphony; Adrian Boult and Malcolm Sargent conducted. Since then the hall has been the home of some of London's major music events.

Royal Fireworks Music, The. Suite for orchestra by Handel (1749). It was written for a mammoth celebration in Green Park, London, on April 27, 1749, for the signing of a peace treaty at Aix-la-Chapelle ending hostilities between France and England. Handel's music proved the only

happy event of this occasion. Some of the fireworks set off a blaze in which the structure was destroyed and sent the people scurrying off in a stampede. The Handel music was preceded by a royal salute for 101 cannon. The suite itself opens with a brief overture. The following brief movements follow: *Largo alla siciliana* (written specifically to celebrate the peace and consequently subtitled *La Paix*); Allegro (expressing the pomp and circumstance of this festival occasion, and named *La Réjouissance*); a bourrée, and two minuets. Handel scored this work for a large band of winds and drums, and later rescored it for a normal orchestra. The suite today is often given in a transcription for orchestra by Sir Hamilton Harty.

Royal Liverpool Philharmonic Orchestra. *See:* Liverpool Philharmonic.

Royal Philharmonic Society of London. England's most venerable symphony orchestra, founded in London in 1813 and originally called merely the Philharmonic Society. Not until its centenary celebration was the title of Royal added to its name. The orchestra gave its first concert at the Argyll Rooms in Regent Street on March 9, 1813, with J. P. Salomon as concertmaster and J. B. Cramer at the piano. Until 1820 the orchestra did not have a conductor as such, the responsibility of training and leading it being shared by the concertmaster and the performer at the piano. But in 1820, on a visit to London, Louis Spohr conducted the orchestra with a baton. From this time on, the orchestra was led by some of the world's leading conductors. Among the prominent musicians, mostly British, who have held the post of principal conductor with this orchestra are Michael Costa, Sterndale Bennett, Arthur Sullivan, Frederick H. Cowan, Alexander Mackenzie, and Thomas Beecham. Many important composers have appeared as guest conductors, including Edward Elgar, Mendelssohn, Weber, and Wagner. From 1894 to 1941 the orchestra played at Queen's Hall. From 1941 to 1951 the orchestra performed at the Royal Albert Hall, and since 1951 it has appeared at the Royal Festival Hall.

Rubato. In tempo the term indicates "stolen" time, or giving some of the time value of longer notes to shorter ones without changing the rhythm.

Rubbra, Edmund Dominic, composer. Born Northampton, England, May 23, 1901. After studying composition with Cyril Scott he received a scholarship for the Royal College of Music, where for four years he was a pupil of John Ireland and Vaughan Williams. He also took lessons in composition from Gustav Holst. His Symphony No. 1, introduced in 1937 in London, made a strong impression. Premières of subsequent symphonies, of which he has produced seven in all, carried him to an imposing position in English music. Besides the symphonies he has written a viola concerto, *Improvisation* for violin and orchestra, *Sinfonie concertante* for piano and orchestra, *Soliloquy* for cello, strings, two horns, and timpani, and an overture for orchestra; also 2 string quartets, 2 violin sonatas, a cello sonata, and a trio. His style is modeled on the free rhythmic writing and lyrical polyphony of the Elizabethan composers. After World War II he became lecturer on music at Oxford and Fellow of Worcester College. He also made many appearances as pianist in recitals and in performances of chamber music.

Rubinstein, Anton, pianist and composer. Born Vykhvatinetz, Russia, Nov. 28, 1829; died Peterhof, Russia, Nov. 20, 1894. After some piano instruction from Alexandre Villoing, he made his concert début as a child prodigy. During a European tour he attracted the interest of both Chopin and Liszt. The latter advised Rubinstein to continue his music study in Germany, which he did with Siegfried Dehn. From 1841 on, he began making extended concert tours of Europe, and from 1846 to 1848 he taught the piano in Vienna and Pressburg. After returning to Russia in 1848 he was appointed chamber virtuoso to the Grand Duchess Helen, under whose sponsorship he wrote three operas. He later held the posts of court pianist and conductor of court concerts in St. Petersburg, and in 1859 he became the conductor of the Russian Musical Society. Notwithstanding these activities,

he managed to make a further intensive study of the piano, from which he emerged a profound artist and fabulous technician. His performances between 1867 and 1870 aroused the adulation of all Europe. In 1872 he toured the United States for the first time, giving 215 concerts. Between 1885 and 1887 he traveled throughout Europe in "farewell concerts." He then returned to St. Petersburg, where from 1887 to 1891 he devoted himself to the direction of the Conservatory, which he had helped to found. In 1890 he established the Rubinstein Prize, an international competition for pianists.

Rubinstein was a prolific composer in all branches of music. Strongly influenced by Mendelssohn, he had a gift for ingratiating lyricism and a sound harmonic technique. But he lacked self-criticism, producing an abundant library of music that lacked originality and that was often prolix. About all that has survived from his immense output is the Fourth Piano Concerto, op. 70, and several smaller pieces for the piano which include the *Melody in F, Kamenoi-Ostrow,* and *Romance.* Nevertheless in his own lifetime Rubinstein was greatly esteemed as composer. For his musical achievements he was the recipient of many honors, including the Order of Vladimir which brought him the rank of nobility, Knighthood of the Prussian Order of Merit, and the title of Imperial Russian State Councillor.

Rubinstein's principal works for orchestra include 6 symphonies (among them the *Ocean* and the *Dramatic*), 5 piano concertos, 2 cello concertos, a violin concerto, *Concertstueck* for piano and orchestra, and numerous overtures, suites, and tone poems (including *Don Quixote, Russia,* and an overture to *Antony and Cleopatra*). In chamber music he produced 10 string quartets, 5 piano trios, 3 violin sonatas, 2 cello sonatas, a quintet for piano and winds, string quintet, piano quartet, string sextet, and piano quintet. His numerous compositions for the piano embrace 4 sonatas, *Portraits* (including *Kamenoi-Ostrow*), *Melodies* (including the *Melody in F*), *Soirées de St. Pétersbourg* (including the *Romance* in E-flat), together with barcarolles, preludes, caprices, mazurkas, polonaises, etudes, serenades, nocturnes, and funeral marches.

See: Barcarolle; Concerto—*Rubinstein.*

Rubinstein, Artur, pianist. Born Lódz, Poland, Jan. 28, 1886. A child prodigy, he made a phenomenal début in Berlin at the age of twelve as soloist with a symphony orchestra. He was immediately engaged to appear with major orchestras in Dresden, Hamburg, and Warsaw. After a period of study with Paderewski, he made major appearances in Paris and London. In January 1906 his American début took place with the Philadelphia Orchestra, followed by a tour in which he gave 75 concerts. After returning to Europe he went into temporary retirement, devoting himself to additional study. He further enhanced his reputation as one of the foremost living virtuosos of the piano upon returning to the concert stage. His first tour of Spain in 1916 was so successful that he had to give 120 concerts instead of the four originally scheduled. In 1919 he appeared again in the United States. Since then he has been heard in all parts of the civilized world, recognized as a Titan of the keyboard. He has established permanent residence in the United States, having become an American citizen after World War II. He has appeared in several motion pictures, including *Carnegie Hall, Night Song,* and *Of Men and Music;* for two others—*I've Always Loved You* and *Song of Love*—he recorded the piano selections on the sound track. Villa-Lobos' *Rudepoêma,* both for orchestra and for piano solo, is a tonal portrait of Rubinstein.

Rubinstein, Beryl, pianist and teacher. Born Athens, Ga., Oct. 28, 1898; died Cleveland, O., Dec. 29, 1952. He studied the piano with Ferruccio Busoni in Germany, among other teachers. In 1916 he made his début as a mature artist in New York City, in a joint concert with Eugène Ysaÿe, several tours of Europe and the United States followed. In 1921 he joined the music faculty of the Cleveland Institute of Music, and from 1932 until his death was its director. He was the author of *Outline of Piano Pedagogy* (1929) and the composer of 2 piano concertos, a string quartet, and many etudes and pieces for the piano.

Rubinstein, Nikolai, pianist and teacher. Born Moscow, Russia, June 14, 1835; died Paris, France, March 23, 1881. After completing his music study in Berlin with Theodor Kullak and Siegfried Dehn, he began his concert career as a pianist in 1858. In 1859 he returned to Russia, where he founded and became head of the Russian Musical Society, an organization that distinguished itself for its performances of outstanding new Russian works, including many by Tchaikovsky. In 1866 he helped organize the Moscow Conservatory, serving as its director until his death; among his many pupils were Alexander Siloti, Emil Sauer, and Taneiev. He appeared as pianist in London in 1861 and in 1878 he conducted four concerts of Russian music in Paris. He died of consumption while en route to Nice for a health cure.

Rudepoêma. For piano solo, and also for orchestra, by Villa-Lobos. He wrote it originally for piano (1926), orchestrating it six years later. "Rudepoêma" means "savage poem." This work was intended as a tonal portrait of the piano virtuoso, Artur Rubinstein. Rhapsodic in style and elastic in structure, this music is filled with rhythmic vitality and dynamic changes of tempo. Its rich-sounding sonorities are calculated to portray the dynamic personality of the famous pianist. The orchestral version was introduced in Rio de Janeiro on July 15, 1942, the composer conducting.

Rudolf, Max, conductor. Born Frankfort, Germany, June 15, 1902. After completing his musical training at Hoch's Conservatory in Frankfort, he was appointed in 1922 coach at the Freiburg Municipal Theater. He held several conducting posts with other opera companies in Germany and Prague between 1929 and 1935. During this period he made several guest appearances with the Berlin Philharmonic. From 1935 to 1940 he was principal conductor of the Göteborg Symphony in Sweden. He settled in the United States in 1940, later becoming an American citizen. On Jan. 13, 1946, he made his début at the Metropolitan Opera, where until 1957 he served as conductor, musical secretary, and finally artistic administrator. In 1954 he made his American début as orchestral conductor with the Dallas Symphony. He was appointed principal conductor of the Cincinnati Symphony in 1958. He is the author of *The Grammar of Conducting* (1949).

Ruggles, Carl, composer. Born Marion, Mass., March 11, 1876. While attending Harvard University, he took courses in music with Walter Spalding and J. K. Paine. After leaving Harvard, he founded an orchestra in Winona, Minn., in 1912. In 1937 he was appointed to the music faculty of the University of Miami, in Florida. After twenty years in this post he went into retirement in Arlington, Vt. He has produced only a handful of compositions, but all are strongly individual, with a partiality for contrapuntal writing in an atonal style. These compositions include *Men and Angels* (later called *Angels*), *Men and Mountains, Portals, Sun Treader, Divinations, Organum,* and *Affirmations,* all for orchestra. He also wrote several pieces for the piano. In 1954 he was elected to the National Institute of Arts and Letters.

Ruhig. Peaceful.

Ruins of Athens, The (Die Ruinen von Athen). Incidental music by Beethoven, op. 113 (1811), for a play by August von Kotzebue. This play, with Beethoven's music, was produced in Pesth on Feb. 9, 1812. The score includes an overture and eight numbers. The most famous of these sections is the fourth, the *Marcia alla turca,* or *Turkish March,* popular in its original orchestral version and in an excellent transcription for violin and piano by Leopold Auer. Beethoven had used the same melody two years earlier in his Variations in D, for piano, op. 76 (1809).

Rumanian Rhapsodies, Nos. 1 and **2.** Two rhapsodies for orchestra by Georges Enesco, op. 11 (1901-1902), first performed in Paris on Feb. 7, 1908, the composer conducting. Both compositions exploit Rumanian folksongs and dances; one tune follows another in rapid succession and without much elaboration or variation. These rhapsodies are of interest not only for their exotic musical content but also for their exciting contrasts and climaxes. The first rhapsody, in A major, is the more popular. A slow, languorous theme for clarinet opens the work. This subject is answered by the oboe, after which the flute, other woodwinds, and strings join in. The tempo is accelerated to become a vivacious dance for the whole orchestra. A second important subject now appears in the strings against a decisive rhythm. This exciting melody soon assumes a melancholy character in the solo viola. After the presentation of a lively dance by first violins and woodwinds, and after the flute indulges in an improvisation, the mood becomes abandoned as one exciting dance follows another. A respite arrives with an oriental melody in the clarinet against a strong rhythm in plucked strings and brass. The rhapsody ends quickly after a last outburst of energy.

The second rhapsody, in D major, is for the most part slow and sensual music. It opens with a declamation in strings leading to a stately subject, also in strings. The mood becomes somewhat melancholy as the English horn presents a second important theme against tremolo strings. After the first section is developed, the solo viola plays a peasant dance. But an earlier somber mood is once again with us, as the rhapsody ends with the poignant voice of a flute.

Russia. Tone poem for orchestra by Balakirev (1884), originally entitled *Second Overture on Russian Themes,* and introduced at a school concert in St. Petersburg on April 18, 1865. When this overture was published it was called *One Thousand Years* in honor of the millennium of Russia, but when Balakirev revised it in 1882 he finally entitled it *Russia.* The tone poem develops three folksongs: a wedding song from Nizhni-Novgorod; a dance from Samara; and a dance from Simbirsk.

Russian Easter Overture (La grande pâque russe). Concert overture by Rimsky-Korsakov, op. 36 (1888), introduced in St. Petersburg on Dec. 15, 1888, the composer conducting. The principal melodic material is derived from the *Obikhod,* a collection of canticles of the Russian Orthodox Church. The slow introduction to the overture presents two of these melodies, *Let God Arise,* in the woodwind, and *An Angel Cried Out* in the solo cello. To the composer, this slow section represented the "Holy Sepulcher that had shone with ineffable light at the moment of the Resurrection." A cadenza for solo violin leads to the main body of the overture, in which these themes are repeated and developed. Trumpet blasts and horn calls introduce a subsidiary section, but the two main melodies are soon recalled, the second preceding the first, separated by a trombone recitative. A development of both melodies rises to a brilliant coda, and the overture ends with a final recollection of the second theme in trombone and strings.

Russian Five, The (or The Mighty Five). A school of nationalist Russian composers prominent in St. Petersburg in the latter half of the 19th century. The acknowledged leader of this group was Balakirev, while the other members were Mussorgsky, Cui, Borodin, and Rimsky-Korsakov. The term "Mighty Five" was coined by the Russian critic Vladimir Stassov in his discussion of a concert in St. Petersburg on May 24, 1867, conducted by Balakirev, in which works of the five composers were featured.

Russian Quartets. *See:* Quartet—*Haydn.*

Russian Sailors' Dance. An orchestral episode by Glière which comes as a climax to the first act of his ballet, *The Red Poppy;* this excerpt is often given at symphony concerts. *The Red Poppy* is one of the first successful Soviet ballets utilizing a revolutionary scenario. The ballet was introduced in Moscow on June 14, 1927.

Its setting is a Chinese port, where the arrival of a Soviet ship has a far-reaching effect on the lives of the exploited coolies.

Russian Symphony Orchestra. *See:* Altschuler, Modest.

Russlan and Ludmilla, Overture to. Overture for orchestra to an opera by Glinka (1842). The libretto, based on a poem by Pushkin, was written by the composer in collaboration with Shirkov and Bakhturin. The opera was introduced in St. Petersburg on Dec. 9, 1842. The principal melodies of the overture come from the opera's finale. After loud chords, the vigorous main theme comes in violins, violas, and woodwinds. The second theme is more melodious and has a folksong-like character; it appears in violas, cellos, and bassoon. Both themes are elaborated, and the overture ends with a gay coda in which a descending bass passage presents one of the first uses of the whole-tone scale in art music, before Debussy.

Rustic Wedding Symphony. *See:* Symphony—*Goldmark.*

Ruy Blas. (1) Concert overture by Mendelssohn, op. 95 (1839), first performed in Leipzig on March 11, 1839, the composer conducting. The overture is based on the drama by Victor Hugo, set in the court of Charles III of Spain. The overture opens in an austere mood with four bars for brass and woodwind. The first theme then appears in first violins and flute. After a recall of the opening mood, the second theme is presented staccato by clarinet, bassoon, and cellos.

(2) *See:* Hugo, Victor.

S

Sabata, Victor de, conductor and composer. Born Trieste, Italy, April 10, 1892. He was graduated from the Milan Conservatory in 1911 with a gold medal in composition. One year later he made his début as a composer with an orchestral suite which, after its successful première in Rome, was given in Paris, Brussels, and Russia. The tone poems *Juventus* and *Gethsemani* added to his reputation as composer. But it is as a conductor that de Sabata is best known. He first attracted attention with orchestral performances with the La Scala Orchestra in Milan and the Augusteo Orchestra in Rome, just before the end of World War I. For many years after that he was active in opera at the Monte Carlo Opera, La Scala, Bayreuth, and Salzburg, among other places. He made his American début as symphony conductor with the Cincinnati Symphony in 1927. This was followed by many appearances with leading American orchestras. He was appointed artistic director of La Scala in 1955.

Saber Dance (Khatchaturian). *See: Gayane.*

Sacher, Paul, conductor. Born Basel, Switzerland, April 28, 1906. He studied music with Karl Nef at the Basel University and with Rudolf Moser and Felix Weingartner at the Conservatory. In 1926 Sacher founded the Basel Chamber Orchestra, which he has since conducted in stimulating programs including numerous premières. In its first quarter of a century this orchestra introduced 75 new works by such masters as Richard Strauss, Honegger, Bartók, Stravinsky, and Hindemith; many of these compositions were written on special commission. Since the end of World War II Sacher has made numerous guest appearances with leading European orchestras and at major festivals. His American début took place in New York on April 3, 1955. Since 1935 Sacher has been president of the Swiss section of the International Society for Contemporary Music; since 1941 he has conducted the Collegium Musicum of Zurich, organized that year; and since 1946 he has been president of the Association of Swiss Musicians.

Sacre du printemps, Le (Stravinsky). *See: Rite of Spring, The.*

Saeverud, Harald, composer. Born Bergen, Norway, April 17, 1897. He received his musical training in Bergen and Berlin. In 1912 he conducted a program of his own works in Bergen. A government pension in 1933 enabled him to devote himself completely to composition. His mature works have been strongly influenced by the scales, rhythms, and contrapuntal techniques of old Norwegian music. They

include 7 symphonies (the most popular being No. 6, *Sinfonia dolorosa*), various concertos, several suites and shorter pieces for orchestra, a divertimento for flute and strings, *Romance* for violin and orchestra, and incidental music to *Peer Gynt*. He also wrote works for piano including sonatas, sonatinas, a suite, and variations.

Safonov, Vassily, conductor. Born Ishterskaya, Russia, Feb. 6, 1852; died Kislovodsk, Russia, March 13, 1918. From 1878 to 1880 he attended the St. Petersburg Conservatory. He made his début as a concert pianist in St. Petersburg on Nov. 22, 1880, then toured northern Europe, Austria, and Hungary. After returning to Russia he held teaching posts at the St. Petersburg Conservatory and from 1885 on at the Moscow Conservatory; the latter institution he served as director from 1889 to 1905. He made his début as a conductor in 1889 with concerts at popular prices in small Russian towns. In 1890 he was appointed conductor of the Russian Musical Society. He made successful guest appearances with the New York Philharmonic in 1904, and from 1906 to 1909 was principal conductor of that orchestra. A notable interpreter of the Russian and German symphonic literature, and especially of Tchaikovsky's symphonies, Safonov is perhaps best remembered as one of the first conductors of modern times to direct performances without a baton.

Saga, En (Sibelius). *See: En Saga.*

St. Francis' Sermon to the Birds (Liszt). *See: Legend.*

St. Francis Walking on the Waves (Liszt). *See: Legend.*

St. John Passion (J. S. Bach). *See: Passion According to St. John.*

St. Louis Symphony Orchestra. A symphony orchestra developed from the St. Louis Choral Society. The Choral Society was organized in St. Louis, Mo., in 1880; one year later an orchestra was added to it, with Joseph Otten as conductor. In 1890 the organization changed its name to the St. Louis Choral Symphony Society; about a decade later the choral functions of the Society were abandoned and the organization devoted itself to the orchestral repertory. Its principal conductors since Otten have been Alfred Ernest,

Max Zach, Rudolph Ganz, Vladimir Golschmann, and Edouard van Remoortel. The orchestra performs in Kiel Auditorium.

St. Matthew Passion (J. S. Bach). *See: Passion According to St. Matthew.*

St. Paul's Suite. For orchestra by Gustav Holst, op. 29, no. 2 (1913). It was written for the school orchestra of St. Paul's Girls' School, where Holst was serving as director. The music, influenced by English folksongs, is in four sections. I. Jig. An exotic atmosphere is here achieved through modal melodies. II. Ostinato. This section has the character of a perpetual motion. III. Intermezzo. The main melody of this movement resembles an English folksong. IV. Finale. Here the composer quotes from two English folksongs, *Dargason* (which is repeated thirty times with various alterations and variations) and *Greensleeves,* used as a contrapuntal background.

Saint-Saëns, Camille, composer, organist, and pianist. Born Paris, France, Oct. 9, 1835; died Algiers, Dec. 16, 1921. He made a remarkable appearance as a child prodigy pianist in Paris on May 6, 1846, and then from 1848 to 1853 attended the Paris Conservatory, where he was a brilliant student. In 1853 his Symphony No. 1 was successfully introduced in Paris, and the *Ode à Sainte-Cécile* received the prize of the Société Sainte-Cécile. From 1858 to 1877 he was organist of the Madeleine Church. In 1861 he also became professor of piano at the Ecole Niedermeyer. He won fresh acclaim as a composer in 1872 with the première in Paris of his tone poem, *Le Rouet d'Omphale,* and a comic opera, *La Princesse jaune.* In 1871 he helped found the Société Nationale de Musique, which became a powerful medium for introducing new French music.

A man of extraordinary versatility, Saint-Saëns was undoubtedly most famous as a composer. He had an extraordinary technique, impeccable taste, and an aristocratic style. He could write in many different styles with equal skill: sometimes music that was a stylistic carryover from a bygone era; at other times, music that bore the local coloration of exotic lands. He was prolific, facile, spontaneous —and at times superficial. But he was also able to bring to his music a winning beauty of sound, an ingratiating grace, a sense of structural balance and symmetry, and clarity.

He enhanced his reputation as a composer between 1872 and 1877 with a succession of important works including the First Violin Concerto, *Danse macabre* for orchestra, and the opera, *Samson and Delilah.* By 1881 his significance in French music was publicly confirmed when he was elected to the Institut de France, an occasion upon which he was described as "the best musician in France."

Saint-Saëns paid his first visit to the United States in 1906, making his American début as piano soloist with the New York Symphony on November 4. He returned to the United States for a second time in 1915. In his 81st year he toured South America and when he was 85 he performed in Greece and Algiers. He made his last public appearance as a pianist on Aug. 6, 1921, and two weeks after that he conducted his last concert. He was on a holiday in Algiers when he died.

The following are his principal instrumental compositions:

Chamber Music: 2 string quartets; 2 piano trios; 2 violin sonatas; 2 cello sonatas; piano quintet; piano quartet; septet; *Havanaise,* for violin and piano; oboe sonata; clarinet sonata; bassoon sonata.

Orchestra: 3 symphonies; 5 piano concertos; 3 violin concertos; 2 cello concertos; *Introduction and Rondo Capriccioso,* for violin and orchestra; various tone poems (including *Le Rouet d'Omphale, Phaëton, Danse macabre,* and *La Jeunesse d'Hercule*); *Suite algérienne; Jota aragonesa; Rapsodie d'Auvergne,* for piano and orchestra; *Carnival of Animals* (*Le Carnaval des animaux*), for two pianos and orchestra; *Ouverture de fête;* incidental music to various plays.

Organ: 3 *Rhapsodies on Breton Themes;* 3 fantasies; 3 preludes and fugues; 7 improvisations.

Piano: Variations on a Theme of Beethoven, for two pianos; *Souvenir d'Italie; Caprice héroïque,* for two pianos; *Feuillet d'album;* bagatelles, etudes, fugues, and so on.

See: Bacchanale; *Carnival of Animals, The;* Concerto—*Saint-Saëns; Danse macabre; Havanaise; Introduction and Rondo Capriccioso; Jeunesse d'Hercule, La; Rouet d'Omphale, Le;* Symphony—*Saint-Saëns.*

Sakuntala Overture. Concert overture by Carl Goldmark, op. 13 (1865), first performed in Vienna on Dec. 26, 1865. This composition, with which Goldmark achieved his first success, was based on the tale of Kalidasa. Somber harmonies in violas, divided cellos, and bassoons open the overture. After a change of tempo, a clarinet and two cellos bring on the main melody, a beautiful song describing the water nymph, Sakuntala. Subsidiary ideas, including a hunting theme, are introduced. Loud chords lead to a return of the introductory section. The work ends with a coda built from figures derived from the main melody and the hunting subject.

Salieri, Antonio, composer and conductor. Born Legnano, Italy, Aug. 18, 1750; died Vienna, Austria, May 7, 1825. A dominant musical figure in Vienna, he was the teacher of Beethoven, Schubert, and Liszt. He went to Vienna in 1766 and in 1770 led the première of his first opera, *Le Donne letterate.* From 1774 to 1778 he was conductor of Italian opera in Vienna. After several years in Paris and Italy, he returned to Vienna in 1788 and he served as court conductor there until 1824. As a composer, Salieri was most famous for his operas, but he also wrote 2 symphonies, various concertos, sonatas, trios, duets, and other instrumental pieces.

He was one of the most celebrated teachers in Vienna. He also featured prominently in Mozart's life—as one of his most bitter rivals and opponents. When Mozart's star first rose in Vienna, Salieri used his influence and power to obstruct performances of Mozart's operas or conniving for their failure. An unfounded rumor was circulated after Mozart's death that he had been poisoned by Salieri; this legend was the basis of a one-act opera by Rimsky-Korsakov, *Mozart and Salieri.*

Salle Pleyel. A concert auditorium on the Faubourg St. Honoré in Paris. It opened in 1926 and has since been the home for the Concerts Lamoureux as well as for chamber-music concerts and recitals.

Salmond, Felix, cellist. Born London, England, Nov. 19, 1888; died New York City, Feb. 19, 1952. For three years he attended the Royal College of Music, then completed his study of the cello with Edouard Jacobs in Brussels. His concert début took place in London in October 1909. During the next decade he made many appearances in England. In 1921 he made his first tour of the Continent. His American début took place in New York on March 29, 1922. Salmond now made his permanent home in the United States, where from 1925 to 1942 he was head of the cello department of the Curtis Institute and from 1942 on professor of cello and chamber music at the Juilliard School.

Salome. (1) A music drama by Richard Strauss, whose libretto was the play by Oscar Wilde in a German translation. The opera was introduced in Dresden on Dec. 9, 1905. For an orchestral excerpt *see: Dance of the Seven Veils.*

(2) *See:* Wilde, Oscar.

Salomon, Johann Peter, violinist and conductor. Born Bonn, Germany, January 1745; died London, England, Nov. 28, 1815. He began his professional career as a violinist by touring several German cities in 1765. He was then appointed court musician for Prince Henry of Prussia. In 1781 Salomon went to London, where he lived for several years, appearing with chamber-music groups and as a concertmaster of several orchestras; he also conducted orchestral concerts in which he introduced to London several of Haydn's and Mozart's symphonies. He induced Haydn to come to London in 1791 and 1794 to conduct two series of orchestral concerts and to write for them a dozen new symphonies. Some of Haydn's last quartets were written with Salomon's violin-playing style in mind; and it was Salomon who suggested to Haydn that he write the oratorio, *The Creation.* In 1796 Salomon resumed his concert activity in London. He helped found the Royal Philharmonic Society in London in 1813, and served as its concertmaster.

Salomon Symphonies. *See:* Symphony—
Haydn.

Salón México, El. Tone poem for orchestra by Aaron Copland (1936), first performed in Mexico City on Aug. 27, 1937, Carlos Chávez conducting. This work was inspired by a visit paid to Mexico by the composer when he was introduced to a popular dance hall called "Salón México." His final stimulation came from browsing through two scholarly works on Mexican songs. Copland explains that he intended to have this music reflect "the Mexico of the tourists, and that is why I thought of the Salón México. Because in that 'hot spot' one felt, in a very natural and unaffected way, a close contact with the Mexican people. It wasn't the music I heard, but the spirit that I felt there, which attracted me. Something of that spirit is what I hope to have put into my music." The work opens with some markedly rhythmic measures which contain the fragments of two melodies. A popular Mexican song, *El Mosco,* is then presented by a solo trumpet. Other Mexican tunes appear in rapid succession; one of these has the rhythm of a tango, and another is a jaunty tune for a clarinet.

Saltando. A method of bowing on a string instrument in which the bow executes a series of leaps from the string while continuing to move in one direction.

Saltarello. A 16th-century Roman dance in quick 3/4 or 6/8 time with lively skips and jumps. The main theme of the finale to Mendelssohn's *Italian Symphony,* the opening subject of Berlioz' *Roman Carnival Overture,* and a subject in the finale of Lalo's *Symphonie espagnole* are all saltarellos. Charles Gounod also wrote a Saltarello for orchestra (1871).

Salzburg Festival. One of Europe's most prominent summer music festivals, held approximately for four weeks from the end of July in Salzburg, Austria (Mozart's birthplace). It developed from a Mozart Festival held there eight times between 1877 and 1910, under many eminent conductors including Mahler, Muck, and Richard Strauss. The present festival came into existence in 1920, organized by Hugo von Hofmannsthal, Max Reinhardt, Franz Schalk, and Richard Strauss. The festival theater (Festspielhaus) was erected in 1926, but a new festival theater was being constructed in 1959. A pattern of activity was established which has continued through the years with minor deviations. Mozart's music holds the central interest. The emphasis is on opera, not only by Mozart, but by other composers as well, with occasional provocative premières. Orchestral, chamber, choral, and solo music are also part of the festival program. Orchestral concerts are given by the Vienna Philharmonic under leading conductors; but at times visiting orchestras from other countries participate. In addition, there are serenade concerts in the courtyard of the Archbishop's palace, and choral concerts in the Cathedral. The Festival suspended operations during World War II, in 1943. It resumed on Aug. 1, 1946, through the cooperation of the United States Army. Since 1956 Herbert von Karajan has been artistic director. Samuel Barber's *Symphony in One Movement* was the first American composition heard at the festival, in 1937; Barber's opera, *Vanessa,* the first American opera performed there, in 1958.

Salzedo, Carlos, harpist and composer. Born Arcachon, France, April 6, 1885. He was graduated from the Paris Conservatory when he was eighteen. After touring Europe as a harpist he came to the United States in 1909 and became first harpist of the Metropolitan Opera orchestra. After World War I he devoted himself to concert work and to appearances with chamber-music ensembles, some of which he had helped to found. He has written numerous compositions in which the technique of the harp has been extended. His first important composition was *Five Poetical Studies* for harp, introduced in 1919. Later harp compositions include *Scintillation, Panorama,* and *Wedding Presents* (all for solo harp), a sonata for harp and piano, several other chamber-music works employing a harp, and a tone poem for harp and orchestra entitled *The Enchanted Isle.*

In 1924 he organized the harp department at the Curtis Institute. He has also been active in promoting modern music. In 1921 he helped organize the International Composers Guild, the first organization in the United States exclusively devoted to the presentation of new music; in 1924 he helped create the Pan-American Association. Among the chamber-music ensembles he helped found were the Salzedo Harp Ensemble, Trio de Lutèce, the Barrère-Salzedo-Britt Trio and the Salzedo Harp Duo. He is the author of *Modern Study of the Harp* (1921) and *Method for the Harp* (1929).

Samaroff, Olga (born **Olga Hickenlooper**), pianist and teacher. Born San Antonio, Texas, Aug. 8, 1882; died New York City, May 17, 1948. She attended the Paris Conservatory from 1894 to 1897, the first American woman to do so. Her piano study was completed in Berlin with Ernst Jedliczka. She made her professional début on Jan. 18, 1905, with the New York Symphony; a tour of the United States followed immediately. In 1908-1909 she toured Europe. She later distinguished herself as one of the most eminent teachers of the piano in the United States. She was head of the piano department of the Philadelphia Conservatory and a member of the faculty of Juilliard School of Music. She also promoted layman's courses in music and lectured on music appreciation. From 1927 to 1929 she was the music critic of the *New York Post*. She was the author of *The Layman's Music Book* (1935), *The Magic World of Music* (1936), and an autobiography, *An American Musician's Story* (1939). From 1911 to 1923 she was married to the conductor, Leopold Stokowski.

Saminsky, Lazare, composer and conductor. Born Gotzulovo, Russia, Nov. 8, 1882; died New York City, July 1, 1959. He studied science and philosophy at the University of St. Petersburg and was a pupil of Rimsky-Korsakov and Liadov at the St. Petersburg Conservatory. His first important work to be performed was *Vigiliae,* in Moscow in 1913 by the Koussevitzky Orchestra. From 1915 to 1918 he conducted symphony concerts in Tiflis, and in 1917 became director of the People's Conservatory there. He came to the United States in 1920, becoming an American citizen, and from 1924 to 1958 he was music director of Temple Emanu-El in New York. From 1936 to 1958 he

conducted there an annual Three Choirs Festival. He has also made many appearances as guest conductor in Europe, South America, and the United States. He is the author of *Music of Our Day* (1932), *Music of the Ghetto and the Bible* (1934), *Living Music of the Americas* (1949), and *Physics and Metaphysics of Music* (1957). His principal works for orchestra include 5 symphonies, *Ausonia, Stilled Pageant, Pueblo: a Moon Rhapsody,* and *Rhapsody on Dunlap's Creek.*

Sammartini, Giovanni Battista (born **San Martini**), organist and composer. Born Milan, Italy, 1701; died there Jan. 15, 1775. As a composer of instrumental music he was a significant precursor of Haydn. After being organist for various small churches in Milan, he served as organist and choirmaster of Santa Maria Maddalena from 1730 to 1770. His early compositions were for organ and for chorus. In 1734 he completed his first symphony, successfully introduced that year in Milan. After that he made rich contributions to instrumental music. Mozart admired him profoundly, and Gluck was his pupil from 1737 to 1741. A prolific composer of over two thousand compositions, Sammartini produced symphonies, quartets, trio sonatas, sonatas, and concerti grossi. His music represented an important advance over that of his contemporaries in logic of structure, elegance of style, and lyricism.

Sammons, Albert, violinist. Born London, England, Feb. 23, 1886; died there, Aug. 24, 1957. He was mostly self-taught. From 1908 to 1913 he was concertmaster of the Beecham Orchestra in London, a period in which he also made many appearances as a virtuoso. From 1907 until 1916 he served as first violinist of the London String Quartet. After the war he concentrated on concert work. For many years he was professor of the violin at the Royal College of Music. He was the author of several theoretical works on the violin. Among his compositions is a *Phantasy Quartet* for strings which won the W. W. Cobbett Prize for chamber music.

Samson and Delilah. An opera by Saint-Saëns, libretto by Ferdinand Lemaire based on the biblical tale. The opera was introduced in Weimar on Dec. 2, 1877. For an orchestral excerpt *see:* Bacchanale.

Samuel, Harold, pianist. Born London, England, May 23, 1879; died there, Jan. 15, 1937. After attending the Royal College of Music, a pupil of Edward Dannreuther and Charles Villiers Stanford, he made his début as pianist at London in 1894. He first became known as an authoritative interpreter of Bach's music in London in 1921, when he devoted a week of daily concerts entirely to Bach. He subsequently made many appearances in cycles of all-Bach programs. His American début took place in 1924 with such a cycle. In 1930 he conducted a special class at Yale University. For many years he was professor of piano at the Royal College of Music and examiner at the Royal Academy, both in London.

San Francisco Symphony Orchestra. An orchestra founded in 1911 in San Francisco, Calif. Its first concert took place on Dec. 29, 1911, with Henry Hadley as conductor. The orchestra's principal conductors after Hadley were Alfred Hertz, Issai Dobrowen, Pierre Monteux, and Enrique Jorda. It gives its concerts at the War Memorial Opera House. When Monteux was engaged in 1934, the orchestra was reorganized, and its financing was arranged under a public tax system.

Sand, Georges (born **Amadine Aurore Dupin**), novelist. Born Paris, France, July 1, 1804; died Nohant, France, June 8, 1876. A prominent figure in the literary and cultural life of France, Sand played an important part in Chopin's life. Her turbulent love-affair with him is partly described in her book, *Un Hiver en Majorca* (1841); *Consuelo* (1842) is also a novel about Chopin. Liszt and his mistress, Mme. d'Agoult, appear thinly disguised as characters in *Les Lettres d'un voyageur* (1836).

Sándor, György, pianist. Born Budapest, Hungary, Sept. 21, 1912. From 1927 to 1933 he attended the Budapest Academy of Music, where his instructors included Béla Bartók and Zoltán Kodály. He made his public début as a pianist at Budapest in 1930, and from 1933 to 1938 he made many concert tours of Europe. His American début took place in New York in February 1939. During World War II he served in the United States Army. Since then he has lived in the United States and become an American citizen. His tours of the United States, South America, Mexico, and Europe brought him international recognition. He has lectured on musical interpretation and piano technique at the University of Mexico City and University of Bogota.

Sanromá, Jesús María, pianist. Born Carolina, Puerto Rico, Nov. 7, 1903. He came to the United States when he was fourteen, then attended the New England Conservatory, winning the Mason & Hamlin Prize for piano performance in 1920. Later study took place in Europe with Alfred Cortot and Artur Schnabel. He was official pianist of the Boston Symphony from 1926 to 1944, a period in which he also made many appearances in recitals and as guest artist with symphony orchestras. In 1951 he was appointed chairman of the music department at the University of Puerto Rico.

Sarabande. A slow and stately dance said to be of Spanish origin, in triple time, with the phrase usually beginning on the first beat. It is often found as a movement of the Baroque suite. Erik Satie wrote three exotic Sarabandes for piano (1887)—slow, grave dances audacious for their harmonic language. In their use of parallel chords and chords of the ninth they anticipate Debussy. Ferruccio Busoni wrote a Sarabande for orchestra, op. 51 (1921), planned as "a study" for his opera *Doktor Faust*. This is a symphonic intermezzo of great lyric interest, intended to forecast Faust's death.

Sarasate, Pablo de, violinist and composer. Born Pamplona, Spain, March 10, 1844; died Biarritz, France, Sept. 20, 1908. A child prodigy, he made his début at the age of six, following this with a tour of Spain. For three years he attended the Paris Conservatory, receiving a *premier accessit* in 1859. He began the first of many extensive tours of Europe in his fifteenth year. In the years that followed he performed in all parts of the civilized world. For about a decade his programs were dominated by fantasias on opera airs, many written by him to exploit his fabulous virtuosity. But a reappearance in Paris in 1872 marked the beginning of a dedication to the more traditional violin literature. From then on he was everywhere acclaimed as one of the world's foremost violinists, who now combined sensitive musicianship with his formidable technique. Many composers wrote major works for him, including Max Bruch, Edouard Lalo, and Saint-Saëns. He himself produced a library of violin pieces some of which became basic in the repertory. These include the *Gypsy Airs* (*Zigeunerweisen*), *Spanish Dances* (*Danses espagnoles*), *Caprice basque, Jota aragonesa, Introduction and Tarantella,* and *Zapateado.*

See: *Gypsy Airs; Spanish Dances* (2); *Zapateado.*

Sargent, Sir Malcolm, conductor. Born London, England, April 29, 1895. He received his first formal music instruction at the organ, becoming an Associate of the Royal College of Organists. In 1914 he was appointed organist of the Melton Mowbray Parish Church. After World War I, he became the youngest musician ever to receive a doctorate in music, from Durham. He made his conducting début in 1921 at a London Promenade Concert in a performance of his own *Impression on a Windy Day.* His first successes as conductor came in performances of music by Gustav Holst and Vaughan Williams; he directed the première of the latter's *Pastoral Symphony* in 1925. After that he made numerous guest appearances with leading English symphony orchestras. He also became principal conductor of the Royal Choral Society in London and shared with Beecham the direction of the Leeds Festival. In 1940 he was appointed principal conductor of the Liverpool Philharmonic, and from 1950 to 1957 was principal conductor of the BBC Symphony. His American début took place with the NBC Symphony in 1945. He was knighted in 1947.

Sarka (Smetana). *See: My Fatherland.*

Satie, Erik, composer. Born Honfleur, France, May 17, 1866; died Paris, July 1, 1925. He entered the Paris Conservatory in 1883, but impatient with its academic attitudes and traditional thinking, remained only a single season. In the ensuing few years he produced several piano pieces, all harmonically unorthodox, and audacious in the precision of their language and economy of form. *Ogives* came in 1886, followed by *Sarabandes, Gymnopédies,* and *Gnossiennes,* all still performed. For a while he worked as a pianist in a Montmartre cabaret, where he met and befriended Debussy, whom he influenced with his provocative ideas about and novel approaches to music. In Satie's own writing, these ideas and approaches grew increasingly quixotic. Besides his continual experiments in rhythm and harmony, he adopted unusual procedures such as barless notation; he gave his pieces such whimsical titles as *Dessicated Embryos* (*Embryons desséchés*) and *Three Pieces in the Shape of a Pear* (*Trois morceaux en forme de poire*); he filled his music with at times impish and at times absurd instructions to the performer. Such idiosyncrasies made him a notorious and provocative figure in French music after the turn of the 20th century.

Dissatisfied with his technique, Satie returned to music study just before his fortieth birthday by attending the Schola Cantorum, where for three years he was a pupil of Vincent d'Indy and Albert Roussel. This training gave him the confidence to undertake more ambitious projects than heretofore, in some of which he successfully utilized idioms of American popular music. In 1917 he wrote the music for a satirical ballet, *Parade,* introduced by the Ballet Russe in Paris on May 18, 1917. A year later he completed the "symphonic drama," *Socrate.*

Satie was no eccentric for eccentricity's sake alone. He was an artist deeply concerned with his artistic purpose: to rid music of all the sanctimonious attitudes, elaborate architectonic structures, and inflated emotions it had acquired from the Romantics and post-Romantics. He deeply felt that what the art of music needed was restraint, simplicity, and objectivity; it had to shed the influences of Wagner, Mahler, and Richard Strauss. Thus Satie was a precursor of the neo-Classical movement.

His influence on his contemporaries can hardly be overestimated. His esthetic theories and his individual techniques were assimilated by Debussy, Ravel, and members of "Les Six." In 1923 he became spiritual leader of still another French school of composers, the "Arceuillists," named after the section near Paris where Satie lived after 1898.

Besides pieces already mentioned, Satie's works for the piano include *Danses gothiques, Quatre préludes, Prélude de la porte héroïque du ciel, Pièces froides, Trois préludes flasques, En habit de cheval, Descriptions automatiques, Croquis et agaceries d'un gros bonhomme en bois, Chapitres tournés en tous sens, Enfantines, Heures séculaires et instantanées, Trois valses du précieux dégoûté, Sports et divertissements, Les Pantins dansent, Avant-dernières pensées, Nocturnes,* and *Premier menuet.* His compositions for orchestra include the ballet suite from *Parade, En habit de cheval, Quatre petites pièces montées,* and *La Belle excentrique.*

See: *Gymnopédies; Parade;* Sarabande.

Saudades do Brasil (Nostalgia for Brazil). Suite of 12 Brazilian dances for orchestra by Darius Milhaud (1921), first performed at Paris in 1921, Vladimir Golschmann conducting, and Loie Fuller interpreting the music in dance. In these pieces, which are also available in a version for piano, the composer nostalgically recalls various types of Brazilian dances he had encountered while living in that country. The dances are not reproduced authentically, but only suggested. The suite was intended as an idealized portrait of the Brazilian dance. The twelve numbers are named after different districts in Rio de Janeiro: I. Sorocaba; II. Botafogo; III. Leme; IV. Copacabana; V. Ipanema; VI. Gavea; VII. Corcovado; VIII. Tijuca; IX. Paineras; X. Sumaré; XI. Laranjeiras; XII. Paysandu.

Sauer, Emil von, pianist. Born Hamburg, Germany, Oct. 8, 1862; died Vienna, Austria, April 28, 1942. From 1879 to 1881 he attended the Moscow Conservatory, a pupil of Anton Rubinstein. After additional study with Liszt in Weimar, he made several tours of Europe and almost at once enjoyed huge success. His first tour of the United States took place in 1898-1899. From 1901 to 1907 he was the head of the piano division of the Meisterschule fuer Klavierspiel in Vienna. From 1908 to 1915 he lived in Dresden. In the latter year he returned to Vienna to resume his former post at the Meisterschule. One of the most distinguished pianists and teachers of his time, Sauer wrote an autobiography, *Meine Welt* (1901), and was the composer of 2 concertos, 2 sonatas, and 24 etudes, all for piano.

Sauguet, Henri, composer. Born Bordeaux, France, May 18, 1901. He went to Paris in his twentieth year, and a year later began an intensive period of music study with Charles Koechlin. At about this time he associated himself with Erik Satie and Roger Desormière and several other young French composers, all of whom formed a new school of composers dedicated to simplicity and economy and called the "Arceuillists." Sauguet's first important work to be performed was an opéra bouffe, *Le Plumet de colonel,* given at Paris in 1924. Success came three years later with a ballet, *La Chatte,* introduced by the Ballet Russe. His mature style is a compromise between Impressionism and medievalism: a marriage of the sensitive atmosphere and subtle suggestions of Debussy with the modal harmonies and esoteric lyricism of plainchant. His major orchestral works include a piano concerto, violin concerto, *Symphonie expiatoire, Stèle symphonique à la mémoire de Chateaubriand, Portraits de Paris, Les Trois Lys, Orphée* for violin and orchestra, and incidental music to many plays and motion pictures. He also wrote a considerable amount of chamber music including 2 string quartets, wind trio, *Dix Images pour une vie de Jeanne d'Arc,* and *Bocages.* Among his piano works are a sonata and two sets of pieces for children.

For many years Sauguet was a music critic for leading French newspapers; he has also been instrumental in founding such important French literary journals as *Candide* and *Hebdomadaire.* He paid his first visit to the United States in the spring of 1953, when an all-Sauguet concert was given in New York.

Saxophone. A keyed brass wind instrument with a conical tube and a single reed. It was designed in or about 1840 by

Adolphe Sax (born Dinant, Belgium, Nov. 6, 1814; died Paris, France, Feb. 7, 1894). In 1845 the saxophone made its first appearance in a French orchestra. The family of saxophones ranges in size from soprano to bass; the ones most often in use are the tenor and alto. The saxophone has achieved considerable vogue in American popular orchestras and jazz bands, and it is part of the orchestration of numerous famous symphonic jazz compositions. It has also been employed in serious music without a jazz content. Henry Brant and Paul Creston have written concertos for the saxophone; Debussy, a rhapsody; Glazunov, a concerto for saxophone, flute, and strings; Jacques Ibert, a concertino; Frank Martin, a ballade for saxophone, string orchestra, piano, and percussion; and Florent Schmitt, a *Légende*. The saxophone appears in Josef Holbrooke's tone poem *Apollo and the Seaman;* Prokofiev's *Lieutenant Kije* suite; Ravel's orchestration of Mussorgsky's *Pictures at an Exhibition;* Shostakovich's Polka from *The Age of Gold;* Richard Strauss' *Domestic Symphony;* Vaughan Williams' Ninth Symphony; and Villa-Lobos' Chôros No. 3. Florent Schmitt wrote a quartet for four saxophones, op. 102.

Scale. An arrangement in a fixed succession of the principal notes of a piece of music, or a passage within the music; the subdivision of an interval, like an octave, into a definite series of tones for melodic or harmonic purposes. The diatonic scale is a division of the octave into five whole tones and two semitones; and the chromatic scale divides the octave into twelve equal intervals. The order in which the five whole tones and two semitones appear in the diatonic scale is called a mode. In the major mode, the half step occurs between the third and fourth notes, and the seventh and eighth notes. In the harmonic minor mode the half-step interval is between the second and third notes and the sixth and seventh; while in the melodic minor mode the half step occurs between the second and third notes. Among other scales sometimes used by composers are the whole-tone (*see* Debussy) and the pentatonic scale (which see).

Scapino. Comedy overture for orchestra by William Walton (1940), introduced in Chicago on April 3, 1941, Frederick Stock conducting. The music was inspired by two 17th-century etchings by Jacques Callot. The picture of Scapino, a character from the Italian *commedia dell' arte,* is vivaciously portrayed at the beginning of the composition by a vigorous *Molto vivace* section. This is followed by a melodic passage for horns and violas, and a quasi-sentimental interlude for cellos against a background of pizzicato violins imitating the sound of strumming guitars. The vigorous opening section returns as a last reminder of Scapino before the overture ends.

Scarlatti, Alessandro, composer. Born Palermo, Sicily, May 2, 1660; died Naples, Italy, Oct. 24, 1725. His greatest contributions were to the stage, where he helped develop the traditions and techniques of Italian opera. Though less important, his instrumental music has historic value. Here will be found some notable early examples of Italian instrumental writing. Scarlatti was one of the first composers to write string quartets, a form in which he produced 4 works. He also wrote 12 concerti grossi, some sonatas and suites for solo instruments and accompaniment, and some pieces for the piano.

He studied with Giacomo Carissimi in Rome, and had his first opera, *L'Errore innocente,* produced at Rome in 1679. From 1682 to 1702 he lived in Naples, where he was maestro di cappella to the Viceroy, and where he wrote many works for the stage. He returned to Rome in 1703 and became at first assistant maestro di cappella, then full maestro, at Santa Maria Maggiore. He was back in Naples in 1709 to resume his old post with the Viceroy, remaining there for the rest of his life. He was the teacher of many eminent composers, including Francesco Durante, Johann Adolph Hasse, and Nicola Logroscino.

Scarlatti, Domenico, composer and harpsichordist. Born Naples, Italy, Oct. 26, 1685; died Madrid, Spain, July 23, 1757. The son of Alessandro (see above), he received his first music instruction from his father; some years later he was a pupil of Francesco Gasparini. He then settled in Rome, where he first became famous for his skill in playing the harpsichord; on one occasion he entered into a competition with Handel, which was judged a draw. From 1709 to 1714 he was employed by Queen Maria Casimira of Poland as maestro di cappella; during this period he wrote some operas. In 1714 he was appointed maestro di cappella at St. Peter's in Rome. The last quarter of a century of his life was spent in Spain as music master to the royal family. Long famous throughout Europe as a virtuoso on the harpsichord, Scarlatti now began writing music for that instrument. These works ushered in a new era for keyboard music. The composer called his pieces "Essercizi," or "Exercises," but they are now labeled "sonatas." These compositions, numbering over 500, represent the first full flowering of homophonic music, the beginning of a modern technique in writing for and performing on a keyboard intsrument. Scarlatti's sonatas have been adapted by several composers into orchestral or ballet suites, among these composers being Arthur Benjamin (Suite for Flute and Orchestra), Alfredo Casella (*Scarlattiana*, for piano and orchestra) and Vincenzo Tommasini (*The Good-Humored Ladies*).

See: Capriccio and Pastorale; *Good-Humored Ladies; Scarlattiana;* Sonata—*Scarlatti.*

Scarlattiana. For piano and orchestra by Alfredo Casella (1926), introduced in New York on Jan. 23, 1927, Otto Klemperer conducting, and the composer soloist. This work is a "divertissement" on themes from Domenico Scarlatti's sonatas for harpsichord.

Scène infernale (Prokofiev). *See: Love for Three Oranges.*

Scènes de ballet. Ballet suite by Stravinsky (1944), commissioned by Billy Rose. Parts were used in a ballet sequence in the Billy Rose Broadway production, *Seven Lively Arts,* produced in 1944; the dancers were Alicia Markova and Anton Dolin. The complete score was introduced in New York on Feb. 3, 1945. The music, as the composer explains, was "patterned after the forms of the classical dance, free of any given literary or dramatic argument. The parts follow each other as in a sonata or in a symphony, in contrasts and similarities." There are eleven sections, played without interruption: I. Introduction; II. Corps de Ballet Dances; III. Variations of the Ballerina; IV. Pantomime; V. Pas de deux; VI. Pantomime; VII. Variation of the Dancer. VIII. Variation of the Ballerina; IX. Pantomime. X. Corps de Ballet Dances; XI. Apotheosis.

Scenes from Childhood (Kinderscenen). Suite of 13 children's pieces for piano by Schumann, op. 15 (1838). The composer here contemplates the world of the child, and reproduces that world through short, descriptive pieces. The approach is always subtle and sophisticated. Undoubtedly the most famous single number in this set is the seventh, *Traeumerei (Dreaming)*, a gentle moody melody which has become one of the composer's most popular pieces of music. No. 4, *Bittendes Kind (Pleading Child)*, No. 5, *Glueckes genug (Perfect Happiness)*, and No. 9, *Ritter vom Steckenpferd (Rocking Horse Knight)* are also popular. Schumann wrote a second set of piano pieces about children, *Album for the Young* (which see).

Schaeffer, Pierre. *See:* Concrete Music.

Scharwenka, Xavier, pianist, teacher, and composer. Born Samter, Poland, Jan. 6, 1850; died Berlin, Germany, Dec. 8, 1924. After attending the Kullak Academy in Berlin he made his début as a pianist at Berlin in 1869; at the same time he joined the piano faculty of the Kullak Academy. During the next decade he combined his duties as teacher with concert appearances. In 1881 he founded his own Conservatory in Berlin, which he directed for a decade; in 1893 this school assumed the name of Klindworth-Scharwenka Conservatory. Scharwenka made his American début in New York on Jan. 24, 1891, in a performance of his own concerto. From 1891 to 1898 he was director of his own Conservatory in New York and from 1898 to 1914 co-director and head of the piano division of the Klindworth-Scharwenka Conservatory in Berlin. In 1914 he organized the Meisterschule for piano in Berlin, which he directed until the end of his life. He was court pianist to the Emperor of Austria.

Scharwenka was a prolific composer, producing a symphony, 4 piano concertos, numerous trios, sonatas, and quartets, and many pieces for the piano. He was the author of a book of piano exercises, and an autobiography, *Klaenge aus meinem Leben* (1922).

Scheel, Fritz, conductor. Born Luebeck, Germany, Nov. 7, 1852; died Philadelphia, Pa., March 13, 1907. After studying the violin with Ferdinand David in Leipzig, he held various posts as concertmaster and conductor in several German cities. He came to the United States in 1893, and conducted concerts in New York and at the Chicago Columbian Exposition. In 1895 he helped found the San Francisco Symphony and was its principal conductor for four seasons. His performances of Beethoven's symphonies in Philadelphia were the stimulus for the founding of the Philadelphia Orchestra in 1900, which he conducted until his death.

Scheherazade. Suite for orchestra by Rimsky-Korsakov, op. 35 (1888), introduced in St. Petersburg on Dec. 15, 1888, the composer conducting. The music is based on episodes from *The Arabian Nights*. Though in four movements, the work is integrated through the continual repetition of two important musical motifs. One is the theme of the Sultan, a strong subject for unison brass, woodwinds, and strings, with which the suite opens. The other is the Scheherazade theme, a tender melody in triplets for violin solo. I. The Sea and Sinbad's Ship. A strong statement of the Sultan theme is followed by soft chords in the brass. The Scheherazade melody is now presented by the solo violin against harp arpeggios. In the succeeding fast section, arpeggio figures present a picture of a swirling sea, while Sinbad's ship is represented by a theme for solo flute. II. The Tale of the Kalendar. This movement opens with the Scheherazade melody in the solo violin. The bassoon then begins the tale of the Kalendar which midway is dramatized by a brilliantly orchestrated and rhythmically dynamic section. III. The Young Prince and the Princess. This is a love song shared by the violins and clarinet. The movement ends with a recall of the Scheherazade theme. IV. The Festival at Bag-

dad; the Sea; the Ship Founders on the Rock. The Sinbad theme introduces the finale. A Bagdad festival is then depicted in a brilliantly orchestrated and richly sonorous section. Suddenly this gay mood is interrupted by the picture of an aroused sea which sends a ship to its doom against a rock surmounted by the bronze statue of a warrior. After this disturbance subsides, the Scheherazade melody returns for the last time to bring the wonderful tales of Scheherazade to their conclusion.

Schelling, Ernest, pianist, conductor, and composer. Born Belvidere, N.J., July 26, 1876; died New York City, Dec. 8, 1939. A child prodigy at the piano, he was sent in boyhood to Europe to study with Theodor Leschetizky, Moritz Moszkowski, and, finally, Paderewski. He then made his first extended tour of Europe, giving 186 concerts in 18 months. In 1905 he made his American début with the Boston Symphony. Neuritis of the hand compelled him to give up the career of piano virtuoso, and soon after World War I he diverted his musical energies to conducting. From 1922 on he conducted children's concerts with the New York Philharmonic, and other major American orchestras. He also appeared as guest conductor in adult concerts. From 1936 to 1938 he was the principal conductor of the Baltimore Symphony. Schelling first achieved success as composer in 1913 with *Impressions from an Artist's Life* for piano and orchestra. His most famous composition came a decade later, an orchestral fantasy entitled *A Victory Ball*. Other works for orchestra include a violin concerto, *Morocco, Suite fantastique,* and *Légendes symphoniques.*

See: *Victory Ball, A.*

Schelomo (Solomon). Rhapsody for cello and orchestra by Ernest Bloch (1915), introduced in New York on May 3, 1917, the composer conducting. The solo cello represents King Solomon; it opens the rhapsody with a declamation against woodwind chords. After another cello monologue, this time unaccompanied, there comes the first of two principal themes: an incisive rhythmic phrase first suggested by the strings, then carried on by horns, finally unfolded by full orchestra. The solo cello, unaccompanied, introduces the second main theme, which finally appears in bassoons and oboes; this is a sinuous melody of oriental character. Both themes are worked out elaborately, as the voice of the cello intermittently injects at times a brooding and at other times a melancholy commentary. The rhapsody ends with the same theme with which it opened.

Schenker, Heinrich, musicologist. Born Wisniowczyki, Poland, June 19, 1868; died Vienna, Austria, Jan. 14, 1935. Schenker evolved a theory of musical analysis with the aim of proving that music obeys certain natural laws. Courses in the Schenker theory have been given in the United States.

Schenker attended the Vienna Conservatory, where he was a pupil of Bruckner. Brahms became interested in him and through his influence Schenker's early compositions were published. He soon abandoned creative work for teaching and research in theoretical studies. He devoted himself to teaching a selected group of dedicated pupils. He formulated his ideas in many publications, of which the most important are the three books collectively entitled *Neue musikalische Theorien und Phantasien* (1906-1935).

Scherchen, Hermann, conductor. Born Berlin, Germany, June 21, 1891. After playing the viola with the Berlin Philharmonic, he made his conducting début with that orchestra in 1911. He was conducting orchestral concerts in Riga when World War I broke out, and he was interned in a Russian prison camp. After the war he became identified in Berlin with the *avant-garde* in German music. To promote contemporary music and contemporary German composers, he helped found the Neue Musikgesellschaft, the journal *Melos,* and the Scherchen String Quartet. He held various conducting posts in Germany between 1920 and 1928, the most important being that at the Museum Concerts in Frankfort. In 1933 he left Germany and became music director of the Swiss Radio. In 1937 he was appointed conductor of the then newly organized Musica Viva Orchestra in Vienna, with which he made many tours. Two years later he established a master class

in conducting in Switzerland. During this period he appeared as guest conductor throughout Europe, and at the festivals of the International Society for Contemporary Music. After World War II Scherchen became known to American audiences through his many recordings. He is the author of *Handbook of Conducting* (1929), *The Nature of Music* (1947), and *Musik fuer Jedermann* (1950).

Scherman, Thomas Kielty, conductor. Born New York City, Feb. 12, 1917. He received his academic education at Columbia University, and his musical training at the Mannes School of Music and the Juilliard School. In 1939 he was assistant to Otto Klemperer with a chamber orchestra in New York. After World War II, he originated an opera program and conducted orchestral performances over radio station WQXR, New York; he also served as assistant conductor of the Opera Nacional in Mexico. In 1947 he founded in New York the Little Orchestra Society which, since then, he has conducted in distinguished concerts in New York and on tour (*see:* Little Orchestra Society). Besides his performances with his own orchestra, Scherman has made guest appearances with major American symphonic ensembles; in 1957 he conducted the Berlin Philharmonic during a German-American music festival.

Scherzando. A term in performance indicating a lively, whimsical, or jovial style.

Scherzi, Gli. *See:* Quartet—*Haydn.*

Scherzo. A piece of music light in character, in a rapid tempo, carrying out the literal meaning of the word as a "joke." Scherzos are found in symphonies where, since Beethoven's Second Symphony, they often appear as a third movement, replacing the earlier minuet. The scherzo, like the minuet, is in 3/4 time, but its form may be more extended, and the mood lighter and more whimsical.

The scherzo also appears in orchestral music outside the symphony—as a self-sufficient composition. Works like Paul Dukas' *The Sorcerer's Apprentice* and Jaromir Weinberger's *Don Quixote* have been designated by their composers as scherzos. The Scherzo from Mendelssohn's *A Midsummer Night's Dream* is one of the most familiar examples of this orchestral form.

The scherzo can also be often found as a movement of a sonata, or as an independent composition for a solo instrument. In the latter category we find Chopin's four Scherzos for piano: B minor, op. 20 (1832); B-flat minor, op. 31 (1837); C-sharp minor, op. 39 (1839); and E major, op. 54 (1842). Chopin here does not observe the traditional meaning of the scherzo as a light-hearted composition; the prevailing mood of these works is somber, and the style is usually powerful and rugged.

Scherzo Capriccioso. For orchestra by Dvořák, op. 66 (1883). This work opens with a motto theme that recurs throughout. Two main subjects follow. The first is for full orchestra, and the second is waltz-like. The trio has an effective melody for English horn, and a subsidiary section for strings and winds. The work ends with a coda built out of the motto theme.

Schiller, Friedrich von, poet and dramatist. Born Marbach, Germany, Nov. 10, 1759; died Weimar, Germany, May 9, 1805. An outstanding figure in German Romantic literature, he was the author of numerous poetical dramas and poems which were the source of instrumental compositions, listed below. (Where titles of compositions are not given they are the same as the dramas or poems.)

Die Braut von Messina: Schumann (concert overture).

Demetrius: Ferdinand Hiller (concert overture); Josef Rheinberger (concert overture).

Don Carlos: Sir George Macfarren (concert overture).

Fiesko: Carl Graedener (concert overture).

Die Jungfrau von Orleans: Johann Philip Christian Schulz (concert overture).

Maria Stuart: George Vierling (concert overture). Incidental music by Vissarion Shebalin.

Die Raeuber: Incidental music by Yuri Shaporin, and Vissarion Shebalin.

Turandot: Incidental music by Carl Maria von Weber.

Wallensteins Lager: Vincent d'Indy (3 symphonic overtures); Josef Rheinberger (tone poem); Smetana (tone poem).

William Tell: Felix Draeseke (piano sonata); Rossini (overture to the opera); Hermann Zopff (tone poem).

In addition to the above, the finale of Beethoven's Ninth Symphony is a vocal setting of Schiller's poem, *Ode to Joy;* and Liszt's tone poem, *Die Ideale,* is based on Schiller's poem of the same name.

Schillinger, Joseph, composer and theorist. Born Kharkov, Russia, Aug. 31, 1895; died New York City, March 23, 1943. After attending the St. Petersburg Conservatory he conducted an orchestra in Kharkov and was professor at the State Academy of Music there. From 1926 to 1928 he was active in Leningrad as composer for the State Academy Theater. He came to the United States in 1929, later becoming a citizen. In the United States he held various posts as teacher and lecturer. Though he wrote several orchestral works performed by major orchestras—including *Airphonic Suite* for Thereminvox and orchestra, *North Russian Symphony* for accordion and orchestra, and a symphonic rhapsody for piano and orchestra entitled *October* —Schillinger distinguished himself primarily as a teacher and theorist. Having been trained as a mathematician, Schillinger formulated a new approach to composition based on mathematical and scientific methods. He evolved a system of exact techniques for writing music in every style, reducing composition to mathematical formulas, and making creation possible through the application of these formulas and through the use of various graphs and rules. His theories, and their application, were formulated in *The Schillinger System of Musical Composition,* published posthumously (1946). After Schillinger's death, the system was taught in several conservatories. It had a far-reaching influence on several contemporary composers, especially in the popular field.

Schippers, Thomas, conductor. Born Kalamazoo, Mich., March 9, 1930. He received his musical training at the Curtis Institute in Philadelphia, the Juilliard School in New York, and privately with

Olga Samaroff. His début as a conductor took place in New York in 1948 with the Lemonade Opera. Gian Carlo Menotti then selected him to conduct *The Consul* during its first Broadway run in 1950, and the première of the television opera *Amahl and the Night Visitors* in 1951. Schippers was engaged as a conductor of the New York City Opera in 1951. He also initiated his career as symphonic conductor with guest appearances with major American orchestras. On March 25, 1955, he made his début with the New York Philharmonic, the youngest musician ever to lead that organization. Late that spring and summer he conducted orchestral performances in Paris, Aix-en-Provence, and Bordeaux. In May 1955 he made his début at La Scala in Milan, and on December 24 of the same year at the Metropolitan Opera, in New York.

Schmitt, Florent, composer. Born Blamont, France, Sept. 28, 1870; died Neuilly, France, Aug. 17, 1958. In 1889 he entered the Paris Conservatory, where his teachers included Jules Massenet and Gabriel Fauré, winning the Prix de Rome in 1900. His first important compositions appeared between 1906 and 1907. They were the *Psalm 47* for chorus, soloists, and orchestra, and *The Tragedy of Salome,* both still popular. His early music was sometimes attacked for its adventurous experimentation with advanced harmonies, compound meters, and modern instrumentation. But the later music is permeated with poetic eloquence, effusive lyricism, and emotional expressiveness. He always, however, promoted the cause of the ultramoderns, and was one of the first in Paris to speak out on behalf of Stravinsky, Satie, and Schoenberg.

Schmitt was director of the Lyons Conservatory from 1922 to 1924. In 1932 he visited the United States, appearing in concerts devoted to his works. In 1936 he was elected a member of the French Academy and in 1957 presented with the Grand Prix in music by the City of Paris.

The following are his principal instrumental compositions:

Chamber Music: Piano quintet; saxophone quartet; string trio; flute quartet; quartet for three trombones and tuba; violin sonata; string quartet.

Orchestra: The Tragedy of Salome (La Tragédie de Salomé), ballet suite; *Trois rapsodies; Légende,* for violin and orchestra; *Antoine et Cléopâtre,* two suites; *Mirages; Ronde burlesque; Symphonie concertante; Trois danses; Janiana; Trois monocantes; Scènes de la vie moyenne;* Symphony.

Piano: Soirs, ten preludes; *Trois valses nocturnes; Pièces romantiques; Crépuscules; Ombres; Mirages.*

See: *Tragedy of Salome, The.*

Schmitz, Elie Robert, pianist. Born Paris, France, Feb. 8, 1889; died San Francisco, Calif., Sept. 5, 1949. He was graduated from the Paris Conservatory with first prize in piano. In 1908 he toured with several famous vocal artists, including Leo Slezak and Emma Eames, as accompanist. In 1912 he founded the Association des Concerts Schmitz in Paris, directing it for two years. After World War I he devoted himself to playing the piano, making several tours of Europe, and his first tour of the United States in 1919. He distinguished himself particularly in the French repertory. Besides his performances in recitals, he was a participating artist with leading chamber-music groups. He was also active as a teacher. In the United States he was a member of the faculty of the Golden Gate College in San Francisco and of the McCune School of Music in Salt Lake City. He issued an edition of Chopin's etudes and was the author of *The Capture of Inspiration* (1935) and *The Piano Works of Claude Debussy* (1950).

Schnabel, Artur, pianist. Born Lipnik, Austria, April 17, 1882; died Axenstein, Switzerland, Aug. 15, 1951. In 1888 he went to Vienna, where he studied the piano with Anna Essipova, Theodor Leschetizky, and Eusebius Mandyczewski. His concert career was then launched in Germany and Austria with recitals and in chamber-music performances with Carl Flesch, A. Hekking, and others. Later performances in all parts of Europe helped establish his reputation as an aristocratic interpreter of the piano works of Beethoven, Brahms, and Schubert. His American début took place on

Dec. 25, 1921, but this first tour of the United States was not successful. His return to the United States in 1933, on the other hand, was a triumph. In 1935 he presented in New York a cycle of seven concerts devoted to all the Beethoven piano sonatas. He later performed this cycle several times in Europe and the United States.

Schnabel was also active as a teacher of the piano, from 1925 to 1933 at the Berlin High School for Music, and after that at his summer home in Tremezzo, Lake Como, Italy. He was the author of *Reflections on Music* (1933) and *Line of Most Resistance* (1942); he was also the editor of Beethoven's sonatas and piano works of Mozart and Brahms.

Schnabel wrote several works for orchestra (including a symphony, rhapsody, and piano concerto), chamber-music ensembles, and piano. Though as a pianist he was a traditionalist who rarely played anything written later than Brahms, in his own music he was an ultra-modernist with pronounced leanings towards the twelve-tone technique.

His son, Karl Ulrich (born Berlin, Germany, Aug. 6, 1909), is also a concert pianist. He attended the Berlin High School for Music, and made his concert début in 1925. Besides appearing in recitals and with orchestras, he gave many performances of two-piano and four-hand music with his father.

Schnéevoigt, Georg Lennart, conductor. Born Viborg, Finland, Nov. 8, 1872; died Malmö, Sweden, Nov. 28, 1947. After attending the Helsinki Conservatory, and studying cello with Julius Klengel in Leipzig and Robert Fuchs in Vienna, he played the cello in a Helsinki orchestra and taught at the Conservatory. He made his bow as a conductor at Riga in 1900. From 1904 to 1908 he conducted the Kaim Orchestra in Munich, and from 1909 to 1920 the Riga Symphony. In 1912 he founded the Helsinki Municipal Orchestra, and in 1919 the Oslo Symphony, directing both until 1927. His American début took place in 1924 with the Boston Symphony. From 1927 to 1929 he was principal conductor of the Los Angeles Philharmonic. In 1932 he became the conductor of the National Orchestra in Finland, which through his efforts became one of the leading symphonic organizations in Scandinavia. Though a versatile conductor, Schnéevoigt was perhaps most famous as an interpreter of Sibelius' symphonies. In 1939 he conducted an all-Sibelius program at the New York World's Fair.

Schneider, Alexander, violinist. Born Vilna, Poland, Dec. 21, 1908. After attending the Frankfort Conservatory he was concertmaster of the Frankfort Symphony from 1925 to 1933, and second violinist of the Budapest String Quartet from 1933 to 1944, and since 1957. Since 1933 he has lived in the United States. In 1950 he helped Pablo Casals establish the Prades Festival, and in 1957 the Puerto Rico Festival. At both of these events, and elsewhere, he has appeared as a conductor, as well as a violinist.

Schneiderhan, Wolfgang, violinist. Born Vienna, Austria, May 25, 1915. He studied the violin with Otakar Ševčik in Prague and Julius Winkler in Vienna, making his public début in Vienna when he was ten, and at eleven touring Europe. In 1932 he was appointed concertmaster of the Vienna Symphony, and later of the Vienna Philharmonic. From 1939 to 1950 he was professor of the violin at the State Academy of Music in Vienna; since 1948 he has conducted master classes in Lucerne, Switzerland. Schneiderhan founded and played in a string quartet bearing his name, and founded and directed the Schneiderhan Orchestra. He made his American début as a violinist in October 1956 with the Boston Symphony. He was the only soloist appearing with the Berlin Philharmonic when it toured the United States that year. He is married to the celebrated singer, Irmgard Seefried.

Schnell. Fast.

Schoeck, Othmar, composer and conductor. Born Brunnen, Switzerland, Sept. 1, 1886; died Zurich, Switzerland, March 8, 1957. The son of a famous painter, he did not decide on a musical career until his seventeenth year. He then studied music at the Zurich Conservatory and privately with Max Reger in Leipzig. In 1917 he was appointed conductor of the St. Gall Symphony, a post retained for more than a quarter of a century. He was, however, most distinguished as a composer, occupying a dominant position among the Swiss composers of his generation. Though best in his operas and songs, Schoeck also produced some distinguished instrumental music, rich in romantic feeling and fresh in lyric content. In his later works, the emphasis in his writing passed from the lyric to the harmonic element. His works for orchestra include various concertos (violin; cello; horn), a suite, *Praeludium, Sommernacht,* and *Festlicher Hymnus.* He also wrote 2 string quartets, 2 violin sonatas, and a clarinet sonata.

Schoenberg, Arnold, composer. Born Vienna, Austria, Sept. 13, 1874; died Los Angeles, Calif., July 13, 1951. He is the creator of the twelve-tone technique (dodecaphony), in which he wrote some of his most provocative works. He began studying the violin and cello at the Realschule in Vienna. Later on, he was a pupil in counterpoint of Alexander Zemlinsky, who subsequently became his mentor, guide, closest friend, and finally brother-in-law. (Schoenberg married Mathilde Zemlinsky in 1901.) For a while Schoenberg played the cello in the Polyhymnia Orchestra directed by Zemlinsky. Then he turned to composition and produced his first ambitious works, including a string quartet, performed at Vienna in 1897. Two years later he completed *Transfigured Night* (*Verklaerte Nacht*) in its first version for sextet. By 1901 he had produced most of the *Gurre-Lieder,* a monumental setting of poems by Jens Peter Jacobsen for soloists, chorus, and orchestra; he did not orchestrate it until a decade later. In these early compositions, Schoenberg showed pronounced Romantic leanings, and an indebtedness to the Wagnerian idiom.

Soon after his marriage Schoenberg went to live in Berlin. There he led a cabaret orchestra, and for a time taught composition at the Stern Conservatory. He was back in his native city by July 1903, concentrating on teaching and composition. He was now beginning to renounce his former Romantic tendencies for greater simplicity and concentration of style and greater elasticity of technique. The Quartet in F-sharp minor, in 1907, was the last time in more than three decades that he was to use a key signature. From 1907 on he began to abandon set tonalities in a search for music freed from dependence on a key center or tonic; at the same time he undertook experiments with various types of dissonance. Now an avowed atonalist, he produced works that shocked and electrified the world of music, and that usually inspired catcalls and sometimes riots when first performed. These works include the Five Pieces for Orchestra, Six Pieces for Piano, and *Pierrot Lunaire.*

There were those in Vienna who believed in him implicitly. A few of his pupils became disciples who formed a clique to promote his creative principles; among them were Alban Berg and Anton Webern. Several older and more famous musicians, including Gustav Mahler and Richard Strauss, used their influence to arouse interest in Schoenberg's theories and works.

The antagonism of the Viennese critics and concert audiences towards his music led Schoenberg to return to Berlin in 1911. There he taught composition at the Stern Conservatory. He also completed the orchestration and final revision of his early *Gurre-Lieder,* which scored a major success when introduced in Vienna on Feb. 23, 1913, Franz Schreker conducting. However, the climate in Vienna had not yet changed completely for Schoenberg. The première of his *Kammersymphonie* on March 31, 1913, provoked fist-fights in the audience, occasioning "the greatest uproar which has occurred in a Viennese concert hall in the memory of the oldest critics," according to a report in the *Musical Courier.*

During World War I Schoenberg served in the Austrian Army. After the war he returned to Vienna, now to evolve that personal technique with which he would henceforth be identified: the twelve-tone row. In an effort to bring discipline to atonality Schoenberg now built his music from the twelve basic semitones within the octave, treating each tone as of equal importance with the others. These twelve tones were arranged according to certain principles into a melody or row, and each composition was built around its own row, which could be manipulated in various ways. Schoenberg had been experimenting with this technique since 1915, but it makes its official appearance in the fourth movement of his *Serenade,* in 1924; it was fully crystallized in the Suite for piano, the Third String Quartet, and the Variations for Orchestra, completed between 1925 and 1928. As precise as a mathematical formula, as coldly logical as a syllogism, this music was often strident and ugly. The increasing individuality of Schoenberg's writing now provoked even greater antagonism. Premières of his twelve-tone compositions inspired violent demonstrations everywhere.

To counter the long-prevailing hostility towards new expression in music, Schoenberg and his disciples created in Vienna, in 1918, the Society for Private Performances, from which critics were barred, and in which their controversial music could be played and heard under favorable auspices.

Until 1933, Schoenberg divided his activities between Vienna and Berlin. In the latter city he became a member of the Prussian Academy of Arts. He left Berlin permanently in 1933 when the Nazis came to power, and for a while lived in Paris. There, as a gesture against the anti-Semitic program of the Nazi regime, he officially returned to the Jewish faith in which he was born but which he had abandoned in 1921. Later in 1933 he migrated to the United States, where eight years later he became a citizen. For a while he taught special classes in composition at the Malkin School in Boston. Then he established his residence in Brentwood, outside Los Angeles, Calif. He taught classes in composition first at the University of Southern California, then at the University of California in Los Angeles. When he was seventy he went into retirement. From then until a month before his death his teaching activity was confined to a few handpicked students.

Schoenberg was creatively even more productive in America than he had been in Europe. In his last works he no longer felt impelled to write exclusively in the twelve-tone technique, and at times he abandoned that technique altogether. These later works included a violin concerto, piano concerto, *Ode to Napoleon,* and *A Survivor from Warsaw.*

In the last decades of his life, Schoenberg found he was no longer a prophet without honor. Premières of his last works became major musical events, towards which audiences and critics proved most sympathetic. His 70th and 75th birthdays were celebrated throughout the United States with performances of his works. In 1947 he was the recipient of a Special Award of Merit from the National Institute of Arts and Letters.

In Thomas Mann's novel, *Doctor Faustus,* the central character is a composer in the twelve-tone style. A note in the first edition of the novel expressed indebtedness to Schoenberg and his technique for much of the musical content of the novel. Despite this explanation, Schoenberg, upset at the "consequences of ascribing my creation to another person which, in spite of being fictitious, is represented as a living man," attacked Mann and his novel in the *Saturday Review* for taking advantage of "my literary property."

Schoenberg was the author of several theoretical texts, the most important being the *Theory of Harmony (Harmonielehre),* published in an English translation in 1948.

Besides compositions already mentioned above, Schoenberg's instrumental music includes the Second and Fourth String Quartets, a quintet for flute, oboe, clarinet, horn, and bassoon, a suite for two clarinets, bass clarinet, violin, viola, cello, and piano, a string trio, *Fantasia* for violin and piano. His orchestral music includes *Pelleas and Melisande,* Suite in G major for strings, Theme and Variations, *Prelude to Genesis,* and a Second Chamber Symphony.

See: Five Pieces for Orchestra; *Kammersymphonie; Ode to Napoleon; Pelleas and Melisande* (2); *Pierrot Lunaire;* Quartet—*Schoenberg; Transfigured Night.*

Schoepfung, Die (Haydn). *See: Creation, The.*

Scholes, Percy Alfred, musicologist. Born

Leeds, England, July 24, 1877; died Vevey, Switzerland, July 31, 1958. He was a music teacher at various English schools, and lecturer on music at Oxford and Cambridge, before he turned to music journalism. In 1908 he founded the periodical *The Music Student*, which he edited for many years; in 1913 he became the music critic of the London *Evening Standard;* from 1920 to 1925 he was editor of the *Radio Times;* and from 1920 to 1927 music critic of the *Observer.* He also made many tours as lecturer, including five of the United States beginning in 1915. In the middle 1920's he made his home in Vevey, Switzerland, where in 1929 and 1931 he organized the Anglo-American Conference of Musical Educators. Among his books are the *Listener's Guide to Music* (1919), *The Book of the Great Musicians* (1920), *The Listener's History of Music* (1923), *The Mirror of Music* (1947), and biographies of Charles Burney (1948) and John Hawkins (1953). He was also the editor of the *Oxford Companion to Music* (1938), *The Concise Oxford Dictionary of Music* (1952), and *Oxford Junior Companion to Music* (1954).

School for Scandal, The. *See:* Sheridan, Richard Brinsley.

Schoolmaster, The. *See:* Symphony—*Haydn.*

Schradieck, Henry, violinist and teacher. Born Hamburg, Germany, April 29, 1846; died Brooklyn, N.Y., March 25, 1918. He studied music at the Brussels Conservatory and with Ferdinand David in Leipzig. From 1863 to 1868 he was professor of the violin at the Moscow Conservatory. For many years after that he was the concertmaster of first the Hamburg Philharmonic, then the Leipzig Gewandhaus Orchestra. In Leipzig he also taught violin at the Conservatory. He later came to the United States, where he became famous as a teacher of the violin. He published several excellent volumes of violin etudes and works on violin technique.

Schreker, Franz, composer. Born Monaco, March 23, 1878; died Berlin, Germany, March 21, 1934. He attended the Vienna Conservatory. In 1911 he founded the Berlin Philharmonic Choir, with which for two years he conducted such provoca-

tive programs of new music that they led to his dismissal. Meanwhile, his first opera to be performed was seen in Frankfort in 1912; it was *Der ferne Klang,* a failure owing to its progressive style and stark realism. Recognition as a composer of operas came in 1918 with *Die Gezeichneten,* given in Frankfort. From then on, his importance in the theater was recognized throughout Europe. In 1920 he became director of the Berlin High School for Music, where his influence as a teacher was profound, and in 1932 he was appointed professor at the Prussian Academy of Arts. He resigned in 1933 when the Nazis came to power. Schreker was at his creative best in his operas. His orchestral music, like his stage works, had a pronounced dramatic feeling, and combined Wagnerian orchestration with French Impressionism. These works include the *Romantic Suite; The Birthday of the Infanta,* ballet suite; *Ein Tanzspiel; Rokoko,* ballet suite; *Fantastic Overture; Kammersymphonie;* and *Little Suite.*

Schubert, Franz, composer. Born Vienna, Austria, Jan. 31, 1797; died there, Nov. 19, 1828. The son of a schoolmaster, Schubert was directed by his father to that profession. But music was not neglected. As a child Franz received instruction on the violin, viola, and organ, and in singing and thorough bass from his father, brother, and a local choirmaster. From 1808 to 1813 he attended the School of the Imperial and Royal Court Chapel, where he was trained for the Chapel Choir. While there he completed a symphony, several chamber-music works, and numerous songs and piano pieces. His teacher, Antonio Salieri, said: "You can do everything, for you are a genius."

Schubert left the Chapel School when his voice broke. In 1814 he became a teacher in a Vienna school owned and directed by his father. He held this job (which he detested) for two years. He wrote music every free moment he could find. In 1814 he wrote an opera, a Mass, 2 string quartets, and many smaller compositions; among the last was his first song masterpiece, *Gretchen am Spinnrade.* In 1815 he completed 2 symphonies, 2 Masses, an opera, 4 operettas, 4 sonatas, some piano pieces, and 146 songs including the celebrated *Der Erlkoenig.*

He abandoned teaching in 1817 to devote himself to composition. Taking up lodgings with a friend, Franz von Schober, he spent the next few years in a happy-go-lucky Bohemian existence, with several bosom friends, including the renowned singer Johann Michael Vogl, Johann Mayrhofer, and Joseph von Spaun. They spent their evenings at parties henceforth known as "Schubert Evenings" ("Schubertiaden"). There many of Schubert's compositions were introduced. They also visited cafes, drank a great deal of wine, and indulged in schoolboy pranks. But gaiety and irresponsible living did not keep Schubert from his work. By 1820 he had produced over 500 works in every branch of music. Of these only a Mass and a single song had been performed publicly. Except to his small and affectionate circle, he was completely unknown, dependent for his subsistence on the charity of friends.

The year 1820 seemed to promise a change of fortune. Two of his operettas were introduced in Vienna: *Die Zwillingsbrueder* on June 14, and *Die Zauberharfe* on August 19. Both were dismal failures. When a year later the first of Schubert's compositions to achieve publication were issued in Vienna (*Der Erlkoenig* with a few other songs) it was once again only the result of the bounty of his friends who had gathered a hundred subscribers in advance of publication.

Frustrations and disappointments continued to haunt him. *Rosamunde,* for which he wrote incidental music, was a fiasco in 1823, largely due to the silly and confused play by Helmina von Chézy. An opera score he submitted to Carl Maria von Weber for criticism evoked the annihilating advice that "first puppies and first operas should be drowned." Except for two summer engagements as a music tutor at the Hungarian estate of Count Esterházy in 1818 and 1824, he was unable to find a job. Penniless and unknown, he succumbed to despair which not even the love of his friends nor the carefree Schubert evenings could dispel. Besides he was suffering a deterioration of health, brought on by a venereal disease; on several occasions he had to go to a hospital.

Yet his formidable creative vitality remained unaffected. Though he had lost all hope of earning a living from his music, or interesting audiences, he continued writing one masterwork after another—song cycles, symphonies, sonatas, string quartets, and so on.

His depression deepened in 1827 when he served as torchbearer at the funeral of a composer he revered above all others— Beethoven. From this time on he repeatedly expressed the wish to be buried next to Beethoven. The tragedy of his daily life, and his preoccupation with death, are expressed in much of the music Schubert wrote in 1827-1828, especially in the song cycles *Die Winterreise* and *Schwanengesang,* the C major String Quintet, the three piano sonatas published posthumously, and the E-flat major Mass.

On March 26, 1828, there took place in Vienna the first concert devoted entirely to Schubert's works. It aroused so much enthusiasm that Schubert and his friends were led to believe that recognition was at hand. Optimistic about his future, Schubert began planning more ambitious works; and to meet the technical demands they would make on him he planned to study counterpoint with Simon Sechter. But he was mortally sick. At the home of his brother, where he was now living, he kept tottering from "the chair to the bed and vice-versa," as he revealed in a letter. On November 18 he became delirious and kept asking if he were lying next to Beethoven. One day later he was dead.

He was buried as near to Beethoven as could be arranged. When a monument was erected on Schubert's grave a few months later, it bore the following epitaph by the eminent Viennese poet, Franz von Grillparzer: "Music has here entombed a rich treasure, but still fairer hopes."

It is not difficult to explain why Grillparzer should speak of "fairer hopes." At the time of Schubert's death, the world of music could hardly be expected to know the full range of his achievements, since few of his works were either pubished or performed. Most of his manuscripts remained for years after his death forgotten on dust-laden shelves in closets, thrown together haphazardly. It took the patient labors of several notable musicians—among them Schumann, Arthur Sullivan, and George Grove—to locate much of this music, which included such treasures as the *Unfinished* and C major Symphonies, the *Rosamunde* music, and innumerable songs, piano pieces, and chamber-music works.

Once the world was introduced to Schubert's music in all its infinite variety, it did not fail to place him among the greatest composers. He was undoubtedly the most inspired melodist of all time. Beautiful lyricism came from him effortlessly; he produced musical beauty as easily as he breathed. There is hardly a major work that is not flooded with the happiest lyrical expression, an expression so fresh and youthful and spontaneous and poetic that it never fails to cast a spell of enchantment on the listener.

He had technical shortcomings, particularly in his larger works. His structures are sometimes diffuse; his orchestration sometimes lacks luster and variety. But so exalted is the inspiration of the lyricism, so rich in poetic content is the best music, so stirring are the emotional outbursts, so enchanting are the lighter moods, and so sure are his instincts for creating an unforgettable passage through an unusual progression, modulation, or harmony—that in listening to one of his masterworks we are conscious only of its immense creative power.

In one field of composition he was preeminent, because this was the field in which his technique could fully meet the requirements of his poetic expression. Since that field is vocal—it is that of the lied, or art song—it does not come within the scope of this encyclopedia. Nevertheless, many of Schubert's songs appear in concerts of instrumental music through transcription and adaptation. Schubert himself borrowed from his songs for material for larger works. Franz Liszt transcribed many of Schubert's best-known songs for the piano.

The following are Schubert's principal instrumental works:

Chamber Music: 15 string quartets; string quintet; *The Trout (Die Forelle)* piano quintet; octet; 2 piano trios; string trio; violin sonata; 3 violin sonatinas; Fantasy in C major for violin and piano; Sonata in A minor for arpeggione (a kind of guitar) and piano (arranged as a concerto for cello by Gaspar Cassadó).

Orchestra: 8 symphonies; 7 overtures (including 2 in the Italian style); incidental music to *Rosamunde; Konzertstueck* for violin and orchestra; German dances, minuets.

Piano: 22 sonatas; *Wanderer Fantasy* (arranged for piano and orchestra by Liszt); minuets, ecossaises, waltzes, German dances, laendler, impromptus, *Moments musicaux.*

See: Ecossaise; Fantasia—*Schubert; German dance; Gastein Symphony;* Impromptu—*Schubert;* Laendler; *Moment musical;* Octet; Quartet—*Schubert;* Quintet—*Schubert; Rosamunde;* Sonata—*Schubert;* Symphony—*Schubert;* Trio—*Schubert;* Waltz.

Schuman, William Howard, composer. Born New York City, Aug. 4, 1910. He studied harmony with Max Persin and counterpoint with Charles Haubiel. Later on he attended the Mozarteum in Salzburg on a scholarship and studied composition with Roy Harris. In 1939 and 1940 he received a Guggenheim Fellowship. His first successes as a composer came with the *American Festival Overture,* introduced by the Boston Symphony under Koussevitzky in 1939, and the Third String Quartet, which won the Town Hall Composers Award. His Third Symphony, first given by the Boston Symphony in 1941, received the New York Music Critics Circle Award and his cantata, *A Free Song,* the first Pulitzer Prize in music in 1943. From 1935 to 1945 he taught at Sarah Lawrence College. From 1945 to 1952 he was director of publications for G. Schirmer, Inc. Since 1945 he has also been president of the Juilliard School of Music. While Schuman's compositions are dynamic in their rhythmic vitality, they are also characterized by expansive lyric lines and expressive contrapuntal writing. A fresh instrumentation and occasionally an infectious sense of humor provide additional interest. The following are Schuman's principal instrumental works:

Chamber Music: 4 string quartets; *Quartettino,* for four bassoons.

Orchestra—6 symphonies; piano concerto; violin concerto; *American Festival Overture; William Billings Overture; Side Show (Circus Overture); Undertow; Judith: A Choreographic Poem; Prayer in Time of War; New England Triptych; Credendum.*

Piano—Three-Score Set; Voyage.

See: American Festival Overture; Credendum; New England Triptych; Symphony—Schuman; Undertow.

Schumann, Clara (born **Clara Wieck**), pianist and wife of Robert Schumann. Born Leipzig, Germany, Sept. 13, 1819; died Frankfort, Germany, May 20, 1896. Besides being the wife of Robert Schumann, Clara is remembered as one of the foremost women pianists of her generation. The daughter of Friedrich Wieck (Schumann's teacher), she received from him piano instruction early and made her concert début in Leipzig when she was nine. She continued playing in public for the next half-dozen years, scoring major successes in Germany, Austria, and France; her programs often included her own compositions and extemporizations. Her turbulent love affair with Robert Schumann is described in that composer's biography; it began in or about 1835 and culminated in marriage in 1840. After her marriage she made numerous concert appearances, sometimes with her husband. She was responsible for introducing and popularizing many of his piano works, including the Concerto in A minor. After Schumann's death she intensified her concert activity throughout Europe, an ardent propagandist for the music of her husband and that of Brahms. She taught piano at Hoch's Conservatory in Frankfort in 1878-1879. She wrote many works for the piano, including a piano concerto and some chamber music. She also prepared cadenzas for piano concertos by Beethoven and Mozart.

Schumann, Robert, composer. Born Zwickau, Germany, June 8, 1810; died Endenich, Germany, July 29, 1856. He started studying the piano when he was six and at eight he formed and led a lit-

tle orchestra; he also made some childhood attempts at composition. His widowed mother, however, wanting him to become a lawyer, discouraged all musical interests. Schumann entered the University of Leipzig in 1828. While there he combined law study (which he detested) with piano lessons from Friedrich Wieck. An acute attack of melancholia dictated a change of scene. He continued his law study at Heidelberg in 1829, but while there he also plunged deeply into musical activity. He completed his first serious works, including the *Abegg Variations* for piano, his first work to be published.

By the end of 1829 he had come to the irrevocable decision to abandon law study for music. Returning to Leipzig, he lived with Wieck and began an intensive period of piano study with him. The determination to become one of the greatest virtuosos of all time led him to devise an artificial method of making the fourth finger as flexible as the others. This method brought on a paralysis of the hand, and brought to an abrupt end all thoughts of a virtuoso career. Schumann now aspired to become a great composer. After studying theory with Heinrich Dorn, he wrote a major work for the piano, the *Paganini Etudes.* He also started work on a symphony. At the same time he engaged in varied musical activities in Leipzig which brought him to prominence. In 1833 he formed the Davidsbuendler, a musical society made up of idealistic young musicians out to destroy philistinism in music. In 1834 he helped found the *Neue Zeitschrift fuer Musik,* a journal dedicated to the highest ideals in music. This soon became one of Europe's most influential musical journals, the medium through which young composers like Chopin and Brahms first achieved recognition.

Between 1833 and 1835 Schumann's creative powers ripened. He produced his first masterworks in *Carnival (Carnaval)* and the *Études symphoniques,* both for piano.

In 1835 Schumann entered upon one of the most turbulent periods of his life when he fell in love with Clara, daughter of his teacher, Wieck. She was sixteen he, twenty-five. She had adored him from the time she was twelve. His love, however, ripened more slowly. But as he came to admire her remarkable gifts as a pianist, and to enjoy her warm and loving company, he recognized how indispensable she had become to his personal happiness.

Clara's father, opposed to Schumann as a son-in-law, did everything he could to keep the lovers apart. For four years, Clara and Schumann had to contrive hurried meetings or surreptitious exchanges of notes. Wieck employed lies and deceptions to poison his daughter against Schumann; also threats of violence against Schumann himself to keep him from Clara. Only one course was finally left to the young composer: the law courts. The trial was long and bitter, with Schumann emerging victorious. On Sept. 12, 1840, he and Clara were finally married.

The personal happiness that followed brought on in Schumann an outpouring of musical creation in fields other than the piano. In the first three years of his marriage he completed about 30 works, including his first symphony, the first version of his piano concerto, 3 string quartets, the piano quintet, the piano quartet, and many fine lieder. At the same time he carried on vigorously his duties as editor of the *Neue Zeitschrift* and as a teacher of piano and composition at the Leipzig Conservatory, which he helped to found in 1843.

In 1844 Schumann was compelled by poor health to give up all activities except composition and teaching. For a few years he lived quietly in Dresden, where he completed several important works, among them his second symphony and the final version of the piano concerto. Between 1850 and 1853 he served as municipal music director at Duesseldorf. But he was not well. All his life he had been subject to minor nervous disorders and melancholia. In Duesseldorf his nervousness and irritability were aggravated; for the first time he revealed lapses of memory. He began hearing voices and musical sounds. His depression deepened, and he once tried drowning himself in the Rhine. One week later he was confined to an insane asylum near Bonn, where he spent the last two years of his life, always haunted by fantasies and tortured by noises and sounds in his mind's ear.

Schumann's career is unique in that, broadly speaking, he concentrated on a single branch of composition at a time. First he devoted himself to the piano, for which he created some of his greatest music. Here he brought a wealth of harmonic, rhythmic, and melodic ideas together with a remarkable virtuosity in polyphony, a poetic fancy, delightful whimsy, and a wide range of moods and feelings. For these richly varied thoughts and emotions he created flexible structures made up of many small sections, but always integrated by a single poetic idea.

This creative process can be said to have ended in 1840, the year of his marriage. In 1840 he entered upon songwriting, producing about 140 lieder in that year. In 1841 he turned mainly to orchestral composition, and in 1842 he directed his energy principally to chamber music.

He was often less successful in the larger orchestral forms than in his songs and piano pieces; the symphonies especially leave much to be desired in the way of orchestration and structure. But he never failed to produce a wealth of the most appealing and expressive lyricism, to create seductive moods often of a radiant beauty, and to fill his music with the most affecting and stirring emotion.

The following are his principal instrumental compositions:

Chamber Music: 3 string quartets; 2 violin sonatas; 3 piano trios; piano quintet; piano quartet; 4 *Fantasiestuecke* for violin, cello, and piano; 3 *Fantasiestuecke* for clarinet and piano; 3 *Romances* for oboe and piano.

Orchestra: 4 symphonies; 4 concert overtures; *Scherzo, Overture and Finale;* piano concerto; cello concerto; violin concerto; Overture and incidental music to *Manfred;* Fantasy in C major, for violin and orchestra; Introduction and Allegro (*Konzertstueck*), for piano and orchestra.

Piano: 3 sonatas; *Abegg Variations;*

Etudes after Caprices of Paganini; Davidsbuendlertaenze; Toccata in C major; *Carnival (Carnaval); Fantasiestuecke; Études symphoniques; Papillons; Scenes from Childhood (Kinderscenen); Kreisleriana;* Fantasy in C major; *Faschingsschwank aus Wien; Album for the Young (Album fuer die Jugend); Waldscenen; Bunte-Blaetter; Albumblaetter;* arabesque, intermezzi, humoresque, *Novelletten, Romances,* marches, fugues.

See: Arabesque; *Abegg Variations; Albumblatt; Album for the Young; Carnival* (2); Concerto—*Schumann; Davidsbuendlertaenze; Études symphoniques;* Fantasia—*Schumann; Fantasiestuecke; Faschingsschwank aus Wien; Kreisleriana; Manfred; Novelette; Paganini Etudes* (1); *Papillons;* Quartet—*Schumann;* Quintet—*Schumann;* Romance; *Scenes from Childhood;* Symphony—*Schumann;* Toccata.

Schuricht, Carl, conductor. Born Danzig, Poland, July 3, 1880. His principal music study took place at the Berlin High School for Music and with Max Reger in Leipzig. After serving his apprenticeship with various German opera companies he was appointed music director at Wiesbaden in 1912; from 1922 to 1944 he was music director there. During the same period he made guest appearances with leading European orchestras, becoming such a favorite in Holland that in 1938 Queen Wilhelmina conferred on him the Order of Orange-Nassau. His American début took place at St. Louis in 1927. In 1944 he settled in Switzerland, and for the next decade was heard in guest performances throughout Europe. He made his return appearance in the United States, in Washington, D.C., on Nov. 4, 1956, with the Vienna Philharmonic, then making its first American tour.

Schuster, Joseph, cellist. Born Constantinople, Turkey, May 23, 1903. He studied the cello with Josef Press at the St. Petersburg Conservatory and Hugo Becker at the Berlin High School for Music. From 1926 to 1931 he was first cellist of the Berlin Philharmonic. He settled in the United States in 1934, later becoming a citizen. His American début took place in New York on March 15, 1935. From 1936 to 1944 he was first cellist of the New York Philharmonic. After that he devoted himself extensively to concert work.

Schwanda der Dudelsackpfeifer (Schwanda the Bagpipe Player). An opera by Jaromir Weinberger, with a libretto by Miloš Kareš based on a folk tale. The première of the opera took place in Prague on April 27, 1927. For orchestral excerpts *see:* Polka and Fugue.

Schwanendreher, Der. *See:* Concerto—Hindemith.

Schwarz, Rudolf, conductor. Born Vienna, Austria, April 29, 1905. He studied the piano and violin with private teachers in Vienna. Between 1923 and 1933 he was conductor at the Duesseldorf Opera, then was removed from this post and later despatched to a concentration camp by the Nazis. In 1945 he settled permanently in England, where he became successful as a symphony conductor. From 1947 to 1950 he was conductor of the Bournemouth Municipal Orchestra, from 1950 to 1957 of the Birmingham Orchestra, and since 1957 of the BBC Symphony.

Schweitzer, Albert, organist, physician, and humanitarian. Born Kaysersberg, Alsace, Jan. 14, 1875. He won the Nobel Peace Prize in 1952. Long before he distinguished himself as a physician and humanitarian in French Equatorial Africa, he was famous as an organist and an authority on Bach. He studied the organ with Ernst Muench in Strasbourg. While pursuing the profession of minister, he completed his organ studies in Paris with Charles-Marie Widor. In 1906 Schweitzer became organist of the Société J. S. Bach in Paris. From this time on he gave performances throughout Europe, acclaimed as one of its foremost organists, and one of the world's greatest interpreters of Bach's organ works. With Widor he edited all of Bach's organ music; he also wrote a definitive biography of Bach (1905). In 1909 he presided over a conference on organ building in Vienna which helped establish international regulations; he also read a paper on the reform of the construction of organs. He then turned to the study of medicine, and as a physician went to Lambaréné, in French Equatorial Africa, to do medical missionary work; in his first nine months there he treated over 2000 cases. From time to time he has left Africa to tour Europe as organist and lecturer, usually to raise money for his missionary work.

Schweitzer wrote his autobiography, *My Life and Thought* (1933), and *On the Edge of the Primeval Forest* (1948). In 1951 he was the subject of a film biography. Often described as one of the greatest men of the 20th century, Schweitzer has been the recipient of many honors.

Schwieger, Hans, conductor. Born Cologne, Germany, June 15, 1906. He attended the Cologne High School for Music, a pupil of Walter Braunfels and Hermann Abendroth. From 1927 to 1930 he was Erich Kleiber's assistant at the Berlin State Opera, and from 1930 to 1937 general music director in several German cities. In 1937 he toured Japan, directing the Tokyo Symphony. He came to the United States in 1938 and subsequently became a citizen. From 1939 to 1941 he was conductor of the Southern Symphony in Columbia, S.C. In 1944 he founded, and from then until 1948 directed, the Fort Wayne Symphony in Texas. Since 1948 he has been principal conductor of the Kansas City Philharmonic. Beginning in 1956 he combined this post with one in Germany as conductor of the Nuremberg Opera and Nuremberg Civic Orchestra.

Scordatura. The mistuning of a string instrument to produce a special effect.

Score (German, **Partitur;** Italian, **Partitura;** French, **Partition**). A series of staves, each with different music, placed one above another so that they can be read simultaneously. The modern orchestral score follows a more or less standard pattern. Reading from top to bottom, the score begins with the woodwind, and proceeds with brasses, percussion, and strings.

Scoring. Apportioning a musical composition to various instruments.

Scorrevole. A term calling for a nimble performance.

Scotch Fantasy. For violin and orchestra by Max Bruch, op. 46 (1880), first performed by Pablo de Sarasate at Hamburg in September 1880. This work was inspired by several novels by Sir Walter

Scott. Bruch makes skilful use of some popular Scottish melodies throughout the four movements: I. Grave; *Adagio cantabile;* II. Allegro; III. *Andante sostenuto;* IV. *Allegro guerriero.* In the first movement Bruch utilizes *Auld Rob Morris.* In the second, the solo instrument presents *The Dusty Miller.* The third movement begins with *I'm a Down for Lack of Johnnie,* in the solo violin, while the finale opens with *Scots wha hae* in solo violin and harp.

Scotch Symphony. *See:* Symphony—*Mendelssohn.*

Scott, Cyril Meir, pianist and composer. Born Oxton, England, Sept. 27, 1879. Scott attended Hoch's Conservatory in Frankfort, then studied privately with Iwan Knorr. In 1898 he settled in Liverpool, where he taught piano and began composition seriously. In 1900 two of his orchestral works were successfully introduced under Hans Richter's direction: the *Heroic Suite* in Liverpool and his first symphony in Darmstadt, Germany. His piano quartet and second symphony, introduced respectively in 1901 and 1903, added to his reputation. Scott has been most effective in writing shorter pieces for the piano, some of which have become extraordinarily popular. Among the most celebrated are *Danse nègre, Water Daffodil, Impressions of the Jungle Book,* and *Lotus Land* (the last transcribed for violin and piano by Fritz Kreisler, and also for orchestra). These and other miniatures are sensitive tone pictures, Impressionist in their harmonies and poetic in mood. But Scott has not avoided experimentation. He was one of the first English composers to use advanced idioms and techniques: shifting meters, unresolved discords, unorthodox progressions and modulations. His orchestral compositions include 2 symphonies, various concertos (piano; violin; cello; two violins); oboe), *Christmas Overture, Two Passacaglias on Irish Themes, Festival Overture,* Rhapsody, *Russian Fair, Souvenir de Vienne,* and Suite for Strings. Among his chamber-music works are 3 string quartets, 2 string trios, piano trio, piano quartet, a suite for string quartet, 2 violin sonatas, cello sonata, clarinet quintet, and *Sonata melodica* for violin and piano. Besides piano pieces already mentioned his works for that instrument include sonatas, suites, etudes, nocturnes, and arabesques.

Scott toured the United States in 1921 as pianist, conductor, and lecturer on contemporary music. He is the author of an autobiography, *My Years of Indiscretion* (1924), and of several interesting books on varied musical subjects including *The Philosophy of Modernism in its Connection With Music* (1917), *The Influence of Music on History and Morals* (1928), and *Music: Its Secret Influence Throughout the Ages* (1933). He also wrote books on adult education and occult philosophy.

Scott, Sir Walter, poet and novelist. Born Edinburgh, Scotland, Aug. 15, 1771; died Abbotsford, Scotland, Sept. 21, 1832. He was the originator of the English historical novel. The following novels were the source of orchestral compositions.

Ivanhoe: John Parry (concert overture).

Land of the Mountain and the Flood: Hamish MacCunn (concert overture).

Lay of the Last Minstrel: John Francis Barnett (tone poem).

Marmion: Dudley Buck (concert overture); Arthur Sullivan (concert overture).

Peveril of the Peak: Edward H. Thorne (concert overture).

Rob Roy: Berlioz (concert overture); W. L. Viner (concert overture).

Waverly: Berlioz (concert overture).

In addition, Max Bruch's *Scottish Fantasy,* for violin and orchestra, was inspired by the reading of several novels by Scott.

Scottish Ballad. For two pianos and orchestra by Benjamin Britten, op. 26 (1941), introduced in Cincinnati, O., on Nov. 28, 1941, Eugene Goossens conducting; Bartlett and Robertson were the soloists. This work is made up of Scottish tunes treated in a highly personal manner. Britten did not seek to produce a potpourri but to evoke ideas and feelings about the life of the Scottish people. The composer explains: "A short introduction (Lento), which consists of a strongly harmonized version of the Psalm tune called *Dune,* leads directly to a Funeral March, in which use is made of the Lament for the Scottish soldiers who fell in the Battle of Flodden, *The Flowers of the Forest.* A short bridge-passage . . . leads to a Reel (*Allegro molto*). After a Scottish military funeral the pipers play the liveliest of tunes. . . . The Reel begins pianissimo . . . and gradually works up to an exciting climax."

Scottish National Orchestra. A symphony orchestra founded in Glasgow, Scotland, in 1893, in competition with the Choral Union Society, with which it merged in 1898. Its principal conductors have included George Henschel, Willem Kes, Wilhelm Bruch, Frederick H. Cowen, Emil Mlynarski, Landon Ronald, Julius Allen Greenway Harrison, Václav Talich, John Barbirolli, George Szell, Aylmer Buess, and Warwick Braithwaite. The orchestra was reorganized in 1949 with Walter Susskind as principal conductor; Karl Rankl succeeded him in 1952, and in 1958 the post was assumed by Hans Swarowsky.

Scriabin, Alexander, composer. Born Moscow, Russia, Jan. 6, 1872; died there, April 27, 1915. His early musical education was so haphazard that for a long time he was unable to read music. Nevertheless so pronounced was his talent that when, in his seventh year, he played the piano for Anton Rubinstein, the latter said: "Let the child develop in freedom. Everything will come out in time."

Formal study took place with George Conus, Taneiev, and Zverev. In 1888 he entered the Moscow Conservatory, where he proved to be a brilliant student under Safonov, Taneiev, and Arensky. Despite an affliction of the right hand, brought on by an overzealous attempt to perfect his technique, he won the gold medal in piano playing. After leaving the Conservatory he embarked upon the career of piano virtuoso. He also published his first compositions. His talent attracted the interest of the publisher, Belaiev, who assumed the direction of Scriabin's career as pianist, beginning with a tour of Europe in 1895-1896. Belaiev also undertook the publication of everything Scriabin wrote, and for many years even subsidized him secretly with an annual grant.

From 1898 to 1903 Scriabin taught

piano at the Moscow Conservatory. He was writing music all the time, attempting increasingly ambitious symphonic structures which he infused with philosophic concepts. *The Divine Poem* was completed in 1903; the *Poem of Ecstasy*, which received the Glinka Prize, followed in 1908. From writing music expressing metaphysical ideas he proceeded to the dream of formulating a new gospel, a world philosophy such as no musician had ever pronounced. He called this dream a "Mystery," planned it as a summation of man's history from the dawn of time to final destruction, and called it the last will and testament of a dying civilization. His "Mystery" was to consist not only of music, but also drama, poetry, dance, colors, perfumes, and even a new kind of language consisting of exclamations. Scriabin not only hoped to create such a "Mystery." He also aspired to have it performed in a temple especially built for it in India. But he did not live to realize his dream. He managed to write only the text, which he entitled *Propylaea*, after the entrance to the Acropolis in Athens. Of the music itself he produced only a few random sketches.

Despite his creative and personal eccentricities he always found people to believe in him and finance him. When Belaiev died, Scriabin interested a new patron: one of his pupils who for several years provided him with a handsome subsidy. Beginning in 1908 he acquired still another generous believer in Serge Koussevitzky, who used his immense influence both as publisher and conductor to promote Scriabin's music, besides endowing him with an annual income.

Scriabin visited the United States in 1906, making his American début in New York on December 21 with the Russian Symphony, in his piano concerto. A tour of the country followed, but it was suddenly and unpleasantly terminated when he decided to leave, to avoid a government charge of moral turpitude: the composer was then traveling with his common-law wife.

During the summer of 1910 Scriabin traveled with Koussevitzky and his orchestra down the Volga, performing his piano concerto in eleven concerts in small towns and villages. Soon after these appearances, composer and conductor quarreled bitterly, a result of their conflicting temperaments. A permanent rift developed between them. But though he bore Scriabin personal animosity, Koussevitzky never allowed his personal feelings to interfere with his interest in Scriabin's music and his efforts to promote it.

In 1914 Scriabin played in England. His last public performance took place in St. Petersburg on April 15, 1915. He succumbed to an infection which brought on a fatal gangrene.

Besides his five symphonies (including *The Divine Poem, The Poem of Ecstasy,* and *Prometheus: The Poem of Fire*) and a piano concerto, Scriabin's principal works were for piano solo. These include 10 sonatas, 89 preludes, 26 etudes, and impromptus, waltzes, and other pieces.

Scriabin's earliest works, influenced by Chopin, are poetic, sensitive, and beautifully constructed. Here he demonstrated that he was one of the most important writers of piano music ever to appear in Russia. Then he began to imitate the harmonic and instrumental techniques, and even some of the mannerisms, of Wagner. From Wagnerism he progressed to mysticism. His writing grew increasingly nebulous; his musical thinking became rambling and episodic; his tonality free. An individual harmonic structure was based on a chord of his own invention, since come to be known as the "Mystery Chord." It was built up by fourths: C, F-sharp, B-flat, E, A, D.
See: Etude—*Scriabin;* Prelude—*Scriabin;* Sonata—*Scriabin;* Symphony—*Scriabin.*

Scythian Suite (Ala and Lolli). Suite for orchestra by Prokofiev, op. 20 (1916). The composer originally wrote this music for a ballet about an ancient race, called the Scythians, and their gods. They inhabited Southeast Europe near the Black Sea before 100 B.C. When Diaghilev, director of the Ballet Russe, for whom Prokofiev planned his ballet, failed to show interest in it, the composer revised his score into an orchestral suite. This was introduced in St. Petersburg on Jan. 29, 1916, the composer conducting. The suite has four movements. I. Invocation to Veles and Ala. This is music of barbaric force and brilliant tone colors, describing the invocation to the sun by the Scythians. II. The Evil God and the Dance of the Pagan Monsters. The Scythians make a sacrifice to Ala, daughter of Veles. The Evil God, surrounded by seven pagan monsters, performs a feverish dance. III. Night. The Evil God inflicts harm on Ala, and the Moon Maidens descend to console her. IV. The Glorious Departure of Lolli and the Cortège of the Sun. Lolli, the Scythian hero, comes to save Ala. The Sun God assists him in his struggle against the Evil God, in which he proves victorious. The suite ends with a picture of a sunrise.

Sea Drift. Tone poem for orchestra by John Alden Carpenter (1933), introduced by the New York Philharmonic in November 1934, Werner Janssen conducting. This is Impressionist music inspired by the Walt Whitman poem. The work is in two sections, each ending with an effective climax. In the first part, most of the principal material is assigned to the horn; in the second, the main theme is a melody for English horn repeated by the strings.

Sea Interludes (Britten). *See: Four Sea Interludes.*

Seashore, Carl Emil, psychologist. Born Mörlunda, Sweden, Jan. 28, 1866; died Lewiston, Idaho, Oct. 16, 1949. He received his education in the United States at the Gustavus Adolphus College in St. Peter, Minn., and Yale University. Until 1902 he taught psychology at Yale. In 1908 he was appointed dean of the Graduate School of Iowa State University, becoming dean emeritus thirty years later. His interest in psychology and music enabled him to arrive at methods of assaying musical talent through tests of intellect, memory, feeling, and imagination with the aid of instruments of his own invention (audiometer, tonoscope, chronograph, and so on). These tests have been extensively employed in American schools to help uncover musical potentialities in children, even though many psychologists remain unconvinced of the validity of Seashore's methods. He discussed his methods in several books, the most important being *The Psychology of Musical Talent* (1919), *The Psychology of Music* (1938), and *In Search of Beauty in Music* (1947).

Seasons, The. (1) Ballet suite for orchestra by Glazunov, op. 67, derived from the score to a ballet, with book and choreography by Marius Petipa. The ballet was introduced in St. Petersburg on Feb. 23, 1900. The four movements of the suite describe the four seasons of the year beginning with winter (Introduction; the Frost, Ice, Hail and Snow). Spring is introduced with a dance by Birds, Flowers, and the Zephyr. Summer has four uninterrupted parts: Waltz of the Cornflowers and Poppies; Barcarolle; Variation; and Coda. The autumn movement consists of a bacchanale and finale.

(2) *See:* Concerto Grosso—*Vivaldi.*

Second. The smallest interval, comprising two adjoining notes. Seconds can be major (for example C-D), minor (C-D-flat), or augmented (C-D-sharp).

Secret of Suzanne (Il Segreto di Susanna), Overture to The. Overture to a one-act "intermezzo," or comic opera, by Ermanno Wolf-Ferrari. The opera, with libretto by Enrico Golsciani, was introduced in Munich on Dec. 4, 1909. The slight and gay little overture sets the mood of vivacity that prevails throughout the opera. The first principal melody is heard at once in violins and woodwinds. After it has been discussed, the second subject is presented by flute and clarinet with string accompaniment. Both subjects are later treated contrapuntally.

Segall, Bernardo, pianist. Born Campinas, Brazil, 1911. After receiving an honorary degree from the São Paulo Conservatory and winning a national piano competition, both in his fourteenth year, he came to New York, where he studied with Alexander Siloti. He gave concert performances in Brazil in 1928 and 1931, and made his American début in New York on Dec. 27, 1936. Since then he has established his home in the United States and become a citizen.

Segno. *See: Dal Segno.*

Segovia, Andrés, guitarist. Born Linares, Spain, Feb. 17, 1893. He attended the Granada Musical Institute, making his début as a concert guitarist at Granada in 1909. In 1916 he gave a series of concerts in Barcelona and toured South America; in 1924 he made his début in Paris; and in 1928 he toured the United States for the first time. Since then he has been heard throughout the world. By developing a new technique of guitar playing and by performing the works of the masters in special adaptations, he has given the guitar significance as a concert instrument. Segovia has also performed many modern works written expressly for him, by Mario Castelnuovo-Tedesco, Joaquín Turina, Alfredo Casella, Manuel Ponce, and Albert Roussel among others.

Segue. Follows.

Sehr. Very.

Seidel, Toscha, violinist. Born Odessa, Russia, Nov. 4, 1899. He studied the violin with Max Fiedelmann in Odessa and Leopold Auer at the St. Petersburg Conservatory. His début took place in Oslo on Sept. 1, 1915, and was followed by a European tour. He made his first appearance in the United States in New York on April 14, 1918. After that he lived in the United States and became a citizen. During the decade following his American début he appeared throughout the world. He subsequently associated himself with radio as advisory director of music of the Columbia Broadcasting System, for which he initiated several important cycles of programs devoted to serious music. During World War II he served in the United States Navy; after the war he settled in Hollywood, where he worked in the music divisions of several major motion picture studios.

Seidl, Anton, conductor. Born Budapest, Hungary, May 7, 1850; died New York City, March 28, 1898. After attending the Leipzig Conservatory he worked with Wagner at Bayreuth, first as copyist, then as assistant conductor. Through Wagner he was appointed conductor at the Leipzig Opera in 1879. After that he toured Europe as conductor of the Angelo Neumann Opera Company in performances of the Wagner *Ring* cycle. He continued to distinguish himself as a Wagnerian conductor at Covent Garden and the Metropolitan Opera in New York. But he was also an eminent symphony conductor. In 1891 he succeeded Theodore Thomas as principal conductor of the New York Philharmonic, remaining in that post until his death, from ptomaine poisoning. In 1893 he presented in New York the première of Dvořák's *Symphony from the New World*.

Sellinger's Round. *See:* Byrd, William.

Semiquaver. Sixteenth note.

Semiramide, Overture to. Overture to a tragic opera by Rossini. The text, by Gaetano Rossi, was based on a drama of Voltaire, and the opera was first performed in Venice on Feb. 3, 1823. A sprightly figure for strings grows in sonority from *pianissimo* to *fortissimo* at the opening of the overture. A stately melody for four horns follows, and is discussed by the woodwind against plucked strings. An orchestral exclamation and a brief woodwind passage lead to a return of the opening crescendo section. The main body of the overture now unfolds, dominated by two lively themes: the first is for strings, and the second for the woodwind. A characteristic Rossini crescendo brings this section to an end. The two lively themes of the main part are now repeated, and the overture ends with another crescendo.

Semitone. A half tone, a minor second. On the piano, a semitone is produced by striking two consecutive keys.

Semplice. Simple.

Sempre. Always.

Senza. Without.

Septet. A composition for seven instruments. This combination is not often encountered. The most familiar Septet is that by Beethoven in E-flat major, op. 20 (1799-1800). It is in the fresh lyrical vein and has the simple structure of Beethoven's first-period music. Scored for violin, viola, cello, double bass, clarinet, bassoon, and horn, it is in six brief movements.

Septolet (Septulet, or Septimole). Seven notes played in the time of four or six notes of the same value.

Sequence. Repetition of a melodic or harmonic phrase at a different position in the scale.

Serenade (Staendchen, or Serenata). Essentially a form of vocal music—a love song sung under a lady's window at evening. The term, however, is also found in 18th-century instrumental music, applied to a composition of light character and consisting of several brief movements. Such serenades were usually written on order for some festive occasion, and they can be found for various combinations of instruments, or for orchestra. In the 18th century the term "serenade" was used interchangeably with "divertimento," "cassation," and "nocturne." All of these are merely suites.

The following are some frequently heard instrumental serenades:

BRAHMS. Brahms revived this essentially 18th-century form with two orchestral works, both coming comparatively early in his career: Serenade No. 1 in D major, op. 11 (1857-1858), and Serenade No. 2 in A major, op. 16 (1859, revised 1875). The first, for full orchestra, is from many points of view the more satisfying artistically, because it has greater distinction of style and structure. The second serenade, for small orchestra, however, has greater audience appeal—it is more characteristically Brahmsian in its Romanticism, and of a more intimate nature.

MOZART. Mozart wrote many delightful serenades. The most famous of these is No. 13 in G major, best known as *Eine kleine Nachtmusik* (which see). But several others are also familiar: No. 6 in D major, *Serenata Notturno,* K. 239 (1776), unusual in that it is scored for two ensembles; Serenade No. 7 in D major, K. 250, known as the "Haffner," because Mozart wrote it in 1776 for the wedding of Elisabeth, daughter of Sigmund Haffner, Burgomaster of Salzburg; Serenade No. 9 in D major, K. 320 (1779); Serenade No. 10 in B-flat major, K. 361 (1781); Serenade No. 11 in E-flat major, K. 375 (1782).

TCHAIKOVSKY. The Russian master revived the serenade form interestingly in his Serenade for Strings in C major, op. 48 (1880). It is in four movements, the most famous being the second, a waltz, one of the composer's best loved melodies.

Serenade for Violin, Strings and Percussion. By Leonard Bernstein (1954). It was commissioned by the Koussevitzky Foundation and was introduced in Venice on Sept. 12, 1954, with Isaac Stern as violin soloist and the composer conducting. This work has five movements: I. Lento; II. Allegretto; III. Presto; IV. Adagio; V. *Allegro molto vivace.* Based on Plato's *Symposium,* it consists of a series of related statements in praise of love. Each movement bears the name of one who engaged in the discussion of love at the home of the poet Agathon: Phraedus, Eryximachus, Aristophanes, Alcibiades, and Socrates.

Serenata Notturno. *See:* Serenade—*Mozart.*

Serial technique. The technique of composing with the twelve-tone row (or series). In some compositions the series principle is extended to cover rhythm as well as melody.

Serious Quartet. *See:* Quartet—*Beethoven.*

Serkin, Rudolf, pianist, born Eger, Czechoslovakia, March 28, 1903. He studied music in Vienna: piano with Richard Robert and composition with Joseph Marx and Arnold Schoenberg. His professional career began at Berlin in 1920, and continued throughout Europe in recitals and appearances in joint concerts with Adolf Busch. His American début took place in Washington, D.C., in 1933. Three years later he returned to the United States to give a distinguished performance of two Mozart concertos with the New York Philharmonic under Toscanini on Feb. 20, 1936. From this time on he was acclaimed in the United States as well as in Europe as one of the most sensitive and poetic piano virtuosos of his time. On the outbreak of World War II, Serkin settled in the United States, of which he later became a citizen. He joined the faculty of the Curtis Institute in Philadelphia, and later on in Vermont (where he had established his permanent residence) he helped found the Marlboro School of Music and create an annual music festival. Serkin is married to Adolf Busch's daughter, Irene.

Sessions, Roger, composer. Born Brooklyn, N.Y., Dec. 28, 1896. He was graduated from Harvard in 1915, after which he studied music at the Yale School of Music and later privately with Ernest Bloch. From 1917 to 1921 he taught theory at Smith College, and from 1921 to 1925 at the Cleveland Institute, of which Bloch was director. For eight years after that he lived mostly in Europe as the recipient of two Guggenheim Fellowships (1926, 1927) and one from the American Academy in Rome (1928-1931). While in Europe he completed several ambitious works, the most important being the Symphony in E minor, introduced by the Boston Symphony under Koussevitzky in 1927. In 1933 Sessions returned to the United States. Since then he has held teaching posts at the Malkin Conservatory in Boston, Boston University, Columbia University, University of California, and most recently Princeton. Sessions is one of the most original and powerful voices in American music. His writing is complex, its emphasis being on harmony and rhythm rather than melody. His music is usually built around more than a single tonal center. Intricate technique is combined with subtle thought to make his mature works difficult to assimilate at first hearing. But their inexorable logic and vigor of speech command admiration. In 1950 he received the New York Music Critics Circle Award for his Second Symphony. His Third Symphony was commissioned by the Boston Symphony for its 75th anniversary season and was introduced by that orchestra on Dec. 6, 1957, Charles Munch conducting. Besides the symphonies, Sessions wrote a violin concerto, piano concerto, the orchestral suite *The Black Maskers, Idyll of Theocritus* for soprano and orchestra, 2 string quartets, a sonata for unaccompanied violin, 2 piano sonatas, and several piano suites. Sessions is the author of *The Musical Experience of Composer, Performer, Listener* (1950), *Reflections on the Music Life in the United States* (1956), and a text on harmonic practice.

Ševčik, Otakar, violinist and teacher. Born Horaždowitz, Bohemia, March 22, 1852; died Pisek, Czechoslovakia, Jan. 18, 1934. He was one of the most distinguished violin teachers of his generation. After attending the Prague Conservatory he was concertmaster of orchestras in Salzburg and Vienna. He made his début as a concert violinist at Vienna in 1873. From 1875 to 1892 he was professor of violin at the Music School in Kiev; from 1892 to 1906, at the Prague Conservatory; from 1909 to 1919 at the Vienna Academy of Music; and from 1919 to 1924 at the Prague Master School. Between 1920 and 1932 he paid several extended visits to the United States to teach the violin and propagandize his methods. He taught over five thousand students during his career, among the most famous being Jan Kubelik, Erica Morini, and Efrem Zimbalist. He devised his own technique of bowing, and originated a "semitone method" calculated to produce greater accuracy in intonation even among beginners. His methods and system are embodied in several valuable volumes of technical studies for the violin. He also edited concertos by Brahms, Mendelssohn, Paganini, Tchaikovsky, and Wieniawski.

Seven Ages, The. Suite for orchestra by John Alden Carpenter, introduced in New York on Dec. 2, 1945, Artur Rodzinski conducting. This work is a musical interpretation of the famous soliloquy of Jacques in Shakespeare's *As You Like It*, Act 2, Scene 7, beginning with the line "All the world's a stage." The suite is in seven uninterrupted sections, each intended to depict a stage of man from "the infant . . . in the nurse's arms" to "second childishness and mere oblivion."

Seven Last Words of the Saviour on the Cross, The (Die sieben Worte des Erloesers am Kreuze). A composition for orchestra by Haydn comprising seven slow movements, or "sonatas," flanked by a slow introduction and a fast movement depicting an earthquake. The seven "sonatas" are: I. B-flat major; II. C minor and major; III. E major; IV. F minor; V. A major; VI. G minor and major; VII. E-flat major. This work was commissioned by the Canon of the Cadíz Cathedral, Spain, in 1785. It was performed there during Lent of 1786. In 1787 Haydn transcribed it for string quartet.

Seventh. An interval between two notes separated by six diatonic notes. Sevenths may be major (C to B-natural), minor (C to B-flat), augmented (C to B-sharp), or diminished (C to B-double flat).

Seventh chord. A chord of four notes, made up of three thirds.

Severance Hall. The principal concert auditorium in Cleveland, O., home of the Cleveland Orchestra. It opened on Feb. 5, 1931, with a concert by the Cleveland Orchestra which featured the première of Charles Martin Loeffler's *Evocations,* written for that occasion.

Sevitzky, Fabien (born **Fabien Koussevitzky**), conductor. Born Vishni-Volotchok, Russia, Sept. 29, 1893. He is a nephew of Serge Koussevitzky. In 1911 he was graduated with honors from the St. Petersburg Conservatory. His professional career began when he played the double bass in the orchestra of the Moscow Imperial Opera. In 1915 he toured Russia as a double bass soloist. He left Russia in 1922 and in 1924 settled in the United States, where he later became a citizen. For a while he played the double bass in the Philadelphia Orchestra. In 1925 he organized the Philadelphia Chamber Sinfonietta, which he conducted until 1937. From 1937 to 1955 he was conductor of the Indianapolis Symphony, besides making numerous guest appearances as conductor in Europe. Since 1957 he has appeared in Europe, the Near East, and in Central and South America.

Sextet. A composition for six instruments. Several of Haydn's divertimentos are for six instruments: string quartet and two horns; or flute, oboe, and strings; or exclusively for winds. One of the few Haydn chamber-music works specifically designated as a sextet is *The Echo,* for four violins and two cellos. Boccherini was the first composer to devote himself extensively to writing sextets, producing sixteen works of this type. Beethoven wrote two sextets now rarely heard: E-flat major, op. 81-b (1795), for strings and two horns, and E-flat major, op. 71 (1796), for two clarinets, two bassoons, and two horns.

The first important works for string sextet (two each of violins, violas, and cellos) were produced by Brahms, who wrote two of these compositions. The Sextet in B-flat major, op. 18 (1860), breathes such youthful ardor, exuberance,

and joy of life (especially in the last two movements) that it has come to be known as the *Spring Sextet.* The Sextet in G major, op. 36 (1865), is called the *Agathe Sextet.* Agathe is Agathe von Siebold, with whom Brahms was in love. He broke off the affair when marriage appeared imminent and apparently sublimated his feelings in the writing of this music. Agathe appears in the principal theme of the first movement (*Allegro non troppo*), in a motif utilizing the notes A, G, A, H (the German equivalent of B-natural), and E. If there is any poignancy at all in Brahms' renunciation of his beloved it is found in the finale, particularly in the *Poco adagio* section and in the concluding coda.

Sforzando. An indication that a note or group of notes is to be emphasized.

Sgambati, Giovanni, pianist, conductor, and teacher. Born Rome, Italy, May 28, 1841; died there, Dec. 14, 1914. He studied the piano first with Amerigo Barbieri and after that with Liszt in Rome. From 1860 on he appeared throughout Italy in piano recitals emphasizing the German literature, including many masterworks then still unknown in his country. He began directing orchestral performances in 1866 at the Dante Gallery in Rome, again introducing German music to Italian audiences. In 1868 he established a free piano class at the Santa Cecilia Academy; in 1877 the government designated it as the Liceo Musicale and it grew into one of Italy's most important schools of music. Sgambati, who came to be regarded as one of Italy's most distinguished piano teachers, taught the piano there until his death. Though he wrote 2 symphonies, a piano concerto, 2 piano quintets, and a string quartet, among other large works, he was best in his smaller pieces for the piano, which include a prelude and fugue, etudes, and nocturnes.

Shake. Trill.

Shakespeare, William, poet and dramatist. Born Stratford-on-Avon, England, April 1564; died there, April 23, 1616. His tragedies and comedies were the source of innumerable instrumental compositions, of which only the most significant or representative are listed below (where titles of compositions are not given they are the same as the play):

All's Well that Ends Well: Incidental music by Arthur Hoerée.

Antony and Cleopatra: Vincent d'Indy (concert overture); Anton Rubinstein (concert overture); Dame Ethel Smyth (concert overture). Incidental music by Henry Bishop, Quincy Porter, Florent Schmitt, and Virgil Thomson.

As You Like It: John Alden Carpenter (*Seven Ages,* symphonic suite); John Knowles Paine (overture). Incidental music by Henry Bishop, Arthur Bliss, Edward German, and Roger Quilter.

Comedy of Errors: Incidental music by Henry Bishop, and Yuri Shaporin.

Coriolanus: Incidental music by Alexander Mackenzie.

Hamlet: Boris Blacher (tone poem); Frank Bridge (*There is a Willow,* for orchestra); Niels Gade (concert overture); Edward German (tone poem); Joseph Joachim (overture); Guillaume Lekeu (*Marche d'Ophélie,* tone poem; *Hamlet,* symphonic study); Liszt (orchestral prelude); Edward MacDowell (*Hamlet and Ophelia,* tone poem); George Macfarren (overture); Bernard Rogers (orchestral prelude); Tchaikovsky (fantasy-overture). Incidental music by Lehman Engel, Karl H. Graun, George Henschel, Arthur Honegger, Darius Milhaud, Stanislav Moniuszko, Gabriel Pierné, Dimitri Shostakovich, Tchaikovsky, and Virgil Thomson.

Henry IV: Edward Elgar (*Falstaff,* symphonic study); Joseph Joachim (overture). Incidental music by Henry Bishop.

Henry V: Edward Elgar (*Falstaff,* symphonic study); Walter Macfarren (overture).

Henry VIII: Incidental music by Lehman Engel, Edward German, and Arthur Sullivan.

Julius Caesar: Mario Castelnuovo-Tedesco (concert overture); Felix Draeseke (overture; tone poem); Schumann (overture). Incidental music by Marc Blitzstein, Hans von Buelow, J. B. Foerster, John Ireland, and Darius Milhaud.

King John: Mario Castelnuovo-Tedesco (concert overture).

King Lear: Granville Bantock (overture for brass band); Antonio Bazzini

(overture); Berlioz (overture); Paul Dukas (overture); Felix Weingartner (tone poem). Incidental music by Balakirev, Debussy, Felipe Pedrell, and Yuri Shaporin.

Love's Labor Lost: Incidental music by Henry Bishop and J. B. Foerster.

Macbeth: Ignaz Bruell (overture); Henry Fry (overture); Smetana (*Macbeth and the Witches,* for piano); Richard Strauss (tone poem); Nikolai Tcherepnin (*Witch's Scene,* for orchestra). Incidental music by Boris Asafiev, Granville Bantock, Walter Braunfels, Norman Demuth, Edgar Stillman Kelley, Aram Khatchaturian, Matthew Locke, Darius Milhaud, and Arthur Sullivan.

Measure for Measure: Incidental music by Dmitri Kabalevsky.

Merchant of Venice: Mario Castelnuovo-Tedesco (overture); George Macfarren (overture). Incidental music by Boris Asafiev, Elliott Carter, Engelbert Humperdinck, Stanislav Moniuszko, Goesta Nystroem, Henri Rabaud, Karol Rathaus, and Arthur Sullivan.

Merry Wives of Windsor: Otto Nicolai (overture to comic opera). Incidental music by Henry Bishop and Arthur Sullivan.

A Midsummer Night's Dream. Mario Castelnuovo-Tedesco (overture); Mendelssohn (incidental music, adapted into suite for orchestra). Incidental music by Henry Bishop, Ernst Krenek, Walter Leigh, Carl Orff, and Erik Satie.

Much Ado About Nothing: Incidental music by Edward German, Benjamin Godard, Tikhon Khrennikov, and Erich Wolfgang Korngold.

Othello: Dvořák (overture); Zdenek Fibich (tone poem); Henry Hadley (overture). Incidental music by Samuel Coleridge-Taylor and Walter Macfarren.

Richard II: Incidental music by Percy Pitt.

Richard III: Smetana (tone poem). Incidental music by Edward German, Arthur Hoerée, and Robert Volkmann.

Romeo and Juliet: Berlioz (symphony); William Boyce (dirge for orchestra); David Diamond (suite for orchestra); Joseph Holbrook (*Queen Mab,* tone poem); Dmitri Kabalevsky (*Pictures for Romeo and Juliet,* suite for orchestra); George Macfarren (overture); Prokofiev (ballet suites for orchestra); Johan Svendsen (overture); Tchaikovsky (fantasy-overture). Incidental music by Henry Bishop, Roberto Gerhard, Edward German, Engelbert Humperdinck, and Darius Milhaud.

Taming of the Shrew: Mario Castelnuovo-Tedesco (overture); Walter Macfarren (overture); Percy Pitt (overture); Josef Rheinberger (overture); Johan Wagenaar (overture). Incidental music by Richard Addinsell.

Tempest: Walter Braunfels (*Ariel's Song,* for small orchestra); Zdenek Fibich (tone poem); Lukas Foss (suite for orchestra); Arthur Honegger (prelude for orchestra); John Knowles Paine (tone poem); Sibelius (suite for orchestra adapted from incidental music); Tchaikovsky (fantasy for orchestra); Egon Wellesz (*Prosperos Beschwoerungen,* for orchestra). Incidental music by Lennox Berkeley, Henry Bishop, Arthur Bliss, Ernest Chausson, David Diamond, Engelbert Humperdinck, Matthew Locke, Willem Pijper, Goesta Nystroem, Sibelius, Arthur Sullivan, and Felix Weingartner.

Timon of Athens: Arthur Sullivan (overture).

Twelfth Night: Mario Castelnuovo-Tedesco (overture); Alexander Mackenzie (overture); Johan Wagenaar (overture). Incidental music by Stanley Bate, Henry Bishop, Walter Braunfels, J. B. Foerster, and Engelbert Humperdinck.

Two Gentlemen of Verona: Incidental music by Henry Bishop.

A Winter's Tale: Mario Castelnuovo-Tedesco (overture); Walter Macfarren (overture); Josef Suk (overture). Incidental music by Friedrich von Flotow and Jaroslav Křička.

In addition to the above, the following instrumental works were inspired by Shakespeare (unless otherwise designated all works are for orchestra); J. B. Foerster's *Suite from Shakespeare;* Manfred Gurlitt's *Shakespeare Symphony;* Gordon Jacob's *Six Shakespearean Sketches,* for string trio; Norman O'Neill's *Two Shakespeare Sketches;* Smetana's *Solemn March for Shakespeare Celebrations.*

Shaporin, Yuri, composer. Born Glukhov, Russia, Nov. 8, 1889. He was graduated from the University of St. Petersburg as a student of law in 1913, and from the St. Petersburg Conservatory in 1918. He was then appointed musical director of the St. Petersburg Drama and Academic Theater, for which he wrote a considerable amount of incidental music for stage productions. His first major work was the Symphony in E minor, introduced in Moscow on May 11, 1933. He later wrote *Humorous Suite: The Flea* for orchestra, 2 piano sonatas, an opera (*The Decembrists*), and a symphonic cantata, *On the Fields of Kulikov,* for which he received the Stalin Prize in 1941.

Sharp. Sign raising a note half a step.

Shaw, George Bernard, dramatist and music critic. Born Dublin, Ireland, July 26, 1856; died Ayot-St.-Lawrence, England, Nov. 2, 1950. The world-famous dramatist who won the Nobel Prize for literature in 1925 was a distinguished music critic early in his career. In 1888-1889 he wrote music criticisms under the pen name of "Corno di Bassetto" for the London *Star.* These were republished in a volume called *London Music* (1937). His criticisms then appeared in the London *World* over the initials G.B.S. from 1890 to 1894. These writings were collected into three volumes entitled *Music in London* (1932). Eric Bentley edited a volume of Shaw's criticisms in *Shaw on Music* (1955).

Shaw, Robert, conductor. Born Red Bluff, Calif., April 30, 1916. While Shaw has become famous as a choral conductor he has in recent years also conducted symphony orchestras. He studied to be a minister, but was directed to music by the popular bandleader, Fred Waring, for whom he worked for seven years as choral director. In 1941 Shaw founded the Collegiate Chorale, and in 1948 the Robert Shaw Chorale. He led both organizations in distinguished concerts, often in collaboration with the foremost symphony orchestras in the United States. For several years, beginning in 1953, he led summer orchestral concerts in San Diego, Calif. In October 1956 he became assistant conductor of the Cleveland Orchestra, and from that time on made many guest appearances with other orchestras. Shaw was choral director at the Berkshire Music Centre in Tanglewood from 1942 to 1945, and a member of the faculty of the Juilliard School of Music from 1946 to 1950. He received a Guggenheim Fellowship in 1944.

Shebalin, Vissarion, composer. Born Omsk, Russia, June 11, 1902. He was graduated from the Moscow Conservatory in 1928. From 1935 to 1942 he was professor of composition there, and from 1942 to 1948 director. He completed his first symphony in 1925, and achieved substantial successes with his third and fourth symphonies in 1934 and 1935 respectively. He also has produced a fifth symphony, two orchestral suites, 2 violin concertos, a cello concerto, Concertino for horn and small orchestra, and several shorter orchestral compositions (*Overture on Mari Themes, Dramatic Overture,* and *Russian Overture*). He has also written 7 string quartets, string trio, piano trio, viola sonata, violin sonata, sonata for solo violin, 2 piano sonatas, and 3 piano sonatinas. In his earlier works he showed pronounced Romantic and at times national leanings. But his later music veers towards Expressionism, with occasional recourse to modal harmonies.

Shelley, Percy Bysshe, poet. Born Field Place, England, Aug. 4, 1792; died (by drowning) off Viareggio, Italy, July 8, 1822. One of England's foremost lyric poets, Shelley and his poetry were the source of several instrumental compositions: Granville Bantock (*The Witch of Atlas,* tone poem); Samuel Barber (*Music for a Scene from Shelley*); George Chadwick (*Adonais,* overture); Edward Elgar (Symphony No. 2); Mikhail Gnessin (*After Shelley,* symphonic fragment); Edward MacDowell (*Winter,* poem for piano in *Four Little Poems,* op. 32); Miaskovsky (*Alastor,* tone poem); Bernard Rogers (*Adonais,* symphony).

Sheridan, Richard Brinsley, dramatist. Born Dublin, Ireland, Oct. 30, 1751; died London, England, July 7, 1816. Samuel Barber wrote a concert overture, *The School for Scandal,* based on Sheridan's comedy of the same name. The following are some of the composers who wrote incidental music to Sheridan's plays: Dennis Arundell (*St. Patrick's Day*); J. L. Dussek (*Pizarro*); James Hewitt (*Pizarro*); Dmitri Kabalevsky (*The School for Scandal*); Thomas Linley, Sr. (*The Camp, The Duenna, Robinson Crusoe,* and *The School for Scandal*).

Shift. In violin music, the shifting of the left hand from one position to another either up or down the fingerboard.

Shostakovich, Dmitri, composer. Born St. Petersburg, Russia, Sept. 25, 1906. He was graduated from the St. Petersburg Conservatory as a pianist in 1923, and as a composer two years later. While studying there he made several appearances at school recitals, featuring his own compositions, including the *Three Fantastic Dances* for piano, his first published work. For his graduation exercise, Shostakovich completed his First Symphony, introduced in Leningrad on May 12, 1926. This symphony achieved world prominence, and is still the composer's most often performed composition. For about a year after leaving the Conservatory, he abandoned composition to reconsider his musical values. Until now he had been concerned with abstract musical ideas presented in a style derived mainly from Tchaikovsky, and occasionally from Prokofiev. Now Shostakovich decided that his role as a Soviet composer was to write proletarian music, to speak through his music to the masses about Soviet ideas. With this goal in mind he completed a second symphony, utilizing a text by Lenin and commemorating the 10th anniversary of the October Revolution; a third symphony, *May Day,* dedicated to the international workers' day; and a satirical ballet, *The Age of Gold.* The last received first prize in a competition among Soviet ballets. Shostakovich now rapidly began to assume a commanding position among Soviet composers, a position solidified by the success of his piano concerto and the ballet *The Bolt.*

Upon several occasions, in his ensuing brilliant career, Shostakovich has fallen from grace with the Soviet authorities. But each time he managed to reestablish himself more firmly than before as a leading Soviet musician. In 1936 *Pravda* denounced his opera, *Lady Macbeth of Mzensk* (which had been a substantial success since its première at Leningrad in 1934), as "crude, primitive, vulgar."

When this attack was followed by another equally savage against his ballet, *The Limpid Stream,* it became apparent that Shostakovich was no longer a favorite with Soviet officialdom. But he soon sprang back to general acceptance and popularity. The première of his Fifth Symphony in 1937 was a triumph. Three years later he won the Stalin Prize for a piano quintet. And during World War II he became a national hero—particularly after his Seventh Symphony (inspired by the siege of Leningrad) was awarded the Stalin Prize and received resounding acclaim when given throughout the free world.

Then once again Shostakovich became the victim of a severe attack. Early in 1948 the Central Committee of the Communist Party denounced most of the leading composers of the Soviet Union for their "decadent bourgeois formalism" and "cerebralism"; for having lost touch with the people through their excursions into ultra-modern idioms and techniques. Shostakovich confessed his guilt and promised to mend his ways by writing music capable of meeting the standards required by the Central Committee. In 1949 he wrote an oratorio extolling Stalin's reforestration plan (*The Song of the Forest*). Together with his incidental music for a motion picture, *The Fall of Berlin,* this work earned the Stalin Prize. And on his 50th birthday, in 1956, Shostakovich received the Order of Lenin. In 1958 Shostakovich was awarded the Sibelius Prize of $22,000, which he turned over to the Finnish-Soviet Friendship Association.

In March 1949, Shostakovich paid a visit to the United States. He came as a member of a committee representing the Soviet Union at the Cultural and Scientific Conference for World Peace in New York.

On more than one occasion Shostakovich has not hesitated to stoop in order to conquer—whether to meet the favor of audiences or to satisfy the esthetic demands of government officials. He has written a great deal of music that is contrived, cliché-ridden, superficial, and trite. But by virtue of his greatest works he is a significant creative figure in contemporary music. He can be witty, ironical, whimsical, or amusing, as in the *Age of Gold,* the first piano concerto, and parts of his Ninth Symphony. A remarkable gift of orchestration, a virtuoso technique, a cogent rhythmic force, and an ingratiating lyricism endow his best music with unflagging interest. But there are also times when he goes deeper than these surface attractions; and at such times—as in many pages of the Fifth Symphony —he has produced music of dramatic power, nobility of expression, and grandeur of spirit.

The following are his principal instrumental compositions:

Chamber Music: 6 string quartets; *Two Pieces,* for string octet; cello sonata; piano quintet; 2 piano trios.

Orchestra: 11 symphonies; 2 piano concertos; *The Age of Gold,* ballet suite; *Ballet Suite No. 1;* Concertino for two pianos and orchestra; violin concerto; *Festival Overture;* incidental music to plays and motion pictures.

Piano: 2 sonatas; 24 preludes; 24 preludes and fugues.

See: Age of Gold, The; Concerto—*Shostakovich;* Prelude—*Shostakovich;* Quartet —*Shostakovich;* Quintet—*Shostakovich;* Symphony—*Shostakovich.*

Sibelius, Jean, composer. Born Tavastehus, Finland, Dec. 3, 1865; died Järvenpää, Finland, Sept. 20, 1957. Though he started piano study at the age of nine, and composition at ten, he did not plan to engage in music professionally. After attending the Finnish Model Lyceum, he enrolled in the University of Helsinki for the study of law in 1885. After a year there he decided to concentrate on music. He now entered the Helsinki Conservatory, where he remained from 1886 to 1889, a pupil of Ferruccio Busoni and Martin Wegelius, among others. Public performances of his string quartet and a suite for strings in 1889 helped bring him a government stipend, as a result of which he continued his music study in Berlin with Albert Becker and in Vienna with Carl Goldmark and Robert Fuchs.

Back in his native land in 1891, Sibelius now deserted the German-Romantic style, to which he had been hitherto addicted, for a national idiom. His first

Finnish composition was *Kullervo,* a suite for orchestra, introduced in Helsinki under his own direction in 1892. In the same year he completed his first national tone poem, *En Saga;* and in 1893, he wrote *Karelia Suite.* By 1900 he had not only completed his first symphony but he had also produced two more national works which made him the foremost musical spokesman of his country and its people. One was the *Four Legends* for orchestra, which include the now-famous *The Swan of Tuonela.* The other was *Finlandia,* more famous throughout the world as the voice of Finland, and its determination to be free, than even its national anthem.

While writing these works, Sibelius taught theory at the Helsinki Conservatory and at the orchestral school of the Philharmonic Society; he also played the violin in a string quartet. But in 1897, by virtue of the first annual government grant ever bestowed by Finland on a musician, Sibelius was able to give up these activities and concentrate on composition. By the beginning of World War I he had completed his first four symphonies, the violin concerto, *Pohjola's Daughter,* a string quartet (*Voces intimae*), and his extraordinarily popular salon piece, *Valse triste.* Just before the war he paid his only visit to the United States, where he conducted a concert of his own works in Norfolk, Conn., on June 4, 1914.

After the war Sibelius made several tours of Europe, conducting performances of his music. After 1924 he rarely left his home in Järvenpää, which he had acquired in 1904. His last completed work was a set of piano pieces, *Esquisses,* op. 114 (1929). For many years after that rumors were circulated that he was working on an eighth symphony, but he never progressed beyond a few sketches.

But by 1929 he had won world recognition as one of the most significant symphonists since Brahms. And in his own land he was accepted as a national hero. Withdrawn from the rest of the world, he became something of a legend. Up to the time of World War II, admirers from all parts of the world made pilgrimages to his home to pay him homage. Finland issued stamps bearing his likeness, an

honor without precedent in that country for a living composer. His 80th and 90th birthdays inspired monumental celebrations in all parts of the civilized world.

Sibelius was one of the major creative figures in 20th-century music; but spiritually he belonged to the 19th century. He started out as a composer imitating the styles of Tchaikovsky and Brahms. Though he finally achieved his own identity, he remained a true Romantic. The new idioms and techniques and concepts arising all around him had little significance for him. He remained faithful to traditional approaches, filling his music with windswept melodies, vigorous rhythms and sonorities, and strong emotion. His own personality emerged in his music only after he had come upon musical nationalism. From then on his music became the voice of Finland: its landscapes, sagas, culture, and people. His music is recognizably Finnish in its alternation between serene pastoral moods and orgiastic outbursts; between austerity and bleakness of atmosphere and surging passion. This music has assimilated some of the elements and temper of Finnish folk music so successfully that it is sometimes believed that Sibelius quoted folk material in his music; but all of Sibelius' melodies are his own.

With successive compositions he acquired greater compactness of structure and a greater concentration of harmonic and contrapuntal language. His early, spacious melodies were replaced by brief, epigrammatic subjects, just as the emotional eruptions in his older works later gave way to introspection and deeply personal utterances. Without seeking for new forms, or inventing new idioms, Sibelius succeeded in achieving originality by speaking simply and directly from the deepest recesses of his heart.

The following are his principal instrumental compositions:

Chamber Music: Voces intimae, string quartet; violin sonatina; *Novelette,* for violin and piano; 11 pieces for violin and piano.

Orchestra: 7 symphonies; violin concerto; *Kullervo; En Saga; Karelia; Four Legends* (including *The Swan of Tuonela*); *Finlandia; Romance; Valse triste;*

Pelleas and Melisande; Pohjola's Daughter; Belshazzar's Feast; Night Ride and Sunrise; In Memoriam; The Bard; Oceanides; Tapiola.

Piano: Sonata; 3 sonatinas; lyric pieces, characteristic pieces, bagatelles.

See: Concerto—*Sibelius; En Saga; Finlandia; Pelleas and Melisande* (3); *Pohjola's Daughter; Swan of Tuonela, The;* Symphony—*Sibelius; Tapiola.*

Siciliana (or **Siciliano**). An old dance said to be of Sicilian origin. It has a pastoral character, is usually in a minor key, and is in a slow 6/8 or 12/8 time. It is sometimes found as a movement of the Baroque suite, as in J. S. Bach's Violin Sonata in G minor or his E-flat major Flute Sonata. Sicilianas for orchestra are also found in many 17th- and 18th-century operas, an example being that in Gluck's *Armide.*

Siegfried (Wagner). *See: Ring of the Nibelungs, The.*

Siegfried Idyl. A composition for orchestra by Wagner. This is the only orchestral composition, not intended for the stage, written by him in his full maturity (1870). He wrote it as a birthday gift for his wife, Cosima, and originally called it *Triebschen Idyll*—"Triebschen" being their home near Lucerne, Switzerland. Its first performance took place there on Christmas morning, 1870. A small orchestra, under Wagner's direction, was grouped on the stairway leading to Cosima's bedroom. Wagner later led a private performance of the *Idyl* in Mannheim on Dec. 20, 1871, and a public performance in Meiningen on March 10, 1877. Described as one of the most eloquent lullabies ever written, the *Siegfried Idyl* is made up of motifs from the music drama *Siegfried,* with the single exception of the lullaby, *Schlaf, mein Kind,* a folksong. The work opens with a tender melody for strings derived from Bruennhilde's awakening music in *Siegfried.* A delicate passage for flute suggests Bruennhilde's slumber. After that come the love music that ends the drama, a quotation of Siegfried's horn call, and the song of the bird.

Siegfried's Funeral Music (Siegfrieds Tod). Threnody for orchestra from Act 3 of Wagner's music drama, *The Twilight of the Gods (Goetterdaemmerung),* from *The Ring of the Nibelungs.* Betrayed by his wife, Bruennhilde, who thinks Siegfried has abandoned her, Siegfried, the hero, is killed by Hagen. His body is lifted by Hagen's vassals, and they carry it back to Gunther's hall, to the strains of majestic funeral music in which the hero's life, career, and heroic exploits are reviewed. The music begins with a timpani roll, a lament in the strings (the "Death" motif) and piercing chords in the orchestra. Various motifs associated with Siegfried are skilfully woven into a fabulous orchestral fabric: the theme of heroism of the Walsungs (brass); the "Sympathy" motif (horns and woodwinds); the theme of "Love" (oboe); Siegfried's sword motif (trumpet); "Glorification of Death" motif (full orchestra); and Bruennhilde's theme (clarinet and English horn). The death motif and the roll of drums concludes the funeral music.

Siegfried's Rhine Journey (Siegfrieds Rheinfahrt). Orchestral interlude between the prologue and Act I of Wagner's music drama *The Twilight of the Gods (Goetterdaemmerung)* from *The Ring of the Nibelungs.* This music accompanies Siegfried's journey down the Rhine in search of heroic exploits. It begins with a descending passage for full orchestra, followed by the "Decision to Love" motif in strings and clarinet, and the Siegfried theme in the horns. After that, in a marvelous tonal fabric, are woven numerous other motifs associated with the hero's life and deeds, a kind of tonal summary of all that transpired in the three preceding music dramas. In rapid succession come the motifs of the "Magic Fire" in strings, the "Rhine" in the brass, the "Ring" in woodwinds and strings, and "Power of the Ring" in the oboes. In the last twenty-one bars the music hastily anticipates some of the action soon to unfold in the last drama, *The Twilight of the Gods.*

Siegmeister, Elie, composer. Born New York City, Jan. 15, 1909. While at Columbia University he attended the sonata and fugue classes of Seth Bingham and studied composition privately with Wallingford Riegger. In 1927 he went to Paris, where he remained four years and was a composition pupil of Nadia Boulanger. In 1935 he attended the Juilliard School on a conducting fellowship. In 1939 he founded the American Ballad Singers, which, for several years, he led in performances throughout the United States. He also did considerable research in American folk music, making many arrangements of indigenous folksongs and editing several volumes of folk music, including *A Treasury of American Song* with Olin Downes (1940). His own compositions, which previously had been somewhat esoteric in style and approach, now became more popular in appeal as they assimilated melodic and rhythmic characteristics of American folk music and sought to interpret the American scene. With these compositions he achieved success in America, Europe, and the Soviet Union. His principal works for orchestra include 3 symphonies, *Walt Whitman Overture, Ozark Set, Wilderness Road, Prairie Legend, Western Suite, Sunday in Brooklyn,* clarinet concerto, *Summer Night, Lonesome Hollow, From My Window,* and Divertimento. He also wrote a violin sonata, string quartet, and several compositions for the piano including the *American Sonata, Children's Day,* and *American Kaleidoscope.*

Since 1949 Siegmeister has been assistant professor of music at Hofstra College in Long Island. He is the editor of *The Music Lover's Handbook* (1943).

Signature. *See:* Key Signature.

Sigurd Jorsalfar. Suite for orchestra by Grieg, op. 56 (1872, revised 1892). It was adapted from incidental music by Grieg for a drama by Bjørnstjerne Bjørnson, first given in Christiania (now Oslo) in 1872. The suite has three sections. I. In the King's Hall. This is a three-part prelude beginning with a theme for clarinet and bassoon against plucked strings. After a trio section, the first part returns. II. Borghild's Dream. An intermezzo, this movement contrasts a sensitive melody for strings with an agitated section. III. Homage March. The finale opens with trumpet fanfares. Four cellos then present the main subject, which has a martial character. The middle part is a trio dominated by a melody for first violins. The first section then returns.

Siloti, Alexander, pianist, conductor, and teacher. Born Kharkov, Russia, Oct. 9, 1863; died New York City, Dec. 8, 1945. He was graduated from the Moscow Conservatory in 1881 with a gold medal in piano; his teachers there included Tchaikovsky and Nikolai Rubinstein. Meanwhile, in 1880, he made his début as a pianist in Moscow. Two more years of piano study were spent in Weimar with Liszt, after which he made sensational appearances throughout Europe, acknowledged one of Russia's foremost virtuosos. From 1887 to 1890 he was professor of piano at the Moscow Conservatory. In 1898 he scored a triumph in his début in the United States. In 1901 he entered another field of musical activity by conducting the Moscow Philharmonic. Two years after that he organized, and for many years directed, the Siloti concerts in St. Petersburg, which introduced a considerable amount of new Russian music.

He escaped from Russia in 1919, finally coming to the United States, where he remained for the rest of his life. There he continued his activities as teacher and pianist; from 1925 until 1942 he taught at the Juilliard School of Music.

Siloti edited or made transcriptions for orchestra of music by Bach and Vivaldi.

Simchas Torah (Bloch). *See: Baal Shem.*

Sinding, Christian, composer. Born Kongsberg, Norway, Jan. 11, 1856; died Oslo, Norway, Dec. 3, 1941. From 1877 to 1881 he attended the Leipzig Conservatory. After returning to Norway he settled in Oslo, where he taught piano and made concert appearances. In 1884 his first published work, a piano quintet, appeared, and on Dec. 19, 1885, he directed a concert of his own works. Success came later with pieces for the piano, the most popular being *Rustles of Spring* (*Fruehlingsrauschen*), the third piece in a piano suite entitled *6 Stuecke,* op. 32 (1896). Throughout the years this composition has been a favorite of salon orchestras and budding pianists. In 1890 a government subsidy enabled Sinding to give up all activity except composing. This subsidy was extended into a munificent life pension in 1915 and was supplemented by a gift of 30,000 crowns on his 60th birthday. Sinding visited the United States in 1921-1922, when he served on the faculty of the Eastman School of Music in Rochester. He was a Romantic composer who cast his ambitious works in epic molds. Much of his writing was national in character, but the nationalism was usually expressed in a Wagnerian idiom. His orchestral music embraces 4 symphonies, 3 violin concertos, a piano concerto, a suite for violin and orchestra, *Épisodes chevaleresques*, *Rondo infinito*, and a *Légende* for violin and orchestra. Among his chamber-music works are 4 violin sonatas, 4 violin suites, 3 piano trios, a piano quintet, and a string quartet. He also produced many piano pieces, including a sonata, a suite, and sundry variations, etudes, waltzes, caprices, and intermezzi.

Sinfonia. In the 17th century any composition for instruments. The term was also applied specifically to the orchestral work that introduced an opera. In the next century it acquired the modern sense of "symphony."

Sinfonia Antartica. *See:* Symphony— *Vaughan Williams.*

Sinfonia concertante. A large work, occasionally for a solo instrument and orchestra, but most often for several solo instruments and orchestra; it is a compromise between a symphony and a concerto. It retains some of the scope and breadth of a symphony without sacrificing the individuality of the solo instruments.

A popular work in this form is Mozart's *Sinfonia concertante* in E-flat major, K. 364 (1779), for violin, viola, and orchestra (I. *Allegro maestoso.* II. Andante. III. Presto). The first movement is in a large design with two sets of themes. The first set appears in the orchestra, the other in the solo instruments. The slow movement is a noble lyrical section consisting of two soaring, emotional melodies, both first presented by the orchestra. The finale, like the first movement, comprises two sets of themes, one for the orchestra and the other for the soloists.

Mozart wrote a second *Sinfonia concertante* that is sometimes given on symphony programs: E-flat major, K. Anh. 9 (1778), for wind quartet and orchestra.

The Polish composer, Karol Szyma-

nowski, wrote an important 20th-century work in this form, the *Sinfonia concertante* No. 2, for piano and orchestra, op. 60 (1932), introduced at Warsaw in May 1937, with the composer as soloist (I. *Allegro moderato.* II. *Andante molto sostenuto.* III. *Allegro non troppo*). The principal themes of the first movement appear at once in the piano against syncopated chords in the strings. The second main theme is played by the flute against chromatic-scale passages. The second movement opens with a flute melody against piano and strings; soon the violas join in with a counter-melody. The poetic mood thus established is maintained with a lyrical second thought for muted horns. A repetition of the first theme provides a transition to the finale, an outburst of energetic dance rhythms.

Sinfonia da Requiem. For orchestra by Benjamin Britten, op. 20 (1940), introduced in New York on March 29, 1941, John Barbirolli conducting. Structurally this work is not a symphony but a suite in three movements. It was inspired by the death of the composer's father. I. *Lacrymosa.* A slow lament presents three motifs. A syncopated subject presented by cellos is answered by a bassoon. After that comes a broad melody based on the interval of the major seventh, and alternating chords in flute and trombones. II. *Dies irae.* The second movement enters without pause. It is in the nature of a dance of death with some passages of quiet marching rhythm; the main melody is presented by the flutes. III. *Requiem aeternam.* The principal motif is a serene melody for flutes against strings and harp. The entire movement is lyrical. The symphony ends gently on a sustained note for clarinet.

Sinfonía de Antígona. For orchestra by Carlos Chávez (1933), first performed in Mexico City on Dec. 15, 1933, the composer conducting. This composition originated as incidental music for Jean Cocteau's play, *Antigone*, based on Sophocles. Chávez's music is a successful blend of Mexican-Indian rhythms and melodies constructed from Greek modes. While the composer disavows a program, the work was intended to interpret the defiance, heroism, and martyrdom of Antigone. There are three important melodies: the first in solo oboe; the second, in violins; the third, in bass flute.

Sinfonia Domestica. *See:* Symphony—*Richard Strauss.*

Sinfonía India. For orchestra by Carlos Chávez (1936), introduced by the Columbia Broadcasting System Orchestra in New York on Jan. 23, 1936. The main interest of this music lies in its exploitation of such authentic Indian instruments as the water-gourd, rasps, rattles, and Indian drums, and in its use of actual Mexican-Indian melodies.

Sinfonia Sacra. *See:* Symphony—*Hanson.*

Sinfonietta. A little symphony. A composition in symphonic form but of smaller dimensions than a symphony, slighter in texture, and less ambitious in scope. An outstanding composition of this type is Leoš Janáček's *Sinfonietta* (1926), which originated as a series of fanfares for outdoor performance in Prague. The composer subsequently amplified it into a five-movement *Sinfonietta,* a version in which it was introduced in Prague on June 29, 1926 (I. Allegretto. II. Andante. III. Moderato. IV. Allegretto. V. Allegro). Much of its melodic and rhythmic material comes from Moravian folk sources. Janáček uses many of these ideas successively; some are of a fragmentary nature, and none receive detailed elaboration. The first movement serves as a prelude to the second and consists of two subjects of folk character. The second section is the most extended in the *Sinfonietta.* Its principal ideas are a vivacious subject for two oboes, and an extended melody first appearing in the horn and lower strings against clarinet arpeggios. There are three motifs in the third movement: a song for muted violins and cellos; a stately subject for the brass; and a theme for trombones. The fourth movement opens with a dance melody for three trumpets. A song for three flutes is the heart of the finale, which ends with a return of a basic thought from the first movement.

Francis Poulenc's *Sinfonietta* (1947) is also an important contribution to this literature. It was first given in London, on Oct. 24, 1948, Roger Desormière conducting. This music is consistently light, and at times satirical, overflowing with ingratiating popular tunes and sprightly dance rhythms (I. *Molto vivace.* II. *Molto vivace.* III. *Andante cantabile.* IV. *Très vite et très gai*).

Singer, Jacques, conductor. Born Prezemsyi, Poland, 1912. His family settled in the United States when he was nine. After making his début in New York in 1925 he attended the Curtis Institute on a scholarship, as a pupil of Carl Flesch. Further study took place with Leopold Auer and Paul Kochanski at the Juilliard School of Music. He became a violinist in the Philadelphia Orchestra in his eighteenth year. In 1937 he was appointed conductor of the recently organized Dallas Symphony, holding that post until 1943. After World War II he became conductor of the Vancouver Symphony in British Columbia. From 1954 to 1958 he held a similar post with the Corpus Christi Orchestra in Texas, and since 1958 with the Buenos Aires Symphony.

Sinigaglia, Leone, composer. Born Turin, Italy, Aug. 14, 1868; died there, May 16, 1944. He attended the Liceo Musicale in Turin and completed his music study from 1895 to 1900 in Vienna with Eusebius Mandyczewski and in Prague with Dvořák. The latter persuaded him to compose in a national Italian style. It was in this vein that he wrote his first success, *Danze piemontesi* for orchestra, introduced in Turin on May 14, 1905, under Toscanini's direction. Later works, which helped establish Sinigaglia's reputation, were also in a national idiom. They included the *Rapsodia piemontese* for violin and orchestra and *Piemonte Suite* for orchestra. Other major works, however, followed German post-Romantic tendencies. Besides compositions already mentioned, Sinigaglia completed for orchestra a violin concerto, an overture *Le Baruffe chiozzotte,* a tone poem *In Memoria d'un giovane artista,* and various compositions for solo instruments and orchestra. In chamber music he produced a string quartet, violin sonata, and cello sonata, among other works.

See: Baruffe chiozzotte, Le, Overture.

Sirènes (Debussy). *See:* Nocturnes.

Sites auriculaires, Les. *See:* Habanera—Ravel.

Sitwell, Sacheverell, poet, essayist, and biographer. Born Scarborough, England, 1897. His writings include several books on musical subjects, among them biographies of Mozart (1932) and Liszt (1934) and *A Background for Domenico Scarlatti*. Constant Lambert's *Rio Grande* was based on one of his poems.

His sister, Edith (born Scarborough, England, 1887), is also a distinguished poet. Her abstractionist poems were used by William Walton for his famous *Façade*.

Six, Les (The French Six). A school of contemporary French composers which came into prominence soon after World War I. Its members were Arthur Honegger, Georges Auric, Darius Milhaud, Germaine Tailleferre, Louis Durey, and Francis Poulenc. This is not a "school" in the accepted sense of the term: composers united by a single artistic purpose. It was, rather, a label invented for this group by a French critic, in a review printed in *Comoedia* on Jan. 16, 1920; in discussing an album of piano pieces by these six composers, Collet compared them to the "Russian Five." The label of "Les Six" persisted for these French composers for several years, even though each one tried to dissociate himself from it.

Six four chord. Second inversion of a triad. The second inversion of the C major triad reads, from the bottom up, G, C, E.

Sixth. The interval between two notes separated by five diatonic notes. A sixth may be major (C to A, for example), minor (C to A-flat), augmented (C to A-sharp), or diminished (C to A-double flat).

Six three chord. First inversion of a triad. The first inversion of the C major triad reads, from the bottom up, E, G, C.

Skilton, Charles Sanford, composer. Born Northampton, Mass., Aug. 16, 1868; died Lawrence, Kansas, March 12, 1941. He was graduated from Yale in 1889, and two years later went to Berlin for music study. In 1893 he became director of music at Salem College in Winston-Salem, N.C., and conductor of the Salem Phil-

harmonic. From 1898 to 1903 he was music director of the State Normal School in Trenton, N.J. In 1903 he was appointed Dean of Fine Arts at the University of Kansas; when he resigned this post, fourteen years later, he remained professor of organ and music history until his death. Skilton first achieved acknowledgment as a composer after 1915 when he had discovered and begun an intensive study of American Indian music. His most popular works were written in that style. These include the following compositions for orchestra: *Two Indian Dances, Suite Primeval* (with the popular *Deer Dance* and *War Dance*), *Shawnee Indian Hunting Dance,* and *American Indian Fantasy* for cello and orchestra. Also in an American Indian idiom are the *Two Indian Dances* for string quartet, the *Sioux Flute Serenade,* and the *Three Indian Sketches* for piano. Other works by Skilton, among them a string quartet, 2 violin sonatas, and an orchestral overture, reveal a European derivation.

Skyscrapers. Suite by John Alden Carpenter adapted from the score to a ballet introduced in New York on Feb. 10, 1926. The composer explains he sought in the ballet "to reflect some of the many rhythmic movements and sounds of modern American life." The setting is Coney Island where a skyscraper is being built, and where there takes place some merrymaking and a rowdy brawl. A Negro, stretching out for some sleep, dreams of his Southern home, which is conjured up for him in song and dance. The factory whistle blows and the workmen return to build the skyscraper. The orchestral suite is made up of the following sections as designated in the score: "Symbols of Restlessness—An abstraction of the skyscraper and the work that produces it— and the interminable crowd that passes by—The Transition from work to play —Coney Island and a reflection of a few of its manifold activities, interrupted presently by a throw-back, in the movie sense, to the idea of work, and reverting with equal suddenness to play—The return from play to work."

This music is in a jazz idiom. The score also quotes several folk and popular tunes, including *Massa's in de Cold, Cold*

Ground, by Stephen Foster, *Yankee Doodle,* and *Dem Goo-Goo Eyes,* and some blues melodies.

Slavonic Dances. Two series of folk dances for orchestra by Dvořák, opp. 46 and 72 (1878, 1886). Dvořák originally wrote them for piano four hands on a commission from the publisher, Simrock. They made Dvořák so famous throughout Europe that Simrock prevailed upon him to orchestrate them. The first set consists of folk dances from Bohemia; the second, of dances from Yugoslavia and Little Russia. The most famous dances in the first set are: No. 1, in C major; No. 2, in E minor; No. 3 in D major; No. 6 in A-flat major; and No. 8, in G minor. In the second set the most popular are: No. 2, in E minor; No. 7, in C major; and No. 8, in A-flat major. The dances are varied in mood and feeling. Some are gay and spirited, some stormy, some sentimental or melancholy, and some suggest whimsy and coquetry. No. 2 in the first set and Nos. 2 and 8 in the second are also familiar in transcriptions for violin and piano by Fritz Kreisler.

Slavonic Rhapsodies. Three rhapsodies for orchestra by Dvořák, op. 45 (1878). The first two were introduced in Prague, and the third in Berlin, all in 1878. The three were played on a single program for the first time in 1879 at Vienna, Hans Richter conducting. The rhapsodies describe old Bohemia: its sagas, knights, fair ladies, and tournaments. The first, in D major, is built out of two melodies, and suggests a knightly tournament. The second, in G minor, depicts a lover's tryst. The third and most famous in the set, in A-flat major, describes a hunt and the service of fair ladies; here the main melody is a vivacious folk dance constructed from a solemn strain with which the rhapsody opens and closes.

Sleeping Beauty, The (La Belle aux bois dormant). Suite for orchestra by Tchaikovsky, op. 66 (1889), adapted from the score to a ballet whose scenario was based on Perrault's famous fairy tale. This ballet was first produced in St. Petersburg, on Feb. 15, 1890. From the 30 numbers in his ballet score the composer extracted for his suite a prologue and three "acts." I. The Lilac Fairy. This is the prologue, and its musical essence is a suave melody for English horn. II. Adagio and *Pas d'action,* or Act 1. A graceful melody appears in the strings. The *Pas d'action* enters without pause, representing this same material with changed rhythm and orchestral color. III. Characteristic Dance and Panorama, or Act 2. The characteristic dance consists of a dialogue in the woodwinds between Puss-in-Boots and the White Cat, occasionally interrupted by chords in the orchestra. The Panorama, which follows without pause, is based on an elegant melody for strings. IV. Valse, or Act 3. This is one of the composer's most celebrated waltzes, a mobile melody for strings preceded by a stately introduction in brass and strings. The waltz is brought to a powerful climax by the full orchestra.

Music from the last act of the *Sleeping Beauty* ballet has been adapted into still another celebrated ballet, *Aurora's Wedding,* introduced by the Ballet Russe and a staple in the dance repertory.

Slonimsky, Nicolas, musicologist. Born St. Petersburg, Russia, April 27, 1894. He attended the St. Petersburg Conservatory and in 1923 came to the United States, of which he eventually became a citizen. After serving on the faculty of the Eastman School of Music in Rochester, N.Y., he settled in Boston. For two years he was secretary to Serge Koussevitzky. In 1927 he founded the Boston Chamber Orchestra, and conducted it in concerts of unusual programs. In 1931 and 1932 he directed performances of contemporary music in New York, Havana, Paris, and Berlin; in 1938, a program of American and Latin American music at the Ibero-American Music Festival in Colombia. He has also taught music at various institutions including the Peabody Conservatory in Baltimore. Among his compositions are *Overture on an Ancient Greek Theme, Four Simple Pieces,* and *Toy Balloon* for orchestra; also many pieces for piano including *Studies in Black and White, Silhouettes, Tintinnabulations,* and *Yellowstone Park.* He is most famous as a musical lexicographer and musicologist. His books are: *Music Since 1900* (1937, revised

1949); *Music of Latin America* (1945); *The Road to Music* (1947); *A Thing or Two About Music* (1948); *Lexicon of Musical Invective* (1953). He has also edited Oscar Thompson's *International Cyclopedia of Music and Musicians* (since 1946) and completely revised Baker's *Biographical Dictionary of Musicians* (5th edition, 1959). He is also the compiler of the *Thesaurus of Scales and Melodic Patterns* (1947), a reference book of over 2,000 melodic and harmonic progressions.

Slur. A curved line above or below a group of notes indicating they are to be connected smoothly.

Smallens, Alexander, conductor. Born St. Petersburg, Russia, Jan. 1, 1889. He came to the United Sates as a child, then attended the Institute of Musical Art in New York. His music study was completed at the Paris Conservatory. From 1911 on he made numerous appearances in America and Europe with major opera companies and was responsible for many important premières and revivals. He also appeared as guest conductor of leading symphony orchestras. From 1927 to 1934 he was assistant, then associate, conductor of the Philadelphia Orchestra. For many years he has conducted annual summer concerts at the Robin Hood Dell in Philadelphia and at the Lewisohn Stadium in New York.

Smetana, Bedřich, composer. Born Leitomischl, Bohemia, March 2, 1824; died Prague, May 12, 1884. The father of Bohemian national music, Smetana interested himself in music from childhood on, but had little early systematic training. In his nineteenth year he went to Prague, where he became a pupil of Josef Proksch. Four years later he became a music teacher in the household of Count Leopold Thun. In 1848 he helped organize the first important music school in Prague and a year later he was appointed pianist to the former Emperor of Austria, Ferdinand I, then residing in the Bohemian capital. From 1856 to 1861 he lived in Göteborg, Sweden, where he taught, played piano, and conducted the city's orchestra. In 1861, back in his native land, he assumed a commanding role in his country's musical life. He became director of the music school in Prague; led an important orchestra and chorus; wrote music criticisms in which he espoused the cause of Bohemian national music; founded and directed a dramatic school for the Bohemian theater; helped organize the Society of Artists.

As a Bohemian national composer Smetana was most successful in his operas, especially *The Bartered Bride,* Bohemia's first and still its greatest folk opera. But the national identity is also strong in his instrumental music, in which his outstanding achievement was the cycle of tone poems collectively entitled *My Country (Má Vlast),* one of which is Smetana's most celebrated orchestral composition, *The Moldau (Vltava).* Thus Smetana became the first composer in Bohemia to demonstrate how to fuse sophisticated approaches to harmony, tonality, thematic development, and form with the basic elements of Bohemian folksongs and dances.

After 1874, Smetana was afflicted by deafness. Despite this infirmity he continued to produce substantial works, including his autobiographical string quartet *From My Life (Aus meinem Leben).* The severe criticisms levelled against his last opera, *The Devil's Wall,* precipitated the composer's physical and mental breakdown. He lost his mind in 1883 and was confined to an asylum, where he died a year later.

His principal instrumental compositions follow:

Chamber Music: Piano trio; 2 string quartets (including *From My Life*); Two Pieces, for violin and piano.

Orchestra: Festive Symphony; Richard III; Wallenstein's Camp; Haakon Jari; Solemn Prelude; My Country (Má Vlast), a cycle of six tone poems that includes *The Moldau,* or *Vltava; The Prague Carnival.*

Piano: Sonata in One Movement; Memories of Bohemia; Dreams; Six Characteristic Pieces; Czech Dances; waltzes, bagatelles, impromptus, and polkas.

See: Dance of the Comedians; Furiant; My Fatherland; Moldau, The; Polka; Quartet—*Smetana.*

Smith, Carleton Sprague, musicologist.

Born New York City, Aug. 8, 1905. He was graduated from Harvard in 1927, and in 1930 received his doctorate from the University of Vienna. After serving as music critic on the Boston *Transcript,* in 1931 he became a member of the faculty at Columbia University in the department of history, where he remained two years. From 1931 to 1959 he was chief of the Music Division of the New York Public Library; since 1948 he has lectured on American music at New York University. In 1959 he became director of the Brazilian Institute of New York University. He has been president of the Music Library Association and the American Musicological Society, has lectured at leading American universities, and has written scholarly articles on music.

Smith, David Stanley, composer, conductor, and teacher. Born Toledo, Ohio, July 6, 1877; died New Haven, Conn., Dec. 17, 1949. He was graduated from Yale in 1900 and after that studied music privately with Horatio Parker, Ludwig Thuille in Munich, and Widor in Paris. In 1903 he joined the music faculty of Yale, where he remained over forty years, twenty of them as dean of the School of Music. For 26 years he was also conductor of the New Haven Symphony. A prolific composer, Smith was a conservative who preferred traditional styles and structures. To these he brought a sound technique, a fine feeling for dramatic effect, and a sensitive harmonic and lyric style. His major works include 4 symphonies, 2 violin concertos, various tone poems (including *Credo* and *The Apostle*), *Prince Hal* overture, 10 string quartets, 2 violin sonatas, a piano quintet, and a cello sonata.

Smyth, Dame Ethel, composer. Born Foots Gray, Kent, England, April 23, 1858; died Woking, England, May 8, 1944. She was England's foremost woman composer. She attended the Leipzig Conservatory, and first gained fame as a composer with a Mass, some chamber music, and an opera, *The Wreckers.* She subsequently produced a considerable amount of orchestral and instrumental music that demonstrated excellent workmanship and a fine lyric and harmonic invention. These include a Serenade and a Suite for orchestra, a horn concerto, *Overture to Antony and Cleopatra,* shorter orchestral works (*March of the Women, On the Cliffs of Cornwall,* and *Two Interlinked French Melodies*), a string quintet, violin sonata, cello sonata, string quartet, 2 oboe trios, and 2 horn trios. In 1920 she was made Dame of the British Empire. She wrote several autobiographical volumes, the most famous being *Impressions That Remained* (1919).

Snares. Catgut stretched loosely across the head of certain drums. When struck, the drums produce an unusual effect by having the catgut vibrate against the head.

Snow Maiden (Snegurochka). An opera by Rimsky-Korsakov with a libretto by the composer based on a play by Alexander Ostrovsky derived from a folk tale. The opera was introduced in Moscow on Feb. 10, 1882. For orchestral excerpt *see: Dance of the Buffoons.*

Société des Apaches. A school of French musicians founded in the early 1900's by Maurice Ravel and several other prominent Parisian musicians. Their aim was to promote innovation and experimentation in composition, with particular dedication to Debussy and the "Russian Five." The earliest members of this group included Maurice Delage, Ricardo Viñes, Leon Paul Fargue, Paul Sordes, M. D. Calvocoressi, and Ravel.

Société des Concerts du Conservatoire. *See:* Paris Conservatory Orchestra.

Society of Ancient Instruments. A society organized in Paris in 1901 by Henri Casadesus (born Paris, France, Sept. 30, 1879; died there, May 31, 1947), who was its director for many years. Its aim was to present the music of the old masters on the old instruments for which it was intended. Casadesus did considerable research in the music of the past, unearthing many long-forgotten masterworks which he reintroduced at his concerts. After World War I, the Society, under Casadesus' direction, made the first of several tours of the United States.

Society of Friends of Music (New York). *See:* Friends of Music.

Soir, Le. *See:* Symphony—Haydn.

Soirée dans Grenade (Debussy). *See: Estampes.*

Soirée de Vienne. Nine valse-caprices for piano arranged by Liszt (1852) from Schubert's waltzes for piano, opp. 9, 18, 33, 50, 67, 77.

Sokoloff, Nikolai, conductor. Born Kiev, Russia, May 28, 1886. He was the youngest student to be admitted to the Yale School of Music. Later music study took place with Charles Martin Loeffler in Boston and with Vincent d'Indy and Eugène Ysaÿe in Europe. In 1911 he became concertmaster of the Russian Symphony. Five years later he organized a string quartet in San Francisco and became conductor of an orchestra. From 1918 to 1933 he was principal conductor of the Cleveland Orchestra, which he had helped to organize. From 1935 to 1939 he served as national director of the Federal Music Project, and from 1938 to 1940 was conductor of the Seattle Symphony. After that he was director of the Musical Arts Society in La Jolla, Calif.

Soldier's Tale, A (Stravinsky). *See: Histoire du soldat, L'.*

Solmization. A system of naming the notes of the scale, "do, re, mi" and so on. It was devised in the 11th century by Guido d'Arezzo, who derived this nomenclature from the first syllable of each line of a hymn to St. John.

Solomon (born **Solomon Cutner**), pianist. Born London, England, Aug. 9, 1902. He does not use a given name. After being prepared for the concert stage by Mathilde Verne, he made an impressive début in London on June 30, 1911. In 1918 he withdrew from the concert stage to devote himself to a five-year period of study. Returning to a concert career, he was then acclaimed one of England's foremost pianists, an outstanding interpreter of the contemporary repertory. He made his American début at the New York World's Fair on June 10, 1939, in the première of Arthur Bliss' piano concerto.

Solomon, Izler, conductor. Born St. Paul, Minn., Jan. 11, 1910. After studying music with private teachers in Kansas City and New York he was appointed in 1928 to the music faculty of Michigan State College in East Lansing. During this period he completed his music study with Michael Press. He made his conducting début with an orchestra he founded in East Lansing on March 17, 1932. From 1936 to 1942 he was conductor of the Illinois Symphony in Chicago and several other symphonic groups. After appearing as guest conductor with major American orchestras, he was appointed music director of the newly organized Columbus Philharmonic in Ohio in 1941. In 1956 he was appointed principal conductor of the Indianapolis Symphony and director of the annual summer festival in Aspen, Colorado. When the Israel Philharmonic toured the United States in 1951, Solomon was one of its conductors.

Solti, Georg, conductor. Born Budapest, Hungary, Oct. 21, 1912. He was graduated from the High School for Music in Budapest in 1930. His début as a conductor took place with the Budapest Opera in 1937. One year later he settled in Switzerland, where in 1942 he won the Geneva Prize for pianists; and in 1944 he became conductor of the Swiss Radio Orchestra. For six years, after the end of World War II, Solti was music director in the city of Munich, Germany, directing both operatic and orchestral performances. Since 1951 he has held a similar post in Frankfort. His American début took place with the San Francisco Opera on Sept. 13, 1953. The following January he gave guest performances with the San Francisco Symphony, and on March 14, 1957, he made his first appearances in New York with the New York Philharmonic.

Solveig's Song (Grieg). *See: Peer Gynt Suites.*

Sombrero de tres picos, El (Falla). *See: Three-Cornered Hat, The.*

Sonata. An extended composition for piano, or for a solo instrument and piano. It is often in three movements, the middle one slow, and the outer ones fast. The first movement is usually in the sonata form (which see). The slow movement is lyrical, often in a three-part song form or in the form of a theme and variations. The finale may be in any one of several forms: rondo, sonata, or theme and variations. Where sonatas have four movements, a minuet or scherzo is interpolated between the slow movement and the finale.

The term "sonata" is found in the 17th century as the instrumental counterpart of "cantata": a cantata was a composition to be sung, and a sonata a work to be "sounded" or played. The sonata da chiesa produced by many Italian composers in the 17th century represents an important step forward in the history of this form, since it consists of several movements. Though the 12 sonatas for violin and accompaniment by Corelli (1700) did not yet crystallize the classic sonata form, they proved of significance in establishing a mature homophonic style. Later Italian masters followed Corelli in writing violin sonatas, among these being Vivaldi, Tartini, and Viotti. In England and Germany, the violin sonata found its masters in Handel and J. S. Bach. Bach made significant progress in the structure of the violin sonata by writing out the accompanying harmonies completely instead of suggesting them with a figured bass has had heretofore been the practice.

One of the first uses of the term "sonata" in clavier literature is found with Johann Kuhnau (1692). Kuhnau published in 1700 a set of 6 biblical sonatas (of which the most celebrated is *The Combat Between David and Goliath*) in three, four, or five brief movements, each episodic in construction, and with little awareness of thematic development. Clavier writing after Kuhnau achieved technical and artistic development with the sonatas of Domenico Scarlatti. Important progress toward a fully developed sonata form was achieved by Carl Philipp Emanuel Bach.

The sonata, whether for solo piano or for single instrument and piano, achieved its classical design with Haydn and Mozart; its emotional and poetical content was intensified by Beethoven. Though the Romantic composers were partial to smaller pieces, the sonata was by no means neglected; and the repertory has also been enriched by the moderns.

The following are some of the most significant works in the sonata literature:

C. P. E. BACH. It is with Carl Philipp Emanuel Bach that the classic piano sonata form is crystallized. He wrote three-movement sonatas in which a slow movement stands between two fast ones. He often suggested the sonata form in his first movements. He employed an aristocratic manner of piano writing, the "galant" style. It is consequently no surprise to find C. P. E. Bach often spoken of as the "father of the piano sonata," acknowledged as such by Haydn and Mozart, both of whom cut their creative teeth on his music. Bach wrote over 60 sonatas. His first set was dedicated to the King of Prussia (1742). Another set is the *Wuerttemberg Sonatas* (1774). His greatest sonatas are found in 6 sets *For Connoisseurs and Amateurs* (*Fuer Kenner und Liebhaber*), published from 1779 to 1787.

J. S. BACH. The 6 sonatas Bach produced for violin and clavier marked a momentous advance in the art and technique of writing sonatas. One of the striking features of these compositions is the independence achieved by the clavier, often no longer just an accompaniment but rather a partner of the violin in the projection of the music. The third movement in the G major Sonata consists entirely of a clavier solo. Another striking feature is the beautiful lyricism of many of the slow movements—those of the E major and F minor Sonatas particularly, in which the homophonic style of a later era is forcefully foreshadowed. A third significant feature is the enriched harmony which displaced the stilted and formal accompaniments of earlier violin sonatas.

All 6 sonatas were written during Bach's Coethen period (1717-1723); they are in the following keys: No. 1, B minor; No. 2, A major; No. 3, E major; No. 4, C minor; No. 5, F minor; No. 6, G major. The first movement of the Sonata No. 4, a Siciliano, is so famous that it is sometimes given independently of the rest of the work.

Bach wrote 6 works for unaccompanied violin. Three are designated Partitas (which see), because dance forms are used for most of the movements. The other three are classified as sonatas. The three sonatas, written in or about 1720 during the composer's Coethen period, are No. 1, G minor; No. 2, A minor; No. 3,

C major. As in the Partitas, the writing for unaccompanied violin is remarkable for its wealth of polyphony and for the organlike, and at times even orchestral, textures. Of exceptional interest is the third movement (Andante) of the A minor Sonata, one of the master's most eloquent slow movements. The first movement (Adagio) of the C major Sonata was transcribed by the composer for the clavier. Robert Schumann wrote piano accompaniments for these three violin sonatas.

Bach also wrote 3 sonatas for cello (originally viola da gamba) and clavier during his Coethen period: No. 1, G major; No. 2, D major; No. 3, G minor. All his cello works, including the 6 suites for unaccompanied cello, were neglected until the turn of the 20th century, when they were rediscovered by Pablo Casals and popularized in his concerts. As with his violin sonatas and partitas, Bach's writing for cello is extraordinary for its polyphonic skill, rich sonorities, and variety of tone colors. In addition all these cello compositions extend the then limited technique of that instrument so that it can be said that with them the cello achieves emancipation as a solo instrument.

BARBER. Samuel Barber's Sonata in E-flat minor for piano, op. 26 (1949), was commissioned by the League of Composers. It is a work of large design in which the virile modern harmonic and rhythmic writing of the first movement is combined with the eloquent lyricism of the third; in which a varied modern idiom is harmoniously blended with a classic structure. As Harriet Johnson wrote, this sonata "encompasses realism and fantasy, conflict and resolution, poetry and power" (I. *Allegro energico.* II. *Allegro vivace e leggero.* III. *Adagio mesto.* IV. *Fuga*).

BEETHOVEN. The 32 piano sonatas of Beethoven elevate the piano to a position of first importance among solo instruments. Here the piano sonata passes from the precise and classical design of C. P. E. Bach, Haydn, and Mozart—with its trim, neat, pleasing but frequently slight ideas —to a monumental structure to which the foremost composers would henceforth consign some of their profoundest feelings and most penetrating musical thoughts. The first Beethoven sonatas definitely belong to the era of C. P. E. Bach and Haydn. They are slender of structure; they are pleasing to listen to, but without much depth of feeling or profundity of thought. The form always dictates the music, not vice-versa. In the first movement of Beethoven's first piano sonata—in F minor, op. 2, no. 1—we even find thematic material that bears a striking resemblance to that found in the first movement of an F minor Sonata by C. P. E. Bach. On the other hand, the last sonatas by Beethoven are almost orchestral in sonority and dynamics, filled with tempestuous moods and emotions; they have epical architectonic structures; their musical contents are often mighty dramas.

Beethoven wrote his first piano sonatas in 1795, a set of three works gathered as op. 2 (F minor, A major, and C major). He wrote three more sonatas before his own dynamic personality began to assert itself: E-flat major, op. 7; C minor, op. 10, no. 1; and F major, op. 10, no. 2. That personality first appears in the slow movement (*Largo e mesto*) of his Sonata No. 7 in D major, op. 10, no. 3, music of such rich expressiveness and such stirring poetry that Romain Rolland remarked that here "the full grandeur of Beethoven's soul is for the first time revealed."

With the very next Sonata, in C minor, op. 13 (1798), we arrive at the first of the composer's unqualified masterworks in the form. With this work the sonata parts company with the 18th century (I. Grave; *Allegro di molto con brio.* II. *Adagio cantabile.* III. Allegro). The tragic accents of the opening Grave section earned for the sonata as a whole the sobriquet of "Pathétique." With such music, with the storm and stress of the succeeding Allegro section, and with the subjective song of the slow movement we are finally carried to the threshold of the Romantic era.

The main point of interest in the Sonata No. 12 in A-flat major, op. 26 (1801), is its third movement (*Maestoso andante*), a stirring funeral march become famous in transcriptions for orchestra and brass bands. This is the first time that a funeral march has appeared within the context of a sonata.

Sonata No. 14 in C-sharp minor, op. 27, no. 2 (1801), is surely one of the composer's most popular compositions for the piano, a perennial favorite (I. *Adagio sostenuto*. II. Allegretto. III. *Presto agitato*). It is familiarly known as the *Moonlight Sonata*, a name bestowed upon it not by Beethoven but by a German critic, Ludwig Rellstab, to whom the serene first movement conjured up a picture of moonlight on ocean waves. Beethoven himself designated this work as a "sonata quasi fantasia." This is because he substituted for the usual first-movement sonata form an unconventional slow and romantic movement (the sonata form is found in the last movement); also because his material is often developed more along the elastic lines of a fantasia than the stricter procedures of the sonata. If it is possible to evoke a picture of a moonlit night in the first movement, such an image is quickly dissipated in the two succeeding movements. The second has a delicate scherzo-like character, while the finale is in a turbulent mood.

The sobriquet *Pastoral* for Sonata No. 15 in D major, op. 28 (1801), is happier than that of *Moonlight* for the preceding work. Once again the descriptive title was not given by the composer himself, but concocted by another, this time the publisher Cranz. A pastoral mood is prominent in the first and last movements (Allegro, and *Allegro ma non troppo*). While the slow movement (Andante) is on the somber side it also manages to suggest an idyllic mood.

The Sonata No. 17 in D minor, op. 31, no. 2 (I. Largo; Allegro. II. Adagio. III. Allegretto) is one of the most dramatic works of Beethoven's stormy middle period; it is sometimes said that this second creative period is actually ushered in with this composition. A majestic Largo, only a bar and a quarter long, leads to a first movement that throbs with conflict and agitation. The drama is momentarily arrested with the contemplative music of the second movement in an abridged sonata form. But the storm erupts again in the finale, in an oceanic surge of triplets and sextuplets.

The Sonata No. 21 in C minor, op. 53 (1804), is most often identified as the *Waldstein Sonata*, because it is dedicated to Count Waldstein. In this music we find the same type of Herculean struggle with fate that we encounter in the Fifth Symphony, also written during this period, especially in the titanic first movement (*Allegro con brio*), which opens with the fury of an unleashed hurricane. In this sonata we also find the introspective Beethoven searching the deepest recesses of his heart, and plumbing emotional depths rarely before encountered in piano literature—in the three-section second movement (*Adagio molto*). Beethoven originally planned quite a different slow movement for this work but wisely rejected it as not in character with the epic proportions of his first movement; he published it separately as *Andante favori*, in F major (1806).

There is remarkable appropriateness in calling the Sonata No. 27 in F minor, op. 57 (1804), *Appassionata*. This is passionate and powerful music, endowed with a nobility and grandeur of expression on the one hand, and with struggle and resignation on the other. But this title was the invention of the publisher Cranz, and not of the composer (I. *Allegro assai*. II. *Andante con moto*. III. *Allegro ma non troppo*). The first and third movements reflect the composer's stormy personality, and like the first movement of the *Waldstein* represent the composer's life and death struggle with Fate. Indeed, the four notes with which Beethoven's Fifth Symphony opens find a counterpart in a persistent four-note motif in the first part of the first movement of the *Appassionata*. The middle movement is a theme and variations, much of it in a peaceful mood. The serenity is shattered by violent chords which herald the arrival of the stormy finale. At the end of the sonata the storm finally subsides. "The spirit has freed itself," explains Ernst von Eiterlein, "and at last the struggle ceases in solemn minor strains."

The Sonata No. 26 in E-flat major, op.

81a (1809), is a rare case in which Beethoven provided his own programmatic titles. In May 1809 Beethoven's friend and patron, Archduke Rudolph, fled from Vienna to escape the invading French. The sonata became a personal testament of the composer's feelings about the Archduke, to whom the work is dedicated. Each of the three movements bears a descriptive heading. The first movement (Adagio; Allegro) is called *The Farewell* (*Das Lebewohl,* or *Les Adieux*); the second (*Andante espressivo*), *Absence* (*Abwesenheit* or *L'Absence*); the finale (*Vivacissimamente*), *The Return* (*Das Wiedersehen* or *Le Retour*). The first three notes of the slow introduction to the first movement is a motto theme recurring throughout the movement; above these three notes, Beethoven wrote the word "Farewell" ("Le-be-wohl"). This movement is touched with a pervading sadness. The feeling of desolation is heightened in the second movement, a monologue with an occasional recitative-like character. The last movement, however, is an outburst of joy at the Archduke's return to Vienna. In the second and third movements Beethoven utilized both Italian and German tempo markings, the first time he had recourse to the German terminology.

The same qualities and feelings that set aside the last string quartets of Beethoven from those that preceded it can be found in his last piano sonatas: a new concept of form which now must be completely flexible in order to contain Beethoven's turbulent feelings and penetrating thoughts; an impatience with the limitations imposed upon him by existing harmonic, contrapuntal, and melodic laws; the need to seek out new avenues of expression, to endow music with new spiritual values. The sonatas of this last period embrace the following epical works: No. 28 in A major, op. 101 (1816); No. 29 in B-flat major, op. 106, the *Hammerklavier* (1818); No. 30 in E major, op. 109 (1820); No. 31 in A-flat major, op. 110 (1821); No. 32 in C minor, op. 111 (1822). The apex of the A major Sonata is the monumental finale (Allegro) towards which the earlier movements seem to reach, especially the

deeply moving and eloquent third movement (*Adagio ma non troppo con affetto*).

The title page of the B-flat major Sonata reads: "Grosse Sonate fuer das Hammerklavier," which is why this work is designated as the *Hammerklavier Sonata.* "Hammerklavier" is the German word for piano, with its percussive action—as distinguished from the earlier clavier with its plucked strings. Fully exploiting the new dynamic range and the enriched colors of the piano, Beethoven produced a work monumental in structure and equally epical in musical content; the writing at times almost achieves a symphonic breadth (I. Allegro. II. *Assai vivace.* III. *Adagio sostenuto.* IV. Largo; *Un poco più vivace*). The alternation of stout-fisted defiance and resignation found so often in Beethoven can be discerned in the very opening measures of the first movement: in the thrust of the loud chords followed at once by a docile lyric response. But it is struggle that is uppermost in this movement, and truly it is a struggle of the gods. Never before had the dynamic resources of the keyboard been so severely taxed. Resignation, however, gains the upper hand in the spacious slow movement, the longest ever written by Beethoven (it requires twenty minutes for performance). The somber and at times dissonant chords, the shifting tonalities, the plunging registers from the highest treble to the lowest bass—all this explores recesses of heart and soul rarely before touched by music. Then like a crown comes the finale with its giant three-voice fugue, and opening with a slow section in a nebulous tonality. There is in this movement a grief almost too terrible to contemplate—in a succession of tortured trills. But here, too, is the proud expression of the will to live and create; and it is with a firm and resounding feeling of optimism that the sonata finally ends in a cascade of trills and gigantic chords.

The last of Beethoven's piano sonatas, the C minor, was also his last work for that instrument. It was almost as if the composer felt he had nothing more to say for the piano; his mighty skein of sonatas came to an end with perhaps the noblest of these works (I. Maestoso; *Allegro con brio ed appassionato*. II. *Arietta: Adagio molto semplice e cantabile*). Once again, as in many earlier works, we find the dual concept of struggle and resignation. Struggle appears in the first movement, which is in three-part song form (A-B-A), much of it in a fugal style. Resignation is found in the second —a slow movement with which the sonata ends and which consists of a series of variations on a stately arietta heard in the opening measures. Perhaps appropriately, it is on a note of resignation that Beethoven has his last say in piano music —almost as if to acknowledge that his troubled heart has finally found peace.

Beethoven produced 10 sonatas for violin and piano, in which the two instruments are regarded as a single artistic unity, and in which each instrument has its own individuality and its own significance in projecting the main thought. No composer before Beethoven had succeeded in achieving such a harmonious artistic partnership.

The most famous of these violin sonatas is that in A major, op. 47 (1803), known as the *Kreutzer Sonata*. That name comes from its dedication to the famous violinist Rodolphe Kreutzer. It is amusing to note that Kreutzer refused to perform it because he found it "outrageously unintelligible." The music of the outer movements is so passionate and dramatic that it served as an inspiration for Tolstoy's story, *The Kreutzer Sonata*. There is, however, little emotional turmoil in the middle slow movement, in which a placid and gentle melody is subjected to a series of more or less formal variations (I. *Adagio sostenuto*; Presto. II. *Andante con variazioni*. III. Presto).

Almost as familiar as the above work is the Sonata in F major, op. 24 (1801), which has such an abundance of joyous lyricism and such an outpouring of exuberant spirits that it has come to be known as the *Spring Sonata*, a name not concocted by the composer.

Two of the three violin sonatas in op. 30 (1802) make for rewarding listening. The second, in C minor, is in the theatrical, emotionally turbulent vein of the *Kreutzer Sonata*, with a robust first movement in which the main subject is a transposition of a theme used by the composer in the opening measure of his Eighth Symphony. The slow movement is a song-like duet for the two instruments, in which the turmoil subsides. But the agitation is back in the ensuing scherzo and finale movements (I. *Allegro con brio*. II. *Adagio cantabile*. III. Allegro. IV. Allegro).

On the other hand, the Sonata in G major, op. 30, no. 3, has the lyrical and pastoral character of the *Spring Sonata*, so much so that one unidentified writer was tempted to call it Beethoven's "second *Pastoral Symphony*" (I. *Allegro assai*. II. *Tempo di minuetto*. III. *Allegro vivace*). In the first movement there is a main theme that sounds almost like a finger exercise for the violin. The sonata has no slow movement, its place being taken by a graceful minuet.

If in his violin sonatas Beethoven occasionally allows the violin the luxury of indulging in virtuosity, in his cello sonatas he is ever concerned with the expressive character of his instrument. He wrote 5 cello sonatas, in all of which the soaring cantabile passages are uniquely suited to the rich mellow voice of the cello. One of Beethoven's most beautiful slow passages is a brief but eloquent song for the cello, the *Adagio cantabile* movement of his Sonata in A major, op. 69 (1808). The opening moods of the Sonatas in C major and D major, op. 102, nos. 1 and 2, are designed to exploit the mellow colors and timbres of the cello in melodies that range from the melancholy to the introspective.

BRAHMS. All 3 of Brahms' piano sonatas came early in his career. Only one is sufficiently individual and indicative of the master's later creative power to warrant survival: the Sonata in F minor, op. 5 (1853). The first movement (*Allegro maestoso*) is notable for its virility and romantic ardor: a brusque first subject is contrasted with a lyrical second theme, and receives an amplitude of development, and a dramatization within the coda, that we are accustomed to encounter in the master's mature compositions. To his second movement (Andante) the composer appended a quotation from C. O. Sternau to suggest the music's mood: "The twilight glimmers, by moonbeams lighted. Two hearts are here in love united, And locked in blessed embrace." After a scherzo, into which vitality is injected through some startling dissonances, an innovation appears in the interpolation of a transition movement, an intermezzo entitled "Retrospect." This is music of such somber character that it has been described as a funeral march. But optimism is restored in the finale, which is characterized by some complex polyphonic writing and which includes two elaborate codas.

Brahms wrote 3 violin sonatas. The Sonata in G major, op. 78 (1879), has been named the *Rain Sonata* because a persistent 16th-note figure that sounds like falling raindrops makes an appearance in the first movement (*Vivace non troppo*) and recurs in the beautiful slow movement that follows (Adagio). In the finale (*Allegro molto moderato*) there is an extended section of serene and meditative character that is as noble a page as can be found in the violin-sonata literature.

The Sonata in A major, op. 100 (1886), is the *Thun Sonata,* so called because Brahms wrote most of it at Lake Thun, Austria, during a summer holiday. The main theme of the first movement (*Allegro amabile*) resembles the famous "Prize Song" from Wagner's opera *The Mastersingers.* Song dominates this sonata, many of whose themes have the spaciousness of lieder. Most of the expressive lyricism is reserved for the middle movement (*Andante tranquillo*). The finale (*Allegretto grazioso*) is in the composer's characteristic Hungarian vein, vitalized by Hungarian folk melodies and dance rhythms.

The Sonata in D minor, op. 108 (1888), is in a key the composer usually reserved for his more tragic utterances. But this sonata is more passionate and febrile than tragic. In the first movement (Allegro) much use is made of a pedal point on the dominant. In the slow movement (Adagio), a tender solo for the violin is contrasted by a gypsy melody. The third movement, a scherzo (*Un poco presto e con sentimento*), opens with forceful

chords in the violin; on its reappearance this theme is heard in a pizzicato version, and in the coda it is heard in double stops. The finale (*Presto agitato*) is in a combined sonata-rondo form.

Brahms completed 2 cello sonatas. The first—in E minor, op. 38 (1862-1865)—was his first published work for a solo instrument and piano. The second sonata, in F major, op. 99 (1886), is the more famous, a fruit of the composer's full maturity. The first movement (*Allegro vivace*) is dramatic, accentuated by the frequent use of tremolos in both instruments. The slow movement (*Adagio affettuoso*) is a long, expressive song notable for its eloquent detail work; a coda serves as a kind of summation of the main material. The vigorous Scherzo (*Allegro passionato*) is even more spacious in form and design than the finale. The latter, in rondo form (*Allegro molto*), has a greater placidity than is usually encountered in Brahms. It opens in a gentle mood. While the music grows more animated, the relaxed mood of the opening measure seems to dominate the entire movement.

CHOPIN. Chopin wrote 3 piano sonatas. The first, in C minor, op. 4 (1827), is an early work and rarely heard. The composer's full maturity is found in the second, in B-flat minor, op. 35 (1839), a masterwork of impressive structural dimensions. This is the work that has for its slow movement undoubtedly the most celebrated funeral march ever written. The solemn, stately tread of its main melody is beautifully contrasted with an elegiac trio. The concept of death is carried out in the other three movements: in the opening theme of the first movement (Grave; *Doppio movimento*), with its short-breathed, abrupt first theme conveying a sense of terror; in the atmosphere of doom, caught in the breathless Scherzo which precedes the funeral march; in the strength and resignation of the finale (Presto), in which death appears to be triumphant.

The third piano sonata, in B minor, op. 58 (1844), suggests melancholy in the first and third movements. The first (*Allegro maestoso*) abounds in musical ideas, while the third is a Largo which, while not a funeral march, has a funereal character. Between them comes a scherzo in a light, whimsical manner (*Allegro vivace*). In the finale (*Presto non tanto*), in rondo form, the music is by turns dramatic and virtuoso, but of such compelling brilliance that Herbert Weinstock said of it that "in subject matter, in handling, in scope, and in sheer sonorous beauty it is one of the major musical achievements after Beethoven."

DEBUSSY. Debussy planned 6 sonatas for various solo instruments and piano which would revert to the forms and approaches of 17th- and 18th-century French instrumental music. He completed only three, the third being a violin sonata (1917). This work was written while the composer was suffering from cancer. The first movement (*Allegro vivo*) has rhythmic vitality; the second movement (*Intermède*) is a scherzo with faun-like grace and a lightness of motion; in the finale the principal theme of the first movement receives prominent treatment.

Another sonata completed by Debussy was for the cello (1915). The main subject, in a declamatory style, of the first movement (Prologue) is recalled in succeeding movements. This Prologue is in an ironic mood, which is successfully carried over into the second movement (Serenade) in which a bantering pizzicato theme for cello is the main thought. The finale is believed to have been inspired by an old French song; a twelve-bar section marked *con morbidezza* has particular melodic interest.

FAURÉ. Of Fauré's two violin sonatas, the first, in A major, op. 13 (1876), is the more famous. This is Romantic music filled with pleasing melodies and harmonies. In its mood and thematic construction it anticipates César Franck's Violin Sonata. There are two principal themes in the first movement (*Allegro molto*), the first energetic and passionate, and the second lyrical. The second movement (Andante) is a melody of classic beauty assigned entirely to the violin. The mood of the scherzo (*Allegro vivace*) is capricious. The finale (*Allegro quasi presto*) is introduced with a passionate subject for the piano. After an agitated section is temporarily relieved by a gentle song for the violin, the movement ends with a vivacious scherzo-like passage for the violin.

FRANCK. César Franck's only violin sonata, in A major (1886), is one of his masterworks. He wrote it for Eugène Ysaÿe, who introduced it. In the first movement (*Allegretto ben moderato*) the first theme is in a reflective vein, and is presented by the violin following a few introductory notes in the piano. The second theme, also pensive, is first heard in the piano. This movement departs from the traditional sonata form in that it has no development section. There is emotional upheaval in the second movement (Allegro), which has a stormy first theme heard in the piano, and an equally vehement subject later appearing in the violin. The third movement, "Recitative-Fantasia" (*Ben moderato*), opens with a dialogue between piano and violin and continues with a rhapsodic elaboration of these ideas. The finale (*Allegretto poco mosso*) maintains a consistent level of spiritual exaltation. The main melody is presented canonically by piano and violin.

GRIEG. The most popular of Grieg's three violin sonatas is the third, in C minor, op. 45 (1887). It represents the composer at the height of his lyrical powers, particularly in the second movement (*Allegretto espressivo alla Romanza*), in which a soaring melody has the introspection of a Norwegian folksong. While the two outer movements (*Allegro molto ed appassionato;* Presto and *Allegro animato; Cantabile; Prestissimo*) abound in delightful thematic material, their interest lies principally in the boldness of the harmonies and rhythms, and in the grandeur of the over-all concept.

HAYDN. Haydn's admiration for the piano sonatas of C. P. E. Bach is reflected in his own sonatas, in their obedience to classical structure, clarity of thematic presentation, and felicitous realization of a "galant" style. Not all of Haydn's more than fifty sonatas for piano are representative of his best creative efforts; indeed, some are even trite and derivative. But there are a few of these works, familiar to all piano students, which are true Haydn in the charm of their lyricism, inventiveness of development, and occasional deviations from the norm. In these Haydn sonatas the piano-sonata form becomes fixed once and for all, ready for the masterful hands of Mozart and Beethoven. The most frequently performed Haydn sonatas are the following: No. 35 in C major (1780); No. 37 in D major (1780); No. 43 in A-flat major (1785); No. 51 in D major (1794); and No. 52 in E-flat major (1794).

IVES. Ives' second piano sonata (1915) is one of the composer's most distinguished and original compositions. Subtitled *Concord, Massachusetts, 1840-1860,* it owes its inspiration to the intellectual heritage of Concord. Each of the four movements is devoted to a famous writer associated with that village. The first movement is dedicated to Emerson's transcendental philosophy. In the second movement, as the composer explained, Hawthorne's "fantastical adventures into the half-childlike and half-fairylike phantasmal realms" are explored in turbulent music. An interesting technical feature of this movement is the use by the performer of a ruler, or other strip of wood, to encompass a two-octave cluster. The third movement is in a more pastoral mood, and is dedicated to the Alcotts. Ives here quotes the first four notes of Beethoven's Fifth Symphony because the Alcott children used to practice Beethoven all the time. The finale is devoted to Thoreau and suggests that a "flute may be played throughout the page" because Thoreau liked to hear a flute play at Walden.

KABALEVSKY. Kabalevsky's Sonata No. 3, op. 46 (1946), is one of the most significant Soviet works for solo piano. Two delightful but subdued themes dominate the first movement (*Allegro con moto*); but a third melody, with a march-like character, provides dramatic contrast. A folk-like melody unfolds in the second movement (*Andante cantabile*), interrupted by a dissonant section. The finale (*Allegro giocoso*) is martial music, opening with a three-note theme answered by two notes in the bass. This movement depends for its main interest on powerful rhythmic surges and sweep. Recollections of the main themes from the first movement emerge in the background; but the movement is primarily dominated by the martial subject, which is eventually built into an exultant climax.

LISZT. The Sonata in B minor (1853) does not follow traditional lines. It is more of a fantasia, or a tone poem for piano, than a sonata. Diffuse, and at times prolix, the work also possesses singular eloquence and power. It is in a single movement in which the introduction presents the principal thematic ideas: a dramatic subject in octaves; a forceful and epical statement; and a *marcato* passage for the bass. Later on religious sentiment is introduced with a stirring chorale; there also appears a lyrical section with a Beethoven-like nobility. A brilliant *prestissimo* section, in which earlier material is reviewed, brings the sonata to an exciting conclusion.

MOZART. Mozart's piano sonatas are significant historically in establishing the sonata form and extending the technique and dynamics of piano writing. Some of them have esthetic interest as well. The Sonata in A major, K. 331 (1778), is one of the most popular. Its opening movement (*Andante grazioso*) is unorthodox in replacing the sonata-allegro with a theme and variations. A graceful melody is here followed by six variations. The second movement is also unusual in that it consists of a minuet (instead of a slow movement), whose trio is filled with romantic feeling. The finale is so celebrated (Allegretto) that it is often heard apart from the other two movements, and in various transcriptions. This is the Turkish rondo (*alla turca*) written in the pseudo-Turkish style so popular in Vienna in the 18th century.

Mozart preferred to have his Sonata in C minor, K. 457 (1785), played in conjunction with his Fantasia in C minor, K. 475 (1785). But they were written separately. (For a discussion of the Fantasia *see:* Fantasia—*Mozart.*) The two works, however, are allied in spirit. The dramatic character of the Fantasia can be found in the first and third movements of the Sonata. In the first movement (Allegro) the main theme is an incisive staccato subject which alternates with an expressive reply. After the Adagio, which has a singing character, and is akin to the gentler pages of the Fantasia, there comes a virile finale (*Molto allegro*) in which a sensitive middle section provides a momentary point of repose.

The Sonata in D major, K. 576 (1789), was the composer's last piano sonata. The opening Allegro has two contrasting melodies: the first is virile, and the second feminine. The slow movement (Adagio) is a lyrical page with tragic implications, particularly in its middle section. The finale (Allegretto) comprises three melodies; this movement has virtuoso brilliance and contrapuntal dexterity.

The Sonata in F major, K. 497 (1786), is for piano four hands. In the opinion of Sir Donald Francis Tovey, among others, this is one of the composer's finest instrumental compositions. It opens in an unusual way, with an Adagio movement of singular beauty and gentle introspection. The slow movement, in sonata form, is one of Mozart's most elaborate polyphonic structures for the piano, and the finale is a vigorous rondo.

The Sonata in D major, K. 448 (1781), for two pianos, was described by Ernest Hutcheson as a "masterpiece of antiphonal writing."

Mozart wrote 42 violin sonatas, the first when he was only eight. Many of his earlier violin sonatas are filled with delightful melodies and enchanting moods; they are so clear in construction and so straightforward in their artistic expression that they can readily be appreciated at first hearing. It is, however, in the late sonatas that we come upon the masterworks. The first such composition is that in G major, K. 379 (1781), the first of a set of 6 violin sonatas written during Mozart's first year in Vienna. In merely two movements, this work opens with a spacious Adagio which soon progresses to a turbulent and dramatic Allegro. The development is remarkably brief (12 bars) and in the recapitulation the intensity and passion of the exposition are recalled. The second movement (*Andantino cantabile*) presents a theme with five variations.

The Sonata in E-flat major, K. 481 (1785), is so free in treatment, spacious in structure, and varied in content that it almost has the scope of a concerto. In the first movement (*Allegro molto*) the two main themes are sharply contrasted. The first is a vigorous subject to which an extended virtuoso passage is appended; the second, presented over a pedal point, is by turns dramatic and tragic. The second movement (Adagio), in rondo form, opens with a stately melody which gains in ardor through several variants. This movement is dramatized by some unorthodox key changes. The finale (*Allegretto con variazioni*) has a sprightly melody followed by five variations; the piano, rather than the violin, here carries most of the musical burden.

PIZZETTI. Ildebrando Pizzetti's Sonata in A major for violin and piano (1919) expresses the composer's feelings during World War I. The first movement (*Tempestoso*) reflects his inner conflicts and personal grief. It begins with a passionate theme in the piano followed by a lamentation in the violin. The emotions become further intensified in the development, so much so that to Mario Castelnuovo-Tedesco this section represents "a grandiose and terrible vision, like that of Dante or of the Prophets. The human soul is torn in this furious tempest." Pizzetti entitled his second movement "Prayer for the Innocents," and appended to the opening measures the following line: "O our Lord, have pity upon all the innocents who do not know why they must suffer." The poignant melody, heard in the violin, is given additional interest through altered rhythms and modern harmonies. In the finale (*Vivo e fresco*) we get a relief from earlier sufferings. The main subject, in the violin, has the simple appeal of a folksong; and the entire movement has an almost joyous quality.

PROKOFIEV. Prokofiev wrote 9 piano sonatas. Three (the sixth, seventh, and eighth) were written under the stimulus of World War II and are consequently known as the "War Sonatas." They are the composer's major achievements for solo piano. Of them the Seventh, op. 83 (1942), is perhaps the most significant; it received the Stalin Prize. This work is sometimes known as the "Stalingrad Sonata," since it was written at the time when the Red Army brought the invading Nazi armies to a halt at Stalingrad, and thus turned the tide of the war

(I. *Allegretto inquieto.* II. Andantino. III. *Precipitato*). The first movement is turbulent, even though the second theme is slow and lyrical. In the second movement a lyrical and romantic subject is subjected to a series of variations which mount to a thunderous climax and then recede to a quiet restatement of the opening melody. The finale has the character of a toccata, and it is here that many writers find expressed and reflected the steel-like resistance of the Red Army at Stalingrad.

Prokofiev's Sonata in D minor, for violin and piano, op. 94 (1943), is music in which humor and whimsy are accentuated, especially in the second and fourth movements. But this work also boasts soaring lyricism in the spacious song that dominates the first movement, and in the introspective brooding of the main melody in the third movement. This work originated as a sonata for flute and piano, and then was rewritten as a violin sonata (I. Moderato. II. Scherzo. III. Andante. IV. *Allegro con brio*).

Another Prokofiev violin sonata, though with an earlier opus number, is actually of later vintage. It is the Sonata in F minor, op. 80, begun in 1938, but completed in its final version in 1946. Once again, as in the D minor Sonata, lyricism is prominent in the first and third movements, while motor energy and satiric attitudes are emphasized in the other two (I. *Andante assai.* II. *Allegro brusco.* III. Andante. IV. *Allegrissimo*).

DOMENICO SCARLATTI. Scarlatti wrote over 500 pieces for the harpsichord which he designated as exercises ("esercizi") but which today are called sonatas. Written early in the 18th century, when the classic sonata pattern had not yet come into existence, they are usually in two-part form, and contain a single basic thematic idea. They often suggest a mood or picture. Nevertheless, though they are not sonatas in the usual sense of that term, they influenced later writing for the keyboard. All kinds of techniques, some of them revolutionary for the early 18th century, are found in these pieces: runs in thirds and sixths; arpeggios; shakes; leaps across the keyboard in intervals greater than the octave; crossing of

hands; broken chords in contrary motion.

Scarlatti filled his music with so much grace, charm, wit, refreshing lyricism, and subtlety of expression that it has never become obsolete. To this day these sonatas have the capacity to enchant audiences. The following are some of the most frequently heard (the number adjoining the letter "L" following each sonata refers to its place in the Longo edition of Scarlatti's sonatas):

E major, *Cortège,* L. 23; B minor, L. 33; D minor, L. 58; C major, L. 104; F major, L. 188; B minor, *Bourrée,* L. 263; G major, L. 286; E major, L. 375, called *Capriccio* by Carl Tausig in his arrangement for piano; E major, L. 375; G minor, *Burlesca,* L. 378; D minor, L. 413, called *Pastorale* by Tausig in his arrangement for piano; D major, L. 461; D major, L. 463; G major, L. 487; G minor, L. 499, known as *Cat's Fugue,* because according to legend its melody was suggested to the composer by a cat running across the keyboard of a harpsichord.

Several composers have adapted some of these sonatas into orchestral compositions: Arthur Benjamin (Suite, for flute and strings); Alfredo Casella (*Scarlattiana,* for piano and orchestra); Vincenzo Tommasini (*The Good-Humored Ladies,* ballet suite).

SCHUBERT. Schubert wrote over 20 piano sonatas, the greatest coming towards the end of his life. The earlier sonatas are usually more interesting in parts than as a whole. They depend for their appeal on their attractive lyricism, freshness of spirit, youthful ardor; but they lack compact organization and a capacity to amplify and vary basic material. Of the earlier sonatas, the ninth in A minor, op. 120 (1819), is one of the most attractive (I. *Allegro moderato.* II. Andante. III. Allegro). In the opening movement the central interest lies in the long sustained melody of the first theme, which spans 19 bars. Transitional material and the development are perfunctory. Once again, in the second movement, lyricism is the main asset, this time a graceful melody bearing a passing resemblance to the famous minuet from Mozart's opera *Don Giovanni.* The finale has the most sustained interest, for its consistently lively tunes and rhythms and its effervescent spirit.

In the last year of Schubert's life (1828) he completed 3 sonatas, all published posthumously. One still accepts the first of these, in C minor, with some reservations, since the material is of uneven quality. Here the first movement is the most striking, for its almost Beethoven-like force and vitality, for its exciting rhythmic drive and unusual modulations.

But the next two sonatas are masterworks, as consistently rich in melodic invention as in emotion, as impressive in structural dimensions as they are epical in concept and execution. The Sonata in A major has the greater dramatic impact, but it also has tragic overtones (I. Allegro. II. Andantino. III. *Allegro vivace.* IV. Allegretto). The first movement achieves its most telling effect in the sweeping second theme, and in the magical transformation achieved by the forceful first theme in the coda. The second movement arrives at an unusual intensity of expression which deepens the usually appealing Schubertian lyricism into profound human experience. There are also echoes of dramatic expression in the trio of the Scherzo and in the finale, which is a structural compromise between the sonata and the rondo. The Sonata ends with a recall of the virile opening theme of the first movement.

The Sonata in B-flat major is in a heroic cast (I. *Molto moderato.* II. *Andante sostenuto.* III. *Allegro vivace con delicatezza.* IV. *Allegro ma non troppo*). The first movement has a spacious melodic line, especially the first theme with its Romantic surge. The high point of this Sonata comes in the second movement, whose heart is a long, poetic, 13-bar melody. The vigorous Scherzo, dramatized by alternations of major and minor, and the powerful finale, which opens startlingly in a foreign key, combine dynamic strength with tumultuous feelings.

Schubert's Sonata for Cello and Piano in A minor originated as a work for "arpeggione" and piano; the "arpeggione" is a now-obsolete six-string instrument combining features of the guitar and the viola

da gamba. This Sonata is today most often heard as a Concerto for Cello and Orchestra in a transcription by Gaspar Cassadó.

SCRIABIN. Scriabin wrote 10 piano sonatas, the first, op. 6, in 1892, and the last, op. 70, in 1913. Sonatas Nos. 1 through 4 are in two parts—an introduction and a main section—and are Romantic in style and poetic in content. They reveal the influence exerted on the composer by Chopin. In this early group the Sonata No. 4 in F-sharp minor, op. 30, is characteristic. It is a programmatic work in that the composer intended the first theme to symbolize Desire, and the second Anguish.

All sonatas after the fourth are in a single movement; Nos. 7 through 10 are without key signatures. As was the case with Scriabin's other piano music—the etudes and preludes, for example—his writing grew increasingly complex, obscure, and nebulous with each later sonata. Sonata No. 9 in F major (1913), known as "The Black Mass," is a popular example of these later compositions. It projects an atmosphere of mystery in the opening bars. Four melodic ideas follow and are developed, after which the mysterious opening returns.

TARTINI. *See: Devil's Trill Sonata.*

Sonata da camera. A "chamber sonata," a form of instrumental music popular in the late 17th century. It consisted of a group of dances, often introduced by a prelude.

Sonata da chiesa. A "church sonata," a form of instrumental music popular in the late 17th century. It usually consisted of four movements, in the pattern slow-fast-slow-fast.

Sonata form. A form found in the sonata, symphony, concerto, quartet, and so on—generally in the first movement, though sometimes in other movements as well. The form comprises three sections. In the first (Exposition) the main themes are presented. Usually there are two such themes, the first in the key of the composition, the other in a complementary key (dominant, or relative major or minor) and of a contrasting mood. In the second section (Development) these themes are amplified, otherwise altered, and subjected to various adventures in various keys. The concluding section (Recapitulation) repeats the themes as first stated in the Exposition, though usually now all in the home key.

Sonatina (or **Sonatine**). A small sonata, less ambitious in structure and content—and less demanding on the technique of the performer—and consequently often valuable for piano instruction. The sonatinas for piano by Muzio Clementi (opp. 36, 37, 38) are familiar to piano students. Similar sonatinas for the piano were written by Anton Diabelli, Jan Ladislas Dussek, and Daniel Frederick Rudolph Kullak, and have been used advantageously for piano instruction. While the two works by Beethoven in op. 49, in G minor and G major (1796), are officially designated as sonatas, they are actually sonatinas. On the other hand, Beethoven's Sonatina in G major, op. 79 (1809), has the amplitude of a sonata. Other sonatinas have also been the medium for a composer's most serious artistic endeavors, notably three highly lyrical sonatinas for violin and piano by Schubert: in D major, A minor, and G minor, op. 137 (1816), and sonatinas for piano by Ferruccio Busoni, Schumann, and Sibelius among others.

The 20th century has produced an important sonatina for the piano by Maurice Ravel (1905). The artistic possibilities of this form are here forcefully demonstrated in a work that is a beautiful fusion of Impressionist style and the Classic form. Precise in its writing, and of graceful outline of structure, this Sonatine is a veritable jewel (I. *Modéré*. II. *Mouvement de menuet*. III. *Animé*). An interesting technical feature is a two-note motif, either a rising or falling fourth, which appears in each of the three movements. Another point of thematic interest is the way in which a descending lyrical figure in the first movement becomes, through a change of rhythm, an effective carillon chime-like melody in the finale.

Sonetti del Petrarca (Liszt). *See: Années de pèlerinage.*

Song form. A term sometimes used for any slight piece of music that consists merely of an instrumental melody and accompaniment. More specifically, however, it is an instrumental form borrowed from vocal music, made up of two or three sections. The two-part form consists of a melody and countermelody and may be designated as A-B; in the three-section form, designated as A-B-A, the original melody is repeated after the countermelody.

Song of Summer, A. Tone poem for orchestra by Frederick Delius (1931), introduced in London on Sept. 17, 1931, Sir Henry J. Wood conducting. This is one of several compositions by Delius completed during his blindness; like all the works of this period, it was dictated by the composer to his friend and amanuensis, Eric Fenby. Delius explained the context of this tone poem to Fenby as follows: "I want you to imagine we are sitting on the cliffs of the heather and looking out over the sea. The sustained chords in the high strings suggest the clear sky and stillness and calm of the scene . . . You must remember that figure that comes in the violins when the music becomes more animated. I'm introducing it there to suggest the gentle rise and fall of the waves. The flutes suggest a seagull gliding by."

Song of the Earth, The (Mahler). *See: Lied von der Erde, Das.*

Song of the High Hills, A. For chorus and orchestra by Frederick Delius (1911), first performed in London on Feb. 26, 1920, Albert Coates conducting. This work is essentially symphonic, the chorus being used as a background. The composer explained: "I have tried to express the joy and rapture felt in the High Mountains and to depict the lonely melancholy of the highest altitudes of the wide expanses. The vocal parts typify Man in Nature."

Song of the Nightingale, The (Le Chant du rossignol). Tone poem for orchestra by Stravinsky (1917), first performed in Geneva on Dec. 6, 1919, Ernest Ansermet conducting. This composition originated as an opera in 1914, in which version it was introduced by the Paris Opéra on May 26; the libretto, by S. Mitusov, was based on a fairy tale of Hans Christian Andersen. Stravinsky later adapted the opera into a ballet for the Ballet Russe. For this purpose he prepared a tone poem for orchestra derived from the opera score capable of being choreographed. The ballet was performed for the first time in Paris on Feb. 2, 1920. The tone poem has three sections played without interruption. I. The Palace of the Chinese Emperor. The Emperor appears at court with pomp and ceremony. The nightingale, famous for its singing, is brought to the Emperor. II. The Two Nightingales. The nightingale sings for the Emperor a song of such beauty that the latter is deeply moved. Then a mechanical bird is introduced, one also capable of beautiful song. The live nightingale, chagrined, disappears, and the mechanical bird displaces it in the Emperor's favor. III. Illness and Recovery of the Emperor of China. The Emperor is dying, and the mechanical bird is called upon to sing and relieve the Emperor's distress. But the mechanism has broken. Suddenly the live bird returns and with his beautiful singing refreshes the Emperor, who now makes a speedy recovery.

Throughout the score the song of the live nightingale (assumed at different times by a solo flute, or an E-flat clarinet, or a solo violin) contributes soaring flights of beautiful melody to an idiom otherwise jarred by discords and shifting tonalities. The music is also generously spiced with satire. The entrance of the Emperor in the first section (to music in the pentatonic scale) mocks at the hollow pomp of court ceremony; in the closing section, there is a tongue-in-the-cheek funeral march when the courtiers appear expecting to find the Emperor dead only to see him alive and sound again.

Songs Without Words (Lieder ohne Worte). Eight books of 48 pieces for the piano by Mendelssohn, opp. 19, 30, 38, 53, 62, 67, 85, and 102 (1830-1845). The "song without words" is a piano form created by Mendelssohn; it refers to a short composition of such lyric character that it can be considered a "song for the piano." Mendelssohn's *Songs Without Words* are descriptive, or sentimental, or atmospheric. Some are of the salon-music variety, ingratiating but unoriginal. Others are imaginative and fresh in their melodic and harmonic content. The most popular instrumental piece ever written by Mendelssohn can be found in this group: the *Spring Song*, in A major, op. 62, no. 6. Other popular *Songs Without Words* are the following: *Hunting Song* (A major, op. 19, no. 3); 3 *Venetian Gondola Songs* (G minor, op. 19, no. 6; F-sharp minor, op. 30, no. 6; and A minor, op. 62, no. 5); *Duetto* (A-flat, op. 38, no. 6); *May Breezes* (G major, op. 62, no. 1); *Elegy* (D major, op. 85, no. 4). With the exception of the *Venetian Boat Songs* and *Duetto*, all of the above titles were concocted not by the composer but by enterprising publishers.

Sonneck, Oscar George, musicologist. Born Jersey City, N.J., Oct. 6, 1873; died New York City, Oct. 30, 1928. He received both his academic and his musical education in Germany, mainly at Heidelberg and Munich. From 1902 to 1917 he was head of the Music Division of the Library of Congress in Washington, D.C., which he helped develop into one of the world's outstanding music libraries. In 1915 he became the first editor of *The Musical Quarterly,* and from 1921 on was vice-president of the music publishing firm, G. Schirmer. His leading books are *Early Concert Life in America* (1907), *Early Opera in America* (1915), *Suum Cuique* (1916), *Miscellaneous Studies in the History of Music* (1921), *Beethoven: Impressions of Contemporaries* (1926), and *The Riddle of the Immortal Beloved* (1927).

Sonority. Richness of sound.

Sophocles, poet and dramatist. Born Colonus, Greece, about 496 B.C.; died place unknown, 406 B.C. One of the great tragic poets and dramatists of ancient Greece, Sophocles wrote a number of dramas, of which the following were the source of orchestral compositions (where titles of compositions are not given they are the same as the drama):

Ajax: Incidental music by William Sterndale Bennett, and George Macfarren.

Antigone: Väinö Raitio (tone poem). Incidental music by Jean Binet (for two pianos and percussion), Carlos Chávez, Mikhail Gnessin, Henry Hadley, Arthur Honegger, Mendelssohn, Willem Pijper, and Saint-Saëns.

Electra: Incidental music by Granville Bantock, and Stanley Bate.

Oedipus (trilogy): Incidental music by Eduard Lassen.

Oedipus Coloneus: Granville Bantock (*Overture to a Greek Tragedy*). Incidental music by George Antheil, Frank Martin, Mendelssohn, and Ildebrando Pizzetti.

Oedipus Rex: Ildebrando Pizzetti (*Three Symphonic Preludes*); Max von Schillings (*Symphonic Prologue*). Incidental music by George Antheil, Willy Burkhard (for wind instruments and drums), Reinhold Glière, Arthur Honegger, and Frank Martin.

Oedipus Tyrannus: Incidental music by Andrea Gabrieli, John Knowles Paine, Charles Villiers Stanford, and Virgil Thomson.

Philoctetes: Incidental music by Elliott Carter.

Trachiniae: Incidental music by Ildebrando Pizzetti.

Sorcerer's Apprentice, The (L'Apprenti sorcier). Scherzo for orchestra by Paul Dukas (1897), introduced in Paris on May 18, 1897. This orchestral work is based on the Goethe ballad, *Der Zauberlehrling*, which, in turn, came from a folk tale. The music follows the story literally. A sorcerer's apprentice emulates his master by ordering a broom to fetch water. Unfortunately, he does not know the formula with which to stop this operation, and he is being submerged under all the water that is being poured. Seizing a hatchet he tries to destroy the broom. Instead he splits it in two, and each half now goes through the routine of bringing in buckets of water. The outcry of the apprentice brings on the master, who utters the incantation necessary for cancelling the spell.

An atmosphere of mystery is evoked in the opening measures, followed by a roguish theme in the double basses which is soon taken over by the full orchestra. This theme describes the sorcerer's apprentice. The march of the broom with the buckets of water is depicted in the bassoons against plucked strings; and arpeggios in the orchestra tell of the pouring water. Chords in the violins hint at the growing misery of the apprentice;

and as the music gains in sonority and intensity we gather that he is unable to stop the broom from doing its duty. At the climax, when the apprentice splits the broom into two, a mocking theme in the bassoon is doubled to portray this operation. A shriek of terror is soon heard in the full orchestra. The master sorcerer now comes upon the scene. The air of mystery with which the scherzo opened now returns to prove that everything has been straightened out, and four notes of the broom theme appear as a conclusion.

Sordino. Mute.

Sospiro, Un. *See:* Etude—*Liszt.*

Sostenuto. Sustained.

Sound post. A piece of wood standing vertically inside the body of a violin, viola, cello, or double bass.

Soupirs, Les (Rameau). *See: Pièces de clavecin* (and *Nouvelle suite de pièces de clavecin*).

Sowerby, Leo, composer. Born Grand Rapids, Mich., May 1, 1895. He went to Chicago when he was fourteen; there he studied piano with Calvin Lampert and theory with Arthur Olaf Andersen, and there his début as a composer took place when he was eighteen with a performance of his Violin Concerto. After World War I he became the first American to receive the Prix de Rome of the American Academy. Returning to the United States in 1924, he became professor of theory and music history at the American Conservatory in Chicago and organist at St. James' Episcopal Church. Sowerby's major works have been represented on the programs of leading American symphony orchestras. In 1946 he received the Pulitzer Prize in music for *The Canticle of the Sun,* for chorus and orchestra, based on Matthew Arnold's translation of St. Francis. His orchestral music includes 4 symphonies, 2 piano concertos, various other concertos (violin; cello; organ), and shorter works (*Comes Autumn Time, Prairie, Fantasy-Portrait, Concert Overture,* and *All on a Summer Day*). He also wrote 2 string quartets, 2 violin sonatas, a cello sonata and a trumpet sonata among other chamber music.

See: Comes Autumn Time.

Spaeth, Sigmund, writer on music. Born

Philadelphia, Pa., April 10, 1885. He was graduated from Haverford College in 1905, and five years later received his doctorate in music from Princeton. For several years he served as music critic for the *New York Mail* and the *New York Times*. He also distinguished himself as a lecturer, especially in programs in which he identified himself as a "tune detective." He has been a prolific author of books on music. The best of these are: *The Common Sense of Music* (1924); *Music for Everybody* (1934); *Great Symphonies* (1936); *Music for Fun* (1939); *Guide to Great Orchestral Music* (1943); *A History of Popular Music in America* (1948); and *Fifty Years With Music* (1959).

Spalding, Albert, violinist. Born Chicago, Ill., Aug. 15, 1888; died New York City, May 26, 1953. He studied the violin with private teachers in New York City, Florence (Italy), and at the Conservatories of Paris and Bologna. From the last of these he was graduated with highest honors when he was fourteen. His début took place in Paris on June 6, 1906, and was followed by successful appearances in London and Vienna. He made his first American appearance as soloist with the New York Symphony on Nov. 8, 1908. One year later he was soloist with the Dresden Philharmonic when that orchestra toured the United States; and in 1920 he appeared with the New York Symphony on its tour of Europe. His performances in all the major music centers of the world gave him a preeminent position among American-born violinists. He was the first American violinist to appear with the Paris Conservatory Orchestra (1922); one year later he was the first American to serve on the jury of the Paris Conservatory to award prizes to the graduating violin class. He announced his retirement after a New York concert on May 26, 1950. He was the author of an autobiography, *Rise to Follow* (1946), and a novel about Tartini entitled *A Fiddle, A Sword and a Lady* (1953). He also made numerous transcriptions for the violin.

Spanish Caprice (Rimsky-Korsakov). *See: Capriccio espagnol.*

Spanish Dances (Danzas españoles, or **Danses espagnoles).** (1) Four volumes comprising 12 Spanish dances for the piano by Enrique Granados (1893). Here every known element of the Spanish folk dance is skilfully utilized with the fullest resources of modern piano technique. The fifth dance, *Andaluza,* is especially popular. The sixth dance, *Rondalla aragonesa,* is a jota. Other outstanding dances in this collection are No. 2 in C minor, *Oriental;* No. 4, in G major, *Villanesca,* and No. 10 in G major.

(2) Four sets of pieces for violin and piano by Pablo de Sarasate. Two dances in op. 21 are among the best-known compositions in the violin repertory: No. 1, *Malagueña;* and No. 2, *Habanera.* Op. 22 contains two other celebrated violin pieces: No. 1, *Romanza andaluza;* and No. 2, *Jota navarra.* The most famous number in op. 23 is the second, *Caprice basque.* The two dances in op. 26 are not titled: No. 1 is in A minor, and No. 2, in C major.

Spanish Rhapsody (Rapsodie espagnole). Suite for orchestra by Maurice Ravel (1907), first performed in Paris on March 15, 1908, Edouard Colonne conducting. This was the composer's first successful work for orchestra, and it has remained a favorite with concert audiences (I. Prélude à la nuit. II. Malagueña. III. Habanera. IV. Féria). In the first movement a recurrent figure appears consistently: four descending notes in muted strings, repeated by other instruments. This figure eventually becomes the accompanying background for two Spanish melodies, the first in octaves for clarinets, and the second in thirds for strings. In the second movement, the rhythm of a malagueña in the basses is used against a malagueña dance tune in bassoons, repeated by muted trumpet. The rhythm of a habanera is presented by the clarinets in the third section against several Spanish melodies, the most important being a rhythmic subject for the woodwind. In the finale muted trumpets present a lively tune which is developed into a powerful climax. After that comes a beautiful Spanish melody for the English horn. (This movement is an adaptation by the composer of his own earlier work, *Habanera* for two pianos, written in 1895.)

A theme from the first movement is hurriedly recalled. Then the music progresses to a climax, which is brilliant in color and thunderous in sonority.

Spiccato. Staccato bowing in a rapid string passage.

Spider's Banquet, The (Roussel). *See: Festin de l'araignée, Le.*

Spinet. Originally a small harpsichord usually in the shape of an oblong. It had only a single string to each note, and a range of about three octaves. The term is now applied to a small upright piano.

Spinning Song (Mendelssohn). *See: Songs Without Words.*

Spirit Trio. *See: Trio—Beethoven.*

Spirituals. Suite for string choir and orchestra by Morton Gould (1941), first performed in New York on Feb. 9, 1941, the composer conducting. Though no folk tunes are quoted, this music derives its mood and personality from American spiritual music, white as well as black. Gould uses a string choir as if it were a vocal chorus, and places it in juxtaposition to the regular orchestra. The work is in five sections. I. Proclamation. This music is rhapsodic and declamatory. II. Sermon. By contrast, the material here is light in mood, with frequent use of syncopated rhythms. III. A Little Bit of Sin. The levity of the preceding movement is maintained, with the aid of a dance orchestra. IV. Protest. The expression now becomes powerfully dramatic. V. Jubilee. Hoe-down music appears in strings. Then a boogie-woogie bass moves against a sustained melody for violins.

Spivakovsky, Tossy, violinist. Born Odessa, Russia, Feb. 4, 1907. After attending the Berlin High School for Music he was appointed concertmaster of the Berlin Philharmonic, one of the youngest musicians ever to hold this post. Between 1933 and 1941 he made many tours of Europe, Australia, and New Zealand as a concert violinist. His American début took place at New York in 1941. From 1942 to 1945 he was concertmaster of the Cleveland Orchestra, a period in which he also made many concert appearances. He resumed his career as a virtuoso in 1945.

Spohr, Louis (Ludwig), composer, conductor, and violinist. Born Brunswick, Germany, April 5, 1784; died Cassel, Germany, Oct. 22, 1859. He studied the violin with private teachers, then launched his career as a virtuoso with a tour of Germany when he was fourteen. He soon found employment in the court orchestra of the Duke of Brunswick, but in 1804 resumed his career as a concert virtuoso, establishing his reputation as a performer of the first rank. In 1805 he began an equally successful career as a conductor by leading the court orchestra at Gotha. In 1812 he settled in Vienna, where he conducted the orchestra at the Theater-an-der-Wien and came into personal contact with Beethoven. In 1817 he was appointed conductor of the Frankfort Opera, which presented several of his works. On March 6, 1820, he appeared as guest conductor of the Royal Philharmonic in London, where he made conducting history by being one of the first to lead an orchestra with a baton (*see:* Conducting). From 1822 to 1857 he was chief Kapellmeister to the Elector of Hesse-Cassel. In 1857 he retired on a pension. A year later, when he broke his arm, he gave up playing the violin. But he continued to appear as a conductor for a few months more. Except for his excellent *Violin School,* still a basic work to violin students everywhere, and one or two of his violin concertos (particularly the eighth in A minor, op. 47, subtitled *Gesangsscene*), Spohr's numerous compositions in all the branches of music are virtually *terra incognita* to the present-day concert-goer. Yet they enjoyed considerable prominence in the composer's lifetime; and some of his contemporaries esteemed his symphonies almost as highly as they did those of Beethoven. Spohr's works are of special interest for their programmatic content and their interesting experiments in instrumentation. His major works include 9 symphonies (the most famous being the fourth, *Die Weihe der Toene*), several overtures, 15 violin concertos, 34 string quartets, 7 string quintets, and 5 piano trios.

Spring Sextet. *See:* Sextet—*Brahms.*

Spring Sonata. *See:* Sonata—*Beethoven.*

Spring Symphony. *See:* Symphony—*Schumann.*

Staccato. Sharp, detached manner of playing.

Stadium Concerts. *See:* Lewisohn Stadium.

Staff. In musical notation the five parallel, horizontal lines on or between which notes are placed.

Stalingrad Sonata. *See:* Sonata—*Prokofiev.*

Stamitz, Johann, composer and conductor. Born Deutschbrod, Bohemia, June 19, 1717; died Mannheim, Germany, March 27, 1757. A predecessor of Haydn, he was one of the first important composers of symphonies. He was also prominent in the early history of orchestral performance and conducting. He studied the violin with his father. In 1742 he made such a favorable impression at the coronation of Emperor Charles VII in Frankfort that a year later he became chamber musician to the Elector of Mannheim, a post he retained until his death. As the conductor of the Mannheim Orchestra he helped revolutionize the art and technique of orchestral performance through his rigid discipline and meticulous rehearsals. He helped create an ensemble whose technical perfection and artistic finish made it one of Europe's foremost orchestras. Stamitz made several tours of Germany with his orchestra. He himself visited Paris in 1754-1755, where he conducted public concerts and the private orchestra of Rameau's patron, La Pouplinière.

Stamitz was the composer of over 70 symphonies. He was one of the first composers to introduce the minuet into the symphony and to establish the principle of contrasting themes in sonata form. He was also one of the first to fill his orchestral writing with contrasts of dynamics and sonorities. Thus he helped to inaugurate an era in orchestral music. Besides his symphonies he wrote 12 violin concertos, 8 flute concertos, 6 harp concertos, 10 orchestral trios, and a considerable amount of chamber music.

His son, Karl (born Mannheim, Germany, May 7, 1745; died Jena, Germany, Nov. 9, 1801), was also an eminent composer and violinist. He played the violin in his father's orchestra in Mannheim, then distinguished himself as a virtuoso throughout Europe. He wrote over 40 symphonies, 20 *sinfonies concertantes,* 7 violin concertos, and many other concertos, string quartets, and trio sonatas.

Stanford, Sir Charles Villiers, composer, conductor, and teacher. Born Dublin, Ireland, Sept. 30, 1852; died London, England, March 29, 1924. While attending Queen's College, Cambridge, on an organ scholarship, he played the organ at Trinity College and conducted the Cambridge University Musical Society. Following his graduation in 1874 he went to Germany for additional music study with Karl Reinecke and Friedrich Kiel. He first achieved recognition as a composer in London between 1876 and 1879 with his first symphony, *Festival Overture,* and incidental music to Tennyson's *Queen Mary.* From this time on he composed abundantly in every branch of music. He is most often remembered for his songs and choral music. In his instrumental compositions he adhered to classical traditions. He was a skilful technician, but not much of this music has survived. His principal instrumental works include 7 symphonies, 5 Irish Rhapsodies for orchestra, various concertos for solo instruments and orchestra, 6 Irish Rhapsodies for solo instruments and orchestra, 8 string quartets, 2 string quintets, and several violin and cello sonatas.

He was most distinguished in the field of music education. In 1883 he became professor of composition at the Royal College of Music, and in 1887 professor of music at Cambridge. His many pupils included Gustav Holst, John Ireland, Vaughan Williams, and Eugene Goossens.

Stanford was also active as a conductor with the Bach Choir, at the Leeds Festival, and in guest performances with important American and European orchestras. He was knighted in 1902. He is buried near Purcell in Westminster Abbey. He was the author of *Musical Composition* (1911), *Interludes* (1922), and with Cecil Forsyth *A History of Music* (1916).

State Fair Auditorium. *See:* Dallas Symphony.

Steinberg, William (born **Hans Wilhelm Steinberg**), conductor. Born Cologne, Germany, Aug. 1, 1899. After studying the violin, theory, and conducting with private teachers in Cologne, he won the Wuellner Prize for conducting in 1919. He then held conducting posts with various German opera houses including the Cologne Opera and the German Theater in Prague. From 1929 to 1933 he was general music director at Frankfort, and in 1937 he became a conductor of the Palestine Symphony. He came to the United States in 1938, and subsequently became a citizen. For several seasons he was Toscanini's assistant with the NBC Symphony. In 1945 he became conductor of the Buffalo Philharmonic, and in 1952 of the Pittsburgh Symphony. In 1958 Steinberg combined his duties in Pittsburgh with the office of musical director of the London Philharmonic.

Stenka Razin. Tone poem for orchestra by Glazunov, op. 13 (1885), introduced at the Paris Exposition in 1889, the composer conducting. Stenka Razin was a notorious 17th-century Cossack who plundered and looted Russian towns and villages and finally met his doom at the hands of the Tsar's army. In his tone poem, Glazunov describes Stenka Razin sweeping down upon the villages of the Volga bringing devastation. In his boat he carries a beautiful Persian princess he has captured. As he is about to meet defeat at the hands of the Tsar's army, he drowns the princess in the Volga. Three main melodies are used. The first, based on the folksong *The Volga Boatman,* speaks for the Volga River; the second, savage and passionate, represents Stenka Razin; the third, sensual and oriental, describes the princess.

Stern, Isaac, violinist. Born Kremenetz, Russia, July 21, 1920. He came to the United States as an infant. After studying violin with Naoum Blinder and Louis Persinger, he attended the San Francisco Conservatory. His début took place when he was eleven, when he appeared with the San Francisco Symphony. He gave his first New York recital on Oct. 11, 1937. From 1939 on, he toured the world with outstanding success. In the summer of 1947 he toured Australia and New Zealand, giving 125 concerts in a ten-month period. Between 1948 and 1952 he made five tours of Europe, including performances at the Prades Festival. In 1953 he

scored a major success at the Edinburgh Festival and in the spring of 1956 he was the first American concert artist to perform in the Soviet Union in ten years.

Stewart, Reginald, conductor. Born Edinburgh, Scotland, April 20, 1900. He received his musical training mainly from Isidor Philipp and Nadia Boulanger in Paris, and Mark Hambourg and Arthur Friedheim in Canada. Having settled in Canada as a young man, he became conductor of the Canadian Opera Society in 1919, and a few years later director of music of the Hart House of the University of Toronto. In 1925 he made appearances as a piano virtuoso in England, and in 1930 as a conductor. In 1933 he organized the Bach Society of Toronto, which he conducted for many years. In 1934 he founded, and for many years after that directed, the Toronto Promenade Symphony. From 1942 to 1952 he was conductor of the Baltimore Symphony and from 1941 to 1958 director of the Peabody Conservatory in that city.

Still, William Grant, composer. Born Woodville, Miss., May 11, 1895. He studied music at first with private teachers, then at the Oberlin Conservatory, the New England Conservatory, and with Edgard Varèse. In 1928 he received the Harmon Award for composition, and in 1931 he achieved world prominence with his *Afro-American Symphony,* successfully given in the United States, throughout Europe, and in Panama. In 1934 he received a Guggenheim Fellowship, and subsequently a Rosenwald Fellowship. His *Festive Overture* won first prize in a nationwide contest sponsored by the Cincinnati Symphony, and his opera, *Troubled Island,* was introduced by the New York City Opera in 1949. He is best known for his compositions based on racial subjects. These include *Darker America, Log Cabin Ballads, From the Black Belt, Africa, A Deserted Plantation, Kaintuck'* for piano and orchestra. *Dismal Swamp, Can'tcha Line 'Em,* and *Archaic Ritual,* all for orchestra. He also wrote 4 symphonies, *Poem for Orchestra, Little Red Schoolhouse* for orchestra, a suite for violin and piano, and *Incantation and Dance* for oboe and piano.

Stock, Frederick, conductor. Born Juelich, Germany, Nov. 11, 1872; died Chicago, Ill., Oct. 20, 1942. He attended the Cologne Conservatory, then for five years played the violin in the Cologne Municipal Orchestra. In 1895 he came to the United States, where he later became a citizen. After he played the violin in the Chicago Symphony for about a decade, Theodore Thomas appointed him his assistant conductor. Upon Thomas' death in 1905 Stock took over the post of principal conductor, retaining it until his death.

Stockholm Philharmonic Orchestra. A major Swedish symphony orchestra, organized in 1902 in Stockholm with Tor Aulin as conductor. Aulin continued to direct the orchestra until 1910. Later principal conductors included Georg Schneevoigt, Václav Talich, Fritz Busch, Carl Garaguly, Schmidt-Isserstedt, and Tor Mann. The orchestra acquired its own auditorium in the 1920's. Besides giving an annual series of concerts there, the orchestra performs regularly over the Swedish Radio as the Radiojanst Symphony.

Stojowski, Sigismund, pianist and teacher. Born Strzelce, Poland, April 8, 1869; died New York City, Nov. 5, 1946. He was one of America's most distinguished teachers of the piano. He studied music principally at the Paris Conservatory, and privately with Paderewski. He then toured Europe as a piano virtuoso; in 1891 he performed his own piano concerto in a Paris concert devoted entirely to his works. He settled in New York in 1906, becoming an American citizen thirty-two years later. He was head of the piano department of the Institute of Musical Art until 1912, and at the Von Ende School of Music in New York from 1912 to 1917. From the end of World War I on he taught piano at the Juilliard Summer School and Mills College in California.

Stokowski, Leopold, conductor. Born London, England, April 18, 1882. He studied at the Royal College of Music in London and at the Paris Conservatory. In 1900 he was appointed organist of St. James, Piccadilly. Five years later he came to the United States, of which country he became a citizen. For a while he served as organist of the St. Bartholomew Church in New York. He was appointed principal conductor of the Cincinnati Symphony in 1909, remaining there three years. From 1912 to 1933 he was the principal conductor of the Philadelphia Orchestra, where his dynamic performances, magnetic personality, passionate dedication to new music, and novel experiments in the presentation of his concerts won him world renown. In 1940 he became conductor of the All-American Youth Orchestra, which he had organized. In 1944-1946 he was principal conductor of the New York City Symphony, in 1946-1947 of the Hollywood Bowl Orchestra, and in 1949-1950 a conductor of the New York Philharmonic. Since 1955 he has been the conductor of the Houston Symphony in Texas. In the summer of 1958 he made his first appearances in the Soviet Union as guest conductor of three major Russian orchestras. He has appeared as himself in several motion pictures, including *The Big Broadcast of 1937, A Hundred Men and a Girl,* and *Carnegie Hall.* In 1939 he collaborated with Walt Disney in the presentation of great music in conjunction with animated films in *Fantasia.* He is the author of *Music for All of Us* (1943) and a distinguished transcriber for orchestra of works by J. S. Bach.

Stradivari, Antonio, violin maker. Born Cremona, Italy, about 1644; died there, Dec. 18, 1737. He was one of the most illustrious makers of violins. To this day some of his instruments are among the finest ever made. He served his apprenticeship with Amati, and in or about 1666 began constructing his own violins. He continued to experiment with instrument-making for many years before he finally achieved violins that were supreme models of form and balance. His best instruments were made between 1700 and 1725. It has been estimated that he built over one thousand violins, violas, and cellos. His sons, Francesco and Omobono, assisted him.

Stransky, Josef, conductor. Born Humpoletz, Bohemia, Sept. 9, 1872; died New York City, March 6, 1936. He studied medicine at the University of Prague, but during the same period received intensive music instruction from Bruckner, Dvořák, and Salomon Jadassohn. By 1898 he had turned to conducting, and from 1903 to 1909 was conductor of the Hamburg Opera. After 1910 he devoted himself to symphonic music, directing orchestral concerts that year in Dresden. From 1911 until 1923 he was principal conductor of the New York Philharmonic, and from 1923 to 1925 of the State Symphony in New York. He then deserted music for a successful career as art dealer.

Strauss, Johann, II, composer. Born Vienna, Austria, Oct. 25, 1825; died there, June 3, 1899. Though Strauss was essentially a composer of popular Viennese music, his best compositions have such artistic merit that they often appear on symphony programs, directed by the foremost conductors. His father, Johann I, was also famous as a composer of dance music and conductor of salon and popular music. The son made his début as a conductor in a Viennese café on Oct. 15, 1844. He soon became an idol of Vienna, the voice and symbol of Hapsburg Austria. In 1872 he appeared in the United States in mammoth performances of his works. The 50th anniversary of his début as a conductor was celebrated for an entire week in Vienna in 1894. Of his many popular waltzes, for which Strauss has been dubbed "the waltz king," the most famous are: *Acceleration Waltz* (*Accelerationen*); *Artist's Life* (*Kuenstlerleben*); *The Beautiful Blue Danube,* (*An der schoenen blauen Donau*), perhaps the most famous waltz ever written; *Emperor Waltz* (*Kaiserwalzer*); *Morning Journals* (*Morgenblaetter*); *Roses from the South* (*Rosen aus dem Sueden*); *Tales from the Vienna Woods* (*G'schichten aus dem Wiener Wald*); *Vienna Blood* (*Wiener Blut*); *Voices of Spring* (*Fruehlingsstimmen*); and *Wine, Women and Song* (*Wein, Weib und Gesang*).

Besides waltzes, Strauss wrote numerous polkas and quadrilles, the most popular being the *Annen-Polka, Pizzicato Polka, Tritsch-Tratsch,* and *Perpetuum mobile.*

Strauss' brothers, Josef and Eduard, were also composers of waltzes and other light Viennese pieces.

Strauss, Richard, composer and conduc-

tor. Born Munich, Germany, June 11, 1864; died Garmisch-Partenkirchen, Germany, Sept. 8, 1949. The son of a horn player who had performed in orchestras conducted by Wagner, Richard was early directed to music. He studied with private teachers in Munich: August Tombo, Benno Walter, and F. W. Meyer. By 1881 he had completed several large works that were performed in Munich, including his first symphony and a string quartet. Hans von Buelow became interested in him and introduced several of his orchestral compositions in Meiningen. Then, in 1885, von Buelow appointed Strauss his assistant with the Meiningen Orchestra; a year later, Strauss succeeded von Buelow as principal conductor. Meanwhile, Strauss continued active as composer. His second symphony was introduced in the United States in 1884, and a piano quartet received the Berlin Tonkuenstlerverein Prize. In all these apprentice works, Strauss adhered to the conventions and esthetics of the German Romantic style, modeling his idiom after that of Wagner and Brahms. But a change of values was not slow in coming. In or about 1885 Strauss befriended Alexander Ritter, a poet, philosopher, and musician. Ritter's personal theories on music reacted on Strauss, as he said, like a "stormwind." Ritter convinced Strauss he must carry on the torch of Wagner by abandoning absolute music and the structures and techniques of German Romanticism; that he must aspire for programmatic, poetic, and dramatic writing along the models already established by Liszt in his tone poems.

With Ritter's encouragement, Strauss deserted his old methods and ideals to enter upon a new creative phase. Soon after he had paid a visit to Italy in 1886, he completed a symphonic fantasy, *Aus Italien,* in which he made his first attempt at programmatic writing, and in which for the first time he resorted to dissonance for greater realism. *Aus Italien* was a fiasco when introduced at Munich in 1887. Far from retreating, Strauss proceeded even more boldly in the new directions he had set for himself. His first tone poem, *Macbeth,* came in 1887. In the next eleven years he wrote six other tone poems, beginning with *Don Juan* in 1888, which electrified the world with their daring, originality, and creative power. These works made their composer one of the most provocative and highly publicized musicians in the world. His realism, luscious orchestration, exciting use of dissonance, sensual style, and fantastic virtuosity in composition were often combined with a grandeur of speech and majesty of expression uniquely his. This was a new era in orchestral music—just as the songs and operas he began writing in the middle 1890's proved a new era for those media.

All the while he was achieving eminence as a composer he was pursuing a second distinguished career in music— as conductor. Here, too, he achieved world eminence, particularly as an interpreter of Wagner, Mozart, and his own music. After holding appointments at the Munich Opera and the Weimar court, in 1898 he was made musical director of the Berlin Royal Opera, where he remained a dozen years. From 1919 to 1924 he was principal conductor and co-director of the Vienna State Opera. Subsequently he made distinguished appearances at major festivals in Munich, Salzburg, and Bayreuth and appeared as guest conductor with the world's foremost symphony orchestras. He made his American début as a conductor with the Wetzler Orchestra in New York on Feb. 27, 1904. During this visit he conducted the première of his *Domestic Symphony*. He returned for a second tour of the United States in 1921.

Though Strauss continued producing major works in all branches of music until the end of his life, he completed most of his greatest compositions before World War I. Many of his later works have charm and technical mastery; but they often lack the passion and inventive power of the earlier ones. On more than one occasion, in these later creations, he took to imitating mannerisms that once made him famous, and idiosyncrasies that had once set his music apart from that of his contemporaries. But though this was a creative decline, Strauss remained a giant figure in music, as both composer and conductor—the dean of

German composers, a master who had lived to see many of his works become classics.

In 1933, when the Nazis first assumed power in Germany, Strauss accepted the post of president of the Third Reich Music Chamber. But a break with the authorities came about when he insisted on collaborating with the Jewish-born writer, Stefan Zweig, on an opera. He then went into retirement in his villa in Garmisch-Partenkirchen, and during most of World War II he lived in Switzerland. After the war he visited London to direct a concert of his music at a Strauss festival held in 1947. In June 1949 his 85th birthday was celebrated throughout the world with festive performances.

The following are Strauss' principal instrumental compositions:

Chamber Music: 2 sonatinas for 16 wind instruments; string quartet; cello sonata; piano quartet; violin sonata; *Duett-Concertino,* for clarinet, bassoon, harp, and strings.

Orchestra: 2 symphonies; 2 horn concertos; violin concerto; *Burleske* for piano and orchestra; *Aus Italien; Macbeth; Don Juan; Death and Transfiguration (Tod und Verklaerung); Till Eulenspiegel's Merry Pranks (Till Eulenspiegels lustige Streiche); Thus Spake Zarathustra (Also sprach Zarathustra); Don Quixote; A Hero's Life (Ein Heldenleben); Domestic Symphony (Sinfonia domestica); An Alpine Symphony (Ein Alpensinfonie); Le Bourgeois gentilhomme,* suite; *Divertimento after Couperin; Metamorphosen* for 23 strings; oboe concerto.

Piano: Sonata; *Five Pieces.*

See: Bourgeois gentilhomme, Le; Burleske; Dance of the Seven Veils; Death and Transfiguration; Don Juan; Don Quixote; Hero's Life, A; Macbeth; Metamorphosen; Rosenkavalier Waltzes; Symphony—Richard Strauss; Thus Spake Zarathustra; Till Eulenspiegel's Merry Pranks.

Stravinsky, Igor, composer. Born Oranienbaum, Russia, June 17, 1882. He was the son of a successful opera singer. Originally directed to law rather than music, he attended the University of St. Petersburg. While there he began studying harmony and counterpoint mostly by himself. He later drew guidance and inspiration from Rimsky-Korsakov, who became his teacher in instrumentation. After being graduated from the University, Stravinsky decided to abandon law for music. Under Rimsky-Korsakov, he completed several large works, including a symphony introduced in St. Petersburg on Jan. 22, 1908, his first work to be publicly performed.

In 1909 two other orchestral compositions were given at a Siloti concert: *Fireworks* and *Scherzo fantastique*. They made a strong impression upon Serge Diaghilev, then planning to organize the Ballet Russe, and he commissioned Stravinsky to orchestrate two Chopin numbers for a ballet planned for his company's initial season. As a second assignment, Diaghilev turned over to Stravinsky a major project, an original score for a new ballet entitled *The Firebird* (*L'Oiseau de feu*), scenario by Fokine. Introduced in Paris on June 25, 1910, *The Firebird* became one of the company's major artistic achievements; at the same time, it presented Stravinsky to the world of music as an exciting new composer of courageous originality and immense gifts.

With succeeding scores for the Ballet Russe, Stravinsky became one of the most provocative and most highly publicized, as well as one of the most significant, composers to appear in Europe since Debussy. *Petrouchka* came in 1911; *The Rite of Spring* (*Le Sacre du printemps*) in 1913. Ever more audacious grew his efforts to uncover new musical sounds and colors and idioms; ever more dynamic grew his partiality for motor energy and rhythmic vigor. So iconoclastic did Stravinsky's writing become that when *The Rite of Spring* was introduced it created an unprecedented scandal in the theater and a bitter controversy in the press.

All the major scores Stravinsky had thus far produced were Slavic in subject and background; so were some of the works that followed *The Rite of Spring*, notably *Mavra* and *The Wedding* (*Les Noces*), produced in 1922 and 1923 respectively. But in the early 1920's there came about a remarkable change of style and personality in Stravinsky's music. He deserted Russian folklore and culture as a source of material and inspiration. At the same time he abandoned his advanced techniques—dissonance, polytonality, polymeters, and primitive rhythms —for a style that was classic in its simplicity, precision, clarity, objectivity, and emotional restraint. He had already begun to reveal such a tendency in *The Story of a Soldier* (*L'Histoire du soldat*) in 1918, and in *Pulcinella* a year later. In the early 1920's his neo-Classic idiom became fully realized, beginning with the Concerto for Piano and Wind Orchestra in 1924.

This artistic change came simultaneously with a decision, in 1919, to change his permanent home and political allegiance from Russia to France. For the next fifteen years he lived in or near Paris as a French citizen.

In 1925 Stravinsky paid his first visit to the United States, making appearances as guest conductor with major orchestras in programs highlighting his principal works. He returned to the United States frequently after that. When he revisited the United States in 1939 it was to find a permanent home in California and to become an American citizen.

In the United States Stravinsky has been richly productive, turning out numerous works for orchestra, ballet, chorus, and the stage. In some of his latest compositions he has made skilful use of the twelve-tone technique, still another radical departure for him from earlier methods and idioms.

In 1949 Stravinsky received the gold medal for music from the National Institute of Arts and Letters. In 1954 the Royal Philharmonic Society of London presented him with its gold medal, and one year after that he was honored with the Sibelius Award.

The following are Stravinsky's principal instrumental works:

Chamber Music: Three Pieces for string quartet; *Ragtime* for 11 instruments; *Concertino* for string quartet; wind octet; *Duo concertante* for violin and piano; *Suite italienne* for violin and piano; *Elegy* for viola solo; septet.

Orchestra: Fireworks (*Feu d'artifice*);

The Firebird (L'Oiseau de feu), ballet suite; *Petrouchka*, ballet suite; *The Rite of Spring (Le Sacre du printemps)*, ballet suite; *The Song of the Nightingale (Le Chant du rossignol)*, ballet suite; *The Story of a Soldier (L'Histoire du soldat)*, suite; *Symphonies for Wind Instruments;* piano concerto; violin concerto; *Pulcinella*, ballet suite; Capriccio for piano and orchestra; *Apollon Musagète*, suite; *The Fairy's Kiss (Le Baiser de la fée)*, ballet suite; *Card Game (Jeu de cartes)*, ballet suite; *Dumbarton Oaks Concerto;* Symphony in C major; *Danses concertantes; Four Norwegian Moods; Circus Polka; Ode; Scènes de ballet; Scherzo à la russe; Ebony Concerto; Symphony in Three Movements; Orpheus*, ballet suite; Concerto for Strings; *Agon*, ballet suite.

Piano: 2 sonatas; sonata for two pianos; 8 easy pieces for piano four hands; *Les cinq doigts;* etudes; *Piano Rag Music; Serenade;* Concerto for two unaccompanied pianos.

See: Agon; Capriccio; *Card Game; Circus Polka;* Concerto—*Stravinsky; Danses concertantes; Fairy's Kiss, The; Firebird, The; Fireworks; Four Norwegian Moods; Histoire du Soldat, L'; Ode; Orpheus* (2); *Petrouchka; Pulcinella; Rite of Spring, The; Scènes de ballet; Song of the Nightingale, The;* Symphony—*Stravinsky.*

Stretto. In a fugue, a statement of the subject, or part of it, in which the various entries overlap.

String Quartet. *See:* Quartet.

String Quintet. *See:* Quintet.

Stringendo. Faster and more agitated.

Strings (or String Instruments). A colloquial term applied to bowed stringed instruments in the orchestra, such as violins, violas, cellos, and double basses.

Stucken, Frank Van der, conductor. Born Fredericksburg, Texas, Oct. 15, 1858; died Hamburg, Germany, Aug. 16, 1929. After completing his music study at the Leipzig Conservatory in 1878, he returned to the United States, where from 1884 to 1895 he was the conductor of the Arion Society, a male chorus in New York. In 1889 he conducted a concert of American music at the Paris Exposition. He was the first conductor to devote entire programs to American music, as he did during his guest appearances with American orchestras. From 1895 to 1907 he was the principal conductor of the Cincinnati Symphony, and from 1906 to 1912, and again in 1923, he was director of the Cincinnati Music Festival. Previously, from 1895 to 1903, he had been the director of the Cincinnati College of Music. After 1908 he lived and made guest appearances in Europe.

Stuttgart Chamber Orchestra. One of Europe's leading chamber orchestras. It was founded in 1946 in Stuttgart, Germany, by Karl Muenchinger, who since then has been its principal conductor. The orchestra made many tours of Europe and has been heard at leading festivals. It made its first tour of the United States in 1954.

Subdominant. Fourth degree in the key.

Subito. Immediately.

Subject. A musical theme or motif; the principal theme in a fugue.

Submediant. Sixth degree in the key.

Suggestion diabolique. For piano by Prokofiev. This is the fourth of *Four Pieces,* op. 4 (1909), the other three being *Réminiscences, Élan,* and *Désespoir. Suggestion diabolique* is in the grotesque style which the composer made famous; it is noteworthy for its polytonal writing and unusual harmonic progressions.

Suisse Romande Orchestra. *See: Orchestre de la Suisse Romande.*

Suite. In the 17th and 18th centuries, an instrumental composition comprising several dance movements (*see also:* Partita). The usual succession was Allemande, Courante, Sarabande, and Gigue, but other dance movements were also employed. Sometimes, for variety, composers interpolated between dances other kinds of movements such as an Air, or Air with Variations, or Trumpet Tune. J. S. Bach prefaced some of his suites with a prelude.

The Baroque suite was developed by Couperin, Purcell, Rameau, and Handel. J. S. Bach brought it to its final development. While the Baroque suite passed out of fashion after the era of Bach and Handel, several interesting attempts were made to revive the form. Two such examples are Grieg's *Holberg Suite* in the

19th century and Ravel's *Le Tombeau de Couperin,* in the 20th.

Beginning with the Romantic period, the suite acquired a new meaning. It became a composition made up of several pieces representing different aspects of a single subject, such as Albéniz' *Iberia,* Bizet's *Arlésienne Suite,* and Debussy's *Children's Corner.*

All suites with specific descriptive titles (for example, Mendelssohn's *A Midsummer Night's Dream* or Grieg's *Peer Gynt Suite*) are discussed under their titles. Some suites that have become basic in the instrumental repertory, and which do not have any identifying title, are commented upon below.

J. S. BACH. Bach wrote 4 suites for orchestra, sometimes also designated as Overtures. Two are often performed. The Suite No. 2 in B minor, for flute and string orchestra, opens with a three-part overture after which come five dances: Rondo, Sarabande, Bourrée, Polonaise, and Minuet. The concluding section is a happy trifle, Badinerie.

The Suite No. 3 in D major is for two oboes, three trumpets, drums, strings, and cembalo. Its most celebrated movement is the second, an Air, one of Bach's most beautiful and moving melodies. This is also famous in a transcription for violin and piano by August Wilhelmj, *Air on the G String.* This transcription, however, has been severely criticized as a mutilation of the original; Sir Donald Francis Tovey once described it as a "devastating derangement." Nevertheless it has retained its popularity in the violin repertory. The Air is preceded by a two-part overture and followed by two Gavottes, a Bourrée, and a Gigue.

The two less familiar orchestral suites are: No. 1, in C major, for woodwinds and strings; and No. 4, in D major, for oboes, trumpets, bassoons, timpani, and strings.

For Bach's Suites for piano *see: English Suites, French Suites,* and *Partita.* For Bach's Suites for violin *see: Partita.*

DOHNÁNYI. Though an early work, the Suite in F-sharp minor for orchestra, op. 19 (1909), is one of Dohnányi's most popular compositions, and one of his best. It is music of romantic ardor, and the personality of its main melodies is reminiscent of Brahms (I. Andante. II. Scherzo. III. Romanza. IV. Rondo). The first movement is a theme and variations, in which a beautiful Brahms-like melody is presented alternately by oboe and strings and subjected to six variations. The scherzo has for its principal theme a capricious subject for the woodwind; the trio is built upon a pedal point. In the slow movement we once again find Brahms-like melodies. One of these is in the oboe; the second, in the cellos; a third, in the English horn. The suite ends with an energetic Rondo, at whose conclusion the Brahmsian melody of the first movement is repeated.

ENESCO. Georges Enesco's Suite No. 2 in C major, for orchestra, op. 20 (1915), is music in a neo-Classic style. It opens with a forceful overture in which the main theme is heard in the woodwind. A dignified Sarabande follows, its main melody appearing in solo violin, flute, and horn. The violins present the principal melody in the ensuing Gigue. After a sedate Minuet comes an Air, in which the melody is first heard in the oboe and then is taken over by flute, clarinet, and solo violin. The suite ends with a Bourrée; a stirring climax is created with the help of the timpani. The Suite was first performed at Bucharest in 1916.

FOOTE. The Suite in E major, for string orchestra, op. 63 (1907), is one of Arthur Foote's most popular works. It was introduced in Boston on April 16, 1909, Max Fiedler conducting (I. Prelude. II. Pizzicato. III. Fugue). The opening eight-bar phrase provides the basic material for the main theme of the first movement. The second movement opens and closes with a dashing pizzicato subject for strings; midway, an *Adagietto* provides a sensitive section for bowed, muted strings. The concluding fugue has for its subject a four-note theme.

HANDEL. Handel wrote 16 suites for the harpsichord, none of them major works. However, the Suite No. 5 in E major has become famous for one of its movements: the fourth, originally entitled *Air and Variations* but now famous as *The Harmonious Blacksmith* (which see).

PURCELL. Purcell's eight suites for harpsichord were intended for pedagogical purposes. While consistently attractive, they are not particularly inventive. Some of the dances in these suites are adaptations of tunes popular in Purcell's day.

ROUSSEL. Albert Roussel's Suite in F major, for orchestra, op. 33 (1926), is a neo-Classic work. It was introduced in Boston on Jan. 21, 1927, Koussevitzky conducting (I. Prelude. II. Sarabande. III. Gigue). The composer explained that the opening prelude is in the style of a toccata. "The main theme is based upon a continued rhythm of rapid eighth notes announced by strings and with rhythmic punctuation by the woodwind and horns." The principal phrase of the Sarabande is found in octaves in the violins. A second main thought is then presented by clarinet and cellos against an accompanying figure by the double basses derived from the first theme. The concluding movement is in rondo form with the violins introducing a lively tune.

TCHAIKOVSKY. The Suite No. 3, for orchestra, op. 55 (1884), was first heard in St. Petersburg on Jan. 24, 1885, Hans von Buelow conducting. The most celebrated movement is the fourth, a Theme and Variations in which a lyrical subject is presented by the first violins and followed by twelve variations. The last variation, a Polacca, brings the work to a dynamic conclusion. The earlier movements included *Elegy, Valse mélancolique,* and *Scherzo.*

Suite Bergamasque. For piano by Debussy (1905). This was an attempt to combine the harmonic and melodic idiosyncrasies of its composer with the grace and refinement of 17th-century French harpsichord music (I. Prélude. II. Menuet. III. *Clair de lune.* IV. Passepied). The third movement is not merely the most famous in the suite but one of the most celebrated melodies in French music, a delicate evocation in a haunting song of a moonlight night.

Suite Italienne (Stravinsky). *See: Pulcinella.*

Suite Provençale. A set of eight dances for orchestra by Darius Milhaud (1936), first performed in Venice on Sept. 12, 1937, the composer conducting. This work is based on 18th-century folksongs from Provence in France. In the first dance (*Animé*) a folk melody is stated by the full orchestra; a phrase from this melody later receives fugal treatment. The second (*Très modéré; Vif*) alternates between a delicate air for strings and a livelier section for the full orchestra. The third (*Modéré*) places a provocative dance rhythm against a folk melody. The fourth (*Vif*) is a folksong in triple time. A brief subject for trumpet introduces the fifth movement (*Modéré*) in which a kind of religious chant is prominent. The sixth (*Vif*) is a dynamic, rhythmic piece, and the seventh (*Lent*) is lyrical. The suite ends with a robust finale (*Vif*), mainly for the entire orchestra.

Suk, Joseph, composer. Born Křečovice, Bohemia, Jan. 4, 1874; died Benešov, Czechoslovakia, May 29, 1935. He attended the Prague Conservatory, where Dvořák exerted a powerful influence upon him. In 1891 Suk helped organize the Bohemian String Quartet, with which he appeared for about a decade in important performances of new Bohemian music. In 1898 Suk married Dvořák's daughter, and soon after that he achieved recognition as a composer with the successful performance of his first symphony in Prague, on Oct. 1, 1900. The *Fairy Tale* for orchestra, and the *Fantaisie* for violin and orchestra added appreciably to his reputation. In his programmatic orchestral music Suk's own creative identity began asserting itself with an exuberant lyricism, vital rhythms, and elegiac moods. During the last decade of his life his music began exploiting ultramodern harmonies, rhythms, and tonalities. Besides works already mentioned, his orchestral music includes a second symphony, *Praga, Tale of a Winter Evening, Maturity of Life,* and *The Legend of Dead Victors.* He also wrote 2 string quartets, a piano quintet, an *Elegy* for piano trio, and many pieces for the piano. In 1922 he was appointed professor at the Prague Conservatory, and eight years later he became director.

Sul Ponticello. *See: Ponticello.*

Summer Day on the Mountain (Jour d'été à la montagne). Rhapsody for piano and orchestra by Vincent d'Indy, op. 61 (1905), introduced in Paris by the Colonne Orchestra on Feb. 18, 1906 (I. Dawn. II. Day. III. Night). The rhapsody presents a pastoral scene at three different times of the day in an Impressionist style. In the first part, nature awakens for the day. The second movement conjures up a picture of a serene countryside, with murmuring breezes and the chirping of birds. In the finale a sunset is depicted, then night envelops the landscape in darkness.

Summer Evening. Tone poem for orchestra by Zoltán Kodály (1930). This is a revision of an earlier orchestral work (1906). The revised version was introduced in New York on April 3, 1930, Toscanini conducting. The tone poem opens with an eight-bar solo for English horn. After some variation of this material, and a subsequent intensification of the feeling, a new melody is heard: this is a folksong for oboe accompanied by a staccato figure in flute, clarinet, and plucked strings.

Summer Night on the River. Tone poem for orchestra by Frederick Delius (1912), first performed in Leipzig on Oct. 1, 1913. This work was planned as a companion piece to the composer's popular *On Hearing the First Cuckoo in Spring.* A picture of a river is drawn by vague chords in the winds, while swirling figures tell of the rocking of small boats. The beauty and mystery of the night emerges in a beautiful melody for cellos. The tranquillity thus created is maintained as the melody is taken over by strings, and then embellished by other sections of the orchestra.

Sun Quartets, The. *See:* Quartet—*Haydn.*

Supertonic. Second degree of the key.

Surprise Symphony. *See:* Symphony—*Haydn.*

Suspension. In harmony, a discord produced by holding one or more notes of a chord while the rest of the notes move on to the next chord.

Susskind, Walter, conductor. Born Prague, Czechoslovakia, May 1, 1913. After studying composition with Joseph Suk and conducting with George Szell, he made his conducting début in Prague in 1932. He was with the Carl Rosa

Opera Company and Sadler's Wells in England, then served as principal conductor of the Scottish Orchestra in Glasgow from 1946 to 1954. In 1954 he was appointed to a similar post with the Victoria Symphony in Melbourne, Australia, and in 1956 with the Toronto Symphony.

Svendsen, Johan, composer. Born Christiania (now Oslo), Norway, Sept. 30, 1840; died Copenhagen, Denmark, June 14, 1911. When he was fifteen he enlisted in the army, where he soon became a bandmaster. Six years later he traveled throughout Europe as the conductor of an orchestra. A government subsidy in 1863 enabled him to study the violin with Ferdinand David in Leipzig. When paralysis of the hand shattered all hopes for a virtuoso career, Svendsen turned to composition, producing several impressive works including a symphony, a string quartet, and an octet. In 1870 he became conductor of the Euterpe Concerts in Leipzig. He returned to his native land in 1872, and for five years conducted the Christiania Philharmonic. Now a musician of recognized stature in his own country, he received from the government an annual pension and a decoration from the king in 1874. In 1883 he became court conductor, and in 1896 musical director of the Copenhagen Royal Theater.

Svendsen wrote a considerable amount of music steeped in the Classical tradition, but his most popular works are those with a national character. His orchestral music includes 2 symphonies, 4 *Norwegian Rhapsodies,* a violin concerto, one for the cello, and various shorter works including *Carnival in Paris, Norwegian Artists' Carnival,* and *Overture to Romeo and Juliet.*

Swan, The (Saint-Saëns). *See: Carnival of the Animals.*

Swan Lake (Le Lac des cygnes). Ballet suite for orchestra by Tchaikovsky, op. 20 (1876). The ballet scenario, by Vladimir Begichev and Geister, concerned the courtship of Prince Siegfried and Odette, the Swan Queen. Despite the wiles and spells of the enchanter, Robart, the Prince finally wins her. The ballet was introduced in Moscow on March 4, 1877. The ballet score is made up of 33 numbers, the best of these in the composer's most ingratiating sentimental vein. When an orchestral suite from the ballet is given at symphony concerts, it is usually made up of various combinations of the following popular sections: Opening Scene; *Pas de trois* (Dance of the Prince); Valse (one of the composer's most famous waltzes); Dance of the Queen of Swans; Dance of the Swans; Spanish Dance; Hungarian Dance (Czardas) and Mazurka.

Swan of Tuonela, The. Tone poem for orchestra by Sibelius, op. 22, no. 3 (1893), introduced in Helsinki on April 13, 1896, the composer conducting. This is the third of *Four Legends,* a suite inspired by the *Kalevala.* The other three are *Lemminkaïnen and the Maidens, Lemminkaïnen in Tuonela,* and *Lemminkaïnen's Homecoming.*

The following program note appears in the published score: "Tuonela, the land of death, the hell of Finnish mythology, is surrounded by a broad river with black waters and rapid currents, on which the Swan of Tuonela floats majestically, singing." The work opens with a gentle subject for English horn describing the swan, accompanied by muted strings and drum rolls. After a muted horn repeats a portion of the swan theme, a telling climax is realized, and is dramatically followed by a *pianissimo.* The swan melody returns for the last time as the violins simulate the sound of the flapping of the swan's wings by tapping the back of the bows on the strings.

Sweelinck, Jan Pieterszoon, composer. Born Holland, May 1562; died Amsterdam, Holland, Oct. 16, 1621. After studying the organ with his father, he succeeded him in 1580 as organist of Old Church in Amsterdam, where his performances made him famous throughout Europe, and attracted to Amsterdam many pupils and disciples. He wrote pieces for the organ and for the harpsichord which helped extend the then limited technical resources of the keyboard style and helped develop such forms as the fantasia, fugue, and toccata.

Symphonia domestica. *See:* Symphony—*Richard Strauss.*

Symphonia serena. *See:* Symphony—*Hindemith.*

Symphonic Dances. Suite for orchestra by Rachmaninoff, op. 45 (1940), introduced by the Philadelphia Orchestra under Ormandy on Jan. 3, 1941. This was the composer's last major composition. These are not actually dances, though the second has the character of a waltz, but rather orchestral music of symphonic dimensions inspired by the dance. The music is devoid of any programmatic implications. Its main interest lies in its rhythmic vitality, particularly in the last movement, where a popular American dance style is suggested (I. *Non allegro.* II. *Andante con moto: tempo di valse.* III. *Lento assai; Allegro vivace*).

Symphonic Etudes (Schumann). *See: Études symphoniques.*

Symphonic Metamorphosis on Themes by Carl Maria von Weber. For orchestra by Paul Hindemith (1943), introduced in New York on Jan. 20, 1944, Artur Rodzinski conducting. Hindemith draws upon several themes by Weber, none of which, he explains, represents "the composer at his best." Consequently, Hindemith allowed himself the liberty of altering the melodies to suit his own purposes. The first melody (Allegro) comes from the fourth of eight piano pieces, four hands, op. 60, *All' Ongarese.* The second (*Scherzo moderato*) is from the overture to *Turandot.* The third (Andantino), like the first, is drawn from *All' Ongarese.* The work ends with two unidentified little march tunes, one in the woodwinds, the other in the horns.

Symphonic poem. *See:* Tone poem.

Symphonic Variations (Franck). *See: Variations symphoniques.*

Symphonie cévenole. *See:* Symphony—*D'Indy.*

Symphonie concertante. *See: Sinfonia concertante.*

Symphonie espagnole. For violin and orchestra by Edouard Lalo, op. 21 (1873), introduced in Paris by Pablo de Sarasate at a Colonne concert on Feb. 7, 1875. The title is misleading. This is no symphony, but a cross between a concerto and a suite. But there is no mistaking its Spanish identity, abounding as it does in Spanish melodies and rhythms, a gesture of tribute on the part of the composer to the violinist for whom it was written. The work is in five sections: I. *Allegro* *non troppo;* II. *Scherzando: allegro molto;* III. Intermezzo: *Allegretto non troppo.* IV. Andante. V. Rondo: Allegro. The first movement presents the main theme, a rhapsodic subject, in the full orchestra. After the solo instrument elaborates on this idea, it presents a new lyrical subject of its own. The second movement consists of a waltz melody for the violin, and a sensual Spanish song with rapid change of tempo and tonality. The third movement is often omitted; for the most part this is a song for the violin. The fourth movement highlights a Spanish melody of improvisational character, presented by the violin after a brief orchestral preface. The finale has for its main subject a saltarello melody in the violin.

Symphonie fantastique. *See:* Symphony— *Berlioz.*

Symphonie liturgique. *See:* Symphony— *Honegger.*

Symphonie pathétique. *See:* Symphony— *Tchaikovsky.*

Symphonie pour un homme seul (Schaeffer). *See:* Concrete Music.

Symphonies for Organ. *See:* Widor, Charles Marie.

Symphony. The most important form in orchestral music. Its structural pattern follows that of the sonata. The traditional symphony is in four movements (though there are works in that form in from one to ten movements). The first movement is generally in the sonata form. The second, traditionally slow, may be in the song form, or a theme and variations, though at times the sonata form may be utilized. In the Classical symphony of Haydn and Mozart, the third movement is a minuet, but Beethoven displaced the minuet with a scherzo. The finale may be in any one of several forms, including the sonata form, rondo, or theme and variations.

The word "symphony" was derived from "sinfonia," a 17th-century term for any piece of instrumental music, even overtures to or interludes within an opera, oratorio, and so on. As an introduction to an opera it acquired towards the end of the 17th century a three-part pattern— fast-slow-fast. With the introduction of the minuet as a fourth movement about the middle of the 18th century the classic structure was realized. Among the earliest important composers of symphonies are Giovanni Battista Sammartini in Milan and Johann Stamitz in Mannheim. The full-fledged symphonic style was finally established by Haydn and Mozart. The symphony grew in structural dimensions, poetic content, and dramatic impact with Beethoven and the Romanticists who followed him.

The following are some of the basic works in the symphonic repertory:

SAMUEL BARBER. The *Symphony in One Movement,* Barber's first symphony, op. 9 (1936), was written while the composer lived in Italy on the American Prix de Rome. It was introduced in that country by the Augusteo Orchestra of Rome, Molinari conducting, on Dec. 13, 1936. The following summer Artur Rodzinski conducted it at the Salzburg Festival, the first time an American symphony was performed there. While in a single movement, this work is actually a four-movement composition, even if in capsule form. In the opening of the symphony, three principal themes are stated and developed; this becomes the traditional Allegro movement in miniature. An acceleration of the tempo of the first of these themes becomes the heart of a scherzo movement, while the second theme in a more leisurely pace takes the place of the slow movement. A crescendo for full orchestra leads to a finale consisting of a passacaglia built upon the first theme.

BEETHOVEN. "The nine symphonies of Beethoven," wrote Hugo Leichtentritt, "represent the highest and noblest type in existence of music that appeals to the mass of people as well as to fastidious connoisseurs." Beethoven was thirty years old before he wrote his first symphony. Here he is still largely subservient to Haydn and Mozart, a fact rather strikingly pointed up by the resemblance of the main melody of the second movement to one in Mozart's G minor Symphony. The Symphony No. 1 in C major, op. 21 (1800), was introduced in Vienna on April 2, 1800, the composer conducting. The Classical structure is adhered to; the melodic material is usually presented simply and clearly; the developments follow accepted procedures; the style is usually in the refined and graceful manner of Haydn and Mozart. Yet there was a good deal here to disturb an audience in 1800, for already Beethoven was proving to be an iconoclast. The twelve-bar slow introduction to the first movement (*Adagio molto*) opens in the key of F, and passes through A minor and G major before arriving at the C major tonality of the symphony, a procedure as shocking as it was novel. Only after this strange digression does the first movement settle down to the formal business of presenting the two main themes, in the *Allegro con brio* section. The second movement (*Andante cantabile con moto*), while in the recognizable graceful lyricism of the period, with a beautiful Mozartean melody for second violins, is also unorthodox in its modulations and in the instrumentation, which calls for trumpets and timpani. (Throughout the symphony Beethoven makes such prominent use of brass and timpani that one enraged critic maintained that this music should have been written for a military band.) In the third movement (*Allegro molto e vivace*) the minuet acquires such vigor and robustness that to Berlioz this was "the one truly original thing in the symphony." Once again there is a fresh approach in the finale (Adagio; *Allegro molto e vivace*), particularly in the opening bars, in which first violins cautiously present an ascending scale passage before the movement finally plunges into the electrifying first theme.

The Symphony No. 2 in D major, op. 36 (1802), was the last time Beethoven clung to the coat tails of Haydn and Mozart. It was introduced in Vienna under the composer's direction on April 5, 1803 (I. *Adagio molto; Allegro con brio.* II. Larghetto. III. Scherzo: Allegro. IV. *Allegro molto*). The enriched orchestration, the replacement of the minuet by a scherzo, the volatile and at times stormy moods of the finale from its very first aggressive bars through its surprising changes of rhythm and tonality—all this again reveals the stirrings of rebellion in Beethoven against accepted symphonic methods. Somewhat more traditional is the beautiful second movement, its main melody a moving hymn for the violins.

After the Second Symphony, Beethoven took a giant leap forward, leaving behind him forever the symphonic practices and concepts of the past. The Symphony No. 3 in E-flat major, op. 55 (1804), best known as the *Eroica*, may well be said to usher in the Romantic era. Certainly this symphony represented an altogether new approach to architectonic construction, orchestration, thematic development, and subjectivity of expression. As Romain Rolland said: "The *Eroica* is a miracle even among Beethoven's works. If later he went further, never did he take so big a single stride. It is one of the Great Days of music. It inaugurates an era."

It was the first symphony in which a poetic idea seized Beethoven, in which he aspired to make his music the voice of that idea. For this reason his writing had to acquire new scope and dimension. He originally planned his symphony as a tribute to Napoleon, when that dictator appeared to be a champion of human rights and freedom. But when Napoleon proved that he was motivated only by ambition and a lust for power by proclaiming himself Emperor, Beethoven angrily changed his dedication to an unnamed hero, a hero of the spirit, a symbol of man's noblest aspirations. And it is such a hero who strides through the massive frame of the symphony (I. *Allegro con brio.* II. Funeral March: *Adagio assai.* III. Scherzo: *Allegro vivace.* IV. *Allegro molto*). The symphony opens forcefully with two mighty chords. A four-bar theme unfolds in the cellos, passes on to other sections of the orchestra, and is thunderously proclaimed by the full orchestra. At this point a beautiful contrasting subject is provided by woodwinds and violins. This is but the calm before the storm. The music now gathers its strength and with overpowering impact arrives at a climax whose peak is a series of piercingly dissonant chords. Now comes a plaintive melody in the woodwind, peace and resignation after a Herculean struggle. The development section that follows is one of the most monumental thus far achieved in symphonic music, sweeping across 250 bars. Not only is earlier material dramatically altered and extended, but new ideas are introduced as a struggle of epic character is projected. A horn passage brings on the recapitulation. Still the creative force has not been spent. Together with variation and enlargement of earlier material there comes a 140-measure coda in which still new light is thrown upon already stated ideas. This is not merely a resumé; this is the final resolution of conflict into victory.

The second movement is a funeral march, the first time such music appears in a symphony, an eloquent threnody for a fallen hero. The march melody is immediately presented by violins, followed by a poignant lament, again for strings. The tragic expression of this first section finds contrast in a serene trio in which a calm review seems to be made of the hero's achievements. The principal subject here is a melody for flutes and clarinets. After a momentary return of the march theme, a powerful climax is realized with a fugal passage whose subject is stated by the second violins. A faltering presentation of the funeral march melody ends the movement on a poignant note. The ensuing Scherzo is a temporary relief from earlier tensions and emotions. The main theme of the principal section is a light, energetic idea for strings; in the trio, a hunting call for horns is prominent. But this light mood is dissipated by the tempestuous opening measures of the finale. There now is heard the main melody in plucked strings. (Beethoven used this theme several times before this, in a set of piano variations, in a *Contredanse,* and in his incidental music to *Prometheus.*) A series of variations on this melody culminate in a fugato. A resounding hymn of triumph is then sounded by the woodwind. After a proud restatement of the main theme of the movement over throbbing triplets, a presto section brings the symphony to a breathless conclusion.

The Symphony No. 4 in B-flat major, op. 60 (1806), is of much more slender proportions. If the *Eroica* is an epic, the Fourth is an idyl. In place of passion, struggle, and triumph we have gentle contemplation, serenity, and what Berlioz called "a heavenly sweetness." The Sym-

phony was first performed in Vienna in March 1807 (I. Adagio; *Allegro vivace.* II. Adagio. III. Menuetto: *Allegro vivace.* IV. *Allegro ma non troppo*). The opening Adagio of the first movement is a gentle reverie. But gay feelings soon erupt with the lively first theme for first violins against a staccato accompaniment; this theme soon receives humorous treatment from the bassoons against violin trills. A lyrical second subject for flute, and a theme treated canonically by clarinet and bassoon, are two other ideas in this movement. The slow movement presents a radiant song for first violins. In the third movement, Beethoven temporarily deserts the scherzo for the earlier minuet form. The symphony ends with an outburst of ebullient spirits, beginning with a gay and rhythmic melody for the violins.

The Symphony No. 5 in C minor, op. 67 (1807), is perhaps the most celebrated symphony ever written. It was first performed in Vienna on Dec. 22, 1808, the composer conducting (I. *Allegro con brio.* II. *Andante con moto.* III. Scherzo: *Allegro vivace.* IV. Allegro). The miracle of this work lies in the first movement, where an elementary opening theme of four notes is developed into a monumental drama. This rhythmic four-note motif has been interpreted as "fate knocking at the door," a programmatic concept never intended by the composer but admirably carried out by the music. This is also the theme which during World War II was known as the Victory motif throughout Europe because its three short notes followed by a long one resemble the three dots and a dash that in the Morse code stand for "V," or "Victory." If the opening theme represents fate knocking, then the second one—a contrasting lyric subject for clarinets, flutes, and violins—may suggest resignation to that fate. The second movement is in the form of a theme and variations, but with two themes instead of one. The first is immediately heard in violas and cellos; the second appears in the clarinets and bassoons against triplet figures in the violas. In the Scherzo an ominous-sounding subject in cellos and basses leads into the main idea, a chattering subject for horns in a rhythmic pattern similar to that of the opening motif of the first movement. The trio section presents an onrushing, dynamic theme which is subjected to fugal treatment; here the double bass is given a prominence it never before enjoyed in orchestral music. The transition from scherzo to finale is a dramatic high point of the symphony. Hushed fragments of the scherzo theme grow and intensify until the finale erupts with a loud and triumphant march-like subject for full orchestra; the second theme, in the woodwind, maintains the exultant character of this music, a character that persists until the final rousing measures.

Beethoven himself entitled his Symphony No. 6 in F major, op. 68 (1808), the *Pastoral*. To each of the movements he appended programmatic subtitles. This symphony expresses Beethoven's profound love of Nature, and, as he explained, it was intended "more as an expression of feeling than as a painting." The symphony was introduced in Vienna on Dec. 22, 1808, the composer conducting (I. *Allegro ma non troppo*. II. *Andante molto moto*. III. Allegro. IV. Allegro. V. Allegretto). The first movement represents "The Awakening of Joyful Feelings Upon Arrival in the Country." These feelings are voiced at once in an exuberant opening theme for violins. The second movement, "The Brook," recreates the serene flow of the brook as the song of the first violins is accompanied by a murmuring subject for second violins and violas. Just before the end of the movement, the rustic picture becomes realistic through imitation of the calls of a nightingale, quail, and cuckoo. The third movement, a scherzo, describes a "Village Festival," with its country dances, merrymaking, and (in the trio) an amusing caricature of a village band. The dance is suddenly interrupted by "The Storm," which receives dramatic presentation in the fourth movement. This is a brief but turbulent sequence which breaks in on the third movement and is a transition to the finale, "The Shepherd's Song." The sun pierces through the clouds. The opening melody in the clarinet, then the horns, and finally the violins, is a hymn of thanksgiving that the storm is over. The entire finale is a portrait of a countryside transfigured and once again radiant.

The Symphony No. 7 in A major, op. 92 (1812), was first performed in Vienna on Dec. 8, 1813, the composer conducting. This work emphasizes rhythm. A single rhythmic figure is highlighted in each of the four movements to create such momentum that the work was described by Wagner as the "apotheosis of the dance," and by Liszt as the "apotheosis of rhythm" (I. *Poco sostenuto;* Vivace. II. Allegretto. III. Presto; *Assai meno presto*. IV. *Allegro con brio*). The first movement opens with an introduction in which the principal motifs are an ascending scale passage for the first violins, and a tender song for oboes and clarinets. A repeated E, intoned first softly, then crescendo, leads to the main body of the movement, whose first theme is an extended melody for the flute. This idea soon receives vital rhythmic treatment. The rhythmic element now remains pronounced throughout the movement, in which there is no contrasting second theme. In place of a slow movement, the symphony has an Allegretto, in which the rhythmic drive of the first movement is continued. After an opening chord, a march-like melody is presented in cellos and basses; when this melody is repeated by second violins, a new subject appears contrapuntally in violas and cellos. After this a fugato section is launched by the first violins. Midway in the movement a lovely melodic idea is presented by clarinets and bassoons, accompanied by violin triplets. The Scherzo is based on a vivacious melody for full orchestra; in the trio a sustained song is chanted by clarinets, bassoons, and horns. In the finale we confront an outburst of demoniac energy that alone could have won for the symphony its designation as the apotheosis of rhythm. An orgiastic melody explodes in the orchestra after some preliminary chords, and from then on the motor energy is never arrested.

Like the Fourth Symphony, the Eighth in F major, op. 93 (1812), is a slender maiden between two giants. The Eighth was introduced in Vienna on Feb. 27, 1814, the composer conducting. Throughout its four movements it maintains a light and happy mood (I. *Allegro vivace e con brio.* II. *Allegretto scherzando.* III. *Tempo di minuetto.* IV. *Allegro vivace*). There is no slow movement here to cast a shadow on the sunny proceedings; and in the third movement a light-hearted minuet, substituting for the more usual Beethoven scherzo, gives assurance of a continuance of the jovial mood. The most famous movement is the second, in which a sprightly little melody appears in violins and cellos with a background of staccato chords in the winds. It has often been claimed that this rhythmically precise series of chords was intended as an amusing take-off on the metronome, which Beethoven's friend Maelzel is supposed to have invented.

Beethoven's last symphony—No. 9 in D minor, op. 125 (1824)—calls for chorus and vocal soloists in the last movement, which is why this work is often designated as the *Choral Symphony.* No symphony took Beethoven so long to write, and none cost him such mental anguish and creative struggle. It proved his most monumental creation within the symphonic mold, a work that he flooded with humanity and compassion (1. *Allegro ma non troppo, un poco maestoso.* II. Scherzo: *Molto vivace.* III. *Adagio molto e cantabile.* IV. Presto; *Allegro assai*). The première took place in Vienna on May 7, 1824, under the composer's direction, an occasion that was one of the most poignant incidents in the life of the master. He was now completely deaf, incapable of hearing the music he was conducting. At the end of the performance Beethoven, a few measures off, continued to beat time. This tragic episode sent an electric current through the audience, which, after a momentary hush, exploded into an ovation. One of the soloists had to turn the deaf composer around to acknowledge the tribute.

The text of the finale was the poetic idea that set Beethoven's creative imagination aflame, and made him seek out in all four movements an ever profounder strain of feeling and thought. That text was by Schiller, the *Ode to Joy,* a stirring paean to the brotherhood of man. For over a quarter of a century Beethoven

had hoped to provide it with a musical setting.

The symphony opens with an air of mystery. Against violin tremolos, the germ of an idea is presented by first violins. Through 16 bars the theme slowly evolves from embryo to full growth and is finally proclaimed by the full orchestra in unison. Fragments of other themes, together with fully stated subjects, follow. Some are proud and defiant, others resigned or suppliant. In both the involved exposition and the titanic development there is a struggle of epic dimensions, "conceived," as Wagner once wrote, "in the greatest grandeur of the soul contending for happiness against the oppression of that inimical power which places itself between us and the joys of earth." Sometimes there is a premonition of defeat: a poignant descending melody for the first violins; or the funereal chant for oboe and clarinet which appears at the end of the movement. But usually the spirit is triumphant, especially in the closing measures, in which the opening subject is proudly promulgated by full orchestra against rolls of the timpani.

Beethoven alters usual procedures by placing the scherzo movement before the slow one. An exultant mood is at once projected with a fleeting staccato theme in second violins. As this theme passes on to other string sections, it is treated fugally. In the trio a more solemn thought is introduced by oboes and clarinets. But the joyous character of the movement as a whole is not affected.

The slow movement is surely one of the noblest pages in any Beethoven symphony. Two important melodies are encountered. The first is given at once by the first violins, and is gentle and reflective. The second, radiant and spiritual, is heard in second violins and violas. As variations of these two subjects unfold, new breathtaking vistas arise continually. Only a mighty tribute to joy and to the highest aspirations of man could fittingly follow music poised on such a plane of sublimity. And it is at this point that Beethoven finally found a place for Schiller's *Ode to Joy.* An agonizing chord and a demoniac outburst of orchestral sound shatter the exalted mood of the Adagio. Then a main thought from each of the three preceding movements is briefly recalled, and rejected. None can serve as a hymn for the brotherhood of man. Suddenly a new melody is softly intoned by cellos and basses. The violas join in; the violins take over. This is the melody Beethoven had been searching for. But before it is presented again, the dramatic agitation of the opening measures is interrupted by stern exhortation by the baritone: "Oh, Friends, no more these sounds continue. Let us raise a song of sympathy and gladness. Oh, Joy, let us praise thee!" Baritone solo, vocal quartet, then full orchestra now offer the song of joy previously suggested by the strings. This is the heart of the finale. This melody is subjected to variations, extensions, repetitions; it becomes now martial, now religious, and now exultant. Other melodic ideas are also interposed: for example, a dramatic pronouncement by the chorus, "O Ye Millions I Embrace You," and an expression of religious exaltation in "Oh Ye Millions Kneel Before Him."

See also: *Battle Symphony; Jena Symphony.*

BERLIOZ. The *Fantastic Symphony* (*Symphonie fantastique*), op. 14 (1829), was first performed in Paris on Dec. 5, 1830, the composer conducting. This is programmatic music, subtitled by Berlioz "An Episode in the Life of an Artist." Actually it was a passionate autobiographical testament, an expression of his then unreciprocated love for Henrietta Smithson. She is the *idée fixe* of the entire work—represented musically by a graceful melody.

Berlioz prepared his own program. The following explanatory note appears in the published score: "A young musician of morbid sensibility and ardent imagination poisons himself with opium in a fit of amorous despair. The narcotic dose, too weak to result in death, plunges him into a heavy sleep accompanied by the strangest visions, during which his sensations, sentiments, and recollections are translated in his sick brain into musical thoughts and images. The beloved woman herself has become for him like a melody, like a fixed idea, which he finds and hears everywhere."

The symphony has five movements. I. Dreams, Passions (Largo; *Allegro e appassionato assai*). The hero meets the ideal woman and their love is born. An introductory Largo, in which a broad melody appears in violins, leads to the main Allegro section, whose basic material is a motto theme, first heard in unison flutes and first violins after a series of abrupt chords. II. The Ball (*Allegro non troppo*). The hero sees his beloved at a ball. This movement consists mainly of a waltz melody which is followed by the motto theme in flute and oboe. III. Scene in the Country (Adagio). A visit to the country reminds our hero of his beloved. This movement has a pastoral character throughout, beginning with an unaccompanied duet for English horn and oboe, and progressing to a delicate melody for flute and first violins. IV. The March to the Gallows (*Allegretto non troppo*). In a nightmare the hero sees himself killing his beloved. He is executed for his crime. This movement opens with a march for full orchestra. The motto theme appears in solo clarinet, interrupted by a crashing chord. After that the march theme returns in broken chords to end the movement. V. Dream of the Witches' Sabbath. The hero attends the rites of a Witches' Sabbath (Larghetto; Allegro). An eerie atmosphere is established by tremolo chords in divided strings. The motto theme, transformed into something grotesque, is played by the clarinet. Chiming bells bring on a burlesque of the *Dies irae* in tubas and bassoons. A demoniac dance is now presented fugally. After a stirring climax, the *Dies irae* returns majestically in brass and woodwind.

Harold in Italy (*Harold en Italie*), op. 16 (1834), is a symphony with viola obbligato commissioned by Paganini, who had become interested in the viola. Inspired by Byron's *Childe Harold*, this symphony is so sensitive in its expression and so subtle in its atmosphere that Paganini, who had expected virtuoso music, rejected it. *Harold in Italy* was introduced in Paris on Nov. 23, 1834, with Chrétien Urhan as soloist and the composer conducting. When, four years later, Paganini heard the work for the first time he was so impressed that he sent Berlioz a gift of 20,000 francs.

From Byron's poem Berlioz borrowed merely the over-all concept: Harold, wandering through Italy, gathering impressions. The symphony is in four movements. I. In the Mountains, Scenes of Melancholy, Happiness and Joy (Adagio; Allegro). The principal theme of the entire symphony, the *idée fixe*, is the Harold subject, first appearing in the woodwinds before reappearing in the solo viola to a harp accompaniment. A second melody is later presented by bassoons and cellos. In the coda, both themes are worked out fugally. II. March and Evening Prayer of the Pilgrims (Allegretto). The main pilgrim theme is given by the violins after several introductory measures. The Harold melody is also heard, to point up the fact that he is watching the procession. III. Serenade of the Mountaineer of the Abruzzi to his Mistress (*Allegro assai*). The serenade is presented by the English horn against frequent allusions to the Harold theme. IV. Orgy of the Brigands (*Allegro frenetico*). Berlioz explained: "In this brigand scene the orchestra becomes a regular pandemonium—there is something positively supernatural and terrifying in its frantic life and spirit. Violins, basses, trombones, drums, and cymbals all sing . . . and roar with diabolical order and concord."

Romeo and Juliet, op. 17 (1839), is a dramatic symphony for soloists, chorus, and orchestra based on the Shakespeare tragedy. It was introduced in Paris, on Nov. 24, 1839, the composer conducting. The symphony is made up of three major sections; these, in turn, comprise twelve smaller parts. The first section concerns the feud of the houses of Capulet and Montague (I. Introduction: Combat—Tumult—Intervention of the Prince. II. Prologue: Choral Recitative—Song—Recitative and Scherzetto). In the second section, Romeo invades the home of the Capulets during a ball and comes upon Juliet. They fall in love (I. Romeo Alone —Sadness—Distant Sounds of Music and Dancing—Festival in Capulet's Palace. II. Calm Night—Capulet's Garden, Silent

and Deserted—The Young Capulets, Leaving the Ball, Pass By, Singing Fragments of the Dance Music—Love Scene. III. Scherzo: Queen Mab or the Fairy of Dreams). The third section recounts the tragic fate of the lovers (I. Juliet's Funeral Procession. II. Romeo in the Tomb of the Capulets—Delirious Joy, Despair —Anguish and Death of Both Lovers. III. Finale: The Crowd Hastens to the Cemetery—Dispute Between the Capulets and Montagues—Recitative and Air of Friar Laurence—Oath and Reconciliation).

Because of its size, and the huge forces involved, the symphony is heard most often through several orchestral excerpts, rather than in its entirety. Two are especially popular. The first is the *Love Music*, a setting of the Balcony Scene, a passionate duet in which Romeo is represented by violas and cellos in unison and Juliet by oboes, flutes, and clarinets. The second is the scherzo, *Queen Mab*, a delicate and scintillating musical picture of Mercutio's description of Queen Mab.

BERNSTEIN. Leonard Bernstein has written two symphonies. The *Jeremiah Symphony* (1942) was his first work for orchestra. It was introduced in Pittsburgh on Jan. 28, 1944, with Jennie Tourel as soloist and the composer conducting; it received the New York Music Critics Circle Award (I. Prophecy. II. Profanation. III. Lamentation). The composer explains: "The first movement aims only to parallel in feeling the intensity of the prophet's pleas with the people." In the second part we get a "general sense of destruction and chaos brought on by the pagan corruption within the priesthood and the people." The third movement is a vocal setting of a biblical text, the lament of Jeremiah at the ruin of Jerusalem after his futile efforts to save it, taken from *The Book of Lamentations*.

Bernstein's second symphony, *The Age of Anxiety* (1949), is scored for piano and orchestra. It was introduced in Boston on April 8, 1949, with the composer at the piano and Koussevitzky conducting. Like the poem by W. H. Auden on which it was based, the symphony is concerned with man's present-day insecurity, and his need of faith. The symphony is in two parts. The first includes a Prologue, The Seven Ages (variations 1-7), and the Seven Stages (variations 7-14). Part two consists of a Dirge, Masque, and Epilogue. Four characters try detaching themselves from their conflicts through alcohol. They review the life of man from the perspective of their own lives in "The Seven Ages" and embark on an inner symbolic journey in search of comfort and security in "The Seven Stages." In "The Dirge" they mourn the loss of their "Colossal Dad" to whom they look for guidance. In the "Masque" the four are found at a party. In the Epilogue each of the four has finally found the faith for which he, or she, has been groping.

BIZET. There is neither subtlety nor sophistication in Bizet's Symphony No. 1 in C major (1855). But there is here a great deal of buoyant lyricism; the symphony bubbles over with the champagne of fresh and spontaneous melodies and pleasing harmonies (I. *Allegro vivo*. II. Adagio. III. *Allegro vivace*. IV. *Allegro vivace*). Written in the composer's seventeenth year, the symphony had to wait eighty years for a performance, which finally took place in Basel, Switzerland, on Feb. 26, 1935, Felix Weingartner conducting. But since then it has been often performed and recorded. It has also been adapted into a ballet, first presented as *Le Palais de Cristal* by the Paris Opéra Ballet on July 28, 1947, and after that as *Symphony in C* by the Ballet Society of New York on March 22, 1948.

BLOCH. Ernest Bloch's *Israel Symphony* is scored for orchestra and two sopranos, two contraltos, and bass (1916); it was introduced in New York on May 3, 1917, the composer conducting. The work was inspired by the Day of Atonement, the holiest day in the Jewish calendar. Though in a single movement, the symphony has three parts. After a slow section in which the main theme is an elegy for solo horn, there comes a vigorous part whose main theme (in flutes, English horn, clarinet, and strings) has a savage feeling. The closing section, described by the composer as "a fresco of Hebrew struggle," begins turbulently; but the music soon lapses into resignation as

woodwinds, violins, harp, and solo viola present a simple hymn. The movement ends with a prayer of atonement.
See also: America.

BORODIN. Borodin wrote three symphonies, the last left unfinished. The most famous is No. 2 in B minor (1876), nicknamed *Bogatyr* because of its heroic character, a "bogatyr" being a giant in ancient Russian epics. The symphony was introduced in St. Petersburg on March 10, 1877, Nápravník conducting. Some of the material here was also used by the composer for his opera, *Prince Igor*. Like the opera, the symphony is oriental in its rhythmic strength, flaming orchestral colors, and in the character of some of the melodies (I. Allegro. II. Scherzo. III. Andante. IV. Allegro). In the first movement the main idea is a powerful melody in unison strings supported by bassoons and horns. After a vital Scherzo movement there comes an Andante which recalled for Vladimir Stassov, the Russian critic, the songs of the ancient Slav minstrels. The main minstrel song is given by the horn. Stassov found the brilliant and at times savage finale to be a description of a hero's banquet in which the sounds of several ancient instruments are featured.

BRAHMS. With his four symphonies, each a masterwork, Brahms became Beethoven's symphonic heir. It was a long time before Brahms dared to venture into a branch of musical composition in which Beethoven had been so productive. Not until he was forty and had produced masterworks in virtually every other instrumental form did he finally write his first symphony, and it took him four years to complete the project. Often described as the greatest first symphony ever written, it is music of surpassing creative power, eloquence, and originality. The Symphony No. 1 in C minor, op. 68 (1876), was introduced in Karlsruhe, on Nov. 6, 1876, the composer conducting (I. *Un poco sostenuto;* Allegro. II. *Andante sostenuto.* III. *Un poco alle-gretto e grazioso.* IV. *Adagio più andante; Allegro non troppo ma con brio*). This is an epic work with tragic implications. The thirty-seven-bar introduction of the first movement is one of the most elo quent pages in the symphonic literature: a soaring ecstatic flight for the violins, with woodwinds in contrary motion, all against a background of dramatic C's in the timpani. In the main body of the movement the first subject is a restless theme for violins which sets a mighty conflict into action. The conflict is temporarily arrested by a poignant second theme in the woodwinds. In the monumental development, these and several new ideas are worked out into a drama of Grecian proportions. The dramatic thrust, and at times the overwhelming pathos, continually remind us of the Beethoven of the *Eroica* and the Ninth, and we begin to understand why many writers refer to this symphony as "Beethoven's Tenth." After the fever and passion of the first movement, the second comes like a gentle benediction. A beautiful melody arises from strings and bassoons without preliminaries and is immediately succeeded by a second equally expressive song for the oboe. The serenity is intensified into passion as a sensual passage engages the strings against a firm, decisive rhythm. But the gentler mood returns, first with a new melody presented alternately by oboes and clarinets, then with a revival of the second theme, this time in horn and solo violin.

The third movement is a playful Allegretto, rather than the kind of robust scherzo we usually encounter in Beethoven. The light and graceful principal theme, almost like a folk tune, is at once presented by a clarinet against a pizzicato background. A much stronger idea is then offered by woodwinds to an answer by strings.

In the finale we once again confront a titanic drama such as only Beethoven's greatest symphonies had previously projected. Chromatic chords in the wind and an exclamation by the strings preface a section that gains in tempo and dynamics, and to which the timpani contributes a throbbing rhythm. A sublime song is then heard in the horn against tremolo strings. After it has been repeated by the flutes, the most celebrated melody of the symphony is joyously sung by the strings, followed by an equally eloquent countermelody. After that, all the resources of a

master's technique in development are enlisted to dramatize this material until a mighty climax is achieved with a resounding restatement of the earlier horn song by the full orchestra.

Largely because of the finale, in which the main melody for strings resembles the *Ode to Joy* melody, Brahms' First Symphony has often been likened to Beethoven's Ninth. It is possible to compare Brahms' Symphony No. 2 in D major, op. 73 (1877), to a Beethoven symphony also, this time the *Pastoral*. In Brahms' Second we desert the storms and conflicts and tragedy of the First and come upon an idyl which has the peace and tranquillity of a country landscape. This symphony was introduced in Vienna on Dec. 30, 1887, Hans Richter conducting (I. *Allegro non troppo*. II. *Adagio non troppo*. III. *Allegretto grazioso*. IV. *Allegro con spirito*). In the first movement a three-note figure in the cellos prefaces a romantic melody for horn; this is the first main theme. The second is a wondrous song for cellos and violas, answered by flutes. As both subjects are structurally enlarged and enriched in instrumentation in the development section, and as all earlier material is recalled in the recapitulation, the serenity is not disturbed. It is still maintained in the coda, in which a horn solo is emphasized.

While the bucolic atmosphere of the first movement prevails in the second, there is in the latter movement a strong undercurrent of melancholy. Three main melodies are all equally poignant. The first is the opening sensitive song for cellos; the second is for flutes and oboes; and the third is an expansive lyric subject for strings. The third movement is more of an intermezzo than a scherzo. In the first part, the main theme is a reflective thought for woodwinds against pizzicato cellos. This melody is repeated after each of the two trios that follow. There is an ominous-sounding introduction in strings in the finale, but optimistic feelings soon erupt with a joyous melody for full orchestra. Two other melodies are subsequently presented. The first is an introspective one for the woodwinds; the second, a proud statement for violins. It is with a lively recall of the opening phrase of this last idea that the symphony ends.

The Symphony No. 3 in F major, op. 90, came six years after the Second (1883); the first performance took place in Vienna on Dec. 2, 1883, Hans Richter conducting (I. *Allegro con brio*. II. *Andante*. III. *Poco allegretto*. IV. *Allegro*). The symphony is the only one in which the composer makes use of an integrating motto theme: the three forceful chords for wind instruments with which the symphony opens. This motto recurs throughout the work, even if at times only as transition material or as a background. After the motto theme, the first movement continues with a sweeping descending melody for violins, with cellos and basses providing the motto subject as a background. A transition, reminiscent of a theme from Wagner's *Venusberg Music*, leads to a sensitive second theme, a melody first heard in the clarinet, and later in the oboe and cellos. The motto theme makes frequent appearances: once in the solo oboe; then in horn and oboe; after that as a transition to the recapitulation; finally as an introduction to the coda.

The second movement opens with a hymn in four-part harmony for woodwinds. The second theme is also highly lyrical, and once again is presented by the woodwind. Two sensual sections for violins are subsequently prominent. A variation of the opening hymn brings the movement to its conclusion. The third movement is a Romanza in which the main melody is a brooding subject for cellos against string arpeggios. A mysterious atmosphere is created for the opening of the finale. A sober thought is presented by strings and winds. After a violently agitated mood, cellos and horns sing out a majestic melody. Towards the end of the symphony the motto theme appears for the last time in soft and resigned accents in the violins.

At the time Brahms was working on his Symphony No. 4 in E minor, op. 98 (1885), he was deep in the reading of Greek classics. It is probable that the Greek drama had a subtle influence upon him, for in this symphony he succeeded in bringing to his music some of the epic character, the sense of doom, the majestic speech of Sophocles. The symphony was introduced at an orchestral rehearsal in Meiningen in October 1885, Hans von Buelow conducting. The Meiningen Orchestra gave it its first public performance on Oct. 25, 1885, the composer conducting.

The Fourth Symphony is prevailingly sad (I. *Allegro non troppo*. II. *Andante moderato*. III. *Allegro giocoso*. IV. *Allegro energico e passionato*). The first movement opens with a soft, sad melody for the violins, with answering phrases in the woodwind. From then on the symphony proceeds not along the formal lines of sonata structure but through a series of thematic ideas and fully stated melodies, some tragic, others dramatic, all built up with tremendous power and sweep. A passionate horn passage leads to a second main melody in woodwinds and horns, the second part assumed by cellos and horns to a pizzicato accompaniment. After a sensual section in which the violins soar ecstatically to the highest registers, there comes the development, which gives prominent treatment to the opening theme. The four notes of the opening theme, but now in augmentation, bring on the recapitulation.

In the second movement, the principal melody, gently touched by a brooding melancholy, appears in the fifth measure in clarinets and bassoons accompanied by plucked strings. Before the second main theme appears, there is heard a surging, passionate section for strings. Then the cellos lift their voices in a song that is surely one of Brahms' supreme lyric efforts. Both themes are discussed in detail in the development, but it is on the second that the composer concentrates in the coda. The third movement is a brief escapade in a lighter mood, with the first theme appearing in the full orchestra, and the second in the first violins. In the finale, Brahms revives the old Baroque form of the passacaglia. Its eight-bar theme is first given by the brass and woodwind, after which come thirty variations of such subtlety, complexity, and technical wizardry that Brahms' friend, Elisabeth von Herzogenberg, complained that "it is more for the lens of a microscope, for the erudite and the scientific than for the average music lover." Nevertheless, even if the average music lover cannot always trace in the variations the evolutions and transformations of the theme, he cannot fail to be swept away by the titanic sweep of the composer's creative force and by the overwhelming impact of the music's inexorable logic.

BRUCKNER. Anton Bruckner (like Beethoven) wrote nine symphonies. The first, in C minor, came between 1865 and 1866; and the last, in D minor, between 1887 and 1896. Only three are given with any degree of regularity. One has remained a perennial favorite: the Symphony No. 4 in E-flat (1874), the *Romantic,* a name bestowed upon it by the composer after he had written the music. This is also the first symphony by Bruckner to be successful at its première performance, which took place in Vienna on Feb. 20, 1881, Hans Richter conducting (I. *Allegro molto moderato.* II. Andante. III. *Bewegt.* IV. *Maessig bewegt*). Except for its slow movement, the symphony is a work of contagious buoyancy and effervescent spirit. It is also a well-knit work, integrated by a continual use of the descending fifth in the melodic material, beginning with the opening horn subject of the first movement; also by the recurrence of a device now sometimes referred to as the "Bruckner rhythm," which consists of two quarter notes followed by a triplet of quarter notes, in 4/4 time. The first movement opens with a bucolic melody for horn against tremolo strings in which the descending interval is prominent. The "Bruckner rhythm" makes its first appearance in the second main theme, presented by the full orchestra. The second movement is the only one in the work with tragic undercurrents; it almost has the character of a funeral march. Two measures of muted chords or strings preface a haunting melody for cellos. A chorale-like subject leads to a second expressive melody, first played by violas against plucked strings. The movement ends on a solemn note, as a tender passage first for strings is allowed to ebb away with only the dramatic beats of the timpani remaining to be heard. In the third-movement Scherzo, a horn fanfare resembling a hunting call plays an important role in the main section, while a vigorous Austrian dance is prominent in the trio. Though the finale introduces some new material, it is essentially a summary of earlier movements. The new material consists of an extended passage for woodwinds and horns with which the movement opens; a thunderous subject for full orchestra; and a sensitive melody for flute and clarinets in octaves against a countertheme in the violas.

The Symphony No. 7 in E major (1883) is a more epic work than the Fourth. It also plumbs greater emotional depths, particularly in its finest movement, the eloquent Adagio. It was long believed that this deeply emotional music was inspired by Wagner's death, but the fact is that the movement was completed four months before Wagner died. The main subject here is a moving hymn for lower strings and tubas, to which other strings provide an answer. A mighty lamentation now arises from the full orchestra after which a new poignant melody appears in the violins, together with an effective return of the first theme. As the movement progresses, this main first theme receives majestic treatment, but other poignant or turbulent subjects are also introduced with compelling effect. The movement ends in an exalted vein with a return of the main melody in tubas and horns against plucked strings.

The Seventh Symphony was first performed in Leipzig on Dec. 30, 1884, Arthur Nikisch conducting (I. *Allegro moderato.* II. Adagio. III. Allegro. IV. *Bewegt doch nicht schnell*).

There are two versions of Bruckner's last symphony, No. 9, in D minor, which he left unfinished, having completed only three of the four movements. One of these is an edited and drastically revised version by his disciple, Ferdinand Loewe; this was first given in Vienna under Loewe's direction on Feb. 11, 1903, more than five years after the composer's death. The second version is Bruckner's own, but this was not heard until April 2, 1932, in Munich, in a private performance sponsored by the Bruckner Society. After Bruckner's version was presented to the world, many discriminating critics

condemned the Loewe edition as a dese-
cration. It is Bruckner's original that is
now preferred over the Loewe adaptation
(I. *Feierlich.* II. *Bewegt lebhaft.* III. *Sehr
langsam feierlich*). The first movement
is made up of four principal themes, each
built to an impressive climax. After the
fourth theme is carried through a powerful crescendo, a free fantasia section develops all four ideas, the first of which
makes its final appearance in the coda.
The second movement is a scherzo with
a pizzicato subject for strings in the first
section, and two melodies in the ensuing
trio. The Adagio, which Bruckner had
planned as a third movement but which
must now serve as the symphony's finale,
is in sonata form. Both main themes are
lyrically expressive, presented by the violins. After an extended development, and
a climactic crescendo, the first theme is
brought back forcefully; but the movement ends on an elegiac note.

CHAUSSON. Chausson's Symphony in B-
flat major, op. 20 (1890), was introduced
in Paris on April 18, 1891; but its great
success did not begin until a year later,
when Arthur Nikisch introduced it in
Germany. This work was influenced by
Wagner, especially in the dynamics and
orchestration; but structurally it owes a
strong debt to Franck's cyclic form (I.
Lent. II. *Très lent.* III. *Animé; Très
animé*). The first movement leads from
a melancholy introduction to the main
section, in which the principal theme is
stated by horn and bassoons, and the
second theme by cellos and clarinet. The
second movement is an elegy, the core of
which is a song for cellos and English
horn accompanied by arpeggios in the
strings. The third movement has a vigorous introduction followed by the principal theme in trumpet and woodwind. A
chromatic scale leads to a chorale for full
orchestra. The introductory section, with
which the movement opened, also concludes it.

COPLAND. Aaron Copland's Third Symphony (1946) received the Boston Symphony Award of Merit and the New
York Music Critics Circle Award following its première in Boston under Koussevitzky on Oct. 18, 1946. It is one of the
most distinguished symphonies by an

American (I. *Molto moderato,* with
simple expression. II. *Allegro molto.* III.
Andante quasi allegretto. IV. *Molto de-
liberato; Allegro risoluto*). Though no
American folk melodies are quoted, this
symphony has a distinct American character. The first movement is constructed
from three principal ideas: the first is
heard at once in the strings; the second
follows in violas and oboes; and the third
is a vigorous statement by trombones
and horns. The second movement is a
scherzo whose main theme is heard three
times, first in horns and violas, then in
unison strings, and finally in lower strings.
In the trio, the main melody is assigned
to the woodwinds before it is taken over
by the strings. The movement ends with
a recollection of the main melody of the
trio given canonically by the full orchestra. The slow movement is made up
of several sections, each blending into the
next. The main theme appears in the solo
flute. The finale enters without interruption, opening with a fanfare the composer had previously used in another
work (*Fanfare for the Common Man*).
A spirited first theme, and a broad song-
like second, are the principal ideas. The
movement ends with a majestic presentation of the opening phrase of the first
movement.

DVOŘÁK. The work now known as
Dvořák's Symphony No. 1 in D major,
op. 60 (1880), was not actually the composer's first symphony. He had written
several earlier ones, but they are apprentice compositions and are never performed; two were never even published.
The Symphony No. 1 in D major is
Dvořák's first mature symphony. It was
introduced in Prague on March 25, 1881,
Adolf Cech conducting (I. *Allegro non
tanto.* II. *Adagio.* III. *Furiant.* IV. *Allegro con spirito*). In the first movement
the main thought appears in flute and
oboe after an introductory measure. The
cellos and first horn later offer a second
important subject of a highly lyrical
nature. A remarkable feature of the development section is the way in which it
is introduced by sustained chords which
serve as a base on which are built fragments of the movement's first theme.
Finally these fragments are pieced to-

gether, and this and other material is skilfully elaborated. The beautiful second movement consists of a broad folk-like melody for first violins and first horn and, after a change of key, of duet for first violins and cellos. The third movement, while a scherzo, is actually an energetic Bohemian dance in triple time. The finale opens with a peaceful subject for strings. But soon a *fortissimo* section erupts with a restatement of this melody *grandioso*. A second main thought is later given by the clarinet.

After the first symphony, Dvořák produced four more works in that form. The Fourth in G major, op. 88 (1889)—introduced in Prague in February 1890, the composer conducting—is consistently exuberant, spontaneous, and light-hearted (I. *Allegro con brio*. II. Adagio. III. *Allegretto grazioso; Molto vivace*. IV. *Allegro ma non troppo*). A pastoral mood is maintained throughout the work, and particularly emphasized in the second movement.

Dvořák's most famous symphony is the last one, the Fifth, in E minor, op. 95 (1893), best known as *From the New World*. Where earlier symphonies were unmistakably Slavic, often incorporating melodies and rhythms modeled after folk sources, the Fifth Symphony was of American inspiration, even if in many details it still can be identified as the work of a Bohemian. It was written in the United States and introduced in New York on Dec. 15, 1893, Anton Seidl conducting (I. Adagio; *Allegro molto*. II. Largo. III. *Molto vivace*. IV. *Allegro con fuoco*). After a solemn introduction, the main theme of the first movement is suggested by lower strings and horns under violin tremolos. A climactic passage leads to the main section, in which a sharply syncopated subject is pronounced by two horns. A transitional subject in flutes and oboes is followed by a poignant melody for flute that resembles the Negro spiritual, *Swing Low, Sweet Chariot*. The heart of the slow movement is an elegiac song for English horn against string harmonies. This is one of the composer's most famous melodies, so similar to a Negro spiritual that many long suspected it was derived from one.

It has also become famous as a song, *Goin' Home*, with lyrics by William Arms Fisher. The scherzo opens with a brief introduction, followed by a lively idea in flute and oboe in imitation, answered by clarinet. A second subject, also in flute and oboe, but over staccato strings, has a gentler personality. There are two different trios in different keys. In the finale, a triumphant subject is sounded by horns and trumpets, with the rest of the orchestra providing a chordal accompaniment. The second theme, in triplets, is introduced by the clarinets against tremolo strings. Both subjects are worked out and there are quick recollections of earlier material from the three preceding movements.

ELGAR. Elgar's Symphony No. 1 in A-flat major, op. 55 (1908), was introduced in Manchester on Dec. 3, 1908, Hans Richter conducting (I. Andante; *Nobilmente e semplice*. II. *Allegro molto*. III. Adagio. IV. Lento; Allegro). The composer explained that he intended this work to express "the innumerable phases of joy and sorrow, struggle and conquest, and especially between the ideal and actual life." The first movement is filled with such powerful and grandiose statements that it was regarded by Basil Maine as a "salute to national heritage and attainment." This and the deeply tragic slow movement are the high points of this symphony.

The Symphony No. 2 in E-flat major, op. 63 (1911), was first performed in London on May 24, 1911, the composer conducting. Where the First Symphony had been by turns powerful and tragic, the Second is filled with the joy of life, even though the score carries a despondent quotation from Shelley's *Invocation* ("Rarely, rarely comest thou, Spirit of Delight"). The work is in four movements: I. *Allegro vivace e nobilmente*. II. Larghetto. III. Presto. IV. *Moderato e maestoso*. In the opening movement the buoyant first theme is heard at once in the orchestra. The second subject, in the cellos, is of a more reflective nature. The first theme is given considerable prominence throughout the movement. The second movement is dominated by a gentle melody for flutes which appears after several quiet chords in the strings. Gaiety returns in the third movement, in form a rondo. The finale opens with a majestic statement for winds and cellos which is followed by two other stately themes. The opening subject of the first movement returns after a development of these ideas.

FRANCK. César Franck wrote only a single symphony, but that one—in D minor (1888)—is a landmark in French symphonic music. Yet when introduced in Paris on Feb. 17, 1889, Jules Garcin conducting, it was a fiasco, condemned by the members of the orchestra (who gave it a slipshod performance), the audience, and many notable French musicians including Charles Gounod. It is in three instead of the usual four movements (I. Lento; *Allegro non troppo*. II. Allegretto. III. *Allegro non troppo*). A majestic subject in cellos and basses appears in the opening measures. The main section is ushered in by a vigorous subject for strings. Two other important ideas are then elaborated upon. One is a yearning melody treated canonically by the strings; the other is a proud statement for full orchestra. At the conclusion of the movement the opening majestic theme receives canonic treatment. In the second movement the main melody appears in the English horn against plucked strings, a fact that disturbed many academicians of Franck's day since the English horn had up to then not ordinarily been employed by symphony composers. An equally expressive subsidiary subject follows in the first violins. After both ideas have been discussed, a scherzo section arrives, beginning with triplets in muted strings. The clarinet then appears with a haunting refrain, soon taken over by the strings. The movement ends with a single harp arpeggio. The finale is a review of previously stated material, together with some fresh ideas. It opens in a playful mood with a jubilant melody for full orchestra, followed by another vigorous idea for brass. A procession of earlier melodies follows with particular attention paid to the beautiful song for English horn of the second movement. The opening phrases of the first movement, but

now optimistic and spirited, bring the symphony to its close.

GLAZUNOV. Of Glazunov's eight symphonies, the fourth and sixth are the ones most often performed. The Symphony No. 4 in E-flat, op. 48 (1893), was introduced in St. Petersburg on Feb. 3, 1894, the composer conducting. It is unusual in that it has no slow movement; instead slow sections are used to preface the first and last movements (I. Andante; *Allegro moderato*. II. *Allegro vivace*. III. Andante; *Allegro*). In the first movement the main material consists of a simple tune for English horn, a lyrical passage for oboe, a graceful scherzando passage for clarinet, and a beautiful song for flute and oboe. In the second movement, a scherzo, a gay tune for two clarinets is prominent; a tranquil trio provides contrast. The finale is consistently energetic and dramatic, with the first theme forcefully presented by the full orchestra, and a secondary idea by violas and oboe.

The Symphony No. 6 in C minor, op. 58 (1896), was introduced in St. Petersburg on Feb. 21, 1897, the composer conducting (I. Adagio; *Allegro passionato*. II. Andante. III. Allegretto. IV. *Andante maestoso; Scherzando*). The main section of the first movement is ushered in with a strongly accented subject for strings; a melodious second theme is then provided by the violins against an accompaniment hinting at the first subject. The second movement is a theme and seven variations, the theme first heard in the violins. An intermezzo movement follows, its main melody found in the woodwind against pizzicato cellos. Following the trio, a second melody is presented by the flute, this time against pizzicato violins. The finale consists mainly of a fiery Russian dance.

GLIÈRE. Reinhold Glière's Symphony No. 3 in B minor, op. 42 (1911), is named *Ilia Mourometz*; it was introduced in Moscow on March 23, 1912, Emil Cooper conducting, and soon thereafter received the Glinka Prize. Its hero is the 12th-century warrior, Ilia Mourometz, whose exploits in peace and war were legendary; he was ultimately converted to Christianity. I. Wandering Pilgrims: Ilia Mourometz and Sviatogor. Mourometz becomes a bogatyr and upon the death of Sviatogor inherits the latter's power. II. Solovei the Brigand. Ilia defeats the brigand and drags him to the palace of Vladimir the Sun. III. The Palace of Prince Vladimir. A mighty feast is taking place during which Ilia cuts off Solovei's head. IV. The Feats of Valor and the Petrification of Ilia Mourometz. Ilia conquers Batygha the Wicked and his pagan army, but in the end Ilia and his bogatyrs are destroyed.

Among the principal themes in this symphony are a chorale-like subject in free meter with which the work opens (*Andante sostenuto*) and which recurs in various guises; at the end of the symphony it is developed into a powerful climax. This theme is intended to suggest the Christian faith which sends Ilia on his exploits. Two other melodies depict Ilia himself in the *Allegro risoluto* section that follows. One appears in strings and bassoons in the low register; the other, in trombones.

CARL GOLDMARK. Goldmark's *Rustic Wedding Symphony* (*Laendliche Hochzeit*), op. 26 (1876), was first performed in Vienna in 1876, Hans Richter conducting. Strictly speaking, this is a suite of five tone pictures rather than a symphony. I. Wedding March (*Moderato molto*). The march theme appears first in lower strings followed by 13 variations. II. The Bridal Song (Allegretto). The main theme is presented by the oboe against the march theme of the first movement. III. Serenade (*Allegretto moderato scherzando*). This is pastoral music, the main melody given by the oboes. IV. In the Garden (Andante). A dialogue of lovers is reproduced by various pairs of instruments. V. Dance (*Allegro molto*). The march melody of the first movement receives fugal treatment.

MORTON GOULD. Gould's Symphony No. 3 is one of his most important works (1947); it was introduced in New York on Oct. 28, 1948, Dimitri Mitropoulos conducting. American popular idioms are freely employed here (I. Rhapsodic and Intense. II. Moderately Slow and Relaxed. III. Moderately Fast. IV. Slowly Moving; Fast). The first movement is made up of two contrasting sections in which the principal material is a long, sinuous melodic line rather than self-contained themes. The movement ends with funeral-procession music. The second movement emphasizes lyricism, the melodic scheme adhering closely to a blues tonality. The ensuing scherzo opens with a jazz fugue, and continues with a loud and humorous trio. The finale is a passacaglia and fugue. The fugue subject is derived from the passacaglia theme. That theme, restated loudly, brings the symphony to its conclusion.

HOWARD HANSON. Among Howard Hanson's earlier symphonies, the Second, or *Romantic* (1930), is the best-known. It was written for the 50th anniversary of the Boston Symphony, which introduced it on Nov. 28, 1930, Koussevitzky conducting (I. Adagio; *Allegro moderato*. II. *Andante con tenerezza*. III. *Allegro con brio*). The composer provides the following analysis: "The first movement begins with an atmospheric introduction in the woodwind . . . The principal theme is announced by four horns with an accompaniment of strings and woodwind . . . A transition leads to a subordinate theme, with the theme itself in the strings and a countersubject in the solo horn . . . The second movement begins with its principal theme announced by the woodwind with a sustained string accompaniment. An interlude in the brass, taken from the introduction of the first movement and interrupted by florid passages in the woodwind, develops into a subordinate theme, which is taken from the horn solo of the first movement. The third movement begins with a vigorous accompaniment figure in strings and woodwind, the principal theme of the movement, reminiscent of the first movement, entering in four horns and later in the basses. The subordinate theme is announced first by cellos and then taken up by the English horn. A brief coda leads to the final fanfare."

The Symphony No. 4 (1943) was the first symphony to win the Pulitzer Prize in music. It was inspired by the death of the composer's father, and introduced in Boston on Dec. 4, 1943, the composer conducting. The four movements bear the titles of sections from the Requiem Mass

(I. *Kyrie—Andante inquieto*. II. *Requies-cat*—Largo. III. *Dies irae*—Presto. IV. *Lux aeternae—Largo pastorale*). In the first movement, the Kyrie theme alternates with dance and song-like sections; a chorale section leads to the coda. The principal subject of the second movement is a scale-like eighth-note theme first heard in the solo bassoon. The third movement is a stormy scherzo, and the finale is partly pastoral and partly turbulent.

The *Sinfonia Sacra*, Hanson's Fifth Symphony (1954), was introduced in Philadelphia on Feb. 22, 1955, Eugene Ormandy conducting. It is in a single movement and interprets the story of the first Easter as recounted in the Gospel According to St. John. But the composer explains that this story is not portrayed programmatically in the music, which tries "to invoke some of the atmosphere of its tragedy and triumph, mysticism and affirmation." The writing is mainly modal, deriving its style and idiom, but never actual material, from Gregorian Chant.

ROY HARRIS. Harris' most popular symphony is the Third (1938), with which he became famous. It was introduced by the Boston Symphony on Feb. 24, 1939, Koussevitzky conducting. Though in a single movement, it has five distinct sections. The first, "Tragic," exploits low string sonorities, the main theme appearing in the violins after a sixty-bar introduction. A flute solo brings on the second section, "Lyric," its extended melody first heard in the ninth bar. "Pastoral" accentuates the woodwind, with several ideas given successively by English horn, oboe, bassoon, and bass clarinet. The fourth part, a fugue, is dramatic, its subject found in the strings. A rhythmic figure leads to the final part, "Dramatic—Tragic," in which the first main theme returns.

Harris' Fifth Symphony (1942)—introduced in Boston on Feb. 26, 1943, Koussevitzky conducting—consists of a Prelude, Chorale, and Fugue. The Prelude is rhythmic and forceful, of a martial character; its main theme sounds like a bugle call. The Chorale, on the other hand, is lyrical with an effective middle

section, Maestoso, for violins. The symphony is concluded with a double fugue.

The Symphony No. 7 (1951) was introduced in its revised and definitive version in Copenhagen on Sept. 15, 1955, Eugene Ormandy conducting. In a single movement, this work has been described by its composer as a "dance symphony." "In another sense," he goes on to explain, "it is a study in harmonic and melodic rhythmic variation. The first half consists of a passacaglia and five variations. The second half is divided into three sections—contrapuntal variations in asymmetrical rhythms . . . and in symmetrical meter. . . . A final variation of the rhythmic materials of the work serves as a coda."

HAYDN. Just how far the symphony progressed in Haydn's time, and largely through his efforts, can best be assessed by comparing his first symphonies with his last. Haydn's earliest works in this form (1759-1760) are actually serenades or divertimentos, made up of several short movements. The scoring is lean (usually strings and two horns, sometimes supplemented by two oboes). His three symphonies, Nos. 6 (D major), 7 (C major), and 8 (G major), written in 1761 are subtitled *Le Matin* (*Morning*), *Le Midi* (*Afternoon*), and *Le Soir* (*Evening*), since they were intended to depict different times of the day. These are actually more like concerti grossi than symphonies, limited in their instrumentation and scope.

In or about 1770, Haydn began writing works that can be considered symphonies, since for the first time they started to conform to the Classical concept of that form. The earliest of these Haydn symphonies still regularly performed is the Symphony No. 45 in F-sharp minor, called the *Farewell* (*Abschiedssymphonie*), written in 1772, and scored for two oboes, two horns, a bassoon, and strings (I. *Allegro assai*. II. *Adagio*. III. *Menuetto*. IV. *Presto*; *Adagio*). The name "Farewell" comes from the finale, in which the instruments gradually drop out one by one until only two solo violins are left. Legend has it that this movement was written as a hint to Haydn's employer, Prince Esterházy, that the annual vacation for the musicians was long overdue. Legend further states that when the symphony was first performed for the Prince, each musician blew out the candle on his music stand and slipped away silently, taking with him his music and his instrument. According to one of Haydn's friends, the composer wrote the *Farewell Symphony* to dissuade Esterházy from his plan to disband the court orchestra. The clarity of the sonata form in the first movement; the expressive nature of the slow movement; the occasional rhythmic irregularities of the minuet; and the already described original format of the conclusion of the finale all set the *Farewell Symphony* sharply apart from earlier Haydn symphonies.

In 1785 and 1786 Haydn wrote a set of six symphonies, Nos. 82 through 87, for the Concerts de la Loge Olympique in Paris. These works are consequently known as the *Paris Symphonies*. Symphony No. 82 in C major is called *The Bear* (*L'Ours*) because the principal theme of the finale is a bagpipe melody with growling, bearlike bass notes. This work is of special interest for its first movement, in which the abundant thematic development betrays Haydn's growing power in varying and extending his melodic material. Symphony No. 83 in G minor is *The Hen* (*La Poule*), whose cackling appears in the finale in repeated notes in the oboe against a decorated tune in the first violins. In this symphony the dramatic slow movement is particularly striking. Symphony No. 85 in B-flat major was a favorite of Queen Marie Antoinette, which is why it is sometimes referred to as *The Queen* (*La Reine*). The slow movement here consists of a charming set of variations on a delightful French melody, *La gentille et jeune Lisette*.

Symphony No. 88 in G major, written about 1787, is one of Haydn's most often performed symphonies (I. Adagio; Allegro. II. Largo. III. Menuetto. IV. *Allegro con spirito*). As in many of Haydn's earlier symphonies, a slow introduction prefaces the fast first movement. The second movement is a song first heard in cellos and oboes; contrast comes midway with loud chords for the orchestra. The minuet has a peasant-like vitality, its trio actually sounding like an Austrian folk dance, whose repeated fifths in the bass make us think of a hurdy-gurdy. Like the minuet, the finale, which is in rondo form, has the vigor and vitality of a peasant dance.

The Symphony No. 92 in G major is called the *Oxford* because it was first performed at Oxford University in July of 1791, when an honorary degree was conferred on Haydn. But the symphony was not written for this occasion. The one Haydn actually wrote (it has never been identified) proved too difficult for performance and an earlier work he had written for Paris in or about 1788 was substituted. The *Oxford Symphony* is deservedly famous (I. *Allegro spiritoso*. II. Adagio. III. Menuetto. IV. Presto). The first movement begins with a slow twenty-bar introduction mainly for strings, after which the first theme is hesitantly presented by the strings. The second subject is more reflective, coming in the strings after the first theme has been amplified. The slow movement is in three-part song form, the first and third sections consisting of a lyrical idea for strings, while the middle part is stormy. The minuet and the finale both have the inviting robustness and at times gaiety of Austrian peasant music.

For his two visits to London, in 1791 and 1794, Haydn wrote two sets of six symphonies each—the *London* or *Salomon Symphonies*, the "Salomon," of course, referring to the impresario who had commissioned them. They are the crown of Haydn's symphonic output, among the greatest symphonies produced before Beethoven. Here Haydn takes a giant step in advancing both the structure and the style of symphonic writing. His instrumentation is richer and more varied, and so is his melodic and harmonic material. The elaboration of thematic subjects is more imaginative than heretofore, and at times even daring. These symphonies, moreover, are filled with a maturity of thought and wisdom of experience we do not often encounter in earlier Haydn symphonies.

Symphony No. 94 in G major has been described as the *Surprise Symphony,* or the symphony *Mit dem Paukenschlag* ("with the timpani stroke"). In the second movement a gentle melody suddenly ends in an abrupt loud chord for full orchestra. The story goes that Haydn introduced this loud chord to awaken his audience who, he felt, habitually fell asleep during slow movements. The first movement opens with a slow introduction, and the main body consists of two gay themes, both for the strings. The second movement has the simple little tune that is climaxed by the "surprise" chord. This melody undergoes five variations. The minuet is formal in style and content, and the finale is a rondo in a vivacious mood (I. *Adagio cantabile; Vivace assai.* II. Andante. III. Menuetto. IV. *Allegro di molto*).

Symphony No. 100 in G major uses bugle calls and percussion instruments, like the drum, cymbals, and triangle, associated in the 18th century with military music. For this reason it is known as the *Military* (I. Adagio; Allegro. II. Allegretto. III. Menuetto. IV. Presto). The percussion can be found midway in the second movement which, otherwise, is dominated by a graceful little melody for first violins and flute. There is nothing particularly martial about this melody, nor for that matter about the other three charming movements.

Symphony No. 101 in D major is the *Clock,* a name derived from the second movement where a soaring melody for strings is set against a staccato accompaniment, whose even, steady rhythm in bassoons and plucked strings sounds like the ticking of a clock. The first movement opens gravely before the entrance of the vivacious first theme. The minuet has special harmonic interest in the trio, where a drone bass gives the impression of dissonance. The opening section of the bright-faced finale becomes the material for a fugue with which the symphony ends (I. Adagio; Presto. II. Andante. III. Allegretto. IV. Vivace).

Symphony No. 103 in E-flat major has for its opening bar a sustained roll in the timpani which recurs later in the movement with amusing effect. This timpani roll has given the symphony its nickname: the *Drum Roll,* or the symphony *Mit dem Paukenwirbel* ("with the drum roll"). The second movement is a theme and variations; the third is a vigorous minuet; and the finale has for its main theme a melody that resembles a Hungarian gypsy dance tune (I. *Allegro con spirito.* II. Andante. III. Menuetto. IV. *Allegro con spirito*).

These are the other memorable works in the two sets of *London Symphonies:* No. 93 in D major; No. 95, C minor; No. 96, D major, known as *The Miracle;* No. 97, C major; No. 98, B-flat major; No. 99, E-flat major; No. 102, B-flat major; No. 104, D major, specifically referred to as the *London Symphony* for a reason never adequately explained.

The Symphony No. 96 is called *The Miracle* because (so goes the story) during the première of the work a chandelier fell from the ceiling of the concert hall, with nobody getting hurt. However, this incident occurred not during the première of this symphony but during that of Symphony No. 102, and no one seems to know why "miracle" should have applied to the earlier work.

Other Haydn symphonies besides those described above have interesting nicknames, though the reasons for these sobriquets are not always clear. Symphony No. 22 in E-flat major is *The Philosopher* (*Der Philosoph*), possibly because of a solemn passage for horns and English horn in the first movement. No. 26 in D minor is known as the *Lamentation.* No. 31 in D major is the *Horn Call* (*Mit dem Hornsignal*) because of the opening theme of the first movement. No. 43 in E-flat major is the *Mercury* (*Merkur*), and No. 44 in E minor, the *Tragic* (*Trauersymphonie*). No. 48 in C major is the *Maria Theresa,* probably owing to its première playing at the Esterházy palace in 1773 during the visit there of the Queen. The intensity of expression in the second movement of No. 49 in F minor earned for it the name of *The Passion* (*La Passione*). No. 53 in D major is *The Imperial* (*L'Impériale*). No. 55 in E-flat major is *The Schoolmaster* (*Der Schulmeister*), possibly because of its slow movement, whose precise and stately tread may resemble the dignified footsteps of a teacher. No. 59 in A major is *The Fire* (*Feuersymphonie*), perhaps because it had been previously used as an overture to a play entitled *The Conflagration*. No. 69 in C major is the *Laudon Symphony* after Field Marshal von Laudon. No. 73 in D major is *The Chase* (*La Chasse*) for its finale, in which a hunting theme for horns and oboes is prominent.

For many years the *Toy Symphony*—a little work in C major for toy instruments—was attributed to Haydn. But it has since proved to be the work of either Leopold Mozart (father of Wolfgang Amadeus) or Michael Haydn (brother of Joseph). *See: Toy Symphony.*

HINDEMITH. Paul Hindemith's Symphony in E-flat major (1940) was introduced in Minneapolis on Nov. 21, 1941, Dimitri Mitropoulos conducting (I. *Sehr lebhaft*. II. *Sehr langsam*. III. *Lebhaft*. IV. *Maessig schnell*). In the first movement there are two main subjects: a loud, rhythmic idea for brass, and a lyrical theme for the woodwind against string pizzicatos. The second of these receives prominent treatment in the coda. The second movement opens with a rhythmic figure in the timpani which soon serves as a background for a melody in English horn, clarinet, and trumpet. The second principal theme of the movement is given by the oboe against chords in the violins. A light scherzo movement precedes the finale, the latter entering without pause. Its main theme is heard in the violins, and a subsidiary theme in the brass. Midway in the movement an intermezzo for flute and piccolo is interpolated.

Symphonia Serena came six years later, commissioned by the Dallas Symphony, which introduced it on Feb. 2, 1947, Antal Dorati conducting (I. *Moderately Fast*. II. *Geschwindmarsch* by Beethoven, *Paraphrase*. III. *Colloquy*. IV. *Gay*). The opening theme of the first movement is a strong subject made up of descending fifths and ascending fourths. Two other themes follow, one marked *grazioso*, and the other in a more sober mood. The second movement utilizes a little march Beethoven had written in 1809-1810. In the third movement the string orchestra is

divided into two groups, the first presenting a slow and eloquent melody, and the other a livelier idea in pizzicato. A recitative-like section for two solo violins, one playing backstage, serves as a transition between the two sections. A brief fanfare introduces the finale, in which appear five themes and their developments. There is also a vigorous restatement of the main subject of the first movement, and some new material in the coda. The coda ends with the fanfare subject that opened the movement.

See also: Harmonie der Welt, Die; Mathis der Maler.

HONEGGER. Honegger's second symphony, the Symphony for Strings, is one of the composer's most personal and deeply felt compositions. It reflects the emotional storms and stresses through which he passed during the turbulent years of World War II. He wrote it in 1941 in Paris, while the Nazis were occupying the city. It was first performed in Basel, Switzerland, on May 23, 1942, Paul Sacher conducting (I. *Molto moderato;* Allegro. II. *Adagio mesto*. III. *Vivace non troppo*). The first movement opens in a despairing mood with an ostinato figure for violas; this subject recurs throughout the movement. Gloom softens into gentle sadness with a lyrical passage for first violins. As the movement develops, it is gloom rather than subdued sadness which gains the ascendency in strident dissonances and complex rhythms. The movement ends, however, with a quiet review of the first theme. The second movement is a passacaglia with eight variations on a ground-bass subject heard in the cellos in the first eight bars. Once again the music passes from restrained sorrow to uninhibited grief. But optimism is injected into the finale, almost as an omen of better days to come. This faith in the future rings out clear and loud in the chorale for first violins and a single trumpet, with which the symphony ends.

The Symphony No. 3, *Liturgique* (1946), was first performed in Zurich on Aug. 17, 1946, Charles Munch conducting. The three movements have Latin subtitles: I. *Allegro marcato—Dies irae;* II. Adagio—*De profundis clamavi;* III.

Andante con moto—Dona nobis pacem.
To Charles Munch this symphony "poses
the problem of humanity vis-à-vis God,"
and speaks of man's revolt against, and
finally his submission to, a higher will.
The Symphony No. 4 (1946) received
its première in Basel, Switzerland, on
Jan. 21, 1947, Paul Sacher conducting.
It is subtitled *Deliciae basilienses* (*Basel
Delights*), since it makes use of old popular songs from Basel (I. *Lento misterioso.* II. *Larghetto.* III. *Allegro*). The
first movement was described by the composer as an expression of a "state of
spirit . . . In the midst of odious and
stupid conditions of life . . . it raises
the hope of an escape from such atmosphere as, for instance, to spend a summer in Switzerland surrounded by affectionate friends." In the slow movement
the Basel song, *Z'Basel an mim Rhi,* appears in its entirety in the horn. The finale contains structural elements of the
rondo and the passacaglia and fugue, and
is in a polyphonic style. Once again a
Basel song is quoted, this time *Basler
Morgenstreich* as a stretto over the principal theme. The slow melody of the second movement is reviewed. A fife fanfare and a coda with six bars of a hardly
audible chorale bring the symphony to
its conclusion.

D'INDY. Vincent d'Indy's *Symphony on
a French Mountain Song* (*Symphonie
cévenole*) makes use of a mountain air
originating in the Cevennes mountain region of France. Scored for piano and
orchestra, this symphony, op. 25 (1886),
was introduced in Paris on March 20,
1887 (I. *Assez lent; modérément animé.*
II. *Assez modéré mais sans lenteur.* III.
Animé). The pastoral mountain air with
which the first movement opens is in the
English horn, and repeated by a flute.
After the entrance of the piano, a contrasting subject is given by flute, horn,
and harp. Piano and strings present the
mountain air with a slight variation at
the beginning of the second movement.
Later it changes character by becoming
first a fanfare for horns against a drum
roll, and then a tender song for muted
horn. In the finale, the initial phrase of
the mountain air becomes an ostinato figure, the background for a march melody

in unison woodwind. After some enlargement of this episode, the clarinet
appears with a lyrical passage. Several
more variations of the mountain air are
presented before the movement rises
majestically to a sonorous climax.

D'Indy's Symphony No. 2 in B-flat major came eighteen years later, introduced
in Paris by the Lamoureux Orchestra on
Feb. 26, 1904 (I. *Extrèmement lent; Très
vif.* II. *Modérément lent.* III. *Modéré;
Très animé*). D'Indy makes effective use
here of the Franckian cyclical form. The
first movement opens with a slow introduction. A dramatic episode ensues. The
principal thematic material, repeated in
later movements, consists of a four-bar
subject in the introduction; a somber melody for cellos and double basses; and a
phrase for flute built from an ascending
seventh. The second movement is an extended song for orchestra, its second
half resembling a funeral march. A folk
melody brings on the last movement, and
is succeeded by an introduction, fugue,
and finale.

IVES. Charles Ives wrote four symphonies, the first in 1896, and the last between 1910 and 1916. The most famous
is the Third (1904), performed for the
first time forty years after its composition
in New York City on April 5, 1946, Lou
Harrison conducting. It was acclaimed
by the critics, received the Pulitzer Prize
in music and the award of the New York
Music Critics Circle. The work was inspired by camp meetings once popular in
Danbury, Conn. Fragments of old New
England hymns are used (I. *Andante
maestoso.* II. *Largo.* III. *Allegro*). In the
first movement, *O For a Thousand
Tongues* receives fugal treatment. The
composer explains that the slow movement describes a game played by children at a camp meeting while their elders
listen to the Holy Word. In the finale,
another old hymn tune, *Just Am I,* is the
principal subject. Stylistically, the symphony is remarkable for its use of cross
rhythms, unusual progressions, and unorthodox tonalities long before it became
a fashion to do so in *avant-garde* musical
circles.

KABALEVSKY. Dmitri Kabalevsky's Symphony No. 2, op. 19 (1934), is one of

his most frequently performed symphonic works. It was introduced in Moscow on Dec. 25, 1934, Albert Coates conducting. The composer intended this work to reflect Soviet ideology through a description of man's salvation by helping to reconstruct society (I. *Allegro quasi presto.* II. *Andante non troppo.* III. *Prestissimo; Scherzando; Molto agitato;* Allegro). The powerful first movement tells of man's triumph in building a new society. The main material is a strong subject for clarinet, and a lyrical episode also for the clarinet. A soft passage for flute opens the second movement. This serene music—dominated by a D-flat major melody heard now in the orchestra, now in the solo trombone, and now in the clarinet—tells of the peace man finds by having achieved his mission. But there is a feeling of triumph as well, expressed in a turbulent finale which begins as a scherzo with a slight staccato subject for two clarinets and grows into a powerful rhythmic finale. Among the melodic ideas used here is the second theme of the first movement, which is recruited to provide the symphony with a brilliant conclusion.

KALINNIKOV. The Symphony No. 1 in G minor by Vassili Kalinnikov is the only work by the composer to survive him. It was written in 1894 and was introduced in Kiev on Feb. 20, 1897. The work is melodious and rich with national colors and rhythms (I. *Allegro moderato.* II. *Andante commodamente.* III. *Allegro non troppo.* IV. *Allegro moderato*). In the first movement, the main subject appears at once in the strings; the second theme is later presented by horns, violas, and cellos against a syncopated figure in flutes and clarinets and pizzicato chords in violins. Towards the end of the development the first measures of the first theme receive fugal treatment. This first theme is also prominent in the coda, reappearing in the oboe and after that in the full orchestra. The lyrical second movement highlights a melody in English horn and violas after eleven introductory bars; there is also a secondary melody in the oboe to an accompaniment of strings and harp. The scherzo opens vigorously, and is contrasted by a placid trio. The principal material of the finale

consists of two vital themes, one for strings, and the other for orchestra. Themes from earlier movements play an important role in the finale, greatest attention being paid to the first main melody of the second movement, with which the symphony ends.

LISZT. *A Faust Symphony* "in three character pictures" (1854-1857) was introduced in Weimar on Sept. 15, 1857, the composer conducting. The three movements are tonal portraits of the three main characters of the epic by Goethe on which it is based: I. Faust (Allegro); II. Marguerite (Andante); III. Mephistopheles (Scherzo). The first movement has a somber opening as Faust contemplates his lost youth. The music brightens; an energetic transitional section in strings and woodwinds brings on the main section. Two principal themes are presented here, the first in horns and clarinets, and the second in the trumpet. Many climaxes are traversed before the movement ends in the same melancholy vein in which it opened. The second movement is a tender song for oboe against arpeggio figures in a solo viola. A second theme in the woodwind speaks of Marguerite's love for Faust. Her growing passion is reflected in ardent music for the strings. Towards the end, the trumpet subject of the first movement is recalled to bring up the image of Faust. The finale is music with ironic overtones. Motifs that appeared in earlier movements are burlesqued. Solemn strains of the organ bring on a male chorus which comments on the vanity of life in an unaccompanied passage. A solo tenor recalls the melody of the second movement, then the symphony ends on a note of triumph.

MAHLER. Of Mahler's nine symphonies (a tenth was never completed), the most frequently performed are the first, second, fourth, fifth, and ninth. The Symphony No. 1 in D major (1888) was introduced in Budapest on Nov. 20, 1889, the composer conducting. At that time the work was described as a "symphonic poem in two parts." When Mahler again conducted the work in 1894 he had the symphony designated as the *Titan* and explained that it had been inspired by a novel by Jean Paul Richter. On that occasion Mahler also provided a program which has served the music since that time. Of the five movements, the first three were grouped under the heading of Days of Youth—Youth, Flowers and Thorns; the last two, under *Commedia umana*.

The first movement (*Langsam*) carries the following heading: "Spring without end. The Introduction represents the awakening of Nature at early dawn." A long introduction is punctuated by the sound of cuckoos. An ascending passage in the basses leads to a main section whose principal theme is a quiet melody for cellos and double basses used by Mahler for the second song of his cycle *Lieder eines fahrenden Gesellen*. A secondary subject appears in the horns and is repeated by the cellos. The second movement, though given by Mahler at the première of the symphony and later, is now never played. Instead we proceed to the third movement, a scherzo entitled *Full Sail* (*Kraeftig bewegt*), a laendler for woodwind. The slow movement that follows is a funeral march touched with irony and entitled *Stranded: A Funeral March à la Callot* (*Feierlich und gemessen*). The funeral melody (a burlesque of the famous *Frère Jacques* tune) is given canonically, and a new section highlights a sensual melody for first violins. The finale, *Dall' Inferno al Paradiso* (*Stuermisch bewegt*) is the tempestuous outcry of a wounded heart, turbulent music in which the thematic material of the first movement is recalled with intensity. The symphony ends triumphantly with a stately subject for seven horns.

The Symphony No. 2 in C minor (1894), the *Resurrection*, requires soprano and alto solos and a chorus as well as the orchestra. The première of the entire symphony took place in Berlin on Dec. 13, 1895, the composer conducting. This work has been described as a tonal allegory of the life of man. In providing a clue to the meaning of his music, the composer wrote: "I have called the first movement *Celebration of the Dead*. It is the Hero of my first symphony whom I bear to the grave. Immediately arise the great questions: Why have you lived? Why have you suffered? Has it all been only a huge, frightful joke? . . . The reply I give in my last movement." In the first movement (*Allegro maestoso*), the problems of life are posed by the basses with an agitated theme that passes on to the woodwind, and after that to the full orchestra. At least a partial optimistic answer is provided by a gentle melody for horn and strings. But the doubts and questions refuse to be silenced as the music plunges into a Herculean struggle. The rhythm of a funeral march is provocatively suggested, leading to a funeral-like chorale. The struggle is finally resolved, as earlier thematic material is worked out and the mood changes from pessimism and struggle to victory. The vehemence of the first movement is succeeded by the charm and grace of the second (*Andante moderato*), its principal subject a laendler-like tune for strings. The timpani usher in the third and fourth movements, played together (*In ruhig fliessender Bewegung*, and *Urlicht—Sehr feierlich, aber schlicht; Choralmaessig*). These are also light interludes reflecting the gayer aspects of life. In the fourth movement the contralto is heard in *Oh, Little Red Rose*, a song based on a text from *Des Knaben Wunderhorn*, an anthology of old German poetry. The finale also enters without a break; it is entitled *The Great Summons*. Like the preceding movement it recruits the human voice—this time a soprano and chorus join the contralto. The text, *The Resurrection*, is by Klopstock, with additional verses by the composer. The music begins violently. Soft-sounding horns then announce the approach of Judgment Day. After the funeral-like chorale of the first movement is recalled, the winds introduce the Resurrection theme which is soon amplified into a grandiose statement for full orchestra. Mighty funeral music follows, and after that radiant music as if from another world. The horns of the Apocalypse announce the voices of saints and heavenly spirits: "You will arise again, My Dust, after a short repose." From then on the music grows increasingly exultant, increasingly triumphant, until a shattering climax erupts in the full orchestra. Tolling bells, and the peal of an organ, join

to bring the symphony to a majestic end.
The Symphony No. 4 in G major
(1900) is one of Mahler's shortest, sim-
plest, most lyrical, and most optimistic
symphonies. Subtitled *Ode to Heavenly
Joy,* it was introduced in Munich on Nov.
25, 1901, Felix Weingartner conducting
(I. *Bedaechtig.* II. *In gemaechlicher Bewegung, ohne Hast.* III. *Ruhevoll.* IV.
Sehr behaglich). The first two movements
are good-humored and easygoing. The
themes are all light, vivacious, at times
droll. The second movement is a scherzo
which features a violin solo that injects
an intriguing air of mystery into the
otherwise gay proceedings. The slow
movement has an ecclesiastical character.
A soprano solo is heard in the finale in
music that sounds like a Bavarian folksong, its lyric coming from *Des Knaben
Wunderhorn:* "The delights of heaven
we're enjoying."

The Symphony No. 5 in C-sharp minor
(1902) is sometimes described as *The
Giant* because of the vastness of its dimensions and its ambitious orchestration.
Its première took place in Cologne on
Oct. 18, 1904, the composer conducting.
There are five movements (divided into
three sections), the most striking being
the first (*Trauermarsch*), mighty funeral
music preceded by an extended fanfare,
and the fourth (Adagietto), a gentle song
for strings.

Mahler's symphonic swan song, the
Symphony No. 9 in D minor (1909), has
been described as a renunciation of life.
It is Mahler's farewell, music in which
the composer has resolved his own doubts
and struggles into victory and finally
found peace of spirit. The symphony was
introduced in Vienna on June 26, 1912,
Bruno Walter conducting. The opening
movement (*Andante commodo*) offers
two contrasting themes, the first, peaceful, appearing in the sixth bar; the second, coming twenty bars later, passionate
and agitated, and sharply accentuated by
trumpet chords. A subsidiary idea injects
a funereal mood with a marchlike subject. The second movement (*Im Tempo
eines gemaechlichen Laendlers*) has the
style of an Austrian peasant dance, but
with sardonic, and at times even bitter,
accents. The third movement (*Rondo

Burleske*) is still in an ironic vein, and
once again consists of light dance music.
Midway a chorale section points up the
solemn dedication of the artist, but this
feeling is soon dispelled by mockery. The
symphony ends as it began, in a solemn
mood (Adagio). This is one of Mahler's
most eloquent and deeply moving pages,
the voice of an artist who has finally
found peace of heart and spirit. The two
opening agitated bars give us a last reminder of earlier struggles. But the radiant music of the Adagio soon begins to
unfold. A second section interrupts the
serenity with passionate outbursts. But
the symphony ends in a mood of quiet
resignation and peace which is beyond
pleasure or pain.

MENDELSSOHN. Though Mendelssohn's
Symphony in C minor, op. 11 (1824), is
listed as No. 1, it is not actually his first
symphony. He had previously completed
a dozen symphonies for string orchestra
which are *juvenilia* and remain unlisted.
Of the listed five symphonies, only the
last three are frequently performed.

The Symphony No. 3 in A minor, op.
56 (1842), is known as the *Scotch,* its
inspiration coming from a visit paid Scotland by the composer. Some of its material is based on Scottish music, and several of its pages evoke Scottish scenes
and backgrounds. This is the last symphony Mendelssohn wrote—the symphonies being numbered according to
their dates of publication rather than
composition. It was introduced in Leipzig, under the composer's direction, on
March 3, 1842 (I. *Andante con moto;
Allegro un poco agitato.* II. *Vivace non
troppo.* III. Adagio. IV. *Allegro vivacissimo; Allegro maestoso assai*). The published score specifies that the symphony
be played without interruption. The first
movement opens with an extended introduction that conjures up a melancholy
Scottish scene; the principal theme is
heard in wind instruments and low
strings. The main body of the movement
begins with a vigorous subject for strings
and clarinet which is subsequently contrasted by an elegiac song for strings.
The Scherzo presents a melody with a
Scottish character for woodwind and
brass; a later melody, also Scottish in feel-

ing, appears in the clarinet. The slow movement alternates between an introspective mood and vigorous march-like music. In the finale, one is once more reminded of Scotland, particularly by the first theme, a brilliant Scottish tune for violins against staccato strings, and by the third subject, a martial melody for full orchestra.

The Symphony No. 4 in A major, op. 90 (1883), is named the *Italian,* once again inspired by a journey. But unlike the *Scotch,* this symphony has little beyond its finale to justify its sobriquet. It was introduced in London on Feb. 8, 1831, the composer conducting (I. *Allegro vivace.* II. *Andante con moto.* III. *Con moto moderato.* IV. *Presto*). The symphony opens vivaciously with a buoyant subject for violins against horns and woodwinds. The second theme, in a more leisurely pace, is brought in by an ascending violin passage, and is assigned to clarinets and bassoons. There is still a third subject, which is developed fugally. The second movement has been described by some commentators as a pilgrims' march. The main melody is presented by oboe, bassoons, and violas, and a subsidiary one by the clarinet. The first section of the Scherzo is dominated by a delicate subject for first violins; the trio opens with a gentle melody for bassoons and horns. It is only in the finale that the Italian character of the symphony is evident. This movement is in the leaping rhythm of an Italian folk dance, the saltarello, heard in woodwinds and strings after a six-bar introduction. The second theme, in violins, is also in the saltarello rhythm.

The Symphony No. 5 in D major, op. 107 (1830)—the *Reformation*—was written to commemorate the tercentenary of the creed of the Lutheran Church, the Augsburg Confession. It was introduced in Berlin on the anniversary of that event, on June 25, 1830, the composer conducting (I. Andante; *Allegro con fuoco.* II. *Allegro vivace.* III. Andante; *Andante con moto.* IV. *Allegro vivace; Allegro maestoso*). In keeping with the religious character of this symphony, the composer interpolates in the first movement a celebrated passage of liturgical

music, the "Dresden Amen"; this melody is projected by the strings soon after the appearance of the movement's first, stately theme in brass and woodwind. The second movement is a formal scherzo, though with the lightness of touch and mobility with which the composer generally endowed such a movement. In the third movement, the religious character of the symphony returns in a second liturgical quotation, this time of the Lutheran chorale, *Ein' feste Burg,* first heard in flutes. It grows in sonority in the development section, and in the concluding part of the movement becomes a majestic utterance in which the brasses join. The finale enters without pause. This movement is marked by skilful contrapuntal writing in which the Lutheran chorale sometimes serves as a background. The chorale is restated several times in the movement, and is presented by the full orchestra to bring the symphony to its conclusion.

MIASKOVSKY. Nikolai Miaskovsky was one of the most prolific composers of symphonies in the 20th century. Of his 27 works in this form, the most celebrated is the Twenty-first in F-sharp minor, op. 51 (1940). It was introduced in Moscow on Nov. 16, 1940, Nikolai Golovanov conducting; it received the Stalin Prize. It is a short work in a single movement, opening with a contemplative introduction in which the symphony's principal material is presented, the most important being a subject for the clarinet. The main section of the symphony develops these ideas with dramatic changes of mood and tempo. A fugal section generates a feeling of power and exultation; but this soon makes way for a return of the more introspective mood with which the symphony had opened.

MILHAUD. Darius Milhaud's first symphony came comparatively late in his career, and when he was at the height of his creative powers. It was completed in 1939, and was introduced in Chicago on Oct. 17, 1940, the composer conducting. His second symphony was written five years later on a commission from the Koussevitzky Foundation and was introduced in Boston on Dec. 20, 1946, the composer conducting. Like the first symphony, the second is for the most part placid music, but unlike the first it is also touched by melancholy and at times agitation (I. *Paisable.* II. *Mystérieux.* III. *Douleureux.* IV. *Avec sérénité.* V. *Alleluia*). In the first movement, the first theme is a gentle subject heard at once in piccolo and flute; a more virile idea is later presented by the trumpet. The second movement is scherzo-like; in it the higher registers of the orchestra—harmonics in the violins, trills in flute and muted trumpet—are exploited with extraordinary effect. Tragedy predominates in the third movement, particularly in a dramatic melody for the oboe. The fourth movement returns to the serenity of the first. The finale opens with a subject for full orchestra, later made the basis of a monumental fugue.

Milhaud wrote the Symphony No. 4 in 1947 on a commission from the French government to celebrate the centenary of the 1848 revolution in France; its first performance took place over the French Radio in Paris on May 20, 1948, the composer conducting. The first movement, *Insurrection* (*Animé*), is mainly martial in character, dramatically scored for brass and percussion. The second, *To the Dead of the Republic* (*Lent*), is a beautiful threnody. *The Peaceful Joys of Liberty Regained* (*Modérément animé*) which follows expresses the joy that comes with the triumph of liberty; the heart of this section is a fugue. The symphony ends with *Commemoration, 1948* (*Animé*), which reverts to the martial character, and to some of the thematic material, of the first movement.

Symphony No. 6 (1955) was written for the 75th anniversary of the Boston Symphony, which introduced it on Oct. 7, 1955, Charles Munch conducting (I. *Calme et tendre.* II. *Tumultueux.* III. *Lent et doux.* IV. *Joyeux et robuste*). The two principal subjects of the first movement appear respectively in the strings and in a fuller orchestra. The second movement is mostly vivacious, but the ending has a subdued character almost as if to set the stage for the poignant and lyrical third movement, which is in three-part song form. A spirited theme for full orchestra provides the finale with an en-

ergetic momentum which continues till the end of the symphony.

MOZART. Mozart wrote some 50 symphonies, the first when he was eight, and the last three just before his death. Most of them are not often heard, but there is hardly one of them—beginning with No. 25 in G minor, K. 183 (1773)—that is not a reservoir of infectious melodies and characterized by beautiful construction, vivacity of spirit, freshness of ideas, enchanting moods, and the best possible taste. These less familiar symphonies may lack the emotional depth and intensity of expression found in the last three masterworks by Mozart in this form, but they are always a delight to hear. They include No. 29 in A major, K. 201 (1774); No. 31, in D major, K. 297 (1778), known as the *Paris* because it was written in a Parisian style on commission from the Concert Spirituel in Paris; No. 34 in C major, K. 338 (1780); No. 36 in C major, K. 425 (1783), known as the *Linz,* since it was written for a concert given in that Austrian city; No. 38 in D major, K. 504 (1786), the *Prague,* written for a concert conducted by the composer in the Bohemian capital.

The earliest Mozart symphony frequently heard on present-day orchestral programs is No. 35 in D major, K. 385 (1782). This is the so-called *Haffner Symphony* (not to be confused with the *Haffner Serenade*), written on order for a party at the home of Burgomaster Sigmund Haffner of Salzburg, probably to honor the ennoblement of the younger Sigmund (I. *Allegro con spirito.* II. Andante. III. Menuetto. IV. Presto). An unusual feature of the first movement, for Mozart, is the use of a single theme, a virile subject for orchestra; where a second theme would ordinarily appear, this theme is repeated in a different key. The second movement consists of a pastoral melody for first violins. There is also a pastoral quality to the trio of the graceful Minuet that follows. Mozart specified that the finale be played as quickly as possible. Both principal subjects are heard in the strings; and the entire movement proceeds with a breathless momentum.

Mozart's last three symphonies (1788)

are his greatest, the most advanced stage of structure, thematic development, and emotional expression the symphonic form had thus far realized.

Symphony No. 39 in E-flat major, K. 543, came first (I. Adagio; Allegro. II. Andante. III. Menuetto. IV. Allegro). The first movement opens with a slow and stately introduction in which new horizons are opened through daring dissonances and harmonic progressions. The main, Allegro section has two graceful themes, the first in the violins, the second shared by violins and clarinets. Two equally beautiful and graceful melodies form the body of the slow movement, and both are for strings. The Minuet theme is virile, but finds contrast in a gentle subject for the clarinet in the trio. A vivacious theme for the first violins in the finale leads to another brisk and jovial subject also for first violins.

The Symphony No. 40 in G minor, K. 550, came next (I. *Allegro molto.* II. Andante. III. Menuetto. IV. *Allegro assai*). The opening movement unfolds for us a vista of incomparable beauty with one of the most eloquent melodies found even in Mozart. This high plane is maintained with a second beautiful theme, divided between oboe and clarinet. A development along expansive lines is rich in dramatic interest and moving for its depth of feeling. The Andante is a song that begins with a melody presented imitatively by the strings, and continues with an affecting lyrical idea for the strings. The Minuet combines a vigorous dance melody in the first section with a tender discourse between strings and woodwinds in the trio. The finale is spirited in feeling, opening with a vital subject in the violins. Momentarily the pace is relaxed with a tender melody in first violins. The movement ends in the same breathless pace with which it began.

The last of this trio of symphonic masterworks produced in a single year is No. 41 in C major, K. 551, known as the *Jupiter,* perhaps because of the Jovian strength and grandeur of so many of its pages. In any event, the name "Jupiter" was coined not by the composer but probably by the English composer-pianist J. B. Cramer (I. *Allegro vivace.* II. An-

dante cantabile. III. Allegretto. IV. *Allegro molto*). The first movement opens with powerful slashing chords to which the strings reply delicately. The strength of these opening bars prevails throughout the movement, even though the second principal theme is a light and graceful air for strings. The development is spacious, prominence being given to the opening triplet figures. The recapitulation is virtually a restatement of the exposition but with effective key changes. Two beautiful melodies appear in the second movement, the first in muted strings, and the second in oboes. The Minuet follows a traditional pattern, with the violins presenting a flowing melody that is the basis of the main section, and the winds and strings sharing the subject of the trio. The finale, in sonata form, gives prominence to fugal writing, here achieved with consummate polyphonic skill. A sensitive subject is given by the violins, the first four notes constituting a motif Mozart had used in several other works. After this subject is taken over by the full orchestra, it is repeated fugally. A second theme is then presented by strings and woodwinds, after which comes the development section in which the fugal style achieves dramatic intensity and strength.

PISTON. Walter Piston's Symphony No. 3 (1947) is the composer's most important achievement in the symphonic form. It was introduced in Boston on Jan. 9, 1948, Koussevitzky conducting. It later received the Pulitzer Prize in music and the Hornblitt Award (I. Andantino. II. Allegro. III. Adagio. IV. Allegro). The first movement is constructed from three themes: the first, for oboe; the second, for horn, clarinets, and English horn; the third, quiet chords in the brass. A three-part Scherzo follows, the main theme of the first section stated imitatively by violas and bassoons. The trio has its main theme in the flute accompanied by clarinets and harp. There are four sections in the Adagio. The first is a statement of the main theme by the strings. The second offers a variation of this theme mainly in woodwinds and harp. In the third part, a subject for basses and cellos is built up and carried to a climax; and the fourth recalls the first main theme in its original form. The finale is in the sonata form. The first main theme is presented fugally midway in the first section; the second theme is a march-like subject which, towards the end of the symphony, is developed into a powerful climax by full brass.

Symphony No. 6 (1955) was written in honor of the 75th anniversary of the Boston Symphony, and its première took place in Boston on Nov. 25, 1955, Charles Munch conducting (I. *Fluendo espressivo.* II. *Leggerissimo vivace.* III. *Adagio sereno.* IV. *Allegro energico*). The composer has explained that "the first movement is flowing and expressive, in sonata form; the second, a scherzo, is light and fast; the third, a serene adagio, has theme one played by a solo cello and theme two by flute; and the fourth is an energetic finale with two contrasting themes."

PROKOFIEV. Of Prokofiev's seven symphonies, three have been particularly successful: the first, or *Classical;* the fifth; and the sixth.

The Symphony No. 1 in D major, op. 25 (1917), was an attempt to reconcile the structure and instrumentation, and the simplicity and economy of style, of the Classical symphony of Haydn and Mozart with modern harmonic and melodic idioms. The old and new are so beautifully synthesized that this symphony—appropriately named *Classical*—is a perennial concert favorite. It was introduced in Leningrad on April 21, 1918, the composer conducting (I. Allegro. II. Larghetto. III. *Non troppo allegro.* IV. *Molto vivace*). A lively tune in strings opens the first movement. A brief transition in the flute brings on the second theme in strings against accompanying bassoons; it has characteristic Prokofievian octave leaps. The slow movement is a graceful melody for strings set against a forceful accompaniment. Midway in the movement, woodwinds present a subsidiary idea. The third movement is an old-style gavotte but in a modern idiom. The vigorous dance melody is stated by the strings; a middle section consists of a pastoral musette. A forceful chord brings on the finale. The fleet main theme

is dashingly presented by the strings. Two subsidiary ideas (one for woodwinds, the other for solo flute) do not restrict the rhythmic momentum and athletic drive of the opening subject.

The Symphony No. 5, op. 100 (1944), is much more spacious in design than the *Classical,* and emotionally much more compelling. Written during the grim years of World War II, the music reflects the profound impact that the Nazi invasion of the Soviet Union had upon the composer. The music first speaks of the tragedy of war, then proudly asserts its faith in the future of Russia. The symphony was introduced in Moscow on Jan. 13, 1945, the composer conducting (I. Andante. II. *Allegro marcato.* III. Adagio. IV. *Allegro giocoso*). The work opens gravely, with a slow section developed out of two themes, contrasted rhythmically and emotionally. In the main body of the movement these two themes are worked out with epical breadth; a feeling of exultation is released in the extended coda. A scherzo-like second movement has so strong a feeling of austerity that to some writers it speaks of the horror of the war. The woodwinds share the first main theme, while in the middle section another significant subject appears in the clarinet. The principal melody of the slow movement is presented in the woodwinds in imitation, then taken over by the strings. As the movement develops, the emotional intensity is heightened, and the tragedy deepens; but the middle section interpolates a brief emotional respite. In the finale all gloom is dispelled. A calm melody for divided cellos and basses invokes for the first time an atmosphere filled with peace. A subsidiary theme in the clarinet carries with it a feeling of optimism, and the music sweeps on from animation to an exultant expression of faith in a peaceful future.

The Symphony No. 6, op. 111, came two years after the Fifth, and was introduced in Leningrad on Oct. 11, 1947. This work is more spare in design, more restrained in emotional content, and lighter in texture and mood than the Fifth (I. *Allegro moderato.* II. Largo. III. Vivace). The first principal theme of the first movement is a vital dance melody, and the second is a lyrical passage with a modal character. The music passes from lyricism to austerity, but the austerity gains ascendancy, and in the development section and the transition to the second movement the music becomes turbulent and dramatic. The second movement is brighter in spirit, a songful page abounding in happy lyricism. In the third movement the composer's natural bent for whimsy and satire finds an outlet. The vitality and gaiety are briefly interrupted by a return to the more reflective mood of the first movement, but they cannot be permanently denied. The movement ends with an outburst of energy.

RACHMANINOFF. The Symphony No. 2 in E minor, op. 27 (1907), was introduced in St. Petersburg on Feb. 8, 1908, the composer conducting. It received the Glinka Prize, and became the composer's most often performed symphony (I. Largo; *Allegro moderato*. II. *Allegro molto*. III. Adagio. IV. *Allegro vivace*). The symphony begins with an extended introduction, a deeply emotional section terminated by energetic chords. In the ensuing Allegro, the principal theme appears in lower strings, clarinets, and bassoon. The second main theme later emerges in the winds, is continued by descending strings, and then is worked out dramatically. After a long diminuendo, the first theme returns in a solo violin. This begins the development section, in which much use is made of the first theme. The second movement is in the form of a scherzo. There are two themes in the first section, the first a vigorous statement for horns, and the second a more lyrical passage for the violins. The trio has a martial character, and is mainly scored for brass and percussion. After a return of the first part, an extended fugue carries the movement to a climax. In the slow movement, the violins enter with a plangent melody. There are some subsidiary ideas after that: one for clarinet; another shared by oboes and violins; and a recapitulation of the slow melody from the first-movement introduction, presented contrapuntally with one of the new themes of the Scherzo. A powerful subject for full orchestra opens

the finale. After a diminuendo and descending pizzicatos in the bass, a new theme appears in the winds—a marchlike melody. The powerful first theme now returns, followed by a lyrical octave passage for strings. Now, as if in summation, material from earlier movements are brought back to carry the symphony to a dynamic conclusion.

Thirty years after the Second Symphony, Rachmaninoff completed Symphony No. 3 in A minor, op. 33 (1936); it was introduced in Philadelphia on Nov. 6, 1936, Stokowski conducting (I. *Allegro moderato*. II. *Adagio non troppo*. III. Allegro). The symphony opens with an introspective, slightly melancholy introduction. Then a headstrong melody is presented by oboes and bassoons. A contrasting second subject, in cellos, is both lyrical and expressive. A ten-bar horn theme opens the second movement; this is the preface to a beautiful melody for solo violin against chords in woodwind and brass. This melody becomes more passionate but before the movement ends the original elegiac and serene mood is restored. A fiery onrushing subject for violins and violas sets the dynamic finale into motion. The fiery energy is maintained and carried to an overpowering climax, despite the intercession of a lyrical passage. An extended fugue is then built from a motif of the first theme.

RIMSKY-KORSAKOV. Rimsky-Korsakov's Symphony No. 2, op. 9 (1868, revised 1875), the *Antar*, is a programmatic work based on an Arabian legend of the 6th century. This tale concerns Antar, who, having saved a gazelle from a monster, falls asleep and dreams he is in the palace of the fairy Guel-Nazar. The fairy, who proves to be the gazelle Antar has saved, offers him the three greatest delights of the world. After he has accepted these gifts, Antar awakes. The symphony was introduced in St. Petersburg in January 1876 (I. Largo; *Allegro giocoso*. II. Allegro; *Molto allegro; Allargando*. III. *Allegro risoluto alla marcia*. IV. *Allegretto vivace; Andante amoroso*). The first movement recreates the story of the legend. The next three movements are each devoted to one of the delights of the world: revenge, power, and love. A motto theme describing Antar courses throughout the symphony; it is first heard in the violas in the introduction to the first movement. In this section there also appears the theme of the fairy, in flute and horns. The Antar theme is prominent in the second movement. The third movement is a heroic march, symbolic of the power of an oriental potentate. The principal love theme of the fourth movement is presented by English horn, and has an oriental character.

ROUSSEL. Albert Roussel's fourth and last symphony, op. 53 (1935), is his finest; it was first performed in Paris on Oct. 29, 1935, Albert Wolff conducting (I. Lento; *Allegro con brio*. II. *Lento molto*. III. *Allegro scherzando*. IV. *Allegro molto*). The symphony opens with a seventeen-bar introduction. A phrase in the sixth bar becomes the germ of the first principal idea of the ensuing main section; the second main subject is subsequently heard in the horn. The slow movement is pervaded by an atmosphere of mystery. The strings play a soft subject. The oboe then quotes a passage from the introduction to the first movement. An agitated section follows, but is dissipated by the opening tender theme, now assigned to the clarinet, the second theme of the movement serving as a counterpoint in the bassoon. These subjects are amplified and dramatized before the opening mysterious mood returns. A lively gigue-like subject in violins and cellos is the heart of the third movement. The finale, in rondo form, opens with a theme for oboe against pizzicato strings. The first violins borrow this subject, after which they present a soaring melody of their own. The working out of this material is spirited, and the movement ends with an exultant exclamation of the movement's opening subject by the full orchestra.

SAINT-SAËNS. The Symphony No. 3 in C minor, op. 78 (1886), for orchestra and organ, is the composer's last and most important work in symphonic form. He wrote it for the Royal Philharmonic of London, which introduced it under the composer's direction on May 19, 1886 (I. Adagio; *Allegro moderato; Poco adagio*. II. *Allegro moderato; Presto;*

Maestoso; Allegro). The composer explained that while this work is divided into only two movements, it embraces the four usual movements of the traditional symphony. He goes on to analyze this music as follows: "After an introductory Adagio of a few plaintive measures, the string quartet exposes the initial theme, which is somber and agitated. The first transformation of this theme leads to a second motif, which is distinguished by greater tranquillity. After a short development, in which the two themes are presented simultaneously, the motif appears in a characteristic form, for full orchestra, but only for a short time. A second transformation of the initial theme includes now and then the plaintive notes of the introduction . . . The second movement begins with an energetic phrase which is followed immediately by a . . . transformation of the initial theme of the first movement, more agitated than it was before . . . A new theme is soon heard, grave, austere (trombone, tuba, double basses). After a vague reminiscence of the initial theme of the first movement, a Maestoso announces the approaching triumph of calm and lofty thought. The initial theme of the first movement, wholly transformed, is now exposed by divided strings and piano (four hands), and repeated by the organ with the full strength of the orchestra. A brilliant coda, in which the initial theme by a last transformation takes the form of a violin figure, ends the work."

SCHUBERT. Schubert wrote his first symphony, in D major, when he was only sixteen. The next two symphonies (in B-flat major and D major) came two years after that. In his first three symphonies, the attraction is the abundant lyricism, always fresh and youthful and spontaneous. There is little subtlety of workmanship, and structurally the young Schubert pays strict obeisance to the Classic structure of Haydn. The first symphony in which any depths are plumbed is the Fourth in C minor (1816), subtitled by the composer himself the *Tragic*. If there is any tragedy in this work at all it is in the opening of the first movement (*Adagio molto; Allegro vivace*), somber music that is far removed from the sunny and joyous expression of his first three symphonies. But once this solemn preface is ended by a loud C minor chord in the full orchestra we are again in a happier world of buoyant Schubertian lyricism, but a world that also has a few surprises for us: the unexpected key of A-flat, instead of E-flat, of the second theme, and the unusual tonality of G minor in the coda. The second movement (Andante) is a soulful song, heard in strings which are later joined by the oboe. This is followed by a virile Minuet (*Allegro vivace*), whose main melody has an interesting chromatic structure and novel syncopated rhythm. The finale, in sonata form (Allegro), abounds in delightful melodies and ends with a prolonged coda in the key of C major.

The Symphony No. 5 in B-flat major (1816) has the youthful ardor and vitality of Schubert's first three symphonies. One delightful melody follows another in profusion, and never is a cloud permitted to obscure the sunny skies. Since Schubert wrote this symphony for an amateur group, it is scored for a chamber orchestra devoid of trumpets and drums (I. Allegro. II. *Andante con moto.* III. *Allegro molto.* IV. *Allegro vivace*). In the enchanting first movement there is a four-bar introduction for woodwind followed by the joyous first theme in the strings. Immediately a second delightful subject is softly chanted by the strings. The second movement is a flowing melody of Schubertian grace and loveliness. The Minuet has some of the vigor of an Austrian peasant dance. In the finale, in sonata form, both main themes are given by the strings, and both are vivacious.

The Symphony No. 7 in C major is the seventh of Schubert's symphonies in order of publication; but it was Schubert's last symphony, completed in March 1828, a half-year before his death. Its first performance took place more than a decade after the composer's death: in Leipzig on March 21, 1839, Mendelssohn conducting. Sometimes designated as the *Great,* and described by Schumann as the symphony "of heavenly length," the Seventh is Schubert's most ambitious work for orchestra, a symphony of immense structural dimensions, technical assurance, creative power, and profound emotional content (I. Andante; *Allegro ma non troppo.* II. *Andante con moto.* III. *Allegro vivace.* IV. *Allegro vivace*). The spaciousness of the symphony is at once indicated by the extended introduction to the first movement, its main melody a stately subject for horns, followed by woodwinds. A crescendo leads to the allegro section, initiated by a vigorous theme divided between strings and woodwinds. This is followed by a delicate melody for oboes and bassoons, the movement's second main theme. A third important idea is found in the development section, a majestic pronouncement by trombones. The working out of these ideas is along epical lines and with a dramatic impact not found in any other Schubert symphony. The melody of the introduction, stated majestically by the full orchestra, brings the movement to its conclusion.

In the second movement, several introductory bars precede an exquisite song for oboe. Then comes a vigorous thought for full orchestra, followed by still another lovely Schubert melody in the strings. This material is recalled and developed, but some striking new material is also introduced. One of these is a subject for trumpet which combines mystery and grandeur; another, an eloquent song for cello against plucked strings and a countermelody by the oboe. The third-movement Scherzo opens with a dance-like idea divided between strings and oboe. Other dance-like subjects include a lilting waltz tune for strings against a counter theme in cellos and a graceful melody first given by the flute. A repeated E in the horns leads to the trio. The finale erupts demoniacally with a vigorous introduction whose main idea 's a triplet figure in strings, a figure that recurs throughout the movement. In the main portion of the movement the first theme is a flowing melody for oboes; the second, preceded by four D's in the horns, is heard in the woodwinds. The symphony ends after dynamic surges of rhythm and powerful outbursts of sonority. A monumental crescendo sweeps across more than a hundred measures before coming to an exultant close.

If the Seventh is the mightiest of Schubert's symphonies, the Eighth in B minor (1822) remains the most popular. It is the *Unfinished Symphony,* unfinished because it has only two instead of the usual four movements. Schubert sketched out over a hundred measures of a third movement but never completed it, and he never tried to write a finale. Why he allowed this work to remain incomplete is a mystery never adequately explained; one theory is that Schubert actually did complete it, but that the last two movements were lost. Like the Seventh, this symphony did not receive its première performance until after the composer's death: in Vienna, on Dec. 17, 1865, Johann Herbeck conducting (I. *Allegro moderato.* II. *Andante con moto).* The first movement opens with a theme arising from basses and cellos. A swaying figure in the violins then becomes the background for the first theme, a haunting melody for oboe and clarinet, in which other winds join. A brief agitation sets in, after which we hear one of the most beautiful melodies in the whole symphonic literature. It is chanted by the cellos against syncopated chords in violas and clarinets, then repeated even more tenderly by the violins. Once again the music becomes dramatic, and once again the storm is disrupted. The development emphasizes the dramatic element, and the recapitulation the lyric. In the coda, the opening subject of the movement is given prominent treatment. The second movement is one of the most exquisite lyric pages in orchestral literature; an exalted mood is sustained throughout. Two beautiful melodies are prominent. The first appears in violins against a background of a descending scale in pizzicato basses; the second is sung by the clarinet to a syncopated string background. Though later on there are some forceful exclamations by the full orchestra, the gentle general character of the music is never seriously disturbed. The concluding coda brings touches of magic as the first beautiful theme is whispered for the last time against a descending pizzicato passage.

See also: *Gastein Symphony.*

WILLIAM SCHUMAN. William Schuman achieved his first widespread recognition with the Symphony No. 3 (1941), introduced in Boston on Oct. 17, 1941, Koussevitzky conducting, and the recipient of the New York Music Critics Circle Award (I. Passacaglia; Fugue. II. Chorale; Toccata). In the first movement the violas in a low register present a passacaglia theme which is then altered rhythmically and melodically; the fugue enters without pause, its four-bar subject presented by horns. The passacaglia theme becomes the basis of a melody for solo trumpet with which the second movement opens. This section fuses naturally with the brilliant virtuoso music of the toccata.

Schuman's Sixth Symphony came seven years later (1948). Commissioned by the Dallas Symphony, it was introduced in Dallas on Feb. 27, 1949, Antal Dorati conducting. The symphony, while in a single movement, has six sections. The principal thematic material is found in the opening Largo. After a marchlike passage, this material is varied and enlarged (*Moderato con moto).* A cadenzalike subject leads to a vivacious third section (*Leggieramente).* A slow passage then yields to a beautiful chorale melody (Adagio). With a violin solo as a transition, we come to a rhythmic and agitated section (*Allegro risoluto; Presto).* But in the end the symphony is brought to rest with slow music touched with mysticism (*Larghissimo).*

SCHUMANN. Schumann's Symphony No. 1 in B-flat, op. 38 (1841), came after he had already produced masterworks for the piano, chamber-music combinations, and the voice. It was written during one of the happiest periods of his life: his first year of marriage with Clara. Subtitled by him *Spring,* this symphony is effervescent music reflecting the vernal season; but it also speaks of the springtime in the composer's heart when he wrote it. So effortlessly, so spontaneously did Schumann's ideas come that he sketched the entire symphony in four days, and completed it a month later. It was introduced in Leipzig, on March 31, 1841, Mendelssohn conducting (I. *Andante un poco maestoso; Allegro molto vivace.* II. Larghetto. III. *Molto vivace.* IV. *Allegro animato e grazioso).* The symphony opens with a slow horn and trumpet call, to be sounded, according to the composer, "as if it came from on high, like a summons to awakening." This call, in accelerated tempo, becomes the first theme of the ensuing Allegro, suggesting to the composer "how gradually everything that belongs to Spring bursts forth." Four bars of horn octaves lead to the second main theme, in clarinets and bassoons. A third subject consists of an ascending staccato passage. In the slow movement all the freshness and beauty of springtime unfold in an eloquent melody first for divided violins, then in the cellos, and after that in oboe and horns. A phrase toward the end of this movement becomes the kernel of the accented main theme of the Scherzo. This, and a sensitive countermelody in woodwinds, is its basic material, combined with two trios. An exultant outburst of joy in the orchestra brings on the finale. But as this movement progresses there is a touch of sadness, for to the composer this music represents "the departure of spring." The principal melody is a gentle dance-like subject for violins; subsidiary material can be found in bassoons and oboes, and in the strings.

The Symphony No. 2 in C major, op. 61 (1846), was introduced in Leipzig on Nov. 5, 1846, Mendelssohn conducting. There are more somber moods and colors in this work than in the First Symphony, for, as the composer revealed, "it recalls to me a dark period in my life" (I. *Sostenuto assai; Allegro ma non troppo.* II. *Allegro vivace.* III. *Adagio espressivo.* IV. *Allegro molto vivace).* The symphony begins with a solemn introduction containing a subject for brass that becomes the motto theme of the entire work. After an acceleration of the tempo, the Allegro section enters with a dynamic statement for orchestra which the composer interpreted as a struggle in himself between body and mind. This is high-tensioned music which finds relief in a poignant melody. The opening motto theme is effectively used by the trumpets in the coda. The Scherzo that follows has for its main thought a sprightly tune in sixteenths for violins. The deep melancholy found in some of the pages of the

first movement permeates the Adagio, whose main material is a moving melody in strings, with oboe and bassoon joining in. An interlude for strings, with horn and trumpet, maintains this elegiac mood, while a fugal section provides a touch of the dramatic. In the finale, an impetuous subject for full orchestra is contrasted with a reflective thought for strings and woodwinds derived from the melody of the preceding Adagio, and with a radiant lyrical passage for the oboe. The symphony ends triumphantly with a last restatement by the brass of the motto theme.

Since the Symphony No. 3 in E-flat major, op. 97 (1850), was intended as "a picture of Rhenish life" it is subtitled *Rhenish.* Its first performance took place in Duesseldorf, on Feb. 6, 1851, the composer conducting (I. *Lebhaft.* II. *Sehr maessig.* III. *Nicht schnell.* IV. *Feierlich.* V. *Lebhaft).* Schumann's exhilaration in seeing the Rhineland during a visit to Cologne is expressed in the buoyant opening theme for full orchestra. A subject of greater sobriety is the movement's second main subject; this is a melancholy melody for oboe and clarinet. The principal theme of the second-movement Scherzo, appearing in cellos, violas, and bassoons, was derived from the happy German folksong *Rheinweinland.* The subject of the trio appears in horns and other winds over a pedal C. The third movement is a Romanza in which the melody is presented by clarinets and bassoons to an accompaniment by violas; the subsidiary subject is first heard in violins and flutes. The fourth movement, known as the Cathedral scene, owes its inspiration to the impression made on the composer by the ceremony installing the Archbishop of Cologne as Cardinal. Trombones and horns play an ecclesiastical melody which is later elaborated upon contrapuntally. In the finale, a picture of a Rhineland festival is presented, and its thematic material is brilliant and vivacious. Toward the end of the movement, the music of the Cathedral scene is recalled, and the symphony ends in an exalted mood.

The Symphony No. 4 in D minor, op. 20 (1841), is the last of Schumann's symphonies only in order of publication. Actually it was written before both the second and third symphonies. But the composer, dissatisfied with the orchestration, decided at first not to publish it. A decade later he returned to it, making radical revisions in the instrumentation. In this final version it was introduced in Duesseldorf on March 3, 1853, the composer conducting. The symphony is played without interruption, and its basic themes recur throughout (I. *Ziemlich langsam; Lebhaft.* II. *Ziemlich langsam.* III. *Lebhaft.* IV. *Langsam; Lebhaft*). The work opens with an arpeggio figure which serves as the motto theme for the symphony. This marks the beginning of a slow introduction whose main melody, in violas and second violins, has a melancholy cast. An ascending figure in first violins, flutes, and oboes leads to the first Allegro, and becomes the heart of the main theme, in the first violins; a secondary theme is a lyrical passage also for first violins. In the second movement, a Romanza, a tender song for oboes and cellos against plucked strings is used conjunctly with the melancholy subject of the first-movement introduction. The third movement, a Scherzo, contrasts a virile, rhythmic subject with a graceful trio. A slow transition, with phrases in the brass recalling earlier material, leads to the vital finale, which erupts with a vigorous marchlike melody, reminiscent of the main theme of the first movement. A lighter second theme, and a free fantasia section follow. The coda introduces some new material, and the symphony ends with a renewed surge of vigor.

SCRIABIN. Scriabin wrote 5 symphonies, the first, in E major, op. 26, in or about 1891. The last three are his most famous. They are not symphonies in the traditional sense, but one-movement programmatic tone poems striving for a fusion of music with mysticism. Here the composer's highly personal and complicated musical language is combined with often abstruse philosophic concepts. The Symphony No. 3 in C major, op. 43 (1903), is best known as *The Divine Poem* (*Le divin poème*). It is in three sections played without interruption. The first, *Struggles,* represents the conflict between man's slavish subservience to a personal god and his striving for freedom. In the second part, *Delights,* man succumbs to sensual pleasure. The finale, *Divine Joy,* finds the spirit freed of its former submission to superior power; the spirit can now surrender to the joy of free activity, the "divine play."

The three principal themes of the first section are a hymn for muted strings, an expressive subject for woodwinds and violins accompanied by the basses, and a melody that resembles the famous *Dresden Amen.* The second section is dominated by a tender song for woodwinds and horns, which receives passionate treatment. The closing section opens with a trumpet call, and continues with a subject for oboes and cellos. The first theme of the opening section is recalled toward the end of the symphony.

The Divine Poem was introduced in Paris on May 29, 1905, Arthur Nikisch conducting.

The Symphony No. 4 in C major, op. 54 (1907), was given its première in New York City on Dec. 10, 1908, Modest Altschuler conducting. It is called *Poem of Ecstasy* (*Le Poème de l'extase*) and was intended to express the joy of creative activity, the ecstasy of unfettered action. Five theosophic motifs are prominent: motif of Yearning (flute); Protest (muted trombone); Apprehension (muted horns); Will (trumpet); and Self-Assertion (trumpet). The music opens with a prologue in which two themes symbolize the pursuit of the ideal and the self-realization of the ego. This is followed by a section in sonata form beginning with a soaring melody descriptive of the spirit's flight. After the two themes of the prologue are repeated, a Lento passage interprets human love. The will asserts itself, and with a trumpet call the creative force emerges.

The Symphony No. 5 in F-sharp major, op. 60 (1910), *Prometheus: The Poem of Fire,* was Scriabin's last work for orchestra. It was introduced in Moscow on March 15, 1911, Koussevitzky conducting. In Scriabin's adaptation of the Prometheus legend, he traced the destiny of man from primitivism when he lacked the Promethean spark; given that spark he was able to assert his creative will. Man is represented by the piano; the Cosmos, against whom Man is set, by the orchestra. Scriabin originally even intended using colors in setting forth his metaphysical concepts, inventing a special keyboard able to project colors on a screen while the music was performed. Colors were dispensed with when the symphony was given its first performance. But when it was played in New York in 1915 conducted by Modest Altschuler, the color keyboard was utilized, but proved so distracting that since then the accompanying colors have been completely dispensed with.

The symphony opens with Scriabin's "mystic chord." A trumpet call then pronounces the assertion of the creative will, the theme of the creative will being projected by the piano. A passionate discourse for orchestra depicts the struggle of good and evil. A turbulent section follows as Humanity merges with the Cosmos. A chorus of mixed voices in a wordless chant brings the symphony to an exultant conclusion as the creative will finally proves triumphant.

SHOSTAKOVICH. Shostakovich first became famous throughout the world of music with his brilliant First Symphony, op. 10 (1926), still his most popular work. He completed it when he was only nineteen as a graduation exercise for the Leningrad Conservatory. It was introduced in Leningrad on May 12, 1926, Nikolai Malko conducting (I. Allegretto; *Allegro non troppo*. II. Allegro. III. Lento; Largo. IV. *Allegro molto*). The first movement begins with a solo trumpet call which is soon taken over by bassoon and clarinet against pizzicato strings. A slight pause separates this introductory material from the main body of the movement. The first principal theme appears in a clarinet, and has a brisk, martial air. In contrast, the second main theme is a sentimental song first heard in the flute, then repeated in turn by clarinet, horn, and bassoon. Agitation now sets in as the music erupts with stormy climaxes. But a final repetition of the opening introductory material, with slight alterations, restores the initial calm.

The second movement is in the composer's familiar attitude of mockery. This is a whimsical Scherzo whose main theme is heard in the strings and repeated by the piano; the subject of the trio is scored for two flutes. The slow movement presents a poignant thought for oboe against tremolo strings. The entire movement is melancholy, as the principal melody, a soulful song, unfolds *pianissimo* in the strings. A crescendo in the side drum brings on the finale without interruption. Its main section is filled with stirring sonorities, exciting climaxes, and irresistible rhythmic motor action. The main material consists of a gay tune for clarinet built up into a stirring climax, and a forceful subject for strings and woodwinds. After a repetition of the second theme in a solo cello, the symphony ends with an exciting outburst of rhythmic energy.

It took several years, and symphonies, before Shostakovich achieved a success again within the symphonic form. This happened a decade after the First Symphony with Symphony No. 5, op. 47 (1936), one of the composer's masterworks; its première took place in Leningrad on Nov. 21, 1937 (I. Moderato. II. Allegretto. III. Largo. IV. *Allegro non troppo*). From its first measures, this symphony has an epical design, with a spacious subject divided antiphonally between low and high strings. A sensitive subject for violins emerges from this texture and flows towards a dissonant climax. The second principal theme of the movement is then presented by violas against a marked rhythm in cellos and basses. A development section of monumental proportions is introduced by a powerful theme for horns—cogent music whose force is finally dissipated in the recapitulation. Two melodies in waltz time—the first in cellos and double basses, and the other in the woodwind—inject levity into the Scherzo. But the third movement plumbs profound emotional depths with an expansive song for violins, and an elegiac melody first presented by an oboe over tremolo strings. In the development, the emotion grows frenetic, particularly when the first song is passionately projected by the strings. The finale presents a robust march melody of Russian character in the brass against timpani rhythms. Midway, a more sober section repeats ideas from earlier movements, but it is the march theme that brings the symphony to a resounding end.

Like the Fifth Symphony, the Symphony No. 7, op. 60 (1941)—the *Leningrad*—enjoyed a tremendous success. It was introduced in Kuibyshev on March 1, 1942, Samuel Samosud conducting, after which it won the Stalin Prize, and was given to formidable acclaim throughout the non-Fascist world. But this success was due mostly to the stirring times and the subject of the work. It was completed during the first year of the Nazi invasion of the Soviet Union in World War II. In its fiery martial spirit—and in its exultant faith in victory and the future—it spoke for the people of Leningrad during the siege of that city. But since the end of the war the symphony, failing to have sustained musical interest, has been rarely performed (I. Allegretto. II. *Moderato poco allegretto*. III. Adagio. IV. *Allegro non troppo*).

The Symphony No. 9, op. 70 (1945), is brighter in spirit and lighter in texture than either the Fifth or Seventh symphonies. Its good humor and wit have gained for it many admirers, following its première in Leningrad on Nov. 3, 1945, Eugene Mravinsky conducting (I. Allegro. II. Moderato. III. Presto. IV. Largo. V. Allegretto). Gaiety prevails in the first, third, and fifth movements; sobriety, in the second and fourth. In the first movement, which is classic in the simplicity of its structure, the first theme is characterized by its rhythmic vitality, and the second by its ironic overtones. The whole movement has an engaging air of buffoonery. The second movement is more subdued, emphasizing as it does an introspective melody. But the third movement is headlong in its rhythmic flight and capricious in the levity of its thematic ideas. The fourth movement is a gentle intermezzo dominated by an improvisational melody for bassoons. Levity returns in the finale, its main theme having the naïveté of a music-hall tune.

Symphony No. 10 in E minor (1953) was introduced in Leningrad on Dec.

17, 1953, Eugene Mravinsky conducting (I. Moderato. II. Allegro. III. Allegretto; Lento; Allegretto. IV. Andante; Allegro). Following its American première in New York it received the New York Music Critics Circle Award. The composer has explained that this music was intended to reflect the thoughts of the Soviet people about, and their aspirations for peace, but no specific program is provided. The symphony opens with a solemn introduction in which is presented a six-note motif in cellos and basses that recurs throughout the work. After a change of tempo two main themes are given, the first in clarinets, and the second in flutes. An energetic scherzo movement is followed by a poetic slow movement whose heart is a Romantic nocturne for horn solo over pizzicato strings. The finale opens with an oriental type of melody for solo oboe and continues with a stirring martial melody for full orchestra and with a recall of some of the material from earlier movements.

Symphony No. 11 in G minor (1957) was written to commemorate the 50th anniversary of the Bolshevik Revolution (I. Adagio. II. Allegro. III. Adagio. IV. *Allegro non troppo*). It was first performed in Moscow on Oct. 30, 1957, Nathan Rakhin conducting. Subtitled "1905," and in the spirit of the revolution of that year, this work makes considerable use of vigorous martial melodies, brass fanfares, and percussion effects; many of the principal themes are derived from Russian folksongs and the songs of the 1905 Revolution. Each of the four movements bears a descriptive title to provide a clue to its meaning: "Palace Square," "January 9," "Eternal Memory," and "Alarm."

SIBELIUS. Few will deny that Sibelius' 7 symphonies are among the most distinguished contributions to symphonic literature by a 20th-century composer. The first two symphonies are entrenched in the German Romantic traditions and reveal the influence of Tchaikovsky. These two works are still popular, and it is easy to see why: they have the ardor, passion, and vitality of youth; they overflow with sensual lyricism and Slavic sentimentality; they are dramatized by compelling climaxes and irresistible rhythmic drive. The composer began to deviate from the traditional symphonic form in his Third Symphony. As he proceeded on towards his Seventh, he achieved greater compression of structure, conciseness of expression, and economy of means. The orchestral forces are reduced. Formerly spacious melodies become episodic subjects, one following another in rapid succession. The harmonic and contrapuntal vocabulary becomes simplified. The symphonic structure is reduced until in the Seventh Symphony it consists merely of a single movement. Unbridled passion and overflowing emotion often yield to poetic introspection and restrained feeling.

The Symphony No. 1 in E minor, op. 39 (1899), was first performed in Helsingfors (now Helsinki) on April 26, 1899, the composer conducting (I. *Andante ma non troppo; Allegro energico.* II. *Andante ma non troppo lento.* III. Allegro. IV. Andante; *Allegro molto*). A slow introduction, dominated by a melody for clarinet, leads to the main Allegro section, whose first theme is a dramatic subject for strings. A subsidiary idea in woodwinds precedes a thunderous climax in which the first theme is exultantly proclaimed by the full orchestra; only then does the second main theme of the movement appear, a sensitive, lyric thought for two flutes. The second movement spotlights a spacious melody with the character of a Finnish folksong, first presented by muted violins and cellos. The serenity is shattered by a passionate outburst by the orchestra, but a solo cello soon restores calm. There is a kind of barbaric ferocity in the Scherzo that follows, but a flute melody in the trio provides an emotional respite. The finale opens with the clarinet theme of the first-movement introduction, but a new subject is soon heard in the woodwind. Following a powerful surge of the orchestra, a second melody unfolds in the strings against a rhythmic background of percussion. A fugato passage based on the first new theme leads to a climax at whose peak this theme receives exultant expression. The second theme is now taken over by different sections of the orchestra, and an agitated coda brings the symphony to its conclusion.

The Symphony No. 2 in D major, op. 43 (1901), was introduced in Helsinki on March 8, 1902, the composer conducting (I. Allegretto. II. *Tempo andante ma rubato.* III. *Vivacissimo.* IV. *Allegretto moderato*). The first movement begins with an eight-bar introduction in which a figure for violins later becomes the accompaniment to the main theme, the latter a pastoral subject for oboes and clarinets. Eight bars of plucked strings lead to a second theme, in woodwinds. The timpani usher in the second movement. Once again a figure is presented that later becomes the accompaniment to the principal subject, a funereal song for bassoons. A second and beautiful lyrical idea appears in the strings after a climactic working out of the first melody. The spirited third movement, a Scherzo, has been described as the awakening of patriotism in the Finnish people. The two main ideas appear respectively in the violins and in flute and bassoon; a tune for oboe is prominent in the trio. The finale enters without interruption, with a forceful theme projected by strings and trumpet. A transition in flute and bassoon brings on the second important subject, presented first by the oboe, and after that by the other woodwinds. The symphony ends with a majestic presentation of the first subject.

In the Third Symphony in C major, op. 52 (1907), the composer begins to depart from the accepted symphonic structure by combining the Scherzo and finale into a single movement (I. *Allegro moderato.* II. *Andantino con moto quasi allegretto.* III. Allegro). This symphony was introduced in St. Petersburg on Sept. 25, 1907, the composer conducting. The first movement alternates between stormy and pastoral moods. The first principal theme is a restless, at times turbulent, subject for lower strings with which the symphony opens; the second, a poetic song for cellos. The second movement has a sustained elegiac mood, built from three episodes: the first, with which the movement opens, is heard in two flutes; the second, in the clarinet; the third, in the cellos. A graceful Scherzo section is dominated by the woodwinds, but a powerful theme for horn provides a transition to the finale proper, in which the music achieves grandeur, particularly in an eloquent passage for divided violas.

The Symphony No. 4 in A minor, op. 63 (1911), was first performed in Helinski on April 3, 1911, the composer conducting. With the Second Symphony, this is one of the most popular of Sibelius' compositions in the symphonic form. But it is a more profound, more subtle, and more poetic work than its predecessor; leaner in structural design; more economical in its material (I. *Tempo molto moderato quasi adagio.* II. *Allegro molto vivace.* III. *Il tempo largo.* IV. Allegro). A ponderous theme for lower strings in the six-bar introduction is the source of the main melody of the movement, an elegiac song for cellos which grows in emotional intensity as other strings join in. A brass fanfare introduces the second theme in the strings; this is touched by a gentle melancholy. A brisk tune for oboe opens the second movement, contrasted by a more sober thought in oboe and clarinet. The slow movement begins with a pastoral melody first in the flute, then continued by the clarinet. After that the main subject of the movement makes its appearance: an expressive song for the cellos built from the whole-tone scale. This melody gains in beauty and emotional intensity as it is taken over by other sections of the orchestra. The coda introduces a new thought in bassoons and clarinets. In a developed form it becomes the main subject of the finale, which is ushered in by tolling bells. Other subjects in this finale include a fanfare, a declamation, and a chorale, none subjected to any extensive development. The symphony ends serenely after earlier material is rapidly reviewed.

The Symphony No. 5 in E-flat major, op. 82 (1915), reflects the sufferings of the composer during the period of World War I. It was introduced in Helsinki on Dec. 8, 1915, the composer conducting. He subsequently revised it, and in its final version it was performed for the first time in Helsinki on Nov. 24, 1919, Sibelius conducting (I. *Molto moderato; Allegro moderato ma poco a poco stretto.* II.

Andante mosso quasi allegretto. III. *Allegro molto).* This symphony is built from episodic subjects rather than fully stated themes. In the first movement these brief ideas consist of the opening ascending passage for first horn, a later idea for the woodwind accompanied by quivering strings, and finally a forceful statement for three trumpets. The Scherzo comes without interruption, its main thought a jaunty subject for the woodwind. A climax is built up leading to the finale, in which the principal material is a viola theme and a powerful exclamation by horns; the second of these is built up with tremendous impact.

The Symphony No. 6 in D minor, op. 104 (1923), was introduced in Helsinki on Feb. 19, 1923, the composer conducting (I. *Allegro molto moderato.* II. *Allegro moderato.* III. *Poco vivace.* IV. *Allegro molto).* The first movement has a rhapsodic introduction, but its main body is characterized by one of the composer's rare excursions into dissonance and unrelated tonalities. The second movement has the simple appeal of folk music, while the two succeeding movements are built from episodic subjects presented in rapid succession and without much development.

The Symphony No. 7 in C major, op. 105 (1924), the composer's last, is in a single movement. It was introduced in Stockholm on March 24, 1924, the composer conducting. An air of mystery is created by rumbling timpani and an ascending figure in the strings. After that there appears a lyrical subject in divided strings. A declamation for solo trombone leads to an acceleration of the tempo and to a scherzo-like section. But the earlier, more leisurely pace is restored with a repetition of the opening thematic material. Several episodic ideas are built up into a formidable climax, after which the earlier trombone declamation becomes a grandiose hymn for the brass. After another climax, unaccompanied strings appear with an emotional passage to which poignancy is contributed by a new subject for flute and bassoon. A last forceful crescendo sweeps the symphony on to a dramatic ending.

RICHARD STRAUSS. The *Symphonia Do-*

mestica, op. 53 (1903), introduced in New York City under the composer's direction on March 21, 1904, is a programmatic symphony, a fragment of musical autobiography. In four sections (played without interruption) it represents a day in his family life. The composer sanctioned the use of the following descriptive material for the respective movements. I. Introduction and development of three groups of themes. The husband's themes: a) easygoing; b) dreamy; c) fiery . . . The wife's themes: a) lively and gay; b) *grazioso*. The child's theme: tranquil. II. Scherzo. Parents' happiness. Childish play. Cradle song. The clock strikes seven in the evening. III. Adagio. Doing and thinking. Love scene. Dreams and cares. The clock strikes seven in the morning. IV. Finale. Awakening and merry dispute (double fugue). Joyous conclusion.

The principal musical subject in the symphony is the child's theme, first heard in the introduction in the oboe d'amore. In 1927 Strauss worked the first three bars of this theme into a symphonic piece for piano, left-hand, and orchestra, entitling it *Parergon to the Symphonia Domestica*. A "parergon" is defined as "a subordinate activity or work, a work undertaken in addition to one's main employment." The first part of this concerto-like work describes the illness of the child, the second, his recovery.

An Alpine Symphony (*Ein Alpensinfonie*), op. 64 (1914), is also a programmatic symphony; it was introduced in Dresden on Oct. 28, 1915, the composer conducting. This composition is more of a tone poem than a symphony, describing experiences during a day in the Alps. Subtitles at different points in the score provide a literal program: "Night—Sunrise—The Ascent—Entrance into the Forest—Wandering Beside the Brook—At the Waterfall—Apparition—On Flowery Meadows—On the Mountain Pasture—Lost in the Thicket and Brush—On the Glacier—Dangerous Moments—On the Summit—Vision—Mists Arise: The Sun Is Hidden—Elegy—Calm Before the Storm—Thunderstorm—The Descent—Sunset—Night." This work calls for an orchestra of 109 instruments. A few of

these are most unusual: a heckelphone (a kind of baritone oboe); wind machine (invented by Strauss for *Don Quixote*); thunder machine (invented by Strauss for this symphony); and herd bells. Strauss also suggests the possible use of "Samuel's Aerophon," a device enabling the woodwind to sustain some of the long notes by means of a bellows operated by foot and attached to the instrument by a rubber tube.

STRAVINSKY. Stravinsky wrote a symphony early in his career, in E-flat major, op. 1 (1905-1907). The first symphony of his full maturity was that in C major (1940), introduced by the Chicago Symphony on Nov. 7, 1940, the composer conducting (I. *Moderato alla breve*. II. *Larghetto concertante*. III. Allegretto. IV. Adagio; *Tempo giusto*). The work has a classical structure and style. The first movement is in sonata form with the two main themes presented, developed, and recapitulated in the symphonic tradition. The second movement consists of a simply projected "Aria." Two old dances—a minuet and a passepied—make up the third movement, which ends in a fugue. The finale opens with a solemn slow section, while the fast section that follows is in concerto-grosso style.

The Symphony in Three Movements (1945) was introduced in New York on Jan. 24, 1946, Stravinsky conducting. The tempo indication is not given for the first movement, which resembles a three-part toccata. The outer sections are chordal, and the middle polyphonic. This movement is made up of episodic subjects, and its interest lies principally in its motor energy and brilliant sonorities. A little intermezzo follows (Andante) in which strings present a classic melody, followed by another attractive lyrical idea, for harp and flute. The third movement enters without interruption (*Con moto*), with a strong-fibered subject for full orchestra. This movement is in three sections, each with the character of a prelude. A fugue, whose subject is first stated by trombone and piano, leads to the final coda.

TCHAIKOVSKY. Tchaikovsky wrote six symphonies, of which the last three are masterworks and among the most popular symphonies ever written.

Symphony No. 1 in G minor, op. 13 (1866, revised 1874), is subtitled *Winter Daydreams*. Symphony No. 2 in C minor, op. 17 (1872, revised 1879), is called *Little Russian* because in its finale the composer uses a familiar Little Russian melody, *The Crane*. Symphony No. 3 in D major, op. 29 (1875), is often referred to as the *Polish Symphony*, its fifth and last movement being a spirited polonaise. The Symphony No. 4 in F minor, op. 36 (1878), is the first of Tchaikovsky's symphonies to hold a secure place in the orchestral repertory. Its première took place in Moscow on March 4, 1878, Nikolai Rubinstein conducting (I. *Andante sostenuto; Moderato con anima in movimento di valse*. II. *Andantino in modo di canzona*. III. *Pizzicato ostinato;* Allegro. IV. *Allegro con fuoco*). To his patroness and "beloved friend," Mme. von Meck, the composer set forth a program for this music. "The introduction is the kernel, the chief thought of the whole symphony. This is Destiny." Destiny is represented by a fanfare for horns and bassoons in octaves, soon joined by trombones and woodwinds. In the main body of this movement, the first principal theme is a syncopated melody for first violins and cellos. After it has been discussed the clarinet contributes a lyrical second theme. The slow movement opens with a poignant melody for oboe against pizzicato strings. Another touching melody is later given by woodwinds, violins, and cellos. Midway in the movement there is a change of pace and mood with a lively subject for clarinets and bassoons. To Tchaikovsky this music represented "another phase of sadness. One regrets the past and there is no desire to begin life anew. There were joyful minutes. . . . There were also sad moments and irrevocable losses." The Scherzo makes effective use of plucked strings. The main section consists of a pizzicato melody in the strings. In the trio a lively tune exclusively for woodwinds displaces the pizzicato music. "Here," said the composer, "are capricious arabesques, elusive images which pass in the imagination when one has tasted a little wine and ex-

perienced the first phase of intoxication." An impetuous theme for strings and woodwinds opens the finale, followed by a quotation in woodwinds of the famous Russian folk melody, *In the Fields There Stands a Birch Tree*. A new subject consists of a majestic statement for full orchestra. To Tchaikovsky this music meant the following: "If you find no pleasure in yourself, look about you. Go to the people. This is a picture of a folk holiday. Rejoice in the happiness of others, and you will be able to live."

In the Symphony No. 5 in E minor, op. 64 (1888), Tchaikovsky occupies himself completely with the problem of Fate. The composer led the première performance, in St. Petersburg on Nov. 17, 1888 (I. Andante; *Allegro con anima*. II. *Andante cantabile con alcuna licenza*. III. Valse: *Allegro moderato*. IV. *Andante maestoso; Allegro vivace*). A theme signifying Fate opens the first movement in the clarinets, and is given detailed elaboration in a thirty-seven-bar introduction; this subject recurs in all ensuing movements to integrate the work into a unified *Fate Symphony*. The main section has three new subjects: a tender melody for clarinets and bassoons; a lyrical passage for violins; and a spacious and sentimental song for violins. A romantic melody, appearing in a horn, is the heart of the second movement; but two subsidiary themes contribute further interest, a melody for the oboe and a Russian folksong for the clarinet. A loud restatement by the full orchestra of the Fate theme of the first movement is followed by repetition of earlier ideas. In the third movement symphonic tradition is sidestepped by a substitution for the usual scherzo of a graceful waltz, whose main subject appears in the violins. The Fate theme, now in clarinets and bassoons, closes this movement; and it also brings in the finale on a note of triumph, transposed from minor to major. The main section opens with a sweeping idea for strings; relaxation soon sets in with a soft melody for woodwinds. After the brass recall the Fate theme, the two subjects of the finale are developed powerfully and arrive at a climactic statement of the Fate theme first in the strings against woodwind triplets, and after that in two trumpets.

Symphony No. 6 in B minor, op. 74 (1893), the *Pathétique*, is a personal document, an uninhibited expression of Tchaikovsky's pessimism. The composer explained that in writing this music he had a specific program in mind but he refused to reveal it. Wherever this program may be, the music is a mirror to the composer's heart at that period, reflecting all his torments, frustrations, and despair. In all probability Tchaikovsky knew that here he was writing his last symphony, his own requiem: in the first movement there is a brief quotation by the first trombone of a phrase from the Russian service for the dead, a phrase that bears no relation to the rest of the music.

The symphony was introduced in St. Petersburg on Oct. 28, 1893, under the composer's direction, less than two weeks before his death (I. Adagio; *Allegro non troppo*. II. *Allegro con grazia*. III. *Allegro molto vivace*. IV. *Adagio lamentoso*). The title of *Pathétique* was conferred on the symphony by Tchaikovsky's brother, Modest, after the première performance.

The symphony opens in a despairing mood with a brooding subject for solo bassoon. After an emotional outburst in the orchestra, the strings present a grief-stricken melody. A second melody, for flute and bassoon, is somewhat less emotional. A piercing chord precedes the agitated return of the melancholy first subject. Now comes the brief quotation from the Russian requiem service. From this point on, the music grows increasingly stormy and gloomy. The movement ends with a solemn theme in the brass against a descending scale in pizzicato strings.

In the next two movements there is an escape from gloom and pessimism. The second movement is a Scherzo in which a delightful dance melody is heard first in the cellos, and then in woodwinds against pizzicato strings. There is a momentary return of brooding in the trio, but the light mood is recalled with the return of the first section. The third movement is a mighty march, in which a single theme is prominent. Its germ appears in the oboe in an eight-bar introduction. This fragment is repeated by other sections of the orchestra before the march melody is finally projected proudly by the full orchestra.

But in the finale all is black despair. This is a monumental lament by one who can bear the cross no more, the lament of one who is face to face with death. An outcry of tragedy opens the movement leading to a plangent elegy for strings. The tragedy almost becomes too intense to be borne any longer, and the movement finally dies out in a whisper.

In addition to the six symphonies, Tchaikovsky produced a seventh work which while not a symphony is designated as such. It is *Manfred*, a "symphony in four scenes," op. 58 (1885), based on the Byron drama. The symphony was introduced in Moscow on March 23, 1886, Max von Erdmannsdoerfer conducting. The four scenes are as follows: I. Manfred Is Wandering in the Alps; II. The Spirit of the Alps Appears; III. Pastorale; IV. The Underground Palace of Arimanes. The work is dominated by a powerful theme heard immediately in bassoons and clarinets, depicting the torment of Manfred. A more lyrical passage for woodwinds represents his poignant appeal for forgetfulness. In the second movement we get a picture of nature in which Manfred invokes the Spirit of the Alps. Here the main melody is a song for first violins accompanied by harp. Into the pastoral mood that predominates in the third movement is injected the powerful Manfred theme, and the more gentle subject of his appeal, both from the first movement. The finale opens with a theme suggesting Manfred's invocation from the second movement. An orgiastic episode follows and is permitted to subside with a repetition of themes from earlier movements. A quotation of the *Dies irae*, accompanied by organ, and a forceful description of Manfred's death, bring the symphony to its conclusion.

TOCH. Ernst Toch's Symphony No. 3, op. 75 (1955), received the Pulitzer Prize in music following its world première in Pittsburgh on Dec. 2, 1955, William Steinberg conducting. The composer described the form of the symphony as a "ballistic curve," explaining that it has "an initial impulse, becomes steady, and then declines in each of its three sections and in the symphony as a whole." The mood of the music is indicated by a quotation from Goethe's *The Sorrows of Werther* appended to the score: "Indeed am I but a wanderer, a pilgrim in earth—what else are you?" The orchestration is unique in that it calls for two unorthodox instruments, played offstage, yielding sounds never before heard in a concert auditorium. One of these instruments (created by the composer) is a tank of carbon dioxide which issues a loud hissing sound through the valve. A second is a wooden box containing croquet balls which are set into motion by a rotating crank. The score also requires a Hammond organ and a pipe organ, an Armonicon (a glass harmonica invented by Benjamin Franklin) and tuned glass balls.

VAUGHAN WILLIAMS. Vaughan Williams' first symphony (1910) was the *Sea Symphony,* based on Walt Whitman, for soprano, baritone, chorus, and orchestra. This work is seldom given. But his second symphony, *A London Symphony* (1913), is basic to contemporary orchestral literature. After its initial presentation in London in 1914, the work was twice revised by the composer. The final, definitive version, and the one now performed, was first played in London on May 4, 1920, Albert Coates conducting (I. Lento; *Allegro risoluto.* II. Lento. III. Scherzo. IV. *Andante con moto; Maestoso alla marcia; Andante sostenuto*). The composer himself prepared a program for each of the four movements. I. London Sleeps. The Thames flows serenely as the city awakens; the varied character of the city is presented, its activity and good humor. The opening section is a tranquil subject for muted strings, clarinet, and horns. The strings then simulate the rhythm of the flowing Thames, while motifs in horns, trumpets, and trombones tell of the city's awakening to a new day. As the city is fully awakened, the orchestra introduces the main body of this movement in which ideas that had been faintly suggested in

the introduction are fully developed. II. Portrait of a Region Known as Bloomsbury. It is dusk, a damp and foggy twilight. Everywhere there is poverty and despair. An old musician outside a "pub" plays *Sweet Lavender.* The gloom deepens, and the movement ends with the musician still playing his tune. A sensitive melody for English horn against muted strings sets the mood for this movement. *Sweet Lavender* is presented by a solo viola. III. Sitting Late One Saturday Evening at the Temple Embankment. On one side of the river are the slums; on the other, the stately majesty of the Houses of Parliament. The Thames flows on serenely. A lively dance in clarinets, repeated by violins and woodwinds, is followed by a less rhythmic subject for cellos and horns. A new thought is then presented by flutes and oboes and carried to a climax. The movement ends with a picture of the fog descending over the Thames. IV. A Picture of the Crueler Side of the City: the Unemployed, the Unfortunate. An energetic introduction prefaces the first main theme, a march melody in violas, cellos, clarinets, and bassoons. After development of this theme, the chiming of Big Ben is imitated by the harp. A momentary pause separates this material from an Epilogue in which themes from the first-movement introduction are heard.

Vaughan Williams' third symphony, the *Pastoral* (1921), was introduced in London on Jan. 26, 1922, Adrian Boult conducting (I. *Molto moderato.* II. *Lento moderato.* III. *Moderato pesante;* Presto. IV. Lento; *Moderato maestoso; Molto largamente;* Lento). In writing a *Pastoral Symphony,* the composer had no intention of presenting a portrait of nature; he meant merely to emphasize a pastoral mood. All four movements are comparatively slow, quiet, introspective. The only rapid passage occurs in the coda of the third movement, and even this is *pianissimo.* The main theme of the first movement is presented by harp, cellos, and double basses; to this a solo violin, soon joined by the oboe, offers a counterstatement. The tranquil mood thus established is momentarily shattered by an outburst in the full orchestra, but a sensitive song for English horn restores the earlier serenity. In the second movement, a melody for solo horn over divided strings once again establishes a peaceful atmosphere. Midway in the movement there occurs a fanfare for a "natural trumpet," or bugle. The third movement was described by the composer as a "slow dance." Three themes are prominent: one for trumpets and trombones; another, for flute against harp arpeggios and string tremolos; the third, for trumpet. A gentle roll of timpani brings on the finale, in which there soon appears a wordless chant for soprano or tenor. The main subject of this movement comes in the woodwinds, harp, and horns after this chant, which is recalled by the orchestra before the main theme is repeated by muted strings. The symphony ends with a last presentation of the wordless chant soaring above the violins.

The Symphony No. 4 in F minor (1932), introduced in London on April 10, 1935, Adrian Boult conducting, is a radical departure for the composer. This is an ultramodern work, dissonant, strident, technically complex rather than poetic and introspective (I. Allegro. II. *Andante moderato*. III. *Allegretto molto*. IV. *Finale con epilogo fugato: Allegro molto*). The heart of the symphony is two astringent themes heard in the opening measures of the first movement: the first is a chromatic four-note theme for violins and woodwinds; the other, a widely spaced, leaping melody for woodwinds and pizzicato strings. This leaping subject brings on the second movement, whose main idea is a folk-like melody in violins against pizzicato cellos and basses. The chromatic idea of the first movement becomes the material from which the third movement, a Scherzo, is constructed. In the finale, the two themes of the first movement receive considerable attention. But there is also some new material here, including a march melody with which the finale opens, and a lyrical passage for horns and woodwinds.

There is a return of serenity in Vaughan Williams' Symphony No. 5 in D major (1942), introduced in London on June 24, 1943, the composer conducting. Though he borrowed for this work

musical material from his opera *The Pilgrim's Progress*, he insisted that except for the third movement this symphony has no relation to the Bunyan allegory. The four movements are all in a contemplative mood (I. Preludio. II. Scherzo. III. Romanza. IV. Passacaglia). The main thought in the first movement is a gentle subject for two horns. In the ensuing Scherzo a sustained meditative melody is heard in the strings. The affinity between the slow third movement and Bunyan is created through the imposition of a quotation from *The Pilgrim's Progress* in the published score: "Upon that place there stood a cross, and little below, a sepulchre. Then he said: 'He hath given me rest by His sorrow and life by His death.' " The finale is in the form of a passacaglia, the theme presented by the cellos.

The Symphony No. 6 in E minor (1947) is one of the composer's most eloquent works. It was first performed in London on April 21, 1948, Adrian Boult conducting. The four movements are played without interruption (I. Allegro. II. Moderato. III. *Allegro vivace*. IV. Epilogue). A majestic chorale for first violins, accompanied by violas, flutes, and English horn, is the heart of the first movement. In the second the main theme is a syncopated subject with which it opens; a figure from this theme is later used for an important statement by trumpets. A theme for English horn leads into the third movement, a Scherzo, which the composer explains is "fugal in texture but not in structure." The finale, much of which is in a contrapuntal style, is played quietly from beginning to end, "the quietest piece of music imaginable," as Dyneley Hussey described it.

The Symphony No. 7 (1952) received its première in Manchester on Jan. 14, 1953, John Barbirolli conducting. Subtitled *Sinfonia antartica*, it is not actually a symphony but an adaptation of the score for a British motion picture, *Scott of the Antarctic* (I. Prelude. II. Scherzo. III. Landscape. IV. Intermezzo. V. Epilogue). The music is a realistic picture of the polar territory, particularly in the third movement, with simulation of the whistling wind by means of a wind machine, and a description of the ice and wasteland with the aid of an instrument called the vibraphone. The second and fourth movements provide thematic representations of penguins and whales, while the first movement and finale present the struggle of man against nature. This symphony utilizes a wordless solo for soprano and a choir of women's voices.

Symphony No. 8 in D minor (1956) was first performed in Manchester on May 2, 1956 (I. Fantasia. II. *Scherzo alla marcia.* III. Cavatina. IV. Toccata). This symphony is structurally interesting because the first movement is a series of variations not on a given theme but on isolated figures. It is melodically outstanding for its lyrical third movement, scored for strings. And it is rhythmically arresting for its finale with its dynamic exploitation of vast percussion forces.

Vaughan Williams' last symphony was the Ninth in E minor (1957), introduced in London on April 2, 1957, Malcolm Sargent conducting (I. *Moderato maestoso.* II. *Andante sostenuto.* III. Scherzo: *Allegro pesante.* IV. *Andante tranquillo).* This symphony was planned by the composer as a summation of his artistic faith and principles. It is music of frustration and despair, a fact fully realized by the composer, who after the concluding bar appended the word "niente," or "nothing." An expressive melody in the first movement recurs throughout the symphony as an integrating element. The critic of the London *Times* wrote that "the first two movements are alike in outlook and thought. There is a menace, acknowledged as such, in the second movement, which is slow, though not very slow. In the scherzo, the elements are externalized. The finale does not end in triumph for this is a stoic symphony."

WALTON. William Walton's Symphony (1934) was first performed in its entirety in London on Nov. 6, 1935, Hamilton Harty conducting. A complex score, this work is constructed from epigrammatic subjects which receive elaborate harmonic and contrapuntal treatment (I. *Allegro assai.* II. *Presto con malizia.* III. *Andante con malinconia.* IV. Maestoso; *Brioso ed ardentemente; Vivacissimo;*

Maestoso). There are three episodes in the first movement, which avoids the usual sonata-form procedures of development and recapitulation. The first episode, heard in the opening measures, is the one that gets the most prominent attention throughout the movement. The second movement is a Scherzo, with overtones of mockery. The slow movement begins with a beautiful melody for flute and continues with several other expressive themes, including one for clarinet. The finale has four sections. The first is in a heroic cast; the second is equally energetic; the third is fugal; and the fourth revives the mood and basic material of the first.

WEBERN. Anton Webern's Symphony for Chamber Orchestra, op. 21 (1925), is in the twelve-tone technique; it was introduced in New York on Dec. 8, 1929, Alexander Smallens conducting (I. *Ruhig schreitend.* II. *Variationen).* This fifteen-minute work is the last word in economy. The thematic material often consists merely of a few unrelated tones; the harmony is always lean and spare; the scoring is for a small ensemble consisting of clarinet, bass clarinet, two French horns, harp, and strings. The first movement is a double canon in which each instrument contributes only one or two tones of the main theme. The second movement offers a precise, brief theme which is followed by seven equally brief variations.

Symphony for Strings. *See:* Symphony—*Honegger.*

Symphony from the New World. *See:* Symphony—*Dvořák.*

Symphony Hall. The leading concert auditorium in Boston, Mass., home of the Boston Symphony. Situated on Huntington and Massachusetts Avenues, it opened on Sept. 15, 1900.

Symphony of the Air. *See:* NBC Symphony.

Symphony on a French Mountain Song. *See:* Symphony—*D'Indy.*

Symphony Society of New York. *See:* New York Symphony Society.

Syncopation. The shifting of the accent from the strong to the normally weak beat.

Synthésistes, Les. A school of young Belgian composers prominent between 1925 and 1930. Among its members were Marcel Poot, Francis de Bourguignon, René Bernier, and Jules Strens. Their aim, in Poot's words, was to "exclude all well determined programs in our music and to work each according to his own temperament but with respect for established forms and traditions."

Syria Mosque. *See:* Pittsburgh Symphony.

Szell, George, conductor. Born Budapest, Hungary, June 7, 1897. After completing his music study in Budapest and Vienna, he made numerous appearances in Germany, Austria, and London as a pianist. On the advice of Richard Strauss he turned to conducting, and through Strauss' influence became first conductor of the Strasbourg Opera in 1917. In the next two decades he became famous as an opera conductor at the Berlin State Opera and the German Theater in Prague. From 1933 on he gave distinguished symphony concerts with leading orchestras in England. At various times he was principal conductor of the Scottish Orchestra, the Czech Philharmonic, and the Residentie Orchestra in The Hague. His American début took place in St. Louis in 1930. From 1942 to 1945 he was a conductor at the Metropolitan Opera in New York. Since 1946 he has been the principal conductor of the Cleveland Orchestra, with which he toured Europe in 1957. In the same year he also assumed the post of a principal conductor of the Concertgebouw Orchestra in Holland.

Szenkar, Eugen, conductor. Born Budapest, Hungary, April 9, 1891. In 1910 he was graduated from the Music Academy in Budapest, and in 1911 he was appointed conductor at the German Theater in Prague. From 1916 to 1920 he was court conductor and director of opera at Altenburg. After 1920 he held several important posts in Germany as opera conductor. He left Germany with the rise of the Nazi regime, and from 1934 to 1937 was principal conductor of the Moscow Philharmonic. He also made guest appearances throughout Europe between 1933 and 1939. In the latter year he settled in Rio de Janeiro, where he founded, and for several years directed, the Bra-

zilian Symphony. After World War II he returned to Europe, and in 1952 became first conductor of the Duesseldorf Opera and Duesseldorf Symphony.

Szigeti, Joseph, violinist. Born Budapest, Hungary, Sept. 5, 1892. After studying the violin with Jenö Hubay he made his début in Budapest when he was thirteen. After that he made many tours of Europe. From 1917 to 1924 he was professor of violin at the Geneva Conservatory. His American début took place in Philadelphia with the Philadelphia Orchestra in 1925. Since that time he has appeared throughout the world with outstanding success, acclaimed especially for his performances of contemporary music, including many works either written for him or dedictated to him. He is the author of an autobiography, *With Strings Attached* (1947).

Szymanowski, Karol, composer. Born Tymoshovka, Ukraine, Oct. 6, 1882; died Lausanne, Switzerland, March 28, 1937. He attended the Warsaw Conservatory, and while still a student there completed a piano sonata, and his first work for orchestra, an overture. From 1906 to 1908 he lived in Berlin, where he absorbed its musical influences and assumed a German-Romantic style in his own writing. He abandoned this manner in 1911 to produce music of a Russian character influenced by Scriabin and the Russian nationalists; after that he allowed himself to be influenced by the French Impressionists. The Russian Revolution left Szymanowski destitute. Settling in Warsaw, he earned his living teaching the piano, and touring Europe as a piano soloist. In 1921 he visited New York. Meanwhile he had finally arrived at his own identity as a composer. This came about soon after the end of World War I when, traveling in the Tatra range of the Carpathian mountains in Poland, he came into contact with Polish folksongs and dances. Fired with the ambition of becoming a Polish national composer who drew his inspiration and material from the folklore of his country, Szymanowski now produced his first masterworks: a folk ballet, *Harnasie,* in 1926, and the *Stabat Mater,* in 1929.

From 1926 to 1929 Szymanowski was director of the Warsaw Conservatory, which he reorganized completely. After 1929 he completed several major works, including the *Sinfonie Concertante* for piano and orchestra and a second violin concerto. He also assumed the office of president of the Warsaw Academy of Music. A victim of chronic tuberculosis, in 1936 he had to be confined to a sanitorium, where he died less than a year later.

The following are Szymanowski's principal instrumental compositions:

Chamber Music: 2 string quartets; violin sonata; *Mythes,* for violin and piano (including the popular *Fountain of Arethusa*).

Orchestra: 3 symphonies; 2 violin concertos; *Sinfonie Concertante* for piano and orchestra; incidental music to various plays.

Piano: 3 sonatas; *Métopes; Masques;* preludes, etudes, mazurkas, Polish dances.

See: Concerto—*Szymanowski;* Etude—*Szymanowski;* Mazurka; *Métopes; Sinfonia concertante.*

T

Tablature. A system of musical notation in which pitch and duration are indicated by letters or numbers or diagrams rather than in the conventional way. This system was prominent between the 15th and 18th centuries. The most important tablatures were for the lute, where each line corresponded to one of the lute's strings. Numbers or letters on the lines indicated whether strings were left open or stopped to raise the pitch by one or more semitones, while the duration was indicated by stems and flags.

Tabor (Smetana). *See: My Fatherland.*

Tabulatura Nova. *See:* Scheidt, Samuel.

Taffanel, Paul, flutist and conductor. Born Bordeaux, France, Sept. 16, 1844; died Paris, France, Nov. 22, 1908. After attending the Paris Conservatory, he was appointed solo flutist of the Paris Opéra Orchestra. He held this post from 1864 to 1890. From 1867 to 1890 he also served in a similar capacity for the Paris Conservatory Orchestra, and from 1890 to 1903 he was its principal conductor. From 1893 on he was an eminent teacher of the flute at the Conservatory.

Takt. German for time, beat, or measure.

Tales of Our Countryside. Suite for piano and orchestra by Henry Cowell (1940),

first performed in Atlantic City, N.J., in May 1941, Stokowski conducting (I. Deep Tides. II. Exultation. III. The Harp of Life. IV. Country Reel). This is one of the composer's most popular works for orchestra, but it originated as a series of pieces for the piano. The four pictures of the American countryside are influenced by the style of American folk tunes and dances. It is romantic music, though discreetly spiced by tone-cluster harmonies.

Talich, Václav, conductor. Born Kroměříž, Bohemia, May 28, 1883. After attending the Prague Conservatory, where he received training on the violin from Otakar Ševčik, he played for several years with the Berlin Philharmonic. He made his conducting début in 1904 with the Odessa Municipal Orchestra. Returning to his native land in 1907, he devoted himself there to teaching, conducting, and playing the violin. From 1908 to 1912 he was conductor of the Ljubljana Philharmonic, a period in which he also continued music study in Germany and Italy with Arthur Nikisch, Max Reger, and Arturo Vigno. In 1919 he was appointed principal conductor of the Czech Philharmonic, which under his direction became one of Europe's distinguished orchestras. Between 1922 and 1935 he made many tours of Europe with that organization. He also appeared as guest conductor of other major European orchestras, was principal conductor of the Scottish Orchestra in 1926, and from 1931 to 1934 was conductor of an orchestra in Stockholm. In 1932 he was appointed to the faculty of the Prague Master School, and three years later artistic director of the National Opera in Prague. He resigned from the Czech Philharmonic in 1935 to devote himself to the National Theater. He withdrew from this post and from his teaching assignments in 1948 owing to the change of the political regime in Czechoslovakia, and became director of a chamber-music ensemble and an orchestra in Bratislava.

Tam o' Shanter. *See:* Burns, Robert.

Tamara. Tone poem for orchestra by Balakirev (1881), introduced in St. Petersburg, March 19, 1883. The work is based on a poem by Lermontov about Tamara, a beautiful but evil queen, who inhabits a high tower on the River Terek and lures travelers to their destruction. Tamara's theme is an ornamented, sinuous subject with which the work opens and which recurs throughout. The music realistically describes Tamara's call to the travelers, their revelry within the tower, and their doom.

Tambourin. A lively dance of Provençal origin, in 2/4 time. It is usually followed by a second tambourin in the minor, after which the first one is repeated. It is sometimes found as a movement of the Baroque suite. One of the most famous pieces in this form is the seventh movement of Rameau's harpsichord suite in E minor, which is derived from Rameau's opera *Les Fêtes d'Hebé.* Tambourins for orchestra are found in numerous 18th-century operas, including Gluck's *Iphigenia in Aulis,* Handel's *Alcina,* and Rameau's *Platée* and *Les Indes galantes.*

Taming of the Shrew. (1) A concert overture by Castelnuovo-Tedesco (1930), introduced in Florence, Italy, in February 1931. This is vivacious and occasionally witty music describing Petruchio. Three

main melodies are used. The first, with which the overture opens, is dramatic; the second follows at once in violins and violas; and the third is presented by two horns.

(2) *See:* Shakespeare, William.

Taneiev, Sergei, pianist and composer. Born Vladimir, Russia, Nov. 25, 1856; died Moscow, Russia, June 19, 1915. He was graduated from the Moscow Conservatory in 1875 with the first gold medal ever presented there. He then made his concert début as a pianist as soloist with the Moscow Musical Society, and toured Russia in joint concerts with Leopold Auer. Later in life he abandoned concert work to concentrate on teaching and composition. In 1878 he became professor of harmony and instrumentation at the Moscow Conservatory, where in 1885 he was elevated to the post of director, which he held for four years. One of Russia's leading authorities on counterpoint, he was an inspiring teacher whose influence was felt by an entire generation of Russian musicians. In his own music he was at his best in songs and chamber music, his style often derivative from Tchaikovsky. His chamber music includes 6 string quartets, a piano quartet, 2 string quintets, and a piano trio. He also wrote 3 symphonies, a suite for violin and orchestra, and *Overture to Oresteia.*

Tannhaeuser Overture and Bacchanale. Overture and opening scene of Wagner's opera, *Tannhaeuser.* With a libretto by the composer, the opera was introduced in Dresden on Oct. 19, 1845. The overture utilizes melodic material from the opera. It opens with the stately *Pilgrim's Chorus* in clarinets, bassoons, and horns. This leads into a solemn melody for strings representing Tannhaeuser's repentance. After a return of both subjects, there appears a portion of the voluptuous Venusberg music in the strings. A climax is achieved with the outburst of Tannhaeuser's song of love in full orchestra. The overture ends with a return of the pilgrim chant. The *Bacchanale* (or *Venusberg Music*) that follows without interruption was written by the composer for the Paris première of the opera in 1861 to cater to the Parisians' love of ballet. This is perhaps the most sensual and orgiastic music ever written, a veritable delirium of emotion. It begins with exciting trills in violins, cries in piccolos and oboes, and the crashing of cymbals. As the bacchanale unfolds, the music grows more and more uninhibited and frenetic in a mad whirl of harmony, rhythm, and color. Then the passions subside and the music passes into languor.

Tannhaeuser, Prelude to Act 3. In the published score this orchestral prelude bears the title, *Tannhaeuser's Pilgrimage.* It opens in a somber vein with the theme of Tannhaeuser's Penitence and a tender subject depicting Elizabeth's intercession. This is followed by a more melancholy idea in violas, followed by the violins, speaking for Tannhaeuser's suffering. Snatches of the *Pilgrim's Chorus* and a powerful presentation of the Heavenly Grace motif in the brass are some later materials. The latter motif, gently repeated by strings, concludes the prelude with a suggestion of Tannhaeuser's final salvation.

Tansman, Alexander, composer. Born Lodz, Poland, June 12, 1897. Planning a career in law, he attended the University of Warsaw. But at the same time he studied music with private teachers in Lodz and Warsaw. In 1919 he won the first two prizes in a competition among Polish composers, and soon thereafter concerts of his works were given in Lodz and Warsaw. He now made his home in Paris, where he found an admirer in Vladimir Golschmann, the conductor, who was responsible for presenting premières of Tansman's major works for orchestra both in Paris and in the United States. In 1926 Tansman began a series of concert tours, appearing as conductor, composer, and pianist. He visited Austria in that year, Germany in 1927, and made his American début on Feb. 29, 1927, as soloist with the Boston Symphony in the première of his Second Piano Concerto. He settled in the United States in 1941, but after World War II he returned to his Paris home. Tansman's first important works were influenced by his contacts with French music: his style is refined, his workmanship elegant, and the logic

of his structure inexorable. A Polish character continually asserted itself in his writing. In his best music the rhythms of Polish dances are prominent, but they are combined with a strong lyricism and a personal harmonic language. He has been a prolific composer. His works for orchestra include 7 symphonies, 3 serenades, 2 piano concertos, a viola concerto, violin concerto, guitar concertino, and a variety of other works including a Toccata, *Triptyque* for string orchestra, *Four Polish Dances, Two Intermezzi, Polish Rhapsody, Symphonic Etude,* Partita for piano and orchestra, Music for Orchestra, *Ricercari, Tombeau de Chopin* for strings, *Sinfonia piccola,* Concerto for Orchestra, Capriccio, and incidental music to many plays. In chamber music he produced 8 string quartets, 2 piano trios, a septet, flute sonata, cello sonata, sextet, violin sonatina, and other compositions. He also wrote 4 sonatas for piano as well as mazurkas, polonaises, and other pieces. He is the author of a biography of Stravinsky (1949).

See: Ricercare; *Triptyque.*

Tapiola. Tone poem for orchestra by Sibelius, op. 112 (1926), introduced in New York City on Dec. 26, 1926, Walter Damrosch conducting. Tapiola is another name for Finland, Tapio being the ancient forest god of that land. Sibelius' tone poem is a musical picture of brooding Finnish forests and the wood sprites that dwell there. A single theme is dominant, a subject for strings which is heard after a brief drum roll and suggests the Finnish forest. This theme is developed and altered as different facets of a forest picture are portrayed. The music is now idyllic, now melancholy, now mysterious, now austere. At its conclusion, the tone poem rises to a powerful climax.

Tarantella (or **Tarentelle**). A fast Neapolitan dance in 3/8 or 6/8 time, a form used in instrumental music by many composers. The following are some tarentellas for piano: Chopin, in A-flat major, op. 43; Liszt's *Venezia e Napoli* in *Années de pèlerinage;* Mendelssohn, in C major, in *Songs Without Words,* No. 45, op. 102, no. 3; and Rossini in *Péchés de vieillesse.* Wieniawski's *Scherzo tarentelle,* op. 16, is a favorite in the violin repertory; César Cui also wrote a tarantella, for violin and piano. A tarantella appears in Tchaikovsky's *Capriccio italien* for orchestra, and César Cui wrote one for orchestra, op. 12.

Taras Bulba. Rhapsody for orchestra by Leoš Janáček (1918), introduced in Prague on Nov. 9, 1924. It is based on Gogol's novel of the same name, the protagonist being the 15th-century warrior Taras Bulba and his two sons, Ostap and Andrii. Andrii falls in love with a Polish girl, joins the Poles in their struggle against the Cossacks, is captured, and finally shot by his own father. Ostap is a captive of the Poles, is tortured before the eyes of his father, who then avenges his son by laying waste to Polish towns. Taras Bulba is finally captured and burned at the stake, where he prophesies the emergence of a czar who will make Russia invincible.

The rhapsody is divided into three sections: I. The Death of Andrii; II. The Death of Ostap; III. The Prophecy and Death of Bulba. In the first part the main subjects are a poignant melody for English horn with string accompaniment, with which the work opens, and a lyrical idea for oboe speaking for Andrii's love for the Polish girl. Ostap's Death opens with a loud, brutal phrase for first violins, which leads to a sustained melody for violins. A majestic melody for violins and solo horn is the basic material of the concluding section. A turbulent section depicts Taras proudly meeting his death at the stake. The coda is an exultant page for full orchestra and organ voicing Taras Bulba's prophecy.

Tartini, Giuseppe, violinist and composer. Born Pirano, Italy, April 8, 1692; died Padua, Italy, Feb. 26, 1770. He received his initial music instruction at the Collegio dei Padri delle Scuole Pie. In 1709 he entered the University of Padua for the study of law, remaining there four years. His secret marriage to his pupil, Elisabetta Premazone, so infuriated the Cardinal that he ordered Tartini's arrest. Tartini escaped to Assisi, where for two years he lived in retirement, devoting himself to the study of the violin and to composition; it was there that in 1713 he completed his most famous composition,

the *Devil's Trill Sonata,* for violin. In 1715 he was permitted to return to Padua. Within a short period his reputation as violin virtuoso became so great that he was invited to compete with the famous violinist, Francesco Maria Veracini. Before this contest could take place, Tartini became convinced of his own technical shortcomings. He withdrew to Ancona for more study, and emerged a master of his instrument. In 1721 he became violinist at the Cappella del Santo in Padua; from 1723 to 1725 he was violinist and conductor in Prague; and from 1728 until his death he was the head of a violin school in Padua that attracted students from all parts of Europe. In 1768 he was afflicted by cancer of the foot which proved fatal.

Tartini was one of Corelli's most important successors as a composer of violin music. His works are more subtle in their expression and more advanced in technique than Corelli's, representing a significant development in 18th-century instrumental music. They include concertos, sonatas, quartets, and trios. For a long time scholars were puzzled by peculiar geometric symbols placed over the movements of some of his compositions. These symbols finally proved to be quotations of poetry, usually love poetry, sometimes ironic and bitter, and sometimes tragic.

The modern Italian twelve-tone composer, Luigi Dallapiccola, wrote two divertimentos for violin and chamber orchestra, entitled *Tartiniana,* based on themes from Tartini's works.

See: Devil's Trill Sonata.

Tartuffe. *See:* Molière.

Tasso: Lamento e Trionfo (Tasso: Lament and Triumph). Tone poem by Liszt (1854), first performed in Weimar on April 19, 1854, the composer conducting. The work was an outgrowth of a concert overture written in 1849 to help celebrate the centenary of the birth of Goethe. Nevertheless, the tone poem was more strongly influenced by Byron's epic poem than by Goethe. Liszt provided his own program for this music: "Tasso loved and suffered at Ferrara. He was avenged at Rome. His glory still lives in the folksongs of Venice. These three elements are inseparable from his immortal memory. To represent them in music we first called up his august spirit as he still haunts the waters of Venice. Then we beheld his proud and melancholy figure as he passed through the festive halls of Ferrara where he had produced his masterpieces. Finally we followed him to Rome, the Eternal City, which offered him the crown and glorified in him the martyr and the poet." The tone poem opens with the Tasso theme, a subject for cellos and double basses. A second principal theme tells of Tasso's suffering; this is a melancholy folksong for bass clarinet against harp and strings, derived from an old Venetian gondolier's song. Tasso's triumph, the opening Tasso theme being transformed into music of compelling grandeur, brings the work to a close.

Taubman, Howard, music critic. Born New York City, July 4, 1907. He was graduated from Cornell University and received his music instruction from private teachers. In 1930 he became a music critic for the *New York Times.* Upon the death of Olin Downes in 1955, Taubman succeeded him as principal music critic there. He is the author of several books, including *Music as a Profession* (1939), *Music on My Beat* (1943), *The Maestro: The Life of Arturo Toscanini* (1951), and *How to Bring Up Your Child to Enjoy Music* (1958).

Tausig, Carl, pianist. Born Warsaw, Poland, Nov. 4, 1841; died Leipzig, Germany, July 17, 1871. He was a favorite pupil of Liszt in Weimar. His début as a pianist took place in Berlin in 1858, and in 1859-1860 he toured Germany. In 1862 he settled in Vienna, where for a while he conducted orchestral concerts, but from 1865 he made appearances throughout all of Europe as a concert pianist. A remarkable technician with a style in the grand manner, and endowed with a fabulous memory, he was everywhere acclaimed a master of the keyboard in a wide repertory. Tausig made many excellent transcriptions for the piano of works by Bach, Beethoven, Berlioz, Schubert, Schumann, Wagner, and Weber. He was also a distinguished

teacher of the piano, the founder of a school of piano playing in Berlin.

Taylor, Deems, composer. Born New York City, Dec. 22, 1885. While pursuing his academic education in New York he took private lessons in piano, harmony, and counterpoint. As a student at New York University he wrote music for student shows, one of which, *The Echo,* was produced on Broadway. After leaving college, Taylor acted in vaudeville, then did editorial work on various magazines, including *Collier's Weekly.* He first became known as a composer in 1919 with *Through the Looking Glass,* for orchestra. From 1921 to 1925 he was music critic of the *New York World.* He resigned that post to devote himself to composition, and in the next few years attracted world attention with two operas introduced at the Metropolitan Opera: *The King's Henchman,* with a libretto by Edna St. Vincent Millay, in 1927; and *Peter Ibbetson,* in 1931. In 1927 he returned to musical journalism by becoming editor of *Musical America,* holding this post two years. In 1931-1932 he was the music editor of the *New York American.* Since then Taylor has distinguished himself as an author, program annotator, master of ceremonies on radio programs, and intermission commentator for broadcasts of symphonic music and operas. He is the author of *Of Men and Music* (1937), *The Well-Tempered Listener* (1940), *Music to My Ears* (1949), and editor of the *Music Lovers Encyclopedia* (1939). His principal compositions are for orchestra and include the suites *Through the Looking Glass* and *Circus Day,* the tone poem *Jurgen, Marco Takes a Walk, Elegy, A Christmas Overture, Restoration Suite,* and *Portrait of a Lady.*

See: *Elegy* (2); *Through the Looking Glass.*

Tchaikovsky, Peter Ilitch, composer. Born Votkinsk, Russia, May 7, 1840; died St. Petersburg, Russia, Nov. 6, 1893. Intended for law, he attended the School of Jurisprudence in St. Petersburg and after that worked for three years as a clerk in the Ministry of Justice. In 1861 he began to study music with Nicholas Zaremba, and in 1862 he entered the newly founded

St. Petersburg Conservatory. Now certain of his direction, Tchaikovsky resigned his Ministry post to concentrate on music.

After completing his studies at the St. Petersburg Conservatory in 1865, Tchaikovsky became professor of harmony at the Moscow Conservatory, which Nikolai Rubinstein had just founded. While holding this post he completed his first symphony, successfully introduced at Moscow in 1868. The following year successful performances were given of his opera *The Voivoda,* and an orchestral fantasy *Fatum;* he also completed an early version of his first masterwork, the orchestral fantasy-overture *Romeo and Juliet,* introduced at Moscow in 1870.

Always extremely sensitive, misanthropic, and neurotic—and already the victim of one nervous breakdown—Tchaikovsky was driven into a period of mental torment through a disastrous marriage in 1877. His wife was a highstrung student, Antonina Miliukova, who had come to him to express her adoration. Though he did not love her he asked her to marry him, probably hoping thereby to silence the rumors already prevalent in Moscow about his sexual aberration. Marriage proved a hideous nightmare; on one occasion Tchaikovsky tried to commit suicide. Then he fled from Moscow and for a year traveled in Europe. He was never again reconciled with Antonina, who, through the years, remained for him a continual source of irritation. Three years after Tchaikovsky's death she was confined to an insane asylum.

An even stranger relationship involved him with another woman, the patroness Nadezhda Filaretovna von Meck. She was his admirer, and wrote to him saying so; he made a grateful response. Thus began a thirteen-year relationship marked by a voluminous exchange of letters. Mme. von Meck became Tchaikovsky's patroness by endowing him with an annual subsidy to enable him to devote himself completely to composition. She also became his dearest friend to whom he confided not only his hopes and dreams but also his darkest torments. Their letters often contained the most passionate expressions of love. Yet during all these thirteen years they never met—a condition Mme. von Meck had imposed on him. Why she stubbornly refused to meet him, while confiding in her letters ardent outbursts of love, is a mystery never satisfactorily solved. Their different social stations may have been one of the reasons; her excessive adoration of her children, another. In any event, through her correspondence she remained generous with her money, advice, affection, and encouragement.

Under such a stimulus, Tchaikovsky produced a succession of masterworks: the fourth and fifth symphonies, the former written for and dedicated to Mme. von Meck; the violin concerto; the opera, *Eugene Onegin;* numerous shorter orchestral compositions including the *Capriccio italien* and the *Ouverture solennelle 1812.* His fame kept pace with his increasing creative powers. In 1884 he received from the Czar the Order of St. Vladimir; and four years after that the government bestowed on him a life pension.

His relationship with Mme. von Meck ended as suddenly as it had begun. While traveling in the Caucasus in 1890 he heard from Mme. von Meck that financial difficulties compelled her to terminate her annual subsidy to him. When Tchaikovsky replied that he was no longer in need of her generosity but hoped that their friendship would continue, his letter went unanswered. All of his later efforts to communicate with her proved futile. Upon returning to Moscow, Tchaikovsky discovered that Mme. von Meck had lied to him about the state of her finances in order to terminate a friendship that had begun to bore her.

In 1891 Tchaikovsky visited the United States, his début taking place in New York on May 5 in conjunction with the opening of Carnegie Hall. When he returned home he lapsed helplessly into a melancholia which smothered his spirits and sapped his strength. In such a mood he completed his last symphony, the *Pathétique,* a work so filled with pessimism that it is often said that Tchaikovsky wrote it as his own requiem, aware he had not long to live. Tchaikovsky himself conducted the première of his symphony in St. Petersburg on Oct. 28, 1893. Less than two weeks later he was dead, the victim of cholera. The fact that he had contracted that dread disease by drinking unboiled water at a time when an epidemic was raging in St. Petersburg, has led to a suspicion that he might have tried to commit suicide.

Tchaikovsky bared his heart in his music, which is always subjective, emotional, and charged with the most personal feelings. His style was elegant, influenced by Western culture and sophistication. Thus Tchaikovsky stood in opposition to the nationalist composers; and thus, too, the "Russian Five" held him in disdain. Nevertheless it was Tchaikovsky, rather than the "Russian Five," who made an immediate impact upon musical audiences of the world. For with his sensitive lyricism and fervent emotions he could not fail to touch the heart and win it permanently.

The following are Tchaikovsky's principal instrumental compositions:

Chamber Music: 3 string quartets; piano trio; *Souvenir de Florence,* string sextet; *Souvenir d'un lieu cher,* for violin and piano (including the popular *Melody in E-flat*).

Orchestra: 6 symphonies; 3 piano concertos (including the famous Concerto No. 1 in B-flat minor); 4 suites (including *Mozartiana*); *Romeo and Juliet; Serenade* for string orchestra; *Marche slave; Manfred; The Tempest; Francesca da Rimini; Swan Lake,* ballet suite; *Variations on a Rococo Theme* for cello and orchestra; violin concerto; *Capriccio italien; Ouverture solennelle 1812; Hamlet; Nutcracker Suite; Sleeping Beauty,* ballet suite; incidental music to various plays.

Piano: Sonata; *Souvenir de Hapsal* (including the famous *Chant sans paroles*); *The Months; Twelve Characteristic Pieces; Dumka; Twelve Pieces of Moderate Difficulty* (including *Chanson triste*); and so on.

See: Barcarolle; *Capriccio italien;* Concerto—*Tchaikovsky; Francesca da Rimini; Hamlet;* Humoresque; *Marche slave; Mozartiana;* Nocturne; *Nutcracker Suite; Overture 1812;* Polonaise; *Romeo and Juliet;* Serenade—*Tchaikovsky; Sleeping Beauty; Swan Lake;* Suite—*Tchaikovsky;*

Symphony—*Tchaikovsky; Tempest, The;* Trio—*Tchaikovsky; Variations on a Rococo Theme;* Waltz.

Tcherepnin, Alexander, composer. Born St. Petersburg, Russia, Jan. 20, 1899. He is the son of Nikolai Tcherepnin, distinguished Russian composer and conductor (born St. Petersburg, Russia, May 14, 1873; died Issy-les-Moulineaux, France, June 26, 1945). After studying music with his father and attending the St. Petersburg Conservatory, Alexander Tcherepnin became musical director of a theater in Tiflis. Soon after the Revolution in Russia, the family went to live in Paris, where Alexander attended the Conservatory. He then began a successful career as pianist with a recital in London and performances throughout Europe. He also soon distinguished himself as a composer with his first piano concerto, introduced at Monte Carlo in 1923, a ballet, *Ajanta Frescos,* successfully presented by Anna Pavlova, and an opera, *Ol-Ol,* given at Weimar in 1928. In 1933 he embarked on a world tour as composer-pianist, paying his first visit to the United States in 1934. From 1934 to 1937 he lived in the Orient, where he became interested in Eastern music, whose style he began assimilating with his own writing. Since World War II he has divided his time between Europe and the United States. He has taught piano and composition in San Francisco, and since 1949 at the De Paul University Music School in Chicago.

Russian and oriental influences are pronounced in his music. A unique technical feature of his writing is the use of a nine-tone scale, which has been especially effective in projecting satirical or grotesque moods. His major works for orchestra include 4 symphonies, 3 piano concertos, a harmonica concerto, Concertino for violin, piano, and strings, *Suite georgienne* for piano and string orchestra, *Nevsky Prospekt, Enfance de Sainte Nino, Symphonic March, Evocation,* Suite, Capriccio, and incidental music for various plays. In chamber music he produced 2 string quartets, 3 cello sonatas, a piano quintet, flute quartet, flute trio, trumpet trio, piano trio, violin sonata; for the piano, a sonata, sonatina, toccatas, etudes, bagatelles, preludes, pieces, and so on.

Teatro Argentina. *See:* Augusteo Orchestra.

Tedesca. Italian for "German." The designation "alla tedesca" (for example, "alla danza tedesca" in Beethoven's B-flat major String Quartet, op. 130) means to be played in the style of a German dance.

Telemann, Georg Philipp, composer. Born Magdeburg, Germany, March 14, 1681; died Hamburg, Germany, June 25, 1767. He was practically self-taught in music, having been trained for the law. After giving up law for music, he was appointed in 1704 Kapellmeister of New Church in Leipzig and director of a theater there for which he wrote several operas. From 1704 to 1708 he was Kapellmeister to Count Promnitz at Sorau. During this period he became acquainted with French music, of which he became such an enthusiast that he soon became one of the first German composers to write operas in that style. He subsequently was employed as Kapellmeister in Eisenach and Frankfort, and as cantor of the Johanneum in Hamburg. He remained in the latter city until the end of his life, organizing there a Collegium Musicum which gave regular concerts and founding one of the first music journals published in Germany. He also wrote a great deal of music, the most important being for the church and the stage. His vast output of instrumental music includes over five hundred overtures; numerous concertos, sonatas, and suites for the violin; trios; and fantasias for harpsichord.

Telmányi, Emil, violinist and conductor. Born Arad, Hungary (now Rumania), June 22, 1892. He received his musical training at the Academy of Music in Budapest. His concert début took place in 1911 with the Berlin Philharmonic in the German première of Elgar's Violin Concerto. Between 1911 and 1919 he toured Europe many times, and in the latter year he made his début in the United States. In 1919 he also made his début as a conductor in Copenhagen, after which he made guest appearances with leading orchestras in Budapest, Paris, Warsaw, and Oslo. In 1929 he founded the Danish Chamber Orchestra in Copenhagen which he conducted for many years. In 1940 he was appointed professor of violin at the Aarhus Conservatory, becoming a member of its board of governors a year later. With Arne Hjorth, a violin maker, Telmányi helped construct a new kind of violin bow combining the advantages of the one used in Bach's time and the modern one. He has demonstrated it in performances of Bach's music. Telmányi has made numerous transcriptions for the violin of works by Chopin, Schumann, Mendelssohn, Brahms, and others.

Temianka, Henri, violinist. Born Greencock, Scotland, Nov. 19, 1906. After attending the Berlin High School for Music and the Curtis Institute in Philadelphia he made many tours of Europe and the United States as a concert violinist. In 1945, under the sponsorship of Mrs. William Andrews Clark, he founded the Paganini Quartet, which made its début at the Library of Congress in Washington, D.C. in a cycle of Beethoven's string quartets. Its members were Temianka, first violin; Gustave Rosseels, second violin; Charles Foldart (later Charles Libova), viola; and Lucien La Porte, cello. The Quartet toured Europe for the first time in 1947, and since then has been heard throughout the world. In 1953 the Quartet toured 60 European cities and scored a major success at the Edinburgh Festival in a presentation of all the Beethoven string quartets. It derives its name from the fact that all four members use Stradivarius instruments originally owned by Paganini.

Temperament. *See:* Equal temperament.

Tempest, The. (1) Fantasy for orchestra by Tchaikovsky, op. 18 (1873), introduced in Moscow on Dec. 19, 1873, Nikolai Rubinstein conducting. The Russian critic, V. V. Stassov, had suggested to Tchaikovsky that he write this work, and when it was written Stassov prepared its program. "The sea. Ariel, spirit of the air, raising a tempest at the bidding of the magician Prospero. Wreck of the vessel conveying Ferdinand. The enchanted isle. The first shy awakening of love between Ferdinand and Miranda. Ariel, Caliban. The enamored pair give themselves up to the magic of love. Prospero divests himself of his power of enchantment and quits the island. The sea." The principal themes, a graceful song for strings and a ponderous rhythmic subject for cellos and basses, describe Ariel and Caliban respectively.

(2) *See:* Shakespeare, William.

Tempo. Time.

Tempo Giusto. Exact time.

Tempo Ordinario. Common time.

Tempo Primo. Return to the original tempo after a change.

Tempo Rubato. *See:* Rubato.

Tendres Plaintes, Les (Rameau). *See: Pièces de clavecin* and *Nouvelle suite de pièces de clavecin.*

Teneramente. Tenderly.

Tennyson, Alfred, Lord, poet. Born Somersby, England, Aug. 6, 1809; died Haslemere, England, Oct. 6, 1892. Tennyson's *Idyls of the King,* a poetic adaptation of the Arthurian legends, was the source of Edward MacDowell's tone poem for orchestra *Lancelot and Elaine,* and of Olivier Messiaen's *La Dame de Shalott,* for piano. The Nocturne, the third movement of Benjamin Britten's *Serenade* for voice and orchestra, and Edward MacDowell's *The Eagle,* for piano, were both based on poems by Tennyson. Charles Villiers Stanford wrote incidental music for *Queen Mary* and *Becket;* Sir Arthur Sullivan, for *The Foresters.*

Tenuto. A direction to hold notes or chords for their full value.

Ternary Form. A pattern consisting of three sections, the first and third being similar.

Terpander, Greek composer and instrumentalist who lived in the 7th century B.C. He is often called the father of Greek music, and is the earliest Greek musician about whom we have any information. He is believed to have won the laurel for music at the Carnean Games in 676 B.C. and subsequently became famous as a composer and a performer on the lyre.

Terrasse des audiences au clair de lune. *See:* Prelude—*Debussy.*

Terry, Charles Sanford, musicologist. Born Newport Pagnell, England, Oct. 24, 1864; died Westerton of Pitfodels, Scotland, Nov. 5, 1936. He received his education at King's College School, and at the St. Paul's Choir School. In 1903 he was appointed professor of history at Aberdeen University. He dedicated himself to research on J. S. Bach and his era, producing a definitive biography of that master (1928); a biography of Bach's son, Johann Christian (1929); *The Origin of the Family of Bach Musicians* (1929); *Bach: The Historical Approach* (1930); *Bach's Orchestra* (1932); and *The Music of Bach* (1933). He also translated the text of all the Bach cantatas into English, edited a three-volume work on Bach's chorales, and translated into English Forkel's biography of Bach.

Tertis, Lionel, violist. Born West Hartlepool, England, Dec. 29, 1876. He attended the Royal Academy of Music, where Alexander Mackenzie persuaded him to take up the study of the viola. Upon his graduation, Tertis was appointed professor of viola there. During the many years he held this post he made frequent appearances in recitals and with major orchestras and chamber-music groups. His first tour of the United States took place in 1923-1924. In 1936 Tertis withdrew from the concert stage, having achieved recognition as one of the foremost violists of his time. He experimented with new designs for and improvements in the viola. He is the author of an autobiography, *Cinderella No More* (1953), and made many transcriptions for the viola, including Mozart's Clarinet Concerto and Elgar's Cello Concerto.

Tetrachord. In diatonic music the two tones and one semitone within the interval of a perfect fourth.

Thalberg, Sigismond, pianist. Born Geneva, Switzerland, Jan. 8, 1812; died Posilipo, Italy, April 27, 1871. Thalberg was at first intended for a diplomatic career. In Vienna he attended the Polytechnic School while studying music privately with Simon Sechter and Hummel among others. Embracing music as a career by 1830, he started touring southern Germany as a concert pianist. In 1834 he was appointed chamber virtuoso to the Emperor of Austria. He went to Paris a year later, making sensational appearances. During the next fifteen years his brilliant technique and beautiful legato playing made him an idol of the music world, his popularity everywhere rivalling that of Liszt. His American début took place in 1856, when he toured in joint concerts with Vieuxtemps. In 1858 he went into temporary retirement, from which he emerged three years later for a tour of Europe and Brazil. In 1864 he withdrew permanently from the concert stage and spent the rest of his life in Posilipo as a winegrower.

Theme. The melodic subject of a movement or composition.

Theme and variations. *See:* Variation.

Theme with Variations According to the Four Temperaments. For piano and strings by Paul Hindemith (1940), first performed in Boston on Sept. 3, 1943, Richard Burgin conducting. The "four temperaments" are the four moods: melancholy, sanguine, phlegmatic, and choleric. Though described as a theme and variations, this work consists of three themes presented in three sections. Each variation appears in the same order as the themes, and is also divided into three sections. First we get a presentation of the three themes: the first in the strings (Moderato); the second in the piano (*Allegro assai*); the third in the orchestra (Moderato). The first variation is "melancholic," with a melody in muted violins appearing against a piano background. After a quick section, the variation ends with a slow march for piano. The second variation is "sanguine," a waltz tune for piano and strings. The third is "phlegmatic," comprising a Moderato theme for strings followed by a brighter Allegretto thought for piano and concluding with an equally vigorous subject for strings and piano (*Allegretto scherzando*). The last variation, "choleric," begins with a forceful series of chords in the piano, answered by the orchestra. A passionate interlude ensues, and the variation ends with a stately section.

Theory. The science of composition.

Theremin, Leon (born **Lev Termen**), scientist. Born St. Petersburg, Russia, Aug. 15, 1896. He is the inventor of the earliest electronic musical instruments, named after him. He studied physics at the University of Leningrad, and music at the Musical Institute. In 1919 he became director of the Laboratory of Electrical Oscillations at the Physico-Technical Institute. There he created his electronic instrument, demonstrating it for the first time at the Electrical Congress in August 1920. Musical sounds were produced by electric oscillations varying in pitch as movements of the hand approached or receded from the instrument. In 1927 he toured the United States. Leopold Stokowski experimented with the Theremin in the Philadelphia Orchestra and Joseph Schillinger wrote for it an *Airphonic Suite.*

Thibaud, Jacques, violinist. Born Bordeaux, France, Sept. 27, 1880; died Mont Cemet, France, Sept. 1, 1953. After attending the Paris Conservatory he appeared as soloist with the Colonne Orchestra in 1898 with such success that he was required to make 54 solo appearances in Paris that same season. He then toured Europe as a virtuoso. On Oct. 31, 1903, he made his American début in New York with the Wetzler Orchestra. When he next made a tour of the United States, in 1913, he was already recognized as one of France's foremost violinists, an elegant stylist. Besides his appearances in recitals and as soloist with orchestras throughout the world, Thibaud played chamber music with Pablo Casals and Alfred Cortot. He was killed in an airplane crash en route to French Indo-China to perform there for French troops.

Third. The interval between two notes separated by two diatonic notes. Thirds can be major (C to E, for example), minor (C to E-flat), augmented (C to E-sharp), or diminished (C to E-double flat).

Thomas, Theodore, conductor. Born Esens, Germany, Oct. 11, 1835; died Chicago, Jan. 4, 1905. He studied the violin with his father, making a public appearance in Germany when he was six. In 1845 he came to United States, which from then on remained his permanent home. After playing the violin in various orchestras, he made his début as a conductor in 1858 at the Academy of Music in New York. He also inaugurated and appeared in chamber-music concerts in New York which took place from 1855 to 1869. From 1862 to 1878 he led orchestral concerts at Irving Hall in New York. In 1869 he established this orchestra on a permanent basis. As the Theodore Thomas Orchestra it toured the United States for almost twenty years, often performing in cities and towns that never before had heard a symphony concert. Intermittently between 1877 and 1891 he was conductor of the New York Philharmonic, and in 1873 he helped organize the Cincinnati Music Festival which he conducted until his death. When the Chicago Orchestra was founded in 1891, Thomas was appointed permanent conductor, retaining this post until the end of his life. Thomas was responsible for introducing to the United States many masterworks never before heard in this country, together with works by many modern American and European composers. He was one of the great pioneers in spreading interest in symphonic music and helping to create a musical culture in the United States.

Thompson, Randall, composer. Born New York City, April 21, 1899. After being graduated from Harvard in 1920 he studied composition with Ernest Bloch and in 1922 received a fellowship from the American Academy in Rome. From 1927 to 1929 he was assistant professor of music at Wellesley College, and subsequently he was on the music faculty of the University of California. From 1939 to 1941 he was director of the Curtis Institute in Philadelphia; from 1941 to 1946 professor of music at the University of Virginia; and since 1948 professor of music at Harvard. As a composer, Thompson first achieved maturity and significance with his Second Symphony, completed in 1931 and successfully introduced by the Rochester Philharmonic on March 24, 1932, Howard Hanson conducting. Other compositions include a third symphony, *Trip to Nahant, The Testament of Freedom* (based on a text by Thomas Jefferson), a string quartet, suite for oboe and piano, *Jazz Poem* for piano and orchestra, a piano sonata and piano suite.

Thomson, César, violinist and teacher. Born Liège, Belgium, March 17, 1857; died Lugano, Switzerland, Aug. 21, 1931. He attended the Liège Conservatory, and completed his study of the violin with Hubert Léonard. After playing the violin in various orchestras in Italy and Germany he served as professor of violin at the Liège Conservatory from 1882 to 1898, and in 1898 succeeded Eugène Ysaÿe at the Brussels Conservatory. All the while he made many appearances in Europe and the United States. He was also founder and first violinist of a distinguished string quartet bearing his name. At the outbreak of World War I he settled in Paris, where he joined the faculty of the Paris Conservatory. From 1924 to 1927 he gave master classes in violin at a Conservatory in Ithaca, N.Y., and at the Juilliard School in New York City. He edited and made many transcriptions for the violin of music by the early Italian school.

Thomson, Virgil, composer and music critic. Born Kansas City, Mo., Nov. 25, 1896. While attending Harvard, he took courses in music with Edward Burlingame Hill and Archibald Davison. After his graduation in 1922 he went to Paris, where he lived on and off for many years and studied composition with Nadia Boulanger. During this period he completed several provocative works including an opera to a text by Gertrude Stein, *Four Saints in Three Acts,* introduced in Hartford, Conn., on Feb. 8, 1934. While living in Paris, Thomson also served as a correspondent for *Modern Music.* From 1940 to 1954, Thomson was the principal music critic of the New York *Herald Tribune.* Thomson has produced many important instrumental compositions. His writing is always direct and simple, often with a pronounced American character. In 1949 he received the Pulitzer Prize in music for *Louisiana Story,* a score written for a documentary motion picture. Thomson is the author of *The State of Music* (1939), *The Musical Scene* (1945), *The Art of Judging Music* (1948), and *Music Right and Left* (1951). Among his principal works for orchestra are 2 symphonies, 2 sets of orchestral *Portraits, The Plow That Broke the Plains, The*

River, The Seine at Night, 2 suites from *Louisiana Story, Wheat Field at Noon, Sea Piece with Birds,* a cello concerto, Concerto for Flute, Strings, and Percussion, and incidental music to many plays. He also wrote 2 string quartets, a violin sonata, sonata for solo flute, *Portraits* for violin solo, *Portraits* for violin and piano, 4 piano sonatas, and many etudes and "portraits" for piano.

See: Louisiana Story; Plow That Broke the Plains, The.

Thorough bass (or Figured bass, or Basso continuo). A system used in the 17th and 18th centuries in which an accompaniment is improvised from a given bass line, which is usually provided with numerals indicating the desired harmonies.

Three-Cornered Hat, The (El Sombrero de tres picos). Suite for orchestra by Manuel de Falla (1919) adapted from the score to a ballet introduced in London by the Ballet Russe on July 23, 1919. The scenario is based on a novel by Alarcón adapted by Martinez Sierra. A miller, his wife, and a governor make up a love triangle. Repelled by the miller's wife, the governor falls into a stream and is forced to remove his clothes and wait in her bed while they are being dried. The sudden return of the miller proves embarrassing to both the wife and the governor. But the miller is philosophical, saying that he can now go off and make love to the governor's wife. Three dances from the ballet score forming an orchestral suite are frequently performed at symphony concerts. The first, *The Neighbors,* presents its main subject immediately in the first violins. The second, *The Miller's Dance,* is built out of a rhythmic and sharply accented melody in the strings which simulates the stamping of feet in a Spanish dance, and a haunting gypsy melody for the oboe. The third, *Final Dance,* is a vigorous jota for full orchestra.

Three Places in New England. An "orchestral set" by Charles Ives (1914), introduced in Boston on Jan. 10, 1931, Nicolas Slonimsky conducting. The inspiration for this music was New England geography. The first number, *Boston Common,* was inspired by the monument to Colonel Shaw and his colored regiment by St. Gaudens. The second part, *Putnam's Camp,* is set in the small park near Redding Center, Conn., which served as winter quarters for the soldiers of General Putnam in 1778-1779. This part quotes American Revolutionary War songs and marches. Amazing use is here made of polyrhythm in a description of two different bands coming into town, each playing a different melody in a different tempo. The third part, *The Housatonic at Stockbridge,* is an impressionist tone painting inspired by Robert Underwood Johnson's poem of that title.

Through the Looking Glass. (1) Suite for orchestra by Deems Taylor (1919). This work originated as a three-movement composition for flute, oboe, clarinet, bassoon, horn, piano, and strings, introduced in New York in 1919. The composer then rescored it for full orchestra and expanded it with additional material. This is the version that became famous, and the première took place in Brooklyn, N.Y., on Oct. 10, 1923, Walter Damrosch conducting. Taylor's suite is based on the beloved children's story by Lewis Carroll and is in four sections (I. Dedication; The Garden of Live Flowers. II. Jabberwocky. III. Looking Glass Insects. IV. The White Knight). The composer has provided the following analysis: "A simple song theme, briefly developed, leads to *The Garden of Live Flowers* . . . The music reflects the brisk chatter of the swaying, bright-colored denizens of the garden." In the second movement, "the theme of that frightful beast, the Jabberwock, is first announced by the full orchestra. The clarinet then begins the tale . . . The battle with the monster is recounted in a short and rather repellent fugue, the double basses bringing up the subject and the hero fighting back in the interludes." The third movement describes "the vociferous *diptera* that made such an impression on Alice—the Bee-elephant, the Gnat, the Rocking-horse fly, and the Bread-and-butter fly." There are two themes in the concluding movement, "the first, a sort of instrumental prance, being the knight's own conception of himself as a slashing daredevil. The second is bland, mellifluous, a little sentimental—much more like the knight as he really was."

(2) *See:* Carroll, Lewis.

Thun Sonata. *See:* Sonata—*Brahms.*

Thus Spake Zarathustra (Also sprach Zarathustra). (1) Tone poem for orchestra by Richard Strauss, op. 30 (1896), introduced in Frankfort on Nov. 27, 1896, the composer conducting. This music was not intended to convey Nietzsche's philosophy in music but, as the composer explained, "the development of the human race from its origin, through the various phases of evolution, religious as well as scientific, up to Nietzsche's idea of the Superman." Strauss explained further that he wanted his music "to embody the conflict between man's nature as it is and man's metaphysical attempts to lay hold of his own nature with his intelligence—leading finally to the conquest of life by the release of laughter." The work is in several sections played without interruption. After a powerful, grandiose introduction describing Zarathustra's invocation to the sun comes *Of The Dwellers in the World Behind Us.* Horns present a Gregorian Credo. *Of Great Yearnings* has a Gregorian Magnificat in the organ. *Of Joys and Sorrows* describes human passions while *Song of the Grave* speaks of death in an eloquent melody for oboe. *Of Science* tries to present a solution to life's riddle through science. This science theme is further developed contrapuntally in *The Convalescent.* Man's quest for earthy pleasure is told in a waltz in *Dance Song.* The concluding section, *The Song of the Night Wanderer,* appears after twelve strokes of the bell announce midnight.

(2) *See:* Nietzsche, Friedrich.

Tie. A curved line between two notes of the same pitch, making of them a single note whose value is the sum of both.

Till Eulenspiegel's Merry Pranks (Till Eulenspiegels lustige Streiche). Tone poem for orchestra by Richard Strauss, op. 28 (1895), first performed in Cologne on Nov. 5, 1895, Franz Wuellner conducting. The complete title of the composition continues: "After the old-fashioned roguish manner, in rondo form." The source of this music is a famous old German legend about a chronic rascal named Till Eulenspiegel who is condemned to death but manages to escape this fatal punishment. In Strauss' tone poem he is relentlessly doomed at the gallows. The tone poem opens with a simple folk tune for strings which seems to say, "Once upon a time there was a rogue named Till Eulenspiegel." The French horn then tells of his bent for mischief in a sprightly tune, while an even saucier subject for small clarinet brings the culprit on the scene. The music now grows agitated, stormy, filled with discord as Till performs his various pranks. He causes panic in the marketplace by invading it astride a horse; he puts on holy garb and mouths pious sentiments. A glissando in the violin tells how he tears off these holy vestments and loud horns describe his rage when he is rejected in love. But Till forgets his frustration by mocking at a group of Philistines and participating in a village dance with the girls. A drum roll suggests Till is about to be brought to justice, and a funeral march conducts him to the gallows. Above the strains of this funeral music can clearly be heard Till's impudent theme in defiance of his accusers. But Till cannot escape his fate, as we are told in a descending major-seventh interval in bassoons, horns, trombones, and tuba. All is silence. Then a return of the folk tune which opened the tone poem, in slightly altered form, reminds us that once upon a time there was a rogue named Till Eulenspiegel.

Timbre. The specific tone-color of a particular instrument or voice.

Time. Tempo, rate of speed.

Timpani. *See:* Kettledrums.

Tintagel. Tone poem for orchestra by Arnold Bax (1917). This is one of the composer's best known works for orchestra, and it was inspired by Celtic poetry and lore. The composer provided the following program: "The work is intended to evoke a tone picture of the castle-crowned cliff of Tintagel and more particularly the wide distances of the Atlantic as seen from the cliffs of Cornwall on a sunny but not windless summer day. In the middle section of the piece it may be imagined that with the increasing tumult of the sea arise memories of the historical and legendary associations of the place, especially those connected with King Arthur, King Mark, and Tristram and Iseult. Regarding the last named it will be noticed that at the climax of the more literary division of the work there is a brief reference to one of the subjects in the first act of *Tristan*."

Tippett, Michael, composer. Born London, England, Jan. 2, 1905. He attended the Royal College of Music, and first attracted attention to his creative talent with the Fantasy Sonata for piano in 1938 and a Concerto for Double String Orchestra a year later. Subsequent works, notably a symphony and his third string quartet, pointed up his technical assurance as well as his growing artistic maturity; in still other compositions, mainly for chorus, he introduced a deep humanitarian feeling. He has also distinguished himself as a conductor of educational concerts and as a teacher of composition at Morley College. Besides works already mentioned he wrote a second symphony, *Fantasy on a Theme by Handel* for piano and orchestra, *Variations on a Theme by Corelli* for strings, *Little Music* for strings, and Suite in D major, for orchestra.

Titan, The. *See:* Symphony—*Mahler.*

Toccata. A form of organ music which has the character of an improvisation and which exploits the virtuosity of the performer through elaborate runs, figurations, and so on. The form was crystallized in the 17th century, with such masters of organ music as Frescobaldi, Froberger, and Buxtehude. One of the most outstanding examples of a toccata in the era preceding Johann Sebastian Bach is Frescobaldi's *Toccata of the Elevation.*

But it was J. S. Bach who brought the toccata to its most advanced stage of structural and artistic development. One of his most celebrated works in this form is the Toccata and Fugue in D minor. This toccata is so spacious in form, rhapsodic in style, windswept in emotional force that André Pirro once described it as a "classic storm." He provides the following additional comment on this music by referring to it as "the dazzling lightning, the clap of thunder, rumbling formidably in the percussions

of a long broken chord, above the crash of a profound pedal; the wind, then the hail." The fugue begins serenely but soon gains in intensity to match the drama of the toccata. This work is also familiar in numerous orchestral transcriptions, notably by Stokowski, Ormandy, and Henry J. Wood.

Another frequently played toccata by Bach is that in C major. This is a three-section work for organ. The first part is the toccata with its emphasis on virtuosity. The middle part is a brief and expressive song. The concluding part is a fugue. Stokowski, Ormandy, and Leo Weiner are a few of those who have transcribed this work for orchestra.

While the toccata ceased to interest composers after Bach's day, there are several isolated pieces in this form by later composers. One is a dashing piece for the piano by Schumann, the Toccata in C major, op. 7 (1834). It is based on a brief, four-note melodic figure which is developed in thirds, sixths, and broken chords with an unarrested momentum. The finale of Ravel's *Le Tombeau de Couperin*, for piano, is a toccata, and so is the conclusion of Debussy's *Pour le Piano*. Prokofiev wrote an excellent Toccata for piano, op. 11 (1912), and Respighi, one for piano and orchestra (1928). Max Reger wrote numerous toccatas for the organ.

Toch, Ernst, composer. Born Vienna, Austria, Dec. 7, 1887. He was trained for medicine. But while attending the University of Vienna he studied music mostly by himself and began composition; an early string quartet, completed when he was seventeen, was performed in Vienna by the Arnold Rosé Quartet. Winning the Mozart Prize in 1909 enabled him to attend Hoch's Conservatory in Frankfort, where he specialized in the piano. In 1910 he won the Mendelssohn Prize for composition, and after that he received the Austrian State Prize for four consecutive times for orchestral and chamber-music works. In 1910 he abandoned his medical studies, and three years later was appointed teacher of composition at the Mannheim School for Music. Performances of his chamber music at major German festivals brought him recognition. That recognition spread to the United States in 1932 when he toured the country in performances of his own works. After the rise of the Hitler regime in Germany, Toch settled in the United States and subsequently became a citizen. In 1937 he went to live in California, where he wrote music for motion pictures and taught composition at the University of Southern California. He later served as visiting professor at Harvard, University of Utah, University of Oregon, and the Berkshire Music Centre. In America, Toch wrote some of his most popular works for orchestra, including *Big Ben Variations,* the concert overture *Pinocchio,* and his third symphony, the last of which received the Pulitzer Prize in music in 1956. Formerly a Romanticist who owed a strong debt to Brahms, Toch developed a personal style in which Classical traditions are skilfully reconciled with modern techniques and idioms. In 1957 he was elected a member of the National Institute of Arts and Letters and in 1958 he received from the West German Federal Republic the Grand Cross of the Order of Merit. Besides works already mentioned Toch has written for orchestra a fourth symphony, 2 piano concertos, a cello concerto, *Bunte Suite, The Idle Stroller, Hyperion, Notturno, Circus Overture, Peter Pan: A Fairy Tale,* and incidental music to various plays. He also wrote 9 string quartets, 2 violin sonatas, a piano quintet, string trio, cello sonata, clarinet sonata, 3 piano sonatas, and many pieces for the piano.

See: Big Ben; Symphony—*Toch.*

Tod und das Maedchen Quartet. *See:* Quartet—*Schubert.*

Tod und Verklaerung (Strauss). *See: Death and Transfiguration.*

Tolstoy, Count Leo, novelist. Born Tula, Russia, Aug. 28, 1828; died Astapovo, Russia, Nov. 20, 1910. Leoš Janáček's String Quartet No. 1 was inspired by Tolstoy's novel, *Kreutzer Sonata,* and Albert Roussel's symphonic prelude, *Resurrection,* by the novel of that name.

Tombeau. A dramatic elegy, as, for example, Maurice Ravel's *Le Tombeau de Couperin* (see below).

Tombeau de Couperin, Le. Suite for piano by Maurice Ravel (1917), written to honor the memory of the composer's friends who died in World War I. This composition pays tribute to Couperin-le-Grand, early-18th-century composer of French harpsichord music. Ravel's suite is in the Baroque form and comprises 18th-century dances and forms: I. Prelude; II. Fugue; III. Forlane; IV. Rigaudon; V. Menuet; VI. Toccata. In style, Ravel preserves the serene and graceful manner of 18th-century music without deserting modern harmony and rhythm; the stately minuet, for example, ends in an unresolved discord. But the fusion of old and new is achieved so naturally that no feeling of incongruity exists. In 1920 the composer orchestrated this suite, using only four of the movements, and omitting the fugue and the toccata. The orchestral version was performed for the first time in Paris on Feb. 28, 1920, Rhené-Baton conducting.

Tommasini, Vincenzo, composer. Born Rome, Italy, Sept. 17, 1878; died there, Dec. 23, 1950. While receiving his academic education at the University of Rome (where he specialized in Greek and philology), he pursued an equally intensive training in music at the Santa Cecilia Liceo and Academy. In 1902 he made an extensive trip in Europe, a period in which he studied with Max Bruch in Germany; he also visited the United States. Maturity as a composer was first achieved with a string quartet in 1910; recognition came three years later with a one-act opera, *Uguale fortuna,* which won first prize in a national competition. Later successes included the tone poem for orchestra, *Chiari di luna,* introduced under Toscanini's direction, and the ballet, *The Good Humored Ladies (Le Donne di buon umore),* presented by the Ballet Russe. In these and subsequent works, Tommasini became a leading figure in the movement in 20th-century Italy to create a revival of instrumental music. He was partial to old Italian forms, and often simulated the style of old Italian songs and dances; nevertheless his melodic and harmonic writing is personal, idea and form always being beautifully integrated. Orchestral works other than those already commented upon include *Paesaggi toscani,*

Prelude, Fanfare and Fugue, Carnival of Venice, Quattro pezzi, Napoli, Three Symphonic Dances, La Tempesta, Duo Concertante for piano and orchestra, and various concertos (violin; string quartet; strings; orchestra with cello obbligato). He also wrote 3 string quartets, a violin sonata, and a harp sonata.

See: Carnival of Venice (2); *Good-Humored Ladies, The; Tuscan Landscapes.*

Tonality. The quality that binds certain chords together as aspects of a single key.

Tondichtung. German for tone poem or symphonic poem.

Tone. Quality of sound.

Tone clusters. A term most often associated with the early piano music of Henry Cowell in which the harmonic writing is extended through the use of simultaneous seconds. These harmonies are played on the piano with fists, forearms, palms of the hand, and occasionally even a ruler. Cowell was responsible for giving this technique the name of tone-cluster, but he did not invent it. Many composers used it before him, including Charles Ives in the United States and Vladimir Rebikov in Russia.

Tone poem (or **Symphonic poem**). A one-movement composition for orchestra, flexible in form, which realistically translates into musical terms a poem, prose text, story, painting, or idea. The tone poem was an invention of Franz Liszt in his effort to bring to orchestral music the dramatic power and esthetic principles of the Wagner music dramas. It was brought to its highest technical and artistic development by Richard Strauss. It is a form favored by many contemporary composers since Strauss.

Tone row. *See:* Schoenberg, Arnold.

Tonic. Principal note of a scale or key.

Tonic chord. A chord built on the tonic.

Toronto Symphony Orchestra. The leading orchestra in Canada, founded in 1906 by Frank S. Weisman, who remained its principal conductor until 1918, when the orchestra passed temporarily out of existence. It was revived in 1923 for "Twilight Concerts" in Massey Hall under the direction of Luigi von Kunits, and in 1927 it resumed its original name of Toronto Symphony. Upon the death of von Kunits in 1931, the direction of the orchestra passed to Sir Ernest Macmillan, under whose guidance the orchestra achieved a position in the first rank. Macmillan resigned in 1956 and was succeeded by Walter Susskind.

Toscanini, Arturo, conductor. Born Parma, Italy, March 25, 1867; died New York City, Jan. 16, 1957. His musical training took place at the Parma Conservatory, from which he was graduated with highest honors in 1885. For a few years he played the cello in various Italian opera orchestras. His début as a conductor was unscheduled, and took place under dramatic circumstances. He was a cellist in the orchestra of an Italian touring opera company performing in South America when its conductor resigned just before a performance of Verdi's *Aida* in Rio de Janeiro on June 25, 1886. Toscanini took over the baton and without consulting the score, which he had memorized, directed with such authority and brilliance that he received an ovation. From then on he was the company's principal conductor during the remainder of the tour, directing eighteen different operas, and all from memory.

Back in Italy he continued conducting operas with such distinction that he was soon acclaimed the outstanding young conductor in the country. He also began conducting symphony concerts, first with the Turin Municipal Orchestra and subsequently with the orchestra of La Scala. But for a long time his field was essentially the opera. In 1898 he received the most important opera post in Italy, that of principal conductor of La Scala, which under his exacting and inspiring leadership entered upon one of its most brilliant eras. His first regime there lasted five years. He returned to his post for another two seasons from 1906 to 1908, and for eight years between 1921 and 1929, when he was also the artistic director of the company. Meanwhile, from 1908 to 1915, he appeared as conductor at the Metropolitan Opera, New York, where he made his American début on Nov. 16, 1908, in *Aida*. On Feb. 21, 1909, he made his American bow as a symphony conductor with a performance of Verdi's *Requiem* in New York, and on April 13, 1913, he conducted a performance of Beethoven's Ninth Symphony. He reappeared in the United States as an orchestral conductor during 1920-1921 with the visiting La Scala Orchestra.

Though he was to give magnificent performances of opera at Bayreuth, Salzburg, and elsewhere in Europe, his immense energies and formidable gifts after 1929 were channelled into symphonic music. On Jan. 14, 1926, he appeared as guest conductor of the New York Philharmonic. For the next decade he served as principal conductor of that orchestra. In the spring of 1930 the New York Philharmonic made its first tour of Europe, with Toscanini as its conductor. Toscanini gave his last concert with the Philharmonic on April 29, 1936. On December 26 of that same year he conducted the first concert of the newly organized Palestine Symphony in Tel Aviv.

In 1937 the NBC Symphony was founded by the National Broadcasting Company to bring Toscanini back to the United States in concerts to be broadcast from coast to coast. For over fifteen years Toscanini served as its musical director; with it he recorded for RCA Victor a rich library of symphonic literature. In 1940 he toured South America with the NBC Symphony, and a decade later the United States.

Toscanini conducted his last public concert, with the NBC Symphony, on April 4, 1954. After that, except for several recording sessions, he went into retirement. Toscanini suffered a stroke on New Year's Day, 1957, from which he never recovered. After his death his body was taken back to Italy to be buried in Milan on Feb. 18, 1957.

Tost Quartets. *See:* Quartet—*Haydn.*

Totenberg, Roman, violinist. Born Lodz, Poland, Jan. 1, 1913. After completing his violin studies with Carl Flesch in Berlin and Georges Enesco in Paris, he made his concert début in 1925 with the Warsaw Philharmonic. For the next few years he concertized throughout Europe, receiving in 1932 the Mendelssohn Prize for violin playing. His American début took place in Washington, D.C., on Nov. 7, 1935, and his first South American tour followed in 1937-1938. Since then he has

appeared throughout the world of music. In 1947 he became head of the violin department at the Music Academy in Santa Barbara, Calif.

Toteninsel, Die (Rachmaninoff). *See: Isle of the Dead.*

Totentanz (Danse macabre). A "paraphrase on the *Dies irae"* for piano and orchestra by Liszt (1853), introduced at The Hague on March 15, 1865, with Hans von Buelow as soloist. The source of Liszt's inspiration is not clear. One version credits Holbein's fifty-three etchings known as *The Dance of Death;* another, the painting, *The Triumph of Death,* attributed to Andrea Orcagna. This composition is a series of variations on the famous *Dies irae* theme, which appears and reappears in various guises. As Richard Pohl has written: "Irresistibly and irrevocably does this threatening motif advance, now clearly brought forward as a subject, now as a counterpoint serving as a bass, now covered over with manifold strange figures and original metamorphoses. And every variation discloses some new character—the earnest man, the flighty youth, the scornful doubter, the prayerful monk, the daring soldier, the tender maiden, the playful child."

The work opens with an austere statement of the *Dies irae* melody in low woodwind, brass, and strings. After a cadenza for the piano, the theme returns in the orchestra, and then is taken over by the piano. Only then do the variations begin, each maintaining the macabre effect of the whole, abounding in glissandi and cadenzas for the piano.

Touch. In keyboard instruments, the weight used to bring the key into action. The term is used for pianists to designate the quality of tone produced.

Tourte, François, maker of violin bows. Born Paris, France, 1747; died there, April 1835. His father and older brother were also celebrated makers of violin bows, introducing a few innovations which have since remained basic. François proved the most important of the Tourtes. He was the first to use Pernambuco wood; by subjecting it to heat he molded it into the most efficacious curvature; he was also responsible for inventing a method of fastening the hairs to the bow.

Tovey, Sir Donald Francis, pianist, composer, and musicologist. Born Eton, England, July 17, 1875; died Edinburgh, Scotland, July 10, 1940. He studied counterpoint with Walter Parratt and piano with Sophie Weisse, early distinguishing himself as a pianist in Bach's music. In 1894 he received the Lewis Nettleship scholarship for Balliol College, Oxford. He was one of the most brilliant students in the history of the College, graduating in 1898 with classical honors. In 1894 he appeared in London in a joint recital with Joseph Joachim. By 1900 he established his reputation as a concert pianist, from then on giving numerous concerts throughout Europe, often in his own works. In the succeeding years he helped organize important chamber music and orchestral concerts in London. In July 1914 he was appointed professor of music at Edinburgh University, entering upon a new and significant career as musical scholar. He wrote brilliant analyses of the orchestral repertory, establishing a standard by which program-note-writing is still measured; these were collected into six volumes entitled *Essays in Musical Analysis* (1935-1939). He was also the author of *A Companion to Bach's Art of the Fugue* (1931), *A Companion to Beethoven's Piano Sonatas* (1931), *A Musician Talks* (1941), *Beethoven* (1945), and *Essays and Lectures on Music* (1949). He wrote a considerable amount of chamber music, including 2 string quartets, a piano quartet, and various trios and sonatas. He also wrote a symphony, piano concerto, cello concerto, and sundry pieces for the piano. Tovey was knighted in 1935.

Town Hall. A major concert auditorium in New York City, situated on 43rd Street between Broadway and Sixth Avenue. It was founded in 1921 by the League for Political Education as an auditorium for debates and lectures. It opened on Jan. 12, 1921, and has since become second in importance to Carnegie Hall as the home for recitals, chamber-music concerts, and so on.

Toy Symphony. A little symphony in C major for toy instruments long attributed to Haydn. It was said that Haydn had written the work after visiting Berchtesgaden, Bavaria, in 1788, where he came upon several toy instruments. The composition he is supposed to have written used only three conventional instruments (two violins and bass) and with it the following toy noise-makers: penny trumpet, quail call, rattle, cuckoo, screech-owl, whistle, a little drum, and a little triangle. The symphony, in three brief and lively movements, was introduced in Vienna as a work by Haydn in 1790. But recent research makes it seem likely that it was written by Leopold Mozart, father of Wolfgang Amadeus, or by Michael Haydn (brother of Joseph).

Tragedy of Salome, The (La Tragédie de Salomé). Ballet suite for orchestra by Florent Schmitt, op. 50 (1907). In its original version this composition was a "mute drama," a setting of a sensual poem about Salomé by Robert d'Humières. In this form it was danced by Loie Fuller in Paris on Nov. 9, 1907. The composer later adapted his score into a ballet suite, a version introduced in Paris on Jan. 8, 1911, and since become one of his most successful works for orchestra. The suite opens with a somber prelude prognosticating Salomé's doom. A sensual dance follows, describing Salomé's joy in receiving some jewels from her mother. But once again an atmosphere of foreboding is suggested in a moody passage. The music soon becomes ecstatic, and after that is filled with terror as Salomé appears with the head of John the Baptist on a tray. She hurls the head into the sea. The waters turn to blood and a bolt of lightning razes Herod's palace and destroys Salomé.

Tragic Overture (Tragische Ouvertuere). A concert overture for orchestra by Brahms, op. 81 (1880), first performed in Vienna on Dec. 20, 1880, Hans Richter conducting. Brahms never disclosed the tragedy he had in mind in writing this music, but its heroic character and the stateliness of the music suggest a Greek drama involving a hero and fate. Two abrupt chords open the overture, followed by a febrile subject for strings. A second theme, appearing later in the woodwinds, is more gentle. Both melodies are worked out as struggle alternates with resignation. The overture ends with the first subject repeated triumphantly by brass and strings.

Tragic Symphony. *See:* Symphony—*Schubert.*

Tranquillo. Calm.

Transcription. An arrangement of a musical composition for an instrument or instruments other than what it was written for.

Transfigured Night (Verklaerte Nacht). For string orchestra by Arnold Schoenberg. It originated in 1899 as a string sextet, op. 4. In 1917 the composer transcribed it for string orchestra, the version in which it is famous. He revised it once again in 1943. This music has also been used for a ballet, *The Pillar of Fire,* introduced in New York by the Ballet Theatre on April 8, 1942.

This romantic and sensual music, influenced by Wagner, was inspired by *Weib und die Welt,* a poem by Richard Dehmel. A man and a woman are walking through a grove. The woman confesses she is about to have a child that is not his. The man understands, and forgives, and they sink into each other's arms. Then they continue their walk through the moonlight.

The composition is made up of two sections: the first, in which she confesses her guilt; and the second, in which she is forgiven. A slow, sensitive tone painting of a moonlit grove opens the composition (this music also serves as a transition between the two sections and as an ending to the entire work). Highly atmospheric and pictorial writing suggests the night, the walk, the confession, the forgiveness, and the transfiguration. The last of these is suggested by a solo violin in the upper register against plucked chords in the strings. Sensual love music follows, soon to be presented jointly with the transfigured night passage. A crescendo tells of a final outburst of passion and subsides to bring back the picture of a tranquil night and a quiet walk through the grove.

Transformation Scene. The solemn, majestic music accompanying a change of scene in Act 1 of Wagner's music drama,

Parsifal. The scene shifts from the forest near Montsalvat to the interior of the Grail Castle. The music begins with an even-rhythmed march, but it achieves an emotional climax with a poignant statement of the "Penitence" motif of Amfortas. This music, punctuated by tolling bells, ends with the approach of Parsifal and Gurnemanz to the Hall of the Grail Castle. Six trombones then pronounce the "Love Feast" motif.

A Transformation Scene also appears in Act 3. As the bells sound louder and louder, the woods of Scene 1 in that act disappear and the Hall of the Grail, from Act 1, reappears.

Transpose. To rewrite or play in another key from the original.

Trauersinfonie. *See:* Symphony—*Haydn.*

Tre Sonetti del Petrarca (Liszt). *See: Années de pèlerinage.*

Treble. The high register.

Tremolo. In string music, the rapid reiteration of a single note while the pitch remains steady.

Triad. A chord of three tones—the root, the third, and the fifth. Also any inversion or inflection of such a chord.

Triakontameron. Suite of 30 pieces in three-quarter time for piano by Leopold Godowsky (1920). The composer adapted the title of his suite from that of Boccaccio's *Decameron;* each of his thirty pieces was written in a single day. The most famous composition here—and Godowsky's most popular work— is *Alt Wien.* Other delightful atmospheric pieces are *Nocturnal Tangier* and *Ethiopian Serenade.*

Triana (Albéniz). *See: Iberia* (1).

Triangle. A percussion instrument of the symphony orchestra, a steel bar bent into the form of a triangle, but open at one angle. It is struck with a steel rod to produce a clear, tinkling sound.

Trill. A quivering sound produced by alternating a note rapidly with another, a major or minor second away.

Trio. (1) The middle section of a minuet or scherzo, usually contrasting with it in theme and texture. In the scherzo, the trio receives more extended treatment than in the minuet.

(2) In general, any composition for

three instruments, but specifically a work in four movements for three instruments which follows the structural pattern of the sonata. The most popular combination is piano, violin, and cello, known as a piano trio. The string trio is also popular, comprising a violin, viola, and cello, or two violins and cello. Less frequently encountered are the clarinet trio (clarinet, cello, and piano) or horn trio (horn, violin, and piano).

The following are some important compositions in the trio literature:

BEETHOVEN. Beethoven's op. 1 is a set of three piano trios (1793-1795). Thirteen years later he published a set of two piano trios, op. 70 (1808). The first of these, in D major, is known as the *Geister* (*Spirit*) *Trio.* This is due to the tremolo piano chords in the *Largo assai* movement which heighten and intensify the atmosphere of desolation and mystery that prevails throughout the movement. Beethoven's most celebrated piano trio is No. 6 in B-flat major, op. 97 (1811). Because of its dedication to Archduke Rudolph, the composer's patron and friend, this work has come to be known as the *Archduke Trio.* The first movement (*Allegro moderato*) is especially interesting for the nobility of the two main themes, the second somewhat reminiscent of the main subject in the first movement of the composer's Fourth Piano Concerto. The second movement (Allegro) is a delightful Scherzo, one of Beethoven's most infectious pieces in that form. The most impressive movement of all, however, is the third (*Andante cantabile*), a set of five variations on a melody of religious majesty. A recitative-like coda leads directly into the finale (*Allegro moderato*), a sprightly rondo.

BRAHMS. Brahms' Trio in B major, op. 8 (1854), is a work filled with youthful ardor, spontaneity, and fresh lyricism but within a structure and in a style often self-conscious and stilted. Thirty-seven years later Brahms revised it, bringing to it a master's technique and maturity of thought without sacrificing its ardent youthful vitality. The greatest interest in this revised trio lies in the radiant opening passage of the first movement, the drama of the coda in that movement, the dramatic intensity of the trio of the Scherzo, and the radiance of the Adagio.

But the Brahms Piano Trio performed most frequently in that in C minor, op. 101 (1886). This is consistently powerful, and at times brusque, music. The first movement (*Allegro energico*) is constructed mostly from a vigorous fournote subject which is evolved with dramatic force in the development. Serenity prevails in the second movement (*Andante grazioso*), and lightness and grace in the ensuing Scherzo (*Presto non assai*). But the robustness of the first movement returns in the finale (*Allegro molto*), which William Murdoch described as "defiant and relentless."

DVOŘÁK. The Piano Trio in E minor, op. 90 (1891), is known as the *Dumky Trio,* since it is made up of a series of elegiac movements. ("Dumka" is a Slavic term meaning musical lament.) This trio has six brief movements, each in a sad, and at times turbulent, mood.

RAVEL. Maurice Ravel's Trio in A minor (1914) is one of the composer's most important chamber-music works (I. *Modéré.* II. *Pantoum: Assez vif.* III. *Passecaille: Très large.* IV. *Animé*). The first movement has especial interest for its original metrical design. Both principal themes here are of a serene character. The Scherzo movement that follows is a "pantoum"—the "pantoum" being a form of Malayan poetry in which two ideas are expressed simultaneously, each pursuing its own train of thought independently. Ravel's first idea is a staccato motif, and the second is a waltz. In the Passacaglia the problem of the opposing sonorities of piano and strings is skilfully solved, and in the finale bright flashes of wit provide sustained vivacity.

SCHUBERT. Schubert produced two remarkable piano trios, both in 1827. The first is in B-flat major, op. 99 (I. *Allegro moderato.* II. *Andante un poco mosso.* III. Allegro. IV. *Allegro vivace*). In the first movement, a strong and impetuous subject is immediately presented in the opening measures; by contrast, the second subject is a melody of transcendent beauty in the violin. The development of both subjects is more sophisticated and subtle than we usually encounter with Schubert, and the recapitulation is brought on with a surprising change of tonality (G-flat instead of B-flat). The second movement once again is a Schubertian melody of singular loveliness; it is first stated by the cello, then the violin, and finally the piano. The second theme, in 32nd notes, offers a welcome change of pace. The main part of the Scherzo has rhythmic vitality, but in the trio lyricism once again is dominant. The finale has the lusty vigor of a peasant dance.

The Trio No. 2 in E-flat major, op. 100, is on the whole more tragic in content (I. Allegro. II. *Andante con moto.* III. *Allegro moderato.* IV. *Allegro moderato*). To Schumann the first movement combined "profound imagination with heartfelt longing"; the most appealing melody in the movement appears, strange to say, not in the exposition section but in the development, where it is transformed by several variations and changed tonalities and is brought to a climactic point. The second movement is like a funeral march, the main theme given to the cello against a march-like rhythm in the piano. In the Scherzo the principal section is soft and restrained while the trio is loud and energetic. The finale is the most extended of the four movements, consisting of three self-sufficient groups. In the first group a simple folk tune is contrasted with a more brilliant passage. The second is dominated by the piano, while in the third the funeral march music of the second movement is recalled.

TCHAIKOVSKY. The Piano Trio in A minor, op. 50 (1881), was written in memory of Nikolai Rubinstein, who died in 1881 (I. *Pezzo elegiaco.* II. *Tema con variazioni.* III. Finale). The first movement is in sonata form with its main melody an eloquent elegy. The second movement is in a brighter mood, intended to describe a happy day spent by the composer with Rubinstein. A spirited melody here is subjected to eleven brief variations, each of the variations said to represent some phase of Rubinstein's career. The finale is distinguished for its contrapuntal dexterity and rhythmic vitality.

Triple concerto. A concerto for three solo instruments and orchestra, as for example Beethoven's Concerto in C major for Piano, Violin, Cello and Orchestra, op. 56.

Triple time. Three beats to a measure.

Triplet. A group of three notes played in the same time as would normally be taken by two notes of the same value.

Triptyque. For string quartet or string orchestra by Alexander Tansman (1931). As a string quartet it was introduced in Paris by the Brosa Quartet in 1931; as a work for string orchestra, in St. Louis on Nov. 6, 1931, Vladimir Golschmann conducting. The work has three parts: I. *Allegro risoluto;* II. Andante; III. Presto. A basic thought in the first is presented at once; it is a rhythmic subject for second violins against an equally forceful cello background. The second theme is based upon a rhythmic play on the interval of the third. The second movement opens with a serene melody which receives fugal treatment in the development. The finale is a kind of perpetual motion interrupted midway by a theme of grave character; the work ends with a solemn subject similar to a Polish hymn.

Tristan and Isolde, Prelude and Love-Death. The opening prelude and the closing scene of Wagner's music drama. The opera, libretto by the composer, was first performed in Munich on June 10, 1865. The prelude opens with a slow phrase in the cellos, soon joined by another in the oboe; these have been designated as the motifs of "longing" and "desire." They are repeated twice, followed by cries of torment in strings and woodwinds. After the eruption of a loud chord, a wonderful song unfolds in the cellos signifying Tristan's love glance. As this melody is developed and given an elaborate polyphonic dress, it becomes increasingly passionate. The return of the "longing" and "desire" motifs ends the prelude. The *Love-Death,* or *Liebestod,* follows without pause. In the music drama this is sung by Isolde over the dead body of Tristan just before her own death; this melody is derived from the love-music of the second act. In the orchestral version, Isolde's moving death-song is taken over by the strings against the somber voice of the clarinet. The music grows more and more ecstatic as the tempo quickens, then is permitted to subside gently as strings provide a quiet and gentle benediction over Isolde's death.

For other excerpts from *Tristan and Isolde see:* Prelude, Act 3 (see below); *Liebesnacht.*

Tristan and Isolde, Prelude to Act 3. An orchestral prelude to the third act of Wagner's music drama, *Tristan and Isolde.* This is a melancholy tone poem describing the garden in Brittany overlooking the sea where Tristan is lying fatally wounded. The prelude opens with a gloomy theme in the low register. An ascending subject for violins leads to another mournful theme in horns and cellos. This material is repeated and elaborated upon with unrelieved gloom.

Triton. A school of young French composers founded in Paris in the 1930's by Jean Rivier and Henri Barraud. Rivier was chairman from 1936 to 1940. The school advocated moderation in composition as opposed to such extremists as the atonalists, neo-Classicists, and mystics.

Tritone. An augmented fourth or diminished fifth.

Trojan Women, The. *See:* Euripides.

Trombone. A brass instrument, lower in register than the trumpet but higher than the tuba. It has a cupped mouthpiece and is manipulated by means of a slide; its tone is solemn. Tenor and bass trombones are used in the symphony orchestra.

Troppo. Too much.

Trout Quintet. *See:* Quintet—*Schubert.*

Trumpet. The highest in register and the loudest in sonority of brass instruments in the symphony orchestra. It has a clear, brilliant tone and is operated with the aid of three pistons; it has a semi-cylindrical bore and a cup mouthpiece.

Tschaikowsky, Peter Ilitch. *See:* Tchaikovsky, Peter Ilitch.

Tuba. The lowest in register of the brass instruments. It has valves, a coiled tube, and a deep funnel mouthpiece. It differs from other brasses in that it is played in a vertical instead of horizontal position. Wagner invented a new kind of tuba to fill in the gap between horns and ordinary tubas. He used four such tubas in his cycle of dramas, *The Ring of the Nibelungs:* two tenor tubas in B-flat, and two bass tubas in F. Other composers since Wagner have used these tubas effectively, including Bruckner in his later symphonies, Richard Strauss, and Stravinsky.

Tuning. Adjustment of an instrument to the correct pitch.

Turangalîla. *See:* Messiaen, Olivier.

Turca. Turkish. "Alla turca" means in the Turkish style, as in "Allegretto alla turca" in Mozart's Piano Sonata in A major, K. 331. *See: Turkish March.*

Tureck, Rosalyn, pianist. Born Chicago, Ill., Dec. 14, 1914. From 1931 to 1935 she attended the Juilliard School, a pupil of Olga Samaroff. In 1935 she received the Schubert Memorial Award, making her concert début in New York on October 18 of that year. She subsequently distinguished herself as a Bach specialist. She gave her first cycle of six Bach concerts in New York in 1937-1938, for which she received the Town Hall Young Artists Award. She has given similar series in Europe, and has made recordings of Bach's clavier music. Since 1935 she has also devoted herself to teaching, mainly at the David Mannes School and after that at the Juilliard School of Music.

Turina, Joaquín, composer. Born Seville, Spain, Dec. 9, 1882; died Madrid, Spain, Jan. 14, 1949. After attending the Madrid Conservatory he lived for a decade in Paris, where he studied composition with Vincent d'Indy at the Schola Cantorum. His early chamber music reflects the impact upon him of French music in general, and d'Indy in particular. However, his association in Paris with his compatriot, Isaac Albéniz, proved a stimulus directing him towards the writing of Spanish national music. His first major work in such an idiom is still one of his best, *La Procesión del rocío* for orchestra, introduced in Madrid in 1913. In that year Turina returned to his native land, to occupy an important position in its musical life. He played the piano in the Quinteto de Madrid; wrote music criticisms for leading publications; taught at the Madrid Conservatory; was a member of the Spanish Academy of Arts. He also continued to turn out significant works. In 1920 his *Sinfonía sevillana* received first prize in a competition held at San Sebastian. This and later compositions were successful projections of the personality, geography, culture, folksong, and dance of his native land. Besides works already mentioned, his orchestral music includes *Evangelio de Navidad, Danzas fantásticas,* and *Rítmos.* In chamber music he produced 2 piano trios, a string quartet, piano quintet, *Oración del torero* for string quartet, piano quartet, *Serenata* for string quartet, and *Circulo* for violin, cello, and piano, among other works. He also wrote prolifically for the piano, including *Sonata romántica, Coins de Séville, Mujeres españolas, Cuentos de España, Jardines de Andalucía, Danzas gitanos,* and *Niñerias.*

See: *Oración del torero; Procesión del rocío, La.*

Turkish March. (1) *See: Ruins of Athens, The* (Beethoven).

(2) *See:* Sonata—*Mozart.*

Tuscan Landscapes (Paesaggi toscani). Rhapsody for orchestra by Vincenzo Tommasini (1922), introduced in Rome in December 1923, Molinari conducting. This rhapsody is made up of popular Tuscan folk melodies. It is in two sections, played without interruption. In the first (*Andante sostenuto*) a melancholy Tuscan melody is heard against a nebulous harmonic background. In the second (Vivace) two lively folk tunes provide a change of mood.

Tutta (or Tutto). All, entirely.

Tutti. Entrance of the entire orchestra after a solo passage.

Tuxen, Erik, conductor. Born Mannheim, Germany, July 4, 1902. After completing his music study in Paris, Berlin, and Vienna, he received his conducting apprenticeship in various European opera houses. In 1936 he was appointed conductor of the Danish State Radio Orchestra, with which he achieved prominence and which he led in performances

at the Edinburgh Festival in 1950. He also appeared as guest conductor of major European orchestras. He made his American début in Philadelphia in the spring of 1951.

Twelfth Night. (1) Concert overture by Mario Castelnuovo-Tedesco (1933), first performed in Rome on Jan. 6, 1935, Vittorio Gui conducting. In this music the composer emphasizes the character of the Shakespeare play rather than the plot. An opening slow section describes Prince Orsino. This is followed by a gay, satirical section for bassoon depicting Malvolio. These two ideas are developed as subsidiary characters (the heroine, the clown) make their entrance. Towards the end of the overture, three old men dance to the melody of an ancient galliard.

(2) *See:* Shakespeare, William.

Twelve-tone row or **technique (Dodecaphony).** *See:* Schoenberg, Arnold.

Twilight of the Gods, The (Goetterdaemmerung). The concluding music drama in Wagner's cycle *The Ring of the Nibelungs.* For orchestral excerpts *see: Ring of the Nibelungs, The.*

Two Gentlemen of Verona. *See:* Shakespeare, William.

Two Jamaican Pieces. Suite for orchestra by Arthur Benjamin (1938), utilizing West Indian melodies. The first piece is *Jamaican Song;* the second, *Jamaican Rhumba.* The latter has become independently popular in a two-piano arrangement by the composer. The gay and saucy rhumba melody is heard against a light staccato accompaniment.

Tzigane. Rhapsody for violin and orchestra, or piano, by Maurice Ravel (1924). It originated as a work for "luthéal" and piano—the luthéal being a violin with an organlike attachment. It was written for the violinist Yelly d'Aranyi, who introduced it in London on April 26, 1924. Ravel orchestrated the accompaniment in 1925, the first performance of this version taking place that year in Amsterdam with Samuel Dushkin as soloist and Mengelberg conducting. The rhapsody is filled with Hungarian gypsy melodies and rhythms. It opens with an extended cadenza for solo violin. A cadenza for harp follows. The main section now unfolds, beginning with a gay gypsy tune for the violin, followed by a second gypsy melody in the clarinet accompanied by harmonies in the violin. Other gypsy melodies are then presented and developed rhapsodically.

The writing for the violin is characterized by effective glissandos, trills, and harmonics. A broad, beautiful song for violin leads to a vertiginous conclusion, whirlwind passages for the solo instrument.

U

Ulalume. *See:* Poe, Edgar Allan.

Una Corda. In string music, a direction that a passage is to be played on one string alone; in piano music, it indicates the use of left or "soft" pedal alone.

Under the Spreading Chestnut Tree. Variations and fugue for orchestra by Jaromir Weinberger (1939), first performed in New York City on Oct. 12, 1939, John Barbirolli conducting. The work is based on a tune popular in England just before World War II. The tune is heard without preliminaries. There follow seven variations and a fugue, with the piano serving as the link between sections. The variations are named: Her Majesty's Virginal; The Madrigalists; The Dark Lady; The Highlanders; Pastorale; Mr. Weller, Senior, Discusses Widows With His Son, Samuel Weller, Esquire; Sarabande. The fugue, with which the work ends, has an eight-bar subject which is finally joined contrapuntally with the popular English tune.

Undertow. Suite for orchestra by William Schuman, adapted from the score to a ballet introduced in New York by the Ballet Theatre on April 10, 1945. The scenario by Antony Tudor is the case history of a psychopath who, a victim of neglect and frustrations, murders a lascivious woman. His soul is finally purged following his apprehension. Schuman's music has caught all the grim drama of this ballet. The orchestral suite has three sections: I. Prologue—Birth and Infancy; II. The City—Adolescence and Manhood; III. Epilogue—Guilt.

Unfinished Symphony. *See:* Symphony— *Schubert.*

Unison. Identity of pitch.

Upbeat. Last beat in an introductory bar; the upward motion of a conductor's hand or baton.

Upper partial. A harmonic.

Utility music. *See: Gebrauchsmusik.*

V

Vaermland Rhapsody, A. For orchestra by Kurt Atterberg, op. 36 (1933), first performed over the Swedish Radio in Stockholm on Nov. 20, 1933. This rhapsody was written to honor the 75th birthday of Selma Lagerloef, celebrated Swedish novelist. Vaermland is the locale of Lagerloef's novel, *Goesta Berling's Saga,* and Atterberg borrowed his musical material from melodies and rhythms indigenous with that part of Sweden. Both principal themes are derived from that source: the first is heard in the first violins, and the second in the clarinet.

Valkyries, The (Die Walkuere). Second music drama in Wagner's cycle, *The Ring of the Nibelungs*. For orchestral excerpts *see: Ring of the Nibelungs, The.*

Valse, La (The Waltz). Choreographic tone poem by Maurice Ravel (1919), introduced in Paris on Dec. 12, 1920, Camille Chevillard conducting. Stimulated by the waltzes of Johann Strauss II, Ravel here planned an "apotheosis of the waltz" to provide a picture of old Vienna. The published score provides the following program: "Whirling clouds give glimpses, through rifts, of couples dancing. The clouds scatter, little by little. One sees an immense ball peopled with a twirling crowd. The scene is gradually illuminated. The light of the chandeliers bursts forth, fortissimo. An imperial court, in or about 1855." A snatch of a waltz melody is presented by bassoons. It is taken over by the other woodwinds, and then the waltz melody itself emerges in strings and oboe before being presented by the full orchestra. Dissonant chords bring the waltzing to an end. When the waltz melody returns it is no longer light-hearted and light-footed, but somber and bitter, touched with despair. The music grows more restless and turbulent, then ends in discord. The gaiety of Vienna in 1855 becomes grim and tragic in the tragic post-war year of 1919.

Valses nobles et sentimentales. A set of waltzes for the piano by Maurice Ravel (1910), inspired by the piano waltzes of Franz Schubert: *Valses nobles*, op. 77, and *Valses sentimentales*, op. 50. Ravel's suite consists of seven waltzes and an epilogue played without interruption. The published score contains the following quotation from Henri de Régnier: "To the delicious pleasure of useless occupation." In the sensitivity of its harmonic writing and in the restrained rhythmic pulse, these waltzes are more French than Viennese. The first waltz is even discordant in its harmonies. Other waltzes are varied in mood and atmosphere, and the epilogue is touched with sentimentality. The composer orches-

trated this work for a ballet, *Adelaide*, introduced in Paris on April 12, 1912. The concert première of this orchestration took place in Paris on Feb. 15, 1914, Pierre Monteux conducting.

Valses romantiques (Romantic Waltzes). Three waltzes for two pianos by Emmanuel Chabrier (1883). The first waltz (*Très vite et impetueusement*) is brilliant and lively. The second (*Mouvement modéré de valse*) has a feeling for the old-fashioned. The third and best waltz in the set (*Animé*) is passionate. This work was orchestrated by Felix Mottl.

Valve. A piston-like mechanism to shorten or lengthen the tube of a brass instrument to permit a new harmonic series.

Van Beinum, Eduard. *See:* Beinum, Eduard van.

Van der Stucken, Franz. *See:* Stucken, Franz Van der.

Van Dieren, Bernard. *See:* Dieren, Bernard van.

Van Hoogstraten, Willem. *See:* Hoogstraten, Willem van.

Van Remoortel, Eduard. *See:* Remoortel, Eduard van.

Van Vactor, David, composer, flutist, and conductor. Born Plymouth, Ind., May 8, 1906. He studied music at Northwestern University and with Marcel Moyse and Paul Dukas in Paris. From 1931 to 1943 he played the flute in the Chicago Symphony. In 1944 he was appointed head of the theory and composition department at the Conservatory of Music at Kansas City. He also directed orchestral performances in that city. In 1947 he became principal conductor of the Knoxville Symphony in Tennessee, and head of the department of Fine Arts at the University of Tennessee. He received a Guggenheim Fellowship in 1957. His works for orchestra include 2 symphonies, 2 *Overtures to a Comedy*, Concerto Grosso, Divertimento, viola concerto, *Three Dance Scenes*, and *Fantasia, Chaconne and Allegro*. He also wrote a piano quintet, string quartet, string trio, flute sonata, and a Suite for bassoon and contrabassoon.

Varèse, Edgard, composer. Born Paris, France, Dec. 22, 1885. Because he originally intended to become an engineer, his early training embraced science and mathematics. In his eighteenth year he turned completely to music, attending the Schola Cantorum. After additional study with Charles Widor at the Paris Conservatory, he led various choral groups in Paris and Berlin; he also made a successful appearance as guest conductor of the Prague Philharmonic in 1914. In 1916 he came to the United States, where he later became a citizen. He immediately identified himself with progressive movements in music. In 1919 he founded and directed the New Symphony Orchestra, and in 1921 he helped organize the International Composers Guild.

In his compositions Varèse has been an innovator in the exploitation of sonorities not usually found in music. His works, which he calls "organized sound," utilize combinations of tones and timbres defying convention. His first work to attract attention and controversy was *Hyperprism*, introduced in 1926 by the Philadelphia Orchestra. In his most recent works Varèse has tried to displace traditional instruments with electrical ones. His principal works for orchestra include *Amériques, Arcana, Ionisation,* and *Deserts.* For various chamber-music groups he wrote *Intégrales, Offrandes, Octandre, Equatorial,* and *Hyperprism.*

Variable meters. *See:* Blacher, Boris.

Variation (Theme and variations). The technique of subjecting a given theme to a series of harmonic, rhythmic, and melodic transformations. Usually the theme is stated before the variations. The form seems to have originated in the 16th century, and it became popular in the instrumental compositions of the English virginal composers of the early 17th century. Instrumental composers of the 17th and 18th centuries made extensive use of this technique, not only in specific theme-and-variations compositions but also in passacaglias and chaconnes. After Bach, many composers used it within the context of such larger patterns as the sonata, symphony, quartet, concerto, and so on. The Romantic and post-Romantic composers devised the theme and variations as an independent composition for the orchestra—for example, Brahms'

Variations on a Theme of Haydn, Elgar's *Enigma Variations,* and Vincent d'Indy's *Istar Variations.*

Variations and Fugue on a Theme by Mozart. For orchestra by Max Reger, op. 132 (1914), introduced in Berlin on Feb. 5, 1915, the composer conducting. The Mozart theme is from the first movement of the Piano Sonata in A major, K. 331, where it is also subjected to variation treatment. In Reger's work, the first part of the theme is heard in oboe and two clarinets, and repeated by strings; the second part appears in oboe and clarinet supported by violins and violas, then is repeated by strings. Eight variations follow. The ninth is a fugue, with the subject appearing in first violins, and answered by the second violins in the eighth bar. The theme is given a final and forceful statement by the trumpets at the conclusion of the fugue.

Variations, Chaconne and Finale. For orchestra by Norman Dello Joio (1947), introduced in Pittsburgh on Jan. 30, 1948, Fritz Reiner conducting. It received the award of the New York Music Critics Circle. This work is of liturgical character, the principal theme in the oboe being derived from the Kyrie of the *Missa de Angelis.* In the first part, following a brief preface, the melody undergoes six variations. The chaconne is built from the first four notes of the theme, but in chromatic form. The finale is spirited and joyous, far removed from the religious nature of the two earlier sections. A loud return of the first four notes of the theme brings the work to a dynamic conclusion.

Variations in F minor. For piano by Haydn (1793), one of his most famous piano compositions. It has a dual theme, the first section in F minor, the second in F major. Two variations follow, then an extended coda, which is improvisatory in character.

Variations on a Nursery Song. For piano and orchestra, by Ernst von Dohnányi, op. 25 (1913). This witty music is based on the old French tune, *Ah, vous dirai-je Maman,* which Mozart had used for a set of piano variations and which in the United States is a melody used for teaching children the alphabet. This theme undergoes eleven variations. The work opens with a stately introduction for orchestra which provides an amusing and unexpected contrast to the statement of the little nursery tune in the piano that follows. The variations pass through a gamut of moods and feelings. In the second variation, the melody becomes military; in the third, a satirical dance; in the sixth, an etude; in the seventh, a Viennese waltz; in the tenth, a ground bass for a passacaglia; and in the eleventh, a chorale. A lively fugue on the theme reaches a climax, following which the tune itself reappears for the last time in a slightly distorted version.

Variations on a Rococo Theme. For cello and orchestra by Tchaikovsky, op. 33 (1876). It was written for the cellist, Wilhelm Karl Friedrich Fitzenhagen, who introduced it in Moscow on Nov. 30, 1877. The "rococo" theme is a graceful 18th-century melody in the style of Mozart; it first appears in the solo instrument after a delicate sixteen-bar orchestral preface. Seven variations follow, separated by orchestral interludes, and each in the light and well mannered style of 18th-century music.

Variations on a Theme of Chopin. For piano by Rachmaninoff, op. 22 (1903). The theme is Chopin's Prelude No. 20 in C minor, given 22 variations, after which an extended transition leads to a coda. Many of the variations are brief, self-sufficient pieces of music suggesting such Romantic piano forms as the etude, nocturne, or prelude.

Variations on a Theme of Corelli. For piano by Rachmaninoff, op. 42 (1931). The theme is that of Corelli's violin sonata, *La Folia,* and receives 20 variations and a concluding coda. The variations section is more cohesive and better integrated than that in Rachmaninoff's earlier *Variations on a Theme of Chopin;* but the relationship with the original theme is often tenuous and elusive.

Variations on a Theme of Frank Bridge. For orchestra by Benjamin Britten, op. 10 (1937). It was introduced at Salzburg in 1937, Boyd Neel conducting. The theme is from the second of Bridge's *Three Idyls.* In Britten's work it first appears in the first violins after a brief introduction. Ten variations ensue. The first (Adagio) consists of soft chords in the strings. The second is a march; the third, a Romance; and the fourth, an *Aria italiana,* a satire on a Rossini type of aria. In *Bourrée classique* and *Wiener Walzer* two other musical styles are caricatured. In *Moto perpetuo* the theme appears in the strings tremolando. Two brief lyrical sections follow, a *Funeral March* and a *Chant.* The work ends with a fugue.

Variations on a Theme of Handel. For piano by Brahms, op. 24 (1861). Brahms took his theme from Handel's Suite in B-flat, a simple melody with elementary harmonies. On such a simple foundation rest 24 mighty variations, crowned by a monumental fugue. The theme is subjected to the most subtle and intricate changes. Frequently the barest rhythmic or melodic suggestion of the theme becomes the starting point for a vast new idea in which it is difficult to recognize the original subject.

Variations on a Theme of Haydn. For orchestra (op. 56a) and also for two solo pianos (op. 56b) by Brahms. The orchestral version came first (1873), the composer's first major work for symphony orchestra; he later transcribed it for two pianos. The two-piano version was introduced by Brahms and Clara Schumann in Vienna in August 1873. The orchestral version was first performed in Vienna on Nov. 2, 1873, Otto Dessoff conducting.

The theme by Haydn comes from the second movement of a comparatively unfamiliar Divertimento. Haydn himself described this theme as the "Chorale St. Antoni," giving rise to the belief that he himself had borrowed it. The Brahms work for orchestra opens with the theme in wind instruments against a pizzicato background. After that come eight variations in which the theme becomes passionate, martial, delicate, lyrical, assertive. The finale begins with a five-bar ground-bass adaptation of the theme and ends with a triumphant promulgation of that theme in the full orchestra.

Variations on a Theme of Paganini. For piano by Brahms, op. 35 (1863). The theme is that of Paganini's Twenty-

Fourth Caprice for solo violin. Thirty-five variations follow, many in the nature of technical exercises; in fact, Brahms described this composition as "studies." The work consists of two sets; it is sometimes the custom of pianists to delete some of the weaker sections of each set and to present all the remaining variations as one set.

Variations on a Theme of Tchaikovsky. For orchestra by Anton Arensky, in E minor, op. 35a. Arensky took his theme from one of Tchaikovsky's *Children Songs*, op. 54—*In the Garden of the Infant Christ.* Arensky's composition originated as the slow movement of his Quartet in A minor, op. 35, for violin, viola, and two cellos. In the orchestral version, which is the composer's most celebrated work, seven variations follow the statement of the beautiful melody by the strings. In the first (*Un poco più mosso*) the melody is distributed among the choirs of the orchestra; in the second (*Allegro non troppo*) the theme is played in unison by violas and cellos against a contrapuntal background of violins. The third variation (*Andante tranquillo*) gaily decorates the melody with accompanying voices. The fourth (Vivace) is mostly a delicate pizzicato section. In the fifth variation (Andante) the theme, given to the lower strings, becomes contemplative; while in the sixth (*Allegro con spirito*) it is vivacious. The poetic seventh variation (*Andante con moto*) is modeled after Tchaikovsky's famous *Andante cantabile* from the Quartet in D major. This work ends with a coda of a religious character.

Variations on a Waltz by A. Diabelli. For piano by Beethoven, op. 120 (1823). This is the master's last work for the piano, and one of his greatest; here he displayed again his extraordinary inventiveness in the use of the variation form. As if to test his powers further, he selected for his theme a trite little waltz melody by Diabelli. Diabelli published a volume in which many composers (including Schubert) were invited to contribute variations on his melody. Beethoven wrote a volume of his own, providing Diabelli with no less than 33 variations on the waltz. Beethoven explored in his variations every possible nuance and feeling of the original subject, always presenting that subject in fascinating new designs and formats. His gamut ranges from the pensive to the dramatic, from Handelian grandeur to the whimsical. No wonder, then, that Hans von Buelow referred to this composition as the "microcosmos of Beethoven's genius." In the last variation Beethoven begins with a Tempo di Menuetto, as if to recall the age of Haydn and Mozart, and proceeds from that point to three more variations described by von Buelow as "a picture of the whole musical universe." The minuet is abandoned for those rarefied musical realms explored by Beethoven himself in his last sonatas. To Schumann this last variation was Beethoven's farewell to his audience.

Variations on an Original Theme (Elgar). *See: Enigma Variations.*

Variations on the Name Abegg (Schumann). *See: Abegg Variations.*

Variations sérieuses. For piano by Mendelssohn, in D minor, op. 54 (1841). This is one of the composer's most important works for the piano. The melody is a gentle song almost in the style of one of his *Songs Without Words.* The 18 variations that follow are of rapidly changing moods—by turns lyrical, dramatic, tragic, and whimsical.

Variations symphoniques. For piano and orchestra by César Franck (1885), introduced in Paris on March 1, 1885, with Louis Diémer as soloist. This is an unusual work structurally, since it does not consist of a theme followed by variations, as is usual with this form. This composition consists of an introduction, a middle section, and a finale. The variation technique is used only in the middle section, while the two outer parts serve to provide varied suggestions of the main theme.

The introduction is a dialogue between strings and piano. A change of tempo brings on the first two phrases of the theme. After a lengthy discourse first by the piano and then by the orchestra—and a recollection of the opening dialogue—the variation section unfolds. A beautiful melody is presented by the piano and is succeeded by six variations.

A lively finale brings this composition to a vivacious close.

Vassilenko, Sergei, composer and teacher. Born Moscow, Russia, March 30, 1872; died there, March 11, 1956. He attended the Moscow Conservatory, where his teachers included Taneiev and Ippolitov-Ivanov. After graduating he was appointed professor of composition there. While holding this post he inaugurated an important series of historical concerts with the Imperial Russian Musical Society. Though his principal works are strongly influenced by Impressionism, Vassilenko never completely abandoned an early enthusiasm for nationalist music. He often made effective use of Russian folksong idioms in his works. Those for orchestra include 2 symphonies (one of them the *Arctic*), suites (*Sappho, Zodiac, Turkmenian, The Soviet East,* and 2 *Chinese Suites*), a violin concerto, a symphony for orchestra and brass band, a tone poem *The Garden of Death,* rhapsodies (*Red Army* and *Slavonic*), *Eight Soviet Dances, Merry Go Round,* and incidental music to many plays. He also wrote 3 string quartets, a piano trio, violin sonata, *Quartet on American Themes* for woodwind, and a *Japanese Suite* for oboe, clarinet, bassoon, xylophone, and piano.

Vaughan Williams, Ralph, composer. Born Down Ampney, England, Oct. 12, 1872; died London, England, Aug. 26, 1958. Vaughan Williams attended the Royal College of Music, a pupil of Hubert Parry and Charles Villiers Stanford, after which he studied privately with Max Bruch in Berlin. Receiving his doctorate from Cambridge in 1901, he was organist at the St. Barnabas Church in London, founded and led a choral and orchestral society, edited an English hymnal, and wrote several minor works. A turning point in his career came in 1904 when he first came into contact with the folksongs of the English Tudor period. The impact of this music upon him was decisive. He joined the Folk-Song Society, which was dedicated to the study of and research in this music. In the next few years he helped to resuscitate many long-forgotten songs which he adapted with fresh harmonizations and helped to popularize throughout the world of music. More important still, he now found a direction and purpose in his own creative work: to write ambitious compositions which might serve as a showcase for this rich folk material. Between 1905 and 1907 he completed three *Norfolk Rhapsodies* for orchestra, which made extensive use of the folksongs native to King's Lynn in Norfolk.

Dissatisfied with his equipment as a composer, Vaughan Williams went to Paris in 1908 and for eight months studied with Maurice Ravel. This period brought him not only technical assurance but perspective as well. He recognized that his aim as a national composer should be to make the folksong the point of departure for his own writing, not the end. After returning to England, he produced his first significant work in 1909, a work still frequently performed, the *Fantasia on a Theme by Thomas Tallis.* This was immediately followed by several other distinguished works, including the opera *Hugh the Drover* and the *London Symphony.*

During World War I Vaughan Williams saw service for three years, first with the Territorial Royal Army Military Corps, then on the battlefield with the Artillery. After the war's end he combined his activity as composer with that of teacher and conductor. He became a member of the faculty at the Royal College of Music, where for over thirty years he headed classes in composition. From 1920 to 1928 he conducted the Bach Choir in London.

His American début took place on June 7, 1922, when he conducted his *Pastoral Symphony* at the Norfolk, Conn., Music Festival. He returned to the United States a decade later to deliver lectures on music at Bryn Mawr College, subsequently published as *National Music* (1934).

As a composer Vaughan Williams continued to be productive until the end of his life, completing large-scale works in all branches of composition. After the death of Elgar he was considered the dean of English composers, in recognition of which fact he was given the Order of Merit in 1935 and the Albert medal of the Royal Society of Arts in 1955. The influence of old English music is evident even in his later works: in his contrapuntal and modal writing; in his serene, contemplative lyricism; in his emotional restraint. To these qualities Vaughan Williams often added modern techniques of harmony and tonality, as well as mysticism and introspection.

The following are Vaughan Williams' principal instrumental works:

Chamber Music: 2 string quartets; piano quintet; *Fantasy Quintet; Household Music* for string quartet; violin sonata.

Orchestra: 9 symphonies; 3 *Norfolk Rhapsodies; Fantasia on a Theme by Thomas Tallis; The Lark Ascending,* for violin and orchestra; *Flos Campi,* for viola, chorus, and orchestra; *Job; Fantasy on Sussex Folk Tunes* for cello and orchestra; *Fantasia on Greensleeves;* Suite for Viola and Orchestra; Partita for double orchestra; *Serenade to Music;* various concertos (violin; piano; two pianos; oboe; bass tuba); incidental music to various plays.

See: Fantasia on a Theme by Thomas Tallis; Lark Ascending, The; Norfolk Rhapsody No. 1; Symphony—*Vaughan Williams.*

Veloce. Swift.

Venusberg Music (Wagner). *See: Tannhaeuser, Overture and Bacchanale.*

Veracini, Francesco Maria, violinist and composer. Born Florence, Italy, Feb. 1, 1690; died near Pisa, about 1750. After studying the violin with his uncle, he went to Venice and joined the orchestra of St. Mark's Cathedral. He achieved such renown that he was invited to engage in a performing competition with Tartini. When Tartini heard him play, the former not only withdrew from the contest but even went into retirement to perfect his own style and technique. In 1714 Veracini went to England, making a sensational début. During the next few years his performances there led Burney to refer to him as "the greatest violinist in Europe." From 1717 to 1722 he was solo violinist and composer for the Elector of Saxony in Dresden. There in 1722, either in a moment of insanity, or in morbidity over a humiliation suffered at

the hands of a rival musician, he threw himself out of a window and became lame for life. He was back in England in 1735, now to enjoy successes as a composer of operas. He is believed to have lost his fortune in a shipwreck en route to Italy. In any event, his last years in Italy were spent in poverty. Veracini made impressive contributions to early 18th-century instrumental music with various symphonies, concertos, and sonatas; some of the last are still occasionally performed.

Verbrugghen, Henri, violinist and conductor. Born Brussels, Belgium, Aug. 1, 1873; died Northfield, Minn., Nov. 12, 1934. He attended the Brussels Conservatory, where he studied the violin with Eugène Ysaÿe. After a decade of playing the violin in major orchestras in England and France, he assumed his first conducting post in 1911, with the Glasgow Choral Union. In 1915 he went to Sydney, Australia, to become director of the Conservatory and conductor of the State Orchestra. In 1923 he settled in the United States and from then until 1931 was principal conductor of the Minneapolis Symphony.

Verdi, Giuseppe, composer. Born Le Roncole, Italy, Oct. 10, 1813; died Milan, Italy, Jan. 27, 1901. Verdi directed his remarkable energies and creative genius almost exclusively to the stage to become the greatest figure in Italian opera. He did, however, complete several works outside the theater. Among his choral compositions is the *Manzoni Requiem,* a masterwork. A lesser product is the String Quartet in E minor (1873), to which the composer himself attached so little significance that for some time he refused to allow it to be published or performed.

See: Requiem—Verdi.

Verklaerte Nacht (Schoenberg). *See: Transfigured Night.*

Verlaine, Paul, poet. Born Metz, France, March 30, 1844; died Paris, France, Jan. 8, 1896. The following works for orchestra are based upon poems by Verlaine: Gabriel Fauré's suite, *Masques et bergamasques;* Charles Koechlin's *Le Nuit de Walpurgis classique* (an adaptation by Verlaine of Goethe); Charles

Martin Loeffler's tone poem *La bonne chanson* (*Poem*); and Percy Pitt's suite, *Fêtes galantes.*

Vetrate di chiesa (Respighi). *See: Church Windows.*

Vibrato. On a string instrument, a vibrating, tremulous tone.

Victory Ball, A. Fantasy for orchestra by Ernest Schelling (1922), first performed in Philadelphia on Feb. 23, 1923, Stokowski conducting. This music is based on a poem by Alfred Noyes describing a ball celebrating victory in the war. This ball is attended by the shadows of dead soldiers. The tone poem opens with a description of the ballroom; the dancing is depicted by fox-trot and tango music. Two trumpet calls interrupt these festive proceedings and introduce a march by the dead hosts. The composition ends with the sounding of taps.

Vidui (Bloch). *See: Baal Shem.*

Vienna Philharmonic Orchestra. The foremost symphony orchestra in Austria, and one of the greatest in Europe. It came into existence on March 28, 1842, with Otto Nicolai leading a concert of the Vienna Royal Opera orchestra in the Redoutensaal at the Hofburg. Nicolai remained principal conductor until 1848, sharing the podium with G. Hellmesberger from 1845 to 1848. After that the principal conductors of the orchestra were: K. Eckert, Otto Dessoff, Hans Richter, Mahler, J. Hellmesberger, Franz Schalk, Felix Weingartner, Wilhelm Furtwaengler, Clemens Krauss, Bruno Walter, Josef Krips, and Herbert von Karajan. The Vienna Philharmonic first appeared at the Salzburg Festival in 1879 (Hans Richter conducting), and since 1925 has been that festival's principal orchestra. It has toured throughout Europe many times, and made its first tour of the United States in 1956. In Vienna, the orchestra performs in the Musikverein.

Vierne, Louis, organist and composer. Born Poitiers, France, Oct. 8, 1870; died Paris, France, June 2, 1937. He attended the Paris Conservatory, a pupil of Franck and Widor. After serving his apprenticeship as organist as assistant to Widor at the St. Sulpice Church in Paris, he became principal organist of Notre Dame in 1900, retaining the latter post until his

death. From 1912 on he was professor of organ at the Schola Cantorum, where his pupils included Joseph Bonnet, Marcel Dupré, and Nadia Boulanger. He made many tours as organ virtuoso, including one of the United States in 1927. His many works for the organ include 6 symphonies and 24 *Pièces en style libre.*

Vieuxtemps, Henri, violinist and composer. Born Verviers, Belgium, Feb. 17, 1820; died Mustaphah-les-Algers, Algiers, June 6, 1881. As a child prodigy he attracted the interest of the famous violinist, Charles de Bériot, who adopted him and gave him instruction until 1831. In 1828, Vieuxtemps made concert appearances with de Bériot in Paris. In 1833 he made a successful tour of Germany and Austria, and soon after that achieved a place of first importance among the violinists of his day. He was a performer with an astonishing technique and an aristocratic style. In 1844 he paid the first of three visits to the United States. From 1846 to 1852 he was solo violinist to the Czar of Russia and professor of the violin at the Moscow Conservatory. From 1871 to 1873 he was professor at the Brussels Conservatory. Paralysis of the left hand compelled him to withdraw in 1873 from all professional activity.

Vieuxtemps wrote 7 concertos for the violin, two of which are still performed: No. 4 in D minor and No. 5 in A minor. He also wrote 2 cello concertos, 3 string quartets, and numerous compositions and etudes for the violin. He also prepared three cadenzas for the Beethoven Violin Concerto.

See: Concerto—*Vieuxtemps;* Polonaise.

Vif. Quick and lively.

Villa-Lobos, Heitor, composer. Born Rio de Janeiro, Brazil, March 5, 1887. He had little formal instruction in music. As a boy he received some cello lessons from his father, and earned his living performing in theater and restaurant orchestras. Since he could not discipline himself to formal study, he acquired a musical education in his own way, and mostly by associating himself with Brazilian popular and folk music. One of his earliest works, *Canticos Sertanejos,* in 1909, is a suite based on popular folk melodies. In

1912 he made the first of several expeditions into the interior of Brazil to acquaint himself with indigenous folksongs and dances and to witness local rites and ceremonies. After these expeditions, he dedicated himself to the mission of writing music that would tap fully the resources and materials of Brazilian folk music. He began writing abundantly, sometimes using unorthodox styles within formal structures, sometimes devising forms of his own invention. In 1915 there took place in Rio de Janeiro the first concert devoted entirely to his works. But widespread recognition was still some years off. When it came, it was the result of the influence of the piano virtuoso, Artur Rubinstein, who made it possible for Villa-Lobos to receive a government grant and spend several years in Europe, most of them in Paris. Villa-Lobos was back in his native country in 1930, from then on to be a dominating figure in its musical life. He became Director of Musical Education, an office in which he helped revolutionize the methods of teaching in Brazil. He also made frequent appearances as conductor of Brazilian orchestras.

Villa-Lobos paid his first visit to the United States in the winter of 1944-1945 and was honored with a "Villa-Lobos Week" in which major orchestras invited him to conduct his works, and major musical organizations presented some of his principal compositions.

Villa-Lobos has been one of the most prolific composers of all time. It is impossible to compute how many works he has written, but the number easily exceeds 1,500 in all branches of composition.

The qualities that characterize Brazilian folk and popular music also identify Villa-Lobos' compositions: the impulsive rhythms and syncopations; vivid orchestration; alternation from the primitive and the savage to the lyrical and sentimental; partiality towards improvisational melodies; extensive use of percussion instruments. Some of his most popular works are in forms of his own invention, the *Bachiana brasileira* and the *Chôros* (which see).

The following are Villa-Lobos' leading instrumental works:

Chamber Music: various *chôros* for different combinations of instruments; 8 string quartets; 3 piano trios; 4 sonata fantasias for violin and piano; 2 cello sonatas; wind quintet; nonet.

Orchestra: 12 symphonies; 5 piano concertos; various *chôros;* various *Bachianas brasileiras;* cello concerto; *Dansas dos Indios mesticos; Rudepoêma* for piano and orchestra; *Legende; Suite paulista; Descobrimento do Brasil; Carnaval de Brasil; Momo Precoce* for piano and orchestra; *Uirapurú;* violin concerto; harp concerto; *Fantasia* for cello and orchestra; *Saudades da juventude; Erosion,* or *The Origin of the Amazon River; Madona; Dawn in a Tropical Forest.*

Piano: Prole do bebé; Poema do menestrel; Rudepoêma; Sul America; Cirandinha; Saudades das selvas brasileiras; Francette et Pia; Ciclo brasileiro; Poema singelo; and so forth.

See: *Bachianas brasileiras; Chôros;* Quartet—*Villa-Lobos; Rudepoêma.*

Village Romeo and Juliet, A. An opera by Frederick Delius with a libretto by the composer and his wife based on a story by Gottfried Keller. The opera was introduced in Berlin Feb. 21, 1907. For an orchestral excerpt *see: Walk to Paradise Garden, The.*

Viñes, Ricardo, pianist. Born Lerida, Spain, Feb. 5, 1875; died Barcelona, Spain, April 29, 1943. He attended the Paris Conservatory, winning first prize in piano in 1894. He maintained his home in Paris after that, identifying himself with the latest tendencies in French piano music. In his many tours of Europe and South America he became recognized as an eminent interpreter of the music of Debussy, Ravel, and Manuel de Falla, much of which he himself introduced.

Viol. A family of string instruments played with the bow, and prominent in the 16th and 17th centuries. While there were many varieties of viol, the following were the most popular, and proved important in the evolution of present-day string instruments: treble or discant viol, antecedent of the violin; the viola da gamba or bass viol, which was held between the knees and developed into the cello; and the bass viol, later to become the double bass.

Viola. A string instrument of the violin family, larger in size than the violin but smaller than the cello. Like the violin it is played under the chin supported by the shoulder. Its strings are thicker than those of the violin. The viola is pitched a fifth lower than the violin and has a mellower tone. Music for the viola is generally written in the alto clef.

Viola da gamba. *See:* Viol.

Viola d'amore. A stringed instrument played like a violin with bow. It was particularly popular in Germany in the 17th and early 18th centuries. Vivaldi wrote a Concerto in D minor for it, and Bach used it in the orchestra for the *Passion According to St. John.* It is similar in construction and size to the treble viol, has six or seven strings and a second set of strings vibrating in sympathy with the others.

Violin. The most important and the most lyrical of stringed instruments. It is played under the chin, supported by the shoulder; has a three-octave range, though higher notes can be produced by means of harmonics. The strings are normally set into vibration with a bow; to obtain special effects, they are sometimes plucked. The violin did not achieve significance, either as a solo instrument or as a basic member of the orchestra, until it had been structurally developed by the Amatis, a family of Italian instrument-makers; further developments in its construction were made by such outstanding instrument-makers as Stradivari and Guarneri. Only then did the violin completely supersede the viol in interest among composers. What is believed to be the first piece of music for solo violin is *Capriccio stravagante* by Carlo Farina (1627) in which various extra-musical sounds (barking dogs, drums, fifes, guitars) were imitated, often through the then novel techniques of trills and double stops. But the history of violin music—both in performance and composition—can be said to begin with Corelli in the mid-17th century. His most significant successors—Torelli and Vivaldi, among others—further developed the technique and style of violin

playing and writing, setting the stage for the first masters of violin music: J. S. Bach, Handel, Haydn, Mozart, Beethoven, and Paganini.

Violoncello. A string instrument of the violin family, tuned an octave below the viola. Its range is about two and a half octaves. It is played in a vertical position, resting on the ground and supported by the knees of the performer.

Viotti, Giovanni Battista, violinist and composer. Born Fontanetto, Italy, May 12, 1755; died London, England, March 3, 1824. He received some musical instruction from his father, a blacksmith. When he was eleven, Giovanni was subsidized by the Prince of Cisterna to study with Gaetano Pugnani. Viotti was fourteen when he wrote his first violin concerto. In 1780 he went with his teacher on a tour of Italy, Germany, Poland, Switzerland, and France. After making a sensational début in Paris on March 15, 1782, he settled in France, soon winning acceptance there as one of the foremost virtuosos of his time. At the height of his fame he suddenly decided to withdraw from the concert platform; the reason for this has never been adequately explained. Nevertheless, he continued giving private performances at his home, and from 1784 to 1792 he served as court musician for Marie Antoinette. In 1792 he went to London, where two years later he resumed his public career with appearances at the Salomon concerts. He also became conductor, then director, of the Italian Opera at the King's Theatre. Accused of being in league with the revolutionary leaders in France, Viotti was forced to leave England in 1798. But he was allowed to return three years later. For the next decade or so he ran a wine establishment, whose collapse forced him to return to musical activities. In 1813 he helped found the Royal Philharmonic Society, which he subsequently directed on several occasions. After that he served as director of the Italian Opera in Paris. Accused of business mismanagement, he was removed from this post and retired on a modest pension. In 1822 he was back in England for the last time, his last two years spent in obscurity and

bitterness. He wrote 29 violin concertos, of which the 22nd in A minor is still popular. He also wrote 10 piano concertos and numerous quartets, trios, duos, serenades, and violin sonatas.
See: Concerto—*Viotti.*

Virginal. A small, oblong keyboard instrument of the harpsichord family. While it was sometimes supported by legs, it was usually no more than a small box that could be held on the lap or placed on a table. It had a single string to each note, set into vibration by quills on jacks. It is believed that it derived its name from the fact that young girls, or virgins, favored it in accompanying themselves in songs. The virginal was popular in the 16th and early 17th centuries. Music written in England for this instrument represents an important milestone in keyboard music (*see: Fitzwilliam Virginal Book*).

Virtuosi di Roma. Italian chamber orchestra of 13 performers founded in 1946 by Renato Fasani, who has since remained its conductor. This organization has made a specialty of early Italian orchestral music and has made many successful tours of England and the United States.

Virtuosity. Display of brilliant technique.

Virtuoso. A person who has acquired complete technical mastery of some musical instrument.

Visions Fugitives. A set of 20 pieces for the piano by Prokofiev, op. 22 (1915-1917). Each is a brief tonal impression. Some of these pieces are technically interesting for their unconventional harmonies and experiments with polytonal writing. Of special interest are Nos. 1, 7, 16, and 20 for their pensive lyricism, often of a Russian nature. No. 19 is restless music, descriptive of a crowd during the February Revolution. The composer himself introduced these pieces in a recital in St. Petersburg on April 15, 1918.

Vite. Quick.

Vitesgrad (Smetana). *See: My Fatherland.*

Vivace. Lively; faster than Allegro. Vivacissimo means extremely fast.

Vivaldi, Antonio, composer. Born Venice, Italy, about 1675; died Vienna, Austria, July 1741. The facts of Vivaldi's life are meager. He received his earliest music instruction from his father, a violinist in the ducal palace in Venice; after that, he received some instruction from Giovanni Legrenzi. When he was fifteen he submitted to the tonsure, and in 1703 was ordained priest. He did not altogether abandon musical activity during this period, perfecting himself on the violin and devoting himself to composition. In 1703 he became a teacher of the violin at the Conservatorio dell' Ospedale della Pietà; in 1709 he was appointed its director. In or about 1720 he became Kapellmeister to Prince Philip of Hesse-Darmstadt in Mantua, a post he held for three years. Later, he spent some time in Germany. In Italy he won renown not only as a violin virtuoso but also for his operas. In 1735 he was back at his old post at the Ospedale della Pietà, now a leading musical figure in Venice, and personally honored by the Pope. Just before his death he went to Vienna, for reasons never explained. There he was apparently forgotten by the world of music. His last years were spent in obscurity and poverty. Upon his death he was given a pauper's burial.

Vivaldi's instrumental output was varied and prodigious. He wrote over 400 concertos, and numerous compositions for small combinations of instruments. It is through his concertos for various solo instruments and orchestra, and his concerti grossi, that we know him best; and it was through this medium that he arrived at greatness. He helped to establish the concerto form by giving it clarity of design and solidity of structure. He taught his contemporaries how to produce a singing lyric line. He pointed the way to contrast of thematic ideas and thematic development. He was one of the early exponents of program music. His influence upon J. S. Bach has been recognized; Bach used to copy out Vivaldi's concertos for his own pleasure and transcribed many of them. Besides the concertos, Vivaldi wrote 23 symphonies and 73 sonatas.

Gian Francesco Malipiero's *Vivaldiana* for orchestra is based on themes from Vivaldi's works.

See: Concerto grosso—*Vivaldi.*

Vivo. Animated.

Vltava (Smetana). *See: Moldau, The.*

Vogler, Georg Joseph (Abbé Vogler), organist, composer, teacher, and theorist. Born Wuerzburg, Germany, June 15, 1749; died Darmstadt, Germany, May 6, 1814. He was ordained a priest at Rome in 1773, and was subsequently made Apostolic Protonotary and Chamberlain to the Pope and Knight of the Order of the Golden Spur. From his childhood on he had been a student of music; he was a pupil in counterpoint of Padre Martini in Bologna. In 1775 he made his home in Mannheim, where he filled the post of second Kapellmeister, wrote operas, and opened a music school. For about twenty years, beginning in 1780, he traveled extensively. In 1786 he went to Stockholm, where he was musical director at the Royal Court and director of a music school; in 1803-1804 he lived in Vienna; and in 1807 he settled in Darmstadt as Kapellmeister to the Grand Duke Louis I; there he established his most successful music school. Vogler made innovations in the building of organs, including the invention of a species of that instrument called the Orchestrion. He also evolved his own system of harmony. Despite the vast amount of music he himself wrote in all branches, he was most important as an organ virtuoso, and as a theorist and teacher. Carl Maria von Weber was one of his pupils. Besides many operas and choral works, Vogler wrote symphonies, concertos, trios, and other instrumental compositions.

Voice in the Wilderness. Tone poem for orchestra by Ernest Bloch (1936), introduced in Los Angeles on Jan. 21, 1937, Otto Klemperer conducting. The work is in six uninterrupted sections with a cello serving as a kind of commentator between parts to discuss briefly what had previously been said. To the composer these six sections represent "meditations,"
and the work as a whole was planned as a description of the "unhappy destiny of man." The composer further explained that the various parts are "sometimes bound together by a barely perceptive thematic relationship or 'reminiscence' but each has its own clearly defined character."

Volante. Light and fast.

Voluntary. A short introductory or concluding piece for the organ, usually extemporaneous.

Von Buelow, Hans. *See:* Buelow, Hans von.

Von Einem, Gottfried. *See:* Einem, Gottfried von.

Von Karajan, Herbert. *See:* Karajan, Herbert von.

Von Klenau, Paul. *See:* Klenau, Paul von.

Von Sauer, Emile. *See:* Sauer, Emile von.

Vorspiel. German for prelude.

Voyage d'Urien, Le. *See:* Gide, André.

Voyageur sans bagage, Le. *See:* Anouilh, Jean.

Vronsky and Babin. A distinguished two-piano team made up of Vitya Vronsky and Victor Babin, in private life wife and husband. Victor Babin (born Moscow, Russia, Dec. 13, 1908) attended the Riga Conservatory and completed his music study in Berlin with Artur Schnabel and Franz Schreker. While studying with Schnabel he became acquainted with Vitya Vronsky, a fellow-student. They were married in 1933 and immediately formed a two-piano partnership. Appearances throughout Europe included a successful performance at the festival of the International Society for Contemporary Music in Amsterdam in 1934. Their American début took place in Baltimore, Md., early in 1937. They have since concertized throughout the world. Babin is the composer of orchestral, chamber, and piano music, including a concerto for two pianos and orchestra.

W

Wagner, Richard, composer. Born Leipzig, Germany, May 22, 1813; died Venice, Italy, Feb. 13, 1883. Though Wagner's great works are all music dramas, he is often represented on symphony programs by orchestral excerpts or orchestral adaptations of episodes from his stage works. In his boyhood, his ambition was to become a writer. However at the Thomasschule he was such a negligent student that he was expelled. He was equally lax in his studies when, as a young man, he attended the University of Leipzig. Only in connection with music did he demonstrate both seriousness of purpose and industry. He learned theory by memorizing a textbook, and in 1829 wrote an overture that was performed in Leipzig. In 1831 he received some formal instruction in theory from Theodore Weinlig, which prepared him for the writing of a symphony, played in Leipzig and Prague in 1833. One year later he completed his first opera, *Die Feen,* never performed in his lifetime. In 1834 he was appointed conductor of the Magdeburg Opera, where two years later he led the première of his second opera, *Das Liebesverbot.* Here, as in all subsequent operas and music dramas, Wagner wrote his own libretto. This opera was such a financial failure that the company was dragged into bankruptcy. After that he led opera performances in Koenigsberg and Riga. In the former city he married Minna Planer in 1836; in the latter, he incurred so many debts that to avoid imprisonment he had to flee to Paris, arriving there in September 1839. For the next three years he lived in appalling poverty, often compelled to do hack work. Nevertheless he managed to complete two operas, *Rienzi* and *The Flying Dutchman (Der fliegende Hollaender).* The latter, when introduced at

Dresden in 1842, was such a success that the following year Wagner was appointed Kapellmeister at the Dresden Opera. He held this post six years, a period in which he wrote *Tannhaeuser* and *Lohengrin.* The former was a failure when given in Dresden in 1845, while the latter had to wait until 1850 for its première.

Involved in the revolutionary movement in 1848-1849, Wagner once again had to flee to avoid imprisonment. This time he made his home in Zurich, where he stayed five years. It was at this time that he began to crystallize his thinking about opera and to evolve his original concepts of the music drama. He expounded his theories in pamphlets and essays, then set himself a life's mission of putting these theories into practice. In 1852 he completed and published the texts of his monumental cycle of four operas, collectively entitled *The Ring of the Nibelungs.* The music of these dramas was to occupy him for a quarter of a century, the score of the last of them being completed in 1874. Meanwhile, by 1859, he had written his mighty love drama, *Tristan and Isolde;* and by 1867, he had produced his comedy opera, *The Mastersingers.*

While involved in such Herculean creative labors, he fell in love with Cosima, wife of his friend, Hans von Buelow, and the daughter of Liszt. In 1865 a daughter was born to them and was named Isolde. After the birth of a second child, Wagner and Cosima set up their home on Lake Lucerne in Switzerland, where the now-divorced Cosima and Wagner were married. It was for Cosima, as a birthday gift, that Wagner in 1870 wrote his only mature purely orchestral composition, the *Siegfried Idyl.*

A pardon for his revolutionary activities of 1848 enabled him to return to Saxony in 1862. Two years after that, Ludwig II, king of Bavaria, became his patron. Through the king's munificence Wagner's music dramas were performed in Munich: *Tristan and Isolde* in 1865; *The Mastersingers* in 1868; *The Rhinegold* and *The Valkyries* of the *Ring* cycle in 1870. On Aug. 13, 1876, Wagner brought a lifelong dream into fruition with the opening of his festival theater in Bayreuth, Germany, where his music dramas could be performed according to his own specifications. The first complete performance of the *Ring* cycle took place there that year. Since then Bayreuth has been the setting of festivals of the Wagner music dramas and operas attracting music lovers from all parts of the world.

Wagner completed one more music drama, the consecrational play, *Parsifal,* introduced in Bayreuth on July 26, 1882. A few months later, while on vacation in Venice, he suffered a fatal heart attack. His body was brought back to Bayreuth to be buried in the garden of his home, Villa Wahnfried.

The revolution created by Wagner in opera in achieving a synthesis of the arts—a single artistic unity out of text, music, poetry, scenery, costuming, stage-craft, and so on—does not come within the province of this volume. But certain observations on his methods and technique are essential for an understanding of the music by which he is represented on orchestral programs. Mention must particularly be made of a device in composition which he introduced in all his mature works, which he perfected with amazing technical virtuosity, and which he exploited with amazing artistic effect. That device is the *Leitmotif,* or leading motif—a specific theme, or melodic fragment, identifying each character, object, feeling, and situation in his dramas. He used hundreds of such themes within his musical texture in various permutations and combinations following the demands of his text.

He brought such enrichment and amplification to his orchestral writing by exploiting the fullest resources of harmony, instrumentation, counterpoint, and

thematic development that he may be considered the last of the Romantics. Those who would be Romantics after him would have to imitate him; those who would retain their identity would have to react so sharply against him that they would have to create an altogether new musical speech. Thus the impact of Wagner, his esthetics, and his music on his own generation, and upon the succeeding one, was cataclysmic.

The following are the excerpts from his operas and music dramas most often performed at symphony concerts:

The Flying Dutchman (Der fliegende Hollaender): Overture.

Lohengrin: Preludes to Acts 1 and 3.

The Mastersingers (Die Meistersinger); Preludes to Acts 1 and 3; *Dance of the Apprentices; Procession of the Mastersingers.*

Parsifal: Prelude; *Good Friday Spell; Klingsor's Magic Garden and Flower Maidens Scene; Transformation Scene.*

Rienzi: Overture.

Ring of the Nibelungs (Der Ring des Nibelungen). I. *The Rhinegold (Das Rheingold)*: *Entrance of the Gods into Valhalla.* II. *The Valkyries (Die Walkuere)*: *The Ride of the Valkyries; Wotan's Farewell and Magic Fire Scene.* III. *Siegfried: Forest Murmurs.* IV. *Twilight* (or *Dusk*) *of the Gods (Goetterdaemmerung)*: *Bruennhilde's Immolation; Siegfried's Funeral Music; Siegfried's Rhine Journey.*

Tannhaeuser: Overture and *Bacchanale;* Prelude to Act 3.

Tristan and Isolde: Prelude and *Love Death; Liebesnacht;* Prelude, Act 3.

Wagner's principal orchestral and instrumental works outside the theater include a symphony, *A Faust Overture (Eine Faust Ouvertuere), Siegfried Idyl,* and various overtures and marches. He also wrote two piano sonatas, and various shorter pieces for the piano including polonaises, *Albumblaetter,* and *Songs Without Words.*

See: *Bruennhilde's Immolation; Dance of the Apprentices; Entrance of the Gods into Valhalla; Faust Overture, A; Flying Dutchman, The; Forest Murmurs; Good Friday Spell; Klingsor's Magic Garden and Flower Maidens Scene; Liebesnacht;*

Lohengrin; Mastersingers, The; Parsifal; Procession of the Mastersingers; Ride of the Valkyries, The; Rienzi; Siegfried Idyl; Siegfried's Death Music; Siegfried's Rhine Journey; Tannhaeuser; Transformation Scene; Tristan and Isolde; Wedding March; Wotan's Farewell and Magic Fire Scene.

Waldesrauschen. *See:* Etude—*Liszt.*

Waldstein Sonata. *See:* Sonata—*Beethoven.*

Waldweben (Wagner). *See: Forest Murmurs.*

Walk to Paradise Garden, The. Orchestral interlude in Frederick Delius' opera, *A Village Romeo and Juliet,* between the fifth and sixth scenes (or, as the composer designated them, "pictures"). This music evokes the gentle, peaceful mood surrounding two lovers as they pause at "Paradise Garden" at a village fair during their elopement. The haunting melody first appears in the cellos, but is soon taken over by the oboe. A powerful climax is a temporary break in the dreamy atmosphere, but the composition ends peacefully.

Walkuere, Die (Wagner). *See: Valkyries, The; Ring of the Nibelungs, The.*

Walkuerenritt (Wagner). *See: Ride of the Valkyries, The.*

Wallenstein, Alfred, cellist and conductor. Born Chicago, Ill., Oct. 7, 1898. After studying the cello in Los Angeles with Julius Klengel among others, he toured southern California as a boy prodigy. In 1916 he played the cello in the San Francisco Symphony, and a year later toured as solo cellist with Anna Pavlova and her company. From 1919 to 1929 he was cellist in the Los Angeles Philharmonic and the Chicago Symphony, and from 1929 to 1936 he was first cellist of the New York Philharmonic. On the advice of Toscanini he turned to conducting, directing orchestral performances over the radio and at the Hollywood Bowl. In 1935 he was appointed music director of radio station WOR in New York, where he initiated several important series of musical broadcasts. After 1936 he made notable appearances as guest conductor of American orchestras. From 1943 to 1956 he was principal conductor of the Los Angeles Philharmonic. In 1947 he was the recipient of the Alice M. Ditson Award for his contributions to American music.

Wallensteins Lager. *See:* Schiller, Friedrich von.

Walsingham Variations. *See:* Bull, John.

Walter, Bruno (born **Bruno Schlesinger**), conductor. Born Berlin, Germany, Sept. 15, 1876. He received his musical training at the Stern Conservatory, then served his conducting apprenticeship in small German opera houses. In 1901 Gustav Mahler engaged him as assistant at the Vienna Royal Opera. During the eleven years Walter worked under Mahler he developed into a mature artist. In 1914 Walter was engaged as general music director in Munich, where his performances of Wagner and Mozart gained him international fame. He also gave distinguished performances annually at the Salzburg Festival. In 1923 he made his American début as guest conductor of the New York Symphony. He returned to the United States for the next two seasons to perform with the same orchestra. When he again appeared in the United States, in 1932, it was with the New York Philharmonic, an association that continued for a quarter of a century. Meanwhile, in 1925, he was appointed principal conductor of the Charlottenburg Opera in Berlin, and in 1930 he became the conductor of the Gewandhaus Orchestra in Leipzig. When the Nazis came to power in Germany, Bruno Walter settled in Vienna, where in 1936 he was appointed principal conductor and artistic adviser of the Vienna State Opera. During this period he also made many appearances throughout Europe, the United States, and in the Orient. After the *Anschluss,* Walter became a French citizen and made his home in Paris, devoting himself now mainly to performances in England and France, and at major festivals in Italy and Switzerland. When France capitulated to the Nazis, during World War II, Walter's French citizenship was abrogated. He then came to live in California, and made his American début as an opera conductor at the Metropolitan

Opera in New York in 1941. After the war he returned to Austria for some guest appearances with the Vienna State Opera and was given a hero's welcome. Walter has written an autobiography, *Theme and Variations* (1946), and a biography of Mahler (1936).

Walton, Sir William, composer. Born Oldham, England, March 29, 1902. After attending the Christ Church Cathedral Choir School, Oxford, he was enrolled in Christ Church, but was expelled for failing to apply himself to any studies other than music. Settling in London, he concentrated on composition, completing a piano quartet, a string quartet, and the provocative *Façade,* which made him famous in 1922. His later works followed a more traditional pattern than *Façade,* attesting to his growing technical mastery and ability to express a wide gamut of feelings within long-flowing melodic lines and complex harmonic, contrapuntal, and rhythmic patterns. His importance as a composer became evident with the cantata, *Belshazzar's Feast,* successfully introduced at the Leeds Festival on Oct. 10, 1931. Further recognition came with his symphony and violin concerto. During World War II Walton wrote music for documentary films. He later wrote the music for several successful motion pictures, including *Henry V, Hamlet,* and *Major Barbara.* He was knighted in 1951. In 1955 he paid his first visit to the United States to attend the American première of his opera, *Troilus and Cressida,* in San Francisco.

The following are his principal instrumental works:

Chamber Music: 2 string quartets; piano quartet; violin sonata; Toccata for violin and piano; Two Pieces for violin and piano.

Orchestra: Façade, suite; *Portsmouth Point; Siesta* for chamber orchestra; *Sinfonia Concertante* for orchestra with piano obbligato; viola concerto; symphony; *Crown Imperial;* violin concerto; *Scapino; Orb and Sceptre;* Partita; cello concerto; *Music for Children; Johannesberg Festival Overture.*

See: Concerto—*Walton;* Façade; Partita; *Portsmouth Point; Scapino;* Symphony—*Walton.*

Waltz. A dance derived from the Austrian laendler and *Teutsche.* It became outstandingly popular in Austria in the late 18th century, then spread throughout Europe. It is in 3/4 time, and though originally slow and sedate, became faster and faster in the 19th century until it was considered by many an obscene dance. Its popularity in Vienna never diminished; by the end of the 18th century, one person out of every four in Vienna danced the waltz.

The waltz has been successfully transferred into serious instrumental music. Waltzes for the piano were written by Haydn, Mozart, Beethoven, and Schubert. Schubert was one of the first to gather several different waltzes into a cohesive and unified work, in *Valses sentimentales,* op. 50 (1825), and in *Valses nobles,* op. 77 (1827); Liszt adapted nine of these Schubert waltzes into his *Soirées de Vienne* (1852). One of the earliest successful works in this extended form was Carl Maria von Weber's *Invitation to the Dance* (which see).

Chopin's 14 waltzes for piano are among his most popular compositions. The most celebrated of these (and few instrumental waltzes have greater grace and salon elegance) are the so-called *Minute Waltz* in D-flat major, op. 64, no. 1 (1847); the Waltz in C-sharp minor, op. 64, no. 2 (1847); the *Grande Valse brillante* in E-flat major, op. 18 (1831); and the Waltz in F-major, op. 34, no. 3 (1838), known as the *Cat's Waltz.*

The title of the *Minute Waltz* does not refer to sixty seconds, the time in which the waltz can be played, but to the French word "minute" meaning "little." The *Cat's Waltz* acquired its nickname from an appoggiatura section which sounds as if a cat ran across the keyboard.

Brahms wrote 16 waltzes for the piano, op. 39 (1865). Originally these were for four hands but the composer later transcribed them for two hands. Though Brahms may be more sedate or austere in other piano compositions, he is here the true Viennese, writing music that is full of the joy of living and dancing. The fifteenth Waltz, in A-flat major, is the most famous of all.

One of the most celebrated waltzes for the piano by Tchaikovsky can be found in a suite entitled Six Pieces, op. 51 (1884). It is the infectious *Valse sentimentale* in F minor, which has been transcribed for various combinations of instruments.

Ravel wrote for the piano a remarkable set of seven waltzes inspired by Schubert and with a pronounced Viennese character: *Valses nobles et sentimentales* (which see).

As a form of orchestral music, the waltz first became popular in the works of the Viennese waltz kings: Josef Lanner, Johann Strauss I, and the greatest of them all, Johann Strauss II. Perhaps no waltz music has enjoyed greater popularity throughout the world than the waltzes of the second Johann Strauss: *The Beautiful Blue Danube, Artist's Life, Wine, Women and Song,* and so on.

Waltzes for orchestra have been interpolated into symphonies (Berlioz' *Symphonie fantastique,* Tchaikovsky's Symphony No. 5); into suites (Tchaikovsky's *Nutcracker Suite,* Suite No. 2 in C major, and Serenade, op. 48); into operas (Richard Strauss' *Der Rosenkavalier* and Tchaikovsky's *Eugene Onegin*).

Wanderer Fantasy, The. Fantasy for piano solo in C major by Schubert, op. 15 (1822). It is most familiar in a transcription by Liszt (1857-1858) for piano and orchestra, introduced in Vienna on Dec. 14, 1861, with J. Egghard soloist and Hellmesberger conducting. Both the piano solo composition and Liszt's transcription are entitled the *Wanderer* because they make use of Schubert's song of that name. The Liszt transcription has four movements (I. *Allegro con fuoco ma non troppo.* II. *Adagio.* III. *Presto.* IV. *Allegro*). The first movement is in sonata form but without a recapitulation. Its main theme, derived rhythmically from the Schubert song, appears at once in the orchestra. The second principal theme appears in the piano (*dolce con grazia*) after a brief cadenza. The second movement enters without inter-ruption. Here the piano presents the song, *The Wanderer,* in a rich harmonization. Several simple variations follow. The next movement is a scherzo, opening with orchestra and piano stating a new theme; a subsidiary waltz-like melody is heard later on in the piano. In the trio, the oboe suggests the main theme before it is actually heard in the piano; after the trio, the first theme appears in varied and developed form. The finale is actually an extended coda in fugal style, the subject first stated by piano alone.

War Memorial Opera House. *See:* San Francisco Symphony.

Warlock, Peter. *See:* Heseltine, Philip.

Warner, H. Waldo, violist and composer. Born Northampton, England, Jan. 4, 1874. He attended the Guildhall School of Music in London. After his graduation he was appointed professor of the viola there. From 1907 on he played in the London String Quartet, with which he toured the world. He also served as first violist in the New Symphony and the Royal Philharmonic. Warner wrote some distinguished chamber music, including a string quartet that won a prize in a competition in England in 1916, and a piano trio that won the Coolidge Prize in 1921. Other works include 2 additional trios, *3 Phantasies* for string quartet, *Pixy Ring* for string quartet, a violin sonata, a viola sonata, and a Rhapsody for viola and string quartet.

Warsaw Philharmonic Orchestra. The leading symphony orchestra in Poland, founded in 1901, its initial concert taking place in Warsaw on November 5, Emil Mlynarski conducting. Mlynarski remained principal conductor for six years. Later conductors included Gregor Fitelberg, Zdzislaw Birnbaum, Henryk Melcer, and Josef Oziminski. In 1947 the orchestra was reorganized and nationalized and renamed the City of Warsaw Philharmonic Orchestra; it was once again reorganized in 1950.

Wasps, The. *See:* Aristophanes.

Water Carrier (Der Wassertraeger, or Les Deux Journées), Overture to The. Overture for orchestra to an opera by Luigi Cherubini, with a libretto by Jean-Nicolas Bouilly, introduced in Paris on Jan. 16, 1800. It opens with a slow section in which there is a suggestion of impending doom. The Allegro section which follows is built from two themes, the first in the strings (repeated by full orchestra), and the second, a tender melody first heard in bassoons and violas.

Water Music. Suite of airs, dances and fanfares for orchestra by Handel (1717) written for a royal water pageant down the Thames. Many barges floated down the river carrying royalty and people of high station. A special barge held the fifty musicians who played Handel's music. The king, George I, was so delighted with this music that he requested that the orchestra repeat it three times. About twenty pieces survive, from which Sir Hamilton Harty selected six and transcribed them for modern orchestra. The first is an overture in French style characterized by fanfares in the horns and ending in a fugal section. A pleasing air, a brisk bourrée, a lively hornpipe, and an attractive Andante follow. The suite ends with a finale (*Allegro deciso*) full of royal pomp and ceremony.

Weber, Carl Maria von, composer. Born Eutin, Germany, Nov. 18, 1786; died London, England, June 5, 1826. His importance in music rests principally on his operas, particularly *Der Freischuetz,* with which was established the foundations of a national German operatic movement. Nevertheless, his best instrumental music is not without merit; when performed, it affords pleasurable listening even while lacking the creative power and originality found in his operas.

When he was eleven he studied for six months with Michael Haydn in Salzburg, and subsequently continued his study in Munich and with Abbé Vogler in Vienna. In 1805 Weber received his first appointment, as conductor of the Breslau Opera, where he stayed three years. He then held two other opera posts, after which he traveled throughout Europe as a concert pianist. From 1813 to 1816 he was principal conductor of the Prague Opera and in 1816 he became the musical director of the Dresden Opera, where he was so successful that his appointment was confirmed for life. While there he led performances of German operas which fired him with the ideal of creating

a national opera, an ideal first realized by him in 1821 with *Der Freischuetz.* His last opera, *Oberon,* was written for and introduced in England in 1826. Weber died in his sleep just before making his journey home from England. He was buried in London, but his body was transferred to Dresden eighteen years later. For this second burial, Wagner wrote special music and delivered a eulogy.

The modern composer, Paul Hindemith, wrote a major work for orchestra based on Weber's music, entitled *Symphonic Metamorphosis on Themes by Carl Maria von Weber* (which see).

The following are Weber's principal instrumental works:

Chamber Music: 6 sonatas (or sonatinas) for violin and piano; piano quartet; clarinet quintet; flute trio; *Nine Variations on a Norwegian Air,* for violin and piano; *Grand Duo Concertante,* for clarinet and piano.

Orchestra: 2 symphonies; *Jubilee Overture; Teutscher* in D major; Andante in D minor for cello and orchestra; clarinet concertino; 2 clarinet concertos; 2 piano concertos; *Andante e rondo ongarese* for bassoon and orchestra; *Konzertstueck* for piano and orchestra.

Piano: 4 sonatas; *Momento capriccioso; Grande polonaise;* 18 *Favorit-Walzer; Air russe; Seven Variations on a Gypsy Song; Rondo brillante;* ecossaises; variations; and so on.

See: Euryanthe; Freischuetz, Der; Invitation to the Dance; Konzertstueck; Oberon.

Webern, Anton, composer. Born Vienna, Austria, Dec. 3, 1883; died Mittersill, Austria, Sept. 15, 1945. He attended the University of Vienna, specializing in music as a research student of Guido Adler and receiving his doctorate in philosophy in 1906. For four years, beginning in 1904, he studied composition with Arnold Schoenberg. His first major work, a Passacaglia for orchestra in 1908, followed traditional concepts of form and style. But Webern soon became influenced by his teacher to write first in an atonal idiom, and then in the twelve-tone technique. His atonal writing was first fully crystallized with Five Pieces for Orchestra, which created a scandal when introduced in Vienna in 1913. He began to use the twelve-tone technique with Three Sacred Songs in 1924. Webern was also active as a teacher of composition, and as a conductor of orchestral and choral concerts in Vienna. He was shot and killed when, soon after the end of World War II in Europe, he misunderstood the order of an American soldier and advanced towards him instead of standing still.

The following are his principal instrumental works:

Chamber Music: Five Pieces for string quartet; Four Pieces for violin and piano; Six Bagatelles for string quartet; Three Pieces for cello and piano; string trio; saxophone quartet; piano quartet; string quartet.

Orchestra: Six Pieces; Five Pieces; symphony for chamber orchestra; Orchestral Variations.

See: Bagatelle; Symphony—*Webern.*

Wedding Day at Troldhaugen (Grieg). *See: Lyric Pieces.*

Wedding March. *See:* March.

Weihe des Hauses, Die (Beethoven). *See: Consecration of the House Overture.*

Weinberger, Jaromir, composer. Born Prague, Czechoslovakia, Jan. 8, 1896. He studied music at the Prague Conservatory and with Max Reger in Berlin. In 1922 he visited the United States, for several years serving as professor of composition at the Conservatory in Ithaca, N.Y. In 1926 he assumed the post of director of the National Theater in Bratislava and of the Eger School of Music. It was in the field of opera that he first achieved recognition as a composer, with *Schwanda the Bagpipe Player* (*Schwanda der Dudelsackpfeifer*), a sensation when introduced at Prague in 1927, and in the next four years given over 2,000 performances in Europe and the United States. After the occupation of the Sudetenland by the Nazis he went to live in Paris; then in 1939 he settled permanently in the United States, where he subsequently became a citizen.

His music passed through several transformations. His earlier works, many of which he destroyed, were influenced by French Impressionism. Then he assumed a national Bohemian style. Since coming to the United States he has tended to derive his inspiration, and sometimes even his musical materials, from American folklore and backgrounds. His principal works, outside the theater, are for orchestra and include *Marionette Overture, Christmas, Six Bohemian Songs and Dances, Overture to a Puppet Play,* Passacaglia, *Under the Spreading Chestnut Tree, Don Quixote, Prelude and Fugue on Dixie, Abraham Lincoln Symphony, Song of the High Seas, Legend of Sleepy Hollow,* and *Préludes religieux et profanes.*

See: Polka and Fugue; *Under the Spreading Chestnut Tree.*

Weiner, Leo, composer and teacher. Born Budapest, Hungary, April 16, 1885. He attended the Budapest Academy of Music, then for a while worked as coach at the Budapest Comic Opera. Winning the Francis Joseph Jubilee Award enabled him to spend several years in Austria, Germany, and France. In 1908 he was appointed to the faculty of the Budapest Academy of Music, where for many years he was a distinguished teacher of theory, composition, and chamber music. He received a government pension in 1949 and the State Kossuth Prize in 1950. His music has paid much less attention to national idioms than has that of his Hungarian contemporaries (though on several occasions he did produce works based on Hungarian folksongs and dances). He prefers to express his pronounced Romantic tendencies in a style more essentially Germanic than Hungarian. His orchestral compositions include a piano concertino, *Carnival, Play at Soldiers, Hungarian Folk Dances,* 3 divertimentos, a suite, *Pastorale,* and *Festive Sounds.* He also wrote 3 string quartets (the second winning the Coolidge Prize in 1922), a string trio, *Hungarian Wedding Dance* for violin and piano, and *Ballade* for clarinet and piano. Weiner has written several excellent texts on harmony and form and transcribed for orchestra works by Bach, Schubert, Liszt, and Béla Bartók.

Weingartner, Felix, conductor and composer. Born Zara, Dalmatia, June 2, 1863; died Winterthur, Switzerland, May 7, 1942. He entered the Leipzig Conservatory in his eighteenth year, remaining there two years and winning the Mozart Prize. In 1884 his first opera, *Sakuntala,* was introduced in Weimar, where Weingartner became a friend of Liszt, who convinced him that he ought to become a conductor. Through Liszt's influence Weingartner became an assistant of Hans von Buelow with the Meiningen Orchestra. In 1891 he became principal conductor of the Berlin Royal Opera, with whose orchestra he also led distinguished symphony concerts. After a period in Munich, where he conducted orchestral concerts with the Kaim Orchestra, he went to Vienna in 1908 to succeed Gustav Mahler as principal conductor of the Vienna State Opera and the Vienna Philharmonic. It was in Vienna that Weingartner first achieved international fame, especially for his performances of the Wagner music dramas and the Beethoven symphonies. From 1912 to 1914 he was principal conductor of the Hamburg State Theater and from 1914 to 1919 he was music director in Darmstadt. He made his American début with the New York Philharmonic on Feb. 10, 1905, and in 1906 he returned to the United States to appear with the New York Symphony, with which he made an extensive tour. After a period as music director of the Vienna Volksoper and principal conductor of the Vienna Philharmonic, Weingartner settled in Basel, Switzerland, in 1927 as director of its Conservatory and a conductor of symphony concerts. In 1935 he returned to Vienna to assume for one season the post of artistic director of the Vienna State Opera. He also appeared as guest conductor throughout Europe and at its leading festivals. He wrote several books, including an important treatise on conducting (1895) and a history of Bayreuth (1896). He also prepared new editions of some operas and orchestrated several important works, including Beethoven's *Hammerklavier Sonata* and Weber's *Invitation to the Dance.* He was the composer of 6 symphonies, various concertos and tone poems, 4 string quartets, 2 violin sonatas, and other chamber music; he was most successful as a composer of operas.

Weinrich, Carl, organist. Born Paterson,

N.J., July 2, 1904. He attended the Curtis Institute in Philadelphia, and studied organ with Lynwood Farnham. In 1930 he was appointed organist of the Church of the Holy Communion in New York, where he gave distinguished concerts of organ music covering virtually the entire basic literature for that instrument. He also appeared in concert performances throughout the United States, acclaimed particularly for his performances of Bach's music. Weinrich has been head of the organ department of the Westminster Choir School in Princeton, N.J., and from 1942 to 1952 was a member of the music faculty at Columbia University. In 1943 he was appointed director of music at the Princeton University Chapel.

Weldon, George, conductor. Born Chichester, England, Jan. 5, 1906. He received his musical training at the Royal College of Music in London, and conducted several English semi-professional orchestras. From 1943 to 1950 he was principal conductor of the City of Birmingham Orchestra, and from 1952 second conductor of the Hallé Orchestra. He has also been heard in guest performances with leading European symphonic groups.

Well-Tempered Clavier, The. Two books of preludes and fugues for the clavier, twenty-four in each book and in each of the twelve major and twelve minor keys. Bach wrote this music as instruction pieces for his wife and children, but also to prove how music could be written effectively for the "well-tempered" or "well-tuned" clavier. Andreas Werckmeister had been one of the pioneers in dividing the octave into twelve equal semitones, called "equal temperament," which made it possible for the first time for each tone to be approximately in tune by distributing the discrepancy in pitch more or less equally among the twelve tones of the octave. This innovation was functional, enabling composers to transpose from one key to another more easily. Bach favored this idea and wrote his *Well-Tempered Clavier* in the twenty-four keys to prove its value. Being a genius, he also succeeded in bringing to functional music a wealth of harmonic daring, an infinite variety of style and expression, and much depth of feeling. These preludes and fugues are surely among the greatest works written for the keyboard, speaking, as William Whittaker wrote, "as no musician ever spoke save Bach . . . One can find music there to meet all needs, to synchronize all states of emotion."

Wellesz, Egon, composer and musicologist. Born Vienna, Austria, Oct. 21, 1885. He attended the Vienna University and studied music privately with Arnold Schoenberg. After teaching music history in Vienna he became a member of the faculty of the University there in 1913, and from 1930 to 1938 professor of music history. When Austria was annexed by Germany, Wellesz went to live in England, where he received a research fellowship at Oxford, and in 1943 was appointed university lecturer in the history of music. During the early part of World War II, he temporarily abandoned composition, with which he had occupied himself since early manhood, to concentrate on research. An authority on Byzantine music, having written a definitive study of it in 1922, he now completed two additional works in that field: *Eastern Elements in Western Chant* (1947) and *A History of Byzantine Music and Hymnography* (1949). Since the end of the World War II, he has returned to composition, completing two symphonies and two string quartets among other works. In 1947 he visited the United States to lecture at Princeton and Columbia Universities, and in 1948 he was appointed reader in Byzantine music at Oxford. In his compositions, Wellesz has been influenced by Baroque styles and techniques. Modal writing and medieval polyphony often give his music an exotic character; but its motor energy also endows it with contemporary interest. His principal works for orchestra include 2 symphonies, a piano concerto, Suite for violin and orchestra, *Festlicher Marsch* and *Prosperos Beschwoerungen*. In chamber music he produced 7 string quartets, sonatas and suites for solo cello, violin, or clarinet, and *Geistiges Lied* for violin, viola, and piano.

Wellingtons Sieg, oder **Die Schlacht bei**

Vittoria (Beethoven). *See: Battle Symphony.*

Wesley, Samuel, organist and composer. Born Bristol, England, Feb. 24, 1766; died London, England, Oct. 11, 1837. He was one of the leading organists of his time, a remarkable interpreter of Bach's music. He studied the organ with his brother, making public appearances as a child prodigy. As a young man he became an enthusiast of Bach's works. From then on he dedicated himself to introducing to English audiences Bach's organ works, many of which were then unknown in England; he also made an arrangement of Bach's organ trios, edited the *Well-Tempered Clavier,* and helped promote an English translation of Forkel's biography of Bach. Wesley was a prolific composer of church and organ music; he also wrote symphonies, organ concertos, overtures, string quartets, and numerous sonatas.

White Peacock, The. A piece for the piano (also for orchestra), by Charles Tomlinson Griffes, op. 7 (1916). It is the first of four numbers in *Roman Sketches,* a suite for piano. This sensitive tone picture, whose delicate mood remains unbroken, was inspired by a poem by William Sharpe beginning with the lines "Here, as the breath, as the soul of this beauty Moveth in silence, and dreamlike, and slowly . . . the White Peacock." Griffes orchestrated this piano piece for a stage production at the Rivoli Theater, New York. The concert première of the orchestrated version was given in Philadelphia, Dec. 19, 1919, Stokowski conducting. The tone poem for orchestra is dominated by a haunting song for a flute.

Whitman, Walt, poet. Born West Hills, Huntington, Long Island, May 31, 1819; died Camden, N.J., March 26, 1892. The following works for orchestra are based on poems by Whitman: John Alden Carpenter's tone poem, *Sea Drift;* Frederick Converse's orchestral fantasy *The Mystic Trumpeter,* and two tone poems for piano and orchestra, *Night* and *Day;* Frederick Delius' *Sea Drift,* for baritone, chorus, and orchestra; Arthur Farwell's *Symbolist Study No. 3.* The poet himself was the inspiration of Gustav Holst's *Whitman Overture.*

Whittemore and Lowe, a duo-piano team made up of Arthur Whittemore and Jack Lowe. Whittemore was born in Vermillion, S.D., Oct. 23, 1916; Lowe, in Aurora, Col., Dec. 25, 1917. Whittemore studied music with private teachers, and in 1934 was graduated from the University of South Dakota. In the same year he received a teaching fellowship at the Eastman School of Music; a year later, he was appointed director of music at the University of Rochester College for Men. There he met and became a friend of Jack Lowe, who had studied the violin with private teachers and at sixteen was a member of the Denver Symphony. At the Eastman School of Music, Lowe concentrated on the piano, and in 1935 he became assistant to Whittemore at the University of Rochester College for Men. Whittemore and Lowe made their début as a two-piano team over the radio in Pittsburgh in 1938, and their concert début in New York in 1940. During World War II they gave over 700 concerts in hospitals, army bases, and in combat zones. Since then they have successfully performed throughout the world, introducing many world premières, including works for two pianos by Vaughan Williams, Quincy Porter, Francis Poulenc, and Morton Gould.

Whole tone scale. A scale made up entirely of whole tones, the octave being divided into six equal parts. The whole-tone scale was first popularized in Western music by Debussy.

Widor, Charles Marie, organist and composer. Born Lyons, France, Feb. 24, 1844; died Paris, France, March 12, 1937. He studied the organ with his father and Nicolas Lemmens. In 1869 he was appointed organist of St. Sulpice in Paris, remaining there until his retirement in 1934. In 1890 he succeeded César Franck as professor of organ at the Paris Conservatory, and in 1896 he assumed there the post of professor of counterpoint, fugue, and composition. Widor distinguished himself not only as one of the leading French organists of his time, but also as a composer. His compositions include operas, symphonies for orchestra,

various concertos for solo instruments and orchestra, some chamber and piano music, and much music for the organ. He was at his best in the last department, making the most important contribution to organ literature by any French composer in his symphonies for the organ. These are not actually symphonies in the traditional meaning of that term, but suites comprising variations, marches, fugues, canons, toccatas, scherzos, slow movements, and so on. The most popular of these works are: Symphony No. 1 in C major, op. 13, no. 1; No. 5, in E minor, op. 42, no. 1; No. 6, in G minor, op. 42, no. 2; No. 9, op. 70, the *Symphonie gothique.*

Wieniawski, Henri, violinist and composer. Born Lublin, Poland, July 10, 1835; died Moscow, Russia, March 31, 1880. For five years he attended the Paris Conservatory, a pupil of Joseph Massart. In 1848 his concert career was launched with successful performances in Paris and a tour of Europe and Russia. From 1859 to 1871 he was court violinist in St. Petersburg. He made his American début in 1872 in joint recitals with Anton Rubinstein. In 1874 he was appointed professor of the violin at the Brussels Conservatory. A heart disease ended his career as violinist and teacher in 1879. Besides being one of the most eminent violin virtuosos of his generation, a formidable technician and an aristocratic musician, Wieniawski was a composer of successful works for his instrument. These include 2 violin concertos (the second, in D minor, being famous), and numerous shorter compositions including *Souvenirs de Moscou,* polonaises, mazurkas, *Légende, Scherzo-Tarentelle,* and *Capriccio-Valse.*

See: Concerto—*Wieniawski; Kujawiak; Legend; Polonaise; Tarantella.*

Wigmore Hall. An important concert auditorium in London, England. It was built by Friedrich Wilhelm Carl Bechstein, head of the German piano firm, on Wigmore Street adjacent to his London showrooms. Originally called Bechstein Hall, it opened on May 31, 1901, with a concert featuring Ferruccio Busoni, Eugène Ysaÿe, and others. The hall was renamed Wigmore Hall in 1917, and re-opened with a concert by Albert Sammons and Safonov. In 1946 it was leased by the Arts Council of Great Britain for a twenty-year period.

Wilde, Oscar, poet, dramatist, and novelist. Born Dublin, Ireland, Oct. 16, 1856; died Paris, France, Nov. 30, 1900. His poetic drama in French, *Salomé,* was the libretto for the celebrated opera of Richard Strauss, whose *Dance of the Seven Veils* is often heard at symphony concerts. Flor Alpaerts, Granville Bantock, and Alexander Tcherepnin wrote incidental music for that drama, while Alexander Krein's tone poem *Salome* is based upon it.

Wilde's story, *The Birthday of the Infanta,* was the source of suites for orchestra by John Alden Carpenter, Mario Castelnuovo-Tedesco, and Franz Schreker. Jacques Ibert's tone poem for orchestra, *The Ballad of Reading Gaol,* and Vassilenko's tone poem, *The Garden of Death,* were also based on Wilde's poems of the same names.

Wilhelmj, August, violinist. Born Usingen, Germany, Sept. 21, 1845; died London, England, Jan. 22, 1908. On the recommendation of Liszt, who described him as "the future Paganini," Wilhelmj attended the Leipzig Conservatory from 1861 to 1864. While still a student there he made sensational public appearances in Leipzig. In 1865 he began the first of many tours of the world. He was immediately acclaimed as one of the foremost violin virtuosos of his day. In 1878 he made his American début, in the course of a world tour that lasted until 1882. In 1882 he temporarily withdrew from the concert stage to found and direct a violin school in Biberich. He returned to concert activity in 1885. In 1894 he became professor of the violin at the Guildhall School of Music in London. Towards the end of his life he interested himself in violin construction; his home in London became a museum of modern violins. He was the author of a *Modern Violin School,* and transcriber of many compositions for the violin, the most popular of these being Bach's *Air on the G String* and Wagner's *Traeume,*

and the *Prize Song* from *The Mastersingers.*

William Tell. *See:* Schiller, Friedrich von.

William Tell (Guillaume Tell), Overture to. An overture to the tragic opera by Rossini, text by Etienne de Jouy and Hippolyte Bis based on Schiller's drama. The opera was introduced in Paris on Aug. 3, 1829. The overture is one of the most popular compositions in the orchestral literature—a tone poem, rich with poetic content and vivid in its programmatic writing. An eloquent slow section highlights a melody for cellos and basses describing the rise of the sun in the Swiss Alps. A realistic description of a mountain storm follows, presented by the full orchestra. Another slow section depicts unforgettably a pastoral scene; a lovely Swiss melody is heard in the English horn. Fanfares in the trumpets shatter this mood and invoke dramatic march music, with which the overture comes to an exciting conclusion, describing the triumphant return of the victorious Swiss troops.

Wind instrument. Any musical instrument in which the sound is produced by the performer's breath.

Winter Daydreams. *See:* Symphony—*Tchaikovsky.*

Winter Wind Etude. *See:* Etude—*Chopin.*

Winter's Tale, A. *See:* Shakespeare, William.

Wittgenstein, Paul, one-armed pianist. Born Vienna, Austria, Nov. 5, 1887. He studied music in Vienna, where in 1913 he made his concert début. He lost his right arm during World War I, then began training himself as a one-armed pianist. His return début took place in Vienna in 1916 with a Concerto for the Left Hand, written for him by Josef Labor. After World War I he concertized throughout Europe, presenting many new works written for him by such eminent composers as Richard Strauss, Maurice Ravel, and Erich Wolfgang Korngold. He made his American début in 1934 with the Boston Symphony in Ravel's Concerto for the Left Hand. After the *Anschluss,* Wittgenstein left Austria and settled in the United States.

Wolf, Hugo, composer. Born Windischgraz, Austria, March 13, 1860; died Vienna, Austria, Feb. 22, 1903. Wolf's was essentially a genius for the art-song (lied). His infrequent excursions into the writing of instrumental music yielded only one gratifying work, the *Italian Serenade* for string quartet and also for small orchestra; but he also produced a string quartet, an intermezzo for string quartet, and various pieces for piano. Except for a brief period at the Vienna Conservatory, Wolf was self-taught in music. In 1884 he became the music critic of the *Salonblatt* in Vienna, and in 1887 he published his first volume of songs. Towards the end of his life he lost his mind and had to be confined to a private hospital.

See: Italian Serenade; Penthesilea.

Wolf-Ferrari, Ermanno, composer. Born Venice, Italy, Jan. 12, 1876; died there, Jan. 21, 1948. Though Wolf-Ferrari is famous for his operas, he wrote several notable instrumental compositions. He studied music mainly in Munich with Josef Rheinberger, and he first achieved recognition with an opera buffa, *Le Donne curiose*, in 1903. From 1902 to 1909 he was director of the Liceo Benedetto Marcello in Venice. He paid a visit to the United States in 1912 to attend the American première of his opera, *The Jewels of the Madonna,* in Chicago. Wolf-Ferrari's orchestral works include a Chamber Symphony, *Suite veneziana, Arabeschi,* Divertimento, and *Idillio* for oboe and string orchestra. He also wrote 2 violin sonatas, a piano quintet, string quartet, and piano trio.

See: Secret of Suzanne, The.

Wolff, Albert Louis, conductor and composer. Born Paris, France, Jan. 19, 1884. He attended the Paris Conservatory for ten years. From 1906 to 1910 he was organist at the St. Thomas Aquinas Church in Paris. In 1911 he became conductor of the Opéra-Comique, and from 1919 to 1921 he was conductor of the French repertory at the Metropolitan Opera in New York. After that he served as principal conductor of the Opéra-Comique and the Champs-Elysées Theater in Paris. Despite his intensive activity in opera, he also distinguished himself as a symphony conductor, being the founder and director of the Concerts Modernes in Paris, a series devoted to the presentation of new music. He also served for many years as principal conductor of the Lamoureux and the Pasdeloup Orchestra. As a composer, he is best known for his opera *The Blue Bird.*

Wolsey's Wilde. *See:* Byrd, William.

Wood, Sir Henry J., conductor. Born London, England, March 3, 1869; died Hitchin, Herts, England, Aug. 19, 1944. He attended the Royal Academy of Music, then for several years appeared as an organ virtuoso throughout England. He made his conducting début in Clapton, England, in 1888. After leading performances with the D'Oyly Carte and Carl Rosa opera companies he was appointed in 1895 principal conductor of the Promenade Concerts at Queen's Hall, London, with which his reputation was established. Wood remained conductor of the Queen's Hall Orchestra (later renamed New Queen's Hall Orchestra) until his death. But he also conducted at festivals in Norwich and Sheffield, and symphony concerts in Birmingham, Cardiff, Manchester, and Liverpool. He was responsible for introducing to England major works by Elgar, Debussy, Schoenberg, Scriabin, and others; and for introducing new English works to Germany, Switzerland, and the United States, visiting the last in 1925. His thirtieth anniversary as a conductor was celebrated in 1938 with a concert at Albert Hall for which Vaughan Williams wrote *Serenade to Music.* Wood was knighted in 1911, and in 1921 he was awarded the Royal Philharmonic Society medal. He made orchestral transcriptions of works by Bach, Handel, Mussorgsky, Purcell, and Debussy.

Woodland Sketches. Suite of 10 pieces for the piano by Edward MacDowell, op. 51 (1896), the composer's most popular work for piano. All ten pieces are delicate mood and nature pictures. Two are especially popular: *To a Wild Rose* and *To a Water Lily.* The other eight are: *Will-o-the-Wisp, At an Old Trysting Place, In Autumn, From an Indian Lodge, From Uncle Remus, A Deserted Farm, By a Meadow Brook,* and *Told at Sunset.*

Woodwind. Wind instruments made of wood, the most common being the flute, oboe, clarinet, and bassoon families, all of which are regarded as woodwinds even though some flutes and oboes are nowadays made of metal.

Wotan's Farewell and Magic Fire Scene (Wotans Abschied und Feuerzauber). The concluding scene of Wagner's music drama *The Valkyries* (*Die Walkuere*), from the cycle *The Ring of the Nibelungs.* Wotan, having banished his beloved daughter, Bruennhilde, from Valhalla, bids her a tender farewell, as a poignant song rises from the strings. He puts her into a deep sleep and surrounds her with a circle of flame to protect her until a hero shall arrive to awaken her. The flames are realistically simulated in the flickering tones of the woodwinds. The motifs of "Bruennhilde's Slumber" and "Fate" are sounded, and the scene ends with the exclamation by the brasses of the "Siegfried" theme. The fire music returns, followed by a brief recall of Bruennhilde's slumber motif.

X

Xylophone. A tuned percussion instrument with a three- to four-octave range; its hard-wood bars are struck by two mallets. Effective use of the xylophone is made in major works by Saint-Saëns (*Danse macabre*), Shostakovich (*The Age of Gold*), Manuel de Falla (*Three-Cornered Hat*), Khatchaturian (*Saber Dance* from *Gayane*), and Stravinsky (*The Firebird* and *Petrouchka*).

Y

Yon, Pietro, organist. Born Settimo-Vittone, Italy, Aug. 8, 1886; died Huntington, Long Island, Nov. 22, 1943. He attended the Conservatories of Milan and Turin and the Santa Cecilia Academy in Rome. After serving as organist at the Vatican and at the Royal Church in Rome, he came in 1907 to the United States, where he lived for the rest of his life and became a citizen. From 1907 until 1926 he was organist of the St. Francis Xaver Church, and from 1926 on at St. Patrick's Cathedral, both in New York. He also made many tours of the United States in organ recitals. Yon was the composer of many pieces for organ, orchestra, and piano, including an oboe concerto, and *Concerto gregoriano* for organ and orchestra.

Young Person's Guide to the Orchestra, The. A set of orchestral variations by Benjamin Britten, op. 34 (1945). It was commissioned by the Ministry of Education in England for a film describing the instruments of the orchestra. Britten utilized a theme-and-variations form. His theme is a vigorous subject by Henry Purcell, a rondeau from the incidental music to *Abdelazar.* Thirteen variations follow in which the different instruments of the orchestra appear in the following order: flutes and piccolo; oboes; clarinets; bassoons; violins; violas; cellos; double basses; harp; French horns; trumpets; trombones; percussion. The work ends with a fugue in which the instruments again enter in the order in which they are first heard in the variations.

Youth of Hercules (Saint-Saëns). *See: Jeunesse d'Hercule, La.*

Ysaÿe, Eugène, violinist, conductor, and composer. Born Liège, Belgium, July 16, 1858; died Brussels, Belgium, May 12, 1931. After attending the Liège Conservatory, he made his concert début at Liège in 1869. Additional study of the violin took place with Henri Wieniawski and Henri Vieuxtemps; the latter arranged for a special government subsidy to enable Ysaÿe to attend the Brussels Conservatory for three years. After appearances in Germany, Ysaÿe was appointed in 1880 concertmaster of Bilse's Orchestra in Berlin, where he gained his first experiences as a conductor. In 1881 he toured Norway, and beginning in 1883 he lived for several years in Paris, where he became intimately associated with Franck, Debussy, d'Indy, and other leading musicians; in 1886 he gave the world première of Franck's Violin Sonata, which is dedicated to him. From 1886 to 1897 he was professor of the violin at the Brussels Conservatory; in that city, in 1894, he founded the Ysaÿe Orchestral Concerts, which he led for several years in provocative programs that included many important premières. He also founded and played in the Ysaÿe String Quartet. In many tours of Europe both with his quartet and as a concert artist Ysaÿe established his reputation as one of the foremost violinists of his generation. He made a highly successful début as a violinist in the United States on Nov. 16, 1894, as soloist with the New York Philharmonic. His American début as a conductor took place in Cincinnati on April 5, 1918. He proved so successful that he was at once engaged as principal conductor of the Cincinnati Symphony, holding this post until 1922. After 1922 he directed orchestral and chamber-music concerts in Brussels. Ysaÿe was the composer of 6 violin concertos, 6 sonatas for unaccompanied violin, several string trios, and numerous pieces for the violin.

Z

Zapateado. A lively Spanish dance with a vigorous rhythm accentuated by the clicking of the dancer's heels. A popular example of this dance in instrumental music is Pablo de Sarasate's brilliant *Zapateado,* op. 23, no. 2, for violin and piano.

Zarlino, Gioseffe, theorist. Born Chioggia, Italy, March 22, 1517; died Venice, Italy, Feb. 14, 1590. He was trained for the church, receiving minor orders in 1539 and ordained deacon in 1541. After going to Venice he studied music with Adrian Willaert, then became maestro di cappella at St. Mark's in 1565. He did not abandon his ecclesiastical duties. In 1582 he was elected canon of Chioggia, and in 1583, bishop. Zarlino wrote some church music, little of which has survived. He is most famous for his theoretical studies. He was one of the first to suggest equal temperament. These writings appeared in three treatises: *Istituzioni armoniche* (1558); *Dimostrationi armoniche* (1571); and *Sopplimenti musicali* (1588).

Zauberfloete, Overture to Die (Mozart). *See: Magic Flute, Overture to The.*

Ziemlich. Rather.

Zigeunerweisen (Sarasate). *See: Gypsy Airs.*

Zimbalist, Efrem, violinist. Born Rostovon-the-Don, Russia, April 9, 1889. He studied the violin with his father and, from 1901 to 1907, with Leopold Auer at the St. Petersburg Conservatory. His début in Europe took place on Nov. 7, 1907, with the Berlin Philharmonic. In his ensuing performances throughout Europe he scored such striking successes that he was invited by the Leipzig Gewandhaus Orchestra to continue a tradition established by Joachim: to appear with that orchestra every New Year's Day. Zimbalist's American début took place on Oct. 27, 1911, with the Boston Symphony in the American première of Glazunov's A minor Violin Concerto. He later decided to live permanently in the United States and become a citizen. In 1914 he married the famous singer, Alma Gluck, with whom he made many appearances in joint concerts; their daughter is the writer, Marcia Davenport. Since then Zimbalist has appeared throughout the world of music. He has also been an important teacher of the violin. In 1928 he became head of the violin department of the Curtis Institute in Philadelphia, and in 1941 director of the Institute. His second wife is Mary Louise Curtis Bok, whose endowment had been responsible for the founding of the Curtis Institute. He has written several large-scale compositions including a violin concerto, Rhapsody for orchestra, a string quartet, and violin sonata.

Zingaresca, Alla. In a gypsy style.

Selected Readings on Music and Musicians

(NOTE: *Only books in English on instrumental music of general interest —either those in print or those readily available in libraries—are listed.*)

ANALYTICAL OR PROGRAM NOTES

Bagar, Robert, and Biancolli, Louis, *The Concert Companion*. New York, Whittlesey House, 1947.

Biancolli, Louis, ed., *The Analytical Concert Guide*. New York, Doubleday, 1951.

Burk, John N., ed., *Philip Hale's Boston Symphony Programme Notes*. New York, Doubleday, 1935.

Ewen, David, *Complete Book of 20th Century Music,* revised ed. New York, Prentice-Hall, 1959.

Ewen, David, *Music for the Millions*. New York, Arco, 1944. (Republished as *Ewen's Musical Masterworks*. New York, Arco, 1958.)

Hill, Ralph, ed., *The Concerto*. London, Pelican Books, 1952.

Hill, Ralph, ed., *The Symphony*. London, Pelican Books, 1949.

Hutcheson, Ernest, *The Literature of the Piano*. New York, Knopf, 1948.

Newmarch, Rosa, *The Concertgoers Library of Descriptive Notes,* 6 vols. London, Oxford University Press, 1928-48.

O'Connell, Charles. *The Victor Book of Symphonies*. New York, Simon & Schuster, 1948.

O'Connell, Charles, *The Victor Book of Overtures, Tone Poems, and Other Orchestral Works*. New York, Simon & Schuster, 1950.

Robertson, Alec, ed., *Chamber Music*. London, Pelican Books, 1957.

Tovey, Donald Francis, *Essays in Musical Analysis,* 6 vols. London, Oxford University Press, 1935-39.

Veinus, Abraham, *The Victor Book of Concertos*. New York, Simon & Schuster, 1948.

HISTORIES

Abraham, Gerald, *A Hundred Years of Music,* 2nd ed. London, Duckworth, 1949.

Abraham, Gerald, *Studies in Russian Music*. New York, Scribner, 1936

Bukofzer, M. F. *Music in the Baroque Era*. New York, Norton, 1947.

Calvocoressi, M. D., and Abraham, Gerald, *Masters of Russian Music,* New York, Knopf, 1936.

Chase, Gilbert, *America's Music*. New York, McGraw-Hill, 1955.

Chase, Gilbert, *The Music of Spain*. New York, Norton, 1941.

Copland, Aaron, *Our New Music*. New York, Whittlesey House, 1941.

Demuth, Norman, *Musical Trends in the 20th Century*. London, Rockliff, 1952.

Einstein, Alfred, *Music in the Romantic Era*. New York, Norton, 1947.

Einstein, Alfred, *A Short History of Music*, 3rd ed. New York, Knopf, 1947.

Hanslick, Eduard, *Vienna's Golden Years of Music: 1850-1900*. New York, Simon & Schuster, 1950.

Howard, John Tasker, *Our American Music*, 3rd ed. New York, Crowell, 1946.

Lang, Paul Henry, *Music in Western Civilization*. New York, Norton, 1941.

Leichtentritt, Hugo, *Music, History and Ideas*. Cambridge, Harvard University Press, 1938.

Leichtentritt, Hugo, *Music of the Western Nations,* edited and amplified by Nicolas Slonimsky. Cambridge, Harvard University Press, 1956.

Leonard, Richard Anthony, *A History of Russian Music*. New York, Macmillan, 1957.

Pahlen, Kurt, *Music of the World*, rev. ed. New York, Crown, 1953.

Reese, Gustave, *Music in the Renaissance*. New York, Norton, 1954.

Rolland, Romain, *A Musical Tour Through the Land of the Past*. London, Kegan Paul, Trench, & Trubner, 1922.

Sachs, Curt, *Our Musical Heritage*, 2nd ed. New York, Prentice-Hall, 1955.

Salazar, A., *Music In Our Time*. New York, Norton, 1946.

Slonimsky, Nicolas, *Music Since 1900*, 3rd ed. New York, Coleman-Ross, 1949.

Slonimsky, Nicolas, *Music of Latin America*. New York, Crowell, 1945.

Strunk, Oliver, ed., *Source Readings in Music History*. New York, Norton, 1950.

Ulrich, Homer, *Chamber Music*. New York, Columbia University Press, 1948.

Walker, Ernest, *A History of Music in England,* 3rd ed., revised and enlarged by J. A. Westrup. Oxford, Clarendon Press, 1952.

MUSIC APPRECIATION AND GENERAL ESSAYS

Abraham, Gerald, *This Modern Music*. New York, Norton, 1952.

Barzun, Jacques, ed., *Pleasures of Music*. New York, Viking, 1951.

Bentley, Eric, ed., *Shaw on Music*. New York, Doubleday Anchor Books, 1955.

Bernstein, Martin, *An Introduction to Music*. New York, Prentice-Hall, 1951.

Boyden, David D., *An Introduction to Music*. New York, Knopf, 1957.

Copland, Aaron, *What to Listen for in Music*, rev. ed. New York, Mc-Graw-Hill, 1957.

Einstein, Alfred, *Essays on Music*. New York, Norton, 1956.

Finney, Theodore M., *Hearing Music*. New York, Harcourt, 1941.

Haggin, B. H., *Music for the Man Who Enjoys Hamlet*. New York, Knopf, 1944.

Kolodin, Irving, ed., *The Composer as Listener*. New York, Horizon Press, 1958.

Machlis, Joseph, *The Enjoyment of Music*. New York, Norton, 1955.

McKinney, Howard D., and Anderson, W. R., *Discovering Music*. New York, American Book, 1949.

Moore, Douglas, *Listening to Music*, 3rd ed. New York, Norton, 1937.

Morgenstern, Sam, ed., *Composers on Music*. New York, Pantheon, 1956.

Rolland, Romain, *Essays on Music*. New York, Allen, Towne & Heath, 1948.

Scholes, Percy, *The Listener's Guide to Music*. London, Oxford University Press, 1947.

COLLECTIVE BIOGRAPHIES

Bacharach, A. L., ed., *Lives of Great Composers*, 4 vols. London, Pelican Books, 1942-57.

Brockway, Wallace, and Weinstock, Herbert, *Men of Music*, 2nd ed. New York, Simon & Schuster, 1950.

Cross, Milton, and Ewen, David, *The Milton Cross Encyclopedia of Great Composers*, rev. ed. New York, Doubleday, 1959.

Ewen, David, *The Book of Modern Composers*, rev. ed. New York, Knopf, 1950.

Foss, Hubert, *The Heritage of Music*, 2 vols. London, Oxford University Press, 1927-34.

Leonard, Richard Anthony, *The Stream of Music*. New York, Doubleday, 1946.

Mason, Daniel Gregory, *Beethoven and His Forerunners*, rev. ed. New York, Macmillan, 1940.

Mason, Daniel Gregory, *The Romantic Composers*. New York, Macmillan, 1930.

Rolland, Romain, *Some Musicians of Former Days*. London, Kegan Paul, Trench & Trubner, date unknown.

Seroff, Victor, *The Mighty Five*. New York, Allen, Towne & Heath, 1948

Zoff, Otto, ed., *Great Composers Through the Eyes of their Contemporaries*. New York, Dutton, 1951.

INDIVIDUAL BIOGRAPHIES

J. C. Bach

Terry, Charles S., *John Christian Bach*. London, Oxford University Press, 1929.

J. S. Bach

David, Hans T., and Mendel, Arthur, eds., *The Bach Reader*. New York, Norton, 1945.

Pirro, André, *J. S. Bach*. New York, Orion Press, 1957.

Schweitzer, Albert, *J. S. Bach*, 2 vols. New York, Macmillan, 1950.

Spitta, Philipp, *Johann Sebastian Bach*, 3 vols. in 2. New York, Dover, 1951.

Terry, Charles S., *Bach: A Biography*, 2nd ed. New York, Oxford University Press, 1949.

Bach Family

Geiringer, Karl, *The Bach Family*. New York, Oxford University Press, 1954.

Barber

Broder, Nathan, *Samuel Barber*. New York, Schirmer, 1954.

Bartók

Fassett, Agatha, *The Naked Face of Genius: Bartók's American Years*. Boston, Houghton, 1958.

Stevens, Halsey, *Bartók*. New York, Oxford University Press, 1953.

Beethoven

Burk, John N., *The Life and Works of Beethoven*. New York, Random House, 1943.

Rolland, Romain, *Beethoven the Creator*. New York, Harper, 1929.

Schauffler, Robert Haven, *Beethoven: The Man Who Freed Music*. New York, Tudor, 1947.

Sullivan, J. W. N., *Beethoven: His Spiritual Development*. New York, Knopf, 1947.

Thayer, Alexander W., *The Life of Ludwig van Beethoven*, 3 vols. New York, Beethoven Association, 1921.

Turner, W. J., *Beethoven: The Search for Reality*. London, Dent, 1927.

Berg

Redlich, H. F., *Alban Berg*. New York, Abelard-Schuman, 1957.
Reich, Willi, *Alban Berg*. London, Dobson, 1954.

Berlioz

Barzun, Jacques, *Berlioz and the Romantic Century*, 2 vols. Boston, Little, 1950.
Berlioz, Hector, *Memoirs of Hector Berlioz*, Ernest Newman, ed. New York, Knopf, 1948.

Bizet

Curtiss, Mina, *Georges Bizet*. New York, Knopf, 1959.
Dean, Winton, *Bizet*. London, Dent, 1948.

Borodin

Abraham, Gerald, *Borodin*. London, Reeves, n.d.

Brahms

Geiringer, Karl, *Brahms: His Life and Work*, 2nd ed. New York, Oxford University Press, 1947.
Latham, Peter, *Brahms*. New York, Pellegrini & Cudahy, 1949.
May, Florence, *The Life of Brahms*, 2 vols. London, Reeves, n.d.
Schauffler, Robert Haven, *The Unknown Brahms*. New York, Dodd, 1933.
Specht, Richard, *Brahms*. New York, Dutton, 1930

Britten

Mitchell, Donald, and Keller, Hans, eds., *Benjamin Britten*. New York, Philosophical Library, 1952.
White, Eric Walter, *Benjamin Britten*, rev. ed. London, Boosey & Hawkes, 1954.

Bruckner

Newlin, Dika, *Bruckner, Mahler, Schoenberg*. New York, King's Crown Press, 1947.
Wolff, Werner, *Anton Bruckner: Rustic Genius*. New York, Dutton, 1942.

Busoni

Dent, Edward J., *Ferruccio Busoni*. London, Oxford University Press, 1933.

Byrd

Fellowes, Edmund H., *William Byrd,* 2nd ed. London, Oxford University Press, 1948.

Chausson

Barricelli, Jean-Pierre, and Weinstein, Leo, *Ernest Chausson.* Norman, University of Oklahoma Press, 1955.

Chopin

Hedley, Arthur, *Chopin.* New York, Pellegrini & Cudahy, 1949.
Weinstock, Herbert, *Chopin: The Man and His Music.* New York, Knopf, 1949.

Copland

Smith, Julia, *Aaron Copland.* New York, Dutton, 1955.

Corelli

Pincherle, Marc, *Corelli.* New York, Norton, 1956.

Couperin

Mellers, Wilfrid, *François Couperin and the French Classical Tradition.* London, Dobson, 1950.

Debussy

Lockspeiser, Edward, *Debussy.* New York, Pellegrini & Cudahy, 1949.
Seroff, Victor, *Debussy: Musician of France.* New York, Putnam, 1956.
Thompson, Oscar, *Debussy.* New York, Dodd, 1937.

Delius

Hutchings, Arthur, *Delius: A Critical Biography.* New York, Macmillan, 1948.
Warlock, Peter, *Delius.* New York, Oxford University Press, 1952.

Dvořák

Robertson, Alec, *Dvořák.* New York, Pellegrini & Cudahy, 1949.
Sourek, Otakar, *Dvořák.* New York, Philosophical Library, 1954.
Stefan, Paul, *Antonin Dvořák.* New York, Greystone, 1941.

Elgar

Chambers, George B., *Edward Elgar: Centenary Sketches*. London, Novello, 1957.

Reed, William Henry, *Elgar*. New York, Pellegrini & Cudahy, 1949.

Falla

Pahissa, Jaime, *Manuel de Falla*. London, Museum Press, 1954.

Fauré

Koechlin, Charles, *Gabriel Fauré*, rev. ed. London, Dobson, 1946.

Suckling, Norman, *Fauré*. New York, Pellegrini & Cudahy, 1951.

Franck

Demuth, Norman, *César Franck*. New York, Philosophical Library, 1949.

Gershwin

Ewen, David, *A Journey to Greatness: The Life and Music of George Gershwin*. New York, Holt, 1956.

Jablonsky, Edward, and Stewart, Lawrence D., *The Gershwin Years*. New York, Doubleday, 1958.

Grieg

Abraham, Gerald, ed., *Grieg: A Symposium*. Norman, University of Oklahoma Press, 1950.

Griffes

Maisel, Edward M., *Charles T. Griffes*. New York, Knopf, 1943.

Handel

Abraham, Gerald, ed., *Handel: A Symposium*. London, Oxford University Press, 1954.

Deutsch, O. E., *Handel: A Documentary Biography*. New York, Norton, 1955.

Flower, Newman, *George Frideric Handel: His Personality and His Times*, rev. ed. New York, Scribner, 1948.

Weinstock, Herbert, *Handel*, rev. ed. New York, Knopf, 1959.

Young, Percy M., *Handel*. London, Dent, 1947.

Haydn

Geiringer, Karl, *Haydn*. New York, Norton, 1946.
Hughes, Rosemary, *Haydn*. New York, Pellegrini & Cudahy, 1950.
Jacob, H. E., *Haydn, His Art, Times and Glory*. New York, Rinehart, 1950.

Holst

Holst, Imogen, *The Music of Gustav Holst*. London, Oxford University Press, 1951.

d'Indy

Demuth, Norman, *Vincent d'Indy*. London, Rockliff, 1951.

Ives

Cowell, Henry and Sidney, *Charles Ives and His Music*. New York, Oxford University Press, 1955.

Liszt

Newman, Ernest, *The Man Liszt*. New York, Knopf, 1935.
Searle, Humphrey, *The Music of Liszt*. London, Williams & Norgate, 1954.

Mahler

Mahler, Alma, *Gustav Mahler: Memories and Letters*. New York, Viking, 1946.
Newlin, Dika, *Bruckner, Mahler, Schoenberg*. New York, King's Crown Press, 1947.
Walter, Bruno, *Gustav Mahler*, rev. ed. New York, Knopf, 1957.

Mendelssohn

Radcliffe, Philip, *Mendelssohn*. London, Dent, 1954.

Miaskovsky

Ikonnikov, Alexandrei A., *Myaskovsky*. New York, Philosophical Library, 1946.

Milhaud

Milhaud, Darius, *Notes Without Music*. New York, Knopf, 1953.

Mozart

Blom, Eric, *Mozart*. New York, Pellegrini & Cudahy, 1949.
Biancolli, L., ed., *The Mozart Handbook*. New York, World Publishing, 1954.
Burk, John N., *Mozart and His Music*. New York, Random House, 1959.
Einstein, Alfred, *Mozart: His Character, His Work*. New York, Oxford University Press, 1945.
King, A. Hyatt, *Mozart in Retrospect*. London, Oxford University Press, 1955.
Landon, H. C. Robbins, and Mitchell, Donald, eds., *The Mozart Companion*. New York, Oxford University Press, 1956.
Turner, W. J., *Mozart: The Man and His Works*. New York, Knopf, 1945; reprint, Garden City, Doubleday, 1954.

Mussorgsky

Calvocoressi, M. D., *Mussorgsky*, Gerald Abraham, ed. London, Rockliff, 1956.

Paganini

De Courcy, G. I. C., *Paganini, the Genoese*, 2 vols. Norman, University of Oklahoma Press, 1957.

Pizzetti

Gatti, Guido M., *Ildebrando Pizzetti*. London, Dobson, 1951.

Prokofiev

Nestyev, Israel, *Serge Prokofiev: His Musical Life*. New York, Knopf, 1946.

Purcell

Holst, Imogen, ed., *Henry Purcell, 1659-1695. Essays on His Music*. London, Oxford University Press, 1959.
Westrup, J. A., *Purcell*. New York, Dutton, 1937.

Rachmaninoff

Bertensson, S., and Leyda, J., *Sergei Rachmaninoff*. New York, New York University Press, 1956.
Seroff, Victor, *Rachmaninoff*. New York, Simon & Schuster, 1950.

Rameau

Girdlestone, Cuthbert, *Jean-Philippe Rameau*. London, Cassell, 1957.

Ravel

Demuth, Norman, *Ravel*. London, Dent, 1947.
Seroff, Victor, *Ravel*. New York, Holt, 1953.

Roussel

Demuth, Norman, *Albert Roussel*. London, United Music Publishers, 1947.

Rimsky-Korsakov

Rimsky-Korsakov, N., *My Musical Life*, 3rd ed. New York, Knopf, 1942.

Rubinstein

Bowen, Catherine D., *Free Artist: The Story of Anton and Nicholas Rubinstein*. New York, Random House, 1939.

Satie

Myers, Rollo H., *Erik Satie*. London, Dobson, 1948.

Scarlatti

Kirkpatrick, Ralph, *Domenico Scarlatti*. Princeton, Princeton University Press, 1953.

Schoenberg

Leibowitz, René, *Schoenberg and His School*. New York, Philosophical Library, 1949.
Newlin, Dika, *Bruckner, Mahler, Schoenberg*. New York, King's Crown Press, 1947.

Schubert

Abraham, Gerald, ed., *The Music of Schubert*. New York, Norton, 1947.
Brown, M. J. E., *Schubert*. New York, St. Martin's Press, 1958.
Deutsch, O. E., *Schubert: Memoirs by His Friends*. New York, Macmillan, 1958.
Deutsch, O. E., *The Schubert Reader*. New York, Norton, 1947.

Einstein, Alfred, *Schubert: A Musical Portrait.* New York, Oxford University Press, 1951.

Hutchings, Arthur, *Schubert.* New York, Pellegrini & Cudahy, 1949.

Schauffler, Robert Haven, *Franz Schubert: The Ariel of Music.* New York, Putnam, 1949.

Schuman

Schreiber, Flora Rheta, and Persichetti, Vincent, *William Schuman.* New York, Schirmer, 1954.

Schumann

Abraham, Gerald, ed., *Schumann: A Symposium.* New York, Oxford University Press, 1952.

Chissell, Joan, *Schumann.* London, Dent, 1948.

Schauffler, Robert Haven, *Florestan: The Life and Works of Robert Schumann.* New York, Holt, 1946.

Sibelius

Abraham, Gerald, ed., *The Music of Sibelius.* New York, Norton, 1947.

Ekman, Karl, *Jean Sibelius.* New York, Tudor, 1945.

Gray, Cecil, *Sibelius,* rev. ed. London, Oxford University Press, 1945.

Johnson, Harold E., *Jean Sibelius.* New York, Knopf, 1959.

Ringbom, Eric, *Sibelius.* Norman, University of Oklahoma Press, 1954.

Shostakovich

Martinov, Ivan, *Shostakovich.* New York, Philosophical Library, 1947.

Stravinsky

Onnen, Frank, *Stravinsky.* New York, Macmillan, 1950.

Stravinsky, Igor, *Stravinsky: An Autobiography.* New York, Simon & Schuster, 1936; reprint, New York, Steuer, 1958.

Tansman, Alexander, *Igor Stravinsky.* New York, Putnam, 1949.

Tchaikovsky

Abraham, Gerald, ed., *The Music of Tchaikovsky.* New York, Norton, 1946.

Bowen, Catherine D., and Meck, B. von, *Beloved Friend.* New York, Dover, 1946.

Evans, Edwin, *Tchaikovsky.* New York, Pellegrini & Cudahy, 1949.

Weinstock, Herbert, *Tchaikovsky.* New York, Knopf, 1946.

Thomson

Hoover, Kathleen, and Cage, John, *Virgil Thomson*. New York, Yoseloff, 1959.

Vaughan Williams

Howes, Frank, *The Music of Ralph Vaughan Williams*. London, Oxford University Press, 1954.

Pakenheim, Simona, *Ralph Vaughan Williams*. London, Macmillan, 1957.

Vivaldi

Pincherle, Marc, *Vivaldi*. New York, Norton, 1957.

Wagner

Newman, Ernest, *The Life of Richard Wagner*, 4 vols. New York, Knopf, 1933-1946.

MUSICAL INSTRUMENTS

Baines, Anthony, *Woodwind Instruments and Their History*. New York, Norton, 1957.

Galpin, Francis W., *A Textbook of European Musical Instruments*. New York, John de Graff, 1937.

Geiringer, Karl, *Musical Instruments*. New York, Oxford University Press, 1945.

Sachs, Curt, *The History of Musical Instruments*. New York, Norton, 1940.

DICTIONARIES AND ENCYCLOPEDIAS

Apel, Willi, ed., *Harvard Dictionary of Music*. Cambridge, Harvard University Press, 1944.

Baker, Theodore, ed., *Biographical Dictionary of Musicians*, 5th ed. completely revised by Nicolas Slonimsky. New York, Schirmer, 1958.

Cobbett, W. W., ed., *Cobbett's Cyclopaedic Survey of Chamber Music*. London, Oxford University Press, 1930.

Grove, George, and Blom, Eric, eds., *Grove's Dictionary of Music and Musicians*, 5th ed., 9 vols. New York, St. Martin's Press, 1954.

Scholes, Percy, *The Oxford Companion to Music*, 9th ed. London, Oxford University Press, 1955.

Thompson, Oscar, *The International Cyclopedia of Music and Musicians*, 5th rev. ed. New York, Dodd, 1949.